The History of the
German Resistance 1933–1945

THE HISTORY OF THE GERMAN RESISTANCE 1933–1945

Peter Hoffmann

Translated from the German by
RICHARD BARRY

The MIT Press
Cambridge, Massachusetts

First MIT Press edition, 1977

This translation of 1970 edition with additional material by the author, first published
in Great Britain © MacDonald and Jane's
Publishers, Ltd., 1977

First published in West Germany under the
title Widerstand, Staatsstreich, Attentat, 1969
© R. Piper & Co. Verlag, München, 1969;
second edition, 1970

Library of Congress catalog card number:
76-0824
ISBN 0 262 08088 5

Printed in the United States of America

Contents

Contents

Author's Foreword

There has always been resistance to authority ever since authority existed. If the possessor of power, based on a traditional or written code of law, abuses his authority, if he does not fulfil the obligations which men have always considered inseparable from power, the victims of such abuse are entitled to consider themselves released from their own obligations. Mediaeval feudal law was based on such a reciprocity of service – protection and livelihood on the one side, obedience and allegiance on the other. In 1530 even the Lutheran princes, despite Luther's doctrine of god-given authority, claimed the right of resistance to the measures of the Emperor. In 1804, with the onset of the Napoleonic hurricane and the end of the Holy Roman Empire in mind, Friedrich Schiller put the following into the mouth of Stauffacher in *Wilhelm Tell:*

> When the oppressed for justice looks in vain,
> When his sore burden may no more be borne,
> With fearless heart he makes appeal to Heaven
> And thence brings down his everlasting rights
> Which there abide, inalienably his
> And indestructible as are the stars.
> Nature's primeval state returns again
> Where man stands hostile to his fellow man,
> And if all other means shall fail his need
> One last resource remains – his own good sword.

Admittedly the right of resistance has never been undisputed. The Roman legal luminaries developed the concept of the majesty of the ruler and the sovereignty of the state, a notion overemphasized in 19th-century Germany by many; this hardly allowed room for any legal resistance. Many of the 17th-century philosophers of natural law, Thomas Hobbes for instance, flatly denied any right of resistance. Others, however, have deduced from the law of nature, from the assumed basic legal state of freedom, a right to resistance which has in practice been exercised over and over again.

There is moreover no lack of examples of the exercise of this right of resistance. In 1649 the English followed the doctrine of sovereignty of the people to its extreme conclusion and beheaded their King, Charles I; in 1688 they refused the throne to one of his descendants. Between 1789 and 1795 the

French sought to assert the concept of the people's sovereignty with terrible consistency and during the 19th century almost all European peoples attempted, by means of more or less coordinated resistance to the established State authority, to obtain for themselves that which the French Revolution had achieved – individual freedom, legal and economic security, the 'rights of man', in short a constitution and a legal definition of the nation's existence. Resistance to a state of affairs felt to be intolerable but nevertheless maintained by the State is therefore nothing unheard-of in the history either of Europe or of Germany.

The resistance which is the subject of this book is in this line of tradition. In broad terms this resistance had already begun before Hitler's seizure of power; in the true sense, however, it began only in 1933 and even then took five years to progress to the stage which is the real hallmark of resistance, dealt with in this book – the attempt at a *coup d'état*. For this the spur provided by the imminent threat of a major war was necessary. In this context, therefore, 'resistance' implies activity designed to bring about the overthrow of the Nazi regime from within; in general terms it was carried on by those groups directly or indirectly involved in the assassination attempt of 20 July 1944.

Active resistance to an unlawful regime can only be demanded from the mass of the people by someone both ready and competent to organize and lead it. In the state constructed by Hitler, with its feared and apparently ubiquitous police, with its social achievements and its apparently brilliant successes, this was not in practice possible and, when catastrophe was visibly approaching, the majority simply wanted to save their skins. In such a society only a few highly-placed functionaries possessed both the essential timely insight into the realities of the situation and the authority to deal with it accordingly by opposition to the government. Only a few were able to make up their minds unequivocally whether and when a sworn oath and pledged loyalty had become meaningless and were only assisting in the destruction of that which they were supposed to protect. Both condemnation and denigration of those who remained faithful to their oath are equally pharisaical. Equally wrong is condemnation of the conspirators, who refused to recognize 'law' based solely on force, when it was destroying life rather than preserving it. Such an attitude elevates the form of the law above its purpose or content. The attitude of the conspirators was the more spiritually creative and fundamentally humane in that it accorded with the principle of life and the preservation of life.

It is now thirty years since the end of the Second World War and during this period innumerable authors have dealt with Germany's most recent past. They have tried to explain how it was possible for a world conflagration to be initiated in which over forty million men lost their lives and which ended in the dismemberment of Germany, the division of Europe, and Russian military hegemony on the continent. Since the war thousands of books and articles have been published purporting to describe what was being done inside Germany, initially against the ruinous policy of the Nazi regime and its consequences, finally with the object of the regime's total elimination. These publications include a considerable number of outstanding works but an even greater number which fail to satisfy the requirements of historical scholarship. All have one failure in common: an inadequate basis of source material for an account of the concrete attempts to overthrow the Nazi regime and do away with Hitler.

There are many reasons for this. Many authors have been and still are today more interested in describing the motives of the resistance than its actual deeds; many who wrote of their own experiences knew and saw only a small section of the whole; for others numerous important sources were inaccessible at the time of writing. In many respects the position in regard to sources was more difficult twenty years after the end of the war than it was in 1945. Numerous witnesses of these events had died; others had either forgotten or preferred to forget the details. On the other hand many of the former German *Reich*'s official files relevant to research on the resistance have meanwhile been returned to the Federal Republic by the western Allies (it is, of course, hardly possible to say what important material is still stored away in the East); moreover discussion of the rights and wrongs of resistance can now take place in a calmer atmosphere than in the years immediately following the war, when 'denazification' and the search for the guilty were the order of the day. Many witnesses have therefore been prepared to give a factual account of their experiences when ten years earlier they would have held their tongues.

My starting point has been the conviction that the resistance movement of 20 July 1944 and its tragic failure can only really be comprehensible if the previous history and course of events are known in detail; I have accordingly been concerned primarily to clarify the course of events connected with those attempts to overthrow the regime or assassinate its leaders which progressed beyond the stage of mere thought and discussion. They culminated in the rising of 20 July, the last attempt of a long series. The well-known books by Hans Rothfels, Eberhard Zeller, Gerhard Ritter, Annedore Leber and others remain the basic secondary works for any character study of the personalities involved or their motives, for any understanding of the overall phenomenon of the resistance movement and for any study of the activities of individuals.

At this point I would wish to thank all those who have assisted me in my extensive researches. It is not possible to list them all individually but at least mention must be made of: the staff of the Federal Archives in Koblenz, that of the Württemberg *Land* Library in Stuttgart, that of the *Institut für Zeitgeschichte* in Munich, of the Central Reference Archive of the Federal Archives in Kornelimünster, of the Central Office of Provincial Judiciaries in Ludwigsburg, of the Berlin Document Centre, of the National Archives, Washington (Messrs Wolfe, Bauer and Taylor were particularly helpful), of the Library of Congress, Washington, of the Hoover Institution in Stanford, California, where Mrs Agnes F. Peterson was a constant and reliable source of assistance, and of the Library of the University of Northern Iowa in Cedar Falls; I should also mention the many people who were involved in these events and who were prepared to tell me what they had seen (their names appear in the 'Notes' and 'Sources'). I am also grateful to the *Militärgeschichtliches Forschungsamt* (Military History Research Office) for knowledge of certain important papers, although I did not succeed in gaining sight of all relevant documents stored there.

Production of this book, which entailed much travel, would not have been possible had it not been for the initiative and generous financial support of the *Hilfswerk 20 Juli 1944* Foundation from 1962 to 1964, of the *Evangelische Verlagswerk* from 1963 to 1965, of the *Volkswagenwerk* Foundation in 1965 and of the University of Northern Iowa, Cedar Falls, from 1966 to 1968. My special thanks are due to all these institutions.

Last but not least I owe the completion of this book and of this third (revised and expanded) edition to the patience, understanding and active assistance of my wife. My thanks are also due to my father, Professor Wilhelm Hoffmann, and to Professor Hans Rothfels for reading the original manuscript and for their encouraging comments.

P.H.
McGill University, Montreal.

PART I/THE BACKGROUND

1 *The Year 1933*

On 30 January 1933 Adolf Hitler was appointed *Reich* Chancellor by President von Hindenburg; he was commissioned to form a government, for which he was to find a majority in the *Reichstag* later. He had therefore come to power by virtue of the provisions of the German *Reich*'s current constitution, although he had been proclaiming for years that he would change both the State and the constitution, through which he had reached his goal, on National-Socialist and authoritarian lines – in other words destroy them.

The Weimar Republic, successor to the Prussian/German empire defeated in the First World War, had not been able to overcome its external or internal weaknesses and contradictions. In particular it had been unable to cope with the continuous and irresponsible attacks of its opponents, both left-wing and 'national' – German-National (*Deutschnationale*), reactionary, militarist and ultra-conservative; even in its early years there had been right- and left-wing extremist *putschs*, with uproar and separatism, with the refusal, primarily by the nationalist elements of the National Assembly, to affix their signature to the Treaty of Versailles and an equal refusal to assume responsibility for their action by forming a government. In the following years the victors too did not allow the young state to recover from the war; society and the economy were ruined and eroded by the burden of reparations and by inflation. When hatred finally began to give way to common sense and a good start had been made with economic consolidation, the reviving republic, in common with all industrial nations, was rocked in 1929 by the most catastrophic economic crisis which the world had ever seen.

Adolf Hitler, born in Austria, stateless from 1924 to 1932 and a devilishly clever demagogue, was the most adroit of all in exploiting this antipathy to the 'Weimar system', which was held guilty of everything; he was largely responsible for fanning this antipathy and finally, with the aid of his following, swollen into a mass party, he was in a position to administer the death-blow to the Weimar Republic.

He had, however, by no means 'seized' power entirely on his own initiative, although this was what he said; it would in any case have been contrary to the legality by which he had ostensibly been setting so much store ever since the miserable failure of his *putsch* in 1923. Instead power had fallen into his lap as the result of the apparently insoluble problems of internal politics, the constitution and the economy. The politicians, whether opportunist, perplexed or dazzled, were at work behind the scenes with their intrigues; 'the people', however, had also played no small part in Hitler's rise to power. Precisely how strong Hitler's popular backing was can hardly be established; certain indications, however, enable some estimate to be made. In the elections of July 1932, 37.4% of all who went to the poll (84%) cast valid votes in favour of the NSDAP (*Nationalsozialistische Deutsche Arbeiter-Partei* – the Nazi party); in November 1932 the Nazi vote was 33.1% in an 80.6% poll. In March 1933, however, when the Nazis had been for a whole month in control of the *Reich* and Prussian Ministries of the Interior and therefore of the entire police force, when they had been terrorizing the population by means of the SA for more than four weeks, they still scored only 43.9% of all valid votes in an 88.7% poll.[1]

The results of these three elections, of course, reflect the popular mood of 1933 only to a limited extent. Hundreds of thousands of people never registered their political views, at least not by going to the polls. The figures certainly require interpretation and must be looked at against the background of the situation at the time.

It will rightly be observed that a thirty to forty per cent vote for a lawless demagogue like Hitler, who made no secret of his views, was too large, in other words that it indicated a degree of extremist and violent nationalism greater than could be carried by a state as young as the Germany of that time. A good illustration of the open acknowledgment of violent crime by Hitler and his Nazis was provided by the 'Potempa case'. In August 1932 some SA men in the Silesian village of Potempa beat and kicked to death before his mother's eyes Konrad Pietzuch, one of their workmates who supported the Communist Party. Sentences of death and life imprisonment were pronounced. Hitler and the other Nazi leaders thereupon explicitly and publicly proclaimed in the Party newspaper, the *Völkischer Beobachter*, their solidarity with their 'comrades', swearing to revenge and release them.[2] Their acknowledgment of violence, crime and lawlessness was unmistakable in August 1932. The criminals were amnestied on 23 March 1933.

Although the 'Potempa case' can justifiably be quoted as a typical example of Nazi methods, an explanation is also to be found in the general political atmosphere of brutality and extremism characteristic of the years 1929–33. Disturbances and violence, political and criminal murder were the order of the day. Wildcat strikes broke out in various places, sometimes simply provoked by the extremists, who stood only to gain from chaos. The wildcat strike of transport workers in Berlin in 1932, for instance, was supported both by the communists and the Nazis.[3]

A further factor was the colossal unemployment; by February 1932 this had reached the terrifying figure of over six million and no effective reduction took place between the winters of 1931–32 and 1932–33. Not until 1933 was there any significant fall in unemployment; in the first six months of that year alone the reduction was over $1\frac{1}{2}$ million.[4]

Despite some small improvement, in 1932 poverty was still very great, in many individual cases almost inconceivable. There were working-class couples paying 10 marks rent per month but receiving only 3.20 marks per week in national assistance, leaving them in theory only 2.80 marks per month to live off. If they were not to die of hunger they had to rely on gifts from relatives and friends or credit in the shops. Another worker with a wife and two children received 9 marks per week in national assistance but was paying 4.50 per week in rent, leaving available for the family 0.16 marks per person per day.[5] In this situation the communists promised class warfare and a better, but distant, future; the Nazis, on the other hand, promised work, bread and good order; since they also presented themselves as patriots, many believed in them rather than the communists who, it was feared, would bring revolution and civil war.

The extent of Hitler's following can therefore largely be explained by the general economic situation and by ill-feeling towards both the victors of the war and the people's own leaders, who were trying to reach some accommodation with the victor powers. On the other hand a very large section of the electorate, over half of the adult population which played any part at all in political life, had not been beguiled by Hitler and National-Socialism. Hundreds of thousands, if not millions, of voters were irreconcilably opposed to the Nazis. Only later, with the new government's growing success, did a broader-based measure of support develop among the masses and even this was coincident with the systematic destruction of all opposition organization by the new regimented (*'gleichgeschaltet'*) *Führer* State and the erection of the 'SS State' in which Heinrich Himmler, leader of an élite Party army, wielded an instrument of thorough domination in his capacity as *'Reichsführer-*SS and Chief of the German Police'. Then it seemed wise to keep quiet, to allow the new government, like the old, just to carry on, and to look for a job; things were now on the upgrade; the masses could see work and food ahead of them; those who behaved with the necessary propriety and were not in some way classified as 'enemies of the state' had no need to fear molestation by the regime.

In the early months of 1933 there was still some form of legal opposition. An incessant stream of prohibitions on meetings and publications, together with other repressive measures, descended upon it but initially neither the Social Democrats nor the communists were banned as organized political parties. Nevertheless, despite all the proclamations and fine words of the preceding years and months, they did not offer any large-scale resistance to the excesses of the Nazi-controlled government.

The Communist Party had long been in the forefront in preparing and arming for civil war against 'fascism'. Yet, when 'fascism' came to power, nothing really significant was done.[6] The German Communist Party was directed by the Communist Party Central Committee of the Soviet Union, and the prevailing view there was that the advent of a fascist government should promote Germany's internal self-destruction and prepare the ground for a communist seizure of power. As we know, Stalin had imposed the principle of 'socialism in one country' in opposition to Trotsky's doctrine of continuing world revolution and he frowned on any attempt to instigate revolutions in neighbouring countries in support of that in Russia. In this it is admittedly difficult to differentiate between Stalin's interest in the elimination of Trotsky and his genuine political convictions. In any case, however, persecution by the regime together with the ideological dissensions and quarrels between the German Communist Party and other left-wing political groupings made any real or effective cooperation between them impossible even in the hour of greatest danger. The call for a general strike on 25 February 1933 organized by the communists and Social-Democrats in concert was almost totally disregarded.

Three days later all previous political developments were overshadowed by the *Reichstag* fire. This enabled the wielders of power to take far sterner action against the communists than they had probably planned to do at this early stage of their rule.[7] On 1 April the Executive Committee of the Comintern (Communist International, the coordinating agency for the work of non-Russian communist parties), which was impotent but never at a loss for tactical subterfuges, decided that, with the ban on the Communist Party, the open establishment of a fascist dictatorship must inevitably assist the masses to discard their democratic illusions; this would release them from Social-Democrat influence and accelerate the tempo of Germany's progress towards the proletarian revolution. Such opportunism does not detract from the heroism of the few Communist Party members who offered resistance. Nevertheless, as a revolutionary and anti-fascist organization, the German Communist Party had proved a failure. Many of its leading functionaries emigrated, leaving the perils of the underground struggle to their subordinate officials and members.

The attitude of the German Communist Party therefore stood in sharp contrast to its previous claims and public pronouncements but it was at least a truer reflection of its real influence on the masses than the reaction of the two largest left-wing political organizations, the Social-Democrats and the trade unions. They remained equally inactive, but there was nothing new or unusual in their inactivity. Ever since 1930, in a broader and more general sense ever since the early 1920s, since the Kapp *putsch,* even since the *Reichstag* vote on war loans in August 1914, the Social-Democrats had abandoned use of revolutionary methods. A legalistic attitude of mind was widespread and deep-rooted in the Party; a refusal to recognize the new government of 30 January 1933 was hardly possible; everything was confused, politically obscure and undefined; no one knew what to do.[8] The leaders were not sure of the support of the working masses and did not think that they could risk a general strike. Inactivity seemed to offer the only chance of survival. In the space of a few weeks the basis of real power had changed radically as a result of the dissolution of the *Reichstag* on 1 February 1933, the electoral campaign, the Emergency Ordinance of 4 February, Göring's terror campaign in Prussia where he was Minister-President, and the rapid widespread muzzling of the press.

The emergency Ordinance of 4 February 1933, which was based on Article 48 of the Weimar constitution, forbade all open-air meetings or parades which might endanger public security.[9] It was now a simple matter to ban all opposition demonstrations or gatherings and confiscate all publications which could be labelled as dangerous to public security and order. Anyone who contravened the Ordinance, anyone who organized some gathering subject to a ban, even a retrospective one, anyone who distributed printed matter, be it newspaper, poster, leaflet or advertisement thought by the new rulers to merit a ban, and even anyone who knew of such things and did not report them, could be punished with imprisonment and consequently arrested. In this way all opponents could be eliminated, ostensibly legally. The timing of the various measures was merely a question of tactics; clearly it was wrong to try to disrupt all opposition groups at one and the same time. The more they could be separated from one another, treated in isolation and, if possible, assaulted individually, while leaving the remainder in hope, the more helplessly they would have to surrender themselves to the wielders of power.

Everything else was designed more for the consolidation than for the seizure of power. The Nazis were as surprised as the communists by the *Reichstag* fire of 27 February 1933. Many of the government's measures were totally unplanned and ill-considered,[10] but it seized the opportunity only five days before elections for a new *Reichstag* to complete its grip on all authority at home. The Emergency Ordinance abolished the basic rights and guarantees of personal freedom established under the Weimar constitution. Almost without restriction, certainly without a court order and without subsequent redress by the courts, people could now be arrested and detained for an indefinite period; theoretically, and largely also in practice, any human utterance, any exchange of information, any publication in word or picture was subject to censorship; periodicals and books could be banned, parties and associations dissolved, meetings forbidden and property confiscated.[11] All this struck at the whole basis of the rule of law in the state and the method used was that designed to save the state, the right of emergency legislation.

The Enabling Law of 23 March 1933, giving the government complete freedom of action without regard to parliamentary or constitutional limitations, was merely the 'legal' culminating point. The government was now explicitly authorized, not only to promulgate laws without the participation of the *Reichstag,* but even to introduce legislation incompatible with the constitution.[12] Shortly after the *Reichstag* elections of 5 March communist deputies were expelled from the House and their Party was banned; they could therefore do nothing against this law. The Social-Democrats fought it bravely but vainly. The Centre Party, the Bavarian Peoples Party and the remaining splinter groups lying between the socialists and the German-National/National-Socialist coalition voted for their own emasculation in the paradoxical hope of saving their existence thereby.[13]

The previous opposition leaders had now been 'cut out', to use an apt technological phrase, and the National-Socialists proceeded to ensure themselves total control over all walks of life by means of *Gleichschaltung*, in other words projecting on to the level of the *Länder* the prevailing political conditions in the *Reich,* elimination of the *Länder* parliaments, assumption of power in the *Länder* by Nazi *Reichsstatthalter* (Regents), penetration of all

official agencies and authorities by National-Socialists and finally the abolition of all parties except the NSDAP and proclamation of the 'Unity of Party
and State'.[14]

Again and again the question has been asked: how was this possible? Why
was there no opposition movement or even any stubborn defence of established rights?

There is no short satisfactory answer. Those who wrestle with this question generally, with some justification, refer to the 'situation at the time'
which, they say, must be understood. Formation of a totalitarian state was
something entirely new; there was no previous experience on which to draw.
Germany had not achieved her form of government as a result of centuries-
long endeavour; it had just 'happened' in 1919 along with military defeat and
the collapse of a once-brilliant empire. Germany had then passed through a
series of severe economic and political crises, for which the people and the
majority of its representatives held not only their ex-enemies but also their
own government largely responsible. Now, after a continuous political,
economic and social crisis lasting since 1930, the country was politically
exhausted. A sense of democracy and republican vigilance would have been
fortunate accidents, certainly not a natural development. Before 30 January
1933, even before the elections of July and November 1932, people knew of the
Nazis' violence, brutality and contempt for the law. But violence and brutality
were attractive; many mistook them for strength and were convinced. On the
other hand in the free elections held between 1919 and 1934 only a minority
had ever voted for the NSDAP. The individual German had no influence on the
events of 30 January, 4 February, 28 February and 23 March, in so far as he
understood them at all. Many even of those who possessed all the necessary
knowledge and information did not believe that the threats to which Hitler
and his adherents were continuously giving vent, were seriously meant; they
genuinely hoped that the Nazis could be tamed if they formed a minority in a
cabinet, and would then be compelled to assume political responsibility.

The problem was therefore not solely lack of the will to resist but equally
lack of comprehension of the nature of Nazism. Uncertainty and loss of the
basic values added to ignorance, led to absence of comprehension and
helplessness in face of the appearance of a totalitarian leviathan which felt
itself bound by no dictates of humanity or law. People did not believe that the
Nazis would obtain an absolute majority in the *Reichstag* to be elected on 5
March – and the Nazis did not; people naïvely hoped that the government
could be held in check by parliamentary methods and by the checks and
balances enshrined in the constitution, and be forced to return to the constitutional ways which from the outset it had rejected. As long as people
thought this, there could be no question of an 'illegal' resistance.[15] For the
Social-Democrats in particular adherence to legality had become an *idée fixe*.
The fact that the *Reichsbanner*, the socialist militant wing, other similar
organizations and many of the workers were ready, even clamouring, for a
fight by means of strikes, demonstrations, disturbances and even an armed
rising, was of no avail. The Social-Democratic leadership remained im-

movable, hopeful, uncomprehending. There were sufficient subjective grounds for inactivity: the *Reichswehr*'s apparent collaboration with the government; the formal legality of the Hitler government and its measures; the threat of the Social-Democratic Party's complete annihilation. Looked at from a distance, the most convincing explanation is lack of comprehension of Nazism and its true nature, despite the fact that there were plenty of warning voices. The courageous speech made in the *Reichstag* by Otto Wels, chairman of the Social-Democrats, protesting against the Enabling Law, should not be forgotten.

'Legal resistance', about which many cudgelled their brains, was an illusion. The electoral campaign preceding 5 March had shown that the Nazis were determined to cling to power 'by all methods'. The press was censored and deluged with restrictions; the radio was almost totally under Nazi control. More than four million adult Germans were quietly allowed to vote communist; then their elected deputies were arrested or forced into hiding and emigration, so that the relative Nazi strength in the *Reichstag* was increased. Finally the German Communist Party was banned altogether. The Social-Democrats were permitted to lead a shadowy existence for a time but on 22 June 1933 their hour of dissolution and proscription struck. By the end of the following three weeks no German political party existed apart from the NSDAP.[16]

Meanwhile the terror increased; all who opposed or fell foul of the authorities were literally clubbed down. As early as February 1933 the Nazis began to misuse the police as an instrument of power and terror, also to transfer auxiliary police functions to uniformed members of the Party and SA.[17]

So the 'legal' door was thrown wide open to arbitrary action and terror. A Party uniform and a white armband were adequate justification for the use of the rubber truncheon or revolver; arbitrary arrest was the rule; people were beaten up on the street, assaulted and kicked by undisciplined uniformed Nazis or 'shot while attempting to escape'. Thousands who survived their first assault were taken to 'wildcat concentration camps' run by the SA. Looting, theft, deprivation of liberty, bodily injury, manslaughter and murder were somewhat out-of-date expressions for measures now called 'police' and therefore 'legal'. Who can be surprised that many were intimidated by such terror?

Despite all this, and often before the terror had reached its full height, resistance to certain of the new government's measures was offered in many places both by official institutions and by individuals. In Bavaria there was widespread and energetic opposition to the *Gleichschaltung* policy; restorationist and even separatist motives and tendencies fused and coalesced with those of the federalists and anti-Nazis. Representatives of the Bavarian Peoples Party acted with special energy. They petitioned the *Reich* President and obtained assurances both from him and from von Papen, the Vice-Chancellor. Heinrich Held, the Party's leader, declared on several occasions in February that no *Reich* Commissar would cross the line of the Main with impunity; if, contrary to Hindenburg's assurances, one of them did enter Bavaria, he would be arrested forthwith. The Emergency Ordinance of 28 February, however, gave the government a 'legal' handle for the seizure of power in the *Länder*, including Bavaria, in so far as 'the necessary measures for the reestablishment of public security and order' had not been taken there.[18] Decision on whether this had in fact been done was the prerogative of the Nazi Minister of the Interior, Dr Wilhelm Frick. Further protests were of no avail; legal methods and procedures could achieve nothing against the ostensible legality of a dictatorship which was in fact violating both the constitution and the law. Here was yet another illustration of the complete change in the location of power, also of the complete misappreciation of the situation by the victims and the protesters.

After the elections, in which the Bavarian Nazis scored 43%, all possible methods were employed to impose *Gleichschaltung* on Bavaria, the last *Land* without a Nazi government.[19] On 9 March 1933 armed detachments of SA and SS dominated the streets of Munich; the swastika flag was hoisted on the City Hall tower; SA leaders in uniform demanded the immediate installation of General Ritter von Epp as State Commissar-General. The Bavarian government, however, remained firm and opened negotiations with the *Reichswehr* on measures to be taken against revolution in the streets. But the *Reichswehr* Ministry in Berlin was discouraging; events in Bavaria, it said, were purely internal political matters, from which the *Reichswehr* must remain aloof; it would remain standing at ease. Heinrich Held, the Bavarian Minister-President, remained unshaken; Ernst Röhm, Chief of Staff of the SA, General von Epp, Adolf Wagner, *Gauleiter* of Bavaria, and Heinrich Himmler, commander of the SS, were sent unceremoniously packing.

What could have been done? For technical reasons effective resistance was barely conceivable. How long would the police obey the orders of the legal Bavarian government? How long could they hold out against the SA and SS? Whom would the *Reichswehr* obey, should it cease standing at ease? Should the population be incited to civil war and revolt against uniformed 'authority'? Resistance would have implied disturbance of public order and so given the *Reich* government the handle for which it had been waiting all along.

'Legal' resistance could achieve nothing in the long run. The SA dominated the streets; there was much disorder and the government was largely powerless. So the inevitable happened; the *Reich* government intervened on the basis of the Emergency Ordinance of 28 February and appointed Ritter von Epp its representative in Bavaria. Protests and telegrams were of no further avail; the President, through Hans Otto Meissner, his State Secretary, replied that application should be made direct to Hitler. Thus the President registered his own impotence.

In other *Länder* men were to be found no less courageous than those in Bavaria. Many of them were executed by the Nazis after 20 July 1944. Dr Carl Goerdeler, the Burgomaster of Leipzig, stopped the swastika flag, which was not yet the national emblem, being hoisted on the City Hall; he also intervened personally to protect Jewish businessmen from molestation by the SA.[20] Such resistance was frequently of short duration; it was offered in ignorance of the perils involved and in the belief that the incident concerned was due to an isolated, or at at any rate temporary, excess of zeal, not to deliberate policy. But in those days all were treated alike; everywhere the Nazis seized power with unexampled brutality. The discussions and parliamentary methods, of which the Social-Democrats were the main protagonists in their efforts to stop the Enabling Law, could no longer achieve anything.

The reader will wonder to what extent the Nazis' partners in the government coalition offered resistance to the progressive totalitarian seizure of power; from the outset, after all, they had joined the coalition with the intention of 'taming' Hitler and his party and confining them to proper legal procedures.

Hugenberg was the one who at least made some move towards a demand for the association of President Hindenburg with those laws due to be promulgated on the basis of the enabling legislation.[21] Meissner, Hindenburg's State Secretary, however, assured him that this was neither necessary nor would Hindenburg wish it. Nevertheless, he said it was for consideration whether Hindenburg's authority should not somehow be 'engaged' in the case of particularly important legislation; moreover the President had in fact 'insuperable objections' to one proposed ordinance whereby the *Reichstag* fire-raising would be punishable with death, a sentence not on the statute book when the fire took place.

The resistance offered by the Nazis' political partners was therefore very small, in fact insignificant. In practice they placidly renounced their support from the President, in effect the whole basis of such influence as remained to them. They had no wish to cause a split by open opposition in cabinet.

Ultimately, therefore, though in face of determined resistance from the socialist parliamentary party, the *Reichstag* was put out of business through the acceptance of the Enabling Law on 23 March 1933. It was a spectacle of opportunism, of desperate attempts by the parties to preserve their existence which in fact they succeeded in prolonging only by a few weeks. This spectacle of the weakness shown by the remnants of a never very robust democracy is undoubtedly both disillusioning and exasperating. In practice a refusal to vote the Enabling Law would have achieved nothing other than to allow the parties to make an honourable exit from the stage. This weakness was general and it applied to all walks of political life.

Parliament did not, of course, agree to the Enabling Law entirely of its own free will. The *Reichstag* met under unconcealed pressure from the Nazi private armies, the SA and the SS, and under pressure and threat from the streets. Well-drilled supporters, who penetrated even into the Chamber, gave notice of violence; in the Kroll Opera House, where parliament had met ever since the *Reichstag* fire, SA and SS uniforms dominated the scene; SA and SS 'stewards' stood menacingly beside the opposition benches; there were shouts of 'Heil', thunderous applause for Hitler, swastika flags, the singing of the national anthem at the end of Hitler's speech – everything designed to create the intended mass-meeting atmosphere.[22] In a famous speech Otto Wels, the

Social-Democratic Party leader, rejected the Enabling Law, defending freedom and democracy. Hitler thereupon replied that 'only for the sake of the law' had they sought from the *Reichstag* something 'which we could have taken in any case'. So the Enabling Law, giving the Nazis a free hand in almost everything, was forced through. In the end, however, the Nazis neither observed nor respected this law which had reached the statute book in so illegal and unconstitutional a manner; they broke it as unscrupulously as they did all their other obligations and promises. With his unconcealed scorn for procedure adopted 'for the sake of the law', Hitler had, as always, given forewarning of his real intentions.

In parallel with the elimination of the parties went that of the trade unions, potentially strong though they were; the major campaign against them, however, did not open until April 1933. Faced with an apparently inevitable choice between *Gleichschaltung* and elimination, the trade unions, despite all earlier brave words and even occasional militant utterances in February 1933, proved as ineffective as the Social-Democratic leaders. One historian describes them as helpless, timid, resigned and fragile.[23]

After the March 1933 elections the SA together with members of the Nazi factory cells began to occupy certain trade union offices. The reply to this was acquiescence instead of resistance. The Committee of the German General Trade Union Federation decided to address a memorandum to Hitler; in this Theodor Leipart, First Chairman of the Free Trade Unions, said that he wished to keep the trade unions out of politics and would accept any regime 'of whatever type'. The Nazis then succeeded in persuading large numbers of trade union members to participate in the May Day celebrations – the day had been declared a paid holiday, thereby forestalling the trade unions. The rest then followed 'blow upon blow'. On 2 May *Gleichschaltung* of the trade unions began with arrests of trade union leaders, occupation of trade union offices by SA and SS, expropriation of trade union banks and the trade union press. Trade union officials were thrown into concentration camps, their previous readiness to compromise being scoffed at as subservient hypocrisy. On the same day formation of the Nazi 'German Labour Front' was announced. All this happened ostensibly without legal backing from the government; it was a purely Party initiative.

In the following months such members of the Social-Democratic hierarchy as had not emigrated suffered a similar fate. On 29 May Party headquarters in Prague announced the start of illegal resistance and underground activity – in fact an admission of the loss of almost all freedom of action inside Germany.[24] Finally a split developed between the Social-Democratic leaders in Berlin and those in Prague; the Party collapsed and was in effect banned by the government at the end of June.

Finally even Hitler's partners, the German-Nationals, were persecuted, bypassed and terrorized, primarily when they attempted to protest against Nazi encroachments and Nazi tutelage. Here again arrests, prohibitions, beatings-up and SA raids were the order of the day.[25]

Were there other spheres, the intellectual for instance, where the Nazis met greater and more determined resistance ? Here too the general picture is one of acquiescence, weakness, opportunism, delusion and error. The hundreds of German professors hastened to acclaim Hitler and National-Socialism; the notorious speech by Martin Heidegger, Chancellor of Freiburg University, on 27 May 1933 was merely a particularly striking, but by no means isolated, instance.[26]

Even the churches were not entirely immune to this conformism, although their whole *raison d'être* was as vitally affected as that of the sciences. They were, however, the only organizations to produce some form of a popular movement against the Nazi regime.

Admittedly in the early days of the regime the churches were hardly engaged in anything like a struggle. No one can deny that Martin Niemöller was the outstanding figure among the leaders of ecclesiastical resistance and that he suffered severely for his courageous stand by long years spent in a concentration camp. Even he, however, in a thanksgiving sermon in the autumn of 1933 spoke of 'calling and status, race and nationality [*Volkstum*]' as inescapable requirements and of the reawakening of the German people.[27] The Nazi regime initially treated the churches with the greatest circumspection; it had no wish to start a battle for the prevalence of a new ideology during its very first months; appeasement was the watchword. On the other side many evangelical pastors who had once been royalist and imperialist and were still patriots, hailed and accepted the spirit of Germany as preached by Luther, heroic piety and even a form of Christian faith 'suited to the times'; many even supported the movement known as 'German Christians' in their opposition to Marxism, Jewry, cosmopolitanism and freemasonry.

Ludwig Müller, the Nazi '*Reich* Bishop', however, was not accepted by the evangelical church despite a public statement by Bernhard Rust, Commissar for Science, Art and Popular Education in Prussia, that the formation in the church of a 'first focus of resistance' was not to be tolerated. Soon such organizations as the 'Pastors Emergency League' and the 'Confessional Church' were formed, initially to combat the 'Aryan paragraphs' in the new German church constitution of 11 June 1933. Led by Martin Niemöller of Dahlem and the young theologian Dietrich Bonhoeffer, they resisted any adulteration of the evangelical faith by Germanistic or other non-Christian ideas. Thousands of pastors now felt themselves, and remained, under an obligation to offer religious resistance to Nazism; an equal number, however, evaded the issue, held their tongues or paid more or less thorough-going lipservice to the regime and 'our *Führer*'. Nevertheless what the Nazis had feared had happened: a 'first focus of resistance' had formed. They were forced to abandon their attempts to regiment and control the evangelical church from within and shifted to brutal control from outside, using the police, the administration and the regulations. The *Reich* Bishop was dropped but refused to resign. At the end of the war he committed suicide in Königsberg.

In general terms the Catholic Church, like the Protestant, had reacted to the seizure of power by recognition of the new regime.[28] After the passing of the

Enabling Law at the end of March 1933, for instance, the Bishops' Conference in Fulda thought it right to express a certain confidence in the new government subject to reservations concerning some 'religious and moral lapses'. In July, only a few days after the dissolution of the Catholic Centre Party, a concordat was concluded between the Vatican and the German government – Hitler's first major international success. The government explicitly guaranteed certain rights and prerogatives of the Church, on which the Catholics were proposing to insist. Catholic schools were not to be touched but, on the other hand, all Catholic organizations of a political, social or professional nature were to be disbanded.

During the course of 1933, however, the Catholic Church too was literally forced to resist. It could not silently accept the general persecution, regimentation or oppression, nor in particular the sterilization law of summer 1933. Over the years until the outbreak of war Catholic resistance stiffened until finally its most eminent spokesman was the Pope himself with his Encyclical '*Mit brennender Sorge*' ('With burning anxiety') of 14 March 1937, read from all German Catholic pulpits. Clemens August Graf von Galen, Bishop of Münster, was typical of the many fearless Catholic speakers.[29]

In general terms, therefore, the churches were the only major organizations to offer comparatively early and open resistance; they remained so in later years. They achieved a certain success, for even during the war the Nazi rulers did not think that they could risk complete destruction of the churches. They were confronted here with barriers which they could not understand – the fortitude and integrity of religious conviction, conscience and a sense of responsibility for one's fellow men which were not to be extinguished by regulations and prohibitions.

There were 'invisible frontiers' which proved to be genuine obstacles in bringing the new rulers to a halt. To the outward eye both religious and intellectual life was regimented and controlled; all intellectual utterances were subject to censorship. The object was to concentrate under unified control the press, the cinema, the radio, literature, the theatre, and mass demonstrations; their 'centralized employment' must be 'absolutely guaranteed', declared Dr Joseph Goebbels, the Minister for Popular Enlightenment and Propaganda; propaganda, he continued, was one of the most important arts by which a people could be ruled; all cultural life must now be concentrated in the service of the National-Socialist concept.[30] The control of the minds of the people, essential for total domination, could only be achieved if these were entirely permeated by the thinking of the rulers and purged of everything else. In this they did not eventually succeed – nor has anyone else anywhere.

During 1933 the following were formed: a *Reich* Chamber of Authorship, a *Reich* Press Chamber, a *Reich* Radio Chamber, a *Reich* Theatre Chamber, a *Reich* Music Chamber, and a *Reich* Chamber of the Visual Arts. All these formed the *Reich* Cultural Chamber, which was subordinate to the *Reich* Ministry of Propaganda. Anyone who wished to pursue these 'registered' professions had to belong to the relevant Chamber. Executive instructions, under which, for instance, only 'Aryan' writers were permitted, laid down the system of control and regimentation in the minutest detail. Brecht, Döblin, Kaiser, Mann, Tucholsky, Zweig, Bergengruen, Borchardt, Hofmannsthal, Lasker-Schüler, Werfel, Hesse, Heine, Kästner and Kafka were declared 'degenerate' authors; on 10 May 1933 thousands of 'degenerate literary works' were burnt on the Opernplatz in Berlin and in the squares of other German cities; students held the torches and suitable speeches were made by professors. During 1933 many people eminent in German intellectual and cultural life were deprived of their citizenship.[31]

All this was accompanied by terror of incalculable brutality, without which the internal German situation would be incomprehensible. Terror was nothing new; it had been used by numerous political groupings in the party struggles of the previous turbulent crisis years. Now, however, it had risen to be an instrument of government policy. The government could easily have dealt with its opponents by the 'legal' means which had meanwhile become available. But Hitler had no intention of putting a brake on the terror – on the contrary. He knew that he could not convert the stubborn non-conformists and so the only alternative was their suppression by force.[32] Terror and violence, no matter against whom, kept the 'movement' going and without movement the masses might possibly come to their senses; the opponents whom Hitler rightly suspected of existing in all walks of life might congeal into an opposition.

The campaign preceding the 5 March elections had already cost sixty or more lives. Göring had urged the police to abandon all political neutrality and not to be afraid 'to use their weapons' when dealing with 'anti-state', in other words left-wing, organizations or when supporting 'national' formations, in other words the SA, the SS and the *Stahlhelm*.[33] These latter three organizations were given the status of 'auxiliary police'; on 20 February Hitler threatened that 'the enemy' would be beaten, either constitutionally through the forthcoming elections, or in battle using other weapons – and this would, of course, mean more casualties. By mid-October 1933 this unequal struggle had cost between five and six hundred lives and over 26,000 people had been deprived of their liberty as 'police prisoners'. The various 'actions' were frequently characterized more by ill-treatment of prisoners in the notorious SA cellars, by sadism and material greed than by any genuine struggle against 'the enemy'. While on the hunt for communists, Jews and other 'enemies', the SA flying squads did not find housebreaking, robbery, looting, violence, kidnapping or blackmail for ransom to be beneath their national dignity. The murders of 30 June and 1 July 1934 were admittedly a terrible culmination of this unconcealed terror campaign, but incomparably more terrible were the sufferings of hundreds of thousands behind prison walls or the concentration camp barbed wire; what was not known was at least suspected by potential victims. The people were now fully regimented (*gleichgeschaltet*); fear prevented almost everyone leaving the well-drilled ranks.

A few figures may perhaps give some vague idea of the extent of the terror and also of the breadth of resistance to it. Over six years the regular courts alone sentenced 225,000 persons in political cases to terms of imprisonment totalling some 600,000 years. In addition there were the far more numerous, but barely calculable cases, in which detainees were thrown into a concentration camp without trial or done to death beforehand by police measures.[34] Official data show that between 1933 and 1945 about three million Germans were held at some stage in a concentration camp or prison for political reasons, some only for a few weeks, some for the whole twelve years; of these approximately 800,000 were held for active resistance.[35]

A *Gestapo* report of April 1939 shows that at that time there were 162,734 persons held in 'preventive custody' for political reasons, 27,369 awaiting trial for political misdemeanours and 112,432 under sentence for political misdemeanours.[36] On the outbreak of war an SS summary showed 21,400 prisoners in six concentration camps; by the end of April 1942 the number in these same six camps had risen to 44,700. In December 1942 there was a total of 88,000 persons in concentration camps and this had risen to 224,000 by August 1943. The total for August 1944 was 524,286, the majority Jews and forced labourers. The peak figure was reached in January 1945 when the total of concentration camp prisoners in Germany as a whole was 714,211.[37]

In the space of fourteen months in 1935–36, 2,197 persons from left-wing circles were arrested in Berlin alone.[38] In 1936, 11,687 persons were arrested throughout Germany for illegal socialist activity. In 1936 the *Gestapo* seized 1,643,200 illicit leaflets distributed by the Communist and Social-Democratic Parties alone and, in 1937, 927,430.

Anyone fortunate enough to be released from a concentration camp involuntarily contributed to an even more sophisticated system of terror, since the ex-prisoner was forbidden to speak of his terrible experiences.[39] His silence alone produced a sinister increase in the fear and horror aroused by these camps. Frequently, however, ex-prisoners did tell their acquaintances of the ill-treatment, starvation, rape, murder and homicide which were the order of the day in concentration camps; his listeners were then subject to the pressure of knowing the truth but being forced to hold their tongues on pain of permanent threat of the concentration camp.

The register of executions kept by the *Reich* Ministry of Justice from 1871 to 1945 was known as the 'murder register' because, until 1933, the death sentence was only exacted for common murder. After 1933, however, it lived up to its name since, by legal principles, many of those executed were merely the victims of judicial murder. It is estimated that between 1933 and 1945 some 32,600 persons were executed in Germany after pronunciation of a death sentence but less than half of these are shown on the 'murder register'.[40] It carries only 11,881 names and does not include those sentenced by court-martial – over 20,000. The list is also incomplete because, particularly in the final weeks of the regime, executions could no longer be recorded centrally. On the other hand it does include the names of common criminals. It is estimated that 'only' 6,927 people were executed on political grounds, of whom 3,137 were Germans.[41] On the other hand, based on files captured after the war, the British estimate at 4,980 the number of people executed for participation in the 20 July 1944 conspiracy alone.[42] This figure, however, undoubtedly includes many executions not connected with 20 July.

All these figures are probably too low. They do not include the innumerable people shot 'while attempting to escape', those starved or beaten to death in concentration camps, the victims of bestial experiments, those shot or hanged under camp 'justice'. Nevertheless, they give only too clearly a picture of the conditions; they prove that, not only was there oppression, persecution and terror, but also widespread resistance to the regime.

A glance at the suicide statistics for Germany will round off the picture. In the periods July-December 1942 and 1943 7,862 and 7,379 persons respectively took their lives; the figures remained constant despite the considerable reduction in population due to casualties at the front and the bombing of cities.[43] The figures for suicides of Jews are particularly illuminating; official statistics show that for the period July–December 1942 the figure was 1,158 but only 49 for the same period in 1943.

Such, therefore, was the setting in which the resistance movement conspired and acted – brave courageous men, all working against Nazism whether or not they knew each other or were in touch with each other; from them sprang that section of the movement responsible for the attempts to overthrow the regime and assassinate its leaders which will be recounted in this book.

2 Forms of Resistance

While pursuing their revolution inside Germany, the Nazis succeeded in scoring victories and gaining respect in the outside world such as had never been vouchsafed to their democratic predecessors. Apparently uninterruptedly, they extracted piecemeal revisions of the hated Versailles Treaty from their former enemies, thus enabling Hitler to fulfil one of his best vote-catching promises. When he reintroduced universal military service in 1935, no one lifted a finger: on the contrary, while Hitler was tearing up the Treaty of Versailles page by page, a stream of prominent visitors made the pilgrimage to Germany and were granted audiences. In 1934 came Jean Goy, President of the French Ex-Servicemen's Association; in 1935 a British Legion delegation arrived and was also received by Hitler. In March 1935 Sir John Simon and Anthony Eden came on a visit and in June of that year the Anglo-German Naval Agreement was concluded, allowing Germany to build warships up to 35% of the strength of the British Navy and submarines on a parity with those of the British.[1] Great Britain had thus given agreement to a partial rearmament of Germany in order to prevent a repetition of the pre-war arms race. How totally were people deceiving themselves! As early as 3 February 1933, only three days after his appointment as *Reich* Chancellor, Hitler had said in an address to senior *Wehrmacht* commanders that if France had any statesmen, she would not allow Germany the time to rearm but would attack the *Reich* in good time.[2]

In December 1935 William Philips, the US Under-Secretary of State, came to Germany, and in February of the following year Lord Londonderry, the British Lord Privy Seal, visited Hitler. A few days later German troops marched into the Rhineland, which had been demilitarized under the Versailles Treaty; as we know, there were no consequences whatsoever apart from empty protests. Hitler, however, now had the freedom he required to construct fortifications in the west and so protect his rear in the event of a move eastwards;[3] moreover he had demonstrated that France and Britain would give way in face of determined action. Nothing was done when Hitler supported Italy during her invasion of Abyssinia. German troops gave even more effective support to Colonel Franco and his Civil War party in Spain; on this occasion new weapons and tactics were tested and, moreover, the line-up in the looming world war now became obvious: the Germans and Italians supported Franco, the right-wing extremist, while numerous French, British and

American volunteers fought on the side of the republicans and communists.

In July 1936 Hitler received Charles Lindbergh, the famous Atlantic flyer; in the same year the Olympic Games were held in Berlin amid incredible pomp and circumstance and were visited by many distinguished foreign guests. On 4 September Lloyd George, one of the Big Four of Versailles, came to Germany, followed in October by the Governor of the Bank of France and the French Minister of Commerce. In May 1937 the Marquis of Lothian, formerly Chancellor of the Duchy of Lancaster and later British Ambassador in Washington, who had already attended on Hitler in 1934, paid a second visit; in the autumn of 1937 even the Duke of Windsor and Lord Halifax, then a Privy Councillor and later Secretary of State for Foreign Affairs, were unwilling to be excluded from the procession of dignitaries. This list is by no means exhaustive but names only the most prominent personalities.[4] Though probably unintentionally, their appearance gave an impression of approval of Hitler's regime, both externally and internally; his opponents were correspondingly discouraged.[5] Hitler seemed to be registering one success after another. The hated Treaty of Versailles was no longer valid; German-speaking areas, such as the Saar, were coming back to the German *Reich*, as were areas which had once formed part of the Holy Roman Empire but had never belonged to the Bismarckian *Reich* and had never been claimed by Bismarck or his successors of the Weimar Republic. Despite all the shortcomings of his regime, therefore, was not Hitler a great German? Who either would or could offer 'resistance' and thereby expose himself to the reproach of being a traitor?

Nevertheless there were men who did exactly this; many of them had begun to resist even before 1933. One was Ernst Niekisch who, in 1926, founded the 'Journal for socialist and national-revolutionary Policy' entitled *Der Widerstand* (Resistance); it campaigned against reparations, characterizing them as blackmail by the capitalist powers; it called for world revolution against world capitalism and so acquired the label 'National-bolshevist'.[6] In 1932 Niekisch published a pamphlet, 'Hitler – a German disaster' (Berlin 1932), and even after 30 January 1933 he continued his journalistic campaign against the regime in *Der Widerstand*. The paper was not banned until the end of 1934 when the *Gestapo* seized all available copies of the November issue.[7] Niekisch himself was allowed to go but in 1937 was accused of treason and sentenced to life imprisonment; he was not released from Brandenburg prison until 1945.[8]

Contact between Niekisch and the communists had come about quite naturally since he championed an 'eastern orientated' German policy, in other words collaboration with Russia which, like Germany, had been isolated since the war and which had waived German reparations payments. Ever since 1932 Niekisch had been conspiring with functionaries of the German Communist Party, using as intermediary Dr Josef ('Beppo') Römer, an ex-Free Corps captain who had joined the Communist Party.

After 1933, however, Niekisch's contacts extended even into extreme conservative and nationalist circles.[9] Through his interest in questions concerning the East he came to know Ewald von Kleist-Schmenzin, an ultra-conservative Prussian monarchist landowner and politician, one of the most determined and uncompromising opponents of Hitler; he edited the *Mitteilungsblatt der konservativen Hauptvereinigung* (Information Journal of the Central Conservative Association) which courageously called a spade a spade until banned in 1933 because of an article Fabian von Schlabrendorff had published in it.[10] From March 1933 Kleist invariably visited Niekisch whenever he came to Berlin; they exchanged information and Kleist would express his scorn for *Reichswehr* officers, such as Rundstedt and Blomberg, for their failure to oust Hitler. In a draft of a leaflet Kleist wrote: 'In future the word will be: "As characterless as a German official, as godless as a Protestant minister, as unprincipled as a Prussian officer".'[11]

Ewald von Kleist was due to be shot during the mass murders of 30 June 1934; he had steadfastly refused to fly the swastika flag or give even a penny to the NSDAP – the Nazi district leader had even been reduced to suggesting that at least he might contribute 10 pfennig. He was warned, however, and escaped in time; Niekisch, the left-wing radical, hid him in his Berlin apartment.[12] Here was one of the remarkable but characteristic features of the anti-Hitler resistance.[13] National-Socialism was not simply a party like any other; with its total acceptance of criminality it was an incarnation of evil, so that all those whose minds were attuned to democracy, Christianity, freedom, humanity or even mere legality found themselves forced into alliance. So after Kleist took refuge in Niekisch's apartment on 1 July 1934, political friends of both of them would meet there – 'left-wing' conspirators in one room, 'right-wing' in another. Kleist was executed after 20 July 1944 for his part in the attempted *coup d'état*.

However heroic the resistance offered by these brave men and however great the number who paid for it with their lives, it seldom had any prospect of success. Soon after 30 June 1934 Elard von Oldenburg-Januschau, the old Court Chamberlain, did succeed in making his mark; by virtue of his great age, his total intrepidity and his commanding presence he contrived to push his way past all the guards and penetrate into Hindenburg's bedroom to tell him of the Nazi murders. Hindenburg, however, was already too old and sick to make any attempt to dismiss Hitler. Nevertheless some of those arrested on 30 June were released on Hindenburg's orders.[14]

Many offered resistance simply by refusing to fly the swastika flag on the prescribed days, by suddenly turning into ardent church-goers, or by studiously failing to hear the cry 'Heil Hitler'. Many deliberately refused promotion to avoid having to join the Nazi Party; they concealed Jews and others on the run; if on the judicial bench, they awarded lenient sentences in political cases. Others joined the army to be safe from Nazi importunities or persecution and to escape the *Gestapo*. Journalists and authors wrote on subjects providing an analogy of the existing situation that was obvious to anyone and that enabled them to criticize in indirect, non-judiciable terms. These methods of resistance were aptly termed 'internal emigration'.[15] The more active forms of resistance, aiming at concrete results, had an equally wide range of possibilities and variations.

For instance, people disillusioned by the ideological and organizational rigidity and conformism of the German Communist Party formed a group led by Walter Löwenheim and known as the 'Leninist Organization'.[16] Ever since 1929 Löwenheim had been recruiting into his organization Social-Democratic and Communist Party members who wished to liberate the forces of socialism from their dogmatic immobility. He had to proceed secretly, since he wished to infiltrate his supporters into all socialist organizations and so ultimately control them or at least guide them back on to the true path of socialism. From the outset, therefore, this group inevitably had to work underground.

Löwenheim, however, only realized somewhat late in the day the true significance of the Nazi seizure of power and its concomitant revolution. Not until the *Reichstag* fire and its accompanying wave of arrests was the group (known as 'The O' for short) convinced of the seriousness of the situation.[17]

Many conspiratorial illusions were suddenly destroyed. It was not possible to produce a clandestine effect from within on workers' organizations which no longer existed or which had been banned and broken up. So 'The O' pinned its hopes on some crisis of the regime. It concentrated on information and on 'education', on under-cover agitation in the factories – 'industrial activity'; it attempted to form a 'unity front' with other class-warfare circles, even including those labelled 'bourgeois-democrat'.[18] Forbidden pamphlets were smuggled in – one written by Walter Löwenheim, for instance, entitled *Neu Beginnen* ('Begin afresh'), published in October 1933 by the Social-Democratic Party Committee-in-exile. This was then re-edited in the form of an advertisement booklet and issued in November by 'Graphia' of Carlsbad under the pseudonym 'Miles' and with the camouflage title 'Schopenhauer – On religion'; 5,000 copies made their way into Germany.[19] As a result the 'Leninist Organization' has frequently been called the 'Miles Group' or the 'Begin afresh Group'. In 1934 English, American and French editions of the pamphlet appeared and the resistance group became one of the best known of all in its time. Its reputation abroad was greatly assisted by the fact that its members had remained in Germany and were not *émigrés*.[20]

Nevertheless, although its underground operations were adroit and it worked for a considerable period without losses, this organization came no nearer overthrowing the regime than had the socialists or communists; all had to relearn the conspiratorial trade. In the light of conditions in a totalitarian state even the first prerequisite for a revolution from below, in other words a mass movement, could not be created.[21] The 'Leninist Organization' in fact went so far as to state that formation of a mass movement was possible in the period following the fall of National Socialism, provided that democratic political structures were allowed enough 'elbow room'.[22] Under the prevailing circumstances, however, no mass movement could possibly be created; organization, however efficient, could do nothing to alter this fact.

The great year of arrests and destruction of the communist, Social-Democrat and trade union underground organizations was 1935. For a time a flood of illegal brochures and pamphlets was produced from secret printing presses in Germany or neighbouring countries and distributed, usually with innocent bindings and titles, presenting the contents as a classical drama or cookery book.[23] At this period the *Gestapo* was still only in process of expansion; gradually its methods improved; the informer service and penetration of opposition organizations began to have their effect. Then came the period of mass arrests and mass trials; on one occasion, for instance, 400 Social-Democrats were placed on trial and on another 628 trade unionists; 232 Social-Democrats were tried in Cologne. In 1935 and 1936 fifty-five members of the little 'Begin afresh' group were arrested; the majority were given prison sentences of two to five years. Fate caught up with the remainder in 1938; in 1939 almost all surviving members of 'Begin afresh' were sentenced to long terms of imprisonment and were only released in 1945.[24]

Most other groups had similar experiences. In Mannheim, for instance, when the Social-Democratic Party was banned, Jakob Ott reformed it underground; by distributing illegal newspapers he held together approximately one thousand members; he had no plan, however, for a *coup* or any other action. Another socialist group, formed by Emil Henk, also existed in Mannheim. It looked for ways of overthrowing the regime and maintained contact with other groups in Mannheim, Eberbach, Stuttgart, Frankfurt, Offenbach, Darmstadt, Worms, Landau, and with the Party Committee-in-exile in Paris. Basically, however, it could do no more than inform, advise and pursue general conspiratorial activities.[25] In late summer 1934 this organization was blown when one of its members had a motor-bicycle accident and the propaganda material he was carrying was strewn all over the street. The organization's officers were arrested and, although the leadership was quickly reconstituted, it was broken up again in 1935. By that year the period of large-scale underground activity was over; the *Gestapo* had annihilated the various organizations. From 1936 many German communists and socialists, including Wilhelm Zaisser, Walter Ulbricht, Alfred Kantorowicz, Ludwig Renn and Willy Brandt, saw in the Spanish Civil War an opportunity of fighting Spanish and German fascism; Hitler was supporting Franco with troops and war material, and they regarded fascism as a class warfare phenomenon, not as a nationalist movement. The majority of these volunteers foregathered in the Thälmann Brigade.[26] With Franco's victory in 1938 this incident in the anti-Hitler resistance was over too. Of some 2,000 German survivors from the International Brigades (out of a total of about 5,000) hundreds next saw each other either in the French internment camps or in the hands of the *Gestapo* or later in the French resistance movement; some even escaped to Mexico or San Domingo. So when war broke out in 1939, apart from isolated groups and cells, there was no working-class underground movement in Germany worth mentioning.[27] Such will to resist as remained on the part of numerous communist groups was, at least temporarily, stifled by the Russo-German pact of 23 August 1939.

War, and the crimes instigated by Hitler under cover of it, led to new forms of resistance, self-sacrificing but mostly impotent and hopeless. Even a semi-exhaustive description of this resistance would fill many volumes but certain outstanding instances can at least be quoted as illustrations.

Communist cells and groups in particular felt it their duty to continue anti-war and anti-regime agitation. In many cases they were even prepared to cross the line between treason against the government and treason against their country and to conspire with prisoners of war. One such group was that led by Dr Theodor Neubauer, a former communist deputy in the *Reichstag*. Neubauer spent five-and-a-half years in Buchenwald concentration camp between 1933 and 1939. On his release he immediately resumed his illegal activity; he drafted leaflets and from his base in Jena organized contacts to Berlin, Leipzig, Eisenach, Gotha, Erfurt, Weimar and the Ruhr. He was once more arrested and finally executed in Brandenburg prison on 5 February 1945.[28] Another group, led by Saefkow, Jacob and Bästlein and directed from the Soviet Union, engaged in similar activities. The organization led by Harro Schulze-Boysen and known as 'Red Orchestra' was primarily concerned with espionage.[29] Other groups, such as the one around Reinhold Mewes which cooperated with the former Free-Corps leader Dr Josef Römer, also became convinced by autumn 1941 that it was in the interests of the working classes to aid the struggle of the Soviet Union against National-Socialist Germany and at the same time to prevent an Anglo-French-American occupation of Germany. Römer, whose name is mentioned far less frequently by East German historians than the names of other communist underground fighters, led a resistance group that was perhaps the largest and best-organized of any operating in Germany under communist auspices. The Schlotterbeck brothers and some of their friends formed a smaller but equally ideologically-based organization; it carried on espionage for the Soviet Union – for political reasons, not for money. Their Russian contact man, however, who had arrived by parachute, fell into the hands of the *Gestapo* and was forced to transmit 'play-back' material, in other words false information, over his radio. As a result the group was destroyed. Friedrich Schlotterbeck alone contrived to escape into Switzerland; nine members of his family were executed on 30 November 1944.[30]

One of the many groups resembling each other both in spirit and in action was that of the Scholls (brother and sister) and their friends; in 1942 and 1943 they prepared and distributed leaflets in Munich calling for resistance to the government and the war. Although they realized that their activities could hardly do any significant damage to the regime, they were prepared to sacrifice themselves.[31] Secretly they may have hoped to produce greater results, but primarily they were ready to stake their lives for the cause. Even Marinus van der Lubbe's act of fire-raising (the *Reichstag* fire) should be looked at in this light – as an attempt to rouse the working class and as altruistic self-sacrifice.

Kurt Gerstein should also be counted as a resister. He had close links with the Confessional Church and had twice, the second time in 1938, been sent to a concentration camp for resistance activity on religious grounds; he had also been expelled from the Nazi Party.[32] He was a mine manager and industrialist, well-to-do and deeply religious, and had also studied medicine; he was convinced that, as an individual, he could only exert some effect from inside the machine. Accordingly on 10 March 1941, when he heard of the start of the euthanasia programme, he joined the SS. The improbable happened. In January 1942 Gerstein became Head of the Technical Hygiene Section in SS Headquarters and was commissioned by the RSHA (*Reichssicherheitshauptamt* – Central Security Department) to obtain supplies of prussic acid; he thus gained an insight into the whole fearful extermination system in the concentration camps. He set about using chemical methods to make his consignments of prussic acid harmless; his main activity, however, was the broadcasting of his knowledge wherever he could; he told over one hundred people what he had discovered. In August 1942, after he had personally attended a mass gassing using the somewhat ineffective method of exhaust fumes from a diesel engine, he told a member of the Swedish embassy in Berlin what had happened, asking him to ensure that the news was passed on to London. Gerstein believed that, once the German people knew of this crime, they would put an end to the regime. This hope proved illusory, partly because it was based on an overestimation of 'the people', partly because the news was inadequately disseminated or alternatively, owing to the enormity of the crime, was received with incredulity. Gerstein's special merit, however, was the fact that he deliberately involved himself in crime, accepting responsibility thereby, in order to discover, to broadcast and, if possible, to sabotage the most secret and most appalling processes. In this he was only partially successful.

The killing of alleged incurables was a different matter, since a far smaller number of potential victims was involved than in the 'Final Solution', the term for the liquidation of the Jews. The latter was carried out primarily on Polish territory, whereas the euthanasia programme was pursued in Germany itself and involved direct interference with charitable institutions, almost all closely connected with one of the two main churches. Knowledge of the murder programme ordered by Hitler on 1 September 1939 was therefore widespread and the leading personalities of the ecclesiastical opposition could count on considerable support. Dr Theophil Wurm, Bishop of Württemberg, and Graf von Galen, Bishop of Münster, both called the programme what it was – murder. By means of petitions and courageous public protests they and other church leaders succeeded, by and large, in bringing the operation to a halt by the end of 1941.[33]

If resistance was to be more promising than this, its focus had to be nearer the centre of power, in the higher levels of the *Reichswehr* for instance. Hindenburg had long since been pushed on one side. During the last days of January 1933 rumours of a *putsch* had in fact circulated here and there. It was whispered that the *Reichswehr* intended to use force to prevent the installation of a government with Hitler as Chancellor. In fact Colonel-General Kurt Freiherr von Hammerstein, Commander-in-Chief of the Army, and Lieutenant-General Erich Freiherr von dem Bussche-Ippenburg, Head of the Army Personnel Office, had had a personal interview with Hindenburg on 26 January and had attempted to dissuade the President from appointing Hitler, emphasizing the dangers.[34] During this interview Hindenburg referred to the 'Austrian corporal' whom he would never appoint as Chancellor.[35] On 29

January, however, Hammerstein and Schleicher agreed that there could be no question of anyone other than Hitler as Chancellor, since, as Hammerstein and Schleicher saw it, a Papen-Hugenberg government would have had to rule with the support of only 7% as against 93% of the German people. Nevertheless they only visualized a Hitler government on condition that Schleicher was *Reichswehr* Minister in it. They had no thought of a *putsch* in their minds.[36] Hammerstein was far more concerned to avoid a general strike and civil war, involving the employment of the *Reichswehr* against the Nazis and the political Left. Rumours of a *putsch* involving an alleged proposal to declare a state of emergency and lay hands on the person of the President seem to have stemmed from circles interested in justifying the formation of a Hitler-Papen-Hugenberg government and extracting Hindenburg's agreement to it.[37] Be that as it may, when Hitler was appointed *Reich* Chancellor, the *Reichswehr* took no action.

Very soon after the 'seizure of power', however, people began to wonder how the Hitler government could be overthrown; Dr Heinrich Brüning, the former *Reich* Chancellor, was involved together with Schleicher and Hammerstein.[38] The true nature of the new regime had naturally become obvious soon enough, but no 'counter-action' was taken. A major obstacle was the new *Reichswehr* Minister, Werner von Blomberg; he was naïve, weak and somewhat unrealistic; he was also favourably disposed to the Nazis. So, in July 1933, Hammerstein found himself deprived both of his influence and command authority in the Army.[39] At the end of 1933 he handed in his resignation and on 1 February 1934 was succeeded by General Werner Freiherr von Fritsch.[40]

With Hammerstein retired the conflict between the SA and the *Reichswehr* became increasingly acute and in the spring of 1934 certain people in Papen's entourage were thinking of seizing the opportunity, when the anticipated SA revolt came, to persuade Hindenburg to proclaim a state of emergency.[41] To bring this about Generals von Witzleben, von Bock and von Rundstedt, who were obviously prepared to act, were to use their troops against the SA and Hitler was to be forced to 'go along'. Tension was to be raised to boiling point by a major speech drafted by Edgar J. Jung, the Munich lawyer and 'young conservative', and actually delivered by Papen in Marburg on 17 June 1934; it was in fact an indictment of the whole course of events since January 1933.[42] Hopes centred on Fritsch; Major-General von Schleicher, Hitler's predecessor as Chancellor, considered that Fritsch must 'under all circumstances strike' as soon as Hindenburg died.[43] Fritsch, however, had been utterly opposed to Schleicher's pre-1933 political activity and subsequently stated spontaneously: 'Politics pass me by totally.'[44] He did not adopt this blinkered attitude merely as a matter of duty; it was in line with his character and his lack of comprehension of the criminal nature of the entire Nazi movement, including its *Führer*.

At this time, therefore, before the bloodbath of 30 June 1934 carried out by the SS, no one 'struck', not even the SA leaders, who perhaps had planned to do so. Hitler was the one who struck and he had two generals shot in the process, an action accepted by the *Reichswehr* without noticeable protest.[45] 'The *Reichswehr*' as such possibly had no objection to the murder of Röhm and his SA leaders; it was perhaps glad to see its competing army thus emasculated and the danger of its encroachment on the *Reichswehr* removed – it numbered, after all, well over three million, many of whom now proposed to enter the *Reichswehr* ranks.[46] It is certain, however, that Hammerstein and other senior *Reichswehr* commanders were pleased by the elimination of Röhm and his friends and, at least initially, raised no objection to the methods used. Hammerstein was only 'much affected' when he heard that Schleicher too had been murdered, saying: 'So they are now starting to murder gentlemen as well.'[47] He went to Blomberg, his immediate superior as *Reichswehr* Minister, in order 'through him to bring about some opposition on the part of the *Reichswehr*'. Even at this point, however, no one was really thinking of an attempt at a *coup d'état*. Blomberg 'did nothing'; he could not even be persuaded to adopt a threatening attitude or make a serious protest. This is not surprising since he had prior knowledge of the planned action against the SA and was in agreement with it.[48] Lieutenant-General Walter von Reichenau, Head of the Ministerial Office in the *Reichswehr* Ministry from 1 February 1934, had also been informed beforehand of the planned preventive action against the SA; he placed no more credence than did Blomberg in the story that a *putsch* had been nipped in the bud. Both in fact knew perfectly well that the SA's attempts to arm itself and its readiness to take precautions were no more than defensive reactions to the military measures ordered by Hitler on pretext of a threatened SA revolt.[49] It may even be assumed that both, and particularly Reichenau who was the more adroit, were among the string-pullers working for an aggravation of the tense situation.[50]

In fact, therefore, both Blomberg and Reichenau, and through them the senior officers of the *Reichswehr*, were indirectly involved, and a significant factor, in Hitler's success on 30 June 1934. Blomberg had given his agreement to the arrest of Schleicher and Reichenau drafted the text of the official announcement saying that Schleicher had been shot when resisting arrest.[51]

With hindsight it is easy to reproach the *Reichswehr* leaders for their attitude on 30 June and thereafter. Undoubtedly, as Helmut Krausnick says, the circumstances and the *Reichswehr*'s position must be taken into account in their entirety.[52] Krausnick is equally correct, however, when he says: 'In fact 30 June faced the army leaders for the first time with the stark choice between obedience and acceptance of partial responsibility, between compliance with orders and their conscience.'[53]

General von Fritsch, the Commander-in-Chief of the Army, and his Chief of Staff, Lieutenant-General Ludwig Beck, can hardly have realized beforehand what Hitler's real intentions were.[54] But later – ? The murders lasted two days and it may be taken as certain that Fritsch and Beck were accurately informed. Even taking account of all the circumstances it is difficult to see any satisfactory explanation for the absence of some determined reaction, not only to these arbitrary murders in general, but to the shooting of Major-Generals von Schleicher and von Bredow in particular.

On the afternoon of 30 June Erwin Planck, the former State Secretary of the *Reich* Chancellery, went to Fritsch and urged him to act in view of Blomberg's failure to do so. Others, including Major-General von Witzleben, his Chief of Staff Colonel von Lewinski (alias von Manstein), General Ritter von Leeb and General von Rundstedt, demanded that Blomberg institute a military inquiry. Blomberg, however, declared that an inquiry was impossible and thus matters remained. Krausnick says: 'Not even at this point could people muster the courage to take action of political significance, still less with a political objective, as was called for by the monstrous nature of the proceedings.'[55]

So the 'non-political army' in reality renounced its neutrality and became both a part and a servant of the National-Socialist system of domination. At the same time 30 June 1934 put an end to the potential bourgeois conspiracy against Hitler. Not until 1937–38 did any real insurrectionist movement reconstitute itself.[56]

The way was now open for a typical *coup d'état* by Hitler himself. Only one prerequisite was still lacking – the death of old President von Hindenburg which was expected daily. It occurred on 2 August 1934 when the President died at his country seat in Neudeck. On the previous day the government had passed a law whereby, on Hindenburg's death, the offices of *Reich* President and *Reich* Chancellor were to be combined. So by unconstitutional methods Hitler obtained constitutional authority over the *Reichswehr*.[57] A 'law' had been passed in January enabling the government to 'lay down fresh constitutional legislation'.[58] The *Reichswehr* had been relieved of the threat of the SA, but it was also brought more fully under the control of Hitler and the Nazi Party.

On the very day of Hindenburg's death Hitler took a further step in the consolidation of his authority over the armed forces of the *Reich*. On 2 August he ordered the entire *Reichswehr* to be sworn in afresh, taking an oath not to the people, the country or the constitution but solely to him by name. Under a law promulgated by the Nazis only a few months before (1 December 1933) the oath read: 'I swear by Almighty God this sacred oath: I will at all times loyally and honestly serve my people and my country and, as a brave soldier, will be ready at any time to stake my life for this my oath.'[59] Now, however, the oath ran: 'I swear by Almighty God this sacred oath: I will render unconditional obedience to the *Führer* of the German *Reich* and people, Adolf Hitler, Supreme Commander of the *Wehrmacht*, and, as a brave soldier, I will be ready at any time to stake my life for this oath.'[60] For soldiers, therefore, loyalty to the constitution or the country no longer existed; there was only loyalty to the *'Führer'*. Henceforth the only valid order or channel of command was that approved by the *'Führer'*; this was now the law. The new legislation met with no opposition of any significance, and Hitler had succeeded in releasing the *Reichswehr* from all previous traditional obligations and in attaching it to himself personally.

This new hurriedly organized oath-taking process was more than a mere *coup* by Hitler, analogous to a *coup d'état*, designed to take the *Reichswehr* by surprise as in the Fritsch crisis of 1938; it was also intended as a powerful obstacle to any form of resistance to the deified 'command'. Of course, many of the generals subsequently took refuge behind their oath when asked to cooperate in an attempt to overthrow the regime. In fact they knew perfectly well that such an oath is only valid if it presupposes some moral and political obligation and loyalty on the part of the man to whom it is sworn; they also knew that this man, Hitler, was guilty of a thousandfold contravention of his obligation to the German people and a thousandfold misuse of his followers pledged to him by oath. For many others, however, this oath constituted a real problem; they still felt themselves bound by it, even when the immorality and illegality of the whole system had long since become clear. Many maintained that its content must be valid, since the form existed and persisted. Form was given precedence over meaning, the meaning being thereby destroyed. Recipients of orders, however, were not permitted to harbour such thoughts; they must think solely on the lines of the 'leadership'.

Having thus laid hands on all important positions of power in the *Reich* (he did not observe till later that the army was unwilling to be his complete tool and he dealt with this situation by removing its Commander-in-Chief), Hitler was able to announce complacently that the National-Socialist revolution was at an end. In a proclamation read by *Gauleiter* Adolf Wagner at the Party Rally in Nuremberg on 5 September 1934 it was stated: 'The violent phase of the National-Socialist revolution is now at an end. As a revolution it has fully accomplished all that could be hoped from it.'[61] All subsequent difficulties could be dealt with as problems concerning personalities.

The expected harmony between Party and *Reichswehr*, however, did not materialize. Hitler had promised the *Reichswehr* that it would be the nation's sole bearer of arms, but from and immediately after 30 June 1934 the SS was further expanded; friction continued between the *Reichswehr* on one side and the Party and SA on the other. Finally the realization that 30 June 1934 had not been an isolated instance of revolutionary over-enthusiasm but could be repeated at any moment helped to clarify the minds of many soldiers. A further factor was the increasingly obvious trend towards a purposeless war which, in the light of Germany's foreign policy successes, was clearly 'unnecessary'.

It took four years, 1934 to 1938, before the true conscientious opponents of Nazism had emerged from the ranks of the fellow-travellers, the indifferent and the undecided. In the administration, in the judiciary, in the teaching profession, in the churches, in factories and offices, in the *Reichswehr*, among the educated, among artists and authors, in other words in all conceivable walks of life, the like-minded formed groups and circles; gradually they learnt not to disclose their views at once but nevertheless to be recognizable to other opponents of the regime. All this required time and the process occupied the years preceding 1938. Greater activity on the part of all these various groupings could obviously only be expected if the impulse was strong enough. The general atmosphere of oppression did not suffice; the anti-Jewish atrocities of November 1938 and Hitler's aggressive war policy during the Sudeten crisis were required to evoke more intensive efforts to overthrow the regime. In addition to the misgivings in military circles already mentioned, however, a number of sincere attempts were made prior to 1938.

Among these must be counted the activities of Edgar J. Jung, the Munich lawyer already referred to; he is usually described as a member of the 'Young Conservatives' group and even before 1933 was an uncompromising opponent of Nazism.[62] After Hitler's appointment as Chancellor he seized every conceivable opportunity to bring about the fall of the regime. In November 1933, together with Herbert von Bose, Vice-Chancellor von Papen's Press Officer, he proposed to use Papen's and Hindenburg's influence to put forward eighty non-Nazi candidates for the next *Reichstag*, the object being to undermine the position of the National-Socialists. When this attempt failed he made feverish attempts to concentrate and coordinate various opposition circles.[63] Jung is generally thought to have been the principal author of the famous speech made by Papen in the University of Marburg on 17 June 1934; it was intended as the signal for a rising and general upheaval, hopes being centred on Hindenburg, Papen and the *Reichswehr*.[64]

In his speech Papen pleaded for religious freedom, rejecting any 'unnatural totalitarian aspirations' in the field of religion; he warned against the use of force and regimentation of the life of the people outside the political sphere, in other words against any attempt to set up a totalitarian state.[65] This warning was not lost on Hitler; publication of the speech was banned, but a number of clandestine copies circulated and it did in fact create a sensation both at home and abroad.[66] Papen protested and offered his resignation, but then allowed himself to be pacified by Hitler.

A few days later there followed the murders of 30 June, 1 and 2 July. Admittedly the SA had been eliminated as a possible competitor of the *Reichswehr*; admittedly violent social upheaval on the lines of Röhm's 'second revolution' had been prevented.[67] At the same time, however, it had been made plain in unmistakable terms to every German what fate awaited him, should he in any way oppose the 'National-Socialist revival'. The warning was clear; in addition to the SA leaders one hundred or more actual and potential oppositionists had been shot, including Jung and Bose. Papen himself was also possibly due to be murdered.[68] Apart from his speech, however, he had not been willing to take part in plans for a *coup*[69] and he came to terms with the Nazis once more. When Jung was arrested on 25 June, he had again protested and again allowed himself to be pacified;[70] when Jung and Bose were murdered, he protested yet again, but nevertheless went off to Vienna as Hitler's special representative. Even in 1938, when Freiherr von Ketteler, his personal assistant, was murdered by the *Gestapo*, he once more allowed himself to be pacified (if indeed he had ever been indignant) and settled with his *Führer* for the post of Ambassador in Ankara.[71] From a man such as this it was clearly futile to expect opposition or even any display of character when confronted with Hitler. Jung and Bose were the victims of their illusions about Papen.

Despite the brutally naked totalitarian threat to which, as a result of these murders, all those in any way displeased with the ruling regime were exposed, many continued to work against the system and the government. In the following year, on 16 April 1935, the poet Ernst Wiechert made a speech against government policy in the Great Hall of Munich University; he protested against the government's attitude to the visual and other arts, against production of poets in 'Poets' Training Camps', which he characterized as equivalent to 'spiritual murder', and against politically-motivated art criticism; he pleaded for truth, freedom, the law, compassion, love and respect. Youth, he said, should not allow itself to be seduced into silence when its conscience commanded it to speak; nothing was more cor-rosive of the essence of man or of a people than pusillanimity.[72] Wiechert was taken forthwith to Dachau concentration camp.

Eight years later, in 1943 the Scholls (brother and sister), Professor Huber and their friends met their deaths for these same ideals. In the mid-1930s, however, the voices raised were primarily those of the older generation. Ernst Niekisch was still active. He was in touch with Otto Strasser, who was one of Hitler's most dangerous adversaries in the 1930s; working from Vienna, Strasser directed a 'Black Front' with adherents inside Germany; primarily, however, he was trying to sabotage Hitler's policy from outside.[73] Rudolf Pechel refers to a 'Markwitz Circle', composed primarily of Social-Democrats, which distributed forbidden literature and assisted in escapes by opponents of the regime threatened with arrest. The entire circle was arrested by the *Gestapo* in May 1935 after an informer had infiltrated himself into its courier service. Some of its members were done to death, others escaped or succeeded in ob-taining release by means of adroit defence before a court. One of these was Dr Mischler, who was arrested but acquitted owing to lack of evidence; he was expelled and emigrated to Prague, where he was again arrested in 1938; once more he was acquitted but was nevertheless confined in a concentration camp until 1942. No sooner was he released than, via the Social-Democratic journalist Theodor Haubach, he made contact with Wilhelm Leuschner and so eventually was one of those involved in the conspiracy of 20 July 1944.[74]

Another group was led by Dr Joseph ('Beppo') Römer, a First World War warrior and commander of the Free Corps 'Oberland'.[75] This man's activities are to some extent, and very understandably, obscure; only a few details are known. Römer was arrested on several occasions, the first time in 1933 and then again after 30 June 1934 when he was held in Dachau concentration camp.[76] On his release in July 1939, which he owed to his regimental fellow-officer General Robert Ritter von Greim, his thoughts immediately turned once more to a *coup* and attempted assassination.[77] Römer was finally arrested on 4 February 1942 and executed on 25 September.[78]

The overlapping which occurred both before and during the war between the Römer group and other resistance organizations was almost incredible. Some 150 other people were involved in Römer's trial before the People's Court, the majority belonging to communist or other working-class-based groups.[79] The most important was that run in the Osram Works by Robert Uhrig, a Berlin worker; it was known as the 'Robby Group'. Uhrig had been expecting war since 1938, and he had prepared his group for communist propaganda activity and for espionage for the Soviet Union through conspiratorial methods.[80] From the summer of 1941 his group was active as a regular part of the war organization of Soviet military intelligence. This involved the group not only in the gathering of military and war-production information, but also in infiltration preparatory to forming governmental structures that were to cooperate closely with the Soviet Union after the defeat or collapse of Hitler's regime.[81] Römer also worked towards this end. With this purpose in mind, he resumed his connections with his friends of the former Free Corps 'Oberland', many of whom favoured national-bolshevist tendencies. Römer also told his communist friends of his good connections with *Wehrmacht* circles, and early in the summer of 1941 he impressed Willy Sachse by his correct prediction of Hitler's attack on the USSR.[82] The 'Robby Group' eventually combined with the Römer circle and another workers' group led by Walter Budeus, an engine fitter; it was broken up by the *Gestapo* in 1942 and 1943 after being infiltrated by informers. Its remnants joined the communist group under Anton Saefkow, Franz Jacob and Bernhard Bästlein, which was directed from the Soviet Union.[83]

Römer was also in contact with a group in the Foreign Ministry, with an industrialist, with the famous 'Solf Circle' and, from 1941, with leading army circles.[84] These people included Nikolaus Christoph von Halem, a businessman and industrialist, who had been in touch with Niekisch via Schlabrendorff even before 1937; he was able to obtain many foreign contacts for the resistance movement and was also largely responsible for turning Josef Wagner, the *Gauleiter* of Silesia, against Hitler.[85] Far to the Right a group had formed around the former industrial entrepreneur, leader of the Party of the Radical Middle Class, and editor, since 1930, of the weekly *Die Parole der radikalen Staats- und Wirtschaftsreform*, Dr Helmuth Mylius. The group was joined by members of *Jungdeutscher Orden, Schwarze Front, Stahlhelm*, the group of the former SA leader Walther Stennes, by one of the murderers of Rosa Luxemburg and Karl Liebknecht, First Lieutenant von Rittgen, and by Captain Ehrhardt. They all agreed that Hitler must go. Ehrhardt and Mylius arranged in 1935 to infiltrate former members of *Brigade Ehrhardt* into the SS and then to organize a *putsch*. Approximately 160 men were thus organized and armed, and information was collected on Hitler's habits and on conditions in the *Reich* Chancellery. But the plan to arrest or assassinate Hitler was never carried out, mainly because the loyalty of the infiltrators seemed dubious to Mylius, and because they were in turn infiltrated by *Gestapo* informers. A friend of Mylius, Oskar von Arnim, was arrested and sentenced to a term in a penitentiary. Mylius himself escaped arrest only narrowly; when the war broke out, he managed to 'emigrate' into the Army, with Manstein's assistance, and ended up as Quartermaster II to General Busch in the rank of a Major on the reserve.

Also far to the Right there were groups of the *Schwarze Reichswehr* and of the *Stahlhelm* such as the *Stahlhelm* University group in Königsberg led by Arnold Bistrick. Bistrick was arrested in 1935 and afterwards only managed to turn over part of his group to Major Wilhelm Heinz in 1938. Heinz had a special plan for the assassination of Hitler during the Sudeten crisis. Bistrick's group also had connections with Dr Goerdeler, who later, in 1943 and together with Count Schwerin von Schwanenfeld, helped Bistrick to join the *Abwehr* regiment 'Brandenburg' which was to be used in the occupation of Berlin during a planned *coup*. This became impossible when most of the regiment was sent into action against the Yugoslav guerrillas early in 1944.

Römer also had contacts with Field Marshal von Bock, Adam von Trott zu Solz, Karl Ludwig Freiherr von und zu Guttenberg; he was later in touch with Catholic circles, Justus Delbrück and during the war, via Schlabrendorff, with the group in Headquarters Army Group Centre.[86] During the war Halem worked in the Ballestrem coal concern in Upper Silesia and was able to give Römer cover in the firm's Berlin office.[87] Through Gertrud von Heimerdinger Römer was also in touch with the Headquarters of the Commandant of Berlin, through which he obtained information on Hitler's travels and movements in 1939 and 1940. His source was Lieutenant-Colonel Holm Erttel, aide to the Commandant, Lieutenant-General Ernst Seifert.[88]

Equally, through Gertrud von Heimerdinger, Römer had a link with the Foreign Ministry. His contacts here included Dr Richard Kuenzer, a Counsellor (*Legationsrat*), who was arrested after 20 July 1944 and murdered by the SS in April 1945.[89] Through Kuenzer the links ran to Albrecht Graf von Bernstorff, a retired Senior Counsellor (*Botschaftsrat*), murdered at the same time as Kuenzer, and to the 'Solf Circle'.[90] Bernstorff was one of the most courageous opponents of Hitler; he concentrated mainly on helping émigrés and Jews to escape and saving their belongings. For this purpose after 1933 he joined an ex-Jewish bank, A. E. Wassermann.[91]

The 'Solf Circle' consisted of a group of like-minded people who simply wished to oppose and counter the oppression, persecution, humiliation and degradation of human beings by the regime. It included Halem, Graf von Bernstorff, Kuenzer, Fanny von Kurowsky, Irmgard Zarden, Dr Herbert Mumm von Schwarzenstein (retired Legation Counsellor), Dr Otto Kiep (Minister in the Foreign Service), Dr Hilger van Scherpenberg (Legation Counsellor) and Elisabeth von Thadden. They used to meet in the house of Frau Hanna Solf, widow of Dr Wilhelm Solf who had been German Ambassador in Tokyo and had died in 1936. They were all arrested in 1944, some as having been present at a tea party given by Fräulein von Thadden on 10 September 1943 when certain statements hostile to the regime had been made, some merely because they were members of the circle. Certain of them were subsequently executed, simply because they had stood up for humanity.[92] Owing to continual postponement of proceedings against them Frau Solf, her daughter Lagi Gräfin von Ballestrem, Dr van Scherpenberg (Schacht's son-in-law) and Irmgard Zarden survived the war; Fräulein von Thadden, Kiep, Mumm and Halem were executed; Kuenzer, Bernstorff and Guttenberg were murdered by the SS.[93] Helped by a recommendation given in all good faith, a *Gestapo* spy, presenting himself as Dr Reckzeh of the Berlin Charité, had wormed his way into the tea party.[94] From this circle, which was in no way really subversive, links ran to the remaining opponents of Nazism in the Foreign Ministry and to other centres of power in the Third *Reich.*

Kiep, who was a Major on the reserve, was Foreign Policy Desk Officer in OKW (*Oberkommando der Wehrmacht* – High Command of the Armed Forces) from 1939.[95] He was therefore one of the most important links to the Foreign Ministry and the resistance existing there. It included Ernst Freiherr von Weizsäcker, the State Secretary (Permanent Secretary) and Ambassador Ulrich von Hassell, together with Dr Fritz von Twardowski, Drs Theo and Erich Kordt, Dr Hasso von Etzdorf, Bernhard von Bülow and Dr Paul Schmidt.[96] Others were Dr Eugen Gerstenmaier, Georg Federer, Gottfried von Nostitz, Albrecht von Kessel, Hans-Bernd von Haeften and Adam von Trott zu Solz – even this by no means completes the list. Further contacts led to the so-called 'Kreisau Circle' which had been in existence, at least as a social group, since 1937; it included Helmuth James Graf von Moltke, Peter Graf Yorck von Wartenburg, Horst von Einsiedel, Carl Dietrich von Trotha, Adolf Reichwein, Hans Peters, Hans Lukaschek, Carlo Mierendorff, Theodor Steltzer, Adam von Trott zu Solz, Hans-Bernd von Haeften, Harald Poelchau, the Jesuit Fathers Augustin Rösch, Alfred Delp and Lothar König, and Theo Haubach, Eugen Gerstenmaier, Paulus von Husen, Julius Leber, Hans Schönfeld and many others on a less intimate and permanent basis.[97] There were further cross-connections to many socialists and trade unionists.

The name of Albrecht Haushofer is also coupled with that of the Foreign Ministry; being in close contact with Rudolf Hess, Hitler's 'Deputy', he was able to alleviate or stop many things.[98] He was a conservative, in many respects more closely allied to the group centred on Popitz and Langbehn; via his pupil Horst Heilmann he was in contact with 'Red Orchestra', a primarily communist-orientated group which had been built up as a Soviet wartime intelligence service under Harro Schulze-Boysen, a Lieutenant in the Ministry of Aviation, and Dr Arvid Harnack, a senior civil servant in the Ministry of Economics. It went into action on the outbreak of war with Russia in June 1941 and by the time it was destroyed in 1942 included numerous groups and cells scattered all over Western Europe. This organization passed its intelligence to Russia by radio; its finds included Hitler's decision to pursue the offensive in Southern Russia in the spring of 1942.[99]

It is not possible to quote all the names but it is clear that, starting in the second half of the 1930s, a complex and widespread conspiracy was gathering.

Whether their names have been quoted or not, all these people 'did' something to sabotage the government and assist in bringing about the fall of the regime. It must also be remembered that many of the subsequent participants in the various plots spent years in prisons or concentration camps – as representatives of those still at large, so to speak. Between 1933 and June 1934 Wilhelm Leuschner was detained for months either by the police or in a concentration camp; his last place of confinement was Börgermoor concentration camp. Immediately on his release he began to work with Jakob Kaiser, the former leader of the Christian trade unions. Their object was to remove Hitler and then form a united trade union, thus eliminating the cleavage between the Marxist and Christian trade unions. Max Habermann, leader of the German White-collar Workers Union, joined them and together they drafted memoranda in 1936 and 1937 addressed to General von Fritsch stressing the degrading and brutal treatment meted out to workers and Jews. Leuschner was executed on 29 September 1944 as a participant in the 20 July plot and died with the call 'Unity' on his lips. Habermann was also executed. Kaiser, who became the focus of many opposition circles and one of Goerdeler's most valuable partners, succeeded in hiding in Berlin after 20 July. He played an important political role in 1945 in connection with the formation of the Christian-Democratic Union and subsequently in discussion with the Russian and their German satellites, finally becoming Federal Minister for All-German Questions.[100]

Carlo Mierendorff was arrested in 1933 and then held in a concentration camp until 1938.[101] Theodor Haubach was arrested time and again between 1933 and 1939 and spent two years in Esterwegen concentration camp.[102] Dr Julius Leber, the former Social-Democrat *Reichstag* deputy, was arrested, ill-treated and released; then, on 23 March 1933, he was once more arrested at the entrance to the *Reichstag* and handcuffed on the spot.[103] He spent many miserable years in prisons or concentration camps between 1933 and 1937.

'Out in the open', however, various groups and individuals such as those referred to above did everything possible to undermine the Nazi tyranny. Pechel refers to a 'Stuermer Group' under Dr Paul Joseph Stuermer, which was active against Hitler from 1932, was then in close touch with the circles centred on Edgar Jung and Dr Römer, and was even an accessory to their plans for an assassination. The group included members of the *Stahlhelm*, a university professor, a Jesuit Father, a Social-Democrat and a number of officers; it had connections in southern Germany where its contacts were Dr Arnulf Klett, Theodor Bäuerle, a government architect named Albrecht Fischer, and the industrialist Robert Bosch.[104]

Admittedly in many cases these people did no more than 'merely' express their abhorrence of the regime and talk about ways and means of dealing with it. According to their rulers, however, even this was tantamount to conspiracy; under the notorious 'Treachery Law' it was a punishable offence, meriting even the death sentence.[105] To understand the courage required, one must always bear in mind what it meant to live under a dictatorship, where the individual had no rights in practice and lived permanently under threat of mental and physical ill-treatment, officially sanctioned and practised, of blackmail, loss of liberty and livelihood and an agonizing death. It is of course unreasonable today to require every opponent of the regime and of Nazism to have been a potential fanatical assassin, if he is to be accepted as a member of the opposition. Only a few possess the capability to translate convictions into action of such intensity. Finally, although before 1938 there were many of the conspirators who regarded the physical elimination of Hitler as the only effective solution, the majority still hoped to bring about his fall by less violent methods, by gradual erosion of the Nazi tyranny, by blunting its edge or stealthily drawing its teeth. Slowly, however, a single colossal danger began to loom – war. So the forces of the resistance became increasingly concentrated on preventing the threatened war and later on ending it. Naturally, therefore, in the first instance those anti-Nazis active in the field of foreign policy played the most important role. Even before the outbreak of war, however, the military element could not long remain aloof from developments.

3 Top-Level Crisis

In 1937 far-reaching changes were under way in Germany, and in the succeeding years they were destined to convulse the world. Hitler's single-minded determination to go to war can be proved with convincing clarity from his own utterances between 1920 and 1945.[1] The important point here is that towards the end of 1937 Hitler made concrete statements showing that he was set on a course of aggressive and violent foreign policy; he actually laid down the stages leading to war; he set the immediate objectives and the methods to be employed to attain them, and these, as he himself explicitly emphasized, led inevitably to war.

On 5 November 1937 Hitler held a conference with the senior *Wehrmacht* leaders in the *Reich* Chancellery; it lasted from 4.15 to 8.30 p.m.; Freiherr von Neurath, the Foreign Minister, was also present. Of the military those present were Field Marshal von Blomberg, Minister of War, and the Commanders-in-Chief of the Army, Navy and Air Force, Colonel-General Werner Freiherr von Fritsch, Admiral Erich Raeder and Colonel-General Hermann Göring; in addition Colonel Friedrich Hossbach, the '*Führer*'s and Chancellor's *Wehrmacht* Aide', who was also head of the Coordinating Section (Personnel Branch) of the Army General Staff, was there. During the meeting Colonel Hossbach had made notes and these he reduced to writing five days later; they were incorporated in the War Ministry files.[2] During his first five years in office it had not been Hitler's habit to expatiate on his day-dreams or fantastic ideas in front of his military entourage or even in personal interviews with Commanders-in-Chief of the Services. On military matters he had shown great reticence when faced with experts. In conferences or discussions he had only rarely expressed his own views and had generally confined himself to listening and giving more or less silent agreement.[3] Up to 1937 he had seldom taken important decisions on military matters without previous discussion with his advisers. Now, however, he had summoned the most senior *Wehrmacht* leaders in order to tell them that he would shortly be leading the German *Reich* into war.

The German people's *Lebensraum*, Hitler said, was too small; in certain important aspects, particularly that of food, self-sufficiency could not be achieved. The German *Lebensraum* must consequently be expanded and this was best done 'in areas immediately contiguous to the *Reich* in Europe and not overseas'. This expansion of territory could only be achieved by 'breaking resistance'; since untenanted areas did not exist, the attacker would always be confronted by those in possession. Such intentions would be opposed by Britain and France; a moment for action must therefore be chosen when Britain and France would be prevented from intervening by other – internal or external – difficulties. In no case, however, should one wait longer than until about 1943 to 1945 since thereafter the potential enemies would have perceived German intentions and would also have armed themselves to resist. If one could be ready by about 1943, Austria and Czechoslovakia must be eliminated with extreme rapidity in order then to be able to face the most dangerous enemy, France, without the flanks being threatened. Should France, however, be paralyzed by something like a civil war, the situation must be exploited at any time in order to 'strike against Czechoslovakia'. It was naturally not possible to say with any certainty how the other powers – particularly Poland, Russia and Britain – would react to such action on the part of Germany. Hitler tried to suggest, however, that they would not intervene before Germany was ready to strike them down also.

According to Hossbach's minutes the reaction of the Commanders-in-Chief to Hitler's disquisition was antipathetic and cold. Blomberg and Fritsch stressed that Britain and France should not be turned into enemies of the *Reich* since, at this point, Germany was in no position to deal with them, not even with France alone; they also emphasized the strength of the Czech fortifications. Hitler countered these objections by expressing his conviction that Britain would not intervene, also with the comment that he did not anticipate tension increasing before about summer 1938. The argument, Hossbach recalls, was 'at times very sharp', primarily between Blomberg and Fritsch on one side and Göring on the other; Hitler listened attentively and was visibly impressed. He saw that 'instead of being met with acclamation and agreement, his political ideas encountered sober, factual objections. He also now knew full well that the two generals were opposed to any warlike development instigated from our side.'[4] No one, however, refused to implement Hitler's plans; no one characterized them as unlawful or criminal. No doubt the soldiers felt that they were not called upon to express an opinion on such matters.[5]

On at least two subsequent occasions Hitler revealed his plans for assaults on Germany's neighbours to a similar, but even larger, military assemblage – on 23 May 1939 in the new *Reich* Chancellery, Berlin, and on 22 August 1939 in the 'Berghof' near Berchtesgaden.[6] He was as explicit as on 5 November 1937. On 23 May 1939, for instance, sentences such as these were to be heard: 'Further successes can no longer be won without bloodshed.' 'It is not Danzig that is at stake. For us it is a matter of expanding our *Lebensraum* in the east.' 'No stock can be taken of declarations of neutrality.' 'Everybody's armed forces or government must strive for a short war. The leadership of the state must, however, also prepare itself for a war of ten to fifteen years' duration.' 'We shall not be forced into a war but we shall not be able to avoid it.' And on 22 August: 'A showdown which one cannot be sure of postponing for four to five years, had better take place now.' 'The moment is now favourable for a

solution [of the Polish Question], so strike!' 'Object: Destruction of Poland . . .
Start: Method a matter of indifference. The victor will not be questioned
afterwards whether his reasons were just. What matters is not to have right on
our side, but simply to win.' 'Execution: Harsh and ruthless! Close your
hearts to pity!' In face of such monstrous self-revelations no objection was
raised, still less were resignations offered or compliance refused.

Apart from the audiences at these conferences only a few knew of the ideas
and intentions revealed by Hitler. Considering it to be his duty, however,
Colonel Hossbach had shown his memorandum on the meeting of 5
November 1937 to Colonel-General Ludwig Beck, Chief of Staff of the Army,
and had also reported verbally on the course of the discussion. Hossbach
records that the effect of his report on Beck was shattering.[7] Beck followed his
usual habit on such occasions; he seized his pen and wrote to clarify his
thoughts. On 12 November he noted that Germany did in fact have a
territorial problem, particularly from the strategic point of view; 'minor
changes' seemed possible, certain revisions of the Treaty of Versailles, for instance; for the sake of these changes, however, 'the homogeneity of the German people, of the German racial core, must not be jeopardized afresh'.[8]
Looking at the situation realistically, Beck then demolished Hitler's reasons
and arguments, saying that his conclusion regarding the necessity of solving
the German territorial problem by 1943 to 1945 at the latest was 'shattering in
its lack of sound reasoning'; France would always have adequate defensive
forces facing Germany; from the point of view of food imports, the economy,
the military and the political situation Germany's position would not be
noticeably improved by the incorporation of Austria or Czechoslovakia.
Then: 'The expediency of dealing with the Czech problem (possibly also the
Austrian) when opportunity offers, of planning therefore and making such
preparations as may be possible is not contested'; but a more thorough and
comprehensive examination must be made of the conditions giving rise to
such an opportunity. In Beck's view as given above, however, such 'conditions' would not obtain. As early as 3 May 1935 he had written to Fritsch
offering to resign should preparations be made for an offensive war against
Czechoslovakia.[9]

Meanwhile the fall both of Blomberg and of Fritsch was being engineered; it
was caused primarily by their negative attitude to Hitler's disquisition of 5
November 1937.[10] Intrigues against Fritsch had long been in progress, as he
observed in a memorandum dated 1 February 1938, looking back over just
four years in office as successor to Colonel-General Freiherr von
Hammerstein.[11] Göring's ambition to become Commander-in-Chief of the
Wehrmacht was well known.[12] The War Minister (Blomberg) had too independent a position, liable to impede Hitler's progress; moreover he had just
raised objections to Hitler's policy. Hitler subsequently made an oblique
reference to the reason for his action:[13] a political leader, he said, could not do
with a Commander-in-Chief who raised not only military but also political
objections to all proposals and so failed to serve the leaders of the State.[14]

Both an occasion and an opportunity to replace by more pliable men the military leaders who had proved so sceptical about Hitler's plans were soon available. During the funeral ceremonies for General Ludendorff on 22 December 1937 Blomberg asked Hitler casually for his permission to marry. Hitler gave his agreement and, together with Göring, appeared as a witness at the wedding on 12 January 1938. Simultaneously, however, rumours began to circulate and eventually documents were found: Eva Gruhn, now the wife of Field Marshal von Blomberg, had a disreputable past; she had been a prostitute and a model for lewd photographs; she was known to the vice squad.[15] Göring played a particularly shady role in this affair; knowing the facts and fully aware of the probable consequences, he had done his utmost to bring about Blomberg's marriage.[16] Immediately after the wedding rumours about Blomberg's wife were circulating in *Wehrmacht* circles; mysterious telephone calls to the *Wehrmacht* Adjutant's Office made action essential; Blomberg himself sought an audience with Hitler. The dictator pretended to be disillusioned and to feel that he had been duped. Perhaps he actually had; in any case he acted accordingly. Blomberg had to go and here was an opportunity to remove Fritsch at the same time.

Hitler may merely have seized his moment and used the refurbished evidence against Fritsch provided by Göring and Himmler as a handy instrument – he had known about it for some time since it was already two years old and, when first produced, he had himself given orders for its destruction.[17] It is not possible to say how far he had simply been searching for an occasion of this nature. False evidence was now to prove that Fritsch was a homosexual and therefore unacceptable as head of the Army or as a candidate for the succession to Blomberg.

The 'witness' against Fritsch was a professional criminal drop-out named Otto Schmidt. He was head of a group of blackmailers and had made his living for years by starting affairs with homosexuals so that he could blackmail them later. On 28 December 1936 he had been sentenced to seven years imprisonment and ten years loss of civil rights for fourteen cases of blackmail and nine cases of contravention of paragraph 175 of the legal code (on homosexuality). He was finally executed in the summer of 1942 while an inmate of Sachsenhausen concentration camp; on 29 July 1942, at the end of a report on Schmidt, Himmler wrote to Göring: 'I request your agreement, dear *Reich* Marshal, that I should submit Schmidt's case to the *Führer* for his authorization to execute'; Göring's marginal comment was : 'Ought to have been shot *long* ago'.[18] Hitler's early relationships with Röhm, whose homosexuality was notorious long before 1934, his nomination of Dr Walter Funk, another notorious homosexual, as *Reich* Minister of Economics on 5 February 1938 (no less), his indifference when the first accusations against Fritsch were made and his order at that time for the destruction of the files – all this was clear proof that Hitler was quite unmoved by the presence or absence of homosexuals among his adherents.[19] Now, however, he had a comparatively convenient opportunity to rid himself, admittedly by the use of extremely underhand methods to which he was not averse, of two subordinates who were primarily desirous of serving their country rather than him; Hitler knew that he had no hope of overcoming Fritsch's opposition to his plans.[20] Moreover he also had an opportunity, which he seized at once, of appointing as successor to the Ministry of War not some more faithful follower but himself and thus very considerably increasing and consolidating his control over the military. During the course of 1938 and 1939 certain successes in the exercise of military command confirmed Hitler in his growing conviction that he knew how to use the armed forces as an instrument of power as well as, if not better than, the experts.

So, on 4 February 1938, the great changing of the guard took place. Blomberg and Fritsch were relieved of their posts, in both cases 'for health reasons'; the *Reich* War Ministry was in effect turned into the *Oberkommando der Wehrmacht* (OKW) which henceforth served as Hitler's military staff under the 'Chief of OKW' who ranked as a Minister of the *Reich*. Hitler himself took over supreme command of the entire *Wehrmacht*; as Commander-in-Chief of the Army he nominated General Walther von Brauchitsch, who was promoted Colonel-General. Göring, already a Colonel-General and Commander-in-Chief of the *Luftwaffe*, was promoted Field Marshal. General Wilhelm Keitel became Chief of OKW.[21] During February, March and April changes were made in more than forty senior command positions; some fourteen generals found themselves summarily retired.[22] In this way the monstrosity of the proceedings was largely camouflaged. Finally, a number of German ambassadors were recalled – Ribbentrop from London, Hassell from Rome, Dirksen from Tokyo and Papen from Vienna. Ribbentrop was appointed Foreign Minister in succession to Freiherr von Neurath who was relieved of his office. This change of Foreign Minister was a particularly striking illustration of the switch from willing assistants to sheer minions; in this sphere Hitler knew his personalities better than he did in the military.

It will rightly be asked why the Army accepted almost without comment the insult administered to its Commander-in-Chief. The main essential for any counter-action was absent, however – the necessary unanimity in the officer corps.[23] Its numbers had increased enormously since 1933; in 1932 there had been forty-four officers of the rank of major-general and upwards; in 1938 (1 October) there were 275, not counting 22 medical and 8 veterinary officers of general's rank. By May 1943 there were over a thousand officers of general's rank.[24] Only one method of opposition seemed possible, the simultaneous resignation of all generals – there was no other legal method; but the necessary conditions simply were not present; the officer corps had not the requisite internal solidarity. Without unanimity, without the participation of at least the majority of senior officers, any measure of protest would have been ineffective and might even have represented a form of mutiny. Ever since the end of the First World War naval officers had been suffering from a sort of trauma; the *Luftwaffe* had been built up by Göring and under the Nazi regime; it was unlikely, therefore, that any significant number of naval or Air Force officers would have joined those of the Army.[25] All this presupposes that the officer corps, and particularly that of the Army, was adequately informed of these happenings, of the accusations made against its Commander-in-Chief and of the scurvy treatment meted out to him. There was, however, an almost complete lack of such information; even senior officers and their staffs had to rely on supposition and such occasional news or rumour as filtered through.[26] By 18 March 1938, when a Court of Honour under the presidency of Göring had pronounced on Fritsch's complete innocence and the mendacity of the evidence against him, Austria had been occupied and an ostensibly major success had therefore been scored with the assistance of the *Wehrmacht*. How, at such a moment, could anyone mutiny against his supreme warlord, to whom moreover he had sworn a personal oath? Concepts of honour, loyalty and morality were blurred and ambiguous, corrupted by an unscrupulous but successful and scintillating government.

Fritsch himself thought long and hard how he might defend himself – in the interests of the Army and the honour both of the officer corps and of himself. But against whom was he, perhaps in concert with senior officers of the Army, to take action? Göring and Himmler worked in the background and were unassailable so long as Hitler covered them and refused to make up his mind. It was, of course, both possible and conceivable that Hitler would realize the absurdity of the case against Fritsch, with its elementary slovenly emendations.[27] But on his own admission to Hossbach on 25 January 1938 he had long known about the file. The point was not whether he did or did not believe Göring, Himmler and the documents, but whether he should be so ready to believe them just at this moment – the opportunity to be rid of a tiresome Army Commander-in-Chief being a favourable one. Fritsch probably felt this but was unable fully to appreciate it. He believed in the *Führer* and his sincerity – 'until this case', as he put it.[28] This was not mere well-bred reticence; it was naïveté. Only considerably later did he realize that Hitler had been consciously and deliberately determined to remove him, using the most despicable methods. Even so, however, the foreboding remained that the use of force to defend his honour and that of the Army might lead to bloodshed and civil war – and that Fritsch did not want.[29] It was a long time before Fritsch really grasped Hitler's villainy, although the latter's refusal to accept his word of honour as even provisional proof of his innocence against a statement by the criminal Schmidt should have been warning enough; it was even longer before he realized that in this crisis his personal fate was largely identical with that of the Army and of Germany. He did realize this at the end of February but then it was too late.

On 13 June 1938, on Barth airfield near Stralsund, Hitler addressed the same assemblage of officers to which he had revealed Fritsch's 'shortcomings' on 4 February. Now he declared Fritsch rehabilitated and both Fritsch and himself to have been victims of a tragic error. Naturally, he said, he could not reinstate Fritsch since he, Hitler, could not expect Fritsch to have further confidence in him; moreover as *Führer* he could not recant before the nation.[30] On 15 June, therefore, Fritsch was simply nominated 'Chief' of No. 12 Artillery Regiment.[31] In September 1939 he took his regiment to Poland, where he was killed in action.[32]

In certain places efforts were indeed made to set in motion some counter-action to the intrigue against Fritsch, but those principally involved were not prepared to act with the necessary energy. Admittedly Fritsch did challenge Himmler, who was suspected of being the main string-puller behind the whole dirty business, to a duel with pistols but the challenge never even reached Himmler. Fritsch was persuaded to withdraw it, since it might have done the Army more damage than all the preceding crisis.[33]

After the war General Wilhelm Ulex, who was commanding XI Army Corps at the time, told of a meeting in May 1938 with Viktor Lutze, Chief of Staff of the SA; Lutze had promised the full support of the SA in the event of action by the Army against Himmler and the SS; should Hitler side with Himmler his life must if possible (but not under all circumstances) be spared. Ulex had asked for concrete proof that Schmidt, the 'witness', had been forced to give false evidence by Himmler; without this, Ulex, said, he could do nothing. Lutze had produced the proof a fortnight later and Ulex had gone to Achterberg to see Fritsch; the latter, however, had refused to do anything, saying that Hitler knew the whole story and so any action against Himmler would be futile. Ulex finally went to Brauchitsch, who merely advised him that 'if these gentlemen want this, then they must do it on their own'.[34]

After the completely inadequate rehabilitation of Fritsch by Hitler in June 1938 a number of generals wished to tender their resignation. At Brauchitsch's request, however, they did not do so; Brauchitsch said that there would inevitably be war over the Sudeten question in the next few weeks and a man could not therefore leave his post. As might be expected, according to Ulex, Fritsch was also of the same opinion.

Rumour was rife and news of the crisis in the higher levels of the *Wehrmacht* filtered through by various channels – via Canaris and Oster in the OKW office *'Ausland/Abwehr'* (Military Intelligence), via Nebe, Director of the *Reich* Criminal Police Office, via Dr Gisevius who had been with the *Gestapo* and was now working in the *Reich* Ministry of the Interior, and via Dr Hans von Dohnanyi, a senior civil servant (*Oberregierungsrat*); as a result several of those who later became resistance leaders attempted to initiate some counter-action, but without success. They all now felt that nothing could be achieved except 'from outside', since at this time (end January 1938) no real leadership existed in the Army any more. Goerdeler, together with Schacht, accordingly visited General Wilhelm List, commanding IV Army Corps in Dresden, Chief of Staff of which was Major-General Friedrich Olbricht; after a brief description of events in Berlin Goerdeler urged List to act at once.[35] The *Gestapo*, he said, must be 'smoked out' and Hitler be faced with a *fait accompli*; this must include the removal of Göring, Himmler and Heydrich to ensure that Hitler was no longer under the influence or even control of these dangerous paladins. Lieutenant-Colonel Oster, who was in touch with Goerdeler either direct or via Gisevius and equally considered that the 'smoking out' of the *Gestapo* and the elimination of Himmler were the first essential measures, thought that Hitler would be most likely to recognize and accept a *fait accompli*; after all, he said, the *Gauleiter* were doing what they liked and getting away with it.[36]

Goerdeler really thought it possible that IV Army Corps would act. In some ways, as with all his subsequent efforts until summer 1944, he was not entirely wrong; a military *putsch* was not quite so difficult as most of the generals approached invariably made it out to be. Wielding an instrument like the Army, however, was not quite so simple as the impetuous Dr Goerdeler thought. For both personal and practical reasons any action from Leipzig was more than unlikely; Olbricht was no go-getter; on the contrary, although those who knew him invariably stressed his extreme intelligence, he tended to be at a loss if rapid and exceptional decisions were demanded of him.[37] General List did not feel able to decide, still less to take revolutionary action, on the basis solely of Goerdeler's report, which in any case was second-hand. When Goerdeler again urged the 'smoking out' of the *Gestapo*, Olbricht replied that in the first instance only the troops around Berlin, in Potsdam, Spandau and Döberitz, could be of any use. To this Goerdeler could only reply that at the time there was no leadership in Berlin. General von Witzleben, who commanded the troops around Berlin (III Army Corps), was sick in Dresden.[38] In fact it was almost inconceivable that the *Gestapo* in Berlin could have been attacked from Dresden, even if General List had been prepared to do it. The Army was no longer a homogeneous, united and reliable instrument; it had been diluted and permeated by reserve, ex-police and so-called replacement (*Ergänzung*) officers and the junior ranks had come from the Hitler Youth. Moreover troops could not in practice be moved to Berlin without the whole affair becoming known. As Lieutenant-Colonel Röhricht, Operations Officer of IV Army Corps, said, the move of a division by rail would take at least three days and in any case it had first to be reported to and approved by Berlin.[39]

Finally List decided to go to Berlin with his Operations Officer and there obtain first-hand information.[40] This produced nothing more definite and all agreed that they were working 'completely in the dark'. Fritsch had of course demanded legal proceedings; the whole affair was obviously a dirty trick. Beck, however, found their suspicions 'incomprehensible'; back-stage work by Göring and Himmler was only a supposition; Hitler's attitude was unknown and no motive could be seen for him to participate in an attack on Fritsch. List and his staff officer therefore returned to Dresden.

In those days following 25 January 1938 other parallel efforts to initiate counter-action were being made. According to Gisevius, Schacht, Goerdeler, Nebe, Graf von Helldorf, the Police President of Berlin, and Gisevius himself were involved together with Beck, Canaris and Oster on the military side. Of this small group only Schacht and Gisevius escaped execution or, in Beck's case, suicide. Again according to Gisevius and a statement by Schacht recorded by Colonel Jodl, head of the OKW Operations Staff, all were quite clear what game was being played and what should happen: the SS was trying to lay hands on the Army; the *Wehrmacht* must therefore forestall the *Gestapo* and occupy its headquarters at No. 8 Prinz-Albrecht-Strasse, Berlin.[41] But how was this to be done?

One can only guess who of all these was primarily responsible for bringing pressure to bear on Brauchitsch. Gisevius made at least one of the many attempts.[42] At times it was said that Brauchitsch was ready to act if backed by a memorandum from the Minister of Justice. As later experience showed, he invariably had some good reason for wishing to 'make sure first'. Nothing, of course, came of it. According to Gisevius, Schacht tried to persuade the Commander-in-Chief of the Navy to act but he said that this was outside his competence; Schacht then enquired of General Gerd von Rundstedt, C-in-C of No. 1 Group Headquarters (Berlin), but all he would say was that everyone knew what he had to do. Again according to Gisevius, people gradually gained the impression that the *Wehrmacht* leaders were allowing the moment for action to slip by. Yet Goerdeler had made the approach to List already referred to; Gisevius himself had gone to Münster to see General Günther von Kluge, commanding VI Army Corps, and Ferdinand Freiherr von Lüninck, the Governor (*Oberpräsident*) of Westphalia. He had urged both the latter and Carl Christian Schmid, the senior government official (*Regierungspräsident*) in Düsseldorf, to bring pressure to bear on Kluge.[43] The object was to bring about a combined *démarche* by commanders of Military Districts (*Wehrkreis*).[44]

Nothing came of all these attempts and all these efforts. They hardly merit use of the term 'plans for a *coup*', although the *Gestapo* refers to them as such in its interrogation reports following 20 July 1944.[45] In February 1938 Fritz-Dietlof Graf von der Schulenburg, then Vice-President of Police in Berlin, negotiated with Witzleben for some intervention on the part of the *Wehrmacht*.[46] Major-General Paul von Hase, then commanding No. 50 Infantry Regiment in Landsberg on Warthe, was prepared to use his regiment against the government in Berlin or at least against the *Gestapo* and SS.[47]

Practical realistic plans were in fact out of the question; none of those involved could be sure what was fact and what was slander; no explanations were given even of the little that was known and Fritsch was guilty of much ineptitude in his handling of the matter. When, on 4 February 1938, Hitler was the one to produce the *fait accompli*, Brauchitsch, the C-in-C of the Army, said that Fritsch's court-martial must now be awaited for the affair to be cleared up.

Brauchitsch proved completely inaccessible to the conspirators.[48] He came with the reputation of being a determined 'strong' man,[49] but all the hopes placed in him by the opposition were doomed to disappointment – this should have been realized. Both by his fellow-officers and by historians he has been accused of lack of determination, weakness, instability and corruption.[50] Brauchitsch may perhaps have succeeded Fritsch 'with mixed feelings' but he did so willingly and, at least at the outset, without any attempt to reject the proposal indignantly or make his decision dependent on the outcome of the proceedings against Fritsch. On 29 January 1938 Jodl noted in his diary that Brauchitsch had told Hitler that he was 'ready for anything'.[51] He allowed Göring and Hitler to help him persuade his wife to agree to a divorce so that he could marry Frau Charlotte Schmidt, an ardent Nazi.[52]

During the critical days from 24 January to 4 February the *Wehrmacht*, particularly the Army, was to some extent leaderless. General Beck, the Chief of Staff, was still firmly in the saddle and still occupied a key position. His attitude was potentially significant. What Beck did in this situation, however, is characteristic both of the state of uncertainty in which senior Army officers found themselves on the subject of their Commander-in-Chief and also of the personality of the Chief of Staff himself.

After Fritsch, at his interview on 26 January, had failed to convince Hitler of his innocence, with Hitler's permission Hossbach had informed Beck during the night and had asked him to come to the *Reich* Chancellery from his house in Lichterfelde.[53] There Beck was told by Hitler of what he (Hitler) regarded as proved and which seemed to Beck highly improbable. Beck thereupon went to Fritsch who indignantly denied all the accusations. Beck returned to the Chancellery the same night and informed Hitler. Hitler remained unconvinced and told Beck that he wished to appoint him to succeed Fritsch. Beck refused and insisted on court-martial proceedings to take place under all circumstances before Fritsch's removal from office.[54]

It was not Beck's habit to act on emotion. Naturally he was now extremely suspicious of Hitler and even more of Göring, Himmler and Heydrich. Yet however strong his inclination to believe Fritsch's protestations – the concept of honour characteristic of the officer corps left him no choice but to do so – he found it equally difficult to believe that men could be capable of so dirty a trick as that constituted by the intrigue against Fritsch. Moreover at the time neither Hossbach nor Fritsch, and perhaps not even Hitler himself, knew the full details of the intrigue or of the web of falsehood woven with the assistance and knowledge of the *Gestapo*. It was therefore all the more difficult for Beck to construct an accurate picture of events. Since his habit was to draw conclusions only after due consideration and exercising great caution on the basis of the available evidence, it was utterly impossible for him to conclude that the whole affair was a trumped-up racket without the smallest basis of truth. In the light of Fritsch's undoubted honesty and Hitler's inconceivable dishonesty he was literally forced to the conclusion that there must be some misunderstanding. Even later, when he had realized the role played by Göring and Himmler, he was still prepared to concede that Hitler had acted in good faith.[55]

This was really the sum total of Beck's attempts to intervene in connection with the Fritsch crisis. In the succeeding weeks he kept himself in the background and concentrated on the initiation of court-martial proceedings, although his relationship with Canaris and particularly Oster became closer and closer.[56] At this time, however, there was no question of Beck considering plans for a *coup d'état*. Lieutenant-General Franz Halder, who was then Deputy Chief of Staff I (Operations) in the Army General Staff, was urged by Oster and others to persuade Fritsch and Beck that, if catastrophe was to be avoided, Hitler and the Nazis must be dealt with by methods other than mere submission of realistic views followed by polite silence and trust in the force of argument and common sense. At the time of the Fritsch crisis Beck had clearly not grasped this.[57] Halder records that when, speaking in the name of his fellow-officers, he asked for an explanation of events during the crisis, Beck replied that people must wait and hold their tongues until informed by him. Halder objected and said that the senior officers of the Army must be assembled now and that it was Beck's duty to do so in place of Fritsch. The argument finally ended with a remark by Beck which has become famous: 'Mutiny and revolution are words not to be found in a German officer's dictionary.'[58] So at this time all efforts to move Beck or to form a group to act against Hitler or at least against Göring and Himmler, failed. Beck's attitude did not change until the start of the Sudeten crisis.

PART II/THE SUDETEN CRISIS AND THE ATTEMPTED COUP OF 1938

4 Operation 'Green'

The court-martial of Fritsch took place almost simultaneously with the move of German troops into Austria. On 12 February 1938 Dr Kurt Schuschnigg, the Austrian Chancellor, visited Hitler on the Obersalzberg and, by means of threats, Hitler forced him to amnesty Austrian Nazis under sentence, to allow much greater freedom of action to National-Socialism in Austria and to appoint a Nazi, Dr Artur Seyss-Inquart, as Minister of the Interior.[1] By this means Hitler thought that he would ensure an internal Nazi seizure of power in Austria. Schuschnigg had no choice but to accept Hitler's demands. Austria was in practice impotent in face of the German *Wehrmacht*; Britain had made up her mind in 1937 not to oppose an Austro-German union and France was torn by government crises.

Despite this desperate situation, however, Schuschnigg attempted to prevent the annexation of Austria. Surprisingly and at short notice, on 9 March he announced a plebiscite in which Austrians were to decide in favour of an independent, social and Christian Austria. Thus in the event of a 'seizure of power' or a German invasion, the rape of Austria would have been plain to all the world; there was no doubt that the result of the plebiscite would be in Schuschnigg's favour. Under renewed massive pressure, both internal and external, however, Schuschnigg abandoned the project. Austria could no longer be saved from annexation.

On 11 March the Vienna government was presented with an ultimatum demanding the immediate nomination of Seyss-Inquart as head of government in place of Schuschnigg; otherwise German troops would march into Austria. Once more Schuschnigg was isolated. Italy, Austria's traditional enemy who had no wish to see an expansion of the German *Reich*, now led by an Austrian, was unwilling to act at this time; as a *quid pro quo* Italian sovereignty over German-speaking South Tyrol was later confirmed. Unless, therefore, Schuschnigg was willing to risk a hopeless war, he could only give way; many would have regarded such a war as an internecine struggle and conflicting loyalties would undoubtedly have led to terrible atrocities. Seyss-Inquart took over the government in Vienna that very evening; nevertheless, on pretext of a call for assistance from the new Austrian government, German troops moved in next day.[2]

Mass jubilation greeted the German troops; a sense of community prevailed and ostensibly brought a happy ending to all external and internal difficulties.

Union of the two countries was announced on 14 March and confirmed by a plebiscite held in both Germany and Austria on 10 April. For Austria disillusionment soon came but it was too late. Hitler had gained an unparalleled success and the *Wehrmacht* had played an important part in this international *coup*. Who was therefore likely to draw any conclusions from the exoneration of Fritsch, which finally took place on 18 March?

Hitler had long had his eye on a 'solution' of the Czech question. Czechoslovakia was a product of the collapse of the Austro-Hungarian monarchy and the Peace Conference of 1919. As a result of the Austrian *Anschluss* the problem was now acute; the Sudeten Germans and the Sudeten German Party under Konrad Henlein were demanding the *Anschluss* of the Sudetenland, which was primarily German-speaking.[3] All Europe was expecting Hitler to press for a solution of this question and none of the great powers could or would come to the assistance of the hard-pressed Czechoslovak State. Britain in particular was largely sympathetic to German demands for a revision of the Treaty of Versailles and for other reasons – economic, political, military and strategic – was not prepared to go to war to preserve intact a multi-nation state which had never worked harmoniously. France was Czechoslovakia's ally but, without British support, was in no position to fulfil the obligations of her alliance. If Germany infringed the territorial integrity of Czechoslovakia, France had no other course but to attack Germany and for this she felt herself too weak; moreover she was far too disunited politically and in practice incapable of acting. In 1935 the Soviet Union also had concluded an assistance pact with Czechoslovakia but subject to the condition that France fulfilled her obligations. Poland wanted to extract from Czechoslovakia the Polish minority together with a sizeable piece of territory; in addition she was by no means willing to allow the Red Army, against which she had fought in 1920, to move across Polish territory. Czechoslovakia was therefore just as isolated as Austria had been before the *Anschluss* and in addition was surrounded by hostile neighbours.

Immediately after the occupation and incorporation of Austria Hitler started preparations for the destruction of the Czechoslovak state. He was not particularly interested in the Sudeten Germans, but their distress (which was real) and the agitation by their extreme nationalist elements provided him with a convenient pretext. On 28 March Hitler personally instructed Konrad Henlein to make unacceptable demands on the Czechoslovak government.[4] On 24 April in its 'Karlsbad Programme' the Sudeten German Party demanded full autonomy for the Sudetenland, removal of all obstacles to agitation and compensation for economic losses suffered since 1919.

Shortly thereafter the Czechoslovak government thought, wrongly, that a German attack was imminent and on 20 May it mobilized its army. Hitler was furious and the world at large thought that the Czechs were in the wrong. Hitler may well have regarded the Czech measures as a challenge or alternatively merely as an extra argument presented to him as a windfall; the fact remains, however, that concrete planning for 'Operation Green', a surprise attack on Czechoslovakia, had started long before 20 May. The main lines of the operation had been laid down with complete clarity and in writing on 22 April 1938, and on 20 May General Keitel submitted to Hitler a fully prepared draft of the strategic directives to be issued.[5] The Czech government's information was therefore to some extent correct. Finally on 30 May Hitler informed the Commanders-in-Chief of the Army, Navy and Air Force in writing that: 'It is my unalterable decision to destroy Czechoslovakia by military action within a foreseeable time.' The time factor was given as 'a suitable moment from the political and military points of view'. All preparations were to be ready by 1 October 1938 at the latest.[6]

Throughout the summer the crisis deepened. In late June Hitler was present at manoeuvres in the Grafenwöhr training area in Franconia, near the Czechoslovak frontier.[7] Construction of fortifications in the west was accelerated and on 22 June compulsory civil defence service was introduced; the press devoted itself to whipping up a war fever.[8] On 10 August, having taken note of a memorandum from Beck opposing the war plan, Hitler held a further conference with his senior military commanders, this time in the 'Berghof'.[9] When Hitler again made known his intentions, certain generals were bold enough to voice doubts about the *Wehrmacht*'s capacity to withstand the anticipated attack from France and even Britain, but this was ill received by Hitler. His answer was an outburst of rage against the 'pusillanimity' of which he accused the General Staff. Jodl's explanation was that the General Staff did not 'in the last analysis believe in the genius of the *Führer*'.[10]

Between 21 and 26 August Admiral Horthy, the Hungarian Regent, paid a state visit to Germany with Kania von Kanya, his Foreign Minister, and Rácz von Nagylak, his Defence Minister. They were told that in no case would Germany accept another provocation from Czechoslovakia and that 'if it should happen tomorrow, it was for them to decide whether they wished to participate or not'.[11]

At the end of August further details of 'Operation Green' were fixed, in some cases under cover of exercises and manoeuvres.[12] For military reasons it seemed advisable that the 'incident' which was to 'give Germany cause for military intervention' should take place on the day before invasion and 'be officially known here by midday on D-1'. On 26 August Jodl noted in his diary: 'If on technical grounds it is desirable that the incident should occur *in the evening*, the following day could *not* be D-Day; it would have to be the day after that.' This, however, would dangerously reduce the level of surprise. In any case, the note concludes, the *Wehrmacht* must learn of the *Führer*'s intentions in good time – 'if the Intelligence Section [of OKW] is not entrusted with organizing the incident'.[13] On the next day Beck handed in his resignation.

But such setbacks were not enough to deter Hitler, particularly seeing that the other generals were carrying out his orders with the utmost alacrity. On 3 September he held a further conference with Brauchitsch and Keitel in the 'Berghof' and again laid down the timing of the attack as end September or early October. During the night of 9–10 September a further discussion was held in Nuremberg; those present were Hitler, Brauchitsch, Halder, Keitel and the aides, Schmundt, Engel and Below. Halder, the new Chief of Staff, explained the plan for 'Operation Green' and expressed confidence in its success.[14] Numerous military measures were then taken, so that foreign intelligence services could have been in no doubt of Hitler's determination. On 15 September the Labour Service was placed under orders of the *Wehrmacht*; the railways were instructed to 'hold large quantities of empty rolling stock available'; a Sudeten German Free Corps was formed under Konrad Henlein to 'protect Sudeten Germans and maintain the series of disturbances and clashes'.[15] During September Hitler made a number of inflammatory speeches, referring to battle more frequently than usual; finally on 12 September he announced to the Nuremberg Party Rally that Germany would no longer tolerate 'the oppression and persecution of three-and-a-half million Germans' in Czechoslovakia; statesmen of other European countries should note that in the case of the Sudeten Germans 'the free right of self-determination' should take the place of oppression by the Czechs.[16] In a speech in the Sports Palace in Berlin on 26 September he emphasized his determination in an intemperate outburst of hate, coupling it, however, with the statement that his claim for the Sudeten area constituted 'the last territorial demand which I have to make to Europe'.[17]

In the light of this growing crisis Chamberlain, the British Prime Minister, took the lead and made every conceivable effort to bring about a peaceful solution. At short notice he proposed that Hitler receive him for a discussion on 15 September, and in fact it took place on the Obersalzberg on that day.[18] The Sudeten Germans' right of self-determination, or to be more precise the German *Reich*'s right to annex the Sudetenland, was recognized by Chamberlain in general terms; France, Czechoslovakia's ally, supported the British proposal. What could the Czechs do other than submit? From 22 to 24 September Chamberlain was in Germany again to settle the problem completely; the Czechs were prepared for far-reaching concessions. The Godesberg conference, however, ended without agreement, since Hitler announced his determination to march in at once, a plebiscite to follow in an area yet to be decided; a German ultimatum in this sense was despatched on 28 September. The Czechs mobilized; France called up reservists; Britain put her fleet on a war footing. World war was at the door.

Finally, however, came the Munich conference of 29 September. At this Hitler, Chamberlain and Daladier accepted a 'mediation proposal' by Mussolini whereby German troops would move into the claimed area by stages between 1 and 10 October. The Czech delegation was simply told of the result of the discussions.

Relief at the preservation of peace was everywhere great, in Germany as much as in Britain and France. The majority failed to perceive that this was no peaceful settlement on a basis of mutual compromise but international blackmail of the first order. In addition to Czechoslovakia, Britain and France were in fact also victims of blackmail, because they did not feel able to arrest the course of events, because to a large degree they had not the means to do so and because they did not possess the will to resist – a will which they were ultimately forced to acquire when they realized that 'the last territorial demand' would always be followed by another one, that their turn would come one day and that Hitler was bent on making himself dictator of Europe.

Those in Germany who raised warning voices against Hitler's policy of brinkmanship in the early days were 'proven wrong'. But they could see further than Hitler either could or would see and in the long term they were proved horrifyingly right. The next point in Hitler's programme was the 'disposal of the remainder of Czechoslovakia', to use his own expression, and thereafter he proposed to demand even more extensive *Lebensraum*.[19] The great war had only been postponed.

5 Foreign Policy and Resistance

It was the threat of war, a war unnecessarily initiated or provoked by Hitler with the object of overthrowing the European order and so inevitably leading to world war, which produced a German resistance movement whose object was to overthrow the regime by *coup d'état* or revolutionary measures and then face the leaders of the regime with responsibility for their crimes.[1] There were a number of politicians, senior officials in various ministries and in numerous other positions, senior army officers and captains of industry who used their influence to curb and restrain Hitler's foreign policy, working both from within and indirectly from outside; resistance to Hitler's internal policy of course continued. It goes without saying that, in Hitler's SS State, all such efforts entailed the greatest danger to life and limb.

The most intensive and extensive activity was displayed by Dr Carl Goerdeler, who subsequently, during the war, was largely recognized as the leader of the resistance movement. He came of a civil service family; his original home was in West Prussia, ceded to Poland in 1919. Goerdeler became a lawyer and administrative civil servant; in 1930 he was appointed Burgomaster of Leipzig.[2] In December 1931 Brüning, the Chancellor, persuaded Goerdeler to become *Reich* Prices Commissioner and, since the German National People's Party, to which Goerdeler belonged, continued to oppose Brüning and refused to support his essential measures aimed at improving the economic situation, Goerdeler publicly resigned from Hugenberg's party. In May 1932 Goerdeler was asked to join the Papen cabinet as Minister of Economics and Labour but he refused; he was incensed by the fall of Brüning and indignant with those backing Papen; Papen himself he regarded as a diplomatic failure without support, competence or political merit. When, therefore, Hitler became Chancellor Goerdeler was soon in conflict with the Nazis; he refused, for instance, to hoist the swastika flag on Leipzig City Hall when it was not yet the national emblem; he personally protected Jewish businessmen against looting by the SA.[3]

Nevertheless it still seemed possible to differentiate between Hitler himself and his followers; many still contrived to believe that various of the regime's manifestations, later proved to reflect its real nature, were no more than aberrations which Hitler would by no means wish to condone. Goerdeler was one of such people; he possessed not only inexhaustible energy but an almost ineradicable optimism, bordering on inability to grasp the evil and depravity of Nazism. Always, until the very day of his execution, he believed himself capable of changing everything, or at least many things, for the better by means of commonsense, argument and explanation.[4] This pronounced characteristic is a possible explanation for the fact that in November 1934, after the murders of 30 June, he was willing to be reappointed *Reich* Prices Commissioner, a position in which he remained until 1 July 1935.[5] In personal interviews with Hitler, Goerdeler did in fact succeed on several occasions in asserting his views against those of the Party bosses and even of Hitler himself and in gaining Hitler's support for them.[6] To the very end these experiences seemed to Goerdeler to provide some rational justification for his optimism; in his later years he even went so far as to think that he could persuade Hitler not to continue with the war.

In practice cooperation with the Nazis soon proved to be impossible. In 1936, on the expiry of his first term of office as Burgomaster, Goerdeler was re-elected for a further twelve years and, since he had had the support of the Nazi Party, he thought that sensible logical ideas would prevail.[7] In his absence, however, behind his back and against his explicit instructions Haake, his deputy, had the Mendelssohn memorial in front of the Leipzig Gewandhaus removed; this was done at the demand of the Nazi Party which refused to rescind the measure despite a threat of resignation by Goerdeler. He accordingly took his leave and retired on 1 April 1937.[8]

Goerdeler now devoted all his efforts to the prevention of war, initially in concert with South German industrialists and opponents of the regime led by Robert Bosch.[9] From this source he drew the financial support without which he could not have undertaken the numerous journeys which were of such importance for his role in the opposition. He left on one such trip as early as June 1937; it took him to Belgium and Britain, back to Berlin and then to Holland, France, Canada and the United States. In March and April 1938 he travelled again to France and Britain, in late summer and autumn to Switzerland, Italy, Yugoslavia, Rumania and Bulgaria. Then in 1939 he visited France, Algeria, Britain, Libya, Egypt, Palestine, Syria, Turkey and returned through Switzerland.[10]

In all these journeys Goerdeler was at pains to explain to the ruling statesmen of the West the dangers which threatened and his ideas for averting them. He preferred to use economic arguments since these best illustrated the 'natural' conditions, in other words the commonsense reasons in which he placed so much confidence. But he had no success.

In Germany his reports served to convince the converted even more firmly that their views were right and they provided ammunition for some of their initiatives. But these had no influence at all on the government in power.

An astonishing number of foreign statesmen received and listened to Goerdeler. In the years before the outbreak of war he talked in Paris to Daladier and Reynaud, in London to Montagu Norman, Governor of the Bank of England, Anthony Eden, Secretary of State for Foreign Affairs, Sir Robert

Vansittart, Permanent Under-Secretary of State in the Foreign Office, Frank Ashton-Gwatkin, a counsellor in the Foreign Office and head of the Economic Department, also to Lord Halifax and Winston Churchill. In the United States he had conversations with Cordell Hull, the Secretary of State, Henry A. Wallace, Secretary for Agriculture, Sumner Welles, the Under-Secretary of State, G. S. Messersmith, Assistant Secretary of State, Herbert Hoover, the former President, Henry Lewis Stimson, later Secretary for War, Henry Morgenthau Jr, Secretary of the Treasury, and Owen D. Young, the industrialist; in Canada he talked with the Prime Minister, William Mackenzie King.[11]

Goerdeler was never regarded as representing a realistic, probable or even desirable policy. The French, British and American governments felt unable to follow up his proposals in any way. Goerdeler's reception in Paris in the spring of 1938 is a good illustration.[12] Dr Reinhold Schairer, a German jurist who had been active in affairs of academic education at an international level and who had been living in London since 1933 and had many connections in France and Switzerland, arranged Goerdeler's most important contacts in Paris. He recommended Goerdeler to Pierre Bertaux, Professor for German Studies, who was at that time *Chef de Cabinet* in the section *Education Nationale* of the French Ministry of Culture. Together with Schairer, Goerdeler was invited to Bertaux's house in Paris early in March.[13] Bertaux listened to Goerdeler's explanation of the reasons why the French government should adopt a firm unyielding attitude on the Czechoslovak question and on all questions involving German territorial demands; he could hold out no hope, however, that such an attitude would be adopted, still less that Goerdeler's warnings would be taken seriously. Apart from this the two were entirely agreed on the dangers threatening Europe.

On 5 April Goerdeler reappeared in Bertaux's office, this time completely unexpectedly, and begged to be put in touch with French government circles. The same day Bertaux obtained for him an interview with the most senior official of the French Foreign Ministry, Alexis Léger the Secretary-General (known as a poet under the name Saint-John Perse); Bertaux was present and the conversation lasted two hours. Goerdeler again urged as unyielding an attitude to Hitler as possible. He stated that he might perhaps exert some influence on German policy, but only provided that he had support and backing from abroad. Léger, however, committed himself in no way; he spoke, Bertaux recalls, like a Radical Socialist from the Midi, without bluster but only in general non-committal terms. Goerdeler was given not the smallest assurance. Bertaux and Léger had no doubts of Schairer's good faith but they knew very little indeed about Goerdeler. It might well be that he belonged to the German resistance movement, but it equally well could be that he merely wished to pump the French government and would immediately report everything he was told to the German government. In addition there was the problem of whether anyone was prepared to take responsibility for initiating a major war in Europe; although France was relatively better prepared in 1938 than in 1939, she was hoping to overhaul Germany shortly in the arms race.

On 7 April Goerdeler and Bertaux dined together and Goerdeler reiterated his urgent request for a firm attitude on the Czech question. Next day, however, Leon Blum's government, which had only been in office since 13 March, resigned and on 10 April Edouard Daladier formed a government; Bertaux went to Toulouse University. Goerdeler's contact with the French government, never very effective anyway, was now severed.

Goerdeler did little better in London. Here at least the ground had been prepared in that Vansittart had not the smallest confidence in the Hitler government's policy. He also placed much trust in Goerdeler, whom he regarded as reliable, honest and patriotic, in fact the sole genuine opponent of Hitler among the many who presented themselves as such.[14] In April 1938, however, talking to Vansittart, Goerdeler demanded the cession of the Sudetenland to Germany, just after Austria had been incorporated in a somewhat unseemly manner; at the same time he urged the British government to adopt a clear consistent policy, since otherwise Hitler's appetite for other people's territory would only be increased. Thus he was involuntarily working contrary to the efforts of the resistance and giving rise to even greater mistrust of the 'other Germany' than was anyway felt by foreign governments.[15]

The British gained the impression that Goerdeler might well be advancing the ideas of leading circles in the German opposition, not merely his own. The various emissaries who appeared during the Sudeten crisis all showed similar revisionist tendencies and their views seemed to tally with those of Goerdeler.[16] Faced with conservatives, Prussians and monarchists on the one hand and on the other with memories of the Wilhelmine era (particularly 1900–14), the invasion of Belgium and the First World War, all now compounded by Hitler's 'neo-Prussianism', views about Germany held in leading influential circles in Britain could differentiate only vaguely between the unattractive alternatives. Such considerations must be remembered.[17]

Finally Goerdeler's demand for cession of the Sudetenland underlined another weakness in the position of the German opposition vis-à-vis the French and British governments; they were not vitally interested in the territorial integrity of the Sudetenland or indeed of Czechoslovakia as such; Hitler, on the other hand, might be satisfied with the German-speaking Sudetenland; after all, he was making no demand for colonies, participation in world policy or maintenance of a large fleet. Why, therefore, should France and Britain resurrect the spectre of imperial Germany and '1914'? To many Western statesmen in fact Hitler seemed the lesser of the two evils. If concessions were to be made, they thought, why not to Hitler? Why help overthrow his government and then grant the concessions demanded to another German government? This seemed both complicated and senseless. The British Ambassador in Berlin, who was obviously highly credible as an informant, contributed largely to these ideas about Germany and Hitler in London.[18]

Quite apart from this, the suggestion that Britain, working from outside and in time of peace, should attempt to overthrow the government of a major

European country was extraordinary. However determined Britain might have been, she would hardly have ventured on so foolhardy a policy; freedom of choice for other people in their own form of government was firmly rooted in British tradition.[19] In international dealings, even with dictators, good faith was assumed. A government which negotiated and communicated with another on a basis of mutual recognition could not at the same time secretly pursue the overthrow of its partner without itself losing all credibility and confidence. In London people were only too well aware of this.[20] From this point of view it was entirely understandable that Vansittart should have said in reply to Goerdeler that what he was proposing amounted to treason.[21] This basically disregarded the ethical motive, the subordination to humanity of loyalty to one's country. Nevertheless Goerdeler's revisionist demands, however well meant, raised an insuperable obstacle to any meeting of minds.

When Chamberlain compared the German opposition to the Jacobites (supporters of James II, exiled in 1688, who were trying to overthrow William of Orange and restore James to the throne by stirring up France against England), he was, of course, missing the point entirely.[22] The German opposition was not primarily interested in its own power or position but in the maintenance of peace. For this purpose they made such proposals as seemed to them effective: they wanted Britain to give an unequivocal 'No' to Hitler's plans for conquest by blackmail. Both sides were agreed on the inadmissibility of Hitler's procedures; British military preparedness was not substantially inferior to that of Germany; equally both were agreed that Germany could not conduct a successful war on two fronts or even a successful war against Britain and France.

From the point of view of the German opposition they were by no means calling upon Britain to risk a world war, which commonsense and a readiness to compromise might well avert, but this might be the impression which they created in Britain. People there did not realize as clearly as did many in Germany that, consistently from the beginning, Hitler was demoniacally headed for war. In any case London could see no vast difference between the Nazi government and one that might possibly be formed by the opposition. Both would be 'nationalist' and revisionist; the British government, therefore, had no wish to deal with the German opposition; they wanted to reach some agreement with the legitimate German government.[23]

The British and French, therefore, failed to appreciate the position in which German opposition politicians were placed if they were to avoid being accused of pursuing a Versailles Peace Treaty policy and betraying their national interests. Goerdeler was fully and painfully aware of this dilemma; on 11 October 1938, after the occupation of the Sudetenland, he wrote to an American friend: 'For myself I could say now: the power and *Lebensraum* of my country constantly increases. As a German I ought to rejoice at this. But I know that these dictators are criminals and that their economic policy leads to bolshevism; Hitlerism is poison for the German soul; Hitler is determined to root out Christianity ... It will not be justice, reason and decency that will determine the world's future but naked force'.[24] Such an attitude was difficult to understand for those in foreign countries, where people were not habitually involved in a conflict between their ethical principles and their patriotism.

The fact remains, however, that Vansittart did advise the British government to adopt a firm attitude towards Hitler, as he had been doing ever since 1930; he referred to previous conversations with Goerdeler in 1937, to memoranda by the German Heavy Industry Association and by Colonel Thomas, head of the War Economy Section in *Oberkommando des Heeres* (OKH).[25] He prepared a report for the cabinet stressing the weakness of the German economic and military potential, the failure of the Four-Year Plan, the shortage of raw materials and the desire for peace in Hitler's military entourage which merited support from outside. But Neville Chamberlain, the Prime Minister of the time, and his cabinet, which had only come to office at the end of May 1937, a few days before Goerdeler's first visit to London, never even received the report. When the draft was submitted to Anthony Eden, the Foreign Minister, he suppressed it and prevented its finalization and submission to the cabinet.[26] Chamberlain was already determined on a policy of compromise as regards Austria and Czechoslovakia and he was confirmed in his view by memoranda from the British Chiefs of Staff pointing out that Britain was in no way prepared for war with Germany.[27] He did not appreciate discussion on British foreign policy before taking his decision; he wished to be solely responsible for deciding what happened.[28] Vansittart's warnings, which gave a very accurate appreciation of the Hitler government, were accordingly disregarded.[29]

Despite all these obstacles to an understanding by either side of the position of the other, many still saw value in warning the British government against Hitler's intentions as often and as emphatically as possible in the hope that an unyielding attitude might still prevent war. Through their own channels, particularly from their Embassy in Berlin and their intelligence services, the British government received a continuous stream of information and warning.[30] There were also numerous contacts with German emissaries.

In July 1938 Captain Fritz Wiedemann, Hitler's personal aide, travelled to London with Hitler's knowledge and talked to Lord Halifax. Through Wiedemann Halifax gave Hitler to understand that a solution of the Sudeten German question by force would not be calmly accepted by the British people. According to his own report Wiedemann indicated that the latest possible date for a solution was March 1939 – he had had the timing laid down by Hitler confirmed by OKW.[31]

On his return from London Wiedemann did not even manage to report in detail to Hitler. Accordingly in August he let the British government know 'through a third party' that Hitler was now determined to solve the Sudeten question 'by force in the immediate future'.

During August 1938 further approaches to London were made by a journalist, Captain (retd.) Victor von Koerber.[32] On at least three occasions, the first time on 6 August, he contacted the British Military Attaché, who reported to his superiors.[33] Koerber said that the colours black-white-red were the only revolutionary colours and spoke about a restoration of the monarchy; he indicated that the overthrow of the regime must of course be brought about from within but could be supported from outside. In his report the Military Attaché opposed these ideas, saying that, should an attempt fail, everything would be worse than before and Hitler's position would merely be strengthened. Moreover Koerber was proposing the Crown Prince as candidate for the throne; he had supported Hitler at the presidential elections of 1932 and did not have a good press abroad.[34]

As a member of the exclusive Casino Club in Berlin, Ian Colvin, a British journalist, had made the acquaintance of Ewald von Kleist-Schmenzin, landowner and conservative monarchist politician. At the end of March or early April 1938 (soon after the German invasion of Austria) Kleist spoke to Colvin, begging him to warn the British government of Hitler's plans for conquest. Hitler would not be satisfied with Austria, he said; he was aiming at world domination; he was mad of course but in full possession of his mental powers. Kleist could see only one possibility of stopping the next planned move against Czechoslovakia – a clear firm 'No' from Britain. For the moment Hitler did not possess the resources to fight Britain; he knew this and had admitted as much himself; the Army General Staff also wished to prevent war but needed a 'sheet anchor', some effective resistance from outside, if they were to restrain Hitler.

In May Colvin passed on Kleist's warning to Ogilvie-Forbes, Counsellor in the British Embassy, and he is convinced that Vansittart received it before mid-May.[35]

In late July 1938 Colvin received word through an intermediary 'from one of the three highest generals in the German High Command' that military action against Czechoslovakia would begin on 28 September.[36] In a letter dated 3 August he reported this to his friend Lord Lloyd, Chairman of the British Council, who on many matters had the ear of Chamberlain and Lord Halifax; Lord Lloyd is said to have passed Colvin's report to Vansittart and certain members of the cabinet.[37] In a covering letter Colvin also announced that Kleist would be visiting London and doing so on behalf of the *Abwehr* with the object, if possible, of obtaining British agreement to intervene against Germany in the event of a German attack on Czechoslovakia.

Kleist did in fact travel to London with the blessing and support of Canaris and Oster.[38] On 16 August even Sir Nevile Henderson, the British Ambassador, himself recommended Kleist as an emissary of 'the moderates in the German General Staff'.[39] As Kleist told Colvin in November 1938, the specific purpose of his mission was given him by General Beck in these words: 'Bring me certain proof that Britain will fight if Czechoslovakia is attacked and I will make an end of this regime.'[40] The 'proofs' visualized were a public declaration of British support for Czechoslovakia and a military demonstration.

On 18 August, therefore, Kleist flew to London, where he stayed in the Park Lane Hotel.[41] Late that afternoon he had a talk with Vansittart and told him that war was a certainty unless Britain, the only country able to do so, stopped it.[42] As Vansittart stated with great clarity in his report to the Foreign Minister, according to Kleist the problem now was not the threat of war but its complete certainty, since Hitler was totally determined to have it. When Vansittart asked for the planned timing of the attack, Kleist laughed and said that the British government had known that for a long time. He knew of course of Colvin's report to Lord Lloyd through Ogilvie-Forbes and therefore of the information which the British government had, part of which came from him.[43] Kleist then said to Vansittart that after 27 September it would be too late and in his report to Lord Halifax Vansittart referred to the letter which he (Halifax) had received from Lord Lloyd and in which 28 September was given as the final date.[44]

As a method of deterring Hitler Kleist proposed some proof which would convince him that Britain and France were not bluffing, if possible a public speech by a leading British statesman including an appeal to all Germans who did not want war. In his report Vansittart added that, as Lord Halifax already knew, this was a proposal which had frequently been made to him in recent weeks by Germans opposed to war; the general political ideas put forward by Kleist were sensible; in Kleist's view, however, no reasonable German policy was to be expected while Hitler was in power; if Hitler suffered a defeat, this would be the prelude to the downfall of his regime – a view also supported by the British Military Attaché in Berlin.[45]

Halifax sent Vansittart's report on to Chamberlain, and the Prime Minister commented upon it in writing on 19 August:[46] That very morning, he said, he had been informed by German military circles through Major-General Lord Hutchinson of Montrose that this time Hitler was not bluffing and must be restrained from taking extreme measures by some form of compromise; this view, he said, ought to be compared with what Kleist proposed! The Prime Minister, therefore, who either could not or would not see the reality, had to struggle hard to resist the obviously great impression made by Kleist's mission, emphasized by the enormous risk to Kleist himself – Kleist had said that he had left practically with a noose round his neck. As already mentioned, Chamberlain then compared Kleist and his friends to the supporters of James II, saying that Kleist was clearly anxious to stir up his friends in Germany to attempt to overthrow Hitler, that he was therefore prejudiced and that a good deal of what he said must be discounted.

The most that Chamberlain eventually declared himself ready to do was to make the gesture of summoning Sir Nevile Henderson, the British Ambassador in Berlin, to London for talks on the Sudeten question. In short Kleist's approach to Chamberlain had achieved nothing.

Henderson, however, whose duty it should have been to report to his government with unvarnished realism, was more of an admirer of the Nazis and of their remarkable organizational achievements than a cautious sceptic.[47] It is true that on 19 August 1938 he wrote to his superiors in London that, if Britain saw any utility in war, now would be the moment to make it rather than later.[48] He knew Chamberlain's views, however, and was certainly not prepared to advise determination and firmness. Telephoning from Berlin to his Foreign Minister on the afternoon of 19 August he urged him not to irritate Hitler unnecessarily or force him to yield further to the 'extremists' in his own ranks; in conclusion he said that objectively the Germans had 'a strong case' over the Sudetenland.[49] After the war he said: 'Nothing but the direct and immediate threat of war would have stopped Hitler at that stage.'[50] War, however, was what people were trying to avoid.

On the evening of 18 August Kleist saw Lord Lloyd again and on the next day Winston Churchill. The meeting with Lord Lloyd does not seem to have led to the anticipated unanimity of view. Kleist was quite frank with Churchill about his own views and those of his friends – restoration of the monarchy and elimination of the Polish Corridor. Churchill did not think it opportune to deal with the Corridor problem, since Hitler himself had shelved it. He promised, however, to send a letter to Kleist giving his views – unofficial of course – on the risk of war which would result from the threatened German attack on Czechoslovakia.[51]

As an opposition leader Churchill could naturally make no binding agreements. In his letter he said that it was difficult for democracies like Britain to commit themselves in advance to a specific policy and on the basis of hypothetical situations. One must consider, Churchill continued, not what might happen in the first few months of a conflict, but where we should all be in the third or fourth year. It would be a great mistake to imagine that even the slaughter of the civilian population through air raids would prevent the British Empire from developing its full war power. All the major nations involved in such a war – and a crossing of the Czech frontier by German troops would undoubtedly entail a new world war – would fight it to the bitter end and Britain would have the support of the greater part of the world. For the moment the attitude of the British government, as Lord Halifax had recently confirmed to Churchill, was that set out by Chamberlain in his speech of 24 March.

With the best will in the world Churchill could not say more. Vansittart, however, was authorized to say that, should the situation deteriorate, Britain would make a naval demonstration and in any case Sir John Simon, the Chancellor of the Exchequer, would make a minatory speech in the next few days. (It was made on 27 August and reiterated that the content of Chamberlain's speech of 24 March was still valid.)[52]

Taken as a whole, therefore, Kleist's mission was unsuccessful and he himself confirmed this.[53] Canaris and Oster, to whom Kleist reported on his return on 24 August,[54] could hardly hope that this would persuade the generals of Britain's will to fight, though Churchill's toughness was convincing enough. The letter found its way into Hitler's immediate entourage and so, whether via Canaris or the Foreign Ministry, reached its destination.[55] Without mentioning the recipient but specifying the author, Weizsäcker included an extract from it in a memorandum dated 6 September on foreign reactions to a possible conflict between Germany and Czechoslovakia.

Meanwhile the opposition renewed its attempts to persuade Britain to adopt a firm attitude. On 18 August, as a protest against Hitler's policy, General Beck, Chief of the General Staff of the Army, had handed in his resignation, which was accepted by Hitler on 21 August.[56] General Halder, his successor, however, continued the efforts to prevent war. Halder assumed office on 1 September and as early as 2 September (the idea seems to have originated about 15 August while Beck was still in office) Lieutenant-Colonel (retd.) Hans Böhm-Tettelbach went to London in a further attempt to influence the British government.[57] His mission, as given him by Halder and Oster, was to press the British government with all urgency to stand firm in face of further demands by Hitler. Halder and Oster visualized Vansittart as the immediate recipient of this message. Böhm-Tettelbach knew nothing of Kleist's mission.[58] As one of the most elementary security precautions members of the opposition seldom knew of any initiative other than their own.

In London Böhm-Tettelbach did not succeed in penetrating into any leading influential circle. All he could do was to talk to Julian Piggott, whom he had known after the First World War and who was now in business, and with a Major of the Intelligence Service. Piggott had been Inter-Allied High Commissioner at Cologne in 1920 and still had some important contacts, but Böhm-Tettelbach's message, which was basically similar to that of Kleist, eventually reached Vansittart via the Major.[59] Naturally this 'warning' was no more effective than its predecessors or successors; Chamberlain's attitude and views were more or less fixed. On his return Böhm-Tettelbach reported to Oster, whom he met in Wuppertal, and Oster passed the report on to Halder.[60]

Hardly had Böhm-Tettelbach returned than a fresh approach was made to London, this time from the Foreign Ministry but once more in collusion with the group centred on Canaris and Oster. Halder seems to have known nothing of it.[61] As in the *Abwehr*, there existed in the Foreign Ministry a group of all ages whose conspiratorial activity was tolerated and to a great extent supported by their superiors, Canaris and Weizsäcker respectively.[62] The Foreign Ministry group included Adam von Trott zu Solz, Otto Kiep, Hans-Bernd von Haeften, Eduard Brücklmeier, Albrecht Graf von Bernstorff, Albrecht von Kessel and the Kordt brothers. Dr Erich Kordt, a counsellor (*Legationsrat*), was on Ribbentrop's staff, first in the 'Ribbentrop Bureau' and then in the Embassy in London; since the spring of 1938 he had been in the Foreign Ministry in Berlin as head of the 'Ministerial Bureau'.[63] He worked closely with Freiherr von Weizsäcker, the State Secretary, both officially and because their views on Hitler and his policy of brinkmanship tallied; Weizsäcker was also in touch with Beck, after the latter's retirement, with Halder and also with Canaris.[64] Theo Kordt was Counsellor at the Embassy in London, where for a time he was acting as Chargé d'Affaires.

As a result of numerous deliberations, contacts and discussions the idea emerged that the Foreign Ministry's influence should be utilized to prevent the outbreak of war. Two possibilities were envisaged: action from within and the exertion of influence from outside.

The first thought was to bring influence to bear on Hitler via Colonel-General von Brauchitsch, the Commander-in-Chief of the Army. At the end of August Oster asked Erich Kordt to seek an interview with Brauchitsch and give him a picture of the external political situation; Brauchitsch, he said, was not politically-minded but he might perhaps be impressed by the views of an expert.[65] Weizsäcker, whom Kordt asked for advice, agreed that he should talk to Brauchitsch. He (Weizsäcker) could no longer do this himself, he said, since in these tense days such action might give rise to the most dangerous and possibly well-founded suspicions on the part of the rulers and also of the public.

Kordt accordingly went to the War Ministry on the Tirpitzufer, where Oster had clearly taken precautions to ensure that no entry should appear in the visitors' book; Kordt was received at the entrance by someone he knew and conducted inside. He told the Commander-in-Chief of the Army that Germany was entirely isolated; there was no justification for the idea that Britain and France would not intervene if the *Wehrmacht* invaded Czechoslovakia. He knew the theory well, he said, and he was aware of its source, but he knew the material on which it was ostensibly founded and on the basis of that material he was forced to the opposite conclusion. He showed certain documents to Brauchitsch, who asked a number of questions; in particular he wanted to know on what Hitler and Ribbentrop based their hopes of victory. Kordt thereupon quoted a circular of Ribbentrop's which said that, should the Western Powers be so deluded as to intervene, seventy-five million Germans would fall upon them as one man and annihilate them.

On Oster's advice, Kordt volunteered no opinion; he simply set out the situation and left it to Brauchitsch to draw his own conclusions. When Brauchitsch asked what Kordt hoped to gain from his visit, he merely said that the fate of the Army and of Germany, and therefore entire responsibility, now lay with Brauchitsch. The General was taken aback.

The Foreign Ministry group considered that the second possibility of preventing war lay in massive pressure from outside and that this would best take the form of unequivocal threats and warnings from Britain. Many approaches had already been made to London for such warnings to be issued. Despite previous negative reactions, however, efforts were pursued.

On 1 September Professor Carl Jacob Burckhardt, the League of Nations High Commissioner for Danzig, passing through Berlin on his way to Berne, visited Weizsäcker to report and discuss the situation with him. Weizsäcker told Burckhardt of the proposal to send Theo Kordt secretly to Chamberlain and Lord Halifax and asked him urgently to act on the same lines as soon as he could. In his memoirs Burckhardt recalls that he was to contact the Foreign Office in London from Switzerland and say that 'with Hitler unambiguous language must be used since only this would deter him. He [Weizsäcker] was thinking some "uninhibited undiplomatic Englishman like some general with his hunting crop" might suddenly confront Hitler; only thus would the latter perhaps listen.' Burckhardt stresses that in so doing Weizsäcker was 'conspiring with a potential enemy for the purpose of preserving the peace – a double game of the utmost peril . . . Even as early as this, Weizsäcker was making no secret of his view that the preservation of peace and the salvation of Germany were only possible if the one ruinous figure, in whose hands all power was concentrated, should disappear.'[66]

Burckhardt drove straight to Karlsruhe via the autobahn and on to Berne, where the same morning he visited Sir George Warner, the British Minister, and spoke on the telephone to Lord Halifax's Parliamentary Secretary, passing on Weizsäcker's request. A few days later Burckhardt was able to explain it all in detail to Ralph Stevenson, specialist for League of Nations questions in the Foreign Office, and the latter passed it on to Sir William Strang, Head of the Central Department, in a letter dated 8 September.[67] This said that the only method of bringing Hitler to see the truth was a letter from the British Prime Minister which should be handed direct to Hitler by a courier;[68] care must be taken to ensure that Hitler was given an accurate translation. In his proposal Weizsäcker had said that he could not, of course, make such a request to the British Ambassador in Berlin and had therefore asked Burckhardt to act as intermediary; it was of the utmost importance that this letter reach Hitler as soon as possible, before the end of the Nuremberg Party Rally.

Finally, in his letter to Strang, Stevenson passed on Burckhardt's impression of the whole affair. Weizsäcker, he said, had undoubtedly told Burckhardt many things which, under normal circumstances, he would have kept secret out of loyalty to his superiors. Burckhardt had been so impressed by his interview that he had driven the 550 miles from Berlin to Berne without stopping in order to report at once to Sir George Warner. At the conclusion of his report and transmission of Weizsäcker's message Burckhardt added that senior officers of the German *Wehrmacht* and all members of the government to whom he had talked, including Göring, were opposed to war against Czechoslovakia. Admittedly the Army would march at Hitler's order, but the first set-back would lead to the collapse of the regime.

Before, however, action through Burckhardt could take effect, the men of the Foreign Ministry had initiated another approach on similar lines. Once more senior officials of the Foreign Ministry warned a potential enemy against their own government's policy and took the risk of divulging information which might produce an unyielding attitude on the part of that enemy to their own government's aggressive demands.

Lieutenant-Colonel Oster urged Dr Erich Kordt somehow to obtain from the British some unequivocal statement, not using the niceties of diplomatic language, but couched in terms which would impress even a semi-educated dictator who thought in terms only of force.[69] If this could be obtained, the military opposition would be in a position to prevent the outbreak of war – 'Then there will no longer be any Hitler. Do you understand me?'

Kordt, of course, knew the position of the British government; he knew that the British were inclined, rather than to use brave words, to act at the right moment, never too early; he knew that Britain's attitude was basically pacific and defensive; finally he knew that a government dependent upon parliament and the will of the electorate could not easily stipulate anything. Kordt and Oster, on the other hand, believed that Halder and his fellow-conspirators were ready for a *coup d'état*: at least they were convinced that Halder would act. Did the British government not know the mood of Germany and the *Wehrmacht* leaders, they argued? Did it not know how weak the Siegfried

Line was? Did it not know that that there could be no more than six to eight divisions facing some fifty French?[70] In 1938, therefore, the German generals had no choice but to lose the war and sink in terrible defeat or, in their own interests, overthrow Hitler. Could one therefore rely upon the generals being prepared for a *coup d'état*? The answer must be 'Yes', the opposition argued, since the generals had no other choice.

Kordt wished to remain as near as possible to the centre of affairs in order to provide a guiding hand if necessary. He therefore asked his cousin Susanne Simonis to learn by heart the message destined for the British government and transmit it verbally to his brother Theo in London.[71] She arrived there on the evening of 5 September.

Previously, on 23 August, in the house of Philip Conwell Evans, Kordt had met Sir Horace Wilson, chief industrial adviser to the British government and actually one of Chamberlain's most important advisers on foreign policy; on that occasion Kordt had implored Wilson to urge Chamberlain to adopt a consistent policy towards Germany as the only method of preventing the outbreak of the war at which Hitler was aiming so ruthlessly.[72] Conwell Evans, who had worked at Königsberg University, had certain leanings towards the Nazi regime but nevertheless played an important intermediary role between the German resistance movement and British government circles.[73]

Kordt now turned at once to Wilson again and they agreed on a meeting which took place on the following day, 6 September. What Kordt had to say seemed to Wilson of sufficient importance for him to ask that it be repeated next day to the Foreign Secretary himself. To avoid attracting unnecessary attention this discussion, at which only Kordt and Halifax were present (Wilson left after having made the arrangements), took place not in the Foreign Office but in Wilson's office in 10 Downing Street. Kordt entered unobserved by the garden entrance.[74]

Kordt told Halifax that he was the delegate of an influential group in German military and political circles which wished to prevent the war with Czechoslovakia planned by Hitler and, subject to certain conditions, had the power to do so.[75] Hitler was planning his attack on the assumption that France would not meet the obligations of her treaty of alliance with Czechoslovakia of 25 January 1924. If Hitler was now allowed to play fast and loose with his policy of force, then no further sensible international European relationships based on trust and good faith would be possible. The group for which he was speaking, Kordt continued, believed that in July 1914 the international situation would not have been so impossible had Sir Edward Grey stated clearly at the time that Britain would not stand aside in the event of a Franco-German war. If this was really the Prime Minister's view, then he must state it publicly and unequivocally so that everyone would realize Britain's determination. It must be made totally clear that war with Czechoslovakia would mean war with Britain. If, in spite of this, Hitler continued with his policy, then the German Army leaders would intervene by force of arms; German patriots saw no other method of stopping the crime of war. The prerequisite for such a step was a foreign policy defeat for Hitler, which the declaration requested would imply; this would in practice signify the end of the Nazi regime.[76]

Halifax promised to inform the Prime Minister and one or two of his cabinet colleagues; the request would be considered, he said, with the greatest care and discretion. Kordt left 10 Downing Street, again through the garden gate, feeling that an unequivocal British declaration would shortly be made. Even when Chamberlain flew to Berchtesgaden on 15 September, Kordt still thought that he was going to tell Hitler some home truths. After the Munich conference, however, Halifax said to Theo Kordt: 'We were not in a position to be as frank with you as you were with us. When you passed your message to us, we were already considering Chamberlain's mission to Germany.'[77]

In the light of all these and other initiatives, including a further warning from Goerdeler whose efforts to oppose Hitler's policy were acknowledged by Vansittart in 1948,[78] what claim can the British government make to have offered resistance when it so definitely cold-shouldered the Kordt brothers?

The British did in fact issue a warning in unmistakable language. Late in the evening of 9 September a British government message to the German Foreign Minister arrived in the Berlin Embassy; it was to be passed immediately to Nuremberg. There the great Party Rally was taking place and Sir Nevile Henderson, who was also in Nuremberg, was instructed beforehand to seek an audience with Ribbentrop.[79] He was to say that, should force be used to solve the Sudeten question and should France, at Czech request, fulfil her duties as an ally, a general conflict must ensue, from which Great Britain could not stand aloof. Ribbentrop was to be asked to pass this message forthwith to Hitler.

Henderson received the message but, in a despatch to Halifax, advised strongly against its delivery, saying that it would not restrain Hitler but merely drive him to ill-considered measures.[80] He stated that he had already spoken to Göring, Goebbels and Ribbentrop and had pointed out the inevitability of British involvement in a general conflict; under no circumstances, however, did he wish to deliver a formal warning which might be reminiscent to Hitler of the *démarche* of 21 May. Halifax accepted this; if Henderson, he replied, had already represented the British viewpoint so unequivocally to Ribbentrop, there was no need for him to deliver the warning of 9 September.[81] On 10 September, in a statement to the press, the British government even denied all reports of an intention to despatch a diplomatic note to the German government.[82]

There was occasional talk of a secret letter from Chamberlain to Hitler, but this never materialized. The British 'warning' to the German government eventually consisted merely of a statement by Chamberlain to the press, which he explicitly described as unofficial.[83] Having thus reduced its effect, the Prime Minister then expressed his great confidence in the method of negotiation and in the discussion of differences; he referred to the British warning of 24 March, reiterated in Simon's speech in Lanark on 27 August: if Czechoslovakia were attacked and France, in fulfilment of the obligations of her alliance, were involved in war with Germany, Britain would not be able to stand aloof from a general conflict. British security was closely linked with that of France.

Erich Kordt was at the Party Rally in Nuremberg when, on 12 September, he received Chamberlain's press statement. He immediately had a translation and copies prepared, also of the much sharper-toned comments by a Foreign Office press officer. Copies of both these documents were immediately distributed to the Party dignitaries staying in the Grand Hotel. Even in the general confusion, however, a Foreign Ministry official remarked on the unofficial character of the press statement and pointed this out to those present. Hitler himself dismissed the whole manoeuvre as sheer bluff.[84] In his closing speech to the Party Rally he was as aggressive as ever, although he avoided totally committing himself.[85]

The British government remained conciliatory and, as already indicated above, continuously made fresh concessions. On 15 September Chamberlain flew to Berchtesgaden; Britain and France volunteered to force Czechoslovakia to cede the Sudetenland, whereupon Hitler raised his demands and insisted on agreement to an immediate move of the *Wehrmacht* into the disputed area. Chamberlain then went to Germany once more – to the Godesberg conference of 22 to 24 September, which ended without result. The Western Powers would now be satisfied if Hitler marched into the Sudetenland, not against their will but with their agreement, and if the Czechs gave up the idea of resistance – so that there should be no war.

6 Beck's Plans

While the members of the German opposition, both inside and outside government service, were attempting to create the external political conditions conducive to the fall of Hitler, the military conspirators were developing plans for a *coup d'état*. Thoughts on this subject went back a long way. During the Fritsch crisis the idea had germinated in the minds of Oster, Gisevius, Schacht, Witzleben, Halder and others. Without the cooperation of the Commander-in-Chief of the Army and his Chief of Staff, however, no military *coup* seemed practicable, and without the military, no *coup* at all. Brauchitsch's ambiguous position has already been mentioned; hopes that he would cooperate were not great.

Beck, however, continued to try to prevent war, at least by means of memoranda. Apart from a chance conversation lasting five minutes in March 1938, he had never had an opportunity to present his views to Hitler in person.[1] Hitler was not willing to receive Beck even to say farewell on his retirement.[2]

The first series of memoranda setting out the reasons why a war would inevitably lead to catastrophe for Germany and all Europe was handed by Beck on 5 May 1938 to his Commander-in-Chief, Colonel-General von Brauchitsch. To understand these and subsequent memoranda a short explanation of their antecedents must be given.

Beck initially hoped that he could influence Hitler and persuade him to moderate his views and this he might be able to do as Chief of the General Staff but not as a private citizen. For this reason he did not resign during the Fritsch crisis despite the fact that Brauchitsch willingly took over Fritsch's post and so became Beck's superior, when all the time unfounded accusations were being made against his former Commander-in-Chief. As we have seen, Brauchitsch made no conditions regarding the reinstatement of Fritsch after the latter's rehabilitation; it would have been mere loyalty had Beck handed in his resignation at that time. On the other hand Fritsch's rehabilitation could only be achieved from inside, not from outside; moreover Beck was convinced that he must remain in order to prevent further Nazi encroachments on the Army. Finally he stayed so that, in so far as lay in his power, he could stop the war announced by Hitler on 5 November 1937.[3]

Beck's attitude was, of course, largely dictated by his character. His custom was to reflect, to check, to consider and finally to take a carefully thought-out decision. His extremely poised and deliberate manner had even earned him the nickname of 'Cunctator'.[4] This is incorrect if taken to mean that he lacked energy, but rapid decision and unorthodox action were not in Beck's make-up. During the Fritsch crisis Graf von der Goltz, Fritsch's defence counsel, said of Beck: 'As regards readiness to act everyone who knew him realized that he could not be persuaded into a "cavalry charge".'[5]

A word should be said here about the position of senior military commanders as such. Particularly during the Nuremberg trials senior officers of the *Wehrmacht* have been accused of failure to use their troops to sweep away the Nazi regime or at least of failure to disobey. This accusation, however, presupposes that there was a clear legal and moral antithesis between the leadership of the state and that of the army and only a few individuals really thought that this situation obtained; in fact this accusation presupposes, not merely a legal and moral, but also a formal and ostensibly insuperable divergence between the leadership of the state and that of the army. In 1938, during the Sudeten crisis, Beck considered that such divergence existed but his superior officer, Colonel-General von Brauchitsch, did not. Brauchitsch wanted no strike by the generals; for this reason and because of the manner in which he evaded Beck's request, Beck accused him of weakness of character. Brauchitsch was not, in fact, a strong character but refusal to consider a strike by the military is only secondarily a question of character.[6]

A strike of all commanding generals was a practicable method of stopping the war, at least temporarily. But there would not have been a strike of *all* commanding generals. There was no question of the Navy and Air Force participating in such a step and 'the leadership' of the Army was not sufficiently monolithic to make it a practicable possibility at this time. Had the 'strike' not been unanimous, Hitler could easily have replaced the refractory commanders. There were plenty of ambitious, efficient candidates not overburdened with scruple; men like Reichenau and Jodl would have been glad of promotion. Moreover in January 1938 Brauchitsch had declared himself ready to accept another Chief of Staff if necessary.[7] Beck and generals who thought as he did were regarded as expendable from the outset; they knew this and were forced to take account of the fact.

Even had the necessary conditions existed, mere refusal to obey could have been no better than a half-measure. At the Nuremberg trial Field Marshal von Manstein said very aptly that a dictator could not allow himself to be coerced since otherwise his dictatorship was at an end.[8] Opinions may vary regarding the methods Hitler might have used to free himself from coercion by the generals but he was not squeamish in his choice of methods and the Army leaders would have had to visualize their own '30 June'. Under all circumstances, therefore, the generals had to be ready for more than a strike, in other words for a *coup d'état*. A collective initiative by the military leaders was sensible only as the signal for the overthrow of the regime. Since, within the Army, the prerequisites for a *coup d'état* did not exist, this whole method was impracticable.

The question why the necessary conditions for a military strike were not present leads on to that of the political and moral responsibility of soldiers. Undoubtedly there is a duty to refuse to obey if soldiers are required to carry out illegal or criminal orders such as the shooting of prisoners of war protected by the Geneva Convention. In this case, for anyone with knowledge of the circumstances, the illegality is clear and unequivocal. Were the generals, however, to assume the right to judge the political leadership? Were they to decide what was legal and what was not in matters of foreign policy, what was a just and what an unjust war? No officer could be expected to rebel merely on a vague feeling that Hitler was in the wrong. Anyone without an overall view had no choice but to obey – assuming that he recognized the existence of military power and military resources as sensible and necessary in themselves. Those generals who could see matters clearly and had some insight into all the factors involved admittedly carried a responsibility in the sense in which Beck considered that he did himself. Even in this conflict between obedience and moral responsibility, however, generals did not necessarily display lack of character if they opted for obedience.

Discipline is the foundation of any military organization and for the relationship between a modern government and its army.[9] Over centuries of history Europe has made up its mind that policy shall be decided, not by generals or insurrectionists, but by the government of the state. If the military are not subordinate to the government, there can only be chaos internally and impotence externally. This is equally valid both for the democratically organized and for the authoritarian states.

This is not to pretend that the German Army contained no opportunist, irresponsible or characterless generals. The post-war trials showed clearly enough that there were plenty of them. Human qualities and human weakness are presumably to be found in the same proportions among military men as in other walks of human society. Too much should not be expected of the so-called 'corps of generals'. In 1938 it was not as obvious as it was in 1944 that the path chosen would inevitably lead to catastrophe; it was by no means clear that every step forward would squander thousands, hundreds of thousands, millions of human lives.

Nevertheless it was clear that the threat of war with Britain and France and, if they were in difficulties, with the United States also, was great; it was also clear that Germany was militarily incapable of dealing with such an eventuality. The danger could be averted by political means, but not by military. The duty of the military leaders was to point this out, and this they did. Hitler complained with astonishment and irritation about the pacifism of the General Staff.[10] Beck was not the only one to emphasize the hopelessness of war against the Western Powers; he received support from many quarters. Having dutifully made their reservations, however, Brauchitsch and the other senior commanders left it to the politicians to draw their conclusions, whereas Beck felt himself compelled to go further.

In his memorandum dated 5 May 1938 Beck pointed out that, owing to the progressive weakening of Japan as a result of her Far Eastern campaigns, Britain and Russia had an increasingly free hand in Europe, that Britain and

Italy were cooperating on many subjects and that Britain and France had come to political and military agreement and were already visualizing the possibility of world war; they were in the process of accelerating their rearmament.[11] Germany was therefore surrounded almost exclusively by potential enemies. However averse Britain and France might be to a new war and however great the efforts they might make to avoid it, they would not tolerate a further shift of power in Europe in Germany's favour. Germany lacked the resources necessary to sustain a prolonged war: the *Wehrmacht* would not be ready for years; the continental foundation for a prolonged war was lacking; raw materials and food were only available, or could only be obtained, in inadequate quantities. A military solution of the Czech question was therefore a bad one; the only acceptable solution was one with which Britain would agree.

Brauchitsch received Beck's memorandum on the afternoon of 7 May. He discussed it with Keitel and, on the latter's advice, submitted to Hitler only the third (military) section. Hitler rejected it indignantly as far too pessimistic.[12] On 28 May Hitler announced to the leaders of the *Wehrmacht* (including Beck), the Party and the State his 'unalterable decision to destroy Czechoslovakia by military action within a foreseeable time'.[13] He spoke of *Lebensraum* and did not even exclude war with the West in order to expand Germany's coastline. Beck reacted at once with a further memorandum to Brauchitsch on 29 May.[14] He still did not wish to push matters to an open breach; he still hoped to convince Hitler and make him change his mind. Beck's campaign was still *for* Hitler (for his comprehension), not *against* Hitler; he therefore went a long way with the dictator in order to make his arguments, which were essentially military, credible. Wolfgang Foerster, Beck's biographer, has aptly said that Beck was trying 'to throw the weight of *military judgment* into the scales of *political decision-making*'.[15]

Beck himself read his new memorandum to Brauchitsch on 30 May. In it he said that it was correct that Germany required further *Lebensraum*, both in Europe (as Hitler had said on the previous day) and in colonial areas. In Europe Germany could only acquire additional territory by war. It was also correct that Czechoslovakia in its present form was intolerable for Germany and should be eliminated as a source of danger to Germany, 'if necessary by a military solution'. In this event (solution by war), however, 'the anticipated success must justify the stake'.[16] It was not correct, however, that, as Hitler had maintained, Germany was stronger today than in 1914 or that she could sustain a struggle against France — a certain opponent of any expansion of German power — and against Britain. Compared to the 1914 army the *Wehrmacht* was inferior in 'personnel, equipment and morale'; territory available was inadequate for a war on several fronts; as regards finance, foodstuffs and raw materials the position was worse even than that of 1917–18; the people were opposed to any war not obviously unavoidable. Internally, therefore, Germany was not very strong and externally she faced a coalition of Czechoslovakia, France, Britain and the United States. In this situation Germany might well win the Czech campaign, but she would lose the war. Even in 1914 Britain and France had been underestimated, though not by the General

Staff. A soldier knew that France and Britain had a vast hinterland available – colonies, dominions, maritime communications, fleet bases and in emergency even the United States; Germany had no comparable operational base. Initial 'blitz' victories might be won, but they should not be regarded as decisive for the war as a whole. These considerations showed that the Supreme Commander of the *Wehrmacht* lacked realistic advice and, if this situation persisted, the fate of the *Wehrmacht* 'and therefore the fate of Germany too' could only be painted in the blackest colours.

On this same day, 30 May, Hitler notified the Commanders-in-Chief of the three Services in writing of his unalterable decision to destroy Czechoslovakia; he instructed them to prepare to carry out this decision by the end of September, so that action could be taken at any time thereafter.[17]

Beck immediately drafted yet another memorandum. In this he confined himself primarily to technical military arguments designed to show that the Supreme Commander's military directive could not be implemented.[18] Brauchitsch received the document on 3 June. In it Beck complained that Hitler's directive had been issued without consultation with the Chief of Staff of the Army and he showed that action against Czechoslovakia based on this directive could only lead to disaster. The Army General Staff, he said, must refuse to take any responsiblity for measures based on these principles. This was clear enough. It concerned matters on which Beck was the expert and with which his position entitled him to deal; he had no need to fear being told to mind his own business and so finding his protest brushed aside.

Beck now took a step designed to bring home to the entire top level of the Army what Hitler's intentions were and to prove that they were both dangerous and impracticable. Instead of the annual General Staff tour he ordered an indoor war game to study the course of a German attack on Czechoslovakia on the assumption that France intervened.[19] In his summing up Beck showed that, although Czechoslovakia had been crushed by German troops, the French Army had meanwhile advanced deep into German territory and that defeat could no longer be averted.[20] Beck's conclusion from this was that the political leadership must be guided in its decisions by military and economic capabilities, otherwise the country would slide into catastrophe.

Brauchitsch did not contradict Beck, but neither did he explicitly agree with him.[21] During the dinner in the 'Esplanade' Hotel, Berlin, given by Beck to his audience at the closing conference, it was clear that his views did not have unanimous support. In particular Major Schmundt, the *Führer*'s *Wehrmacht* aide in succession to Hossbach, and Lieutenant-Colonel Hans Jeschonnek, later Chief of Staff of the *Luftwaffe*, described Beck's views as antiquated and obsolete, saying that, like Graf von Schlieffen, he had not kept pace with technical progress.[22] The warning voices, however, seem to have been in the majority; people pointed out that the world would never permit German continental hegemony, that Russia represented a vast and grossly underestimated threat and that, because he talked sense, Beck would probably soon share the fate of Fritsch.[23]

On 15 July Beck took up his pen once more. In a further memorandum to

Brauchitsch (the final draft carries the date of 16 July) Beck insisted with even greater emphasis than before on the dangers of a general European, and probably worldwide, war.[24] Daladier's latest speech on 12 July, he said, must have convinced all the sceptics of France's determination. All available information showed that the people did not want war and did not understand its purpose; the Army was once more a people's army and would have no confidence in leaders prepared to risk another general war. Even before the outbreak of war this popular mood might have dangerous consequences for the fighting value and morale of the troops. Moreover, once Britain and France had intervened to defend Czechoslovakia, they would no longer be satisfied with mere restoration of Czech territory; it would be '*a life and death war with Germany*'. Germany lacked the resources for effective defence in the West.

Beck concluded his politico-military arguments with these words: 'In the light of my previous statements I regard it as my duty today – in full knowledge of the significance of such a step but conscious of the responsibility laid upon me by my official assignment for the preparation and conduct of a war – to put forward the following urgent request: *the Supreme Commander of the Wehrmacht must be induced to halt the war preparations which he has ordered* and to postpone his proposed solution of the Czech question by force until the military conditions therefor have radically changed. At present I can see no prospects of success and this my view is shared by all my subordinate Deputy Chiefs of the General Staff and heads of General Staff sections, in so far as they are concerned with preparation for and conduct of war against Czechoslovakia.'[25]

Beck's deep-rooted sense of ethical responsibility emerges clearly from these sentences. Admittedly it was not officially his province to judge the moral rectitude of strategic plans and military operations; for this reason he invariably confined himself to military arguments. This was why he said that 'at present' Germany was not yet ready for war. His estimate of the military forces, however, was based upon a political estimate, which was strictly not his province, as he himself recognized when he said that he was conscious of the significance of his step: Beck assumed that Britain and France, probably also the United States, would intervene. Under such conditions Germany would never be 'ready' for war, since her defeat would be certain from the outset.[26]

Finally Beck urged upon his Commander-in-Chief the production of a sober unanimous appreciation of the situation resulting from discussions with and incorporating the views of Commanders-in-Chief and commanding generals of the Army and of the Commanders-in-Chief of the other two Services. Then Hitler should hold a conference with commanding generals, who must be agreed beforehand on the views which they would put forward. This would be the famous 'collective step' – the generals should tell Hitler that they were opposed to war. The Commander-in-Chief of the Army and his Chief of the General Staff could not, by themselves, hope to gain the ear of their Supreme Commander. In Hitler's eyes they were expendable. Would he not, however, be forced to abandon his plans, if he found that the vast majority of the military commanders were also opposed to war?

This memorandum was submitted to Brauchitsch on 16 July and on the same day Beck discussed it with him; this enabled Beck to set out his proposal for a collective initiative with much greater clarity: the senior commanders of the *Wehrmacht*, he said, should *force* Hitler to halt his war preparations and, if he would not be coerced, they should resign from their posts in a body. Beck's papers include a record of his discussion with Brauchitsch.[27] He explained the moral responsibility of the high-ranking soldier in even sharper and clearer terms: '*Vital decisions for the future of the nation are at stake. History will indict these commanders of blood guilt if, in the light of their professional and political knowledge, they do not obey the dictates of their conscience. The soldier's duty to obey ends when his knowledge, his conscience and his sense of responsibility forbid him to carry out a certain order.*'[28] If, he continued, the military commanders' warnings and advice were not heeded, then they had both the right and the duty before their nation and before history to resign from their posts. If they did this as a body war would be impossible and the Fatherland would be saved from ruin. High-ranking soldiers should not confine themselves to their purely military task but must be conscious of their supreme responsibility to the people as a whole – '*Exceptional times demand exceptional measures.*'

Beck was well aware that, even if successful, the proposed collective step must have internal political repercussions. He thought that there would be '*serious internal political strains*'; Hitler, he knew, intended in any case to rid himself as soon as he could of the old generals, in other words those so far immune to Nazi ideology – he is supposed to have said that he would conduct the war against the Czechs with these people, but would have a new breed of commanders for that against France and Britain. Beck therefore concluded that 'we must make up our minds that simultaneously with or immediately after this protest there must be a thorough-going showdown between the *Wehrmacht* and the SS. In other words the collective protest could only be successful if simultaneously or immediately thereafter the Nazis were deprived of their own instrument of power, and that implied a *coup d'état*. Even if he remained Chancellor, Hitler would not be a dictator if the *Wehrmacht* no longer obeyed him and his Party army had been disarmed.[29]

On 19 July Beck reiterated his proposal for a collective protest even more emphatically. Again he stressed the 'consequences' of such a step and the opportunity for a 'showdown with the SS and the Party bosses' which he described as essential for the 'reestablishment of the rule of law'. In the record of this particular discussion with Brauchitsch which Beck drafted, however, appears the sentence: 'There can and must be no doubt that this struggle is conducted for the *Führer*.'[30] Perhaps for the last time, he continued, destiny was offering an opportunity 'to the German people and the *Führer* himself to liberate themselves from the nightmare of a Cheka and domination by Party bosses who, by influencing the attitude of the people, will destroy both the existence and welfare of the *Reich* and enable communism to revive'.

The key to this phrase lies in the reference to communism, which was by no means reviving at the time, and in Beck's situation when making these statements. Undoubtedly he knew that Hitler was not the tool of some devil's advocate. He had to remember, however, that all soldiers had sworn a personal oath to Hitler as Supreme Commander and he knew that the majority, including Brauchitsch, were not prepared to brush this oath aside. If Brauchitsch was to be persuaded to act, this could only be done through the fiction of liberating Hitler from the evil influences of the SS and corrupt Party bosses. The references to the Party bosses, whom the military hated, the arrogant competing army of the SS and the spectre of communism were calculated to influence Brauchitsch's military mind.

It is easy to say now that nothing could be achieved by such arguments; today we know that to be true. At the time, however, no other course was open to a man like Beck who, as Chief of Staff, had no troops under his command. Beck knew his Army officers well. He knew that, however much they might dislike the man and his actions, they were not to be persuaded to revolt against the Head of State: 'There must not be even the smallest suspicion of a plot.'[31] Nevertheless Beck visualized the situation in which Hitler would be placed if faced with a collective protest by the generals: therefore 'the most senior military commanders must stand united *behind this step under all circumstances*'. These last words applied to the foreseeable eventuality that Hitler might not simply give way. In that event it was necessary to look further and visualize the situation once the spark had been lit. Consequently: 'Short, clear slogans: For the *Führer* – against war – against the tyranny of the Party bosses – peace with the church – freedom of expression – away with Cheka methods – back to the rule of law in the *Reich* – reduction of all levies by half – no more building of palaces – housing for the people – Prussian honesty and simplicity!'[32] That was his programme. It implied nothing less than the removal of the Nazi tyranny with everything characteristic of it.[33]

Remarkably enough another memorandum or minute exists, the background to which is still unexplained. It is dated 17 July and was written by Vice-Admiral Günther Guse, Chief of the Naval Staff. It puts forward entirely similar thoughts: In a war of European proportions Germany must inevitably be defeated and it was to be feared that such a conflict might develop from an attack on Czechoslovakia; it was therefore the duty of Hitler's responsible advisers, not merely to carry out his orders, 'but also to exert the full force of their personality, accepting all the consequences, in order to arrest a development threatening the existence of the *Reich* while there is still time'.[34] As the means of doing this Guse proposed 'combined representations by the heads of the three Services' or at least by those of the Army and Navy if Göring would not participate. Like Beck, Guse proposed to battle not against but for and about the *Führer*, and to prevent advisers closer to the *Führer* than the Commanders-in-Chief calling the tune entirely. Like Beck, however, he wished to 'go to the limit', in other words not merely to protest but, if necessary, to take resolute action against Hitler.

Captain Helmut Heye, Guse's senior Operations Officer, also gave vent to similar ideas; again paralleling Beck, he urged reestablishment of the rule of law at home and stoppage of the persecution of the churches and the Jews. There was now a crusading spirit abroad in Europe, he said, or at least an antipathy to Germany. An attack on Czechoslovakia would inevitably act as the spark, and intervention by the Western powers would mean loss of the war by Germany.[35]

Only gradually did the would-be struggle *for* Hitler turn into open struggle *against* him. For Beck the turning point seems to have been 28 July, on which day he received detailed information on Hitler's reaction to Wiedemann's report on his London mission.[36] As he recorded in a note on that day, Beck's conclusion from Hitler's persistent determination to use warlike methods was this: 'The moment seems to have passed, or at least it has become considerably more difficult, to wean him away from these ideas by reasoned argument and warnings.'[37]

On the following day, 29 July, Beck had a further interview with Brauchitsch and pressed him even harder than before. It was now urgent, he said, to consider 'whether and at what moment the Commander-in-Chief of the Army with the Army generals solid behind him should present himself to the *Führer*'. Brauchitsch should say to Hitler, he continued: '*The Commander-in-Chief of the Army, together with his most senior commanding generals, regret that they cannot assume responsibility for the conduct of a war of this nature without carrying a share of the guilt for it in face of the people and of history. Should the Führer, therefore, insist on the prosecution of this war, they hereby resign from their posts.*'[38] This statement, he said, should be made in the sternest and most brutal terms and the most suitable moment was probably the latter half of September.[39] The intoxication of the forthcoming Party Rally would have evaporated by that time; the anticipated notes from the French and British governments would have arrived and they should 'make the situation far clearer'. At about this time the financial situation would compel the Finance Minister to protest to Hitler against continuation of his policy.[40] A few days later, however, Beck had become convinced that there was no more time to lose and that action must be taken before the Party Rally, the best opportunity being 15 August when Hitler had ordered a gathering of senior generals in the Jüterbog training area.[41]

Beck was now equally clear on the 'internal strains' to be expected. These must be anticipated 'in any case', no matter whether Hitler gave way or not. Clearly, therefore, he appreciated realistically the situation which would arise as a result of a strike threat by the generals. He set out its sequel quite plainly: 'It will thereafter be necessary for the Army to be prepared, not only for possible war, but also for upheaval at home which it should be possible to confine to Berlin. Issue orders accordingly. Get Witzleben together with Helldorf.'

No further proof is therefore required of Beck's readiness to initiate a *coup d'état* 'in any case'. At this time Witzleben was commanding III Army Corps and Military District III (Berlin); Graf von Helldorf was Police President of Berlin. These two together had sufficient force to occupy all key positions in Berlin. The transition had therefore been made from mere protest, even though that included a threat of resignation, to concrete planning for a *coup d'état*. On Beck's instructions and in collaboration with Witzleben, Lieutenant-General Karl-Heinrich von Stülpnagel, Deputy Chief of Staff II in the Army General Staff, was already busy working out detailed plans.[42]

About this time Beck wrote a draft of the speech to be made by Brauchitsch to group commanders and commanding generals giving them the background and urging them to participate in the protest.[43] In essence it consisted of the arguments and opinions already put forward by Beck in his memoranda and his interviews with Brauchitsch. On 15 August Hitler was proposing to assemble army group commanders-in-chief, commanding generals and others of similar rank in Jüterbog. There Beck hoped that, when Hitler explained his ideas, the generals would support Brauchitsch; they were also to give the necessary information and instructions to such other officers under their command as might be invited by Hitler in the next few weeks to the Obersalzberg or on board the yacht 'Grille'.[44]

Now it was for Brauchitsch to make up his mind. But the Commander-in-Chief of the Army could not bring himself to take up a definite attitude. He thought that both Hitler and Beck were right. He knew that Beck's views were correct in the long term but he was incapable of drawing the necessary conclusions from that knowledge.

At Beck's suggestion Brauchitsch summoned army group and corps commanders to a conference in Berlin on 4 August.[45] Beck's major memorandum of July was read to the meeting.[46] Invited by Brauchitsch, General Adam then described the totally inadequate condition, defensive capability and manning of the Siegfried Line. Brauchitsch agreed and instructed Adam to say precisely the same to Hitler.[47]

The other generals were then invited to put forward any differing views. There was almost unanimous agreement with the appreciation prepared by the Army High Command. Only two people, General von Reichenau commanding Army Group 4, and General Ernst Busch, commanding VIII Army Corps, struck a divergent note; the *Führer* would do the right thing, they said; one must have confidence in him and maintain discipline. Opposition was so small that, at the end of the conference, Brauchitsch announced unanimity. He had not, however, delivered the speech drafted by Beck. The assembled generals heard not a word about the collective protest and its probable consequences; no one was asked to declare his readiness to 'fight for Hitler'.

Nevertheless a few days after the 4 August conference Brauchitsch submitted Beck's memorandum to Hitler; subsequently, moreover, when the crisis was at its height about mid-September, Brauchitsch asked corps commanders to 'support him in opening the *Führer's* eyes to the adventure into which he has decided to plunge', saying that he himself no longer had any influence with Hitler – as Jodl noted in his diary on 13 September.[48] Even before Beck's resignation, however, Brauchitsch had begun to work more and more with General Halder, the Deputy Chief of Staff, and less and less with Beck. Finally he remained placidly at his post when General Ludwig Beck, Chief of the General Staff of the Army and his principal adviser, resigned.[49]

On 10 August Hitler convened group commanders, their chiefs of staff and other high-ranking officers at the 'Berghof', and addressed them for several hours after lunch, talking about his unalterable decision to smash Czechoslovakia, and about other ideas he had for the future. When Generals von Wietersheim and Adam voiced misgivings about the inadequacy of defences in the West, Hitler began to scream and said the position there would not merely be held for three weeks but for three years.[50] On the whole, however, Hitler remained calm and polite, and finally concluded his remarks by saying he knew that his soldiers would not let him down and he hoped that neither would the generals and the General Staff.

Hitler sent word to Beck through Brauchitsch that he refused to accept political disquisitions; he alone knew what he had to do. This and Brauchitsch's insincere vacillating attitude inevitably left Beck feeling that he had been disowned; he had no other choice, therefore, but to resign. 'Brauchitsch left me in the lurch!', he would often say later in tones of anger and indignation. His proposals and preparations for measures following the collective protest, his advocacy of collective action and finally his utterances after his ultimate resignation show that Beck placed little hope in the possibility of his resignation preventing war.[51] He was now determined not to carry a share of the responsibility; he could no longer stop anything. His fellow-officers and collaborators such as Weizsäcker advised him to remain – but in vain.

Having heard Hitler's speech in Jüterbog on 15 August, which included a reiteration of his announcement that he would solve the Sudeten German question by force that autumn, on 18 August Beck applied to his Commander-in-Chief to be relieved of his office. Three days later, on 21 August, he was told that Hitler had approved.[52] On 24 and 26 August Beck had further talks with Brauchitsch and the latter told him that, for foreign policy reasons, Hitler did not wish his retirement publicized for the time being. Beck complied. On 27 August he handed over his duties to his successor, General Halder, saying farewell only to his immediate staff, the deputy chiefs of staff and heads of section.

Initially Beck was appointed to command First Army which was to concentrate in the West in the event of war. On 19 October, when the crisis was over, on Hitler's instructions he asked to retire, which he did on 31 October, being simultaneously promoted Colonel-General.[53] During the crisis he was not closely involved in Halder's, Witzleben's and Oster's plans for a *coup*.

Beck did not allow himself to be deluded by Hitler's success over the Sudeten question; he was still convinced that pursuance of Hitler's policy would inevitably lead to war with the Western Powers. In November, at greater leisure now since his retirement, he once more reduced his thoughts to writing. Since 1914, he said, great wars were total wars, in other words wars absorbing the entire resources of a people – men, raw materials, industry, labour, research, pertinacity and moral conviction. 'The defensive capacity of a people stems from a combination of spiritual, physical and industrial strength. The armed forces are only a component of this strength which will carry them to victory over the enemy. Representatives of the new-born *Wehrmacht* must recognize the relationship between defensive capacity and the armed forces and be as solicitous for the one as they are for the other. This summarizes the great lesson of the World War.'[54] This was written to Beck by Ludendorff in 1935; it was Beck's view also. Beck's thoughts led him to the conclusion – precisely as before – that, comparing Germany's total resources with those of her certain enemies, she had no prospect of winning a war. The requisite foundations must first be laid by a judicious economic and alliance policy so that both strategy and war economy rested on secure foundations. This had to take place in peacetime. On the other hand, with her new *Wehrmacht*, Germany was now so strong that no attack need be feared; an aggressor would be taking too great a risk.[55]

As a soldier Beck did not believe that war could be avoided for ever. There would always be enemies, he said; a people and its leaders must insist on a policy which served its vital (and accepted) interests and, if all other methods failed, war remained as the final arbiter. Moltke, for instance, held war to be part of the divine world order but, even in victory, he thought it a national misfortune.[56] 'We cannot abolish war,' Beck wrote. 'Whenever one reflects on the imperfection of mankind as decreed by God, one invariably reaches this conclusion.'[57] But he went on: 'Although it must be assumed that the goal of eternal peace can never be fully reached', a new moral idealism 'should make possible never-ending progress, bringing us nearer and nearer to it.'[58] Basically Beck was an opponent of war in any form.

7 Halder's Plans

Beck's successor was the former Deputy Chief of Staff I in the Army General Staff, General Franz Halder. Those who knew him describe him almost unanimously as religious, conservative, an outstanding staff officer in the best tradition with an 'inexhaustible capacity for work', correct, sober but sensitive too, with a pronounced sense of responsibility and rooted in the tradition of military discipline.[1] Though no one is prepared to eulogize Halder in the same terms as Beck, no one has voiced serious doubts about his antipathy to Hitler. Nevertheless his attitude as regards resistance is the subject of controversy and will remain so.

Halder succeeded Beck with the latter's agreement and he left Brauchitsch in no doubt that he was firmly determined to continue to oppose Hitler's war policy.[2] Nevertheless events cast a shadow over Halder.

Why did he remain after the abortive attempt at a *coup* in autumn 1938 and after Hitler's breach of treaty by the invasion of the 'remainder of Czechoslovakia'? Why did he still remain when he must have known that Hitler would attack Poland? Why did he help prepare Hitler's war? There is no clear answer to these questions.[3] After the Sudeten crisis Halder must have known that Britain, though not yet prepared militarily, was ready to fight if agreement could not be reached; he must also have known that Hitler's bloodless victories were at an end, seeing that he was not prepared to change his methods. Halder was well informed at all times about conditions at home, about the tyranny of the *Gestapo*, later about the murders in Poland and finally about Hitler's crazy strategic ideas; his own diary proves as much.[4] No one seriously pretends that Hitler was not in the habit of implementing his threats; at the latest by the time of the move into Prague it was clear that the opposite was the case. To a soldier the honest conviction must be conceded that resignation *in wartime* is a form of desertion and dereliction of duty. Halder, however, can hardly be credited with the intention, which kept Weizsäcker in office, of remaining in order to prevent and restrain as much as he could. Halder could neither foresee nor stop the 'liquidations' in Poland and Russia nor the strategic and tactical blunders coupled with the name Stalingrad. Beck's fate shows what prospects of success a protest had and, once the guns were firing, there was little more that could be stopped.[5]

This is not to say that in 1938 Halder's opposition was not serious. He allowed himself to become so deeply involved in preparations for a *coup* that there can be no doubt of his sincerity and courage. The reasons for his failure are only partially to be found in his character.

Even before becoming Chief of Staff Halder was in close touch with Weizsäcker, State Secretary in the Foreign Ministry; Beck had introduced them and paved the way; from end August 1938 Halder kept in closer touch than ever, despite the fact that direct correspondence between the two offices was explicitly forbidden.[6] The exchange of information, communications and agreements between Halder and Weizsäcker was largely channelled through the OKW office *Ausland/Abwehr* (Military Intelligence) under Admiral Canaris. This excited no comment since it was as natural that the Foreign Ministry and Canaris' office should correspond as it was that Canaris and the Army Chief of Staff should do likewise. During Canaris' frequent absences his place was taken by Oster, whom Halder knew already from the time when he had been Chief of Staff of *Wehrkreis* VI in Münster and Oster had been one of his staff officers.[7]

The central and most active role between all the various groups was played by Oster; he was the driving force and at the same time the intermediary.[8] Gisevius was also actively involved in preparations for a *coup*; Dr Hjalmar Schacht, the President of the *Reichsbank*, took part in vital discussions and was available for political tasks.[9]

The first discussions on details of a *coup* seem to have taken place at the very end of August; it is not possible to establish a precise date. Beck's and Halder's efforts overlapped; those of Oster and his immediate associates, together with Gisevius' probings, ran in parallel.[10] When Halder assumed office on 27 August (a Saturday), he already knew of Beck's intentions. As before, Oster continued to make every effort to prevent war. At the end of August Schacht and Gisevius met in their quest for men with military power of command who were also prepared to 'act'. At the same time, on Beck's advice, Halder turned to Oster, asking him what technical and political preparations for a *coup* had been made.[11] At that time Oster could only refer in general terms to the readiness of certain personalities such as Schacht and Goerdeler to collaborate and participate on the political level.[12]

Halder had no wish to be in contact with Goerdeler; he did not know him and Goerdeler had too great a reputation as an 'anti'. Schacht, on the other hand, seemed more balanced; he was still in office and highly respected; contact with him seemed less perilous and prejudicial. Halder had already met Schacht at a *Reichsbank* reception in the winter of 1937–38, to which he had been taken apparently by Colonel Eduard Wagner, head of Section 6 (Quartermaster section) of the Army General Staff.[13] Shortly after his first talk with Oster, Halder visited Schacht in his house.[14]

Halder was insistent that a *coup* must not lead to chaos or civil war, but must result in the quickest possible reestablishment of stable political conditions. Accordingly at this very first encounter he asked Schacht – and it was nothing less than high treason – whether he would be prepared to play a leading part in a new government to be formed after the regime had been overthrown by the Army. A *coup*, he said, was unavoidable if Hitler pushed matters as far as war.[15] Schacht gave general consent but no political programme was discussed in detail.[16]

To settle questions concerning use of the police in the event of a *putsch*, first Oster and then Schacht referred the Chief of Staff to Dr Gisevius. He was a *Regierungsrat* (counsellor) in the Ministry of the Interior; between 1933 and 1936 he had been in turn – with the *Gestapo*, in the Prussian Ministry of the Interior, in the *Reich* Ministry of the Interior, in *Reich* Criminal Police headquarters and finally, until May 1937 on the staff of the *Regierungspräsident* in Münster dealing with price control; since then he had been on unpaid leave but had remained in somewhat nebulous touch with the *Abwehr*.[17] It was arranged that Gisevius should visit Halder in the latter's apartment in Berlin-Zehlendorf, and this meeting took place shortly after Halder's talk with Schacht.[18]

At the meeting Halder was totally frank about his antagonism to Hitler; he was a blood-sucker and a criminal, he said, and should be done away with. It was hard, however, extremely hard, he continued, to explain to other generals in plausible terms this and Hitler's patent intention to initiate war.[19] The widespread view among the generals was that Hitler was merely preparing a colossal bluff, but not war. Hitler knew perfectly well, they thought, how dangerous war would be for the success of German policy and perhaps even for the existence of the *Reich*; they believed that some form of arrangement existed between the Western Powers and Hitler leaving him a free hand in the east.[20] One could not be sure of the mass of the people either. So long as it was not made tangibly clear to them that continuation of the present policy was bound to lead to bloodshed, so long they and the mass of the Army would support Hitler; should a *coup* be attempted, therefore, one must reckon with civil war. The best remedy for this situation was perhaps to wait until the actual outbreak of hostilities or at least until declaration of war by the Western Powers.[21]

Halder was sceptical on this point too. No one could say with complete certainty at what point the Western Powers would proceed to war, though the probability was verging on certainty that this would happen as soon as some country was occupied by warlike as opposed to 'peaceful' methods – as in Austria's case. It could, however, be said with certainty that they would very quickly counter any further expansion of German power or conquest by Hitler. Halder, however, wanted to know this for sure and the most certain knowledge would come with the outbreak of war. As Schacht put it, Halder was searching among those around him for the assurance which he could not find within himself. He realized what had to be done and he did not lack determination, but his weakness and lack of self-assurance prevented him taking the step from decision to action.[22] Halder himself must have realized the enormous peril of such procrastination. As did Gisevius he visualized that on the outbreak of war there would be immediate air raids on industrial areas and he also thought, like Beck, that the Western Powers would achieve a strategic break-through.[23] Anyone who remembered the First World War and who, like Beck and Halder, thought the British and French armies to be superior to the

German, could not foresee the 'phoney war' of 1939.

Understandably Gisevius did not exactly gain the impression that Halder was a go-getter. One could hardly rely, Gisevius reported, on this pedantic, over-cautious, though very clever, man. On his side Halder had not been particularly attracted by Gisevius.[24] One reason for this was the proposals which Gisevius put to the Chief of Staff and which he considered foolhardy, not without some justification. Gisevius had said that the regime must be attacked as criminal, in other words that indictment should be based on the *Gestapo*, the SS in general and the concentration camps. The criminal nature of these institutions was in fact obvious and action against them required no special justification. In this way Hitler could, to some extent, be kept out of the affair. Anyone so minded, Gisevius said, might think that Hitler was being protected against the worst of his thugs and the great advantage was that this would circumvent the problem of the oath sworn by the soldiers to their Supreme Commander. This would create a situation in which the *Wehrmacht* would have to reestablish order.[25]

Such a procedure Halder regarded as dubious. What would happen if the *Wehrmacht* were subsequently accused of having broken the law when its whole ethic was exactly the opposite? Gisevius knew a way out of this too: within a few hours of the occupation of *Gestapo* headquarters, he said, he would have secured evidence and proof of the crimes of Heydrich, Himmler and Göring; this would demonstrate the legality of the purge.[26] These documents could not, of course, be obtained beforehand. Halder was not sure about this either; he preferred that there should first be some foreign policy or even military set-back.

The fact remained that Halder was not willing to use the Army against the regime — at least that was the impression which he gave Gisevius during this visit. According to Gisevius' report he was thinking of a bomb attack on Hitler's train which could be represented as an enemy bombing raid.[27] Halder had certain scruples about an assassination attempt which might be ascribed to the Army.[28]

The same night, after this unsatisfactory evening talk, Gisevius met Oster and gave him his somewhat unflattering impressions of Halder. Oster was taken aback. The next day, however, there was cause for fresh hope: Halder instructed Oster to cooperate with Gisevius in preparing all police measures for the *coup d'état*.[29]

Gisevius, Oster and Schacht were now confronted by four main tasks. In the first place a plan for the *coup d'état* must be worked out at once and in full detail; secondly an immediate attempt must be made to win over other senior officers, particularly formation commanders; thirdly every effort must be made to persuade Halder that the code-word which he intended to issue only in the event of war, should in fact be broadcast much earlier; finally, in order to provide Halder with some basis for his decision other than an invasion order by Hitler, he must be kept continuously informed of all foreign policy developments. This last was done primarily by Oster with occasional help from Schacht and Weizsäcker. Halder's instruction to work with Gisevius on police matters gave Oster the office to proceed on the first point. A number of days passed before progress could be made on the other two points.

On 5 September the Party Rally opened in Nuremberg; its motto was 'Greater Germany'. For a week everyone waited tensely for Hitler's closing speech scheduled for 12 September, when he proposed to 'square the account' with Czechoslovakia.[30] In fact Hitler did threaten to intervene in Czechoslovakia to enforce his demands and those of the Sudeten Germans 'by hook or by crook'.[31] But he did not commit himself.

Some time passed before preparations for the *coup* really got under way. Schacht and Gisevius were uneasy and impatient. They wanted to establish whether Halder would keep his word and whether he was making the necessary preparations; primarily, however, now that war seemed increasingly probable, they wished to press him to issue the signal for the *putsch* before the outbreak of hostilities. Schacht accordingly expressed a wish to visit Halder and this was arranged by Oster. Gisevius accompanied him, uninvited and unannounced, which did not please Halder very much.[32]

In fact, when Schacht and Gisevius appeared in Halder's house, they found him no longer as resolute as before.[33] Oster also could only tell his co-conspirators that Halder was 'nearly decided'.[34] Halder was apparently hoping that, despite everyone's fears, the Western Powers would allow Hitler a free hand to annex the Sudetenland provided that this could be done peacefully, in other words without bloodshed.[35] On the other hand Halder did now seem ready to stop a war and to do so before the outbreak of hostilities. He was prepared to give the signal for a rising as soon as Hitler issued the order to march.[36]

Halder was also able to reassure Schacht and Gisevius on another important point: Hitler could not make a surprise move leaving the opposition no time to act. The military plans, Halder said, were so designed that the Chief of Staff 'would know whether he [Hitler] was planning something' at least seventy-two hours before an attack.[37] An irrevocable order must be issued twenty-four hours before H hour, after which an attack could no longer be halted.[38]

On 8 September Lieutenant-General Karl-Heinrich von Stülpnagel, the Army Deputy Chief of Staff I who knew of the plans for a *coup* and had taken part in working them out, asked OKW in writing for an assurance that OKH would be told five days beforehand if 'an action' was to take place.[39] Colonel Jodl, head of the OKW Operations Staff, gave this assurance with the proviso that any major change in the weather might lead to alteration in the intention and issuance of the order to march up to two days before the time of movement, in other words up to D-2. During the night 9/10 September Halder had an interview with Hitler in Nuremberg about preparations for mobilization. The discussion was evidently stormy and a few days later General Keitel told Jodl of his disappointment with the attitude of certain generals. There had been reports from the *Abwehr* and a memorandum from the Economic Defence staff on the great strength of the British arms industry, lack of confidence in the *Luftwaffe*, doubts voiced by Brauchitsch and Halder owing to the danger of the overall strategic situation, particularly if the Western Powers intervened. Though Jodl himself shared these doubts at the time, all this must have enraged Hitler.[40] Hitler was especially unwilling to have his hands tied by military arguments about the time interval between D Day for the assault and issue of the final order. Though previously he had apparently accepted Halder's reasoning, on 28 September he laid down that decision on the final order must be taken 'by midday on the previous day'.

Schacht was opposed to this insistence on waiting until the last moment for the *coup d'état*, but Halder was adamant. Schacht and Gisevius increasingly gained the impression that no reliance could be placed on Halder.[41]

This disillusioning realization decided Gisevius and Schacht, together with Oster to whom they reported, that greater efforts must be made to win over other military personalities. The obvious course was to turn first to the commander primarily responsible for carrying out the orders which it was hoped that Halder would issue; this was General von Witzleben, commanding Military District III.[42] He had been Oster's commanding officer for a time and was now commanding III Army Corps (Military District III) with headquarters at No 144 Hohenzollerndamm, Berlin.[43] He was not interested in politics and frequently said that he understood nothing about them. It was enough for him to know that the time had come to do away with Hitler's illegal regime and that he could make a major contribution to this. Witzleben has been described as typical of the honest, unbureaucratic, uncomplicated, energetic commander, rooted in the best military traditions – a straightforward person who invariably kept his word.[44]

In the first half of September Oster approached Witzleben, asking him whether he would be prepared to participate in a *coup* if necessary and Witzleben agreed at once, not without certain conditions, however. In the first place Witzleben wished to know whether there would really be war if Hitler attacked Czechoslovakia; he was sufficiently politically-minded to realize that he could hardly oppose Hitler if the latter was in process of winning another major bloodless victory on the lines of the invasion of Austria.[45] Some risk was unavoidable, he said, but foolhardiness was not and the troops should not be expected to do the impossible. Oster and Gisevius said that Schacht was the politician best qualified to give information on the foreign political situation. The result was a visit by Witzleben to Schacht in his country house at Gühlen.[46]

Witzleben was accompanied by Major-General Walter Graf von Brockdorff-Ahlefeldt, Commander of 23 (Potsdam) Division, and Gisevius was also present. As far as can be established this meeting took place between Halder's visit to Schacht and the latter's return visit, in other words between 4 and 14 September.[47] Schacht and the generals quickly reached agreement; Schacht spoke most convincingly on the external political situation and the imminent intervention of the Western Powers; Witzleben and Brockdorff agreed that all methods must be used to prevent war. Witzleben gave his word that he would act with, or if necessary without, Halder's agreement.[48]

Preparation of detailed measures now forged ahead. Schacht was to think out a list of members of the political directorate to be formed; Graf von Brockdorff-Ahlefeldt was to work out and prepare the military measures; Gisevius was to draft detailed plans for the use of the Berlin police and the neutralization of police and SS units elsewhere in the country.[49]

Ideas on what was to be done after a successful *putsch* were naturally vague and varied. No one could know precisely what political forces would emerge after a *putsch*, how quickly trade unions and political parties would re-form, who would be prepared to cooperate and on what conditions, which of the previous functionaries might have to be accepted. Halder and many other generals after him have complained bitterly about this uncertainty. Halder later maintained that he was always being urged to act but had never been given 'a clear plan or satisfactory idea' of what was to happen after a *coup* either by Goerdeler or by Beck, Canaris, Oster or Schacht.[50] After the war Halder tried to ascribe the failure of the resistance movement to this alleged shortcoming: 'The *putsch*, the assassination of Hitler, is only the negative side. Anyone interested in the fate of his people must look at the positive side. What was to happen afterwards? I was never given a glimpse of this positive side. The soldiers were asked to "clean the place up" like housemaids, but no one, neither Beck nor Goerdeler, told me what was then to be served up. Herein lies the overriding weakness of this entire resistance movement.'[51] This was true only in so far as no one could know whether or not there would be civil war; Halder, of course, knew perfectly well what the *aims* of the *coup* were.

On certain things people were agreed in September 1938: in the first place a military dictatorship or military state of emergency of the shortest possible duration would be declared.[52] Thereafter a provisional civil government would be formed, fresh elections being called based on the old Weimar constitution.[53] Schacht even mentions a form of preliminary parliament elected from 'shop foremen'.

There was no agreement on the question whether certain of the Nazi functionaries could be used, at least initially. Many senior officers, however, and many ordinary people thought that they could see in Göring a conservative moderate who could somehow be utilized as mediator or to facilitate the transition.[54] Though many people were fascinated by Göring's highly colourful personality, Gisevius thought any participation by him to be particularly dangerous; he also thought that in the early stages tactics vis-à-vis Hitler should be flexible. In his view the correct course was to create a confused political situation with, for instance, the slogan 'An SS *putsch*; the *Wehrmacht* is reestablishing order'; this would avoid any conflict of conscience about the removal of Hitler while at the same time clear military orders could be issued.[55] Moreover, he thought, it would not be difficult to fill senior posts in the administration with fresh uncompromised people. This was in any case a matter which could be left to the future government.[56]

Availability of the necessary military forces and preparation for their use constituted a considerably more difficult problem. In the first place it became clear that, contrary to current ideas, by no means every general was in a position to issue marching orders to teeth-arm units. Even the Chief of the General Staff could not do so without the authority and backing of his Commander-in-Chief – he was not a 'commander' but merely adviser to the Commander-in-Chief of the Army.[57] Should a genuine 'commander' be found, it must be made easy for him to take the planned action: he must receive no counter-orders from the other side; he must not be confronted with resistance from units similar to his own, in other words Army units as opposed to the SS and SA; there must be no clash with the police. In any other event the action might all too soon wear an air of illegality, something regarded with much apprehension by many officers and capable of affecting the loyalty of the troops before the aim had been achieved. It was bad enough that in all probability an occasional clash with uniformed 'dignitaries' could not be avoided. Effective military and moral authority was essential to see the matter through and by no means every general could lay claim to this.[58] Under these circumstances all action obviously had to be very rapid to deprive the other side of any possibility of issuing counter-orders. There was no hope that the majority of the Army could be persuaded to act against the regime; not even a single division could be prepared for movement unnoticed. Unless the War Ministry was on their side the leaders of the military *putsch* could not even hope to proceed undisturbed during the first few hours.[59] According to Gisevius' report, however, Witzleben was determined to act at the correct moment even without a signal from Halder, should the latter refuse to give one; he was prepared, if necessary, to occupy the War Ministry and have the top-level Army leaders arrested.[60]

At the latest by early September, therefore, Witzleben was ready to act by force. He could rely totally on Major-General Graf von Brockdorff-Ahlefeldt, commanding the Potsdam division.[61] Early in September Witzleben went to Halder to tell him that he was planning a *coup* which, so he assured the Chief of Staff, would only be initiated by the C-in-C or Chief of Staff of the Army.[62] The role to be played by Brauchitsch in issuing the 'starting orders' and during the subsequent upheaval remained obscure until the very end. No one could tell how he would decide at the vital moment.[63] Apart from a few hints Halder had not even informed his Commander-in-Chief. Later he said that he had wished 'to leave the Commander-in-Chief personally' out of the 'business in hand'[64] – 'One can risk one's own neck but not that of someone else'.[65] Halder only wished to 'bring in' Brauchitsch at the very last moment – but how and for what purpose remained obscure.[66]

In cooperation with Schacht, Witzleben, Brockdorff-Ahlefeldt and Gisevius now began detailed planning; Nebe, the director of the *Reich* Criminal Police Office and Lieutenant-Colonel Oster provided them with the necessary material.[67] Gisevius was allotted a conference room adjoining Witzleben's office in *Wehrkreis* headquarters as a place of work; the General told his aide that Gisevius was a relative who was arranging family papers.[68]

Gisevius first worked out where SS units were located all over Germany, Nebe and Oster providing the information. It emerged that, not only were they concealed and camouflaged in a most sophisticated manner, but that the regular police (*Schutzpolizei*) and the criminal police were not in general housed with the *Gestapo*.[69] It was of importance to lay hands on all police offices as rapidly and as completely as possible. It was also vital to occupy at once radio transmitters and telephone and telegraph installations together with the Post Office repeater stations through which the police telephone and teleprinter circuits were routed.[70] Thereafter, if possible simultaneously, the *Reich* Chancellery, the most important ministries and what Halder called 'the more important Berlin agencies run by Party people' could be occupied.[71] At the same time the provinces had to be brought under control. Every *Wehrkreis* commander was to be told what offices to occupy and whom to arrest; martial law regulations had to be issued to implement the state of emergency.[72] In the process Gisevius made an astounding discovery: since 1934 there had been no valid regulations for the introduction and implementation of a state of siege.[73] Every individual order had to be drafted afresh.

Once Halder had been won over to the idea of a *coup*, it was possible to pre-plan for the use of troops other than Brockdorff's division. No 1 Light Division under Lieutenant-General Erich Hoepner was to be placed under Witzleben on orders from Halder.[74] The division had been on the move since 5 September, ostensibly on autumn manoeuvres lasting until 23 September but in fact with the object of positioning it in the area Greiz-Plauen-Chemnitz for an attack on Czechoslovakia.[75] From this position it would, if necessary, be able to bar the Berlin road to the elements of the 'SS Leibstandarte Adolf Hitler' stationed in Grafenwöhr training grounds.[76] In the course of the various moves Halder proposed to bring certain other units nearer to Berlin so that they could intervene there.[77]

Halder felt sure of support from the group and corps commanders of the formations concentrating in the south-east and west. Colonel-General Fedor von Bock was commanding Eighth Army in the Bayerischer Wald, Colonel-General Gerd von Rundstedt was in Silesia with Second Army and in the west General Adam was C-in-C of Army Group 2 with headquarters in Frankfurt; it included First Army commanded by General Beck who took part in discussions on 2 September, only a few days after his resignation.[78] Halder was convinced that he could count upon support from all these as soon as the *coup d'état* began; as a precaution, however, he had not let them into the secret beforehand.[79]

In addition to Brockdorff-Ahlefeldt, Witzleben had special reasons for confidence in Major-General von Hase, commanding 50 Infantry Regiment in Landsberg on Warthe. Witzleben summoned him during September and, since Hase had already been prepared to take armed action against the regime during the Fritsch crisis, he needed little persuasion to participate in a *putsch*; henceforth he held himself in readiness.[80]

The majority of the measures planned for Berlin were the responsibility of Major-General von Brockdorff-Ahlefeldt. Early in September he drove with Gisevius to the Wilhelmstrasse, Göring's palace, the 'Leibstandarte's' barracks in Berlin-Lichterfelde, Sachsenhausen concentration camp and the main radio transmitter in Königswusterhausen to obtain a precise idea of the troops required to occupy these various objectives.[81] To avoid attracting attention they were driven in her private car by Frau Strünck, whose husband worked in the *Abwehr* during the war. Witzleben told Hossbach before 15 September that military preparation for the *coup* was complete.[82]

The attitude of the Berlin police was a particularly thorny problem. Gisevius had many police contacts but of course no authority. Even Nebe, Director of the *Reich* Criminal Police Office, had influence only over his own force, not over the regular police or the *Gestapo*. Since summer 1937, however, Fritz-Dietlof Graf von der Schulenburg had been Vice-President of Police in Berlin.[83]

Schulenburg had joined the National-Socialist Party in 1933 while still a *Landrat* in East Prussia; he had hoped that the word 'Socialist' implied a fresh revolutionary start and rallying of forces and he had believed in the ideals of National-Socialism. Subsequently, however, he had turned against all that he regarded as signs of degeneracy in the movement[84] and in February 1938, under the impact of the Fritsch crisis, he had finally broken with Nazism and joined the fight against the regime.[85] He was now in contact with opposition members such as his old friend Cäsar von Hofacker, Graf von Üxküll, Yorck von Wartenburg, Berthold Graf Stauffenberg and Ulrich Wilhelm Graf Schwerin von Schwanenfeld; he was also in touch with Albrecht von Kessel, the counsellor who was personal assistant to Weizsäcker, with the group centred on Halder and Witzleben and with Friedrich Wilhelm Heinz and Hans Oster in the OKW office *Ausland/Abwehr*.[86]

The goodwill of Schulenburg, however, was not enough if the Police President himself, Wolf Heinrich Graf von Helldorf, did not participate, but a few days before the proposed initiation of the *putsch* he too was won over to the conspiracy. Helldorf and Schulenburg proposed to ensure that, at the very least, the police in Berlin remained neutral.[87]

The next point to be considered was what to do with Hitler himself. Gisevius proposed that, at least in the early stages of the *coup*, tactics vis-à-vis Hitler personally be kept flexible; Göring, he considered, must go under all circumstances. If necessary, Gisevius said, Hitler might be declared misguided which would be the course most acceptable to public opinion.[88] As soon as Hitler could be secured, however, he should be killed. In the circumstances tyrannicide was a moral necessity.

Halder was opposed to assassination pure and simple but not opposed to the elimination of Hitler. He preferred to have him murdered by some unobtrusive method rather than arrest him, since this would conceal the part which he and the Army might play in overthrowing Hitler and would prevent the birth of a dangerous Hitler myth, which he feared so much.[89] He thought it best to blow up Hitler's train and then give out that he had been killed in an air raid, but this of course meant waiting until the outbreak of hostilities.[90] There is no evidence that any concrete planning was done on this subject.

Many of the conspirators, Beck in particular, were convinced that Hitler must be taken alive and brought to trial so that his crimes could be made clear to the entire people. This, they hoped, would prevent the birth of a new 'stab-in-the-back' legend. Dr Hans von Dohnanyi, a Judge Advocate involved in the conspiracy, and Oster wished to arrest Hitler and then have him declared insane by a panel of doctors. The chairman of the panel had already been found in the person of Dohnanyi's father-in-law, Professor Karl Bonhoeffer, the psychiatrist; Dohnanyi was also preparing a trial of Hitler, for which he had been collecting evidence in a special secret file ever since 1933.[91]

There was, however, a group of younger conspirators who were by no means willing to 'by-pass' Hitler in the first instance, to declare him insane or to adopt flexible tactics in so far as he was concerned. The driving force behind this group and the source of its ideas was Major Friedrich Wilhelm Heinz, an ex-*Stahlhelm* commander.[92] In deliberate opposition to Beck, Canaris and even Witzleben he and certain officers of the *Abwehr* developed an assassination plan – as far as is known the first to issue from those circles which later gave birth to the conspiracy of 20 July 1944.

For some time, but particularly since early August, a group of anti-Nazis including Heinz, Oster, Schulenburg and temporarily also Goerdeler, had been occupied with planning a constitution and thinking about the formation of a new government after the fall of Hitler. They had been opponents of Hitler from the outset, long before the danger of war appeared imminent; they were working for the fall of Hitler from fundamental political conviction. The threat of war acted as a spur but it was not their primary motive. They were prepared for far-reaching changes and they had their own particular ideas on the reconstitution of Germany. They thought that a new government must acquire some outward expression of greater strength than would be provided merely by the reinstatement of a President and Chancellor in a reestablished parliamentary democracy on Weimar lines. Like other groups, they were bent on learning and drawing the consequences from the errors and weaknesses of the pre-1933 period. Instead of emblems, mass organizations, mass parades, seas of flags and other demonstrations of authority, they wanted to found a modern democracy organically linked to the forces of tradition, in other words 'a clear-cut democracy under a monarchical Head of State standing above party' on the British model.[93] According to Heinz, Goerdeler knew of this idea and agreed with it – he had told John Wheeler-Bennett in 1937 that he favoured a monarchist restoration.[94] As candidate for the throne, however, he proposed Prince Louis Ferdinand of Prussia, second son of the former Crown Prince; Heinz and his friends preferred the elder son Prince Wilhelm of Prussia. They thought Prince Louis Ferdinand too similar in character to his grandfather, the former Kaiser Wilhelm II, whereas Prince Wilhelm had precisely the personality which Germany required to lead her – just, distinguished, amiable, humane, disinclined to adventure and prepared to allow free rein to democracy. Under no circumstances was this group (SchmidNoerr – Liedig – Heinz) prepared to see an empire reestablished on 1871–1918 lines.[95] Goerdeler was eventually persuaded by the arguments adduced in favour of Prince Wilhelm – greater attraction as a symbol and deep roots in the Army – and did not insist on his own candidate, who nevertheless repeatedly figured in later discussions. With the outbreak of war Prince

Wilhelm ceased to believe in the possibility of a restoration and in 1940 he was killed on active service.[96]

In mid-September or a few days later (about the 20th), there took place a discussion in Oster's house at which Heinz, Lieutenant-Commander Liedig, General von Witzleben and also Goerdeler were present.[97] Witzleben declared his intention to go to the *Reich* Chancellery surrounded by officers of his headquarters and with a further escort of reliable officers seek out Hitler and demand that he resign. At the same time units of III Army Corps, which would have been previously alerted, would occupy Berlin and crush the anticipated resistance from the SS. Since Witzleben would not readily be able to gain access to Hitler, the purpose of his escort was clear. There would be scuffles, he said, possibly shooting; all sorts of unforeseen things might occur. Witzleben and Goerdeler supported by Canaris insisted that Hitler should be arrested; Heinz, however, thought this naïve and quietly continued to prepare more drastic measures.

Witzleben and Oster commissioned Heinz to form a raiding party as escort for General von Witzleben. Heinz had been a member of the Ehrhardt (Free Corps) Brigade and also a *Stahlhelm* commander; he still had good contacts with the so-called Young *Stahlhelm*, the former *Stahlhelm*'s youth organization, and to its 'Langemarck Student Circle'.[98] His task was not, therefore, difficult, particularly since the *Abwehr* could assemble members of the *Wehrmacht* unobtrusively on pretext of 'special training courses'. Twenty to thirty young officers were collected, but in addition there were some workers and anti-Hitler students. The trade union leaders Wilhelm Leuschner and Hermann Maass were, at the very least, involved in the discussions; Heinz had introduced them to Oster after the Fritsch crisis.[99] From this point onwards contact was also established with circles only indirectly involved in the planning and discussion of autumn 1938; they included Gustav Noske, the ex-*Reichswehr* Minister, Julius Leber, Klaus Bonhoeffer, Otto John, Richard Künzer of the Foreign Ministry and Ernst von Harnack.[100] Among the leaders of the raiding party was Lieutenant Hans-Albrecht Herzner; later, at the start of the Polish campaign, he led an *Abwehr* 'commando', the task of which was to seize the Jablunka Pass and hold it open for the advancing German troops. Another was Wolfgang Knaak, also from the *Abwehr;* he was killed in 1941 during a raid on a bridge over the Duna. Finally there was Lieutenant-Commander Liedig already mentioned.[101] Preparations for the formation of the raiding party were begun in the first half of September; it was assembled after 15 September and held ready in certain Berlin apartments, one of which was No 118 Eisenachstrasse.[102]

The formation of this raiding party and the preceding constitutional discussion showed that certain tendencies existed which were by no means in accord with the ideas of Beck, Schacht and Goerdeler; Heinz's and Liedig's ideas on the actual operation also differed from Witzleben's. As Heinz aptly remarks, therefore, there was a conspiracy within the conspiracy.[103] The raiding party was in fact intended not merely to 'escort' Witzleben for his vital approach to Hitler and force an entry into the *Reich* Chancellery if necessary, after which

Witzleben would confront Hitler with his demand for resignation. Instead its members were determined to provoke an incident and shoot Hitler in the process. Even Oster had been won over to this plan. Admiral Canaris commissioned an *Abwehr* officer, Major Groscurth, to obtain and hold ready weapons and explosives.[104] The word went round that Hitler was to be shot, come what might, even if, contrary to expectations, the SS offered no resistance.[105] This was the only method of producing a clear-cut situation at the outset and thereafter no one need worry about any oath sworn to the Head of State. On this point Heinz's and Liedig's group undoubtedly thought more realistically than the older, more highly-placed, conspirators who were inclined to conservatism.

Preparations were more thorough and prospects of success greater than at any subsequent period. The members of the raiding party had been provided with weapons by the *Abwehr* and were on call in their quarters; proclamations were ready; provision had been made for the occupation of radio stations.[106] Witzleben, Brockdorff-Ahlefeldt and Gisevius had worked out military and police precautions to ensure that the capital was brought under control. Halder reserved to himself the issue of the 'starting order'[107] – he, after all, would inevitably be the first to know of Hitler's order to march against Czechoslovakia and this order would be followed by declarations of war from France and Britain. Everyone now waited for these conditions to become actual – for the moment in fact when war would be inevitable unless Hitler fell.

Chamberlain's surprise visit to Hitler in Berchtesgaden on 15 September, in effect an open admission that Britain was backing down, produced confusion and in some cases consternation among the conspirators.[108] In their view the British statesman had been doing homage to a gangster and so, subjectively, they felt that he had let them down. In this they were right in so far as they ascribed his action to overestimation of the German war potential and failure to recognize the nature of Hitler's policy; they were wrong, however, in so far as they thought that the British government was in any way obligated to act on proposals and assurances from the German opposition.[109] It now looked as if the conditions for a *coup* were not going to obtain.[110]

Then, however, it proved that tension did not relax but in fact increased considerably, for, instead of showing moderation now that satisfaction of his allegedly last territorial requirements was imminent, Hitler became ever more demanding.[111] He still wished to seize the whole of Czechoslovakia and he wanted to do so now.[112] When Chamberlain, after consulting his cabinet and the French, returned to Bad Godesberg from 22 to 24 September to settle the details, Hitler raised his demands: he would not agree that there should first be a plebiscite in the Sudetenland and areas of mixed population; he would not agree that there should first be negotiations on the line of the future frontier; he insisted, as the first and immediate step, on the move of the *Wehrmacht* into the areas demanded. If this was not conceded, he said, war against Czechoslovakia would begin on 1 October.[113]

At last people in France and Britain began to grasp the fact that Hitler clearly wanted much more than the fulfilment of his 'last territorial demand'.

The attitudes of the British and French governments stiffened; mobilization measures were ordered; France recalled reservists; on 25 September Britain placed her fleet on a war footing; Czechoslovakia also mobilized.[114] Hitler became increasingly aggressive, the Western Powers increasingly unyielding.

Finally came the development for which the German opposition had striven so long: on 26 September the British government issued a press statement to the effect that if, despite satisfaction of his original demands on Czechoslovakia, Hitler should start a war, France would fulfil the obligations of her alliance and Britain and Russia would assuredly side with her.[115] Here at last was the 'firm attitude'.

Hitler, however, pursued his warlike measures. Much points to the fact that, at this moment, he was not seriously trying to avoid war with France and Britain. Much gives one to suspect, however, that he gradually weakened in his resolve and finally gave way. In the first place he realized that the people were totally unprepared for war – a propaganda march by motorized troops through the government quarter of Berlin on the evening of 27 September was received in glacial silence;[116] secondly, about midday on 27 September Sir Horace Wilson told him that, unless he abandoned his warlike intentions, France and Britain would open active hostilities;[117] thirdly, on the morning of 28 September he received news that the British fleet had mobilized;[118] finally Mussolini intervened and advised conciliation.[119] Many regard Mussolini's intervention as the decisive factor in dissuading Hitler from war – temporarily; many ascribe the change to the effect of the Franco–British threats. The vital point, however, is whether the prospect was war against Czechoslovakia alone, for which Hitler was fully prepared, or a simultaneous war against the Western Powers.[120]

In the light of Hitler's statement on 22 August 1939 that he hoped that some swine would not appear again with a proposal for mediation, there is much to be said for the theory that Hitler's about-turn was caused by Mussolini's refusal to go to war.[121] The remark, however, throws no light on Hitler's mental and emotional processes: why should a mediation proposal cause him to waver and raise doubts in his mind which had not been provoked by tangible, and on this occasion obviously genuine, threats? Rational explanation may not, of course, be applicable to Hitler's mental processes. It is possible that after his weeks of bluster he began to waver, that at that moment a series of obstacles appeared and that he seized upon the one most likely to give him a way out, save his face and allow him to register a triumph at the same time.

The opposition was working on the assumption that Hitler would not recoil even from the threat of world war and until midday on 28 September they knew nothing of any tendency to yield on Hitler's part; all they knew was that military preparations were continuing.[122] They were convinced that the final order to march would be issued on 28 September.[123] At 13.20 on 27 September Jodl noted in his diary: '*Führer* approves the forward move of the first attacking wave so that it can be in its assembly areas on 30.9';[124] and at 13.30: 'Passed to General Halder by telephone.' That evening Hitler approved mobilization of the 'five active divisions in the West (26, 34, 36, 33, 35) and the fourteen *Landwehr* divisions'.[125] Announcement of general mobilization was anticipated for 2 p.m. on 28 September.[126]

The extent to which, in his heart of hearts, Hitler regarded all this as bluff, one can only surmise. It is barely conceivable that he, the First World War veteran, did not have some anxieties concerning the shortcomings in German preparations as compared to the potentialities of the Western Powers. On many subsequent occasions, however, Hitler was to show indifference about the prospects of success of his policy. Be that as it may, Halder and the opposition assumed that Hitler would not recoil from war with the Western Powers. When visiting Colonel-General von Hammerstein on his sixtieth birthday on 26 September Halder said: 'There will now be action unless Hitler abandons his plans.' Even at this stage Hammerstein had doubts of Halder's determination.[127]

Late on the evening of 27 September Oster succeeded in obtaining a copy of Hitler's reply, given that afternoon, to Chamberlain's last mediation proposal;[128] it had been drafted by Weizsäcker, who had tempered its language somewhat, but it was a rejection. On the morning of 28 September Gisevius took the copy to Witzleben in *Wehrkreis* headquarters on the Hohenzollerndamm; Witzleben went forthwith to Halder in Army Headquarters on the Tirpitzufer and showed him the paper as 'proof' of Hitler's determination to make war. Halder seemed to be convinced; he hurried off to Brauchitsch with the paper while Witzleben waited in Halder's office. After a few minutes Halder returned and said that Brauchitsch was persuaded; he too now advocated an 'action'.[129]

The partial British mobilization had in fact made Brauchitsch most uneasy.[130] His remark that the moment for an 'action' had now arrived did not, however, mean much. As he admitted after the war, he had never made up his mind to issue the order for a *coup* himself.[131] Witzleben had telephoned him from Halder's office, had told him that everything was ready and had begged him for God's sake to issue the order now. But Brauchitsch wanted to reassure himself first that Halder and Witzleben were right, that the decision for war had been taken. To find out he went to the *Reich* Chancellery.[132] In addition Schulenburg was despatched to the Foreign Ministry to obtain a report on the foreign political situation for Brauchitsch.[133]

Meanwhile the raiding party was all ready for its assault on the *Reich* Chancellery. With Schulenburg's assistance Kordt proposed to ensure that the great double doors behind the sentry at the entrance were open, thus paving the way for the raiding party; he had also obtained a plan of the *Reich* Chancellery for Oster. No extraordinary security precautions had apparently been taken, as might have been expected in the light of the situation.[134] Halder was merely waiting for Brauchitsch's return; Witzleben had hurried back to his headquarters, where Gisevius was still waiting.[135] Any moment now, everyone thought.

That afternoon arrived the news that Mussolini had intervened and that a conference had been called for the next day in Munich at which both Daladier and Chamberlain proposed to be present in person.[136] Both the Western Powers and Hitler made concessions. The Western Powers conceded to Hitler his brutal demand for military invasion; Hitler, however, temporarily renounced his intention to seize any opportunity offered him by Czech resistance or engineered incidents[137] to 'destroy' the whole of Czechoslovakia. The danger of war had been averted for the moment. So the ground was cut from under the feet of the most promising attempt to overthrow Hitler; the measures prepared could not be carried out. On 6 October 1938 Henderson, the British Ambassador, wrote to Lord Halifax, the Foreign Secretary: '. . . by keeping the peace, we have saved Hitler and his regime . . .'[138] This, of course, does not imply that the Western Powers had stabbed the German resistance movement in the back, although subjectively this was the way things looked to those involved.[139]

PART III/PLANS FOR A
COUP 1939–1940

8 Before the Outbreak of War

The Munich Conference and the abandonment of Czechoslovakia by the Western Powers administered to the anti-Hitler opposition a blow from which it could not recover. The public at large did not know what had really gone on and, from their position, it was hard for the resistance leaders to judge realistically on this point. Hitler had been proved right: the Western Powers had no wish to fight — any other view of the situation inevitably seemed unrealistic. Could he not similarly be proved right in the future? Who could deny that, thanks to his perspicacity and sleight of hand in foreign policy and politico-military matters, he had been successful? Today we know when the Western Powers finally lost patience but at the time no one could know.

For the moment Hitler proceeded almost unchecked on his career of conquest. Britain accelerated her rearmament but Hitler could nevertheless carry on with what he cynically termed 'dealing with the rump of Czechoslovakia'. He ordered military preparation for this action as early as 21 October 1938. In the spring of 1939 the Czechoslovak state, sapped by its own weaknesses and the separatist tendencies of the Slovaks, collapsed under Hitler's pressure. Threatened with transfer to Hungary should Slovakia fail to divorce itself from Prague, on 14 March 1939 the Slovak provincial parliament declared the sovereignty of Slovakia and placed the country under the protection of the German *Reich*.[1] The very same day Emil Hácha, the President of Czechoslovakia, was summoned to Berlin. He arrived late on 15 March to be told that German troops were already moving on Prague and that the city would be bombed, should the Czech army resist. Like Schuschnigg a year earlier, Hácha was now faced with the choice between honourable but bloody defeat and the passive surrender of his country, blackmailed by a mighty enemy and abandoned by its friends but at least preserved physically. He chose the latter alternative.

On 16 March, from the Hradshin in Prague, Hitler announced the formation of the 'Protectorate of Bohemia and Moravia'. After less than six months he had broken the Munich Agreement. Apart from protests the Western Powers took no action. Poland would be the next victim.

On 31 March 1939, however, the British government promised unrestricted support to Poland, should she have to defend her national integrity and independence. Similar assurances were given to Greece, Rumania and Turkey.[2] Hitler was given to understand that his next step would meet armed resistance from Britain. Had he any reason to believe this, however? After all in the autumn of 1938 Britain, in her weakness, had bought him off his real purpose, the conquest of Czechoslovakia, at the price of a bloodless invasion of the Sudetenland and the partial disarmament of Czechoslovakia through the loss of her western fortifications. In any case, as Hitler well knew, months would pass before Britain could help Poland militarily; it was hardly conceivable that a British expeditionary force could be shipped through the Baltic to Poland; without an Anglo–Russian alliance effective aid to Poland was not possible. Subsequently, in autumn 1939, France and Britain did not even launch a diversionary attack in the west, still less produce effective support.

The Western Powers realized the key position of the Soviet Union as well as did Hitler and he set about neutralizing Russia. Meanwhile in May 1939 Germany signed a formal alliance with Italy; in March the Rumanian economy was brought largely under German control by means of a trade treaty; Denmark, Esthonia and Latvia were neutralized by non-aggression pacts. On the other side the Western Powers opened negotiations with Moscow in April; the main obstacle to agreement proved to be the Polish refusal to allow Soviet troops to move across Polish territory. In the light of Poland's history and her relations with Russia this attitude was entirely comprehensible. Poland clearly had to choose between possible neutrality vis-à-vis the two blocs or holding her western frontier against Germany assisted by an Anglo–French offensive in the west. Russian 'assistance' would almost certainly entail loss of independence.

On 23 August 1939 the world was told that a pact between Hitler and Stalin had been concluded and signed by Ribbentrop in Moscow. Ever since April Stalin had been negotiating simultaneously with the Western Powers and with Hitler. Hitler had no scruples in paying the price demanded by the Soviet Union: in addition to the official non-aggression pact a secret supplementary protocol was signed in which the partition of Poland between the two states and the delineation of 'spheres of interest' in the Baltic were agreed. Hitler could now proceed to attack Poland, which he did on 1 September 1939, after a postponement of a few days as a result of intervention by Mussolini. Britain and France now entered the lists and declared war on Germany on 3 September. The Second World War had begun.

After the Munich Agreement and the occupation of the Sudetenland Hitler felt himself so strong that he let loose a vast anti-Jewish pogrom such as had not been seen since the Middle Ages; thousands of Jewish businesses and synagogues were looted, demolished or set on fire. The resistance movement was a well-nigh helpless spectator of all this. Many members of the opposition did all in their power to help Jews and victims of the regime in general; they assisted them to emigrate; they protected property; they provided shelter and refuge – moral and material assistance of all sorts in fact.[3] But none of this provided a basis for the overthrow of Hitler.

The Western Powers had been regarded as natural allies in the struggle against Hitler. Now his opponents felt – wrongly from the objective point of view – that they had been betrayed. The opposition crumbled; the ties between the civil and military resistance groups loosened or were severed.[4] Admittedly the core of the opposition remained – Beck, Oster, Schulenburg, Gisevius, Witzleben, Schacht, Halder, Goerdeler, to name only a few, had not abandoned their aim of overthrowing Hitler. But in the atmosphere and situation following Munich they could see no possibility. Without resources of power any attempt was hopeless; no one at that time thought that the dictator's authority was in any way shaky; any attempt to overthrow him, therefore, would lead to an upheaval verging on civil war; consequently the removal of Hitler would not of itself solve the problem. After Munich, moreover, the military could no longer be persuaded into a *coup d'état*. None of the opposition leaders believed that an occasion such as the occupation of Prague would produce adequate support in the Army for a further attempt at a *coup*. The 'destruction of the rump of Czechoslovakia' did not even give rise to a real crisis, let alone a situation as dangerous as that of the Sudeten affair. Hitler had used force with impunity and his further 'bloodless victory' merely aggravated the paralysis of the opposition.[5]

Even had the key figures involved in the preparations of September 1938 still been in their old positions in the spring of 1939, most of them would hardly have been able to concoct fresh plans since there was no acute danger of war. But many of the key figures were either not available at all or at least not in Berlin. In November 1938 General von Witzleben, the most important commander, had left Berlin to assume command of Group Headquarters No 2 (Frankfurt on Main) in the west.[6] Major-General von Sodenstern was appointed as his Chief of Staff in December. After only a few conversations both were agreed that Hitler's policies, despite all temporary successes, could in the end only lead to a world war greater even than that of 1914, and finally to the destruction of Germany.[7] They also agreed that, this being so, they had come to the limits of military obedience and that whoever continued to obey shared responsibility for the consequences. They did not think that they should consider resigning and escaping into private life. This left only one alternative: to fight Hitler. It was clear that other determined officers and civilians who could assume administrative responsibilities were needed; the forces working against the regime had to be consolidated. Witzleben had kept up his connections with Dr Goerdeler and Lieutenant-Colonel Oster; in his own staff Colonel Vinzenz Müller was taken into confidence. Witzleben and Sodenstern thought there was ample time; a war was inevitable if Hitler continued his policies, but it was not expected to come before 1940. In June or July 1939, Witzleben and Sodenstern agreed on a long-term programme: No generals' *putsch*, no *putsch* at all as long as the socialist masses were marching solidly behind the swastika flag and a general strike could paralyse a *coup d'état* completely (the Kapp *Putsch* was obviously in Witzleben's and Sodenstern's minds); formation of reliable conspiratorial groups in all *Gau* capitals so that all *Gauleiter* might be arrested at once, all radio transmitters be seized, and the press be tightly controlled; Dr Goerdeler hoped to win over the former trade-union leaders and through their influence to prevent a general strike in the event of the *coup d'état* (he too hoped to have accomplished this by spring of 1940); then, early in 1940, the conspirators were to meet again to agree dates and first steps for the *coup*. But in late summer of 1939 the war broke out; Witzleben and Sodenstern were completely taken by surprise. They had been so isolated that during the peak of tension before the attack on Poland, Witzleben had asked Oster to send him Gisevius to fill him in on what was happening in Berlin.[8] The most basic preconditions for any action against the regime obviously did not exist.

Other commanders who had been ready to act during the Sudeten crisis were similarly isolated or unavailable. Lieutenant-General Graf von Brockdorff-Ahlefeldt was still commanding the Potsdam division but he did not think that he could carry out a *coup* alone.[9] General Curt Haase (not to be confused with Lieutenant-General Paul von Hase, later Commandant of Berlin), Witzleben's successor as commander of *Wehrkreis* III in Berlin, was regarded by Halder as 'incapable of conspiracy'.[10] Lieutenant-General Fritz Fromm, head of the *Allgemeines Heeresamt* (AHA), who was destined to play a fateful role on 20 July 1944, was approached by Halder to see whether he might be willing to participate in preparations for a *coup*, but he refused.[11] Halder himself was in favour of waiting; early in 1939 it was not even possible to extract vague promises from him.[12] Shortly before the move into Prague, which many of the initiated knew was coming, he was not even prepared to discuss contingency measures since he was convinced – rightly – that the Western Powers had long since abandoned Czechoslovakia.[13] He was not to be persuaded into any conspiratorial activity, however hard Gisevius, Oster, Beck and Canaris pressed him.[14] Production of the so-called timetables towards the end of 1938 created further difficulties in planning for any future *coup*.[15] Hitler had ordered these tables to be drawn up so that at any time precise details could be given of the moment at which orders for movement or attack from a concentration area must be issued irrevocably.[16] Such minute preparations were necessitated by Hitler's strategy of surprise attack and sudden move, but even more by his habit of waiting until the very last moment before finally deciding on military measures. He did not hold with the traditional methods of mobilization and, if planning an attack for instance, wished to have German troops available at any time to move into the country he intended to occupy within twelve hours of the issue of his order.[17]

The top-level military, of course, knew beforehand which units were to be used in any attack and which would remain located in Germany and where. This fact did not necessarily make the opposition's planning more difficult. But the interval between the issue of orders to move and the actual opening of major hostilities was now so short that it was increasingly difficult for the conspiracy, working in secret, to assemble and move their forces. Not until 1943 did they discover a vehicle for unobtrusive but far-reaching planning. This was the famous Plan 'Valkyrie'.[18] In addition no one could be certain that a movement order from Hitler really meant war. On 25 August 1939 he issued the order at midday and cancelled it in the evening; by using every signal circuit and with a vast expenditure of labour every unit on the move had to be stopped and turned round. Brauchitsch merely backed up Hitler in this; when asked by Hitler what consequences cancellation of the movement order would have, he replied that it made no difference at all. Surprise effect would be lost, he said, but they would gain the advantage of more thorough preparations for mobilization. Brauchitsch could well have seized this opportunity to counsel moderation, using military arguments, but he did not do so.[19]

So the interval between issue of the order for war and the actual start of the war was reduced practically to zero.[20] It was, in fact, conceivable that Hitler might cancel an order for attack only an hour or two before the first shot was fired. He could always excuse himself or offer compensation for isolated operations or frontier violations which it had been impossible to stop. His 'enemies', after all, were not particularly bellicose. At any rate, in so far as concerned the military element of the conspiracy, in other words the Army units which might have been persuaded to participate in a *coup*, this was the view of the situation taken in 1939 by the highest-ranking military conspirator, the Chief of Staff of the Army.

After the end of the Polish campaign the opposition was no longer confronted by the question whether there would be war or not, but whether the offensive against France (which the General Staff considered suicidal) would actually take place or not. Basically, therefore, the problem remained the same.

Hitler's convinced opponents had long ago recognized his demoniac thirst for destruction and felt sure that the war would continue. Searching for some fresh starting point, individual groups continued to foregather, but nothing positive could be achieved. One meeting during the winter 1938–39, however, is worth mentioning, since it was the start of a development which ended only with 20 July 1944. It took place in the house of Ernst von Harnack, the Social-Democrat government representative (*Regierungspräsident*) in Merseburg, dismissed in 1933, and there were present the socialists Leuschner, Leber and Noske together with Dr Richard Künzer, a Foreign Service counsellor, Klaus Bonhoeffer and Otto John. They discussed the possibilities of resistance activity with a view to overthrowing the regime and concluded that progress might be restarted by formation of a 'Unity Front' combining all opposition tendencies, both civil and military, without regard to party political background.[21] For such a group this was a significant step away from tradition; it implied a readiness to cooperate with forces which would otherwise have been labelled nationalist, conservative and reactionary. After prolonged hesitation Leuschner declared himself ready to cooperate in anything, provided that the generals made a concrete proposal. Accordingly in early autumn 1939 permanent contact was established between the Kaiser-Leuschner-Habermann group and Oster's in OKW *Ausland/Abwehr* via Dr Josef Wirmer, a lawyer who was a passionate anti-Nazi.

Here was illustrated the great weakness of the early stages: there were no forces and the generals in key positions were not prepared to act against the regime. Albrecht von Kessel records an attempt which he made together with Adam von Trott zu Solz to persuade Lieutenant-General Alexander von Falkenhausen, later Commander-in-Chief Belgium and Northern France, to act.[22] Falkenhausen was an old acquaintance of Trott's from his days in China where he had been Military Adviser to Chiang Kai-shek; on 1 September he was due to take over from Lieutenant-General von Schwedler as Commander of *Wehrkreis* IV. In July or August Kessel and Trott went to Dresden where Kessel explained his plan to the General: Hitler was to be invited to inspect the fortifications hurriedly constructed on the Bohemian frontier; he was to be separated from his entourage in a bunker and faced with the choice of committing suicide or being killed forthwith; in the latter case Falkenhausen was to toss in a grenade. The General was somewhat astonished by this unusual proposition – 'so this is what comes from the Foreign Ministry nowadays', he remarked – but though he listened approvingly, he doubted that the thing could be done, and he does not seem to have made any move to try it.

The reasons are all too obvious; even for the go-getting Witzleben, be it noted, the elimination of Hitler at the height of his success was too risky a proceeding. None of the generals wanted civil war.

Accordingly the opposition devoted its initial efforts primarily to prevention of the outbreak of war. As already mentioned far fewer generals were prepared to participate than in 1938; there was no alternative, therefore, but to work primarily in the foreign policy field. In the first place efforts were made to obtain support for the internal movement by declarations of goodwill towards any non-Nazi government which might be formed; secondly it was hoped to persuade the Western Powers to give some clear proof of their determination not to give way again, not to permit any further blackmail or conquest by Hitler and to issue unmistakable threats should this take place.

After his resignation as Burgomaster of Leipzig Goerdeler had become a part-time employee of the firm of Bosch. His real job was to hold the opposition groups together, to expand and consolidate them and to provide financial support to some of the members.[23] Through an intermediary, he was at pains to explain to Cordell Hull, the American Secretary of State, that Hitler must be warned against war in the clearest possible terms; the United States would certainly be drawn in if a conflict should develop between Germany on one side and France and Britain on the other.[24] At the same time, based on information and impressions acquired during his journeys abroad, he attempted to influence Hitler's foreign policy through Göring, warning him that British patience would shortly be exhausted and that the might of Russia would undoubtedly be allied to that of the Western Powers.[25]

During the winter 1938–39 Goerdeler transmitted to his American friends a 'peace programme' visualizing international cooperation based on a liberal economic and social policy, tolerance and freedom of the individual under the rule of law, rejection of bolshevism, Marxism and fascism of all colours.[26] Being an incurable optimist, he inevitably thought that his peace proposals would have some effect and that Hitler would be subjected to adequate threats. Since the Munich Conference, however, even he realized that there was no real foundation for such an idea. Since war now seemed almost inevitable, he hoped for a quick end to it as a result of Germany's inevitable exhaustion which he thought must come after, at the most, a year. Like Beck,

Goerdeler grossly over-estimated France's war potential and will to fight; he was also a victim of self-deception over the capacity of the Nazi government to mobilize the energies of the German people for their own purposes.

The inactivity of the Western Powers after the occupation of the 'rump of Czechoslovakia' (*Rest-Tschechei* in Hitler's terminology) acted as a spur rather than a discouragement to Goerdeler; his activity was feverish and a veritable flood of memoranda from him descended on Paris, London, Rome and Washington.[27] Again and again he demanded that Hitler be publicly exposed and attacked on the international stage as the great disturber of the peace. The whole world, he said, must call upon the German nation to decide between the disturber of the peace and the forces of peace. He hoped that the Pope might open the campaign with a suitable call to the German and Italian peoples to overthrow their dictators. Simultaneously the dictators should be precluded from making war by an embargo on vital raw materials; until peace was assured Hitler should be diplomatically isolated and personally cold-shouldered by foreign ambassadors; no congratulations should be sent for his fiftieth birthday on 20 April 1939.[28]

Goerdeler, the optimist, also believed that his own frankness and honesty would be realized and given their due weight. Only in this light is his continuous repetition of demands for territorial revision comprehensible. He proposed settlement of the Polish Corridor question, cession of a large overseas colonial area to Germany, opportunities for German settlers to immigrate into British and French colonial territories, reestablishment and neutralization of Czechoslovakia but without the Sudetenland; all this was intended to contribute to a relaxation of tension. Removal of the injustices of the Treaty of Versailles, he thought, would take the wind out of the sails of German revisionism and nationalism and eliminate smouldering antipathies.[29] Such concessions, however, must be made to a law-abiding peaceful German government, not to the blackmailer Hitler; only in that case would they serve the cause of peace – this was the purpose of Goerdeler's demands. As a *quid pro quo* Germany would abandon her drive for hegemony in South-East Europe, become a co-guarantor of the status quo in the Mediterranean, use her military, economic and political resources to help the Western Powers reestablish their influence in the Far East and participate in an international stabilization of currencies, limitation of armaments and a disarmament agreement under international control. This would bring about an alliance between Germany and France and constitute a first step towards the later formation of a general federation of European states. War should be banned for all time as a result of voluntary cooperation.[30]

Within the opposition attempts were made to arrive at an agreed definition of their views for the benefit of the Western Powers, but Schacht in particular was at odds with Goerdeler's ideas which he regarded as illusory.[31] Schacht proposed to persuade the Western Powers to stand firm, not by telling them of the weaknesses of the German economy and German Army but, on the contrary, by warning them of the dangers of growing German strength.[32] The lack of unanimity in the opposition's views undoubtedly did not increase its standing abroad; equally certainly, it did nothing to change the well-known attitude of the Western Powers.[33]

Shortly after the German move into Prague Schacht, Gisevius and Goerdeler met Dr Reinhold Schairer in Ouchy near Geneva. Schairer must be regarded as one of the principal middlemen between London and Paris on one side and the ideas of the Schacht-Goerdeler circle on the other; he had already arranged for Goerdeler to meet Bertaux and Léger.[34] The talk turned around the old question: not how to overthrow Hitler (they had long known that) but how finally to persuade 'the generals' to do it.[35] Once more they reached the conclusion that a revolt in Germany was only possible if it was made crystal clear from abroad that Hitler's next attempt at conquest would be the prelude to major war.[36]

Much optimism was required to believe this possible after the experiences of Munich and Prague. An increasing number of people in Germany thought that Hitler had luck on his side or was intuitively right and that he would continue to succeed. Abroad, however, Hitler's 'successes' had the opposite effect: each additional 'success' filled the cup fuller and brought nearer the time when it would overflow.

In fact the situation was hopeless; even the sternest threats had little prospect of penetrating, although they did give many Germans and some of the generals food for thought.[37] Efforts to influence matters were nevertheless pursued.

In Switzerland Schacht met his friend Montagu Norman, Governor of the Bank of England who was also a close friend of Chamberlain, and urged that some warning be sent to Hitler.[38] Schairer finally went to London and probably also to Paris with a general commission to sound a warning against the unbridled ambition and bellicosity of the dictator; his objective was not merely Danzig and the Corridor but the whole of Poland and more.[39]

In May 1939 Goerdeler himself went to London where he had an interview with Churchill but their talk was of little significance.[40] This was hardly surprising since Goerdeler had nothing to offer apart from his own honest opinion. Until signature of the Russo–German pact a continuous stream of anxious conspirators warned the British government of Hitler's nefarious intentions and tried to persuade it to take suitable counter-measures.[41]

The next emissary was Adam von Trott zu Solz.[42] Even before the Sudeten crisis he had tried to work for coexistence between ideologies, hoping that the totalitarian system in Germany might be changed without a new world war. His idea was that Britain should make clear to Hitler that there could be no second Munich. He was in London from 1 to 8 June. Officially he had been commissioned by the Foreign Ministry to use his private contacts as an ex-Rhodes scholar to find out the British attitude to Germany. Trott had talks with Lord Astor, proprietor of the *Observer* and Chairman of the Royal Institute of International Affairs whom he had known since his student days in Oxford, also with Lord Halifax, Lord Lothian and Neville Chamberlain.

At this time Trott was wondering whether he should leave Germany for the duration of the Nazi regime which he loathed, or whether he could fight the regime in some way. The latter he could only do, he thought, if he could obtain for himself some suitable position within the system. Foreign policy he regarded as his calling and so, in 1940, he joined the Foreign Ministry permanently in order to work for the resistance movement. In 1938 he had already written to his friend, David Astor, that he wished to return to Germany (from a trip he was taking at the time) with the single purpose of devoting himself entirely to working against Hitler. Outwardly, of course, he had to obey his superiors' instructions and try to appear to them as a man with useful contacts. When in London in June 1939 Trott was already playing this dual role – this much is clear from the tone of his official report. The report is full of warnings aimed at Hitler about determination to fight and about Anglo–American community of interests and solidarity; the report includes explicit references to the absolute British rejection of the use of force against other nations and of the violation of Belgian neutrality in 1914. Lord Lothian had said that the British regarded both events – Belgium 1914 and Prague 1939 – as equally significant and undoubtedly he was right. On the other hand, in a special confidential interview Lord Lothian had also said that reestablishment of Bohemian and Moravian independence would disarm the British totally; this should not be too difficult for Hitler, he said, since he had achieved his strategic and undoubtedly essential purpose of destroying Czechoslovakia; moreover it could not be disputed that *economically* Germany's *Lebensraum* already extended far outside her present frontiers. If this principle were generally recognized in Eastern and South-eastern Europe and supported by Great Britain, then solutions would also be found for the problems of Danzig and the Corridor. Chamberlain expressed himself similarly to Trott at an interview on 8 June.

In his report, therefore, Trott did the exact opposite of what he was later accused of doing by certain circles. He did not try to soothe and pacify Britain; in fact he used every conceivable argument to dissuade Hitler from further conquests. In the hope of taking the right psychological line with Hitler, Trott even explained that as a result of the German action in March, of which Britain had had to be an inactive spectator, she now felt so humiliated that she was ready to fight; the real way to humiliate Britain, however, was to give the Czechs back their national independence since then the role of protector assumed by Britain would end in pitiable collapse.

Naturally Trott's mission did not have the success intended. It did not produce the desired effect on Hitler nor did it lead to any readiness on the part of the British government to cooperate with the German resistance movement. Efforts were nevertheless continued.

During the summer the two lawyers Fabian von Schlabrendorff and Helmuth James Graf von Moltke also visited London; their background was similar to that of Trott.[43] Talking to Lord Lloyd, Schlabrendorff advised that the British make their determination to fight abundantly clear and he warned of the imminent conclusion of a pact between Hitler and Stalin. With Schlabrendorff's agreement Lord Lloyd passed this on to Halifax. At about the same time Schlabrendorff visited Churchill at his country house near London and told him of the existence of a German opposition, of the imminence of war with Poland and the almost certain conclusion of a Hitler–Stalin pact. Churchill had long known that a German resistance movement existed, at least since summer 1938, but he did not think much of the conspiracy since 'it had shown neither the will to act nor the courage to come into the open'.[44] To Churchill's question whether Schlabrendorff could guarantee a successful *coup* by the opposition,[45] he naturally had to reply in the negative. In such matters there can be no guarantee of success.

Moltke fared no better than Schlabrendorff. He warned his British friends of Hitler's immediate intentions but he was hardly in a position to make proposals for collaboration. Wheeler-Bennett, with some justification, asks what these emissaries really thought that they could achieve.[46] He answers the question himself: they hoped, by means of British and French declarations and actions, to make clear to the generals something that Chamberlain, Daladier and Hitler already knew – that there could be no repetition of Munich. If this could be done, they thought, there was still perhaps some hope of a *coup* before it was too late. This was the object of all the conspirators with contacts abroad; they included Rudolf Pechel who went to London in March, April and May 1939 to warn against Hitler's depredations, Gerhard Graf Schwerin von Schwanenfeld, who was in London on 6 July, and Ulrich von Hassell who drafted a penetrating article on Nazism for publication in a Swiss newspaper; he hoped that the world would listen while there was still time, but no Swiss paper was willing to print it.[47]

In the summer of 1939 Erich Kordt also went to London to try to stop the Hitler–Stalin pact. This he did with the backing of Weizsäcker who throughout July and August was trying to sabotage Hitler's and Ribbentrop's foreign policy by warnings and procrastination. In August, among other things, he reiterated his request of summer 1938 to the British government that a general be despatched to Hitler who could talk to him privately 'man to man', in other words issue a threat which would be unmistakable and credible even to Hitler.[48] At the same time the Kordt brothers were hoping to give the generals proof that this time there really would be world war and that the prior overthrow of Hitler was therefore essential. Kordt flew to London in the second half of June and was met by his brother at the airport. Next day they both met Robert Vansittart in the house of Philip Conwell Evans. To the consternation of the German opposition, for which the Kordt brothers were specifically authorized to speak, Vansittart's news was placatory. London was counselling moderation in Warsaw, he said; there was no risk that the Poles, relying on the British promise of assistance, would overcall their hand; there was no need to worry about Russia; the Western Powers, not Hitler, would conclude a pact with Stalin.

Weizsäcker and the Kordt brothers, however, took a different view of the situation and they continued their warnings. On his return from a visit to Berlin in August Theo Kordt again met Vansittart in Conwell Evans' house and again urged him to accelerate the Franco–British negotiations in Moscow and persuade the Italians to intervene with Hitler.[49] Both Hitler and

Mussolini, he said, were still not clear that war with Poland could not be localized but that this time the Western Powers would assuredly intervene.[50]

Then, however, Hitler did conclude his pact with Stalin. From 23 August he could be certain that, if he attacked Poland, no other power would directly stand in his way. Hitler now only had to defeat Poland quickly and then calmly await developments; France and Britain would not attack immediately even if, contrary to expectations, they formally declared war.

It was now no longer possible to talk of immediate danger to the *Reich* in the event of war with Poland.[51] Though some people were still seriously considering and urging a military *putsch*, in such a situation it was out of the question.[52] Oster had hoped that the situation would develop similarly to that of September 1938 and, as a precaution, had told the members of the raiding party formed at that time to hold themselves in readiness. In Frankfurt Witzleben and Major-General von Sodenstern, his Chief of Staff, had drawn up a plan for a *coup*; Goerdeler had assisted them and the plan was to be ready for execution by the spring of 1940. It included: formation of reliable activist groups within the Army with numerous resistance cells and representatives in every *Wehrkreis*; support from a wide section of the workers arranged by Goerdeler with the assistance of Christian and socialist trade union leaders; simultaneous arrest of all *Gauleiter* at the start of the *coup*; occupation of radio stations and control of the press; formation of reliable groups of conspirators in the capital of each *Gau*.[53] After the conclusion of the Russo–German pact, however, not even Oster thought it possible to stop the outbreak of war.[54] On 20 August 1939 Leuschner wrote to a friend abroad: 'I fear that there will be war this autumn and that it will last for years . . . Tell our friends over there, particularly Walter Citrine [Secretary-General of the T.U.C.] that we are still what we were. But we are completely incapable of preventing the catastrophe. We are inmates of a great prison. To rebel would be as suicidal as if prisoners were to rise against their heavily armed gaolers.'[55] Despite this desperate situation efforts continued, primarily aimed at the preservation of peace.

In order to warn the Western Powers and the world in general against Hitler – the real demoniac Hitler capable of any madness – Beck passed to Louis Lochner, Associated Press correspondent in Berlin, a copy of the intemperate speech delivered by Hitler on 22 August. It was transmitted by Hermann Maass who had frequently been used as a channel since 1936.[56] Lochner took the copy to Kirk, the American Chargé d'Affaires, but he did not want to have anything to do with it, saying: 'Oh, take this out of here. That is dynamite . . . We have had so many troubles already, I don't want to get involved.' The copy finally landed in the British Embassy whence it reached London on 25 August.

Before conclusion of the Russo–German pact Weizsäcker warned Henderson, the British Ambassador, advising that the British negotiations be accelerated. Even the Nuremberg Court, which condemned him as a war criminal, admitted that, after conclusion of the pact, he did not abandon his efforts to preserve peace.[57] Assisted by Theo Kordt he attempted to persuade the Italians to divorce themselves from Hitler's war policy. This, together with the conclusion of the Anglo–Polish treaty of alliance, had the desired effect but, owing to Hitler's irrationality and propensity for brinkmanship, it was only temporary; shortly before 6 p.m. on 25 August, after a report from Schmundt, Hitler's chief aide, Jodl noted in his diary that Hitler was 'no longer quite sure whether Britain was not in earnest this time; but he does not want a showdown with Britain'.[58]

Even after conclusion of the Russo–German pact Theo Kordt continued to talk to Vansittart, on some occasions in the latter's house. Even as late as 31 August Kordt and Vansittart were still concerting their efforts, but in vain; they agreed, however, to remain in touch. Theo Kordt was, if possible, to obtain a transfer to some neutral country – which should be possible with Weizsäcker's help – whence he would send a prearranged innocent postcard as a signal of his arrival and availability for secret discussions.[59]

Meanwhile Oster's group had not remained inactive. They had found an important and influential ally – at least any sensible person would have thought that, in his position, he would have had some influence – in Major-General Georg Thomas, head of the 'Economics and Supply' Group in OKW (rechristened Economics and Armaments Office in November 1939).[60] They now approached Thomas asking him to do all he could think of to prevent war. Gisevius even refers to Thomas as the spokesman of the group at this time; Thomas himself says that the members of the group were Popitz, Goerdeler, Beck, Hassell, Schacht, Erwin Planck (retired State Secretary), Oster, Wittke (senior civil servant) and Gisevius.[61]

After exhaustive discussions the conclusion was reached that, primarily for the reasons given above, there could be no question of action by force at this time; on the other hand there still seemed to be slight hope that if the absence of the economic conditions necessary for war against the Western Powers could be demonstrated, Hitler might be dissuaded from running so great a risk. As we now know, Hitler thought on quite different lines. He considered that war itself would create for him the necessary economic basis for war, primarily in Eastern and South-eastern Europe. This was the object of the trade treaties of recent months. Thomas knew that commonsense arguments did not achieve much with Hitler. Nevertheless it was essential to try.

With Schacht's assistance, therefore, Thomas drafted a memorandum in which he explained that an attack on Poland would inevitably lead to world war, in other words a long war of attrition, and that without strong allies Germany could not sustain it owing to her inadequate reserves of raw materials and food. In mid-August Thomas submitted this memorandum to Colonel-General Keitel, his superior officer as Chief of OKW. Keitel, however, cut Thomas short, saying that there was no danger at all of a world war; the French were a degenerate pacifist people and the British too decadent to help the Poles; the United States would not send a single man to Europe to fight for Britain, still less Poland. This was Hitler's view and anyone who did not share it was blind to Hitler's greatness. The memorandum never got further than Keitel.

A second attempt made by Thomas after he had heard from Canaris that the date for the invasion of Poland had been postponed was somewhat more successful, at least procedurally. Thomas drew up tables and comparative graphs illustrating the economic warfare capacity of Germany and the other great powers, from which Germany's inferiority clearly emerged. Schacht and also Goerdeler had assisted in their production. Thomas submitted his tables and graphs to Keitel on Sunday 27 August.[62] This time Keitel took them to Hitler but Hitler sent Thomas word that, since Russia was now on Germany's side, there was no need to fear world war and his warnings were therefore groundless.

Attempts were then made to bring Keitel together with Schacht or Goerdeler; Schacht also wished to speak to Brauchitsch or Halder; first Thomas and then Canaris were to arrange these meeetings – but all without success.[63] Since conclusion of the Russo–German pact the order for attack on Poland might be expected any day, in fact at any moment. Brauchitsch and Halder, who of course knew this well, remained unapproachable.

Meanwhile Schacht and Gisevius together with Thomas and Oster decided to try once more in what Gisevius calls 'one last desperate step'.[64] During the interval between issue of the order for attack and the actual start of the shooting Schacht, Gisevius, Thomas and Canaris proposed to drive to Army Headquarters in Zossen and demand to see Halder and Brauchitsch. Schacht was still a Minister of the *Reich* and it was thought unlikely that his car would be stopped.

Late on the afternoon of 25 August the conspirators met in the *Abwehr*'s offices on the Tirpitzufer. They proposed to confront Halder and Brauchitsch with an ultimatum: the decision to go to war was unconstitutional since it had not been discussed in cabinet (of which Schacht was a member); either, therefore, troops were to be placed at Schacht's disposal to preserve the rights of the *Reich* government or Brauchitsch and Halder should have all those present arrested; they were to be deterred from adopting the second course by threat of disclosure of all previous conspiratorial agreements, plans and discussions.[65] While Schacht, Gisevius and Thomas, however, were waiting for Canaris, Oster arrived instead with the news that Hitler had lost his nerve and called off the war. Now, they thought, Hitler would have forfeited the generals' respect and no war would be possible for decades.

Peace seemed assured, Canaris said, for at least twenty years, but not as a result of the efforts of the opposition or even of the 'moderates' in Hitler's entourage, not because of Mussolini's refusal to participate, still less because of any threat exerted by the Anglo–Polish alliance, but simply because of the failure of the dictator's nerve.[66] Gisevius thought that this was just the moment for the opposition to overthrow Hitler, but Canaris was convinced that Hitler was more or less 'finished' and that everything else would happen automatically; by acting now, he said, they might only make the generals stubborn once more and spoil everything. Oster and Hassell supported this view.[67] So when, six days later, the order to attack was reissued and war actually began on 1 September, hardly anyone was expecting it. Surprise and, until the start of shooting, uncertainty as to whether this was really now the actual thing, in general condemned the opposition to inactivity. On the afternoon of 31 August Canaris said to Gisevius with tears in his eyes: 'This means the end of Germany.'[68]

9 Plans, Probings and Memoranda

Once more, on 31 August, Weizsäcker and Hassell attempted to save the peace, making representations to Göring, Henderson and Josef Lipski, the Polish Ambassador.[1] During the last few days before the French and British declarations of war Schlabrendorff too was indefatigable in maintaining contact between the opposition and the few British diplomats still in Berlin.[2] These last-minute efforts proved to the civilians something which the soldiers had often heard from Hitler himself but had never quite believed: that Hitler, Ribbentrop and some of the other hangers-on actually *wanted* war. There were perfectly genuine possibilities of satisfying Hitler's demands by peaceful means, in other words without bloodshed; not only did he fail to seize them, but he purposely and deliberately rejected and sabotaged them.

Halder was busy with the war against Poland and the other generals involved lacked either the opportunity, the time or the will to do anything. Meanwhile, however, an unexpected opportunity presented itself with the appointment of Colonel-General von Hammerstein-Equord to command Army Detachment A in the west. When questioned by Rudolf Pechel early in the summer of 1939 he said: 'Just give me some troops and I won't fail you.'[3] Schlabrendorff had always been convinced that Hammerstein would be given a command on the outbreak of war and then, provided opportunity offered, would be prepared to arrest Hitler. On 3 September he said as much to Sir George Ogilvie-Forbes whom he met preparing to return to England.[4]

Hammerstein certainly made his mistakes but he had been an opponent of Hitler from the outset and he was a man of whom even so severe a critic as Wheeler-Bennett could say with confidence that, if Hitler had ever come within range of him, he would have struck him down quickly and without more ado.[5] When subsequently told that none of the generals approached by the conspirators could be persuaded to participate in an attempt at a *coup* even when given descriptions and documents on the terrible mass murders in Poland, he said to his friend Rudolf Pechel: 'Doctor Pechel, I am an old soldier but these people [his fellow-officers] have turned me into an anti-militarist.'[6]

Hammerstein was appointed to command Army Detachment A on 9 September; it was stationed on the Lower Rhine with headquarters in

Cologne and planning started immediately. Contact between Schlabrendorff's friends in Berlin and Hammerstein was maintained by Colonel Stern von Gwiazdowski and Nikolaus von Halem. The idea was that, if it were possible to do away with Hitler, major war might perhaps still be avoided; a new German government would restore Poland and Czechoslovakia and, though insisting on certain demands for revision, would only seek to obtain these by negotiation.

Hammerstein tried to persuade Hitler to visit his Army Detachment, arguing that German defence preparedness in the west must be demonstrated during the Polish campaign. Hitler contemplated a visit but then called it off, so that Hammerstein was unable to carry out his plan. Shortly thereafter Hammerstein was relieved of his command and placed on the retired list once more. In the autumn of 1939 Hitler did make several visits to the Polish front; in the west, however, he did not show his face until the end of the year when he inspected front-line troops in the Hunsrück and Saarbrücken areas from 23 to 25 December.[7]

No action against Hitler could therefore be taken during the period of uncertainty before the Polish war had been won and while the danger of French intervention across the Rhine was still acute. After Hitler's victory over Poland, however, the opposition was really at its wits' end.[8]

No one knew what to do now. The generals were rejoicing in victory so would certainly not participate in a *putsch*; many of those who were ready to do so or who realized the necessity of a *coup* in the light of the terrible mass murders in Poland by the SS or police *Einsatzgruppen* (task forces) thought it too bold a step, first because of their concepts of loyalty and commitment to their oath, to which particularly strict standards applied in wartime, and also because of the uncertainties of the strategic situation.[9] It had to be assumed that any internal upheaval would be exploited by the Western Powers to launch an offensive; anyone who thought otherwise was naïve. The opposition accordingly devoted its efforts to obtaining the necessary assurances from the British government (without these the French would be unlikely to do anything) and exploring possibilities of halting the war.

The soundings made by Adam von Trott zu Solz in London and Washington were primarily designed to serve this second purpose. With some justification it was expected that, quite apart from other motives and weighty reasons, President Roosevelt would not be averse to playing the role of saviour of world peace. Accordingly in September 1939 Trott set off for the United States, well camouflaged by an invitation to the conference of the Institute of Pacific Relations in Virginia Beach and a mission for the Foreign Ministry. Officially the purpose of his journey was to deliver an address to the conference, thus assuring Germany of a place among the countries represented in the Institute – tantamount to a considerable prestige victory for the German government.[10] The British maritime blockade created difficulties but, after an adventurous journey, Trott reached New York towards the end of October.

There he met and talked on several occasions with Paul Scheffer, the former editor of the *Berliner Tageblatt* who had emigrated. Scheffer had been told of

Trott's official mission and initially, therefore, was cautious. At their second meeting, however, the truth came out and they then discussed exhaustively the prospects of exploiting the present fluid situation between the end of the Polish war and the anticipated opening of hostilities in the west. Scheffer explained his ideas and Trott asked him to put them down on paper.[11] A draft was quickly available in the form of an article written by Scheffer for the *Atlantic Monthly* but it was never published. On reading it Trott was impressed; he agreed with it all, apart from one point dealing with the question whether the opposition would prefer a military defeat of Germany to continuance of a victorious Nazi regime.[12]

Although, apart from one or two final comments added by Trott, Scheffer was the sole author, it was agreed that the paper should be presented as stemming primarily from Trott, since a journalist's ideas would not have carried so much weight. Support and signatures were to be canvassed from prominent German émigrés including Dr Brüning, Hans Simons, Kurt Riezler (formerly secretary to Bethmann Hollweg) and Dr Hans Muhle.[13] This seems to have taken place; in any case consultations on the paper were held.

On 13 November the memorandum reached G. S. Messersmith, Assistant Secretary of State in the State Department, via W. T. Stone, a member of the Washington Foreign Policy Association. The same day Messersmith passed a copy to Cordell Hull, the Secretary of State, and the next day told Sumner Welles, the Under-Secretary of State, of Trott's arrival and of the gist of the memorandum. Welles had already seen it, however.[14] Lord Lothian, the British Ambassador in Washington, also received a copy. Undoubtedly the memorandum was given an unfortunately wide distribution; Scheffer recalls that it was duplicated in twenty-four copies.[15]

The memorandum took as its starting point the well-known dictum by President Woodrow Wilson in 1917 that after the war there should neither be victors nor vanquished and that men must learn not to regard military victory as the basis of a lasting peace.[16] It was absolutely necessary, the memorandum continued, that the Allied war aims should now be announced clearly and publicly; before deciding on these war aims, however, there must be definition of the historical role to be played by Germany. If Germany was regarded as the perpetual and incorrigible disturber of the peace, then there was no alternative but to dismember and finally disarm the country. Those who thought this way presumably regarded the Treaty of Versailles as insufficiently severe rather than too severe. Announcement of war aims on this basis, however, could only do harm since practically every German would support even the present regime if the alternative was the total destruction of Germany. If, however, the present German state were considered to be, not the natural manifestation of the German national character, but an unnatural aberration caused by extraordinary crisis conditions stemming from the Versailles Treaty, in other words if the purpose was not to destroy and dismember Germany but to integrate her into a new European order as soon as she was liberated from the present tyranny, then the earliest possible announcement of the Allied war aims would be of decisive significance. The establishment and announcement of moderate war aims would encourage and strengthen the opposition and so contribute to the overthrow of Nazi domination.

The memorandum stressed that there was already widespread opposition among all classes of people; only the middle and lower-middle classes would follow any violent mass movement more or less unthinkingly. The upper classes, on the other hand, placed their hopes on the Army officers and they did not think that Germany could sustain a major European war; they must be convinced that Hitler alone was standing in the way of an honourable and acceptable solution. The Germans might well liberate themselves from the Nazi tyranny if the necessary psychological conditions could thus be created.

To produce an effect the Allied peace demands must be precise. Naturally every detail could not be laid down but in no case should Germany be confined to an area smaller than in 1933. To achieve all this the United States Government should throw into the scales the great respect in which it was held and bring diplomatic pressure to bear on Britain and France to announce reasonable war aims.

When Trott visited Messersmith on the morning of 20 November,[17] he modified the ideas in the memorandum to some extent, saying that it was perhaps too early for a *public* announcement of Allied peace conditions; the worst that could happen would be some premature agreement leaving the present German regime in power. This would be a catastrophe not only for Germany but for the rest of the world and would mean the end of all prospects for the German resistance movement. The danger of compromise was real enough, Trott said, since there was still a powerful group in Britain desirous of some such settlement. Nevertheless it was highly important for the 'conservative elements' in Germany, in other words that section of the opposition which he represented, to be informed of the Allied war aims as soon as possible. Their efforts were hampered by uncertainty.

Messersmith regarded the memorandum as important; Scheffer even recalls that he was enthusiastic and urgently recommended Sumner Welles, the Under-Secretary of State, to read it. During the following weeks, however, doubts about the credibility and reliability of Trott began to grow. On 20 November Messersmith did write to Sumner Welles saying that Trott had been strongly recommended to him by Brüning as a thoroughly 'honest man' who could be regarded as spokesman for those circles in Germany from which a non-Nazi government would have to be formed; when Trott had visited him in the State Department, Messersmith said, he had made a very good impression and he thought Brüning's estimate was correct. A few days later, however, he was saying that anyone who could leave Germany and return could hardly be a free agent; in addition the FBI had established that, while in the United States, Trott had had contact with 'certain persons here who are acting directly or indirectly for the present German government'. This may have been the price, he said, which Trott had to pay for the freedom of movement permitted him. On 8 December Trott was able to see Messersmith once more,[18] but suspicion was in the air. He was shadowed by FBI agents and a file was opened on him entitled: 'Subject: Espionage Activities, Adam von Trott in US' (Case No 862.20211).[19] This man was thought to be a spy.

During his interview Trott asked Messersmith to treat both his memorandum and his statements as confidential since in effect they put a noose round his neck. Nevertheless the memorandum was duplicated (Paul Scheffer recalls twenty-four copies) and one of them reached Felix Frankfurter, a member of the United States Supreme Court whom Trott had known at Oxford. Frankfurter had been highly suspicious of Trott from the outset; he had been warned of Trott and, according to Messersmith's report to Sumner Welles, he took care to spread this suspicion. The meeting with Frankfurter, at any rate, was a catastrophic failure.[20] Trott himself knew that certain Oxford circles had denounced him as an 'appeaser', in other words one of those who would really like to bring about a compromise with Hitler.[21] This was certainly not his purpose now. This reproach is justified only insofar as in 1938 Trott had pleaded for a firm but non-aggressive attitude on the part of the Western Powers, thinking that an external conflict would prevent any solution of what he called the social and economic crisis in Germany.[22] An external conflict would force the Germans on to the defensive, he believed, and therefore on to the side of the Nazi system. Trott also hoped to avoid an armed conflict between the ideological camps, believing that a bloody victory of one over the other was unnecessary.[23]

American officialdom was apparently unable to follow the somewhat complicated process of thought which could lead a German patriot to refuse to accept any form of solution leaving Hitler and his regime in power. Through his American contacts Trott wished to prevent the Allies committing themselves to a war of annihilation against Hitler–Germany and so forcing on to Hitler's side all those elements which were beginning to coalesce to overthrow him; this was the argument Trott put forward to the chief editor of the *Washington Post* on 19 November.[24] It would have been of importance for the opposition to have some indication of the conditions which the Allies would guarantee to a Germany liberated from Hitler. It would have been stupid, however, at this point publicly to announce peace terms which might have seemed acceptable to Hitler. That might well have made his overthrow impossible.

About the same time (November or December 1939) a further memorandum from Trott reached Lord Halifax via Charles Bosanquet, one of Trott's British relatives.[25] In this Trott stressed, much on the lines of Scheffer's paper, the conditions regarded as important for any success by the anti-Hitler opposition: the largest possible number of Germans must be convinced that this time Britain did not want a Versailles or something worse; otherwise decent Germans would be forced to defend Nazism in order to save Germany from destruction. British propaganda, he said, must go deeper and wider; non-Nazi (and therefore silent) opinion in Germany must be *convinced* that Britain aimed at peace and justice in Europe. The most respected and unassailable personalities in all the countries concerned must work in this direction; anything which was 'sheer propaganda' should be avoided; only honesty would convince.

At the end of December 1939 or early in January 1940 yet another memorandum reached London, this time from and through Wheeler-Bennett, who was in New York at the time and had been present at many of Trott's discussions with his German and American friends. At the end of December 1939 Trott wrote to his friend David Astor that Wheeler-Bennett understood many aspects of the German situation better than anyone else in Britain and that he should be listened to carefully; he had asked Wheeler-Bennett, he said, to pass to Astor his memorandum of 28 December 1939.[26] In this Wheeler-Bennett had produced almost the same ideas as Trott: as Chamberlain himself had said, Britain was fighting, not the German people but its tyrannical regime; in some sense, therefore, the war was one for the liberation of the Germans. In this struggle the democratic powers had allies inside Germany whose aim was equally the destruction of the Nazi regime and reestablishment of a state based on the rule of law. These elements must be so far strengthened and encouraged that they could take the initiative themselves. This they could only do, however, if they could be sure that a new Germany would be treated with justice and generosity by the democratic powers. It was therefore essential, not to establish and announce the Allied war aims in detail now, but to give more definite assurances which would seem to the German opposition to justify action against Hitler. A declaration should be made as soon as possible by Britain, France, Poland and the British Dominions at war with Germany guaranteeing: no political division or dismemberment of Germany; collaboration with a new Germany; large-scale trading facilities, access to raw materials, economic agreements and limitation of armaments.

Trott returned to Germany via Japan early in 1940, having achieved no visible success from his mission as a whole. His messages had almost certainly reached their addressees in Britain; that they did so in America can be proved from the files. But the Allied announcements urged by Trott and his friends were never made nor did any form of cooperation with the internal German opposition take place via Trott. The fronts solidified; men were set in their well-worn ways. The human and material sacrifices claimed by the war were indescribable. Yet paradoxically it was easier to accept them than to make the necessary mental and political efforts to cooperate with the German resistance movement. The only meagre result of all Trott's efforts, for which he was risking his life, was an instruction from the State Department to Alexander Kirk, American Chargé d'Affaires in Berlin, telling him to listen to what Trott might have to say and report thereon to Washington.[27] The suspicions not only remained, but were more intense, and reached the highest levels.[28]

From San Francisco, before he left the North American continent, Trott wrote to Justice Frankfurter on 9 January 1940: 'Dear Justice Frankfurter, I cannot leave this country without at least sending you a brief note of farewell. I understand and respect the reasons why it has not this time been possible to reestablish more than a purely human contact. You will not, I hope, consider my feeling of its continued existence presumptuous – since, I am afraid, there is now no more opportunity left to confirm it.'[29] There are a number of likely and plausible reasons for Trott's lack of success. Trott himself believed he had made a serious mistake by suggesting to the sensitive Justice Frankfurter that it would be better if American Jews did not engage in anti-National-Socialist propaganda too prominently.[30] Apart from this, misunderstandings and suspicions assumed almost grotesque proportions, and appearances were against Trott who was formally a part of the National-Socialist bureaucracy. On 17 January 1940, the President of the United States wrote to Justice Frankfurter: 'For Heaven's sake! Surely you did not let your Trott friend get trotted out of the country without having him searched by Edgar Hoover. Think of the battleship plans and other secrets he may be carrying back. This is the height of indiscretion and carelessness on your part!'[31] Whereupon Frankfurter wrote acidly he had been under the impression that someone other than himself was Hoover's boss but now he saw great opportunities opening up.[32]

Trott foresaw the tragic consequences of his failure. Casablanca and the demand for unconditional surrender proved him right. Nevertheless he did not cease trying till the very end. His subsequent efforts will be referred to later.

After the Polish campaign and while Trott was busy in New York and Washington, the resistance movement took up the threads again through other channels. With the help of Weizsäcker, Dr Theo Kordt had arranged to be transferred to Berne and from there he regained contact with London, his primary object being to find out what the British attitude would be in the event of an internal German *coup*.[33] Contact was not established until the end of October when Conwell Evans brought over a document containing statements by Chamberlain.[34]

In his broadcast of 4 September 1939 Chamberlain had already said that the fight was not against the German people but solely against the tyrannical regime which had betrayed its own people and the whole western civilization.[35] This sounded encouraging to the opposition; Chamberlain knew of its existence and aims and so its members felt that his words were addressed to them. All the other prerequisites for a *coup*, however, were lacking; the generals were unlikely to be satisfied with such vague statements.

Then, on 6 October, Hitler delivered his *Reichstag* speech with its peculiar peace offer – possible reestablishment of a truncated Poland but settlement of all questions connected with Poland solely between Germany and Russia, the partitioning powers. He did not seriously believe that Russia would relinquish, in order to create a 'rump-Poland', that part of Polish territory which she had seized, and he would not make territory available alone; at least this seemed to be the implication when he continued that such an arrangement would best suit the existing situation. There was therefore really no object, he said, in carrying on war in the west in order to revise this situation. Instead people should recognize that the Treaty of Versailles was finished and abolished and should return the German colonies. Based on a new territorial division of Europe and 'creation of a *Reich* frontier which – as already stressed – is in line with historical, ethnographic and economic conditions', a new system of peace and security should be possible.[36] Creation of a *Reich* frontier corresponding to economic conditions was merely another way of expressing the brutal policy of conquest which Hitler was clearly proposing to continue, not so much in the West as in the East.

The Western Powers did not react in the manner expected or desired by Hitler and so the dictator lost patience. In his 'Directive No 6 for the Conduct of the War' dated 9 October 1939 he announced his decision to take the offensive in the west unless it became evident in the near future that Britain and France were disposed to bring the war to an end.[37] OKH had known of Hitler's intention to go over to the offensive ever since 25 September and in a discussion with Halder and Brauchitsch on 27 September he had said that immediate preparation for an attack on France was necessary.[38] Directive No 6 was the formal order. Twelve days later, on 21 October, he told the *Reichsleiter* and *Gauleiter* assembled in the *Reich* Chancellery that in a fortnight's time he would be ready to open a major offensive in the west; once France and Britain had been forced to their knees, then he would turn east again and put matters in order there.[39]

In a further speech on the next day he made another peace offer – not seriously meant. Meanwhile the *Wehrmacht* leaders were debating the pros and cons of a western offensive in general and an autumn offensive in particular.[40] These discussions became academic, however, when on 27 October Hitler assembled the *Wehrmacht* leaders and laid down the date of the offensive in the west — 12 November.[41]

So the well-known situation had arisen again: the outbreak of real war with the Western Powers was imminent. Since it could not be won, its outbreak must be prevented by a *coup*.[42] At least the conspirators could now put this argument forward with some conviction. Preparations for a *coup* were restarted with renewed energy.

Meanwhile, in a speech in the Commons on 12 October, Chamberlain had answered Hitler's peace offer.[43] He had spoken of his conviction that, like all other European peoples, the German people were longing for peace; British policy, he said, had no vindictive purpose but was simply in defence of freedom. Peace could only be assured, however, if account was taken of the just claims and needs of all countries.

This was the situation when contact was finally reestablished between Theo Kordt and Conwell Evans. Evans brought over a copy of a statement by Chamberlain; it was in fact the relevant extract from the speech mentioned above but Kordt and his friends took it as a message from Chamberlain explicitly addressed to the opposition. Conwell Evans described the document as a solemn commitment by Chamberlain which would be honoured in dealings with any trustworthy non-Nazi German government.[44] In addition Conwell Evans brought a message from Sir Robert Vansittart sent on behalf of Chamberlain and Halifax; it said that the British government could not enter into any form of negotiation 'with Hitler or his like'; 'it was the job of the German opposition to produce a German government capable of negotiating and on whose word the British could rely.'[45]

Admittedly this did not amount to much; for the conspirators, who undoubtedly already knew of Chamberlain's speech, it contained nothing new.

Owing to the circumstances, however – war, *coup* preparations, conspiratorial activity, danger – and the secrecy surrounding their transmission, both the documents and the statements they contained came to be regarded as something special and were given greater weight than their contents justified. There was not even a hint of an armistice or strategic standstill during an internal German *coup*. In addition the 'message' apparently never reached Halder, the most important addressee at the time. The conspirators could not persuade the generals to act without guarantees and the Western Powers were not willing to give guarantees without prior assurance, by actual deeds, that the conspirators were in earnest. Their suspicions were reinforced rather than aroused by the famous Venlo Incident.

At the end of September 1939 Captain S. Payne Best and Major R. H. Stevens, two members of the British Intelligence Service working in The Hague, contacted a German émigré who told them that he was in touch with German officers belonging to a military anti-Hitler conspiracy. This seemed plausible, particularly in the light of the many reports reaching Britain. After checking with London the two were authorized to meet the German. The meeting took place on 21 October, on Dutch territory and in the presence of a Dutch secret service officer, but it proved that the German was only of junior rank. On condition that a more senior officer in a more important position would appear a further meeting was agreed for 30 October in The Hague.[46]

Three further meetings took place with the Germans who were in reality members of the SS *Sicherheitsdienst* (SD – security service) and the *Gestapo* – on 7, 8 and 9 November, on each occasion in Backhus near Venlo. Ostensibly a senior officer representing the German opposition was to appear but in fact the German representative was Walter Schellenberg, head of Section IV E (*Gestapo* Counter Intelligence) in the *Reichssicherheitshauptamt* (RSHA, Central Security Office). At the last meeting on 9 November the two Englishmen and the Dutchman were lured close to the German–Dutch frontier and, with the assistance of a few SS men, they were kidnapped.

Hitler and Himmler apparently assumed at once that the British Secret Service, which had shown itself so willing to contact an alleged resistance movement designed to overthrow Hitler and his regime, was also behind the assassination attempt made in the *Bürgerbräukeller*. This was anyway a good propaganda point in such a favourable concatenation of circumstances. Any previous willingness on the part of British agents and their superiors in London to contact the German opposition, however, was inevitably markedly reduced after the Venlo incident.

Meanwhile efforts continued in Germany to build up an internal opposition front. On 10 October Hassell and Goerdeler discussed matters in Munich.[47] They agreed on minimum external demands which included annexation of the German parts of Poland, reestablishment of the rest of Poland as an independent state, reorganization of Czechoslovakia and armaments agreements; such demands are of course only comprehensible in the light of the situation at the time, though they appear most immoderate today. It was taken for granted by most Germans that Germany had not started an unnecessary war in 1914 but had merely defended vital interests that were being threatened, and that consequently the Versailles Treaty constituted an injustice and the rape of a nation not only in form but in content, too. Now, in autumn 1939, Germany was in fact the strongest military power on the continent and she actually controlled the territories whose disposal might have been discussed, and which could not be wrested from Germany without a long war and huge sacrifices in blood. However, a European concert and community could hardly be founded on the basis of possession through use of sheer force, and even if Germany had had better legal claims to the acquired territories, the method of acquisition would appear to have reduced the validity of the claim. There is no indication in Hassell's diary, moreover, that he and Goerdeler considered the method an obstacle to rightful possession.

The idea that Göring might have a seat in a government to be formed after the fall of Hitler is also only explicable in the light of the situation at the time. Nazism was strong and had scored great successes both at home and abroad. A *coup*, even if conceivable at all, could only take place on grounds of the threatened expansion of the war which was generally considered, even by many Party members, to constitute an immense danger to everything so far achieved. At the end of October Göring himself, admittedly with Hitler's knowledge, had held conversations with a Swedish emissary who wished to act as intermediary for peace negotiations with Britain.[48] Having heard that even Beck would be prepared to go along, Hassell told Goerdeler that he would agree to the retention or inclusion of Göring; they were agreed, however, that this could only be a transitional solution. There was no satisfactory basis for action, however; Hassell referred to the whole affair as 'still somewhat unmatured'. The necessary forces were not even on the horizon.

During this autumn following the Polish campaign Hassell held further talks with Goerdeler, Beck, Hammerstein, Weizsäcker and even with Grand Admiral Raeder, the Commander-in-Chief of the Navy, also with Popitz, indirectly with Schacht and again on several occasions with Goerdeler.[49] But what good was it all? Hassell and Popitz were both equally clear: nothing was to be done so long as 'the main factor still failed them – the general prepared to act'.[50] Witzleben was thought to be the most capable but he had really no opportunity since he was now located in Bad Kreuznach, far away from Berlin.[51]

Towards the end of October it became increasingly clear that Hitler was determined to seize the military initiative and order a move through Belgium and Holland; opposition activity reached a feverish pitch.[52] After the Polish campaign Klaus Bonhoeffer, Otto John and Hans von Dohnanyi had reestablished contact with Ernst von Harnack, Leber, Jakob Kaiser, Habermann, Wirmer and Leuschner. Dohnanyi had been Personal Assistant to Gürtner, the *Reich* Minister of Justice, until 25 August 1939, then judge of the *Reich* court in Leipzig and was now a *Sonderführer* (approximately equivalent to major) in OKW *Amt Ausland/Abwehr* under Admiral Canaris and Colonel Oster; owing to his central position he played a key role in the reestablishment of these contacts. The object was to win Brauchitsch, Halder and other commanders over to the idea of a *coup* before the western offensive.[53]

Though basically the generals who were approached held the view that the western offensive would result in catastrophe and must be stopped, most of them thought that there would be inadequate support for a *coup* among the people and that it could, therefore, easily lead to civil war. It would then hardly be surprising, they said, if Germany's enemies exploited the situation to score some military victory or propose unacceptable peace conditions. The idea of the 'stab-in-the-back' and their oath to Hitler also figured largely in the commanders' counter-arguments.

The group referred to above accordingly tried to demonstrate to the generals the real attitude of mind of the workers – like other sections of the population they wanted to have nothing to do with the war. In fact since the Polish campaign and particularly since Hitler's speech of 6 October a rumour was going round, which people were only too glad to believe, that peace negotiations were under way and the war was really at an end.[54] To provide Beck, the leading conspirator, with the necessary arguments and also to promote cooperation both before and after the *coup*, after much effort the group referred to, in particular Ernst von Harnack, Klaus Bonhoeffer, Otto John and Dohnanyi, arranged a meeting between Beck and Leuschner.[55] Leuschner and his friends promised that, in the event of a military *putsch*, they would call a general strike. As a precaution emissaries were despatched to the more important headquarters of the workers' underground movement to prepare the ground for the planned action.[56]

It was also thought possible that the public might be convinced of the necessity and justification for a *coup*. For months Dohnanyi and Oster had been collecting material and evidence on the crimes of the Party, the SS and the Nazi leaders, on corruption in Party organizations, on criminal and immoral practices in the Hitler Youth and the SA, on profiteering, infringements of the law, brutalities, cases of rape, ill-treatment of prisoners, atrocities in Poland and anti-Jewish pogroms. The evidence was intended to be used, not only to open the eyes of the generals but also subsequently for legal proceedings against the culprits and to show the people what their leaders were like.[57]

The opposition's arguments were only some of those with which 'the generals' were assailed. From all interested quarters arrived memoranda explaining what a catastrophe would result from a western offensive and how it could be stopped. The spectre arose once more of a static war of attrition lasting for years with vast useless battles. The unfavourable state of the weather and ground in the autumn – mist, rain and mud – it was argued, would make it all even more catastrophic; the Navy could not operate properly in fog; the *Luftwaffe* would be practically paralysed and the advantage of the Army's motorization, the major step forward since the First World War, in particular of the tanks, would largely be lost.[58] Moreover its own commanders regarded the German Army as inferior to the French.[59] From all points of view, it was said, preparations were totally inadequate; a western offensive now would be a completely irresponsible project, doomed to failure from the outset.

Beck had already, at the end of September, written a memorandum headed 'On the war situation after conclusion of the Polish campaign'; it was intended for the Commander-in-Chief of the Army and his Chief of Staff.[60] Beck warned against any underestimation of the Western Powers' determination after the German victory over Poland. A war with Great Britain must always be conducted as a world war since the British operational base consisted, not of the British Isles alone but of India, Canada, Africa and Australia as well. Germany would in any case be facing the economic might of the United States in the form of economic and material support to France and Britain. This could easily be followed by military support. The French and British, the memorandum continued, had not attacked because they were preparing a vast war of attrition which would be characterized by enormous 'gun-power and ammunition expenditure, barrages of incalculable duration and infantry assaults conducted on the principle: "the artillery gains the ground, the infantry occupies it".' The war would be conducted by the Western Powers with the object of wearing Germany down and starving her out; a defensive battle of unlimited duration must be visualized; no possibility of a *military* decision in the west was to be seen. There were only two possibilities of forcing a decision and turning the anticipated position warfare into a war of movement: either by abandoning the Siegfried Line and possibly larger areas of Germany (endangering the Ruhr area) – which was too risky; alternatively by violating neutral territory, when the disadvantages (an increase in the number and bitterness of Germany's enemies) would outweigh the advantages. No one should count on a 'miracle' such as had saved Frederick II in 1762.

In a further memorandum of 10 October entitled 'The German peace offer of 6 October 1939 and the possible future course of the war'[61] Beck developed the ideas on length of war, attrition and the nature of real world war at which he had only hinted in his previous paper. World war, he said, would not be decided on land or even on a single continent and it had not yet even begun. To judge by all expert experience a German victory in the west was improbable, no matter whether an offensive or defensive strategy was adopted.

During this period, however, serving soldiers too were to be heard voicing the same doubts as Beck.

Since 1 September 1939 the Commander-in-Chief of Army Group C in the West had been Colonel-General Wilhelm Ritter von Leeb, of whom Etzdorf said to Hassell on 27 January 1940 that of all the senior commanders he was 'the only one with whom something might be done'.[62] On 7 October 1939, with Hitler's speech of the 6th fresh in his mind, Leeb noted: 'All instructions... indicate that it is proposed to launch this crazy offensive, violating the neutrality of Holland, Belgium and Luxemburg. Hitler's speech... was therefore merely a sop to the German people.' On 11 October he despatched to the Commander-in-Chief of the Army a comprehensive 'Memorandum on the Prospects and Effects of an Attack on France and Britain violating the Neutrality of Holland, Belgium and Luxemburg.' A copy went to Halder and the paper was shown to Colonel-

General Fedor von Bock, Commander-in-Chief of Army Group B.[63] In a covering letter to Brauchitsch Leeb said that in his anxiety for the future of Germany 'in this grave hour which will perhaps decide on the fate of our people for decades', he must address himself once more to his Commander-in-Chief with a summary of his views, since an attack on France through neutral countries was clearly in course of preparation.

In general the views put forward by Leeb were similar to those of Beck. The traditional object of any war, a favourable peace, he said, was not attainable. Militarily it was impossible to inflict such a defeat on France and Britain that they would be ready to sue for peace. There followed detailed arguments and evidence to show why, in the circumstances, an offensive in the west must fail in face of French and Belgian defensive measures. The result would be exhaustion and at the best position warfare. The availability of tanks would not alter this situation; the French and British were also well provided with tanks and anti-tank guns. Ultimately the side to hold out the longest would be that possessing the greater reserves of men and material – and that was the Western Powers.

Leeb then turned to the political consequences of an offensive in the west. He reached the same conclusions as Beck: the offensive could only lead to catastrophe since Germany would place herself in the wrong by the planned violation of Belgian neutrality and all those not yet ready to do so would be prepared to fight. Germany would be isolated, without allies and surrounded by enemies. Evil effects were also to be feared at home. The majority of the German people were confident that the *Führer* wanted peace and so would be sadly disillusioned by the offensive and the consequential casualties. The people wanted peace, not offensives, and at any time this mood could quickly spread to the Army.

Against these weighty disadvantages of the offensive, Leeb continued, the immeasurable advantages of the defensive should be considered. If the German Army in the west remained on the defensive, it was unassailable. The enemy could only attack at the price of enormous casualties and even then would not achieve his minimum objective, the destruction of the German defence capability. The economic advantages were also important. Production could continue undisturbed and thus Germany would be equipped for a long war, for which she must now be prepared. The great political advantage, however, was that the people would realize that only the unyielding attitude of Britain was keeping Germany in a state of war. People would therefore understand the purpose of the war effort and support it accordingly.

On 31 October Leeb wrote once more to Brauchitsch.[64] The military position was clear, he said – German forces were totally inadequate. Much of the artillery was so badly trained that it constituted 'a greater menace to its own troops than to the enemy'. It was impossible at present to annihilate the British, the French and the Belgians militarily but there was no other military method of achieving peace. Moreover there was no necessity to attack. Germany already held Poland as a bargaining counter and could calmly await an enemy attack; this equally had no prospects of success; the enemy could not achieve his object by an offensive. From the bottom of their hearts the people were longing for peace. If Hitler were now to conclude peace on more or less

125

acceptable terms, such as reestablishment of an autonomous Czech state and a truncated Poland, no one would regard this as a sign of weakness; he would be hailed as a prince of peace. Leeb had begun his letter with the emphatic warning that 'in the next few days the fate of the entire German people' possibly depended on Brauchitsch. He concluded with the significant sentence: 'In these coming days I am prepared personally to range myself solidly behind you, accepting any consequences which may be desirable and necessary.'

Even before Leeb Colonel-General von Bock had sent to Brauchitsch a memorandum of his own, in which, using military arguments, he warned against violation of Belgian, Luxemburg and Dutch neutrality.[65] Bock discussed his views with Halder on 9 October.[66]

Equally on 31 October Colonel-General Gerd von Rundstedt, Commander-in-Chief of Army Group A, also located in the west, handed in a memorandum. All the senior commanders in the west had now therefore protested against the offensive which they were to conduct.[67] Like Bock, Rundstedt deliberately avoided any political arguments and confined himself entirely to 'the soldier's sphere of responsibility'. He hoped, justifiably, that he would thereby have better prospects of making an impression on Hitler. Numerically, he said the strength ratio between the German forces and those of the French, British and possibly also Belgian and Dutch was unfavourable to Germany and would become critical in the event of a costly offensive. The Polish campaign had shown how greatly the troops were dependent upon their commanders in the attack since they lacked the necessary impetus on their own; losses in officers must therefore be expected to be very high and this again would reduce efficiency.[68] In the long term, therefore, superior leadership could not compensate for the strength ratio. The advantage of surprise had long since been lost.

Finally Rundstedt was unable altogether to forego adducing political reasons. Germany had already miscalculated once, he said, in assuming that France and Britain would not enter the war. Since this had now happened she must be prepared for a long war and conserve her strength until the decisive moment. It was therefore better to leave the onus of attacking to the enemy; particularly in the case of the French, this would submit their determination to a test which it would not be able to withstand. Moreover, if their offensive was to have any prospect of success, the Western Powers would also have to move through Belgium. If they did so, they could be met there with the advantage that Germany would not have put herself in the wrong. Admittedly one could not wait for ever, otherwise Britain would have time to complete her preparations to an undesirable level. If necessary, therefore, the enemy must be forced to attack; this would assure Germany the advantages of the defensive and offer the best prospects of separating France and Britain. The Army having defeated Poland, it was now the task of the Navy and the *Luftwaffe* to take the necessary steps against Britain.

On 14 October Halder noted in his diary: 'Exhaustive discussion with C-in-C on overall situation. C-in-C three possibilities: Offensive, wait, fundamental changes. No overriding prospects of success for any of these, particularly not for the last since it is basically negative and produces moments of weakness. Apart from above, duty to present military views realistically and support any peace possibility.'[69] Halder had discussed the two courses of action with his Commander-in-Chief and also the anxieties voiced by Rundstedt, Bock and Leeb, the three Army Group commanders, about the western offensive, now set for November. They had discussed possible alternatives. They did not like any of the three possibilities but they thought that the third offered the least prospects of all. 'Offensive' offered practically no prospect of success; 'wait' until Britain and France attacked entailed great risk. 'Fundamental change', however – and in this context they cannot have meant external change – they regarded as 'basically negative' and productive of 'moments of weakness'. The word 'negative' here means 'not conservative' or 'revolutionary'. They feared a vacuum, the destruction of the existing order. Halder had always been afraid of civil war and it was highly improbable that the Western Powers would fail to exploit the internal situation in Germany during a *coup* and launch an offensive. So, as soldiers, they decided to do their military duty, invariably to present the military situation realistically and, as far as possible, work for peace.[70]

Bock, Rundstedt and Leeb continued their efforts to stop the western offensive. Bock reiterated his objections in a personal interview with Hitler on 25 October.[71] Even Colonel-General von Reichenau, reputed to be a Hitler follower and now commanding Sixth Army in Army Group B, tried to talk Hitler out of his plans.[72] He told Halder on 15 October that he had been commissioned to do so by Brauchitsch.[73] When he first heard of the plan for the offensive on taking over his command on 10 October, Reichenau had described it as 'downright criminal'.[74] Reichenau was thought to have influence with Hitler and he did in fact try to use it. In an interview with Hitler on 25 October (the same at which Bock was present) Hitler maintained that, if they did not strike now, the British would secretly move into Belgium and so prevent any possible German victory; Reichenau's reply was that he would prefer that; it was better that, if it must be, the British rather than the Germans should be the first to violate Belgian neutrality. This naturally made no impression on Hitler. Reichenau was so convinced of the necessity of stopping the offensive through Belgium and Holland, however, that he did something which no one would have expected of him: he had recourse to the same method as Oster and warned the Belgians of the German attack.[75] At the end of October Leeb also made further urgent representations.

Brauchitsch seems to have made one attempt, perhaps only half-hearted, to dissuade Hitler from his intentions. In an interview on 16 October he put forward reasons against the offensive, but Hitler had an answer to everything. Halder did what he could but his scope was limited by his temperament, his character and his political views. Perhaps his conspiratorial activity was no more than the normal action of a General Staff officer in producing a contingency plan which was then pigeonholed when no executive order arrived – one can only speculate.

10 Halder's New Plan

Since August 1939 Major (later Lieutenant-Colonel) Groscurth had been working in OKH as liaison officer from *Ausland/Abwehr* of OKW. At the same time he formed the main link between the circle of conspirators in the *Abwehr* and the anti-Hitler officers in OKH; he also worked closely with Weizsäcker's liaison officer in OKH, Counsellor and Captain (Reserve) Dr Hasso von Etzdorf. On 20 October, writing in his office diary about attempts then under way to bring about a peace settlement through Swedish or Vatican intermediaries, he noted: 'In all peace negotiations one is confronted by the categoric demand for the removal of Hitler and the reestablishment of Czecho in some form.'[1] This must therefore be the object. The removal of Hitler from power was as important as stopping the western offensive. The one would follow from the other.

Halder knew perfectly well the role being played by Groscurth, his two staff officers Major Werner Schrader and Captain Fiedler, by Etzdorf and also General von Stülpnagel, Deputy Chief of Staff I and Halder's official deputy. Others already involved in the conspiracy by this time were Major-General Fellgiebel, Colonel Eduard Wagner and Lieutenant-Colonel Henning von Tresckow, head of the Army Operations Section.[2] Halder agreed with what his fellow-officers were doing and encouraged them; he did not wish, however, to play an active part himself unless 'the Fatherland was in danger', a general phrase never more precisely defined. On one occasion when Halder objected that the psychological climate was unfavourable, Beck replied that, according to information from Leuschner and Kaiser, the workers were extremely opposed to the war and in favour of a *coup*; a general strike was being prepared in support of it. Halder answered ill-humouredly that, if that were so, then the workers should initiate the *coup* from below.[3]

Nevertheless Halder continued to plan and prepare for a *coup*, risking his neck in the process, as he well knew. He was convinced, however, that it could not be carried out without his Commander-in-Chief. In this, the events of 20 July 1944 proved Halder partially right. Stauffenberg was then Chief of Staff of the Replacement Army and his orders were not carried out because they lacked the backing of his Commander-in-Chief; a Chief of Staff alone had no command authority over the troops. If Brauchitsch would cooperate, well and good; plans were ready and could be carried out. The murder of Hitler might pave the way both for the *coup* itself and for Brauchitsch's participation but, if

Brauchitsch refused, he, Halder, could do nothing. As Chief of Staff only some outstanding personality of exceptional energy and authority could possibly have by-passed his Commander-in-Chief and himself seized command authority. Halder was no such personality. He deserves credit rather than blame for recognizing the fact.

In autumn 1939 and on many occasions until summer 1942 Halder wondered whether he should murder Hitler.[4] For weeks, during his visits to the *Reich* Chancellery, he carried a loaded revolver in his pocket in order to shoot Hitler. He told Groscurth so at the time and confirmed it later, though only when confronted with Groscurth's diaries. Groscurth wrote in his private diary on 1 November 1939: 'With tears in his eyes H[alder] said he had been going to see Emil [Hitler] with a pistol in his pocket for weeks in order possibly to shoot him down.' Yet he was never even near making up his mind to use his weapon – this is characteristic of Halder's whole attitude during all *coup d'état* preparations. In his heart he was against assassination but he knew perfectly well that it could not be done any other way. He carried a loaded revolver around with him but never fired it. He complained to Oster that someone should have murdered Hitler long ago but equally that this should not be regarded as the duty of a man in a senior official capacity; in other countries, he said, some private individual or desperado would have been commissioned to do it. In 1942 Halder told Etzdorf that, to assassinate Hitler, one had to be born to be an assassin, and he had not been born to be one.[5] Such was his dilemma – and his tragic inconsistency.

During the weeks following 14 October Halder became increasingly convinced of the necessity of a *coup* involving use of force. Finally, certainly no later than 31 October or 2 November, Halder and Stülpnagel gave Groscurth and his group the go-ahead for preparation of a *coup*.[6] They revived the 1938 plans and modified them to suit the changed circumstances. As in 1938, the capital was to be surrounded and occupied by troops; Party, *Gestapo* and SS headquarters were to be raided; radio transmitters and studios and all telegraph offices were to be occupied. General Hoepner was to move a Panzer division to Berlin.[7] General von Falkenhausen, who had been in command of Military District IV (Dresden) since the end of August, had agreed to participate with the forces he could control.[8] Guderian, commanding XIX Corps, was also to participate.[9] Halder himself later recalled having held two or three Panzer divisions back east of the Elbe so that they could be used for the *coup*.[10]

Among the plans kept in a safe in Army Headquarters, Zossen, was a 'study' by Oster.[11] It was a plan of action for the revolt and included lists of leading personalities and officials of the regime who were to be done away with, together with names for the new government to be formed.[12] Hitler, Ribbentrop, Himmler, Heydrich, Göring, Goebbels and 'Dietrich' (presumably Sepp Dietrich, commander of the 'SS Leibstandarte') were to be arrested; provisional governmental authority was to be exercised by a triumvirate led by Beck.[13] Among those involved were listed the following: Witzleben, Hoepner, 'Geyer' (probably Lieutenant-General Geyr von Schweppenburg, commanding a Panzer division), Falkenhausen, Reichenau,

Schacht, Goerdeler, Fritz-Dietlof Graf von der Schulenburg, Josef Wagner the *Gauleiter* and Helldorf. Troops to be used consisted of 9 Infantry Regiment (Potsdam), 3 Artillery Regiment (Frankfurt on Oder) and 15 Panzer Regiment stationed in Sagan.[14] Concentration of these units was far more difficult and far less certain than in 1938.

Dohnanyi prepared proclamations, approved and redrafted by Beck and Oster, for the information of the public.[15] They said that Hitler had ordered an offensive in the west involving violation of Belgian and Dutch neutrality and this could only bring enormous misery to Germany. To prevent this Colonel-General (retd) Ludwig Beck had decided to resume active service and he had taken over the office of Commander-in-Chief of the Army, offered him by Brauchitsch, and also command of the entire *Wehrmacht*. The *Führer* was ill and had been badly advised by his staff; he would temporarily withdraw from official business. Ribbentrop, Himmler and Göring had been arrested because they had themselves attempted to arrest the officers responsible for the present measures. Göring had embezzled millions out of the taxes paid by workers; Himmler had imprisoned thousands of innocent people; proofs were available and would be published shortly. The *Gestapo* and Propaganda Ministry were to be abolished; Beck would shortly call fresh elections; as proof of the genuine efforts being made for peace, the black-out was to be lifted. Oster had also compiled a list of people who were to be involved from the outset; it included: Goerdeler, Hassell, Schacht, Gisevius, Nebe, Helldorf, Fritz-Dietlof Graf von der Schulenburg, Liedig, Heinz, Witzleben, Hoepner, Olbricht and Reichenau. One of the drafts (in Canaris' handwriting) emphasized that the *coup* should not be declared too soon as being directed against Hitler and the story should be spread that criminal and corrupt elements in the Party had formed a conspiracy which had now been frustrated by the *Wehrmacht*.

Despite all these preparations and, indeed, explicit commitments Halder and Brauchitsch remained the major doubtful factors in the conspiracy. In October Canaris noted in his diary that he saw no further possibility of influencing Halder; he invariably listened to everything and then produced threadbare reasons for doing nothing.[16] Other members of the conspiracy were equally sceptical.[17] Meanwhile the indications multiplied that Hitler would insist on his western offensive. Rapid action was therefore necessary. The question was: what action, so long as the military would not cooperate.

This wait-and-see attitude seemed to the civilians both impractical and irresponsible, so they used the only weapon available to them and drafted memoranda. Ernst von Harnack and Otto John drafted one, intended for Brauchitsch, setting out the real opinion among the people.[18] It was in effect a manifesto from Popitz and Goerdeler for the conservative Right, from Josef Wirmer and Jakob Kaiser for the Catholic bourgeoisie, from Bernhard Letterhaus for the Catholic working class, Ernst von Harnack and Julius Leber for the underground socialist party and Wilhelm Leuschner for the trade unionists showing that they were all united behind Beck. In a letter to Beck Prince Louis Ferdinand declared that he was ready, if called upon. Like

Halder, however, Brauchitsch maintained that if the workers were really so anti-Hitler, then they should overthrow him by means of a general strike. When Leuschner heard this from Dohnanyi he was furious and said that these gentlemen, the officers, would then, of course, open fire on the workers – they had always fired on the Left but never on the Right.

About this time Kordt and Etzdorf together with Groscurth drafted an impressive memorandum entitled 'The threatening calamity.'[19] It said that if Hitler clung to his decision to attack in the west and invade Belgium, this would mean the end of Germany. The offensive would be halted owing to the weather and the strength of the enemy; if German troops invaded French territory, the French will to fight would increase rather than decrease; the United States and countries now still neutral would enter the war; Italy would move over to the enemy side; Russia would help herself in areas where no one could stop her. Neither the German war economy nor morale could withstand such a coalition; the results would be the collapse and bolshevization of Germany or at best her dismemberment. Consequently: 'Steps must be taken to stop the invasion order reaching the execution phase. This can only be done by an early *overthrow* of the Hitler government. Experience has shown that it will neither adjust its plans nor give way as a result of argument, protest or threat of resignation from the military leaders alone.'

It was not a valid objection, the memorandum continued, that Hitler had scored many successes so far. They were spurious successes or alternatively the result of some natural development which would have taken place sooner or later without Hitler. This applied to Germany's recovery of her sovereignty in military matters, to the Austrian *Anschluss* and to the 'inclusion of Czechoslovakia in the German sphere of influence'. The occupation by force of the rump of Czechoslovakia had brought severe disadvantages to Germany. Had this not happened, the Polish campaign could have been conducted without provoking the Western Powers to support the Poles – a remark clearly intended for military ears. Hitler's prognostications had proved wrong. Britain and France had entered the war and Italy had revoked.

Hitler's internal political successes should also not be adduced as an argument against his overthrow. In 1929–32 unemployment had been a problem common to all industrial states; similarly the post-1932 recovery had not been confined to Germany; most other countries, however, had achieved it without the enormous mortgaging and dissipation of the national assets which had occurred in Germany. It was equally useless to say that all was now in order and petty quarrels of the political parties had disappeared. Instead of a single national authority there were now numerous semi-independent rulers; alongside the *Wehrmacht* there were several defence formations neither controlled nor influenced by the national armed forces; instead of a unified administration there was now dispersion of authority as a result of duplication of authority between Party and State and the chaos of semi-independent local potentates; instead of good order there was demoralization, indiscipline and corruption; instead of the rule of law, arbitrary action. In reality, therefore, Germany had never been so close to bolshevism as she was now; she had even been prepared to hand over twenty million men in Eastern Europe to Russian domination.

Equally it should not be argued that neither the people nor the Army nor officialdom 'up to stupidity level' would understand a *coup* because of the *Führer*'s successes and consequent great hopes for the future. Time-honoured experience showed that a debacle was only recognized when it happened – '*Then* admittedly a *coup* would be popular but it would be too late to avert the calamity into which, with our fine Polish laurels, we should all be plunged, whether with Hitler or without him. Once loosed from its cage, the Fury of war cannot be tempted back again by reason. War obeys its own inexorable laws and every army primarily wants to win, in other words in present-day terms to annihilate.' The indisputable fact had to be faced that the conspirators were engaged in overthrowing a government which was *at present* victorious – '*The comparative unpopularity of the venture must therefore be faced with the necessary degree of civil courage.*' After the fall of Hitler the public would be so clearly informed of the crimes which he had committed and was planning that they would accept the *coup*.[20]

Finally the objection that a soldier must abide by his oath was entirely fallacious. The soldier's oath had long since lapsed since Hitler had not observed his own obligations but was in process of sacrificing Germany to his own crazy purposes. A soldier's loyalty could therefore only be given to his country. An example of a German patriot placing his conscience and his duty to his country above the formal requirements of his oath was that of General Yorck at Tauroggen in 1812 when he concluded a treaty of neutrality with a Russian general, although his King was still at war with Russia.

If, therefore, people wished to work towards the conclusion of peace, action must be taken soon. An acceptable and honourable peace could only be concluded while Germany still possessed some weight militarily. 'Action by those desirous of preserving the country', in other words a conservative *coup*, only had prospects of success provided military defeat could be avoided. Thereafter it would be too late; a successor government to a defeated one could no longer obtain good terms. An honourable peace was still obtainable on the basis of the Munich Conference, establishment of overland communications between the *Reich* and East Prussia and incorporation of the eastern Upper Silesian industrial area. Therefore it was not necessary to forego the fruits of the Polish victory. By such a solution, on the other hand, Germany would not be 'burdened with foreign nationalities' and at the same time would retain 'overriding influence in the rump of Czecho and the rump of Poland'. The victories won with the sword need not therefore be marred by the pen-pushing of the diplomats. Moderation in the conclusion of peace was at least as important as military victory in the campaign, as Bismarck had shown at Nikolsburg in 1866.

The situation was therefore clear and the necessity of a *coup* had been proved. The only remaining question was how to carry it out. The programme for this was only given in outline in the memorandum:[21] Conclusion of an honourable peace; reestablishment of the rule of law primarily by guaranteeing personal liberties and the disbandment of the *Gestapo*; honest administration on traditional Prussian lines; popular participation in the determination of political aims; measures for 'just and genuinely German (Prussian) socialism' and for 'Christian moral regeneration'. To implement this programme local military commanders were to assume executive authority, news media such as the radio and press to be controlled, telephone installations and power stations to be occupied and 'purges' carried out.

With its perilously frank speaking this memorandum was a rousing document. It was submitted to a number of generals including Halder, Brauchitsch and Witzleben.[22] But what effect did it have?

Halder had known since 22 October that Hitler proposed to order the offensive in the west for Sunday 12 November; so for the first time there was a definite date.[23] Two days later Halder was told by senior Army commanders that the date was unacceptable. Brauchitsch made every effort to explain the obstacles and difficulties to Hitler.[24] Naturally the conspirators also quickly learnt of the date; Oster in particular was an official recipient of such information and on 25 October he discussed it in Zossen with Stülpnagel, Deputy Chief of Staff I in OKH.[25]

On 25 October Hitler interviewed Halder and Brauchitsch in the *Reich* Chancellery and details of the opening situation for the offensive and the lines of attack were discussed.[26] There was apparently no argument but at a subsequent meeting with Hitler that afternoon Bock and Reichenau raised objection on the grounds of inadequate preparation and the weather.

About 1 p.m. on 27 October, a Friday, Brauchitsch, Halder, ten generals, one colonel, one lieutenant and one 2nd lieutenant were received by Hitler in the *Reich* Chancellery and all were decorated with the Knight's Cross.[27] After lunch Brauchitsch and Halder held a discussion with Hitler when they unsuccessfully attempted to dissuade him from the date ordered. Hitler insisted on 12 November. Brauchitsch was 'exhausted and downcast'.[28] At 10 a.m. next morning Halder attended on Hitler once more and explained all kinds of difficulties, but Hitler adhered to his viewpoint.[29]

That afternoon Halder discussed with Stülpnagel the results of his interviews with Hitler and on the 29th he decided to send Stülpnagel on a tour of front-line units.[30] Stülpnagel had asked Halder simply to lock Brauchitsch up and act on his own, should Brauchitsch refuse to cooperate; his task now was to establish whether 'people like von Bock . . . Manstein and Rundstedt' would obey Halder, should he appeal to them.[31] Halder did not think they would, but Stülpnagel wished to see what might eventuate. The official purpose of the journey was to inform senior commanders of changes in the concentration plans and intentions in the west.[32]

On Halder's own admission the result was negative.[33] Rundstedt and Bock, the Commanders-in-Chief of Army Groups A and B, were admittedly against the western offensive but they were a long way from cooperating in a *coup d'état*. Rundstedt was afraid that his officers would not follow him, or at least not as a whole, and that the instrument with which he had been entrusted would break in his hand.[34]

Colonel-General von Leeb, commanding Army Group C, on the other hand, declared himself unreservedly ready to participate and explicitly reiterated this statement later. Witzleben, whose First Army belonged to Army Group C, was also ready.[35] But this was not enough for Halder.

It was still conceivable that some of Leeb's troops could be sent to Berlin or possibly that the *coup* could be attempted solely with troops available in the vicinity of the city. This, however, would have necessitated the support of General Fromm, Commander-in-Chief of the Replacement Army, or at least his cooperation in authorizing the necessary movements. He had already replied in the negative to a similar question, however, in 1938. Now during one of his regular visits to Zossen on 31 October or in the first few days of November Halder specifically drew Fromm's attention to the necessity of stopping the western offensive.[36] He, Halder, he said, was proposing, with the assistance of a reliable division, to arrest Hitler and the *Reich* government and remove them in order to bring about a peaceful settlement. Fromm gave him no answer and returned to Berlin. He asked Lieutenant-Colonel Kurt Haseloff, his Chief of Staff, what he made of Halder's remarks; Haseloff replied that Halder had evidently at last made up his mind to initiate a *coup* and was ready to commit treason. Fromm nodded and told Haseloff to note the matter in his office diary. A few days later Fromm told Brauchitsch of the incident and thenceforth considered the affair ended as far as he was concerned.[37] So Fromm held aloof, covered up both ways but still did not betray his fellow-officer. He was entitled to assume that Halder would not have made such proposals without the knowledge of his superior. Brauchitsch never mentioned the matter to Halder.[38] Fromm's refusal to participate in a *coup*, however, showed Brauchitsch and Halder what the prospects were, for without the agreement, in fact the cooperation, of the Replacement Army troop movements inside Germany were scarcely conceivable in wartime. All this merely reinforced Brauchitsch in his attitude of non-cooperation or caution.

Another of Halder's fears could neither be dissipated nor refuted. What would be the reaction of the people, particularly the workers, to a *coup*? Beck and others were telling him that the people would understand; Dohnanyi and Oster had assembled material from which they could produce rapid and effective propaganda. Their information was certainly still applicable in autumn 1939. Halder, however, as he later admitted, preferred to believe his chauffeur's father and others not directly involved in the conspiracy. They told him that the people were not yet ready.[39] Admittedly it might be too late when they finally were. What Halder found so disturbing in connection with the entire enterprise, however, was its incalculability. In the General Staff one could plan, calculate and make the necessary forces and resources available. If an operation went wrong, one could calmly examine the mistakes and perhaps avoid them next time. But with a *coup d'état* there would be no next time; one was risking one's neck. And if one was not sure of a thing, was not one risking too much? Civil war – unpreparedness of the masses – these were simply phrases expressing uncertainty.

Halder was not, of course, totally wrong when he said that no one could know whether the Western Powers would not exploit the momentary weakness caused by a *coup* to carry out an offensive, also when he maintained that he had no assurances of any sort. Dr Müller's negotiations in Rome had so far produced no result.[40] He had adequate reasons for thinking the *coup* impractical. But – and herein lay the inconsistency stemming from his character and the highly ambiguous situation as viewed by an officer – he did not abandon all idea of some 'action'.[41]

Meanwhile the planned date for the offensive drew nearer. Brauchitsch and Halder were due to leave for a tour of inspection of the front but before this Beck came up with a further memorandum dated 31 October and entitled 'Breathing space after the failure of the German peace offer.'[42] It is hardly likely that either Halder or Brauchitsch had read it before they left.[43] In any case they probably regarded this stream of memoranda more as unwelcome interference in their official business than as a reinforcement of their views.

Once more Beck attempted to show, with all possible emphasis, what catastrophic effects continuation of the war must have. Though this statement had often been made before, he said, highly important, in fact decisive proof of its accuracy had meanwhile appeared: on 27 October the United States Senate had followed the House of Representatives in lifting the arms embargo imposed as a result of the US declaration of neutrality on the outbreak of war.[44] France and Britain could now be supplied. For political, economic and strategic reasons (the blockade), however, Germany was barred from deliveries of arms and war material. The accuracy of another forecast was also daily becoming clearer – the isolation of Germany in Europe. The Franco–Anglo–Turkish pact of 19 October[45] was proof of that. The pact would tie Italy's hands in the eastern Mediterranean, reinforce the position of the Western Powers in the Middle East and encourage the peoples of Southeastern Europe to resist Russian expansionist policy with the result that all these countries would be lost to Germany as partners. Finally by abandoning the Baltic States and Finland Germany had forfeited both these and the Scandinavian countries. Germany now stood alone in Europe while the threat of a European anti-German coalition was growing all the time. All this was followed once more by thoughts on the prospects of a German offensive in the west leading to the well-known negative conclusions.

Beck concluded with an unequivocal demand: 'It becomes daily more urgent to draw the political conclusions from such a situation'; if this was not done, he said, and if 'the military instrument' should suffer a reverse, it would be threatened with demoralization.

Whether or not Brauchitsch and Halder had read Beck's memorandum they basically reached the same conclusions as a result of their tour of inspection. They left on the evening of 1 November; they spent 2 November in Army Group B's area, the morning with Sixth Army in Düsseldorf and the afternoon with Fourth and Second Armies in Cologne; the next morning they were in Army Group A's area with Twelfth Army in Mayen and in the afternoon with Sixteenth Army in Bad Bertrich.[46] Result: 'An offensive with extensive objectives cannot be carried out at this time . . . *None* of the senior headquarters regard the offensive ordered by OKW as likely to succeed. From the point of view of land warfare a decisive victory cannot be anticipated.'[47]

On 4 November Halder discussed 'future measures' with Brauchitsch.[48] On the afternoon of that day he interviewed General Thomas who submitted data showing the great risk to the supply of war material and food in the event of attack in the west. Thomas also showed Halder a memorandum containing far-reaching warnings, in the compilation of which Oster, Dohnanyi and Gisevius had been involved. It also dealt with the initial optimistic reports from Dr Josef Müller on his soundings in the Vatican.[49] Halder agreed with Thomas and referred to the murder of Hitler as the most practical solution.

On 31 October Halder had already passed a form of codeword to Oster through Groscurth; Goerdeler and Beck were asked to hold themselves in readiness. To Groscurth Halder expressed the hope that arrangements could be made for Hitler, Göring and Ribbentrop to meet with 'fatal accidents'.[50] Groscurth said to Halder and Etzdorf, if only some Macedonians could be found and a hatred of Hitler could be generated in them through some Macedonian gravamina, some money and alcohol added and the belief in a 10 per cent chance of survival – then the assassination of Hitler would be a foregone conclusion.[51]

Groscurth, Oster, Etzdorf, Fiedler and other conspirators at once set to work on the immediate preparations; they assumed that Halder had at last made up his mind since he had told his deputy Stülpnagel, who had also just returned from a tour in the west, that preparations should now proceed. On return from his own tour Halder seemed even more determined than before and on 4 November he reiterated his instructions, this time to Oster as well, that the previous year's plans should be refurbished and completed. In addition to Beck and Goerdeler, Schacht was also asked (through Colonel Eduard Wagner) to hold himself in readiness.

All sorts of rumours were circulating, including one to the effect that Hitler was to be arrested on 7 or 8 November while reviewing troops in the neighbourhood of Berlin.[52] Meanwhile, without Halder's direct knowledge, an assassination attempt on Hitler was being planned. Erich Kordt had made up his mind to do it, having reached the conclusion with Oster that, if the support of the generals was to be obtained for a *coup*, they must be freed from the inhibitions associated with their oath and from their fascination with the dictator's sleepwalking sureness of touch. Kordt was to be given the necessary explosive by Oster on 11 November but the project came to nothing since, after the assassination attempt in the *Bürgerbräukeller* on 8 November, the material could no longer be obtained.[53]

At midday on 5 November, shortly after his return from his tour of the front, Brauchitsch had an interview with Hitler. This was a vital day for the opposition since everyone hoped that, if Hitler clung to his timing for the offensive, Brauchitsch would decide in favour of the *coup*. The decision had to be taken by 1 p.m. that day since the timetable was one still demanding seven days warning.[54] The interview lasted twenty minutes and was heated if not stormy on both sides.[55] Brauchitsch once more put forward his view that owing to inadequate preparation and in view of the unfavourable conditions a western offensive at this time would not be successful but would probably be catastrophic. When he said that the attitude and morale of the troops left much to be desired and could not be compared with that of the men of 1914, Hitler began to rage and wanted evidence and proof forthwith showing units in which cases of indiscipline had occurred and the number of death sentences pronounced – as if morale could be expressed in figures. He wanted to fly to the front himself that very night and convince himself; he did not believe Brauchitsch (who had in fact exaggerated somewhat).

Hitler equally refused to accept the Commander-in-Chief's other arguments, rejecting them in insulting and humiliating terms. The Army just did not wish to fight, he said; this was why rearmament had progressed so lackadaisically; this was why they were not ready now. The weather would be just as unfavourable in the spring and in any case it rained not only on our own troops but on the enemy as well. As Halder noted on hearing Brauchitsch's account, it was simply not possible to talk to Hitler on these matters. Finally Hitler simply left the General standing and went out of the room. Brauchitsch returned from the *Reich* Chancellery, his face white with anger and humiliation.[56]

In his almost uncontrollable rage over the recalcitrance of his generals Hitler poured scorn on the 'spirit of Zossen' which he said was tantamount to cowardice. It almost looked as if he suspected the existence of a conspiracy and in fact a fairly large group of those planning the *coup* were located in OKH. Sweeping judgements were not unusual with Hitler but it was impossible to tell how much he knew and he must at least have realized that an attempt was being made to persuade him to avoid further bloodshed.[57]

Hitler now immediately (1.30 p.m.) issued the order expected for 1 p.m. By the afternoon or early evening of 5 November it had reached Zossen in writing. Troop movements continued for two full days before they were once more called off.[58]

Halder took to heart Hitler's threats against the 'spirit of Zossen'. No one had forgotten 30 June 1934 and Hitler was thought quite capable of repeating the procedure. Halder, however, seemed to forget that he himself was wanting to engineer a *putsch* precisely because such a thing was possible under the existing system. He was seized with panic. The most elementary precautions now seemed to demand the destruction of all evidence which might confirm Hitler's suspicion. The *Gestapo* might be in Zossen in a few hours, perhaps even sooner. Immediately on his return to Zossen Halder ordered the destruction of all papers connected with the *coup*.[59] Much was destroyed but many papers were saved through the efforts of Dohnanyi and Groscurth.[60] Towards evening and during the next few days it became obvious that Hitler was in complete ignorance and the dreaded purge did not take place.[61]

Shortly after 3 p.m. on 5 November, after Brauchitsch's 'initiative' had failed, Halder, now back in Zossen, told Groscurth of the outcome of the interview; the offensive in the west must now go forward, he said; there was nothing to be done about it.[62] The *coup* could not take place. Groscurth recorded Halder's words: 'Thus the forces who had been counting on us are no longer under obligation. You understand what I mean.' The only explanations for the change in Halder's attitude are panic, inability to make up his mind, insincerity or the belated realization that he could not count on Brauchitsch, who had command authority over the troops.

Conditions for the *coup* were favourable. Halder had in fact been determined to strike if Hitler insisted on the offensive in the west and this had now happened. If for a time he felt that without some special protective force he was sitting in Zossen defenceless against an incursion by the SS, it soon proved that there was to be no such incursion. Moreover a guard unit could have been obtained, as subsequently became clear.

By the afternoon Brauchitsch had more or less recovered his equanimity and he was still of the opinion that the offensive must be stopped. How this was to be done, however, he now expressly left to others; he told Halder that in any case he himself would not embark on anything, not even if someone else did so, but he, Brauchitsch, would not resist 'if someone else does it'.[63] Thereupon Halder plucked up courage once more. As already mentioned, one can only speculate why he did not at last initiate the *coup*; all the conditions were favourable; the *Gestapo* and SS did not appear and Brauchitsch had explicitly given him freedom to act. Gisevius was proved right in his scepticism regarding Halder's determination.[64]

Nevertheless at 5 p.m. Halder spoke to Groscurth once more and commissioned him to tell Canaris of the state of affairs, asking him at the same time to have Hitler removed by assassination. Groscurth had fulfilled his mission by 8 p.m.[65]

Canaris was incensed at this buck-passing by Halder – rightly but to the detriment of the opposition.[66] He was a sensitive man and detested assassination and suchlike methods; he wished to run his secret service 'decently'.[67] He accordingly sent word to Halder that the possibilities of a military *putsch* must first be explored and it was for Halder himself to assume both the initiative and the responsibility.[68]

The following day, 6 November, Etzdorf went to Halder while Oster also visited Zossen to discuss with Stülpnagel and Wagner whether the old plans for action against the SS and *Gestapo* could not be revived on the pretext of an SS *putsch* against Hitler. Gisevius was already revising the relevant drafts.[69] Halder had recently stated that he would gladly engineer a *coup d'état* but without Witzleben he was unfortunately powerless.[70] When Oster heard of this he put through a call from Zossen to Witzleben in Bad Kreuznach suggesting that he (Witzleben) ask for a visit from him (Oster) so that the matter might be discussed in more detail.[71] Witzleben accordingly called Groscurth in Zossen and asked him to get Canaris to send Oster down to him for a 'consultation'.[72]

Oster was authorized by Canaris to go to Witzleben and take Gisevius with him.[73] They first went to General Thomas (after Oster had warned Sas, the Dutch Military Attaché, of the proposed date of attack) and discussed plans with him. Thomas declared himself ready to go to the three Army Group Commanders in the hope of winning them also over to the project.[74] Finally Beck was also informed; he had heard of Brauchitsch's remark that he would not stand in the way of a *coup* and had declared himself ready to assume command of the Army.[75]

The journey to Bad Kreuznach had to be broken in Frankfurt. There Oster spoke to Lieutenant-Colonel Vincenz Müller, Colonel-General von Leeb's Operations Officer, and tried to persuade him to participate but with only limited success. On 8 November Oster and Gisevius arrived at Witzleben's headquarters, explained the situation and put forward their proposals.[76] At almost the same time Witzleben had to halt the troop movements already in progress. Witzleben was very pessimistic over the prospects of a *coup*. No further hopes could be placed on Brauchitsch and Halder, he said; he had seen them during their tour of the west and there was no further object in talking to them about a *coup*.[77] Moreover the junior officers were far too prejudiced in favour of Hitler; no one could tell whose orders they would carry out.[78] If the Army Group Commanders refused to carry out the order to attack, then things might be got on the move again. This was the only conceivable solution. Oster and Gisevius pressed Witzleben to go to Halder and talk to him, but he refused to do so on his own initiative. Finally, however, he said he was ready to do so, provided that Leeb, his Commander-in-Chief, agreed. Oster and Gisevius then drove back to Frankfurt where again they had to spend the night. On 14 November Halder received Witzleben's request for an interview but the meeting never took place.[79]

Instead, on 13 November, Stülpnagel arrived in Frankfurt and held a discussion with Witzleben. Both were agreed that efforts must be pursued. Simultaneously Lieutenant-Colonel von Tresckow of the Operations Section in OKH was working on his uncle, Colonel-General von Bock, and Stülpnagel on corps and divisional commanders such as Lieutenant-General Geyr von Schweppenburg — but without success. In addition ever since 5 November Halder had been systematically dismantling the preparatory measures for the *coup*, although he did not openly admit it. Later Halder told General Thomas it was not possible 'to act' against Hitler, firstly because it was against tradition, secondly because there was no successor, thirdly because the younger officers were not 'reliable', fourthly because the mood among the population was not ripe for it, fifthly because Germany must not be a people of English helots, and sixthly that he, Halder, was not afraid of history's judgement concerning the forthcoming offensive, for Ludendorff, too, had conducted an offensive in 1918 against everyone's advice and the judgement of history was not against him.[80]

Owing to unfavourable weather conditions the earliest date for the opening of the offensive was then postponed to 19 November. Hitler went off 'on tour' in order to deliver his annual speech in Munich on 8 November commemorating the 1923 *putsch*; he therefore suddenly became inaccessible, particularly to foreign diplomats.[81] He had no wish to be bothered by the peace mediation offer made on 7 November by the King of the Belgians and the

Queen of the Netherlands, a development to which (without his knowledge) three of his officers had contributed – Reichenau, Oster and Colonel Warlimont. Without knowing of Oster's contacts Reichenau and Warlimont had gained touch with certain Dutch, Belgian and Danish agencies; Oster had not only warned Sas, the Dutch Military Attaché, but on 6 November had despatched Albrecht Graf von Bernstorff to the Dutch Legation with news of the intended attack in the west.[82]

On the evening of 8 November while, as the military say, there was 'nothing to report', Groscurth was sitting by his radio and listening to Hitler's speech in the *Bürgerbräukeller* on the Rosenheimer Strasse, Munich; it ended at 9.07 p.m.[83] What happened thirteen minutes later Groscurth only learnt at two minutes before midnight when he received a call from Section III (Counter-intelligence and Counter-espionage) of the OKW *Ausland/Abwehr* in Berlin: at 9.20 an attempt had been made to assassinate Hitler; he had escaped, apparently by accident, because he had left the building immediately after his speech.[84] The assailant, a lone wolf named Georg Elser, had come so incredibly near to success that all sorts of extravagant rumours began to circulate. First a foreign secret service was said to be behind it, then some dissatisfied Party members and finally even the *Gestapo* was held responsible. One version was that the attempt stemmed in some way or other from within Hitler's own ranks but that he had been warned in time; it was therefore possible that it was a propaganda trick and on 9 November this was thought by the *Abwehr* in Berlin to be the most likely explanation. Groscurth heard of it on the afternoon of that day and noted it down in his diary.[85]

There was vast confusion. Many of the conspirators thought that the attempt had come from resistance circles, from within their own ranks; for obvious reasons they seldom knew precisely what groups other than their own were doing. Many Germans, on the other hand, simply did an about-turn and Hitler became the object of a wave of sympathy; the atmosphere was one of irrational reaction. When, on 9 November, the British agents Stevens and Best were kidnapped on the Dutch frontier and taken into German custody, many people simply added two and two together. Everything fitted – the Dutch–Belgian offer of mediation, now exposed as a dishonest swindle by the capture of British agents working on Dutch soil with Dutch officers, the assassination attempt and now the arrest of the agents. For others, however, confusion became even greater.[86]

Meanwhile the western offensive had merely been postponed (to 19 November from 9 November), not abandoned; efforts to stop it and end the war therefore had to continue.[87] On 10 November, via Groscurth, Gisevius submitted a thesis to Halder in which he explained that this was the moment for the Army to take Hitler under its 'protection'; the SS had clearly proved itself incapable of doing so, and in any case much connected with the assassination attempt pointed to murky machinations by Party circles; the opportunity for something on the lines of a *coup d'état* was now particularly favourable.[88] Halder was naturally no more inclined towards adventures of this nature than before. When Groscurth submitted Gisevius' memorandum to him on 12 November, he said that he would tear it up unread. When Groscurth saw it still lying on Halder's desk next morning, however, Halder gave him to understand that, not only had he read it but he agreed with Gisevius' ideas and had also shown the memorandum to Brauchitsch. The latter was basically in agreement with Gisevius' views but this did nothing to change his vacillating attitude.[89]

Halder felt that he was being pestered by the conspirators. In addition, however, to his embarrassment at having left his fellow-conspirators in the lurch, he had further cause for vexation. He had heard that, when visiting Bad Kreuznach and Frankfurt, Oster had gone around somewhat imprudently with copies of the proclamations to be made by Beck after the *coup*.[90] Witzleben had been horrified that Oster should be carrying anything like that in his car; a traffic accident could have blown the whole conspiracy. Lieutenant-Colonel Müller had been equally taken aback and, when shown a copy of the proclamation, had made Oster burn it in an ashtray before his eyes. Oster, however, had at least one other copy with him. When Oster and Gisevius had spent the night in Frankfurt on the return journey, that evening Oster had launched into such a tirade against the regime in the mess that his friends had had to push him into another room to avoid a major scandal. Such things did not redound to the credit of the conspiracy. Halder and Brauchitsch now had adequate reason (or excuse) to keep their distance from the opposition. Disillusionment grew.

Colonel-General von Leeb too had made little progress with his efforts. Major-General von Sodernstern, his Chief of Staff, arranged a meeting of the Commanders-in-Chief of Army Groups A, B and C at the headquarters of Army Group A in Koblenz for 9 November.[91] Oster had some hope that this would result in a threat to Brauchitsch of concerted resignation by the Commanders-in-Chief. In fact they merely agreed to continue to do what they could to postpone the opening of the offensive by means of arguments and objections in order to give the diplomats time to reach, by negotiation, the agreement which they hoped for and thought possible.[92] Rundstedt and Bock refused to agree to a more far-reaching proposal by Leeb that the three Commanders-in-Chief together should demand that Brauchitsch intervene once more with Hitler against the offensive and, if he refused, should all three resign.[93]

On 7 November motorized movement was provisionally halted until the evening of 9 November; at the same time the earliest date for the offensive was laid down as the 15th and two days later as the 19th.[94] On 13 November Hitler's decision was again postponed to the 16th which meant that the attack could not start before the 22nd. On the 16th the decision was again postponed to the 20th, putting the earliest date of attack at 3 December.

The generals tolerated without objection this senseless hithering and thithering, these announcements and cancellations of the offensive, and the disorderly procedure or the impatience of their Supreme Commander. Hitler, however, was sick of hearing continuous arguments against the offensive. Accordingly, in the space of seven hours on 23 November, he delivered three addresses in the New *Reich* Chancellery to leaders of the *Wehrmacht*.[95]

Hitler made his first, and major, speech at midday to Commanders-in-Chief of the Army, Navy and *Luftwaffe*, Army Groups, Armies and Air Fleets, Corps Commanders and their Chiefs of Staff and the corresponding ranks in the Navy and *Luftwaffe* together with a number of staff officers from OKH and OKW. In all 180 people were present.[96] He began by recounting his successes. From his exit from the League of Nations through to the Polish campaign the prophets had always croaked and warned, but nevertheless all had gone well. He drew the strength to make his decisions from the realization that the only purpose of the state was to serve the 'substance' of the people, in Germany's case that of 82 million men. Battle was the destiny of all creatures; no one could avoid it; he who did not fight was condemned to ruin beforehand. There could therefore be no thought of adapting the size of the population to its *Lebensraum*; that was cowardice, weakness, genocide and ruin. Instead *Lebensraum* must be adapted to the size of the population. Consequently there must be battle – 'I have long wondered whether I ought to strike first in the east and then in the west. I have not set up the *Wehrmacht* in order not to use it. The decision to strike has always been in my bones. Sooner or later I wished to solve the problem.'[97]

At present, he continued, the situation was unique. Ever since 1870 Germany had had to reckon with a war on two fronts but now, for the first time since the foundation of the *Reich*, she could fight the West without having to fear an intervention from Russia. No man could tell how long this would continue. In every respect time was working for the enemy who was accelerating his rearmament. Meanwhile, however, he (Hitler), who was irreplaceable, might fall victim to assassination. He had recent experience of the dangers of a statesman's life. The fate of the *Reich* depended on him alone; he would attack and never capitulate.

Hitler was, of course, unable to advance really convincing foreign policy reasons for his views, since there were none. His arguments were those of the fiendish nihilist revolutionary. He had to have all or nothing – he would never capitulate – he would stand or fall in this struggle – he would not survive the defeat of his people – dark, threatening, sinister words which the *Führer* was to repeat in April 1945 shortly before his suicide. It is striking how frequently he spoke of capitulation while initially he scored victory after victory and prophesied more. His road was the road to destruction, as he said himself – he would recoil from nothing – he would annihilate anyone who was against him – an internal revolution against his regime was as unthinkable as capitulation to the enemy.

The warning was clear and the generals took it to heart. They were no weaklings and it would be unjust totally to condemn them. Nevertheless they were facing a man who was far ahead of them in determination, ruthlessness and cruelty. It was easier not to face up to the destruction of Germany to which Hitler had admitted, in so many words, that he was indifferent. There was their oath, command authority, military discipline in wartime, the external threat; with all this weighing in the balance, they did not perceive the extent to which they were taking refuge in argument to avoid facing the apocalyptic threat which they did not comprehend.

On the afternoon of the same day Hitler addressed a number of senior Army officers in his study. He partly repeated his warnings and exhortations but he also went into detail of the planned operation.[98]

Brauchitsch and Halder had meanwhile returned to Zossen but hardly had they arrived before they were summoned to Hitler once more. At 6 p.m. the dictator gave them a piece of his mind again.[99] Many generals, he said, were left-overs from a rotten upper class and had not grasped the spirit of the times. He, Hitler, knew of the spirit of resistance in the Army, the 'spirit of Zossen', and he would annihilate it. In face of this accusation of pusillanimity Brauchitsch asked to resign – but Hitler refused and Brauchitsch complied.

There was no follow-up to Hitler's monstrous statement that he was interested only in conquest and to hell with the justification for it. Rundstedt, Reichenau and other generals were incensed but nothing happened. Halder simply accepted the accusation of pusillanimity[100] and Brauchitsch allowed himself to be insulted by Hitler but did not insist on resigning.

Although officially 3 December was now the next date for the offensive, hardly anyone thought that it would take place that year. In October representatives of OKW had been deliberately conducted over ice-covered roads in the Eifel, littered with abandoned vehicles. There was now no longer any need for special efforts to point out that it was winter.[101] Halder himself considered that 23 November 1939 marked, at least provisionally, the end of both official and unofficial efforts to postpone the western offensive.[102] It had to be assumed that Hitler knew something about the unofficial efforts.

Nevertheless on 27 November General Thomas made another urgent request to Halder for an interview.[103] He expounded the views of his friends and besought Halder to press Brauchitsch to prevent a world war and arrest Hitler. Halder replied that that was impossible. He later explained that he had to obey and also that there was no great man capable of carrying out a *coup d'état*. In an office minute he noted that the German Army and in particular the officer corps would not participate in a *coup*. Hugo Stinnes, the industrialist, had received a similar reply (also recorded in an office minute) when he had visited Brauchitsch in the first half of November.[104]

The conspirators did not realize at the time that Halder was not sincere in his negotiations with them. When asked by Peter Bor after the war whether the possibility of a *coup* had been discussed subsequent to the Sudeten crisis, Halder replied: 'It was discussed over and over again. I had long been clear, however, that it was no longer possible to embark on anything decisive without calling the existence of the Fatherland in question as the result of a war at home.'[105]

What could be done? No *coup* was possible without the Army but the Army would not march without orders. Only Brauchitsch could give the order; subordinate commanders' forces were located where they could be of no use to the conspiracy, in other words at the front. Quite apart from this, they would not act without orders from Brauchitsch. None of them were adventurers; they had to have some 'assurance' that the Western Powers would not stab the conspiracy in the back or refuse favourable peace terms after a *coup*. In the light of such apparently insuperable obstacles only those who had joined the conspiracy out of the deepest moral and religious convictions pursued their efforts. Hassell, for instance, went round making every conceivable effort to rouse 'the generals' from their lethargy but even Goerdeler, the incurable optimist, began to give up hope. On 30 November Hassell went to Canaris and talked very straight to him, but Canaris placed no further hopes in resistance from the generals and said that there was nothing further to be done and attempts were useless. On the evening of the same day Hassell visited Beck; he could only say that everything possible had been done but unfortunately without result.[106]

11 Further Efforts

On 20 November Beck had submitted a further memorandum designed to win Brauchitsch over to the conspiracy.[1] He said that since the end of the Polish campaign the situation had changed greatly to Germany's disadvantage. The victory over Poland had been nullified by Russia's advance westwards; the anticipated Russian military support for Germany had not been forthcoming and Russia was merely pursuing her own interests; German methods of conducting war in Poland had had a devastating effect on world public opinion; relations between Germany on the one hand and Spain, Japan and Italy on the other had cooled visibly and Italy in particular would ultimately divorce herself from Germany altogether. The barrier formed in the south-east by the Anglo–Franco–Turkish pact was a set-back. The smaller countries of South-east and Northern Europe would be forced increasingly on to the Allied side, the former to protect themselves against Russia and the latter from fear of a German invasion. In France and Britain determination to fight was increasing and the anti-German attitude of the United States was becoming more and more obvious.

Even more than before therefore, Beck continued, Germany now stood alone; the number of her enemies was increasing. The Western Powers were pursuing their preparations and so the prospects of the offensive, now almost inconceivable anyway, were deteriorating. The requirement 'to liquidate, and the sooner the better, a world war which had always been hopeless', was therefore increasingly attractive. Responsible military leaders now faced the duty of 'exerting intellectual self-discipline and pursuing their path to its logical conclusion . . . of doing what commonsense dictated'. He himself, Beck continued, had said as much in a speech in October 1935[2] and had been 'conspicuously applauded by the *Führer*'. If, therefore, this requirement was still justified, the path of duty for the military leaders was clear: 'At a time of grave crisis the limits of their responsibility, particularly that of the most senior military commanders, are set solely by their own conscience, by their sense of responsibility towards the Army and the people and by the judgement which history may be expected to pronounce.'

On 2 January 1940 Beck set out his views once more.[3] Germany could never win a world war, he said, but even the German press was now talking of world war and the *Führer* was speaking of a life and death struggle for the German people. What levity, what nihilism were evidenced by such words, since there was no compulsion either to begin or continue the war. Since Germany could not now defeat her principal opponents, self-preservation was the only war aim remaining to her and it was more than doubtful whether even this could be achieved; the final result would therefore be 'a Germany bled white, doomed to surrender unconditionally'. To prevent this was both the right and the duty of those possessing responsibility and knowledge. All other considerations must be subordinated to the preservation of the nation.

Early in December another memorandum reached OKH stemming from very different circles from those of Beck. It was headed 'Implications of the Russo–Finnish conflict on Germany's present Situation' and it came from Captain (Navy) Liedig.[4] In it Liedig declaimed against Hitler's opportunism and his betrayal of his own ideological aims. Hitler had always wanted to reach agreement with Britain, Liedig said, and to save Europe from her enemy Number One, Red Russia; on both counts he was now doing exactly the opposite. Russia was in process of carrying out a vast expansion and was being largely assisted therein by the nihilist policy of the Nazis. Germany, however, was heading for a disaster of unparalleled proportions as a result of Hitler's unprincipled policy. Britain was still waiting but Russia was not; she had already begun her march westwards. Now was the great opportunity for Germany to obtain from Britain a just and generous peace, confirmation of her present frontiers in so far as they were co-terminous with areas of German settlement and recognition of her predominance as a continental power. The prerequisite for this was for Germany to place her armed forces at the disposal of Finland and of Europe, both of which were threatened (Finland had been attacked by Russia at the end of November 1939), and, together with Britain, turn against the bolshevist danger. Both the *Reich* and Christian Europe could still be saved; the die was cast only for Hitler and his followers; their fate was irrevocable but not that of Germany.

There could be no mistaking Liedig's call for a *coup* as the only alternative to the frightful chaos resulting from Russia's penetration into the heart of Europe. His ideas bore a close relationship to those of the circle centred on Heinz and SchmidNoerr; they included certain romantic imperialist notions. Liedig's proposal for combined Anglo–German action against Russia was fantastic but his prophecies proved true, not because he had correctly appreciated the Russian communist menace but as a result of Hitler's limitless thirst for conquest.

Brauchitsch, however, was not to be convinced either by Liedig's political arguments or by the expert appreciation of the situation by his fellow-officer Beck. His attitude was dictated by his personality – he did not lack the necessary knowledge. The opposition group centred on Beck and Oster continued to lose ground both with Brauchitsch and with Halder. Both were too weak to follow matters to their logical conclusion and adopt a definitive attitude. They could not make up their minds either to fulfil their military duty in the true sense of the word or to do their ethical and moral duty. They really wanted to do both but then again they wanted neither. It was all too uncertain and too risky.

In view of this weakness and vacillation the opposition attempted once more to bring influence and pressure to bear from another quarter. The idea of combined action by the Commanders-in-Chief in the west was revived, as so often in subsequent years right through until summer 1944. This time Groscurth made the journey to the west. He left on 18 December, on 19 and 20 December he visited the headquarters of Army Group C (Leeb) in Frankfurt am Main and Witzleben in Bad Kreuznach; on the 21st he went to Army Group A (Rundstedt) and Army Group B (Bock).[5]

The only reaction in any way favourable came from Leeb. He was concerned over the 'difficulties of the internal situation' as he put it in his diary, and wrote a letter to Halder.[6] At the time there was widespread indignation over the actions of the SS and police *Einsatzgruppen* in Poland. Colonel-General Johannes Blaskowitz, Commander-in-Chief East (*Oberost*), had protested energetically.[7] During his tour of the west Groscurth had made a special point of the atrocities committed in Poland in order to persuade the generals to revolt; he had with him the necessary evidence, including a detailed, highly secret report from Blaskowitz, from which certain of the Chiefs of Staff took excerpts.[8] Groscurth wrote in his private diary on 21 December: 'So now we have aroused the most important sections of the western front. Successfully, it is to be hoped! – It will be continued!' But it was all of no avail. Even in the light of these crimes committed on the orders of their Supreme Commander the Commanders-in-Chief were not to be persuaded to take concerted action against him.

The stream of memoranda urging some action never entirely dried up. The warnings, however, increasingly came to be considered as tiresome and unrealistic. On 1 January 1940 Dr Etscheit, a Berlin lawyer who had been working with the *Abwehr* and Admiral Canaris ever since autumn 1939, submitted via Groscurth a memorandum to Major-General Kurt von Tippelskirch, Deputy Chief of Staff IV; it was entitled 'The external and internal situation'; Tippelskirch read it on 3 January and then passed it back to Groscurth.[9] In it Etscheit protested against collaboration with Soviet Russia, the hereditary enemy; he also showed how the atrocities committed by the SS and police in Poland reinforced the impression that people under the power of the present German regime were treated as serfs just as much as those under the Soviet regime.

Admittedly, the memorandum continued, 'the parliamentary democratic institutions of other countries did not represent a system of government suited to the German people'; on the other hand it had also been shown that dictatorship was not the solution. People were now increasingly beginning to recognize the necessity of 'conservative institutions and methods capable of preserving the country'; stern methods would be accepted if they guaranteed justice.[10] Power carried with it responsibility but the present leadership had failed because it had not kept its promise to guarantee peace to Germany. As a result of the mighty victory in the Polish campaign the power of the military leaders had grown to such an extent that it was now their responsibility to 'solve the crisis which had arisen'. Meanwhile, by his continuous expansion of the SS, Himmler was undermining the position of the *Wehrmacht* and its leaders.

In the light of these considerations, the memorandum continued, external affairs were of significance. The German economy could not long withstand the British blockade; a military decision in Germany's favour leading to a peace treaty was not to be anticipated during the short period available before Germany's economic exhaustion. The internal German situation was inseparably bound up with the prospects for peace because the Allies would never conclude peace with Hitler unless Germany had been victorious. On the other hand they were entirely prepared to come to some agreement and had not closed their minds to the necessity for some suitable concessions: 'It is recognized abroad that the overthrow of the government would only be possible and justifiable if those in power in Germany [after the overthrow] could rely on some guaranteed agreement with our enemies which would ensure, not only an honourable peace but also a combined effort to make good the damage meanwhile done in Europe.'

There is here a clear reference to the talks being held at this time by Dr Josef Müller in Rome. Only a few days later, on 8 January, Halder referred in his diary to conversations with the Pope reported to him by Etzdorf. On the same day he received information from Tippelskirch about Groscurth's and Goerdeler's activities and about peace feelers.[11] It could be anticipated therefore, Etscheit's memorandum continued, that Greater Germany would be preserved 'on condition that fresh provision be made for the Czechoslovak people and state' and that the errors and extravagances of Versailles would not be repeated. Particularly in Britain people were convinced that Germany was indispensable for the maintenance of the European economy and culture; they would certainly not object to a German economic hegemony over the smaller countries of eastern Europe.

While for the moment there was still some possibility of agreement, time was working against Germany. Popular support for a *coup* was obviously desirable and this might come about as a result of hardships and set-backs; at the same time, however, these would reduce the other side's readiness to come to some accommodation and the great confidence at present felt in the military leadership. The readiness of the masses to accept resolute action should not be underestimated.[12] If action were taken now it was still possible to preserve the positive achievements of the National-Socialist State and prevent the destruction of Europe.

In this memorandum Dr Etscheit had said nothing but the patent truth. Too many people saw things this way at the time for the excuse to be valid that no one could know that things would turn out 'thus'. In his own handwriting, however, Tippelskirch noted on this memorandum: 'This treatise presents things too gloomily. It takes too much account of the views of the German intellectuals who have always been prophets of gloom. I very much doubt whether the British and French would treat us any more leniently if we acted as stupidly as in 1918. The threat of the destruction of Europe seems to me a method of pressure at least as effective in paving the way for the conclusion of peace as an agreement predicating an internal upheaval. T.'

What a gulf was fixed between the opposition and military men such as Tippelskirch! The implication of the final sentence is that the threat of the destruction of Europe could be used to force the enemy to conclude peace and end a war unnecessarily begun. This can be no alibi for Tippelskirch's loyalty to the regime. The mere fact that he participated in such considerations turned him into an accomplice in attempted treason.

The continuous postponement of the date of the offensive, though not un-expected in knowledgeable circles, was a wearing process and it had now been going on since November; in the light of this and of the inertia of the top-level Army leaders the opposition took refuge in all sorts of fantastic plans. There was an idea that, with the assistance of certain divisions in transit from west to east, Witzleben should arrest Hitler in Berlin and have him declared incapable of governing. Beck was then to go to Zossen and seize command of the Army from the flaccid hands of Brauchitsch.[13] Unfortunately no divisions were on the move eastwards; they were waiting in the west for the order to attack. Even had there been any on the move, they would certainly not have obeyed Witzleben's orders unless he had been properly appointed as their commander. Concentration of troops round Berlin was impossible without the assistance of the C-in-C of the Replacement Army (which had been explicitly refused). Bold though he was, Witzleben was no adventurer and, weak though he was, Brauchitsch would have resisted any attempt to seize command authority from him. The concocter of this plan, which Hassell noted in his diary on 30 December, was Popitz, the Finance Minister of Prussia; he was no military expert and clearly had only the haziest ideas of what was practicable in this field.[14]

Despite this gloomy outlook efforts continued. Continuous attempts were made to arrange a meeting between Witzleben and Beck. At the end of December Goerdeler visited Witzleben and told Hassell that he thought he had succeeded – 'Witzleben would soon come to have a final talk with Beck.'[15] Lacking a concrete basis to work on, the 'action', to which Beck also now referred with increasing frankness, never advanced beyond the discussion stage. Nothing could be done without troops and for the moment none were available.

The more frequent the postponement of the offensive, the more marked became the absence of the vital prerequisite – the generals' conviction that attack in the west could lead to nothing other than colossal catastrophe. Militarily they were now far better prepared and who was to say whether the offensive would ever take place? Week by week it was postponed; how could anyone take it seriously?

The period of comparative calm was unexpectedly prolonged as a result of the capture of two German airmen who force-landed at Mechelen in Belgium on 10 January 1940; they were carrying papers from which the German operational plans could be deduced.[16] Despite this unfortunate incident, on 11 January Hitler decided, in the light of a favourable weather forecast, that the offensive should take place on the 17th. On the 13th came an unfavourable forecast and he postponed it once more. Then came alarming news of increased Belgian and Dutch defence preparation, demonstrating the importance of the loss of the Mechelen documents, and this had its effect on Hitler. On 16 January he decided definitely to postpone the offensive to the spring and meanwhile to have the plans totally revised in order to recover both secrecy and surprise.

The opposition now renewed its efforts to persuade Halder. On his return from a tour of the western front from 3 to 6 January he was shown reports of the Rome talks and about the middle of the month was at last persuaded to have a discussion with Beck; it took place on 16 January immediately after a conference with General Thomas.[17] Halder later recalled how he and Beck had paced the empty streets of Berlin-Dahlem in order to avoid the attention which would inevitably have been aroused had one visited the other.[18]

Beck put forward to Halder his well-known viewpoint that Germany could not sustain a war against the West either from the military or economic points of view; America would not long remain aloof and no one should be deceived by possible initial victories. Hitler had lost all confidence abroad and this government, therefore, had no prospect of ending the conflict by diplomatic methods.[19] Halder recalled that, when he asked Beck how the people would react to a *coup d'état*, Beck became impatient and told Halder that, as an experienced horseman, he should know that he had to throw his heart over the fence.

Halder now became irritated. He was a long-standing and bitter opponent of Hitler, he said, but since he was in a responsible position, he had to consider the consequences of his action and could not simply charge on and carry out a *putsch*.[20] Among the consequences might well be civil war and the collapse of the Army.[21] A month later (14 February) Halder saw Witzleben in Bad Kreuznach and Witzleben voiced his opinion with some violence on the necessity of resistance to Hitler; Halder's reaction to the moral argument was similar – he took refuge in formal excuses and finally ordered Witzleben kindly to do what he was told by OKH.[22]

Halder therefore remained inactive. He could not even be roused by a letter from Goerdeler. Admittedly he replied to it at the end of March[23] but he merely repeated that the *Wehrmacht* could do nothing. The war must now run its course first, he said.

During January Halder was increasingly evasive in face of opposition attempts to influence him. He remained irritated with Beck and Dr Müller's talks in Rome made little impression on him. Then clouds began to gather around the head of Lieutenant-Colonel Groscurth who occupied so vital a position in OKH.

In fact Halder and Groscurth thought alike and, provided he was not pressed too hard, Halder was not basically opposed to Groscurth's activities – protection of people subjected to persecution and preparation for a *coup*. Even on 13 January Halder and Groscurth had held an hour-long discussion of a report by Helldorf describing among other things the conditions in Poland.[24] Halder told Groscurth that he was in favour of the necessary fight against

England which was forced upon Germany and sooner or later inevitable in any case. After the victory the Army would be strong enough to call the tune at home; before the fight there was 'no basis for attack [upon Hitler]; troops still believed in the *Führer*'. Those who wanted to engineer a *putsch* did not agree among themselves, and they were also reactionaries, said Halder, who wanted to turn back the wheel of history. The 'revolution was still in progress, however, and nothing could be gauged by the traditions that are sacred to us'. Apparently this last remark referred to the atrocities committed in Poland. Halder remarked, with regard to Groscurth's efforts to make them known to the military commanders at the western front, that 'one must not burden the front with unnecessary worries'. Thus Halder may well have acknowledged that Hitler's regime was illegal and immoral – but he was obviously not prepared to deny what he believed were the regime's successes. He also failed to enlighten Groscurth how Hitler could have fewer supporters among the troops after the expected success 'against England' (France was not mentioned; perhaps her position depended so clearly on that taken by Britain). What Halder was really saying was that he was going to run the war, and that he was not going to participate in any *coup*.

On 5 January, however, when Halder was away on tour, Colonel-General Blaskowitz asked Brauchitsch 'why his report on the East had become known in the West'; he was referring, of course, to the report which Groscurth had used when visiting Army Group Commanders in December.[25]

Groscurth had then been heavily involved in efforts to bring about cancellation of a decree issued on 28 October 1939 by Himmler with Hitler's explicit approval which had evoked much indignation and many protests in the *Wehrmacht*.[26] In this Himmler had urged SS men in particular but also all men 'of good blood' to mate with women 'of good blood', whether their own wives, someone else's wife or an unmarried girl, and produce as many children as possible in order to provide the population urgently required for the conquest of *Lebensraum* and the replacement of war casualties. Since no one either could or would do much about the horrible shootings in Poland – Blaskowitz complained bitterly that officers were too flabby and 'no one had the humanity to stand up for those subjected to unjust persecution'[27] – attention had turned to this immoral SS decree.

Groscurth had made himself highly conspicuous in all this and the conflict with Himmler finally took a threatening turn. At the latest by 23 January 1940 Halder was trying to get rid of Groscurth and find a replacement for him.[28] Meanwhile, however, Groscurth refused to give way; he submitted a number of drafts to Halder commenting on the SS decree and tried to spread the news of SS crimes in Poland.[29] He knew, of course, that his position had become untenable; he regarded his draft on the SS decree as providing the occasion for his 'fall'. In a letter of 17 February to Graf Schwerin von Schwanenfeld, Witzleben's aide who had tried to arrange a posting for him to 75 Division which was in Witzleben's Army, Groscurth said: 'People are still sore about my trip to the west. In this connection, however, conditions in the east have become far *worse*. I may not say more on this subject – and even this much is forbidden.'[30] On 1 February Groscurth was told that he was to be relieved; Colonel Heim, his successor as head of the Special OKH Section under Halder, reported for duty on 20 February.[31] A vital post was lost to the opposition.

Halder invariably gave as his main reasons for the impracticability of an army *coup* the fact that opinion among the population and the younger officers (major and below) was not 'ripe' and also the lack of assurances from abroad about the attitude of the enemy in the event of an internal German *coup*.[32] Nothing could be done about the 'unfavourable' public opinion. It would only become 'ripe' when Germany had already been plunged into catastrophe, by which time it would be too late for a *coup* to save the situation; public opinion would only change with major military defeats, which at the moment were not in prospect. The opposition therefore hoped to achieve more by obtaining 'assurances' in the form of binding agreements with the Western Powers.

12 Soundings Abroad

Efforts to obtain assurances from abroad had been in progress ever since the Sudeten crisis of 1938 and they never entirely ceased until just before 20 July 1944. The probings of the Kordt brothers and Adam von Trott zu Solz, have already been referred to. Now, in the period when the western offensive was continually being postponed, efforts to this end were reintensified, though using very different methods.

On 4 January 1940 Ewald von Kleist-Schmenzin had a talk with the Swedish Minister in Berlin and gave him a detailed picture of the internal German situation.[1] In addition he said that the western offensive was at present scheduled for 15 January but might be further postponed at any time owing to the weather or for other reasons. In any case, he said, the majority of the generals regarded an attack in the west as hopeless. If it bogged down, this would create the conditions for the overthrow of Hitler by the senior military commanders. In this connection it was vital for the opposition to know whether, if necessary, it could count on peace mediation from some neutral quarter and whether this would be more likely to occur with a new German government than with the present one.

In mid-January Eivind Berggrav, the Bishop of Oslo, travelled to Berlin and had discussions with Weizsäcker. Weizsäcker was in despair at the apparent futility of all efforts for peace, but he encouraged Berggrav and his colleagues in Britain, France and the Scandinavian countries to pursue their endeavours – during the ecclesiastical conference at Zilven in Holland early in January they had gone on record with peace proposals.[2] However hopeless it might seem, Weizsäcker said, it was their responsibility to try everything possible and conceivable.

On several occasions during the autumn of 1939 Goerdeler attempted to obtain assurances from Britain on the basis of the German 1914 eastern frontiers, but without tangible success. Early in March 1940 he had discussions in Berlin with Sumner Welles and probably also in the same month with the King of the Belgians.[3] The only result of these, however, was to establish that, although practical bases for peace existed, no one would consider further negotiations with Hitler.[4] At the same time the Beck-Goerdeler group made use of their contacts in Switzerland in order to gain touch with the British government; these produced some more concrete reaction and showed that the British government was extremely interested in the possibilities offered by encouragement of the German opposition. Professor Siegmund-Schultze, for instance, who had emigrated to Zurich was in constant contact with the German resistance and Dr Josef Wirth, the German ex-Chancellor who also lived in Switzerland, was equally available as an intermediary.[5]

Early in 1940 Dr Wirth wrote a letter to Chamberlain which was taken to London by Dr Schairer. In it Wirth pointed out that an opposition group of considerable strength existed in Germany and it would be greatly assisted if it knew that the Western Powers would not exploit a *coup* to the military detriment of Germany.[6] Thereupon, in mid-February, two representatives of the Foreign Office appeared in Switzerland; they were personal friends of Vansittart. A meeting in Lausanne-Ouchy was arranged with Dr Wirth and a certain gentleman accompanying him who was known to both the Englishmen. The meeting took place.[7]

The British representatives put forward a number of proposals on behalf of the Prime Minister; they were said to be valid until the end of April 1940. The principal assurance was that 'the British government will not, by attacking in the west, use to Germany's military disadvantage any passing crisis which might be connected with action by the German opposition'. Moreover the British government was prepared to work with a German government in which it could have confidence, in order to ensure lasting peace. Further individual assurances – the question of German frontiers was not mentioned but was undoubtedly meant – could only be given in agreement with the French government. Should the German opposition 'wish their action made easier through a diversion by the Western Powers,' the British government was ready to do this in so far as it was able.[8] To the question what sort of a German government would be regarded as trustworthy, the verbal reply was that no member of the present government should belong to it, not even Göring.[9]

On 24 February Chamberlain expressed himself similarly in a speech in Birmingham. The implication was clear: if the Germans showed goodwill and were prepared to abandon the principle that might was right, they must be ready to give some proof of this and then they would be met with goodwill on the other side; under their present government, however, there could be no security for the future.[10]

At last, therefore, there was now some concrete assurance, though not in writing. The opposition, however, could hardly expect an official British government document stating its attitude to a German government which did not yet exist and whose aims and ideas were not entirely above suspicion.[11] This being so, the 'proposals' handed to Dr Wirth must be considered far-reaching. Unfortunately, so far as is known, they never reached the Beck-Goerdeler resistance group.[12]

The contact between the German opposition and the British government established through Theo Kordt and Philip Conwell Evans was maintained and utilized further.[13] On 15 November Groscurth noted in his diary: 'Halifax has sent word to Kordt that peace is still possible on the basis of the ethnographic frontiers.'[14] Kordt and Conwell Evans met in Berne on 18

December 1939 and 27 January 1940. People in London were losing patience, Conwell Evans said. Kordt thereupon went to Berlin to find out what was happening. On 16 February he met Conwell Evans once more in Berne; Evans said that, as proof of the new government's goodwill, it was expected that Poland be evacuated immediately on the fall of the Nazi regime.[15] Kordt handed over a letter to Vansittart. He could naturally give no firm assurances and, as far as Poland was concerned, he followed Beck's instruction that after a *coup* Poland would be evacuated as soon as there was no longer a threat from Russia (which had meanwhile attacked Finland). He said that his friends in Germany realized that there could be no negotiation with Hitler; they were therefore endeavouring 'with all the force at their command to provide a negotiator on the German side who could bring about the just peace they wanted'.[16] The British side, Kordt continued, had created the necessary conditions by the Prime Minister's promise not to exploit an upheaval to the military detriment of Germany. He and his brother Erich 'had done all that was humanly possible to convince our friends of the absolute reliability of this promise'. He hoped that the *coup* might still take place before major operations opened in the west; if not, however, they must still continue to strive for peace. Under no circumstances must one allow oneself, as Vansittart had done when talking to Kordt a few days before the outbreak of war, to lapse into a mood like that of Samson in the Bible when he tore down the pillars of the palace and buried everything in the ruins. Possibly prospects for an internal German *coup* might be even better after a German attack in the west.

This did not amount to much and understandably it was not enough for the British; from their point of view they had more than sufficient reason to be cautious and suspicious vis-à-vis a German opposition which in their eyes was only nominal. On their side the opposition wanted, not only a guarantee that there would be no military action but written conditions on which the British government would be prepared to conclude peace.[17] Such demands could not be met.

About this time, late autumn 1939 and early 1940, there was to be found in Rome an amateur diplomat and peripatetic adventurer named James Lonsdale Bryans; he had a contact to Lord Halifax and was on the look-out for an opportunity to play the part of mediator between the warring parties.[18] In November 1939 he happened to make the acquaintance of Dr Detalmo Pirzio Biroli, who was later to become Hassell's son-in-law and whose German contacts seemed interesting. Lonsdale Bryans laid siege to Biroli and in the course of some forty conversations picked up hints about the existence and aims of the German opposition. This fired his ambition to arrange contact between the Germans and the British Foreign Minister.

About the turn of the year, at Bryans' request, Biroli wrote a letter to Halifax vouching for the amateur diplomat and urging Halifax to make some overture.

On 8 January Lonsdale Bryans passed the letter to Halifax, who was impressed. Unofficially he commissioned Bryans to pursue the matter but he gave him nothing in writing.[19] Bryans thereupon returned to Rome and told

Biroli who, using the cover of family correspondence, arranged a meeting between Hassell and Bryans in Arosa, Switzerland.

On 22 and 23 February discussions took place between these two representatives. Hassell's pretext (naturally only a pretext) for his presence in Arosa was to visit his son who was ill in a sanatorium there. As a result of this contact Bryans proposed to obtain an official binding declaration from the British government about their attitude in the event of a possible internal German *coup* and the peace terms which they would regard as acceptable. Such was 'Mr X's' aim and he had already set the wheels in motion in Rome. The proposal, of course, went much further than all previous requests by the opposition to the Western Powers but Hassell had not put it forward himself and he could naturally only express support for Lonsdale Bryans' hope that it would be successful.[20]

To provide some basis for the British declaration Hassell drafted a statement which he gave to Lonsdale Bryans to pass to Halifax, adding verbally that the proposal was only valid provided that agreement could be reached before the opening of major military operations in the west. He could not give names of the other leaders of the conspiracy, he said, but Sir Nevile Henderson, the former British Ambassador in Berlin, was 'well-informed' on the circumstances and personalities; a change of regime and the resignation of certain persons in Germany were matters of purely German concern and should not be made the subject of demands from non-German quarters (to avoid any defiant patriotic reaction or an understandable revival of memories of 1918 – Wilson's demands and the jettisoning of the Kaiser). Should no authoritative British statement along these lines be forthcoming, Hassell concluded, there was no prospect of any change of regime in Germany which would help towards a compromise peace.

In his 'Statement' Hassell said[21] that this mad war should be stopped as soon as possible, otherwise Europe was in danger of complete destruction and also of bolshevization (as a result of the advance of Russia now already under way and the social and political extremism to be anticipated following the war). Europe, he said, was 'for us' not a military arena or a base of power but a magnified form of Fatherland, in which a healthy Germany was an indispensable factor, particularly with an eye to Soviet Russia. The object must therefore be permanent pacification, reestablishment of Europe on a solid base and security against a renewal of warlike tendencies. The Austrian *Anschluss* and the annexation of the Sudetenland should not be called in question; the German–Polish frontier should be 'more or less' that of 1914 and there should be no change in the 1937 status of Alsace-Lorraine, which should remain French. The following principles should be universally accepted as the basis of future peace: the principle of nationality with certain modifications deriving from history; reestablishment of an independent Poland and of 'a Czech Republic'; general reduction of armaments; reestablishment of free international economic cooperation; recognition of the principles of Christian ethics, of justice and law as fundamental elements of public life, of social welfare as a '*leitmotiv*', of popular control of government, of liberty of thought, conscience and intellectual activity.

In the light of the situation of 1945 Hassell's principles and requirements sound fantastic, if not intemperate; they were largely in accord, however, with those of Liedig, Etzdorf and others, also trade union leaders such as Jakob Kaiser.[22] It must also be remembered that the union of Austria with Germany had not been seriously disputed and that the annexation of the Sudetenland had taken place with the help and explicit approval of the Western Powers, sealed by an agreement.

As regards Poland and the 1914 frontier, the opposition's case rested solely on power, in other words on the fact that German armies were occupying Poland. In the areas primarily populated by Germans which had become Polish after 1918, the problem could perhaps have been settled by plebiscite but, apart from this, it was hard to justify the 1914 frontier. On the other hand reestablishment of the territorial position of August 1939 would not have been a satisfactory basis for lasting peace, since it would have left outstanding the problem of the Corridor and the question of minorities. It was highly questionable, moreover, whether Russia would relinquish her conquests made at Poland's expense and on the basis of the Russo–German pact. The Polish question therefore remained unsolved. There was thus a clear contradiction between the declared determination to reestablish the rule of law and a return to the paths of peaceful agreement, and the claim to retain at least part of Hitler's conquests.[23]

Looking at the statement through British spectacles, Britain, having declared war on Germany specifically to preserve the integrity of Poland within her August 1939 frontiers, could derive but little encouragement. No commitment for the removal of Hitler was made; it was even demanded that the subject should not be raised; at the same time there was a clear desire to maintain Germany's predominant position in Eastern Europe and retain part of Hitler's conquests. How else could the demand for the 1914 frontiers and the offer of reestablishment of a 'Czech Republic', presumably still divorced from Slovakia, be interpreted?[24] Admittedly Germany was still powerful and she had greatly extended her influence. The opposition's demands, however, seemed to place far too great reliance on that fact; they inevitably sounded like the demands of nationalism rather than nationality. The excuse that in no other way could 'the generals' be persuaded to act, only made the whole thing more suspect.[25] Those points in Hassell's programme which could not be implemented without the removal of Hitler did little to mitigate this.

Lonsdale Bryans went back to London to fulfil the other half of his mission, procurement of an official British declaration. But he was not even received by Halifax and saw only Sir Alexander Cadogan, the Under-Secretary of State, who thanked him for his pains and allowed him to go to Switzerland once more, but only to take leave of Hassell and formally conclude his mission.[26] A written declaration was unobtainable. The venture had failed.

Talking to Cadogan Lonsdale Bryans had stressed the German opposition's main requirement – a declaration that Britain would not make military use of a *coup d'état* against Hitler and would embark forthwith on peace negotiations with a non-Nazi Germany. Without such a declaration, he said, it was inconceivable that the military could be persuaded to act. Cadogan, however, refused to issue a British declaration of this nature. It had already been done a week earlier, he said, through another channel, by which he may have meant either the message to Dr Wirth or the assurance to Dr Müller that the British standpoint was still the same as at end January 1940.[27]

On 14 April Hassell and Lonsdale Bryans met again in Arosa.[28] Meanwhile, on 9 April, the German invasion of Denmark and Norway had begun; much was therefore now out of date and the overall situation had greatly changed. Lonsdale Bryans told Hassell (which on his own admission he was not authorized to do)[29] that he had passed Hassell's message to Halifax who had shown it to Chamberlain; Cadogan had also been informed. Halifax was most grateful and in agreement with the principles set forth; he could not, however, give a written assurance since such had been given through another channel just a week before. Hassell thought he knew what this channel was and said as much to Lonsdale Bryans. He knew Brauchitsch's and Halder's reaction to the Rome talks and he had little hope when he asked whether, after the latest developments, London was still prepared to conclude peace with a 'respectable Germany'. Lonsdale Bryans replied in the affirmative but at a further meeting next morning Hassell gained the impression that 'Halifax and his group had no real faith in the possibility of attaining peace in this way, that is through a change of regime in Germany.'[30]

In effect, as a payment on account without which they were unwilling to do anything, the generals wanted a firm statement of future British policy vis-à-vis a government which did not yet exist and of which practically nothing was known. They were afraid that they would be badly treated later. Even if assurances were given, it was hardly to be expected that the other side would be full of such goodwill that they would accord Germany generous treatment. In 1918–19 the hopes placed on such declarations, specifically on Wilson's Fourteen Points, had proved false. Political and military weight was what counted in the achievement of acceptable peace conditions; this was the criterion by which views were judged at the negotiating table. The example of France showed this clearly enough. Who ever asked about France? Everyone turned to Britain. It was from Britain that the assurances and payment on account were demanded, obviously on the assumption that French decisions would be dependent on those of Britain. Britain, on the other hand, with far greater justification was demanding first to see a *coup*, the removal of Hitler and his hangers-on from the government and the assumption of responsibility by the other 'respectable Germany'.[31]

From the conspirators' point of view the only successful contact with the British government came about because an intermediary of the necessary influence and reputation was available. This was the Vatican.

As early as end September 1939 Dr Josef Müller was commissioned on behalf of the military conspirators to gain contact with the British government using the Vatican as a channel.[32] As a strict Catholic Dr Müller had belonged to the anti-Hitler opposition more or less from the outset.[33] Until the outbreak of war he worked as a lawyer in Munich; he then agreed to be called up into the Army as a Second Lieutenant and was posted to the *Abwehr* Office in Munich.[34] In their very first conversation Oster had told him what his mission was – to use his good relationships with the Vatican for the benefit of the German opposition.[35] Cover was provided by giving him an intelligence assignment – discovery of the intentions of the enemy and of the Italians. Although interrogated on over two hundred occasions by the *Gestapo*, Dr Müller stuck to this story: he had been introduced, he said, to Pacelli, formerly Cardinal Secretary of State and now Pope, and had the *entrée* to the crypt of St Peter's in Rome; he had accordingly been officially commissioned by the *Abwehr* to exploit the Vatican sources of intelligence.[36] That he was doing so for the benefit of the opposition he did not of course reveal. Credibility was given to this cover by the reports sent to Berlin by Dr Müller on developments within the Italian government, on the Italian attitude to Germany, Britain and France, and on the question of Italian entry into the war. One of these reports (dealing with the period 6–12 November 1939) has survived among the Groscurth papers, and a considerable body of correspondence on the Vatican contacts between the German opposition and His Majesty's Government exists in the files of the Foreign Office in London.[37]

Dr Müller's first task at the end of September 1939 was to establish the necessary contact and to find out whether, in general terms, the Vatican was prepared to mediate.[38] He accordingly went to Rome, where he stayed at the Hotel 'Flora'.[39] He gained contact with the Jesuit Father Leiber, the Pope's Private Secretary. Dr Müller never dealt with the Pope personally since this would have been far too conspicuous and dangerous and might well have spoilt the whole affair.[40] After a short time he received word that the Vatican was ready to provide the machinery for mediation.[41] He was regarded as a representative of Colonel-General Beck, clearly an important condition for the Pope's commitment since no one among the opposition leaders was so well known or so highly respected as Beck.[42]

At the end of September or early October Müller reported to Berlin on his initial soundings.[43] With Beck's approval he was commissioned by Oster, Canaris and Dohnanyi to ask Pius XII to discover whether the British government might be prepared to enter into peace discussions with the German opposition which proposed to overthrow Hitler and form a new government.[44] He returned to Rome and regained contact with Father Leiber. Through Sir Francis d'Arcy Osborne, the British Minister, the Vatican sounded out the British government and was told that they were ready to negotiate with the German opposition's representative provided that he was vouched for by the Vatican.[45] Dr Müller carried this information to Berlin on 18 October. On 20 October Groscurth made a reference to it in his office diary.[46]

The Pope now channelled questions and answers in both directions between Müller and Osborne, Father Leiber once more acting as intermediary between Müller and the Pope.[47] Information, messages and the results of the soundings were almost invariably transmitted verbally, but on several occasions Father Leiber left some missive for Müller in his hotel, if he had failed to meet him or if the information was urgent. All these papers were immediately destroyed by Müller with the exception of one of Father Leiber's visiting cards and a sheet of paper with the Vatican watermark, on which was set out a summary of the British negotiating conditions. Both these were used as proof for General Halder of the authenticity of the reports about the talks being conducted in Rome.

The talks proceeded on the premise that while they were in progress no major military operations would take place in the west and furthermore that substantive negotiations would only be conducted with some responsible government which would have to replace the Hitler regime.[48] The talks took place in an atmosphere of tension, for the German offensive in the west might start any day; particularly on the British side they were conducted with extreme caution, as was only to be expected since the whole affair was conspiratorial in character and dubious from the point of view of international law. The Venlo incident led to a six-week interruption and the fact that the British were prepared to resume talks at all was due primarily to the efforts of the Pope and the respect in which he was held. Chamberlain and Halifax set great store by the Pope's readiness to mediate.[49] On 27 January 1940 Bishop Berggrav visited Lord Halifax; this may well have influenced the British government to give a favourable reply to Müller's soundings two days later.

Dr Müller's negotiations in Rome dragged on into February 1940. Pius XII summoned the British Minister, Osborne, on 11 January and related to him the position of the German military opposition.[50] This information reached the British Government in London:

'A grand German offensive [the Pope told Osborne] has been prepared down to the last detail for the middle of February, or possibly even earlier. It will be violent, bitter and utterly unscrupulous. But it need never be delivered. If the German generals could be assured of a peace with Great Britain (France was not mentioned) which would neither be another Compiègne, i.e. like the Great War armistice, nor Wilsonian in nature, they were prepared to replace the present German Government by a *"Verhandlungsfähige Regierung"* – a government with which it was possible to negotiate – and then to reach a settlement in eastern Europe with the British Government. This settlement would include a restoration in Poland [sic] and Czechoslovakia (no details given) and would also deal with Russia (this was even more enigmatic, but seemed to imply the fact or menace of action against Russia). There could, however, be no concession over the existing *Anschluss* with Austria.' Thus Osborne had reported to Halifax on 12 January 1940, and he had continued: the Pope had expressly not adopted these ideas, but indicated that his conscience forced him to transmit them to Osborne. Osborne had replied to Pius XII that the whole matter was hopelessly vague and dangerously reminiscent of the Venlo incident. The Pope was not at all comfortable in his role as mediator, but he did say in conclusion that the German principals were in no way connected with the NSDAP.

Halder's remarks to Groscurth even in those days show how justified were the Pope's reservations. On 13 January, Halder told Groscurth that he agreed that the fight against England was a necessary one and that the basis for a *coup* was lacking in Germany.[51] Osborne's doubts concerning the reliability of the German contacts and assurances, too, were not unfounded, and of course he did not hesitate to report his misgivings to Halifax.

On 16 January the British War Cabinet discussed the matter and adopted Osborne's opinion that they could not take up such nebulous overtures. If the German opposition were serious, they might, as a first step, do away with the present government, and then talk of peace. It was further decided to inform the French Government.[52]

It is not yet clear whether or not Osborne immediately transmitted the reply he received from London to the Pope nor even if Osborne had received such a reply at this time. On 6 February Pius XII summoned him for 7 February and Osborne reported on his conversation with the Pope to Halifax on the same day. The Pope had had in front of him about four typed pages in German and said the conspirators in Germany wanted to replace the present government by a democratic, conservative, moderate, decentralized and federal one. He had been asked to find out if the continued union of Austria with Germany could be guaranteed as a basis for peace negotiations; Poland and non-German Czechoslovakia were to be independent. Pius XII repeated that he felt uneasy about transmitting such information, but that his conscience forced him to pursue even the smallest chance of saving human lives, and once again Osborne made no secret of his own doubts as to the sincerity or genuineness of the German overtures. However, this time Chamberlain and Halifax decided to reply, and not to inform the French Cabinet. In the communication from London to Osborne of 17 February there were the following statements: 'It must be clear from the outset that His Majesty's Government can take no step in this matter except in conjunction with France. If His Majesty's Government were convinced that the intermediaries who approached His Holiness represented principals in Germany who had both the intention and the power to perform what they promised, His Majesty's Government would be willing to consider with the French Government any enquiries that those principals might make. But His Majesty's Government could not broach this question with the French Government on the basis of ideas emanating from undisclosed sources and so vague in character as those which have been conveyed to you. If any progress is to be made, a definite programme must be submitted and authoritatively vouched for. In examining any such programme, and in framing their own conditions, what His Majesty's Government would look for above all, in addition to reparation of the wrongs done to Germany's smaller neighbours, would be security for the future. . . . In this connexion the suggestion of a decentralized and federal Germany is of interest, and might be held to go some way towards a solution of this problem.'

A few days later, around 20 February, the Pope received a written communication from Osborne in which the position of the British Foreign Minister and Prime Minister was set forth. The Pope had the contents of Osborne's note communicated to Dr Müller at once.[53] So far, nothing except

Dr Müller's own reports indicated that the Pope had said more to him than Halifax's instructions to Osborne contained. On the other hand the Pope, who knew the wishes and conditions of the opposition for the *coup* against Hitler's regime, seems to have counted on the *coup* as late as the middle of March 1940, as he told the French diplomatic envoy on 13 March, and the American envoy on 18 March.[54] But then hope began to fade quickly, the more so, as the Pope told Osborne on 30 March, since 'he feared that any prospect of favourable developments from the approaches made through himself were vitiated by the fact that other similar approaches had reached His Majesty's Government through other channels . . . He added that, according to his understanding, His Majesty's Government were not very hopeful of any results from these communications nor enthusiastic about their receipt.'[55] Obviously the use of several channels at the same time reduced their relative value – even if the opposition had, as they certainly had not, presented the same programme and stated the same conditions for action on each occasion.

Understandably, what Dr Müller was able to report home earlier in the year was quite useful, and it must have sounded more favourable to the opposition than it would have had they seen Halifax's instructions to Osborne.[56] Still, it did not differ fundamentally from the British position in those details which may be regarded as confirmed on the basis of sources available to date. The German opposition were assured by the British Government that, should there be no German western offensive and should the German dictatorial regime be replaced by a democratic one within a reasonable time, the Western Powers would not take the offensive during the *coup*; further that in the peace settlement the *Reich* frontiers of 1937 would be left intact and the question of Austria's union with the *Reich* would be settled by a plebiscite in Austria. As Halifax put it to Osborne on 17 February 1940: 'Under any Federal plan [for the reorganization of Germany] it would be in our view right that Austria should be allowed to decide whether or not she wished to enter the Federation.'[57]

On the retention of the Sudetenland by the *Reich* available sources are less clear. In contrast to Austria, on this point Dr Müller and his principals could base their case on a formal international treaty, the Munich Agreement. Nevertheless the question was a difficult one and not even an outline solution emerged from the Rome soundings. Hitler had long since broken the agreement and the other signatories were no longer totally bound by it.

Reporting on his talks in Rome between 6 and 12 November, Müller was able to say that Noots, the (Belgian) Abbot of the Premonstratensian Order, who was always meeting diplomats, had told him that among Germany's enemies there was a general desire for a just peace, always provided that there was a change of regime.[58] *Entente* diplomats were always saying that it only needed the reestablishment of a Czech state, perhaps also of Slovakia and a 'Polish Poland' which was not more closely defined. Germany could keep everything else, possibly even Austria, although there was an increasing tendency in favour of a federal monarchy including both Germany and Austria.[59] As far as Dr Müller remembers the terms transmitted to him and intended solely for him and his principals were: Reestablishment of Poland, Germany not being responsible for the area occupied by Russia; subsequent negotiations on Danzig and frontier rectifications with Poland; other territorial questions in the east to be solved by plebiscite.[60] The Sudetenland does not seem to have been specifically mentioned in the communications received by Müller. The German frontiers in the west were not even a subject of discussion.[61]

The communications and assurances received in Rome appeared in Berlin as minutes and reports by Dr Müller and notes by his principals and friends. Many of them simply repeated what Müller had found out in Rome. Others, however, in particular one known as the 'X Report' because Müller was referred to therein as 'x', were intended to be used solely to influence 'the generals', in other words Halder and Brauchitsch. There were a number of drafts of the 'X Report' before it was finalized but none of these papers have been found since the war.[62] One may venture a cautious reconstruction of the contents of the 'X Report' based on certain evidence, such as diary entries and memoirs, which are not invariably accurate or reliable; it is possible, however, to establish the *minimum* concrete statements which the 'X Report' must have contained.[63] These were points which, in the light of Germany's actual situation, had to be conceded and on which all those involved in the 'X Report', its preliminary drafts and supporting documents, were in agreement.

These points included: No German offensive in the west; a change of regime; reestablishment of the rule of law; peace negotiations with a new non-Nazi government; settlement of the relationship between Germany and Austria by mutual agreement, possibly by a plebiscite in Austria; a settlement acceptable to Germany of problems in the East.[64]

General Thomas, moreover, says that, while under interrogation after 20 July 1944, he was shown a minute showing that the 'report from Rome' included agreement to the settlement of all eastern questions in favour of Germany.[65]

Halder goes even further than Thomas. From what he remembers the 'X Report' did not contain a specific demand for a change of regime but only for the removal of Hitler and 'if possible' of the entire National-Socialist regime. The Czech region[66] should remain in a German 'sphere of influence' and moreover, not only should the German eastern frontier of 1914 be reestablished but also the western 1914 frontiers. This is so ludicrous as to cast doubts on the authenticity of everything else. We shall never know whether this is perhaps the key to Halder's remarkable feats of memory.[67] In any case a document such as that described by Halder could never have produced the desired result.

At the conclusion of the Rome talks, around 20 February 1940, Dr Müller told his opposite number in Rome, Father Leiber (as Father Leiber later related), that his principals regarded the results as so favourable that they were now prepared to act; the *coup d'état* was now scheduled for a date in February.[68] Father Leiber does not say on what authority Müller made this pronouncement but in any case it proved over-optimistic. Halder did not receive the 'X Report' and other papers about the Rome talks until 4 April.[69]

Why had Beck, Oster and Dohnanyi let slip the rest of February and March? No one can say. Possibly they were hoping for some diplomatic solution, for which Sumner Welles' mission may have given grounds for hope. Possibly also, after the fruitless talk between Beck and Halder, the two opposition centres were out of touch, not only technically but in identity of purpose.[70] Certainly Beck's group did not now think that the western offensive or the war situation in general need be taken any less seriously. On the contrary – the crimes committed in Poland, on which further reports had been reaching the opposition particularly since the end of January, continued to demonstrate that the overthrow of the regime was essential.[71]

Admittedly people were wearied with waiting. It was difficult to penetrate to Halder; the continual visits must have been tiresome to him at a time when he was so preoccupied with preparations for the western offensive and when, moreover, he had neither the hope nor the desire to persuade his Commander-in-Chief to participate in a *coup*. When Hassell reached Berlin on 14 February, Goerdeler told him that Brauchitsch must be written off entirely.[72] Talking to Hassell the next day, Popitz, the Prussian Finance Minister, referred more optimistically to 'the generals' but confirmed Goerdeler's opinion that there was little hope of a decision before the visit of Sumner Welles, the American Under-Secretary of State.[73]

During the second half of February Hassell, at least, placed all his hopes on Sumner Welles' visit. Among others he spoke to Alexander C. Kirk, the American Chargé d'Affaires in Berlin, and urged him to arrange for Sumner Welles to meet men like Planck and Popitz.[74] Hassell then went to Arosa for his second meeting with Lonsdale Bryans. He was back in Berlin in the second week of March. Sumner Welles' visit had taken place meanwhile (1–5 March) and, from the opposition's point of view, had produced nothing. It is understandable, however, that hope revived when Sumner Welles postponed his departure from Europe on receipt of the news of Hitler's and Mussolini's meeting on the Brenner on 18 March.[75]

The imminence of the western offensive now became a subject of discussion once more. From a cousin of Brauchitsch Hassell learnt that, if Hitler so instructed, Brauchitsch would issue orders for the offensive and would conduct it in order to reach a 'military decision' – or in order thus to evade a decision. At heart, however, he was uncertain, the cousin said, and, although he would not undertake a *coup* himself, he would stand by if he was relieved of responsibility for it by someone else.[76] On 11 March Hassell was back in Ebenhausen, returning to Berlin on the 15th.[77]

Again and again people tried to persuade Brauchitsch to play an active part in a *coup*. When Popitz visited him between 10 and 15 March, Brauchitsch gave the impression of 'an inwardly broken man'. Nevertheless he had asked whether there was any prospect of a 'decent peace'. Popitz, who was obviously not familiar with the details of the peace soundings, particularly of the Vatican talks, even if he knew of them at all, could only reply that he believed so.[78]

There is so far nothing definite to show why Popitz had not been told of the details and commissioned to deliver the 'X Report'. It was, of course, a particularly hot potato, since, technically at any rate, it amounted to treason. Who had the courage to show these papers to Halder when he risked being arrested or thrown out? The ground had first to be tested. In addition the military situation had changed. The Army was now far better prepared than in the previous autumn and the people much less alarmed. The allegedly essential psychological basis was totally lacking.[79] Finally it had to be remembered that ever since November Halder had become unapproachable for the opposition; he had refused all requests; he was at cross purposes with Beck; Groscurth had been removed from his vital position – from every point of view the opposition had been losing ground with Halder all the time.

Nevertheless the backers of Dr Müller strove to get the 'X Report' to Halder and Brauchitsch. On 17 March Goerdeler succeeded in obtaining an interview with Halder but no one gave him the report to take with him.[80] On the other hand it was now decided to let Hassell into the secret and show him the results of the Rome talks. He was an experienced diplomat and an expert who, in addition, had formerly been Ambassador in Rome. He was the man to give the necessary authenticity to these unsigned documents and lend weight to the background arguments which might be obscure to the uninitiated. On 16 March, therefore, Hassell was asked by Gottfried von Nostitz, a Counsellor in the Foreign Ministry, on behalf of Oster and Dohnanyi to meet Beck that afternoon at No 9 Goethestrasse, Berlin–Lichterfelde; Oster and Dohnanyi appeared there some time later.[81] They read to Hassell the papers prepared by Dr Müller which showed that what was called a 'decent peace' was still perfectly obtainable, as the British government had explicitly stated. The main points were: a change of regime; 'acknowledgement of Christian morality' (which could be taken to mean a return to the rule of law); decentralization in Germany and a plebiscite in Austria (an idea also ventilated in connection with a federal organization for the German–Austrian area). All this was now divulged to Hassell, firstly to have his opinion as a foreign policy expert and secondly to ask him to be the channel to Halder 'because no other intermediary had much chance of success'.[82]

Hassell was ready to act and on 18 March he discussed the matter again with Dohnanyi and Oster in the latter's house. It was decided first to see what news Goerdeler had.[83] He had seen Halder on Sunday 17 March and for two hours had discussed 'the necessity for peace before the start of a showdown by force' and 'the possibility of a favourable settlement', as Halder noted in his diary less laconically than usual.[84] Goerdeler had had to promise to tell no one about his talk. He therefore merely told Hassell that at the last moment Halder had been unable to receive him but that he had 'received from another source the assurance that understanding was growing in that quarter'.[85] Halder, he said, now wanted to talk to Hassell. When Goerdeler had besought him to initiate the *coup* Halder had given the well-known reply, difficult to refute, that he had neither the forces nor the necessary backing.[86]

Goerdeler urged Hassell to hurry, saying that he must see Thomas the very next day and discuss with him preparations for his interview with Halder.

Hassell had not actually wanted to stay in Berlin so long but he postponed his departure and on 19 March went early to see Thomas and discussed with him the best arguments to use with Halder and the basic political proposals.[87] During their talk it emerged that Goerdeler had in fact seen Halder; Thomas confirmed that Halder wanted to talk to Hassell but not until after Easter, after 24 March in other words.[88]

For the moment, therefore, Hassell was free to return to Ebenhausen. There he remained and heard nothing more until 2 April when, becoming uneasy, he returned to Berlin. There he was told by Goerdeler that Halder had 'got cold feet' and had called off the interview with Hassell. Goerdeler showed him a letter he had had from Halder.[89] Halder refused to take action at this time, using arguments which Hassell characterized as naïve in the extreme. After all, Halder had said, Britain and France had declared war on Germany and the war must now be fought out. The *Wehrmacht* could not act on its own to overthrow the government or at least only in extreme emergency, in other words after severe defeats or in face of imminent defeat. This was in fact naïve and worse – it was irresponsible.

From what Goerdeler said Hassell drew the conclusion that it was now too late altogether; the invasion of Denmark and Norway was imminent; Halder and Brauchitsch had obviously decided to have nothing more to do with ideas about a *coup d'état* and to carry out Hitler's orders instead.[90]

Time was pressing. After three months of preparation, minute-writing and vacillation the date for the invasion of Denmark and Norway had been settled on 27 March; it was to take place on 9 or 10 April.[91] OKH had been at high pressure for weeks; there were tactical and technical questions to be dealt with; arms and ammunition production had to be raised; a 'bottleneck' in rubber production had to be overcome by an order against fast driving; there were tours of inspection and conferences of all sorts. According to the mid-February Order of Battle the field Army now numbered 3.3 million men. The mere administration of such a mass of men entailed a mountain of work quite apart from the preparation of two or three offensives at the same time.[92] On 12 March Halder went to a conference in Koblenz, from which he did not return until the morning of the 14th; on 15th and 16th he had conferences with Hitler.[93] After the excitement about Sumner Welles' visit had died down – it is mentioned several times in Halder's diary – came Hitler's meeting with Mussolini on the Brenner. It is astounding, therefore, that on 17 March Halder found the time to talk to Goerdeler for two-and-a-half hours.[94] When he made time to write to Goerdeler over Easter he was clearly hoping to be left in peace thereafter. His letter was obviously intended as a brush-off for the opposition. The opposition, however, could not leave him in peace while the *Führer* monster was still there.

On 27 March, in a long conference with Brauchitsch, Halder, Leeb, Witzleben, General Dollmann and Lieutenant-General Felber, Hitler announced the date for 'Exercise Weser', the invasion of Norway. The state of preparations and the weather now no longer constituted obstacles as in the previous autumn and hardly anyone could doubt that this time it was the real thing. Preparations were stepped up and completed; activity became even more hectic. On the evening of 30 March Halder went to Frankfurt to confer with Leeb; he did not return to Berlin until the morning of 1 April. On the afternoon of 2 April OKH issued the codeword 'W-7' — Exercise Weser minus seven. This meant that movement must now begin for the invasion of Denmark and Norway in seven days' time.[95]

Finally on 4 April, in the midst of this whirl of preparations, General Thomas penetrated to Halder with the 'X Report' and Dr Müller's assurance from Rome that the Allies were still firm in their views as set out therein. The entry in Halder's diary is buried among notes on shortages of vehicles, rear services including bakeries, the fuel situation, Hitler's field headquarters 'Felsennest' (Crag's Nest), the move of OKH on the afternoon preceding the offensive, a pioneer battalion and so on and so on; it merely says: '*Gen. Thomas:* Glimpse of intelligence material.'[96] Small wonder if, so soon before the invasion, after so many preparations and war games, with everything so fully ready, when all this labour was at last about to come to fulfilment, Halder was seized by the soldier's thirst for battle. In April even the calm composed General Fromm was 'touched by the war fever'.[97]

Halder read the 'X Report' and showed it to Brauchitsch that evening. Halder maintains that, as set out in these papers, the terms on which Britain was prepared to conclude peace included not only the retention of Austria and Czechoslovakia (sic) under German influence, but also reestablishment of the 1914 frontiers of Germany both in east and west. Hitler and 'if possible' his entire Nazi regime, however, must be removed. Later Halder recalled that, having read the papers, Brauchitsch said to him next morning: 'You should not have shown me this. What is happening here is sheer treason. Under no circumstances can we be involved in this. We are at war; in peacetime you can talk about contacts with a foreign power, but in wartime soldiers cannot do that. Moreover this is not a struggle between governments; we are concerned with a contest of ideologies [sic]. Removal of Hitler would therefore achieve nothing.' Brauchitsch expressed himself similarly to Dr Otto John after the war.[98] Brauchitsch then demanded to know who had brought the paper to Halder; he would have him arrested, whereupon Halder replied: 'If anyone is to be arrested, you had better arrest me.' Naturally that did not occur.

In his diary Halder does not mention his Commander-in-Chief's outburst of indignation; he merely records his actual objection — or pretext — which was also his own — this despite the fact that the papers had made so great an impression on him that he had submitted them to Brauchitsch, thereby showing that he took them seriously. The objection read: 'Where did material come from to be able to make use of it. (Thomas.)'[99] After the war Halder explained that the papers were unsigned and that one had to be suspicious of such extraordinary concessions as the 1914 frontier in the west. But would the reactions of Brauchitsch and Halder have been any different had the 'X Report' or the British terms been handed over on notepaper of His Britannic Majesty's Embassy to the Holy See, signed, sealed and perhaps with an official stamp? Would they not then have suspected a simple forgery? Who can blame them for being suspicious about the contacts that had been made through such dark channels – of which Osborne, Halifax and Chamberlain were equally suspicious?[100] By the same token, however, who can blame them for the fear that Britain would use the moment of an internal upheaval in Germany for a military attack? After all, Britain and France had declared war on Germany, and such action would have been entirely appropriate and in fact what one would have expected. Why should Britain and France assume that new German leaders would be more conciliatory than the old ones? The success of a *coup d'état*, in short, cannot be guaranteed any more than can that of a war. Halder and Brauchitsch had considered both and to a certain extent prepared both; they then implemented one of them, not because it offered more assured prospects of success but because it was more official. They carried the responsibility in any case but, if they executed 'lawful' orders, they were sticking to the generally recognized rules of the game, irrespective of the fact that the rules would multiply the loss of human life by millions. Everything had its proper place. The conspirators who were ready to embark on a *coup* to save human life could be labelled as traitors; the general who sent millions to their death was 'doing his duty' and so was honourable.

Word was received from Halder that he hardly thought that Brauchitsch would change his attitude.[101] And so it proved. On 14 April Brauchitsch even urged on Hitler early issue of orders for 'Operation Yellow', the attack in the west, saying that nothing was to be gained by waiting longer.[102] Nine days later Halder referred angrily in his diary to the 'absence of planning' in the *Reich* Chancellery, saying: 'Operation Yellow apparently not urgent at the moment.'[103] He had tried everything, Halder said after the war, but he could understand why his Commander-in-Chief 'was not eager to tread on this thin ice'. That is a subtle way of putting it. Naturally, had the 'X Report' included that which Halder recalled later – agreement to the 1914 frontiers both in east and west – its effect would have been disillusioning and rightly so. But this was not the reason given by Brauchitsch. It is known that Halder wavered; he must be given credit for the fact that he was the victim of a severe conflict between formal military discipline and his duty on the one side and his ethical humanitarian duty on the other. In his letter to Goerdeler he is supposed to have summarized his attitude thus: 'The Army will do its duty to the country, even against Hitler's government if the situation so requires.'[104] When would it require? On 5 November 1939 none of the conditions for the *coup* prescribed by Halder were lacking and Brauchitsch had explicitly given him a free hand. 'The situation' was not, therefore, the real obstacle. Now victory and fame were beckoning and the war prospects were good. And thus it was. Halder's tragedy was characterized by weakness, devotion to military duty and formalism – combined with simultaneous realization of the criminal nature of Hitler's orders.

The group centred on Oster, Dohnanyi and Hassell still tried to persuade a number of army leaders, including Leeb, Witzleben, List and Kluge, to make a combined *démarche* to Brauchitsch and refuse to carry out the offensive.[105] Nothing came of it, however; the attack rolled forward and the occupation of

Denmark and Norway proved a brilliant military manoeuvre. No wonder that many of the conspirators, General Thomas for instance, were a prey to deep discouragement and considered that fate must now be allowed to run its course for a time. It is all the more astounding that others such as Beck, Hassell, Popitz and Goerdeler still felt that they should not relax their efforts for an instant.

Inevitably the German opposition now fell into disrepute abroad. For so long it had roused hopes of an internal German *coup* and people had long waited for it in vain. Now, instead of overthrowing Hitler, 'the generals' had occupied Denmark and Norway and administered an ignominious defeat to the western Allies. Naturally it was not known in London how little OKH, still the only available centre of power for a *coup*, had had to do with the invasions nor that Norway was the first 'OKW Theatre' of the war. But this made little difference. There was nothing to show that Brauchitsch and Halder would not have carried out Hitler's orders with the same alacrity as Keitel and Jodl.

To avoid losing all credibility, to keep the contact open and to demonstrate loyalty to their Rome opposite numbers who had risked themselves unselfishly, Oster and his associates decided on a final mission for Dr Müller. At the end of April,[106] as in November 1939, he was despatched to Rome to explain that the vital condition governing the British concessions, a *coup* in Germany, could no longer be fulfilled since the generals were unable to make up their minds to act. The western offensive was now certainly imminent.[107]

The question will invariably be asked whether, either objectively or subjectively, this was treason. In the first place it should be observed that the western offensive had long since ceased to be a secret; everyone knew that preparations had been made. Secondly no one apart from Hitler, and perhaps not even he himself, could tell with any certainty what he would do. What was therefore being 'betrayed'? Legally, on the other hand, an intent or deliberate act designed to damage one's own country constitutes treason.[108] Poland showed whither Germany's path was leading and men like Oster, Dohnanyi, Canaris, Müller, Hassell, Beck and Goerdeler knew this only too well. In trying to prevent Hitler's offensives succeeding by warning the enemy, they were in fact trying to save not only the enemy but equally their own people from inconceivable suffering and bloodshed, in fact from their destruction as a nation. This is the antithesis of treason. Finally there is the right of self-defence, transcending nationality and common to all men. When so monstrous, devilish and erratic a criminal as Hitler appears, both willing and able to subjugate a whole continent, national boundaries in the strict and formal sense lose their significance; the interests of all peoples then become similar.

In this spirit Oster took the ultimate and most extreme action open to anyone to prevent the western offensive taking place or at least succeeding. As soon as he knew it himself, he told the Dutch government of the date ordered by Hitler for the attack on Belgium and Holland. He did this from hatred of a regime which he regarded as criminal, from a realization of the monstrous injustice about to be perpetrated and as the result of a particularly clear and logical process of thought which the majority of other conspirators could not bring themselves to follow.[109]

Moreover those patriots and opponents of Hitler who were determined to fight him to the end were not alone in their decision to take action technically classifiable as treason. Even General Reichenau, usually condemned as a careerist and Nazi general, who commanded first Tenth Army and then Sixth Army, had the courage not only to oppose Hitler openly but also to warn the Netherlands of Hitler's planned invasion.[110] On 6 November, in the house of Fritz Elsas, he met Goerdeler, whom he had known since 1934, and he told him of Hitler's plan, which he said was 'completely crazy'. The Dutch must be warned, he said, so that they could put their defences visibly in order, particularly the dikes and canals; this would show that the advantage of surprise had already been lost. Elsas was in fact able to transmit Reichenau's message to London both via Copenhagen and Stockholm and via Switzerland, but the plan had already become known there through other channels. Reichenau's motives in doing this were undoubtedly honourable; that he, of all people, should be capable of it emphasizes the stress of conscience under which patriots such as Oster were acting who had fought against Hitler from the outset.

Towards the end of the Polish campaign Major (later Colonel) G. J. Sas, the Dutch Military Attaché in Berlin, had himself come to the conclusion that Hitler would launch an offensive on France through Belgium and Holland. On 28 September 1939 he warned his government accordingly. In mid-October this was confirmed to him by Oster, whom he had known since 1932; they had been good friends since 1936. On 7 November Oster told Sas for the first time the date of the planned attack — 12 November. A few days later, about 12 November, Dr Müller passed a similar warning to Belgium through his Rome contacts. Thereafter, as soon as he knew it himself, Oster told Sas on each occasion the date to which the offensive had been postponed.

Hardly any of Sas' superiors put faith in his initial report; many of them regarded him as a joke.[111] The longer the series of announcements and cancellations, the less seriously was Sas taken by his government. The process in fact demonstrated Hitler's disorderly methods and his impatience; it produced, perhaps deliberately, an artificial state of permanent tension and hectic activity; it continuously threw the *Wehrmacht* into confusion but it was typical of Hitler's style of government. To the Dutch agencies in The Hague it was totally incomprehensible.

In addition to this unintentional side-effect the repeated changes of date did something else: both Berlin and Zossen began to realize that German operational intentions were leaking.[112] Oster continued to pass information to Sas, thereby increasing the mortal danger in which he had placed himself in any case. But of this he took no account.

On 3 April 1940, via Dr Müller (the Vatican channel) and via Sas, Oster attempted to warn the Danish, Norwegian and British governments of the attack planned for 9 April. The warning reached the Danes but they were helpless in any case; it did not reach either the Norwegians or the British who could have made better use of it.[113] Early in May Oster told the Dutch Military Attaché, as before, of the imminence of the western offensive; the date, however, had not been entirely fixed. When information reached The Hague from the Vatican and Sas was asked for confirmation by telegram, Oster advised him to wait before saying anything further to his government. On Oster's advice Jonkheer H. M. van Haersma de With, the Dutch Minister in Berlin, gave the approximate date as 'the middle of next week', in other words about 8 May.

On 9 May Hitler fixed the opening of the offensive for 10 May at 5.35 a.m.[114] At 7 p.m. on Thursday 9 May Oster met Sas and told him of the latest development; nothing could now be stopped failing a counter-order by about 9.30 p.m. Oster checked that no such order had been issued and shortly before 10 p.m. told Sas that the offensive would definitely open next morning.[115] Sas passed the message forthwith to The Hague and also to the Belgian Military Attaché in Berlin whom, as a precaution, he had summoned to the Legation in the Rauchstrasse.

About midnight Sas received a call from the Dutch Director of Military Intelligence who, with little attempt at concealment, asked whether there was now to be no change in arrangements for the 'operation on your wife'. People in The Hague were still doubtful whether the information was correct. Sas' reply was: 'It takes place tomorrow morning at daybreak.'[116]

Oster's disclosures had no noticeable result. The Dutch did not really believe the news and were taken totally by surprise when the attack actually began; the Belgians alerted their troops at 3 a.m. on 10 May, far too late to be effective.[117] The well-worn statement, therefore, that Oster's treachery cost thousands of German soldiers their lives, is quite wrong; it is not of major significance, however, for any assessment of Oster's behaviour.

Oster was well aware of the danger that his betrayal might result in the loss, not only of his own life but that of many other German soldiers. He calculated that, should the *Wehrmacht* suffer an initial defeat as a consequence of his warnings, casualties might amount to 40,000. Wrestling with his conscience, however, he concluded that such casualties must be accepted in face of the certainty that, failing an initial defeat, the war, with its millions of victims and untold misery and destruction, would almost certainly be a long one. His reasoning, accepted with all its consequences by Beck, was as follows:[118] formal legal scruples could no longer carry weight in a fight against a demon of destruction like Hitler, to whom the word 'humanity' meant nothing; the object must be to prevent as much damage, misery and death as was possible. Membership of the military machine carried with it at least a share of the responsibility; every effort must be made to mitigate this load of guilt which no excuses put forward by those of feeble conscience could remove. Like Beck, Witzleben and, at least until early 1940, Brauchitsch and Halder also, Oster was convinced that the western offensive would fail and be brought to a halt with catastrophic losses; it should therefore be stopped and not merely be caused to fail after it had begun.

The most effective method of preventing Hitler carrying out his plan was to demonstrate to him that the Dutch and Belgians had taken far-reaching counter-measures in good time; this would imply loss of the surprise factor and make a rapid advance impossible. Hitler always wanted quick success; patience and caution were not in his nature.[119] If, however, in spite of everything the offensive took place, and there was every indication that it would, then the anticipated defeat must be brought about as soon as possible and with the smallest number of casualties; otherwise the longer the war dragged on, the greater would be the casualties and destruction on both sides, the stronger and more unyielding would be the enemy front and the smaller the prospects of a reasonable peace.

Oster's purpose was not to damage the *Reich* or his country. It was precisely the opposite. Neither actually nor theoretically can there therefore be any question of treachery. Hitler had begun and was pursuing a vast bloody war of conquest which according to the dictates of common sense and any realistic appreciation of the situation could only do damage to Germany; of this all knowledgeable experts were convinced and their conviction was confirmed by events. Objectively, therefore, there can be no question of Oster's 'treachery' having done damage to Germany.

Opinions about Oster will continue to range from condemnation to approval. The question is one of a man's conscience and of assessing his action in a wider context than that of formal legality and the nation-state. After the war the Western Allies were only too ready to accuse the German people, including the military leaders, of lack of moral courage because they had done nothing to overthrow Hitler, had not emigrated abroad or had not fought against the regime; yet even the Allies regarded Oster as a morally despicable traitor.[120] General Winkelman, the Dutch Commander-in-Chief, described Oster as a 'miserable fellow', whereupon Colonel Sas replied that he had never met so bold or courageous a character.[121] As these two remarks show clearly, the question is whether one is thinking in terms of men or organizations. Oster was only too well aware of this problem when he said to Sas: 'People may well say that I am a traitor but in reality I am not. I regard myself as a better German than all those who are trotting along behind Hitler. It is both my purpose and my duty to liberate Germany, and with her the world, from this plague.'[122]

PART IV/INTERNAL POLITICAL PLANS

13 SchmidNoerr

One of the earliest constitutional drafts came from the circle centred on Oster, Heinz and Liedig. It was produced in the summer of 1937 by Professor Friedrich Alfred SchmidNoerr.[1] Its centrepiece is the 'community of the people' (*Volksgemeinschaft*) – 'the community is above everything except the law of morality'. In the preamble alone *Volksgemeinschaft* appears more than forty times, practically in every sentence. The community, the draft says, is linked to the European Christian tradition and aims at peaceful coexistence with all peoples. Freedom for all forms of belief and thought is guaranteed but only 'in so far as it is compatible with the spirit and existence of the community'. Anyone 'of German origin as to one quarter of his blood' belongs to the community but 'respect and a guarantee of their rights' is promised to 'resident minorities of foreign race or origin'. The German *Reich* is defined as the contiguous area inhabited by Germans; it should be divided into regions (*Gaue*) 'which would be largely self-administering'.

The constitution was to be corporative in form, the *Reich* consisting of the independent *Reich* corporations* (ecclesiastical, administrative including legal, defence including the police) and the independent state corporations (farmers, workers, craftsmen, business and industry, commerce, education, science and the arts). Women, whether married or single, formed a corporation of their own. All corporations possessed equal rights and were 'royal'; they were to be self-administering but were responsible to the community and the *Reich*. The corporations had 'limits' but these could be exceeded in any direction by the members provided certain regulations were observed. The right of all forms of association was explicitly guaranteed, but equally explicitly, political parties formed the exception to this. Formation of any association was to be under the supervision of legally established bodies representing the corporation and of overseers designated by them or of authorities appointed by the associations themselves.

The three *Reich* corporations were represented only in the *Reich* House of corporations, the state corporations only in the Regional Chambers of Corporations; the latter, however, were to send ten representatives, at least one from each state corporation, to the *Reich* House of Corporations. The tasks both of the Regional Chambers and the *Reich* House were self-administration

* In this Part the word 'corporation' has been used to translate the German word '*Stand*' (pl. *Stände*). Its meaning is similar to that of the word 'estates' in its mediaeval sense. [Translator]

and 'advice to the *Reich* administration'. A sort of Upper House was to be formed from a 'meritocracy', a personal, not hereditary, aristocracy. Members of this aristocracy were to be elected for life by their corporations and, after a two-stage process of recommendation, confirmed in office by the 'People's King' (*Volkskönig*). They constituted a Council of State which was 'the supreme supervisory authority of the *Reich*', could act for the People's King and at the same time formed both the electoral college and source of candidates for future Kings (the latter not necessarily). It was not, however, clear how the People's King was to be elected.

The monarch was the 'incumbent of the supreme office in the State and administrator of the *Reich*'; he was to be sworn in to the community (not to the constitution); 'since he carries responsibility for the administration of the *Reich*, he is, in this capacity, head of the community'. No corporation could therefore control him or call him to account; if, however, the Council of State raised objection to the actions of the monarch on three occasions, he became 'subject to the law of the community which elected him'. In principle he was elected for life but could be deposed. He must be over forty years of age on assuming office.

Like the People's King the *Reich* Corporations owed their duty to the community; they swore their oath to the community, never to an individual, not even the People's King. The oath could only be invalidated in one way – if a member of a *Reich* Corporation was expelled from the community, either with his consent or as a punishment. The community was the guardian of the law; it would permit no exceptional proceedings outside the law; it guaranteed work to all citizens and, so far as possible, freedom to make their way and prosper; corporations had no special prerogatives. Freedom of the press and public disputation were guaranteed but they must remain within the limits set 'by the spirit and continuance of the community and by the security provisions against treason towards the community evidenced by any attempt to disturb, reduce or otherwise weaken it'. Any attempt to form a party, for instance, would constitute treason; any form of extraordinary or secret association and any attempt to obtain special rights or privileges was foreign to the concept of the community of the people.

The object therefore was to do away with the pluralist society, with the parliamentary system, in which special-interest groups could legally be represented or irresponsible demagogues come to power, with the system of 'party reaction', with disunity, and to substitute a community without conflicts.[2] Absolutism at the top and egalitarianism in the community of the people – both were unrealistic, the draft said, and so rotten at the roots. Whither the ideal of majority rule had led, it continued, could be seen by all.

The draft evidenced a clear aversion to anything inefficient, anything which did not function smoothly and well. It failed to explain, however, how the new arrangements to be set up in place of the old, could function. How were corporations to be prevented representing their own interests or even allying themselves with other corporations against third parties? This would be tantamount to formation of a party and that would be treason. Since the monarch was not fully independent, the constitution would inevitably be enforced by the Council of State acting as a dictatorial body. The ideal of the community of the people in which there would be no majority, no conflict and no political parties remained an ideal and unattainable.

This constitutional draft is a particularly glaring example of the political ineptitude of many of Hitler's opponents. Nevertheless rejection of the past while retaining that which suited the German character, and the ideal of freedom from conflict were very widespread ideas. This should not surprise — pragmatists deal with each situation as it arises rather than planning for the future; their voice was hardly likely to be heard in this context. The draft also evidenced, however, the reliance which had to be placed on authoritarian procedures in order to achieve this absence of conflict, at least in theory. Admittedly the rights of assembly and association were guaranteed but only in so far as they did not 'disturb' the community. In no other way could 'harmonious living' by the community of the people be substituted for party strife.

14 Hassell

A draft prepared in January and February 1940 by the former Ambassador, Ulrich von Hassell, after discussion with Beck, Goerdeler and Popitz, is not quite so radical as that of Professor SchmidNoerr but its basic ideas are similar.[1] Others contributed at least as much as Hassell – Professor Johannes Popitz, the Prussian Finance Minister, Dr Jens Peter Jessen, Professor of Political Science (who worked in the Army General Staff during the war) and Dr Erwin Planck, former State Secretary and then director of a steel firm.

The first point announced in Hassell's 'programme' was the determination of the (new) German government to continue the war until peace, the existence and independence of the German people and also 'the old *Reich* frontier' with Poland were assured. This is only comprehensible in the light of the situation of 1940 and against the background of the blitz victory over Poland – not welcomed by Hassell but a fact nevertheless. His other conditions for peace were freedom of the individual and his legitimate activities, integrity of justice and the law, a state based on the rule of law, observance by the administration and the police of the principles of morality, respect for human life in general and of minorities in particular. The positions and functions usurped by the Party bosses must return to the civil service; the State must cease squandering money; a sensible foreign policy must be adopted aimed at reduction of armaments and cultural and economic exchanges.

The idea of unity figured largely in Hassell's programme. Many Germans considered the unity of the 'community of the people' to be one of National-Socialism's main achievements; it was not merely for this reason, however, that Hassell wished to safeguard it but because it was desirable in itself. The Nazi Party with all its branches was to be dissolved and its property confiscated; the Labour Service, however, should continue in a different form and the Labour Front should be reorganized, not abolished. The various social groupings were by no means to be left free to organize cooperation between themselves.

These were to be the guiding principles for the initial transitional period of regency; they were not, however, dictated by considerations of temporary expediency, as further study of the programme shows. The regency was to set up a constitutional council under the chairmanship of the Minister of the Interior; this was to work out organizational proposals based 'on the principle of a unified German state'. There must be 'cooperation by the people' in the political life of the *Reich* and 'control of the state based on local and corporate self-government'. There was no mention of a parliamentary system nor any provision for universal, equal, secret and free elections in future. There could therefore be no question of democracy nor is there any mention of it. The draft does not reveal how future governments were to be brought into being; it merely says that, if dictatorship by a group or an individual is to be avoided, something like a 'meritocracy' must be created.[2] The emphasis placed on the professional civil service as opposed to political officialdom, which had turned into rule by Party bosses under the Nazi regime, seems to point in this direction.

The liberties enshrined in all liberal constitutions are not explicitly guaranteed in Hassell's and Popitz's drafts; instead they refer to 'true freedom'. Admittedly they propose to reestablish at once a state based on the rule of law. The *Wehrmacht*, however, was to take its oath, not to the state nor even to the community but to the regency and regional commanders were to have full executive powers. With the best will in the world therefore, this amounted in practice to a military dictatorship.

Science and teaching were declared free from restraint, as was also the press during the post-war period. The limits of freedom, however, were to be those imposed by the 'requirements of state security'; in the case of the written and printed word, the people's security was even invoked in addition to that of the state – 'after the war the security of the state and nation shall be protected by legislation against abuses in the literary field'. Moreover, as already pointed out, these are no emergency measures but plans and principles applicable to the period after the end of the emergency.

However well meant these proposals, however sincerely men like Beck and Hassell must be credited with the determination to establish justice, the rule of law and humanity, they were certainly not liberal. So long as they themselves were in power, perhaps in association with Goerdeler, their regime might have been tolerable; but what might happen afterwards? Not even an attempt was made to provide assurances against abuses, though it is, of course, true to say that unless the people, the electors, the press and the public in general, are willing to exert some control any constitutional instrument given them, however good, is of little value.

15 Popitz

A 'Provisional Basic Law' drafted primarily by Popitz and also originating about the turn of the year 1939–1940, followed somewhat similar lines.[1] According to this 'the supreme law of action' was to consist of the 'rules of propriety and good morals'. In view of the appalling brutalization and the murderous perverted savagery of the Nazi regime, this was undoubtedly called for. But habits and ideas concerning what is 'proper' can change considerably. Who is to decide whether and when it is 'proper' to shoot a fugitive, to suppress an opposition campaign or marry a divorcee? Would it be 'proper' to accuse the government of corruption or a mistaken foreign policy? If the rules of propriety and good morals were to constitute the 'supreme law of action', it may be useless promising in the next sentence 'independence of the judiciary and the protection of personal liberty, of the family and of property', quite apart from the potential contradiction between protection of the family and protection of personal liberty.

There followed further 'laws of action': 'Every German must so comport himself that the good of the community is not affected and no damage done to the good name of Germany'. Every man had a right to 'a way of life worthy of a human being', to an old age pension, to 'sickness and unemployment benefits' and to housing permitting a decent family life – but all this only applied to those 'who did their duty to the people and the state'. The economy as a whole was to be state-directed; in the case of agriculture the object was a distribution of property conducive to 'the highest possible yield'; schools and other 'educational establishments of all grades' were charged with instilling into the younger generation destined 'for service to the state, the churches, the sciences, art and industry' the necessary knowledge combined with the principles of 'physical fitness, character and morals'; religious instruction in the schools was described as an 'indispensable method of education'. There was therefore no freedom either of learning or of conscience despite the dictum that 'research, teaching and art' were to be 'restricted only in so far as was necessary for external and internal security and as was required by the necessary respect for the spiritual and moral heritage of the people'. Even the wording threw the door wide open to arbitrary interpretation.

On this point the courts might conceivably intervene but Popitz, the lawyer, says remarkably little on this subject, although he makes a point of stressing the independence of the administrative courts. Apart from this, however, the judiciary is only mentioned in passing and in the same breath as the administration of, for instance, taxes, customs, railways and the post office. Naturally judges were civil servants; this was taken so much for granted that it is not even mentioned; they were to be appointed by the government, in other words by the head of state with the agreement of the Chancellor, or possibly merely by the minister responsible. There are numerous methods of bringing to heel judges who are too 'independent' – always assuming that the law allows them to be so. They can be moved frequently or passed over for promotion. Since there was to be no parliament, abuses would be difficult to deal with; alternatively their elimination would depend almost exclusively on the goodwill of the central 'authority'.

This presages a strong, centralized system. The *Länder* (provinces) were to be regions of the *Reich* administratively and only secondarily 'local self-governing bodies'. 'At the head of the *Land* as an administrative region of the *Reich* is the Regent [*Statthalter*]'; he was at the same time *Reich* Government Commissar 'supervising the *Land* in its capacity as a local body'. This puts an end to any question of independent self-government; the *Statthalter* or *Reich* Commissar, and through him the *Reich* government, had the last word on affairs in a *Land*. The *Landeshauptmann* (lit: *Land* headman – senior minister in a *Land*) as 'supreme self-government authority of the *Land*', was in a miserable position compared with the *Statthalter*. Here again there was to be no elected parliament, so that self-government was a total illusion.

The *Länder*, already designated as administrative regions of the *Reich*, were to be further combined into governmental regions, which again were administrative regions of the *Reich*. Subordinate districts and boroughs were to be both 'administrative areas and local self-governing bodies'. This ran counter to any idea of federalism. The *Reich* government and *Reich* administration were fully centralized and their unity explicitly emphasized.

At the top level of the *Reich* distribution of power was little better. There was to be a provisional Head of State known as Regent of the German *Reich*; this left open the possibility of restoring the monarchy which, as Otto John says, at least between 1938 and 1941 formed part of Beck's, Popitz's, Goerdeler's, Oster's and Dohnanyi's programme and, subject to a plebiscite, was also accepted by Wilhelm Leuschner and Jakob Kaiser.[2] In practice the Head of State was to have the prerogatives of a monarch: he represented the *Reich* internationally; he was Commander-in-Chief of the *Wehrmacht*; he could appoint or dismiss the Chancellor (no parliament had anything to do with this); he could appoint and dismiss civil servants and military officers; he had the right of pardon and bestowal of titles and decorations. It is not, therefore, clear what purpose was served by the provision that 'for all orders and instructions' the Head of State required the counter-signature of the Chancellor or relevant minister. Anyone who refused to counter-sign could be dismissed. In the exercise of his military command, moreover, apart from the appointment and dismissal of officers the Head of State did not even require a counter-signature.

The Chancellor and government were therefore primarily executive agencies of the Head of State. They *promulgated* laws after hearing the views of the Council of State and Head of State. The government's budget was controlled only by a Chamber of Accounts (whose officials were to be appointed by the Head of State).

The Council of State was a body of notables since it consisted of 'men who had shown themselves worthy of the people's confidence by their achievements, their ability and their personality'. They did not have actually to possess this confidence; they were not elected but appointed by the Head of State. Under this constitution no one was elected; the word election does not even appear. Apart from these 'worthies' all *Reich* ministers and *Statthalter* belonged to the Council of State (but not the senior ministers of the *Länder* – that would have smacked of federalism). The Council of State was to 'represent the people in its entirety' but not by election; hopefully its motives were to be a sense of propriety, goodwill and the dictates of conscience. Only to a limited degree could the Council be said to represent the people's interests. Later a 'broad-based body representing the people' was to be instituted; here again, however, there was no mention of elections and it was distinguished from the Council of State only in the breadth of its base – whatever that may mean.

As the logical sequel to all this, not only was the Nazi Party proscribed but the 'formation of new political associations' was flatly forbidden. Where elections and representative bodies did not exist, parties were unnecessary.

The general trend of the draft is therefore clear. Ritter has rightly described it as an expression of an enlightened absolutism, an instrument of 'dictatorship by senior officials remote from the people'.[3] Ritter maintains that, as a transitional solution, the draft was good, implying that a more democratic constitution would have been introduced later, but there can be little confidence in this. Admittedly, before the *coup* had even taken place, there was little purpose in drafting ideal constitutions; thought had to be concentrated on dealing with the immediate situation. When that had been done, since planning was the order of the day, something could be drafted dealing with the more distant future. But Popitz did not do this. His draft contained no provisions or promises holding out hope of democracy in the future. He was not even prepared to cancel forthwith the anti-Jewish discriminatory legislation and regulations, but only to suspend them 'until the final settlement'. Of course, Popitz did not have in mind what the Heydrichs and Himmlers referred to as the 'final solution'; but he seems to have wanted to expel at least a great number of Jews.[4]

The picture of an authoritarian illiberal regime is completed by Popitz's 'Guidelines for application of the law on the state of siege' – the draft of the actual law has been lost.[5] For the period of the state of siege plenary powers were granted to *Wehrkreis* (Military District) commanders, as was inevitable. To provide the necessary counter-weight, civil servants were to be attached to them. *Gauleiter*, Nazi District Leaders, senior SS and police commanders were to be arrested. The specious, discredited idea of 'protective custody', however, so misused by the Nazis, was not considered suitable for this purpose especially since it was also to be employed for persons who were actually threatened.

In late 1939 and early 1940 Popitz's draft came near to being implemented. It was not – for the reasons given in Part III above. Subsequently other drafts seemed more likely to provide the guidelines for German political developments. In 1943 and 1944 the plans of the so-called 'Kreisau Circle', in which many of the younger members of the opposition met, seemed quite as likely to provide the decisive influence as those of Dr Goerdeler, so long the undisputed civilian leader of the opposition. Initially, however, Goerdeler's plans were in the forefront of people's minds, although Popitz's draft still had much support in his own immediate circle.

16 Goerdeler

Goerdeler's ideas are recorded in numerous memoranda and drafts. The two most important, 'The Aim' written late in 1941 and 'Thoughts in the condemned cell — September 1944' have been fully or partially published and at least parts of many others are in print.[1] Goerdeler has frequently been accused of being a reactionary. To some extent this results from the vehemence with which differing points of view were often argued between the various political tendencies in the opposition. In Goerdeler's case the accusation is unjustified. Admittedly he, like Popitz, wished to avoid the pitfalls of mass democracy; he was concerned to form an élite (whereas Popitz simply assumed that an élite would exist); he looked for 'de-agglomeration' and some stable form of authority. This he wished to achieve, however, through liberalism and decentralization; his stable authority should be so constructed that it guaranteed rather than suppressed freedom.[2] In working out the ideas set out in 'The Aim' Goerdeler was in contact not only with Hassell and the 'Freiburg Circle' headed by Professors Constantin von Dietze, Adolf Lampe and Gerhard Ritter but also with Trott, Yorck and Moltke of the 'Kreisau Circle'; later, from the end of 1941 he was in touch with socialists like Leuschner, Kaiser and Habermann. Goerdeler was always ready to compromise and he adopted many of his friends' ideas. He had his own ideas too, however, and they were anything but reactionary, although the machinery for implementing his plans was not always entirely practical.

Popitz together with Hassell and Jessen was violently opposed to Goerdeler's plans; the great difference between them and those of Popitz is clearly to be seen in 'The Aim'. Like Popitz, Goerdeler wishes to reestablish the rule of law and propriety, but he also wants freedom. In the early paragraphs on the principles of internal policy is to be found this: 'All restrictions on freedom of intellect, conscience and research will be lifted *forthwith*.'[3] This is clear and unequivocal — no mere vague future paradise. Further: 'In principle the press and literature will be free. Failure to grant such freedom indicates a pusillanimous government or a stupid people.' The only exceptions to the grant of this freedom were 'the criminal and the good-for-nothing'. Under the provision for administration of the law, however, only the regular courts could decree who should be included in such categories. Similarly, in his 1944 draft, Goerdeler thought that the press should be entirely free, subject to a binding obligation to tell the truth.

Goerdeler placed great hopes in the educational value of the truth and of responsibility. Almost every sentence on the subject of education emphasizes this. Religious instruction is indispensable, he says; but it must be given by people – schoolmasters, clergy or the laity – who practise what they preach. Textbooks must *forthwith* be cleared of every form of untruth. In education the truth must take the place of propaganda and party indoctrination. In industry hourly wages should be replaced by piecework; it was more 'genuine' and better calculated to produce responsibility and efficiency. Instead of the automatic sickness benefits and old age pensions paid for out of taxes as advocated by Dr Robert Ley, Leader of the German Labour Front, there should be adequate insurance schemes which workers and employees should, at least partially, finance themselves.

In addition to veracity and responsibility self-government was one of the basic concepts in Goerdeler's constitutional ideas. As far as possible, he considered, parishes (*Gemeinden*) and districts (*Bezirke*) should run themselves, not however without some supervision by the state; the same applied to colleges and student bodies and even the churches, which to this extent were to be divorced from the state and would have to fend for themselves, though they were still to retain the right to levy church taxes. In Goerdeler's view, however, they should be sparing in the use of this right to avoid large-scale walk-outs. He did not commit himself on the question whether the state should continue to collect taxes for the churches or not. Divorce of church and state would, of course, be neither possible nor complete so long as the official tax offices continued to support the church with their authority, the dread which they inspired and their punitive and executive powers more or less backed by the authority of the law.

There are certain other deficiencies in Goerdeler's constitutional plans. The main point is, however, that they were liberal and attempted to avoid the errors of the Bismarckian and Weimar periods, as also of course those of the Nazi regime. Confidence in freedom, in educational precepts and in the effect of public dissemination of the truth is as essential as a good constitution. According to the 1941 draft the Nazi Party with its affiliated organizations was to lose all its prerogatives including that of carrying arms, all its official functions and all its rights but was not to be banned – 'Opinion must and will soon make itself clear spontaneously.' This confidence is the hallmark of both constitutional drafts, that of late 1941 and of September 1944. Men, Goerdeler said, must want and actively seek to attain that which their constitution could hold out to them and give them; alternatively they must learn to want it – 'There is no such thing as a constitution which works *automatically*.'

In Goerdeler's view the right people would only be found in the right places if the state were built up from below; this was to be achieved by a complicated electoral system, partly direct and partly indirect. At the lowest level only the direct system applied, since only in his own restricted circle did the elector 'know' his candidate well enough. Parishes (*Gemeinden*) were to be divided into the smallest possible areas, in each of which four candidates should stand and the one who amassed the most votes be elected. Candidates must be at least thirty years of age and be resident in their area; trade unions and professional associations should each put forward one candidate and 'political movements' two. The candidate elected then became a councillor of the parish.

After the parish council the next rung was the district (*Kreis*) council; its members were elected by parish councils. Members must live in the district but need not be members of the parish council.

Members of district councils in turn elected their representatives for the *Land* (provincial) and *Gau* (regional) councils; to be eligible they must have been members of a parish or district council for five years 'to guarantee administrative experience'.

Finally the regional council elected their chairman (*Landeshauptmann*); as head of the administration in a region, however, he possessed little of the power wielded by either the present-day or previous minister-presidents. He had no cabinet, no seat on any *Reich* body and was under the supervision of a *Reich Statthalter*, a sort of centrally-appointed governor. He (the *Landeshauptmann*) was assisted by 'provincial councillors' (*Landesräte*), chosen, however, not by him but by the regional council. Both he and his assistants required confirmation by the *Reich Statthalter*.

Finally members of regional councils elected 150 deputies to the *Reichstag* out of a total of 300; these 150 had to be 35 years of age, have spent five years in some official unpaid capacity and be resident in their region. They need not therefore necessarily be members of their regional council but·whence they were to come is not made clear. The remaining 150 candidates were to be elected, as those for parish councils, by majority vote, any German over twenty-five years of age being eligible to vote. For these elections to the *Reichstag* 150 constituencies were to be formed, distributed throughout the *Reich*; candidates had to be residents of their constituencies.

In addition to the *Reichstag* which was thus elected half directly and half indirectly, there was to be an Upper House known as the *Reich* Chamber of Corporations (*Reichsständehaus*). It consisted of 'leaders of *Reich* groups (industry)', in other words professional organizations, presidents of *Reich* Chambers of Commerce (all presumably elected by their Chambers), three Evangelical and three Catholic bishops, rectors of universities and a number of trade union council members equivalent to that of the industrial and professional representatives. Finally there were to be fifty Germans of repute drawn from any source; they had to be fifty years of age and be appointed by the Head of State.

Whether this was liable to produce a good distribution of powers can only be judged by examining the attributes and methods of the various individual bodies. This shows that, despite the stress laid upon them, the responsibilities of the regions (*Gaue*) were in fact limited and the *Reich* was comparatively highly centralized. The regions administered universities, welfare and health services, land improvement schemes, regional district courts, regional roads, certain other functions on behalf of the districts or delegated by the *Reich* and finally their own property. There is no mention of taxes and so, apart from revenue produced from their own property, regions, districts and parishes were dependent on the *Reich* for money. *Pecunia nervus est rerum* – without some independent source of money there could be little question of self-government. Goerdeler almost certainly overestimated the benevolence of the future *Reich* Treasury.

The *Reich* and the central government were to be solely or primarily responsible for law, economic policy including social and labour legislation, internal policy, foreign policy, financial policy, basic principles for educational and church affairs (again calling in question the reality of the divorce between church and state), principles for reconstruction and public works, *Reich* railway, postal and air communications and finally for defence.

The *Reich* government was headed by the Chancellor; ministers who did not approve his general policy must resign. The cabinet did not have to enjoy the confidence of the two representative houses but the Head of State was called upon to dismiss the cabinet and nominate a new government should this be demanded by a simple majority in the *Reichstag* and *Reich* Chamber of Corporations or by a two-thirds majority of the *Reichstag*, a new cabinet being appointed at the same time. Laws could be promulgated by the government with or without the agreement of the *Reichstag*; cancellation of legislation promulgated without agreement required majorities similar to those for dismissal of the cabinet – a simple majority of both Houses or a two-thirds majority in one. One is tempted to say with Hans Mommsen that this was an emergency constitution intended to operate in normal circumstances; many other aspects also invite criticism.

Goerdeler was never one to cling rigidly to formulae, although he almost invariably laid stress on economic principles and their application to constitutional questions. He never over-emphasized consistency and was invariably optimistic and liberal. In his 1941 draft strikes and lock-outs were forbidden; at the same time, however, he emphasized that life in general, and particularly in industry, was a struggle, in this case a competitive struggle. In this draft no provision was made for the nationalization of certain industries; the working class as such was only to be permitted to participate in public life to a limited degree. Participation in industry was to be granted to the workers, this being one of the fundamental demands of the trade union leaders. According to Dr Elfriede Nebgen, a close associate of Jakob Kaiser, they did not want any more institutionalized form of participation in public life since they were opposed to anything tending to introduce corporatism.[4] However the trade union leaders had long striven for a single united union; although of itself it would not have led to the institution of a corporate state, it would have been a step in that direction.

In his 1944 draft, however, Goerdeler proposed large-scale participation in public life by the workers and their organizations, at least during the electoral process; he put them on a parity with the representatives of the employers and professional groups. He also proposed to nationalize mineral resources and monopoly concerns serving the economy as a whole such as the railways, postal services and producers of electricity, gas and water. Trade unions were encouraged to run their own economic undertakings.

All this was to be brought about primarily through the formation of the united trade union which the trade union leaders wanted. They proposed to organize it in units embracing each profession. After working with trade union leaders during the years 1941 to 1944 Goerdeler adopted these ideas as his own.[5] Goerdeler may therefore have been more inclined towards a corporate system than the trade union leaders, though both tended that way, whether they consciously admitted the fact or not. Nevertheless the large political parties restricted in number which the trade union leaders wanted would have formed an effective counterweight to any corporate developments. At one point, however, Goerdeler seems to have wished to replace the political parties entirely by a 'popular movement' encompassing all classes and regions.[6]

It is clear that Goerdeler, particularly under the influence of his socialist and liberal-democrat friends from southern Germany like Robert Bosch, was fully prepared for change, concessions and new developments. In his draft of September 1944 he says in so many words: 'This is the approximate form of the *Reich* constitution and administration.' Subsequent changes in the electoral system were equally allowed for. The idea of avoiding the formation of political parties as long as possible is unrealistic; the draft, however, leaves open the possibility of formation of groups representing socio-economic and political interests.

Under Goerdeler's constitution obstacles to the overthrow of a government were considerable. It was highly unlikely that this would be demanded by a majority of the *Reich* Chamber of Corporations and equally unlikely that the *Reichstag* would muster a two-thirds majority. On the other hand there was no advantage in merely making it easier to overthrow the government, as France's example in the pre-war period had shown.

None of this is crucial, however. Had there been a successful *coup* in 1941–44 a constitution on Goerdeler's lines would probably not have come into force. There could easily have been a military dictatorship against which Goerdeler's idealism would have been impotent; had things gone more smoothly a constituent assembly might quickly have asserted its rights; had none of this happened, Goerdeler's own comment remains valid – that the best constitution does not automatically guarantee justice and democracy; the principal requirement for a democracy, if it is to function properly, is the goodwill of its citizens.

Goerdeler's draft should not, therefore, be taken too literally but regarded as a basis for discussion put forward by a man recognized as one of the leaders of the opposition but with no great backing in any of its groups, and whose military backing depended on Beck. Nevertheless under Goerdeler's draft there was at least adequate opportunity for a democratically-minded parliament insistent on its rights to keep the government under control. In particular it prescribed that the government invariably required 'the agreement of both Houses' for its budget, taxation legislation, treaties with foreign countries and customs regulations. No government can rule without money and if parliament insisted on control of expenditure and of short-term legislation on the subject, the government would be forced to render account of every step it took before it could get further money. If, added to this, resources for long-term requirements were forthcoming only on a case-by-case basis, the government could not afford to behave undemocratically.

The tentative nature of Goerdeler's drafts is further emphasized by the position allotted to the Head of State. For the first five years the position was to be filled by a Regent-General proposed by the government and elected by the Upper House. Elections would not be possible until after demobilization but a Head of State was required forthwith and he should be the most popular figure possible to ensure that the *coup* was acceptable to the public. The next Head of State would be elected by the *Reichstag* and the Chamber of Corporations.

The idea of a restoration of the monarchy was put forward on many occasions before 1944 and a wide variety of candidates was discussed. Jakob Kaiser referred to Prince Rupprecht of Bavaria as a possible *Reich* Regent; Goerdeler looked to Fritz, Kaiser Wilhelm's grandson in England; Colonel-General von Hammerstein and Beck insisted on the legitimate successor in the event of a restoration of the House of Hohenzollern.[7] Finally Klaus Bonhoeffer and Otto John were continually putting forward the name of Prince Louis Ferdinand and arranged meetings between him and Jakob Kaiser, Leuschner, Wirmer, Ewald von Kleist-Schmenzin and Ulrich von Hassell. The Crown Prince refused to be a candidate and early in 1943 Prince Louis Ferdinand also withdrew.

Goerdeler thought a hereditary monarchy to be the best solution but neither could nor would commit himself. The important point seemed to him to be that the Head of State or monarch should not rule but should carry out representative functions and be the guardian of the constitution.

In the so-called racial question Goerdeler's position was one in favour of separation. In his memorandum, 'The Aim', he wrote:[8] 'A new order for the position of the *Jews* appears necessary in the entire world; for there are movements afoot everywhere that cannot be stopped without some organic order; they will lead to injustices, inhuman treatment and at least to an unsatisfactory disorder, unless an organic structure is found. It is a matter of course that the Jewish people belong to a different race . . . But the world can come to rest only if the Jewish people are given a realistic opportunity to found and maintain their own state. An appropriate territory with acceptable physical conditions could be found easily enough in Canada or in South America. Once this issue is settled through the cooperation of the Powers, there will be a natural development of the German position: The Jew is a citizen of his Jewish state, and an alien in Germany: as such he has the same right to engage in trades and commerce as any other alien. But, just as any Englishman or Frenchman, he cannot be a public servant, nor can he be elected to sit in popular representative assemblies or vote in such elections.' This is followed by a number of exceptions; exceptions are suggested on the basis of military service during World War I, and on the basis of the possession of German citizenship before 1914 and, with further modifications, before 1871. Thus the majority of those falling under the restrictions would have been Jews who entered Germany since 1914, mostly from East European countries.

Goerdeler did not change his views on the 'racial question' in the light of the abominable crimes committed against the Jews since 1938, perhaps rather the contrary: what he was looking for was a realistic and permanent settlement that would make such crimes impossible in future.[9] He wrote in the belief that Jews living amongst other peoples in great numbers would always, again and again, become victims of persecution. It can be debated whether special discriminatory laws and the resulting separation were the best method. It is a fact, however, that even the most liberal and democratic nations, such as the Swiss or the British, have not found it possible in the 20th century to do without special legislation aimed at certain groups of foreigners; and it is another fact that leading members of the Alliance against Germany finally founded the Jewish state and thus implemented a proposal that many besides Goerdeler had advocated for decades. In addition to eliminating the possibility of future troubles, Goerdeler wanted to make restitution for injustices done, so far as that was possible: 'In the past years [he wrote in autumn of 1941] an injustice has been done in Germany by expropriation and destruction etc. of Jewish property and life that we *cannot* condone before our conscience and our history. The possibilities of a new order can only be examined and entered into when the full scope of this injustice has been determined. It will then be seen that we must take the initiative in seeking a method of healing, with a view to our position in the world as well as to our own conscience.' It was taken for granted, Goerdeler concluded, that all discriminatory regulations aimed at Jews in such matters as rationing of food and housing, in cultural activities, in the style of personal names, must be suspended immediately, and living conditions in the ghettos of the occupied territories had to be raised to a level fit for human beings.

However averse one may be to Goerdeler's draft and however insistent on pointing out the contradictions therein, the fact remains that he himself did not regard it as final and it would not have been so in practice. Argument, proposal, counter-proposal and compromise are the essence of politics and democracy. Goerdeler's draft offered adequate opportunities for opposition if anyone wished to take them.[10] Those who say that, under Goerdeler's draft, opposition would have been practically impossible, are refusing in advance to place any confidence in the democrats of the future; alternatively they are looking for a sealed-pattern solution which, by providing the perfect democratic constitution, will create the perfect democratic citizens. Real life is never so abstract as a constitutional draft. Ritter has said aptly that, had a Prince of the Hohenzollerns like Louis Ferdinand placed himself at the head of the German resistance movement and publicly staked his life against tyranny, Germany would have looked quite differently both at the monarchy and the House of Hohenzollern and 'the painful memories of November 1918 would have vanished abruptly'.[11] In any case some trust in the goodwill and capacity for adaptation both of rulers and ruled is indispensable. Alternatively does anyone think that the comparatively favourable development of post-1945

West Germany has been due to more trustworthy direction and supervision than could have been provided by Germans? This would be justification for those constitutional drafts from the resistance movement which were far more authoritarian than those of Goerdeler.

17 The Kreisau Circle

As a result of numerous meetings and discussions a number of drafts were produced by the 'Kreisau Circle', the most important in July 1941, May and October 1942 and June 1943;[1] they must be regarded as having the same provisional character as those of Goerdeler and judged accordingly; they were even further removed from reality. Although the 'Kreisau Circle' was at one on a number of principles, these were so broadly stated that much was left in the air, primarily for the sake of agreement. The Circle was so named after Graf von Moltke's estate where the group frequently met. It had no established leader, however, and more often met in Berlin, though not in full conclave; it consisted of highly independent personalities holding views of their own. They were both able and willing to compromise, for they knew that politics without compromise are impossible. In the discussion phase, however, they clung to their own views. Until the very end of opposition differences of view within the group remained on such important questions as the expropriation of real estate and heavy industry, support for an attempted assassination, the build-up of the post-war administration and confessional or interdenominational schools. Since the *coup* failed, the pressure of events required to bring about some practical consensus on such matters never materialized.

It is seldom possible, therefore, to refer to the views or attitude of the 'Kreisau Circle' as a whole without being guilty of major over-simplification; the alternative is to restrict oneself to those proposals on which, at least for a time, the majority of the Circle were agreed. This is what I propose to do here.[2] I do not propose to deal in detail with the political, economic and social views of the Circle. For the purposes of this book it is more important to examine the attitude and influence exerted on the attempted *coup* and its preparation by the personalities involved in the Circle. I shall be reverting to this subject in Chapter 39 below.

Different though they were in many respects, there were many parallels between Goerdeler's ideas and those of the 'Kreisau Circle'.[3] In both stress is laid on Christianity as the basis of society, of the reestablishment of the rule of law and of freedom of belief and conscience. On some points, however, the principles of the Circle were even more far-reaching but in the process they forfeited a considerable degree of realism and practicality. In the 1943 draft, for instance, entitled 'Principles of Reorganization' it is laid down that the dignity of man must be inviolable and also that the right to work and own property must be 'under state protection without regard to race, nationality or belief'. How was the right to work and own property to be guaranteed in practice? What would people say if foreign capital obtained a decisive or even dominant influence in branches of German industry or the economy? The question is not meant to imply that such a development is essentially bad, merely that it would produce long faces followed by counter-measures which could be regarded as restrictions of the right to hold property. A further tendency to a sort of utopian socialism is to be seen when it is said that not only must the family as an institution be taken under state protection but also its daily requirements such as 'food, clothing, housing, a garden and health'.

The principles enunciated on work and the citizen's political activity, on the other hand, are very similar to those of Goerdeler – 'work must be so organized that it promotes a ready acceptance of responsibility'. This entailed professional continuation training and sharing of responsibility in the factory and the economy as a whole. The object was to reduce 'agglomeration' and give back some meaning and purpose to the life of the individual within his social environment. Similarly in the exercise of his personal political responsibility the individual should participate in the administration of small manageable communities. Working upwards from this point, elected representatives should participate in the build-up of the state and a community of peoples. The sequence led from the family to the parish and thence to the *Land* and the *Reich*, the principles and methods of self-government being applicable at each stage. According to a draft by Fritz-Dietlof Graf von der Schulenburg the *Länder* should not be too large in order to ensure that they were manageable; in any reorganization, however, account must be taken of the historical and cultural background.[4]

In contrast to that of Goerdeler, the electoral system provided for direct elections up to parish and district levels. Anyone over twenty-one could vote; fathers of families were entitled to an additional vote for each child (Goerdeler had only allowed one additional vote for a minimum of three children). Electoral districts were to be kept small to keep them within the purview of the electors. Nothing was said on the important questions of nomination of candidates, their number or their source; an unspecified number of electors was to agree on the subject. The draft equally contains nothing on the majority required – relative, absolute or other proportion.

At the level of the *Land* and the *Reich* elections were indirect. *Land* parliaments were elected by parish and district councils. A similar procedure was envisaged for large cities; there the district councils elected the borough council. Apart from military personnel any citizen over twenty-seven years of age could be elected; political officials, however, could not be candidates for borough councils, *Land* parliaments or the *Reichstag*. Moreover at least half of the representatives so elected might not be members of the parish or district councils which elected them.

The local government bodies produced by this somewhat obscure electoral system, however, were allotted, at least on the surface, far greater responsibilities than those of Goerdeler. In the Kreisau draft, for instance, the *Land* parliament had the right, not only to administer *Land* property but also to raise taxes; it drew up a budget and could promulgate laws; it chose the *Landeshauptmann* (senior minister of the *Land*) and the *Landesverweser* (*Land* administrator) who headed the *Land* administration for a period of twelve years. The senior minister headed a government composed of councillors. The *Land* administrator had to be confirmed by the *Reich* Regent (Head of State); he supervised the entire administration in the *Land* and appointed the *Land* officials – no mention of any elected body being entitled to propose them; he was responsible that *Reich* policy was implemented in his *Land*. He was Chairman of the *Land* Council, the composition of which was not explained but was presumably analogous to the Upper House at national level which was composed of leaders of industry and the professions and possibly also of trade union and community leaders. The *Land* administrator, therefore, constituted a powerful counter-weight to the senior minister. The federalism which might seem to be implied by the right to raise taxes and issue legislation, was perhaps unintentionally not of great importance in practice.[5]

The *Land* parliaments nevertheless retained a certain influence over *Reich* policy since they elected the members of the *Reichstag*. The procedure was highly complicated; its primary purpose was not to bring the will of the majority of citizens to bear on *Reich* policy but to place in leading positions the maximum number of men able and willing to accept responsibility. Goerdeler, with his requirement for five years' administrative experience, had laid far greater stress on this aspect; no such qualifications appeared in the Kreisau draft. This merely said in general terms that *Land* parliaments were to elect the *Reichstag* and that at least half of those elected – no figures were given – might not belong to *Land* parliaments. No indication was given of the source from which they were to be drawn.

Thus elected, the *Reichstag* was responsible for decisions on taxes, the budget and laws of the *Reich*. Again no clear or definite provisions were made for the production of legislation. The *Reich* government was under obligation to produce a draft – of the budget, for instance, but the *Reichstag* had only 'power of decision' on it. In the event of disagreement, therefore, was the government to act like Bismarck in 1862 or to resign? Nothing was said on this subject or on the vital question of the frequency of *Reichstag* sittings. The *Reichstag* could only ask questions and then decide. It chose the *Reich* Regent, the Head of State, but not the *Reich* government; this required only 'assent' from the *Reichstag*.

The implication is that the majority in the *Reichstag* should (or must) be in agreement with the Chancellor nominated by the *Reich* Regent. The point is not made clear. The departmental ministers who, together with the Chancellor, formed the government, were to be proposed by the Chancellor and appointed by the *Reich* Regent. They did not even require 'assent' from the *Reichstag*; there was therefore no parliamentary responsibility. A complicated procedure was designed to ensure that a Chancellor and his government could not remain in power for ever, even if backed by the Head of State.

The Chancellor could be dismissed by the Regent and his removal could also be requested (a binding request?) by the *Reichstag*; this required a 'qualified majority' and a simultaneous proposal for a new Chancellor. If the *Reich* Regent refused to appoint the Chancellor proposed, the result was an impasse.

In addition to the *Reichstag* there was an Upper House, the *Reich* Council (*Reichsrat*); it consisted of the *Land* administrators, not the senior ministers of the *Länder* who could have represented their regional interests, but of functionaries whose duty it was to represent the interests of the *Reich* in the *Länder*. Other members of the *Reich* Council were the President (Speaker) of the *Reichstag*, the President of the *Reich* Chamber of Commerce and an unspecified number of counsellors nominated for a term of eight years by the *Reich* Regent with the agreement of the government.[6] The Council was empowered to make proposals for the election of the *Reich* Regent and make recommendations to the *Reichstag*; it was also to act as a 'disciplinary court of appeal against the government or *Land* administrators'. It is not clear whether this implied that it was to act as a constitutional court or merely ensure observance of government regulations.

In this case too, as with all somewhat original constitutional arrangements, much would depend on how its provisions were interpreted, how they were used, what procedures were developed spontaneously, by case law, by reference to tradition or by habit, and how strong the tendency was to return to the old ways provided they proved effective. On the other hand there was a tendency, not always quite clear owing to imprecise drafting, to authoritarianism and concentration of political power; this must inevitably carry with it certain dangers and temptations. It is more than doubtful, for instance, whether the *Reich* Council, being independent of the electorate, could have acted as an effective counter-weight.[7]

Finally the Head of State, the *Reich* Regent, was elected by the *Reichstag* for a term of twelve years on a proposal from the *Reich* Council. He represented the *Reich*, he signed legislation, he was Commander-in-Chief of the *Wehrmacht* and Chairman of the *Reich* Council. He also had the vital prerogative of appointing and dismissing Chancellors. It is not stated whether he could dissolve the *Reichstag*, but since there was no other way out of an impasse, he presumably could. Although, therefore, the *Reichstag* had considerable, though not clearly defined authority, there was great concentration of power in the hands of the Regent. He could appoint and dismiss Chancellors and, if the general tenor of the draft has been correctly understood, he had no need to take account of the *Reichstag* in doing so; in the event of conflict he could disregard it. Since the Regent was elected for a defined term, there can have been no thought of a monarchy. Nevertheless twelve years is a very long period of office.

The Kreisau draft is really a draft of principles for a draft constitution. Its tendency is towards a strong central *Reich* authority produced and perpetuated by an élite. The emphasis is on authority and an élite.

For purely practical reasons the 'Kreisau Circle' thought it impossible to return to the parliamentary system immediately after a *coup*.[8] Everything implied by the word 'Weimar' in its negative sense was to be avoided, particularly its multiplicity of parties and self-interested unscrupulous party warfare, which could only do damage to the country, as had indeed been shown. The possibility of reconstruction of parties was left open till a later stage but it was not proposed to allow it initially. The first parliament was to be formed without participation by parties, by election of individuals and the principle of delegation from the bottom upwards.

These drafts were designed to set out principles and guidelines, not to produce a constitution which could be introduced immediately. Their aim was a special and probably unrealistic one. They were intended to contribute towards the creation of a new mankind. This was to be done by the combination and cooperation of all intellectual, political and social forces willing to carry responsibility, from the trade unions to the churches. Party and individual interests were to give way to the interests of the community and humanity as a whole and this was to result, not from coercion but from voluntary cooperation in the attainment of a common aim. 'Integration' was the key word; Moltke and most of the 'Kreisau Circle' thought the essential to be 'an attempt to replace the former party coalitions by a new spiritual *integration*'.[9] The foundation of this integration was to be the Christian religion; without a common foundation it was, of course, not possible.

In the discussions from 1942 to 1944 Dr Gerstenmaier opposed these ideas as utopian. He was not quite so flatly against them at the time as he is today (he now thinks that they were totally impractical) – they were, after all, only drafts, he says, and not matters of life and death. The 'Kreisau Circle' knew as well as anyone else that in practical politics compromise and therefore coalition were unavoidable and that, after a *coup*, they would probably have to reach agreement with Goerdeler.[10] There would have been many arguments – on questions of the churches (Goerdeler's divorce of church and state), of schooling (confessional or community schools), of agriculture (major estates or medium-size farmer-owned properties) and on economics (direction of competition, a planned economy on the Kreisau side,[11] controlled liberalism and nationalization on Goerdeler's). In any case there was no unanimity on these questions within the 'Kreisau Circle'.[12]

The 'Kreisau Circle' and Goerdeler were at one in their efforts to reduce 'agglomeration' and thus, at least to some extent, in their search for a new mankind. Both wished to give men back some organic relationship and at least temporarily to eliminate political parties as being soulless engines of power. Goerdeler laid stress on the use of the most suitable people with previous administrative experience, the 'Kreisau Circle', and Moltke in particular, on integration and restoration of an élite.[13] Understandably, however, neither had that confidence in the electorate and the citizenry by which they set such store. They intended their proposals to produce citizens who would justify that confidence. Until then they intended to impose their ideas, as the Weimar experience had shown was essential.

Well-meaning though these drafts were, their general trend was illiberal, as Hans Mommsen has pointed out with some asperity in his comprehensive study on 'Social Ideas and Constitutional Plans of the German Resistance'. At the same time, however, he emphasizes how greatly planning must have been affected by the pressure of danger and by intellectual isolation in a totalitarian state and how great was the lack of practical political experience, particularly in the 'Kreisau Circle'.[14]

The forces which would have emerged had a *coup* succeeded would not have been solely those whose political views and ideas have been set out in this Part. Goerdeler, Beck, Hassell, Moltke and Yorck would certainly have played important parts, but the Stauffenberg brothers and certain liberal democrats too would have made their voices heard. Claus Graf Stauffenberg in particular had his own peculiar political views, on which he proposed to insist.[15] No doubt practice would have looked very different from theory.

18 Socialists

Constitutional drafts by socialists who were involved in the opposition to Hitler have not so far appeared. Perhaps this is due in part to a better understanding of conspiratorial principles. Moreover, Social-Democrats such as Dr Leber saw little value in joining the ranks of those who were busily manufacturing too many drafts and programmes as it was.[1] Social-Democrats had good reason to avoid political prominence in the first hours after a *coup*: after they had formed the Republic in 1918–19, and after they had been forced by an Entente ultimatum to sign the Versailles Treaty (while the nationalist opposition refused to form a government and take responsibility for insisting that the Treaty not be signed), the Social-Democrats received no credit for saving the fatherland, for preventing foreign occupation and for bringing the troops home. They were merely denounced and held in contempt as traitors.

Leber occasionally spoke to his friends of the 'positive goal' that must be set up in answer to National-Socialism, but he said that he had not yet put it down formally. He used to refer to the ' "new state", for which we must find a new positive content and a convincing formulation.' One may infer however, from existing documentation, that the basic programme of the Social-Democrats as written during the 1920s had not changed greatly, although the tactics could no longer be the same as those that had, after all, allowed Hitler and the National-Socialists to seize power. Thus it was indeed questionable whether this important sentence from the 1925 Programme could still be considered valid: 'The democratic republic is the best basis on which to wage the struggle for the liberation of the working class and thus for the realization of socialism.'[2] No Party Convention could discuss this after 1933, but certain statements of leading socialists may shed light on the issue.

The traditional basis of Social-Democracy was the conviction that general and equal adult suffrage must lead to right and just representation of all classes in parliament, and that thus the interests of the most numerous class would be adequately represented. To make this effective, parliament and the central government responsible to it needed full authority, and while self-government on lower administrative levels was desirable, unity of the central government down to provinces and communities had to be stressed. Decentralization and federalism tended to strengthen provincial and local forces, that is forces of oligarchic, agrarian-patriarchal, clerical, establishment, or even monarchist tendencies. Bavaria was a clear example of this danger. A unitary republic was the only framework in which the influence due to the working class from its numbers could be secured and maintained. Conservatives often denounced this socialist position as egalitarianism and as apt to make the masses even more faceless and rootless, therefore more mobile, politically volatile and dangerous, than they already were; but for socialists, the unitary republic and centralism were basic necessities for the practical realization of their goals. As long as there were remnants of local authority in administration, in the judiciary, in provincial and community government, or in rural economic and social conditions, there could be no equal rights.

Dr Leber demanded in 1944 a 'purely socialist solution' for the reorganization of Germany after Hitler's fall. In conferences with co-conspirators, he developed 'a radical socialist programme,' and he refused 'to throw overboard important principles of traditional Social-Democracy for the sake of unity [among the conspirators].'[3] But in reality, Leber went beyond the traditional concepts of Social-Democracy in his demand for a 'purely socialist solution' for this could hardly mean a return to a democratic republic as 'the best basis on which to wage the struggle for the liberation of the working class and thus for the realization of socialism'. It could only mean that all forces of political life were *not* to be given 'equal' starting conditions within a liberal framework, but that to a great extent socialism must be built into the reorganization and must be codified in a new constitution.

Naturally Leber was under heavy pressure to compromise with somewhat more conservative leaders in the conspiracy in the interest of the immediate tactical aim of the overthrow of Hitler's regime, particularly when a proclamation was discussed to start a 'popular movement' for a new order.[4] Goerdeler also rejected a new state with the old political parties; he said he wanted one without parties and in their place unity of all classes, strata and regions through a 'popular movement'. On this somewhat nebulous basis he seems to have agreed with the socialists, although he certainly did not mean what they meant when he rejected a state including parties. The proclamation that was discussed and more or less agreed upon before the *coup d'état* in any case contained declarations not only for the socialization (nationalization) of basic and key industries, but also for inalienable rights of liberty, for toleration in 'questions of race, faith and class', and even for German culture and for the Christian heritage of the German people.[5] This last point, particularly, had provoked a sharp attack by Leber. There was never any definitive agreement concerning the proclamation for the 'popular movement' that was to unite all parties from the Social-Democrats through the Centre to the German-Nationals, as Graf von Schwerin put it, although Goerdeler and Leber, with very different motives, wanted a state without political parties.

Religion stood in the way of unity, especially in the negotiations between leaders of the Christian trade unions and the leaders of the Marxist labour organizations. In the interests of the overthrow of Hitler, the problem was smoothed over for the time being, but of course it was a fundamental one. Marxist socialists were definitely in favour of toleration in religious and racial matters, and they declared themselves in favour of the 'restoration of the rights of Jews', but they were strictly against mixing government activities with religion in any form.[6] Therefore Leber rejected sharply the proposed formula 'of the divine mission of the Christian church in the secular state'. Religious and pseudo-religious principles were not to govern conditions in the new state, such as inequality of the sexes, sanctity and permanence of matrimony, legal discrimination against persons born out of wedlock, or revenge and retribution in the administration of justice. In the new state, rational and objective principles must be applied putting the interests of society as a whole before class interests. Such principles included among others, the participation of lay judges in trials in courts-of-law, the subordination of individual property rights to the rights and needs of society, equality before the law for men and women, for children born in or out of wedlock, easier divorce, abolition of the death penalty, humane methods of punishment aiming at resocialization, and generally in the administration of justice the principles of education, resocialization and protection of society instead of the principle of retribution.[7] All of this would serve to help remove class differences and inequalities, and to reduce the power of traditional authorities and of the haves over the have-nots.

A number of other tenets of the Social-Democrat programme of 1925 were held, with more or less variation, by the socialists in the conspiracy. The right of labour to participate in economic decisions was emphasized here and there, the working class were to take part in the planning of the economy through their own structures of self-government and through labour organizations, and production cooperatives and national shops were to be fostered and expanded.[8] Basic and key industries were to be nationalized, likewise all mineral wealth.[9] The old demand that all land be nationalized, however, seems to have been abandoned, and state socialism was rejected in principle; the free market economy based on private initiative was to be restored in all but basic and key industries.[10] Goerdeler accepted these ideas.[11]

There were also some points in which the new concepts went beyond the old programme. They were based on the experiences of the last fifteen to twenty years. During the Great Depression, the workers had found that they were almost entirely at the mercy of government and industry – a traumatic experience they did not wish to be repeated. Therefore, social insurance and social administration, the administration of unemployment, old age and sickness benefits were to be transferred entirely to the control and authority of the workers.[12] On the issue of narrowing the gaps between classes, Leuschner wanted to see education emphasized more than changes in the distribution of wealth and in control of the means of production.[13] Undoubtedly, the mere improvement of the material conditions of workers was not enough to raise for them the quality of life, even if a government had managed to distribute material benefits equitably. But participation in overall economic management, in decisions in the factory, in the cultural life of the nation were not possible without a fairly high level of general education, nor could the feeling of being socially low-class be removed without it. Ignorance and lack of education meant less power, fewer rights, and fewer opportunities for self-fulfilment. Leuschner therefore laid particular emphasis on nine years of compulsory schooling, in the same type of standardized school for everyone.[14] It is obvious that this would have a tremendous levelling effect.

Equal opportunity, but also unity and solidarity, were fundamental tenets of socialism at all times. Only by concentrating and institutionalizing their potential power could labour secure and safeguard an influence proportionate to their numbers. Again, it was the bitter experiences of the Weimar years that had taught leaders like Leber and Leuschner to insist on the organizational unity of the labour movement. The *Einheitsgewerkschaft*, a unified association of trade unions, was a point on which they refused to compromise. The National-Socialists had united the trade unions in the *Deutsche Arbeitsfront* (German Labour Front), but only after removing all power from them, making them an instrument of control for the dictatorship. Leuschner wanted to retain the unity, but reshape the *Deutsche Arbeitsfront* into 'a real political instrument of the German worker', in other words, into an *Einheitsgewerkschaft*.[15] For reasons of unity and of concentration of power in the hands of the workers, Leuschner was forced to oppose Mierendorff's demand for factory unions instead of trade unions.[16] Unity was the key word; federal and soviet structures could have no place in a Social-Democrat system. Leuschner told his *Gestapo* interrogators on 18 August 1944: 'It was my desire to form a unified trade-union movement, and I continued my efforts to this end when I negotiated with representatives of the NSDAP in spring of 1933. The principles that guided my actions then have not changed.'[17] And Leber told the *Gestapo*: 'Leuschner was appointed leader of the German *Einheitsgewerkschaft*. The other [white-collar and Christian] unions were to delegate a deputy each (these were Kaiser and Habermann). *With this, the unification of the unions (!)* was virtually *accomplished* in February of 1944.' On the day before his execution, Leuschner told trade-union friends in Tegel prison: 'Tomorrow I shall be hanged. Create the unity.'[18]

If the conservative leaders had more detailed plans for the constitutional reorganization of Germany after Hitler's fall, the ideas of the socialists, particularly the Social-Democrats, seem to have had better chances of being adopted in the weeks before 20 July 1944. As Stauffenberg gained more and more complete control of the conspiracy, his friend Leber gained more influence on post-Hitler planning, while Stauffenberg's own ideas were not exactly clear.[19] It is not known what Stauffenberg promised his friend Leber, the reserve officer decorated with the Iron Cross First Class in World War I and member of the *Wehrausschuss* (Armed Forces Committee) of the *Reichstag* in the Weimar years, with respect to social reorganization. But the fact is that both Leber and Leuschner were given key positions on all cabinet lists drawn up by the opposition after January 1943. On such lists, Leuschner always figured as a candidate for the Vice-chancellorship under Goerdeler as Chancellor; in discussions in 1944, either he or Leber was put forward as successor to Goerdeler, and some even proposed the elimination of the interim Goerdeler government. Leber always appeared as a candidate for the ministry of internal affairs (sometimes with Gayl and Fritz-Dietlof Graf von der

Schulenburg).[20] If Leber and Leuschner collaborated closely with Stauffenberg, they certainly did so in the conviction that this was the best way to ensure realization of their ideas and plans – even if this was not entirely clear to Stauffenberg. As Leber once told Otto John, whatever could be done after the overthrow of Hitler remained to be seen once that situation had arisen, but it would not be likely to conform to what Goerdeler had in mind; meanwhile, said Leber, Stauffenberg must be supported since he represented the only remaining hope for action by the military.[21] It is therefore not surprising to find that Popitz, Professor Jessen and Hassell were opposed 'to the thorough integration [into the conspiracy] of the trade unions by Goerdeler', and that Helldorf declared the *Einheitsgewerkschaft* dangerous.[22] Popitz stated: 'It was clear to me that with the *Einheitsgewerkschaft* a power centre of the first rank would be created, especially if the trade unions were given control of the assets and installations of the *Arbeitsfront*. I had the impression that pressure was being applied to which Goerdeler believed he had to give in.'[23] Jessen voiced similar misgivings and feared that the trade unions would become a state-within-the-state, and Helldorf, Gisevius and Strünck agreed there was a danger of being 'overrun by the workers' if too many concessions were made.[24] Stauffenberg, however, who had at first also opposed trade unions, hoped to 'win over' the workers and thus stave off communism.[25] Leber and Stauffenberg held in common the belief that the most important point was being there in the 'free moment' which would follow Hitler's death.[26]

PART V/CONTACTS WITH THE ENEMY 1940–1944

19 Albrecht Haushofer
1940–1941

During the winter 1939–40 contacts with the enemy had either failed to materialize or had come to nothing; there had followed the victorious German offensives against Norway, Holland, Belgium and France. It had all been a great triumph and it would have been surprising had many been found in the summer of 1940 to lift their voices in favour of the removal of the *Führer* and Chancellor of the German *Reich*. Yet the determined opponents of Hitler did not relax for a single moment. Moltke in particular did not swerve from his attitude or his views, even in face of this apparently unbroken run of victories, the fruits of which any moderate regime could have retained. In December 1940 he made this quite clear to Lord Lothian, the British Ambassador in Washington.[1] He also contrived to maintain his contact with Alexander C. Kirk, the American Chargé d'Affaires in Berlin.[2] Admittedly, so long as there was no real prospect of a *coup*, such contacts had little purpose, however dangerous they might be for those involved. In 1940 the generals were less in favour of a *coup* than ever, a situation which only changed when the attack on Russia was imminent. Meanwhile, however, contacts had to be nursed and maintained so that they might be there when needed.

One of the first attempted contacts after the French campaign is associated with the name of Albrecht Haushofer. His father was the First World War general, Professor Karl Haushofer, regarded as the founder of the science of geopolitics in Germany. The son taught Political Geography and Geopolitics at the Berlin School for Politics from 1934 and at Berlin University from 1939; he was at the same time on the staff of the Foreign Ministry.[3] Through his father Haushofer was in close touch with Rudolf Hess, the '*Führer*'s Deputy and *Reich* Minister without Portfolio', who had been assistant to Professor Karl Haushofer for a short time in 1922; despite Hess' inadequate intellectual abilities a close and lasting friendship had formed between the two.[4] During the 1930s, thanks to his extensive knowledge of Britain, Albrecht Haushofer frequently had opportunity (or the duty) to act as adviser to Hess and so indirectly to Hitler. He tried to use his influence to prevent Ribbentrop's appointment as Foreign Minister but with so little success that he felt forced to issue urgent and outspoken warnings – also without success.[5]

Politically Haushofer inclined towards the Right. He advocated a liberal-bourgeois but authoritarian monarchy. He was opposed to Nazism and Hitler's policy from the outset but because of his parents (his mother was half-Jewish), his connection with Hess and his conviction that he could only work from the inside, he decided not to make an open break with the regime.[6] He did not propose, as he wrote to his mother in December 1939, to leave 'this limping ship which is already on fire at several points and is largely run and steered by criminals and fools,' to jump into the water where he would quickly sink; he intended to wait and try 'perhaps to give the tiller a favourable twist'.[7] During the war he was in contact, not only with the Hassell–Popitz–Langbehn group, but also with the 'Kreisau Circle' and leading members of the so-called 'Red Orchestra', Harro Schulze-Boysen and Wolfgang Hoffmann-Zampis.[8]

Under the Nazi dictatorship his non-conformist views and clear outspoken opinions were as great a danger to Albrecht Haushofer as his mother's Jewish blood; so long as Hess retained his influence, however, and was prepared to protect the family, the threat could be averted. In August 1937, for instance, Haushofer wrote in the *Zeitschrift für Geopolitik* that everyone from San Francisco to Washington knew 'that the United States could not be a passive onlooker if Britain was fighting for her existence'. The common interests of the two powers went so deep that, even if not bound by treaty they would both pursue a policy consistent with an indissoluble alliance. 'Anyone who comes into collision with Britain should know that he will have America too among his enemies – despite all the laws of neutrality.'[9] In October 1938 Haushofer proclaimed, again in the *Zeitschrift für Geopolitik*, that despite his sixty years Chamberlain had three times climbed into an aeroplane to 'explain to Hitler, man to man, that the British Empire is just as unlikely to mobilize its fleet to no good purpose as Germany is her army.'[10] In other words war had only been avoided on that occasion because Hitler had given way in face of the British threat. When Haushofer realized how little Hitler understood the situation or wished to understand it and how his intemperance and megalomania were growing, he raised his voice again and again to warn that Britain and France were determined not to retreat one single step further. In June 1939 he said so quite explicitly in the *Zeitschrift für Geopolitik*.[11] At the time hardly anyone in Germany could publicize such views as freely as Haushofer – he was protected by Hess; at the same time he was able to maintain contact with Popitz, Beck and Hassell.

With his intimate knowledge of Britain Haushofer sensed that, once war had broken out, this time the Western Powers would fight on until Germany had been defeated finally and unmistakably. Nevertheless he still searched for ways of persuading them to meet Germany halfway, always provided that a *coup* had taken place first. After his victory over France Hitler was also interested in getting rid of his British enemy and, since Hess thought that he should follow Hitler's lead, Haushofer had an opportunity to play it both ways. Hess wished to help Hitler conclude peace with Britain; Haushofer wished to exploit the resulting possibilities of contact for the benefit of the opposition, to create the external conditions for a *coup d'état*.[12]

About 1 September 1940 Hess approached Professor Karl Haushofer asking whether he could think of any method of preventing the assault on England which was now ready; the Professor took this as a hint really addressed to his son; he said that Albrecht might be able to meet competent British personalities in Lisbon. In a letter of 3 September 1940 he asked Albrecht whether he could not gain contact with Sir Ian Hamilton or Douglas Douglas-Hamilton, Duke of Hamilton.[13] Armed with this letter Albrecht Haushofer went to Hess and on 8 September discussed the whole question of peace mediation in detail with him in Bad Gallspach.[14]

Albrecht Haushofer made a note, dated 15 September, on his talk with Hess, including in it his own view of the project. He sent the paper, labelled 'Most Secret', to his parents for safe custody.[15] Hess had said that it must be possible to find someone in a responsible position in Britain who would be prepared to accept Hitler's desire for peace, but Haushofer had replied that 'practically all Englishmen in this position regarded any treaty signed by the *Führer* as a worthless scrap of paper'. Hitler had broken too many treaties to be considered trustworthy; in the Anglo-Saxon world he was regarded as 'Satan's representative on earth' who must be fought. When Hess pressed his point and asked Haushofer whether he personally saw any opportunities for contact, Haushofer adroitly replied that it might be possible, via the British Ambassador in Washington, to convince the British that an insecure peace was still better than war. This presupposed, however, that Britain had been deprived of all hope of American aid and this could only be established in Washington, not working from Germany. In addition, he said, it was conceivable that something might be achieved by a meeting on neutral territory with the Duke of Hamilton since he had access both to Churchill and to the King. Hess finally said that he would think the matter over, which Haushofer took to mean that he intended to talk to Hitler.

The next move came from Hess with a further letter to Karl Haushofer on 10 September: he had reflected on the matter and now thought it best if Karl Haushofer or his son Albrecht could contact their friend (he can only have meant the Duke of Hamilton) through non-official channels; they should seek to discover whether the friend could come to some neutral country or alter- natively where he might be in the near future.[16] Owing to postal delays Haushofer did not receive Hess' letter until 18 September.

Although, owing to the increasingly close relationship between Britain and the United States, Haushofer had practically no hopes of success, he nevertheless did what Hess asked. On 19 September he wrote a letter to the Duke of Hamilton and another to Hess. On the same day he sent copies of both letters together with his notes on his talk of 8 September to his parents asking that they be kept safely.[17] The letter to the Duke of Hamilton was despatched via Hess' brother but not until 23 September; in it Haushofer asked whether the Duke could pay a short visit to somewhere like Portugal for a highly important discussion, the subject of which the Duke could easily guess from his previous contacts with Haushofer.[18]

In the letter to Hess Haushofer explained how he proposed to ensure that his letter reached the Duke of Hamilton and indirectly recommended that he himself should be the contact man on the German side since 'like many Englishmen H is extremely reserved with people he does not know personally'. Haushofer also suggested that the channels already mentioned via Lord Lothian in Washington or Sir Samuel Hoare in Madrid offered somewhat better prospects than that via the Duke of Hamilton, though 'admittedly from the political point of view they are more difficult to use'.

Were Haushofer to confront the Duke of Hamilton as an official representative with adequate cover against suspicions at home, his prospects of success were very meagre. If, however, he was to achieve anything either through Lord Lothian or Sir Samuel Hoare, he could under no circumstances appear as a representative of the Hitler government. Not only, therefore, must he have secure governmental cover (through Hess) but he must be able to appear to his British opposite numbers as a non-official emissary whose mission had nothing to do with official policy or official agencies. He would then be able to reveal himself secretly as a representative of the resistance movement and explain to the British the conditions required for an internal German *coup* without fear of being disowned.[19]

Since Hess had been prepared to sponsor the letter to Hamilton but not a journey by Haushofer, the latter was forced to do something which, from the opposition's point of view, he regarded as useless. He received no answer to his letter, although it reached its destination.[20] Then for a long time nothing happened. The assault on England faded into the background and increasingly intensive preparations were made for the Russian campaign.

Not until April 1941 did Haushofer have a further opportunity of making contact.[21] He suggested to Hess that Professor Carl Jacob Burckhardt would be a suitable intermediary to the British, his object being to get sent to Switzerland himself.[22] While in Geneva on 30 January 1941 Hassell had been approached by Burckhardt who had told him that he had received private word from London that people there were still ready to conclude a negotiated peace with Germany – apart, however, from Anthony Eden who had joined the cabinet as Foreign Secretary in December; it would be somewhat on the following basis: reestablishment of Belgium, Holland and some form of Poland minus the former German provinces; Denmark and the Czech area to remain German spheres of influence; the former German colonies to be restored. None of this could be done with Hitler, however, whose word no one believed any more.[23] On 10 March 1941 Hassell met Albrecht Haushofer in Popitz's house and discussed with him how his (Hassell's) connections in Switzerland could be used to obtain assurances from the Allies in the event of a change of regime in Germany.[24]

On 28 April Haushofer had a discussion with Professor Burckhardt in Geneva. The result was not encouraging. In the situation of early 1941 the generals, faced with the prospect of a war on two fronts – a mortal sin in their eyes – were once more becoming approachable, but when he returned to Berlin on 8 May,[25] Haushofer was unable to bring with him the assurances which might have persuaded them to act. He hoped, however, to maintain this contact and perhaps achieve more if he continued to present himself as a man with good connections. At about this time he hoped that a lecture invitation might provide a pretext for a journey to Spain.[26] During the night 9–10 May news arrived via the Foreign Ministry in Berlin that Haushofer was to address the Academy of Sciences in Madrid on 12 May.[27] There seemed therefore to be a possibility of a meeting with Sir Samuel Hoare.

On 10 May, however, Rudolf Hess, the *Führer*'s Deputy, embarked on his astounding flight to Britain where he proposed to contact the King through the Duke of Hamilton and arrange peace.[28] Haushofer had nothing to do with it; for him this mad foolhardy flight was a catastrophe. The Haushofer family had now lost their protector; they gradually fell into increasing disfavour and Albrecht Haushofer was finally murdered in April 1945 by an SS squad. All the steps taken so far and Albrecht Haushofer as their initiator lost all credibility and authenticity both in Hitler's eyes and abroad.

Early on the morning of 12 May Haushofer was arrested in Berlin and taken forthwith to Hitler on the Obersalzberg where he was interrogated.[29] That evening he wrote a report on his British contacts and the efforts he had made together with Hess to use them for peace mediation.[30] In this situation his object was naturally not to provide some accurate document for the historians; he presented the efforts which he and Hess had made in as innocent a light as possible from the regime's point of view and cast himself in the role of faithful recipient of orders. With remarkable calm and presence of mind he tried to emphasize his own indispensability for further missions.

According to this report an influential Englishman had recently expressed to Professor Burckhardt 'the desire of important British circles to explore the possibilities of peace' (which was not true); he (Haushofer) had suggested to Burckhardt that he arrange a properly authenticated contact with British personalities of the necessary authority. For this purpose, as he had told Professor Burckhardt, he would probably be able to come to Geneva again. As regards possible peace terms, the report continued (again largely untrue), Burckhardt's impression was that moderate circles in Great Britain were only notionally interested in East and South-east Europe with the exception of Greece; they would, however, insist on reestablishment of 'the West European order of states'; on the colonial question they would certainly be forthcoming provided that German demands were confined to her former possessions. The only point supported and agreed by Burckhardt was of course that dealing with the reestablishment of Western Europe; Haushofer, however, had to try to obtain Hitler's authorization for further negotiations with Britain in order to exploit them for the purposes of the opposition and perhaps at the last moment stop the war against Russia. Burckhardt did in fact think that Britain was still prepared for peace on a sensible basis but, as Hassell put it: '1. not with our present rulers and 2. perhaps not for much longer.'[31] Haushofer then repeated – basically entirely correctly – an alleged statement by Burckhardt that all relationships between Germany and Britain were overshadowed by the difficulty of finding 'a basis of personal confidence between Berlin and London'; he followed this by adroitly phrased remarks about the 'indigenous plutocratic section' and the 'non-indigenous, primarily Jewish element'. All this was designed to convince Hitler of his loyalty, honesty and innocence.[32]

But no one paid any attention to Haushofer. The reward of his friendship with Hess was eight weeks of *Gestapo* arrest in the Prinz-Albrecht-Strasse, Berlin, and after his release the permanent mistrust of the regime. Meanwhile, on 22 June 1941, the war against Russia began and demolished all hopes of peace and understanding with Britain. The United States became increasingly committed in Europe and, as Haushofer had prophesied in his report to Hitler, was no longer to be deterred from the aim of crushing Germany. Great Britain could now face the future calmly. Germany's defeat was certain.

20 Hassell 1941–1942

Among the German opposition too people were beginning to think that defeat was inevitable. Two months after the invasion of Russia it was generally thought by those in touch with Hassell, Popitz and Goerdeler that the enemy could now foresee the total overthrow of Germany and that not even 'a decent government would still receive an acceptable peace'.[1] This, however, did not preclude further soundings regarding the truth of this statement and perhaps the possibilities of negotiation.

On 14 August 1941, from a British battleship in the north-east Atlantic, Churchill and Roosevelt proclaimed the Atlantic Charter, a general agreement on war aims. It created a new situation. America was not yet in the war but her entry was clearly only a question of time and occasion. The Charter was a declaration in favour of freedom for all nations, but, commenting on the Charter, Churchill said that it implied no commitment in so far as enemy countries were concerned; it therefore applied only to neutrals and allies. Neutrals needed no assurance of territorial integrity; for the Allies such an assurance was a matter of course seeing that no western government had accepted the annexations of territory at the expense of Poland and the Baltic States.[2] There was therefore little substance in the Charter, apart from the threat to the enemy.[3] The opposition accordingly concluded that the generals would now be able to say that the enemy was determined to crush, not only Hitler, but Germany as such and to render her defenceless. Once again, therefore, it seemed essential to take soundings and obtain clarification in London.

An opportunity presented itself through Dr Langbehn, the lawyer. Professor Burckhardt was in Germany on Red Cross business and was then to go to Britain for a similar purpose. On 18 August Burckhardt, Hassell and Langbehn met near Munich. Hassell explained the 'national German' viewpoint: the other side must not demand a change of regime; this must remain a matter for the German opposition; threats such as those contained in the Atlantic Charter destroyed every reasonable chance for peace; 'national Germany' made moderate demands but some of them they were not prepared to renounce.[4]

On or shortly after 20 January 1942, during the return journey from a lecture in Paris, Hassell went to see Burckhardt again in Geneva.[5] Burckhardt said that peace with Hitler and his system was no longer possible, but, in the view of government circles close to Lord Halifax and Churchill, could still be concluded with 'a decent Germany'. He had been asked again and again about the generals; there was much scepticism about the possibility of a *coup* in Germany. The 1914 frontiers, however, seemed a perfectly practical basis for peace talks.[6]

Hassell also had a contact to the American government via the New York businessman, Federico Stallforth.[7] Stallforth was especially interested in trying to maintain the fragile peace between Germany and the United States; he wished to talk to responsible members of the German government. He was in Germany in the summer of 1940 and talked with Göring who outlined to him the following peace-plan (turned down immediately by both the British Prime Minister and the American President, when presented to them subsequently): '(1) British Empire in status quo, except certain colonies for Germany. (2) Political independence for France, Belgium, and Holland (except Alsace-Lorraine and Luxembourg to Germany). (3) Germany to have free hand in the East, including Poland and Czecho-Slovakia.'[8]

In May 1941 Stallforth was again in Germany, but he did not get to see Göring this time. He talked with many old and new acquaintances instead, among them Udet, Brauchitsch and Keitel, and also a group of high-ranking officers of all branches of the *Wehrmacht* on the occasion of a rather formal lunch to which he had been invited. At the lunch, some officers expressed their confidence that Russia would be defeated, but added that it was hoped that a war with the United States could be avoided. Stallforth replied that neither the United States nor Britain would make peace with the present German government, whereupon he was asked: but what if Hitler and Göring were no longer there? Stallforth then suggested that probably the whole regime would have to be replaced by a constitutional one before the United States and Britain would be ready to talk peace. When asked: what about a monarchy? Stallforth said he believed this was a possibility, maybe something like the British monarchy.

On the following day, Stallforth had a visit from one of those who had attended the lunch who asked him whether the Army would be acceptable as a negotiating partner if it seized power in the *Reich*. Stallforth said he thought it possible, and the officer then stated these conditions: '(1) No double crossing of Germany, as happened after Germany's acceptance of Wilson's Fourteen Points; (2) The army to remain in control to avoid chaos and thus of course disarmament could not be immediate.' Stallforth said it should be possible to reach agreement on this basis, and he mentioned the names of Donovan, Willkie and General Wood as possible negotiators (he thought it advisable to indicate by this choice of names that America would be quite united in such matters). The German officer mentioned as likely negotiators on the German side Falkenhausen, Halder, Stülpnagel and Hassell. He added that there was no time to lose before resentment against the United States became too strong; undoubtedly the German people would accept the overthrow of Hitler once they saw that the change meant peace; all action against Hitler and the regime would have to come from within Germany to avoid all appearance of a *coup* engineered from outside. When the officer expressed his fear that

Churchill and Roosevelt might be so full of hate against Germany that they would reject the proposals just outlined out of hand, Stallforth said this was absurd. Concerning territorial arrangements, the officer finally said the Army would be ready to evacuate all territories except Austria.

Hassell attempted to obtain further political and economic assurances in the event of a *coup*; in October he was told by Stallforth, who had meanwhile returned from America, that 'the "proposition" had been well received'.[9] Hassell's proposals, approved by Beck and Hammerstein, sounded most moderate. The United States could not speak for London, however, and Stallforth failed to see Roosevelt. Then, on 7 December, came the Japanese attack on Pearl Harbor and destroyed everything.

21 Lochner 1941–1942

About the same time and also because of the obviously imminent entry of the United States into the war the opposition approached Louis P. Lochner, the press correspondent and head of the Associated Press Bureau in Berlin. Lochner had been in touch for years with Hermann Maass, ex-Director of the *Reich* Committee of German Youth Organizations, and with Colonel-General Beck. In August 1939 Maass had arranged through Beck to pass to Lochner a copy of Hitler's speech of the 22nd. Lochner was present on occasions at secret meetings of the opposition.[1]

In late September 1941 a preliminary talk took place in Otto John's house between Lochner and Ernst von Harnack. Then, one night in November 1941, Lochner was taken to a meeting of twelve to fifteen people in the house of Dr Josef Wirmer, former Centre Party deputy in the *Reichstag*. Jakob Kaiser was in the chair and there were present: representatives of the old trade unions (M. Habermann, B. Letterhaus), of the Confessing Churches, of certain democratic parties of the Weimar period (Centre Party, Social-Democrats, German People's Party) together with J. Delbrück, Otto John and Klaus Bonhoeffer on behalf of Canaris and Beck. Lochner knew the President of the United States and both were friends of Prince Louis Ferdinand of Prussia who had been received in the White House in 1938. Lochner therefore seemed specially qualified to act as intermediary between the opposition and President Roosevelt.

This assembly in November 1941 requested Lochner, who was shortly due to return to the United States, to tell the President at once and in the greatest detail of the opposition's composition, aims and activities. He was also to ask the President to say something on the form of government America would prefer for a Germany liberated from Hitler. To facilitate subsequent agreement the conspirators gave Lochner a secret radio code, the object being to establish radio communications between the American President and the opposition.

Lochner promised to do all in his power but in fact could not keep his promise until June 1942 since, like many of his colleagues, he was interned in December 1941 when Germany declared war on the United States. When he finally returned to the United States he immediately sought an audience of President Roosevelt saying that he had personal and confidential messages from Prince and Princess Louis Ferdinand of Prussia and secret information on resistance groups in Germany which he might not confide to anyone else. All attempts to obtain an audience with the President failed, however; he wrote from Chicago but received no answer. Finally, through the Washington office of the Associated Press, he was informed that there was no desire to receive his information and he was requested to refrain from further efforts to transmit it.

The explanation of the American attitude is obvious. The government in Washington was already well informed on the German resistance movement. Adam von Trott zu Solz had established contact in 1939. In November 1942 Allen Welsh Dulles, later Director of the CIA, was sent to Berne for the express purpose of establishing permanent contact with the German opposition. He informed his masters of all developments and Washington had a vast amount of information on resistance in Germany.[2] Viewed from Washington, however, the United States was not merely fighting the Nazi regime but a people permeated by an illiberal inhuman ideology who had learnt nothing from a fearful defeat in another similarly imperialist war. In face of Hitler's claim to total power a total victory must be won. Looked at in this light, the American government, as Lochner was informed, could only be embarrassed if it learnt and was forced to acknowledge that an anti-Hitler opposition existed in Germany capable of taking over the government.

In addition there was the relationship between the United States and her allies. No assurances could be given to the resistance without consultation and this would have amounted to betrayal of the opposition. Finally, had Stalin learnt that the Americans were negotiating 'with Germans', he might have tried to forestall them and conclude a separate peace with Hitler. There was at least a risk of the Western Powers losing Russia as an ally, leaving the United States, almost alone, to carry the burden of the war against both Japan and Germany.[3] Even at the Yalta Conference in 1945, Roosevelt was urging Russia to enter the war against Japan as soon as possible after the end of the war in Europe – no one then knew what the effect of the atom bomb would be.

22 Trott, Bonhoeffer, Schönfeld 1942

Throughout the war numerous contacts existed between members and friends of the 'Kreisau Circle' on the one hand and neutral or Allied countries on the other. Only the most important can be dealt with here.[1]

The entry of the United States into the war was a turning point which led to fresh thinking and renewed efforts in many quarters, including the 'Kreisau Circle'. Trott, together with other members of the Circle, in particular Dr Hans Schönfeld and Dr Eugen Gerstenmaier who had worked with Trott in the Foreign Ministry in 1939 and 1940, drafted a memorandum which may be regarded as the outcome of this new thinking. At the end of April 1942, when in Geneva, Trott handed it to Dr W. A. Visser't Hooft, Secretary-General of the Ecumenical Council of Churches;[2] it was intended for Sir Stafford Cripps, the British Lord Privy Seal.

In writing this memorandum the object of Trott and his friends was to keep alive any tendency in Britain which might help to bring about the *coup d'état* through an encouraging statement of some sort. Equally, however, he wished to show that the opposition, in line with Moltke's thinking, understood the position of the western world to which Germany *together with* France, Britain and all other 'western' states belonged, acceptance of a common responsibility in other words.

At present, the memorandum said, destruction of human life and economic resources was on so vast a scale that, after the war, even the victors would suffer from extreme poverty. Owing to the pressures of war totalitarian control was increasing even in liberal countries; at the same time there was a tendency to anarchism and the abandonment of all established civilized standards. Everywhere the threat of bolshevization was increasing owing to the victories of the Red Army and the consequent expansion of communist underground activity throughout the western world. The German anti-Hitler resistance movement had no wish to make excuses for the resulting situation but acknowledged its share of responsibility for it. In the light of its own struggle, however, it felt justified in appealing to the solidarity of the civilized western world. The best way of expressing this solidarity was to refrain from decrying in public the statements and appeals of the German opposition.

The first most important step towards the prevention of a catastrophe in

Europe was the overthrow of the present German regime. There were two possibilities of doing this, both intimately connected with affairs outside Germany. The first possibility lay in a Soviet victory; if Hitler fell as a result of this, the outcome would be catastrophe for all Europe and ultimately world revolution brought about by military methods. The success of the second possibility, formation of a German government prepared to return to the standards of civilized Europe, however, was also dependent on conditions outside Germany, in other words on the final renunciation of nationalism in Europe, particularly in its militaristic form.

Anti-Nazi forces in Germany, the memorandum continued, consisted of significant sections of the working class, of influential circles in the Army and administration and of militant groups from the churches. Names and details naturally could not be given. The aims of this widespread resistance movement were as follows: self-government and decentralization in Germany achieved by breaking down the mass society into local self-governing bodies and groups and the application of 'modern socialist principles in all fields of political and economic existence'; an organic link between a self-governing federated Germany and a federal Europe including Great Britain; close international cooperation with other continents; reestablishment of free access to overseas raw materials instead of national autarky; reorganization of Europe on the basis, not of a return to the status quo, but of concentration on creating social and political security; international cooperation in solving the Jewish problem.

The questionable nature of certain of these points leaps to the eye. It must be remembered that, when the memorandum was drafted, Germany's military situation was not *completely* hopeless – as Schönfeld said to the Bishop of Chichester on 31 May 1942 the German Army was then occupying territory 1,000 miles into Russia;[3] moreover account had to be taken of certain 'national' elements in the resistance movement, particularly in the Army. Such general statements, however, as 'the rights of *all* nations to self-determination within the framework of a European federation' and reestablishment of 'a free Polish and a free Czech state within their ethnographic frontiers' could not satisfy the British government. On 25 August 1939 that government's predecessor had guaranteed Poland, as she then stood, all support including immediate military assistance in the event of attack by a third power.[4] According to the memorandum, however, Poland would have been required to renounce without compensation considerable areas, perhaps even her access to the Baltic. It was doubtful whether a purely Czech state was viable and here too previous international obligations existed under the Munich Agreement, if nothing else. Finally the principle of self-determination would have been unacceptable to France if applied to Alsace and Lorraine.

The resistance movement's objectives were not primarily material; basically they wished to reestablish the dignity and the natural inalienable rights of man. Nevertheless they proposed to achieve these aims, as the memorandum explained, by the seizure of political power in Germany. But there were a number of obstacles to this: continuance of warfare in the east, essential for national defence against the Soviet Union and against 'anarchic developments'; the ubiquitous power of the *Gestapo* in Germany and the danger of Nazi revolts after the *coup*; the complete uncertainty about the British and American attitude to a change of regime in Germany; the problem of controlling the anticipated outbursts of hatred in the territories occupied by German troops. These last two problems could only be solved by international cooperation and this was the purpose of the appeal.

Sir Stafford Cripps read the memorandum and was very attracted by it. He gave it to Churchill who thought it 'very encouraging', as he noted in the margin. But that was all.[5] In August 1950, at the Consultative Assembly on the Council of Europe in Strasburg, Gerstenmaier reminded Churchill of the memorandum. Churchill 'remembered and regretted the course of events'.

Closely connected with this memorandum passed by Trott to Visser't Hooft were the conversations conducted in Stockholm in May 1942 by Hans Schönfeld and Dietrich Bonhoeffer with the Bishop of Chichester, George Kennedy Allen Bell.[6] Dr Hans Schönfeld was Director of the Research Section of the Ecumenical Council in Geneva and had known the Bishop of Chichester since 1929. Dr Dietrich Bonhoeffer was a pastor who had been in charge of the German Evangelical community in London from 1933 to 1935; he was a theologian of independent unorthodox views; from about August 1940 he had been working with Dohnanyi in OKW *Ausland/Abwehr* and at the end of October was seconded to the *Abwehr* office in Munich.[7]

In February 1941 Bonhoeffer was commissioned by Oster and Dohnanyi to go to Zurich and Geneva to reactivate the church contacts, which had lain idle since Dr Müller's talks in Rome in 1939–40 and to find out Allied ideas on peace aims.[8] His journey produced little as far as reestablishment of contact was concerned. In September 1941 Bonhoeffer went to Switzerland again and had talks with Visser't Hooft and others.[9] He urged his friends, particularly those in the Ecumenical Movement, to use their influence to ensure that the Allies would call a halt to military operations during the anticipated *coup* in Germany. But Visser't Hooft and Bonhoeffer received no definite answer to their queries in London. Too few people in influential positions believed that there was a really serious opposition in Germany. There was also an obvious misunderstanding between Bonhoeffer and many of those to whom he talked, who thought that he himself, and still more his masters, insisted on maintenance of the German 1939 frontiers. From about 11 to 23 May 1942 Bonhoeffer was in Switzerland again but, to his disappointment, met neither Visser't Hooft (he had meanwhile gone to London with Trott's memorandum), nor Schönfeld nor the latter's assistant Nils Ehrenström.[10]

It had long been known that Bishop Bell proposed to visit Sweden in May 1942 and, independently of each other, Schönfeld and Bonhoeffer planned to meet him there.[11] In preparation Bonhoeffer, through his brother Klaus and the latter's friend Dr Otto John, asked Jakob Kaiser, Wilhelm Leuschner and Max Habermann to give him a memorandum on their plans for the period following the overthrow of Hitler. But the trade union leaders refused and would only allow Bonhoeffer to give their names. They did not set much store by political soundings abroad so long as the Germans themselves had not succeeded in eliminating Hitler.

The Bishop arrived in Stockholm on 13 May 1942 and first visited various places in Sweden, returning a fortnight later to Stockholm where he stayed at the British Legation.

On 26 May he and Dr Schönfeld met at the headquarters of the Student Movement. Schönfeld gave a detailed account of the German opposition and its aims, in general on the lines of Trott's memorandum. Efforts to overthrow Hitler were under way, he said, possibly making use of a *putsch* by Himmler, whereupon the Army would seize power. The question now was whether Britain and America were prepared to negotiate with a post-Hitler or post-Himmler government and whether their attitude would differ from that of Versailles. Unless they could offer some encouragement in this respect, there was no hope of a *coup*.

When the two met again on 29 May Schönfeld reported primarily on the opposition from the churches and, at the Bishop's request, promised to reduce his report to writing.

In this *aide-mémoire* Schönfeld enumerated the main groups of conspirators: those in the *Wehrmacht* and the administration; leaders of the former trade unions and other working-class representatives; leaders of the Evangelical Church under Bishop D. Theophil Wurm and of the Roman Catholic Church under the Fulda Bishops' Conference. The leaders of these groups, he said, were now ready to seize the next opportunity to do away with Nazi domination, including the SS, the *Gestapo* and the SA. As Schönfeld explicitly emphasized, therefore, power would be seized, not by a military junta but by a government comprising all these three main groups.

Schönfeld gave the following three points as the main planks in the political programme of these groups (their similarity to those in Trott's memorandum is unmistakable, though they were not given in such detail): reestablishment of the rule of law and social justice in Germany with far-reaching self-government in the provinces; reconstruction of the economy 'according to truly socialistic lines'; instead of autarky close economic cooperation between free nations as the best guarantee against European militarism; a European federation of free countries including Great Britain, a free Polish and a free Czech state, with a common executive and a European Army. At present, he said, the situation in Germany was developing favourably for a *coup* by the Army and other opposition forces. A declaration by the Allies that they would enter into peace negotiations with a government formed by this opposition and on the basis of the points outlined above would assist and accelerate this development. Should the Allies, however, insist on fighting on till victory, as announced in the Atlantic Charter, then even the members of the conspiracy would continue to fight in the Army until the bitter end. In addition the opposition had information that the SS under Himmler was planning its own *coup* in order to save itself and its power. If, when the anticipated approach took place, the Allies would encourage the SS to do this, it would materially assist to set in motion the whole process of a change of regime; the Army would then have a welcome opportunity to eliminate Himmler and the SS.[12]

On 31 May the Bishop went to Sigtuna for talks with Harry Johansson, Head of the Nordic Ecumenical Institute, and Dr Manfred Björquist, Head of the Sigtuna Foundation. There, to his astonishment appeared 'another German pastor – Dietrich Bonhoeffer'. As Bonhoeffer records, the idea that he should go to Sweden to see Bishop Bell had originated from Oster and Dohnanyi. He had talked it over with them and they had consulted Beck, without whose agreement they would do nothing since he had been 'constituted coordinator' at the end of March.[13] Soon 30 May, only a few days after his return from Switzerland, Bonhoeffer was provided, through the good offices of Canaris, with 'Courier Pass No 474' from the Foreign Ministry and flew to Stockholm.[14] There he heard that the Bishop was in Sigtuna and immediately followed him.

In a private discussion Bonhoeffer gave an account of the opposition similar to that of Schönfeld. The Bishop told him of Schönfeld's visit and said that, dangerous though it was, he would be greatly assisted in countering the suspicion of his report which he anticipated from the British government if he could give a few names of leaders of the opposition. Although Bonhoeffer was obviously uneasy at this enormous responsibility, he gave the names of Beck, Hammerstein, Goerdeler, Leuschner, Jakob Kaiser and Schacht, describing the latter, however, as an opportunist; he indicated that Field Marshals von Kluge, von Bock, von Küchler and von Witzleben were 'trustworthy'.

Dr Schönfeld then arrived in Sigtuna. Bishop Bell, Johanssen, Björquist, Bonhoeffer, Schönfeld and his assistant Nils Ehrenström now all sat down together and discussed the possibilites of a *coup* in Germany, but in more general terms and without mentioning names. Bonhoeffer emphasized that they were not looking for an easy escape since Christians could not wish to escape punishment or even chaos if that was what God willed for them. When Visser't Hooft asked what he was praying for in the present situation, Bonhoeffer replied: 'If you want to know, I pray for the defeat of my country, for I think that is the only possibility of paying for all the suffering that my country has caused in the world.'[15] Schönfeld agreed – with certain provisos – that Berlin must be occupied by Allied troops; his reasoning was less fundamental, in other words more political, than that of Bonhoeffer. The question of a restoration of the monarchy under Prince Louis Ferdinand was also touched on.

Finally Schönfeld and Bonhoeffer urgently reiterated their view that 'there was little purpose in the resistance movement accepting all the perils to which they were exposed in pursuit of their aims if the Allied governments intended to mete out to a Germany purged of Hitler and his minions exactly the same treatment as to a Hitler-Germany'.[16] They asked Bishop Bell to obtain information on this subject from the British government and, if possible, inform them of the results. Should the reaction be positive, they proposed Adam von Trott zu Solz, a friend of Cripps' son, as participant in further talks. Information in both directions was to be passed via Geneva.

The Bishop returned home on 11 June. On 18 June he visited Mr Warner in the Foreign Office who suggested to him that he write to Anthony Eden, the Foreign Secretary. The Bishop wrote the same day, explaining briefly that the subject was connected with the memorandum which Eden had received through Visser't Hooft and asking for an interview. Eden fixed this for 20 June. He seemed highly impressed with the Bishop's comprehensive report but envisaged the possibility that, without their knowledge, the two pastors were being used by the German government to put forward peace feelers; similar attempts to gain contact were being made, he said, in Turkey and Spain. With an eye to Russia and the United States, however, the British government could not give even the smallest impression of negotiating with the enemy. Such was, and remained, the attitude of the western Allies to all attempts at contact by the German opposition.[17]

At the same time the Bishop handed over a secret memorandum, which he had drafted himself, on his talks with Schönfeld and Bonhoeffer. In this he gave an outline, similar to that of Schönfeld in his *aide-mémoire*, of the resistance movement and its aims: representatives of the Army and administration, of the former trade unions, of the Protestant and Catholic Churches all wanted to eliminate the Hitler regime including Himmler, Göring, Goebbels and the heads of the *Gestapo*, the SS and the SA. Would Britain advocate a monarchy? If so Prince Louis Ferdinand should be considered. The new government would renounce aggression, repeal the Nuremberg laws and cooperate in an international solution of the Jewish question; German troops would withdraw by stages from the countries which they had attacked and occupied; Germany would not further support Japan and would assist the Allies to end the war in the Far East; she would cooperate with the Allies in reconstruction of areas destroyed or damaged during the war. On behalf of the opposition Schönfeld and Bonhoeffer then asked whether, under these conditions, the Allies would negotiate peace with a new German government on the following basis: (1) Formation of a state based on the rule of law and on the principle of federalism together with far-reaching local self-government; (2) the closest possible international economic relations in Europe both as a matter of justice and as the most effective possible guarantee against militarism; (3) formation of a representative federation of free nations or states including a free Polish and a free Czech nation; (4) formation of a European army to control Europe; the German Army to be incorporated into it under centralized European command.

The opposition, Bell's memorandum continued, had complete confidence in the Army; should the Allies refuse to negotiate with a new non-Hitler government, it would fight to the bitter end. The opposition warned, however, against the millions of deaths which this would cause; for Europe it would be a suicidal struggle in fact. The opposition was strong enough to carry out a *coup*; it had groups and supporters in all important centres of power. Bell repeated the names given him by Bonhoeffer – Beck, Hammerstein, Goerdeler, Leuschner, Kaiser. The opposition knew that Himmler was planning his own *coup*; this might be a first step, but no more than that. The opposition wished to sweep away the entire present regime, including Himmler's SS. At the same time the opposition wished to pledge their goodwill. German troops would cooperate with Allied and neutral military units in the maintenance of order in Germany and in the territories now occupied by German troops. Some form of occupation of Germany was therefore already accepted.

Now, however, the memorandum continued, the opposition representatives with whom the Bishop had talked asked what encouragement the Allies could give the opposition leaders to enable them to set the *coup* in motion. Would, for instance, the Allied governments let the opposition know privately that they would be prepared to negotiate with a new government on the basis of the above principles? Alternatively could the Allies announce publicly and unequivocally that, after the fall of Hitler and his entire regime, they would be ready to negotiate with a German government on the basis of these principles?

Eden promised to consider the Bishop's report and memorandum. Meanwhile, on 13 July, the Bishop met Sir Stafford Cripps who gave an enthusiastic account of Trott and his memorandum transmitted through Visser't Hooft. Cripps had told Hooft to encourage Trott 'but on the basis of a defeated Germany'. The Bishop then showed Schönfeld's memorandum to Cripps who was so impressed by it that he proposed to show it to Eden. He accepted the argument that encouragement of the opposition could do no harm (to Britain) and in the best case might do much good.

On 17 July Eden wrote to the Bishop to say that he had examined these interesting documents with care and had no wish to question the honesty of the two Germans; he had, however, come to the conclusion that it would not be in Great Britain's national interest to reply. Thereupon Bell wrote back on 25 July saying that he was glad that Eden had given such careful attention to the papers and did not doubt the honesty of the two German pastors; he must, of course, bow to the Foreign Secretary's decision. Reading between the lines it is clear that, in view of the credibility of the two emissaries, the Bishop found the decision incomprehensible. He reemphasized his hope that the Foreign Secretary would be able 'in the near future to make it plain in an emphatic and public way that the British Government (and the Allies) have no desire to enslave a Germany which has rid itself of Hitler and Himmler and their accomplices'. There was, as he had said, a clear difference between Nazis and other Germans; the opposition was urgently awaiting recognition of this difference, with all its consequences, on the part of the British government. On 13 May 1940 Churchill had proclaimed Great Britain's purpose as 'war against a monstrous tyranny, never surpassed in the dark lamentable catalogue of human crime'.[18] Support of an internal German opposition pursuing the same aim was the obvious course if Great Britain, as Churchill had equally said, wished to achieve victory at any price. Nothing could be expected from the opposition without such support, in other words without a statement that there was no intention to enslave Germany and that anti-Nazis would not be treated exactly like Nazis. Otherwise the opposition would be forced to believe that

Lord Vansittart's remarks, which breathed hatred, represented official British policy.

Eden replied on 4 August. No one could believe in the opposition, he said, until it had taken active steps to remove the regime. So far the opposition had given 'little proof of its existence'; it had not shown itself in active operations like the resistance movements in the occupied countries. Under these circumstances it was not possible to promise Germany more than 'a place in a future Europe' after the war. The longer the German people tolerated the Nazi regime, the greater became its responsibility for the crimes which the regime committed in its name.

The Bishop replied on 17 August pointing out that resistance movements in occupied countries were fighting under different conditions; they had been promised liberation which had been explicitly refused to the Germans. They were the exception under the Atlantic Charter.

There was no purpose in arguing further with Eden. The Bishop was undeterred, however, and unwilling to end the correspondence without going on record once more in favour of the German anti-Hitler resistance. He explained that the longing for legality and justice, for removal of the Nazi regime and the hope that a better Germany could find a place in a future Europe were potent factors which might enable the opposition to come increasingly into the open.

After so hopeful a start the British government's refusal even to reply to the opposition's questions came as a severe disillusionment to Schönfeld and Bonhoeffer, as also to the Bishop, who had done all he could. On 30 July he had also passed copies of the documents given to Eden to John G. Winant, the American Ambassador in London, and had given him a detailed account of the opposition in Germany. Winant promised to inform the State Department but the Bishop heard no more from him. Undeterred, however, he continued his campaign, both in parliament and the press, for the formulation and announcement of reasonable peace aims applicable to Germany.

When Beck was told of the results of Bonhoeffer's and Schönfeld's efforts, he ordered a report to be prepared and passed to the Vatican. This was done.[19]

Trott, who had been named by Schönfeld and Bonhoeffer as a contact man for possible talks with representatives of the British government, visited the Swedish contacts from 18 to 28 September 1942, despite Eden's negative reaction to the overtures of Schönfeld and Bonhoeffer.[20] In his conversations there, Trott emphasized the danger of bolshevization of Germany from within, and he searched for ways of generating understanding on the British side for the efforts and aims of the German opposition and of producing some sort of statement of policy towards a Germany that had liberated itself of Hitler. But as he was about to leave Sweden, Trott wrote to Harry Johansson on 26 September 1942: 'I feel that you have fully understood that we do *not* intend to plead for support or even encouragement from friends on the other side – but that we wish to repose our faith in the necessity of some movement springing from like-thinking minds in the whole of Christian Europe to make salvation possible.'

It is fair to ask if the many misunderstandings Trott encountered were not at least partly caused by his tendency to reason and argue on very varied levels. It was certainly pointless to try to deal with Britain on any level other than that of practical politics, and the suggestion of a possible bolshevization of Germany from within, or of a solidarity movement for the salvation of Europe, were not obviously on this level. Had Trott forgotten that Britain wanted no part of the Holy Alliance of 1815, and that the danger of the bolshevization of Germany in 1919, when this was a much more unknown and horrifying quantity, had not caused Britain to do her utmost to modify the Treaty of Versailles in order to make it more acceptable to the German people? At this point Britain was inevitably more anxious to keep the anti-Hitler coalition going, and to win the war. The bolshevization of Germany would depend on the will of the occupation powers much more than on the wishes of the German people, and Trott's suggestions looked suspiciously like an attempt to split the coalition. Moreover, a certain amount of contradiction in Trott's statements could not be overlooked, and it was not at all clear whether Trott was speaking for a group able and willing to overthrow Hitler, or for a group that expressly did not wish to do so.[21]

23 Moltke 1943

Despite Allied refusals to deal with them the active members of the opposition continued their efforts even after Roosevelt and Churchill had agreed on the formula of 'Unconditional Surrender' in Casablanca in January 1943.

In the same month Trott went to Switzerland, where he met Dulles through the good offices of Gero von Schulze-Gaevernitz who was on Dulles' staff. Trott tried to explain to Dulles how essential it was for the enemy to differentiate between Germans and Nazis if the resistance movement was to have any possibility of action.[1] People in the resistance movement began to feel that 'the Anglo-Saxon countries are filled with bourgeois prejudice and Pharisaic theorizing. There is a strong temptation to turn East. The reason for the eastward orientation is the belief in the possibility of fraternization between the Russian and German peoples, although not between the present governments. Both have broken with bourgeois ideology, both have suffered deeply, both desire a radical solution of social problems which transcends [sic] national limits ... Fraternization between Germans and imported foreign workers is also an important element.'

Even if there had been on the American side any willingness to recognize the opposition and acknowledge the difference between Germans and Nazis, Trott's somewhat woolly and inaccurate statements, together with the threat of turning East, were not likely to further such an attitude on the part of the American government. Dulles maintained that 'to stop short of total military victory, to allow Germany any doubt of its total defeat, would have been unthinkable on our part'. From summer 1943 Langbehn could only report from Switzerland that 'the Anglo-Americans have absolute confidence in victory and are determined to see it through to the end'.[2] The longer the opposition failed to show itself by 'deeds' – nothing was known in the West, of course, about the assassination attempts, that of March 1943 for instance – the greater became the suspicion of its sincerity. Before the war, Dulles said, people had wanted to appease the devil; now no one would trust any German.[3] But since the opposition was opposing as a matter of conscience, they could not simply resign themselves to failure. They pondered over possible success but it was not the overriding factor.

In June 1943 Trott was officially despatched to Turkey by the Foreign Ministry to discover what the Turkish attitude was; secretly he probed the possibilities of establishing fresh contact with the Allies.[4] It is not clear what progress he made. But immediately thereafter Moltke also travelled to Turkey, having been given the opportunity by Canaris who commissioned him to enquire into the case of certain ships which had moved from the Danube into the Sea of Marmora. In Istanbul Moltke discussed the prospects of agreement between the opposition and the Allies with Professor Hans Wilbrandt whom he had known from earlier days, and with Professor Alexander Rüstow, a friend of Wilbrandt's who was in touch with the American secret service.[5]

Moltke proposed that an officer of the German General Staff with all necessary information and full authority be brought over to England to agree with the Allies on free passage for Allied troops through the German front in the west, the eastern front against Russia continuing to be held. He wished to discuss this with Alexander C. Kirk, the American Minister in Cairo. His object was to obtain acceptable peace conditions and withdrawal of the demand for unconditional surrender; as a *quid pro quo* the Western Allies were to occupy Germany. He rejected an attempt at assassination and an internal *coup* using force.[6]

Rüstow, however, said that there could be no question of withdrawal of the hated formula and, if Moltke insisted on this, he could not undertake to mediate further. Moltke thereupon gave way.[7] The journey to Cairo never took place and Moltke had to return to Germany without having made any form of contact with the Western Powers. Wilbrandt and Rüstow, however, promised to pursue the matter.

Finally, in November 1943, Moltke received news that contact had been established and Kirk would come to Turkey secretly for a discussion. Once more assisted by Canaris, Moltke went to Istanbul in December prepared, if the American reaction was positive, to offer himself as mediator and arrange for the German and Allied military commands in the West to cooperate. But Kirk was not in Istanbul after all. Moltke, who was under imminent threat of arrest, was sadly disappointed. He did meet Major-General R. G. Tindall, the American Military Attaché in Turkey, but the encounter was fruitless; both sides were suspicious and the American merely wanted military information from Moltke.

Shortly thereafter General Donovan, Head of OSS (Office of Strategic Services) himself brought to New York an offer of negotiation from the resistance movement. What he had was a letter written on the paper of the German Embassy in Ankara and signed by Dr Paul Leverkuehn who had been in Washington before the war as German representative on the Mixed Claims Commission. This document was submitted to Professor Karl Brandt of Stanford University, California, who was in New York on business. He knew certain leading members of the opposition personally and Trott had visited him in Palo Alto in December 1939.[8] With elaborate security and secrecy precautions Professor Brandt was asked to go at once to General Donovan's office in Rockefeller Centre, New York, examine the document with the utmost care and give an opinion on it. There was to be a discussion with President Roosevelt next morning to decide whether to follow the offer up or not.[9]

The letter said that the opposition could not guarantee that the entire western front would remain inactive in the event of an Allied invasion; it had, however, sufficient influence with important German Army and some *Luftwaffe* commanders to ensure that counter-measures against an Allied landing would at least be delayed. If this were to happen the Western Powers should be prepared to negotiate with a German government formed by the opposition after a *coup*. Professor Brandt acknowledged the offer to be genuine; he already knew of these ideas and he also knew that OSS was very well informed about the German opposition. That night the document, together with Brandt's opinion on it, was taken to Washington under strict guard by Mrs Emmy Rado, General Donovan's assistant (who later worked for OSS in Military Government, Berlin, with the rank of Colonel). Brandt later heard from Mrs Rado that, based on his opinion, Donovan had advocated acceptance of the offer but that President Roosevelt had flatly declined to negotiate with 'these East German Junkers'.

Before leaving Turkey Moltke had written a letter to Alexander Kirk, whom he had known since 1936.[10] In it he said how much he wished to talk over the possibilities of ending the war more quickly and dealing with the resulting problems; he offered to come to Istanbul again, at the earliest in February 1944 and at the latest in April. Kirk replied on 10 January 1944 saying that the war could be ended by nothing other than the unconditional surrender of the German *Wehrmacht*. This information reached Moltke's friends in Istanbul,[11] but it did not reach Moltke. He was arrested on 19 January 1944.

24 Trott 1943–1944

Until the very last moment, only a few days before 20 July 1944 in fact, Trott was still pursuing his efforts to establish contacts and obtain assurances. As did a number of other members of the opposition from the 'Kreisau Circle' and their friends (Eugen Gerstenmaier for instance), Trott visited Sweden in the autumn of 1943 (27 October to 3 November) and in late October had an exhaustive discussion with Dr Ivar Anderson, editor of the *Svenska Dagbladet*.[1] The subject of their talk was the establishment of some contact with Allied diplomats. The opposition urgently needed outside help for their *coup* and without delay; otherwise, in the light of the meagre forces and resources at the disposal of the resistance movement, the danger of counter-action by the regime and of civil war was great. The major obstacle was the demand for unconditional surrender. In reply to a question by Trott Anderson said that the prospects of outside help were extremely small, whereupon Trott said that they could only wait. This was of course highly dangerous, he added, because it might mean that Russia would win the game.[2]

Anderson finally arranged meetings for Trott with Christian Günther, the Swedish Foreign Minister,[3] and Sir Walter Monckton, then Under-Secretary in the British Ministry of Information.[4] Both meetings were fruitless, as also was a contact with members of the British Embassy in Stockholm arranged by a Swedish lady.[5] Trott received no answers apart from assurances that his information would be transmitted to London.[6]

About the time of his visits to Sweden Trott wrote certain comments on the peace programme of the American churches, which was presented to the Ecumenical Council in Geneva in November 1943.[7] In these comments Trott emphasized the necessity of international federal organizations based on the rule of law instead of that of force; a measure of self-government should ensure the cultural autonomy and equality of all peoples and racial groups. He acknowledged 'the inadequacy of the sovereign nation-state as the ultimate international authority' and the necessity for some limitation of national sovereignty, without which the problems of central and eastern Europe could not be solved. Without some restriction of national sovereignty, moreover, effective limitation of armaments and prevention of the recurrent misuse of armed force were not possible; in this connection, however, too great hopes should not be placed on measures of enforcement. Disarmament applied to the defeated countries alone would deprive the new international organization in advance of its quality of objective legality and would create second-class nations – 'international cooperation burdened from the outset with mistrust of entire peoples cannot be lasting'. In the long term peace could not be guaranteed solely by an international police force and reduction of armaments; rather one must look to the effects of 'continuous practical and constructive cooperation between nations', of 'desuetude' of suspicion, hatred, fear and enmity in relations between peoples and a gradual change in traditional ways of behaviour. Compromise and agreement are the keynotes of this memorandum. It also dealt with the economic aspect, stressing freedom of the masses from want and the necessity to restrict the monopoly position of individual states, not in order to deprive them of something but to assist the development of the less powerful. Free trade was an obvious ideal provided that the smaller nations were not prevented from expanding their exports by currency and other restrictions and provided that access to the raw materials of rich countries did not remain theoretical. The Christian way of life was another central concept running through the entire memorandum and this was contrasted with 'the agglomeration of humanity' and its evil results. Nothing is known of any reaction to this document.

Trott was in Stockholm again in March 1944 and yet once more for a period of several days between 19 June and 3 July.[8] As with many other probes from the German side, both from Himmler's entourage and anti-Nazi circles, the primary object was to obtain withdrawal of the demand for unconditional surrender and its replacement by clear acceptable armistice terms and an assurance that negotiations would take place after the end of hostilities. In this instance, however, Trott took pains not to request any modification of the 'unconditional surrender' formula *before* the overthrow of Hitler by the opposition.[9]

Roosevelt's view was that there could be no deviation from the principle of total victory over Germany as a whole, that there was no desire to annihilate the Germans as human beings but that he was not prepared to say that the German nation would not be destroyed in so far as, for the Germans, the words 'nation' and '*Reich*' and all that they implied were one and the same thing. The Germans should be allowed to live, he said, and should quietly place their trust in the generosity of the Americans; the errors and failures of the post-1918 period, however, must not be allowed to happen again; the Germans must divest themselves of their warlike and aggressive nature. This might take two generations but anyone who thought otherwise must realize that, after a time, there would be a third World War.[10]

After much hesitation Roosevelt eventually drafted a proclamation to the German people and all those who sympathized with them; it was to be published in the name of the three major Allies shortly after the planned Allied invasion of the European continent.[11] In it he reiterated that the Allied aim was not 'total destruction of the German people' but 'total destruction of the philosophy of those Germans who have announced that they could subjugate the world'. In the long term the Allies wanted individual, political, religious and intellectual freedom together with greater social and economic justice. The victory of the Allies was assured. It was unintelligent of the Germans to carry on the war; every additional casualty was an unnecessary one. Admittedly the Allies would also suffer losses if the war continued, but their reserves and population were so incomparably larger that, as the war went on, the sufferings of the German people, of every family in fact, would be by far the greater.

For the Germans this proclamation was highly encouraging. In their desperate situation of 1944 they would inevitably have regarded it as a significant departure from the principle of unconditional surrender. But the proclamation was never made, for it could not be done without Churchill and Stalin. On 25 May Churchill wrote to Roosevelt that 'considerable concern was expressed' in the British cabinet 'at the tone of friendship shown to the Germans at this moment when troops are about to engage'.[12] One could hardly proclaim at this moment that the Allies and the Germans were divided by little more than the latter's 'evil philosophy'. There would then hardly be sound reason for continuing the struggle. Almost all Europe was crying for vengeance against the brutal tyrant. How would the total disarmament of Germany, on which they were agreed, be carried out in practice? How was Poland to be compensated for the cession of the Curzon Line to Russia if she was not given East Prussia and certain areas reaching to the Oder? In short, in this form and at this time Churchill and the cabinet could not agree to the proclamation.

The next day Stalin replied in similar vein: the nature of the Germans held out little hope of success; the uncertainties of the military situation immediately before the invasion constituted a further factor against the proposed proclamation.[13] There may have been fear that the opposition might be encouraged by such a proclamation, that they might succeed in overthrowing the regime, and that then the Western Allies might deal with them separately after all. Finally, the communists had at this time not yet entered into any negotiations with the opposition – had they had any chance of influencing a post-*coup* government, it might have been a different proposition.[14] Roosevelt gave way; he could say with a clear conscience that his hands had been tied.

The difficulties were insuperable. There could be no agreement between the Allies and the German opposition because of mutual suspicions between the Allies, because of the excessive number of persons involved, each with their opinions, their convictions and their rancours, and finally because of the imminence of the invasion. Before the Second Front had scored its first great victory and before the success of a great new Russian summer offensive Stalin had no wish to cause the Germans to lay down their arms. He was not very concerned with human life and the further the Red Army advanced, the better. Churchill put the dilemma thus: 'I think myself that the message might conceivably be taken as a peace feeler and that the Germans might reply that they accepted your [Roosevelt's] note as a basis for further discussion.'[15] In this situation Trott's missions had no prospect of success. He did not, of course, know of the exchange of views between Washington, London and Moscow but he was the victim of the results.

Johnson, the American Minister in Stockholm, had sent to his government detailed reports on both Trott's visits to Sweden.[16] During his March visit Trott had hoped to reactivate the British Embassy contact established early in November 1943 and possibly obtain from London the answer of which there had seemed to be some hope at that time. Through the same Swedish lady who had acted as intermediary in the autumn of 1943, he indicated to the British Embassy that there was now somewhat greater probability of an understanding with the Russians; they were fighting very hard at the front whereas the British and Americans were merely killing German civilians by bombing. As agreed with his backers – it is not clear whether these were the Beck-Goerdeler group, the Kreisau group, or the circle around Stauffenberg that included elements of both[17] – however, Trott now asked for nothing in advance except a gesture. (On his next visit to Sweden in June, Trott once again requested a qualification or retraction of the 'unconditional surrender' formula.[18]) The leaders of the conspiracy had now become convinced that the *coup* must be attempted under all circumstances, with or without external political 'assurances'.[19] Trott proposed that, on the fall of the Nazi regime, the British should cease their air raids on Berlin and so indicate their approval of the *coup*.

Stauffenberg, who was by this time the practical leader of the opposition, was apparently firmly convinced that the position of the Western Allies was strategically catastrophic and that they could not afford to treat Germany badly; they would have urgent need of her in face of the menacing Russian superiority on the continent.[20] Trott thought this an illusion. Both were right. Stauffenberg, however, assumed that the policy of the Western governments would be dictated by their own interests and their view of the future, whereas Trott knew that this was not so.

In answer to Trott's question the British Embassy replied that they were interested in his information but had nothing to say on the subject. The Embassy was prepared to take at their face value Trott's assurances that he was acting on behalf of the opposition, though fruitless attempts were made to find out who its members were. The Foreign Office, however, inclined to the view that Trott was an agent of the regime – there were plenty of them going around on behalf of the now somewhat pitiable German super-man.[21] Policy was made in London, not in the Embassy in Stockholm.

After this abortive attempt Trott was extremely downcast and discouraged. Germany's situation was so desperate, however, that every effort, however hopeless, had to be made to persuade the Allies to make some positive gesture. In many of his reports from Berne Dulles urged that something be done on these lines.[22] Eisenhower and General Bedell Smith, his Chief of Staff, also took the view that the demand for unconditional surrender should be abandoned since it merely raised the fighting morale of the Germans. Quite apart from these concrete and pressing considerations, however, in Trott's view (and here he was in full agreement with Moltke and the 'Kreisau Circle') some progress would have been registered had there been any form of cooperation at all – for the future, after the end of the slaughter.[23]

In April 1944 Trott paid a further visit to Switzerland where he met Dulles' assistant, Schulze-Gaevernitz. Trott pointed out that Russian influence in Germany was growing all the time – owing to the 'Free Germany National Committee', the mass of forced labourers in Germany, the presence of Russian prisoners of war and even more the continuous stream of constructive ideas for the post-war period issuing from Russia. In comparison the West had nothing to offer as regards the future of central Europe. The working-class leaders feared that, if present developments continued, the present dictatorship would be replaced, not by democracy but by another dictatorship.

They therefore urged: 1. Some encouraging declaration to the working class from the democracies; 2. a declaration that Western business interests would not seek to influence the organization and development of the German labour movement; 3. a statement of the degree of self-government to be granted to Germany with emphasis on self-government in the *Länder* and in parishes; 4. a declaration that the Allies would not set up a puppet government; 5. a message of encouragement specifically aimed at the socialist leaders; 6. leaflets, which would best be drafted in agreement with the resistance movement so as to fit the psychological situation, to be distributed in such quantities that the *Gestapo* could not collect and destroy them; 7. establishment of active contact 'between the German socialist labour movement and progressive forces in the West' as a counter-weight to the links between Russia and the German communists; 8. restriction of air raids to military and industrial targets in order not to promote the proletarianization of central Europe.

These were not terms or conditions to be fulfilled before the *coup* could take place. They were simply proposals for the prevention of the anticipated Russian hegemony in Europe. The Russian armies were advancing inexorably, while France, Holland and northern Italy were still under German domination. Nevertheless, however sympathetic Dulles was to Trott's ideas and however genuinely he recognized their strategic validity, he could do no more than report to his superiors. To Trott he had to say that he should not rely on anything.

Trott had agreed to meet Albrecht von Kessel in Geneva at the same time but the meeting did not take place. The two were able to spend a few days together in Venice, however, in the second half of May. In the company of his friend and in these beautiful surroundings Trott recovered from his deep depression and regained some of his strength.

In June Trott made a further attempt to make contact in Stockholm.[24] On 21 June Trott talked with a fairly high-ranking British diplomat who was also a member of the secret service, David McEwan.[25] McEwan said that the Allies were planning a new and comprehensive bombing offensive against industrial centres in western Germany and that they might consider dropping the idea if the opposition was strong enough to help them end the war quickly. Trott promised all required information on condition that the Allies revoke or qualify their demand for unconditional surrender. In a memorandum Trott wrote at the request of McEwan, he described, without mentioning any names, the political situation of the German militant opposition to Hitler. It was psychologically and politically impossible for these men, Trott wrote, 'to shoulder the burden and blame of Hitler's defeat unless they can hope to offer the people some improvement or advantage in their situation compared to what would follow Hitler's own defeat. Accepting unconditional surrender now, they would feel unable later on to counteract the mass slogan of having "stabbed in the back" our fighting forces.' That in turn would make it impossible for them to gain political control in Germany and to establish a new system on broadly socialistic lines, but it would probably bring to power strongly nationalist or communist elements. Trott was unable to offer assurances of action, however, in exchange for 'some qualification of the term "unconditional surrender",' but merely stated that 'it is recognized, however, that the opposition must first act and establish itself . . . provided that some qualification of the term "unconditional surrender" is forthcoming' – in other words, without such qualification there was not likely to be any action.[26]

On 22 June he told a Swedish intermediary who was in touch with the American Legation, that the 'Free Germany National Committee' was now active on Germany territory; the Russians had dropped organizers by parachute. Trott's resistance group, he said, had no scruples about working with the 'National Committee'; they wished to have contacts both with the Russians and with the 'Anglo-Americans'. They had not, however, yet contacted the 'National Committee' because a friend in the *Gestapo* had warned them that it had been penetrated by spies. His group, he said, was composed of bourgeois, Catholic and Social-Democrat elements and was in touch with certain officer circles. They hoped to emerge as a political force after the fall of Hitler and were preparing a *coup* against the Nazis. At that time, Trott also attempted to contact Mme Alexandra Michailovna Kollontay, the Soviet Ambassador in Stockholm.[27]

This contact did not materialize perhaps owing to lack of time. As is well known, Russian officials invariably have to ask for instructions from Moscow and their freedom of action is severely limited. Moreover the implied threat, voiced with increasing frankness by Trott, clearly missed its mark. This was not the way to persuade the Western Powers to come out openly in favour of the opposition. They had no wish to tie their hands and sensed, with some justification, an attempt to split the alliance. The Russians were extremely suspicious; Roosevelt and Churchill were very strict in their observance of their obligation to consult their ally; they immediately informed each other and Stalin of any peace feelers received.[28] Allen W. Dulles, the OSS representative in Berne, had reported back to Washington that Gisevius and another emissary of the opposition, Waetjen, had approached him with a proposal from Beck and Goerdeler to mastermind a *coup d'état* on condition that the opposition group 'would deal directly with the Western Allies alone after overthrowing the Nazi regime . . . excluding the USSR from all negotiations . . .' This information had been transmitted to the British and Soviet Embassies in Washington dated 24 May 1944.[29]

On 23 June, through the Swedish senator Professor Gunnar Myrdal, Trott met John Scott, the correspondent of the American periodicals *Time* and *Life*. He made it abundantly clear that the demand for unconditional surrender was a powerful reinforcement to German fighting morale and was playing straight into Goebbels' hands. Until it was withdrawn there would be no hope of a successful *coup* in Germany; the Germans would continue to fight because they could see no alternative. In the later stages, however, the Russians would occupy part of Germany and most of the well-disposed anti-Nazis would gravitate thither because they could clearly expect more sympathetic treatment and a better understanding of their sense of dignity from the Russians than from the Americans. For his part, Trott said, he would act this way. Trott enumerated the following points as important for the treatment of Germany if the Western Allies wished to avoid the dangers described above: (1) Demobilization to be carried out by German officers and not too quickly in order to avoid total chaos with the resulting threat of revolution; (2) Maintenance of a certain degree of German sovereignty.

On 3 July Trott was back in Germany. He wished to go to Sweden once more in July but could no longer obtain a travel permit.[30] Alexander Werth, a member of his staff in the Foreign Ministry, accordingly undertook the journey. It was as fruitless as the rest.

25 Gisevius

In autumn of 1939 Dr Hans Bernd Gisevius began his career as 'diplomat' of the opposition when he smuggled a letter from Dr Schacht to George Frazer, the banker and former president of the Bank for International Settlements, in Switzerland.[1] Gisevius also played a role in connection with the talks in Rome conducted by Dr Josef Müller in 1939–40.[2] At the instigation of Oster and Canaris, Gisevius was called up to serve in the Army, more precisely in the *Amt Ausland/Abwehr*, and in summer of 1940 he was installed in a counter-intelligence post under the *Abwehr* in the German Consulate General in Zurich where he was appointed vice-consul.[3] Gisevius' work included shielding other members of the German underground who had connections in Switzerland and who were frequently in danger of being discovered by agents of the *Gestapo* and SD (SS Security Service) operating in Switzerland. In his key position Gisevius was aware of and in some way a participant in most opposition activities that were channelled via Switzerland, including Bonhoeffer's 'mission' to Sweden and other efforts of the German Evangelical and Confessing Churches and their ecumenical contacts. For instance, he also took part in the drafting of a letter by the Rev. Asmussen in 1942 which became a basis for the 'confession of guilt' of the German Evangelical Church proclaimed in Stuttgart in 1945. In Zurich he was to maintain contact with the enemy on behalf of the opposition. In war, such contacts are best maintained through secret-service methods and channels; but in any case really useful contact could not begin to be established before the end of 1942, the first time there had been any serious prospect of an opposition *coup* since spring of 1940; it was then that Allen W. Dulles, who knew the American President well, came to Berne.[4] Dulles' closest assistant, Gero von Schulze-Gaevernitz, was a friend of Gisevius and told him that one could talk with Dulles not only on the secret-service level but also 'on a purely political level' (by which phrase he meant primarily diplomatic contacts). Gisevius then obtained authorization from Beck, Canaris and Oster to build up and solidify the contact from January 1943 on – at about the same time Trott transmitted to Schulze-Gaevernitz his first memorandum for Dulles.[5]

Gisevius' first object was to convince Dulles that America should concentrate on halting the advance of the Bolshevik world revolution rather than on winning a war.[6] On this premise, he pleaded again and again for an arrangement between the opposition and the Western Powers that would provide for continuation of the war in the east. At first Gisevius met only lack of understanding on the American side; then he was forced to acknowledge the realities of the coalition against Germany.[7]

Dulles' answer was always the same: separate arrangements were out of the question, the war would be ended by the United States only in concert with her allies, and peace would not be concluded without them.[8] It was probably not unimportant in this connection that the American government was concious of a race between the United States and the German *Reich* for the production of operational atomic bombs. At any rate, even though the Americans were undoubtedly convinced of their industrial and military superiority in the long term, it would have been frivolous to risk losing their Russian ally's assistance in defeating Germany and, in future, perhaps Japan, when the compensation for such a risk was as uncertain as the statements coming from the German opposition. The invasion of France had not yet been carried out, the effectiveness of the atomic bomb as an instrument of war was not yet known, Japan was still in control of a vast area of Asian mainland and the struggle against the Japanese was at least as bloody, cruel and hard as that against Germany. Not only Trott and John, but also Beck, through Gisevius, Waetjen and Strünck, were brought up against some of these realities again and again when they made their overtures, or harboured illusory hopes.

In March 1944, despite all the negative reactions from the Western Allies received so far, and despite his deep insight into the overall strategic position, Beck once more wanted 'clear information': Did the Allies want a constructive, that is to say conservative reorganization of post-war Germany? Did they want to 'eliminate the Nazi system in collaboration with the *fronde*, or were they now prisoners of ideological, diplomatic and strategic considerations?' Gisevius was instructed to put these questions to Dulles, acting as Beck's representative.[9] If Gisevius had reported to Beck the negative attitude of the Western Allies as early as January 1943 (then underlined by the Casablanca Declaration), and again and again later, as he and Dulles and Hassell all say,[10] it is difficult to see what the useful function of the opposition's outpost in Berne was, since the basic and obvious results of its work were not accepted in Berlin. Admittedly it seems that Gisevius himself was not fully convinced of the inflexibility of the Allied position for about another year after January 1943.[11] During this time he may therefore have kept alive unrealistic hopes on the part of Beck. But from about February 1944 Gisevius' prognostications hardly differ from those of John with whom he takes issue so sharply.[12]

No doubt the overtures of John, Trott and others in Madrid, Stockholm and also in Switzerland did not make Gisevius' life any easier; he felt justified in considering himself the 'legitimate' representative of the opposition led by Beck and Goerdeler, especially from March 1942 when Beck had been recognized by most groups as their central authority.[13] It was probably naïve to think that a variety of contacts would help rather than damage the prospects of the opposition, that it would be useful to have contacts, and not merely contacts but serious communication, in Stockholm, in Madrid, in Geneva, in

Istanbul, and wherever American and British diplomats and intelligence agents could be approached. There were enough reasons for caution and suspicion on the Allied side as it was, without this confusing variety of contacts. From the Allied point of view, it could not be ruled out that the opposition was involved in the Venlo affair; the action promised in the autumn and winter of 1939–40 had never materialized although the British had gone quite a long way in trying to encourage the opposition; Trott was always in an ambiguous position carrying out official business for the German Foreign Office as well as his diplomacy for the opposition – it was not far-fetched to suspect that he could be an *agent provocateur* whose purpose was to elicit some British statement that could be used to 'prove' that Britain was negotiating with the Germans behind the Russians' backs; it was often not at all clear for whom in Germany the various emissaries were speaking – did they represent a group that was able and determined to overthrow Hitler, or one such as the 'Kreisau Circle' that in contrast was opposed to any attempts at overthrowing the dictator? But the desire of the conspirators to leave no avenue of contact unused is also understandable. Moreover, the different groups had different concepts for the reorganization of Germany, and these they wished to bring to the attention of the potential occupation powers. Trott was talking about the application of modern socialistic principles in all fields of political and economic life in 1942;[14] in the same year, Schönfeld said in a memorandum that the German economy must be reorganized 'according to truly socialistic lines' after the war;[15] in his June 1944 memorandum Trott referred to a group that had now been formed to lead the fight against Hitler, potentially representative of 'the two churches, the moderate as opposed to the violently communist working-class organizations, the conservative and progressive elements in the bureaucracy and army'.[16] The objections to inclusion of trade-union leaders, and, indeed, to any opening to the left, voiced by Gisevius and Helldorf among others, at first also by Stauffenberg and as late as 15 July 1944 by Strünck have been mentioned.[17] In the face of such important disagreements on long-term planning, members of various opposition groups who had an opportunity to travel abroad felt obliged not to leave contact with the Allied Powers entirely to another representative of another group who might be pursuing a different post-war concept, even though a united front abroad would undoubtedly have served the opposition better.

In 1943 Gisevius was sucked into the vortex which developed around the arrest of Bonhoeffer, Dohnanyi and Dr Müller, and he escaped arrest only by a precipitate departure for Switzerland.[18] As Gisevius was now threatened and so less useful, and since he could no longer travel easily to Germany and back to Switzerland, another contact man was installed in the German Consulate General in Zurich: the lawyer Dr Eduard Waetjen. Captain (res.) Dr Strünck, who also worked for the *Abwehr*, was the principal courier who carried information and instructions back and forth between Zurich and Berlin. He visited Gisevius four times in 1944: on 15 February, 4 May, 6 June, and 8 July.[19]

With Waetjen Gisevius went to see Dulles in April 1944, on express instructions from Beck, Goerdeler and their group (not on Stauffenberg's instructions, therefore). They declared that Beck and Goerdeler were ready and willing to lead a *coup d'état* against Hitler, as Dulles reported to Washington on 12 April 1944 and again after another contact, on 16 May 1944.[20] Dulles continued, however: 'Such action would be contingent upon assurances from Britain and the United States that, once the Nazis had been overthrown, negotiations would then be carried out solely with the Western Powers and under no circumstances with the USSR. The essential conservatism of the group's planners was stressed, but also its willingness to cooperate with any available elements of the Left except for the communists. The group expressed its anxiety to keep Central Europe from coming under Soviet domination. If the capitulation were to be made primarily to the Soviet Union, the negotiations would have to be carried on by another group. Such *Wehrmacht* commanders in the West as von Rundstedt and Falkenhausen, the declaration maintained, would be ready to assist the Allied landings once the Nazis were removed from power.'

Gisevius and Waetjen had then actually been instructed to offer secret peace or armistice negotiations between the opposition and the Western Allies. These would obviously not remain secret for long and would inevitably lead to the break-up of the coalition of the Western Powers with the Soviet Union. Since all were agreed that it was only a question of months before the final victory of the Allies, this can only be taken seriously as an attempt to persuade the Western Powers to join forces with a non-Nazi Germany against the Soviet Union, the vanguard of the World Revolution.

Gisevius, however, could not report anything much different from what Trott and John had told the groups for whom they had made their contacts. As Dulles wrote to the head office of the OSS in Washington on 12 April 1944: 'To these overtures the OSS representative said little beyond expressing his strong conviction that the United States would never act without previous consultation with the USSR.'[21] Nevertheless, Gisevius and Waetjen again approached Dulles, on instructions from the Beck-Goerdeler group which claimed Rundstedt, Falkenhausen, Heusinger, Olbricht and even Zeitzler as members, with a plan to end the war in the west while continuing it in the east. Dulles wrote to Washington on 16 May 1944:[22] 'The group was reported ready to help Allied units get into Germany if the Allies agreed that the *Wehrmacht* should continue to hold the Eastern Front. They proposed in detail: (1) three Allied airborne divisions should land in the Berlin region with the assistance of the local army commanders, (2) major amphibious landings should be undertaken at or near Bremen and Hamburg, (3) landings in France should follow, although Rommel cannot be counted on for cooperation, (4) reliable German units in the area of Munich would isolate Hitler and other high Nazis in Ober Salzburg.[23] The opposition group is reported to feel that Germany has lost the war and that the only chance of avoiding Communism in Germany is to facilitate occupation of as large a section of Europe as possible by American and British forces before collapse of the Eastern Front.'

This time, Gisevius and Waetjen added that they believed the request for separate arrangements excluding the Soviet Union was unrealistic, and that they were reporting to Beck and Goerdeler accordingly.[24] The time for negotiations had definitely passed, Gisevius wrote to Beck and Hansen in letters carried by Strünck.[25] Gisevius further told Dulles in May that the most important thing was the early occupation of Germany by British and American troops, and if they knew some way of carrying out such an occupation quickly, 'the Allies might do well to ignore their [the opposition group's] propositions', because he, Gisevius, had no confidence in the political courage of the German generals.[26]

When he reported to Berlin, the only instruction Gisevius received was to do nothing more.[27]

Then, on 8 July 1944, Captain Strünck came to Switzerland again. Gisevius learnt of his arrival on 9 July.[28] Strünck said that the collapse of Army Group Centre in Russia and the invasion of Normandy had galvanized the opposition activists. General Fromm, Commander of the Home Army, had joined them. But the opposition still planned to begin the liquidation of the war by withdrawing on the western front and by throwing the best divisions against the Red Army. Since this information came from Colonel Hansen via Strünck, it can be assumed that it had been approved by Stauffenberg.[29] Dulles reported on these latest contacts on 12, 13 and 18 July and concluded 'that a dramatic event might take place up north'. On 11 July Gisevius and Strünck travelled to Berlin to be at hand for the *coup d'état*.

26 Miscellaneous Contacts

Until the final days preceding 20 July 1944 all possible contacts were kept open and some fresh ones created. As late as 15 July Dr Theodor Steltzer, a prominent member of the 'Kreisau Circle', passed a memorandum to Moltke's British friends, Lionel Curtis in particular, giving the situation and views of the 'Circle'; the object was to prevent the Allies taking ill-considered post-war measures.[1]

In September 1943 Goerdeler told Hassell that he still had a line to Churchill through Jakob Wallenberg. He went on to say, however, that Churchill had passed word that London would 'look with benevolent interest' upon a German opposition government. This seemed somewhat improbable.[2] An inquiry designed to elicit such a response from the American government made via the American Minister in Stockholm, Herschel V. Johnson, remained without any reply.[3]

There is much to show that in June and July 1944 Stauffenberg had one or two contacts of his own to Western military agencies. In the winter of 1943–44 Berthold von Stauffenberg and Captain (Navy) Alfred Kranzfelder (both were working in naval Headquarters) had been sent to Sweden on duty and while there they had tried to establish touch with Churchill through the Wallenberg brothers.[4] Trott told the *Gestapo* that, when he visited Sweden in the summer of 1944, he had been commissioned by Stauffenberg to find out 'what the attitude of Britain and the USA would be if, in the short term, Germany found it necessary to open negotiations'.[5] In mid-August Goerdeler told the *Gestapo* that in June Stauffenberg had suggested Graf Bismarck to him as an intermediary to Churchill.[6] Goerdeler was vexed by this since Wallenberg was in the habit of visiting Bismarck when in Berlin; Goerdeler accordingly suspected that Stauffenberg was trying to take over his contact without previous discussion. It is not possible to say whether this is correct or merely a story told to the *Gestapo* pending the availability of further documentary evidence.[7] In his memoirs written in prison in November 1944 Goerdeler also records that Stauffenberg told him on 18 July that Churchill was in possession of his (Stauffenberg's) demand that in the event of 'an action' all German territory must remain within the *Reich*. No more is known and allowance must be made for Stauffenberg's obvious optimism; the nature and effectiveness of his contacts, however, will remain obscure until the British and American files become available.

Throughout the war contact was maintained between German and non-German resistance movements, the closest being that to the Norwegians and Dutch. The 'Kreisau Circle' was particularly active in this respect.[8] In contrast to the connections described above, the purpose here was not to come to some accommodation with the enemy, but to prepare the ground for the European Federation to be formed after the war, thereby eliminating nation-states and nationalism. Additional aims were to alleviate the oppression of the population in the occupied territories, to give timely warning of acts of vengeance, anti-Jewish measures, punitive expeditions, deportations and if possible arrange for persons to be released from arrest.[9] As a subsidiary but important issue, through the contacts between the German and non-German resistance movements, the Allies received better and more reliable information on the German resistance.

Steltzer, Moltke, Dietrich Bonhoeffer and Canaris arranged for Bishop Berggrav's release from arrest in April 1942 and naturally made use of the contact thereby established to ask the Norwegians to intervene with the Allies and urge them to gain touch with the German resistance movement.[10] The Norwegians, however, thought that the time was 'not yet ripe'.

In Belgium General Alexander von Falkenhausen, the Military Governor, was himself in touch with the local resistance movement. In France Professor Carlo Schmid, a senior administrative officer (*Kriegsoberverwaltungsrat*) in Lille, had been acting as intermediary between Moltke and the French resistance since early 1942.

Moltke had contacts in Denmark from his time in Silesia before 1933. These he used in October 1943 and, working through Georg Ferdinand Duckwitz, adviser to Dr Werner Best, the *Reich* Plenipotentiary, helped to save most of the Danish Jews who were due to be taken to an extermination camp on an express order from Hitler. When Moltke arrived in Copenhagen and heard that the *Wehrmacht* was to support the SS in their anti-Jewish manhunt, he went at once to General Hermann von Hanneken, the *Wehrmacht* Commander-in-Chief, and said to him (approximately): 'You must have gone mad. You'll pay dearly for this one day. Don't you understand that?'[11]

Contacts with Holland were particularly active. Dr Schönfeld, Dr Paul Collmer and Trott were frequent visitors there.[12] A particularly good line led through Colonel Wilhelm Staehle.[13] He intervened successfully on many occasions on behalf of Dutchmen and so came in contact with the Dutch underground. At the end of 1943 he told his Dutch contacts of the German opposition's plans for a *putsch* and discussed with them how best to arrange for a smooth transition from the existing administration under Seyss-Inquart to a German military regime and thence back to Dutch self-government. He readily agreed to the Dutch terms – dissolution of the Dutch Nazi organizations and return of forced labourers. When asked about the Jews, however, he could only reply in a whisper: 'They are no longer there.'

Staehle told his Dutch contacts that he himself would probably head the transitional regime in Holland after the *coup*. He warned members of the Dutch resistance who were in danger of arrest, but otherwise simply kept his contacts open. Early in 1944, however, the Dutch government-in-exile in London, after consultation with the British government, forbade anything which could be regarded as negotiation or treating with the enemy. Staehle himself was arrested on 12 June 1944. The *Gestapo* could find out very little about his activities, however, and the People's Court, one of whose members was General Reinecke who knew all about Staehle's views and activities, only sentenced him to two years imprisonment. On 23 April, however, he was murdered by a *Gestapo* squad led by the notorious Police Inspector Stawizki.[14]

27 'Eastern Solution'?

Since the Western Allies were turning a deaf ear to all attempts at contact and the situation in the East was becoming increasingly menacing, voices were to be heard both in Hitler's entourage and among the opposition in support of a separate agreement between Germany and Russia. From the opposition point of view a factor in its favour was a declaration by Stalin in February 1942 when he differentiated between Hitler and his clique as transient figures on the one hand and the German people as a permanency on the other.[1]

Quite apart from the removal of Hitler it was in Stalin's interest to allow fresh Russo–German agreements to appear not altogether improbable; they could be used as a means of pressure to impose his territorial demands in Europe. Such was the position in Moscow in November 1943, in Teheran in December 1943 and in Yalta in February 1945 when the Americans were urging Russian entry into the war against Japan and Stalin consequently held the trumps. President Roosevelt and his advisers, moreover, looked upon Russia as a future world power with which they wanted to be on good terms and they were therefore ready to make numerous concessions. They systematically sacrificed German interests to the friendship for which they hoped.[2] At the same time, since July 1943 Stalin had been trying to gain touch with the German opposition through the 'Free Germany National Committee', formed of prisoners of war and émigrés. The contacts between the underground German Communist Party and the socialists Reichwein and Leber were another attempt to influence the opposition and potentially post-war conditions in Germany; probably they were also a reaction to the offers made to Dulles in Berne by the Beck-Goerdeler group to negotiate with the Western Powers alone, without their Russian ally.[3] The opposition's ideas about an 'eastern solution' must be looked at in the light of all these factors, not from an ideological standpoint and still less through the spectacles of the post-1945 Cold War and the Adenauer era.

This is the background to many misunderstandings and accusations, to which admittedly numerous fanciful ideas originating from the opposition have contributed. The 'Kreisau Circle', for instance, toyed with ideas about a sort of anti-fascist world revolution and even Stauffenberg is said by some to have become imbued with enthusiasm for them.[4] There may be something in this but nothing like as much as many have thought; Stauffenberg has been called a national-bolshevist because, quite rightly, he believed that the war with the Soviet Union could not be won *against* the Russian people but only with its support.[5] But in 1944 such opportunities had long since disappeared. German policy towards Russia had turned defence of the Soviet system into a patriotic duty for all Russians, because this system alone represented the interests of their country. Early in 1944 Stauffenberg explicitly rejected any cooperation with the 'Free Germany National Committee', saying: 'What I am doing is treason against the government, but what they are doing is treason against the country.'[6]

Trott's message to Dulles in January 1943 has already been mentioned. This referred to the possibility that Germany might turn eastwards and that the two peoples, having abandoned bourgeois concepts and set their sights on radical social solutions, might march arm in arm.[7] The question is whether these statements should be regarded as seriously meant. If so, Trott was a champion of romantic unrealistic ideas; in the light of their relative strengths the Russian and German peoples could only have 'marched arm in arm' under Russian leadership and with Stalin's agreement. In his biography of Goerdeler Ritter says that Trott put forward these ideas as a method of exerting tactical pressure.[8] Rothfels on the other hand says that in his January 1943 message Trott expressed the hope that the West would support an anti-communist anti-atheist popular movement.[9] What Trott hoped to obtain from Dulles and his government, except perhaps some attempt to prevent the development which he forecast, Rothfels does not say. The 'originator (or at least instigator)' of Trott's message to Dulles in April 1944 was probably Leber. This too Ritter regards as a genuine effort to collaborate with the West by giving warning of communist underground activity and of the growing trend to the Left. In practice it is impossible to distinguish between hope of collaboration with the West against the world menace of communism and the expectation that the danger of Russo–German collusion might persuade the West to act. No one can believe that Trott was so naïve as to have thought of the one but not the other. There was nothing in Trott's statements as reported by Dulles that could justify Gisevius' impression (which he says he received in talks with Trott in April 1944)[10] that Trott advocated an 'option for the East' or a 'rejection of the West'. There were admittedly many fanciful ideas and much disappointment over the attitude of the Western Powers which may have led Trott on occasions to make extreme statements.[11]

Opposition hopes of western readiness to come to some agreement rose and fell. When Trott returned from his visit to Sweden in the autumn of 1943, he was forced to report that Britain was not so prepared.[12] If that were so, was it not essential to try one's luck with Russia? Nothing should be left untried in order to stop the war, the slaughter and the destruction. In August 1943 Hassell had said that, if necessary and as an expedient, an attempt must be made to convince either Russia or the Western Powers that the preservation of Germany was in their interests and, if the Western Powers would not cooperate, accept agreement with Russia.[13] Trott was in full agreement with him – he was realistic in other words. If the Western Powers rejected the German offers, particularly those coupled with a hint of possible understanding with the East, then there was no alternative but to implement the threat unless one was to remain totally isolated and helpless. In autumn 1943 Trott had accordingly tried to contact Mme Kollontay, the Soviet Ambassador in Stockholm, but without success.[14] In order to initiate talks with Stalin, Goerdeler and Tresckow seem to have thought of infiltrating through the German lines Werner Graf von der Schulenburg, the former German Ambassador in Moscow.[15] Goerdeler certainly had doubts; the plan clearly originated from Tresckow.[16] In April 1944 Albrecht Haushofer and Hassell put forward the idea that the best place to contact the Allies was Stockholm because from there it might be possible to talk to Stalin, should the Western Powers be unwilling to negotiate after a successful *coup d'état.*[17]

In contrast to the Western Powers there were definite indications that Russia was ready to negotiate. Trott and Graf Schulenburg knew all about the feelers and offers of negotiation which the Russians had been putting out to Hitler ever since the end of 1942 through Peter Kleist, a desk officer in the Foreign Ministry and for a time also in Rosenberg's Ministry for the East.[18] The German Minister in Stockholm Victor Prinz zu Wied received a Russian peace feeler at the end of 1942 or beginning of 1943, and so did Ambassador von Papen in Ankara in May 1943.[19] The Soviet government had expressed a wish to conduct peace negotiations with Schulenburg but Hitler had invariably refused. Schulenburg was regarded as the only diplomat capable of negotiating with Stalin. Moscow in fact had a high opinion of him and people there knew what they were doing when they suggested him as a negotiating partner. Schulenburg had invariably warned against war with Russia.

There was, in fact, no serious contact between Hitler and Stalin or between the German opposition and the Soviet government. According to Franz von Sonnleithner, who acted as Ribbentrop's representative in Hitler's headquarters during the later years of the war with the rank of Minister, contact between the opposition and the Russian government through Schulenburg did not materialize because the Russians thought that the opposition did not intend to make an honest deal but was merely trying to use them as a pawn in their chess-game with the West; Schulenburg, on the other hand, 'visualized Germany occupying a genuine intermediate position between East and West and had no intention of deceiving Stalin'.

Let it be said once more: in the light of the situation the resistance movement had no alternative but to consider an arrangement with the East *as well*, although they would have preferred one with the West. In contrast to their contacts in Western capitals, those with the East never progressed further than the deliberation stage. No one in the opposition was 'east-orientated', apart of course from the communists.[20] The opposition wished to open negotiations with all sides as soon as possible; for contact they placed their hopes on Gisevius in Berne, Weizsäcker and Kessel in Rome, Goerdeler's link to Wallenberg in Stockholm, Trott's reputation in London and Schulenburg's in Moscow and finally on Dr Otto John's contacts in Madrid.

28 Otto John 1944

Dr Otto John was a lawyer, legal adviser to the German *Lufthansa*. From pre-war days he had been working with the opposition group in *Amt Ausland/Abwehr* and from February 1944 with Canaris' successor Colonel Georg Hansen in particular. His brother Dr Hans John was scientific assistant to Dr Rüdiger Schleicher, a senior civil servant (*Ministerialrat*) in the *Reich* Ministry of Aviation and Head of the Institute for Aeronautical Law in Berlin University.[1] In his position with *Lufthansa* Otto John had been able to carry out intelligence missions for the *Abwehr* and he used both these and his position as cover for conspiratorial opposition activities. In April 1942 and also between November 1942 and January 1943 John was in Madrid ostensibly on business for *Lufthansa*; he tried on behalf of Goerdeler to establish contact between Prince Louis Ferdinand and President Roosevelt but without success.[2] In November 1943 he was commissioned by Captain Gehre to find out whether communications permitting rapid contact could be established to General Eisenhower's headquarters through the United States Embassy in Madrid. John flew there and was soon able to send a coded message to Berlin that the link had been established and could be used. He waited daily for orders to activate it after a planned assassination of Hitler during his inspection of a new uniform. But John found this waiting too prolonged; it was embarrassing and might have drawn the attention of SD and *Gestapo* agents to him. On 16 December he flew back to Berlin to find that Hitler had called off his inspection.

In January 1944 John met Stauffenberg in Werner von Haeften's house and in the first week of February he flew back to Madrid with the task of establishing a link to Eisenhower and Montgomery. Colonel William Hohenthal, his contact in Madrid, was willing to see what he could do. John reported back to Berlin and on 17 April flew to Madrid again to develop the contact.

In his politico-military reports sent to Colonel Hansen from Madrid and Lisbon early in 1944 John dealt in particular with the planned and anticipated invasion which was to create a second front against Germany. The Italian front, he said, had practically nothing to do with the case and was only a secondary front. Preparations for a major invasion from the British Isles were in full swing. In March 1944 he reported that the location of the invasion had been decided and that it would be somewhere between Bordeaux and Hamburg; with Eisenhower's appointment as Supreme Commander all further decisions would be in the hands of the military; the operation would take place, he said, some time in June.

John was also able to confirm something which the opposition's emissaries had always been saying but which Trott, for instance, would not believe: that the Allies, the British and Americans, were completely united in their determination to impose unconditional surrender by military means.[3] Nevertheless, in his contacts with Sir Ronald Campbell, the British Ambassador in Lisbon, John had the impression that there was still a distinct possibility of armistice negotiations following a military *coup* in Germany.[4] Many of John's masters were confirmed in this view by a message from Roosevelt's entourage received by Canaris at the end of 1943 or early 1944 to the effect that offers of peace negotiations should be addressed to Eisenhower.[5]

By this time Stauffenberg was in command of preparations for the *coup* and was working closely with Julius Leber. Early in June 1944 he and John met one evening in Leber's house. Stauffenberg expressed the view that invasion was possible this year but not probable.[6] The question was how much time remained available for preparation of the *coup d'état*. Stauffenberg thought that, if the invasion took place at all, there was a fifty-fifty chance that it would be thrown back into the sea.[7] If it were abandoned or defeated, prospects of negotiation would be better. According to later testimony from his friend Professor Fahrner, Stauffenberg knew very well that the Western Powers had explicitly refused to give any support to a German rising and that they preferred to defeat Germany totally rather than have any contact with the German opposition.[8] He hoped, however, that after the *coup* he would be able to talk to General Eisenhower 'as soldier to soldier'.[9] On the German side he wished to exclude 'the politicals'.[10] He may not have realized the extent to which Allied military commanders were, or rather were not, empowered to take political decisions. In any case he agreed with Leber that the new situation could only be judged after the *coup* when action would be taken accordingly.[11]

All these ideas were overtaken by the invasion of 6 June 1944 and its immediate success. The landing was on a vast scale and had succeeded; the situation could not be reversed; the Allies were far superior to the Germans both in fire-power and in the air, over France as well as over the Channel and Atlantic. The *Luftwaffe* was so weak that not only was it practically helpless against the bombing of German cities but during the days and weeks preceding 6 June it had been unable to provide any useful enemy intelligence.[12]

After this Stauffenberg had little time to bother with the foreign policy side and on 10 June he commissioned Hansen and John to take the necessary steps with a view to negotiations with the enemy in the West. John had tried in vain to convince Stauffenberg and Hansen that the war could only be ended by unconditional surrender. Later, on 20 July, John reproached himself for his failure to get his view across particularly with 'the generals' although, as he himself admitted, they were then less ready to negotiate than ever.[13] On 10

June Hansen emphasized to John the necessity of a link to Eisenhower cutting out 'the politicals', in particular Goerdeler and his group. In a 'soldier to soldier' talk, he said, agreement would quickly be reached. John was commissioned to establish a contact to be used immediately following the *coup*.

John flew to Madrid on 19 June. He was successful in so far as he obtained an assurance that all his messages and information would definitely be passed to General Eisenhower but he could obtain no guarantee of an answer. He now waited in Madrid for authority to act from the shadow military headquarters under Witzleben; this was to be passed to him by Hansen after the *coup*.[14] The key phrase, however, was still 'unconditional surrender' and John was forced to report to Berlin that the Allies would insist on this, no matter who was ruling in Germany.

Meanwhile Stauffenberg too had become convinced that unconditional surrender was unavoidable even after a successful *coup*.[15] At a meeting in Strünck's house during the night 12–13 July he told Hansen and Gisevius that it seemed too late for any accommodation with the West; Stalin would be in Berlin in a few weeks' time, and was not one therefore *forced* to deal solely with the East on political matters? On 13 July Beck also said to Gisevius that Germany was defeated and total occupation could now no longer be avoided.[16]

Naturally John also was convinced that the only prospect of negotiations lay in the earliest possible initiation of the *coup d'état*. He wished to fly back to Berlin in order to urge speed but, in answer to his question, was told that he would have to count on being arrested. Leber had been arrested meanwhile. John therefore sent his message to Hansen and Stauffenberg via Gerhard Lindenberg, a colleague in the *Lufthansa* office in Madrid who was flying to Berlin on 10 July. The answer received by Lindenberg was that John should come to Berlin for a day or two; the *coup* was now definitely to be made and John was to hold himself available to carry messages from the *putsch* government.

Accordingly on 19 July John flew to Berlin and held himself in readiness. On the evening of the 20th he believed that the rising had succeeded but the arrests began that very night so John had nothing further that he could do. On 24 July he escaped to Madrid in a *Lufthansa* aircraft.

PART VI/ASSASSINATION ATTEMPTS 1933–1942

29 The Early Days

As the war went on influential opposition circles came to realize that the removal of the dictator in person, his murder in other words, was an essential prerequisite to the success of any attempted *coup*. A sacred oath had been sworn to him; in strict legal terms and in the minds of the unthinking citizenry and soldiery, the majority in fact, he was the legally established warlord and Supreme Commander. Unless, therefore, its Supreme Commander were first removed, the Army could not be counted upon; yet it was the sole instrument with which a *coup* could be carried out. The majority of the opposition realized this comparatively late; some of them, however, held this view from the outset and the events of 20 July 1944 proved them right.[1] A number of attempts at assassination had been made, however, long before 1943, some by the sort of people who invariably try to assassinate rulers, some from those resistance circles which were later the protagonists of the attempt of 20 July 1944.

As early as May 1933 a preliminary legal investigation was necessary 'owing to a planned attack on the *Reich* Chancellor'.[2] Königsberg communists led by a shipwright named Kurt Lutter planned a bomb attack on Hitler for his expected appearance at an electoral meeting on 4 March. The conspirators held two secret meetings in February and on 3 March the police acted. Since no evidence could be produced, however, towards the end of 1933 Lutter was 'released from investigation'. Also in 1933 an attack on Hitler was planned by a group led by Dr Helmuth Mylius but nothing came of it.[3]

On 8 March 1937 Helmut Hirsch, an architectural student, was condemned to death by the Second Chamber of the People's Court and beheaded in Plötzensee on 4 June. He was a Jew originally from Stuttgart, had been active in the Youth Movement and had emigrated to Prague where he had got in touch with Otto Strasser and the 'Black Front'. He felt some responsibility for his fellow-Jews in Germany and wished to ensure that they would be well treated by Strasser after his 'seizure of power'; he also wished to show that Jews had the courage to fight and so was persuaded into making a bomb attack on a building in the Nuremberg Stadium, on Julius Streicher or even on Hitler himself. Strasser's purpose was to demonstrate his power and avenge his brother who had been murdered in 1934.[4] On 20 December 1936 Helmut Hirsch went to Stuttgart; he was due to take over the explosive in Nuremberg on the 23rd. His name was known to the *Gestapo*, however, from a previous visit to Stuttgart and his arrival form, which he filled in correctly in his lodging, inevitably gave him away. One of his fellow-conspirators had already been arrested on crossing the frontier and he handed the explosive, together with full information, over to the *Gestapo*.

In 1938 two men named Döpking and Kremin were supposed to have made a similar attempt. On 12 October 1940 Karl Hoffmann, Erich Schulz, Wilhelm Tosch and Hermann Chill from Danzig were beheaded in Plötzensee for 'preparation of treason against the government and crimes involving explosives', and on 30 January 1942 Bernhard Rust and Ludwig Schmitt suffered the same fate for the same reason, also in Plötzensee. In several of these cases Otto Strasser, brother of Hitler's former rival for leadership of the Party, was suspected, not without reason, of being behind the would-be assassins.[5] Early in March 1937 the *Gestapo* received a tip that a bricklayer named Max Kostriba was planning to come to Germany from Czechoslovakia to attack Hitler;[6] he had had issued to him a passport from police headquarters in Troppau on 27 February.[7] There were frequent manhunts after foreign assassins. Early in April 1938 the *Gestapo* office in Koblenz suspected that 'certain Jewish circles abroad are trying to find persons ready to carry out assassination attempts in the *Reich* with the object of eliminating the *Führer* and other leading figures in Party and State'. This led to a hunt for twenty-four named Jews, almost all of whom were said to have entered from Czechoslovakia.[8] In August 1938 the head of the SD Sub-Region in Koblenz passed on to his out-stations a message received from Wilhelmshaven to the effect that criminals arrested in Paris had given the names of no fewer than twenty-two people said to be planning attacks on Hitler; the names were listed on an attachment to the SD memorandum.[9] In 1939 Colonel Mason-Macfarlane, the British Military Attaché, suggested in all seriousness to his government that he should himself shoot Hitler from a favourably placed window of his apartment on No. 1 Sophienstrasse, near the Charlottenburger Chaussee, Berlin. He did not try because the British government would have nothing to do with such methods.[10]

One or two attempts were made from Switzerland. In 1935 a certain David Frankfurter, a medical student of Jugoslav nationality living in Berne, son of a Jewish pastor, was ready to attack Hitler. Since he could not get near him, he shot Wilhelm Gustloff (Hitler's Party representative in Switzerland) in Davos.[11] In 1938 a committee with the specific purpose of preparing an attack on Hitler was formed under the chairmanship of Dr Wilhelm Abegg, a former State Secretary in the Prussian Ministry in Braun-Severing's time.[12] This 'Committee A' recruited ten Prussian ex-police officers who had been ransomed with Swiss funds from German concentration camps. As many as possible of Hitler's potential successors in the event of his death were to be killed at the same time. It was planned to dress the assassins up as Italian courier officers carrying important intelligence. For various reasons, for instance alleged difficulties in the production of the bomb, the attempt was postponed until 1942 and then it was said no longer to be necessary since certain circles in the German *Wehrmacht* were meanwhile preparing an attack.

Also in 1938 Maurice Bavaud, a Swiss Catholic student of theology, attempted to attack Hitler.[13] Marcel Gerbohay, a Frenchman attending a theological college in France, had formed the *Compagnie du Mystère* with ten of his fellow-students; its object was to fight and destroy communism. Bavaud was commissioned to persuade Hitler to attack the Soviet Union and to kill him if he refused. However this may be, in October 1938 Bavaud went to Germany and in November attempted to murder Hitler in Munich. He was arrested, condemned to death by the People's Court on 18 December 1939 and finally executed on 14 May 1941.

Mention has already been made of Captain Josef (Beppo) Römer, the ex-Free Corps commander.[14] He too wanted to kill Hitler and from 1939 to 1942 kept himself permanently *au fait* with Hitler's comings and goings through Lieutenant-Colonel Holm Erttel, aide to the Berlin City Commandant.[15] He was in close touch with people like Halem, Schlabrendorff, Niekisch and Guttenberg as also with members of the so-called Solf Circle. In the summer of 1938 Halem parted from his friends Albrecht von Kessel, Peter Graf Yorck von Wartenburg and Botho von Wussow because, as opposed to them, he was one of the few who had realized from the outset that Hitler must be murdered if his regime was to be overthrown.[16] He also thought that regular Army officers were not in a position, either individually or collectively, to attempt assassination and he therefore rejected Fritz-Dietlof Graf von der Schulenburg's plans on these lines as fanciful. The mental attitude and moral concepts of German officers, Halem thought, made anything like this impossible and what was required was a sort of professional thug. Römer was not, of course, a thug but for a long time Halem thought that he had found in him an underling capable of carrying out the assassination. The opportunity never presented itself and in February 1942 Römer was arrested together with many of his contacts, including Halem and the Sachse-Uhrig group. He was executed in September as were some forty other conspirators, some earlier, some later.

Hitler knew perfectly well that he was in constant danger of assassination. He calculated that there had been a total of seven attempts on his life, as one of which he included the Röhm affair. Elser's attempt was not the first to show him 'how easily death can strike down a statesman'; he once said: 'There will never be anyone in the future with as much authority as I have. My continued existence is therefore a major factor of value. I can, however, be removed at any time by some criminal or idiot.'[17] This he said in August 1939; on 23 November that year, after the Elser affair, he said: 'Attempts at assassination may be repeated.'[18] He also expressed his conviction that 'no one is safe against some idealist of an assassin who ruthlessly stakes his life for his purpose'.[19] When Heydrich was murdered in Prague he said that men of such political stature, himself even more so of course, 'must realize that people are lying in wait for them like some wild beast'; it was mere stupidity if such people did not take the elementary security precautions and, for instance, in order to show their courage, travelled in an open car.[20]

Hitler does not seem to have suspected that there might be some 'idealist of an assassin' among the soldiers or officers; in 1942 he referred to the 'fact' that 'all German idealists were either risking their life at the front or were expending all their efforts for the victory of Germany either in the arms factories or at their normal places of work'.[21] He was contradicting himself but this can be explained by the different meanings which he attributed to the word 'idealist' – characteristic of his disdain for *any* form of idealism. He did not think that true idealists, in other words people who would risk their lives, were to be found among the 'bourgeois and Marxists'. The only dangerous people, therefore, were 'assassins whipped up by the black crows in confessionals or patriots from the countries now occupied by our troops'.[22] In Germany these 'dunderheads', as Hitler called them, numbered a few hundred thousand including 'all leaders of opposition tendencies and particularly those of political Catholicism', inmates of concentration camps and 'all criminal elements, no matter whether they are now in prison or at liberty'. In the event of a 'mutiny', Hitler said, he would simply assemble these few hundred thousand men 'within three days for execution and have them shot'.[23]

The reference to 'dunderheads', to the few hundred thousand, including the leaders of Catholicism and the idealists, shows Hitler up for the unreasoning tyrant that he was. His remarks about assassination and its likelihood, however, also show the depth of the man's cunning. For him there was nothing sinister or mysterious about it. For anyone who lives dangerously the sense of danger becomes more acute. Not only was Hitler living dangerously but he relied more on intuition and impression than on rational thought. Moreover, since he wished to be protected as far as possible against assassination, he thought a great deal about how it might occur.[24]

30 *Attempts of 1938–1942*

When General von Witzleben together with General Halder, the Chief of Staff of the Army, were planning the overthrow of Hitler in September 1938, the majority of the conspirators did not yet think it essential for the success of the project that Hitler should be killed immediately. A small number, however, led by Lieutenant-Colonel Oster and Major Heinz, agreed about 20 September that they would kill Hitler even without the agreement of the other conspirators.[1]

It was proposed to adopt the following simple plan: While Berlin was occupied by troops of III Army Corps under Witzleben's command, Witzleben himself and certain of his staff officers would go to the *Reich* Chancellery and demand that Hitler resign. An additional group of officers under Major Heinz would accompany him as an 'assault squad' in order to ensure his entry into the Chancellery and assist in the arrest of Hitler and his entourage. They had to pass several sentries, first at the entrance and then in a large anteroom. Hitler's room was reached through a marble hall from which led a long corridor and in the middle of this was the door to Hitler's study.[2] Once they had reached Hitler wherever he might be, Heinz and his officers intended to provoke an incident during which Hitler would be shot. This of course would only be necessary if, contrary to expectations, the SS did not resist.

For the reasons given in Chapter 7 above the confrontation never took place.[3] We have already seen how the conspiracy was paralysed after the Munich Agreement and acquiescence in the occupation of the 'rump of Czechoslovakia'; the conditions for an attempted assassination synchronizing with a *coup d'état* no longer existed. The great victory over Poland was a further factor; after that no general would take part in a *putsch*.

The preparations for the attack on France and the British Expeditionary Force, planned to take place through the neutral countries of Belgium and Holland, gave fresh impetus to the planning for a *coup* and attempted assassination. Once more catastrophe, a fearful defeat for Germany, seemed inevitable and in the view of many conspirators a situation had arisen in which a *coup* would be understood and might succeed.

Then, coupled with the preparations for a *coup* being made in late October and early November 1939 in the Army General Staff, the OKW *Amt Ausland/Abwehr* and the Foreign Ministry, Dr Erich Kordt, a Counsellor (*Legationsrat*) and Foreign Ministry spokesman, offered to assassinate

Hitler.[4] Majors Heinz and Groscurth had long been discussing the possibilities of a further attempt and General Halder encouraged the group in the *Abwehr* to try. On 1 November 1939 Oster said to Kordt: 'We have no one to throw the bomb which will liberate our generals from their scruples.' Kordt replied: 'All I need is the bomb.' Oster said: 'You will have the bomb by 11 November.'[5] In his capacity as assistant to Freiherr von Weizsäcker, the State Secretary of the Foreign Ministry, and as Ribbentrop's *Chef de Cabinet*, Kordt had always accompanied the Foreign Minister to the *Reich* Chancellery like a shadow; he was not at all conspicuous even when he came alone, he was no longer subject to identity checks, he had the *entrée* to the Chancellery at any time and could wait about in the main anteroom until Hitler appeared. In the next few days he went to the Chancellery as often as possible in order to accustom the sentries even more to seeing him. Groscurth obtained plans of the Chancellery.[6] Kordt told his cousin Susanne Simonis, Hasso von Etzdorf and Albrecht von Kessel what he proposed to do; he recorded it in a statement of which copies were earmarked for Alexander Kirk, the American Chargé d'Affaires, and Dr Kappeler, a counsellor in the Swiss Legation.

Oster was certain that he could obtain explosive and detonators for Kordt, but he had not yet got them. Accordingly, early in November, he summoned to his office Major Lahousen, head of Section II (Sabotage) in the *Abwehr*; two other *Abwehr* conspirators, Dohnanyi and Heinz, were already there. Straight away Oster asked Lahousen whether he could obtain explosive and detonators for an attack on Hitler; the assailant had already been found.[7] It was not so simple as it might seem to obtain explosives. All such material was held by Group T (Technical) of Section II and even the Section Head could not remove any without sound reason. Lahousen asked for time to think it over.

Meanwhile, on 5 November, Hitler and Brauchitsch had had their quarrel about the western offensive and Hitler had insisted on his date of 12 November. Kordt heard of this from Etzdorf on 7 November and told him that, with the explosive promised to him, he would stop the offensive.

On the evening of 8 November, however, Hitler only escaped by a hair's breadth from the assassination attempt by Georg Elser in the *Bürgerbräukeller*, Munich. On 10 November Kordt and Oster discussed the project once more and decided to adhere to the plan for 11 November; as a result of the stricter vigilance following the Elser affair, however, the difficulties of obtaining explosive, great enough anyway, were so vastly increased that Oster was forced to abandon the idea.[8] Lahousen was in no position to remove the necessary explosive from Section II's laboratory; in view of the strict supervision being exercised, the *Gestapo* would have known at once. As a result both Lahousen and Oster as the recipient of the explosive would have been in an extraordinarily dangerous position because, with the best will in the world, they could have given no good reason for going about with explosives; moreover, owing to the excessive risk of premature detection the entire project had really become hopeless. On 10 November Lahousen was forced to issue 'further strict instructions' to Major Marguerre, the head of the laboratory, 'to proceed with great caution in the issue of detonators and explosives'. Marguerre thereupon stated that a precise record was kept in the laboratory but that, once something was issued, he could no longer be responsible for its whereabouts.[9]

When Kordt visited Oster in his house in the Bayrische Strasse, Berlin-Wilmersdorf, late on the afternoon of 11 November in order to fetch the explosive, Oster had to tell him that it had not been possible to obtain it. All laboratories now had to render precise reports on every ounce of explosive and the use to which it was put.[10]

The western offensive had meanwhile been postponed to 19 November so that more time was available for the attempt. Kordt now wished to try with a revolver but Oster dissuaded him. Kordt would not be able to see Hitler alone, he said, and he had no chance in the presence of aides, orderlies and visitors. Before the offensive finally took place Kordt visited Oster on two further occasions when the decision seemed imminent; he also asked Groscurth for help in obtaining the necessary explosive. In fact, towards the end of November Lahousen did succeed in bringing to Berlin a quantity of explosive previously held in Sweden by *Abwehr* II for use against targets in Norway; intensive preparations were then under way for 'Exercise Weser'. Kordt did not get any of it, however. Plans for a *coup d'état* were no longer top priority; less reliance than ever could be placed on Halder and Brauchitsch and efforts were being made to reactivate them by means of Allied assurances. Unless there were a simultaneous *coup* assassination seemed purposeless; Göring, Goebbels, Himmler and Heydrich would presumably survive; the SS and *Gestapo* would remain intact. The conspiracy would therefore almost certainly be crushed and the regime would not have been eliminated.

Georg Elser, who was responsible for the assassination attempt in the '*Löwenbräu*' (formerly '*Bürgerbräu*') restaurant in the Rosenheimer Strasse, Munich, was connected to no other opposition circles. He had temporarily belonged to a communist organization but made his attempt on his own. His care, perseverance and skill brought him remarkably near success.[11] On 8 November 1939 the annual commemorative ceremony of the ill-starred *putsch* of 1923, at which a number of 'Old Fighters' had lost their lives, was due to be held; between early August and this date Elser succeeded on many occasions in spending the night unnoticed in the '*Löwenbräu*' hall where there were few security precautions; it was used partly as a historic site for visitors and otherwise as a restaurant. The pillars were of stone and cement, panelled with wood, and in one of these, against which Hitler made his annual speech, Elser inserted an explosive charge, connecting it to a detonating mechanism including two Westminster clocks. Some of the explosive (Donarit) he had stolen from a quarry, in which he had taken a job specifically for this purpose. In addition he used for his bomb military explosive from a 75 mm shell together with black powder. It took him thirty to thirty-five nights to prepare the chamber in the pillar which was one of the main supports for the roof.

As far as is known there was no one behind Elser. He was uneducated but technically intelligent; during his subsequent interrogations, which included beatings, hypnosis and other methods of 'intensified interrogation', he proved to be merely an opponent of the Nazi regime who in particular felt that ever since autumn 1938 it had been heading for war. By murdering Hitler he thought that he would be doing something great and good.[12]

Since the country was at war in 1939, 'a considerably reduced' programme was planned for the usual ceremony. Hitler did not intend to make a speech himself and instead Hess was to broadcast over all German stations at 7.30 p.m. on 8 November.[13] On 7 or 8 November, however, Hitler decided that he would nevertheless make a speech and on 8 November the *Völkische Beobachter* carried an announcement dated the 7th that Hess would speak on the 9th, not at 7.30 on the 8th. Finally it was announced on 9 November that there would be no speech by Hess since Hitler himself had spoken on the 8th.[14] On that day Hitler flew to Munich. Because it was frequently foggy in November and take-off for the return journey might therefore be delayed, he decided to return to Berlin the same evening by train (although he had originally intended to stay until the 9th). Regular trains for Berlin left for Munich at 9.45 and 10.20 p.m., but Hitler used his special train leaving at 9.31 p.m. and therefore had to leave the hall at the latest at 9.10 p.m.[15] By 6 p.m. on 8 November the hall and balconies of the '*Löwenbräu*' were packed tight; among the 'notables' present were Bouhler, Himmler, Rosenberg, Frank, Goebbels, Ribbentrop and Sepp Dietrich. The Badenweiler march was played and the 'Blood Banner' borne in. Then the *Führer* arrived to the enthusiastic applause of the three thousand people present. Previous custom had been that Hitler began his major speech about 8.30 p.m. ending about 10 p.m., but owing to the short time available, the start had been advanced by half an hour. Hitler arrived on the stroke of 8 p.m. and made his speech, ending at 9.07 p.m.[16] The explosion took place at 9.20 and the roof fell in killing eight 'Old Fighters' (one of them died later in hospital) and injuring more than sixty.

That same evening Elser was arrested in Constance as he was trying to escape into Switzerland. He had all sorts of incriminating material on him, including a '*Bürgerbräu*' postcard, technical drawings of shells and detonators, distinguishing marks of ammunition boxes, parts of a detonator and in the lining of his coat a membership card of the former 'Red Front Fighters League'.[17] It was first assumed that foreign secret services were behind the attack but investigation results were meagre and there was no proof; during the war, therefore, no great trial of Elser was staged. As the end of the *Reich* drew near in spring 1945 '*Gestapo* Müller' extracted via Himmler Hitler's decision 'concerning the special prisoner "Eller",' the cover-name under which Elser was held. On 5 April 1945 Müller wrote to *SS-Obersturmbannführer* Weiter, camp commandant of Dachau: 'During one of the next terror raids on Munich or the neighbourhood of Dachau "Eller" is to meet with a fatal accident. I request, therefore, that when such a situation arises "Eller" be liquidated in an entirely unobtrusive manner. Report of completion should be rendered to me as follows: "On ... on the occasion of the terror raid on ... among others Eller, prisoner in protective custody, was fatally injured".'[18]

After the opening of the western offensive in May 1940 concrete planning for a *coup d'état* by the opposition was at a standstill. Both externally and internally conditions were unfavourable and no cooperation from the Army could be counted upon. Conditions were even more unfavourable after the great victory over France. Field Marshal von Witzleben for one declared any attack on Hitler something that could not even be considered in view of the victories over Poland and France. For the time being he abandoned hope of a *coup d'état*.[19] Nevertheless individuals were still to be found ready to risk their lives against the dictator even when he was winning victories. Among them were Dr Eugen Gerstenmaier and Fritz-Dietlof Graf von der Schulenburg.[20]

Gerstenmaier had been scientific assistant in the External Ecclesiastical Office of the Evangelical Church since 1936; from the outbreak of war he worked in the Information Division of the Foreign Ministry. Until the western offensive Schulenburg remained as Government Representative (*Regierungspräsident*) in Silesia, but in May 1940, as a Lieutenant on the Reserve, he reported to the Training Regiment of the famous No 9 (Potsdam) Infantry Regiment, to which four of his brothers had belonged. Schulenburg was then thirty-eight years of age but he reported not, as he said at the time, to spend his war in training recruits but 'to go on active service as soon as I was considered fit for it'. From earlier days he knew many officers in the regiment and soon reached a position in which he could work for a *coup*; 9 Infantry Regiment would have a vital part to play. At the same time Schulenburg was 'emigrating' into the Army; the imminent dismissal of the *Gauleiter*, Josef Wagner, would have made his position in Silesia untenable. He joined the regiment on 1 June and remained in the Army until his execution.

Gerstenmaier and Schulenburg proposed to assemble a group of officers of about company strength and arrest Hitler in Berlin. If, as expected, resistance was offered, Hitler would be shot. They were never able to approach their victim despite many attempts – they considered, for instance, attacking Hitler during the planned victory parade in Paris but on 20 July 1940 it was finally called off. Postings, official duties and other circumstances invariably stood in their way. Hitler did in fact go to Paris once, on 23 June 1940, but he flew in unannounced very early in the morning, landing at Le Bourget at 5 a.m.; he at once made a tour of the city visiting the Champs-Elysées, the Opéra, the Louvre, the Eiffel Tower and the Invalides including Napoleon's tomb; about 8 a.m. he was back at the airfield and flew off to his headquarters 'Tannenberg' near Freudenstadt. In discussion with his aide during the tour Hitler decided against a victory parade.[21]

In 1941 a similar plan was worked out by the staff of Field Marshal von Witzleben who was C-in-C West with headquarters in Saint-Germain near Paris until March 1942; being a member of the conspiracy, he was always on the look-out for people prepared to attack Hitler.[22] At this time Captain Graf von Waldersee, operations officer on the staff of the Commandant of Paris, was ready to do it, as were Major Hans-Alexander von Voss and Captain Graf Schwerin von Schwanenfeld, both of Witzleben's staff.[23] Goerdeler and Hassell were heavily involved since both were invariably trying to goad Witzleben into action. In January 1941 Hassell visited General Otto von

Stülpnagel, the Military Commander France, but he seemed in no way equal to the situation and was in fact relieved at the end of that month.[24] Goerdeler was in Paris several times in 1941 and on each occasion sought out Graf Waldersee and implored him to do something.[25] Waldersee assured him that Hitler would be arrested or killed as soon as he set foot in Paris; the necessary steps only had to be taken in Berlin and everything in Paris was ready.

In May 1941 a parade of German divisions down the Champs-Elysées was planned. Supposedly the troops had already been assembled and a saluting base had been set up near the Place de la Concorde; Brauchitsch, the Commander-in-Chief of the Army, was coming to Paris anyway and it was expected that Hitler would be present.[26] Hitler was to be shot by two designated officers while at the saluting base. Graf Schwerin, Witzleben's aide, had also pledged himself to throw a bomb at Hitler if opportunity offered, perhaps from a hotel balcony. But Hitler did not come.[27] Meanwhile, in April the Jugoslav and Greek campaigns had begun; on 10 May Hess flew to England and on 22 June the war against Russia began.

In 1942 an attempt was made to produce another plan to kill Hitler during a visit to Paris but it was not possible to persuade him to come. On this occasion Field Marshal von Rundstedt, Witzleben's successor as C-in-C West, was involved together with *SS-Sturmbannführer* Hans-Victor von Salviati and Major Achim Oster.[28]

Prospects of success were very meagre, however; a sharp watch was being kept. In March 1942 the *Gestapo* and Customs Service were hunting for two Montenegrins named Iovan Kovacevis and Iovan Vukovic who had allegedly been recruited by 'England' as 'fanatical elements' for attacks on 'highly-placed European personalities'. Early in May Hitler was warned by the RSHA of a murderous attack planned on him; it was to be made by 'an Austrian officer' who was either a Major or Lieutenant-Colonel, so an 'informer' had told the RSHA; he was of 'non-Aryan origin' and had served in the Austrian Army. He proposed to go to the *Führer*'s headquarters as a courier and there shoot Hitler. He was backed by 'Jewish-bolshevist agents working hand in glove with the English Secret Service'.[29] In those days Hitler was continually referring to assassination attempts, both past and potential; on 27 May Heydrich fell victim to the well-known attack. All this was no encouragement to Hitler to pay visits to the front, particularly if announced beforehand.

PART VII/TRESCKOW AND ARMY GROUP CENTRE

31 Preparations

Not only Brauchitsch and Halder but also many other generals who had previously been in close touch with the opposition or had belonged to it, had increasingly taken refuge in strict military duty. They shut their eyes even to what they were *forced* to see and know – the daily shootings in hundreds, primarily in German-occupied Poland, of Jews, doctors, professors, writers, architects, engineers, librarians, teachers, communists and alleged partisans or gipsies. Colonel-General Blaskowitz's courageous protest in late 1939 awoke no echoes; in the spring Brauchitsch and Halder accepted Hitler's removal of the SS and Police units, in particular the so-called *Einsatzgruppen* (action groups) from the jurisdiction of the Army, which had had full authority in the occupied areas.[1] So the Army was enabled to stand aloof from 'these things'.[2] Acquiescence in this sort of 'division of powers' was monstrous enough. When, however, in the spring of 1941 Hitler broke this agreement and issued the notorious 'Commissar Order', Brauchitsch and Halder still remained at their posts.

The so-called 'Commissar Order', issued from the *Führer*'s headquarters, carried the date of 6 June 1941 and was authenticated by the Chief of OKW. It was entitled 'General instructions on the treatment of Political Commissars' and its preamble included this: 'You are requested to limit distribution to the Commanders of Armies or Air Fleets [air force territorial commands] and to arrange for further communication to lower commands by word of mouth.'[3] A key sentence in the instructions ran: 'In the struggle against bolshevism, we must not assume that the enemy's conduct will be based on principles of humanity or of international law.' This did not come very well from men who were guilty of or had tolerated the gruesome crimes in Poland, quite apart from the fact that they had initiated the war against bolshevism of their own free will. The order continued: 'Political commissars have initiated barbaric, Asiatic methods of warfare. Consequently they will be dealt with immediately and with maximum severity. As a matter of principle they will be shot at once, whether captured during operations or otherwise showing resistance. The following regulations will apply: ... on capture they will be immediately separated from other prisoners on the field of battle ... After they have been segregated they will be liquidated.'

Apart from some feeble protests Brauchitsch and Halder accepted even this without demur. The criminal nature of the Commissar Order was clear; it flew in the face of everything connected with European civilization, irrespective of whether Red Army Political Commissars were accorded prisoner of war status or not. They were quite simply to be murdered. No attempt was to be made – the instructions are quite clear on this point – to establish or prove individual guilt for war crimes or other offences before they were 'liquidated'. Nevertheless Brauchitsch and Halder did mitigate the effect of the Commissar Order by a special army order stressing that the duty of the troops was fighting and that this would usually allow no time for special search or mopping-up operations; under no circumstances were individual soldiers to act arbitrarily; they must always act under the orders of an officer.[4]

The two most senior officers of the Army, therefore, remained at their posts with the praiseworthy intention of 'preventing something worse'. They undoubtedly saved thousands of lives in that by their attitude, their comments and their supplementary orders they made it clear that strict execution of criminal instructions was not desired. Nevertheless the question arises how much evil a responsible senior officer should do in order to prevent something worse. Participation in crime, even in the hope perhaps of sabotaging it, is always questionable. In any case this could only be done with the cooperation of those more junior generals who were candidates for the succession. That being so, the contention that after the resignation of Brauchitsch and Halder no one would oppose crime, is not valid. Insubordination may not have been in the make-up of men like Brauchitsch and Halder – but no more was the execution or toleration of criminal orders.

Nevertheless there was widespread indignation in the Army over the crimes committed by the SS in the occupied territories and over the Commissar Order which turned many soldiers into accomplices. Enthusiasm for the regime declined in many circles. At the same time the will to resistance grew – by no means everywhere but at least in many important staffs and headquarters. This, be it noted, was at a time when Hitler was still scoring major victories and his advance seemed irresistible. The initial impetus to resistance did not come from the defeats of 1942 and later, although they largely contributed to the obliteration of the prestige which Hitler had won through his military victories.[5] Gradually there formed groups of resistance – to the Commissar Order, to atrocities, to the regime in general. Such centres of resistance already existed in Berlin and Paris; now they appeared on the eastern front as well. By far the most active was a group in headquarters Army Group Centre.

Army Group Centre was the descendant of the former Army Group 2. On 1 September 1939, as Army Group North, it advanced into Poland under Colonel-General (later Field Marshal) Fedor von Bock; on 5 October 1939 it was rechristened Army Group B and transferred to the western front where it took part in the French campaign. In September 1940 it returned to Poland; its headquarters was in Poznan.[6] On 1 April 1941, in preparation for the Russian campaign, it was renamed Army Group Centre and in the summer of that year advanced on Moscow. Field Marshal von Bock was still Commander-in-Chief; Major-General Hans von Greiffenberg was Chief of Staff and the senior operations officer was Lieutenant-Colonel Henning von Tresckow.[7]

Tresckow came of an old Prussian officer family; in 1918 he was a platoon commander. Then he travelled for a bank, going round the world; in 1924 he rejoined the *Reichswehr*, sponsored by Hindenburg. His original unit was the 1st Prussian Regiment of Foot Guards; from 1936 he served in the famous 9 Infantry Regiment, dubbed 'I.R. von 9' by the malicious. He attended the Staff College as a Captain in 1932 and joined the General Staff of the Army in 1936.[8] During the war he was considered by his superiors to be an outstandingly capable officer, far above average, very hard-working and exceptionally capable of taking decisions.[9] Tresckow could not abide anything mean or unjust and there was plenty of both under Hitler's regime; over the years his opposition became more deep-rooted. In the summer of 1939 he told Fabian von Schlabrendorff that 'both duty and honour demand from us that we should do our best to bring about the downfall of Hitler and National-Socialism in order to save Germany and Europe from barbarism'.[10]

Ever since Hitler's intention to attack Russia had become clear Tresckow had set about methodically assembling on to the staff of Army Group Centre men who would help to turn it into an instrument for a *coup*. He assumed that Germany would be rapidly defeated in Russia and that this would materially assist his plans; in this he found himself sadly disappointed, as he had been over the French campaign. Hitler's order of December 1941 that the front was to be held at all costs prevented a catastrophic retreat of colossal proportions and so concealed the seriousness of the strategic situation.[11]

Among the conspirators in Army Group Centre upon whom Tresckow could count without more ado was Lieutenant-Colonel (later Colonel) Georg Schulze-Büttger, Tresckow's Operations Officer from December 1941 to end February 1943; he had been Beck's aide from August to October 1938.[12] At the end of February 1943 he became Senior Operations Officer to Field Marshal von Manstein in Army Group South and was promoted. Tresckow placed considerable hopes in this posting as also in the influence of Stahlberg, Manstein's aide, but owing to Manstein's strictly military attitude they were not realized. In the summer of 1944 Schulze-Büttger became Chief of Staff to 4 Panzer Army. His part in the conspiracy was discovered and he was executed on 13 October 1944.

His successor as Operations Officer in Army Group Centre in February 1943 was Lieutenant-Colonel Hans-Alexander von Voss, who had previously been Training Officer with the rank of Major. He had served on the staff of Field Marshal von Witzleben, Commander-in-Chief West, and, as son-in-law to General Joachim von Stülpnagel, he had good contacts; moreover he also came from 9 Infantry Regiment. Those who knew him invariably emphasized his uprightness of character and his sense of realism. He committed suicide on 8 November 1944. His successor as Training Officer in Army Group Centre was Major Hans-Ulrich von Oertzen who also committed suicide on 21 July 1944 when on the staff of *Wehrkreis* III, Berlin.[13]

A most important member of this group was Army Group Centre's Supply Officer, Lieutenant-Colonel Berndt von Kleist who, like Tresckow, came from the 1st Prussian Regiment of Foot Guards. Schlabrendorff described him as the essence of nobility and integrity and this was the background to his political attitude. He had lost a leg in the First World War but was now serving again. He did inestimable service by maintaining contact with Goerdeler and other conspirators in Berlin; his personality and far-seeing judgement exercised a decisive influence throughout the circle.

Another most important member was Colonel Rudolf-Christoph Freiherr von Gersdorff; he was a cavalryman and served as Intelligence Officer to Army Group Centre from April 1941 to February 1944 when he became Chief of Staff to LXXXII Corps; he was posted to Seventh Army at the end of 1944. He was well known for his industry, his tact and his assured, winning manner. Those who knew him could not speak highly enough of his clarity of mind, sureness of judgement, chivalrous attitude, great courage and solid, upright character.[14] Many of the conspirators owe their survival to his circumspection, ability and discretion.

The aides to Field Marshal von Bock and, from mid-December 1941 when Bock relinquished his command, to Field Marshal von Kluge had a most important part to play. It was hoped that they would influence their commander and 'keep him on the level'. Major (later Lieutenant-Colonel) Carl-Hans Graf von Hardenberg and Lieutenant Heinrich Graf von Lehndorff did all they could, but unhappily without success. In June 1942 Lieutenant Philipp Freiherr von Boeselager became Kluge's aide. In January 1943 his brother Georg, who had been awarded the Oakleaves to the Knight's Cross and was then a tactics instructor, began, in agreement with Kluge, to form the 'Boeselager' cavalry unit in the area of Army Group Centre; it will be referred to later. One of his assistants in this was Captain Walter Schmidt-Salzmann. Georg Freiherr von Boeselager was killed in action in Poland in late August 1944; he was posthumously promoted Colonel and awarded the Swords to the Oakleaves to the Knight's Cross.

Others who played a decisive part in the conspiracy in headquarters Army Group Centre were: the lawyer and Reserve Lieutenant Fabian von Schlabrendorff, aide to the head of the Operations Section, and one of the principal liaison officers between the Army Group and the centre of the conspiracy in Berlin; Major Schach von Wittenau, 3rd aide to the Commander-in-Chief; Lieutenant Graf von Berg, aide to the Chief Signals Officer; Captain Graf von Matuschka; Major (later Lieutenant-Colonel) Horst Pretzell, operations officer from January 1941 to March 1942 and intelligence officer from March 1942 to February 1943. Kluge's aide from August 1943 was Lieutenant (later Captain) Eberhard von Breitenbuch, who had been aide to Witzleben in 1940; he continued with Field Marshal Ernst Busch who commanded Army Group Centre from October 1943 to the end of June 1944.[15]

Taken as a whole, therefore, the strongest opposition group yet formed was that in headquarters Army Group Centre. This was the aim which Tresckow had pursued from the outset in his personnel policy and he was given much assistance by his friend Rudolf Schmundt, senior Army aide to the *Führer* and Supreme Commander of the *Wehrmacht* and from October 1942 also head of the Army Personnel Office, who of course had no notion what purpose he was serving. Tresckow thought that, if the German offensive failed – he thought first of that against France and then of that in Russia – it would be possible to strike against Hitler with some prospects of success. Psychologically he thought it would be impossible to persuade a victorious German Army to act against Hitler.[16] The resistance of Tresckow and his friends to the Commissar Order may be regarded as a prelude to their efforts to overthrow the regime.[17]

The Commissar Order reached the field headquarters in June 1941 during preparations for the Russian campaign.[18] It had been preceded by a 'Decree concerning the application of military law in the area of Operation Barbarossa and special measures to be adopted by the troops', dated 13 May 1941, forbidding courts martial and summary proceedings.[19] This prescribed that 'guerillas' were to be 'shot down without mercy' on the battlefield or while trying to escape, also that 'all other attacks by enemy civilians against the *Wehrmacht*, its members or ancillary services' were to be 'crushed immediately by the most stringent measures including summary execution'. Included under 'other attacks' were theft, bribery or suspicious movement. Since suspects were not to be made prisoner, they had to be shot on mere suspicion as they might otherwise continue their alleged activity. At the same time 'action against enemy civilians taken by members of the *Wehrmacht* and its ancillary services' was exempted from disciplinary proceedings; only acts affecting the troops and their discipline – unnecessary destruction of habitable 'dwellings' for instance – remained punishable. This was a gruesome order which could be interpreted, like the Commissar Order, as legitimizing crimes committed by members of the German Army; against it, however, could be set Brauchitsch's supplementary order of 24 May 1941. This laid down that the troops' primary task was to move and fight, not to search and mop up; the *Führer*'s decree, it said, applied mainly to serious cases of hostility by enemy civilians; arbitrary action by members of the Army should under all circumstances be prevented.

When these instructions were followed in June by the Commissar Order, 'a storm of indignation arose from all senior headquarters'.[20] When the order reached Gersdorff he went at once to Tresckow, who was acting as Chief of Staff that day, and the two then went on to the C-in-C. Tresckow suggested to the Field Marshal that concerted action be taken by the three Army Group Commanders but Bock would do no more then send Gersdorff, the first recipient of the order, by air to see General Eugen Müller, General on special assignment attached to the Commander-in-Chief of the Army. Tresckow's view was that Germany would forfeit her honour if this order were not unanimously rejected and he urged Bock to fly to Hitler himself together with Rundstedt and Leeb. But Bock only replied: 'He'll chuck me out.'[21] Gersdorff was told by Müller that Brauchitsch had already done all he could against the Commissar Order; he had 'twice been thrown out by Hitler without succeeding in getting this order withdrawn or changed'.[22] Brauchitsch's order of 24 May, Müller said, was designed to maintain the discipline of the troops and put a spoke in the wheel of the Commissar Order. Gersdorff was unable to speak to Brauchitsch himself since he was not there. When he returned to Poznan to report, Bock was at dinner; he merely said: 'Gentlemen, you see I have made my protest.'[23] For him the subject was closed.

In fact the Commissar Order was only partly implemented. Gersdorff and the intelligence officers of other army groups and armies who were primarily responsible, agreed that it should not be carried out. If questions were asked, fake reports on alleged shootings of commissars were rendered to superior headquarters, but in practice no check was made.[24] Finally Bock himself contacted other commanders and discussed with Kluge, Weichs and Guderian among others, what should be done. Verbal agreement was reached that corps commanders be told that execution of the orders for restriction of military law and the shooting of commissars was not desired.[25]

Nevertheless these orders roused in the minds of decent officers a feeling of abhorrence against Hitler and his murderous minions; they could not remain inactive in face of the shootings of Jews carried out by the SS and Police *Einsatzgruppen* in the narrow strip behind the combat zone over which army commanders now had no jurisdiction. The head of *Einsatzgruppe B*, however, working in Army Group Centre's area (but not under Army Group headquarters) was Arthur Nebe, Director of the *Reich* Criminal Police, and he had been on the opposition's side ever since 1938. He undoubtedly tried to stop the usual mass executions carried out by the *Einsatzgruppen*, while invariably reporting that orders had been completed. He had only gone to Russia against his will, having been persuaded to do so by his friends Oster and Gisevius in order to retain his position in the centre of SS power, so vital for the opposition. He hoped that after a short period of fulfilment of his 'duty', which Himmler also demanded from other senior police officials, he would be able to return to Berlin; he had some idea of what awaited him, whereas his friends had not an inkling.[26] Finally, in the summer of 1942, the Commissar Order officially became inoperative when it had been clearly shown that its effect on the fighting morale of the Red Army was a positive one; final proof was apparently a propaganda manoeuvre when commissars who were taken prisoner or deserted were promised their lives and good treatment and an unusually large number of captured commissars was reported.[27]

In spite of all this there occurred the horrifying incident of Borissov, of which first Gersdorff and then Tresckow and Bock were told by Graf von Hardenberg. He had flown low over Borissov during the 'action' and he had seen a Latvian SS unit herding together several thousand Jews from the ghetto and murdering them in a most bestial manner.[28] The order presumably had been issued by one of Nebe's SS officers acting for another who was on leave. Nebe was at once informed by headquarters Army Group Centre and immediately flew to Borissov himself but by then it was too late. Bock demanded that the SS officer responsible be most severely punished but no one ever heard what happened.

Gersdorff was not afraid to write in Army Group Centre's war diary: 'In all the protracted conversations which I have had with officers I have invariably been asked about these shootings of Jews without bringing the question up myself. I have the impression that there is almost universal detestation in the officer corps for these shootings of Jews, prisoners and commissars, the latter most of all because it increases enemy resistance. These shootings are regarded as a stain on the honour of the German Army and in particular of the German officer corps.'[29] Yet in autumn 1941 a senior officer like Colonel-General Busch, commanding Sixteenth Army in Army Group North, could listen from his hotel to salvos of shots mowing down Jews in Kovno and not be disturbed, merely saying: 'Well, I can't do anything about it; these are political matters which don't interest us, or rather they interest us but we shouldn't do anything. These things don't concern us.'[30] No cases are known in which commanders who protested against such crimes suffered anything worse than removal from their command.

In late August or early September General Thomas paid a series of personal visits to army groups trying to initiate preparations for a *coup*, but the moment was unfavourable.[31] In the spring of 1941 Hassell, Popitz, Goerdeler, Beck, Oster and their circle had hoped that army commanders would refuse to carry out the orders for brutal measures in Russia and that this might bring about the downfall of the regime.[32] But commanders were only prepared to make somewhat half-hearted attempts at evasion as described above and then became completely engrossed in their offensive. The period of mobile warfare was no time for *coup d'état* planning; the winter was more suitable.

The military victories and the hectic activity at the front and in the staffs were not, however, the only factors standing in the way of the *coup*. In fact planning, which had been largely in abeyance since the start of the French campaign, was resumed after the eastern offensive opened.[33] Berlin, however, was not yet looking eastwards but still towards the west and Tresckow's group had no real organizational link with the centre in Berlin.

Since the beginning of the eastern campaign Schlabrendorff had been to Berlin several times in order to talk to Oster, from whom he learnt that Witzleben was wondering whether something could not be done against the regime from France.[34] Both in Berlin and on Witzleben's staff, however, people were uncertain what the attitude of the troops fighting in the east would be. Schlabrendorff could not give an encouraging account of Bock but he did say that Tresckow was still hoping to be able to carry his commander along. [35] This was reported to Witzleben and towards the end of January 1942 he sent Major Hans-Alexander von Voss, who was still on his staff at this time, to Halder to discuss possible measures of coordination.[36] Halder said that he agreed with everything that Witzleben was planning but that he could do nothing himself since he was alone and nobody around him would cooperate.[37]

At the end of September 1941 Tresckow sent Schlabrendorff to Berlin to discuss matters with the headquarters of the conspiracy, 'to find out whether opposition was crystallizing at home' and to assure them that in the staff of Army Group Centre 'one' was ready for anything.[38] It would be good, Tresckow said, if one could count on a benevolent attitude from Britain after a change of regime. Armed with this message Schlabrendorff went to Hassell. He could naturally guarantee nothing and could only assure Schlabrendorff that 'a respectable Germany would always have a very considerable *chance* to get peace and an acceptable peace at that'. Hitler, on the other hand, he said, could certainly get no peace unless Britain and America had been knocked out.[39] This, as Hassell noted, was the first initiative to come from the front and from the Army at all and so constituted an entirely new factor in the opposition. The incident illustrates both the unique character and the revolutionary drive of the group of young officers assembled around Tresckow.

After this talk Hassell went on tour to Bucharest, Budapest and Brazzà on business for the 'Central European Economic Council'; he returned shortly after the middle of October and saw Popitz, Jessen and Goerdeler. General von Falkenhausen, the Military Commander in Belgium and Northern France, and General Thomas had meanwhile visited Brauchitsch who 'comprehended what beastliness is rampant' and was 'gradually awakening to the fact that a share of the responsibility was his'. It was planned to send Hassell once more to Witzleben via Falkenhausen and fresh hopes were now placed in Brauchitsch and Halder.[40] Contact was established with the 'young circles' centred on Trott, Yorck and Moltke and basic questions concerning a change of system were discussed. Then, on 19 December 1941, after the winter catastrophe in Russia had become obvious and the United States had joined Germany's enemies, came the severe blow of the dismissal of Brauchitsch. Hitler himself took over command of the Army.[41] There was nothing more to be hoped for from Brauchitsch; four years of fruitless effort had ended.

In January 1942, as agreed with Popitz, Goerdeler, Beck, Jessen, Planck, Oster and Dohnanyi, Hassell went via Brussels (Falkenhausen) to visit Field Marshal von Witzleben in Paris. On 17 January he had a long talk with Graf Schwerin von Schwanenfeld and Witzleben and in the evening lectured to the officers of the military administration on '*Lebensraum* and Imperialism'. On 19 January he had another meeting with Witzleben, at which Schwerin was again present.[42] They were all agreed on the necessity for the *coup*, but both the commanders thought Beck's and Goerdeler's proposal, that the *coup* be initiated by a *putsch* in the west under Witzleben and Falkenhausen, to be utopian. They had not the fighting troops and there were sufficient other reasons against it. The result would be a struggle for power approximating to civil war which the Nazis might easily win through use of their auxiliary forces, their hold on the actual reins of government with its consequent prestige, their popularity and their methods of mass indoctrination. Unless simultaneous action were taken against Hitler himself and his immediate entourage, no *putsch* had a hope of success.

Early in February Hassell reported to Popitz, Jessen, Beck and Planck on his tour, which had in fact been without tangible result.[43] Once more everything was at a standstill. It was learnt that Popitz and Hassell were both under strict surveillance by the SD; for the moment it seemed impossible to do anything against Hitler; Witzleben was seriously ill and was eventually relieved of his command.[44] He retired on 15 March 1942.

Admittedly towards the end of March the Beck–Hassell–Oster–Olbricht group decided, with the agreement of Goerdeler and Jessen, that Beck should in future hold all the strings of the conspiracy. Beck was officially 'constituted as the headquarters' and from July 1942 Army Group Centre was in permanent touch with Beck and Goerdeler through Schlabrendorff.[45] Hassell himself, however, described the prospects for any form of action as very meagre. Expressions such as 'nothing to be done', 'hardly a hope' and 'little to be done' frequently appear in his diary of this period.

Tresckow had meanwhile attempted to make use of the shock caused by the winter crisis to persuade his Commander-in-Chief to act against Hitler. But when Bock realized what Tresckow was aiming at he shouted: 'I will not allow the *Führer* to be attacked. I shall stand before the *Führer* and defend him against anyone who dares attack him.'[46] As a result Army Group Centre was temporarily out of the running as the focus for a *coup* and Tresckow had to start from the beginning with Kluge, the new C-in-C who took over on 19 December 1941.[47] Eventually the indefatigable Tresckow succeeded in winning him over but it took years of effort and no one other than Tresckow could exert any influence on Kluge.[48] A particular opportunity of exerting pressure on the vacillating Kluge arose when he accepted a gift of 250,000 marks from Hitler in October 1942.[49] It was explained to Kluge that he could only justify his acceptance before history if he could show that his purpose was to remain at his post in order to work for the *coup d'état*.[50]

Schlabrendorff maintained and improved communications to Beck, Goerdeler and Oster, in the process meeting Dohnanyi, Freiherr von Guttenberg and Justus Delbrück of Oster's staff, also Captain Ludwig Gehre and the John brothers. Nevertheless during the hectic period of summer operations any real preparations for a *coup* were inevitably forced into the background. They could not be resumed until the autumn of 1942 and in the shadow of a fresh, even greater, military catastrophe.[51]

In October or November 1942 Goerdeler visited Kluge and Tresckow in Smolensk.[52] In August he had been in Königsberg and had there talked with Field Marshal von Küchler, C-in-C Army Group North; on his return to Berlin Schlabrendorff had asked him to go to Smolensk.[53] His talk with Kluge was such a success that the Field Marshal gave certain general assurances and thereafter was regarded as having been won over to the conspiracy.[54] Whenever Kluge wavered Goerdeler and Tresckow succeeded in winning him over again. But in January 1943 Tresckow was forced to communicate to his friends in Berlin a discouraging reply from Kluge to a request for a decision. Captain Hermann Kaiser of Fromm's staff noted in his diary: '1. No participation in any Fiesco operation. 2. Nor in any operation against Pollux [Hitler]. 3. Will not be in the way when action begins.'[55] Towards the end of 1942 or early in 1943 Schlabrendorff met General Olbricht of the AHA (*Allgemeines Heeresamt* – General Army Office) through the good offices of Captain Hermann Kaiser who was his permanent contact to Goerdeler. All this eventually led to a meeting in Berlin between Goerdeler, Olbricht and Tresckow, at which Olbricht pledged himself to organize a *coup* using the Replacement Army in Berlin, Vienna, Cologne and Munich.[56] But even Olbricht had to be 'worked on' constantly, as Tresckow told Captain Kaiser on 6 February 1943:

'You must do everything to strengthen O[lbricht]'s resolve.'[57] Doubts about Olbricht's ability or will to take the initiative kept recurring.[58] There was still a question whether the main blow against the Nazi centres of power would be struck by the Field Army or the Replacement Army.[59] It was decided to compromise, certain specialized formations being constituted as raiding parties.[60] It was not until the summer of 1943 that, through the efforts of Stauffenberg, emphasis swung towards use of the Replacement Army. From the end of 1942, however, everyone was agreed on the question of initiation of the *coup*: under all circumstances this must come from the Field Army. At the time only Tresckow and his group were either able or resolute enough to kill Hitler.[61]

Tresckow considered various methods of eliminating Hitler – arrest, shooting by a single assailant or by a group, a raid on the *Führer's* headquarters. Even after deciding on a certain method he kept the others in mind in an attempt to make use of every sort of opportunity. He felt it important, however, to have every conceivable assurance that the attack would succeed. Without such assurance the danger to the conspiracy was too great; a single abortive attack might lead to the annihilation of the entire opposition.[62] For these reasons Tresckow decided on a bomb attack. His preference for a bomb had nothing to do with the safety of the assailant; depending on the circumstances, even with a bomb attack he might have to sacrifice himself if he was to succeed.

The danger that 'innocent people' might be involved or even killed was greater with a bomb attack than, for instance, attack with a pistol, although even in this case people other than the intended victims might be killed or wounded in the shooting match which would probably ensue. The conspirators wrestled most seriously with this problem. Men prepared to be the assailant were in any case aware that they would subsequently be labelled as traitors, even if the result of their act was salvation and the end of the war; they knew that in accordance with current laws and ideas they would be committing murder.[63] Tresckow in particular held the view that this must be considered in the light of the magnitude of the task and that this applied both to the sacrifice of the assailant, perhaps of his family, and the danger caused to 'innocent persons'. The object was to save a whole nation, he said, and prevent suffering for millions of human beings; a pistol attack was out of the question owing to the high probability of failure, in which case it would achieve the exact opposite of that intended; there was therefore no alternative between inactivity and non-involvement of the 'innocent' on the one hand and action entailing risk on the other.

Eventually the members of the opposition decided – whether or not they had a right to do so – that those who might be endangered could not be considered entirely 'innocent'. Some people will undoubtedly protest violently but they should consider that even the assailants themselves did not think that they were entirely 'innocent', quite apart from their plans for murder and a *coup d'état*. Hardly anyone who knew about the Nazi crimes and held his tongue could claim 'innocence'; anyone, for instance, who knew about the Commissar Order and said nothing was morally partially responsible and anyone who protested in vain and then felt himself innocent was in fact guilty. There was no black and white in this business, only grey, and even the conspirators felt themselves to be in that category.[64] Certain people had long lived in close proximity to Hitler – his immediate entourage such as Jodl, Keitel, the SS aides, Himmler's and Ribbentrop's liaison officers (from a distance and from outside the many lesser aides hardly made an impression among the mass of SS and Party dignitaries and were not considered by the conspirators). After all that had become known to the outside world about Hitler's way of life and the group with which he was surrounded, the members of the immediate entourage could certainly not call themselves 'white'. The question must remain problematical but it applies to assassinations and *coups d'état* at any time.

In the summer of 1942 Tresckow commissioned Lieutenant-Colonel Freiherr von Gersdorff, Intelligence Officer of the Army Group, to obtain the equipment suitable for an assassination. The explosive should be of the smallest possible volume with the greatest possible effect, he said; the ignition mechanism must provide for the setting of various time delays but above all it must be silent.[65] Tresckow did not say why he wanted this explosive but Gersdorff understood very well. He went off to the depots maintained by *Abwehr* Sections I, II and III which were under his orders and in that of Section II (Sabotage) he found what he was looking for.[66]

Gersdorff asked to see all available explosive material and to have some of it demonstrated to him. He hinted that he was thinking about anti-partisan warfare and wished to equip Russian volunteers serving in 'Front-Reconnaissance Detachment No 103' or the newly formed 'Boeselager' cavalry unit with it. He was shown a small quantity of British plastic explosive which, fastened to a railway line, cut it clean through. In another test with between $\frac{1}{2}$ and 1lb of this explosive the turret of a Russian tank was blown off and hurled some twenty yards. Gersdorff said that he wished to show this interesting material to the Field Marshal and collected a specimen of the explosive and detonators after having been shown precisely how to handle it. As he was about to go Lieutenant Buchholz, commanding the depot, came running after him and demanded a receipt. On the numerous subsequent occasions when he took some explosive Gersdorff invariably had to sign a receipt. Some of this explosive came from containers dropped by the British for sabotage purposes or for the French resistance and had been discovered through 'radio play-back games' and other methods; some had been captured as a result of the British commando raids on Saint-Nazaire and Dieppe in the summer of 1941.[67] Considerable quantities were stored in ammunition depots in Silesia and many Army agencies, particularly intelligence sections, carried out tests and could then order what they wanted. The explosive taken by Gersdorff was primarily the British 'Plastic C' consisting of 88.3% hexogen and the rest axle grease and other additives to prevent crystallization and hardening. It could be kept for two to three years before becoming hard and crumbly; it could only be used in temperatures between 0° and 40°C; below 0° it became too brittle and above 40° too oily and greasy. This explosive was used in many tests subsequently carried out in fields near the Dnieper by Tresckow, Schlabrendorff and Gersdorff.

The British fuses were the most suitable and of these there were several types. In many of them, on removal of a pin a spring acted on a strip of soft metal until it parted, releasing the firing pin on to the detonator. Others worked by acid: a spring was held under tension by a wire encased in cotton wool and above it was a capsule of acid. If the capsule was crushed the acid escaped into the cotton wool and after a predetermined time ate through the wire; this released the spring which in turn drove a firing pin on to the detonator causing the explosion.[68] There were fuses with delays of 10, 30, 60 etc. minutes, each marked by different coloured rings. Timings were calculated on a constant temperature of 65° Fahrenheit (18°C). Tables gave the timings anticipated for different temperatures but Tresckow would not rely on them and drew up his own tables after making tests. It proved that at 0°C ignition time was doubled. These British fuses were not only particularly suitable for use with the plastic explosives but they were also completely silent. German fuses of this type were not available; those in use hissed or, with hand grenades for instance, had to be pulled. Tresckow did not feel that he could accept either noise or a conspicuous pulling motion if he was to be sure of success.[69] The possibility of instantaneous silent ignition through an electric battery appears not to have been considered.

As the months went by Gersdorff took delivery of several pounds of explosive and hundreds of chemical fuses – each time signing his receipt. From time to time new forms of bomb appeared and were tested for suitability. One day during this process the conspirators stumbled upon a small British adhesive mine which seemed to them particularly handy.

This little bomb, which was excellent for sabotage purposes, was known by the British as the 'clam'. A black plastic casing, rounded at the corners, was screwed on to a base plate; in the base plate were four recesses housing magnets which, however, did not project above the surface of the plate.[70] The mine was flat and the pencil-shaped fuse was inserted through an opening in the narrow side of the mine and held in place by a clip. The whole thing was about the size of a small thick pocket bible; measurements were $5\frac{3}{4}'' \times 2\frac{3}{4}'' \times 1\frac{1}{2}''$. The standard filling for a 'clam' was 55% tetryl and 45% TNT. This explosive was so powerful that a single 'clam' could penetrate a 1″ steel plate, twist a railway line or crack a cylinder block. 'Clams' delivered empty were best filled with a plastic explosive known by the British as 'Compound B'; it consisted of 60% hexogen and 40% TNT and its effect was approximately the same.

It is almost impossible to foretell the effect of an explosive unless it is used in a completely solid enclosed area, a bunker for instance. The effect may be far greater at a distance of three feet than at four inches or vice versa. The point is what 'blanketing' takes place, in other words what resistance is met by the bullet-shaped explosion wave, also whether the object is to produce a pressure or expansion wave. It can also be that under similar conditions (blanketing, air temperature, flooring) a target which is highly resistant at a distance of ten yards may be completely demolished at a distance of eight inches and completely intact at a distance of three feet.

Too great confidence, therefore, could not be placed in these small magnetic mines. It was not certain, for instance, that one of them would be enough not merely to wound but to kill a man in an unblanketed space and at short range. There were therefore obvious limits to experimentation but on the basis of trials success seemed likely enough. In any case it was now proposed to attempt the assassination in an entirely different manner; a demolition charge of four 'clams' was prepared for concealment in Hitler's car; if this did not work, the charge was to be smuggled into his aircraft. The quantity of explosive used would certainly have been fatal in a car since Hitler would have been sitting immediately next to it. In an aircraft the effect would at least have been enough to cause the machine to crash.

While Tresckow pursued his preparations for the attempt on the eastern front, the Berlin conspirators were working to create the conditions for the *coup d'état*. Olbricht was playing his part, preparing measures to be taken in Berlin, Cologne, Munich and Vienna, of which Berlin was naturally the most important. He proposed to use troops located in Frankfurt on Oder to occupy the eastern half of Berlin. Units of the 'Brandenburg' Division were to be used to cordon off the SS Artillery School near Jüterbog, occupy the western half of Berlin and isolate the *Führer*'s headquarters, 'Wolfschanze' (Wolf's Lair) near Rastenburg in East Prussia, where Hitler was to be found at the time.[71]

The history of the 'Brandenburg' Division was as follows: in mid-October 1939, on orders from Canaris, Captain Theodor von Hippel of Section II of the *Abwehr* formed 'No 800 Special Construction-training Company' which was expanded into a battalion a month later. The unit was located in Brandenburg on the Havel and its duty was to prepare for 'special operations'. No 1 Company was composed of expatriate Germans originally intended as a reservoir of informers; this company later became the 'Kurfürst' Regiment. The other companies were stationed at the Quenz estate on the Quenzsee and given general infantry training and special training in sabotage. After the French campaign the battalion was expanded into 'No 800 Special Construction-training Regiment' with No 1 Battalion in Brandenburg and Nos 2 and 3 in Vienna and Aachen, later Düren. In October 1940 the unit was rechristened the 'Brandenburg' Regiment. At the end of October 1942 it was further expanded into a division directly subordinate to OKW *Ausland/Abwehr* and commanded by Colonel Haehling von Lanzenauer. At the turn of the year 1942–43 parts of the division were put into action on threatened sectors of the front in southern Russia where they suffered heavy casualties. Early in 1943 they returned in some disorganization and had to be re-formed. Colonel Haehling was sick and died shortly thereafter.

Canaris now looked for a new divisional commander with the necessary qualifications and front-line experience but also likely to be reliable from the opposition's point of view. Oster suggested Colonel Alexander von Pfuhlstein, a man who had shown himself an outstanding regimental commander and had been awarded the Knight's Cross; on 1 February 1943 Oster summoned him to Berlin. He had numerous talks in his own house with Pfuhlstein, probing and instructing; Pfuhlstein was also on good terms with Olbricht. Oster indicated that he was speaking on behalf and with the agreement of Olbricht and Canaris. Jodl wanted to organize the division as an OKW reserve force and in the succeeding period Canaris had only a limited say in its employment. However this did not prevent Oster charging Pfuhlstein to organize the division as a mobile force specially for use in a *coup d'état*. It was to be ready for action by the end of April.

Pfuhlstein was given certain officers who were members of the conspiracy, including Captain Graf Schwerin von Schwanenfeld and Lieutenant-Colonel Heinz.[72] He was officially appointed commander of the 'Brandenburg' Division on 1 April 1943.[73] According to his own account formation of No IV Regiment in Brandenburg under Heinz was not complete until the end of April. The entire division was under the authority of the OKW Operations Staff, partly because the bottom of the barrel was being scraped for troops to hold the front and partly because in spring 1943 the *Abwehr* had fallen into disfavour.[74] While Haehling von Lanzenauer was sick Colonel Lahousen had temporarily commanded the division so that it would have been available for a *coup* during a critical period in March 1943. What would have happened is, of course, difficult to estimate. There were different opinions about the suitability of the division, particularly about No IV Regiment which was the unit in question; it contained many volunteers who were supporters of the regime and also some completely unreliable adventurer types. Nevertheless in March Heinz, the regimental commander, stated that it was ready and on call for the conspirators.[75]

On the eastern front formation of a special '*coup d'état* force' was considerably more successful. As with the 'Brandenburg' Division the first consideration was formation of a unit for war and, again like the 'Brandenburg' Division, it was used accordingly. Army Group Centre had formed a 'Cavalry Regiment Centre' and in 1943 and 1944 this was involved in heavy, costly fighting. At the same time it was hoped that by judicious selection of officers and certain organizational measures the unit could be made suitable for use in a *coup*.

The opportunity presented itself at the end of 1942. Lieutenant Philipp Freiherr von Boeselager had been aide to Field Marshal von Kluge since June 1942; his brother Georg was a tactics instructor with the Rumanian troops. During the winter 1942–43 Georg visited his old squadron which was with 6 Infantry Division in Army Group Centre's area and Philipp asked the Field Marshal whether his brother, whom the Field Marshal knew from his Münster days, might visit Army Group headquarters. Kluge agreed and invited Captain Georg Freiherr von Boeselager to accompany him as his aide on a duty flight. During such flights Kluge used to shoot foxes from the air if he had time and opportunity.[76]

The weather was bad for flying, however, and Georg von Boeselager spent several days in Army Group headquarters. On several occasions he talked cavalry problems with Tresckow who had not met him before. Boeselager wanted to withdraw cavalry squadrons from infantry divisions since they were frequently misused and 'burned up', as the saying was, to no good purpose; he wished them to be independent and to be used in their proper role. He was a cavalryman heart and soul and was trying to save the cavalry from the threat of abolition hanging over it. He accordingly proposed to the Field Marshal that a cavalry unit be formed to act as a sort of fire brigade available for mobile operations in the Army Group area, seeing that reserves were invariably inadequate. Kluge agreed and told Boeselager to discuss details with Tresckow. In discussion with Tresckow Boeselager placed himself unreservedly at the disposal of the conspiracy. In January 1943 Georg Freiherr von Boeselager was officially appointed to form the 'Boeselager' cavalry unit with the energetic support of Tresckow and of Colonel Stieff, head of the Organization Section in the Army General Staff since late 1942. High-class equipment was provided and a first-rate unit formed consisting of two battalions each of five squadrons of 220 men. Some 650 men were Russian cossacks. In late March 1943 Philipp von Boeselager took command of one of the two battalions; on 7 April 1943 Georg Freiherr von Boeselager was appointed commander of 'Cavalry Regiment Centre' which in practice he had been since mid-March.

Army Group Centre now had available a highly mobile specialized force whose officers were largely members of the conspiracy or at least 'reliable' people and which had been specially formed for exceptional employment. There was reason to hope that, at the right moment, it could be flown to Berlin and used for the *coup*. As with the 'Brandenburg' Division, however, people were under no illusions about some of the troops. On 21 May 1943, in reply to a question from Tresckow about the retention of Russian volunteers Boeselager wrote: 'One must realize that these people are only fighting on our side because they are better fed that way. Moreover they hope, if possible, to come out of this war alive.'[77]

32 Projects of 1943

About the turn of the year 1942–43 something like a sense of catastrophe spread through Germany and in some cases to the front.[1] Stalingrad and the annihilation of Sixth Army were fearful blows, from which the German Army never recovered. At the same time the demand for 'unconditional surrender' was announced from Casablanca implying the abolition not only of the Nazi regime, which was more or less detested in any case, but of German sovereignty as a nation. The failure of the opposition's attempts at contact abroad in the spring and summer of 1942 had made the Allied attitude clear; now Germany was faced by it with utter clarity. In this situation, defeat and failure on one side, confidence in victory on the other, a near-revolutionary atmosphere spread in Germany. The demonstration of the Scholl group in Munich University was an expression of this mood, a flash quickly extinguished by the ubiquitous *Gestapo* and general fear.[2]

As already mentioned, about the turn of the year Tresckow had met Georg Freiherr von Boeselager; he had been awarded the Oak Leaves, was known throughout the Army as one of the best pentathlon athletes and early in 1943 committed himself to the opposition. Tresckow now asked whether he thought that he could shoot Hitler at short range with a pistol. This method could only be tried, Tresckow said, if one could be sure of killing with a single shot.

A lone assailant's chances of success were small in any case and, moreover, Boeselager was not sure that he had the necessary *sang froid*.[3] It is one thing to shoot an anonymous enemy and quite another deliberately to kill a man when all the sociological and psychological factors associated with a battle situation are absent. It does not matter who the man is; the point is whether he is an anonymous 'enemy' or a fellow human being, personally recognizable.[4] In any case it was generally thought among the conspirators that, to guard against attempts at assassination, Hitler wore a bullet-proof waistcoat and cap. Tresckow and Gersdorff had been told as much by Schmundt, Hitler's *Wehrmacht* Adjutant; Gersdorff had once lifted Hitler's cap and had remarked on its extraordinary weight.[5]

The next plan, therefore, was that Hitler should be shot by a whole group of officers in the Army Group headquarters mess during a visit to the front which it was hoped to persuade him to make in view of the desperate situation. Captain Schmidt-Salzmann and Colonel von Kleist declared themselves ready to do it together with ten officers from No III Battalion of the 'Boeselager' unit which was still in process of formation. Shortly before Hitler's visit, however, the project had to be abandoned because Field Marshal von Kluge, who would inevitably have been present at the time, could not bring himself to accept the idea. He had to be informed so that he might keep himself out of the line of fire. Kluge said that it was not seemly to shoot a man at lunch and there would also be a risk to a number of senior officers (including himself) who would have to be there and could not be spared if the front was to be held.

Meanwhile, as efforts to persuade Hitler to visit Army Group Centre in Smolensk continued, the *Führer* did pay a visit to the headquarters of Army Group Don in Saporozhe.[6] On 17 February 1943 he left his headquarters near Rastenburg in his Focke-Wulf 'Condor' and flew via Vinnitsa to Saporozhe. This was a snap decision and he took off at 2 a.m. He was accompanied among others, some travelling in two further 'Condors', by General Jodl, head of the OKW Operations Staff, and General Zeitzler who had relieved Halder as Chief of Staff of the Army. In Saporozhe Hitler conferred with Manstein.

In headquarters Army Group B commanded by Field Marshal Maximilian Freiherr von Weichs, however, it had been hoped that Hitler would go there, in other words to Poltava, where General Hubert Lanz and his Chief of Staff Major-General Hans Speidel were prepared to arrest him.

Lanz had been commanding 'Army Detachment Lanz' in the Kharkov area since the end of January; it had been formed after the collapse of the Italian Eighth Army and consisted of the 'Hausser' SS Corps, the SS 'Leibstandarte Adolf Hitler' under Sepp Dietrich, the SS Division 'Reich' under Keppler, the SS Division 'Totenkopf' under the ex-Inspector of concentration camps *SS-Gruppenführer* Theodor Eicke, parts of the 'Grossdeutschland' Division under Lieutenant-General Walter Hörnlein, two other corps, one of which was commanded by Lieutenant-General Erhard Raus, and 24 Panzer Corps. In a late-night briefing conference in 'Wolfschanze' on 26 January Lanz had been instructed by Hitler to hold the area and city of Kharkov against any attack – an almost impossible mission since the strength ratio in the area was 1:4. The next morning, in a snowstorm, Lanz flew to Kharkov, where he found the few available troops in a desperate position. Hitler then held him responsible for the catastrophic situation and its subsequent developments, although he could hardly exert any influence on them at all. His only available reserve was the 'Grossdeutschland' Panzer Regiment under Colonel Graf von Strachwitz in the Poltava area.

While Strachwitz was in hospital recovering from a wound received at Stalingrad he was told by Colonel Wessel Freiherr von Freytag-Loringhoven of the crimes committed by the SS behind the German lines. From the beginning of 1942, Strachwitz had become more and more convinced that Hitler must be removed from the military and political leadership of Germany. On 8 February Strachwitz discussed the employment of his regiment with General Speidel, who asked him what he thought of the situation; Strachwitz replied that, if everything people said was true, then Hitler must go. Speidel said that he thought so too. The same evening General Lanz summoned Strachwitz; he had meanwhile been told of Strachwitz's views by Speidel and now asked him to repeat what he had said to Speidel. This first talk between Lanz and Strachwitz took place in the village of Valki between Kharkov and Poltava, where the Army Detachment's headquarters were located. In this hopeless military situation, in which Hitler was in effect demanding that entire armies sacrifice themselves, Lanz and Strachwitz soon found that their views were identical on the high command in general and Hitler in particular – in short they agreed that Hitler was a criminal and must be removed. This was the origin of the 'Lanz Plan'. Through Dr Strölin, burgomaster of Stuttgart, Field Marshal Erwin Rommel, commanding the 'Afrika Korps', was informed of the plan, though in fact he could hardly have made much contribution to its success.

Strachwitz repeatedly assured his partners that he could rely totally on his tank regiment. It was accordingly decided that Hitler should be arrested by selected sections of the regiment under the personal leadership of Strachwitz, if possible on landing in Poltava or alternatively during a conference in the headquarters. The situation being what it was, the unit could easily be moved over the comparatively short distance necessary without attracting attention; troops were always on the move to and fro.

Weapons were only to be used 'in the event of serious resistance' according to Lanz or 'if it came to a fight' according to Strachwitz. Both were to be reckoned with, however, since Hitler was invariably accompanied by members of the *Reichssicherheitsdienst* (RSD, police bodyguard in SS uniforms), his personal SS Escort (*SS–Begleitkommando*), and officers of OKW; the Operations Staff and aides were usually present. Assassination was not, therefore, intended but its possibility was accepted; under the circumstances and according to current ideas this would not have amounted to sheer murder. Undoubtedly, however, the soldiers would have preferred to arrest Hitler if at all possible. Strachwitz then proposed to hand him over to Kluge.

On 17 February, when Hitler made his sudden visit to the front, however, Army Group B and Field Marshal von Weichs had already moved from Poltava and Hitler visited Saporozhe instead of Poltava. On the third day of his visit he ran into a highly dangerous situation, although in this case the opposition had nothing to do with it. Russian tanks were driving along the road to Saporozhe which ran alongside the airfield, and were only two hours away while Hitler was still in the town.[7] Baur, his pilot, drove into town forthwith to urge him to hurry and, as the three 'Condors' took off, the Russians had already reached the eastern end of the airfield, where, however, they took up positions in a kolkhoz. As Hitler and his entourage flew off two six-engined German 'Giants' came in carrying anti-tank guns, of which there were none in Saporozhe. The Russians had not attacked the airfield because they had run out of fuel.

Meanwhile preparations had been proceeding in Berlin; Schlabrendorff had been there again in February.[8] But the measures were not yet fully decided. Olbricht hoped to be ready by 1 March but Pfuhlstein thought that it would be

April. Captain Kaiser noted in his diary after a conversation with Schlabrendorff on 19 February: 'Deadline 1 March 43'.[9] Dr Gisevius spent many days in January and February 1943 in an office in Bendlerstrasse that Olbricht had made available to him and revised the old 1938 plans.[10] New data on the location of SS garrisons were procured, liaison was established with police commanders and, tentatively, with some field marshals. It made little sense now to wait, if an opportunity presented itself. To a certain extent all was, in fact, ready; postings and other developments could always upset the best-laid plans; much would have to be improvised in any case. At the end of 1942 Olbricht had told Tresckow that he wanted eight more weeks. When these were up, Schlabrendorff had a talk with Olbricht who said to him: 'We are ready; it is time for the flash.'[11] This was at the end of February. Naturally it was true only within the limits indicated above. There had been a discussion, for instance, of the question how to cut all communications to the outside world from 'Wolfschanze', the *Führer*'s headquarters, which also housed the whole of OKW and its Operations Staff when Hitler was there; General Fellgiebel, the *Wehrmacht* Chief Signals Officer, said quite rightly that few preparations could be made since it would be necessary to occupy the repeater stations and trunk exchanges. Without ensuring the assistance of the Post Office no preparations could be made; in this case, therefore, 'action' could only be taken when the 'flash' had taken place.[12]

A certain degree of coordination and agreement, however, between the focus of action on the eastern front and headquarters in Berlin, was essential. For this purpose, on 7 March 1943, Canaris flew to Smolensk with a considerable staff on pretext of holding a general intelligence conference. He brought with him Major-General Oster, head of his Coordination Section, Colonel Lahousen, head of Section II, his special assistant, Dr von Dohnanyi – and a box of explosive.[13] This was handed over by Gersdorff to Section II of the *Abwehr* Detachment.[14] Tresckow and Dohnanyi talked late into the night and agreed on a code to coordinate measures taken by the Berlin group and that at the front. Tresckow declared that the 'flash' would take place at the next available opportunity and accepted an assurance that all necessary preparations for the *coup* had been made in Berlin.

So eventually Hitler arrived in Smolensk on 13 March 1943 on his way back to East Prussia from Vinnitsa. The situation at the front was so precarious and his anxiety on this score so great that he was prepared to make the journey in spite of his fright at Saporozhe.[15] He wished to discuss the Kursk offensive, both pros and cons, and, as for his visit to Saporozhe, brought with him Generals Jodl and Zeitzler together with his RSD and SS escort, doctors, photographers, aides, Party dignitaries, his personal cook and his driver.

Hitler and his entourage again arrived in three 'Condors'; immediately on landing at Smolensk airfield he drove to headquarters Army Group Centre nearby.[16] Kluge and Tresckow had gone to the airfield to meet Hitler; he did not use an Army Group vehicle, however, but departed in his own car driven by his personal driver, Erich Kempka. During the war four motorcades were stationed at various points in Germany, in the west, on the eastern front (at this time in Vinnitsa); they were moved as necessary wherever Hitler might need them. Other security measures were very comprehensive. Rail traffic on a section of line which crossed the road between the airfield and the headquarters was halted for the duration of the visit. Wherever Hitler went SS men with sub-machine-guns at the ready were to be seen.[17]

These security measures were offset by Lieutenant-Colonel von Boeselager who deployed a group of officers and non-commissioned officers from Cavalry Regiment Centre willing to assassinate Hitler.[18] Several squadrons of Boeselager's regiment were used on that day to set up a wide security cordon around the headquarters of Army Group Centre. No. 1 Squadron under Major König had to guard the road from the airfield to the forest in which the headquarters buildings were situated; from the edge of the forest the visitors and their hosts proceeded on foot, and this path was also lined by men from No. 1 Squadron with sub-machine-guns. Some of these, who were led by Major König personally, were collectively to shoot Hitler as he walked back to his car. It is not clear why the plan was not carried out, although König hinted a few weeks afterwards that Hitler had not followed the path originally planned. This is not unlikely; Hitler himself claimed that this sort of thing was an effective security precaution.[19] It is also possible that Tresckow considered an attempt with explosives more promising and less incriminating for the Army.

A conference was then held at which in addition to Hitler, there were present Jodl, Zeitzler, Schmundt and others of the entourage, Kluge and Commanders of Armies included in the Army Group, with their Chiefs of Staff. Following this came lunch in the Army Group headquarters mess. According to the earlier plan Hitler was to be shot during this lunch and this would have been perfectly possible, though the others present would have been in some danger. During lunch Tresckow asked Lieutenant-Colonel Heinz Brandt of the OKH Operations Section, who was accompanying Hitler, to take a package for Colonel Stieff in OKH; Brandt willingly agreed since there was nothing unusual in this.[20] The package to be carried by Lieutenant-Colonel Brandt, however, was to contain a live bomb.

That morning, in accordance with the agreement reached with Dohnanyi on 7 March, Schlabrendorff had called Captain Ludwig Gehre, a member of the *Abwehr* in Berlin, and given him the codeword indicating that the 'flash' was imminent. After lunch Kluge and Tresckow once more accompanied Hitler and his entourage to the airfield and this time Schlabrendorff followed with the package of explosive. He waited until Hitler was about to board his aircraft, activated the fuse by pressing the acid capsule through the wrapping with a key and, on a signal from Tresckow, passed the package to Lieutenant-Colonel Brandt who boarded the same aircraft as Hitler. After all three 'Condors' had taken off with their fighter escort, Schlabrendorff hurried back to the headquarters and called Gehre again; this time he gave the codeword meaning that the 'flash' had been sparked off. Gehre passed the information to Oster via Dohnanyi.

The 'bomb' constructed by Tresckow consisted of two pairs of British 'clams' held together by their own magnets and also bound round with adhesive tape. Wrapped up, they could pass for two bottles of Cointreau. The fuse was set for thirty minutes and it was thought that the aircraft would crash after 125–150 miles, shortly before reaching Minsk.

Hitler in fact flew first to Vinnitsa and thence to Rastenburg so that the crash might have been expected before he overflew Kiev. A few hours later, however, those waiting in Smolensk heard that he had landed in Rastenburg.[21]

Schlabrendorff at once called Gehre yet again and gave him the codeword for failure of the attempt. He then discussed with Tresckow how to save the situation. The first consideration was to lay hands on the package again somehow before a catastrophe occurred; no one could tell whether it might not still explode and Stieff, its addressee, knew nothing at all. Tresckow therefore called Lieutenant-Colonel Brandt and asked him to keep the package, saying that there had been a mix-up. Next morning Schlabrendorff flew by normal courier aircraft to East Prussia, went to see Brandt in OKH's camp 'Mauerwald' and exchanged the package for one really containing Cointreau. Then he took the bomb into his sleeping compartment in a train in Korschen siding which served as overnight accommodation for visitors and carefully opened the package with a razor blade.[22] He found that the fuse had functioned correctly up to the moment when the acid had eaten through the wire and released the striker on to the detonator which should have set off the explosion; the striker had struck correctly, the detonator cap was burnt and the detonator black on the outside. But the explosive had not ignited, probably due to the excessive cold.[23]

Schlabrendorff kept the 'clams' and took the night train to Berlin where he arrived on the morning of 15 March. He went at once to Gehre and Oster and showed them the detonator. The disappointment of all those involved was great; all the dangers and nervous tension associated with keeping and transporting explosives in so mysterious and clandestine a manner and in close proximity to Hitler had been in vain. Already, however, they were thinking of some fresh occasion.

In a few days time the ceremony of 'Heroes Memorial Day' was due to take place; this year it was to be held on 21 March, not around the 15th as usual. On 14 March, two days before the date proposed, Hitler had postponed the occasion to the 21st. He hoped that some visible victory would be won on the eastern front meanwhile, as in fact happened with the recapture of Kharkov by SS troops.

Colonel Freiherr von Gersdorff had a chance to be present at the 1943 ceremony and, when asked by Tresckow, he declared himself ready to use it to make an assassination attempt.[24] He had to be prepared to blow himself up with Hitler; he had been a widower since January 1942 and, in view of the object, his own life did not seem to him too great a sacrifice. Naturally he wished to know whether, if the attempt succeeded, the *coup d'état* would proceed according to plan. The sacrifice of his own life must serve some purpose and be justifiable before history. Tresckow assured him that a fully prepared organization existed which would 'swing into action'; agreements had been concluded with the Western Powers for a separate surrender in the west, while the eastern front would be held in order to safeguard the existence of the German *Reich* and ensure that a democratic form of government was set up.

Gersdorff's opportunity to be present at this annual ceremony arose from the fact that on this occasion it was to be coupled with an exhibition of captured war material to be provided by Army Group Centre and organized by Gersdorff's Intelligence section. Gersdorff therefore had an excellent pretext for being present in order to explain the various exhibits to Hitler when he made his opening visit. Gersdorff having declared himself ready to make the attempt, Schlabrendorff was told by Tresckow to remain in Berlin and, when Gersdorff arrived, hand him the British 'clams' which remained 'over' from the last attempt.

On 20 March Gersdorff flew to Berlin with Field Marshal Walter Model, Commander-in-Chief Ninth Army; the Heroes Memorial ceremony was due to take place next day. Hitler had actually wished Kluge to be present and he would have come as well. Tresckow's group, however, felt that they could not spare him since they placed great hopes on his collaboration after Hitler's death and he would have been in considerable danger during the assassination attempt. With great difficulty they dissuaded him from going and they had even more difficulty with Frau von Kluge. They could not possibly tell Kluge that an attempt was planned since, owing to his oath of allegiance which he took very seriously, he might have felt compelled to report the fact.

Model wanted to go on to Dresden on the 20th to see his wife and only return to Berlin the next morning. This meant, however, that he must know as accurately as possible when the ceremony would begin. Model and Gersdorff therefore went to Schmundt who had also arrived in Berlin on the 20th with Hitler and the usual entourage. Here two major difficulties presented themselves at once.

In the first place Schmundt was not willing to say when the ceremony would start or how it was intended to proceed. This was remarkable and indicated that special security precautions were being taken. In recent years the ceremony had always opened with Hitler's arrival at the same time, on the stroke of midday. When Model pressed Schmundt he revealed the timetable on pain of the strictest secrecy and with repeated references to 'the death sentence'. Schmundt and Gersdorff were old friends even though Schmundt had some suspicion that Gersdorff and also Tresckow, of whom he was an even older friend, did not love the *Führer* anything like as much as he did. In any case, in this instance he overcame his scruples. From what he said it could be inferred that about half an hour had been allotted for Hitler's visit to the exhibition.

The second difficulty arose when Schmundt said that the list of those attending the visit to the exhibition had been drawn up in detail and that under no circumstances could Gersdorff be there. Here Field Marshal Model came to Gersdorff's assistance – without of course realizing that he was assisting an attempt at assassination. He insisted that Gersdorff must be there since he,

Model, would be highly embarrassed if he was unable to answer a question from Hitler about one of the exhibits. Gersdorff, he said, must definitely be at his side and available to explain. After much hesitation Schmundt once more gave way.

The normal programme of the ceremony, which took place in the Unter den Linden Armoury, now a museum, was this: Hitler drove from the *Reich* Chancellery via the Wilhelmstrasse and Unter den Linden, both of which were lined, to the museum where he would arrive at midday. He was received at the entrance by the Commanders-in-Chief of the three Services (only two from the end of 1942 since Hitler himself had taken over command of the Army) and by the Chief of OKW. From the entrance he went through lines of war-wounded into the great hall of the museum where he took the first chair in the front row immediately to the right of the centre gangway. To his right, in order, sat Field Marshal Freiherr von Böhm-Ermolli representing the Imperial Army, then Dönitz and Göring, Keitel, General (retd) Reinhard, Head of the ex-Servicemen's Association, and *SA-Obergruppenführer* Oberlindober, Leader of the War-Wounded. The hall was decked with flags and an orchestra played solemn music. Hitler then made his usual speech and the national anthem was played. Then the guard battalion, the official guests, the war-wounded and the standards took up position in front of the memorial.

While all this was happening, in order to occupy the ten minutes or so required for the move from indoors into the open, Hitler would visit an exhibition arranged for the purpose in the side-rooms of the museum. On a special signal Hitler would leave the exhibition and emerge through the main entrance with a small following of *Reich* dignitaries, inspect the guard battalion and lay a wreath on the memorial. The guard battalion then had to move off to form up for the march-past, which entailed another pause of some five minutes, during which Hitler conversed with the war-wounded of the First and Second World Wars. After the march-past (two minutes) Hitler drove back to the Chancellery; the rest of the company dispersed and departed.

During the afternoon Gersdorff examined the inside of the museum and checked 'his' exhibition. At the same time he looked for possibilities of concealing a bomb and was forced to admit that there were none. The only place where Hitler would certainly be a target, where he would be for a sufficient length of time in other words, was the speaker's rostrum. The great hall of the museum, however, was large, high and roofed with glass; the blanketing effect would be far too little for a comparatively small bomb and there was no way of either obtaining or concealing a large one. Moreover Gersdorff's information about the timetable was not sufficiently precise to enable him to set a time fuse. Finally that afternoon the museum was full of workmen laying out chairs and setting up staging and the whole place was so closely watched by uniformed and plain clothes SS men and police that there could be no question of concealing a bomb. Even had he succeeded in doing so, it would have had to be fused the next day before Hitler's arrival and this was even less possible. Gersdorff could therefore only make his attempt during Hitler's inspection of the exhibition because only then could he be sure of being close to Hitler for a sufficient length of time. A pistol attack had not been seriously considered for the reasons we already know, so there was no question of anything other than a bomb. This, as Gersdorff knew from Tresckow, Schlabrendorff had in his possession from the last time.

During the night 20–21 March Schlabrendorff took the British 'clams' to Gersdorff in the 'Eden' hotel, but major difficulties then arose in finding a suitable fuse. The type used for the 13 March attempt was out of the question. In the first place it had a 30-minute delay and secondly it had not functioned. The best would have been an instantaneous fuse but in the time available none could be found which fitted the 'clam'. Both Schlabrendorff and Gersdorff tried to obtain other fuses through Oster; Gersdorff had brought along from Smolensk some fuses with a 10-minute delay in the hope of finding circumstances favourable for an attempt relying on such a time-span; Schlabrendorff had been in touch with Oster about this problem before Gersdorff's arrival. Explosives experts who served in the German Army in the Second World War say that German pioneer explosives in 100 gram or 200 gram slabs could have been procured easily, and fuses to fit them as well.[25] But the fuses would have to be activated by a pull, and such a conspicuous motion seemed to be a serious danger for the success of the attack (although Axel Freiherr von dem Bussche was of another opinion, as will be seen below). The German fuses also did not fit the 'clams'. In short, the difficulties in procuring exactly the right kind of explosives and fuses for the opportunity at hand seemed insuperable to the conspirators in their situation at the time.

Even enquiries had to be made with extraordinary caution, particularly so soon before one of Hitler's rare public appearances. Even at the front, where partisans had to be fought and sabotage squads equipped, Gersdorff had not found it easy to obtain explosives and detonators; for Oster, tied to his desk, it was far more difficult, quite apart from the security precautions which were very tight. It was not easy to produce a plausible explanation of a general's need for fuses.

The great difficulty, however, was that there were no fuses which would fit into the British 'clam' giving a delay of less than 10 minutes. The fuse of the German hand grenade gave a delay of $4\frac{1}{2}$ seconds but, even accepting its hissing noise, it would not fit into the 'clam' any better than any other German fuse, as comparison of the measurements shows. The attempt had to be made with the 10-minute fuses which Gersdorff had brought with him. The museum was unheated but Gersdorff hoped that the low temperature would be compensated by his body heat through the pockets of his greatcoat so that the delay would, at worst, be only a little over 10 minutes.

On 21 March Gersdorff went to the Unter den Linden museum about midday. From what Schmundt had said the ceremony was due to begin about 1 p.m. though this was only made known to the general company at the last moment. In contrast to previous years the *Völkischer Beobachter* did not even publish the timing afterwards.[26] In the great hall of the museum the orchestra was in place together with twenty-seven flags of the Imperial Army, three of the Imperial Navy and thirty of the new *Wehrmacht* and *Waffen-SS*.

Representatives of the Army, Navy, *Luftwaffe* and *Waffen-SS* were assembled together with three hundred war-wounded; numerous generals, admirals, ministers, Party dignitaries and state secretaries were also present. Hitler drove up to the front of the museum in his open Mercedes, got out and greeted at the main entrance *Reich* Marshal Göring, Field Marshal Keitel, Grand Admiral Dönitz, Himmler the *Reichsführer–SS,* Field Marshal von Bock, Field Marshal Milch and Oberlindober, head of the War-Wounded Association; he was accompanied by Goebbels.

All then went into the great hall and took their places in the front row. The orchestra played the first movement of Bruckner's Seventh Symphony and Hitler made his speech, lasting 12–14 minutes. Its theme was: 'The danger has now been averted.' Kharkov had been recaptured on 14 March and Sepp Dietrich had been awarded the Swords to the Knight's Cross of the Iron Cross with Oakleaves; the crisis had been overcome and now at last he, Hitler, could leave his headquarters for a few moments, although his duties at the front had necessitated the postponement of Heroes Memorial Day. Now, however, victory was assured over bolshevism, capitalism, the hordes of Asiatic barbarians and the criminal warmongers, Churchill and the Jews. Hitler then moved away to inspect the exhibition. His speech had been exceptionally rapid and short, as even the monitoring service of the BBC noted. The entire ceremony was broadcast over all German stations including the Forces networks throughout Europe, so that Tresckow in Army Group Centre could follow the proceedings on the radio.

Gersdorff had stationed himself meanwhile near the entrance to the exhibition.[27] He could not know how long Hitler would speak nor how great a pause there would be between the speech and the visit to the exhibition, otherwise he would have fused his bombs beforehand; he had one in each greatcoat pocket. Field Marshal Model and a director of the museum[28] were with him at the entrance to the exhibition. Hitler approached; Gersdorff, Model and the museum director gave the Hitler salute with the right arm, Gersdorff keeping his left hand in his greatcoat pocket and squeezing the capsule of the fuse. He did not press the fuse of the bomb in his right-hand pocket to avoid arousing suspicion by too many movements; on one occasion, when visiting Hitler, a fellow-officer's arm had been seized by an SS man when he was merely trying to take out his handkerchief.[29] He also thought that, being so close, the left-hand bomb would set off the other.

Gersdorff had had only a superficial impression of the presence of SS uniforms everywhere he looked when he had inspected the exhibition the day before. In fact security precautions were far more elaborate than Gersdorff ever suspected. Twenty-four hours a day during a specified period before, during and after Hitler's announced public appearances, all sites and approach routes were under close surveillance by hundreds of *Gestapo* and other police agents, preventive arrests were made, building experts and watchmakers, electricians and explosives specialists had searched for hidden devices, and elaborate procedures of admission to the sensitive areas were in force. All security precautions, while under the general direction of SS and police chiefs, were subject to review and modification by *SS-Gruppenführer* Hans Rattenhuber, Hitler's personal security chief, and sudden and unannounced changes often added to security by unpredictability. But only a search of the persons of all those admitted to the Armoury on 21 March 1943 could have prevented Gersdorff's assassination attempt. If it was technically feasible in itself, the attempt of an insider such as Gersdorff had every chance of success.

As Hitler reached the entrance of the exhibition rooms with his small following – Göring, Keitel, Dönitz, Himmler, a few aides and bodyguards – he turned and asked Field Marshal von Bock to accompany him – to Gersdorff's consternation; Bock was accompanied by his aide Graf von Hardenberg who was a friend of Gersdorff, belonged to the resistance movement but had no knowledge that an assassination attempt was under way.

Once Hitler had entered, Gersdorff tried to keep as close to him as possible, which he could do without attracting attention since in a sense it was his duty. Then something remarkable occurred: Hitler stopped nowhere; he literally *ran* through the exhibition, not even glancing at the objects displayed. Model and Gersdorff tried to show him and explain this or that exhibit but in vain. Göring then took a hand and began to tell Hitler of a proclamation by the Patriarch of Moscow, showing once more how the churches were anti-Hitler and so forth. Even this favourite subject, however, failed to interest the *Führer*. If anyone says that Hitler must have had some presentiment or 'smell' of danger, this need not be brushed aside as ridiculous. Men who live so much on their emotions and so dangerously as Hitler do not possess supernatural qualities as a result but their senses are highly perceptive and sharp. The possibility that Hitler sensed Gersdorff's nervousness and took warning from it is not so far-fetched. It is sufficient, however, merely to establish the facts of what happened.

Hitler cannot have spent more than two minutes in the exhibition. The announcer reported his emergence from the museum with surprise; those responsible for the arrangements were taken aback and the programme became somewhat confused. Listeners on the radio noticed, as did the BBC monitoring service which noted the incident and the words of the announcer: ' "The Führer goes into the Exhibition. We shall come back to report on the placing of the wreath on the Memorial." Interval of a few seconds [sic]; shouting of orders; drums. At the Memorial in Unter den Linden we hear again orders shouted. Reporter says: "The Führer has left the Zeughaus. Lt./Col. Jehreke [Gehrke], bearer of the Knight Cross, reports the guard of honour." '[30] Hitler inspected the parade and laid his wreath on the memorial. Then he turned to talk with the war-wounded; a major reported 286 present. Hitler asked some of them where they had been wounded and shook their hands as he sombrely repeated the replies: 'At Yukhnov.' 'At Sebastopol.' At Kalinin,' 'Where were you wounded?' 'In France.' 'In France' – how?' 'Air raid.' 'Air raid.'

Gersdorff was no longer able to follow Hitler. At the end of his short visit to the exhibition he deserted his entire entourage. The attempt had failed. The main point now was to remove the fuse quickly and unobtrusively and an opportunity presented itself in a lavatory near the western exit from the museum.[31] Hitler mounted a small platform together with Göring, Keitel, Dönitz and Himmler and took the salute of the guard battalion as it marched past. He then returned to the Chancellery while the crowd gave him only muted applause in view of the solemnity of the occasion.

Gersdorff's assassination attempt was not foiled by regularly instituted security precautions, nor by any sudden changes ordered by security men. It was foiled, in part, by an internal weakness of the plan, namely the lack of an instantaneous fuse, and, in part, by Hitler's own often intentionally unpredictable behaviour.

Gersdorff returned to his hotel and then to the front. He remained an active member of the opposition but never made another assassination attempt. In the autumn of 1943 he hid the British 'clams' in his brother's house in Breslau when he was there for a stomach operation.[32]

33 Abortive Plans

Henning von Tresckow continued his efforts with undiminished energy but he seemed to be tilting at windmills. He tried to influence Manstein, the Commander-in-Chief Army Group South (known as Army Group Don up to 14 February 1943),[1] but did not expect any 'initiative' from him.[2] In the winter of 1942–43 Beck had written to Manstein saying that the war could not be won and that something must be done, but Manstein had replied that a war was only lost if one considered it lost.[3] Captain Kaiser noted in his diary on 6 April 1943, after a conversation with Tresckow, that Manstein must be written off once and for all. In the summer of 1943 Gersdorff went to Manstein's headquarters in Saporozhe carrying letters from Goerdeler and Popitz and with the backing of Tresckow on behalf of Kluge.[4] Tresckow had his contacts there, Colonel Schulze-Büttger, head of the Operations Section, and Stahlberg, the aide, so the Manstein-Gersdorff meeting was well prepared. Gersdorff was only to hand over his letters, however, if it seemed that they would do some good and would not endanger their authors; if Major-General Theodor Busse, the Chief of Staff, was present he could only discuss military matters.

Manstein did not insist on his Chief of Staff being present and so Gersdorff was able to talk frankly about the 'top level'. The Field Marshal agreed that 'a change' was essential but said that he himself could not suggest this to Hitler since he was not in high enough favour; Kluge or Rundstedt were the only people who could do it. He rejected the idea of concerted action by all the Field Marshals saying that 'Prussian Marshals do not mutiny'. Gersdorff replied that they were not very taken with the idea in Army Group Centre either and were looking for a solution in another direction. Manstein understood at once and said: 'You want to kill him then.' Gersdorff said: Yes, indeed; that was what they proposed. Manstein then became indignant and said: 'I will not go along with that; it would ruin the Army.' Gersdorff therefore did not hand over his letters and merely passed on Kluge's request that, in the event of a successful *coup*, Manstein be prepared to assume office as Chief of Staff of the *Wehrmacht*. To this Manstein replied with a slight bow: 'I shall always be loyally at the disposal of the legitimate government.'[5]

Later Manstein took refuge in the assertion that he was concerned only with military matters and had merely done his duty. Nevertheless he could of course see quite clearly that Germany was heading for ruin and he admitted as much. Beck thought that Manstein's attitude stemmed more from his character than from his (alleged) conviction that everything must be done to keep the Russians away from the German frontier and that, in the event of a *coup*, this would be difficult if not impossible. In fact the surest way of bringing the Russians into Germany was to prolong the war and this would certainly happen if there were no *coup*.[6]

Tresckow's efforts with Kluge were only superficially more successful. When out for a walk with Kluge in July 1943 Tresckow and Gersdorff discussed 'the situation' with him and demanded the removal of Hitler.[7] Kluge said that he could not bring himself to do it. Tresckow then said that walking by his side was a man who had already tried – which Gersdorff confirmed. This was the only way, Tresckow said, to save the German *Reich* and people from total ruin. Kluge thereupon said: 'Children, you've got me!' But he did not keep his word. Kluge always remained the same – lacking initiative, as Captain Kaiser noted in his diary early in April 1943 after talking to Tresckow.[8]

From early April Tresckow was frequently in Berlin trying in some way or other to set the *coup* in motion but, despite all his efforts, he encountered only set-backs and mishaps.[9] In May and again in July he gave himself prolonged periods of leave. The first he spent probing and discussing, the second in preparing the *coup d'état*, living with his sister in Neubabelsberg.[10] On 25 July he was transferred to OKH command reserve and became available for posting by the Army Personnel Department; from 1 August to the beginning of October he stayed in Berlin; on 10 October 1943 he took up his new appointment as commander of 442 Infantry Regiment.[11]

Meanwhile efforts had been made in Berlin to bring about 'a change' at 'top level'. The idea was to persuade Hitler to give up supreme command in the east so that the war might once more be run on sensible lines and possibly ended. There were thoughts of making Kluge Chief of Staff of the Army and Manstein Commander-in-Chief, a suggestion aired by Tresckow in May.[12] Somewhat later Gersdorff made a similar proposal to Manstein but with the appointments the other way round. Hopes were still placed in Zeitzler and Olbricht, even in Fromm and Guderian; any of these, it was thought, might go to Hitler, open his eyes to realities and demand a 'change'. Goerdeler obtained an introduction to Guderian through General von Rabenau.[13] But it was all in vain.

Hammerstein was then approached once more; early in March it was hoped to persuade him to go to Fromm. But Hammerstein refused. If he had a division, he said, he would be prepared to fetch that devil (Hitler) out of hell, but he had not got one. Those able to do something would not and the willing ones could not.

Meanwhile Goerdeler, with incredible optimism and an intrepidity worthy of respect, continued his efforts to keep things moving. In February 1943 he tried to galvanize the generals by presenting them with an ultimatum – from the end of the month he would no longer be available.[14] He remarked that the workers 'did not want to wait any longer', and he saw 'indications of [impending] revolution or uprising without the forces of the intelligentsia'. He soon abandoned this idea of threatening, however. A memorandum dated 26 March 1943 and intended for the generals exists but it is not clear who received it. Tresckow, in any case, thought it useless and advised urgently against it.[15] On 17 May Goerdeler wrote a letter to General Olbricht saying that he had been thinking about the generally-held view that the correct psychological moment must be awaited for a *coup* and had come to the conclusion that 'we must not await the approach of the "correct psychological" moment but must *create* it'.[16] The leadership's crimes were colossal, he said; the number of civilians executed was over a million. Popular tolerance of this was incomprehensible and explicable only by terror and the protection afforded to lying and crime. This would change at once, however, 'if the people saw that terror had been brought to book, an end put to corruption and candour and truth established in place of secrecy and lies'. If no other way was open he, Goerdeler, was ready to seek an interview with Hitler and tell him that his resignation was necessary in the vital interests of the people. It was possible, though not probable, that Hitler would realize this; if he did not, in other words if the interview ended 'nastily' for Goerdeler, then he must have the assurance that 'action would be taken immediately'. Olbricht thought the idea of an interview with Hitler completely illusory and advised urgently against it.[17] Then Goerdeler wanted to go and see Keitel, with Captain Kaiser strongly advising against it. Kaiser put in his diary: 'He often seems to me to be a dreamer after all.'

Meanwhile, despite all its activity since autumn 1942, the opposition had suffered a continuous series of setbacks. Early in March 1943 Beck fell seriously ill and had to undergo an operation.[18] At about the same time Colonel Fritz Jäger, commanding II and XXI Panzer Replacement units, was arrested together with his son who was serving as a lieutenant in Frankfurt on Oder.[19] Colonel Jäger had long been a member of the conspiracy and later, on 20 July 1944, had an important part to play. Various highly incautious remarks by the son had now brought the conspiracy into great danger; he had said, for instance, that the balloon would soon go up, his father would take over the Guard Battalion and so forth and his listeners had not kept these comments to themselves. All went well for both father and son, however; the case was closed in July – not without active assistance from Captain Kaiser and a number of kindred spirits in the Army Legal Department. About the same time Fritz-Dietlof Graf von der Schulenburg got into trouble. The word went round that he was looking for reliable young officers for the Potsdam battalion and a certain lieutenant connected this with the current rumours about a *coup* – the time was shortly after the Stalingrad catastrophe and the affair of the Scholls in Munich. Accordingly on 2 April Schulenburg was interrogated; he was nevertheless released, although naturally it was true that he was looking for 'reliable' officers and for the purposes of the *coup* too.[20] Since January 1943 he had been a member of General von Unruh's special staff which was screening agencies and headquarters for men fit for service.[21]

These set-backs were comparatively easily overcome but the same could not be said of the direct assault launched by Himmler's RSHA on OKW *Amt Ausland/Abwehr*; major damage to the opposition resulted.[22] The *Abwehr* office in Munich had become involved in a private currency affair, the culprit being one of its informers, Dr Wilhelm Schmidhuber, an exporter and Portuguese honorary consul. The *Abwehr* could not cover him in this case and he was therefore arrested and interrogated; this led to investigations inside the *Abwehr* which had long been a thorn in the flesh of Himmler and the head of his Section VI, the SD external intelligence service.

During these investigations a further 'scandal' was uncovered: to assist certain Jews considerable sums in foreign currency had been paid as illegal compensation for confiscated property and for this Dr Hans von Dohnanyi, specially employed officer (*Sonderführer B*) in Oster's coordinating section, was responsible.[23] Dohnanyi was now in difficulty from two points of view. In the first place he was of partially Jewish origin, a so-called 'half-caste second grade'. This had long been known and on 14 October 1936 Hitler had issued a special dispensation permitting Dohnanyi to retain his civil service status and be treated as a German; he could not be accepted into the Party, however.[24] Now he seemed likely to lose the personal protection of the man who was Germany's supreme judge in 'racial questions' as in everything else. Secondly, backed and supported by Canaris and Oster, Dohnanyi had been using Jews as 'agents' abroad for years, thereby saving them from 'special treatment' and murder. Moltke, who was also working in the *Abwehr*, had warned Dohnanyi that he was in danger of arrest.

On 5 April 1943 a senior Judge Advocate (*Oberstkriegsgerichtsrat*), Dr Manfred Roeder, appeared in Canaris' office and told him that an investigation was being initiated. He then went to Oster and asked him to be present at the arrest of Dohnanyi. Oster immediately assumed responsibility for anything of which Dohnanyi was accused, but this did not help since the case concerned private, not official, misdemeanours, involving misuse of the office.

Dohnanyi wished to conceal certain papers lying on his desk. They dealt, among other things, with information to be transmitted to Rome by Dr Josef Müller about the failure of the attempt of 13 March 1943 and were marked with an 'O'; they were camouflaged as 'intelligence material', in other words misleading information to be fed to the enemy – nothing unusual in the secret service. Dohnanyi wished to indicate to Oster that the papers should be treated as if they were really what they were supposed to be, official 'intelligence material'. While Roeder was searching the safe Dohnanyi whispered something to Oster which the latter misunderstood. When Oster tried to sweep the papers up into his coat pocket, he was observed by Sonderegger, a *Gestapo* official who was also present, and from then on matters became much worse. Oster's behaviour naturally increased suspicion of his entire group – the authorities had long been on the look-out for 'insecure agencies'. The central group around Oster had been warned early in 1942 that the *Gestapo* was on its trail and since the arrest of Schmidhuber in October every security measure had been taken. All these precautions, however, were cancelled out by this mishap over the papers; it took months for Dohnanyi, sending messages from prison, to persuade Oster to change his attitude and treat the papers as official. The suspicions of the *Gestapo* were only gradually allayed.[25]

On the same day Dr Müller, Dietrich Bonhoeffer and his sister, Frau von Dohnanyi, were also arrested. Oster was placed in cold storage; initially he was sent on leave and placed under house arrest; then, on 19 June 1943, he was transferred to 'leadership reserve'. On 16 December 1943 Keitel wrote forbidding him to have 'any official or non-official contact with the *Abwehr* or its members', it having been reported that Oster was still maintaining 'more or less official relationships' with the *Abwehr* and certain officers of the 'Brandenburg' Division.[26] Finally, with effect from 4 March 1944, he was released from active service. From this point until 20 July 1944 Oster and his friends, including Beck, were under permanent surveillance by the *Gestapo*.

The blow suffered by the opposition was so devastating and so dangerous that for the moment all thoughts of further action had to be abandoned. An effective headquarters in Berlin had to be reconstituted first. It is characteristic of Beck that his first order was for an account of the incidents to be passed to the Pope, who had been involved on several occasions in peace feelers. This was the only way of maintaining the somewhat precarious confidential link between papal circles and the German opposition. Gisevius was accordingly entrusted with this mission by Canaris and despatched to Rome to see Father Leiber.[27]

For two reasons other people did not become involved in the *Gestapo*'s investigations against Oster, Dohnanyi, Bonhoeffer and Müller. In the first place the accused held their tongues and were able to mislead the *Gestapo* for a long time and secondly Canaris succeeded in putting a major spoke in the wheel. During an interrogation of Dohnanyi towards the end of 1943 Roeder, the investigating Judge Advocate, had described members of the 'Brandenburg' Division as draft-dodgers and this came to the ears of Canaris. He summoned the divisional commander, Major-General von Pfuhlstein, an impulsive, difficult but highly courageous character, and suggested that Roeder had merited a lesson.[28] Pfuhlstein took a witness with him, went to Roeder, dressed him down for his remark and then floored him with a smack in the face. This was on 14 January 1944, by which time Roeder had become highly dangerous. Meanwhile Roeder had been bragging about his case to people outside who had nothing to do with it; Kanter, another Judge Advocate and a friend of Dr Karl Sack, head of the OKH Legal Department, lodged a complaint against Roeder who replied with a counter-complaint for slander and demanded disciplinary proceedings. The result was such a tangle of proceedings and complaints that Roeder finally asked for a transfer, which he was given.[29] Try as he might, Sack had not been able to engineer Roeder's removal earlier.

Canaris was able to maintain his position for a while, although the *Abwehr*'s work was largely at a standstill owing to the *Gestapo* investigations. In February 1944, however, the RSHA finally achieved its object and succeeded in abolishing or incorporating the entire OKW *Amt Ausland/Abwehr*. The occasion was the defection to the British of a certain Dr Vermehren who had served in the *Wehrmacht* and been seconded to the *Abwehr* office in Istanbul. Canaris was suspended from office and placed under house arrest. His successor, Colonel Hansen, belonged to the resistance movement and so the *Abwehr*'s highly useful contacts were maintained until 20 July 1944. The *Abwehr* itself, however, was incorporated into the RSHA as '*Amt Mil*' and after 20 July 1944 was subordinated to Section VI under Schellenberg.

For the opposition 1943 was the great year of plans and attempts. The increasingly desperate war situation finally produced the 'correct psychological' moment for which they had waited so long; many of the generals were more prepared to participate and support them. Even people like Himmler realized that the end could not be far off. The cruel fanatical lord of Hitler's black praetorian guard, the director of all the efforts made to maintain the so-called purity of the German race, the head of the National-Political Academies for toughening young National-Socialists, of the 'Ancestral Heritage' and 'Spring of Life' associations, of the concentration camps and mass extermination of the 'racially inferior' – this man was in fact weak, unstable and submissive, without loyalty or character. He could never quite make up his mind between his own interests—desertion for which he had not the courage– and his loyalty to the Nazi movement. He vacillated until the last day of his life; until he bit on his cyanide capsule he was still hoping to save his own skin. He ordered his SS to stimulate the fighting spirit of the Army by the most extreme and barbaric atrocities such as hanging from meat-hooks soldiers who gave vent to 'defeatist' views during the closing months of the war; yet at the same time, ever since 1942 and finally early in 1945, he was repeatedly trying to negotiate with the enemy through Swedish intermediaries, not in order to save Germany – for that it was really too late – but to save himself. Hitler eventually heard of these machinations and on 29 April 1945 expelled Himmler from the Party and stripped him of all his official functions. Finally the mass murderer, whose confidence depended solely on his position and his uniform, tried to disguise himself as a private soldier and, so to speak, creep into a mouse-hole.[30] The lord of the concentration camps was even prepared to enter into negotiations with the German resistance movement and, if necessary, sacrifice his *Führer* for them. But he first obtained authorization from Hitler.[31]

Those of the opposition who entered into communication with Himmler were rewarded neither by success nor gratitude; all they did was to confirm long-standing suspicions against their right-wing, ultra-right-wing, political tendencies. They deserve recognition, however, although it is difficult to say whether they or Himmler harboured the more astonishing illusions. The removal of Hitler would not have made a better man out of Himmler nor could he himself have been removed with certainty. The Allies would have occupied Germany and put Himmler on trial.

Popitz, Langbehn and Jessen believed that they could exploit the differences inside the Nazi leadership and bring about a split. The contact man was Langbehn who acted as Himmler's lawyer although long before the war he had become a committed opposition member, as Himmler well knew.[32]

Since May 1943 he had been in touch with *SS-Obergruppenführer* Wolff who later, in 1945, following Himmler's line conducted treasonable negotiations with Dulles over the capitulation of German troops in Italy. Langbehn told Wolff that his enquiries abroad showed that without Hitler an acceptable peace might still be obtained, whereas clearly Germany could no longer win the war. He wanted to bring Himmler and Popitz together for negotiations. Olbricht first arranged a meeting between Popitz and Tresckow, at which Langbehn was also present: it took place in Popitz's house in August 1943. Tresckow seems to have given the project his blessing. Marie-Louise Sarre, a secretary in the staff of Army Group Centre and a determined opponent of the regime who did occasional courier service for the opposition, reports a conversation with Field Marshal von Bock in July 1943: 'Bock believed a *putsch* carried out by *Wehrmacht* generals only was bound to fail. He consented to participate only on the condition that the *putsch* would be made *with* Himmler. Only if the SS participated could it succeed.'³³

On 26 August Popitz had an interview with Himmler in the *Reich* Ministry of the Interior, which Himmler had just taken over. Adroitly he suggested that Himmler assume the role of guardian of the true Holy Grail of Nazism; someone was required to reestablish order, both at home and abroad, after all the corruption and the unhappy conduct of the war by a single overloaded man. The war could no longer be won, he said, but it would only be lost if it continued to be conducted on these lines. In view of the bolshevist menace Great Britain and the United States were still ready to negotiate, but not with Ribbentrop. As a precaution Popitz did not go further; in the anteroom, however, Langbehn was saying to Wolff that he hoped that Popitz would speak quite frankly.

Immediately after the interview it was clear that Popitz had not gone very far and it was agreed to arrange a further talk. But it never happened. In September 1943 Langbehn was arrested by the *Gestapo*. Some Allied message (Dulles insists that it was neither British nor American) was deciphered by the Germans and gave away Langbehn's Swiss contacts. It was shown to Himmler and he had no choice but to act, though he contrived to avoid ordering a trial. Popitz was still at liberty but he was completely isolated since his previous co-conspirators felt it too dangerous to consort with him. Langbehn said nothing about his talks with Wolff or the wider ramifications of the conspiracy. Only after 20 July 1944 did it become clear that Popitz and Langbehn were members of a wide-spread plot. At their trial their contacts with Himmler were presented as a minor, comparatively insignificant but insidious aspect of their conspiratorial defeatist activity.

It is questionable whether this foolhardy contact with Himmler would have taken place, had the opposition in Berlin not been so lacking in firm leadership, particularly since the dismissal of Oster. Canaris had always worked cleverly in the background acting as a protective screen for the conspirators; Beck was sick; Witzleben was a warrior, not a conspirator or politician, and was also sick; Tresckow had both the energy and determination to lead but neither the position nor influence. He had only been on leave when in

Berlin in the summer of 1943 and the fact that he was able still to work so intensively for the opposition from his positions as regimental commander and then Chief of Staff of an army was due more to his ability and determination than to the circumstances. Olbricht was nearer the potential centre of power but he had neither the initiative nor drive to act. Without Fromm, C-in-C of the Replacement Army, he could do little apart from planning; he had no command authority and Fromm remained unapproachable and always ambiguous in his attitude,[34] The name of Colonel-General Freiherr von Hammerstein was sometimes heard but he was also sick and now had neither influence nor position.[35] He died on 24 April 1943.[36] Hopes placed in Guderian's cooperation proved to be false.[37] Then there seemed to be another chance to have Keitel fired at the end of May. Zeitzler wanted to talk to Hitler about it and propose Kluge as Keitel's successor; Tresckow tried to help things along behind the scenes by getting Heusinger to agree to the plan, and on 28 May Tresckow informed Olbricht of his efforts.[38] These were what was described to the *Gestapo* after 20 July 1944 as 'changes in leadership'.[39] Some of those interrogated claimed that this was all that was ever discussed in these treasonable conversations. Olbricht immediately considered the consequences, as Captain Kaiser noted: '[Olbricht] sees clearly two ways: 1. After change of leadership political demands to be made legally. 2. Zeitzler and the 6 section chiefs to make the demand: Heusinger, Wagner (QMG), Stieff (org), Berendt (foreign sect.). Gerke (Chief Troop Affairs), Fellgiebel (Signal C.). They must be unanimous. Z[eitzler's] demands now that A[dolf] H[itler] replace Keitel by a new man.'[40] But by 9 June, these hopes too had been dashed: 'The five chiefs in the last resort do not wish to torpedo things and to push Pollux [Hitler] out of the saddle.'[41] Finally, in July 1943, Witzleben had to go to hospital with a gastric ulcer.[42]

At the same time fear began to grow that little more time remained available for the *coup* since the tide of war was running so strongly against Germany. The Kursk offensive in the summer of 1943 failed and by mid-July the Red Army was counter-attacking. On 25 July Mussolini fell and Italy prepared to cut loose from the Third *Reich*. Only an incurable optimist like Goerdeler could still think that the Allies would be persuaded to halt operations in the event of a *coup* in Germany. He received no reply to an approach in this sense made via Sweden in May 1943.[43]

On 25 July 1943 Goerdeler wrote a letter to Field Marshal von Kluge.[44] Once more he emphasized the material, economic and moral devastation caused by the war both in Germany and Europe as a whole, the mad crimes which otherwise decent young men were persuaded or compelled to commit and the hopelessness of the regime's political and military situation. If Kluge knew any way, he said, to keep Russia out of Europe and compel the United States and Britain to stop their devastating air raids on German cities, then he must tell the people so openly. 'If there can be no victory continuation of the war is just criminal, since the aim must never be the heroic end of a nation but always the possibility of continuing life.' The prospect of a favourable peace was still open, Goerdeler added, as he had recently established (he did not say that he had had no answer to his approach in May). In view of this situation and the fact that this was clearly the last chance he begged Kluge – and he assured him that he would not do so again – to take action against Hitler. Goerdeler could assure him of the support of the majority of the working class, civil servants and leaders of industry; if thought wise, he could persuade Goebbels and Himmler to ally themselves with Kluge or any other general willing to act; they had long since realized that with Hitler they were lost.

The letter to Kluge was never despatched; Goerdeler's friends, including Olbricht, dissuaded him. They were afraid that Kluge would be offended by its candid emphatic language; Goerdeler was often reproached for offending the generals when he told them the truth.[45] All this took place at the time when Langbehn was trying to arrange the meeting between Popitz and Himmler. In general, therefore, the resistance's affairs were at a standstill. People still irrationally hoped that 'the generals', 'the Josephs' as Hassell called them in his diary, would take some initiative but they did not. On 20 February 1943, referring to Olbricht and Fromm, Captain Kaiser wrote in his diary: 'One wants to act when he gets the order and the other wants to give the order when someone else has acted.'[46]

Although by 1943 it was clear that the war was lost, although therefore psychologically the situation was as favourable as it ever could be, the opposition found itself well-nigh paralysed by these set-backs, particularly the *Gestapo*'s invasion of the very focus of activity centred on Oster. Between 5 April when Dohnanyi, Bonhoeffer and Müller were arrested and 1 October when Stauffenberg officially became Chief of Staff to Olbricht in the AHA the whole headquarters of the conspiracy had to be reconstructed. Many of the conspirators thought that, even had one of the two attempts at assassination succeeded in March, the *coup d'état* would probably not have gone smoothly.[47]

On several occasions, early in April and at the end of May 1943, Tresckow had been in Berlin; in July he took leave with the object of reactivating the planning, ensuring coordination between preparatory measures at the front and those at home, and providing some better basis for further plans for the assassination and the *coup*.[48] He lived with his sister in Neubabelsberg and gave some impetus to the preparations. Increasingly he became the leading brain of the military conspiracy.[49] He was convinced that there was no time to lose; early in August he met Goerdeler and told him that by 1944 the Red Army would be on the borders of East Prussia.[50]

The conspirators now decided to use the Replacement Army for the *coup*, if necessary without Fromm's cooperation.[51] It could not, however, act on its own; the initiative must come from one of the high-ranking front-line commanders. Further efforts were therefore made to persuade Kluge.[52] To ensure the widest possible cooperation, particularly from the armoured forces, attempts were made to arrange a neeting between Olbricht and Colonel-General Guderian, who had been Inspector-General of Armoured Forces since 1 March, but nothing came of it.[53] Kluge was thought to be 'committed' but once again this proved to be a pipe-dream. On 2 August Schulenburg came to Olbricht from OKH with the news that Zeitzler was prepared to cooperate and possibly take the initiative. Then it was discovered that further 'softening up' was required before Kluge would participate in the plan; the proposal was that he should issue an order to C-in-C Replacement Army and, in the event of non-compliance, arrest him and act in his stead, both of which things Olbricht was willing to do. The 'softening up' consisted primarily in the compilation and despatch of a letter from Olbricht to Kluge backed up by a further letter on 3 August.[54] Stieff was despatched to Kluge as an emissary[55] and finally Zeitzler was to be given a directive to act if 'the action' misfired.

Early in August Tresckow told Goerdeler that Manstein, Kluge and Küchler now realized that something must be done and that even the SS generals Sepp Dietrich and Hausser would 'go along'.[56] The question is, however, what these people meant by 'doing something'. They were perhaps thinking more of the famous 'change at top level' than of a *coup d'état* using force. Possibly Goerdeler misunderstood Tresckow or he was again giving way to his optimism when he assured his friend Wallenberg in August that a *putsch* would take place in September.[57] It is equally possible that a *putsch* within a *putsch* was being planned to force the hand of the front-line generals and of Zeitzler rather than persuade them.

In the summer of 1943 Colonel (Major-General from February 1944) Helmuth Stieff became heavily involved with the opposition. At the time he was head of the Organization Section of the Army General Staff; he had long been an opponent of Hitler and Nazism, ever since the early 1930s, and his antagonism had increased all the time.[58] Tresckow had already approached him on several occasions, both in Smolensk and in OKH in East Prussia, and had finally said to him in February 1943 that Hitler must be removed. It was the historic duty of general staff officers, he said, to act in the interest of the people and prevent the loss of the war;[59] would Stieff be prepared to participate in an assassination and a *coup*? During meetings in the *Führer*'s headquarters he, Tresckow, had convinced himself that Hitler could be killed during one of his briefing conferences.

Early in August Stieff paid a short visit to Berlin where he met Olbricht and they were joined by Tresckow and Beck who had just been released from hospital.[60] On 6 August Stieff wrote to his wife saying that he had decided to join the conspiracy: 'I maintain that the point of view to which I have come during the last few days is the right one, in other words that one should never evade any responsibility with which one is faced by destiny. With this statement you must content yourself. I should be ashamed of my whole existence if I did not do my real duty at the moment of emergency. I will do nothing dishonourable – of that you may be sure.'[61]

Stieff thereupon returned to the east. He suffered his first disappointment in OKH. Colonel Thomale, Chief of Staff to the Inspector-General of Armoured Forces, told him that Guderian would not participate in any action directed against the *Führer*. Stieff then went to Army Group Centre and on 13 August handed Olbricht's letter over to Kluge.[62] During a long discussion with Stieff Kluge did at least say that he would work for 'a change' in the military leadership;[63] Stieff, however, evidently had reason to hope for much more. On 27 August he met Kluge again, this time on Rastenburg airfield, and in September he gave a detailed report to Olbricht.

During this same month Kluge also visited Berlin where he held discussions in Olbricht's house with Beck, Goerdeler, Olbricht and Tresckow.[64] From the foreign policy point of view Kluge wanted to know from Goerdeler what the prospects were for ending the war, at least in the west. Goerdeler said that only war against Germany had forced Britain and Russia together. To secure her empire Britain must always require a strong Germany as a counter-weight to Russia. Agreement must therefore be reached with Britain. This was possible on the following basis: 1914 frontiers in the east, Austria and the Sudetenland to remain German and also South Tyrol and Eupen-Malmédy, Franco–German negotiations on a definitive solution of the Alsace–Lorraine question, full preservation of German sovereignty, no reparations, economic fusion between the countries of Europe excluding Russia.[65] After Goerdeler had then referred briefly to the essential internal political reforms Beck and Kluge withdrew for a private discussion. When Goerdeler was called in again Kluge said to him that, since Hitler would neither take the necessary decisions nor be acceptable to the West as a negotiating partner, there was no alternative but to remove him by force. Goerdeler opposed this and said that one must speak frankly to Hitler; reason would always prevail. Kluge rightly questioned this, but he could not suggest to Goerdeler to take any initiative. Kluge admitted that the initiative must come from the military and promised to discuss with his fellow-commanders. Goerdeler, he said, should ensure that the Anglo-Saxons subsequently behaved 'correctly'. At last the *coup* seemed to be imminent; Goerdeler, the optimist, told Wallenberg that it was 'firm' for September.[66]

It did not occur at this time, not so much because the opposition was once more dogged by misfortune – on 12 October Kluge had a serious car accident and was temporarily out of the running – but because a number of essential ingredients were still lacking.[67] Tresckow had to take over a regiment at the front and did not occupy an influential position in Army Group Centre until two months later when he became Chief of Staff to Second Army; Kluge's successor as C-in-C of the Army Group was Field Marshal Busch, a Hitler disciple, so the 'initial flash' could no longer be expected from that quarter. Had this change not occurred, the *coup* might have taken place in October 1943, but probably not, for the most essential ingredient was still lacking, the assassination. So far no one had been found who was ready to do it and had access to Hitler – the most obvious among the conspirators were Colonel Stieff and Colonel Meichssner, head of the Operations Section in the OKW Operations Staff, who both occasionally attended the briefing conferences. In October 1943 Stauffenberg thought for a time that he had Stieff's agreement but either he misunderstood or the agreement was withdrawn again.[68] Only in late autumn were young officers found with sufficient courage to sacrifice themselves and for whom access to Hitler might be engineered. Meanwhile other essential preparations continued and in general terms were completed.

34 'Valkyrie'

For some time the idea had been mooted that the Replacement Army should be used to take over power in Germany but all such projects had so far been checkmated because Colonel-General Fromm, Chief of Army Equipment and Commander-in-Chief Replacement Army, refused to cooperate.[1] A further obstacle was the highly involved chain of command governing military districts in Germany. The title of the local commander in Stuttgart, for instance, was: Commanding General Rear Headquarters V Army Corps and Commander *Wehrkreis* V. The first part of this indicated that as 'Deputy' Commander V Corps he commanded the static, replacement and training units of the corps while the fighting troops were in the field; in this capacity he was responsible to Colonel-General Fromm as C-in-C Replacement Army. The second part of the title indicated that he was a territorial military commander in his own right and as such was responsible direct to OKW, in other words to Keitel or Hitler.[2]

In 1943 the idea was conceived that the Replacement Army should be set to work, if necessary without Fromm. General Olbricht promised either to compel Fromm to participate or alternatively to arrest him and issue the necessary orders himself. To avoid, however, having to improvise everything and to ensure that Army units stationed in the *Reich* would intervene smoothly, rapidly and by surprise, certain preparations were necessary to ensure, first that orders were issued without loss of time and secondly that they were obeyed without too much doubting and questioning. These requirements seemed best to be met by Plan 'Valkyrie'.

In mid-December 1941 the German Army's situation in the frozen expanses of Russia was a desperate one. The object of the campaign, the enemy's overthrow and occupation of his industrial and political centres, had not been achieved. The German divisions were now hundreds of miles from their operational base, without winter clothing, weapons partially useless, without adequate supplies and facing an enemy preparing a major counter-offensive in defence of his country. The German Army's losses in killed during the Russian campaign had by that time risen to 162,799 officers, NCOs and men.[3] On 15 December 1941 Colonel-General Halder, Chief of Staff of the Army, discussed with Colonel-General Fromm, Chief of Army Equipment and C-in-C Replacement Army, how the gaps were to be filled.[4] Fromm, however, had prepared the necessary orders as early as the summer of 1941, precisely in order to be prepared for the emergency situation that materialized by the end of the year. The codewords 'Valkyrie' and 'Rheingold' signified a raid on the reserves consisting of training cadres still in Germany, sick and wounded who had recovered, workers and employees to be withdrawn from industry and the economy.[5] In the spring of 1942 the 'Valkyrie' measures were revised, this time under the codewords 'Valkyrie I' and 'Valkyrie II'; in July 1942 the 'Valkyrie' units were called upon to fill gaps in the field Army for the second time. Up to this time there had been no thought of using 'Valkyrie' units for internal disturbances. Even in the succeeding months their use inside Germany was only a side-issue, not the main purpose of the plan.

On 31 July 1943, however, C-in-C Replacement Army issued fresh 'Valkyrie' instructions which were to be implemented with the utmost speed. Copy No 83 (out of a total of 220) together with five additional copies was received by the headquarters of *Wehrkreis* XVII in Vienna; in addition to its 'Top Secret' stamp it carried the following in large letters: 'Forward immediately by special courier', 'Most Urgent', 'Submit at once.' The headquarters date stamp of *Wehrkreis* XVII shows 2 August 1943. Addressees were to report completion of the preparations ordered by 12 August.[6] The *Wehrkreise* had to become familiar with the new instructions and carry out exercises. The haste is understandable in view of the war situation; but it is not likely that the orders were also considered possible *putsch* instruments at this early stage. At any rate, Olbricht's operations officer and predecessor of Stauffenberg in this position knew nothing of such a secret purpose although he had to do a great deal of work in connection with the orders.[7]

The object of these instructions was not merely the rapid assembly of reserves from the *Reich* but, if necessary, suppression of 'internal disturbances'; these might be caused by organized large-scale sabotage either directed from abroad or carried out by parties of agents dropped into Germany, by raids by airborne troops or by a rising on the part of the millions of foreign workers and prisoners deported or 'conscripted' into Germany.[8]

Basically the 'Valkyrie' orders prescribed concentration into combat groups and into reinforced battalions, of all recruiting and training units in the *Wehrkreis* and of all soldiers in schools or on courses; battalions were to include all available arms of the service. The whole process was to take place in two stages: 'Valkyrie Stage 1' signified 'Ensure combat readiness of all units (company strength) within six hours' but without issuing an alert order. 'Valkyrie Stage 2' meant 'Concentration of Stage 1 units into combat groups ready for action'. The time limit for Stage 1 was laid down as six hours; Stage 2 was to take place with the greatest possible speed depending on local conditions – locations, road conditions, mountains, availability of vehicles. Rail transport was only to be used for unit concentrations under Stage 2 if other methods of transport would entail considerable delay or vehicle movement was not possible.

In detail the following was laid down: readiness for action rather than paper regulations was to constitute the criterion for the equipment of combat groups; armoured and armoured infantry units together with their schools, courses and demonstration units were to be concentrated into special combat groups alongside the regular infantry; signals, transport and administrative troops were only to be included in combat groups as the strength of the latter required, in other words not all the available troops of this type were to be included to avoid overloading the combat groups with useless personnel.

In addition to the combat groups alert units were to be formed. For this purpose mobile battalions and companies were to be used together with schools and courses, demonstration units, recruiting detachments and 'various' units. Under 'schools and courses' were included those for officers, cadets and senior cadets, medical and veterinary academies, the research section and medical officers of the Mountain Medical School, officers of the Medical Training Section, Army NCO Schools, the Army Pyrotechnical School in Berlin-Lichterfelde, Ordnance Schools I and II, the Army Signals School II, the Army Riding and Driving School, the Pioneer School in Karlshorst, the Technical Fortifications School in Sternberg, No 1 Railway Engineers' School in Rehagen-Klausdorf, administration and maintenance courses. Training and recruiting units included were: No 3 Pioneer Training Battalion in Rosenheim, the Fortress Training Section in Althöfchen, the Decontamination Training Company of the Medical Training Section, the Training Battery for Gas-tracker Dogs and the Postal Recruiting Section. Under 'various' were included such important units as the Signal Traffic Section HQ Replacement Army, the Guide Dogs for the Blind Detachment, the Special Army Patrol Service, the Train-control Section, the Welfare Service, the Army School for Female Signals personnel with its corresponding training sections, emergency squads of female signals personnel, ordnance issue offices, vehicle parks, medical sections, remount depots, depots for other arms, AAMG posts, AA batteries and the security service in factories. Only the permanent staff of all the above units was to be available for 'Valkyrie'; the remainder were to provide replacements for the combat groups.

In addition to preparation and planning of these combat groups and their rapid availability *Wehrkreis* headquarters were to prepare and organize 'protection of vulnerable points in emergency'. In many *Wehrkreis* the troops stationed there already had specific tasks such as dealing with parachute or airborne troops and coastal defence; in such cases 'Valkyrie' was to form the basis for these duties also.

The 'Valkyrie' units also had to maintain their regular duties – correspondence and personnel papers, welfare of recruits and convalescents as they arrived including accommodation, feeding and clothing, guarding of buildings and any equipment left behind in the event of combat duty. Personnel allocated to these tasks were to be reduced to the minimum.

In principle all personnel available in the area of the *Wehrkreis* were to be used for 'Valkyrie' including such recruits under training as were suitable and men on leave, not however personnel of mobile companies and battalions in process of formation. Weapons, equipment, ammunition, vehicles, tanks and horses were to be provided from the overall stocks of units located in the area; independent camps and parks, however, were only to be used on instructions from C-in-C Replacement Army. On instructions they might be used to provide the entire equipment for the combat groups and alert units. If available stocks of vehicles and horses were inadequate, it might be necessary to resort to requisitioning but this was under no circumstances to be discussed with other agencies, those responsible for agriculture for instance; otherwise horses and carts would no longer be there when wanted.

A supplementary order dated 6 October 1943 and signed by Olbricht produced a significant reinforcement of the forces available for 'Valkyrie'; it was now to include units of the field Army located in the 'Home Forces area' while forming, recuperating or reorganizing. To the extent that their armament, mobility and other equipment permitted, they were to form combat groups or alert units like the rest on issue of the relevant codeword. They were invariably to form independent units and not be combined with other troops from the *Wehrkreise*. All alert units were to be ready within six hours as for the combat groups.

Finally on 11 February 1944 Stauffenberg, who had by that time been Olbricht's Chief of Staff for some months, issued an instruction designed to streamline and standardize the formation of combat groups. He also made it possible, if 'Valkyrie' or a state of alert was ordered, to concentrate forces at vital points more or less unobtrusively. Combat groups were reorganized as 'reinforced grenadier regiments'; they were to consist of regimental headquarters and headquarters company, two to three battalions, an infantry gun company, one to two anti-tank companies, an artillery detachment of two or three howitzer batteries and a pioneer company.

Stauffenberg's directive continued: '3. Above-mentioned gren. regts will, if necessary, be alerted in accordance with para 2 above by calling out the units required from various *Wehrkreise* to avoid excessive strain on any particular *Wehrkreis*.' This was perfectly sensible and legitimate. By this method one or two of these reinforced grenadier regiments could quickly be made available for operations. Equally however, under cover of this instruction, it was possible to move or concentrate particularly suitable units in the event of an attempted *coup*. It was not necessary to order 'Valkyrie' throughout the *Reich*, entailing a lapse of at least six hours before the majority of units were ready to move. It was now possible, as necessary and required, to concentrate, say, one or two mobile (motorized) and well-equipped anti-tank companies from the surrounding *Wehrkreise* near, for instance, Munich or Berlin or round some SS barracks without setting the entire and somewhat slower machinery in motion. Particularly in Berlin action had to be so rapid that the normal 'Valkyrie' procedure, expeditious though it was, would be too ponderous. Exercises and similar measures provided an additional reinsurance.[9]

The 'Valkyrie' plans were, of course, of the highest security grading; special emphasis was laid on this: 'The number of people involved in these preparations is to be kept as small as possible. Under no circumstances may agencies or individuals outside the *Wehrmacht* be told of these plans and preparations' – not the Party, therefore, nor the SS. *Waffen-SS* units in any case could not be included in the preparations since in practice they were not subject to the territorial command authority of *Wehrkreis* Commanders.[10] In some *Wehrkreise* Party and SS formations were numerically far stronger than those of the Army. Moreover on 6 July 1944, at the first briefing conference at which Stauffenberg was present with a briefcase full of explosive, Hitler decided that, should operations take place within Germany, the military commanders would have plenary powers; the political authorities – the *Gauleiter* in their capacity as *Reich* Defence Commissars – were to have only an advisory function. This now applied particularly to any 'Valkyrie' operation.[11]

With the 'Valkyrie' orders and their supplementary instructions the conspirators had now created, by perfectly legitimate methods, an instrument with which they could, if conditions were right, set in motion all available mobile military forces in Germany with the exception of the SS. The orders were perfectly sensible and suitable for an emergency; on the face of it they were neutral and non-political. If initiated, they only acquired political significance through their object, in other words if directed against the Party and the SS instead of foreign workers and prisoners of war. This was a particularly vital aspect of their suitability for a *coup*. The weak point was the problem of initiation.

'Initiation' meant in the first place the concentration of available troops into combat groups or reinforced grenadier regiments and the formation of alert units; this took place on issue of a codeword, possibly in two stages. Codewords could be modified by certain additions; for instance ' "Valkyrie" Stage 1 for *Wehrkreis* V' meant that only those units located in the Stuttgart *Wehrkreis* were to be ready for operations within six hours; an alert could be ordered by means of the code: ' "Valkyrie" alert for *Wehrkreis* V.' The difficulty was, however, that the codeword had to be issued by C-in-C Replacement Army; this was explicitly laid down. 'The codeword as in para (a) above will be issued by C-in-C Replacement Army. Receipt will be acknowledged immediately by teleprint.' Militarily this was obvious; orders were issued by the commander. If the commander became a casualty he had to be replaced according to the rules. Since, however, C-in-C Replacement Army was still Colonel-General Fromm, an extremely unhappy situation might arise unless the fullest precautions had been taken to cope with his 'unreliability' (from the conspirators' point of view). This situation did in fact arise on 20 July when addressees did not merely acknowledge receipt but asked increasingly pressing questions and demanded to speak to Colonel-General Fromm.[12]

To ensure that Colonel-General Fromm would cooperate, it was essential to create a situation in which he would recognize that cooperation was the only correct course. The most important step in this direction was undoubtedly the removal of Hitler. A great impression would be made on Fromm, however, and it would be of major significance for the success of the entire enterprise, if the measures prepared could proceed smoothly, quickly and apparently uninterruptedly. We shall be dealing later with the question how the main body of the Replacement Army could be mobilized against the regime; here too a situation had to be created – by facts and circumstances as well as propaganda – in which it would seem natural and socially acceptable to obey the orders of the conspirators.

Preparations on the spot, where orders actually had to be executed, were possible only to a limited extent, but here too considerable efforts were made. Attention was concentrated primarily on two methods: recruitment of allies in the right places; under-cover preparation and rehearsal of measures for the *coup*.

During the critical period, from summer 1943 to 20 July 1944, the conspiracy had its members or supporters in various positions in a number of *Wehrkreise*. The list of arrests after 20 July gives a very complete picture, since almost all those who showed any form of willingness to obey the orders from Berlin were arrested. Later, after Stauffenberg had taken over the organization, these contacts fell into two categories: 1. Occupants of important posts in *Wehrkreis* headquarters; 2. Members of the conspiracy in the most varied positions appointed to act on D Day as liaison officers between the *Wehrkreise* and the AHA, the centre of the *coup* in Berlin; they were to be responsible that Berlin's instructions were correctly executed.[13]

Members or adherents in the various *Wehrkreise* were as follows:

Wehrkreis I (Königsberg): Lieutenant-Colonel Hans Otto Erdmann, Operations officer.

Wehrkreis II (Stettin): Major-General Siegfried von Stülpnagel, Commandant of Stettin; Colonel Friedrich Jäger, commanding Panzer Replacement units II and XXI (in April 1943 he had been earmarked by the conspirators as commander of the Berlin Guard Battalion).

Wehrkreis III (Berlin): Major-General Hans-Günther von Rost, Chief of Staff until posted early in May 1944; his aide, Lieutenant Heinz-Günther Albrecht; his successor, Major-General Otto Herfurth (previously Chief of Staff in Stuttgart); Gräfin von der Schulenburg, secretary to C-in-C Replacement Army; a number of officers in the numerous schools and training areas round Berlin.

Wehrkreis IV (Dresden): General Viktor von Schwedler, Commander; his staff officer (personnel), Colonel Wilhelm Sommerlad.

Wehrkreis V (Stuttgart): no one available after the departure of Herfurth.

Wehrkreis VI (Münster): Major Hermann Pünder (not very influential as Q Ops); Lieutenant-Colonel Martin Bärtels (fully informed and prepared to assist a revolt).

Wehrkreis VII (Munich): Colonel Max Ulich, Chief of Staff; Lieutenant-Colonel Bruno Grosser, Operations Officer.

Wehrkreis VIII (Breslau): no member in a position of importance.

Wehrkreis IX (Kassel): Major-General Ludwig von Nida, Chief of Staff, and his successor from spring 1944, Colonel Claus-Henning von Plate; Colonel Fritz von Vethacke (Operations) and Lieutenant-Colonel Hans Beck (Intelligence).

Wehrkreis X (Hamburg): Karl Kaufmann, the *Gauleiter* (at least partially initiated and committed); Captain (Navy) Herbert Wichmann, Intelligence Officer (no effective command authority).

Wehrkreis XI (Hannover): no one in a position of importance.

Wehrkreis XII (Wiesbaden): Major-General Erwin Gerlach, Chief of Staff (would certainly pass on the 'Valkyrie' order).

Wehrkreis XIII (Nuremberg): Colonel Viktor Kolbe, Chief of Staff; Colonel Hans Liphart, Personnel (participation of both officers being hoped for).

Wehrkreis XVII (Vienna): Colonel Heinrich Kodré, Chief of Staff (a member of the conspiracy and in active touch with the Austrian resistance and independence movement); General Hans-Karl von Esebeck, Deputy Commander; Colonel Rudolf Graf von Marogna-Redwitz, Intelligence (until his posting to the AHA).

Wehrkreis XVIII (Salzburg): Colonel Wilhelm Freiherr von Salza und Lichtenau, Chief of Staff. (The commander, on the other hand, General Julius Ringel, was an extremely loyal follower of the regime.)

Wehrkreis XX (Danzig): Lieutenant-Colonel Hasso von Boehmer, Operations (recruited by Tresckow).

Wehrkreis XXI (Poznan): apparently no one.[14]

Prague: Colonel Kurt Engelschall, Operations, was probably informed.

C-in-C West (Paris): a situation similar to that in Army Group Centre – a whole series of important posts occupied by officers who were either members of the opposition or strongly in sympathy with it.[15]

Those senior staff officers in the *Wehrkreise* to whom Stauffenberg and his fellow-conspirators made known their plans hoped or were expected to actively assist in the execution of orders issued from Berlin on the day of the *coup*. Contacts could not be found or 'installed' in every *Wehrkreis*, however; postings could always upset the liaison at short notice; signal communications might fail; for overriding reasons the amount of information passed to these contacts was often small. Additional liaison arrangements between the centre and the *Wehrkreis* were therefore desirable and so special representatives were nominated who were to present themselves to *Wehrkreis* headquarters on D-Day as liaison officers from OKH. They were members of the inner circle of the conspiracy; they knew the plan, the prerequisites and the aims; they were to be responsible for correct, rational and rapid execution of the orders from Berlin in the various *Wehrkreise*.[16] Their names, together with those of the Political Representatives detailed to advise *Wehrkreis* commanders, will be given in Part VIII since their recruitment and briefing took place mainly in the Stauffenberg era.

It was naturally impossible, without arousing suspicion, to arrange rehearsals in all or even many of the *Wehrkreise* for the *coup d'état*, now camouflaged as a 'Valkyrie' operation. Nevertheless this was done in Berlin since the city was plagued by Anglo-American air raids and frequently plunged into a catastrophic situation. Here Major-General von Rost, the Chief of Staff, organized his *coup* preparations with a thoroughness unknown elsewhere and camouflaged his opposition activities with great sophistication.[17]

General Joachim von Kortzfleisch, commander of *Wehrkreis* III (Berlin), was an honest and extremely efficient officer, but he held Nazi views and so Rost could not work with him on anything to do with the *coup*. Instead Rost adopted a bombastic manner, held important discussions with official and Party representatives, gave himself an air of self-importance, organized large festivities in his mess and involved himself in such a whirl of activity that the uninitiated thought that this was what he was really like. He was generally thought to be an ambitious general who had returned from secondment to the Vichy regime in France thinking himself a diplomat and a genius. Behind this façade, however, Rost concealed his real activity. Unfortunately on one occasion he made a 'mistake' when he pleaded for a minimum-existence food ration for Russian prisoners of war. This did him great damage and was a contributory factor in his posting.

In late summer 1943 Stauffenberg and Oertzen spent several days in *Wehrkreis* HQ, Berlin, working out the special plans for 'Valkyrie' in that area and Rost was of great practical assistance to them. He made it his business to acquire information on the functioning and importance of SS and Party agencies in Berlin and on security precautions taken at radio stations and similar installations. Accordingly, accompanied by his aide, he paid frequent visits to these places, where he was naturally received by dignitaries of equivalent rank. On each occasion precautions against all forms of catastrophe taken by the agency concerned were discussed at length and so he found out what they were. Rost was in general satisfied with broad sweeping statements while his aide, Lieutenant Albrecht, dealt with the details. As often as he could Rost also visited barracks, schools and training areas belonging to the *Wehrkreis* and, if possible, cautiously briefed commanders or members of their staff on the possibility of a *coup* and the duties that would fall to them. He had a particularly reliable and knowledgeable ally in Major Meyer, commanding 9 Training Battalion in Potsdam, and his adjutant, Lieutenant von Gottberg. In autumn 1943 Major-General Helmuth Schwierz, commanding No 1 Pyrotechnical School in Berlin-Lichterfelde, after some hesitation also promised to cooperate.

The results of these investigations were passed on to Stauffenberg. Based on them and on his own discoveries during his visit to *Wehrkreis* headquarters, he then issued General Staff directives for the various preparatory measures.

There could be no end to all this work owing to the repeated changes in the situation, continuous fresh air raid damage and the resulting rearrangements. It continued until a few days before 20 July 1944, though with diminished energy after the departure of General von Rost. The repercussions of the war, however, which were always upsetting the preparations also enabled continuous changes to be made in plans to cope with a catastrophe and therefore plans for the *coup*. During 1943, for instance, and particularly after the start of the very heavy air raids on Berlin in the summer, it was found that inadequate emergency preparations had been made by the responsible agencies such as Goebbels in his capacity as *Reich* Defence Commissar and his subordinate offices. *Wehrkreis* HQ thereupon leapt into the breach and General von Rost ordered special emergency plans to be worked out within the framework of 'Valkyrie'. With this official cover troops could be moved about quite openly, sometimes to the discomfiture of Party headquarters.

Naturally the emergency plans made by *Wehrkreis* headquarters did not merely serve as preparations for the *coup* but were also valid for catastrophes in the normal sense and were in fact successfully implemented on several occasions. At the same time the planners were entitled to regard these operations as general rehearsals. This happened, for instance, when a particularly heavy air raid took place in November 1943. The government quarter was badly hit and Rost moved in troops from the Armoured School in Krampnitz, also alerting 9 Infantry Training Battalion. Goebbels thereupon called Kortzfleisch indignantly and demanded to know 'what fighting vehicles were doing in the government quarter'. From the time of alert the troops had taken barely over an hour to reach the centre of Berlin.

As already mentioned, the 'Valkyrie' orders had no political implication. Theoretically it was possible to issue them and set the troops on the move but it was a far cry from that to the occupation of government, SS and Party offices, SS barracks, radio stations and telegraph offices, to the arrest of ministers, *Gauleiter* and SS commanders. Even if orders were carried out with the blind obedience ascribed to German soldiers – as a matter both of praise and blame – doubts and set-backs would certainly arise if resistance was offered, if someone like the voluble Goebbels refused to comply with this 'nonsense'. From early August 1943 Colonel von Tresckow was wrestling with this problem and at latest by the end of that month he was being assisted by Lieutenant-Colonel Graf von Stauffenberg who had more or less recovered from his serious wounds and, when asked by Olbricht in the summer of 1943, had placed himself unreservedly at the disposal of the conspiracy.[18]

Understandably the procedures, ideas and activities of Tresckow and Stauffenberg during these weeks in August and September 1943 remain somewhat obscure. Both met their death on 20–21 July 1944; the surviving participants never knew everything and seldom much. Everything else has largely vanished in the upheavals of those days, the continuous revisions of plans and proclamations and the consequential imprecision of people's memories.[19]

This much can be established with certainty: about 10 August Stauffenberg came back from sick leave, begun at the end of June and spent in Lautlingen; he went to Munich for an operation preparatory to the fitting of an artificial hand. This had to be postponed, however, because a bone splinter in his right arm began to fester. Also in August Stauffenberg had meetings in Berlin with Olbricht, Tresckow and others; then he returned to Lautlingen where he discussed problems of the *coup* with his brother Berthold and Professor Rudolf Fahrner. The artificial hand operation due to be performed by Sauerbruch was first postponed for a month but early in September Stauffenberg called it off completely and went to Berlin. There he worked with Tresckow, whom he had known since 1941, primarily on political directives and proclamations.[20]

Two sets of questions had to be answered: How much detail of the measures to be taken in the *Wehrkreise*, particularly in and around Berlin, could be laid down beforehand? What would be the most convincing explanations and motivations for the initiation of 'Valkyrie' on the day of the *coup*?

To settle the details Tresckow and Stauffenberg contacted officers whom they could trust. These matters could not be dealt with quickly or impetuously. Inevitably weeks passed before, for instance, some member of the conspiracy in an Army school or garrison knew what some new man in Berlin was thinking and had decided whether he could trust him – and even then cooperation in emergency was not assured. Stauffenberg in particular had been working indefatigably on this problem ever since September 1943 and his engaging soldierly character had brought him considerable success. The main work of coordination and establishment of a command channel, however, was not done until late 1943 and early 1944.[21]

In answer to the question of the explanation to be given for the initiation of 'Valkyrie' the first proposal was to spread the story of a *putsch* by the SS.[22] This was certainly a possibility; Himmler's peace feelers have already been mentioned. It was not proposed to announce Hitler's death immediately, although his death was considered essential to trigger off the *putsch*. In the autumn of 1943, however, it was still thought best, at the outset of the *coup*, to adhere to the story that the struggle was *for* Hitler not *against* him. This sprang from a realistic estimate of the mood both of the Army and the people but what practical impact the story would have was still in doubt. It is questionable, moreover, whether it would not have been more effective to lay all the cards on the table at once, as Goerdeler was always demanding, and announce both the assassination and the *coup* as the work of the Army.[23] One thing is certain however – and this is not mere hindsight – doubts, insincerity and ambiguity on the part of the commanders concerned were unlikely to lead to resolute action.

The early drafts of orders and proclamations produced in August and September were continuously revised and changed right up to 20 July 1944; so far none of them have been discovered. The orders actually issued on 20 July are still available since there was little difficulty in collecting them from the various addressees. The *Gestapo* managed to lay hands on only a few of the originals of these orders and still fewer of the autumn 1943 drafts; those they had were probably destroyed at the end of the war.[24] This much, however, is known with certainty about the contents of these orders: They proclaimed a state of emergency and the assumption of plenary powers on the territory of the *Reich* by the *Wehrmacht* under overall command of C-in-C Replacement Army, subordination of all authorities and agencies of the *Reich*, the Party and the SS, incorporation of the SS into the Army, occupation of supply, traffic and communications installations, arrest of all senior Party and SS functionaries, occupation of the concentration camps and a ban on all arbitrary acts of revenge.[25]

Proclamations to the general public described and condemned the behaviour of the Party leaders, explained the imminence of catastrophe and set out plans for a transitional government formed to save the Fatherland;

peace would be concluded as soon as possible and any further sacrifices would be demanded solely with that end in view, not for the purpose of further conquests; henceforth legality and justice would rule; the crimes of the previous regime would be punished and order reestablished. Such was the content of a proclamation to the general public. A similar call was made to the soldiery and a third directed particularly at women asking them to use their own special influence for healing, compromise, love and reconciliation.[26]

Fair copies of the drafts were made under incredible conditions by Fräulein Margarete von Oven (later Gräfin von Hardenberg) who had been secretary both to Colonel-General von Hammerstein and Colonel-General von Fritsch, by Frau von Tresckow and by Gräfin von der Schulenburg (later Gräfin von Rantzau) who worked in Berlin *Wehrkreis* headquarters.[27] Tresckow, Stauffenberg and their secretaries would meet at various points in the Grunewald to discuss and exchange papers. At this time neither Tresckow nor Stauffenberg had their own offices. Stauffenberg's predecessor, Colonel Hellmuth Reinhardt, was present for the hand-over throughout the month of October and he was not a member of the conspiracy. Major difficulties were continually being caused by air raids, absence of transport, the necessity to avoid attracting attention and the impossibility of using either the telephone or post. On one occasion, after meeting Tresckow and Stauffenberg in the Grunewald, Fräulein von Oven was going down the Trabener Strasse with them with drafts of the orders under her arm when a car full of SS men drew up sharply beside her. The SS men jumped out – but took no notice of the three conspirators and disappeared into a house.[28] Fräulein von Oven worked in gloves to avoid leaving fingerprints on the papers; her typewriter was carefully hidden after use. Out-of-date drafts were destroyed with the utmost care. Destruction of large quantities of paper was always a problem since it might easily attract attention. On 29 October 1943 Nina Gräfin von Stauffenberg took a whole rucksack full of drafts from Berlin to Bamberg for burning. *Wehrkreis* headquarters on the Hohenzollerndamm was centrally heated, so papers had to be burnt sheet by sheet in a lavatory pan, the ashes flushed down and the blackened edges of the pan then wiped clean.

On the day of the rising Field Marshal von Witzleben was to be asked to assume supreme command of the *Wehrmacht* and sign the orders proclaiming a state of emergency. When Tresckow showed and explained the drafts to him in the summer or early autumn, he affixed his signature to them without hesitation.[29] It was a far cry to their publication, however.

PART VIII/STAUFFENBERG AND THE REPLACEMENT ARMY

35 Stauffenberg's Career

Claus Schenk Graf von Stauffenberg was born in Jettingen on 15 November 1907; his family was Catholic and belonged to the ancient Swabian nobility. His father was a high-ranking official in the court of Württemberg and later became Marshal of the Court to King Wilhelm II of Würrtemberg. His mother, née Gräfin von Üxküll, was a great-granddaughter of Gneisenau and a considerable personality in her own right. The castle named Stauffenberg near Hechingen can be traced back to 1262. The brothers Berthold Schenk Graf von Stauffenberg and his twin Alexander were two years older; Berthold was later closely involved in the conspiracy and in many respects a leading spirit in it.[1] The three brothers went to the Eberhard-Ludwig-Gymnasium in Stuttgart for a secondary education emphasizing classical studies. Berthold became a lawyer, Alexander a historian and Claus a regular Army officer.

Berthold Graf Stauffenberg studied law and political science and the ease with which he did so was the envy of his fellow-students.[2] Later he wished to enter the diplomatic service. After passing his law examination and serving his term at court, he joined the Kaiser Wilhelm Institute for International Law in Berlin and in 1931 the International Court of Justice in The Hague. In 1934 he returned to the Institute in Berlin and devoted himself to research. Gradually he specialized in military, particularly naval, law and so, when war broke out, was posted to Naval Headquarters as International Law Adviser. His influence there was considerable; all questions submitted to him were answered with the firm assurance of the legal expert and he contributed in no small degree to stemming the increase of savagery in the conduct of naval warfare.[3]

Claus von Stauffenberg first thought of becoming an architect but, after matriculating in 1926, he joined 17 (Bamberg) Cavalry Regiment as a cadet. He was commissioned as 2nd Lieutenant on 1 January 1930 and promoted Lieutenant on 1 May 1933. He attended the Staff College from 1936 to 1938 and was then posted as Ib (Staff officer–Supply) to 1 Light Division in Wuppertal under Lieutenant-General Erich Hoepner. In the autumn he took part in the occupation of the Sudetenland, a year later in the Polish campaign and in May 1940 in the French campaign. On the outbreak of war 1 Light Division had been reorganized as 6 Panzer Division. In May 1940 Stauffenberg was posted to the Organization Section of the Army General Staff where he remained until early 1943. From February to April 1943 he served in Africa where he was severely wounded, losing his right hand, the two little fingers of his left hand and his left eye. After months in hospital followed by sick leave which, though long, was too short for real recovery, he was posted on 15 September 1943 as Chief of Staff to the AHA under General Olbricht; he took up his duties on 1 October.[4]

Only a short summarized account of Stauffenberg's personality will be given here. Theodor Pfizer, who was a school and college friend, has produced a sympathetic eye-witness account of the Stauffenberg brothers' development and background in their young days; to Eberhard Zeller we owe a more comprehensive but equally sympathetic and attractive study; Joachim Kramarz and Christian Müller have done careful research and have cleared up many points.[5] The picture of Stauffenberg, however, is still obscured by misunderstandings and well-meant silences and so it cannot be left to the biographers alone. One or two important points will be enough.

From expressions used by Stauffenberg many of his colleagues concluded that he welcomed and supported the Nazi regime; not until after 20 July did they wonder whether he had spoken from conviction or to camouflage his real ideas. Stauffenberg always liked discussing political, social or historical questions; he had had a penchant for Greek philosophy since his school days. His fellow-officers had other interests; they were simpler characters and at times were sickened by his continuous political talk which they found pretentious and tiresome.[6] Many who subsequently became opponents of the regime initially placed their hopes in 'the movement' and gave it their support – Fritz-Dietlof Graf von der Schulenburg, for instance. Even so determined a subsequent opponent of the National-Socialists as Colonel Albrecht Ritter Mertz von Quirnheim was carried away by the SA in 1932–33 and only became more balanced in the mid-1930s under the influence of Colonel Max von Viebahn in 5 Infantry Regiment; Mertz von Quirnheim's eyes were finally opened in the last years before the war.[7]

Claus Graf Stauffenberg was attracted to the platform of the National-Socialist Party initially, as were both his brothers, Alexander and Berthold, his uncle Nikolaus Graf von Üxküll, and many others among his numerous Franconian and Swabian relatives and in-laws.[8] It was to them natural to be in favour of many things strongly advocated and apparently likely to be achieved by the National-Socialists: they were all in favour of a 'national policy', of removing the restrictions on national sovereignty imposed by the hated Versailles Treaty, of ending reparations, of re-armament to a level comparable to that of the other great nations, of soldierly virtues and values, of *Volksgemeinschaft*, of an end to political strife, of order and integrity in administration and in every-day life as well. There was little if any mention of conquest and war, of winning new *Lebensraum*; but probably most Germans believed that Austria and the Sudetenland ought to be part of the *Reich*, and that Germany had certain territorial claims in the east. Such ideas were not the exclusive property of the National-Socialists.

It has often been said that on 30 January 1933 Stauffenberg, in uniform, placed himself at the head of an enthusiastic crowd which marched through

Bamberg.[9] This is pure legend; the incident never took place. On the evening of 30 January 1933 there was a torch-light procession through Bamberg organised by the Nazi Party but Stauffenberg did not participate; in any case, as a soldier, he was not permitted to take part in Party demonstrations.[10]

The story apparently started with mess gossip and seems to have been based on the following actual occurrence:[11] On 31 January 1933, not on the day of the 'seizure of power' therefore, No 5 Squadron of 17 Cavalry Regiment under command of Captain (as he then was) Hasso von Manteuffel was riding back to barracks from an exercise. Its route led through the town past the town hall where the swastika flag had been hoisted; Manteuffel had been told that the swastika had been raised to the status of national emblem (which was not true) and so he ordered his squadron to ride to attention as they passed it.[12] Manteuffel was given a sharp reprimand, rightly he thought since he had omitted to check whether what he had been told was correct.

This comparatively innocent affair, therefore, turned into the legend of Stauffenberg, the enthusiastic National-Socialist. Many officers of 17 Cavalry Regiment, especially the younger ones, approved wholeheartedly of Hitler's 'seizure of power' at the time, and of policies to restore the prestige of the *Reich*, to expand the Army, and to improve armaments.[13] Stauffenberg agreed with such policies, too, but it was characteristic of him to view things critically, and to voice an opinion running contrary to whatever happened to be the predominant opinion, often for good cause, but often for the sake of dialectical argument.[14] On the occasion of a change in *Wehrmacht* uniforms decreed by the National-Socialist government, Stauffenberg raised the question 'most seriously' whether 'even worse things might not follow this measure'.[15] This does not mean that Stauffenberg did not follow Hitler's rise to power and his victory with interest, was not indeed fascinated by them.[16] He was attracted by the new drive which appeared to have 'broken through the crust of bourgeois habits' and opened the way to fresh arrangements; he was also attracted by the '*völkisch*' ideal, in other words a community of the people, united and working for the common good, in which conflict would either cease or be muted by knowledge of the community's requirements and a sense of 'togetherness'. Reconciliation between nationalists and socialists was equally an aim with which it was difficult to disagree.

A man of Stauffenberg's background and education could not easily be a Nazi in the 'movement' as led by Hitler. Among his ancestors, of whom he was very conscious, were the Prussian Field Marshals Graf Neidhart von Gneisenau and Johann Graf Yorck von Wartenburg; his family was not excessively proud of its title but it was conscious of its tradition. He had been a pupil at the Eberhard-Ludwig-Gymnasium in the liberal and democratic atmosphere of the royal capital of Stuttgart and had inherited the spirit of the school's famous graduates. He had learnt Latin and Greek; he had read classical history, philosophy and poetry. In 1924, as a seventeen-year-old, he had joined Stefan George's circle.[17] Four years before that, writing to Stauffenberg's mother about a photograph of the three brothers, Rainer Maria Rilke had said that they were 'in many ways lads with a future'.[18] Despite a certain undeniable affinity between George's intellectual antecedents and those of many ideas which the Nazis claimed as their own, George and his circle were worlds apart from Nazism as it manifested itself in practice. Certain peculiar aberrations in the George cult which have occasionally been reported, moreover, did not really originate with George himself but rather from certain 'disciples'.[19] The Stauffenberg brothers in particular were opposed to anything false or sham.[20] Stefan George himself evaded the adulation to which he feared that he might be subjected on his sixty-fifth birthday on 12 July 1933. He left Bingen on 8 July and went first to Berlin. Thence he travelled to Wasserburg on Lake Constance, then to Heiden im Appenzell and finally in September to his usual winter resort, Minusio near Locarno. When he died there on 4 December 1933 the three Stauffenberg brothers with eight of their friends were present at his deathbed.[21]

The most dangerous affinity between the ideas of George and those of the National-Socialists existed in the vague and irrational concept of *das Völkische* and *die Volksgemeinschaft*. It may be surprising, but it is symptomatic not only in Germany but in the rest of the world that not merely irrational nationalists and uprooted mercenaries but also young men of the well-to-do middle classes, in this case of the Frankish-Swabian nobility, brought up on humanist, Catholic or other principles of basic respect and regard for every human being were receptive to such xenophobic ideas. They were anti-humanist and anti-Christian concepts which the twentieth century had inherited from the nineteenth: blood and soil; *Lebensraum*; whoever will not work shall not eat; or the social-Darwinist theory of life unworthy of preservation. In the 'racial question', also an anti-Christian concept, Stauffenberg, who was a devout Catholic, and his brothers agreed in principle with the idea of control, separate existence and the essentially foreign, non-German character of the Jews, though they objected to extremism and physical cruelty.[22] As Berthold Graf Stauffenberg told his *Gestapo* interrogators after 20 July 1944: 'The basic ideas of National-Socialism were almost all turned into their opposites by the way the regime implemented them.'[23]

This is not the place to pursue the inconsistency of approving a theory while objecting to its implementation and its consequences. But the rejection of the regime's methods by Stauffenberg must be noted. Soon after the 1934 purges he must have revised his opinion of Hitler and begun to think about the change or removal of the regime.[24] He often referred to Hitler as 'the wallpaper hanger' and said repeatedly that it was impossible for him to be the subject of a petit-bourgeois.[25] Though approving of the *Anschluss* with Austria, he disliked the method by which the Sudetenland was annexed and he strongly disapproved of the invasion of Prague and of 'Rump-Czechoslovakia'. He considered this *hubris* and said to Professor Fahrner: 'The fool is heading for war.'

When war actually broke out in September 1939 Stauffenberg bought himself a stock of books, including the works of Leibnitz, which he took with him to the field. He said to his bookseller in Wuppertal that, despite the horrors of war, it was a relief to be on the move; war, after all, had been his family's trade for centuries.[26]

When, contrary to all expectations, the Polish and French campaigns were so brilliantly successful, Stauffenberg once again revised his opinion of Hitler. He acknowledged Hitler's part in these military successes and spoke with respect if not admiration of him. After the battle of Dunkirk he said to his wife: 'That man has got a nose for military matters. In contrast to the generals he *knew* that the Maginot Line could be pierced . . . He made a mistake in the enveloping movements at Dunkirk – he won't repeat that.'[27] While on leave he visited his Wuppertal bookseller who found the apparent change in the young officer incomprehensible and said that always before he had been so ready to curse this petit-bourgeois; Stauffenberg replied: 'That man's father was not a petit-bourgeois; that man's father is war.'[28]

About this time, after the Polish campaign, Stauffenberg was visited by his uncle, Nikolaus Graf von Üxküll, and by Fritz-Dietlof Graf von der Schulenburg, whom he had known before; they told him of what was happening in Germany and behind the lines in Poland and tried to persuade him to take an active part in the opposition. He should try, they said, to obtain a position from which he could intervene. But Stauffenberg was not responsive.[29]

For the time being, Stauffenberg devoted himself fully to the profession he had chosen in 1926: soldiering. He was a soldier first, and he meant to contribute his part to winning glory for the German arms.[30] Gradually, however, after his transfer to OKH in 1940, he became more and more sceptical and finally condemned both the regime and Hitler himself.[31] During the first winter of the Russian campaign, he seems to have seen matters as did many soldiers to the very end: every effort should be made for victory or for a stalemate achieved by force of arms; that was mere patriotic duty, but it would also set the stage for successful armistice negotiations after a *coup*.[32] This duty Stauffenberg did to his very last day with every ounce of his energy, even after he had long begun to conspire against his *Führer* and Supreme Commander in order to save his country. When Moltke was looking in 1941 or early 1942 for influential officers who might join the resistance movement, he asked Hans Christoph Freiherr von Stauffenberg if anything could be done with his cousin in Army Headquarters.[33] Freiherr von Stauffenberg then asked Berthold von Stauffenberg who replied a few weeks later. According to this report Claus von Stauffenberg replied that the war must first be won and then the brown-shirted plague would be swept away. Until shortly before 20 July 1944 Stauffenberg invariably insisted on the necessity for a military decision.

Because Stauffenberg was essentially a soldier he was disgusted by the inefficiency of the *Wehrmacht*'s leadership as he saw it at close quarters in the General Staff. He was particularly infuriated by Göring's fallacious promises about the capabilities of the *Luftwaffe* which were never fulfilled.[34] He now thought that the war could no longer be won but in 1942 was still hoping that defeat could be avoided, at least in the east, by a well thought-out arms policy and sensible military leadership. As the hopelessness of the situation became clearer towards the end of 1942 and his despair became greater, he was relieved to be posted to the front.[35] On one occasion about this time, when Hitler was being discussed and someone asked how his methods of command could be changed, Stauffenberg replied 'Kill him'.[36] He had already said something similar in the summer of 1942.[37]

Stauffenberg also tried to persuade senior commanders in appropriate positions to offer determined resistance, if necessary by concerted action.[38] But no one was willing to do anything although all admitted the necessity for some 'action'. In January 1943 he visited Field Marshal von Manstein in Taganrog and put to him the necessity for a *coup d'état*.[39] Manstein refused for the well-worn reasons – the eastern front would collapse and mutiny would ruin the Army. After the war he said that, had he thought a *coup* to be either possible or necessary, he would have done it himself.

Soon after this Stauffenberg was transferred to the 'Afrika Korps'. He left Munich about 8 February 1943 to become Staff Officer (Operations) of 10 Panzer Division. Both the divisional commander and Stauffenberg's predecessor had driven over a mine on 4 February; Lieutenant-General Wolfgang Fischer was dead and Colonel Wilhelm Bürklin badly wounded.[40] On 7 April 1943 Stauffenberg himself was severely wounded in a low-level air attack near Gafsa. Even at the main dressing station his right hand had to be amputated above the wrist and so did the third and fourth fingers of his left hand; the left eye also had to be removed. Three days later he was taken to hospital in Tunis and thence to Italy on one of the last transports to leave (his division went into captivity in May). On 21 April he arrived in a Munich hospital where a middle ear operation was performed and later an operation on a knee joint. From the end of June to early August he was on sick leave in Lautlingen; about 9 August he returned to Munich where a preparatory operation for the fitting of an artificial hand was to take place, but a bone splinter began to fester in his right arm and the operation had to be postponed. Twice during August Stauffenberg visited his wife in Bamberg on his way to or from Berlin, finally returning for a second stay in Lautlingen where he had discussions with his brother Berthold and Professor Fahrner. From the autumn of 1943 to 20 July 1944 Stauffenberg was the real driving force behind the attempt to assassinate Hitler.

Many of his acquaintances were struck by the fact that, after his wound, Stauffenberg seemed to be consumed by an urge to intense activity which some took for ambition.[41] In July 1944 Stauffenberg seemed to Colonel Hansen to be nervous, moody and 'burnt out', which Hansen ascribed to his severe wounds; in the summer of 1944 Ferdinand Sauerbruch, the surgeon, also thought that Stauffenberg's state of health totally precluded a project such as he had in mind. Stauffenberg himself was convinced that only through a stroke of fortune had he survived such severe wounds. From his early youth he had felt that he was destined for something out of the ordinary and this, he felt, had now been strikingly confirmed. He told his wife that he felt that he must now do something to save the *Reich* – but not only that; to Peter Sauerbruch, the surgeon's son, he once said: 'I could never look the wives and children of the fallen in the eye if I did not do something to stop this senseless slaughter.'[42] Gerhard Ritter thinks that Stauffenberg had 'a streak of demonic thirst for power'; he adds that 'without Stauffenberg's determination the opposition movement would have been stuck fast in helpless passivity'.

What Stauffenberg wanted was to save Germany, to end the war with its millionfold deaths and its destruction. His vision of the future is given in the words of an oath which was intended to bind the members of the conspiracy together; it is quoted by Zeller: 'We wish there to be a new order of society, which will make all Germans supporters of the state, guaranteeing them justice and right, but we despise the lie that all men are equal, and accept the natural ranks. We wish to see a people with its roots deep in the soil of its native country, close to the forces of nature, finding happiness and satisfaction in labouring in the status into which it has been called, and proud to overcome the base emotions of envy and ill-will. We wish to see leaders from all classes of society, bound to the divine forces, taking the lead on the grounds of their highmindedness, virtue and spirit of self-sacrifice.'[43]

This was phrased in general terms, but it indicates Stauffenberg's will, documented elsewhere as well, not only to fulfil the obligations of nobility as he saw them, but also to secure for the nobility a significant position in the new social structure of post-war Germany.[44] Until late in 1943 or early 1944, Stauffenberg seems to have had little sympathy for the socialist demand for strong trade unions, and when he adopted it he probably did so for tactical reasons rather than out of conviction. He hoped 'to win over' the workers, and to stave off communism.[45] In the weeks preceding the assassination attempt of 20 July, he still appears to have made only minor concessions to the Social-Democrats when he told the former Bavarian envoy to Berlin, Franz Sperr, on a visit to Bamberg on 6 June 1944: 'The goal was a *federal state with very considerable autonomy of the member states*, with much autonomy in administration, with social reforms, with participation of workers in settling wages, working hours and holidays, and the like.'[46] It must be noted that Sperr was one of the leaders of a Bavarian separatist opposition group; certainly the terms of Stauffenberg's remark are so vague that there was still plenty of room to manoeuvre and to make sure that differences of 'natural ranks' would be respected. But the realization of his or anyone else's ideas depended much less on his convictions than on the political situation after the war.

36 Assassination Attempts – Bussche, Kleist, Breitenbuch

On 1 October 1943 Stauffenberg assumed duty as Chief of Staff to the AHA, Berlin, under General Olbricht. Working unofficially during the summer, he had briefed himself on the 'Valkyrie' plans; he was familiar with the subject, having written a prize-winning article 'Thoughts on Home Defence against Enemy Parachute Troops' which probably had some influence on his planning.[1] Shortly after Stauffenberg had officially assumed duty Colonel von Tresckow had to take over a regiment, which more or less divorced him from the centre of the conspiracy. Stauffenberg now applied himself to the creation of conditions for initiation of 'Valkyrie', in other words the 'initial flash'.

For the moment plans for the *coup* were so far advanced that at the end of October Stauffenberg thought that it could be launched about 10 November.[2] He now thought it irresponsible to wait longer or try to win the war first. Force must be used, he said, to put an end to the Nazi regime and its leaders who had lost all sense of proportion and without a qualm were leading the German people to their destruction.[3] But the question remained – how?

Two possibilities were under discussion: (1) Hitler could be made prisoner or killed by capturing his headquarters from outside. (2) Some brave man who had an official *entrée* to the headquarters could assassinate him. There was little prospect of a successful attack during one of Hitler's rare 'public' appearances during the latter war years; preparations would almost certainly have been detected and the essential coordination with the *coup d'état* measures would have been impossible.

In his position and with his contacts Stauffenberg had no great difficulty in keeping informed of Hitler's whereabouts at any particular time. In most cases, however, it was impossible to tell *beforehand* when or where Hitler would move.

Looking for a man who might be prepared to be the assassin, Stauffenberg first thought of Colonel Stieff. He was head of the Organization Section in OKH and so might have access to Hitler. When new weapons and equipment were shown to Hitler, Stieff was standing immediately next to him on several occasions; he was not, however, regularly present at the briefing conferences.[4] In late October Stauffenberg approached Stieff in the OKH camp 'Mauerwald' and asked him whether he could make an attack on Hitler. After profound thought Stieff refused; he kept the explosive, however, which Stauffenberg had brought with him. To the *Gestapo* and in court Stieff naturally said that he personally had refused to attempt murder and his letters to his wife indicate the same. Nevertheless for a time Stauffenberg must have thought that Stieff would make the attempt – at least he told Professor Fahrner so.[5]

The next to be approached was Colonel Joachim Meichssner of the Organization Section of the OKW Operations Staff. He also refused or could see no possibility. He too was not a regular attendant at the briefing conferences, but he had to accompany General Buhle a good many times, and in the summer of 1942 he attended Hitler's late-night teas together with Buhle on several occasions.[6] To admit to the *Gestapo* that his irregular attendance was the reason for refusal would naturally have been suicidal; it was better to give reasons of principle as Stieff and most others did. After his transfer to the Organization Section of the OKW Operations Staff in Potsdam-Eiche Meichssner had no official access to Hitler's conferences, but he had to report to Warlimont, Jodl or sometimes to Keitel. Early in 1944, somewhere between the end of February and the end of May, Stauffenberg himself tried to persuade Meichssner to make the attempt but either he did not wish to or had thought better of it.[7]

Stauffenberg therefore had to look further. He was not a candidate himself because he had no access to the briefing conferences before becoming Chief of Staff to Fromm and then only occasionally – he was seconded with effect from 20 June and finally appointed with effect from 1 July 1944. But he knew nothing of this until Summer 1944. Then Fritz-Dietlof Graf von der Schulenburg, who was serving in 9 Infantry Training Battalion, came to his assistance.

During the war Schulenburg was one of the mainsprings of the resistance movement and he acted with characteristic intrepidity. Some time in August 1942 he approached Lieutenant von Gottberg; he had been severely wounded, had spent months in hospital emerging as 'fit for home service only' and was Assistant Adjutant of 9 Infantry Training Regiment from May 1942 and Adjutant from September. Schulenburg outlined to him the project of removing Hitler by force and received an assurance of readiness to participate.[8] Another member of the battalion was Lieutenant Ewald Heinrich von Kleist, also a member of the conspiracy and one of Schulenburg's protégés.[9] Finally a much-decorated officer, Captain Axel Freiherr von dem Bussche, also came from 9 Infantry Regiment and was a friend of Schulenburg's.

For some time Schulenburg had been 'looking around' and in the spring of 1943 had run into serious difficulties for doing so. The rumour had gone round that Schulenburg was looking for 'reliable' officers and at a most unsuitable time – shortly after the Stalingrad catastrophe and the trial of the Scholl group, when the assassination attempts in Smolensk and Berlin had miscarried and the opposition's active centre in the *Abwehr* had been destroyed by the removal of Oster, Dohnanyi and others; rumours were rife and even Himmler was beginning to turn towards conspiracy. Schulenburg was forced to submit to an unpleasant interrogation but fortunately was not further harried.[10] He refused to be intimidated and now, in the autumn of 1943, was once more actively assisting plans for the *coup*. He arranged a meeting between Stauffenberg and Bussche.

Bussche was a soldier – and a very good one, as he had proved himself to be on innumerable raiding operations; he wore the Iron Cross 1st and 2nd Class, and the German Cross in Gold; in 1944 he was awarded the Knight's Cross and the Golden War-wounded Badge. Coming from 9 Infantry Regiment he had learnt and imbibed the old solid military principles and ideals of chivalrous warfare and human decency. Like many of his fellow-officers, therefore, he was basically opposed to the regime, an attitude in which he was naturally confirmed by Hitler's explicit ban on any form of chivalrous conduct.[11]

Having been wounded in the lung in the spring of 1942, Bussche was classed as unfit for front-line service and became adjutant of 23 Reserve Regiment in Potsdam. He was personally commissioned by General Olbricht to ensure that, as far as possible, the regiment had no Nazis among its officers. In the summer of 1942 considerable parts of the Replacement Army were moved to Russia as occupation forces and Bussche unexpectedly found himself first in the Ukraine and then in the Crimea as adjutant of his scattered unit. On 5 October 1942 he was present on Dubno airfield in the Ukraine when the mass shooting of some five thousand Jews took place. The experience affected him most deeply.

Bussche was present quite by chance and saw everything: the Jews were herded along by Ukrainian SS men, compelled to strip and then to lie face downwards on top of dead or still writhing Jews who had dug the pit and had then been shot; the newcomers were then also killed by a shot in the nape of the neck. The SS men did all this in a calm orderly fashion; they were clearly acting under orders. Bussche had already heard of these things; he knew enough about discipline under a dictatorship to realize that all this must be happening on orders from above, in fact from the highest quarter; moreover it was no isolated incident. But here, for the first time, he was seeing it with his own eyes. He grasped what he had seen: mass murder ordered by the government whose orders he was carrying out, to which he had sworn an oath and which ruled his country. Bussche remembered the wording of the emergency paragraph, No 227 in the code of common law, which had been taught to recruits in his regiment; it laid down the right of self-defence in emergency 'to defend oneself or another against unlawful attack'. The phrase 'unlawful attack' was obviously applicable in this case; it was inconceivable that all these men, numbering several thousands, had been lawfully condemned to death. They could not be partisans since there were many women and children among them.

Bussche's first thought was to invoke the emergency paragraph and call a halt to the operation, but he realized at once that this was impossible. Even if the SS men had taken any notice of him, which seemed improbable, the 'special treatment' of the Jews would have continued next day both in Dubno and elsewhere. In other words this was a symptom and a mere captain, even a much-bemedalled one, could do nothing about it. Removal of the supreme mass murderer would be more effective.

Later, after much thought, there occurred to Bussche another answer to the existential question with which he had been faced in Dubno, the answer of the Christian. He now thinks that he ought to have stripped like the Jews, joined the death queue and lain down in the grave to be shot with the Jews. He would thus have demonstrated that all those involved, the Jews, the murderers and he himself, the captain present by chance, were first and foremost human beings. He would certainly not have been shot and perhaps the 'special treatment' would have been suspended on this occasion; perhaps senior commanders would have come to their senses or a spontaneous resistance movement have developed in the Army. More probably Bussche would have been despatched to a lunatic asylum or a concentration camp. In practice the answer of the Christian – to share the sufferings of others – would have been ineffective.

After what he had seen in Dubno in the autumn of 1942, however, Bussche was so eager to do something against Hitler that all he wanted was an opportunity. He was still in this state of mind in October 1943 when Schulenburg arranged the meeting between him and Stauffenberg in Düppel camp, Berlin-Zehlendorf; a further talk followed in November. Stauffenberg asked Bussche whether he was prepared to attempt the assassination of Hitler and Bussche said that he was.

The possibility of a pistol attack was discussed only briefly. The two men agreed that it was too risky and the chances of success too small. The risk of discovery was great; a straight shot could not be guaranteed and there was the belief that Hitler wore a bullet-proof waistcoat. Bussche, of course, had no access to the briefing conferences but Stauffenberg had another plan.

In 1942 and 1943 various types of new equipment and uniform were being developed, particularly winter clothing for the fighting in Russia. It should be possible, Stauffenberg thought, to find an opportunity of demonstrating equipment to Hitler using a resolute officer ready to make the attempt and if necessary sacrifice himself – and this could be Bussche. He should conduct the demonstration using three or four soldiers as models, himself explaining the properties of the material and equipment. While doing so he would be carrying a bomb which he would fuse and then jump upon Hitler and clasp him until the explosion took place.

Bussche had many advantages which made him the ideal candidate for this sort of demonstration, quite apart from his sense of obligation to do something. He had fought all over the eastern front from Leningrad to the Crimea; he had all the necessary experience and was much bemedalled; moreover he looked 'nordic', a quality much valued at the time.

One idea was that Bussche should carry the bomb in his briefcase together with the papers for the demonstration, but this method was not certain enough. A few weeks later Schulenburg was saying to Kleist: 'You must tie that round your stomach.'[12] There was no question of demonstrating an 'assault pack'. Critics of the opposition later liked to say that some 'poor innocent' ignorant 'private soldier' was to have a bomb planted on him and it would then be secretly ignited; but this is a nonsensical story spread by the *Gestapo,* by Himmler (in his speech to *Gauleiter* on 3 August 1944), by Roland Freisler, President of the People's Court and by Goebbels. During cross-examination of Major-General Stieff before the People's Court on 7 August 1944 Freisler maintained that this was the plan for the attack in which Stieff was involved; Stieff denied it but Freisler cut him short.[13] The plan was obviously technically impracticable. How was the bomb to be ignited without the soldier noticing and precisely at the unpredictable moment when the group was summoned to Hitler? Who could ensure that at the moment of explosion the dictator and the bomb-carrier were close enough together? It could only have succeeded by chance.

In order that he might make further preparations and obtain the explosive Stauffenberg devised some official pretext for Bussche to visit the OKH camp 'Mauerwald' near Lötzen in East Prussia, some ten miles from the *Führer*'s headquarters 'Wolfschanze'. There he discussed all major questions of principle with Stieff and technical details with Major Kuhn. The latter offered him a pack of British plastic explosive with a chemical ten-minute fuse. Its great advantage was that the fuse was completely silent and the explosive extremely powerful, far more so than the normal German explosive. Bussche, however, was not familiar with British equipment; he had no first-hand experience of its effect and was not prepared to rely on second-hand reports. Moreover a delay of ten minutes seemed to him to introduce too many factors of uncertainty. He therefore preferred to use the normal German Army explosive which he knew; this would also eliminate one ambiguity inherent in the use of British explosive. The available stock had in fact been captured during the war and there was no question of it having been 'delivered by the British'; public opinion could easily be deceived on this point, however, as in fact happened after 20 July 1944.

Bussche accordingly asked Stieff for a kilogramme pack of German pioneer explosive, a yard of fuse, a complete German hand grenade with $4\frac{1}{2}$-second fuse and a personnel mine, all for trial. Bussche, Stieff and Kuhn agreed that a metal-cased bomb was far better and more effective than mere explosive. They suspected, however, that there were concealed electronic devices in the *Führer*'s headquarters which could detect any large-size metal object or weapons. This was also a reason against use of a pistol.

Stieff and Kuhn were not able to meet Bussche's requirements at once; procurement of the German explosive and accessories necessitated various cautious manoeuvres.[14] Kuhn, who was working under Stieff in the OKH Organization Section, was concerned primarily with procurement of the explosive. In November 1943 a certain Major Gerhard Knaak passed through 'Mauerwald' on duty; he had been a friend of Kuhn's since 1936 and was now commanding 630 Pioneer Battalion located on the Dnieper east of Orscha, some 2–3 miles behind the front line; the battalion formed part of IV Army Corps which came under Army Group Centre.[15] Kuhn asked Knaak whether he could obtain explosive for an attack on Hitler and Knaak said that he would. On his return journey to the front Knaak was found a lodging in Minsk by Major von Oertzen.

In December Knaak received warning of a visit by Lieutenant von Hagen, who worked under Kuhn in the Organization Section, and he arrived shortly afterwards.[16] Hagen had certain official duties to perform on this trip, but he had also been instructed to take delivery of a quantity of normal Army explosive from Major Knaak. Hagen returned two days later with a standard 1-kilogramme charge used for bridge demolitions and a length of fuse.[17] Hand grenades were not held by pioneer units.

Bussche took the explosive and fuse and returned to Potsdam. There he obtained a hand grenade through his friend Lieutenant von Gottberg who was on the staff of 9 Infantry Training Battalion. He preferred to use the $4\frac{1}{2}$-second hand grenade fuse in spite of its hissing rather than the ten-minute time fuse which was silent. He thought that he could cover the few seconds of noise by clearing his throat and coughing, whereas in ten minutes all sorts of unpredictable things might happen. With the chemical fuse he would have been to a certain extent the prisoner of a machine instead of controlling it.[18]

The procurement of a hand grenade was nothing like so simple as it sounds; in fact it was a most dangerous operation. What should a headquarters officer in a training battalion in Germany want with hand grenades? Gottberg took the risk, went to Sergeant-Major Knodel who was in charge of weapons and equipment and asked for two hand grenades. Knodel asked, as he was bound to do, what they were wanted for but accepted the explanation that they were required for certain purposes. Knodel was tactful enough never to refer to the subject again, not even after 20 July and certainly not to the *Gestapo*.

Gottberg took the hand grenades home and Bussche visited him there. Together they extracted the fuses from the grenades. The next day Gottberg and Kleist threw the remains of the hand grenades into the Havel off the Glienicke Bridge. Helped by Gottberg, Bussche then constructed a fuse mechanism which he thought suitable for his purpose. He sawed the haft of the hand grenade in two, leaving the part containing the fuse, and he unscrewed the primer. He shortened the draw-thread which ran down inside the haft, leaving the pull-button so that there was very little play between the button and the haft. In this way only a very small pulling motion would be required instead of the more extensive movement normally necessary. The hand grenade fuse fitted well into the pioneer charge. The whole thing could well be concealed in one of the deep pockets of the wide trousers then normally worn. Bussche was not afraid of having to make too obvious a motion when fusing the bomb since some gesticulation with the hands would be natural when demonstrating and explaining the uniforms. The $4\frac{1}{2}$ seconds during which the fuse would hiss was not a long time. After clearing his throat and coughing he would jump on Hitler and hold him until the explosion occurred. To guard against a failure he would carry a long thin knife in his boot.

When all was ready and an approximate date had been set for the demonstration of uniforms – Hitler was hardly ever willing to be tied to precise dates – the Berlin conspirators and many others in Germany were given a 'preliminary warning'. Major-General Rost had only to sign and issue orders already prepared in order to be in occupation of all Berlin in a very short time.[19] Arthur Nebe, head of the *Reich* Criminal Police Office, received his first request to hold in readiness the criminal police officers ear-marked for the *putsch*.[20] From 23 or 25 November Bussche was ready, waiting for a call from OKH. It must be remembered, however, that the procedure would have been approximately as follows: Speer, the Armaments Minister, or Field Marshal Keitel suggests to Hitler an inspection of equipment and tries to obtain a date; Hitler agrees but says: not this week, perhaps early December. This would produce a 'schedule' and efforts would then be made through Hitler's Personal Aides to obtain something more precise. In fact this did not produce a date but merely an approximate time envisaged. Apart from commitments which he could not alter such as 30 January, 1 May, 20 April and 8/9 November Hitler was not in the habit of fixing dates. If he agreed to something, he was punctual but as far as possible he avoided firm commitments.

One day, while waiting for the summons to the demonstration, Bussche was called to Stieff who told him that the equipment earmarked for the demonstration (it was to come from Berlin) had been destroyed or severely damaged in a burnt-out railway truck during one of the recent heavy air raids. It could not be replaced quickly.[21] Stieff said that it would now be best if Bussche returned to the battalion which he commanded on the northern sector of the eastern front. He would be recalled in January when replacement equipment had been obtained.[22]

In fact in January 1944 Bussche did receive a telephone call from Stauffenberg asking him to be present for the demonstration which had been re-scheduled. At the same time Stauffenberg sent a teleprint from the AHA asking for Bussche for official duties. But when Bussche asked his divisional commander, who was not in the conspiracy, for leave to go, the general said that he would not have his battalion commanders acting as models for demonstrations of uniforms in East Prussia. Stauffenberg tried again to get Bussche released but the general again said 'No'. A few days later Bussche was severely wounded and lost a leg. He was in hospital for weeks and any active role in the conspiracy was out of the question for him. The little box containing the 'bomb' accompanied him through various hospitals until eventually he managed to throw it into a lake in the autumn of 1944.

The next in line for an attack on Hitler was Lieutenant Ewald Heinrich von Kleist. After Bussche's efforts had ended in failure and he had been so badly wounded Stauffenberg asked Lieutenant Ewald Heinrich von Kleist whether he was prepared to make the attempt. Kleist asked advice of his father, Ewald von Kleist-Schmenzin, the landowner who had been one of the most resolute opponents of Hitler ever since the start of his dictatorship and had always refused to be intimidated. His answer to his son was that under no circumstances must he miss this opportunity of fulfilling so vital a duty – and anyone who takes the trouble to think out the situation and its implications must realize what that answer must have cost him.[23]

Stauffenberg's approach to Kleist was at the end of January 1944. The presentation of uniforms was due to take place early in February, about the 11th. After talking to his father Kleist told Stauffenberg that he would do it. Stauffenberg, however, wished to have someone else available with a bomb in case Kleist should fail. Stauffenberg had explosive, and the idea was to use the same type of fusing arrangement as Bussche's, with a hand grenade fuse.

Meanwhile preparations for the *coup*, particularly in Berlin, were checked through once more. Olbricht and Stauffenberg met Major-General Rost and Lieutenant Albrecht in Olbricht's office.[24] Stauffenberg said that the 'flash' was imminent, whereupon Rost replied that the moment was highly unfavourable; he even threatened to withdraw his support but Olbricht and Stauffenberg managed to persuade him. Olbricht said that Germany's military situation was in fact totally hopeless but it might still be possible to save the country's existence; he saw no way other than the *coup* of avoiding the coming catastrophe. He knew perfectly well, he said, what the consequences of failure would be for him and his family but he was nevertheless prepared to risk his neck. Stauffenberg said that the uniform demonstration had been re-scheduled by the Armaments Ministry and this would provide an opportunity of attacking the 'Numbers One to Three' (Hitler, Göring and Himmler). As soon as it took place the codeword would be issued by telephone. After this meeting Rost and Albrecht returned to the office of the City Commandant, where they held prolonged discussions on details of the measures proposed with Lieutenant-General von Hase and Lieutenant-Colonel Hermann Schöne, his operations officer.

But everyone in Berlin waited for the codeword in vain. For reasons still unexplained this demonstration, too, did not take place. The original plan was to carry the explosive in a briefcase with reports on the trials of the uniforms and equipment, but it was then decided that it should be attached to Kleist's body since, as Schulenburg had remarked, this was by far the surest way. In contrast to Bussche, however, Kleist never actually saw his 'bomb'.

The uniform demonstration finally took place at Klessheim Castle near Salzburg on 7 July.[25] Stieff was present but made no attempt at assassination.[26]

Meanwhile Tresckow had been trying in vain to get himself a position offering access to Hitler which would give him the opportunity of making the attempt himself. He first tried to persuade Schmundt to create a new office to be run by him (Tresckow) to assemble, evaluate and forward 'on up' psychological and political information.[27] Nothing came of this. Tresckow then renewed his earlier efforts to be nominated deputy and potential successor to Major-General Heusinger, head of the OKH Operations Section.[28] In December 1943 Schlabrendorff flew to OKH from Minsk carrying a letter from Tresckow to Heusinger, but Heusinger refused even to discuss the subject.

One more plan and one more attempt are known of before Stauffenberg himself assumed responsibility for carrying out the assassination. In late January Lieutenant Werner von Haeften, who had been severely wounded, was unfit for front-line service and was now Stauffenberg's aide, thought that he might be able to shoot Hitler with a pistol.[29] His brother, Hans-Bernd von Haeften, however raised the most serious objections, asking whether Werner was sure that this was a task given *him* by God and saying that gangster methods should not be used even against gangsters, so Werner von Haeften did not pursue his plan.

The last attempt other than Stauffenberg's own and the last for which the initiative stemmed from Tresckow was to be made by Eberhard von Breitenbuch. It was originally intended to be a bomb attack but after much reflection Breitenbuch decided to try with a pistol.[30]

In 1940 Breitenbuch had been aide to Witzleben; from August 1943 he occupied the same position with Kluge until Kluge had his car accident. He was now aide to Field Marshal Busch who had taken over Army Group Centre.[31] In the summer of 1943 when Breitenbuch arrived, Tresckow said to him that he had not been posted there merely to go around with the Field Marshal but because his political views were known; it was his job to influence the Field Marshal so that, not only would he tolerate an attack on Hitler, but at the right moment make one or engineer one himself. Breitenbuch had known of all the various attempts and plans ever since summer 1943; he had prearranged codewords with which he warned his wife when some plan was imminent.

On 9 March 1944 Colonel-General Zeitzler, Chief of Staff of the Army, telephoned Busch to say that he was required to brief Hitler at a conference in the 'Berghof' on 11 March.[32] As aide to Busch Captain von Breitenbuch had to make the necessary arrangements such as stop-off accommodation in Breslau and accommodation for the crew of Hitler's Focke-Wulf 'Condor' which was to fetch the Field Marshal; finally he had to accompany Busch.

Shortly after this telephone call, during the lunch break, Major-General (he had been promoted in January) von Tresckow and Major von Oertzen appeared in Breitenbuch's office which adjoined that of C-in-C Army Group Centre. They wished to speak to him alone and all three went into Breitenbuch's bedroom. Tresckow had heard that Breitenbuch was to fly to the *Führer*'s headquarters in two days' time and had hurried across with Oertzen from headquarters Second Army. He now asked Breitenbuch whether he realized what a responsibility he would be carrying that day. He would be holding Germany's fate in his hand; it would depend on him whether this miserable war with its air raids on women and children and its hundreds of thousands of casualties was to continue. At the end Oertzen smilingly produced a 'bomb' from his briefcase. This type, Oertzen explained, was a complete certainty and this single specimen had been obtained with great difficulty from Switzerland. It should be concealed underneath the tunic, against the chest and between two buttons; at some suitable opportunity he should ignite the bomb and clasp Hitler until it exploded.

Well prepared though he was, Breitenbuch was taken aback by the proposal but he was ready to have the 'bomb' explained to him. It was of metal and looked like a small grenade, $8\frac{1}{2}$ ins long and 3 ins in diameter; it weighed about $\frac{3}{4}$ lb, much the same as a hand grenade.[33] The fuse was set in the base and by turning the base cap could be set for three timings – 1 second, 3 seconds or 3 minutes. Oertzen suggested that it be set at 3 seconds which would be done beforehand, not necessarily at the time of igniting.[34] At the right time the fuse was set off by a small button.

Breitenbuch was sceptical. He would have no opportunity of testing this bomb or finding out its effect. Since he would be sacrificing himself, it seemed important to have every assurance of success. He foresaw difficulties in igniting the bomb unobtrusively in Hitler's presence. Based on his own experience and attempts Tresckow had long since reached the conclusion that no method could be more sure than a bomb with a preset time fuse and that a pistol attack by an individual had virtually no hope of success. On the other hand, in the same way as Bussche had had his own ideas about his bomb, Breitenbuch was only willing to risk and sacrifice his life in a way which he thought reasonable and this Tresckow had to accept. Breitenbuch decided that, being a good pistol shot, he would try that way. He would have to leave his service revolver with his belt in the cloakroom before going into the conference and so he proposed also to carry a loaded 7·65 mm Browning in his trouser pocket. Tresckow pointed out to him that he must aim only for the head or neck since Hitler wore protective clothing against pistol shots.

On 9 March 1944 Busch and Breitenbuch flew in Hitler's 'Condor' piloted by Hans Baur from Minsk to Breslau, where Busch spent 10 March with his family. On 11 March they flew on to Salzburg where they arrived about 10 a.m. Tresckow had meanwhile passed a 'preliminary warning' to the conspirators in Berlin. From Salzburg the Field Marshal and his aide were driven to the 'Berghof' in Hitler's super-charged Mercedes. There was plenty of time before the briefing conference which never took place before midday. Breitenbuch used the interval to send to his wife, as agreed, his valuables such as his rings and wristwatch.

As it so happened, on 11 March Field Marshal Busch, Colonel von der Gröben, his operations officer, and Captain von Breitenbuch were the only officers summoned to the briefing conference from the front. Usually on such occasions several Commanders-in-Chief and their aides were assembled. Breitenbuch was therefore the only aide from the front who was present. Shortly before the time announced there gathered in the anteroom to the famous great 'hall' of the 'Berghof': Busch, Breitenbuch, Gröben, Keitel, Jodl and Goebbels. Breitenbuch had taken off his cap and belt with his 8 mm service pistol but he still had his loaded Browning in his trouser pocket. Under his arm he carried a briefcase containing the papers which the Field Marshal would need for his briefing and which, as the aide, he would produce as called for.

Finally the doors to the conference room opened and a man in SS uniform announced that Hitler invited the gentlemen to enter. Breitenbuch moved towards the door with his briefcase, the last in line as the most junior. The SS man, however, held him by the arm and said that aides were not to be present at the briefing conference that day. Breitenbuch protested and Busch turned round saying that he needed his aide at the briefing. But it was all to no avail; Breitenbuch was not allowed in and Busch had to deal with his papers himself.

Even before this Breitenbuch had not exactly been calmness itself but he now became a bundle of nerves. He was alone in the great anteroom where from time to time, obviously deliberately, an SS man appeared, did something trivial, took along a drink or simply passed through. From previous experience Breitenbuch knew that these SS men were always to be seen near Hitler and he had some knowledge of the security precautions. In contrast to previous occasions, however, this time he had a loaded pistol in his pocket – very difficult to explain if discovered – and he had intended to shoot Hitler. In his state of mind any glance in his direction by an SS man seemed to indicate that his plan was known or suspected. How else could his unusual exclusion from the conference be explained? He was convinced that his plan must have been betrayed or discovered. All he wanted now was to get rid of his useless but dangerous pistol as soon as he could; his plan was clearly impracticable. Whether in fact or in his imagination, however, the watch kept on him was too strict.

At last his vigil was over. Busch emerged from the conference and Breitenbuch drove with him to Klessheim Castle near Salzburg where they dined. Then they flew back to Minsk. There Breitenbuch found Tresckow waiting for him in headquarters Army Group Centre and his first words were: 'Well, Breitenbuch, the thing was blown'.[35] Tresckow assumed that one or other of his telephone calls to Berlin had aroused suspicion and led to a tightening of security precautions.

Soon after 11 March Breitenbuch had to go to the Obersalzberg once more with Field Marshal Busch but he never even considered making another attempt. Later he said: 'One can only do that sort of thing once.'[36] He did not think that he could stand the nervous strain again and in fact Stauffenberg was the only one of all the potential assassins to do so. Breitenbuch's last visit to Hitler's headquarters with Busch was in Berlin between 15 and 20 April 1945; after talking to the *Führer* Busch came out saying that the 'great turning point' would come soon and the war would then be won.

37 Procurement of Explosive

March, April and May 1944 were comparatively 'quiet' months for the conspiracy since no real opportunity for an assassination attempt presented itself. They were more than fully occupied, however, with all sorts of other endeavours and preparations. The conspirators were patriotic Germans and very good soldiers; they had no wish to damage their country or its Army; their object was to save both from ruin. They therefore took their official duties most seriously and did their utmost to fulfil them. They could only discuss or deal with plans for the *coup* in greater or less haste, during short momentary intervals or when they would otherwise have been sleeping or resting. This fact must always be remembered since it had a definite influence on the quality of the preparations.[1] Obviously no one could wait until he had more time. The object was to bring the senseless slaughter and destruction to an end, in the interests both of Germany and of mankind and to save the German *Reich*. So the work went on; but it was a labour of Sisyphus because something was always happening to upset the carefully constructed house of cards.

One of the major difficulties was the procurement of explosive, curious though this may seem for a conspiracy so closely connected with the military; it was even more difficult to keep it. Danger of discovery was great and the conspirators were taking an enormous risk. None of the officers who handled the various 'bombs' could legitimately have them in their possession for more than a day or two. Such things were governed by strict regulations and it would have been difficult to explain, for instance, why Major-General Stieff should be keeping explosives and fuses in his house for weeks at a time. The constancy of all those involved after 20 July explains why the *Gestapo* were only able to establish roughly the origin and history of the explosive used on that day. Of the attempt of March 1943 the *Gestapo* knew nothing at all and so never even looked for the bomb intended for use then.

As already mentioned,[2] the British 'clams' used by Tresckow and Schlabrendorff for the attempt on 13 March 1943 were recovered in OKH by Schlabrendorff before they had been discovered, were exchanged for a parcel really containing liqueurs and then defused. Schlabrendorff took them to Berlin, where he handed them to Gersdorff during the night 20/21 March. After his own abortive attempt Gersdorff took them back to Army Group Centre and gave them to Tresckow. The *Gestapo* knew nothing of all this.

Equally they never knew that, from September 1943 to January 1944, Gersdorff kept a package of British plastic explosive in the guest room of his brother's house in Breslau and eventually took it away with him.[3]

As far as can be discovered today, between September 1943 and June 1944 three or four 'major deliveries' of explosive designed for assassination purposes took place. The Commission of Inquiry formed by *Amt* IV of the RSHA (the *Gestapo*) was really only able to discover two to three.[4] They only made progress, in fact, when lying had become useless and would only lead to unnecessary torture, when, for instance, other precise evidence was available or suicides, such as those of Schrader and Freytag-Loringhoven of the *Abwehr*, gave them a lead. Actually only two 'deliveries' were discovered – or three counting one consignment which was discovered, 'officialized' and then recaptured by the conspirators. At least two others were never discovered at all. The prisoners – primarily Stieff, Hagen, Klamroth and Knaak – only admitted what could be extracted from them by torture or otherwise proved to them. Thanks to the steadfastness of their fellow-conspirators the *Gestapo* never suspected that (for instance) Philipp Freiherr von Boeselager, Fabian von Schlabrendorff, Freiherr von Gersdorff or Freiherr von dem Bussche were involved in the procurement of explosive.

It seems that the first consignment was a package of captured British plastic explosive in its original wrapping marked 'Hexogen'; this was taken to Berlin by Tresckow in late September or early October 1943 and given to Stauffenberg in October. Stauffenberg personally handed it to Stieff in 'Mauerwald' camp at the end of that month.[5] Stieff kept some of it in his quarters and some in his office in the headquarters in East Prussia. Some time before 20 November Stieff passed the explosive and fuses to Major Kuhn and during the night of 20 November he, together with Lieutenant von Hagen, hid them near a wooden watchtower of 'Mauerwald' camp. The two were seen, but not recognized, by a patrol of 631 Field Security Police Unit. The two made off and the police let loose a tracker dog which located the explosive but then took the trail to the wrong hut, where the search was abandoned.[6] The police handed the explosive over to the Counter-espionage Group of OKH. Lieutenant-Colonel Schrader, the head of the Group, and his Section Head, Colonel Radke, took no action and in December suspended enquiries; the search for the identity of the two officers and the source of the explosive therefore petered out. The head of No 12 Section of the Army General Staff at this time was Colonel Hansen; after discovery of the explosive he summoned Major Kuhn and told him that, via the dog and the patrol, two packages of explosive had landed up in his office; he would have to keep one for the SD. The other he handed back to Kuhn with one or two suitably sarcastic comments.

In June 1944 Colonel Wessel Freiherr von Freytag-Loringhoven became head of the Staff Duties section. At the end of the month he took over the explosive and fuses from Schrader and passed them on to Stauffenberg.[7] Stauffenberg kept them, together with other explosive and fuses, partly in his office and partly in that of Lieutenant-Colonel Fritz von der Lancken in the headquarters of Potsdam District (*Wehrbezirk*). They were usually returned there in between the various assassination attempts in July.

When Bussche had volunteered to make an attempt, Stieff had offered him the British explosive, the same which Kuhn and Hagen had buried. Bussche preferred German material and, through Kuhn and Lieutenant-Colonel Bernhard Klamroth of the OKH Organisation Section, Hagen was commissioned to obtain some from Major Knaak, commanding 630 Pioneer Battalion, then located east of Orscha and forming part of IV Corps under Army Group Centre. Hagen flew to Minsk where he was met by Knaak's car, took delivery of the goods and flew back to East Prussia. The consignment consisted of a number of 'grenade fuses, fuse lengths, a box of detonators and two standard explosive charges' which Hagen handed over to Stieff.[8] Stieff kept the explosives in a drawer of his office desk in 'Mauerwald' until March 1944 when the headquarters moved to Berchtesgaden; the fuses he kept in a desk in his quarters. Before the move he took the explosive also to his quarters in East Prussia. At the end of May he made use of a duty trip by Klamroth and Hagen to send everything to Berlin,[9] where it was delivered to Stauffenberg.[10] It is not clear whether this was solely the material obtained from Knaak or whether it included the explosive which had been buried and recovered.

A cousin of Colonel von Tresckow, Arnold von Tresckow who worked in *OKH/Heereswaffenamt/WaPrüf 5* (OKH/Army Weapons Dept./Weapons Testing 5) had also procured explosives of both British and German origin. At the end of 1943 he brought home with him a briefcase full, and later, in April or May 1944, someone sent by Colonel von Tresckow picked it up.[11]

On 20 July 1944 Stauffenberg and his aide, Werner von Haeften, had with them two packages of plastic explosive. On the drive from 'Wolfschanze' back to the airport Haeften threw one package out of the car; it was later discovered by a pioneer unit and the *Gestapo* described it as German material, though they originally thought that the explosive actually used in the attack was British. *Gestapo* reports, however, are not completely definite about the material discovered, referring to it somewhat vaguely as 'a combination of German and British explosive'.[12] The officials of the Technical Institute of Criminology under the *Reich* Criminal Police Office of the RSHA had no wish to report too precisely; some of them were only too ready to shield those not yet involved in the investigations.[13]

The Technical Institute eventually concluded that both the explosive in the package thrown out by Haeften and the explosive actually used were of German manufacture and the fuses were of British origin. It may well not have been obtained by any of those referred to above or anybody questioned by the *Gestapo*. In the spring of 1944 WASAG Chemicals Ltd had begun manufacture of an explosive entitled 'Plastit W' in their factories at Reinsdorf and Sythen. After the capture of considerable quantities of the British plastic WASAG had been commissioned to develop something similar and even better for the German Army. The result was 'Plastit W' consisting of 64% hexogen, 24% dinitrotoluene, 9% mononitronaphtaline, 3% collodium wool and a small quantity of dinitronaphtaline. This explosive had certain very desirable qualities; its effect was great and combustion was almost complete. Possibly, therefore, the conspirators thought that they now had a miracle explosive of almost unlimited efficacy.[14]

No one after 20 July 1944 ever definitely established who had obtained the explosive used by Stauffenberg or whether, as seems probable, it had been ordered and manufactured specially for the assassination of Hitler. Equally it is not known whether any significance should be attached to the fact that Willi Fromm, manager of the WASAG factory in Reinsdorf, was a cousin of the Colonel-General.[15] In any case Arthur Nebe seems to have been heavily involved in the procurement of explosive. Early in 1944 he asked a chemist in his office what weight of explosive was required to give maximum combustion and blast; he was proposing to construct a bomb 'for an attack on Stalin'. The answer was that 5 kilogrammes (ca. 10 lbs) would be adequate but that less than 2 kilogrammes (ca. 4 lbs) was no good at all.[16] A fortnight before Stauffenberg's attack a number of British time fuses of the type which he used were ordered and collected from the Technical Institute by an official of *Amt* IV A II in the RSHA.

38 Communications Planning

Even since the opposition had seriously considered killing Hitler in his headquarters or, as the phrase was, 'cordoning off' the headquarters, much thought had been given to the technical signals problem of cutting the headquarters off from the outside world. If Hitler was only to be arrested there was no hope of success unless it could be so cut off; he would have been able personally to issue counter-orders and make speeches; hardly anyone would have listened to the conspirators. Even if Hitler were dead, however, his remaining entourage might create many difficulties. Keitel, Jodl and Dönitz in particular were loyal followers; Göring and Himmler were less loyal but no less dangerous. If they were present in the headquarters when an assassination attempt was made, but not at the briefing conference, they could probably rapidly take control of the entire machine. If the *coup* was to succeed, therefore, if the measures taken in Berlin, other German cities and the occupied territories were not to be subjected to pressures from the old rulers, it was essential that technical signals precautions be taken to isolate the headquarters, at least for the first few hours.

For this the conspirators could count on active assistance from a number of outstanding experts in the Army signals service. The most important was General Erich Fellgiebel; both his fellow-officers and his subordinates had an extraordinarily high opinion of him; he was regarded as a highly-educated, sensitive soldier, upright and human, well versed in the natural sciences with a bent for philosophy and an outstanding expert in everything to do with communications.[1] Even before the war Fellgiebel had been an outspoken critic of the regime, although he knew that his telephone had been tapped before 1938. He also knew, however, how indispensable he was; he remained fearless and straightforward. He loathed Hitler as an unintelligent inhuman tyrant; in wartime he loathed him even more as a militarily incompetent, culpable instigator of destruction. In his capacity as Chief of *Wehrmacht-Nachrichten-Verbindungen* (WNV, *Wehrmacht* Communications) and at the same time Chief of *Heeres-Nachrichten-Wesen* (HNW, Army Communications) Fellgiebel had undisputed authority over all Army communications provided he remained within the directives of his military superiors (Hitler, Keitel and until December 1941 Brauchitsch). Despite his title of Chief WNV, however, his authority over *Wehrmacht* communications was limited to those running to the so-called OKW theatres of war and he had no authority over those of the Navy and *Luftwaffe*. In their case he had no right even to know about their system and the same applied to the SS.[2]

Fellgiebel's Chief of Staff in his capacity as Army Chief Signals Officer was Colonel Kurt Hahn and his Chief of Staff as Chief WNV was Lieutenant-General Fritz Thiele; both were members of the conspiracy, were ready actively to assist the *coup* and knew all about it. Fellgiebel and Hahn were located with OKH, usually in 'Mauerwald' camp, but when the *Führer*'s headquarters was in the 'Berghof' they were often in Berchtesgaden. Thiele had his permanent office in the Bendlerstrasse, Berlin.

Other members of the conspiracy in the Army Signals Directorate were: Major Heinz Burchardt, head of the Coordination Group (Personnel); Major Höpfner, head of Group IV (Radio communications) and from 10 July head of Group I (Operations, organization, training); Major Binder, Höpfner's successor as head of Group IV; Lieutenant-Colonel Maultzsch, Höpfner's predecessor as head of Group I (on 10 July 1944 he was posted as a regimental commander in II Corps where Tresckow was Chief of Staff); Major Degner, head of Group V (Transport communications). In July 1944 some of these were still in 'Mauerwald' and some in 'Zeppelin' camp near Zossen since at that time OKH was in process of transfer to 'Maybach' camp, Zossen. To ensure a smooth change the exchanges and circuits existing in East Prussia had been precisely reproduced in Zossen; even the nomenclature was retained with the addition 'Bu' (bunker). Thus 'Anna' ('Mauerwald') in East Prussia became 'Anna-Bu' in Zossen, 'Emma' (Lötzen) became 'Emma-Bu', 'Nora' (Angerburg) 'Nora-Bu' and so forth. The move was cancelled when the *Führer*'s headquarters remained in 'Wolfschanze' after 20 July.[3] Finally another conspirator must be mentioned – Colonel Kurt Hassel, Chief of Signals to C-in-C Replacement Army and in this capacity a subordinate of General Olbricht.

In spring or summer 1943 a meeting took place in Olbricht's house at which Beck, Goerdeler and F. D. v.d. Schulenburg were present. Fellgiebel told them that, when the proposed attack and *coup* happened, he would 'secure' the signals communications for the use of the conspiracy, in other words 'all necessary orders and information from the conspirators would be passed through smoothly, while other subscribers would be cut off'. Some weeks before 20 July and again early in that month he reiterated his promise to Stauffenberg. On the other hand he never promised that he would destroy or cause to be destroyed any signals installations.[4]

Four means of communication were available to the *Führer*'s head-quarters: telephone, teleprinter, radio (both speech and morse), a courier service by land and air. If telephone communications failed, the teleprinter was still available; both used the same cables, exchanges and repeater stations, however, so if the circuit was broken, by cable-cutting for instance, teleprint communications would fail also. Even then the radio and courier services still remained.

The courier service could only be interrupted by physical force, by cordoning off the headquarters, and this would have to be done by 'reliable' units stationed in the immediate vicinity. This would take at least one to two hours, however; only in the later stages could one hope to have the necessary number of troops available and even then there was likely to be fighting with neighbouring SS and Police units which were under the orders of Himmler. In the first few hours, therefore, couriers might get through, though their chances of achieving anything were small.

Equally it was almost impossible to interrupt radio traffic from the headquarters by anything other than force and this the handful of conspirators would not have available in the first few hours. There were sets in Hitler's special train known as 'Brandenburg' and the special trains 'Braunschweig' (Keitel) and 'Franken I and II' (OKW Operations Staff). The trains were parked outside the restricted areas and were not normally accessible; again soldiers would be required to enforce wireless silence. Moreover, when parked in stations, the trains were always connected to the telephone and teleprinter network. Other sets were located on Rastenburg airfield, in the headquarters of Göring, Himmler and Ribbentrop and in that of *Führer* Air Communications Detachment; the main headquarters radio station was at Heiligenlinde, some 12 miles from 'Wolfschanze'. The *Reich* Press officer had his own set in the headquarters and no one knew precisely what Martin Bormann had, but he certainly had his own telephone and teleprinter lines. Similar radio facilities were available in Berchtesgaden, Berlin and Vinnitsa in the Ukraine.

In practice, therefore, radio communications could only be stopped on orders. Bormann, Himmler and Ribbentrop were unlikely to obey orders given by Fellgiebel and he would have no troops with which to enforce them. Nevertheless he was justified in hoping that, in the first few hours when surprise and confusion would reign, radio might prove too complicated for any effective counter-action by the regime. Where the wave-lengths concerned were known or could be monitored, they could be jammed. Older officers (in the *Wehrkreise* for instance) might be as sceptical about a radio message coming suddenly over the air as they proved to be about the telephoned orders from the Bendlerstrasse in Berlin given by unauthorized officers. Asking questions over the radio was difficult and private conversation impossible. The most important means of communication, therefore, remained the telephone and teleprinter.

In this field Fellgiebel really was the master, always provided that his directives accorded with those of his superiors. At the time in question the *Führer*'s headquarters might be in either 'Wolfschanze' or the 'Berghof' and both were connected by telephone and teleprint to: all Army Group headquarters, headquarters of *Wehrmacht* C's-in-C and commanders in the occupied territories, ministries in Berlin or in their emergency location, the RSHA, *Wehrkreis* headquarters, Himmler's, Göring's and Ribbentrop's headquarters in the field and so forth. The exchanges in the 'Berghof' were connected or 'looped' to these various stations via repeater stations in Au (and thence to

Salzburg) and Bad Reichenhall-Rosenheim. The 'Wolfschanze' exchanges were looped via Rastenburg and Angerburg. Later (from end 1942/early 1943) there was an additional cable via Rhein and Lötzen.[5] Apart from Bormann's secret lines, therefore, an order from Fellgiebel should have been enough to isolate either of the headquarters; all he had to do was to instruct the repeater stations to pass no long-distance traffic. This was, of course, no small matter and depended on cooperation by the technicians in the repeater stations since no destruction of installations was being considered.

For normal telephone traffic 'carrier frequency output circuits' were installed in the repeater stations. The low speech frequency was transposed on to one of 160,000 cycles per second used by the transmitter and separated at the receiving end. This produced better range and cable load than with a lower frequency. The low-frequency lines were retained, however, and used for service communications between the repeater stations. If carrier frequency traffic was interrupted, therefore, the low-frequency lines between repeater stations would still be available; to put these out of action the cables would have to be cut at distribution points.

Communications could, therefore, be blocked by issuance of orders, but not completely. It would be complete enough, however, if the previous rulers were prevented from issuing orders by other means or if their orders were no longer being obeyed. Fellgiebel hoped that his great authority would be enough to ensure that his orders were obeyed even by the SS; of course they would not do so out of sympathy for him or the *coup*, but he hoped to convince them that nothing but damage to the regime's interests could result if news of the *coup* were allowed to penetrate to the outside world. This was one of the reasons in favour of spreading the story that the regime was being protected against a *putsch* by the Party or SS.

There remained the secret circuits and connections (there were no actual secret *lines*). Bormann had a secret teleprint circuit running from his bunker in Area I to the teleprint exchange in Area II, by-passing the telephone exchange; this enabled him to send and receive teleprints direct from his bunker. His circuits were naturally routed through the repeater stations but the Post Office officials there did not know exactly *how* they were routed (i.e. through which terminals and switchboard positions) nor therefore how they could be cut. To be certain they would have to disconnect *all* terminals and positions and this would take a long time, at least a whole day if no damage was to be done; there was therefore no object in it. Moreover it would have taken an equally long time to put the repeater stations back to normal. In addition to Bormann's there were probably other secret circuits around the headquarters; Himmler very probably had one and possibly also Göring and Ribbentrop.

Unless, therefore, lasting damage was to be done by cutting cables in the repeater stations, these circuits could not be interrupted; the only alternative was to find Post Office officials who would cooperate and it was obviously improbable that an adequate number could be found and persuaded. For the mere issuance of his orders Fellgiebel would have had to divulge much that could not have been kept secret. He could therefore only rely on the knowledge and goodwill of the Post Office people. Fellgiebel's successor, General Albert Praun, who did not know all the details, criticized the preparations made by Fellgiebel and his fellow-conspirators as inadequate and imprecise; at the same time, however, he admitted that it was not practical to give junior and medium-level personnel the information necessary for thorough preparation.[6] Major Wolf, commanding the *Führer* Signals Detachment, described the situation as follows: 'Technically it would have been easier for two or three junior Post Office officials to isolate 'Wolfschanze' than it was for Fellgiebel or Hahn. For them it was almost impossible to find the assistance essential for their project. Had the *coup* succeeded, of course, there would have been a good chance of their orders being executed.'

The primary object on the day of the *coup* was not to stop all communication between the *Führer*'s headquarters and the outside world but to gain control of the *Wehrmacht* and the apparatus of military command as quickly and smoothly as possible. Fellgiebel's orders and his precautions should have been adequate for this, always provided that the assassination attempt succeeded. Other existing secret channels such as those of the SS, the Party, perhaps the *Gestapo*, the SD and the Foreign Ministry could have been brought under control after the first two or three hours. This could have been done by supervision and checking in the repeater stations. A complete stoppage of communications was not in the interests of the conspiracy. The newly-to-be-formed government would wish to end the war as quickly as possible but it would not wish simply to allow the fronts to collapse; it needed the existing command apparatus to ensure an orderly withdrawal, particularly in the west, and maintenance of the front in the east. Both from the military and technical points of view any destruction or prolonged paralysation of communications would have been madness.

Particularly in the immediate post-war years Fellgiebel has been presented as the man who, next to Stauffenberg, was responsible for the failure of the *coup*. The main reason for the collapse of the *coup d'état*, it was said, was the failure of the assassination attempt, but all could still have been saved had Fellgiebel done his job and blown up the telephone exchange in 'Wolfschanze'.[7] It was even maintained that the second package of explosive which Stauffenberg and Haeften had with them, was intended for this purpose (in that case why did they take it away again and throw it away?).

These criticisms of Fellgiebel stem, not from first-hand witnesses but from hearsay. No primary sources say that Fellgiebel promised personally to destroy the telephone exchange in 'Wolfschanze', Area I. To some extent the idea that on the day of the *coup* Fellgiebel was supposed to destroy certain signals installations is based on his and Hahn's statements to the *Gestapo*; they said that they had agreed 'to *act when the coup took place*. There was therefore no need for much preparation'.[8] This was misleading and was intended, as in fact it did, to save the lives of other conspirators and people with knowledge of the secret.

In fact the preparations made by Fellgiebel, Hahn and Thiele were as comprehensive as they could possibly be. In no less than five sections of the Army Chief Signals Officer's office were leading members of the conspiracy or semi-initiated supporters.[9] Fellgiebel therefore merits no criticism. It cannot be overemphasized that destruction of the telephone communications in 'Wolfschanze', Area I, was impossible in the first place and senseless as well.

The signals bunker in 'Wolfschanze', Area I, was proof against the heaviest bomb then in use in any air force. Even if an explosion had been set off inside it (and Fellgiebel would never have done this without first clearing it of any occupants, which again would have made success questionable), the damage would have been very limited. There would have been a great tangle, the switchboards and keys would have been destroyed, numerous wires cut and the interior of the vital Area I exchange wrecked. Nevertheless within at most half an hour a repair squad would have been able to reestablish some form of communication and it would have been possible once more to telephone from the exchange bunker.

If entry into the bunker was inadvisable, for fear of further explosions for instance, there were sufficient other possibilities. Outside the bunker were cable inspection pits, one on the north and one on the south where there was an annex to the bunker. Technicians could easily have reestablished communications using emergency equipment. Fellgiebel would therefore have had to blow up the pits as well but that would have required a total of three charges and an equal number of accomplices. The inspection pits were nearly bomb-proof and were fitted with heavy steel and concrete manhole covers which could only be lifted with special gear stored in the bunker – a further difficulty in placing the charges. All wires would probably not have been cut so that one or two telephones could quickly have been reconnected.[10] In the improbable event that damage to the pits had made this impossible or impracticable a number of cable check-points existed throughout the headquarters installation where access to the cables (3–6 ft underground) was possible without digging them up. Finally there were connections at 'Görlitz' station, already mentioned; this was outside Area I but still only a few hundred yards from the centre of the *Führer*'s headquarters.

Detailed examination, therefore, shows that, even using force, it was almost impossible to eliminate the Area I signal centre for more than half an hour – to do so Fellgiebel would have had to arrive with a regular demolition party and systematically blow up everything. In any case, owing to the decentralization of communications within the headquarters, such an operation would not have been effective. Allowance had been made for the loss of one signals bunker and so the telephone exchange had been located in Area I and the teleprinter exchange in Area II. It would have been possible, without great difficulty, to telephone from the teleprinter exchange, at least to the most important points in all German-controlled territory including Berlin and the *Wehrkreis* headquarters. This could also have been done from Bormann's bunker in Area I (the necessary equipment could have been quickly produced) since, as already mentioned, Bormann's secret teleprinter circuit ran direct to the teleprinter exchange, by-passing the Area I exchange. Bormann and the

Reich Press Officer also had direct circuits to Berlin for normal newspaper teleprint traffic.[11]

Finally there was a further security precaution which would have prevented the total isolation of the *Führer*'s headquarters, even had the destruction of both exchanges been practicable. In autumn 1943, to guard against just such an eventuality, construction of a 'tented camp exchange' had been planned and it had been tested on 1 and 2 October.[12] The test had shown that, even if the entire *Führer*'s headquarters were destroyed, construction of a full tented camp with *all* essential communications would not take more than four to five hours. If the headquarters had not been totally destroyed, of course, less time would be required.

The opposition did not, therefore, really need or want the destruction of specific bunkers or exchanges. What they required was some procedure which, during the first few hours of the *coup*, would prevent the previous regime using the communications but allow the conspirators to do so. This was the solution towards which Fellgiebel and his associates were working and they were continually discussing the problem and its implications with Stauffenberg, Stieff and General Wagner, the Deputy Chief of the General Staff of the Army. The best method was to gain control of the East Prussian repeater stations, Rastenburg, Angerburg, Allenstein and, in the case of OKH, Lötzen. These were the vulnerable points through which all the 'Wolfschanze' communications ran. Secondly control must be established over the exchanges in the OKH camp 'Zeppelin' near Zossen and in the Bendlerstrasse, Berlin.

Starting in spring 1943, if not earlier, Hahn was primarily responsible for recruiting officers in important posts and he also engineered a number of postings.[13] As planning proceeded it naturally became clear that, if the headquarters in question were to be completely cut off, a considerable organization and highly complicated preparations were required.[14] For a time the conspirators wondered whether to recruit NCOs as well as officers but eventually abandoned the idea since most NCOs had been in the Hitler Youth and were not, therefore, so firm or 'reliable' in their attitude or views as the officers.[15]

Should the assassination attempt take place in the 'Berghof', the repeater stations in Berchtesgaden, Salzburg, Bad Reichenhall and Rosenheim would be blocked. Munich too was of major importance in the south and would have to be paralysed, although it could be by-passed through other stations. Fellgiebel did not rate the importance of radio communications and 'secret lines' very high; the lines were in fact only circuits in the repeater stations and their effectiveness for military purposes was very limited.[16] On 22 May 1944 Fellgiebel told his aide, Lieutenant Arntz, of the plan in broad terms; should the *coup* take place in the south Arntz was to be responsible for 'securing' the repeater station in Salzburg; Berchtesgaden, Bad Reichenhall and Rosenheim were to be dealt with by others whom Fellgiebel did not name. He himself intended to take over the telephone exchange in the 'Berghof'.

Instructions for 'Wolfschanze' were similar. Once Hitler had been killed,

Fellgiebel proposed to order the repeater stations in Rastenburg, Lötzen and Angerburg to switch off. As a security precaution they were camouflaged and, in Rastenburg for instance, were not invariably located in the post office; their position was known, however, to the army signals authorities.[17] Here again Arntz was commissioned to go to Lötzen on the day in question in a motorcycle and side-car and pass on orders from Fellgiebel or Hahn to disconnect all terminals; he was only given his detailed instructions, however, on the morning of 20 July. In OKH Hahn was to do the necessary and silence station 'Anna'.

In addition Hahn attempted to draw someone in 'Wolfschanze' into the conspiracy – Lieutenant-Colonel Sander, the *Wehrmacht* Signals Officer. Despite orders to the contrary from Lieutenant-General Schmundt, at Hahn's request Sander kept Fellgiebel continuously informed of Hitler's movements and any planned shift of the headquarters. But he would go no further. When Hahn tried to persuade him to install secret teleprinters in his own office and that of Hahn in 'Mauerwald', Sander was not prepared to do so; so large a machine, he thought, would certainly attract the attention of visitors and others in the headquarters; there were already enough in Area II and he needed no more. It would, of course, have been of great advantage to the conspirators to have a more or less private circuit available.

All Fellgiebel's plans were based on the assumption that Hitler would be successfully assassinated. Otherwise he would still be tied to Hitler's and Keitel's orders which he could only contravene for a very short time without being relieved of his office. There was therefore no plan to cater for the failure of the attempt; if this happened, nothing could be done. This seems curious since it means that, if the attempt failed and was then discovered, all was lost. Action should not have been entirely dependent on the success of the attempt; at least some effort should have been made to proceed with the *coup d'état* or to show the world that the opposition was active and prepared to stake everything – as indeed it did. But there was no plan to do so; it would have been a plan for failure. The conspiracy as a whole did not deal in alternative plans.[18] Such things could only be discussed, if at all, in the inmost circle. Success was dependent on numerous waverers and, had there not been an air of complete confidence, they could not have been carried along; everything, therefore, had to be based on the certainty of success. It seems, however, that even in the inner circle everyone was convinced that the bomb would do its work – provided it went off. For them failure meant primarily failure of the bomb to explode and this did not necessarily entail detection. They had already lived through a bomb failure followed by non-discovery. On the other hand they had no experience of the effect of the explosive under the actual conditions in which the attempt would be made; there was a limit to the amount of testing that could be done.

In Berlin preparations were concentrated on the 'Zeppelin' exchange near Zossen, the Bendlerstrasse office block and naval headquarters. No access to or control over *Luftwaffe* communications seemed possible. In autumn 1943 Berthold Graf von Stauffenberg, Captain Alfred Kranzfelder and Dr Sydney

Jessen, all of naval headquarters, joined the conspiracy and they approached Captain Kupfer, head of the signal section in naval headquarters; he agreed to ensure that, when the *coup* took place, teleprinter messages from the conspirators would be passed without delay and that his channels would be closed to any counter-orders. Towards the end of November 1943, however, naval headquarters was dispersed to various localities outside Berlin such as camp 'Bismarck' near Eberswalde and camp 'Koralle' near Bernau and Kupfer had consequently to withdraw his promise. Central control of naval communications no longer seemed possible.[19] Colonel Hahn was more successful in his efforts to control the exchange and repeater station in Zossen.

From autumn 1943 cautious hints were dropped to Majors Burchardt, Degner and Höpfner, the heads of the Signals Sections, about a possible 'happening'. From October 1943 they were more or less in a state of permanent alert, awaiting developments. They and other officers were only gradually let further into the secret early in 1944, particularly between March and June, when various talks were held, some in East Prussia and some in the Strub barracks near Berchtesgaden.

On 19 March 1944 Colonel Hahn came into Degner's office in 'Mauerwald' and said: 'Stalin's on his deathbed'. Hitler was then in Berchtesgaden but was expected back in 'Wolfschanze' in one or two days time. It was anticipated that he would fly and, according to Hahn's information, the aircraft was to be shot down over the Böhmerwald. But Hitler came by train.[20] As on future occasions, Hahn's remark indicated to Degner that within his sphere, in other words in 'Mauerwald', he should ensure that communications remained open to the conspirators but were blocked for the previous rulers as soon as the assassination took place.

As long as OKH, and therefore Fellgiebel's staff, were still in 'Mauerwald', this was not too difficult. Degner worked out the necessary measures and was ready to enforce them at any time. After the move to Zossen in mid-July 1944 he had to make fresh preparations and with speed. This he succeeded in doing; he was soon on such good terms with the Post Office officials in charge of the cable and switching stations (whom he knew already) that he was given a pass to enter Post Office premises. He was thus able to locate the important terminals where the main lines linking 'Zeppelin' and 'Wolfschanze' should be cut.

Similarly, as time went on and they talked further with Fellgiebel and Hahn, Burchardt and Höpfner became increasingly involved with the opposition and were given more details of the plans. On 13 or 14 July 1944 they were fully briefed by Hahn in Zossen largely on the lines of what actually happened on 20 July.[21] When the moment came, Thiele in the Bendlerstrasse was to issue the necessary orders to Zossen. Codewords were agreed which Hahn was to pass to Zossen from East Prussia. 'The signals equipment is leaving on the 15th' meant 'The attack will take place on the 15th'. 'The signals equipment has left' meant 'The assassination has taken place'.[22]

In addition to the preparations made by Fellgiebel and Hahn General Olbricht took a hand in the control of communications and initiated the necessary measures. Unfortunately there was a certain lack of cooperation between Colonel Hahn, Chief of Staff to the Army Chief Signals Officer, and Colonel Hassel, Chief Signals Officer (from 30 November 1943) to C-in-C Replacement Army.[23] As head of the *Wehrmacht* Communications Group of OKW Lieutenant-General Thiele was a direct subordinate of Fellgiebel who in turn, in his capacity as *Wehrmacht* Communications Officer was under the OKW Operations Staff; Thiele therefore had Chief of Staff status, although Fellgiebel had formally no staff dealing with *Wehrmacht* communications; Colonel Hassel, on the other hand, was the most senior signals officer in HQ Replacement Army and was directly subordinate to the head of the AHA, General Olbricht.[24] Thiele had the wider command authority; he commanded two High-Command Signals Regiments and the following staff sections: Radio Communications, Long-distance Communications, Special Duties, Codes and Ciphers, Technical Signals Resources.[25] Colonel Hassel was in charge of the Signals Units Section (Inspectorate, one of the 'arms' sections in AHA), of the Signals Service Section, Signals Equipment Section and Female Personnel Section.[26] As part of the Signals Service Section under Colonel Köllner, Hassel was in charge of the signal centre in the Bendlerstrasse but he had no authority over the OKH centre in 'Maybach' camp near Zossen which was known as 'Zeppelin' and primarily served the field Army. Colonel Köllner's office was in the rear wing of the Bendlerstrasse block; behind and adjoining this wing was the exchange which was concrete-protected and had therefore turned into a bunker.[27] Hassel's office, on the other hand, had been evacuated and was in Düppel camp in Zehlendorf.

On 21 November 1942, when the Stalingrad army had been surrounded, Hassel was present at a meeting in Thiele's office with Fellgiebel and certain others.[28] Fellgiebel outlined the war situation, concluding with the statement that the war was clearly lost. Somehow, he said, the leadership must be 'changed'.

The next day Hassel had to report to Olbricht. They agreed that the military situation was bad and Olbricht seized the opportunity to instruct Hassel to compile a list of vulnerable communications points to be guarded in the event of internal disturbances. There were so many foreign workers in and around Berlin, he said, and disturbances were possible at any time; 'Valkyrie' units had, of course, been earmarked for vulnerable points but more should be done for particularly sensitive signals installations; finally not only the *Wehrmacht* communications were important but also those of the SS, the RSHA and the Propaganda Ministry. Hassel suggested in addition the main telegraph office, the Foreign Ministry, the radio stations at Nauen, Strausberg and Rangsdorf airfield and certain other agencies located around Berlin. Hassel compiled a list and brought it to Olbricht who put it in his safe. The list also showed troops required for the protection of each 'vulnerable point'; for the main broadcasting station, for instance, a company was earmarked.[29]

On 1 May 1943 Hassel was posted as Signals Officer of Sixteenth Army but he returned to Berlin on 1 November and was appointed Signals Officer to C-in-C Replacement Army on the 30th. Olbricht and Stauffenberg frequently discussed plans for the *coup* in Hassel's presence; he was regarded as a member of the conspiracy. Olbricht said to Hassel that, now he was back, they must work together as they had before. This applied mainly to the organization for 'vulnerable points', to changes in the plan made necessary by various moves and assembly of the necessary troops to occupy repeater stations, telegraph offices and radio installations near Berlin.[30] Early in July 1944 Hassel arranged for a party of twenty officers to deal with certain important communications objectives on the day of the *coup*. On the evening of 14 July he was given a definite date for the first time – 15 July. Thiele summoned Hassel to his house to tell him.[31] Hassel ordered the officers concerned, including Major Kempe, to remain on call during the weekend.

39 *Internal Political Planning*

A word must now be said about the final preparations in the field of internal politics. Here non-military personalities and groups dominated the scene and the differentiation between the civilian side of the opposition and the special interests of the military is quite clear. Since the first few hours of the *coup* were inevitably governed by the military action and the revolt never progressed beyond this stage, the next part of this book necessarily deals primarily with soldiers and their activities; nevertheless the decisive, fundamental importance of the civilian element in the opposition must not be forgotten. In the preparatory phase it played the major role in deciding the aims of the movement and, when resistance was being hounded to its doom, it once more achieved a tragic prominence through the number of its victims.

We have already seen that the opposition's work in preparing the rising was never-ending owing to continuous changes in circumstances. In view of the rapidly deteriorating war situation, the Allied landing on 6 June 1944 and the approaching end to the war, the conspirators' ideas and plans were thrown into a state of flux again and again.

Final amendments were made to the proclamations held ready ever since October 1943 – to the German people, the Army and to women. In the closing days of June Stauffenberg summoned Professor Fahrner to Berlin once more from Athens.[1] Fahrner was in Berlin from 28 June to 5 July; he spent two days in the naval camp 'Koralle', in the same hut as Berthold von Stauffenberg, taking over the room of Kranzfelder who was on leave; the rest of the time he was in Berthold's flat in the Tristanstrasse, Wannsee, together with Colonel Mertz von Quirnheim and Claus von Stauffenberg. Changes to the earlier drafts were made primarily to take account of Beck's requirements; the proclamation to women was dropped but certain points in it were carried over into the new drafts of the other proclamations. For security reasons only two copies of the proclamations were made and were kept, one in Berthold von Stauffenberg's safe in 'Koralle' and the other in Claus' safe in the Bendlerstrasse.[2]

Briefing of both old and new liaison officers in the *Wehrkreis* HQs continued until shortly before the assassination attempt. Several officers recall that during a commanders' conference called by General Fromm in Krampnitz near Potsdam on 10 July Stauffenberg approached them asking whether they were prepared to participate. Olbricht was also active, primarily dropping hints about the possibility of proclamation of a state of emergency in the near future.[3] Close touch was, of course, maintained with the City Commandant's office and *Wehrkreis* HQ.

This cautious and very limited briefing and preparation of individual officers in the *Wehrkreise* provided no real assurance that the measures necessary for the *coup* would in fact be carried out. The majority of *Wehrkreis* commanders spent a large part, if not the greater part, of the year on tours of inspection and their subordinates too were frequently on the road. There could be no guarantee even that members of the conspiracy would actually be present in the headquarters on the vital day. Uncertainty was increased by postings and other wastage. For this reason and to tighten up communications, Stauffenberg, Olbricht and their co-conspirators double-banked by appointing contact men for the *Wehrkreise* – the OKH liaison officers and the provisional government's political representatives.

In autumn 1943 Beck had demanded a list of political representatives, saying that until it was produced the military neither could nor would act.[4] Towards the end of 1943 F.D.v.d. Schulenburg also demanded a list (Dr Elfriede Nebgen who worked with Jakob Kaiser says that he sent an 'ultimatum') and Goerdeler came up with a similar request. Schulenburg told Kaiser and Dr Josef Wirmer that action would only be taken against Hitler when the list had been handed over. Kaiser found it hard to decide to do so.

The list was complete by the end of 1943 and was handed over in Elfriede Nebgen's house to Graf Schwerin von Schwanenfeld, Beck's representative, Wirmer and Kaiser being present.

The list was drawn up by Stauffenberg himself. The main duty of the liaison officers was to ensure that Berlin's orders were carried out, that instructions issued on D Day were understood and executed and that headquarters was kept continuously informed on the situation in each *Wehrkreis*. The list of OKH liaison officers was continually being altered to cater for changed circumstances. Since both the liaison officers and political representatives were to be briefed on their duties from the conspirators' headquarters, the list was found by the *Gestapo* on 20 July in the Bendlerstrasse signal centre together with other teleprinter messages issued by the opposition.[5] On that day it was as follows:[6]

Wehrkreis I (Königsberg): Lieutenant (res.) Heinrich Graf von Lehndorff (not available for frontline service).

Wehrkreis II (Stettin): Major Hans-Jürgen Graf von Blumenthal, head of Replacements and General Service Section.

Wehrkreis III (Berlin): Major Ulrich von Oertzen.[7]

Wehrkreis IV (Dresden): Major-General Hans Oster (posted to 'OKH Command Reserve' from spring 1943).

Wehrkreis V (Stuttgart): no appointment.

Wehrkreis VI (Münster): no appointment.

Wehrkreis VII (Munich): Major Ludwig Freiherr von Leonrod, reception centre for officer candidates for 17 Cavalry Regiment, Bamberg — engaged by Stauffenberg in December 1943;[8] in reserve from 17 June to 1 July Captain Max Ulrich Graf von Drechsel-Deuffenstetten.[9]

Wehrkreis VIII (Breslau): Captain (res.) Friedrich Scholz-Babisch — commissioned by Stauffenberg in December 1943.[10]

Wehrkreis IX (Kassel): Lieutenant-Colonel Ulrich Freiherr von Sell, Military Assistant to Chancellor Bethmann Hollweg before 1914, at the time in the *Abwehr* censorship office in *Wehrkreis* III.[11]

Wehrkreis X (Hamburg): no appointment.

Wehrkreis XI (Hannover): Colonel Siegfried Wagner, at the time section head in OKW Staff Duties section, Berlin, previously section head in the AHA.

Wehrkreis XII (Wiesbaden): Captain (res.) Hermann Kaiser, War Diary officer in HQ Replacement Army.

Wehrkreis XIII (Nuremberg): Captain (res.) Dietrich Freiherr Truchsess von Wetzhausen, approached by Stauffenberg in January 1944, apparently did not consent explicitly.[12]

Wehrkreis XVII (Vienna): Colonel Rudolf Graf von Marogna-Redwitz, specially employed on staff of AHA.

Wehrkreis XVIII (Salzburg): Colonel Otto Armster, head of Vienna intelligence area, previously head of the *Abwehr* office in *Wehrkreis* XII.[13]

Wehrkreis XX (Danzig): Lieutenant-Colonel Hasso von Boehmer, head of Operations Section in *Wehrkreis* HQ.

Wehrkreis XXI (Poznan): Major (res.) Georg Konrad Kissling.[14]

Wehrkreis Bohemia-Moravia (Prague): Colonel Nikolaus Graf von Üxküll-Gyllenband, an uncle of Stauffenberg, serving in Rear HQ III Corps.[15]

Members of the conspiracy were to be found at several points outside Germany proper and it was proposed to use them on D Day according to their capabilities. Major-General von Tresckow, for instance, was to be brought to Berlin from the eastern front; General Eduard Wagner, Deputy Chief of Staff of the Army, proposed to send an aircraft for him.[16] Tresckow also proposed to ensure that the equivalent of a regiment drawn from 31 and 32 Cavalry Regiments belonging to 3 Cavalry Brigade was flown to Tempelhof for use during the *coup*. All preparations had been made a few days before 20 July and the troops had been alerted, but owing to the failure of the attempt the move was never made.[17]

Certain special features distinguished the preparations and recruitment of associates in Paris and Vienna. Until 6 June 1944 Paris was the only major *Wehrmacht* headquarters where comparative calm reigned and where planning could be done free from the continual demands of the fighting. At the same time the senior Army staffs in and around Paris contained more opposition supporters than most other centres. Conditions in Vienna were somewhat similar in that it was still relatively quiet and at the same time the centre of an indigenous national resistance movement of non-*Reich* Germans.

Fritz-Dietlof Graf von der Schulenburg formed the first link between the Beck–Goerdeler group and the regime's opponents in the staffs of C-in-C France and Field Marshal von Rundstedt, C-in-C West. As a member of General von Unruh's staff Schulenburg had to screen all headquarters and agencies in Paris and elsewhere for available personnel fit for service at the front. He had paid several visits to Paris since June 1943 and the result had been the formation of cells and groups in various headquarters ready to participate in a *coup* and making the necessary preparations in their area.[18] General Karl-Heinrich von Stülpnagel, C-in-C France, had long been a member of the conspiracy. As Deputy Chief of Staff I in 1939 he had played an active part in Halder's plans and he was ready to serve his old master, Colonel-General Beck, in a *coup*; he had his doubts, however, about the planned assassination attempt. The Commandant of Greater Paris, Lieutenant-General Freiherr von Boineburg-Lengsfeld, had assured Witzleben of his willingness to take an active part in the conspiracy as early as spring 1942 when he was still commanding 23 Panzer Division. In July 1943 he placed himself at Stülpnagel's disposal for the same purpose and began preparations for the rising in Paris, together with his Chief of Staff, Colonel von Unger. On 17 July 1944, Stülpnagel told Boineburg to have all SS and SD leaders in Paris arrested when the code-word 'Valkyrie' came through.[19] on the administration staff Lieutenant-Colonel Cäsar von Hofacker, who had long been a friend of Schulenburg, also belonged to the conspiracy. He had been in touch with Beck's group for some time and was the real mainspring of all conspiratorial activities in Paris.[20]

As early as summer 1943 Schulenburg had tried to initiate 'action' from the west, considering that not enough was happening in Berlin. In Paris people thought that this could only be done after the anticipated Allied landing in France; they had some difficulty in dissuading Schulenburg.[21] In France, however, argument continued until well into the spring of 1944 as to whether it was better first to strike with the Army in the communications zone and in Germany, remove the Nazi regime and *then* arrest and shoot Hitler or whether to start by assassinating him.[22] In autumn 1943, after Stauffenberg had taken the lead in the technical preparations, Berlin once more decided in favour of assassination.

Little or nothing of value for the opposition's plans happened in Paris during the winter 1943–44 but it was reinforced by the arrival on 1 January 1944 of Field Marshal Erwin Rommel as C-in-C Army Group B with headquarters in La Roche-Guyon; he asked for, and on 15 April 1944 was given, Lieutenant-General Dr Hans Speidel as Chief of Staff. The war situation, his experience of Hitler's unscrupulous dilettante leadership and the arguments of Dr Strölin, Burgomaster of Stuttgart who was in close touch with Goerdeler, had turned Rommel from Hitler's 'favourite' general into a resolute opponent, although he was not won over for a *coup* until after the beginning of the invasion of Normandy.[23] Meanwhile, a continuous stream of visitors from Germany passed through Rommel's headquarters in France, all of them anxious to reveal to Rommel their grave concern and fear for the future of Germany and to ask his help in seeking a way out of the increasingly hopeless situation.[24] Those around Rommel encouraged some of this activity. Speidel had long been an active opponent of Hitler and had been involved in 'Plan Lanz' in February 1943.[25] General Alexander Freiherr von Falkenhausen, C-in-C Belgium and Northern France, was also a sympathizer of the opposition but he was relieved on 14 July after he had refused to conscript all Belgians born in 1925 for forced labour in Germany at the request of Sauckel, Minister for the Mobilization of Labour. On 18 July he handed over to a successor.[26] In Paris and La Roche-Guyon Falkenhausen was considered absolutely reliable but Beck and Witzleben were much opposed to him because of his notorious affair with a lady.[27]

Speidel established the necessary underground contact between Rommel and Stülpnagel as early as April 1944 but the two commanders could not arrange a private meeting until 15 May.[28] Also in May Wagner, the Deputy Chief of Staff, arrived in France to coordinate preparations for the *coup* with Rommel. He gave an account of the previous attempts on Hitler but Rommel was opposed to assassination. He was afraid that Hitler would be turned into a martyr and that the public would therefore fail to realize his guilt and total responsibility.[29] To some extent Rommel was the natural leader of the opposition in France and so his aversion to assassination could not simply be brushed aside. Nevertheless the chateau in La Roche-Guyon now became another centre of active opposition in continuous communication with the Berlin headquarters. Rommel also succeeded in drawing into his orbit certain realists who had hitherto been 'on the other side' such as Dr Julius Dorpmüller, the Minister of Transport, and Karl Kaufmann, *Gauleiter* of Hamburg.[30]

Speidel conferred with Dr Strölin and with the former Foreign Minister Freiherr von Neurath in Freudenstadt on 27 May 1944, acting on Rommel's behalf.[31] Speidel described the hopeless inferiority of the German forces in face of the anticipated invasion; Neurath and Strölin emphasized that no truce and thus no salvation for Germany was possible unless Hitler and Himmler were removed, and that Rommel, on the other hand, commanded almost limitless confidence among the German people, that his fame and prestige had legendary proportions. They asked Speidel to transmit their appeal to Rommel to make himself available. It was agreed that the war in the west should be ended through secret negotiations in Madrid, Lisbon and Switzerland. Strölin mentioned his contact with Goerdeler who was at the head of the conspiracy together with Beck. Speidel then reported to Rommel on his conversations, and Rommel consented to further preparations. Speidel also informed General Blumentritt, Chief of Staff to C-in-C West, of his contacts and their results.

Speidel gives an account of the plan agreed between Rommel, Stülpnagel and Rundstedt. It took the form of a 'mobilization timetable': armistice negotiations with Allied commanders in the west (Eisenhower and Montgomery) without reference to Hitler; their basis was to be evacuation of German-occupied areas in the west and withdrawal of German forces behind the Siegfried Line; immediate cessation of bombing of Germany; then peace negotiations. Unconditional surrender does not, therefore, seem to have been considered; it was assumed that the Allies would welcome the chance of achieving a large part of their war aims without further bloodshed. At the same time all Western radio stations were to explain to the German people, without mincing words, the real political and military situation and the crimes committed by their leaders. In the east fighting was to continue for the moment and a reduced front to be held from Memel along the Vistula to Lvov, the Carpathians and thence to the mouth of the Danube. As far as Germany was concerned, Rommel's plan provided for the arrest of Hitler either by the OKH resistance group or by an armoured force concentrated round the *Führer*'s headquarters. Hitler was then to be tried and a new government formed under Beck, Goerdeler and Leuschner; there should be neither dismemberment nor a military regime but Germany should work for 'a creative peace within the framework of a United States of Europe'.[32]

For months everyone awaited Hitler's inspection of the prospective invasion front in the west but, though the visit was continually being requested and had long been scheduled, he kept on postponing it. Not until 17 June, eleven days after the start of the invasion did he finally pay a flying visit to France at his headquarters 'Wolfschlucht II' near Margival.[33]

It is questionable whether Rommel had really made up his mind to arrest Hitler, as Wilhelm von Schramm says; Speidel says nothing on the subject. However, no practical opportunity seems to have presented itself on 17 June. Hitler's headquarters were 125 miles behind the front and apparently no troops suitable to make the arrest were available – and troops would have been essential to overpower the SS who had sealed off the whole area shortly before Hitler's arrival. Moreover Hitler had only announced over the telephone on the evening of 16 June that he wished to confer with Rundstedt and Rommel at 9 a.m. next morning. Rommel received the news at 3 a.m., only six hours before the conference and when he had just returned from a tour of the front lasting twenty-one hours. He had to leave at once to drive the 125 miles.[34]

At this 'conference' Hitler did little more than abuse local commanders, the inefficiency of the *Luftwaffe* and other scapegoats. In reply Rommel objected that so far no senior officer from the *Führer*'s entourage or any of the Service headquarters (*Wehrmacht, Luftwaffe* or Navy) had been to the front to get a true picture of the situation; orders were continually issued from an office stool without regard to realities. The conference was interrupted by an air raid alert and Hitler, Lieutenant-General Schmundt, his senior aide, the two Field Marshals and their Chiefs of Staff went into the protected accommodation of the *Führer*'s bunker. Rommel seized the opportunity to point out to Hitler that the Normandy front would inevitably collapse, the Allies break through into Germany and the Italian front disintegrate, leaving Germany totally isolated politically. Hitler rebuked him saying that his business was to deal solely with his invasion front.[35]

Finally Hitler agreed to visit the headquarters of Army Group B in La

Roche-Guyon and this was fixed for 19 June. On 18 June, however, when Speidel started to discuss details with General Blumentritt, Chief of Staff to C-in-C West, he received 'the astonishing news that Hitler had returned to Berchtesgaden on the night 17–18'. A V weapon had gone off course and fallen near his headquarters; it had done no damage and could certainly not have penetrated his bunker, but it had frightened Hitler off.[36] For soldiers his behaviour was incredible.

Speidel does not say that Hitler would have been arrested had he paid this visit but the opportunity was obviously there.[37] After Hitler's departure, however, this unique opportunity was not likely to recur.

Preparations for the *coup* proceeded until the very last day. On 25 June Colonel Eberhard Finckh, the new Deputy Chief of Staff to Army Group B, reported to Rommel and told him that Stauffenberg was planning to assassinate Hitler; Rommel was still against it.[38] On the other hand more and more commanders gave their support to Rommel's plan; they included Lieutenant-General Gerhard Graf von Schwerin commanding 116 Panzer Division, and Lieutenant-General Heinrich Freiherr von Lüttwitz, commanding 2 Panzer Division.[39] It was still uncertain, however, how the most powerful formations on the western front, the SS tank troops, would react.

On 9 July there appeared in Rommel's office Lieutenant-Colonel Cäsar von Hofacker, specially employed officer on General von Stülpnagel's staff. Rommel had been serving under Hofacker's father in the First World War when he won the *Pour le Mérite* (the German V.C.). On behalf of Stülpnagel Hofacker asked for an appreciation of the situation which could be passed to Beck and Stauffenberg.[40] Rommel said that the front should hold for another two to three weeks – in fact the Americans broke through at Avranches on 1 August.[41] Hofacker's particular job was coordination of the *coup d'état* measures in Paris with those in Berlin. On 13 July Stülpnagel reported that preparations in his area were complete; he would deal with the SD in Paris and in France.[42] Rommel, who had been to the front on 13, 14 and 15 July, did not anticipate difficulties from SS units in the west. On 15 July he dictated his famous message to Hitler giving him in peremptory terms a last 'chance' to avoid disaster; Hitler, he said, should immediately draw the conclusions from the desperate situation in the west.[43] According to Speidel, if Hitler did not react, Rommel was quite determined to take action on his own. Two days later, however, Rommel was severely wounded. The message was never sent and Field Marshal von Kluge, Rommel's successor (he had taken over from Rundstedt as C-in-C West on 2 July), pigeonholed it although he told General von Falkenhausen as late as 26 July that he was in full agreement with its contents.[44]

About 12 July Kluge had once more veered towards the opposition's viewpoint.[45] But he was not prepared to take the initiative even though the American breakthrough was bound to come soon, as he told Colonel Georg Freiherr von Boeselager who visited him on behalf of Tresckow between 7 and 12 July.[46] He was ready to place himself at Beck's disposal as soon as Hitler had been removed, he said, but he could not promise more; he was not yet sure either of his troops or his staff and his armies were involved in heavy defensive fighting.[47] On 20 July Kluge kept precisely to the limits of this agreement.

Preparations and developments in Vienna were as much a special case as in Paris. In Austria political groupings were similar to those of Germany – socialists, communists, Christian-socials, liberals, conservatives. In this case, however, responsibility did not rest solely on officers acting from motives of conscience and determined to put an end to injustice, murder and destruction simply because something must be done to avoid the ruin of everything. In Austria there were Austrian nationalist tendencies, more pronounced since the *Anschluss* than ever before. As a historian of the 20 July movement in Austria says, with the *Anschluss* there began 'a rediscovery of themselves by the once so divided Austrians'. Austrian opposition to Hitler was a 'special trend'; 'its ultimate object, despite much confused planning and thinking, was reestablishment of the Austrian state'.[48] Nothing else was seriously considered after the Moscow Declaration of 1 November 1943 which promised the Austrians their independence and did not load them with the same responsibility as the Germans for the crimes committed by Nazism.[49] Talking to Wilhelm Leuschner in early summer 1943, Dr Adolf Schärf, later the Social-Democrat Vice-Chancellor of Austria, said: 'The *Anschluss* is dead; all love of the German *Reich* has been eradicated among Austrians.'[50]

The 'German' opposition leaders took it as a matter of course that Austria would remain with the *Reich*, although they were prepared to guarantee a greater or lesser degree of regional independence; to the Austrians, however, their independence was equally a matter of course. Goerdeler, Graf Schulenburg, Graf von Üxküll (Stauffenberg's uncle), Albrecht Haushofer, Wilhelm Leuschner and Jakob Kaiser all thought that Germany and Austria should remain united; many even hoped that Austria could intercede with the victors on Germany's behalf and would be more likely to be listened to. At the latest by 1940 Jakob Kaiser, who had been in close touch with Austrian trade unionists before the *Anschluss*, had contacted Austrian politicians and he was followed by Max Habermann, Wilhelm Leuschner and Goerdeler; their main contacts were Alois Weinberger and Dr Felix Hurdes, subsequently leaders of the Austrian People's Party and both members of post-1945 Austrian governments, Otto Troidl, the Christian-social politician, and Dr Schärf, the Social-Democrat already mentioned. But they could agree only on one thing – the necessity to overthrow Hitler, and even for this limited purpose there was no real cooperation between the politicians.[51] From about 1942 Austrian politicians were fairly categorical in their rejection of Austro–German unity, although some were prepared to accept a loose form of connection between an autonomous Austria and Germany.

Nevertheless, in his last talk with Jakob Kaiser, Weinberger put forward the names of Karl Seitz and Josef Reither as reliable trustworthy representatives of the Austrian workers and peasants and they were included by the conspirators in the list of Political Representatives.[52] For the Salzburg area they accepted Dr Franz Rehrl, the former *Landeshauptmann,* (senior minister) and for Tyrol *Hofrat* (court counsellor) Dr Anton Mörl, formerly

Director of Security. There is no knowing whether, had the *coup* succeeded, the Political Representatives in Austria would really have cooperated with the Berlin headquarters.

On the military side preparations for the *coup* in Vienna and in Austria differed little from those in other *Wehrkreise*. A few were in the know and it was hoped that, under the circumstances, others would obey the order given them. The leading members of the conspiracy in Vienna were Colonel Rudolf Graf von Marogna-Redwitz, a Bavarian, head of the *Abwehr* office in Vienna (on 20 July he was in Vienna as special AHA representative) and Captain Karl Szokoll, an Austrian, head of the Supply Section (Organization) in HQ *Wehrkreis* XVII; the latter had been personally briefed by Stauffenberg in early summer 1944 and had spent weeks organizing the 'Valkyrie' measures such as the occupation of post and telegraph offices, and arranging postings.[53] Szokoll was a champion of Stauffenberg's plans and ideas, describing them as 'both brilliant and dangerous'. The main military liaison officer between Berlin and Vienna was an Austrian, Lieutenant-Colonel Robert Bernardis, head of a group in the AHA.[54] He tried to recruit Colonel Kodré but both were extremely cautious and so the contact remained somewhat non-committal.[55] Austrian national sentiment was not very pronounced among officers as may be judged from the fact that two Austrians played a leading part in the action which liquidated the *putsch* on the evening of 20 July – Lieutenant-Colonel Karl Pridun of the AHA Operations Section, and SS-*Obersturmbannführer* Otto Skorzeny.[56]

The military liaison officers in the *Wehrkreise* and other military headquarters were primarily responsible for correct and rapid execution of the military measures; civilian advisers were attached to them, for this was no normal military *putsch*. The civilian element was to be represented at all stages since it was the real driving force of the conspiracy and the military invariably refused to act without its support; it was better qualified to carry the flag of rejection of dictatorship and authoritarianism and return to more civilized methods of government. Moreover most officers were politically inexperienced and often needed advice.

The list of Political Representatives resulted primarily from the efforts of Goerdeler with assistance from Jakob Kaiser, Leuschner, Wirmer, Letterhaus and Fritz-Dietlof Graf von der Schulenburg; like that of the liaison officers it originated in autumn 1943. Kaiser, Wirmer and Habermann proposed Letterhaus, Kaschny, Tantzen, Kossmann, Sümmermann and Reither; Leuschner nominated Voigt, Noske, Frölich, Lüdemann, Böhme and Schwamb; Leber proposed Gustav Dahrendorf and the others were nominated by Goerdeler and Schulenburg. Kossmann, a lawyer, belonged to Jakob Kaiser's group; Dr Tantzen had been recruited by Wirmer. All were told of the project in general terms and of what they were expected to do, but were seldom given details. Even Goerdeler did not know all details of the plans although he was the man who recruited the majority of the Political Representatives as a result of laborious, dangerous and often discouraging negotiations; frequently they were men whom he had not even known before autumn 1943 – proof of his courage in risking his life. In any case details changed frequently; the timing was not certain even on the day before the attempt and Goerdeler did not wish to burden people with unnecessary knowledge.[57] Should the attempt fail or be discovered, therefore, people could say that they were involved in the conspiracy against their will and that their names appeared on lists or in teleprinter messages without their agreement. One of the *Gestapo* reports, for instance, says: 'Interrogation of the Stauffenberg group (primarily Schulenburg) and material evidence assembled (orders, instructions etc) leave open the *possibility* that a large number of the Representatives and liaison officers had *not* in fact been briefed.'[58]

The following is the list of persons designated as Political Representatives and advisers to the liaison officers and *Wehrkreis* Commanders on the day of the *coup*:[59]

Wehrkreis I (Königsberg): Major-General (retd) Heinrich Burggraf and Graf zu Dohna-Schlobitten, owner of Tolksdorf;[60]

Wehrkreis II (Stettin): Achim Freiherr von Willisen, senior forestry officer in Schwerin (for Mecklenburg);[61] Ewald von Kleist-Schmenzin as deputy – he was in fact responsible for Pomerania and his title did not therefore imply subordination;[62]

Wehrkreis III (Berlin): no appointment;

Wehrkreis IV (Dresden): Walter Cramer, a Leipzig manufacturer who had offered his services to Goerdeler in 1943;[63]

Wehrkreis V (Stuttgart): Albrecht Fischer whom Goerdeler had pressed into service in 1944;[64] deputy in Karlsruhe, Reinhold Frank, a lawyer;[65]

Wehrkreis VI (Münster): Captain (res.) Bernhard Letterhaus, in Section IIb of the *Abwehr* since 1942 and then in the OKH Military Office, Belinde;[66] deputy – Felix Sümmermann, a district magistrate;

Wehrkreis VII (Munich): Otto Gessler, formerly *Reichswehr* Minister;[67]

Wehrkreis VIII (Breslau): Dr Hans Lukaschek, a lawyer and former *Oberpräsident* of Silesia;[68] Fritz Voigt, Police President of Breslau as deputy for Lower Silesia;[69] Adolf Kaschny, a lawyer and formerly Burgomaster of Ratibor, as deputy for Upper Silesia;[70]

Wehrkreis IX (Kassel): Gustav Noske, ex-*Reich* Minister and former *Oberpräsident*;[71] deputy – August Frölich, ex-Minister-President of Thuringia, Social-Democrat and trade union official;[72]

Wehrkreis X (Hamburg): Gustav Dahrendorf, ex-Social-Democrat *Reichstag* deputy;[73] deputy – Dr Theodor Tantzen, ex-Minister-President of Oldenburg;[74]

Wehrkreis XI (Hannover): Dr Arthur Menge, Burgomaster of Hannover;[75] deputy – Hermann Lüdemann, Social-Democrat, ex-Prussian Finance Minister, *Regierungspräsident* in Lüneburg, *Oberpräsident* in Breslau – had spent much time in concentration camps since 1933;[76]

Wehrkreis XII (Wiesbaden): Ludwig Schwamb, Social-Democrat, lawyer, ex-Councillor under Wilhelm Leuschner when Minister of the Interior in Hesse;[77] deputy Bartholomäus Kossmann, lawyer, ex-official of the Centre Party;[78]

Wehrkreis XIII (Nuremberg): Georg Böhme, ex-trade union official, in Nuremberg-Fürth;

Wehrkreis XVII (Vienna): Karl Seitz, Burgomaster of Vienna 1923–34;[79] deputy – Josef Reither, former *Landeshauptmann* of Lower Austria, Minister for Agriculture and Forestry, President of Austrian Farmers' Association;[80]

Wehrkreis XVIII (Salzburg): Dr Franz Rehrl, Christian-Social politician, former *Landeshauptmann* in Salzburg, recruited by Graf von Moltke;[81] deputy – Dr Anton Ritter Mörl von Pfalzen zu Mühlen und Sichelburg, director of security in Tyrol 1933–38;[82]

Wehrkreis XX (Danzig): Hermann Freiherr von Lüninck, Major (res.) and *Stahlhelm* leader, former *Oberpräsident* of Westphalia, also considered for Ministry of Food;[83]

Wehrkreis XXI (Poznan): Ernst Vollert, Colonel (res.) and senior civil servant, residing in Prague;[84]

Wehrkreis Bohemia-Moravia (Prague): no appointment.

The compilation of cabinet lists and 'coalition negotiations' undoubtedly forms one of the more extraordinary aspects of the conspiracy. For years people discussed who should occupy what position later and what political, social, economic and administrative principles and ideas should be translated into action; meanwhile no one achieved the essential prerequisite to all this, the removal of Hitler and his government. From this point of view Moltke and many of his 'Kreisau' friends were being realistic when they tried primarily to plan for the period 'afterwards'; the Allies would put an end to Hitler if the Germans did not do it themselves – of that there was no doubt. The numerous false starts and attempts ever since 1938 had achieved nothing; the almost desperate enterprises of late 1943 and early 1944 had failed, some for mysterious reasons. The fact that in July 1944 an attempt was finally made and that the same man had tried at least twice before, was both unexpected and improbable; it is explicable only by Stauffenberg's personality and his extraordinary revolutionary energy. Without him nothing even approaching rational planning would have been done; without him it is possible that, in the words of Gerhard Ritter already quoted, 'the opposition movement would have been stuck fast in helpless passivity'.[85]

This endless planning and preparation for an event which never took place is an easy target for subsequent scorn and abuse; but this does not do justice to the subject. Extreme secrecy is naturally the stock-in-trade of any conspiracy; laborious planning and deliberation, drawing up of lists, writing of diaries and notes do not help; energetic, resolute purposeful action is more important than the most careful planning for the 'day after'. But the 'civilian' members of the conspiracy had nothing else to do but plan for the period 'after' (the word 'civilian' is used here in inverted commas because the formal distinction between civilian and military had long since become blurred – many had 'emigrated' into the Army or had been called up). The regime could only be overthrown physically by the military.

The real basic justification for all these plans, discussions and negotiations, however, was the determination to avoid a repetition of '1933' – a political catastrophe resulting from errors, unintelligence and social, political, constitutional and ideological blunders. The opposition felt themselves to be the representatives of the many Germans who only vaguely realized that, by a stroke of misfortune, their state had fallen into the hands of a criminal clique which represented the most destructive and nihilistic tendencies to be found in the German people; the opposition received support for this view among many officials, officers and others from all sections of the population. This is some explanation for the conspirators' lack of caution which has so often been criticized: the criminal clique were 'outsiders'; particularly in the Army, the *Gestapo* and the Party had hardly made an impact; moreover many who were in no way involved in the opposition felt and acted as they did. There can be no other explanation for the incredible fact that 'so many of the high and highest officers in the Army, including a row of Field Marshals, should for years have known of the existence of a civil and military conspiracy without betraying it'.[86]

In the conspirators' eyes there was another aspect which justified, even necessitated, all this planning, making of notes and drawing up of lists: there must at all times be documentary evidence to show that Hitler had fallen victim, not to some military *putsch*, but to an opposition stemming from the 'other', the real, Germany over which he had been exercising his tyranny.[87] This was no archivist's whim; in the opposition's view it was a requirement of the first order. Naturally they knew that, in doing so, they were risking their necks – they were not as naïve as all that. They did it nevertheless in the belief that it was their responsibility to their country and to humanity. Of course there were imprudencies and stupidities as in all enterprises of this nature. But records such as Hermann Kaiser's diary or that of Ulrich von Hassell (which was not discovered by the *Gestapo*), Goerdeler's lists, Schulenburg's scheme of appointments (which has been lost) or Moltke's letters to his wife (also undiscovered) were not written light-heartedly.[88] For attainment of the conspiracy's immediate aims they were not necessary; but today they are indisputable evidence of the spirit of the opposition, of its humanist ethical character; in addition to their political or even literary value they illustrate the dynamism of personalities such as Schulenburg, Goerdeler, Stauffenberg or Moltke. The conspirators lacked the sophistication of normal criminals or traitors; they were self-sacrificing and heroic rather than cunning. Anyone, therefore, who tries to write off the conspiracy as naïve culpable imprudence is guilty of failure to recognize its true worth or level. The conspirators were fully aware of the danger of what they were doing; they knew that they were risking their necks, as Tresckow once said to Schlabrendorff in words already quoted: 'None of us can complain of his lot. Whoever joined the resistance movement, put on the shirt of Nessus. The moral worth of a man is certain only if he is prepared to sacrifice his life for his convictions.'[89]

At the end of November Beck himself asked Goerdeler to compile a formal list of ministers.[90] Activity had been intense ever since January 1943, the object being to be ready for the *coup* in March or April. In January Gisevius came specially to Berlin from Berne to participate in the planning. On 8 January 1943, according to Hassell's diary, 'a great discussion between "young" and "old" ' took place in Peter Graf Yorck von Wartenburg's house, No 50 Hortensienstrasse, Berlin-Lichterfelde. The real argument was between Goerdeler and his associates on the one hand and members of the 'Kreisau Circle' on the other (they in fact met more often in Berlin than in Kreisau). Present at this discussion were Beck, Goerdeler, Hassell, Popitz and Jessen on one side and Moltke, Yorck, Trott, Schulenburg and Gerstenmaier on the other. Carlo Mierendorff and Theo Haubach should also have been there but had to refuse because they were too closely watched by the *Gestapo*.[91]

This discussion was urgently necessary if the opposition was to work together, for numerous points of disagreement had arisen. Anyone who knew Goerdeler was soon convinced that his views were right and liberal but those who had only heard of his background and activities from third parties or by rumour could easily misunderstand him. Many of the 'Kreisau Circle' such as Moltke, Haubach and Mierendorff tended towards revolutionary organic reform and so Goerdeler seemed to them to be reactionary; Moltke even tried to keep Eugen Bolz and Bernhard Letterhaus away from Goerdeler. According to Dr Elfriede Nebgen the Jesuit Father Delp was also involved in these intrigues for a time.[92]

The meeting could only be arranged with considerable effort and after weeks of preparation. Jakob Kaiser, Leuschner, Habermann and Letterhaus held a preparatory meeting with Father Delp in Berlin shortly before Christmas 1942; Schulenburg was an indefatigable intermediary in finally bringing about the great meeting.

The members of the 'Kreisau Circle' wanted a fundamental discussion of their views. Neither their aims nor their attitude were conducive to a diplomatic search for compromise; they wished to discuss problems in depth. They wanted change; they wanted to do away with the regime, but they thought that they could best contribute by formulating principles for reconstruction. Goerdeler, on the other hand, was looking for more immediate practical possibilities of achieving his object. A clash was to be expected, therefore, not only because of the generation gap but because of differing political and social views and differing methods of pursuing the various objectives.

In fact, as far as the 'Kreisau Circle' were concerned and for different reasons Goerdeler too, the 'great debate' was both disappointing and promising. As Hassell noted in his diary, the 'Kreisau Circle', whom he refers to as 'the young', presented a united front with the exception of the more realistic Schulenburg; Moltke was evidently their intellectual leader. Their unity lent 'the young' that weight which 'the old', represented by such independent and highly respected personalities as Beck, Hassell, Goerdeler, Popitz and Jessen, already possessed. Foreign policy problems were discussed with Adam von Trott zu Solz acting as spokesman for the 'Kreisau Circle' and giving an *exposé* on their desire for a European federation. Hassell noted in his diary that he by no means agreed with Trott's views on all points. Yorck then spoke on administrative reform and Moltke on the opposition's overall position and the necessity for cooperation between the churches and trade unions. Finally Gerstenmaier developed the 'Kreisau Circle's' views (not entirely supported by all members) on the relationship between church and state and on social policy. Beck chaired the meeting but did not express an opinion on the problems raised.

Moltke wanted a fundamental discussion of their differences; Hassell and Goerdeler, on the other hand, were trying to bridge existing gulfs; they wanted to achieve the quickest possible agreement and cooperation for the attainment of the immediate goal of everybody, the overthrow of Hitler. For the younger members of the group, who clung resolutely to their convictions and thought more in terms of principle, this looked like evasion or even a patronizing attempt to mollify them. Even Hassell thought that Goerdeler had tried to obfuscate rather than bridge the differences. 'The young' were suspicious, for they thought that 'the old', who were mostly conservatives, had hardly shifted their point of view at all and as soon as they came to power would slide back into the old ways. For the period immediately following the *coup* both sides agreed that a semi-authoritarian regime would be necessary, but Hassell, Popitz, Beck and Jessen did not seem to visualize an element of social change and Goerdeler's statements probably provided little evidence of such ideas. The 'Kreisau Circle', on the other hand, visualized a far-reaching social revolution; their ideas on the integration of classes and interests and elimination of social discord were romantic and idealistic – hardly compatible with a search for compromise and coalition politics.[93]

Moltke was furious with all attempts to evade the issue and avoid the real discussion which, in his view, should have followed explanation of the various points of view. He wanted enthusiastic acceptance of ideas, not portentous head-nodding, not polite registration of each other's viewpoint, not the conclusion of a marriage of convenience coupled with expressions of mutual respect. He wanted a programme for renewal, not a coalition manifesto. Moltke was so provoked by Goerdeler's *exposé* of his constitutional and social programme that he gave vent to an offensive interjection; while Goerdeler was talking he murmured under his breath 'Kerensky'.[94] Gerstenmaier, who was sitting next Moltke, was also irritated by Goerdeler's 'pedagogic obscurement of the issues' and replied in 'sharply antagonistic' terms, but he was not the only one to have heard Moltke's remark and the atmosphere became very tense; at least for the moment the ideas of 'the old' were overshadowed by their indignation at the presumption of 'the young'. Nevertheless they were able to rise above such differences and they knew that they were at one with the 'Kreisau Circle' in their determination to revolt against injustice and crime. In conclusion Beck said that he must now see 'how strong the forces actually available were'. All were agreed on the necessity of the *coup* taking place as soon as possible.

This was a highly important meeting and, although not entirely satisfactory, it did mean the beginning of cooperation between the more active members of the 'Kreisau Circle' and the Beck-Goerdeler group; it also meant that the 'Kreisau Circle' was now in closer touch with the military planning. Fritz-Dietlof Graf von der Schulenburg and Graf von Yorck were the main and most active intermediaries.[95] So far there had been no cooperation between the 'Kreisau Circle' and 'the generals', although Moltke and Yorck had been urging action upon 'the generals' ever since 1941.[96] Their hopes were centred first on Halder and then, after his dismissal in late 1942, on Kluge; when travelling on duty Moltke was continually discussing a *coup* with generals. In 1943 he was still hoping but at times wondered whether defeat was not inevitable in the first place and secondly essential in order to purge Germany both spiritually and politically.[97] Cooperation was finally achieved after all, in the period from autumn 1943 up to July 1944, not least by the arrival in the conspiracy of another 'Count' and 'youngster' – Stauffenberg.[98]

At latest from autumn 1943, therefore, the 'Kreisau Circle' was not merely in contact but in close touch. Trott's and Moltke's efforts in the foreign policy field were aimed solely at creating conditions for the *coup*; 'the generals' and many other non-military patriots wanted assurances from the Allies that they would not insist on unconditional surrender if Germany liberated herself from Nazism.[99] Members and adherents of the 'Kreisau Circle' were associated in the planning for the seizure of plenary power in the *Wehrkreise*; their names were included in the lists of liaison officers and Political Representatives.[100] There was no further question merely of some vague connection.[101]

In view of the mass of evidence to the contrary it is almost incomprehensible that people can still say that in the 'Kreisau Circle' people were 'merely thinking', as Moltke wrote in a letter from prison, that they planned only for the period 'afterwards' and simply wanted Germany to be defeated, as Moltke's letter to Lionel Curtis has been taken to imply. Moltke was not the only one to realize that Germany could not win; generals and field marshals, led by Beck, were continually saying the same thing both before and during the war. If a negotiated peace was not possible – and with the existing regime it was not – a desire for a rapid end to a senseless and hopeless war logically implied a desire for Germany's defeat. Moltke was not the sole representative of the 'Kreisau Circle'. Many others of its members adopted far more extreme points of view in one direction or the other.[102] Inevitably, therefore, members of the 'Kreisau Circle' cooperated in the formation of a future governmental team and in planning for the *coup* despite the fact that many of them had no liking for the word 'coalition'. Indeed, the 'Kreisau Circle' was responsible for establishing contact between the opposition and the communists who received their directions from elsewhere. There could be no better illustration of the Circle's vital importance.

In his draft programme of June 1943 Carlo Mierendorff had already proposed formation of a popular movement which should be above party and include the communists; the 'Kreisau Circle' seriously considered inclusion in a post-*coup* cabinet not only of the ultra-socialist Julius Leber but also representatives of German communism.[103] Reichwein was the protagonist but Moltke and finally Leber also supported the idea. Leuschner had been suspicious of communists ever since his time in a concentration camp because they included many *Gestapo* informers; he and Jakob Kaiser tried in vain to dissuade Leber. Leber said that he proposed to probe the motives and ideas which had led the communists for some time now to seek contact with the opposition. In 1943 Horst von Einsiedel und Trotha had been in touch with Arvid Harnack and Hans Peters with Schulze-Boysen of 'Red Orchestra'. Further efforts to gain contact followed through the Moscow 'Free Germany' Committee and their liaison officers in Germany.[104] Insofar as these contacts were inspired by Moscow, the knowledge that the Beck-Goerdeler group was seeking separate negotiations for an armistice with the Western Allies must have been an important factor. Moreover, the war was drawing to an end and it was time, from Moscow's point of view, to gain an influence on any postwar German government.[105] It was not until 1944, however, that these contacts aimed at concentrating forces for the *coup d'état*.

Several preliminary discussions starting in January were without result. A certain Ferdinand Thomas from the communist students' union acted as intermediary between Leber and Reichwein on one side and the (underground) Central Committee of the Communist Party on the other. Thomas had been sent down from Berlin University in 1933 because of his membership in the communist youth and students' association there, and as a 'half-Jew'; in 1936 he had been sentenced to three years in a penitentiary for alleged preparation to commit treason against the government. His contact with Reichwein was through common friends in Jena. Finally, after prolonged to-ing and fro-ing on the evening of 22 June 1944 a meeting took place with the knowledge and apparently with the approval of Stauffenberg, Yorck and Fritz-Dietlof von der Schulenburg.[106] The meeting place was the house of a Berlin doctor, Rudolf Schmid. The agreement was that Leber and Reichwein would appear and two members of the Central Committee, but Thomas, who introduced the communists, brought three people with him. It was also agreed that no names would be given and no introductions made; one of the communists who knew Leber, however, exclaimed: 'Oh you, Leber.'[107] Two of the visitors were in fact communist party functionaries, Anton Saefkow and Franz Jacob. The third, who like Dr Schmid apparently stayed outside the room in which the functionaries were meeting, was a *Gestapo* agent named Hermann Rambow who had wormed his way into the confidence of the Central Committee and was brought to the meeting as assistant.

Leber took charge of the discussion. Credentials as spokesmen for the Communist Party or Social-Democracy were exchanged and then the two sides felt their way cautiously towards each other. The communists showed themselves far readier to meet Leber's views than he had expected – in some respects they were even further 'right' than he was himself. They were in favour of liberal democracy, land ownership, the bourgeoisie and private property, also of large firms and capital; they were not over-rigid on church matters. One of them then asked what Leber proposed to do to bring about 'D Day'. Leber replied that he could say nothing on that subject.

With this the discussion ended but enough common ground had emerged to make another meeting seem worth while. This was fixed for 4 July but Leber had already become suspicious, primarily because of the forthcoming communist attitude, and he refused. Reichwein went and was arrested together with the communists. Leber was pulled in by the Gestapo next day, 5 July. This was the end of the conspiracy's collaboration with communists.

In politics it is unavoidable to negotiate constantly, to coordinate views and programmes, to form coalitions, to find support, although advocates of authoritarian dictatorial 'unity' are invariably tempted to pour scorn on such efforts.[108] Of course, Goerdeler could see no other way to create a broad basis for the *coup* except negotiations, and so he continued them almost down to the last day. There was no problem with Hassell and Beck; they had worked together for a long time; but touch with Popitz gradually became less close, particularly after the arrest of Langbehn in autumn 1943 which exposed Popitz' involvement in conspiracy with Himmler. There had long been suspicion of Popitz and his authoritarian views and this was increased by his contact with Himmler. Popitz for his part accused Goerdeler of having lost his way, by which he meant his alliance and agreements with the socialists.[109]

After the estrangement between Goerdeler and Popitz following the latter's conversation with Himmler Popitz made several attempts to talk matters out with Leber and Goerdeler. During the winter 1943–44, at Popitz' request, Dr Otto John tried to arrange such a meeting. Although he was under strict observation, Popitz insisted that Leber come to him but Leber refused. Popitz then asked John to arrange a meeting for him with Field Marshal von Witzleben, which John was well able to do since he was a close friend of Graf Lynar, Witzleben's aide on whose estate in the Spreewald Witzleben was then living. Then, however, Popitz thought this too dangerous, for he was undoubtedly under observation since his talk with Himmler; instead he proposed to send Dr Günter Gereke, the ex-*Reich* Commissar for Labour, to talk to Witzleben. A long delay followed since Witzleben went to Bad Kissingen for a cure and John flew to Madrid.[110]

Dr Hans John then took over as intermediary and on 18 July, the day before Otto John's return from Madrid, the meeting between Witzleben and Gereke took place.[111] The whole thing was, of course, an unsavoury intrigue by Popitz who hoped to reestablish his ideas, if not himself, in the centre of the stage, bypassing Beck, Goerdeler and Stauffenberg, the recognized focus of resistance. Through Gereke he even tried, with some success, to persuade Witzleben to take over the chancellorship after the coup, with Popitz, Goerdeler and Leuschner as advisory '*Reich* Government Commissars'. This would have been pure military dictatorship. Leuschner, however, who had been warned against the danger of collaborating with officers by Professor Ludwig Bergsträsser, thought that the united trades union, on which he, Kaiser and Habermann, were agreed, would provide an adequate guarantee against this.[112]

There was, therefore, never any real show-down between Goerdeler and Popitz with his right-wing followers. Meanwhile Goerdeler had his hands full with the socialists, with whom he had been working ever since 1941. Ultimately he advanced so far to meet them that the manifestos and proclamations which he had drafted for the *coup* contained so many other people's ideas as barely to be recognizable. Goerdeler consequently later refused to acknowledge them before the People's Court.[113]

About 15 May 1944 a meeting took place in Dr Josef Wirmer's house between Goerdeler, Leber and Leuschner, at which there was a serious clash between Leber and Goerdeler. Leber maintained that the total occupation of Germany could not be avoided even by a change of government, whereas Goerdeler thought that it could very well be done. The *Gestapo* report clearly only gives extracts from the discussion and other matters were undoubtedly raised. It is clear, however, that there was a not surprising difference of opinion between Leber and Goerdeler.[114]

On 26 May 1944 Stauffenberg and Goerdeler met in Captain Hermann Kaiser's office in the Bendlerstrasse.[115] They discussed the foreign policy and military prospects. Stauffenberg was apparently still hoping that an Allied invasion of France could be defeated. He gave Goerdeler a firm promise that he would use force against Hitler. On Goerdeler's insistence he agreed that Goerdeler should be the main negotiator with Leber, Leuschner and their representatives. Goerdeler had already written a letter to Stauffenberg, transmitted through Kaiser, protesting against Stauffenberg negotiating independently with trade union leaders and socialists. This was, in fact, a violation of the hitherto recognized principle that the soldiers confine themselves to the technical side of the *coup* and the civilian character of the opposition be preserved. This meant that Goerdeler should play the leading role in all non-military questions, as Beck was still insisting as late as July 1944.[116] This he did not so much from suspicion of Stauffenberg as from aversion to exaggerated concentration of power. Moreover Stauffenberg was politically inexperienced; his views were vague; goodwill and idealism by themselves generally only do damage in politics. The fact that he was risking his life did not give Stauffenberg the right to claim power of political decision; Goerdeler and Beck were risking their lives too. The ability to murder Hitler was no adequate justification for assuming the role of political leader.

Stauffenberg's entry into the conspiracy in the summer of 1943 led to a number of strains and disputes about spheres of authority, but there were other reasons. The military, external and internal political situations were all becoming more desperate; slaughter and murder at the front, in the concentration camps and in the cities continued unchecked; one after another centres of German culture were reduced to rubble – and still nothing happened to overthrow Hitler. Then appeared this young impetuous officer with a highly military exterior and began to take upon himself all preparations and planning – and still nothing visible occurred. Goerdeler inevitably wondered what this young officer, thirsting for action and burning for revolution, would make of the opposition; perhaps he might ruin it; alternatively, despite all his energy, he might achieve as little as Tresckow had before him.[117] There was a deep cleavage between the two characters and it was not to be explained merely by the generation gap and quarrels about responsibilities. It is hardly surprising that, writing his memoirs in prison in November 1944, Goerdeler lamented that Stauffenberg had 'subsequently proved to be a cranky obstinate fellow who wanted to play politics'.[118] He continued: 'I had many a row with him but greatly esteemed him. He wanted to steer a dubious political course with the left socialists and the communists and gave me a bad time with his overwhelming egotism.'[119]

Certain tactical problems, comparatively unimportant though they were, added fuel to the fire. For security reasons Stauffenberg did not tell Goerdeler all details of his plans and Goerdeler did likewise over the recruitment of Political Representatives.[120] On the other hand Goerdeler's bustle, despite his combination of courage and extreme caution, must have made Stauffenberg uneasy; moreover for the good of the cause he deliberately accepted the criticism to which his activity (which was important) gave rise. In 1943 and 1944 Goerdeler frequently complained bitterly about alleged attempts to out-wit or by-pass him. He remained an incurable optimist; he clung to his belief that Hitler could be arrested without attempting assassination, that power could then be seized by means of a speech over the radio or even that Hitler could be persuaded to resign. Such ideas, when continually put forward by Goerdeler during discussions of the assassination attempt and the *coup*, mere-ly acted as an irritant and seemed to call in question what the other con-spirators were doing.

In the nervous tension of those months strains, irritability and mutual reproaches were understandable. They were not as serious, however, as the variously motivated descriptions of them both by the conspirators when un-der arrest and by the *Gestapo* would have us believe.

Beck (who invariably supported Goerdeler), Schulenburg and others acted as mediators and continually succeeded in reducing friction and tension; cooperation proceeded even between Goerdeler and Stauffenberg. Stauffenberg repeatedly warned Goerdeler to hold himself in readiness when 'the date' was imminent – on 10 July, for instance, for the 11th and again for the 15th. Goerdeler replied that it was essential to go ahead and effect a breakthrough.[121] Goerdeler and Stauffenberg met many times alone to discuss the *coup* measures, and as late as 18 July, when Goerdeler's arrest was immi-nent, Stauffenberg had a personal discussion with him.[122]

Coordination was the primary object of numerous other meetings. About 28 May Theodor Steltzer, Yorck and Trott met in Berlin;[123] about 15 June, probably on the 16th, Leber, Goerdeler, Wirmer, Habermann and Jakob Kaiser met in the 'Esplanade' Hotel to discuss the future government programme.[124] On 21 June Leber met Lukaschek, Husen and Yorck of the 'Kreisau Circle' in Yorck's house; they discussed the important question of church or state schools and Leber accepted the right of parents to choose. Leber gave an account of his contacts with the communists. Lukaschek and Husen at first advised against this but Leber said that he knew the people con-cerned; he had lain in the same bunk with them for years in a concentration camp.[125] In June or July a meeting, for which Fritz-Dietlof Graf von der

Schulenburg had been pressing, took place in Wannsee between Kaiser and Stauffenberg. Kaiser was much impressed by the personality of Stauffenberg who described Hitler as 'the incarnation of evil'. Stauffenberg then said: 'But, Kaiser, there must not be a restoration.' Kaiser replied: 'Whom are you saying that to?' He was somewhat taken aback, however, and was not sure whether the warning was intended for Goerdeler or whether this indicated ideas stemming from Stefan George's and Rudolf Fahrner's circle.

Starting in 1943 a cabinet list gradually emerged from all these discussions and negotiations. In so far as it can be reconstructed it is given here, together with some of the earlier or proposed appointments:[126]

	Jan '43	*Aug '43*	*Jan '44*	*July '44*	*Undated — from the Gestapo*
Head of State (regent, hereditary or elected monarch)	Beck			Beck	Beck, possibly later Leuschner
State Secretary					Schwerin von Schwanenfeld
President of Reichstag				Löbe	
Chancellor	Goerdeler		Goerdeler	Goerdeler, Falkenhausen or Witzleben (Popitz tried to promote)	Goerdeler, later Leuschner or Leber
Vice-Chancellor	Leuschner		Leuschner	Leuschner	Leuschner
Press					Kiep
State Secretary				Gisevius	Yorck
Foreign Minister	Hassell	Brüning or Hassell	Hassell	F.W.v.d. Schulenburg or Hassell	F.W.v.d. Schulenburg or Hassell
State Secretary				W.v.d. Schulenburg or Hassell	
Min. of Interior	Gayl Leber	F.D.v.d. Schulenburg	Leber	Leber	F.D.v.d. Schulenburg or Leber
State Secretary					possibly F.D.v.d. Schulenburg

	Jan '43	Aug '43	Jan '44	July '44	Undated – from the Gestapo
Chief of Police					temporarily Helldorf, then Tresckow
Security Police					Kanstein
Min. of Finance	Schniewind then Loeser	Popitz	Loeser	Loeser	Popitz, later possibly Schwerin von Krosigk or Loeser
State Secretary					Helfferich
Pres. of Reich Court	Koch			Koch	
Pres. of Reich Court Martial				Oster	
Min. of War		Beck		Olbricht	Hoepner
State Secretary					Olbricht or Stauffenberg
C-in-C of Wehrmacht					Witzleben
State Secretary					Helfferich
Armaments					Speer to be canvassed
Post Office					attached to Transport; if independent, Fellgiebel
Transport		Königs	Stegerwald		Herrmann
State Secretary					Königs
Culture	Popitz		Bolz	Bolz	Bolz, Schuschnigg or Reichwein, temp. Popitz
State Secretary			Lenz (proposed)		H. Kaiser

	Jan '43	*Aug '43*	*Jan '44*	*July '44*	*Undated – from the Gestapo*
Propaganda					only in war; possibly Mierendorff or Haubach
Reconstruction				Letterhaus (Min. w/o portfolio if not appointed)	
Public Relations				an Austrian	
President of Reischsbank	Blessing				Blessing or Lejeune-Jung
Vice-Pres. of Reichsbank	Wedel				
Prices Commissioner					Blessing
Min. of Economics	Loeser, then Schniewind		Lejeune-Jung	Lejeune-Jung	Blessing or Lejeune-Jung
State Secretary					Ernst
Min. of Food			Hermes		Blessing or Lejeune-Jung; temp. F.D.v. d. Schulenburg, also proposed Schlange-Schöningen, Lüninck or Hermes
Min. of Agriculture				Hermes	
Min. of Labour				Lejeune-Jung	Blessing or Lejeune-Jung
Min. of Justice	Langbehn	Wirmer(?)	Wirmer	Wirmer	temp. Sack, later Kriege
State Secretary					temp. Kriege

At no time was this list more than a working document. At the moment of the *coup* power would have been in the hands of the military and it may be doubted whether they would have been prepared rapidly to relinquish it to civilian politicians. As already mentioned the manoeuvrings, in fact the intrigues, continued until shortly before 20 July; no combination of names can be regarded as final. Popitz canvassed for Witzleben as Chancellor and had previously thought of Falkenhausen. Jakob Kaiser wanted to include Schuschnigg as being an Austrian but got little support. Stauffenberg did not want to keep Goerdeler as Chancellor for long and wished to replace him quickly by Leuschner or Leber. In any case the thoughtful, such as Hassell, realized that the first opposition government could only be of a transitional nature and would have to accept the military defeat and occupation of Germany. It would therefore be expended quickly.

Once these people had been initiated into the plans for overthrowing the government and setting up a new order, they became involved in active planning for the *coup*, inconceivable without the assassination of Hitler. Nevertheless in the summer of 1944 there were still some who were opposed to political murder but yet wished to exploit the resulting situation. Logic and rationality do not necessarily go with courage and a spirit of self-sacrifice.

Goerdeler was still opposed to assassination early in 1944 and even in July when he knew that Stauffenberg was about to try; he continued to think it wrong even in prison. When he first saw Dr Elfriede Nebgen after 20 July (on 25 July while on the run), his first words to her were: 'Doctor, thou shalt not kill.' Initially he had hoped to remove Hitler by force with the assistance of front-line generals but without murdering him; Moltke had at least considered this in the summer of 1943 but after the Allied landing in France Goerdeler had been forced to admit that there was no hope of this solution. In May 1944 he had tried in vain to contact General Zeitzler, the Chief of Staff of the Army, and had written him a letter which, however, was never delivered. Stauffenberg hinted to Goerdeler that Zeitzler had long been 'in the picture'.[127] Goerdeler's political argument that a stab-in-the-back legend must be avoided, Hitler brought to trial and his crimes exposed to the whole world was not lightly to be brushed aside.[128] On the other hand it cannot be denied that in the event this would have led to interminable delays in the 'action', thus defeating its purpose.

Consistency is no virtue in itself. It is futile to turn one's back on the world and politics because one is in a situation brought about by a method of which one disapproves. Put shortly: Goerdeler was opposed to political assassination, but he longed and was impatient for the situation that would result from Hitler's assassination in order to become politically active; he rejected any responsibility for helping to bring about the desired conditions, but he was more than willing to make use of them.[129] If, however, one respects a man's conscience when it forces him to resist and commit treason, one must also respect it when it rejects murder, however illogical this may seem under the circumstances. Goerdeler was a courageous man and he did not oppose assassination for reasons of personal weakness or timidity.

There were also a number of generals who were at one with the resistance movement in their conviction that Hitler must be removed, who participated in all the preparations, but who then, despite their deadly trade, could not bring themselves to commit political murder or even approve it. Beck had been against assassination, but after careful consideration he had agreed that it was the only feasible method of removing the regime; since February 1943 he had not opposed assassination of Hitler.[130] But the reasoning of such men as Kluge and Rommel is difficult to comprehend; they were not against killing as such, only against killing their Commander-in-Chief, even though they knew that he deserved death. The excuse of the oath is a sophistry when a man is involved in conspiracy and treason and yet clings to a formula of loyalty. Forms are valuable in human society, they have an important regulatory function. Not everyone of course can be entirely independent in his thinking or be more than a functionary of his society. In the case of most generals who were plagued by scruples, therefore, good faith must at least be conceded. This does not reduce one's disillusionment at their naïveté.

In fact the men of the 'Kreisau Circle', who have so often been reproached for being solely talkers and 'thinkers' without the logicality to act, were the more logical.[131] Mierendorff, Gerstenmaier, Yorck, Delp and Moltke, to name only a few, worked for years to bring about the *coup* and most of them actively supported Hitler's removal by assassination.[132]

Certain people never overcame their doubts and scruples. Hans-Bernd von Haeften, for instance, remained opposed to assassination primarily on religious grounds; he even argued against his own brother Werner who thought that he had a chance of making the attempt himself when serving as aide to Olbricht and Stauffenberg in the AHA; even when talking to members of the 'Kreisau Circle' in July 1944, he was still arguing against political murder on grounds of Christian morality.[133] For a time Werner von Haeften shared his brother's doubts and was opposed to assassination.[134]

Dr Steltzer also never abandoned his conviction that the ethical and religious laws of Christianity must be strictly observed, so strictly that in his view it was not permissible to lie even when under interrogation by the *Gestapo* or People's Court; both the *coup* itself and political murder he considered immoral.[135] He certainly followed this rule in so far as he himself was concerned; when about to be arrested in July 1944 he refused to escape to Sweden although he could easily have done so, and obeyed his instructions to return to Berlin from Norway.[136]

Alongside these determined opponents of assassination on religious or ethical grounds, however, were many more practical-minded laymen and also priests, both inside and outside the 'Kreisau Circle', who thought assassination necessary and supported it. Among them were the Jesuit Father Delp, Eugen Gerstenmaier and Dietrich Bonhoeffer, the latter two from early 1942 at the latest.[137]

Moltke was initially entirely opposed to assassination and even to the *coup* itself.[138] But by the time of the Stalingrad catastrophe, not *because* of it or from nationalist motives, his opposition was no longer so rigid. In late 1943 he still said to Wilhelm Ritter von Schramm that Hitler must be kept alive and made to carry the entire responsibility for the catastrophe with his Party.[139] As far as he and the majority of the 'Kreisau Circle' were concerned, he found the question academic since they were in a position to do neither the one thing nor the other. But Moltke's hands-off-the-*coup* attitude was also based on moral grounds and Steltzer did his best to stiffen him with religious arguments.

Moltke's attitude must be regarded primarily as the antithesis to the ruling regime, a rejection of all force and brutality even in counter-measures. He could be influenced, however, since there was no element of fanaticism in his make-up, only a certain naïveté as regards what the Allies – both Eastern and Western – would do after Germany's defeat. He thought that, after victory, the Allies would hold one or two parades in Germany and then, out of boredom, quickly withdraw again leaving the Germans to reconstruct the country internally. Since the Stalingrad catastrophe and the increasingly appalling destruction of German cities, however, he had had to revise his ideas – as Gerstenmaier had repeatedly forecast during some of his heated debates with Moltke on renunciation of force in 1940 to 1942.

Since the winter 1943–44, Moltke had ceased advising against the *coup* and assassination.[140] According to General Alexander von Falkenhausen, in September 1943 Moltke said to him in Brussels: 'Despite all our scruples we have no alternative but to eliminate Hitler physically.'[141] Writing to his wife from Tegel prison in January 1945, he said: 'We only deliberated . . .' but in this he was merely paraphrasing the judgement of the People's Court.[142] The next day, 11 January 1945, he wrote again to his wife: 'I was removed at the very moment when there was a danger that I might have become involved in active *putsch* preparations – Stauffenberg came to see Peter [Yorck von Wartenburg] on the evening of the 19th [January 1944]; I therefore am and remain free of any association with the use of force.'[143] He was removed by a dispensation of providence in the form of his arrest; it seems certain that otherwise he would have played an active part. Providence enabled him to abide by his principles which otherwise he would have forsaken. At about the same time he had a last talk with Gerstenmaier, arranged for him by two warders in Tegel, and his attitude then was similar. He made no effort to counter Gerstenmaier's argument that in this case assassination was in accord with Christ's commandment to love and declared himself explicitly and unreservedly in agreement with the attitude of his friends of the 'Kreisau Circle'.[144]

40 Stauffenberg's First Two Assassination Attempts

The decision to attempt assassination did not come easily to Stauffenberg, but he reasoned more logically than those who wanted a *coup* and the murder of Hitler as its essential condition but could not bring themselves to do anything about it. At the latest by the beginning of 1943 he was clear in his mind that a *coup* must be preceded by the murder of Hitler.[1] Once decided that assassination was the prerequisite for everything else, the question whether he should do it himself or not was no longer a matter of primary importance. For him, the decision in favour of the *coup* carried with it the decision to attempt the assassination if opportunity offered and the situation so demanded.[2]

On the other hand, in the first weeks of July 1944 the end of the war seemed very near; the purpose of the *coup* was therefore questionable. When Tresckow despatched Lieutenant-Colonel Georg Freiherr von Boeselager to Field Marshal von Kluge (C-in-C West since 2 July) to propose free passage for the enemy through the front in the west, Kluge replied that this was unnecessary since the enemy would shortly break through in any case.[3] Meanwhile the Russians had destroyed Army Group Centre and surrounded Army Group North; Russian tanks were operating little more than sixty miles from Hitler's headquarters in East Prussia.[4] Would it not therefore be more adroit politically to let Hitler charge on into the abyss alone, visible to all as solely responsible? Would this not be a better guarantee for future generations against similar demons of destruction? Was this guarantee not worth the sacrifice of further thousands, perhaps hundreds of thousands of men? On the other hand – how was the nation to regain its self-respect after the war, to continue to exist and to build anew, to occupy its proper place in the world unless it had itself made some visible effort to cleanse its own house? The consequences might be a resurgence of self-deception and a fresh excursion into irrationality.

No calm reflection could provide the answers to these terrible questions. Only conscience could dictate and Stauffenberg's conscience demanded every conceivable effort to save thousands, probably hundreds of thousands, of human lives, to save the *Reich*, to purge the nation and salvage its honour.[5] Whether the prospects of success for assassination and the rising were good or bad was not the most decisive factor. In mid-June Claus von Stauffenberg said: 'Now it is not the *Führer* or the country or my wife and four children which are at stake; it is the entire German people.'[6] On 1 July 1944 he met his friend Thiersch, a sculptor and now an artillery lieutenant, for whom he had arranged a posting to the Bendlerstrasse; he said to Thiersch that the shame and paralysing effect of a lapse into inactivity were worse than failure; only action could produce freedom, externally and internally.[7] Berthold von Stauffenberg was reported as saying on 14 July: 'The worst thing is knowing that we cannot succeed and yet that we have to do it, for our country and our children.'[8] Equally a few days before 20 July Claus von Stauffenberg said: 'It is now time that something was done. But he who has the courage to do something must do so in the knowledge that he will go down in German history as a traitor. If he does not do it, however, he will be a traitor to his conscience.'[9]

Prior to June 1944 the idea had never seriously been mooted that Stauffenberg himself might or should be the assassin. Quite apart from his lack of access to Hitler, no one would have expected it of a severely wounded man who had lost his right hand, two fingers of his left hand and an eye.[10] Moreover the plans for the *coup* provided that, immediately after the attempt, the news of it would be passed to Berlin so that the measures camouflaged under the codeword 'Valkyrie' could be set in train at once. Stauffenberg, however, even before his appointment as Chief of Staff to Fromm, was considered indispensable for this stage. Olbricht did not think he could run the *coup* himself; in the summer of 1943 he had met Beck and Stauffenberg in the house of Ferdinand Sauerbruch, the surgeon (when Beck and Stauffenberg were introduced); afterwards he had said to Sauerbruch: 'Stauffenberg! He's the man we need.'[11]

It was therefore considered to be out of the question that Stauffenberg should both direct the *coup* in Berlin and make the attempt in the 'Berghof' or 'Wolfschanze'. At that time, too, he and his fellow-conspirators were hoping that approximately between the beginning of October and the middle or end of November 1943 the headquarters group would be prepared to take action; Stauffenberg was counting on Stieff and Meichssner, possibly also on Fellgiebel. When it became evident that they either could not or would not act, the attempts with the uniform demonstrations were initiated; the last of these failed in February 1944, as did Breitenbuch's effort in early March.

So an impasse had been reached. The young front-line officers prepared to sacrifice themselves were either no longer available or the opportunity provided by a uniform demonstration was lacking. Nevertheless about March Stauffenberg tried to persuade Meichssner to make the attempt but he found that Meichssner had not the strength and was no longer willing.[12] A solution to the impasse was provided by Stauffenberg's acting appointment as Chief of Staff to Colonel-General Fromm, giving him access to Hitler.[13] But the dilemma was that he would have to play two roles – assassin and leader of the *coup* – which had to be played almost at the same time; a time-lag of about two hours between the assassination and Stauffenberg's return to Berlin was inevitable, quite apart from all the other uncertainties such as Stauffenberg's ability to leave the headquarters after an explosion involving Hitler.

One indication of the time at which Stauffenberg began to toy with the idea of making the attempt from Berlin or even of doing it himself is the moment when he instructed Hagen and Klamroth to bring him the explosive which Stieff had been keeping; this was at the end of May 1944.[14] As early as March 1944 Stieff had told Klamroth, 'Stauffenberg is engaged in preparation of an assassination attempt'. Now, at the end of May, Stauffenberg told Hagen that he was planning an attack on the *Führer*. In June he told Stieff, according to the latter's evidence to the *Gestapo*, that he proposed to avail himself of the next opportunity to make an attempt; Stieff said that he tried to dissuade him.[15] Not until after 20 June, however, did Stauffenberg have any real prospect of doing it.

Berthold von Stauffenberg told the *Gestapo* that his brother had decided to make the attempt himself some four weeks before he did so, in other words when appointed acting Chief of Staff to Fromm, because he had previously had no opportunity of getting near Hitler.[16] At the end of June Stauffenberg told Graf Yorck that he would try to go to the *Führer*'s headquarters in the near future in order to make a bomb attack.[17] Two or three weeks before 20 July Werner von Haeften, Stauffenberg's aide, wrote to a friend: 'Claus is now thinking of doing the thing himself.'[18]

The war situation became more pressing; the day came ever nearer when it really would be too late for any attempt at liberation from inside; to anyone who did not know the background it already hardly seemed possible. Captain Kaiser noted in his diary that about 24 June, summing up a briefing, Stauffenberg said that 'the personnel replacement situation was such that it must all be over shortly'.[19] In mid-June Tresckow from the eastern front had urged rapid action. A few days after the Allied landing in France Tresckow and Schlabrendorff were at an Army commanders' conference in OKH in East Prussia; Stauffenberg sent a message by Graf Lehndorff-Steinort asking whether, now that invasion had begun, the assassination and attempted *coup* had any purpose.[20] On the eastern front preparations for the *coup* had been made insofar as Tresckow could make them. Parts of Cavalry Regiment 'Centre' and of a neighbouring Rifle Division had been earmarked to be flown to Berlin on *coup* day; trucks were ready, and the airfield and the road to it had been decided upon.[21] Tresckow sent word back to Stauffenberg through Lehndorff: 'The assassination must take place *coûte que coûte*. Even if it does not succeed, the Berlin action must go forward. The point now is not whether the *coup* has any practical purpose, but to prove to the world and before history that German resistance is ready to stake its all. Compared to this, everything else is a side-issue.' This is the view which Stauffenberg took from now on, as is clear from his remarks quoted above. At the same time Tresckow advised Stauffenberg to go himself to General Speidel, Chief of Staff to Field Marshal Rommel, and persuade him to open the western front to a breakthrough by the Allies; otherwise, he said, the Russians would shortly overrun the whole of Germany.

Beck also now took the view that action must be taken without regard to the likelihood of success. On the morning of 20 July Habermann brought him a letter from Goerdeler urging rapid action; he and Habermann agreed that 'action must be taken without regard to unconditional surrender'.[22] 'The only point now,' Beck said, 'is that action against this criminal regime should come from within the German people. Germany must suffer the consequences of all that has been done and not been done.' Even if action were not successful, he continued, it would imply some alleviation of the people's fate.

Stauffenberg's determination became firmer. On the evening of 4 July, just before he heard of Reichwein's and Leber's arrest, he had yet another talk with Professor Fahrner, who was proposing to leave Berlin next day.[23] They discussed the question 'whether, if all other possibilities failed, Claus himself should make the attempt since, as Chief of Staff to Fromm, he now had access both to the headquarters and to Hitler. Yet his presence seemed essential to direct affairs after Hitler's fall ... When Claus put this question to me direct, I was faced with the most difficult decision.' Fahrner's answer was Yes and from this moment, in so far as a moment can be fixed, Stauffenberg felt himself under an obligation. He continued to consider all other possibilities, however.[24]

There is much to indicate that, until 7 July, Stauffenberg was still placing his hopes in Major-General Stieff. That was the day on which the much-postponed uniform demonstration finally took place in Klessheim Castle near Salzburg.[25] Stieff told the *Gestapo* that, when he was in Berchtesgaden on 6 July, Stauffenberg showed him his briefcase saying: 'I've got the whole thing here.'[26] Whether he left the bomb with Stieff or took it away again is not known. In any case 7 July passed without an alert from Berchtesgaden.[27]

There were also other obstacles. Early in July Sauerbruch's house was again 'the scene for an assembly of generals and politicians'.[28] Stauffenberg remained behind when the others left; he seemed tired. Sauerbruch had a long talk with him and suggested that he take a few weeks leave, but Stauffenberg refused, saying that he had no time – he had an important mission to fulfil. Sauerbruch understood and was appalled. Under no circumstances, he said, should Stauffenberg have anything to do with such plans; it was irresponsible; he would not be fully restored to strength for a long time; he might make serious errors in his plans and calculations; his nerves might give way. At first Stauffenberg was offended but then he listened to all Sauerbruch had to say. It did not affect his resolution to act, however.

It is not possible to say what purpose the inscrutable General Fromm had in mind when he appointed Stauffenberg, though there are certain indications. It may be that he simply wanted to have this brilliant officer as his Chief of Staff. He knew, however, what Stauffenberg was planning, at least in its broad lines though not in full detail; Stauffenberg had told him when he assumed office.[29] Dr Georg Kiessel, head of the evaluation section of the *Gestapo*'s '20 July Special Commission' (*Amt IV* of the RSHA) reported the results of his investigations as follows: on assuming office, at the latest by 1 July therefore, Stauffenberg had said to Fromm that 'in this war a total defeat could be prevented only by making every effort in the political field', meaning a *coup d'état*; this he was compelled to tell Fromm for reasons of loyalty; Fromm had listened and had then said to Stauffenberg that he was grateful for his candour and that he was to go ahead with his work.[30] In passing, however, Fromm himself once said: 'For God's sake don't forget that chap Keitel when you make your *putsch*.'[31]

In fact Fromm did not credit any of his subordinates with the energy or determination to do anything revolutionary – except perhaps Stauffenberg.[32] He indicated to his secretary that he had taken Stauffenberg away from Olbricht because he was 'under bad influence' there. Both explanations are conceivable – that by his posting of Stauffenberg Fromm wanted either to prevent or to assist the *coup*. Long before the war Fromm was fond of saying: 'We are always perfectly all right.'[33] Early in 1943 Ulrich von Hassell characterized Fromm as a 'weather-vane' and an 'opportunist'.[34] Similarly in February 1943 Fromm's war diary officer noted: 'Fromm will only do something when all is assured and arranged. Order. The one [Olbricht] is willing to act if he gets the order, the other [Fromm] to issue the order if action has been taken.'[35] Provided, therefore, that the conditions for it had been created by others, the conspirators did not have to assume that Fromm would oppose a *coup*.[36] In February or March 1943 Fromm visited the ailing Colonel-General Hammerstein-Equord and admitted to him that the war could no longer be won. Asked how he visualized the future, Fromm replied: 'In the last resort the *Führer* will not wish his own person to be a barrier to a solution.'[37] On 20 and 21 April 1944 Botho von Wussow visited Stauffenberg with Graf Schwerin von Schwanenfeld and Dr Brücklmeier, a military administration officer; Stauffenberg indicated that Fromm was on the side of the conspiracy, saying: 'You don't have to worry about Fromm. Just don't tell him we propose to do away with the Army, but you can talk quite frankly to him.'[38] Allen Dulles reported to Washington from Berne on 13 and 15 July 1944 that Fromm had joined the conspiracy, according to information received.[39]

In so far as the *coup* was concerned, therefore, Fromm's attitude was ambiguous. His behaviour on 20 July is explicable only by a desire to wait and see and cover up both ways. Nevertheless his general demeanour was such that, though they had their doubts, the conspirators hoped that he would participate in some way.[40] At his own trial before the People's Court on 7 March 1945 Fromm admitted that on 3 July 1944 he said to Graf von Helldorf that it would be best if Hitler committed suicide.[41] It is also striking that during the proceedings of the People's Court on 7 and 8 August 1944 none of the accused showed any sympathy for Fromm; Hoepner in particular accused him indirectly of cowardice and duplicity.[42] One thing is certain: had Fromm been prepared to play an active part at the right time, the *coup* would have had better prospects of success.

On 5 July Leber was arrested. Not only had the conspirators lost a friend and an indispensable helper but the entire conspiracy was threatened. No one doubted Leber's extraordinary capacity for resistance but he was only human and, if the *Gestapo* used adequately sophisticated methods, they might torture him sufficiently to produce a breakdown. Only if their methods were crude would he lose consciousness or die before saying anything. But others had already been arrested and no one could really tell how much the *Gestapo* already knew about the conspiracy. Over a year earlier Popitz and

Langbehn had been in contact with Wolff and Himmler; Langbehn had been arrested in the autumn of 1943 and he knew a great deal. The entire conspiracy was therefore in a highly precarious position; Himmler might decide to strike any day and people were in fact surprised that he had not done so long ago. Arthur Nebe, Director of the *Reich* Criminal Police Office, was a member of the conspiracy and so some warning could be anticipated, but this was not certain.[43] In any case Leber's arrest provided an additional reason for attempting assassination as soon as possible. Talking to Trott between 5 and 20 July Stauffenberg repeated several times with emphasis: 'We need Leber; I'll get him out; I'll get him out,' and on 18 July he passed word to Frau Leber: 'We are aware of our duty.'[44]

In addition rumours about an imminent assassination attempt were circulating. Rumours, allegations, denunciations, false reports and suppositions are stock-in-trade, particularly under a dictatorship and particularly in Germany's situation of 1943 and 1944; the country was swarming with millions of prisoners of war and foreign workers, both conscripted and voluntary; bombs, leaflets and sabotage material were being dropped all the time; the course of the war was highly unfavourable and even the ruling caste was beginning to lose heart. So there was much talk and much suspicion. Many statements to the effect that the SS knew of the *putsch* plans, 'knew everything' and were only waiting for the right moment to strike, were the natural outcome of such rumours, though without substance. On the other hand, in a dictatorship such as that in Germany at the time, the rulers must inevitably have had the possibility of an attempted *coup* in mind. There is much to indicate that by 1943 the RSHA knew enough about the conspiracy to arrest at least its leading members.[45] Dr Müller's soundings in Rome had been discovered by the SD as early as 1939 and the names of some of the principals such as Beck, Halder and Hammerstein were known; Canaris had only been able to legitimize the matter and prevent a catastrophe by adroit manoeuvring. Beck, Hassell Goerdeler and others had long been under observation. In November 1941 Heydrich and Himmler knew that Hassell had been trying 'to arrange talks on peace negotiations with leading Americans'.[46] Dietrich Bonhoeffer, Dohnanyi and Müller had been arrested in the spring of 1943 after Oster had received warnings in 1942; Langbehn had been arrested in September 1943 and the 'Solf Circle', Moltke and Kiep in January 1944; Graf Yorck von Wartenburg had been under well-founded suspicion since 1943.[47] On 12 June 1944 Colonel Staehle was arrested, on 4 July Reichwein and on 5 July Leber.[48] Stauffenberg became increasingly alarmed.[49] Himmler and his *Gestapo* were not squeamish in such matters; men had been sent to concentration camps or executed for trifling offences; they must therefore have good reasons for their failure to arrest known 'enemies of the state'.

If the *Gestapo* were taking their duties in any way seriously, they must inevitably assume that these 'enemies of the state' were planning a *coup* and an assassination attempt; it was hardly to be expected that they would wait until overwhelming evidence was available and they could arrest all the members of the conspiracy – unless they themselves were hoping to profit from the assassination or the *putsch*. Himmler's earlier and later attempts to divorce himself from Hitler, particularly his negotiations with Langbehn and Popitz, indicate that this was a possibility.[50] Himmler's own involvement in the conspiracy must have impelled him either to strike or to assist the *coup*; had it been discovered by the other side he himself would have been labelled as a traitor. But he clearly could not muster the resolution to do either one thing or the other. It is certain that Himmler knew a great deal about the conspiracy – Goerdeler's arrest was planned for July;[51] on the other hand, on 20 July he held the SS back and only really took action *after* the *coup* had failed.[52] His alibi was a good one – that it was preferable to let the Army itself deal with mutiny in its own ranks.[53]

By 1943 the machinations of the senior SS leaders were so obvious that they were known even to people in foreign countries not in contact with members of the opposition such as Dr Schönfeld or Dr Langbehn. Secret services reported SS contacts with the conspiracy, conferences with conspiratorial circles and the SS's own plans – a Swiss secret service under Hans Hausamann, for instance, which worked for the Swiss military authorities during the war and sent reports to General Guisan's headquarters.[54] The secret services, however, saw only the superficial aspect and knew little of what was going on inside the opposition or of its motives. Their informers talked of German-nationalist and military-conservative groups and looked primarily for motives based on power politics and opportunism.

Peter Burckhardt, the Swiss Military Attaché in Berlin, was better informed; his information came from another Military Attaché who in turn was kept informed by people in touch with Beck.[55] On 14 July 1944 he reported to his government that the German regime was now in such difficulties that 'far-reaching changes must be anticipated' within the next two to three weeks. In his report on the attempted *coup*, written on 21 July, he referred back to his report of the 14th forecasting the *coup*. He also reported that in the last ten days a total of three attempts had been made including that of the 20th. As the location of the attempt, however, he gave Berchtesgaden which was correct only in one case; he corrected himself on this point on 25 July.

During the weeks preceding 20 July, therefore, talk of plans for assassination and a *coup* was current in many circles; many of the rumours had some basis in fact. With this mass of rumour and speculation flying hither and thither, in various countries of Europe, over to the United States and throughout Germany and the German-occupied territories, it was inevitable that the *Gestapo* would hear of it and this would add to the knowledge they already possessed.[56] The conspiracy was in the greatest danger and its members knew it. On 9 July Gisevius in Zurich was told by Strünck of the forthcoming attempt and of the anxiety lest the *Gestapo* strike; they knew a great deal, he said.[57] Then came a rumour which apparently never got further than the opposition's inner circle but its leaders did not know this. It emerged on 16 July and was passed on to Stauffenberg on the 18th.[58]

Undoubtedly action was accelerated by these rumours, the arrests and the increasing threat of destruction of the opposition; possibly it might otherwise have 'fizzled out'. But the overall war situation was an equally important factor. If the German fronts were only able to hold for a few more weeks, then not a single day must be lost. There was no point in hoping that preparations could be improved; they were being upset daily by war developments, postings and troop movements.[59] It is therefore incorrect to say that the *coup* was badly prepared and 'hastily' carried out because of these rumours and arrests. The mere emergence of Stauffenberg as a man who had access to Hitler's briefing conferences, was more important than all other factors in accelerating action. Without him it is unlikely that an attempt would have been made at all. The reasons for failure, therefore, are connected only to a very small extent with these rumours and arrests; the real reasons are to be found elsewhere – as we shall see.

On 7 June 1944 Stauffenberg for the first time accompanied Colonel-General Fromm to a briefing conference in the *Führer*'s headquarters in the 'Berghof'. So far, on 30 May 1944 for instance, he had only been in Berchtesgaden on occasions for discussions with Keitel and General Walter Buhle, head of the OKW Army Staff; he had never been in Hitler's presence and never in the 'Berghof'.[60] Fromm had been in disfavour for two years owing to his urgent warnings about the replacement situation but now, as the result of a particularly brilliant study by Stauffenberg, Hitler had once more summoned him to the headquarters.[61] Stauffenberg observed that 'in the *Führer*'s immediate entourage one had considerable freedom of movement'.[62] This was not surprising. The main difficulty for an assassin had always been the approach to Hitler. Now, however, Stauffenberg had an opportunity to spy out the land himself – far more satisfactory than any second-hand reports.[63] When asked by his wife afterwards what impression Hitler had made on him and whether his eyes had been impressive, Stauffenberg replied: 'Not at all. Nothing! . . . as if veiled!' Hitler had shuffled the maps around with a trembling hand, continuously glancing at Stauffenberg; Göring had been wearing make-up. The whole atmosphere was rotten and degenerate.

On 3 July General Wagner, the Deputy Chief of the General Staff, General Lindemann, Director of Artillery on Fromm's staff, Major-General Stieff and General Fellgiebel met in Wagner's room in the 'Berchtesgadener Hof' Hotel; they discussed details of the planned attack. It was established that Stauffenberg had the necessary explosive and fuses; a further check was made of Fellgiebel's preparations to cut the communications of government agencies.[64]

On 6 July Stauffenberg was in the 'Berghof' again, for the first time in his capacity as Chief of Staff to C-in-C Replacement Army. He was present at two hour-long 'special conferences' with Hitler, Himmler, Speer, Buhle and others in which Hitler announced the creation of fifteen new 'blocking divisions' to stabilize the eastern front. The first meeting took place between 5 and 6 p.m.; the second lasted from shortly before midnight until close to 1 a.m. on 7 July.[65] These were not regular briefing conferences, at which Himmler's presence had usually not been required. Now, however, Himmler participated because he was to supervise the training of, initially, six and, a few days later, all of the new divisions.

It is not certain whether Stauffenberg intended to make the attempt on this occasion. In any case he had the bomb with him.[66] Frau Hilde Mertz von Quirnheim, who had joined her husband in Berlin on 4 July after a stay in the Black Forest, noted in her diary in connection with the failure of 15 July: 'This was the third time since I have been in Berlin that Stauffenberg has gone down this horrible road in vain.'[67] It is not known, however, whether he was still hoping that Stieff would do it since he himself would be required in Berlin at the time or whether he did not set off his bomb because Göring was not there. The much-postponed uniform demonstration was scheduled for next day however and Stieff was due to be present at that.[68] Stieff did not use this opportunity for an assassination attempt.

On 11 July Stauffenberg flew once more to the *Führer*'s headquarters in Berchtesgaden. His aide, Lieutenant von Haeften, was not available and so he took with him Captain Friedrich Karl Klausing of the AHA staff.[69] According to the shorthand record Stauffenberg was present at the 'morning briefing' from 1.07 to 3.30 p.m. He had the bomb with him and Klausing ensured that all was in order for the return journey. Klausing himself waited in front of the 'Berghof' with the car and the He 111 was ready to take off for the return flight to Berlin.

But Stauffenberg did not set off his bomb because Himmler was not there.[70] He and if possible Göring too were to be killed at the same time as Hitler because it was believed that they might keep the regime going after Hitler's death and suppress the revolt. Field Marshals Kluge and Rommel had both emphasized to Beck that not only Hitler but Himmler and Göring too must be eliminated.[71] A remark made to Stieff by Stauffenberg indicates that before the conference began (Stieff was not present) he knew that Himmler would not come – 'Good God, ought one then not still do it.'[72]

There was never any certainty that Himmler or Göring would be present at the briefing conferences; neither of them attended regularly. They were usually represented by their liaison officers who reported to them; they themselves came comparatively seldom. Sometimes Himmler and Göring had no personal contact with Hitler for weeks; at other times one or the other would attend several conferences with Hitler daily. It was quite reasonable to expect, however, that Himmler would be present at any of the next conferences with Hitler at which Stauffenberg also had to report, since both Stauffenberg and Himmler were immediately concerned with the organization of the new 'blocking divisions' for the eastern front.[73]

After the briefing conference Stauffenberg, Stieff, Fellgiebel and Lieutenant-Colonel Klamroth met for lunch in the Frankenstrub barracks.[74] They discussed yet again the 'screening' of the repeater stations which had recently become complicated owing to heavy air raids on Munich; Fellgiebel had spent two days inspecting the installations in the Munich area under the administration of the Munich G.P.O. Stauffenberg arrived back in Berlin late that evening.

In Berlin a number of preparatory measures had been taken based on telephone conversations with Berchtesgaden but they had then been cancelled again. Goerdeler had been asked by Stauffenberg to hold himself in readiness.[75] On 10 or 11 July Schwerin von Schwanenfeld telephoned Field Marshal von Witzleben, who was on a cure in Bad Kissingen, asking him to return as soon as possible. Schwerin did not, however, fetch him until 12 July.[76] According to plan criminal police officers were held ready to make the initial arrests; as agreed with Helldorf the remainder of the police were to be neutral, stay in their barracks and refuse to carry out orders from the regime.[77] Three young officers of 9 Infantry Reserve Battalion in Potsdam, Ewald Heinrich von Kleist, Georg Sigismund von Oppen and Lieutenant von Widany, who were earmarked for certain duties, were ordered by Graf von der Schulenburg to go to the Deputy Chief of Staff's office in the Prinz-Heinrich-Strasse, where they reported to Graf Schwerin. After waiting for an hour and a half they were told that they could go again.[78]

On 14 July Stauffenberg was again ordered to accompany General Fromm to the *Führer*'s headquarters on the 15th and again he took Captain Klausing with him as aide.[79] Hitler had moved back to East Prussia on 14 July.[80] Once more Stauffenberg had the bomb with him. Fromm, Stauffenberg and Klausing landed at Rastenburg airfield about 9.35 a.m. on the morning of 15 July and were met with a car by Lieutenant Geisberg of the Headquarters Commandant's staff. They then went for breakfast to the 'Kurhaus' mess in Area II.[81] In addition to Fromm, Stauffenberg and Klausing there were present Lieutenant-Colonel Streve, the Headquarters Commandant, Captain Pieper, his operations officer, and Captain von Möllendorff and Lieutenant Geisberg of his personnel section. About 11 a.m. Geisberg drove Fromm, Stauffenberg and Klausing to Field Marshal Keitel in Area I. Stauffenberg had meanwhile telephoned Stieff and Fellgiebel in 'Mauerwald' camp.

About 1 p.m. Fromm, Stauffenberg and Keitel went to the 'morning briefing' in the so-called briefing hut; this was in the special restricted area (see Annex) where was also the so-called visitors bunker in which Hitler was then living.[82] Stauffenberg and Keitel were talking to the *Luftwaffe* General Karl Bodenschatz in front of the entrance when Hitler, accompanied by Rear-Admiral Karl Jesko von Puttkamer, his naval aide, and an RSD official, came out of his bunker and shook hands with the three officers.[83] The briefing conference was a short one, lasting only from 1.10 to 1.40 p.m. This was followed immediately by a 'special conference' on rear positions and straggler organization lasting until 2.20 and then another 'special conference' with General Fromm until 2.25 p.m.[84]

Obviously Stauffenberg had had no opportunity of fusing his bomb before the briefing conference. Possibly he had not even been able to transfer the bomb to his briefcase in which he had had to have ready the papers he required for his discussions with Buhle and Keitel.[85] It is hardly likely that Stauffenberg wanted only to fuse his bomb when actually in the conference room, in other words when he was sure of Hitler's presence. Since he only had three fingers of one hand he had to use a pair of pliers and this would certainly have been seen. Picture the scene: Stauffenberg bends down to his briefcase and laboriously opens it with his three fingers – someone would certainly have come to his assistance, lifted it on to the table and helped him take out the papers – impossible then to search round for the pliers, squeeze the fuse and put the briefcase back on the floor.

Five days later, on 20 July, Stauffenberg started the fuse *before* he went over to the briefing hut.[86] He had to create the opportunity for this by a pretext. By then he had not only learned from his experience on 15 July, but he was also sure that Hitler had entered the briefing room. But on 15 July Stauffenberg was standing in front of the briefing hut, as the photograph taken at the time shows, waiting with others for Hitler's arrival; Hitler came up while they were waiting. This must have been the first of the three conferences listed by the head stenographer, Dr Peschel, in his report of 22 July as those in which Stauffenberg had participated. From the context it is clear that Hitler was present at each of the three conferences.[87] But Stauffenberg could be no more certain than anyone else that Hitler would be there before he actually came, even if he was definitely expected. Therefore Stauffenberg could not stand waiting in front of the briefing hut with the fuse going. For a number of reasons the impractical method with delay-ignition had been preferred to instantaneous ignition; now Stauffenberg was to some extent the prisoner of the chosen method and could not ignite until he could be as certain as humanly possible that he could place the bomb with the fuse started in the immediate vicinity of Hitler's person.

It is not entirely clear how Stauffenberg intended to proceed if he judged an opportunity to exist, once he was in Hitler's presence. Did he have the bomb with him? Would he not have needed two briefcases, impossible for him to carry? What if he had only the one with the bomb, not yet fused, and was called upon to give a report and to take papers out of his briefcase? To avoid being caught in such a situation with only a bomb in his briefcase, covered by a shirt,[88] he had to have either both, bomb and papers, or only the papers. Then he would have had to rely on an opportunity to slip away to get the bomb, perhaps with the assistance of his aide, or perhaps with the help of Stieff.[89] Since precise information on these points is not available, a number of explanations why the attack was not made on 15 July are possible.

Himmler was not at any of the conferences attended by Stauffenberg. On 15 July he had a private meeting with Hitler on formation of the new Army units among other things. They also discussed such problems as 'Parachute attack on the *Führer*'s Headquarters' and 'Hungary – Jewish question' but this last item naturally not in the presence of Fromm, Stauffenberg or other officers who were not directly concerned in 'these things', as they were known in the headquarters.[90]

Himmler's absence as the reason for not making the attack on 15 July may be difficult to accept in retrospect. Yet there is evidence that cannot be dismissed out of hand to the effect that this was the reason for not going ahead, at least initially.[91]

The alert ordered by Olbricht and Mertz on the morning of 15 July for the Guard Battalion and the Army schools near Berlin at least two hours before the earliest expected time of the assassination of Hitler[92] was a very grave risk and a major step before confirmation of the attack; if Hitler was not killed, if he did not appear at all, it had to be cancelled. The alert before the assassination was rationally defensible only if the attack was made regardless of whether Himmler was there or not, even though it was reasonable to expect that he would be present at one of the next conferences with Hitler to which Stauffenberg was summoned. Perhaps Himmler's importance was overrated by the conspirators; but they must have known that they could not alert the Army schools near Berlin and the Guard Battalion every time there was some hope of finding Hitler, Himmler and Stauffenberg with his bomb in one place.[93]

Nevertheless there were those who insisted that the attempt must not be made unless Himmler was present. General Eduard Wagner for one insisted on 14 July 'that the attack should be made only if the *Reichsführer SS* was there'.[94] He told Colonel Hahn who was in Zossen that day to be sure and tell General Fellgiebel of this; Hahn arrived back in East Prussia on 15 July, apparently having flown with Stauffenberg, and he told Fellgiebel and Stieff of Wagner's demand. General Olbricht and Colonel-General Beck also expressed themselves in favour of acting only if Himmler was there, and they did so on 15 July in response to Stauffenberg's question, by telephone from 'Wolfschanze', whether he should go ahead or not in the absence of Himmler.[95]

There is ample evidence for this and another telephone call by Stauffenberg from 'Wolfschanze' to the Bendlerstrasse between 1.0 and 2.0 p.m. on 15 July.[96] Why did he make them? He must have known that Olbricht and Mertz had alerted the schools and the Guard Battalion. Is this why he wanted to report that he had not been able to bring the bomb with him to the first conference? Had he wanted to warn his friends that there was very little chance of success since he himself would have to give a report? Or had he wanted to know if he should act in the absence of Himmler, although he must have known that it would hardly be possible to repeat the advance alert on another day, and although this question must have been answered one way or another in advance?[97] More and more questions arise: When Stauffenberg called the Bendlerstrasse from 'Wolfschanze', why was there (as will be seen below) a time-consuming discussion? Why did not Beck cut this short and make a decision? Why did the conspirators run the risk of squandering the tremendous effort that the advance alert constituted?

There is some evidence to suggest that Stieff actively interfered to prevent the attack on 15 July. He claimed during *Gestapo* interrogations and in his trial on 7 August 1944 that he prevented the attempts of 6 and 11 July, and that he had implored Stauffenberg not to act 'during his first visit on 15 July' (referring either to the first conference, or to Stauffenberg's first visit to 'Wolfschanze' as Fromm's Chief of Staff and would-be assassin).[98] There is no cogent reason to doubt Gisevius' account based on what Beck told him on 17 July 1944: that Stauffenberg, just back from 'Wolfschanze', had told Beck on the evening of 16 July that Stieff had actually removed Stauffenberg's briefcase with the explosive from the conference room while Stauffenberg was making one of his telephone calls.[99] Notwithstanding Stieff's subsequent claims, however, this may well have been intended to protect Stauffenberg and the other conspirators against discovery, rather than to prevent the attack; there is no suggestion anywhere that the fuse had been set off.

In addition to second- and third-hand accounts given to courts and to the *Gestapo*, the only information available on the telephone calls so far has been Helldorf's eye-witness account related by Gisevius. Now another second-hand account has appeared that is very close to the event and confirms Helldorf's story in its essential points. Colonel Mertz von Quirnheim telephoned his wife on the afternoon of 15 July to say that the attack was off, and in the evening he told her all that had happened. Frau Mertz von Quirnheim noted some of this in her diary immediately and expanded her notes a year later. Here is what she relates of Mertz's account:[100]

'Stauff[enberg] had called him after the start of the conference with the *Führer* to say that Himmler again was not there. A[lbrecht Mertz von Quirnheim] reported this to Olbricht, Beck and the other gentlemen who were waiting there together. There had ensued a rather long, and, as A[lbrecht] thought, deliberately prolonged exchange of opinions and additional telephone calls, all of which gave A[lbrecht] the depressing feeling of finding himself alone when the courage and determination to take the plunge were required. So he was forced to tell Stauff[enberg] after a valuable half-an-hour had elapsed that the generals were opposed to carrying out the attack if Himmler was not there. But Stauff[enberg] had replied: "Ali, you know that in the last resort it is only a matter between you and me – what do *you* say?" And Albr[echt] had answered: "Do it." From that moment on he had waited, with [his friend] Siebeck, in maddening suspense, until finally the news came from St[auffenberg] that the conference had just ended as he had returned to it. This was the third time since I had been in Berlin that Stauffenberg has gone down this horrible road in vain'[101]

Thus it may be assumed that Stauffenberg made his first call to the Bendlerstrasse during or immediately after the first of the three conferences. The one described as just ended when he returned may have been the first or the second one, more likely the second. It cannot have been the third, for two reasons. The third conference is described by the stenographer as one with Colonel-General Fromm; Stauffenberg as his Chief of Staff certainly had to be present, probably also to give a report. Secondly, Stauffenberg must have meant the last and final opportunity in reporting to his brother, as Berthold Graf Stauffenberg said to the *Gestapo* on 22 July: 'My brother told me that a conference had suddenly been called at which he had to give a report so that he had no possibility of carrying out the assassination.'[102] It would be meaningless to give this as a reason for the failure of the attempt if it referred not to the final but to the second-but-last opportunity. It should also be noted that this explanation is supported by the accounts given by Helldorf and by Mertz, and that Stauffenberg was not likely to conceal the decisive reason from his brother with whom he was very close, particularly in all matters pertaining to the *coup*.

It may be concluded that the attempt failed first of all because fusing before the first conference was not possible for a number of reasons, perhaps including information that Himmler was not to be present; then a telephone call to the Bendlerstrasse intervened; after that, it is not clear whether the first or also the second conference took place while Stauffenberg was telephoning and waiting for a decision from conspiracy headquarters; if only the first one was over by the time he returned, there is more room for some speculation about Stauffenberg's determination to go through with the attack than his question about Himmler already suggests; there is also the possibility that Stieff interfered by keeping the explosive out of Stauffenberg's reach at a critical moment, during the first or second conference; finally, in the third conference Stauffenberg had no opportunity to make his attempt because he had to give a report and because, assuming that he could have fused the bomb without too much trouble before this conference, and that he could have with him both papers and bomb, he would still have lacked a chance to get away before the explosion and then he could not have assumed his other role which was deemed essential to the success of the *coup*, that of leader of the revolt in Berlin. No other would-be assassin made more than one attempt; it does not detract from Stauffenberg's merit and self-sacrifice if certain indications that his nerves were somewhat less than steady in those days are noted.[103]

Disturbing questions still remain, particularly with regard to the apparent unclear thinking among the leaders of the conspiracy. Did Stauffenberg and Mertz really think they should take over the reins themselves? Was this a conspiracy within the conspiracy? Then it is even more difficult to see why Stauffenberg did not concentrate first and foremost on the assassination of Hitler without waiting for Himmler. Did the presence of Fromm have any influence on Stauffenberg's decisions? Why was there discussion of an assassination attempt which was practically in progress? Stauffenberg probably referred to this confusion when he told Beck on 16 July that some things had not gone smoothly in Berlin either.[104] If the insistence of some of the conspirators on Himmler's presence must be seen as a stalling device, perhaps employed half-unwittingly, the unauthorized procedure of Stauffenberg and Mertz appears quite defensible in view of the goals of the conspiracy and in view of the interminable procrastination of the older generals; but Stauffenberg's apparent wavering because of Himmler's absence does not.

After the second 'special conference' Fromm went off in the direction of Area I, leaving the *Führer*'s enclosure. Stauffenberg remained in front of the briefing hut for a time; Geisberg was waiting for him to help him carry his briefcase in view of his disabilities.[105] When Stauffenberg had finished his discussions outside the briefing hut he 'finally', in other words after some time, went to the car park where the car allotted to him and Fromm was (a four-seater Opel 'Admiral'). Klausing was already waiting there. Geisberg had to look after Fromm as well and find out where he was; he was distressed by his protégés' failure to remain together since he must now inevitably abandon one of them. Fromm had gone off with Keitel to the special train known as

'Braunschweig' and to lunch.[106] Stauffenberg meanwhile was talking to Stieff and Fellgiebel in the car park near bunker 88/8.[107] Then he telephoned to Berlin; this must have been about 3.0 p.m., certainly not much earlier.[108]

Stauffenberg, Klausing and Geisberg then drove to Keitel's special train; lunch had already begun so the three of them ate in an adjoining dining-car.[109] The 'Ju 52' aircraft in which Fromm, Stauffenberg and Klausing had arrived was ordered from Rastenburg airfield to Lötzen and after lunch Fromm went to 'Mauerwald' by car with General Buhle, Stauffenberg and Klausing. Geisberg had to remain behind because there was no more room in the car. Fromm then flew back to Berlin from Lötzen; Stauffenberg and Klausing, however, took the courier train.[110]

In Berlin people had banked on 'the flash' taking place this time. As on 11 July Stauffenberg had asked Goerdeler to hold himself in readiness for the 15th and Goerdeler had again urged the 'breakthrough'.[111] As on 11 July Nebe had earmarked a number of criminal police officers to arrest Nazi dignitaries in Berlin such as Goebbels, Ley and others. On receipt of a codeword from Helldorf, the Police President, on 15 July Nebe alerted them on pretext of a major hunt for gangs of foreign criminals.[112] Hayessen, who was to play the role of liaison and operations officer with General von Hase on the day of the *coup*, was given instructions and had coordinated the anticipated measures during the morning with Bernardis, Oertzen and Hase.[113] The young officers from 9 Infantry Reserve Battalion, Potsdam, had once more gone to the Prinz-Heinrich-Strasse. Widany, who had been posted to the front, was replaced this time by Lieutenant Ludwig Freiherr von Hammerstein; he and Lieutenant Georg Sigismund von Oppen waited in the 'Esplanade' hotel while Lieutenant von Kleist reported to Graf Schwerin. After some time, however, about 4 p.m. Schwerin said that there was nothing in view and dismissed him and the others; Hitler had left the conference unexpectedly, he said.[114]

As already mentioned, Olbricht had been so certain that the attempt would be made that day that he had alerted the Army schools near Berlin and the Guard Battalion beforehand; this he had done about 11 a.m.[115]

When it became evident that the attempt had not been made, the Army schools had to be de-alerted and the whole matter camouflaged as an exercise. The alert could neither have been issued nor cancelled had Fromm been in Berlin instead of East Prussia.[116] Olbricht was not only relieved to be able to handle the alert as a practice, but also apparently that the assassination had not taken place.[117] About 3.0 p.m. Olbricht drove off with Major Fritz Harnack, one of his staff officers, and Major Ulrich von Oertzen to inspect the units which had been alerted in the Infantry Cadet School, Potsdam, the armoured schools at Krampnitz and Glienicke and the Infantry School, Döberitz. The 'exercise' had gone off very well; Olbricht thanked the commanders, telling them and their staffs that in the present situation emergency operations by the Replacement Army must be anticipated, either in the east or against enemy airborne troops or to deal with internal disturbances which might well break out, particularly in Berlin, in view of the presence of so many foreigners. Olbricht then took the salute of the units on parade and cancelled the alert.

Of course, Olbricht could only review the units on parade, not their deployment and action, otherwise he might have noticed some flaws. In Döberitz, for instance, the vehicles had not even been loaded, armed and filled with petrol by 4.30 p.m. when Olbricht arrived.[118] The hasty praise that Olbricht handed out and the cancelling of the alert led several officers to smile or quietly shake their heads, knowing of the serious shortcomings of the alert measures. But before 20 July some important improvements were made.

On Sunday 16 July Stauffenberg visited Beck in his house to tell him about the mishaps of the previous day.[119] Stauffenberg reported, as Beck told Gisevius the next day, that Stieff had taken the briefcase with the explosive out of the conference room while Stauffenberg was making one of his telephone calls; Stauffenberg added that in Bendlerstrasse not everything had worked out satisfactorily either and that his inner circle, that is primarily Mertz, were dissatisfied with Olbricht's performance. Olbricht admitted on 18 July that there had been flaws.[120] On the evening of 16 July, Stauffenberg, his brother Berthold, Fritz-Dietlof Graf von der Schulenburg, Trott, Hofacker, Mertz von Quirnheim, Schwerin von Schwanenfeld, Yorck and Hansen met in the Stauffenberg flat in Wannsee about 7 p.m.[121] According to statements made to the *Gestapo* by those involved they discussed the possibility of other solutions in view of the failure of attempts at assassination so far. There were strong arguments, stemming partially from Goerdeler and Gisevius and to which Beck was not altogether opposed, for transferring the main weight of the *coup* to the west.[122] The Normandy front was about to crack (in Rommel's view this would inevitably happen in about a fortnight) and a Russian invasion of Germany had to be prevented; an obvious solution, therefore, was to withdraw the western front and at the same time turn it into the lynchpin of the *coup*, particularly seeing that both Rommel and Stülpnagel were prepared to participate and do exactly this.[123] After an exhaustive discussion with Rommel, his Chief of Staff and with Field Marshal von Kluge, C-in-C West, Hofacker had come to Berlin on his own initiative to coordinate between Berlin and the west.[124] On 15 July Rommel had drafted his memorandum giving Hitler an ultimatum, describing the catastrophic situation at the front and begging him to draw the consequences therefrom immediately. But the document was shelved and never reached Hitler before Rommel was wounded.

Hofacker gave a detailed report on the views of Rommel, Kluge, and Stülpnagel, saying that they were ready to do all in their power in the west. Trott then dealt with peace negotiations, saying that in his view they should be possible both with the East and the West after a complete change of regime; 'soldier to soldier' negotiations offered the best prospects of success.[125]

They then discussed whether initiation of the *coup* should be left entirely to the west, the commanders ordering a cessation of hostilities on their own authority and withdrawing German troops to the Siegfried Line. This, it was thought, might produce a common front against the Soviet Union. Hopes were based on the assumption that the Western Allies would be guided by political expediency and cold calculation. Though this assumption was wrong, it was understandable in the light of the opposition's isolation and the optimism of its leaders such as Goerdeler and Stauffenberg. Subject to its effects on the eastern front, this 'western solution', as it became known, had certain prospects since both Rommel and Stülpnagel were prepared to act, although no one could ever be sure of Field Marshal von Kluge.

This is how Stauffenberg summed up the alternatives: '1. The "western solution": The military leaders there could capitulate to the enemy's military leaders without authorization. 2. The "central solution": One could murder the *Führer*! 3. The "Berlin solution": The High Command of the Home Army could cut off the *Führer*'s headquarters from all communications for a short time and meanwhile order all fronts to retreat into a "consolidated resistance area"; the *Führer* could then do nothing other than accept the *fait accompli*. 4. If the western front collapsed so rapidly that the assassination of the *Führer* came too late, then one could combine the "western" and the "Berlin" solutions!!!'[126] In this case, Adam von Trott and a general were to be sent to England for negotiations.

If the 'western solution' depended on the willingness of the enemy to negotiate, which they could not afford except at the risk of losing their Russian ally whom they thought they needed in the struggle against Japan once Germany was defeated, the 'Berlin solution' also depended on conditions that were not very likely to exist, namely the removal of the entire Nazi leadership including particularly Hitler, Keitel and Jodl, and possibly also Himmler, Dönitz and Göring. The course of events on 20 July proved that communications could be cut only for a few hours, under unusual circumstances, and not at all against the will of Hitler. Fellgiebel had always made clear to his fellow-conspirators that communications could not be controlled before Hitler's death.[127]

After prolonged discussion the previous plan, known as the 'central solution', was adhered to and the murder of Hitler remained as the essential prerequisite to everything else. This plan had, after all, been prepared down to the last detail; it could and should be combined with the initial stages of the 'western solution', the withdrawal of the front.

Whether some of those involved were seriously hoping to achieve their aim without the assassination it is not possible to say. There were tendencies this way: Rommel was opposed to assassination, in favour of arresting and condemning Hitler and prepared to do his part in the 'western solution';[128] according to Gisevius Beck, advised by Goerdeler, Hansen and Gisevius himself, was willing to try the 'western solution'.[129] It was not surprising that many began to have doubts about the assassination succeeding; Stauffenberg could only propose; he could not guarantee. Much that, for instance, Berthold von Stauffenberg and Fritz-Dietlof von der Schulenburg said at this time should be regarded not only as an expression of determination to sacrifice themselves in fulfilment of a moral duty without great prospect of success but also as evidence of disillusionment with the repeated failures.[130]

On 17 July a number of things happened to influence the course of the conspiracy, though by no means so decisively as is sometimes supposed.[131] The starting point for all further developments was the next opportunity for an attempt at assassination; this was to be seized under all circumstances – as on 15 July. When this would be depended on when Stauffenberg would have access to another briefing conference. There is nothing to show that the conspirators had any influence on the date of Stauffenberg's next summons to headquarters and in fact no conceivable development could have caused him to make an 'over-hasty' attempt. He was determined to do it by hook or by crook; after all he had not gone around for weeks with a briefcase full of explosives for no good reason.

About 4 p.m. on 17 July Rommel, who was travelling without an escort, was severely injured in a fighter-bomber attack while on his way back from a visit to the front. The conspiracy had thus lost its vital man in the west, someone who would not merely talk about action but, once having taken a decision, have the strength to put it into effect.[132] Stülpnagel did what he could within his limits but Kluge had neither the spirit nor determination to rise to the occasion on 20 July (although he must have realized that he was too deeply involved to escape scot-free).

At midday on the same day senior officers of the RSHA discussed the proposed arrest of Goerdeler: since the victim was a prominent person Himmler had to be asked first. As with Dohnanyi, Bonhoeffer, Müller and Moltke, the alleged reason was trivial. An opponent of Hitler on the outskirts of the conspiracy was supposed to have referred to Goerdeler as the future chancellor. Heinrich Müller, head of the *Gestapo* (*Amt IV* of the RSHA), however, thought this adequate reason to enable him at last to take action against this 'enemy of the state' who had long been under suspicion.[133] If Goerdeler were arrested, then the *Gestapo* would have made inroads into the very centre of the conspiracy twice within a fortnight (Leber's arrest was the first). Undoubtedly this was an alarm signal.

Equally on 17 July Graf von Helldorf, the Police President, told Gisevius that he had serious doubts about Major Remer, commander of the Berlin Guard Battalion; he was an ex-Hitler Youth leader and had been awarded the Knight's Cross. Moreover, Helldorf said, he did not yet know what Lieutenant-General von Hase, Commandant of Berlin, planned to do in the event of a *coup*.[134] Gisevius did not know either; he had just returned from abroad.[135] Beck too was uneasy about Remer, obviously after talking to Gisevius.[136] He spoke to General Olbricht that same evening about this and other 'deficiencies' in the preparations. Olbricht admitted the 'deficiencies', including, no doubt, some of his own failings especially in connection with Stauffenberg's telephone calls on 15 July, and he agreed to put things right; he proposed to arrange a meeting between Hase and Helldorf, adding that he was entirely at Beck's disposal but was prepared only to provide technical resources; he was no real *putschist*.[137] Stauffenberg had already tried to reassure Beck about Remer,[138] but even in Hase's own staff there were some who were suspicious of Remer. On 18 July, following a conference regarding possible 'internal unrest' between Hase, Remer, Lieutenant-Colonel Erttel

and Lieutenant-Colonel Heinz, the latter two warned Hase that Remer constituted a danger for the *coup* and that it would be best to send him off to some
place, perhaps to Italy, on some military business.[139] But Hase shrugged this off.

Hase's view was that Remer would obey orders received from his superiors;
he had received some of the highest decorations for bravery, and he was, after
all, a soldier, and nothing else.[140] If necessary, Hase said, he could be arrested.
He could not have Remer posted since he had only just arrived; having proved
himself at the front and won the Knight's Cross, he had been given this distinguished appointment so that he might recover his strength. Efforts to have
him posted would only result in disagreements, intrigues and undesirable
notoriety. Hase had already had experience of Remer and knew what he was
saying. At the end of June the Guard Battalion had been parading for a solstice
festival under Goebbels while Berlin was burning furiously after a heavy air
raid. When Hase heard that most of the Guard Battalion had taken no part in
the fire-fighting and rescue operations, he administered a sharp rebuke to
Remer and ordered him to send all his available men into action at once.[141]
Remer was offended but had complied without further ado. Hase felt that he
could be dealt with like any other major and in fact Remer did initially carry
out all his orders without question.

An improvement in the preparations made on 17 July was the introduction
of a 24-hour state of alert in the 'Zeppelin' telephone exchange in Zossen
camp.[142] Majors Degner and Burchardt worked in shifts. On the same day
Major von Oertzen, on behalf of General Olbricht, visited the 'Grossdeutschland' Armoured Infantry Reserve Brigade in Cottbus, some sixty miles south-
east of Berlin; the object was to establish how quickly the 'Valkyrie' units to
be formed there would be ready to move in the event of 'internal disturbances'.[143] The next day Lieutenant-Colonel Hans-Werner Stirius, commanding the Brigade's Armoured Infantry Reserve and Training Regiment,
representing the brigade commander who was away, was asked to appear on
19 July for a conference with the Chief of Staff, Replacement Army.[144]

On the morning of Tuesday 18 July Goerdeler returned to Berlin from Leipzig. He had taken leave of his family and was now told by Captain Kaiser that
an arrest warrant was almost out against him.[145] Stauffenberg also arrived
and Goerdeler once more raised the idea of the 'western solution'; he proposed
to fly to Kluge together with Beck but Stauffenberg told him that he and Beck
now thought this inpracticable. Goerdeler and Stauffenberg finally agreed on
an emergency address, Rahnisdorf estate near Herzberg, where Goerdeler
could be reached. Goerdeler could, therefore, have been in no doubt that
Stauffenberg intended to make a further attempt at assassination. He spent
the night in Potsdam and from there wrote a further letter to Beck begging
him to do what he could to obtain rapid action. Jakob Kaiser visited Goerdeler
in Potsdam and took the letter with him, also one to Captain Strünck in which
Goerdeler asked for a false passport. The letter to Beck arrived on the morning
of 20 July via Habermann.

On the afternoon of 18 July Stauffenberg seems to have been fairly certain
that he would be summoned to the briefing conference in 'Wolfschanze' on the

20th. In any case about 5 p.m. Colonel Mertz von Quirnheim told Schulenburg that the 20th was the next date; Bernardis, Yorck, Wagner, Klausing, Schwerin von Schwanenfeld, Kleist and Ludwig Freiherr von Hammerstein were also informed on the 18th. Lieutenant-Colonel Klamroth learned from Stauffenberg himself on 18 July that he intended to make the attack on the 20th. During Hitler's evening briefing conference of 19–20 July the wish was expressed that Fromm come to 'Wolfschanze' next day. A call was immediately put through to him but he said that there were reasons which made it impossible for him. As a result it was decided that Stauffenberg should go alone.[146]

On 18 July Stauffenberg heard of a rumour, current since the 16th, that during the week the *Führer*'s headquarters would be blown up. Obviously this must have reinforced him in his determination.

The story was as follows: Anton Graf von Welsburg was a garrulous young man who spent much time in Frau von Bredow's house in Potsdam and was friendly with one of her daughters, Diana; he had apparently heard that an assassination attempt was imminent. This was probably due to some indiscretion on the part of Werner von Haeften, Stauffenberg's aide, who was also friendly with one of the Bredow daughters. Now Graf von Welsburg carried the rumour back, so to speak, to its source in that on Sunday 16 July he regaled it in the Bredow house in the presence of Dr Sydney Jessen who was in the enemy intelligence section of Naval Headquarters and closely involved in the conspiracy.[147]

Jessen was appalled when he heard the Hungarian count naïvely telling this story. Naturally he did not like to ask precisely where the tale came from, since it never occurred to him that it was so close home and he did not know Welsburg. Jessen could have no inkling that, far from being the talk of the town, the rumour was totally, or almost totally, unknown outside the Bredow house. But if someone like Welsburg, whom Frau von Bredow had described as innocent, if not simple, could blab this out, Jessen inevitably thought to himself that it could only be a question of hours, or at the most days, before the *Gestapo* followed the affair up.[148] Stauffenberg had to be warned.

On 17 July Jessen told Berthold von Stauffenberg and Kranzfelder what he had heard on Sunday and on the 18th Kranzfelder went over to the Bendlerstrasse, Berlin, and reported to Stauffenberg. He returned to the naval camp 'Koralle' about 5 p.m. that day (Tuesday).[149] Though Stauffenberg needed no further goading into his decision, it is conceivable that, on hearing Kranzfelder's news, he made a special effort to be present at one of the next briefing conferences. Undoubtedly he was reinforced in his conviction that, in the light of the numerous leaks and arrests of recent days and weeks, there should be no further delay.[150] Kranzfelder told the *Gestapo* what Stauffenberg's answer to his warning of 18 July was: 'So there is no longer an alternative. We have crossed the Rubicon.'[151] In an article written in 1946 Jessen said: 'He [Kranzfelder] returned and said that, on the basis of this report, Claus Stauffenberg had decided to make a fresh attempt forthwith. He had emphasized that he would act now even if Himmler was not present at the meeting – a consideration which had hitherto caused him not to fuse his bomb. Claus Stauffenberg had added that this would be his final attempt. He had arranged to give a briefing in Rastenburg on the 20th.'[152]

At 10 a.m. on 19 July Lieutenant-Colonel Stirius, acting commander of the 'Grossdeutschland' Reserve Brigade arrived from Cottbus for the scheduled conference.[153] Stauffenberg asked Stirius (Haeften was present) about the strength and organization of his brigade and the results of the 'Valkyrie' exercise held on 15 July.

Stirius gave the strength of his brigade as 7–8,000 men; numbers and training were adequate for operations in the field; morale and fighting spirit were good. There were many volunteers in the brigade. During the 'Valkyrie' exercise they had checked the timetable for the 'Valkyrie 1' and 'Valkyrie 2' measures, had moved by road, according to instructions, to a concentration area south of Berlin and returned under peacetime conditions. Early on the day of the exercise the units concerned had reached their allotted areas around Schulendorf – Marienfelde – Lichtenrade some six miles south of Tempelhof airport. There they had come across camps full to bursting with foreign workers; the sudden appearance of the brigade's heavily armed units, their discipline and their alert bearing (no longer a normality in the summer of 1944) had made a great impression.

The conversation was interrupted on several occasions; Stauffenberg was continuously being called away and twice had to ask Stirius to wait in the outer office. There Stirius met an old acquaintance who had been a battalion adjutant with him in the 'Grossdeutschland' Division until he lost a leg and who was now serving as aide to General Fromm – Captain Heinz-Ludwig Bartram. Stirius asked why everything was so hectic but Bartram could tell him nothing. Bartram still had no inkling of what was afoot when that afternoon he called Captain Pieper, operations officer to the Camp Commandant of the *Führer*'s headquarters, asking him to meet Stauffenberg and look after him.[154]

Finally Stauffenberg asked Stirius the surprising question how long it would take the brigade to move by road in battle order to an area south of Hamburg; he hinted at the possibility of British landings at the mouth of the Elbe. After a quick calculation – the distance was some 225 miles – Stirius said that the main body of the brigade could arrive at Bergedorf south of Hamburg eighteen hours from the order to move. Stauffenberg seemed very pleased, also when told that the brigade would undoubtedly be able to put a stop to any attempts to land in cooperation with other formations, the *Luftwaffe* and the Navy. Stauffenberg wished the brigade every success.

Apart from the Tank School in Krampnitz, the 'Grossdeutschland' Brigade was undoubtedly the most powerful Army formation in the neighbourhood of Berlin; its equipment and training were particularly good; it had covered itself with glory at the front and parts of it had the distinction of wearing an armband '*Führer* Escort Battalion "Grossdeutschland".' It was an adroit move by Stauffenberg to make sure of this particular formation. On the same day Mertz von Quirnheim telephoned Major-General Thomale, the Chief of Staff to the Inspector General of Armoured Forces, to ask that the transfer of tank training units from Krampnitz to East Prussia be postponed for a few days because the troops were needed for a 'Valkyrie' exercise. Thomale obtained the approval of the Inspector General, Colonel-General Guderian, who was at that time in Allenstein, and told Mertz that the request had been granted.[155]

On the afternoon of 19 July Stauffenberg conferred for some two hours with about thirty officers of the headquarters.[156] At the same time Witzleben, Hoepner, Hase and others, including selected officers of 9 Infantry Reserve Battalion in Potsdam and Ludwig Freiherr von Leonrod in the Tank School, Krampnitz, were requested to be ready for the following day or alternatively to come unobtrusively to Berlin. Witzleben arrived in Berlin on the 19th and was told by Schwerin von Schwanenfeld: 'Field Marshal, preparations are to be made for tomorrow.'[157] Witzleben then returned to Seesen; Hoepner, who had also arrived in Berlin on the 19th, stayed overnight in his father-in-law's house in Wannsee.[158] About 4 p.m. Major Hayessen of Olbricht's staff visited Lieutenant-General Hase in the City Commandant's office. Hayessen said that the assassination attempt was to be made next day and discussed once more with Hase the measures which the City Commandant's headquarters were due to take.[159] That evening Hase met Olbricht for the same purpose.

During the afternoon Corporal Karl Schweizer, Stauffenberg's driver, was ordered to fetch a bricfcase from 'a Lieutenant-Colonel in Potsdam'; this was Lieutenant-Colonel Fritz von der Lancken, an officer of Olbricht's staff.[160] Schweizer was told to take the briefcase to Stauffenberg's apartment at 8 Tristanstrasse, Wannsee, and leave it there ready for the journey next morning; he accordingly placed it by the bed in the bedroom next to Stauffenberg's room. All Schweizer knew was that the briefcase weighed a good five pounds and contained one or two packages tied up with string; he knew nothing of Stauffenberg's plan. The *Gestapo* later discovered that between Stauffenberg's various attempts the explosive had been held by Lieutenant-Colonel von der Lancken. The briefcase contained the 'bomb'.

About 6 p.m. Stauffenberg saw the Deputy Chief of the General Staff of the Army, General Eduard Wagner, at his Zossen headquarters. The two conferred privately for about an hour.[161] Nothing is known about the subject of their discussion although it can be surmised. Wagner's aide, Graf von Kanitz, noticed that Wagner's mood was relaxed as usually before important decisions and events. Wagner ordered coffee for three which was taken in the ante-room with Kanitz; then Kanitz remarked that the General might perhaps wish to shoot some rabbits and offered his shotgun. But Wagner preferred to have Kanitz shoot the rabbits while he and Stauffenberg enjoyed driving the animals out of the bush behind the bunker-like buildings like experienced beaters. After about half-an-hour of this, Stauffenberg left.

That evening Stauffenberg met Trott zu Solz.[162] About 9 p.m., on the way back to Wannsee, he asked his driver to stop at a church where a service was being held; he went in for a time and was then driven straight home.[163] Later that evening Berthold von Stauffenberg arrived and remained with his brother till next morning.[164]

PART IX/20 JULY 1944

41 'Wolfschanze'

About 7.0 a.m. on 20 July Corporal Schweizer drove his master, Colonel Claus Schenk Graf von Stauffenberg, with his brother Berthold to Rangsdorf airfield.[1] On the 19th, after receiving his summons to headquarters, Stauffenberg had contacted General Eduard Wagner, Deputy Chief of Staff of the Army, and he had made available a Heinkel 'He 111' for the return flight.[2] On the outward flight Stauffenberg presumably used the normal courier aircraft, a Junkers 'Ju 52'.[3] Stauffenberg's aide, Lieutenant von Haeften, was waiting at the airfield; he and Stauffenberg got in and Schweizer placed the briefcase containing the bomb near his master in the aircraft. Haeften told Schweizer to while away the time before fetching him and Stauffenberg that afternoon by getting himself a new uniform from the clothing store in Spandau. When Schweizer asked what he wanted a new uniform for, Haeften replied that he would be getting much more than that. Berthold von Stauffenberg went back from the airfield to the naval headquarters in 'Koralle' camp near Bernau.

Captain Pieper, one of the Camp Commandant's staff officers, had sent a courier car to Rastenburg airfield. When Stauffenberg and Haeften landed about 10.15 a.m., therefore, they were able to leave at once and drive the four miles to 'Wolfschanze' along the country road towards Lötzen as far as Queden Farm and thence northwards into Area II.[4] Major-General Stieff was with them, having apparently been in the same aircraft.[5] Stieff went on to 'Mauerwald', taking Haeften with him for the moment; Haeften was to meet Stauffenberg later in 'Wolfschanze'; Stauffenberg went to No 2 Mess in Area II which was in the 'Görlitz Kurhaus'. Here there was not only a dining room and mess for the *Führer*'s headquarters and the OKW Operations Staff but accommodation for certain members of the headquarters, among them Dr Erich Walker, the senior medical officer.

A table was laid for breakfast under an oak tree outside the mess; in addition to Stauffenberg there were present Captain Pieper, Dr Wilhelm Tobias Wagner, head of the dental clinic, Dr Walker and Captain von Möllendorff, personnel officer in the Camp Commandant's Staff. Lieutenant-General Henning von Thadden, Chief of Staff in *Wehrkreis* I (Königsberg), with a staff officer had arrived in the headquarters between 8.0 and 9.0 a.m. and they were already sitting over coffee when Stauffenberg arrived.[6] The official reason for Stauffenberg's visit was the formation of two new East Prussian divisions from the older home-guard reservists (*Landwehr*), with younger and experienced officers, which Hitler had ordered on 19 July to help prevent the Red Army advancing further into Poland and East Prussia, into *Wehrkreis* I therefore. Thadden had been ordered to the headquarters specially to hear Stauffenberg's briefing.[7] During breakfast Pieper and Möllendorff were continuously on the telephone; Stauffenberg also tried to arrange his meetings and himself telephoned to Major John von Freyend.

About 11.0 a.m. Stauffenberg went to the OKW Operations Staff hut in Area I for his first meeting – with General Buhle; Lieutenant-Colonel Lechler was waiting for him. Lieutenant Jansen, the Camp Commandant's duty officer, accompanied him and carried his briefcase.[8] At this point Haeften joined Stauffenberg in Area I. Lieutenant-General Henning von Thadden was also present at the meeting with Buhle.[9]

About 11.30 Buhle, Thadden, Stauffenberg, Haeften and Lechler went across to Keitel in the building opposite Jodl's.[10] The remaining problems and their submission to Hitler at the briefing conference were discussed once more and this took about three-quarters of an hour. Time was now pressing since, owing to Mussolini's expected visit that day, the briefing conference had been put forward from 1.0 p.m. to 12.30. Linge, Hitler's valet, called Keitel about midday to remind him.[11] Shortly after midday the shuttle railway car between 'Wolfschanze' and 'Mauerwald' arrived bringing Lieutenant-General Heusinger for the briefing conference. John von Freyend saw this and told Keitel that Heusinger was already there whereupon Keitel got up and urged everyone to hurry.

Meanwhile Haeften was in a waiting room in the same building – when he was not pacing up and down nervously in the corridor.[12] When the meeting with Keitel broke up and Keitel, Buhle and John von Freyend prepared to leave for the briefing conference, Stauffenberg asked Keitel's aide where he could have a brush-up; he also wanted to change his shirt, he said. He accordingly went to the lavatory and in the passage met Haeften; both went into the waiting room and began to rearrange the briefcases and their contents.[13] Keitel, Buhle, John von Freyend, Lechler and Thadden were waiting outside the building, Keitel uneasy and impatient. At this point General Fellgiebel called the OKW bunker and sent a message to Stauffenberg asking him to call back. There was now no time for this, of course; John von Freyend, who had taken the call, sent Sergeant-Major Vogel to Stauffenberg in the anteroom to tell him of Fellgiebel's call and also urge him to hurry.[14]

Vogel left the door open and stood waiting in the corridor, looking into the room. He could see, as he reported to John von Freyend that evening, how Stauffenberg and Haeften were busy with a wrapped object which Vogel had noticed previously in the passage of the hut. When Vogel asked Stauffenberg to hurry, the latter replied crossly and abruptly that he was coming straight away. But Vogel remained standing there until Stauffenberg came out. At that moment John von Freyend called from the entrance: 'Stauffenberg, come along, please!'

Stauffenberg and Haeften had now packed the bomb into the briefcase in which Stauffenberg had had his papers for the conference; Stauffenberg had with him a pair of pliers specially twisted so that he could use them with the three fingers of his left hand (parts of the tool were later found where the bomb had exploded), and with these he squeezed the acid capsule of the fuse. But Stauffenberg and Haeften had been disturbed. If they had intended to stow *both* bombs, each weighing about two pounds, into Stauffenberg's briefcase, they now did not find it possible to do so.[15] Stauffenberg hurried off to catch up with Keitel, who had already gone on ahead; meanwhile Haeften stowed the other bomb and papers back into his briefcase and then turned his attention to the car in which they would both drive away. John von Freyend accompanied Stauffenberg.

Buhle went straight off towards the briefing hut, Stauffenberg talking to him briskly. Lechler went part of the way and then turned off towards the mess after offering to carry Stauffenberg's bag, as did John von Freyend; with his one arm both of them wanted to help him but Stauffenberg refused.[16] On the way they encountered an aide, Albert Bormann, who had just escorted Hitler to the briefing hut.[17] Just before reaching the hut Stauffenberg accepted John von Freyend's offer to carry the bag, saying: 'Could you please put me as near as possible to the *Führer* so that I catch everything I need for my briefing afterwards.'[18] Possibly he was referring to his hearing which had been affected or to his requirement to have his data handy, but in any case he needed some pretext to place himself near Hitler *forthwith*; the weather being warm, the fuse might act some ten minutes after the acid capsule had been broken.[19]

Meanwhile the briefing conference had already begun. Just before 12.30 Colonel von Below, the *Führer*'s aide on duty, invited officers waiting or arriving to enter the conference room; a servant had placed a stool for Hitler against the long north-facing side of the great table and laid out his spectacles ready and cleaned. Punctually at 12.30 the *Führer* appeared and opened the conference.[20] General Warlimont had waited outside the door; Jodl was not yet there; he often came a little late because he disliked unnecessary standing around. When Hitler arrived, however, Warlimont went inside and Jodl came soon afterwards.[21] Göring and Himmler had not come; not much time was available and Hitler's aides had told them that numbers were to be kept as small as possible; thereupon Göring and Himmler had sent regrets.

Lieutenant-General Heusinger began by giving the situation on the eastern front and he was still speaking when Stauffenberg, Buhle and John von Freyend entered, five to ten minutes after the start of the meeting.[22]

Keitel introduced Colonel von Stauffenberg who had come to report on the new formations; Hitler shook hands with him and turned back to Heusinger's briefing which had been momentarily interrupted.[23] John von Freyend helped Stauffenberg to a place on Hitler's right, asking Rear-Admiral Hans-Erich Voss, the Naval C-in-C's representative in the headquarters, to make room since Stauffenberg was so crippled; Voss willingly did so and moved to the other side of the table. Only some six people could comfortably find room at the long side of the table.[24] John von Freyend placed the briefcase down about where Voss had been standing, between Lieutenant-General Heusinger and his staff officer, Colonel Brandt.

Stauffenberg had to elbow his way forward a little in order to get near enough to the table and he had to place the briefcase so that it was in no one's way. Despite all his efforts, however, he could only get to the right-hand corner of the table. He accordingly took the briefcase and placed it under the table. Had he tried to push his way between Heusinger and Brandt so as to place his case on the inside of the table-leg immediately at Hitler's feet, this would undoubtedly have given rise to difficulty. He could do no more than place it under the table at its end. If the briefcase was not completely under the table, it is possible that it was in Brandt's way who then pushed it further under the table, on the right (outside) of the table-support, as indeed he said to Heusinger shortly before his death; he did not, however, move it from the inside to the outside of the table-pedestal.[25] Stauffenberg murmured or whispered something and went out of the room. As he moved slowly back from the table he signalled to John von Freyend who went out with him into the passage. There was no difficulty in finding an excuse for leaving and no one would be startled if Stauffenberg went out to telephone during Heusinger's briefing. There was continual coming and going during the briefing conferences; people were always being called out or finding it suddenly necessary to telephone some office. A few moments later, for instance, when Stauffenberg's bomb went off, Ribbentrop, the Foreign Minister, was on the telephone to the briefing hut wishing to speak to his liaison officer, Dr von Sonnleithner.

Out in the passage Stauffenberg asked John von Freyend for a call to General Fellgiebel who had asked him to call back. John von Freyend asked the telephone operator, Sergeant-Major Adam, to put through the call, Stauffenberg took up the receiver and John von Freyend went back into the conference room. Stauffenberg thereupon simply put the receiver down and went out.[26]

Outside the briefing hut Stauffenberg met Lieutenant-Colonel Borgmann on his way in.[27] Stauffenberg, however, went straight to a building about two hundred yards away consisting of bunkers and reinforced huts where were the Private Office, doctors, the Army Personnel Office and the *Führer Wehrmacht* aides and where Lieutenant-Colonel Sander, the *Wehrmacht* Signals Officer, also had his office.[28] Finding himself unable to speak to Stauffenberg before the start of the conference, Fellgiebel had asked Sander to call the briefing hut and tell Adam, the sergeant-major on duty, to ask Stauffenberg to go to Sander as soon as the conference ended.[29] Stauffenberg had received Fellgiebel's message while still in the OKW building; timing had been very tight during the morning and all details could not be planned and discussed beforehand. Stauffenberg's main object now was to find Haeften and the car and as a result of Adam's message he knew where to go.

The positioning of the car had proved somewhat difficult and had only been possible at the last moment. Shortly after Stauffenberg had gone to the conference Haeften had appeared in Sander's office where Fellgiebel also was and, in a great state of agitation, had demanded a car at once, none being available.[30] Apparently the car allotted to Stauffenberg had been withdrawn again by the Camp Commandant. Stauffenberg had a lunch appointment with Streve, the Camp Commandant, and in view of his injuries had a claim not to be forced to walk.

Fellgiebel could do nothing about obtaining a car; outside his own field he had no authority in 'Wolfschanze' where he was a guest and visitor. Sander, on the other hand, was a permanent inmate of Area I, where he was officially on duty; he was therefore entitled to bring in visitors and provide them with passes and cars.

Sander telephoned at once to the Commandant's office; it must have been about the time when Stauffenberg entered the briefing hut.[31] The Commandant's office asked Sander to remind Stauffenberg about his lunch date with Streve; a car was made available.

Meanwhile Stauffenberg himself appeared and reported to Fellgiebel while Sander was still telephoning. Stauffenberg and Fellgiebel went out to the front of the building and Sander followed them to say that a car was on its way. Stauffenberg, however, replied that he already had a car; unnoticed by Haeften, 2nd Lieutenant Kretz, the driver, had waited for Stauffenberg.[32] A few moments later the explosion took place in the briefing hut; Stauffenberg gave a violent start and Fellgiebel was clearly alarmed but Sander said that this often happened; animals were always treading on the 'Wolfschanze' minefields.

Stauffenberg now quickly took his leave, saying that he would not go back to the conference as he had intended but straight to lunch with the Commandant. Haeften got into the back of the 8-cylinder 'Horch' with Stauffenberg in front beside the driver.[33] Kretz pointed out to Stauffenberg that he had forgotten his cap and belt but Stauffenberg told him ill-humouredly to drive on and not bother about that. The car drove off towards Guard Post 1 of Area I. As they drove past, Stauffenberg and Haeften could see through the trees a great cloud of smoke over the briefing hut, burnt scraps of paper swirling about and men running hither and thither carrying out the wounded.[34]

Since Stauffenberg and Haeften had driven off immediately after the explosion, the alarm had not yet been given when they reached Guard Post 1. The men on duty, however, had naturally heard it and had seen where it had taken place. The lieutenant in charge ordered down the barrier on his own initiative.[35] Stauffenberg and Haeften were in luck, however. Both had valid passes; Stauffenberg evoked respect with his mutilations suffered in Africa and his aristocratic commanding exterior; he said that he must go to the airfield at once, perhaps murmuring something about 'Führer's orders'; after all he was a General Staff Colonel. After a short pause the Lieutenant let him go.

From Guard Post 1 the car proceeded west for a short distance and then turned down the road leading southwestward to the southern exit from the camp. Here they encountered considerable difficulties before being allowed to go. The barrier was down and Kolbe, the sergeant-major on duty, would let no one through; the alarm had meanwhile been given on the outer circuit.[36] Stauffenberg demanded with extreme insistence and in a parade ground tone of voice to be allowed through immediately since he had to go to the airfield, but Kolbe was not to be bounced and remained unimpressed. Stauffenberg had to go into the guardroom and telephone the Commandant's office where he spoke to Captain von Möllendorff. Möllendorff knew Stauffenberg and had no second thoughts about letting him go, though this was undoubtedly beyond his authority once the alarm had been given. Möllendorff did not yet know what sort of an explosion he had heard and in any case saw no reason to connect it with Stauffenberg in particular. Sergeant-Major Kolbe allowed himself to be convinced by Möllendorff that Stauffenberg might pass, but he nevertheless called in Kretz, the driver, and told him to 'look out', though he did not specify what he meant.[37]

Stauffenberg urged Kretz to drive as fast as he could; the road was narrow and winding.[38] Nevertheless in his mirror Kretz saw Haeften throw some object out of the car (an open one); it looked like a parcel. He reported later what he had seen and the package was found. It contained 975 grams (2 lbs 2 ozs) of explosive, two detonators and a 30-minute-delay fuse; the whole was wrapped in brown paper.[39] They passed Queden Farm at high speed and about half a mile further on turned down the road leading west to Wilhelmsdorf Farm where was the airfield. At the final barrier in front of the airfield huts Stauffenberg and Haeften got out and covered the last hundred yards to the aircraft on foot. The driver turned straight round and drove back and so did not notice whether the engines were running.[40] The aircraft left Rastenburg for Berlin-Rangsdorf at 13.15 – as the on-the-spot commission discovered the same day.[41]

Shortly after Stauffenberg left the briefing room General Günther Korten, Chief of Staff of the *Luftwaffe*, and Major Herbert Büchs, *Luftwaffe* staff officer attached to the OKW Operations Staff, who had been delayed, arrived and went into the conference room. They had not met Stauffenberg.[42] At about the same time a point was raised in Heusinger's briefing on which Stauffenberg could have provided the necessary information, as General Buhle observed.[43] But Stauffenberg was missing. Buhle went out into the passage to look for him but in vain. It was vexing both for him and Keitel that this brilliant colonel with a great reputation whom they had brought to the briefing, should not be there at the very moment when someone wished to ask him something. Buhle went out into the passage a few times and asked Adam, the telephone operator, but could discover no more than that Stauffenberg had gone. Then the bomb went off under the great table. The time was between 12.40 and 12.50 p.m.[44]

When the explosion took place there were twenty-four people in the conference room. Their positions can only be established with approximate accuracy. There was no regular placing and, apart from Hitler and whoever was giving the briefing, people were always on the move owing to the frequent coming and going.[45]

Hitler was standing in the centre of one side of the table with his back to the door. He was leaning across the table supporting himself on an elbow with his chin in his hand. To his right stood General Heusinger who was giving the briefing; General Korten, the *Luftwaffe* Chief of Staff, was just leaning forward to point out the locations of enemy air attacks on the German positions.[46] On Heusinger's right was Colonel Brandt, senior staff officer of the Army Operations Section, who was holding ready for presentation the maps and other data required by Heusinger, the head of the Section. A little behind Brandt and about at the corner of the table was General Karl Bodenschatz, Göring's liaison officer with the *Führer*. Further right-hand and at the head of the table was Lieutenant-General Schmundt, senior *Wehrmacht* aide to the *Führer* and head of the Army Personnel Office, and next him the *Führer's Wehrmacht* aide (Army) Lieutenant-Colonel Heinrich Borgmann. Somewhat away from the table in this part of the room were General Buhle and Lieutenant-Colonel Waizenegger, Jodl's senior staff officer. Buhle was pacing up and down in a fury because he had been unable to find Stauffenberg. Waizenegger was preparing the maps for Jodl's briefing.

On the opposite side of the table close to the corner was Dr Berger, the shorthand writer, and behind him, leaning against the window-sill, Rear-Admiral Karl Jesko von Puttkamer, the *Führer's Wehrmacht* aide (Navy). On Berger's right was Captain (Navy) Heinz Assmann, senior naval staff officer in the OKW Operations Staff and on his right Major John von Freyend, Army aide to the Chief of OKW (Keitel); next to him was the *Führer's* representative for the compilation of the military history of the war, Major-General Walther Scherff. To Scherff's right and approximately opposite Hitler Rear-Admiral Voss, the Naval C-in-C's permanent representative at the headquarters, had found a place and behind him and to his right were *SS-Hauptsturmführer* Otto Günsche, one of the *Führer's* personal aides, and Colonel Nicolaus von Below, his *Wehrmacht* aide (*Luftwaffe*). The other shorthand writer, Heinz Buchholz, was at the foot of the table. In the area behind him, in other words against the north wall, were Major (*Luftwaffe*) Herbert Büchs, second grade staff officer in the OKW Operations Staff and *SS-Gruppenführer* Hermann Fegelein, *Waffen-SS* liaison officer with the *Führer*.

To the left of Hitler on his side of the table were Field Marshal Wilhelm Keitel, Chief of OKW, Colonel-General Alfred Jodl, head of the OKW Operations Staff, General Walter Warlimont, deputy head of the OKW Operations Staff, and Dr Franz Sonnleithner (Minister 1st class), the Foreign Minister's Permanent Representative with the *Führer*.

The effect of the explosion on all those present was of a powerful pressure wave with a yellow or blue flame and a deafening crack. In many cases hair was lifted by the explosion and set on fire; almost all suffered damage to their eardrums. Everybody's breeches or trousers were more or less in ribbons; normal long trousers without jackboots − worn by Hitler for instance − were hanging down in long shreds. Those near the windows had their pockets full of glass splinters. Dr Sonnleithner came to his senses knee-deep in fibre glass. Almost everybody was thrown to the ground by the explosion but no one was hurled out through the window, as has sometimes been reported.[47] Everyone did, however, try to escape from the smoke-filled room as soon as possible − no one wished to suffocate or be a victim of the next explosion; there could well be other bombs still to come, or the heavy concrete roof might come down.

In the room damage was considerable. The wall and ceiling panelling of white plasterboard hung down in strips; window frames were distorted, curtains torn; fibre glass was strewn everywhere; papers lay around; chairs were smashed and the great table collapsed with its top more than half shattered. There was a hole 18 ins in diameter where the briefcase had stood. The pressure wave had clearly made its way into the cavity between the floorboards and the clinker foundation and had done considerable damage to the rooms at the end of the hut; the absence of windows and the resilience of the walls had produced a greater blanketing effect there.

Those still near the windows after the explosion first tried to get out into the open. In so far as their injuries allowed, they then ran round the hut and tried to help others. John von Freyend, for instance, helped to rescue Colonel Brandt, who was severely wounded, and cut Lieutenant-General Schmundt, also severely injured, out of his boots.

Immediately the cry rang out: 'Where is the *Führer*?' It came from Keitel and almost immediately he had found Hitler in the smoke-filled wreckage of the room and supported him as he left the scene of destruction.[48] *SS-Gruppenführer* Julius Schaub, Hitler's personal aide, had meanwhile hurried along from his room in the briefing hut and Hitler's valet, *SS-Haupsturmführer* Linge, also arrived; they accompanied the somewhat shaken *Führer* to his bunker where he immediately undressed and was examined by his doctors. Linge first fetched Professor von Hasselbach from his office near that of Sander and he put on the first emergency dressings; then Professor Morell took over further treatment while Hasselbach drove to Karlshof hospital near Rastenburg to deal with the severely wounded. Meanwhile more medical personnel and cars arrived and the RSD began to cordon off the area round the briefing hut.[49]

The experts were later unanimous that in the first place in a true bunker the amount of explosive brought into the conference room by Stauffenberg would have killed everybody and secondly that double the amount, in other words all that Stauffenberg and Haeften had brought with them into the *Führer*'s headquarters, would have had the same effect.[50] Under the conditions prevailing in the briefing hut, however, the blanketing effect and therefore the injuries suffered by those present were comparatively minor.

Hitler had suffered a contusion of the right elbow but the joint still functioned normally; he had superficial abrasions on the back of his left hand. The long black trousers and long white pants beneath them were in shreds; he had burns on both thighs and the hair on his legs was singed. His hearing was not noticeably affected, although both eardrums had been pierced and there was a great deal of blood in the right ear.[51] The *Führer* was in a great state of agitation but at the same time relieved. He kept saying that he had always known that there were traitors around him and now there was a possibility of rooting out the whole conspiracy.[52] He was sorry to lose his new trousers.[53]

The severely wounded were Berger, Brandt, Korten and Schmundt. Berger had lost both legs – he was exactly facing the bomb – and died that afternoon. Brandt and Korten died of their wounds in hospital on 22 July; Brandt had lost a leg and Korten had a large splinter of wood in the abdomen. Schmundt was severely wounded in the thigh and died in Karlshof hospital on 1 October.[54] Bodenschatz, Borgmann, Scherff, Heusinger, Assmann, Puttkamer, Buhle, Waizenegger and Jodl suffered moderate, though considerable injuries. Most of them had to spend some time in hospital. All the remainder, except Keitel and Hitler, were suffering from concussion and everybody, except Keitel, had their eardrums pierced.[55]

The nature of the injuries and damage done indicates that the short-range effect of the bomb was considerable, despite the small resistance encountered by the pressure wave all round. It shattered the table and of those standing in the immediate vicinity only Bodenschatz and Assmann remained alive; the one had been some distance from the table and the other on the opposite side. Heusinger was a little further away and, like Hitler, was protected by the massive table legs.

The would-be assassin could not be sure that at the moment of explosion the briefcase would be near Hitler. Accordingly the explosive should have been so calculated as to kill everybody present. Clearly the bomb was not adequate to do this.

Later the driver who had driven Stauffenberg and Haeften to the airfield was questioned and as a result it was discovered that during the drive through the woods Haeften had thrown a parcel out of the car. A pioneer unit was ordered to search for it and they found, wrapped in brown paper, a lump of 975 grams of plastic explosive, two detonators (tetryl initiation charges) and a British time pencil with a 30-minute delay.[56]

Various suggestions were made as to the reason why this second parcel of explosive had been brought; in many people's opinion it was intended to blow up the telephone exchange in Area I or to kill Himmler.[57] Either Fellgiebel or Stieff were supposed to be going to blow up the exchange; it has already been shown that this would have been useless and was not intended.[58] No one has suggested how anyone could have approached Himmler with a bomb set with a 30-minute time delay, *after* an explosion intended to kill Hitler; in any case this presupposes that he was in 'Wolfschanze' but not at the conference.

The only explanation which is not invalidated by some source or evidence is that Stauffenberg was disturbed by the entry of Sergeant-Major Vogel while repacking and preparing the bomb and that he consequently felt prevented from doing all that he intended. Under the circumstances he probably hoped that half the intended amount would be enough to produce the desired effect. One must try to visualize Stauffenberg's situation at this moment: he was proposing to kill a group of men who constituted a considerable proportion of the top-level leadership in a war of colossal size; while packing and fusing his bomb, he was disturbed by someone about ten minutes before the explosion was due to take place and this followed at least two abortive attempts in the last two weeks; can anyone doubt that his nerves were quivering. Had the Sergeant-Major gone away at once and if Stauffenberg could have felt certain that some thirty seconds additional delay would not have made him too conspicuous, Stauffenberg would have been wrong to leave the other package out.

Each bomb measured $12\frac{1}{2} \times 3 \times 2$ ins, so both could have been stowed in a briefcase.[59] But Sergeant-Major Vogel did not go away and the danger of discovery if Stauffenberg delayed further must have seemed too great. Who would have believed him in Berlin, had he returned having failed again? The conspiracy would probably have collapsed.[60]

The first necessity after the attempted assassination seemed to be to summon the top-level leaders of the *Reich*. No one knew the background – whether this was the work of a lone wolf (Hitler at first suspected some 'Organization Todt' worker, of whom there were hundreds employed on construction in Area I every day)[61] or of a conspiracy; possibly parallel attacks on Göring and Himmler had been prepared. More important still, no one yet knew how successful the attempt had been, how seriously Hitler, Keitel, Jodl, Schmundt and other important personages had been injured or how, therefore, military and political leadership was to be maintained. It would not be surprising if, in a company like this, there was a certain mistrust of Göring, Himmler and perhaps also Ribbentrop; people knew or felt that they were capable of anything; moreover the interests of Germany and the German people demanded an end to the war. In any case it was in the leaders' interest to keep news of the attempt away from the outside world; it might be the signal for disturbances.

Colonel von Below's injuries were comparatively minor, though his face was full of glass splinters and covered in blood; he realized at once the necessity of imposing a communications black-out. Naturally he did not know the full story but he had seen that important officers like Lieutenant-General Schmundt were out of action and that Hitler had gone to his bunker having suffered some injury. He accordingly crossed the path at once to the exchange bunker. He must have arrived some three minutes after the explosion. Below himself could not order the signals personnel to impose a black-out. They had to take orders from their superior officers and Below had no command authority in their sphere. His object, therefore, was to summon Lieutenant-Colonel Sander, the senior signals officer in the headquarters. Shortly thereafter Lieutenant Hans Hornbogen, officer in charge of signal traffic, appeared; he had been taking a teleprinter message to General Buhle's office.[62] Some four or five minutes must now have elapsed since the explosion; it would therefore still be before 1.0 p.m. Hornbogen was ordered to call Lieutenant-Colonel Sander, the *Wehrmacht* Signal Officer, at once and this he did. Sander hurried across to the exchange bunker; Fellgiebel followed at a somewhat slower pace and arrived later.

It is possible that Fellgiebel telephoned once more to Colonel Hahn in 'Mauerwald' and told him that the explosion had happened before he followed Sander and this would give the impression that he had been slow in reaching the exchange bunker. Fellgiebel had already telephoned Hahn, however, as soon as he knew that Stauffenberg had gone into the conference if not earlier, and had told Hahn that the attempt would be made. He now had to try to ensure that the conspiracy controlled communications. A communications black-out *after* the attempt – whether successful or not – was justifiable and could be presented as being imposed on the orders and for the purposes of the leaders. The order that nothing should be allowed out did in fact come from one of Hitler's circle. After an unsuccessful attempt the fact that advance steps had been taken for a black-out would have to be kept secret – and measures to isolate the *Führer*'s headquarters in 'Wolfschanze' nevertheless had been inititated *before* the explosion.

Colonel Hahn had already telephoned the conspirators in the 'Zeppelin' signals centre in Zossen either at Fellgiebel's instigation or according to a previous agreement; 'about midday' he had passed to Major Burchardt, who was on telephone duty, the codeword: 'The signals equipment is leaving.'[63] This was not the final codeword signifying that the attempt had been made; that was: 'The signals equipment has left.'[64] Major Degner, who was also a member of the conspiracy and was also working in 'Zeppelin', recalls that the second codeword arrived about 11.0 a.m.; Burchardt, however, says that the first, or preparatory, codeword arrived about midday. In any case Degner and Burchardt both agree that, before the attempt, some codeword was received which led them to take preliminary measures for a black-out. Burchardt passed Hahn's message from 'Mauerwald' on to Degner and Höpfner at once. The *Gestapo* never found out anything about this advance warning.[65] Fellgiebel and Hahn, also Thiele and Hassel, the Bendlerstrasse signals officers, in so far as they knew about it, saved the lives of other conspirators by keeping their mouths shut; moreover it was hardly possible to execute all the experts if the war was to go on.[66]

It is not possible to say when Fellgiebel telephoned Hahn for the second time. He may have done so from Sander's office or from the exchange bunker, perhaps from the switch-room where no one would necessarily have noticed.[67] Both Sander in 'Wolfschanze' and Arntz, Fellgiebel's aide in 'Mauerwald', reported only the *second* conversation when Fellgiebel told Hahn that Hitler was still alive.[68]

While Sander was still on the way from his office to the exchange bunker Below asked to be put through to Himmler; the connection was made and Sander then arrived. Below ordered a communications black-out, barking out at Sander: 'Attempted assassination on the *Führer* – *Führer* alive – nothing to get out – personally order the *Reich* Marshal [Göring] and the *Reichsführer-SS* [Himmler] to the *Führer*.'[69]

Sander ordered the signals personnel to take all plugs out of the terminals and move their chairs back a yard from the tables to ensure that the black-out was operative. All conversations in progress were ruthlessly cut off; the other signals personnel were forbidden access to the manual exchange. Sander then spoke to Himmler and asked him to come to the headquarters but without giving the reason. Himmler immediately asked whether all security precautions had been taken, which Sander found somewhat surprising; but Himmler must have had some hint about the attempt from Below who presumably handed the receiver to Sander as he arrived since, with his damaged eardrums, he could barely hear. Sander replied to Himmler that, as far as communications were concerned, everything necessary had been done.[70]

Sander then called Göring and demanded to speak to the *Reich* Marshal himself; this led to some argument with the aides but eventually he was put through. Göring was also asked to come to 'Wolfschanze' at once.

After giving his initial orders Below went back to Hitler's special enclosure, the '*Führer* enclosure'. Martin Bormann had meanwhile arrived at the scene of the explosion. Below reported the measures he had taken and the information which he had passed on and then headed for the sick bay in Area II to have his wounds dressed. Near the exchange bunker in Area I he encountered Fellgiebel who had arrived meanwhile and, after making a short telephone call from the bunker, was pacing up and down the path between the *Führer*'s enclosure and the communications bunker trying to find out what was happening.

At this point Sander was summoned to Hitler, who wished to know how soon arrangements could be made for him to broadcast. He had meanwhile changed and ordered his bunker to be searched for bombs. He was now walking about in his enclosure and this Fellgiebel saw. Sander, however, was vexed since he had once been told by Schmundt to prevent Hitler meeting Fellgiebel who was labelled as a defeatist and had only been retained because he was indispensable. With some difficulty Sander piloted Fellgiebel away from the path and back into the exchange.

Sander told Hitler that preparations for his broadcast could be made by 6.0 p.m.[71] The necessary equipment was available in the *Führer*'s headquarters but extensive preparation was necessary to ensure that Hitler's speech would be broadcast simultaneously over all German stations and that he would not have to speak twice owing to possible equipment failure or jamming. Sander had to get in touch with the National Radio station in Berlin and with the Propaganda Ministry; this he could only do when the communications blackout imposed by the conspirators had been lifted; subsequently certain other difficulties arose both in the Propaganda Ministry and the broadcasting station when the conspirators tried to lay hands on them. At the same time as it was broadcast over the National Radio and Königsberg Radio, Hitler's speech was to be recorded both in East Prussia and in Berlin so that it could be re-broadcast as necessary. The speech was to be transmitted to the National Radio staion and to Königsberg Radio station via three separate lines in each case ('broadcast stage 3'). In any case Sander wished to use a transmitting van of the headquarters signals unit and have a recording made by them, and also to have a recording and transmitting van sent from Königsberg and it was agreed that this should be done at once. But the crew had gone to Cranz for a bathe in the Baltic and for other reasons too the broadcast had to be postponed – Mussolini's visit occupied the whole afternoon, Hitler's, Dönitz' and Göring's speeches had to be drafted and approved and everywhere including the 'tea house', where Hitler eventually made his broadcast, a search for further bombs was going on.

Shortly after the explosion, the naval officers present at the conference being more or less out of action, Captain Ulrich Meier, assistant to Rear-Admiral Voss, appeared in the Area I telephone exchange. Voss had asked

Below to inform Grand Admiral Dönitz and Below had clearly passed this on to Meier.[72] The call reached 'Koralle' about 1.15 p.m.: Dönitz was to go to the *Führer*'s headquarters at once; no reason was given. Dönitz was annoyed because he could not make his usual meticulous preparations if he did not know what the business in hand was. He flew off to Rastenburg at 2.50 p.m. with his Special Assistant, Rear-Admiral Gerhard Wagner.

Meanwhile Fellgiebel appeared in the telephone exchange and was told of the black-out which had been ordered and which he approved. Communications were not completely cut, of course, but only as required. Nothing was to be allowed out, but in the case of senior officers such as Keitel, Jodl or Fellgiebel himself it was assumed that they would observe secrecy of their own accord. They could still telephone despite the ban – insofar as the ban was imposed from 'Wolfschanze'. Fellgiebel ordered Sander to call Lieutenant-General Thiele in Berlin but he could not be found at once. A secretary was on the line and Sander told her to tell Thiele that there had been an attempted assassination of Hitler but that he had survived. Fellgiebel took the receiver out of Sander's hand and impressed on the secretary the importance of this news and that she must under all circumstances pass it on.

A few minutes later (Sander must have gone out again because he knows nothing of this) Fellgiebel got in touch with Thiele himself. He reiterated the news of the attempt and its failure; he must also have indicated that it was essential to carry out the proposed measures nevertheless. The only witness to this conversation between Fellgiebel and Thiele (and he remembers the scene vividly) can give no information about what was said; the conversation was carried on in code-language apparently agreed between Fellgiebel and Thiele and was totally incomprehensible to him.[73]

After his talk with Thiele Fellgiebel called Hahn in 'Mauerwald' and told him the results of his investigations at the *Führer*'s enclosure. He was forced to assume that Hahn would inevitably hear of the failure and might either cancel the measures initiated or fail to carry them out. Fellgiebel said to Hahn: 'Something fearful has happened – the *Führer*'s alive.' Hahn replied, 'What are we to do?' Fellgiebel said: 'Block everything' – in other words communications with 'Wolfschanze' were to be blocked although the attempt had not succeeded. Fellgiebel, therefore, appears to have had the presence of mind, and courage to do the only right thing in the existing situation: to proceed consistently with the attempted *coup* which had now begun. The conspiracy, even its wider ramifications, was now bound to be discovered but success could still be achieved by resolute action.[74] A little later Fellgiebel drove back to 'Mauerwald'.[75] Major Wolf had had some difficulty, in view of the increased security measures, in escorting Fellgiebel out of Area I and to his car outside the fence, near the eastern guard post. As Fellgiebel and Wolf came out of Area I, Himmler and his aides were just arriving. Hahn meanwhile called Thiele in Berlin and told him personally what he had heard from Fellgiebel.[76] Soon after 1.0 p.m., therefore, Thiele had heard from at least two sources that the attempt had failed.

Stauffenberg had naturally been missed after the explosion but at first the

409

confusion was too great for anyone to draw any conclusions. Some time before 2.0 p.m. Sander went back to the briefing hut to get an idea of the repair problem on the signals installations there. He found that Sergeant-Major Adam was still there, although he had really nothing to do. This Sander pointed out with the customary military asperity but Adam had something to report. He was one of those men who observe everything whether it is their business or not and are determined to put their discoveries to good use. He now told Sander that Stauffenberg must be the assassin since he had left in a hurry without his briefcase, cap or belt.[77] So far Adam had evidently been unable to get anyone to listen to his story. The only answer he had got from Major Wolf was: 'If you think you should report that, then do it.' He was now shouted at by Sander for voicing so monstrous a suspicion against such a distinguished officer. Sander wished to hear no more of the story and said that, if Adam thought that he must report it, he should go to Högl of the RSD. Adam thereupon went to Martin Bormann with his tale and Bormann took him to Hitler.[78] Adam's information soon proved to be accurate. The zealous soldier was promoted, granted a reward of 20,000 marks and given a house in Berlin.[79]

Steps to apprehend Stauffenberg were therefore set in train between 2.0 and 3.0 p.m. but they were still not very energetic. All exits being closed, it was at first assumed that he was still in the headquarters. Enquiries of Sander elicited the reply that he had left to lunch with Streve, the Camp Commandant, and his departure from the headquarters only emerged gradually. Enquiries at the airfield showed that he had taken off for Rangsdorf.[80] This did not mean that he had necessarily landed there. In any case Stauffenberg was not arrested on arrival in Berlin; not until late afternoon did an SS man appear in the Bendlerstrasse with a request for the Chief of Staff of the Replacement Army to go to the RSHA for a 'discussion', failing which he was to be arrested.

The official communications black-out ordered in 'Wolfschanze' remained in force for the moment. Incoming calls were not accepted and only the most senior officers in the headquarters were allowed to telephone.[81] Later a number of RSD officials arrived to supervise the telephone exchange; Sander instructed them in their duties. Understandably accounts about the length of the communications black-out in 'Wolfschanze' vary considerably. At the top level there were in fact no restrictions, although even incoming calls from the front were cut off for a time, at least half an hour, on the pretext that lines were out of order. On the lower level communications were cut for upwards of two hours, although this did not apply to internal 'Wolfschanze' calls. Calls from Berlin or elsewhere in Germany were not accepted for some time – at least an hour. About 3.0 p.m., with Himmler's approval, Sander lifted the 'Wolfschanze' black-out.

The black-out ordered from within the headquarters, therefore, which Fellgiebel himself had checked and approved, was as complete as it could be. It was imposed in the interest and at the behest of the regime still in power but, in the interests of the conspiracy, Fellgiebel had done what he could to assist it. It was impossible to put the 'Wolfschanze' signal centre out of action completely; even blowing up the Area I exchange would only have produced temporary disturbance and would have left the Area II exchange totally intact. Any attempt to use force to cut 'Wolfschanze' off entirely was neither sensible nor possible, as has been shown in the description of the detailed preparations for the *coup*.[82] Since the seat of power and command authority had in no way been changed, Fellgiebel could issue no orders running counter to the intentions of the existing regime.

Something else, however, contributed to produce an impression of an effective, comprehensive, though not total, black-out. As previously agreed, in his two conversations with Hahn, Fellgiebel had ordered the repeater stations through which the 'Wolfschanze' communications ran, to be put out of action and shortly after 1.0 p.m. an attempt was made to do this.

As soon as Hahn heard from Fellgiebel that the assassination attempt had taken place he ordered Lieutenant Arntz to disconnect stations 'Anna' in 'Mauerwald' and 'Emma' in Lötzen.[83] Arntz immediately called both stations and, speaking for Fellgiebel, ordered all calls to be cut off, the stations to be switched off and all terminals to be disconnected. He despatched Captain Jahnke to 'Anna' and after checking with Hahn, who had meanwhile heard of the failure of the attempt from Fellgiebel, went himself to Lötzen ('Emma') in a motor-cycle and side-car and had all terminals disconnected. Arntz remained there from about 2.0 to about 5.0 p.m. when he was relieved by an *Abwehr* officer despatched by Colonel Freytag-Loringhoven who ordered resumption of communications. When Arntz returned to 'Mauerwald' about 6 p.m. he found Fellgiebel, Hahn and Freytag-Loringhoven in the mess; they were talking on the telephone to Berlin.

Fellgiebel himself dealt with the black-out of the Insterburg and Rastenburg repeater stations but he was apparently only partially successful.[84] In any case at no time were communications between 'Wolfschanze' and Berlin *totally* cut; they merely became extraordinarily difficult.

Finally the partial blockage of communications to 'Wolfschanze' which was initiated from Zossen, had its effect and increased the impression of total black-out. This was kept in force until late afternoon.[85]

Fellgiebel and his fellow-conspirators in East Prussia had done what they could. At the latest by 1.30 p.m. Berlin had been told what had happened in 'Wolfschanze'. It was now up to the Berlin headquarters to seize the initiative.

42 Berlin: The Coup

Shortly after 1 p.m. the knowledge was available in the Bendlerstrasse that the attack on Hitler had been made. But apparently only two of the conspirators possessed this knowledge, Lieutenant-General Thiele and General Olbricht, and both remained inactive for the time being. The measures prepared and partially rehearsed on 15 July should have been set in motion immediately, but nothing was done.[1]

The principal reason for this inactivity was, of course, the failure of the assassination attempt. Obviously, this had been considered most unlikely. The thinking must have been: either there is no explosion and then there will not be a *coup* (since Hitler's death was a *conditio sina qua non*); or, there is an explosion and everyone in the room including Hitler will be killed. Incomprehensible as it is, there seem to have been no arrangements made for the possibility of Hitler's survival after an explosion. Soldiers know that this can happen, that sometimes men close to an explosion survive others who are farther away, that explosions are fairly unpredictable except in the most closely enclosed and controlled systems. Moreover, it was always possible that Hitler for some unforeseen reason might move away from the 'bomb' before it had exploded – with the use of delay ignition, one had after all relinquished a great deal of control. Unless one assumes therefore that Thiele or Olbricht or both lost their nerve, the explanation for their inactivity seems to be that they were totally unprepared for and surprised by the unlikely case that had now materialized. Of course, the truth may be more complex.

Fellgiebel had telephoned the news to Berlin in somewhat vague terms: 'Something fearful has happened, the *Führer*'s alive.'[2] If he said no more, if there was no clear agreement on the code-words in case of an explosion that did not kill Hitler, Thiele and Olbricht were not entirely wrong if they suspected that there had not been any attack. After all, this was the third or fourth time that Stauffenberg had taken the 'bomb' to Hitler's headquarters, and he had not exploded it before. The 'fearful' thing that had happened could be his premature discovery by the security service, or he might have shot himself when he was discovered, or he might have been killed by Hitler's bodyguards. If the assassination attempt had failed and had become obvious, however, and if Stauffenberg knew this (how could he not know?), then it was reasonable to expect him to take his own life. The conspiracy might then not be discovered at all, and it was best to do nothing.

412

In the light of such considerations, one could not take irrevocable and open steps unless one was prepared to go all the way. Advance alerts could not again be camouflaged as 'practice alerts', and even without the false start of 15 July, advance alerts would have been impossible this time: Fromm, whose position was always uncertain but who would certainly not take any risks in such an ambiguous situation, had stayed in Berlin this time. Against or without him, there could not be a 'practice alert'; he had been furious at the events of 15 July.[3] It would have been necessary either to win over Fromm, which seemed out of the question, or to arrest him and then give the orders. But Thiele and Olbricht might have found themselves giving orders without being obeyed by anyone – neither Fromm nor Stauffenberg would back them up, nor was the *Führer* dead, in which case unorthodox procedure might have been plausible to those who had to carry out the orders.

Olbricht and Thiele saw no alternative to inactivity. As Olbricht told Gisevius that same night, they decided it was best to wait and to do nothing, to behave 'routinely' and to follow their everyday habits. So they both went to lunch and did not return until about 3.0 p.m.[4]

General Fellgiebel, however, does not seem to have regarded his message from 'Wolfschanze' to Berlin as vague or ambiguous. When he became aware of what was going on, or rather not going on, in Berlin about 4.30 p.m., he told his aide: 'Thiele's making a mistake if he thinks that he can get out of it that way.'[5]

The information given by Colonel Hahn to the waiting signal staff officers in camp 'Maybach II' near Zossen was also unequivocal, and it was understood correctly at once. About 1.30 p.m. at the latest Hahn spoke to Thiele on the telephone, having been ordered by Fellgiebel to proceed as if the attempt had succeeded; he then called Major Burchardt in 'Maybach II'. Burchardt accordingly received the codeword 'the signals equipment has left' and at the same time the order to keep all communications to 'Wolfschanze' from and through Zossen temporarily blocked. Telephone calls were still permitted only to certain specified people, among whom were Olbricht, Wagner and Stauffenberg; teleprinter messages were only to be passed if they carried the signature of one of these people; if they did not, they were simply to be logged in; in cases of doubt enquiry was to be made of Fellgiebel or Hahn.[6] In so far as he could, therefore, Fellgiebel had done precisely what he had promised the conspirators: communications were kept open for them and closed to the other side. The lines between 'Zeppelin' and 'Wolfschanze' were blocked and those between 'Zeppelin' and 'Mauerwald' open only on a restricted basis.[7]

Major Burchardt remained at his post and passed on Hahn's orders to Majors Degner and Höpfner. On receipt of the preparatory codeword 'the signals equipment is leaving' Degner had already disconnected the 'Wolfschanze' terminals in the cable switchroom (he had prepared them for simple manipulation); other officers were forbidden to enter the room; the alternating current station was ordered to cease monitoring long-distance communications until further notice. At the same time the secret exchange was taken into service. At 3.55 p.m. Lieutenant-Colonel Beichele, head of the Line Communications Group in 'Zeppelin' (Zossen), noted: 'Höpfner passes on telephone message from Colonel Hahn: all private conversations to be blocked forthwith. With immediate effect, only conversations authorized by officers to be conducted through stations "Anna-Bu", "Emma-Bu", "Nora-Bu" and "Alarich".'[8]

All conversations now had to be controlled and monitored; other rank signals personnel, whether male or female, were not allowed to put through calls on their own. Female personnel had to leave the long-distance positions and sit against the opposite wall; the three special positions (for priority calls) were still worked by the men on duty but under the special supervision of officers. The entire exchange was now under officer supervision. The whole process took about five minutes. Officers now answered all incoming calls and said that for the moment the connection could not be made. In the 'Zeppelin' repeater station all lines to 'Wolfschanze' were under permanent supervision by a captain listening in through the volume regulator. Lieutenant Büchner, in charge of signal traffic, was told to ask Colonel Negendanck, Major Hoch, Lieutenant-Colonel Kecker and Major Poppe to come to the senior signals officer's office for a conference. Simultaneously Beichele passed on Höpfner's order to Poppe, the signal traffic officer, and two other officers. Having given these orders Höpfner went off to General Eduard Wagner, the Deputy Chief of Staff, who had been told of the attempt by Hahn about 1.30 p.m. in these words: 'An accident has happened in Wolfschanze. The *Führer* is alive, thank God, as are Keitel and Jodl. Several wounded. Otherwise no information to be had.'[9]

Senor Wille, a Chief Inspector of Telegraphs, had also been summoned to the conference in 'Zeppelin' which was conducted by Lieutenant-Colonel Beichele and Colonel Negendanck. Beichele told him of the order received from Fellgiebel: all outside conversations from the transit exchange were to be blocked; all repeater stations were to be occupied by the military. Negendanck then asked Wille to cooperate technically in carrying out this order. Wille, however, refused saying that he could only accept orders from his Post Office supervisors provided that they could be reached by telephone; he asked, therefore, that the necessary instructions be obtained from them. This was not, of course, possible; the Post Office bureaucracy would have reacted too slowly or not at all and would in any case have asked questions of agencies which the assembled officers wished to keep in the dark. The Post Office under its Minister, Ohnesorge, was regarded as fairly rigidly Nazi; the conspirators had invariably and with good reason been averse to including Post Office officials in preparations for the *coup*. On the other hand only the cooperation of Wille could guarantee full success in blocking communications; the *Wehrmacht* had no direct control over the Post Office communications network of which the lines to 'Wolfschanze' from and through 'Zeppelin' formed part and the same applied to the lines from Party and SS agencies, the terminals of which were known only to the Post Office technicians. A number of long-distance lines, therefore, could neither be cut by signals officers nor monitored by the *Wehrmacht*. Pressure was therefore brought to bear on Wille and he eventually proposed a compromise to which Negendanck and Beichele agreed: Wille would forthwith instruct an inspector to monitor all telephone traffic over Post Office lines and meanwhile await instructions from his superiors. The black-out was not, therefore, complete but no more could be done; in this obscure situation use of force did not seem advisable.[10]

Wille applied direct to his superiors in the Ministry of Posts who passed the matter on upwards until it eventually reached the Minister. Late in the afternoon he decided that the long-distance office in the Winterfeldstrasse should switch the Bendlerstrasse on and off during alternate hours, but before this judgement of Solomon had run its course for the first time, the radio had announced that Hitler was alive, the fact that a *coup* was in progress had been realized and normal working had been reestablished.

The people in 'Zeppelin' had therefore done what they could. The communications black-out was maintained until clear orders to the contrary were received about 4.0 p.m.; in accordance with Hahn's instructions, however, the radio stations and telegraph offices were not occupied in so far as this was to be done from 'Zeppelin'.[11]

About 3 p.m. or a little later Lieutenant-General Thiele suddenly reappeared on the scene. He called Major Degner and asked whether there was any interference on the lines to 'Wolfschanze'. Degner said there was and Thiele ordered him: 'See to it that the lines are put in order again.' He then put down the receiver. Degner wanted some explanation since he had just received a precisely contrary order from Colonel Hahn, his superior in 'Mauerwald'. He therefore called back to Thiele in the Bendlerstrasse saying that he had not quite understood. But Thiele merely said to him: 'Do as I tell you' and put his receiver down again. In fact Fellgiebel, not Thiele, was in command of the 'Zeppelin' exchange. Thiele had of late clearly been trying to get control of it but all he had achieved was to muddy the command channels.[12]

Degner now heard from Burchardt that 'the signals equipment has *not* left'. He went straight to Burchardt to talk to him, during which time Hahn called 'Zeppelin' and could not get Degner at his extension, as Beichele noted.

The black-out was never complete; from somewhere between 3 and 4 p.m. it was not strictly enforced in either direction – with Hitler still alive and the Bendlerstrasse headquarters doing nothing it could no longer be maintained. About 4.05 p.m. Colonel Hahn called again from 'Mauerwald' and lifted the black-out. Lieutenant-Colonel Beichele noted: '16.05. Colonel Hahn – normal traffic. Garrison exchange Zossen out of action. Garrison exchange Wünstorf, position 02 blocked. Our position J2 [the line to 'Wolfschanze'] also blocked. Lieut. Gebhard goes to the sub-exchanges and checks (15.56). 16.05 – official calls to be passed forthwith (spot tests). Fegelein (Wolfschanze) – Jüttner: "...[indecipherable words]... Similar as in Munich. *Führer* all right".'[13] From just after 4.0 p.m. all interference ceased. As a result of the conversation between Fegelein and Jüttner, which was monitored, 'Zeppelin' at least now knew what had happened in 'Wolfschanze'. It did not know what was

415

happening in Berlin – what was just beginning to happen and with small prospects of success.

Stauffenberg's flight from Rastenburg to Berlin lasted about two hours.[14] Since he took off about 1.15 p.m. he must have landed in Berlin between 2.45 and 3.15, probably at Rangsdorf airfield. Schweizer, his driver, waited in vain for Stauffenberg at Rangsdorf, and perhaps Stauffenberg landed in Tempelhof or in Gatow but this does not seem likely; Schweizer may have missed him.[15] On landing Stauffenberg told his aide to call the Bendlerstrasse, announce his arrival and ask how measures were progressing.[16] For the first time someone told the waiting conspirators in the Bendlerstrasse that Hitler was dead.[17] Stauffenberg then obtained a car and arrived at the Bendlerstrasse with Haeften about 4.30 p.m.[18]

By about 3 p.m., despite the communications black-out, certain indications and details about events in 'Wolfschanze' had filtered through to the Bendlerstrasse by various means. Since 1.15 p.m. Nebe, Director of the Criminal Police Office, had known that the attempt had been made, because Kaltenbrunner and Dr Wehner had been ordered to the *Führer*'s headquarters; General Wagner had heard the news through Colonel Hahn and Major Höpfner; it was probably also known in Colonel Meichssner's office in Potsdam; Lieutenant-General Thiele reappeared in the Bendlerstrasse about 3 p.m. It is highly probable that there had been some touch between the 'Zeppelin' centre and one or more of the above offices.[19]

The generals in the Bendlerstrasse continued to manoeuvre with cautious circumspection. About 3.15 Thiele told Olbricht and Colonel-General Hoepner, who just returned to the Bendlerstrasse from lunch, that a communiqué was to be expected from the *Führer*'s headquarters. He suggested that they switch on the radio but the communiqué did not come. Thiele was ordered to call the *Führer*'s headquarters once more and ask for the gist of the communiqué. Olbricht also tried to obtain some clarification.

All this time, Mertz von Quirnheim had tried feverishly to get things moving. He had sent out some of the alert orders shortly after 2 p.m.,[20] and time and again he had tried to push the hesitating Olbricht into action. Finally he acted without Olbricht's authorization and signed and issued the first written orders.[21] Olbricht had hesitated and delayed action on 15 July, he had 'played dead' on 20 July between 1.0 and 3.0 p.m., and he now still did not display any energy and determination, at first not even after Stauffenberg's assertion that the *Führer* was dead. Olbricht really did not want to start *coup* measures at all on 20 July. He later told Gisevius: 'Mertz has railroaded me.'[22] Fritz-Dietlof Graf von der Schulenburg told the same story to the *Gestapo*.[23] If Olbricht believed Stauffenberg, there was no cause for further hesitation. If he did not believe him, he could either wash his hands of the affair, completely and consistently, as Fromm was doing, or he could try to pull it through with determination now that the conspiracy had shown its hand. But Olbricht knew Stauffenberg's enthusiastic manner of dealing with difficulties, and Fellgiebel had said 'the *Führer* is alive'. There was considerable room for doubt, after all, and if Stauffenberg had shot himself, the conspiracy might not be discovered. Olbricht also knew that this hope was vanishing quickly. Later he said to Gisevius: 'We cannot deny it now, can we?'[24]

For the time being and not without further prodding from Mertz, Olbricht decided to accept the *Führer's* death as the basis for further action. When Thiele came to him, he told him that Hitler was dead. Thiele said there had indeed been an explosion during a conference in the *Führer's* headquarters in which a large number of officers had been severely injured.[25] This he had just learned in a telephone conversation with the *Führer's* headquarters, but could not get more details.[26]

Mertz, pushing on relentlessly, finally got Olbricht to agree to take from the safe the orders prepared and present them to Fromm for his signature.[27] Then Mertz called together the senior officers of AHA[28] and told them that Hitler had been assassinated; the *Wehrmacht* under command of Field Marshal von Witzleben had taken over full powers for the preservation of law and order and pursuance of the struggle against the external enemy; Colonel-General Beck had assumed overall leadership of the *Reich*. Major Harnack of the AHA Operations Section, the responsible officer in this case, was ordered to issue the codeword 'Valkyrie Stage 2' by telephone and teleprint to all *Wehrkreise* and in particular to the training and replacement establishments in the neighbourhood of Berlin. This was done.[29]

Also just before 4 p.m. Major von Oertzen was despatched to the headquarters of *Wehrkreis* III on the Hohenzollerndamm with the relevant orders, including those for the initiation of 'Valkyrie'.[30] Before departing Oertzen took five manuscript orders which he had drafted himself for the City Commandant's office to Lieutenant-Colonel Bernardis and asked him to issue them in the name of Colonel Mertz von Quirnheim; Bernardis gave the necessary instructions. The 'Valkyrie' orders were in fact issued to the schools by Harnack and Bernardis just before 4.0 p.m. or thereabouts and they only came through somewhat later from *Wehrkreis* headquarters. This was undoubtedly wise since they were not in all cases carried out with great energy; on the other hand it was liable to lead to confusion. Owing to the somewhat complicated command channels, however, this was not altogether avoidable. The liaison officers – Oertzen for *Wehrkreis* headquarters and Hayessen for that of the City Commandant – were intended to help straighten out such difficulties.

Shortly before 4.0 p.m. Olbricht himself called Lieutenant-General von Hase, the City Commandant, in his office at No 1 Unter den Linden. Major Hayessen of the AHA staff was earmarked to coordinate measures to be taken by the Commandant and act as OKH liaison officer; at noon he had announced that he would present himself during the afternoon. Hase had already taken the necessary agreed measures, however, before Hayessen arrived at 4.30.[31] The alert order reached the 'Grossdeutschland' Guard Battalion at 10 Rathenowerstrasse, Moabit, at 4.10 p.m.

Having issued their orders and instructions just before 4.0 p.m., Olbricht and his Chief of Staff then went to their commander, Colonel-General Fromm. According to Hoepner this was almost exactly at the moment when Haeften called the Bendlerstrasse announcing Stauffenberg's return.[32] Hoepner was in favour of waiting until Stauffenberg arrived and could clarify the situation but Olbricht thought that this could mean waiting half to three-quarters of an hour and that that was too long.[33] Olbricht accordingly reported to Fromm that the *Führer* had been assassinated; he had heard it from Lieutenant-General Thiele who had the news from General Fellgiebel in 'Wolfschanze'. He, Olbricht, now proposed that the codeword for internal disturbances be issued and the Army assume executive authority.

Fromm was not convinced. Five days before Olbricht had issued the 'Valkyrie' codeword to the schools on his own initiative and equally on the assumption that Hitler was dead or shortly would be. Fromm knew enough to realize what the background to that alert had been. But Olbricht was sure of his facts, at this point he obviously believed what Stauffenberg had reported, and to prove it to Fromm he arranged an urgent telephone call between him and Keitel.

About 4.0 p.m., therefore, Fromm spoke to Keitel and asked him what was happening in the *Führer*'s headquarters; all sorts of rumours about the *Führer*'s death were current in Berlin, he said.[34] Keitel said that the rumours were nonsense; an assassination attempt had indeed been made but Hitler's injuries were only minor. Where was Colonel Graf Stauffenberg, Fromm's Chief of Staff, Keitel asked. Fromm replied that he was not yet back.[35]

Olbricht, who had listened to this conversation, could hardly be surprised at Fromm's decision to do nothing 'for the moment' and not to issue the codeword to the static corps headquarters in the *Wehrkreise*. Olbricht, however, was now determined to act and use all his energies to carry the *coup* to success. Even if unsuccessful, it would at least show the world and Germany that there existed men ready to sacrifice themselves, who drew the consequences from their abhorrence of the war and the regime's crimes and were ready to make their contribution to the salvage of the German people's honour and self-respect. Fromm's subsequent behaviour showed that he was no Hitler loyalist by conviction. This becomes clear through a remark that Fromm made to Hoepner a little later, just as Hoepner came into Fromm's office to take over his position.[36] Moreover, Fromm only took really energetic counter-measures when the *putsch* had long since failed, and he removed by summary execution those of his staff who knew most about his own involvement in the conspiracy.

Olbricht went back to his office where Hoepner was waiting and said: 'Fromm won't sign.'[37] Meanwhile, however, action proceeded. Captain Friedrich Karl Klausing of the AHA staff had been ordered to act as duty officer to Colonel Mertz von Quirnheim that afternoon and he was handed a number of teleprint messages for despatch. About 4.30 p.m. he hurried along with the first of these to the office of Lieutenant Röhrig, the Signal Traffic officer, which was on the same (2nd) floor. On the opposite side of the passage was a steel door leading to the signal centre which, like certain buildings in 'Wolfschanze', was concrete protected. Klausing rushed in to Röhrig, threw his message on the table and said: 'For immediate despatch.'[38]

Röhrig wondered why Klausing seemed so wrought up and then he saw the first sentence: 'The *Führer* Adolf Hitler is dead.' This then really was no ordinary message; but, Röhrig recalls, it carried neither secrecy grading nor priority. The Traffic Officer was often required to despatch the most trivial messages about equipment deliveries or replacement requirements on the highest priority and security grading and here was something as important as this which was apparently neither secret nor urgent. It only occurred to him later that a security grading was unnecessary since, with all the precautions in the world, it could not have been kept secret. However he ran after Klausing, caught up with him at the end of the passage and asked whether the message should not have the highest security grading and priority. Klausing replied gruffly: yes, yes; would Röhrig insert them. Röhrig accordingly marked his copy 'Most Immediate', the highest priority, and 'Top Secret', the highest security grading. He then passed the message into the 'security room' where the security teleprinter was, worked by four female operators under the supervision of an NCO. Despatch was started immediately.[39]

Despatch was slow because each message had to be sent individually and the first one alone was more than a printed page long.[40] Fräulein Ziegler and Fräulein Lerche, Olbricht's secretaries, had to type additional copies. Had the message been less secret it could have been despatched simultaneously to all twenty addressees using a 'round-robin' circuit; using the sensitive secret machine, however, a single wrong electrical impulse could garble the text and the danger of error was too great. The broadcast method could only have been used had all lines been 'quiet' and this could not be guaranteed.[41]

This missive opened with the statement that Hitler was dead and that, in this situation, 'an irresponsible clique of Party leaders divorced from the front' had tried to stab the hard-struggling Army in the back and seize power. Accordingly the *Reich* government had proclaimed a state of military emergency and had entrusted to the signatory, Field Marshal von Witzleben, the supreme command of the armed forces and full executive powers. These Witzleben delegated, for the home area to the Commander-in-Chief, Replacement Army, who was simultaneously appointed C-in-C Home Forces, and to the territorial (*Wehrkreis*) commanders.[42] In the various occupied territories plenary powers were granted to the relevant Commanders-in-Chief. The following were placed under the orders of the holders of executive power: all *Wehrmacht* agencies and units in their area; the *Waffen-SS*; the Labour Service; the 'Organization Todt'; all public authorities; the entire police force; the Nazi Party with all its affiliated formations and branches; all supply and communications agencies. The immediate tasks of the holders of plenary powers were: maintenance of law and order; security of communications installations; elimination of the SS Security Service (the SD). All commanders were charged with giving full support to the holders of plenary power. Fulfilment of the historic task, the salvation of Germany, depended upon the energy of the German soldier, the message concluded.

Despatch of this message through the teleprinters took two girls at least three hours, allowing for a preparatory period of fifteen minutes. According to the official report from the AHA signal centre Lieutenant Röhrig, the Traffic Officer, began to have doubts about the legitimacy of these messages about 6.0 p.m. and from 6.30 these doubts were 'reinforced' by the broadcasts of the radio about the *Führer*'s survival of an attempt to assassinate him.[43] Nevertheless the same report records that this message and several of its sucessors were in process of despatch until about 9.0 p.m. Despite repeated radio announcements and increasing confusion in the Bendlerstrasse, therefore, the Traffic Officer placed no serious obstacle in the way of despatch of these teleprints.[44]

Shortly after handing in the first message Captain Klausing reappeared with a second one, also for immediate despatch.[45] This carried the name of Colonel-General Fromm (without his knowledge) and was countersigned by Stauffenberg. It consisted of instructions to implement the first general order. They included: military protection of all buildings and installations of the 'Post Office/*Wehrmacht* signals network' including radio installations, repeater stations, main exchanges, major radio stations, long-distance telephone and telegraph offices, amplifier and battery rooms, traffic offices etc; arrest of all *Gauleiter, Reichsstatthalter,* Ministers, Provincial Governors, Police Presidents, Senior SS and Police Leaders, senior *Gestapo* officials, heads of SS offices, Nazi District Leaders and heads of Propaganda Offices; 'rapid' occupation of concentration camps, arrest or confinement to barracks of camp commandants and guards, and maintenance of order; arrest of all *Waffen-SS* commanders who were disloyal or suspected of disloyalty and if necessary disarmament of their units; occupation of *Gestapo* and SD offices; contact and as necessary combined action with naval and air force commanders. Political Representatives were announced (and in later messages nominated) for all *Wehrkreise*; they were to work with *Wehrkreis* commanders and 'assume the duties of head of administration until further notice'; they were to be responsible for 'dealing with all political problems arising from the state of military emergency'. To ensure reciprocal exchange of information and intentions a liaison officer from the staff of C-in-C Home Forces would be attached to each *Wehrkreis* commander.[46] Finally no arbitrary or revengeful acts were to be tolerated in the exercise of plenary power; the population 'must be made aware of the departure from the arbitrary methods of their former rulers'. This implied a *coup d'état* and revolution, not a struggle on behalf of the regime against its internal opponents.

This raises a number of unanswerable questions: would a greater and more telling effect have been achieved if this sentence had appeared at the beginning of the message instead of, somewhat bashfully, at the end? Was it realistic, in face of the 'previous rulers' who had no scruples, to attempt to use methods so sharply differentiated from their own? Ought this not to have been postponed until the post-*coup* period? Many such as Gerstenmaier and Gisevius answered this question with an emphatic affirmative but they could not gain their point in face of those whose humanity condemned them to fight the battle against inhumanity at a disadvantage.

At about the same time as this message was despatched 'Valkyrie Stage 2' was ordered for all *Wehrkreise*; on the copy attached to the *Gestapo* reports the time is shown as 6.15 p.m.[47] In the case of *Wehrkreis* III the order was sent by courier, though in fact it had been received much earlier. Most other *Wehrkreise* had started to receive 'Valkyrie' orders about 4.0 p.m. in the form of telephone or teleprint messages despatched by Major Harnack.

There then followed an order from Field Marshal von Witzleben appointing Colonel-General Hoepner as C-in-C Home Forces; next came a teleprint denying the broadcast announcement that Hitler was still alive and urging that the measures ordered be carried out 'with the utmost speed'. Finally five martial law regulations were issued banning assemblies and demonstrations of all sorts; they also included detailed instructions for the conduct of the administration, a ban on any activity by Party functionaries or organizations, confiscation of Party and other records, a threat of punishment for resistance to measures ordered by military commanders and for incitement to disturbance or looting; finally powers of military courts were extended to cover a number of civil offences. The fifth, or last, regulation seems never to have been despatched; the copy available carries no despatch stamp. According to the report by the Army Signals Department the second regulation also was never despatched but the copy is franked '20.20'.[48]

Lieutenant Röhrig conscientiously carried out the orders of his temporary masters. Neither at the outset nor in the early stages was he sluggish in transmitting the conspirators' orders, as he and Colonel Köllner later adroitly maintained in their defence; on the other hand, as soon as he began to have his doubts (at the latest between 5.0 and 6.0 p.m. after the first broadcast), he displayed no particular energy or sense of urgency.[49] Ultimately all the teleprinter messages were not despatched simply because they piled up and the operators could not deal with them; they merely lay pending and when their turn came the *putsch* was long since over. When, however, some six teleprinter messages were left 'over', not having been despatched, naturally attention was drawn to them and it was said that they had been 'held up' and deliberately left pending.

When Röhrig became really uneasy after 6.0 p.m., he telephoned his brother who was a lieutenant in the anti-aircraft artillery and was on a battalion commanders' course at the Infantry School, Döberitz.[50] The brother asked what was up, saying that in Döberitz they were ready to move, 'Valkyrie' having been ordered between 4.0 and 5.0 p.m.; he was hoping for information from the fountain-head. Röhrig was very agitated, saying that all hell was loose and orders flying hither and thither to the effect that Hitler was dead, which might mean an early end to the war. The brothers spoke to each other again between 7.0 and 8.0 p.m. when Dr Röhrig in Döberitz gained the impression that his brother was caught between two opposing groups in the Bendlerstrasse and was in considerable danger; he advised the utmost caution. This Röhrig displayed; he did not actually sabotage the conspirators, with whom he sympathized, but he ensured that in everything he did he had the backing of Colonel Köllner, his superior officer. He took no initiative or decision on his own but faithfully carried out all orders from his superiors.

Röhrig was not in the secret of the conspiracy and he now suddenly found himself confronted with conflicting statements; some people said that Hitler was dead, others that he was not and that anyone who said so was an enemy of the state. Apart from Klausing and Haeften Röhrig never set eyes on any of the conspirators; for him one side was as nebulous as the other but that representing the regime was notoriously dangerous. He had a healthy fear of losing his head and felt no call to heroism. He did not, therefore, set out to help or hinder either side; he was neither responsible nor semi-responsible for the failure of the *coup*; he was not even a factor in accelerating it.[51]

Meanwhile Stauffenberg and Haeften arrived in the Bendlerstrasse just before despatch of the first teleprint carrying the news that 'The *Führer* Adolf Hitler is dead', in other words about 4.30 p.m.[52] They went first to Stauffenberg's office where they found Fritz-Dietlof von der Schulenburg, Berthold von Stauffenberg, Colonel Jäger, Kleist and Fritzche.[53] Without so much as a 'hello' Stauffenberg walked in and said: 'He is dead. I saw how he was carried out.'[54] Stauffenberg and Haeften then went to Olbricht's office where Hoepner was still waiting. At Olbricht's request Stauffenberg gave his account of the result of the attempt; he was convinced that Hitler must either be dead or mortally injured: 'I saw the whole thing from outside. I was standing outside the hut with General Fellgiebel. There was an explosion inside the hut and then I saw large numbers of medical personnel come running up and cars being brought along. The explosion was as if the hut had been hit by a six-inch shell. It is hardly possible that anyone could be alive.'[55] Stauffenberg was therefore convinced that his bomb had had the effect intended.

With the knowledge that the attempt had succeeded the *coup* could now proceed at full steam. Olbricht told Stauffenberg that Fromm was refusing to participate and was proposing to arrest Colonel Mertz von Quirnheim, Olbricht's Chief of Staff, for his issue of the codeword 'Valkyrie'. They must talk to Fromm once more, he said. Stauffenberg and Olbricht went together. Olbricht said that Stauffenberg had confirmed the death of Hitler, to which Fromm replied: 'That is impossible. Keitel has assured me to the contrary.'[56] But Stauffenberg had an unanswerable counter to this: 'Field Marshal Keitel is lying as usual. I myself saw Hitler being carried out dead.'[57] Olbricht added that, in the light of this situation, they – he said 'we' – had issued the codeword 'Valkyrie' to the *Wehrkreise* to guard against internal unrest.

This was too much for Fromm. After all he was the Commander and giving commands was the commander's prerogative. His subordinates were simply doing what they liked here, he said, and Hitler was probably not even dead at all. He banged his fist on the table and shouted that this was sheer insubordination, revolution and treason; the penalty for this was death; who had given this order, anyway? Olbricht said Mertz, his Chief of Staff, had given it. Thereupon Fromm declared that Olbricht, Stauffenberg and Mertz (who had been summoned to confirm issue of the 'Valkyrie' codeword) were hereby arrested; they would see what happened next. Stauffenberg calmly replied however, that the tables were now turned; it was Fromm who was under arrest; he had set off the bomb himself, he said, and knew for certain that

Hitler was dead. Fromm replied that in that case Stauffenberg must shoot himself at once since the attempt had miscarried.[58] When Stauffenberg refused coldly, Fromm jumped up in a rage and rushed at him with flailing fists; Kleist and Haeften, the two aides, drew their pistols and intervened; Kleist pressed the muzzle of his pistol into Fromm's stomach whereupon Fromm immediately ceased all resistance. Stauffenberg said: 'Colonel-General, you have five minutes to think it over'; then he and the others left the room. Five minutes later Olbricht went back and asked Fromm for his decision. Fromm said: 'Under the circumstances I regard myself as in baulk.' He and Bartram, his aide, were pushed into Bartram's office and kept there under guard. The telephone was disconnected and both exits from the room placed under temporary guard. Fromm allowed all this to happen without resistance. The time was about 5.0 p.m.

Olbricht told Stauffenberg that the codeword 'Valkyrie' had been issued and orders for the assumption of plenary powers by the Replacement Army had been despatched to the various addressees. For the moment, therefore, there was not much to do but wait for the arrival of the troops summoned to Berlin. Colonel-General Beck had meanwhile appeared, having been driven along by Graf Schwerin von Schwanenfeld. He had deliberately come in mufti to avoid giving any impression of a military *putsch*.[59] Hoepner's right to wear uniform had been withdrawn but he had brought it with him to the Bendlerstrasse and wore it during the evening. A short exchange of information took place and the various duties were distributed. Olbricht said that Hoepner was now the commander in place of Fromm with the title of 'Commander-in-Chief in the home war zone'; he even handed him a written order to this effect and Hoepner set himself up in Fromm's office. He went to Fromm and said that he was sorry that events had turned out thus. Fromm replied: 'Well, Hoepner, I am sorry, but I have no choice. In my opinion the *Führer* is not dead, and you are in error.'[60] Heopner had nothing else to do for the moment; the orders were just going out.

Stauffenberg meanwhile called General Wagner in Zossen and told him that Hitler had been assassinated. He, Stauffenberg, had just returned from 'Wolfschanze'; he would now pass the call to Colonel-General Beck.[61] Beck said to Wagner that he had 'today assumed command' and asked that his instructions be obeyed; Field Marshal von Witzleben, the new Commander-in-Chief, he continued, would come to Zossen shortly and take over (the Bendlerstrasse, being occupied primarily by agencies of the Army was nothing like as suitable a command post as the Zossen headquarters; the Bendlerstrasse had only become the headquarters of the *coup d'état* because the C-in-C Replacement Army was located there). Wagner claimed in his own subsequent report that he had reacted negatively to all of Beck's information and requests, and that he had been equally unforthcoming when Mertz told him somewhat later that the Army had assumed full powers and that 'Valkyrie' had been initiated.[62] Shortly thereafter Major-General Stieff called Wagner and said that he had heard of the proclamation of plenary power from HQ Replacement Army and considered it total madness; according to Stieff

Wagner instructed him to tell Keitel at once all about it, including the various telephone calls which he, Wagner, had received from the Bendlerstrasse.

Then, about 5.0 p.m. Graf von Helldorf, the Berlin Police President, appeared accompanied by Gottfried Graf von Bismarck, *Regierungspräsident* of Potsdam, and Gisevius, the vice-consul and *Abwehr* operative. Helldorf had been summoned by Olbricht.[63] Olbricht gave Helldorf a short formal declaration saying that Hitler had been assassinated; the *Wehrmacht* had assumed executive authority, the Berlin police was hereby placed under the authority of OKW and the necessary measures were to be taken forthwith. Helldorf was about to go when Beck spoke up: Helldorf should know, he said, that the *Führer*'s death was being contested by his headquarters. Olbricht wished to stop any discussion and interrupted several times saying that these were lies by Keitel. But Beck had his reason for his insistence on warning Helldorf: the other side might shortly succeed in publicizing their version over the radio, by telephone or by telegraph and it was necessary for the *putsch* group to agree on their reaction to such announcements beforehand. Beck himself was quite clear: 'For me this man is dead.' Everything must proceed as if this were so, whether the assumption were correct or not. The *Führer*'s headquarters would not be able to produce proof to the contrary for some hours and by that time action must have been completed and power actually taken over.[64] Helldorf promised to call the Bendlerstrasse every twenty minutes and returned to his command post in the Karlstrasse; there he alerted the Security Police but, as agreed, did not yet set them in motion.[65] Major Hayessen had already visited Helldorf about midday to confirm that Criminal Police officials had been earmarked to make the initial arrests.[66]

From about 4.0. p.m. the process of summoning the other conspirators and helpers to the headquarters began. About 4.30 Klausing called the 'Esplanade' hotel where some of the younger officers were waiting; Oppen came on the line and was requested to come to General Olbricht in the AHA forthwith together with Kleist, Captain Fritzsche and Ludwig Freiherr von Hammerstein. They had been waiting for this call since 1.0 p.m. and went straight to the Bendlerstrasse. Shortly before reaching the OKH building complex, they were passed by the car carrying Beck and Schwerin. They were taken to Klausing's office first and then assigned functions as duty officers. By the time they arrived Graf von der Schulenburg, Graf Yorck von Wartenburg, Berthold von Stauffenberg (in blue naval uniform) and Colonel Fritz Jäger, commanding XXI Armoured Unit were already there.[67] As already recorded, Kleist was involved in the arrest of Fromm; Fritzsche was placed on guard outside Fromm's door, responsible also for security in the corridor. Colonel-General Hoepner was going in and out of Fromm's office still in civilian clothes. Fritzsche had been ordered by Stauffenberg to give Beck the general's uniform coat that was in a locker, but Fritzsche did not know Beck, thought Hoepner was Beck and helped Hoepner into the uniform.[68]

Goerdeler should have been summoned but for some time no one could be found who knew where he was. He had had to go into hiding and the passage of information, a dangerous business anyway, did not always go smoothly.[69]

Eventually, however, it was decided not to fetch him along; it was thought to be 'too early'; the initial stage of the *putsch* had not yet been successfully completed and Goerdeler could contribute nothing until at least the radio station had been occupied; before that he would only be exposed to unnecessary danger if brought to the Bendlerstrasse.[70]

During the afternoon Dr Otto John called the Bendlerstrasse from his office in the Tempelhof airport building and asked whether Colonel Hansen, who was his main contact, was there. Stauffenberg's secretary said that neither Hansen nor Stauffenberg were there and asked John to call back between 5.0 and 6.0 p.m.[71] When he called the Bendlerstrasse again shortly after 5.0 and asked for Stauffenberg, Haeften came on the line and said: 'We have executive authority; come straight over here.' John informed Dr Klaus Bonhoeffer who worked with him in Lufthansa and they agreed to keep in touch by telephone.[72] John was the fourth civilian to arrive in the Bendlerstrasse that day to play his part in the *coup*; the others were Beck, who deliberately emphasized his civilian status, Gisevius and Bismarck (Schulenburg, Yorck, Kleist and others were, of course, not professional soldiers and therefore basically civilians too). John was not a little taken aback when, on reaching the second floor, he encountered Colonel Fritz Jäger without cap or belt and flanked by two sentries in steel helmets with fixed bayonets and with an SS officer. The latter was *SS-Oberführer* Dr Humbert Achamer-Pifrader who had been sent to the Bendlerstrasse from the RSHA in order to arrest Stauffenberg but had himself been arrested by Jäger. Captain Cords, in charge of identity checks at the building's main entrance and with orders to allow only those carrying an orange identity card signed by Stauffenberg or otherwise authorized to pass, had intercepted the *SS-Oberführer* and had called Jäger to fetch him. He was later disarmed with the assistance of Hammerstein and Kleist.[73] Apart from this there were no visible counter-measures by the SS. About 3.0 p.m. *SS-Obergruppenführer* Jüttner, commanding the SS Operational Headquarters and therefore the General SS (*Allgemeine SS*) and *Waffen-SS*, had issued the codeword 'Scharnhorst' alerting all SS training and replacement units in Germany and forming them into operational troop units.[74] SS teleprinter communications were functioning. The units alerted remained on call.

John enquired about the situation and asked for Colonel Hansen. Haeften said: 'Hitler is no more. Keitel maintains that he's not dead but only slightly wounded. It's not true.' Schwerin von Schwanenfeld gave him a quick briefing; the National Radio had broadcast a report that Hitler was not dead; counter-orders were coming from the *Führer's* headquarters but Beck was determined to see the matter through. Schwerin asked if John had news from Lisbon. He had not, John said, but he would rather tell Beck himself. He had no wish, particularly at this moment, to produce the discouraging words 'unconditional surrender'. He thought of going to see Popitz but remained in the Bendlerstrasse as being apparently the centre of energetic activity.

Between 5.0 and 5.30 p.m. Graf Yorck called Dr Eugen Gerstenmaier, the theologian and head of the Ecumenical section in the External Ecclesiastical

Office of the Evangelical Church, who had been in close touch with the conspirators in the Foreign Ministry and the 'Kreisau Circle' (Yorck and Gerstenmaier shared a house in Berlin–Lichterfelde); Yorck asked him to come to the Bendlerstrasse, saying that 'the thing had come off'.[75] Had not the attempt miscarried, Gerstenmaier asked, as had just been announced over the radio? No, Yorck said, that was a false doctored statement. Gerstenmaier accordingly set off, travelling by street car since no vehicle was available; in the Bendlerstrasse Colonel-General Hoepner appointed him Military Plenipotentiary for Cultural and Church Affairs.

Morale was already becoming somewhat low but Stauffenberg and his aide were now continuously on the telephone, using all their energy to set the *coup* in motion in the *Wehrkreise*. Yorck and Schulenburg briefed Gerstenmaier on the situation: apparently the assassination attempt had miscarried, they said, but the *coup* would proceed and so far everything was going according to plan. Gerstenmaier thought (as did Gisevius) that the conspirators were being far too gentle with their opponents. He himself had a pistol in his pocket as well as his bible. On a day like this, he said, and if one was proposing to revolt against people like the Nazis and the SS, there must be shooting; caution could only unnecessarily endanger both the success of the *coup* and the lives of the conspirators. But the conspirators were prisoners of a dilemma; their purpose, based on humanity and justice, was to remove a regime which had trampled on justice. In taking action to this end they were inhibited by their own principles and purposes.

In general terms, however, everything was going well in the Bendlerstrasse; the units earmarked had been alerted and called out; initial measures were being taken in the *Wehrkreise* and in Paris. About 5.0 p.m. Mertz von Quirnheim called his friend Colonel Eberhard Finckh in Paris and told him that all was under way in Berlin; he asked him to inform Field Marshal von Kluge. The codeword for the *coup* had already been passed to Paris somewhat earlier.[76]

General Joachim von Kortzfleisch, commander of *Wehrkreis* III, had gone to the Bendlerstrasse as a result of a request from Olbricht transmitted by Oertzen. His appointment was actually with Fromm, whom he now demanded to see, but this of course was not possible; he was intercepted by Hoepner, Beck and Olbricht. When they proposed that, owing to the *Führer*'s death, 'Valkyrie' should be ordered for the troops in *Wehrkreis* III, Kortzfleisch refused, saying that a *coup* was clearly being attempted and he wished to have no part nor lot in it. He kept on shouting: 'The *Führer* is not dead; the *Führer* is not dead.'[77] He then made as if to go but noticed that he was being held back on various pretexts and was unobtrusively guarded. Suddenly he escaped from the room next to Olbricht's office and ran down the corridor. Lieutenant-Colonel von der Lancken, Olbricht's assistant, rushed in to Olbricht shouting: 'The General's off.' Freiherr von Hammerstein who was with Olbricht, ran out shouting 'Watch out at the exit!' Kleist and a 'reliable' NCO were at the exit and held the general up with their pistols. Hammerstein conducted the general, somewhat out of breath, back to the room allotted to him and had to stand guard over him for the rest of the evening. Kortzfleisch raged around for a while, shouting about his oath, but eventually calmed down and said that he could not be expected to take part in a *coup*; he was not up to such a thing; he would rather go home and pull weeds in his garden, and if he was going to have to spend the night in the Bendlerstrasse, preparations had to be made for him.[78] All this took place between 6.0 and 7.0 p.m.

In place of Kortzfleisch the conspirators appointed Lieutenant-General Karl Freiherr von Thüngen to command *Wehrkreis* III; he was Inspector of Recruiting in Berlin, was a member of the conspiracy and had arrived in the Bendlerstrasse between 4.0 and 5.0 p.m. Thüngen did not go to *Wehrkreis* headquarters on the Hohenzollerndamn,[79] however, until after 7.0 p.m. and on arrival there did nothing very much.

Meanwhile, about 5.30 p.m., in addition to the 'Valkyrie' orders for schools and other units, the conspirators' orders transferring plenary power to the Army had arrived in *Wehrkreis* III headquarters. The 'Valkyrie' instructions had arrived at least twice, once via Major Oertzen and again by teleprint, probably even before that via Major Harnack.[80] Oertzen now handed in a list of the most important SS, governmental and Party agencies to be occupied. Addresses and numbers corresponding to those on the town plan were given.[81] At the head of the list were SS agencies ranging from the RSHA to the SS radio station; then came the senior Party offices including its printing and publishing houses and the ministries of Propaganda, Interior, Posts and the Prussian Ministry of State, top-level SA agencies, *Gau* headquarters and those of the Hitler Youth, the Labour Front and the SD in Berlin; then came targets of secondary importance ranging from the Foreign Ministry to the 'Motor Group East', the City Administration, the Presidency of Brandenburg and the Press office. Even the 'Research Office' for telephone tapping and the headquarters of the 'Senior SS and Police Commander' had not been forgotten.

Major-General Otto Herfurth, Chief of Staff to *Wehrkreis* III, was somewhat out of his depth, although he had Oertzen with him. He did not think that he could issue such orders without his commander. He had neither been given information nor persuaded to join the conspiracy and General von Kortzfleisch had deliberately been told nothing before going to the Bendlerstrasse. Herfurth was afraid that these orders were 'not genuine' or based on false premises but he eventually decided to issue them nevertheless.[82] Admittedly in the first instance troops were not available to occupy the targets listed. Between 6.0 and 7.0 p.m., however, confirmation arrived from the schools and units that everywhere the troops were ready to move.[83] Colonel von Wiese und Kaiserswaldau, the personnel officer, who had come to Berlin to get signatures from his commander and whose section was located in the Uhlan Barracks, Fürstenwalde, was ordered to alert units stationed there by telephone. Many of the schools noted that they had already received identical orders from the AHA; the commander of the 'Grossdeutschland' Armoured Infantry Reserve Regiment in Cottbus remarked that the order received from *Wehrkreis* III was countersigned by General Olbricht, head of the AHA, although territorially the regiment was under *Wehrkreis* III.[84] Despite such doubts, which in many cases seemed more important in retrospect, by 6.0 p.m. action was in train in so far as the *Wehrkreis* headquarters was responsible.

In the City Commandant's headquarters in Berlin the initial measures were taken with notable energy and this illustrated how much more valuable personalities could be than the much-trumpeted 'blind obedience'.[85] In any case the troops under the Commandant's command were nearer and could therefore be brought into action more quickly.

According to the timetable Lieutenant-General von Hase should have received the order for a 'Valkyrie' exercise on the day before the *coup*, but after the experience of 15 July this was not, of course, possible.[86] Hayessen had looked up Hase in the morning, had gone through the details once again with him and had informed him that the attempt on Hitler's life would be made probably about noon. Then Hayessen had gone to Helldorf to talk over the details of providing Criminal Police officers for the raiding parties which were to arrest the *Reich* ministers. Helldorf had summoned Gisevius to take part in this conversation. It was agreed once again that Helldorf was to keep the Police alerted but in their barracks. The second order was issued to Hase over the telephone about 4.0 p.m.; it proclaimed a state of emergency and the assumption of plenary powers by the Army and ordered the Guard Battalion to move at full strength to the Commandant's headquarters at No 1 Unter den Linden. The Commandant himself was ordered to go to the Bendlerstrasse to receive his orders from C-in-C Replacement Army. Meanwhile all units of the Berlin garrison, including the Spandau garrison and the Army Schools of Pyrotechnics and Ordnance, were to be alerted; a transport capacity of 270 tons was available in Bernau. Order No 3 included details of the cordoning-off measures which the Guard Battalion later carried out, listed the streets to be closed and prescribed the arrest of Goebbels.[87] The Guard Battalion's cordons were soon to be reinforced by units from the Armoured School and the Commandant was to provide further reinforcements from the Spandau garrison and the Army Schools of Pyrotechnics and Ordnance.

The original plan provided for this third order to be issued and explained in the Bendlerstrasse. This idea was abandoned, however, since Major Hayessen, who had witnessed the arrest of Fromm in the Bendlerstrasse, was already with the Commandant and able to explain everything.[88] Hase accordingly issued the orders direct from the Commandant's headquarters. He summoned the commanders of the units to be employed, first Major Remer, then the commanders of the Pyrotechnical School, the Ordnance School and the territorial units stationed in Berlin.[89] The government quarter was to be cordoned off primarily by the Guard Battalion, reinforced later by troops from the Armoured School, Krampnitz; the other units under command of the Commandant were required to occupy the main *Reich* agencies, the communications, newspaper and press installations. Objectives were shown on the list prepared for *Wehrkreis* III, to which specific reference was made in the order issued to Hase. Exceptions, reserved for occupation by troops of the *Wehrkreis*, were the radio transmitter at Tegel, the radio masts and Broadcasting House in the Masurenallee.

The police were instructed to cooperate with the Army and set up barriers and controls on the Berlin circular autobahn. As soon as the City Commandant had sufficient troops available – the Ordnance School was to occupy the Castle and the Pyrotechnical School the Arsenal – thirty raiding parties were to be formed. They were to be led by Criminal Police officers earmarked and provided by Nebe and to be despatched to individual agencies of the *Reich* where they were to arrest the most important functionaries and dignitaries. Signals officers were, of course, to be used for the communications installations; they were also to report to Hase; ten were to be made available by Lieutenant-General Thiele from OKW and ten by Colonel Hassel from OKH. When Thiele refused to take part owing to the failure of the assassination attempt, Hassel arranged to send the Commandant twenty officers from his command instead of ten.[90] Finally fifty men of the 'Brandenburg' Division were to be brought in by road.

The *Waffen-SS* and the 'Hermann Göring' Regiment which was stationed in Tegel, were also not forgotten. This same Order No III laid down that a general with a raiding party should go to the SS Garrison Commandant's office in Berlin and issue him with the order incorporating the *Waffen-SS* into the Army. The *Wehrmacht* City Commandant was to order the 'Hermann Göring' Regiment to remain in its barracks in a state of alert and summon the commander and his adjutant to receive further orders.

At 4.15 p.m., on issue of the codeword 'Valkyrie', those parts of the 'Grossdeutschland' Guard Battalion which were in Moabit and had not already left for guard duty, were alerted. One platoon of No 4 Company was on duty in the Bendlerstrasse and the other platoons at various points in Berlin or off duty. The battalion commander, Major Remer, drove to the Commandant's office at No 1 Unter den Linden as ordered and reported to Lieutenant-General Hase.[91] Hase told him that the Army was taking over plenary powers and the duty of the Guard Battalion was to cordon off the government quarter bounded by the Potsdamer Platz, Saarlandstrasse, Anhalter Strasse, Wilhelmstrasse, Kochstrasse, Friedrichstrasse, Dorotheenstrasse and Hermann-Göring-Strasse. The police had been ordered to assist, Hase said; individuals were not to be allowed to pass for the moment (until the arrests were completed); public transport must be diverted or might be allowed through empty. The first three companies were to be used for this operation and the fourth held as a mobile reserve at the Lustgarten. This last company was not available, however, since it was elsewhere on guard duty.

Remer said: 'Very good, Lieutenant-General' and drove back to Moabit with Lieutenant-Colonel Franz Wilhelm Wolter of the Supply Section, HQ Replacement Army, whom Hase had attached to him.[92] Remer assembled his officers and, with the aid of a town plan, allotted his companies to the area to be cordoned off. According to those immediately involved – Remer himself, Hagen and Schlee – they already had a horrid suspicion that all this was part of a *putsch*. Between 3.0 and 4.0 p.m., while on his way to give an ideological lecture to the battalion on behalf of the Propaganda Ministry, Hagen thought that he had seen Field Marshal von Brauchitsch driving through Berlin in full uniform; this had seemed to him both serious and suspicious; Major Remer and Lieutenant Schlee were apparently uneasy about the whole matter from the outset. They knew, of course, when they reported all this later on that their necks were in danger.

Initially, however, they conformed. The companies embussed and drove to the city centre where they took up their positions cordoning off the government quarter; Remer drove back to the City Commandant's office. The cordon was complete by 6.30 p.m.; Remer himself checked the various control posts.

The original plan was that Remer should be responsible for the arrest of Goebbels but this was abandoned when Lieutenant-Colonel Schöne, the Commandant's operations officer, pointed out to Hase that Goebbels was Honorary Colonel of the Guard Battalion and that this would be asking too much of the troops. Hase proposed to have Goebbels arrested by some other officer still to be designated.[93] When Remer returned from his tour of inspection he overheard Schöne and Hase talking about this in low tones. As he reported later, the planned arrest of Goebbels seemed to him 'particularly suspicious' but, as before, he did what he was told. He reported to Hase that the cordon was complete and pointed out that the posts in the Anhalter Strasse near the RSHA required reinforcement.

Remer, therefore, was clearly acting straightforwardly; alternatively he was not thinking very much and simply carrying out orders. Lieutenant (Dr) Hagen, on the other hand, soon had really serious doubts.[94] After the officers had been briefed in Moabit he told Remer that he had seen Brauchitsch drive by in the city and the whole thing seemed fishy to him. What was Brauchitsch doing in Berlin anyway? He wished to go to Dr Goebbels, his minister, and find out.[95] This obviously suited Remer. He was a soldier and had to carry out the orders of his superior officer, in this case Lieutenant-General von Hase. At this time (5.0 p.m.) he could not tell whose orders were legal and whose were not or whether illegal orders were being issued; Hagen's initiative might perhaps clarify the situation. Hagen therefore went off to Goebbels and was received by the minister by 5.25 p.m. Over an hour passed before Hagen, after talking to Goebbels, succeeded in summoning Remer, on Goebbels' orders, to the Minister's private apartment. Remer did not arrive there until between 6.35 and 7.0 p.m. when he had his famous telephone conversation with Hitler. This ended all vacillation in the drama of the Guard Battalion. The sequel will be told in Chapter 45.

In Cottbus the 'Grossdeutschland' Reserve Brigade received the 'Valkyrie' order just before 4.0 p.m. Lieutenant Kurt Delius, adjutant of the Brigade, took the telephone call from Lieutenant-Colonel Bernardis: the *Führer* was dead – there was a danger of internal unrest – 'Valkyrie' was in force – the Army was taking over plenary power. The Brigade was to occupy the National Radio station near Herzberg, the transmitters in Königswusterhausen and all major road junctions and bridges in the Cottbus area. The commander and adjutant were to report forthwith to HQ *Wehrkreis*

III on the Hohenzollerndamm.[96] Colonel Hermann Schulte-Heuthaus, the Brigade Commander, was on the road attending brigade exercises. Delius therefore passed the information to Lieutenant-Colonel Stirius, commanding the Armoured Infantry Reserve and Training Regiment and deputy brigade commander; he first called Berlin back to confirm Bernardis' order and then at 4.25 p.m. contacted Stirius at home.

Stirius arrived back in barracks about 4.45 p.m. and the order, which had meanwhile been received in writing from OKH and deciphered, was submitted to him. He also received an instruction to move the main body of the brigade to the concentration area in Berlin South, as in the 'exercise' of 15 July. Stirius issued the order at once and set the brigade on the move but he was disturbed by the fact that the order was signed by Olbricht and came from the AHA instead of from *Wehrkreis* III, which was territorially the brigade's superior headquarters.

A quarter of an hour later the commander of the Radio Company reported as ordered to Lieutenant-Colonel Stirius; he was ordered forthwith to take a mixed company consisting of two platoons of armoured engineers and a platoon of radio operators to the National Radio transmitter in Herzberg and occupy it. He was to take command of any guards, particularly if they belonged to the SS and if necessary disarm them. He was then to gain contact by radio and telephone with the brigade and report completion of his task personally to the commander. A little later, about 5.15 p.m., the commander of No 4 Battalion stationed in Guben was given a similar order to occupy the transmitters in Königswusterhausen. Between 5.15 and 6.0 p.m. the other commanders were given their marching orders by Stirius as they arrived from their various garrisons. Everything worked excellently. The local Party and SA leaders together with the SS units placed themselves under the orders of the 'Grossdeutschland'.[97]

Meanwhile the Brigade Commander arrived back from his tour of inspection. In effect, however, Stirius retained command of the brigade since, as soon as the troops had moved off, the Commander had to go to *Wehrkreis* HQ in Berlin. Colonel Schulte-Heuthaus and Delius departed about 6.0 p.m. They reported to Major-General Herfurth but the situation was very obscure; the *Wehrkreis* Commander, General von Kortzfleisch, was in the Bendlerstrasse and no one knew why he had not returned. There was confusion and general suspicion.

About 6.0 p.m. Major von Oertzen called Cottbus to ask how 'Valkyrie' was going. He was given all details but, when asked about the situation in Berlin, could only say that information would be forthcoming later. About 6.45 the commander of the Radio Company reported from Herzberg that the National Radio station had been occupied; he had taken over without difficulty from the SS guards and Hitler (!) would later issue a proclamation to the German people. About 8.0 p.m. No 4 Battalion reported from Königswusterhausen that it had occupied the transmitters, relieving a security force from Armoured School II. From the point of view of the rank and file, who of course knew nothing, however, from about 6.0 p.m. indications began to accumulate that an attack on Hitler had been made and was being exploited to attempt a *coup d'état*. From this point command of the brigade slid back almost automatically into the hands of the Nazi rulers.

In the Infantry School, Döberitz, things did not go quite as smoothly as in Cottbus. Owing to a funeral the Commander, Lieutenant-General Otto Hitzfeld, was not there; he was represented by Colonel Ringler, tactics instructor on the regimental commanders' course.[98] Between 4.0 and 5.0 p.m. it became known that 'Valkyrie' had been launched and the 'Valkyrie' units were alerted. Due to improved preparations made since 15 July, advance reconnaissance parties led by officers moved out shortly after 5 p.m. Then, however, the lieutenant-colonels and colonels could not agree on what should be done next. Some of the commanding officers had requested written orders when they had been told that the *Waffen-SS* would probably be integrated into the Army and that resistance was to be broken by force of arms. But they were denied written orders on the pretext that the matter was too urgent and there was not time.[99] News of the assassination attempt came over the radio; some wished to move off as ordered; others advised against it. Units from the School were ready to move from about 6.0 p.m. but when Colonel Wolfgang Müller of OKH, whose office was in Döberitz, returned from a duty trip to Berlin about 8.30 p.m. they were still standing around.

Major Jakob, a highly decorated officer (the Knight's Cross) and a tactics instructor, was in the school at the time and he was told of the orders received by Colonel Ringler who he thought (though he was not quite certain) was representing the Commander. Jakob was ordered verbally to occupy Broadcasting House in the Masurenallee and report completion by telephone to a number which was given him. He was to stop all broadcasts and gain contact with an OKH signals officer due to arrive there.[100]

Jakob drove with his men in trucks, fully armed; they even had machine guns and mortars.[101] On the way they encountered troops camping in the open.

The occupation of Broadcasting House presented no difficulties. Jakob simply went in with a couple of officers and told the guard that he had been charged with the security of the place and that the guard was temporarily under his orders. An SS officer wanted to telephone but Jakob would not allow it. Some ten Post Office officials in SS uniform were just cleaning their weapons and remained docilely in their room. Jakob placed two soldiers beside the two SS sentries outside the building and, since he had to defend it against all comers, positioned machine guns outside and mortars in the inner courtyard.[102]

As ordered, Jakob demanded that the superintendent stop all broadcasts and he agreed. Jakob was conducted into the main switchroom and told that everything had been switched off. Since he understood nothing of radio and the OKH signals officer had not arrived, he could not check the accuracy of this statement. In fact broadcasting was never interrupted. The central switchroom and studios were no longer in Broadcasting House but in an adjoining bunker which looked like an air raid shelter.

Dust was therefore thrown in the eyes of Major Jakob. The occupation of

Broadcasting House would have had some effect only had it been done by experts or alternatively by ruthless and determined conspirators who knew what they were about. Major Jakob knew nothing of his role in the plan for the *coup* and was therefore soon 'turned round'. Unless practically all commanders involved had been initiated and converted (which was not possible), everything depended on Hitler's death.

The experts possessing the necessary military authority should have been the signals officers to be despatched by Colonel Hassel and Lieutenant-General Thiele. About 4.15 p.m. Colonel Hassel, head of the OKH Signals Group in the AHA, had ordered the ten signals officers whom he had earmarked, to present themselves at the City Commandant's office.[103] Since Thiele refused to play his part and equally send ten officers, Hassel ordered twenty officers to report to Hase.[104] In addition to the transmitters and Broadcasting House they were to assist in guarding and securing the most important telegraph and long-distance telephone stations. But on arrival in the Commandant's office, owing to the general confusion and indecision, they were not given clear orders. Hase told the leader of the party, Lieutenant-Colonel Redlich to see Hayessen, and Hayessen gave Redlich a disorderly-looking file marked top secret containing instructions for the occupation of the main telegraph office, for making available liaison officers, etc. Redlich looked it over and decided there were jobs there for no more than three officers and he told Hayessen this, and that he would take the rest back to the office. Hayessen very nervously said it was all right.[105] Redlich had a feeling, however, that all was not right here in general, and he lost no time in returning to his office in Düppel. Having arrived there he learned that the three officers he had left in the City Commandant's office had since been arrested and had never been despatched on their missions. They also had not heard of the initial successes in occupying Broadcasting House and the transmitters at Nauen and Tegel.[106]

At the overseas transmitter in Nauen and the transmitter in Tegel the same scene was reenacted as in Broadcasting House. On receipt of the 'Valkyrie' order during the afternoon a battle group was formed in Döberitz from Training Staff 1; it was a reinforced battalion consisting of three rifle companies, one machine gun company, one mortar company, one anti-tank company and a personnel reserve company; between 7.0 and 8.0 p.m. it was ordered to occupy both stations and stop all broadcasting pending the arrival of signals officers.[107] The SS guards were to be disarmed and placed in custody, the stations organized for all-round defence and held against any attack. These orders were carried out and by 9.0 p.m. both stations were in the hands of the battle group. The broadcasting studio, which was empty, was occupied and guards were posted. The Döberitz commanders naturally could not be sure that broadcasting had actually been stopped and the signals officers did not arrive. About midnight the units were ordered by telephone to return to their quarters in Döberitz.

Meanwhile General Fritz Lindemann, General of Artillery in HQ Replacement Army, was in General Wagner's office in Zossen upon Wagner's request ready to read the first proclamation to the public at large.[108] Once the *coup* had begun he was to come to Berlin and meet Dr Fritz Theil, a radio commentator belonging to the Propaganda Ministry who had been working closely with Hofacker, Schulenburg and Trott. They were to go under police and military guard to Broadcasting House, where Theil was to read an announcement. During the afternoon he had worked over his draft once more with Trott in the Foreign Ministry and then, when the cordoning-off of the government quarter began, at Trott's request had gone to the Foreign Press Club on the Leipziger Platz so as not to be stopped by barriers at the vital moment. But the car due to fetch Theil did not arrive; Trott reassured him over the telephone from time to time until finally, about 9.30 p.m., he advised him to make good his escape at once.[109] In view of the failure of the *coup* General Lindemann remained in Zossen until about 7.0 p.m. when Wagner despatched him to the Bendlerstrasse to 'find out what was up in Berlin'.[110] According to an account given to an officer of his staff the next day, Lindemann found in the Bendlerstrasse 'considerable disquiet, but no clarification of any sort'; he had seen Olbricht, Hoepner, Beck, Stauffenberg and a number of younger officers, but no one had paid any attention to him and so he had 'returned to General Wagner to tell him that he had not been able to complete his mission successfully'.

By 8.30 p.m., when Colonel Müller returned to Döberitz and did his best to assist the *coup*, it was really already too late. The officers of the school were inclined to hold a council of war; they could not agree whether or not to execute the orders still outstanding from the Bendlerstrasse. Müller established that the School had been ordered to occupy the Nauen and Tegel transmitters forthwith and also Oranienburg I and II concentration camps. He attempted (without authority) to assume command but met some resistance; he did not discover that Nauen and Tegel had already been occupied. Colonel Ringler then called Hitzfeld in Lörrach and was told not to allow himself to be pressurized by Müller unless the latter could produce written orders. Further conversations with Hitzfeld ensued; he was briefed on the situation and eventually instructed that the Bendlerstrasse's orders, which he regarded as legal, be carried out and energetic action taken against the alleged SS *putsch*. At last, therefore, the troops moved off, but not very far. About 9.30 p.m. Colonel Müller and his aide, Lieutenant Goedecke, went to the Bendlerstrasse to obtain from General Olbricht the necessary written authority to assume command of the Döberitz troops. But by the time he returned it was too late for any further action.[111]

The recipient of orders in Armoured School II in Krampnitz should have been Colonel Gorn but on 20 July Colonel Glaesemer was commanding instead; Gorn was due to take over command of 561 People's Grenadier Division on 21 July.[112] About 4.0 p.m. [113] Major von Oertzen called the school and transmitted the order: internal disturbances — state of emergency — the Army in full control. The commander of the school with its own three 'Valkyrie' battalions and the other units under his command was to move by road at once to the area Tiergarten-Bendlerstrasse near the Victory Column, Berlin; the 'other units' consisted of a battalion of five companies from the Infantry Cadets Training Course, Potsdam, and a battalion of three companies from the NCOs School, Potsdam. A scout car company and a grenadier company 'under energetic leadership' were to assault and occupy the transmitters at Königswusterhausen and Zeesen; any resistance from the *Waffen-SS* company at Zeesen was to be broken; political broadcasts were to be stopped pending the arrival of reinforcements. Additional vehicles for the move were to be collected from Kanin, fifteen miles south-west of Potsdam.[114] Finally the Commander was ordered to precede his troops and report to C-in-C Replacement Army in the Bendlerstrasse.

Here he was to receive the second order.[115] Two of his battalions were placed under command of the City Commandant to reinforce the Guard Battalion's cordon round the government quarter; the main body from the Armoured School was to take over protection of the Bendlerstrasse offices and be available to *Wehrkreis* III as a mobile reserve; contact was to be maintained with *Wehrkreis* III's operations section; the troops were to reconnoitre southwards towards the SS barracks in Lichterfelde and Lankwitz; any SS movements were to be reported and if necessary stopped. One company, with scout cars if possible, was to be on call to escort the C-in-C Replacement Army from Tempelhof airport (on the assumption that Fromm would have been with Stauffenberg in the *Führer*'s headquarters). Finally one company with heavy weapons was to be held ready for despatch 'as an assault force against the headquarters of the SS Garrison Commander, Berlin'.

When the news of Hitler's supposed death arrived in Krampnitz, Colonel Harald Momm, commanding the Riding and Driving School, Krampnitz I and senior officer of the garrison, had shouted: 'Orderly, a bottle of champagne; the pig's dead.'[116] Colonel Glaesemer was by no means so enthusiastic but he nevertheless carried out all the orders, though somewhat hesitantly. Major Rode who commanded the armoured-infantry training group did not wish to carry out the orders from Berlin at all; he felt that in view of their importance transmission by telephone was not sufficient. Telephone calls were made; finally Rode was put on the line to talk to Olbricht himself; Olbricht threatened to have Rode shot under martial law, and then Rode submitted.[117] He drove off with his column, still wondering why the lead-car was to carry a sign that said 'Driving School'. Reconnaissance at the SS barracks showed that all was quiet. Rode was then ordered to advance to Grosser Stern square; later in the afternoon the first elements of the armoured-infantry battalion led by Major von Nagel also arrived there. Colonel Glaesemer meanwhile, sometime after 7 p.m., reported to the Bendlerstrasse in which direction a group of the tanks had also departed. Late in the afternoon Colonel Momm was called by Major John von Freyend, Keitel's aide, and told that orders from the Bendlerstrasse were invalid and nothing was to be done.[118] Although Momm himself was only too ready to carry out the orders for the *putsch*, movement was delayed because Colonel Glaesemer (who was under command of Momm as senior officer of the garrison) wished to have this extraordinary order hinting at an SS *putsch* confirmed by the next senior officer Colonel Ernest Bolbrinker, section head in the Inspectorate of Armoured Forces on Fehrbelliner Platz and Chief of Staff to the Inspector in AHA.[119] A technical officer had already protested since certain new equipment was to be used. Colonel-General Guderian, Inspector-General of Armoured Forces, was on a tour of inspection or alternatively at Deipenhof, his country house, and difficult to contact.[120] Bolbrinker therefore told Glaesemer to wait until he had asked Olbricht, to whom his section was responsible. A little later Glaesemer was informed that the order was genuine and should be obeyed. On the way he heard the news that Hitler was still alive but he nevertheless drove on to the Bendlerstrasse, ordering the 'Valkyrie' units from the Armoured School to follow.[121]

In the Bendlerstrasse Glaesemer went to Olbricht and asked him what was really going on. Olbricht confirmed that Hitler was dead and said that Glaesemer would get further orders from Colonel Mertz von Quirnheim. Glaesemer, however, refused to cooperate further. This was a stab-in-the-back like 1918, he said, and Germany would be plunged into military defeat. Mertz replied at once that they no longer required Glaesemer's services and that he was to remain in a room on the fourth floor allotted to him. Meanwhile the armoured troops remained fairly inactive. Bolbrinker also appeared later to see Mertz and demanded to know what the meaning of the radio broadcast was and what ought to be done. Mertz sent him back to his post at Fehrbelliner Platz.[122]

In the Army Ordnance School No 1 in Berlin-Treptow, which was under command of the City Commandant (of Lieutenant-General von Hase therefore), the commander, Major-General Walter Bruns, had long known about the conspiracy and had promised his active participation. At 4.15 p.m. on 20 July he was called to the telephone and Hase himself gave him the alert: 'Valkyrie' had been ordered; Hitler had met with a fatal accident. Major-General Bruns at once ordered his troops to prepare to move and ordered up the eighteen trucks earmarked for this eventuality which were to be made available by the Commandant's headquarters. He himself then drove to the Commandant's office on Unter den Linden in a motor-cycle and sidecar.[123]

When Bruns reported to Hase, the latter was extremely busy; there was great activity in the headquarters; unit commanders were just being briefed. Bruns, however, knew what he had to do – occupy the Castle; so, once having reported, he had only to drive straight back to the school. There he found that two companies were on the barrack square ready to move but the trucks had not arrived. The first company had moved off without waiting for the transport and attempted to reach the city by public transport, primarily the street-car. Towards 7.0 p.m. Bruns called Hase and asked about the trucks. Hase said that he had ordered them and did not know where they were, but other things had gone wrong too; he had now been ordered to the Ministry of Propaganda.

Bruns thereupon ordered the three companies which were still waiting to move to the Castle on foot and by all available means, in other words the street-car once more. He himself drove back in the School's only motor-cycle and sidecar to the Commandant's headquarters, where he arrived at 9.0 p.m. or later.[124] The headquarters was already occupied by units of the 'Grossdeutschland' Guard Battalion.

The three Ordnance School companies marched on. About midnight Nos 2 and 3 companies arrived at the Castle and occupied it in face of protests from officers of the Guard Battalion. No 1 Company had arrived in Berlin earlier, but just before reaching the Castle, shortly after 9.0 p.m. had been diverted to the Bendlerstrasse by a General Staff officer; it arrived there about 9.45.[125] Captain Cords asked and was given command of the Ordnance School troops in the Bendlerstrasse, but the situation became complicated when only some five minutes later parts of Remer's Guard Battalion arrived.[126] Soon the place was swarming with soldiers, and Cords persuaded the leader of the Ordnance School troops that nothing could now be saved from the wreck, that there was no point in engaging in fighting with the Guard Battalion, and that it might be better to move out.

Colonel Helmuth Schwierz, commanding the Army Pyrotechnical School in Lichterfelde, heard the news about the same time as Major-General Bruns. He was addressing No 18 Cadets Course when Captain Hradetzki, his adjutant, informed him that Lieutenant-General von Hase had called out the 'Valkyrie' units and requested that he go at once to the Commandant's headquarters. There Schwierz found that Major-General Bruns had already arrived, also Major Remer who was called in by Hase first. When Schwierz's turn came, Hase told him that Hitler had met with a fatal accident; internal disturbances were to be anticipated in Berlin and the Army had taken over full powers; the detachment earmarked from the school was to be despatched forthwith under a senior officer.[127] Schwierz drove back to Lichterfelde at once. The plan for disturbances or catastrophe agreed with Hase and Major-General von Rost, who had been Chief of Staff to *Wehrkreis* III until May, provided for the operational sections of the school to move forthwith to the street leading from the Arsenal to the Unter den Linden War Memorial and report arrival to the Commandant's headquarters. When Schwierz arrived back in Lichterfelde between 5 and 6 p.m., however, he heard that the assassination attempt had failed. Hase had deliberately referred only to a fatal accident to avoid unnecessarily implicating anyone in knowledge of the *putsch*; this later saved many lives.

In the Pyrotechnical School barracks ten squads of thirty men each had been paraded ready for movement meanwhile.[128] The remaining officers and men were to remain in the barracks to guard it in view of the proximity of the ss 'Leibstandarte Adolf Hitler' in the former Cadet Academy. Though certain officers, Major Korff in particular, had doubts and their own ideas Colonel Schwierz set the troops on the move; he himself remained in the barracks where, contrary to expectation, everything remained quiet. The mobile squads were commanded by Major Korff and Captain Maître.

At about 6.0 p.m. they reported, with their men, at the City Commandant's headquarters at the same time as certain officers similarly summoned. They had to note down on pieces of paper which were subsequently collected the numbers of men and weapons which they had with them. Then a colonel wearing the Knight's Cross came up to them and asked them to come outside.[129] He took each of them aside in turn and with an air of mystery gave them their assignment: the ten squads were to surround, occupy and clear the Propaganda Ministry, the Minister included. In conclusion the colonel said 'A difficult order, but orders are orders.' The colonel left Korff and Maître in some consternation. Maître was left to carry out the order, Korff being in charge of the operation as a whole.

Korff had other orders to give and assembly areas to reconnoitre. Two of the Pyrotechnical School squads were to occupy Broadcasting House. Maître and the main body therefore proceeded alone into the Wilhelmstrasse. On nearing the Propaganda Ministry he left his men on the alert and himself went into the Ministry to reconnoitre. He had no wish to act precipitately since the first shot might lead to catastrophe. He discovered that the Minister was in his private apartment in the Hermann-Göring-Strasse[130] and so he went there. With some difficulty he penetrated through the Guard Battalion's cordon and eventually found out that an officers' *putsch* was taking place and that Major Remer had been nominated Commandant of Berlin by Hitler in person.[131] He thereupon placed himself under command of Remer who was overjoyed at this reinforcement. His unit was held in readiness in the park opposite the Minister's apartment adjacent to the Tiergarten until it moved off next morning.

Meanwhile Korff had a somewhat similar experience.[132] While units of the Pyrotechnical School were taking up positions in the Wilhelmstrasse, Korff went to the Ministry to find Goebbels. He finally found him sitting at a desk in his apartment and said that he had to arrest him on orders from the Commandant. Remer then arrived and said that the attack on Hitler had been made, not by Goebbels and the Party leaders but by men some of whom were to be found in the City Commandant's headquarters. Korff wished to check with the Commandant's office but could not contact anybody either there or in Lichterfelde. Remer then said that he was guarding the Ministry against outside attack and Korff decided to do the same. In this way he thought that he would both be carrying out the Commandant's orders which he regarded as formally binding on him and avoiding a confrontation with other Army units, Remer's Guard Battalion in particular. Shortly thereafter Remer spoke to Hitler on the telephone and Korff heard Hitler order the suppression of the *putsch* in Berlin. From this point neither Korff nor Remer had any doubts who was issuing the legal orders.

Another attempt to arrest Goebbels also petered out. Colonel Jäger was despatched from the Bendlerstrasse to the Commandant's headquarters where he was to take command of two strong raiding parties of the *Wehrmacht* Patrol Service, Berlin, whose commander was Lieutenant-Colonel Heinz, and then arrest Goebbels. By 7.0 p.m. the two raiding parties, reinforced by territorials and men of the Pyrotechnical School, were assembled at the corner of Lindenstrasse and the Wilhelmstrasse.[133] But the territorials and the Pyrotechnical School men placed themselves under command of Major

Remer and so Jäger's operation came to nothing for lack of troops.

During the late afternoon, therefore, the story was everywhere the same: at first the Bendlerstrasse's orders were carried out fairly willingly, particularly if they were transmitted via the Commandant's or the *Wehrkreis* headquarters; the same applied even if they were signed by Fromm and he could not be contacted to confirm them. In Berlin and *Wehrkreis* III, therefore, the *coup* had been successfully started. Almost everywhere, however, the news of the failure of the assassination attempt and the regime's rapid counter-measures deprived the movement of its impetus in its early stages.

Both the broadcast announcement of the failure of the attempt and the counter-measures initiated primarily by Keitel came almost simultaneously with the action launching the *coup*. The original copy of a radio message exists from Keitel to General Schellert, commanding *Wehrkreis* IX (Kassel) saying that Hitler was alive and in good health, that orders from Fromm, Witzleben and Hoepner were not to be carried out and that Himmler had been appointed C-in-C Replacement Army; the message was franked '1615 hours' by Major Wolf, commanding the *Führer* Signal Detachment in 'Wolfschanze'.[134] From the outset there was uncertainty in the Bendlerstrasse about Hitler's death, particularly after Fromm had telephoned to Keitel just before 4.0 p.m. when Olbricht had first proposed to launch 'Valkyrie'. Despite Stauffenberg's assurances to the contrary the uncertainty persisted; it was fed and spread by the repeated radio announcements.

As far as many witnesses to these events remember the first announcement from a German radio station that an abortive attempt to assassinate Hitler had been made was broadcast about 5.0 p.m.[135] The monitoring service of the BBC intercepted the first announcement from the Home Service of the German News Bureau at 5.42 p.m. British double summer time which was equally 5.42 German summer time, then in force in Germany.[136] This first announcement, however, could not be heard on normal radio sets. The next announcement came at 6.28 p.m. on the Home Service of the German Radio; it was broadcast simultaneously in the telegraphic service for the Far East and again at 6.38 and 6.42 p.m. The announcement was broadcast in the Netherlands service at 7.0 p.m., again in the German service at 7.01 and at the same time in an English-language broadcast beamed on Africa. The German Home Service broadcast it again at 7.15, the Far East telegraphic service at 7.16, the European service in Portuguese at 7.30, the English-language service for Great Britain also at 7.30, the Arabic service from Athens at 7.40, the European service in Turkish at 7.45, the German Home Service again at 8.0, the German telegraphic service for the Far East at 9.21, the European service for Denmark at 9.45, the German Home Service yet again at 10.0 and so forth. At the latest from 5.42, therefore, the news could be heard over and over again. This explains the differing recollections about 'the first' radio announcement. It also shows that the news was quickly and convincingly broadcast. Had it not been for this, the *coup d'état* would not have failed so quickly.

43 The Coup in the Provinces

As in Berlin and *Wehrkreis* III, in the majority of the other *Wehrkreise* the first measures connected with the *coup* were taken not so much in ignorance of the failure of the assassination attempt as in spite of it and despite receipt of orders to the contrary from the *Führer*'s headquarters. The conspirators did not realize that, from 4.0 p.m., most of their teleprinter messages were not only going to *Wehrkreis* headquarters but were also being routed through 'Wolfschanze'.[1] His telephone conversation with Fromm told Field Marshal Keitel what was brewing in the Bendlerstrasse, even if he had not already heard it from Lieutenant-General Thiele or Major-General Stieff.[2] Professor Percy Ernst Schramm, war diary officer of the OKW Operations Staff, concludes a note on the outcome of the search for Stauffenberg (who had already landed back in Berlin) with these words: 'First suspicions were aroused by a query from General Stief [sic], head of the Army Organization Section; he reported that C-in-C Replacement Army wished to proclaim a state of emergency and asked what was to be done. This gave the impression that the C-in-C was trying to form a new government. Further information showed that Field Marshal von Witzleben was to assume command of the *Wehrmacht* and General Höppner, ex-commander 4 Panzer Army, to become C-in-C Replacement Army ... The *Führer* thereupon invested the *Reichsführer-SS* with command of the Replacement Army. A directive was issued that the Replacement Army was to accept orders only from the *Reichsführer* or the Chief of OKW. Calls were put through to all commanders in the Home Forces area, from which it emerged that they had already received orders of a different nature.' Command of the Replacement Army was transferred to Himmler that afternoon, about 4.0 p.m.[3] Between 4.0 and 5.0 p.m. Major-General Stieff telephoned from 'Mauerwald' to General Wagner in 'Zeppelin' and said that a message, signed by Colonel-General Fromm, had been received from HQ Replacement Army announcing the assumption of plenary powers; he asked whether Wagner knew anything more. Wagner told Stieff that Stauffenberg and Beck had telephoned to say this and that Stieff should at once report everything to Keitel.[4] Stieff seems to have thought the *coup* was lost fairly early in the afternoon and tried to prevent rather than promote action.[5] Later that evening Stauffenberg said that Stieff, too, was now a defector.[6]

From 4 p.m. Keitel's aides systematically put through telephone calls to all *Wehrkreis* HQs; in some cases information was sent by radio. At 4.15 p.m., for instance, a message from Keitel was despatched to Commander *Wehrkreis* IX (Kassel); it demanded confirmation of personal receipt – normally only requested in the most highly important cases – in addition to the usual acknowledgement of arrival; it read: 'Most Immediate. Radio message. To: Commander *Wehrkreis* IX, General Schellert, Kassel. The *Führer* is alive and in good health. *Reichsführer-SS* now C-in-C Replacement Army. Only his orders valid. Orders from Colonel-General Fromm, Field Marshal von Witzleben, Colonel-General (retd) Hoepner not to be executed. Contact to be maintained with *Gauleiter* and senior police officers. Keitel, Field Marshal, Chief OKW.'[7]

Wehrkreis I (Königsberg). The first teleprints from Berlin were received about 5 p.m. (actually by the Signals Officer of the Air Region); confirmation or explanation was sought, not from Berlin, but from near-by 'Wolfschanze' and HQs of neighbouring *Wehrkreise*. Officers recruited by Stauffenberg were available, Lieutenant-Colonel Hans Otto Erdmann, the Operations Officer, and Major Roland Richard von Hösslin, a wearer of the Knight's Cross and Commander of the Armoured Reconnaissance and Training Detachment in Meiningen. Erdmann was to ensure that Berlin's orders were carried out in Königsberg and *Wehrkreis* I; Hösslin's special duty was to occupy the *Gau* headquarters, 'the government', the telegraph office and other official buildings in Königsberg; for this purpose his unit was to be reinforced by a company from 413 Armoured Infantry Battalion in Insterburg.[8] News of the failure of the attempt, however, arrived simultaneously with or even before the teleprinter messages announcing Hitler's death and the assumption of plenary powers by the Army.

About 5.0 p.m. Colonel Herbert Kandt of the Personnel Section received a call from the Signals Officer of the Air Region asking him to come and fetch a particularly important teleprinter message. Erdmann was not a General Staff officer and so, in the absence of Major-General Henning von Thadden, the Chief of Staff, Kandt was acting as his deputy. Thadden had not yet returned from his visit to 'Wolfschanze' where he had taken part with Stauffenberg in discussions about emergency divisions for the eastern front which had come dangerously close to the boundaries of East Prussia. Initially Kandt said that he was not a postman and the Signals Officer should send a courier. Then, however, the *Luftwaffe* officer gave him the news of the attack on Hitler and convinced him of the importance of the matter. Kandt accordingly drove over. While he was still in the Air Region's teleprinter centre discussing who might have done it with the Signals Officer (like the latter he suspected Himmler), another teleprint arrived nominating Graf von Dohna-Tolksdorf as OKH liaison officer and Graf von Lehndorff as Political Representative for *Wehrkreis* I. Kandt took this with him as well.

On return to *Wehrkreis* HQ Kandt put through a call to 'Wolfschanze' to inform his Chief of Staff and possibly obtain further details. Before the call came through, however, Thadden returned with news of the attempted assassination and of the suspicion against Stauffenberg. Shortly thereafter Keitel called Königsberg and demanded despatch to 'Wolfschanze' of a broadcasting vehicle from Radio Königsberg. The crew had gone to Cranz to bathe, which Keitel was not told, and so numerous enquiries about the vehicle were made during the course of the afternoon. During his first call Keitel gave an assurance that Hitler was alive and that 'Wolfschanze' knew about the teleprinter messages from Berlin; the orders contained in them were not to be obeyed, he said.

General Albert Wodrig, Commander of *Wehrkreis* I, had gone out hunting that afternoon. Kandt tried to contact him somewhere by telephone but initially without success. Meanwhile Thadden called the neighbouring *Wehrkreis* HQs, II in Stettin, XX in Danzig and XXI in Poznan. The orders had been received but nothing had been done in any of them. Thadden and Kandt had already agreed that Berlin's orders could not be carried out in *Wehrkreis* I. The only available troops in Königsberg were a Pioneer Reserve Battalion of two companies and a weak Guard Battalion. The remaining reserve and replacement units of the *Wehrkreis* were on operations in the partisan-infested areas – the *Wehrkreis* included the Polish areas of Zichenau, Bialystok and Grodno. News soon arrived that Erich Koch, the *Gauleiter*, had alerted his SA and a special armoured force which he commanded had been moved into the town. Civil war would have been inevitable; moreover the conditions justifying execution of Berlin's orders, the death of Hitler and a *putsch* by a Party conspiracy, did not obtain.

After some time, towards 6.0 p.m., the Commander was contacted and he came straight back to headquarters. Having been shown the teleprints, he called Keitel who explained the situation and confirmed that only orders from OKW were valid.[9] About this time Stauffenberg called from Berlin. He asked first for Thadden and then for Kandt but both refused to speak to him and so he talked to Erdmann, who could only say, however, that Hitler was still alive and nothing could take place in *Wehrkreis* I.

Before Wodrig's return Thadden and Kandt had asked the *Gauleiter* to come to the HQ for a conference. But Koch was wary and did not trust them. After briefing himself General Wodrig decided to go to the *Gauleiter* himself with Kandt; they exchanged assurances that Berlin's orders were regarded as invalid. Kandt was commissioned to ask Field Marshal von Küchler, who was living in retirement in the *Wehrkreis*, to send a loyal telegram to Hitler, but Küchler refused.[10] In Königsberg, however, any attempt at revolt was already at an end; it had never really begun.

Wehrkreis II (Stettin). The first proclamation from Berlin – 'The *Führer* Adolf Hitler is dead. An irresponsible clique of Party leaders, far behind the fighting front, have tried to exploit this situation and to stab the hard-pressed Army in the back ...' – was received through naval headquarters since it possessed the cipher machine used for top secret messages. The message was brought to *Wehrkreis* HQ by Captain Karau between 5.0 and 6.0 p.m. and delivered to Colonel Hans-Heinrich Staudinger, the Chief of Staff. General Werner Kienitz, the Commander, was with Franz Schwede-Coburg, *Gauleiter* of Pomerania, who was celebrating his ten years of service.[11] Staudinger wondered whether to inform his Commander; it might place him in a difficult position vis-à-vis the *Gauleiter* or even cause the latter to take immediate counter-measures. The teleprint, after all, prescribed that all Party functionaries were now subordinate to the military commanders. While Staudinger was still wondering he heard the radio announcement of the failure of the attempt. This made it advisable to exercise even greater caution vis-à-vis the *Gauleiter* and first clarify the situation.

He accordingly first called the neighbouring *Wehrkreise* to find out whether they had received similar orders and what they proposed to do. Such contacts were almost universal; they did not imply indecision but were according to regulations. To the south the nearest neighbour was *Wehrkreis* III; there Staudinger was told that General von Kortzfleisch, the Commander, had gone to the Bendlerstrasse and Major-General Herfurth, the Chief of Staff, could not be contacted. All that General von Schwedler, Commander of *Wehrkreis* IV (Dresden), could say was that the situation was obscure and that for the moment nothing was being done. The answers from *Wehrkreis* X (Hamburg) to the west and *Wehrkreis* I (Königsberg) to the east were similar. There was nothing to do but wait.

Shortly after the first radio announcement, after 6.30, the long teleprint No 2 from the Bendlerstrasse arrived in Stettin. It contained the executive instructions following Message No 1 – communications installations were to be occupied, *Gauleiter*, *Reichsstatthalter*, Ministers, *Oberpräsidenten*, Police Presidents, senior SS and Police Commanders, heads of *Gestapo* and SS offices and Party District Leaders were to be arrested. Assuming that the radio announcement of the attack on Hitler and his survival were correct, it was now clear that a revolt involving use of force was in progress.

Colonel Staudinger decided not to call his Commander away from the *Gauleiter*'s festivities but to wait until he returned of his own accord. Meanwhile he summoned all general officers and regimental commanders to the headquarters at 8.0 p.m. and drafted orders to garrisons prescribing an increased state of alert and acceptance of orders solely from the Commander *Wehrkreis* II.

General Kienitz left the *Gauleiter*'s festivities shortly after 8.0 p.m.; news of the attempted assassination had arrived and been discussed there. Kienitz went home, to be visited shortly thereafter by Staudinger and Major Schubert, his operations officer. Before they arrived, however, Kienitz had received a telephone call from Keitel in 'Wolfschanze', saying: 'Stauffenberg made the attempt'. There followed a long tirade clearly intended to remove any doubts Kienitz might have had and ending with the remark that he would 'hold Kienitz to his guns'. Kienitz was not prepared to accept such an insult and Keitel had to apologize.

In any case Kienitz was now fully informed when soon after Colonel-General Hoepner telephoned asking whether the orders had arrived. Kienitz had not yet seen them and told Hoepner so; he also said that Keitel had just called. Hoepner then handed the receiver to Olbricht who tersely insisted that the orders from Berlin be carried out. Kienitz could only say that he had precisely contrary information and orders from Keitel, a far more senior officer.[12] While Kienitz was talking to Hoepner and Olbricht, Staudinger and Schubert came with the orders from Berlin decoded. Kienitz went with them to *Wehrkreis* HQ, trying to make up his mind on the way as to the attitude he would adopt. He later noted that these were the saddest hours of his life and had broken his spirit; he had said to his officers: 'It is frightful to be on one side at heart but on the other as far as one's mind and one's duty are concerned.' On the way to his headquarters he made up his mind that 'things being as they were', any involvement in the *putsch* was 'quite impossible', though he found it 'terribly hard to leave old friends in the lurch at this desperate moment'.

On arrival in the headquarters Kienitz explained to the assembled general officers and commanders the situation and his decision, which was accepted.[13] He ordered everyone to be on the alert and await developments.

Shortly thereafter Simon, the Deputy *Gauleiter*, appeared in the headquarters as an emissary of the *Gauleiter*. Contrary to custom he was in civilian clothes, although that afternoon he had attended the *Gauleiter*'s festivities in full Party uniform. He wished to know what orders had been received from Berlin. Kienitz said that he had received counter-orders from Keitel and that for him only these were valid; he would visit the *Gauleiter* later. Meanwhile during the evening other teleprinter messages arrived from the Bendlerstrasse, including one insisting that Hitler was dead, another containing Martial Law regulation No 1 and finally, late at night, a message from Fromm saying that he had resumed command. This was followed by a message from Himmler saying that Fromm's message had no validity.

Some time after midnight Kienitz and Staudinger went to the *Gauleiter* but did not take the Berlin messages with them. The *Gauleiter* never forgave them; he felt it to be a slight and a trick. They were, however, Top Secret messages and he had no right to see them. Kienitz did show the *Gauleiter* Keitel's order and took care to maintain a correct military attitude without a trace of hostility; eventually he divulged part of the contents of the Berlin orders.[14]

Kienitz, Staudinger and the *Gauleiter* listened together to the speeches of Hitler, Dönitz and Göring, and then Schwede-Coburg suddenly demanded a declaration of loyalty from Kienitz. Kienitz felt this to be humiliating but saw no alternative if he was to save himself and others from the wave of persecution now beginning.

Wehrkreis IV (Dresden). The first teleprint announcing Hitler's death arrived between 5.0 and 6.0 p.m. after the office was closed. Most of the staff had gone home or were on the road. In the headquarters the message was received by a duty officer described by his brother-officers as of somewhat limited intelligence. Naturally he could decide nothing but he called together all the headquarters officers whom he could contact; he also informed the

Gestapo by asking them what the message meant. It was Top Secret and therefore no business of the *Gestapo*. The duty officer should not have given the contents of the message over the telephone to Lieutenant-Colonel Werner Bühlmann, head of the Operations Section; but when Bühlmann insisted on knowing why he had to come back to the office, the duty officer told him that Hitler was dead.[15]

General Viktor von Schwedler, the *Wehrkreis* commander, was a highly respected, distinguished, good-natured person and basically in favour of removing Hitler; via Kunrat Freiherr von Hammerstein, acting on behalf of Goerdeler, he had been so far informed about the conspiracy that he inevitably grasped the import of the message immediately; Major-General Wilhelm Kirchenpaur von Kirchdorff, his Chief of Staff, and Colonel Hans Reinheckel, head of the *Abwehr* office, were also in the secret. Briefed by his Chief of Staff, General von Schwedler ordered 'Valkyrie' alert measures: the headquarters office building was secured by additional sentries and troops were placed on alert.[16] Otherwise nothing happened, however; no buildings were occupied, no arrests made and no major troop movements took place.

More or less simultaneously with the arrival of the first teleprint from Berlin General von Schwedler received a call from Keitel. During the next few hours he would receive a number of mysterious teleprinter messages, Keitel said, to the effect that Hitler was dead and that Witzleben had assumed command of the *Wehrmacht*; all this was false and he should not allow himself to be hustled into over-hasty action. Somewhat later, about 6.0 p.m., Schwedler telephoned the AHA in the Bendlerstrasse and the neighbouring *Wehrkreise*, where a 'wait-and-see' attitude was being adopted. All this – the premature warning to the *Gestapo*, Keitel's telephone call, the discouraging news from Berlin and the inactivity of the other *Wehrkreise* – inevitably convinced Schwedler that there was no object in carrying out Berlin's orders. Things being as they were, the only outcome would have been a short-lived civil war in *Wehrkreis* IV – nothing more. The radio announcement of the failure of the assassination attempt completed the tale of woe.

By the evening it was clear that the revolt was collapsing and so Colonel Sommerlad, the personnel officer, suggested to Schwedler that he get in touch with *Gauleiter* Mutschmann, the *Reich* Defence Commissar of the *Wehrkreis* and go to him to ensure that no false suspicions arose. Schwedler refused, saying that he had done nothing for which he had to render account to the *Gauleiter*. Later, after he had given a most thoughtful address, tinged with the deepest despair, to his headquarters officers, Schwedler was nevertheless forced to go; the *Gauleiter* had summoned him. This he felt to be a humiliation but it showed clearly where the power lay.

Towards midnight, therefore, General von Schwedler with his assistant, Colonel Sommerlad, drove over to Mutschmann, whose villa was swarming with men in SS uniform. The visitors had to leave their weapons in the cloakroom and then wait while *SS-Gruppenführer* 'Bubi' von Alvensleben, the Inspector of Security Police who appeared to be directing investigations at this stage, telephoned and was given directives. He returned to the two officers and said that of course there had never been any doubt of the completely impeccable attitude of General von Schwedler; mutual assurances of loyalty were exchanged. Then the Chief of Staff was summoned and compelled to stand up and be questioned; he was not trusted. He was faced with a demand for cancellation of the alert for replacement units; in some cases this had already been done; in others it was now ordered. A few days later the Chief of Staff was arrested and subsequently expelled from the officer corps. Colonel Reinheckel of the *Abwehr* also had to appear at the *Gauleiter*'s villa and was asked to compile a list for Alvensleben of officers in the headquarters who were unreliable from the Nazi point of view; he replied acidly that there were no such officers.

This was the end of the attempted *coup* in *Wehrkreis* IV. The next day all teleprinter messages received were confiscated by the *Gestapo* from Lieutenant-Colonel Bühlmann. A demonstration of loyalty by Party organizations was held on the Elbwiesen in Dresden and General von Schwedler with his personnel officer was forced to be present – in the midst of a seething mob of brownshirts, who ten months later, equally seething but without their brown shirts, carried the red flag through the ruined streets of Dresden; the city was then occupied by the Red Army.

Wehrkreis V (Stuttgart). Among officers of the *Wehrkreis* HQ discussion of the situation and the impossibility of winning the war had always been as frank as elsewhere. Major-General Herfurth, now Chief of Staff in *Wehrkreis* III, had previously been Chief of Staff in Stuttgart and his views were well known. Colonel Kurt Adam, his successor, however, was not in the secret of the conspiracy. The only thing known about General Rudolf Veiel, the *Wehrkreis* Commander, is that he was later relieved of his command.[17] The orders from Berlin arrived during the evening but in No 11 Olgastrasse, Stuttgart, doubts about the *putsch* arose very soon and so developments were very pedestrian.

When the office closed at 6.0 p.m. nothing had happened at all. The officers of the staff left the headquarters as usual. The Commander's personnel officer, Colonel von Tümpling, went to the Hotel 'Zeppelin' for dinner and there was told of the assassination attempt by the head waiter – to his great astonishment as can be imagined. Even then Tümpling felt no call to action; he simply went home to find out more over the radio. No one called him from the headquarters. Late that night, however, Tümpling received a call from 'Wolfschanze'. Lieutenant-General Burgdorf was on the telephone and wanted to know what Tümpling was doing just now. He replied that he was busy with the formation of the People's Grenadier Divisions in Münsingen. Burgdorf, who had clearly been unable to contact anybody in *Wehrkreis* HQ, then told Tümpling to say to his Chief of Staff that any orders received from Berlin were invalid and that those responsible for them had already been shot.[18]

Tümpling thereupon called Colonel Adam and the operations officer, Colonel Steiger. Adam had long since been informed and said that there was nothing to be done anyway – 'during the attempt to obtain clarification the failure of the enterprise became known'.[19] This was the end of the matter. No unit had been alerted and the office routine had barely been disturbed. Next day General Veiel paid a courtesy call on *Gauleiter* Murr which passed off most pleasantly.[20]

Wehrkreis VI (Münster). Here the day was equally ordinary. Late in the afternoon Lieutenant-Colonel Bernardis called his friend Lieutenant-Colonel Martin Bärtels, intelligence officer in Münster. He had previously discussed the possibility of a revolt with him and now wished to know whether all would go smoothly in Münster; Bärtels promised to do his best. General Franz Mattenklott, the *Wehrkreis* Commander, was not in the secret and so Bärtels tried to persuade him to go on a tour of inspection.[21] Soon afterwards, between 4.0 and 5.0 p.m., the first order – 'The *Führer* is dead' etc – arrived from the Bendlerstrasse. A little later the second order arrived prescribing the arrest of *Gauleiter, Kreisleiter* and SS commanders. Doubts soon arose because the order was signed 'The Commander-in-Chief of the *Wehrmacht* von Witzleben, Field Marshal'; the next was signed 'Commander-in-Chief Home Forces', an appointment not hitherto in existence and apparently made by Witzleben. People in Münster were confused and could think of nothing to do but wait.

Meanwhile, however, all exercises in progress were called off and the troops ordered back to barracks. Then an attempt was made to contact OKH in Berlin and OKW in 'Wolfschanze'. Colonel Kuhn, the operations officer, tried to speak to Lieutenant-Colonel Sadrozinski, head of Fromm's operations section, but Stauffenberg came on the line and asked whether the orders were being carried out. The second order dealing with the arrests apparently had not yet arrived and so Kuhn seemed not to understand what the orders concerned were. Then, as far as he remembers, Stauffenberg said: 'So you too have not got the order referred to . . . there is no relying on these signals people. The order explaining everything is on the way and will reach you shortly. Then you will understand "Commander-in-Chief". I rely on you to see that everything is carried out promptly.'

Shortly thereafter the call to 'Wolfschanze' came through, though whether in this case it was Keitel's call or that of the *Wehrkreis* is not certain. Keitel explained that Hitler had only been slightly injured and would speak on the radio that evening; the assassin was to be sought in HQ Replacement Army, he said, and orders from there should not be carried out. A member of the Münster staff aptly summarized the situation as follows: 'Situation thereby clarified . . . *Führer*'s headquarters one jump ahead of Bendlerstrasse. No orders issued by this HQ on lines of those from Replacement Army (assassins).' The note ends with the statement that the teleprinter messages which kept coming in from Berlin were now of historical interest only.

Wehrkreis VII (Munich). None of the orders from Berlin were received before the collapse of the revolt. The heavy air raids of the previous days had left communications partially or totally destroyed apart from one or two exiguous radio links.[22] A number of other *Wehrkreise* had received the codeword 'Valkyrie' without really knowing what to do about it since in many cases it arrived after the radio announcement and counterorders from Keitel; Munich never received it at all. In late afternoon Lieutenant-Colonel Grosser received a most urgent telephone call from Berlin asking him to call Stauffenberg in the Bendlerstrasse at once. The conversation never took place, however, 'since meanwhile the failure of the revolt had been announced over the radio'.[23]

Although, therefore, considerable preparations had been made, the *coup* in Munich was a non-event. A few days earlier Colonel von Linstow, Chief of Staff to C-in-C France, had told Grosser that the revolt might be launched in the next few days. As a precaution, therefore, Grosser had moved the available infantry, pioneer and armoured units to the Starnberg-Berg area for field training. Owing to the air raids *Wehrkreis* HQ had moved to Kempfenhausen on Lake Starnberg and was therefore close to the troops. But the conditions for action had not been created. Hitler was still alive and in command; any action would have been mutiny and, most officers thought, would probably have led to the collapse of the Army.

During the evening Keitel called agitatedly from 'Wolfschanze' asking about the situation in *Wehrkreis* VII. He was assured that all was quiet. Telephoning took place, however, to the neighbouring *Wehrkreis* XIII (Nuremberg) and a cautious exchange of questions showed that nothing was happening there either. The main point now was to erase all trace of preparations and get the units which had been concentrated, back to their barracks as unobtrusively as possible.

Wehrkreis VIII (Breslau). Like *Wehrkreis* I this covered an area near the front where partisans and gangs were active; sometimes in units of up to 300 men they moved about the country on armed plundering expeditions assaulting isolated farms. The static Army units in the *Wehrkreis* were very short of clothing, equipment, weapons and ammunition. Many sentries did not even have a greatcoat in winter. Karl Hanke, however, the *Gauleiter* and Governor (*Oberpräsident*) of Lower Silesia, who was appointed *Reichsführer-SS* in Hitler's last will and testament on 29 April 1945, kept 90 heavy machine-guns with their ammunition in the cellar of his office building; in 1944, after a bitter struggle with General Rudolf Koch-Erpach, the *Wehrkreis* Commander, he released half of them to the Replacement Army but only against a certificate of loan. This man, therefore, who later defended Breslau without mercy or scruple and then himself escaped by air, constituted as much of a problem to Koch-Erpach as did the partisans and gangs.[24]

Major-General Ludwig Freiherr Rüdt von Collenberg, the *Wehrkreis* Chief of Staff, heard the radio announcement of the abortive attempt on Hitler at 6.30 p.m. but at that time had no knowledge of any orders having arrived in the headquarters. He did not think it likely that the *Wehrkreis* would be directly affected; there was therefore nothing to be done. The Commander was on a tour of inspection – nothing unusual, in 1943 he spent 265 days away from Breslau – and could not be contacted while in his car. He did not return to Breslau until 11.0 p.m. when he went to the headquarters where he also had his quarters.

The first order from Berlin must have arrived in Breslau about 5.0 p.m. or soon afterwards but the Chief of Staff did not see it until much later. Between 7.0 and 8.0 p.m., when he had still not seen it, Stauffenberg called from Berlin and said that the OKH order was to be carried out at once; he clearly meant the message issuing the codeword 'Valkyrie Stage 2'.[25] Rüdt von Collenberg, however, had to say that so far he had received no order whatsoever, whereupon Stauffenberg said that it must arrive at any moment. He said nothing about its contents over the telephone since it was a Top Secret matter. Immediately after this conversation Lieutenant-General Burgdorf called from the *Führer*'s headquarters and said that Stauffenberg had been responsible for the assassination attempt and only orders issued by Himmler were to be carried out.

According to regulations Rüdt von Collenberg then telephoned in all directions in order to find out the situation in neighbouring *Wehrkreise*; he also contacted certain military agencies in Berlin and was given information by the Chief of Staff of *Wehrkreis* General Government in Cracow.[26] The news was the same everywhere: the assassination attempt had failed; Hitler was still alive and nothing was being done. The Armoured Replacement Division in Liegnitz had even received a precautionary instruction from the Inspector of Armoured Forces not to obey orders from *Wehrkreis* HQ.

At last, after 8.0 p.m., the first order from Berlin, signed by Witzleben, was decoded and submitted to Rüdt von Collenberg. On reflection he reached the conclusion that 'the outcome had been decided in the *coup*'s disfavour before I or any other member of the headquarters had heard the first word about it'. No action could therefore be taken on Witzleben's order since the necessary conditions did not obtain and the resources were not available; in fact they were in the hands of the other side since special SS formations, arms depots and other SS units were particularly strong in *Wehrkreis* VIII.

General Koch-Erpach returned about 11.0 p.m. and his Chief of Staff reported. The *Gauleiter*'s office had called several times asking urgently for the Commander. It had been indicated to Rüdt von Collenberg that the *Gauleiter* expected Koch-Erpach to wait on him immediately on his return. Following an attempted assassination and revolt against Hitler from within the Army, Army commanders were suddenly in a bad position; moreover the methods used by the *Gestapo* and Party rulers were only too well known. General Koch-Erpach accordingly went immediately to the *Gauleiter* with his operations officer, Major Fritz Roos; each put a Browning pistol in his pocket. Not until he reached the *Oberpräsident*'s office in the city centre did Koch-Erpach learn further details of the attempted *coup*. The *Gauleiter* already knew about the orders issued by the Bendlerstrasse. At the latest from 8.0 p.m. Bormann had been sending teleprinter messages from the *Führer*'s headquarters to all *Gauleiter* keeping them informed of events and developments and of the ramifications and background to the revolt.[27]

Koch-Erpach was not told why he had been summoned in such a hurry; there was nothing urgent to discuss since the outcome had long since been decided. While he was in the *Oberpräsident*'s office it was proposed to arrest

Captain Scholz-Babisch who had been named as liaison officer by the conspirators; Koch-Erpach objected strongly since, for disciplinary matters, Scholz-Babisch was under his command as *Wehrkreis* Commander. For the moment no action was taken but Scholz-Babisch was arrested during the night. Efforts to contact Dr Lukaschek, the Political Representative named by the *coup* leaders failed.[28] Koch-Erpach was not allowed to return to his headquarters until about 2.0 a.m.

Here the view of the situation taken by the responsible officers was that execution of the orders received from the conspirators would only imply mutiny and a hopeless local civil war. Real power was in the hands of the *Gauleiter*, not of the military Commander.

Wehrkreis IX (Kassel). When the attempted *coup* began in Berlin General Otto Schellert, the *Wehrkreis* Commander, was also travelling on duty.[29] He was not in the secret of the conspiracy and had no notion of the extent of preparations for the *coup* made by some of his staff.

The brothers Hermann and Ludwig Kaiser, who had been serving on the staff of C-in-C Replacement Army or the head of the AHA respectively since 1940 and had long been active members of the opposition, came from Kassel. Ever since 1935 they had been in touch with Major-General Ludwig von Nida, who had been Chief of Staff *Wehrkreis* IX until March 1944. In the summer of 1943, in view of the catastrophic consequences of the bombing of the Eder Valley dam, they had tried to extend the 'Valkyrie' plans to include a formal agreement between *Wehrkreis* HQ and the *Gauleiter* of Hesse for the transfer of plenary powers to the *Wehrkreis* Commander in the event of repetition of such a disaster. But the *Gauleiter*'s office had sent the proposal to the Senior SS and Police Commander, Prince zu Waldeck, and he had characterized the plan as attempted treason. A whole series of reports and memoranda were required to extricate the military from this fiasco. Nevertheless on 20 July *Wehrkreis* IX was better prepared than most other *Wehrkreise*. Colonel Fritz von Vethacke, the operations officer, had been let into the secret by Nida and he had adapted the 'Valkyrie' plans as far as possible to suit the conspirators. Colonel Claus-Henning von Plate, Nida's successor as Chief of Staff, was a contemporary of Stauffenberg and knew him well. Though he did not know about the *coup*, Stauffenberg felt that he could rely on him and moreover Nida was still living in Kassel. He (Nida) would have become Commandant of Kassel but had had to spend almost three months in Kassel-Lindenberg hospital as a result of diphtheria and its after-effects.

The first news of the attempted assassination of Hitler reached Colonel von Plate about 6.0 p.m. or a little later. He was in conference with other officers of the *Wehrkreis* on an exercise which had just been held at the Eder Valley dam. About 7.30 p.m. he was shown the first long teleprint from Berlin opening with the announcement of Hitler's death; the codeword 'Valkyrie' had not yet been received in Kassel. Plate telephoned at once to Stauffenberg to confirm the validity of the message. Stauffenberg assured him that Hitler was dead. Plate thought that there were two opposing parties: Göring and Himmler on one side, Witzleben and Fromm on the other. He did not doubt for one moment which side he and his headquarters would be on, as he later told Lieutenant-Colonel Beck, the *Wehrmacht* liaison officer to non-military agencies in the *Wehrkreis*. First, however, he tried to contact his Commander, who was on the road. This was no sign of hesitancy but perfectly correct procedure in view of the importance of the decisions to be taken. Plate believed Stauffenberg's assurances and so would have been within his rights in carrying out his instructions. Before the Commander's return, however, no orders were actually issued by the *Wehrkreis*, though all preparations were made.[30]

When General Schellert returned to his headquarters about 9.0 p.m. Colonel von Plate briefed him at once and recommended that Berlin's orders be carried out forthwith. But Schellert could not make up his mind. Various developments did not come to Plate's ears until about 8.0 p.m.: the radio bulletin and Keitel's message that Hitler was alive and 'in good health', the nomination of Himmler as the new C-in-C Replacement Army, the instruction that orders from Fromm, Witzleben and Hoepner were invalid and the order to Commander *Wehrkreis* IX to keep in touch with the *Gauleiter* and the Senior SS and Police Commander. Since the radio message was despatched from the *Führer*'s headquarters, at 4.15 p.m., as was the teleprint from Berlin, there must have been some delay in the *Wehrkreis* signals centre. Plate then tried to telephone again to Stauffenberg or Mertz von Quirnheim but could not contact them; they were said to be in conference.

Obviously Plate could not simply conceal this message and the radio bulletin from his Commander; he did not think it necessary either since, after his talk with Stauffenberg, he was convinced that they were false. He now presented the situation to his Commander and urged him to decide. Schellert was inclined to go to the *Gauleiter* and ask his advice. Plate, on the other hand, convinced that Stauffenberg's information was correct, thought that all three *Gauleiter* resident in *Wehrkreis* IX, Sauckel, Sprenger and Gerland, should be arrested. Pressed by Plate, Schellert eventually gave his agreement, though with considerable hesitation.[31]

About 9.0 p.m., therefore, Plate and Vethacke in concert issued the necessary orders: certain replacement units located in the *Wehrkreis* were ordered to prepare to move; special guards from 163 Infantry Reserve Battalion were placed on the headquarters building; preparations were made to arrest the *Gauleiter*, Party functionaries and the Senior SS and Police Commander and to guard communications; the Labour Service and the General Labour Leader Wilhelm Neuerburg, were placed under command of the *Wehrkreis*. Lieutenant-Colonel Witzel passed the order and the codeword 'Valkyrie' to No 300 Armoured Experimental Training and Replacement Unit in Eisenach and a company with about fifteen tanks under Major Wollschläger was alerted. Its equipment included radio-controlled armoured minelayers, a highly dangerous weapon. As far as Lieutenant-Colonel Beck remembers the armoured forces were 'on their way to Kassel' but according to later reports from military and Party agencies in Erfurt, though they prepared to move, the troops did not leave their barracks. This is confirmed by Major Wollschläger.[32] Similar measures were taken in other garrisons but, though troops were mobilized, they did not move except in Frankfurt where postal and telegraph offices, the main railway station and the radio station were occupied. It was already very late when the orders were issued and so it was not long before they were cancelled.

As it happened the *Waffen-SS* commander in *Wehrkreis* IX with many of his staff officers was in *Wehrkreis* headquarters; he had taken part in the conference already mentioned and had remained for dinner; he was now in the mess where he was detained. The *Gauleiter* of Hesse could not be arrested; he and his senior officials were all on the Wasserkuppe in Rhön; neither Sprenger, the *Reichsstatthalter*, nor Sauckel were arrested.

In fact everything was going well but an increasing number of queries were coming in from the *Wehrkreis* as to whether all this was in order. The news of the attempt's failure was repeatedly being broadcast and discussed; the absence of further orders from Berlin, in particular the lack of concrete directives for action, finally made Plate suspicious. Could this be a *putsch* and could its prerequisite, stated by Stauffenberg with such certainty, not be a fact? Moreover, despite all efforts, it proved impossible to reestablish contact with the group under Field Marshal von Witzleben in Berlin. Finally an attempt was made, equally without immediate success, to telephone the *Führer*'s headquarters. Plate now advised General Schellert to cancel his orders for the moment and await clarification of the situation.

About 10.30 p.m. Keitel called Kassel himself. Schellert was on another telephone, so Plate took the call. He still had his doubts when Keitel told him that Hitler was alive, that Stauffenberg, Witzleben, Hoepner and the others were traitors and that any orders issued on their instructions should be cancelled forthwith. Then, however, Plate enquired of fellow-officers whom he could trust both in Dresden and Wiesbaden and discovered that they had long since been obeying orders only from 'Wolfschanze' or the new C-in-C Replacement Army. Then the *Gauleiter* returned to Kassel about 11.30 p.m. and began to take a hand. From 11.0 p.m. onwards, after his talk with Keitel and his other enquiries, Plate rang round all headquarters to which he had issued orders, cancelling his instructions and above all putting a stop to any arrests.

Plate had not concealed from Keitel his doubts about Keitel's description of the situation and even of Keitel's own truthfulness; Keitel had not taken this amiss. To authenticate his statements he had said that Hitler would speak over the radio at 11.0 p.m. This did not occur, however, and Plate felt himself corroborated in his doubts. In *Wehrkreis* IX, therefore, orders had been countermanded but uncertainty persisted.

After midnight Plate managed to contact a certain Lieutenant-Colonel Weiss of the Army Personnel Office in Berlin and at last find out the situation: Stauffenberg and some of his brother-officers had been shot; the *putsch* had collapsed. All alerts in Hesse and Thuringia were now hurriedly cancelled.

After midnight the *Gauleiter* with a brown-shirted escort appeared in

Wehrkreis headquarters and demanded to speak to the Commander. Schellert was cross-examined on his reasons for issuing the alert orders; Plate took upon himself the responsibility for issue of the majority of them. Gerland then wished to see the teleprints and other orders received from Berlin and background documents for the instructions issued from Kassel. Lieutenant-Colonel Beck contrived to keep him long enough for Colonels Plate and Vethacke to remove the more dangerous of the orders, particularly those appointing Lieutenant-Colonel Freiherr von Sell as Liaison Officer and the ex-minister Gustav Noske as Political Representative. This in fact did no good since Plate's telephone conversations had been monitored by the Party or SD since 7.0 p.m. and because all documents available in the Bendlerstrasse were confiscated early on 21 July. The conspirators in Berlin may have burnt a great deal before they were arrested but they could not touch papers already in the teleprinter centres.

Wehrkreis X (Hamburg). Both the Commander, General Wilhelm Wetzel, and his Chief of Staff, Major-General Friedrich-Wilhelm Prüter, were absent from the headquarters building in the Knochenhauerstrasse when the first teleprinter messages from Berlin arrived. The Commander was in Munster-Lager and the Chief of Staff had gone home.[33] Colonel Völckers, the Commander's personnel officer, called both of them and asked them to come to headquarters at once as their presence was urgently required.

When Prüter arrived in the Knochenhauerstrasse about 7.0 p.m. Völckers handed him the two messages from Berlin, the first of which began with the statement that Hitler was dead.[34] The second ordered certain security measures and arrests.

The first thing Prüter did was to put through a call to Colonel-General Fromm for confirmation. It came through very quickly; an aide was on the line and said that the C-in-C was not available but the orders were valid and must be carried out at once. Prüter therefore called all senior Party and SS officials in Hamburg and asked them to come to *Wehrkreis* HQ forthwith. The majority of them, however, together with other dignitaries, were attending a lecture by Dr Naumann, Goebbel's State Secretary, in the ballroom of the 'Atlantic' Hotel. Karl Kaufmann, the *Gauleiter*, was also there. Prüter despatched Major-General Kurt Heyser, Garrison Commander Hamburg, to the hotel to fetch the *Gauleiter*.

Having taken these precautions, Prüter ordered two replacement battalions stationed in Hamburg to parade at *Wehrkreis* headquarters, ready for all emergencies. In fact only one of them came; the other had meanwhile heard the radio bulletin, had checked with certain low-level Party agencies and thereupon refused to march to the Knochenhauerstrasse. Other garrisons outside Hamburg were alerted; in Rendsburg, for instance, the Commander made preparations to occupy the Post Office.[35] The Party District Leader (*Kreisleiter*), however, had immediately contacted the Deputy *Gauleiter* and taken counter-measures; for an hour or two, therefore, there was an explosive situation but this soon passed when the orders given to the Commander were withdrawn. Prüter then talked to the Chiefs of Staff of neighbouring

Wehrkreise and discovered that nothing was happening except in Berlin and even there measures taken had already been cancelled. By this time it must have been between 7.0 and 8.0 p.m.

Before beginning his lecture Dr Naumann had been able to give the *Gauleiter* some sketchy information about the attempted military *putsch*; he himself still knew no details. The lecture began punctually, apparently between 4.0 and 5.0 p.m. Naumann had hardly begun, however, when he was called to the telephone; he returned and continued his lecture but a little later was called out again. Goebbels was on the line and said that he was at home, surrounded by troops; Naumann was to return to Berlin at once. He accordingly cancelled his lecture and flew back to Berlin in a *Luftwaffe* aircraft; he was back with Goebbels before 8.0 p.m.[36] The assembly in Hamburg was not dismissed straight away but the *Wehrmacht* Garrison Commandant soon appeared and asked the *Gauleiter* in a whisper to accompany him to *Wehrkreis* HQ. Kaufmann wanted to know why but Heyser himself did not know precisely and could only say that an alert had been issued.

When Kaufmann reached the Knochenhauerstrasse the other recipients of the invitation were already arriving: Georg Ahrens, State Secretary; Georg-Henning Graf von Bassewitz-Behr, Senior SS and Police Commander; Retzlaff, head of the Security Police; Herbert Fust, Commander of the Hamburg SA; the leader of the NSKK (Nazi Party Motor Corps); the heads of the main Party agencies; Vice-Admiral Lohmann, Naval Commander in Hamburg; Colonel Laicher, Chief of Staff, Air Region XI. All, including the *Gauleiter*, were asked to await the arrival of the Commander. In answer to a question from Kaufmann, Prüter said that 'Valkyrie' had been ordered from Berlin and mysterious teleprinter messages had been received. Before the Normandy invasion *Gauleiter* Kaufmann had been discreetly approached by Field Marshal Rommel with a view to his possible cooperation in a change of government and the relationships between him and *Wehrkreis* HQ had always been good and businesslike; without more ado, therefore, Prüter told the *Gauleiter* and the others present of the content of the messages received. All now learnt that they were due to be arrested.

It would have been surprising had they not all felt that they had fallen into a trap; even the *Gauleiter* inevitably had this impression. When Kaufmann, however, humourously remarked that Prüter had better discharge his duty, Prüter replied at once that he would prefer to leave the decision to his Commander. He tried to ease this somewhat unpleasant period of tension by offering everyone a glass of vermouth or sherry; meanwhile he followed the *Gauleiter*'s advice and called the Bendlerstrasse once more.[37] The result was a conversation between Prüter and Stauffenberg who confirmed that Hitler was dead and that Field Marshal von Witzleben had taken over command of the *Wehrmacht*; he insisted that the orders be carried out. As proof of his goodwill to those present, however, Prüter refused to move from his decision to await the arrival of his Commander.[38]

General Wetzel did not keep them waiting long. When he arrived he greeted the *Gauleiter* as affably as ever. Having been briefed by Prüter and having realized with consternation what the messages received implied, he went up to Kaufmann and said: '*Gauleiter*, the two of us are not going to shoot at each other.'[39] Kaufmann was immediately permitted to talk to Bormann in the *Führer*'s headquarters and from him he heard details of the abortive assassination attempt and was ordered under all circumstances to prevent the orders from Berlin being carried out in Hamburg. This was entirely unnecessary, however. General Wetzel had as little sympathy as the *Gauleiter* with so miserably a mismanaged attempt at a *coup d'état*.

When Kaufmann left *Wehrkreis* HQ he placed all Party agencies, the police and the administration on medium alert. *Wehrkreis* HQ, however, cancelled the few instructions issued by the Chief of Staff.

Wehrkreis XI (Hannover). The arrival of the conspirators' first two teleprinter messages during the late afternoon and evening was as great a surprise as in the majority of other *Wehrkreise*. The first said that Hitler was dead and plenary powers had been assumed by the *Wehrmacht*; the second, an hour later, gave detailed instructions for the take-over by *Wehrkreis* commanders including the alerting of troops, the arrest of the *Gauleiter* and a number of senior Party and SS functionaries and the occupation of radio, telegraph and telephone offices. Major-General Rudolf Kütt, the Chief of Staff, and Colonel Kroeger, the operations officer, immediately submitted the teleprints to their Commander, General Benno Bieler.[40]

Initially the General asked to be left alone; he wished to think over the situation and make up his mind. He called Stauffenberg in Berlin and put to him roughly the following questions: 1. Who had the power of government and military command? 2. What was the attitude of Himmler, Goebbels and Göring, the most dangerous supporters of the regime apart from Hitler? 3. What were the new government's intentions regarding prosecution and ending of the war?

Stauffenberg was naturally in a hurry and impatient. All he wanted was to ensure that the orders were carried out; he knew that the *coup* was doomed unless rapid and energetic action was taken; he had no time for discussion. Not surprisingly, therefore, the Commander in Hannover found his explanations unsatisfactory. From his point of view it was all very surprising; he was suddenly expected to take part in a *putsch*, the background to which he did not know and on which he had not even been sounded out beforehand, despite the fact that he had had a long talk with Stauffenberg a fortnight before during a commanders' conference in Potsdam. The leaders of the *coup* did not seem very suitable to Bieler; Stauffenberg could not tell him what the attitude of the SS and police would be. Both in *Wehrkreis* headquarters and replacement units the staffs contained many Nazis, whether members of the Party or not, and this too had to be taken into account. Stauffenberg pleaded urgently for execution of the orders received, but Bieler could foresee that, if he alerted his troops and set them on the move, he would meet resistance.

Shortly thereafter, somewhere between 8.0 and 9.0 p.m., Keitel called Hannover. He was in a great state of agitation and said, almost in a scream, that Stauffenberg had been responsible for the assassination attempt (it had meanwhile been announced over the radio), Hitler was in perfect health, military action was already in train against the mutineers in the Bendlerstrasse and they would soon be 'rendered harmless'. Under no circumstances were orders from the previous commander of the Replacement Army to be obeyed.

So this was not the military versus the remnants of a regime deprived of its *Führer*; it was a group of conspirators within the staff of the Replacement Army versus the whole of the rest of the *Wehrmacht* and the leadership of the Third *Reich* which was still completely intact. This was something quite different. To be certain General Bieler called Berlin once more during the evening and asked what the situation was there. A signals officer told him that shooting was going on in the building and there was general confusion and commotion.

This decided Bieler that 'active participation in the Berlin revolutionary movement was no longer sensible and might be disastrous for all those actively involved'. He accordingly ordered that 'troops were not to be alerted and that the *Wehrkreis* would await further developments'. He informed the commanders of neighbouring *Wehrkreise* X (Hamburg) and IX (Kassel), who agreed with his views.

Wehrkreis XII (Wiesbaden). The situation was very similar to that in Stuttgart and Hannover. The Berlin teleprints arrived late; decoding took some time and the revolt had already collapsed before decisions could be taken. If the 'Valkyrie' order was received at all during the late evening, it could no longer be implemented. Enquiries of Stuttgart and Hannover showed that the attitude there was the same.[41]

Wehrkreis XIII (Nuremberg). Here somewhat more occurred. After 20 July General Mauritz von Wiktorin, the Commander, Colonel Victor Kolbe, Chief of Staff, and Colonel Hans Liphart, personnel officer, were all removed from their posts for over-enthusiasm in carrying out Berlin's orders.[42] Here too the teleprints announcing Hitler's death and assumption of plenary powers by the Army and ordering the arrest of Party and SS functionaries were received during the late afternoon; as elsewhere the first action was to check with Berlin. After talking to Stauffenberg, however, Colonel Kolbe, the Chief of Staff, issued the necessary orders and instructions without hesitation.

Meanwhile Colonel Liphart was telephoning to neighbouring *Wehrkreise*. Munich had already decided against execution of the orders – it must have been 7.0 p.m. or later by this time; the *Führer*'s headquarters was the only authority, Liphart was told. In Stuttgart preparations were being made but a wait-and-see attitude adopted, as a conversation with Colonel Wolf von Tümpling, the personnel officer, showed. Wiesbaden on the other hand was apparently unwilling to obey Berlin's instructions.

Efforts were now made to speak to General Fromm but he could not be contacted and so a call was put through to the *Führer*'s headquarters. The Commander himself spoke to Keitel who told him brusquely that Hitler was alive and would speak on the radio that evening; only his (Keitel's) orders were to be obeyed. Liphart then called Berlin again and himself spoke to Stauffenberg who said to him: 'Liphart, this is a smoke-screen. The *Führer is* dead. The orders of C-in-C Replacement Army are to be carried out.'

The situation now seemed so obscure that action would have been irresponsible, particularly seeing that other *Wehrkreise* were doing nothing whatsoever. Without unanimity of views and action the affair was obviously hopeless. How was anyone in Nuremberg to decide which of the two sides was telling the truth? Was Nuremberg to be the solitary *Wehrkreis* in South Germany to start a civil war and so stab the front in the back, even for a worthy but hopeless cause? Obviously no one wanted that and so: 'In view of these contradictory orders *Wehrkreis* XIII adopted a wait-and-see attitude.' As a precaution two officers, under Liphart's supervision, burnt the orders prepared and put them down a lavatory.[43]

Wehrkreis XVIII (Salzburg). Here the Commander, General Julius Ringel, was regarded as staunchly loyal to the regime; he never even saw the orders from Berlin since he was on a tour of inspection that day.[44] By 6.0 p.m. they had not reached Colonel Glasl, the Chief of Staff, either. When the office closed Glasl went back to his room in the Hotel 'Bristol', Salzburg; as he entered the porter called him to the telephone. It was Lieutenant-General Burgdorf from 'Wolfschanze', who asked whether orders from Berlin had been received in Salzburg. Glasl replied that they had not and Burgdorf then said that an attack had been made on Hitler but he was unharmed; orders from the Bendlerstrasse in Berlin were unauthorized and were not to be obeyed.

It was now just before 6.0 p.m. Glasl went back to the headquarters where a signals officer showed him the two teleprints which had just arrived. The first began with the words 'The *Führer* Adolf Hitler is dead'; the second contained instructions for the immediate arrest of the *Gauleiter*, SS commanders and other functionaries. This precisely contradicted Lieutenant-General Burgdorf's instructions. At about 6.0 p.m. Colonel Ryll, the personnel officer, called Glasl in the headquarters; he had received a call from Major John von Freyend, Keitel's aide in 'Wolfschanze', saying that an attack had been made on Hitler but had miscarried; a mutiny had broken out in Berlin and orders from that quarter were not to be obeyed. All this Ryll passed to Glasl who said that he had just received on his desk a pile of inexplicable teleprints; they were clearly outdated by the news from 'Wolfschanze'. He asked Ryll to come to the headquarters at once.

In the absence of his Commander Colonel Glasl had to take the decision alone. His obvious course was to do nothing and not only because his information was contradictory. From the political point of view *Wehrkreis* XVIII was one of the most uninteresting; it had hardly any replacement units; the major installations and agencies associated with the *Führer*'s headquarters in Berchtesgaden were independent or directly under OKW; security was primarily the responsibility of the SS. All available forces in the *Wehrkreis* were operating against the partisans in the frontier areas of Steiermark and Slovenia.

The 'Valkyrie' plans for *Wehrkreis* XVIII provided for the formation in emergency of a reinforced regiment; on 5 July *Wehrkreis* HQ had asked Stauffenberg for authority to form this regiment so that it might be used in anti-guerilla operations. Stauffenberg authorized this and during the telephone conversation concerned told Glasl to keep the regiment firmly under his own control. Nevertheless, on formation it was immediately allotted to Rösener, the Senior SS and Police Commander. *Wehrkreis* HQ, therefore, had available no units of any significance. Owing to the proximity of the 'Berghof', moreover, there were so many SS units in the *Wehrkreis*, particularly in the neighbourhood of Salzburg, that implementation of Berlin's orders hardly merited serious consideration. In addition General Ringel, the commander, wore the Golden Party Badge. Under these circumstances it was hardly surprising that no one in *Wehrkreis* headquarters had been told of the preparations for the *coup* apart from Colonel Wilhelm Freiherr von Salza und Lichtenau, the previous Chief of Staff, who had meanwhile been posted.

Lieutenant-Colonel Rendel, operations officer of *Wehrkreis* XVIII, heard of the attack on Hitler about 7.0 p.m. while in the mess in the 'Europa' Hotel, playing dice with some of his section officers, as they did every week; they were playing the well-known 'Hindenburg' game.[45] They continued undisturbed. Somewhat later, about 8.0 p.m., a lieutenant arrived with the news of receipt of the teleprinter messages. Rendel tried to call Glasl but could not contact him and finally went back to the office where a number of further teleprinter messages arrived during the evening.[46]

General Ringel returned to *Wehrkreis* HQ about 8.0 p.m. He had no action to take, however, since no orders had been issued and there was therefore nothing to cancel. The only remaining action was to ensure that the existing good relations with the *Gauleiter* were maintained. Glasl had already called his headquarters.[47]

Dr Scheel, the *Gauleiter*, was in Heidelberg on 20 July giving a lecture in his capacity as *Reich* Student Leader; while driving back over the Schwäbische Alb he heard the news of the attack on Hitler over his car radio. He stopped and called Salzburg from a service station on the autobahn to find out what the situation there was. Then he drove on to Salzburg as fast as possible. He arrived about or soon after 8.0 p.m. and went straight to his house. A noticeable number of soldiers were standing in front of it; they turned out to be escorts for the people summoned by Dr Scheel, primarily General Ringel and SS-*Obergruppenführer* Rösener. Assurances were exchanged that the orders from Berlin had no significance. As far as Scheel remembers also present were: Schulz, representing the Senior SS and Police Commander; Dr Laue, the Governor (*Regierungspräsident*) andthe Commander of the Security Police, but this may have been somewhat later.

Glasl and Rendel both remember quite definitely that officers of *Wehrkreis* HQ did not visit the *Gauleiter* in his house but that the *Gauleiter* came to the headquarters where he was shown the teleprinter messages received; this, of course, remains a possibility. Dr Laue, on the other hand, says that he discussed the situation with General Ringel, apparently without the *Gauleiter*, and while he was doing so the teleprint arrived ordering 'Valkyrie Stage 2'. Dr

Scheel does not remember going to *Wehrkreis* HQ.

One thing is certain: on 20 July the relationship between the headquarters of the *Wehrkreis* and the *Gauleiter* in Salzburg was in no way ruffled. No military units were alerted or even placed on stand-by alert. On the contrary, the Innsbruck and Graz garrisons were ordered not to obey any orders which did not come from *Wehrkreis* HQ; they both had their own radio stations and so it was conceivable that they might receive orders direct from Berlin. At the end of the day the failure of the *coup* was celebrated in the *Gauleiter*'s house with one or two glasses of wine, General Ringel, if not others, from *Wehrkreis* HQ being present. Together they listened to the speeches from Hitler, Dönitz and Göring.

Wehrkreis XX (Danzig). Here there was a member of the conspiracy in an important post: Lieutenant-Colonel Hasso von Boehmer was operations officer. The Commander, however, was General Bodewin Keitel, a brother of the Field Marshal.[48] Moreover the *Wehrkreis* was now almost in the combat zone.

On 20 July General Keitel was on a tour of inspection with his assistant; while in Graudenz he heard over the radio of the attack on Hitler. They drove back to Danzig at once. There the Commander contacted *Gauleiter* Forster and also his brother. The usual teleprints had arrived from Berlin and the remainder came in during the evening. None of the conspirators' orders from Berlin were carried out.

Wehrkreis XXI (Poznan). The course of events was similar. The *Wehrkreis* was more or less in the combat zone, if for no other reason because of the partisans; there were practically no static units which might have been used. On 20 July an inspection of certain Labour Service camps was taking place, at which a large number of senior Army and SS officers were present; as a result the more important officers could not be contacted at the critical moment. In any case no one in this area seems to have been in the secret.[49] It was after 6.0 p.m. before the teleprints from Berlin arrived, even later than 8.0 p.m. according to the receipt stamps on copies submitted to the *Gestapo*. Before the second message had been decoded a call came from *Wehrkreis* I (Königsberg) which showed that the orders from Berlin were not being obeyed there.[50] The Chief of Staff accordingly enquired of the *Wehrkreis* HQs in Danzig, Breslau and Wiesbaden in order to find out whether the situation was any different there – and it was not. A fruitless attempt was made to contact Colonel-General Fromm. Clearly the revolt had collapsed and during the evening Lieutenant-General Burgdorf called from 'Wolfschanze' and informed the Commander that Hitler was alive and the revolt had been suppressed.

The Government-General Wehrkreis (Cracow). Here also the orders from Berlin arrived but produced no more action than in neighbouring *Wehrkreise*. General Siegfried Haenicke, the Commander, was on a tour of inspection and the orders were received by Major-General Max Bork, his Chief of Staff, about 9.0 p.m.[51] But he had received the radio news as early as 6.45 p.m., and at 7.20 and 7.30 p.m. respectively he had expressed 'his thankfulness that the *Führer* had been saved' before the officers and then before the enlisted men of the

Wehrkreis headquarters. The teleprinter messages from Berlin did not even arrive until 9.0 p.m. About 10.0 p.m. a call came through from Major-General Stieff who told Bork that no orders from Replacement Army headquarters in Berlin were to be accepted but only orders from the *Reichsführer SS* who had been appointed Commander-in-Chief Replacement Army as of today; Bork should decline even to talk to Hoepner, Witzleben, Fromm and Stauffenberg; Colonel-General Guderian was deputizing for General Zeitzler, and Lieutenant-General Wenck for Lieutenant-General Heusinger. When Burgdorf called a short while later, he was told that the orders from Berlin had arrived about an hour ago, but thanks to Stieff's call the necessary dispositions had already been made. At 10.16 p.m. a *Wehrkreis* order went out 'that all military installations were to be occupied immediately in close consultation with the local SS and police leaders', particularly communications installations, barracks and armaments factories. Also after 10.0 p.m. Bork telephoned to Bormann and Keitel and informed the Governor General and the Senior SS and Police Leader East, both of whom had not yet learned anything of the events of the day. At 11.50 p.m. Bork spoke to the Chief of Staff *Wehrkreis* XX, Colonel Saal, who told him that the orders had arrived there, and also the counter-orders, and that the *Wehrkreis* was 'firmly in the hands of the *Führer*'. Nine minutes later Bork was told the same by Lieutenant-General von Thadden in Königsberg about *Wehrkreis* I, and at 12.05 a.m. by Major-General Rüdt von Collenberg in Breslau about *Wehrkreis* VIII. Rüdt was also able to tell Bork that *Wehrkreise* II, III and IV were 'equally all right'.

In general, therefore, the situation was the same in all *Wehrkreise*: counter-orders from 'Wolfschanze' arrived almost simultaneously with, sometimes even before, the orders from Berlin. Where this was not the case or at least not definitely so, the radio bulletins and the obscure situation in Berlin, where there was obviously uncertainty and in some cases indecision, simply produced confusion in the *Wehrkreise*. Here and there measures were taken and troops moved, though this is nowhere recorded and senior staff officers could not remember – subsequently no one wanted to have had anything to do with it and many actions were successfully covered up. After 10.0 p.m. nothing but counter-orders issued even from the Bendlerstrasse. Even those commanders and staff officers in the *Wehrkreise* who supported the revolt could do nothing when the essential conditions were not there – the death of Hitler and effective seizure of command over the *Wehrmacht* by the conspirators. The others could only have been carried along had the conspiracy effectively seized command; they could not be while the authority of the *Führer*'s headquarters remained intact. Stauffenberg and Mertz had hoped in vain that most or at least many of their brother-officers would join in support of the *coup* of their own accord as soon as it had been declared.[52]

44 Prague, Vienna, Paris

Special conditions obtained in three areas in which the 20 July resistance movement was more successful than in the majority of *Wehrkreise*. In Prague the German troops were in the midst of a hostile Czech population; the Protectorate of Bohemia and Moravia was increasingly becoming a combat zone infested by partisans. Here the position of all *Wehrmacht* and SS units was so precarious that they could not give even the slightest sign of disunity or weakness. It was hardly to be expected, therefore, that the orders issued from Berlin on 20 July would be carried out and yet in large measure they were. Austria too regarded itself as an occupied country; no one in Vienna was interested in supporting the regime in any way and yet this was precisely what the orders from Berlin apparently demanded. Since few in Vienna were in the secret and realized the real implication of the orders, it is somewhat astounding that here too they were largely obeyed. Finally the situation in Paris was similar – a communications zone in an increasingly hostile country and threatened by an imminent break-through by the American forces in Normandy. Admittedly the higher staffs in France contained a particularly large number of opposition supporters but in the circumstances the attempted *coup* was a particularly bold manoeuvre.

Prague (Wehrkreis Böhmen und Mähren). In May 1942 SS-*Obergruppenführer* Reinhard Heydrich, Acting *Reich* Protector for Bohemia and Moravia, had been murdered by Czech patriots. His successor, the German Minister Karl Hermann Frank, had the village of Lidice destroyed and all male inhabitants shot.[1] Frank and the SS were almost undisputed rulers in Bohemia and Moravia and this situation persisted when Dr Wilhelm Frick, ex-Minister of the Interior, became Protector in 1943. The military commander was General Ferdinand Schaal; in his capacity as '*Wehrmacht* Plenipotentiary accredited to the German Minister of State and Commander of the *Wehrkreis* Bohemia and Moravia' he had to coordinate with Frank, though not with Frick; as *Wehrkreis* Commander he was responsible to the C-in-C Replacement Army, Colonel-General Fromm, as *Wehrmacht* Plenipotentiary to Field Marshal Keitel, Chief of OKW.[2] Schaal did his best to cooperate with Frank but the latter was first and foremost an SS man, so tension and suspicion were inevitable.

The first teleprint to arrive in *Wehrkreis* HQ Prague from Berlin carried a despatch time '16.45 hours' but it was not received in Prague until about 6.30

p.m. Frank, the Minister, General Schaal, the *Wehrkreis* Commander, and many other personages were at a ceremony for the opening of an SS Cadet School; it was held in the Institute of Technology on the Wehrmachtplatz, Prague. While the company was drinking a glass of beer before dinner the school adjutant came in with the news of the attempted assassination which had just been broadcast over the radio. A little later between 6.30 and 7.0 p.m. both Frank and Schaal were asked over the telephone to return to their offices.[3]

At about 7.0 p.m., therefore, back in his headquarters, Schaal read the first teleprint from Berlin. The radio had announced that the assassination attempt had failed and now here was Field Marshal von Witzleben, long since retired, taking over plenary powers as Commander-in-Chief of the *Wehrmacht* and ordering *Wehrkreis* commanders to eliminate all SS and Party organizations. This was no simple matter but in Bohemia and Moravia with an underground movement and a hostile population hesitation, delay or restraint were not possible. Whatever shifts of power there might be inside the German leadership, in Bohemia and Moravia security measures were essential; the mere news of the assassination attempt might produce disturbances. These were the factors which General Schaal had to consider in deciding on his attitude.[4]

In Bohemia and Moravia the codeword instituting security measures for important military buildings, bridges, signals installations and power stations was 'Odin' instead of 'Valkyrie'. General Schaal issued this codeword shortly after 7.0 p.m.[5] To be doubly sure that he was right and was acting in accordance with his superiors' wishes (if there were two sets of superiors, in accordance with the wishes of the right ones) he put through a call to his immediate commander in Berlin, Colonel-General Fromm. His object was to find out whether full powers had really been delegated to *Wehrkreis* commanders as the teleprinter message said. The call came through quickly but Fromm was not available. At 7.13 p.m. Schaal spoke to Stauffenberg instead of Fromm; Stauffenberg confirmed that Fromm had transferred plenary powers to *Wehrkreis* commanders; a teleprinter message to this effect was on its way, he said (Schaal had apparently not said that he had it already). According to Schaal Stauffenberg then said: 'The *Führer* is dead; I was there myself. Communiqués already broadcast and any which may come are false. A new government is being formed. Measures ordered against the SD should be carried out with all speed.'[6]

Having received this confirmation Schaal took further action in accordance with the orders from Berlin; at the same time, however, he had in mind the perilous position of the Germans in Bohemia and Moravia. He confirmed the alert for Army units in the *Wehrkreis*. In view of the exceptional situation in Prague, however, before issuing the codewords applicable to SS units – 'Götterdämmerung' and 'Feuerzauber' – he wished to discuss the situation with Frank, the German Minister of State. This was therefore the object of his next telephone call.

Frank was no longer in his office when Schaal called. He had left the ceremony at the same time as Schaal and gone directly to his office in the Czernin Palace; there he had briefed his immediate staff and ordered a state of alert. Then he had driven to his country house, Jungfern-Breschan.[7] Schaal, therefore, could only contact Frank's deputy, *SS-Standartenführer* and *Ministerialrat* Dr Gies. Schaal asked him to come to *Wehrkreis* headquarters. Dr Gies set off, obviously after checking with Frank.

Gies arrived in *Wehrkreis* headquarters about 7.45 p.m. and was briefed by General Schaal who said that he had assumed plenary powers in Bohemia and Moravia. Gies was requested to wait in the office. At about the same time Schaal contacted Frank in his country house, described the situation similarly to him and asked him to come to *Wehrkreis* headquarters for further discussion and coordination. Frank agreed.[8]

Meanwhile, at 8.10 p.m., the second teleprint arrived from Berlin ordering the arrest of *Gauleiter*, *Reichsstatthalter*, Ministers, Governors, Police Presidents, Senior SS and Police Commanders, heads of *Gestapo*, SS and Propaganda Offices and Party District Leaders. This meant that both Dr Gies and also Frank were to be arrested.

Frank meanwhile had gained the impression that the *Wehrkreis* Commander might not be entirely 'reliable'. Gies had not returned and he suspected that he had been arrested. He ordered a call to be put through to Schaal recalling Gies but this resulted in nothing. Schaal on his side had ordered the senior SS commanders to his office. *SS-Gruppenführer* and Lieutenant-General of Police Hitzegrad accordingly appeared and learnt from Gies that he had been detained and could get no definite information from Schaal. Schaal then invited Hitzegrad into his office and in the presence of Lieutenant-General Wilhelm Thomas, Commander of 539 Prague Territorial Division whom he had already summoned, showed Hitzegrad the teleprints received from Berlin ordering the arrest of certain persons. Schaal and Hitzegrad, however, agreed that, in view of conditions in Prague, this should be avoided if possible. On the other hand, Schaal said, for some time he had been trying in vain to contact Colonel-General Fromm to confirm his appreciation of the situation and his decision not to make these arrests. It was unthinkable and highly dangerous to allow the Czech population to see any signs of disunity among their German rulers.

After discussion with Lieutenant-Colonel Kurt Engelschall, his operations officer, General Schaal ordered special precautions for the security and supervision of signals installations; on enquiry from Colonel Ruprecht, his chief signals officer, he exempted the Czernin Palace from supervision and did his best to come to some understanding or 'gentleman's agreement' with Frank.[9]

Schaal made another attempt to speak to Colonel-General Fromm and put through a call to the Bendlerstrasse. Fromm was still not available and instead, about 8.45 p.m., Colonel-General Hoepner (dismissed in 1942) came on the line. The teleprint announcing his appointment as C-in-C Home Forces had not yet arrived in Prague but Hoepner himself confirmed that he was in authority. Schaal accordingly described the situation in Prague and asked for authorization to cooperate with Frank. Hoepner gave it provided that the

Commander retained plenary power in his own hands. Colonel-General Beck was forming a new government, he said, and everything was still in the early stages.[10]

Meanwhile Dr Gies was making increasingly strenuous efforts to get out of *Wehrkreis* HQ. He ought to have told his Minister about the situation long ago and the Minister had already telephoned asking for him. Since, however, Frank had not kept his word about coming to *Wehrkreis* HQ, Schaal did not propose to let this trump card out of his hand. He did not trust the SS and before letting the Minister's deputy go wished to be clear whether they were with him or against him. He accordingly refused to allow Gies to return to Frank and Gies had to consider himself as under arrest.[11]

About 8.50 p.m. Schaal telephoned Frank asking him to come as agreed, but Frank answered evasively, saying that the situation was not what Schaal thought. Schaal, on the other hand, believing that he had been invested with plenary power, could not very well go to Frank himself since, for the moment at any rate, he considered Frank to be under his orders. Frank, however, said that he had information and orders direct from the *Führer*'s headquarters to the effect that he was directly responsible to the *Führer* and therefore had no need of any orders from Schaal.[12] Schaal called Frank once more about 9.0 p.m. and was told by his office that the Minister was on his way to see him. But nothing happened.

At about 9.05 p.m. arrived the teleprinter message from Berlin in which the 'C-in-C Replacement Army and C-in-C Home Forces' (name not given) announced that, contrary to the radio bulletins, the *Führer* was dead and that the measures ordered were to be carried out 'with the utmost dispatch'.[13] Schaal was convinced that Hitler was dead and he could see a struggle for power starting. He felt, however, that this struggle must be decided in Berlin, not in the hostile foreign territory of Prague, where in any case the SS were in such superior numbers that they could certainly defeat the Army – an intolerable thought.[14] Although, seen from Prague, the attempted *coup* seemed to have some prospect of success – Schaal had heard nothing at all from OKW in 'Wolfschanze' – it was essential to avoid any clash, whether in the interests of the previous regime or the new government allegedly being formed.[15]

At about 9.45 p.m. Schaal tried once more to speak to Fromm but again could only get Hoepner.[16] Hoepner, however, had so little to say about the situation, unusual though it was – he merely said that there was nothing fresh – that Schaal decided to act on his own initiative and finally arrange a meeting with Frank.[17] Lieutenant-General Hitzegrad acted as intermediary; it was agreed to meet in a 'third place', the headquarters of *SS-Brigadeführer* Graf von Pückler, *Waffen-SS* commander in the Protectorate of Bohemia and Moravia; mutual assurances of safe conduct were exchanged. General Schaal had acknowledged the actual power ratio, for the safe conduct promised by the SS meant nothing. At the same time Dr Gies was released from arrest.

General Schaal thereupon set off to see Frank but was called back by his aide when, at 10.10 p.m. a telephone call came through from General Burgdorf in 'Wolfschanze'. He said that 'von Witzleben, Fromm, Hoepner, Olbricht and the rest were traitors', all orders issued by them were invalid, Himmler was now C-in-C Replacement Army and the only valid orders were those from Himmler and Keitel. At the same time Schaal was shown a similar teleprint from Keitel, received from 'Wolfschanze' at 10.0 p.m.[18]

Schaal arrived at Pückler's 'command post' between 10.15 and 10.40 p.m. and there at last met Frank.[19] Frank demanded immediate cancellation of all alerts ('Odin' and 'Johannes') and Schaal's word of honour that he regarded himself as Frank's political subordinate. If Schaal refused, Frank said, he would have to arrest him. Schaal had placed himself in Frank's power and there was now no question of safe conduct. Schaal, however, was now convinced that Hitler was not dead and that the reason for calling the alerts, the threat of disturbances as a result of Hitler's death, no longer applied. He had every reason to meet Frank's demands. He was thereupon allowed to return to his headquarters. Frank asked him to come and see him again next morning and to go with him to a concert or the theatre next evening to show the world that the German rulers were still at one.

There was no visit to a concert, however. When Schaal returned to see Frank at 11.0 a.m. next morning Frank had had an order from Himmler to arrest him. There was talk of honourable arrest of short duration but Schaal was in fact held prisoner until the German collapse in April 1945.[20]

Vienna (*Wehrkreis* XVII). The office had long since closed when the conspirators' first teleprinter message arrived from Berlin, but one or two officers were still there, including Colonel Heinrich Kodré, the Chief of Staff, and Captain Karl Szokoll of the Supply Section (Organization). The Commander, General Albrecht Schubert, had left early in July for a cure in Slovakia.[21] General Hans-Karl Freiherr von Esebeck had been appointed acting commander by the Army Personnel Office and he had arrived in Vienna at the beginning of the month. He knew Stauffenberg since the time when they had served together in 1 Light Division in 1939.[22]

The first Berlin teleprint arrived in Vienna about 6.0 p.m. and was taken to the Chief of Staff by the duty officer, Fritz Bollhammer, about 6.20. Bollhammer had been told of its arrival about 6.0 p.m. and, since it was Top Secret, had asked the Chief of Staff and Szokoll to wait for it before leaving the office.[23]

No sooner had Kodré read the message than he ordered the duty officer to recall General von Esebeck to the office from the 'Army House', since 'something "big" has happened'. A platoon of the Vienna Guard Battalion in full battle order with one heavy machine gun was ordered up to guard *Wehrkreis* HQ; after some hithering and thithering it arrived at 8.20 p.m. under a sergeant-major and took up position. Shortly thereafter the second teleprint ordering the arrests arrived. Colonel Kodré forthwith drew up a list of officers to be summoned to *Wehrkreis* HQ for an urgent conference at 7.0 p.m. Bollhammer, the duty officer, was ordered to inform them, but, since time was short, Kroehl, the duty corporal, had to assist and Kodré himself made one or two calls. Captain Szokoll was ordered to set the 'Valkyrie' measures in motion. All this was nothing so unusual in *Wehrkreis* XVII;

alerts of this nature had taken place on several occasions when replacements were urgently required at the front.[24] Szokoll began at once informing the various garrisons in *Wehrkreis* XVII according to plan.

Meanwhile General von Esebeck arrived in the headquarters at No 1 Stubenring and was immediately briefed by Kodré. After reading the messages he agreed with Kodré's view that the orders should be carried out. They both thought that the messages and the information they contained were 'genuine' and therefore official.[25] Regulations did not require them to be confirmed by Berlin but, in view of the unusual nature of the orders and the surprising fact that one of the messages was signed by Witzleben as C-in-C of the *Wehrmacht*, Esebeck thought it wise to obtain confirmation before making a final decision. As Chief of Staff, therefore, Kodré called Stauffenberg, his opposite number in Berlin; he confirmed that the messages were correct and pressed for rapid execution. Kodré reported this to Esebeck who thereupon approved the measures proposed and already partially initiated by Kodré. The Commander and his Chief of Staff then discussed how the arrests were to be made. Kodré proposed that 'the gentlemen concerned be invited to *Wehrkreis* HQ', that they be told the contents of the teleprints and requested to 'make themselves available'. Force was only to be used in emergency. Esebeck agreed and the 'gentlemen concerned' were informed.[26]

Meanwhile the officers who had been summoned were gradually arriving at No 1 Stubenring, the old War Ministry. If unable to come at once they had been told to arrive as soon as possible. There assembled: Lieutenant-General Adolf Sinzinger, commandant of Vienna and a recipient of the Nazi Party Golden Badge; Captain Schram and Captain Sedlmayr representing Major-General Erich Müller-Derichsweiler, commanding 177 Division, absent on duty; Majors Meyer and Futter representing Lieutenant-General Adalbert Mikulicz, commanding 417 Division, also absent on duty; Captain Morell representing Major-General Hans Koelitz, commander Armoured Forces in *Wehrkreis* XVII, who was in Döllersheim; Colonel Otto Armster, head of the Vienna Report Centre and a member of the conspiracy; Colonel Seiffert, operations officer *Wehrkreis* HQ; Colonel Marx, supply officer; Colonel von Dobeneck, Chief Signal Officer; Captain Sandau, operations section; Captain Szokoll, supply section; Captain Ammon, headquarters commandant and air raid precautions officer; Major Neumayr, intelligence officer. Being called at such short notice the conference did not begin punctually and was postponed to 7.20 p.m. All were quickly briefed by Colonel Kodré in his office with General von Esebeck present; they were ordered to issue an alert for their areas. In his capacity as City Commandant General Sinzinger was ordered to arrest the local Party dignitaries; this order he accepted without demur.[27] Meanwhile the military measures in the various garrisons and localities were under way; readiness for action and the occupation of certain buildings were reported to Captain Szokoll.[28]

The gentlemen to be arrested had been invited to *Wehrkreis* HQ for 8.0 p.m. Almost all those present in Vienna came along unsuspectingly: *SS-Brigadeführer* Karl Scharizer, acting *Gauleiter* in the absence at a funeral of

Baldur von Schirach, the *Reichsleiter* and *Gauleiter* of Vienna; *SS-Obersturmführer* Ludwig representing Major-General Goedicke, *Waffen-SS* Garrison Commander, absent on duty; *SS-Obersturmführer* Köhler, assistant to Dr Hugo Jury, *Reichsstatthalter* of the Lower Danube *Gau*, also absent; *SS-Obergruppenführer* Rudolf Querner, Senior SS and Police Commander in *Wehrkreis* XVII, with his aide; Lieutenant-Colonel Frodien, Chief of Staff to the Commander of the Regular Police, who arrived later. Eduard Frauenfeld, head of propaganda in the *Gau*, also arrived later.

Some of these gentlemen arrived armed and full of suspicion, Scharizer the deputy *Gauleiter* with his two aides, for instance. In many cases they were only persuaded to enter the building with some difficulty. It fell to the lot of Lieutenant-Colonel Robert Prince von Arenberg of the *Abwehr* office to arrest *SS-Standartenführer* Dr Rudolf Mildner, head of the *Gestapo* and SD in Vienna, together with his deputy, *SS-Obersturmbannführer* Dr Karl Ebner; Arenberg was to reconnoitre all concentration camps in the area of the *Wehrkreis*.[29] In contrast to the majority of those present in *Wehrkreis* HQ, Lieutenant-Colonel Wackerhagen, head of Group III, had heard the radio bulletin about the failure of the assassination attempt before he arrived; he thought the situation obscure and decided to go back to his hotel and put on uniform. In the hotel he met Colonel Armster, ate a quick supper and then went back to the HQ with Armster. Arenberg was therefore alone and, as he says, went about his job with satisfaction and pleasure. Since he did not know where to find either Mildner or Ebner, he told an officer of the *Waffen-SS* who had arrived meanwhile to invite them to come along. Time passed and they did not come; Arenberg knew that the guards on the building had been reinforced and he was afraid this might scare his victims away, so he went out on to the street to look for them. He discovered Mildner a little distance away beside a car; not knowing him, he had to establish his identity by asking. He accordingly missed Ebner whom Mildner had sent on ahead and who could now no longer get out, since the sentries were not allowing anyone not in *Wehrmacht* uniform to leave. With some difficulty Arenberg overcame Mildner's suspicions and persuaded him to come in and see General Esebeck; Ebner joined them at the guard room. Then, however, Arenberg conducted them, not to Esebeck, but to a special room where, despite their violent and vocal protests, they were politely arrested and disarmed.

The remaining SS and Party leaders assembled in Kodré's office, where were also General von Esebeck and his personnel officer Colonel Hermann Dyes. They listened to the Acting Commander's statement without serious protest. He had orders, he said, to arrest them; he would prefer, however, to avoid so drastic a step and he therefore asked them to remain until the situation clarified. All acknowledged the teleprinter messages which Esebeck showed them, as legal and valid; no one demanded, for instance, to ring up OKW or Himmler. Querner did not even wish to see the messages; he had no reason, he said, to doubt the General's word.[30] Finally all were served brandy and cigarettes; they were allowed to keep their pistols but, initially at least, were allotted different rooms. Though these measures were not as energetic as the conspirators might have wished, at the least the most powerful potential opponents in Vienna were now under lock and key and in any case much more progress had been made than in most other *Wehrkreise.*

Meanwhile outside in Vienna, in Wiener-Neustadt, St Pölten and other localities, troops of the Replacement Army were on the move; they occupied military objectives and in some cases post offices and railway stations. General Sinzinger, City Commandant of Vienna, personally disarmed *SS-Brigadeführer* Leo Gotzmann, the Police President of Vienna; the regular police were placed under the *Wehrmacht* and the *Waffen-SS* almost so – Querner had, after all, admitted to Kodré that the Berlin orders were legal.[31] At the same time, however, the current began to flow in the reverse direction.

Between 8.0 and 9.0 p.m. *Wehrkreis* XVII received the teleprinter message appointing Seitz and Reither as Political Representatives and Colonel Graf von Marogna-Redwitz as OKH liaison officer.[32] Kodré was not in the secret of the *coup*, but he knew at once what sort of people these were: Seitz was a socialist and ex-Burgomaster of Vienna; Reither was a Christian-Social farmers' leader; Marogna-Redwitz was 'an extreme conservative, much under clerical influence' – at least that was Kodré's view. The appointment of these three as leading politicians or coordinators suddenly showed that everything that had happened that evening was directed against the entire previous regime. The appointment of Seitz, Reither and Marogna-Redwitz, Kodré thought, could not be explained by Army measures against a Party *putsch*.[33]

About this time, or at least between 8.30 and 10.0 p.m., Kodré and Esebeck spoke to Hoepner, having tried in vain to contact Colonel-General Fromm. When they told him of the contradictory information which they had, Hoepner said that, if they could not make up their minds, they might as well act as ordered by Keitel.[34] This was hardly calculated to clarify the situation.

Colonel Kodré took the teleprints appointing the Political Representatives and the liaison officer to General von Esebeck and described to him the people concerned. Hitherto it may not have been clear how far Esebeck had been prepared to recognize the *putsch* for what it was or what risks he was ready to take for it, but his reaction to these teleprints was unequivocal: he summoned Scharizer, the acting *Gauleiter* to talk to him about Seitz and Reither.[35] Scharizer's attitude is not the important point here; he was apparently manoeuvring with caution since there is no evidence that he protested (as did other functionaries of the regime); what is important is that Esebeck, without information and in doubt, remained on the side of the legal regime. Soon after Esebeck's and Scharizer's talk Frauenfeld, the *Gau* propaganda leader, appeared; he had been suspicious from the outset and said to Kodré: 'Colonel, I do not believe it [Hitler's death]; there is something up.' Kodré replied that he knew as little as Frauenfeld and they could only await further developments.[36]

Then came a fourth teleprinter message denying the radio bulletin: Hitler *was* dead, it said, and all measures were to be carried out 'with the utmost despatch.'[37] This also Kodré took at once to Esebeck, who was still conferring with Scharizer and Frauenfeld, and told him what it said. Frauenfeld went up to Kodré, struck an attitude, beat on his breast and said: 'Colonel, that is definitely not right; the *Führer* is alive; one feels this.' In the *Wehrkreis* the military measures still proceeded but doubts were growing; some confirmation that all this was a 'mystification' would suffice for everything to be put into reverse at once.

Now a call came through from the *Führer's* headquarters. Lieutenant-General Burgdorf was on the line and then Field Marshal Keitel spoke to Kodré. It must have been about 10.0 p.m.[38] Keitel let loose such a torrent of words that Kodré could not get a word in edgeways – had he gone mad – he would be court-martialled etc. Kodré was taking the call in Esebeck's office and Esebeck came in at the moment; Kodré simply held out the receiver to him and when Esebeck came on the line, Keitel 'clarified'. Hitler was not dead, he said; the orders from Berlin were not valid and must be cancelled at once.

Immediately after this conversation Stauffenberg called from Berlin: 'Kodré, what's up? You don't want to climb out now, do you?'[39] He assumed that Kodré had realized that the measures ordered implied an attempt at a *coup d'état* and that he was in favour of them. Kodré, however, only had time to tell Stauffenberg that Keitel had just called when they were cut off.

After the talk between Esebeck and Keitel, Captain Szokoll had arrived in the Chief of Staff's office with orders ready for signature incorporating the SS into the *Wehrmacht* and announcing the take-over of political administration by Seitz and Reither; through the babel of voices both from prisoners and gaolers he heard that Keitel had just said that it was all treachery, Hitler was alive and a *putsch* was going on in Berlin.[40] Szokoll dashed back to his room and put through a call to Stauffenberg. Stauffenberg's voice sounded tired and discouraged and when he heard that Esebeck had 'defected' after Keitel's call, he said: 'You won't give up too, will you'; then they were cut off. Szokoll was still wavering but when he later saw Kodré and Esebeck apologizing to the SS and Party functionaries, he was forced to abandon all idea of continuing the revolt.

Between 10.0 and 11.0 p.m. Esebeck and Kodré put through calls to Field Marshal von Witzleben in Berlin, General Schaal in Prague and General Ringel in Salzburg. Though made on the highest priority the call to Witzleben never came through; General Ringel did not return to his office until after 11.0 p.m. and then called Vienna himself.[41] Inquiries were made of Burgdorf; about 10.40 p.m. he confirmed that the orders from Berlin were invalid. All measures were then hurriedly cancelled.[42]

General von Esebeck summoned the arrested functionaries and dignitaries in turn to express his sorrow at the unhappy turn of events and to apologize formally. Nobody complained and nobody reproached the Commander. The first to leave was Scharizer, the deputy *Gauleiter*, first asking humorously whether his 'artillery' could be returned to him from the safe of Captain Bollhammer, the duty officer; Querner and his aide departed a quarter of an hour later. *SS-Obersturmführer* Köhler, aide to *Gauleiter* Jury who could not be reached, had already left to look for Dr Gruber, Governor (*Regierungspräsident*) of the Lower Danube *Gau*; he had not returned.

Frauenfeld, continually emphasizing that he had never believed it, remained with Kodré for a while and was then called urgently back to his office; instructions from Bormann had presumably arrived meanwhile.

Dr Mildner and Dr Ebner then appeared in Kodré's, office. They were the only ones to have taken their arrest much amiss and they loudly demanded an explanation.[43] Kodré gave them the teleprinter messages to read and they were then both in a great hurry to get back to their office. They first telephoned from Bollhammer's office and ordered the *Gestapo* to activate the emergency card-index and arrest Seitz and Reither at once.

Finally Esebeck, Kodré and Dyes sat together over a glass of brandy in Dyes' house and listened to Hitler's speech. The attempted revolt in Vienna was at an end and no one wished to have anything more to do with it. Orders had been issued which had been thought legal but had proved to be false and so they had been cancelled. That was all.

The next morning, however, General Schubert appeared, having interrupted his cure, and said that, had he been present, such a mess would never have occurred. As a precaution General Esebeck wished to clear himself with *Gauleiter* von Schirach; Lieutenant-General Sinzinger had the same object and so he went too. Esebeck may have hoped that, with the help of this Nazi Party 'Old Fighter' who carried the Golden Party Badge, he would succeed but he was doomed to disappointment. Schirach was furious and with his own hands tore the Golden Badge from Sinzinger's tunic.[44] For Esebeck and Kodré a long *via dolorosa* through *Gestapo* prisons and concentration camps began, ending only with their liberation by the Allies.

Paris. News that the assassination attempt was to take place that day arrived during the morning of 20 July. It came to Colonel Eberhard Finckh, Deputy Chief of Staff West, from the office in Zossen of General Wagner, Deputy Chief of Staff of the Army.[45] The codeword was 'Exercise' and this was the third occasion on which it had come through during the last fortnight; it meant that preliminaries for the attempt were under way; 'Exercise finished' meant that it had been successfully carried out.

Finckh took from his safe the documents, lists and orders all ready prepared; then he called the Hotel 'Majestic' and passed the codeword to Lieutenant-Colonel Cäsar von Hofacker, specially employed officer on the staff of General von Stülpnagel.

Sometime after 2.0 p.m. Finckh received the second codeword, again from General Wagner's office; the exercise was 'finished'.[46] Finckh drove from his office in the Rue de Surène to St Germain, headquarters of C-in-C West and reported to General Günther Blumentritt, the Chief of Staff. There had been a *Gestapo putsch* in Berlin, he said; Hitler had been assassinated and Field Marshal von Witzleben, Colonel-General Beck and Dr Goerdeler had formed a new government.[47]

Blumentritt was not in the secret but, when Finckh said that he had the news from C-in-C France, he believed it; he rang up La Roche-Guyon, Army Group B Command Post, at once. Field Marshal von Kluge had moved his own headquarters there so as to be nearer the front. Kluge himself was up at the front so the call was taken by Lieutenant-General Speidel, Chief of Staff Army Group B. Blumentritt gave him some inkling of the news and then drove to La Roche-Guyon himself. The time was now about 5.0 p.m.[48]

Conditions in Army Group B were exceptional since Rommel had been wounded on 17 July and Kluge had taken over command of the Army Group only on the evening of the 19th. The news of the assassination attempt caught Speidel unprepared. Kluge had started in a state of optimism, suffering from 'Berchtesgaden euphoria', highly irritating to his staff and induced by Hitler's power of persuasion; gradually, however, he had come round to Rommel's view that the front could hold only for a short time and would then collapse. Although Kluge had once more become increasingly prepared to consider plans for a *coup*, in the short time available Speidel had not been able to brief him on current plans or the action already taken by Rommel. Speidel himself had received none of the previous preliminary warnings nor that for 20 July. Moreover it was questionable whether Army Group B could do much and not only because Rommel was not there. With or without Hitler the front had to be held; if it collapsed the enemy would be unlikely to negotiate even with a Beck-Goerdeler government but would press on into Germany. There was therefore nothing for Speidel to do except await the return of Kluge and the arrival of Blumentritt.[49]

In the headquarters of C-in-C France in the Hotel 'Majestic' Lieutenant-Colonel von Hofacker received a call from Stauffenberg sometime after 4.0 p.m.; Hitler was dead, Stauffenberg said, and the *coup* was under way. Hofacker immediately passed this on to his Commander and Freiherr von Teuchert who in turn informed Bargatzky and others in the know.[50]

General von Stülpnagel, C-in-C France, acted at once. He summoned his principal staff officers: Colonel von Linstow, his Chief of Staff, Lieutenant-General Eugen Oberhäusser, Chief Signal Officer, and Dr Michel, head of military administration, and Lieutenant-General Hans Freiherr von Boineburg-Lengsfeld, Commandant of Paris who was largely already in the secret and prepared. Boineburg with his Chief of Staff, Colonel von Unger, arrived between 5.0 and 6.0 p.m. and was ordered by Stülpnagel to arrest all SS personnel with their officers including *SS-Gruppenführer* Oberg, the Senior SS and Police Commander; any who resisted were to be shot.[51] Stülpnagel handed them a map, brought up to date in the last few days, showing all accommodation occupied by the SS and SD.[52]

While still in the Hotel 'Majestic' Boineburg alerted No 1 Regiment of 325 Security Division which was under his command and made the necessary preparations (he and his chief of staff had already largely briefed themselves on the locations of the SS and SD in Paris); he ordered the operation of arresting and disarming both organizations not to start before 11.0 p.m. to avoid presenting the French unnecessarily with the spectacle of fighting between Germans and to ensure that all those to be arrested would be back in their billets.[53] Lieutenant-Colonel von Kraewel, commanding the Security Regiment, was to direct the operation. He had already left his office and first had to be found.

Shortly after 6.0 p.m. Beck called Stülpnagel from Berlin. Stülpnagel assured him that he would use the troops under his command to the full and 'whatever happens', although Beck said that the blow had fallen but details of its success were not yet known. Stülpnagel could not tell Beck what Kluge would do and thought it best that Beck himself should telephone; he had the call transferred to La Roche-Guyon.[54]

A few minutes later, at about 6.15 p.m., after Beck had spoken to Kluge, Speidel called Stülpnagel to say that Kluge wished him and his chief of staff to come to Army Group B's command post at La Roche-Guyon at 8.0 p.m. for an important conference. Colonel von Linstow, the chief of staff, remained behind so that a responsible representative should be in the headquarters. Stülpnagel drove off soon after 7.0 p.m. accompanied by Lieutenant-Colonel von Hofacker, Dr Horst (Speidel's brother-in-law) and Dr Baumgart, his personal aide.[55]

Field Marshal von Kluge returned from his tour of the front towards 6.0 p.m., took a quick snack and set to work again at once. He was briefed on the more important reports of the day by Speidel, his chief of staff. Speidel gave him some news from the front and then told him of the assassination attempt. Blumentritt and Hofacker had reported it over the telephone about 5.0 p.m., he said, and meanwhile the radio had announced that the attempt had failed.[56] Kluge must have returned between 6.0 and 6.10 p.m. at the latest because shortly thereafter the conversation between him and Beck took place.[57] Beck said that Hitler was definitely dead; a state of military emergency was being declared in Berlin and throughout Germany; he asked whether they could count on Kluge's cooperation and added imploringly: 'Herr Kluge, the fate of Germany is at stake!' Kluge said that he must first think it over and would call back. Blumentritt arrived soon afterwards.

Blumentritt had been responsible for the news, which he now repeated, that Hitler was dead but the radio was saying the opposite and so the conspirators evidently did not control that. Kluge accordingly called Major-General Stieff, head of the Army Organization Section in 'Mauerwald' whom he knew well. He asked whether Hitler were dead and Stieff, apparently breathing heavily, replied: 'No. Major Ferber, one of my staff officers, spoke to him an hour after the attempt.'[58] Kluge then called the Bendlerstrasse and Stauffenberg answered. Kluge asked for Fromm; Stauffenberg said that he was no longer available; he would pass Kluge over to Fromm's successor, Colonel-General Hoepner. Hoepner said at once that reports and statements about the failure of the attempt were machinations of the SS; orders for Army Groups were already on the way by teleprinter. At this point they were cut off and Kluge specifically refused to be reconnected.[59]

Then came a call to Kluge from General von Falkenhausen, ex-Commander Belgium and Northern France who had been dismissed on 14 July; he had already been called by Beck. Kluge said to him that he too had received a call from Berlin; he did not believe that Hitler was dead.[60]

Towards 8.0 p.m. the well-known teleprinter messages from Berlin arrived in La Roche-Guyon, forwarded from St Germain by Colonel Bodo Zimmerman, the operations officer. The first announced the assumption of plenary powers by the *Wehrmacht* and ordered commanders to take command of all *Waffen-SS* units, the Labour Service, the 'Organization Todt', all authorities, officials and branches of the Nazi Party and its affiliated formations in their area, to secure signals installations and eliminate the SD. There also arrived in La Roche-Guyon the message denying the radio bulletin and insisting that Hitler was dead. This made an impression on Kluge and he wavered once more – for him everything depended on whether Hitler was alive or not. Now he believed Hitler dead and he said to Blumentritt: 'A historic hour has arrived.' He then discussed with Blumentritt detailed steps to bring about a cease-fire in the west. By this time it was 8.0 p.m.[61]

Then came the teleprint from Keitel in 'Wolfschanze' saying that, all statements to the contrary notwithstanding, Hitler was alive and in perfect health. Kluge at once wavered again and told Blumentritt to telephone everywhere until he had found out what the real truth was; meanwhile everything remained in *statu quo*.[62]

Blumentritt could contact neither Keitel, Jodl nor Warlimont in 'Wolfschanze'. After a prolonged wait he was told that Warlimont was in conference with Keitel and could not telephone. He thought this odd, as did Kluge. Blumentritt then called Oberg, the Senior SS and Police Commander in France, but he too knew nothing except for the radio announcement. Stieff in 'Mauerwald', on the other hand, reiterated that Hitler was alive. So perhaps the radio was right. Stieff asked Blumentritt where the news of Hitler's death had come from. Kluge himself seized the receiver and said: 'By teleprinter,' to which Stieff replied: 'No. Hitler is alive.'[63]

Kluge changed sides again, saying to Speidel and Blumentritt: 'Well then, it's just a bungled assassination attempt.' A half-baked affair, that's what it was, he would have no part nor lot in it. Whether the *coup* was under way or not, he was convinced that, as long as Hitler was alive, it could not succeed.[64]

What curious twist of logic – apart from the prospects of success – allowed Kluge to feel that it would be permissible to treat with the enemy after Hitler was dead but not while the tyrant was alive, it is impossible to say; perhaps it was the mercenary's loyalty to his condottiere. Kluge's heart was certainly with his troops, but less because they were human beings with a right to live than because they were the instrument of war-making and of power. Field Marshal von Kluge was no strong independent character; that had already been shown by the affair of the estate and large gratuity which he had accepted from Hitler.[65] But Kluge was ambitious. If he dared to take up the cudgels against Hitler, he might come off second-best and lose his command. When C-in-C Army Group Centre he had been very proud of the fact that he was commanding one of the largest armies ever to be placed under a single general. He had then had to leave his Army Group in Russia in a terrible state of defeat and dissolution to take Rommel's place on the Normandy front, a double-edged distinction about which he must have had mixed feelings. There were other considerations such as the threat of civil war. Kluge was certainly no cynic; he had the courage to take personal risks; he was not afraid of physical danger. But Kluge did not possess the independence of mind essential to sound reasoning; his duty to Germany was not in the forefront of his mind. Now that the *coup* had failed, therefore, he did not wish to have anything to do with it, its consequences or its leaders. He told Blumentritt that he had been called and urged to participate in the *coup* by 'a voice he did not recognize from somewhere in Germany – he did not know where'.[66]

Towards 8.0 p.m. Field Marshal Hugo Sperrle, C-in-C of Air Fleet 3, appeared in La Roche-Guyon. Kluge had asked him to come but there was not really much to discuss. Sperrle knew nothing of the *putsch* apart from the radio bulletins. After a quarter of an hour he drove back to his headquarters in the Palais Luxembourg, Paris.[67]

Shortly thereafter Stülpnagel and his companions arrived. At the initial meeting there were present Kluge and Blumentritt, Stülpnagel, Hofacker and Dr Horst. Hofacker spoke for fifteen minutes, describing the plan and course of the *coup d'état* and his own role as liaison officer between Beck and Stauffenberg on one side and the group centred on Stülpnagel in Paris on the other. He ended with an urgent passionate appeal to Kluge to cut free from Hitler and assume leadership of the liberation movement in the west.[68]

There was no visible reaction from Kluge. Finally he merely said: 'Yes, gentlemen, just a bungled affair.' When Stülpnagel said that Kluge knew all about it, he replied sharply: 'No ... I had no idea.'[69] Stülpnagel was boiling with rage and disappointment but he knew that meanwhile action was being taken in Paris and a situation of fact created. Perhaps Kluge might still change his attitude when he knew.

Kluge invariably observed the proprieties, even though for the others the tension was intolerable. He invited them into the next room for dinner; Lieutenant-General Speidel was also present. Later in the meal Stülpnagel asked the Field Marshal for a private talk and the two went into the adjoining room. A few minutes later Blumentritt was called in. Kluge was furious over Stülpnagel's unilateral action and told Blumentritt that Stülpnagel had ordered the arrest of the entire SD together with Oberg, the Senior SS and Police Commander, without asking or even reporting to his superior officer, the Commander-in-Chief West, him, Kluge. It was intolerable. Blumentritt was to cancel Stülpnagel's order forthwith.[70] Blumentritt telephoned to Colonel von Linstow, Stülpnagel's chief of staff, who could only express regret, saying that the troops were on the move and nothing could be changed now.

Dinner was resumed; the civilities were still observed but conversation ceased completely and the atmosphere was even more oppressive than before.[71] Kluge rose from the table about 11.0 p.m. and, as he accompanied Stülpnagel outside, said that he should now drive straight back to Paris and release those arrested (no other measures had yet been taken). Stülpnagel replied that there could be no going back now and Hofacker made one more appeal to Kluge, using all his eloquence. But Kluge remained unmoved.[72] Stülpnagel should regard himself as suspended from duty, Kluge said, and finally, as they reached the car, the man known in the Army as 'Clever Hans' delivered himself of this piece of advice: 'Get into civilian clothes and disappear somewhere.'[73] This was not Stülpnagel's way and Kluge himself would hardly have done so.

In Paris meanwhile the SS and *Gestapo* had been overpowered without a hitch. Officers in command were clearly more resolute than in Berlin, their solidarity was greater and outside influence less strong. The radio bulletins did not shake any of the commanders responsible to Stülpnagel in their conviction that the SS was engaged in an anti-Hitler *putsch*, whereas in Berlin it was quickly realized that this was not so. Telephone calls from 'Wolfschanze' or protestations from Dr Goebbels did not penetrate to Paris. In addition both Lieutenant-General von Boineburg-Lengsfeld, Commandant of Paris, and Colonel von Unger, his Chief of Staff, were largely in the secret.[74]

Major-General Brehmer, wearer of the Nazi Party 'Blood Order' of 1923, placed himself at the head of the troops detailed to arrest the senior SS leaders.[75] Boineburg stood with his aides at the corner of Avenue Foch and Boulevard Lannes and supervised the operation.[76] At 10.30 p.m. whistles blew and the troops moved off from the Avenue du Bois de Boulogne.[77] A few moments later, with submachine guns and pistols at the ready, all SD and SS quarters were taken by surprise and occupied; there were no scuffles or shooting except for a single shot discharged by mistake which hit no one. All those in quarters were arrested; anyone not in quarters despite 'retreat' (10.0 p.m.) was summoned by alarm siren and arrested. The prisoners, some 1200 men, were loaded on to lorries and incarcerated in the *Wehrmacht* prison at Fresnes and the old Fort de l'Est, St Denis. *SS-Gruppenführer* Oberg was arrested by Major-General Brehmer in person.[78] When told that the SS was carrying out a *putsch* in Berlin, Oberg ceased to protest and merely said that there must be some misunderstanding. *SS-Standartenführer* Knochen, the senior SD officer, was recalled by telephone from some night-club by a junior officer and arrested by Lieutenant-Colonel von Kraewel in SD headquarters in the Avenue Foch. He was held with other senior SS officers in the Hotel 'Continental' in the Rue Castiglione.[79]

Surprise had therefore been complete. Some of the junior SD officers however had managed to escape through back doors and gardens. They informed *SS-Oberführer* Meyer, commander of 12 SS Panzer Division 'Hitlerjugend', and he in turn informed *SS-Obergruppenführer* Sepp Dietrich, commander of I SS Panzer Corps; others contrived to send a teleprinter message to the RSHA, one of the SD teleprinter stations having been overlooked. This had no effect on the course of events in Paris, however. Sepp Dietrich could only pass the information on to higher authority and the RSHA did not react until 2.0 a.m. on information from its representatives in Paris.[80] Meanwhile summary courts martial were to be held during the night to decide on the guilt or innocence of those under arrest. Around midnight sandbags were piled up in the courtyard of the École Militaire, the barracks of No 1 Security Regiment, to act as butts for the executions by shooting expected to be ordered by the courts martial.[81]

Meanwhile the Paris group of conspirators was waiting in the Hotel

'Raphael', where the staff of the Military Commander France had its mess and many of its officers were quartered, for General von Stülpnagel and the outcome of his efforts with Field Marshal von Kluge. About 10.0 p.m. Colonel von Linstow had reported that nothing had yet been decided but that all was going well in Berlin. Then sometime after 10.0 p.m. Stauffenberg called him from Berlin and said that it was all over; his executioners were already hammering at his door![82] Linstow telephoned at once to General Blumentritt, who was still in La Roche-Guyon and who said that action against the SD must be called off. Linstow replied that this was already in train. Then he told Teuchert, Bargatzky and the others. The sequel was merely the liquidation of the revolt.

General von Stülpnagel left La Roche-Guyon shortly after 11.0 p.m. and drove back to Paris, arriving at the Hotel 'Raphael' mess with Hofacker, Baumgart and Horst soon after midnight. He found there Boineburg and Linstow in not very optimistic mood. When asked about Kluge Stülpnagel replied that he had asked to think it over until next morning.[83] This, of course, was not true but it was better than telling the truth and perhaps Stülpnagel was still hoping to carry the affair through himself. At about 1.0 a.m. the speeches by Hitler, Dönitz and Göring were broadcast. Since some who were not in the secret were present, Stülpnagel had to put a good face on it and listen. Between 1.30 and 2.0 a.m. Colonel von Unger called and told his master, Lieutenant-General von Boineburg, that Admiral Theodor Krancke, C-in-C of the Naval Group Headquarters West, who had more than 1,000 marines at his disposal, had threatened to liberate the SD men with his own troops unless the arrests were cancelled at once.[84]

The first Berlin teleprint, signed by Witzleben, had arrived in Krancke's headquarters at 9.20 p.m. Krancke immediately called Grand Admiral Dönitz in the *Führer*'s headquarters who told him that Hitler was alive and the only orders to be obeyed were those of Himmler.[85] Krancke then tried to telephone Kluge but was told that the Field Marshal was in conference and could not come to the telephone. General Blumentritt then called and exchanged information with Krancke. Blumentritt said that C-in-C West had also received the teleprint but Warlimont had briefed him on the real situation and 'all was in order'. At 11.0 p.m. a teleprint from Dönitz arrived, the gist of which had already been passed by telephone: a conspiracy had taken place in which Fromm and Hoepner were involved; Himmler had been appointed C-in-C Replacement Army; the Navy was placed on alert; only orders from the Naval C-in-C or other senior naval officers were to be obeyed; the requirements of the *Reichsführer-SS* were also to be met; long live the *Führer*. Soon afterwards, at 11.40 p.m., a teleprint in the same vein arrived from Field Marshal Keitel. At midnight the officer in charge of naval signals installations ordered full-scale alert; if necessary fire was to be opened.

By 12.30 a.m. Krancke knew that Army units had taken the SD personnel into custody and he immediately called Kluge once more. Kluge thanked him for the information and promised to put matters right. At 12.45 a.m. Krancke nevertheless ordered his troops to prepare for operations. When he tried to call

Kluge yet again, he was told that Kluge was not available and he became highly suspicious. At 1.07 a.m. Admiral Hoffmann, Krancke's Chief of Staff, contacted Lieutenant-Colonel von Kraewel commanding No 1 Security Regiment and explained to him that he was the victim of a serious misunderstanding. Kraewel proposed to speak to the Commandant of Paris at once. Immediately after Dönitz' speech at 1.11 a.m. Krancke ordered his Chief of Staff to call Blumentritt and say that he had been unable to contact Kluge and that Kraewel had arrested Oberg and the entire SD.[86] Blumentritt replied that he had orders to remove Stülpnagel from his post and to release Oberg. He would do this very shortly.

But Krancke was still not satisfied. At 1.37 a.m. he tried to call Lieutenant-General von Boineburg but could not contact him; he contrived to tell Colonel von Unger, Boineburg's Chief of Staff, however, what he had to say: if Oberg and the SD men were not released on the instant, he, Krancke, would liberate them with his own men; Stülpnagel had been dismissed and what was the game anyway. Unger replied that he could obey orders only from Stülpnagel. The industrious Krancke then got in touch with Colonel von Linstow and he was able to avert the threat. No 1 Security Regiment, he said, had already been ordered to release Oberg and the SD men; there had been a misunderstanding; the Military Commander's headquarters had thought that a *Gestapo putsch* was taking place.

Action by the marines and the consequential potential bloodshed was therefore averted. This was also the case with a headquarters company of the *Luftwaffe* which General Hanesse, *Luftwaffe* commander in Paris, alerted about midnight in order to free the SD men. Colonel von Unger heard of this and called Hanesse to say that the SD had been surprised, not by men of the *maquis*, as Hanesse thought, but by German soldiers and he would 'hear still stranger things before the night was out'.[87] This action, too, was thus averted. Pressure from the Navy and *Luftwaffe* on the Army officers responsible to the Military Commander increased but it was not the decisive factor in the turn of events.

General von Stülpnagel heard of Krancke's threat between 1.30 and 2.0 a.m. in the Hotel 'Raphael'. He gave himself half an hour to think it over. He did not hear until nearly 2.0 a.m. and that from Blumentritt himself, that he had been relieved of his office and that Blumentritt had been appointed his acting successor.[88] A little reflection, however, showed him that all was lost: Hitler had broadcast in person so the news from Berlin must be correct and now the Navy was threatening to shoot at the Army. Quite apart from the consequences of this, it was questionable how long his troops would go on obeying him. He could do nothing, therefore, other than cancel his previous orders to avoid useless bloodshed. Boineburg, who pleaded for pushing on with the *putsch*, was nevertheless ordered to release Oberg and the others and when Krancke called Linstow soon afterwards, Linstow was able to tell him that the order for their release had been issued. Just before 2.0 a.m. Krancke reduced the level of alert for his marines.[89]

Lieutenant-General von Boineburg drove to the Hotel 'Continental', preserving his dignity; with a polite smile and eyeglass still in eye he told the arrested SS leaders that they were free and asked Oberg to go straight to the Hotel 'Raphael' with him to see the Military Commander. Oberg was indignant but went.[90] Oberg's minions were then also released amid significant scenes. Many of the SS men refused to leave their prison saying: 'We're not coming out of here. We know that tale – shot while attempting to escape!'[91]

Meanwhile Otto Abetz, the German Ambassador, had also arrived in the Hotel 'Raphael' and as a result of his diplomacy Stülpnagel and Oberg actually shook hands. In France there was neither blind fanaticism nor that brand of opportunism shown that evening in Berlin by Fromm and some of his staff officers; in a hostile occupied country the atmosphere was rather one of solidarity even between Army and SS, particularly under present circumstances when it was clear that neither side had covered itself with glory. The point now was to smooth things over, calm things down as far as possible and play down the importance of what had happened. Soothing words from Abetz won the day and accord was then sealed over glasses of champagne. Soon everyone was sitting relaxed in the mess discussing the events of the day.

Blumentritt, C-in-C West's Chief of Staff, had reached his headquarters in St Germain about 1.0 a.m. Shortly afterwards he had a telephone conversation with Kluge. Blumentritt said: Apparently the Army patrols had orders for 'some arrests or something. I believe the Security Forces are a little misled there. I suggest I act as Military Commander for a short time to put things back into shape.' Kluge said: 'I hereby order you to talk the matter over and to tidy it up and to get it back to normal.'[92] Then Blumentritt, now also Acting Military Commander France, had driven on to Paris shortly after 2.0 a.m., arriving there with Dr Knochen (now released) at 2.45 a.m. On the way he stopped at the office of the Senior SS and Police Commander and there heard that Oberg and Knochen had been set free; he made another stop at naval headquarters in the Bois de Boulogne for any necessary coordination and discussion. People there were drinking the *Führer*'s health.[93] Finally he stopped at the SD office in the Avenue Foch and thence drove to the 'Raphael' with Dr Knochen. On the way Knochen uttered the magic 'formula' which was gratefully seized upon by the staffs both of the Military Commander and the SS Commander. An identical account of developments was to be presented in all reports.[94] In the early hours of 21 July there was hand-shaking all round in the Hotel 'Raphael'; SS men and Army officers sat together and celebrated. Next day Lieutenant-General von Boincburg-Lengsfeld issued an invitation to the SD to which Oberg replied with a beer evening. Soon after 1.0 a.m. Kluge agreed to a telegram expressing loyalty and congratulations to Hitler, as proposed by Blumentritt.[95] The revolt in Paris was at an end. In contrast to Berlin persecution of the conspirators did not begin until a little later.

45 Collapse in Berlin

Shortly before 4.0 p.m. the conspirators in the Bendlerstrasse, Berlin, had started to issue the 'Valkyrie' codeword to the Army schools in and around Berlin. The first orders had reached the Berlin Guard Battalion by 4.10 p.m. Teleprinter messages to the *Wehrkreise* and Military Commanders in the occupied territories were being despatched from the signal centre from 4.45 p.m. Stauffenberg had arrived back in the Bendlerstrasse between 4.0 and 5.0 p.m. and since then had worked indefatigably, answering the numerous questions from the *Wehrkreise* and insisting that the orders be carried out. Beck, Hoepner, Schulenburg, Gisevius, John, Gerstenmaier, Yorck and other members of the conspiracy had assembled in the Bendlerstrasse and were awaiting the arrival of the troops and the occupation of radio stations and signals installations.

At about 5.0 p.m. General von Kortzfleisch, Commander of *Wehrkreis* III (Berlin), had come to the Bendlerstrasse at Olbricht's request for a conference with Fromm. Meanwhile, however, Fromm had been arrested by the conspirators and so Kortzfleisch was initially detained too; between 6.0 and 7.0 p.m., when he refused to order 'Valkyrie' in his *Wehrkreis*, he was arrested as well. Lieutenant-General von Thüngen, Inspector of Recruiting in Berlin, was appointed Commander *Wehrkreis* III in his place. This led to delays and uncertainties. In view of the absence of his Commander Major-General Herfurth, Chief of Staff *Wehrkreis* III, could only make up his mind about 6.0 p.m., after some hesitation and questioning, that the orders he had received to occupy certain important offices and agencies in Berlin, were 'genuine'. The orders were carried by Major von Oertzen and Herfurth at first tried to make him responsible for their execution; then he asked Colonel von Wiese, the personnel officer, and Lieutenant-Colonel Mitzkus, his operations officer, to go into an adjoining room with him for a discussion; there he sank down on a camp bed and said that he was ill. Orders such as these simply could not be carried out, he said; there was no certainty that this was not a *putsch*; he had already enquired of OKH and Colonel Mertz von Quirnheim, Olbricht's Chief of Staff, had confirmed that the orders were correct. Finally he managed to decide that the orders should be regarded as binding, comforting himself with the thought that the troop movements would take some time and by then one might have more information.[1] As soon as *Wehrkreis* HQ had troops available – in particular the tanks from Krampnitz and the armoured infantry from

Cottbus – Herfurth was to order the occupation or 'securing' of all SS offices including the RSHA and SS radio stations, the top-level agencies of the Party, the Party printing press, the most important ministries, all SD offices and the telephone-tapping 'research office'. But the troops were not yet there; it had all begun too late. Lieutenant-General von Thüngen, appointed Commander *Wehrkreis* III by the conspirators, did not reach the headquarters until between 7.0 and 8.0 p.m. and even then he did not act with much energy.[2]

In the initial stages the only commander in Berlin capable of taking any action was Lieutenant-General von Hase, the City Commandant (headquarters at No 1 Unter den Linden). His troops were earmarked to occupy the objectives which also figured on the *Wehrkreis* HQ list with the exception of the radio transmitter in Tegel, the radio towers and Broadcasting House in the Masurenallee. Between 4.0 and 5.0 p.m. Hase set about carrying out these orders energetically, but they had arrived disastrously late. Hase summoned the commanders of the Guard Battalion and the 'Valkyrie' units from the Army Pyrotechnical School, Army Ordnance School and the territorial battalions in the Berlin area; as the troops arrived, assault squads were formed, to be led by police officers detailed by Nebe, Director of the *Reich* Criminal Police Office, to arrest the most important functionaries of the regime in Berlin. Nothing of importance had been forgotten and the necessary orders were issued.

To some extent these orders were carried out. Major Remer surrounded and cordoned off the government quarter with units of the Guard Battalion; in this respect Hase's orders had been implemented by 6.30 p.m. Remer himself checked the road blocks. Soon afterwards, however, Dr Hagen, National-Socialist 'leadership officer', (*Nationalsozialistischer Führungsoffizier* – NSFO) managed to arrange a meeting between the Guard Battalion commander and his minister Dr Goebbels; as *Gauleiter* of Berlin, *Reich* Defence Commissar and one of the most important and influential *Reich* ministers Goebbels had widespread powers in the capital. As a result the vital chain of command, running solely through military channels, was severed.

Even while Remer was issuing orders to company commanders at about 5.0 p.m. in Moabit, Hagen – according to his own account – had voiced a suspicion that the whole affair was not in order. He then persuaded Remer to allow him to go to Goebbels and find out the situation. Remer gave him a motorcycle and driver and Hagen was driven to the Ministry of Propaganda.[3] In the Minister's office there he found Dr Heinrichsdorff, a government counsellor (*Regierungsrat*) whom he knew and, by telling him about the possibility of a military *putsch*, persuaded him that he be allowed to go at once direct to Goebbels in his apartment on the Hermann-Göring-Strasse. Hagen briefed Goebbels at about 5.30 p.m.; when he reported the orders given to the Guard Battalion, Goebbels jumped up and shouted: 'But that's impossible.' Hagen pointed out through the window where a lorry-load of soldiers was just rolling past.[4]

Hagen proposed that Remer be summoned and issued with counter orders, but Goebbels was suspicious and initially somewhat at a loss. Only when Hagen said that he would stake his life on Remer's loyalty did Goebbels agree to the suggestion. He alerted the SS *'Leibstandarte* Adolf Hitler' in Berlin-Lichterfelde but ordered it not to move for the present. Goebbels trusted the SS hardly more than the Army and no risk of fighting between SS and Army was justifiable except in extreme emergency.[5]

Between 5.0 and 6.0 p.m. Goebbels telephoned Hitler and discovered that a military *putsch* was under way throughout the *Reich*; he took the situation very seriously and put one or two poison pills into his pocket as a precaution. By continuous telephoning he established the fact that troops were on the move to Berlin from all directions; his inability to contact Himmler on the telephone at this time made him particularly suspicious. On the other hand he had been able to contact Speer, the Armaments Minister, who was under some suspicion since his duties entailed cooperation with Colonel-General Fromm; at Goebbels' request Speer had hurried along to the apartment at once. On 17 July Stauffenberg had invited Speer to lunch on the 20th for a discussion with Fromm afterwards; Speer had only refused because he had to address ministers and state secretaries in the Propaganda Ministry at 11.0 a.m. that day. Although not in the secret and in no way involved, it was thus only by chance that Speer was not in the conspirators' headquarters when the *putsch* took place.

Hagen drove back to Moabit. As he passed the Brandenburg Gate he briefed Lieutenant Blumenthal (Knight's Cross) commanding No 1 company of the Guard Battalion, telling him that this was all treachery and he should act only in accordance with the wishes of the legal regime. He did not find Remer in Moabit and so drove back to the City Commandant's headquarters, where Remer meanwhile had set up his command post.

Major Remer, another wearer of the Knight's Cross, was carrying out without question the orders of his superior officer, the City Commandant; some of those present say that he was doing so with enthusiasm.[6] He himself says that on two occasions he personally checked his road-blocks, once between 6.0 and 6.30 p.m. and again soon after 6.30.[7]

The original intention was that Goebbels should be arrested by a platoon of the Guard Battalion; Remer was present when the question was discussed about 6.0 p.m. in the Commandant's headquarters by Hase and Lieutenant-Colonel Schöne. The next proposal was that the Minister be arrested by soldiers from the Pyrotechnical School under Major Korff and Captain Maître, but before this could be done Remer had swung over to Goebbels' side. At about the same time that Major Korff and Captain Maître set off came another idea – that Goebbels be arrested by two squads of the *Wehrmacht* Patrol Service reinforced by soldiers of a territorial battalion and the Pyrotechnical School, all under Colonel Jäger who had been sent specially from the Bendlerstrasse for the purpose.[8] Everything he saw and heard seemed 'dubious' to Remer, as he said later, but he continued to carry out his orders.

At first Hagen had difficulty in regaining contact with Remer. He arrived in the Commandant's headquarters about 6.0 p.m. but did not meet Remer.[9] He informed Second Lieutenant Buck of the Guard Battalion, ordering him to tell Remer a *putsch* was in progress, that the old government was still the legal one and that Remer should come to Goebbels at once. When Buck did this, Remer was, of course, flabbergasted but it is doubtful whether he immediately recognized that 'the situation had totally changed', as he said a few days later. In any case he did not propose to act without the consent of his superior officer.

Remer accordingly went in to Lieutenant-General von Hase's headquarters with Buck. As a precaution Remer made Buck himself report what he had heard from Hagen – that 'the situation had changed' and that Remer was to go to Goebbels.[10] Remer still seemed to be a loyal recipient of orders, though clearly he was now no longer an ignorant one.

In view of the indecision about the arrest or 'protection' of the Propaganda Minister Remer suggested that he himself go to Goebbels. Hase and the other conspirators were still insisting on the story that they were protecting the legal government against a *putsch* by certain Party and SS circles; there was therefore no certainty which side Goebbels was on. Remer could not tell whether Goebbels was one of those who, according to Hase, were trying to overthrow Hitler or whether Goebbels was on the side of the legal government and Hase on the 'wrong' side. We shall probably never know what Remer really thought at the time but he must be given credit for the fact that he was faced with a most difficult decision between an apparently legal order from his superior officer and a summons, apparently also legal, from a minister to whom he was only indirectly responsible. With his basically naïve attitude, however, Remer would hardly be likely to act on behalf of Hase and the conspiracy when actually faced by Goebbels; probably he already knew of the radio announcement about Hitler's survival; he was not the man for Hase to send to Goebbels. Hase said to him: 'Remer, you stay here.'[11]

Remer left Hase's office and went out on to Unter den Linden. He told Second Lieutenant Siebert, his adjutant, of the cleft stick in which he found himself: 'My head's at stake. There seems to be a military *putsch*. Hagen has sent me word that I should go to Goebbels. The General has forbidden me to do so.'[12] It was still not clear whether Hase had right on his side or not. Remer walked off a little way to think it over. After a time he decided to go to Goebbels. Meeting some of his officers in front of the Commandant's headquarters he 'briefed them in turn', individually, and told them to be very much on their guard.[13] Since Remer did not feel secure either on one side or the other, he gave instructions lest he be detained against his will. Then he drove off to Goebbels.[14]

Remer arrived in the Hermann-Göring-Strasse between 7.0 and 8.0 p.m. and was taken in to Goebbels at once by Hagen.[15] Remer said that he had orders to cordon off the government quarter because a *putsch* against the *Führer* was in progress and he was said to have been mortally wounded.[16] Goebbels was at first unwilling to believe what Remer said (or so it seemed to him); he had himself talked to the *Führer* on the telephone only a few minutes ago, he said. He asked whether Remer was a National-Socialist. Yes, Remer said, very much so. He then wanted to know from Goebbels the truth about what had happened to the *Führer*. Goebbels told him, but Remer was still suspicious and asked Goebbels whether *he* was a National-Socialist and whether he was on the *Führer's* side. Goebbels said that he was and gave Remer his word of honour; on 22 July 1944 Remer reported: 'The Minister assured me that he was acting on behalf of the *Führer*. The *Führer* had not been injured at all.' The whole affair, Goebbels went on, was an underhand military *putsch* against the *Führer* by certain officers. Remer said that under all circumstances he would do his duty as a decent officer, 'faithful to his oath to the *Führer*'.[17] He asked whether he could speak to the *Führer*.

In 'Wolfschanze' there had been much speculation as to who was behind the explosion; real suspicion did not fall on Stauffenberg until about 2.0 p.m.; even then no one had an inkling how widespread and dangerous the conspiracy was. Then, at 2.30 p.m., Mussolini and his entourage arrived for a visit to the *Führer's* headquarters and was received by Hitler at Görlitz station. Hitler showed him the devastation in the briefing hut. There was still much confusion; people were still discussing this unheard-of occurrence; the meeting of the two dictators was an eerie one.[18] At times Hitler, Göring and Ribbentrop completely forgot their visitors; they discussed the affair in violent terms and even started to quarrel, while Mussolini and his escort sat there embarrassed. When Colonel-General Fromm called about 4.0 p.m., however, and asked whether he should issue 'Valkyrie', everyone pricked up their ears and very soon realized that a *putsch* was being attempted from Berlin. Proof was soon forthcoming from the teleprinter messages arriving in 'Wolfschanze'; the picture was completed by the fact that from about 4.30 p.m. Fromm could not be contacted and enquiries began to be made by the *Wehrkreise*; now came the news from Goebbels that troops were on the move.[19] Clearly rapid and resolute counter-measures must be taken,[20] and counter-orders were issued by Keitel and his aides. Perhaps the most important of them were now given to Remer.

Goebbels immediately put through the call for which Remer had asked and about 7.0 p.m. Hitler himself spoke to Remer. He asked whether Remer recognized his voice and said that he was completely unharmed. Remer said that he recognized Hitler and he was then given his orders: he was to be directly responsible to the *Führer* until the arrival in Berlin of the *Reichsführer-SS* who had been appointed C-in-C Replacement Army. Meanwhile Remer was to be responsible for the security of the capital and was to use all means at his disposal to deal with any resistance.[21] Remer promised to obey these orders.

Now the ice between Remer and Goebbels was really broken. Understandably, Goebbels later did not emphasize how near he had been to arrest; authors of other accounts had no wish to embarrass so powerful a man. Until Remer's talk with Hitler, however, matters had been on a knife-edge.

This was not so, however, in so far as the *coup* as a whole was concerned. Remer's decision certainly prevented much confusion and perhaps bloodshed, but the dice had been loaded against the conspiracy long before – as a result of Hitler's survival, of the publication of this news at the very moment when the orders for the *putsch* should have been in course of execution, of the almost simultaneous arrival of counter-orders from 'Wolfschanze' and the resulting uncertainty in the minds of commanders not only of the Guard Battalion but of all troops involved in the *coup*. All this took place before Remer could exert any influence. A further factor was the proliferation of command channels which Hitler had introduced into the *Wehrmacht* over the course of the years.[22]

Remer drove back at once to the City Commandant's headquarters on Unter den Linden to give the necessary orders and brief his officers about the real situation. He proposed to telephone Goebbels every twenty minutes. Then he ordered the entire Guard Battalion to withdraw from its road blocks and assemble in the garden of Goebbels' house at 20 Hermann-Göring-Strasse. Commanders of territorial units or troops from the Pyrotechnical School and the Patrol Service located near the Commandant's headquarters were similarly briefed and placed themselves under Remer's orders. General von Hase was no longer in his office when Remer arrived about 8.0 p.m.; he had gone over to *Wehrkreis* HQ on the Hohenzollerndamm.[23]

Remer then returned to Goebbels in the Hermann-Göring-Strasse and asked him to speak to the soldiers assembled in the garden. He ordered Second Lieutenant Buck to stop all units approaching the Brandenburg Gate and direct them to him (Remer) in the Hermann-Göring-Strasse. Goebbels spoke to the men of the Guard Battalion and Remer explained to them that he had been ordered by the *Führer* in person to suppress any attempted resistance ruthlessly.[24] He then ordered two companies reinforced by units from the Pyrotechnical School to organize for defence the block of buildings bounded by the Hermann-Göring-Strasse, Wilhelmstrasse, Vosstrasse and Unter den Linden.[25] Remer also ordered up the other units from the schools which had been posted near the War Memorial, and the remainder of the Guard Battalion, particularly the headquarters company, which had remained behind in Moabit. Troops diverted from the Brandenburg Gate, those of the Ordnance School for instance, gradually arrived; large quantities of ammunition were assembled. Officers, as they arrived, were briefed by Remer as to the true situation and requested to inform their commanders. Remer posted officers of the Guard Battalion on the main approach routes to inform and instruct units as they arrived.[26] Between 8.0 and 9.0 p.m., therefore, the road blocks and guards around the government quarter were withdrawn and the available troops concentrated and positioned afresh.

Difficulties at first arose with the armoured troops from Krampnitz when Hagen tried to persuade them to gain contact with Remer. According to an order from HQ *Wehrkreis* III transmitted by Major von Oertzen the 'Valkyrie' units from the school had moved off towards Berlin, heading for the Victory Column. The commanding officer, Colonel Glaesemer, had checked Olbricht's order through his immediate superior, Colonel Ernest Eberhard Bolbrinker, head of the Armoured Forces section in the AHA.[27] An armoured unit had taken up position in the Tiergarten, only a few hundred yards west of Goebbels' house. Colonel Glaesemer had then gone to Olbricht in the Bendlerstrasse but, when he heard that Hitler was not dead and that the SS were not engaged in a *putsch*, he refused to carry out further orders. Colonel Mertz von Quirnheim thereupon confined him in a room on the fourth floor of the Bendlerstrasse. There he was discovered by one of his officers, Captain Graf von Rothkirch und Panthen, who told him that the troops had now reached the Victory Column but that Colonel Bolbrinker had ordered them to be withdrawn immediately to the Fehrbelliner Platz and that Olbricht's orders were not to be obeyed. This was about 9.30 p.m. These in-structions were said to be based on orders from Colonel-General Guderian, Inspector-General of Armoured Forces. Guderian's Chief of Staff, Major-General Thomale, had indeed called Bolbrinker from 'Mauerwald' and had told him what had happened at 'Wolfschanze', that Hitler was alive, and that the conspirators' orders must not be obeyed.[28] Colonel Glaesemer managed to escape from the Bendlerstrasse on some pretext and reach his troops on the Fehrbelliner Platz.[29] Colonel Bolbrinker had gone there, too, after his telephone conversation with Thomale; now he sent Colonel Mildebrath and Lieutenant-Colonel Abraham, who worked under him, to meet the armoured troops marching towards Grosser Stern with orders to return at once to their barracks.[30] This did not end all the confusion but it did end all chances for the conspirators to gain control of armoured troops.

Meanwhile Hagen reached the armoured force and made as if to give them instructions; but he was told that they had been ordered to concentrate on the Fehrbelliner Platz by Colonel-General Guderian and anyone who did not do so would be shot. Hagen's rejoinder that Remer had been charged by the *Führer* personally with the maintenance of order had no effect. Only Guderian had authority to issue orders to the armoured forces, Hagen was told.[31]

With this Hagen returned to Remer in Goebbels' house. Then Lieutenant-Colonel Gehrke, ex-commander of the Guard Battalion, appeared and offered to act as liaison officer to the Fehrbelliner Platz and, in Remer's words, find out 'on which side the armoured force was, since I was not clear as to the at-titude of Colonel-General Guderian'. Gehrke soon returned and reported that the armoured force was fully on the side of the *Führer*.[32] Meanwhile Remer had called the Armoured Replacement Brigade in Cottbus and had asked for heavy weapons and tanks, to be used, if necessary, against Guderian's force if this should prove to be on the side of the conspirators. A battalion from Cott-bus was placed at Remer's disposal but was eventually halted near Rangsdorf, the loyalty of Guderian and the troops from Krampnitz having been es-tablished meanwhile.[33]

Part of the Guard Battalion was on guard duty in the Bendlerstrasse. At 4.15 p.m. the guard detachment under Second Lieutenant Arnds was alerted on orders from General Olbricht and ordered to open fire on any SS troops which might arrive; the *Führer* was dead, the order continued, and the Army had taken over full powers.[34] When Remer, from the City Commandant's office, was trying to concentrate his forces, he ordered Lieutenant Rudolf

Schlee, who had hitherto been checking the outlying guard posts and road blocks, to contact the guard in the Bendlerstrasse.[35] He explained to Schlee that a military *putsch* was in progress but that he should say nothing about the actual situation. Schlee accordingly drove to the Bendlerstrasse where he had only recently checked the guard and gave Second Lieutenant Arnds 'instructions on our future attitude', primarily that no orders other than those of Remer were to be obeyed.[36] Since, however, Remer had issued no orders, this at first made little difference to the attitude of the guard.

On the way back to the Commandant's headquarters Schlee saw men of the Guard Battalion assembling in front of Goebbels' house. He discovered that the battalion's command post was now here and arrived just as Goebbels was addressing the men in the garden. Schlee was now 'clear' for the first time. He was then ordered by Remer to bring the guard from the Bendlerstrasse to No 20 Hermann-Göring-Strasse.

For the third time, therefore, Schlee drove to the Bendlerstrasse and passed on the order to Arnds. A captain (probably Helmuth Cords) on duty at the entrance, however, persuaded Schlee to go first to General Olbricht since Remer's order did not agree with those of Olbricht.[37] In Olbricht's anteroom Colonel Mertz von Quirnheim ordered him not to carry out Remer's instructions and for the moment to remain where he was; when Mertz went in to Olbricht, however, Schlee escaped and was able to leave the building unchallenged. A captain ran after him and said that he had noticed that the Guard Battalion officers had realized the true situation; he was the OKW Signals Officer, he said, and was occupying the signal centre with a few men; the leaders of the *putsch* were in the OKW building and he had not passed on their orders.[38] Lieutenant Schlee hurried back to Major Remer with his news – the conspirators' headquarters was in the Bendlerstrasse.

Remer was with Goebbels but, at Hagen's instigation, Schlee was taken straight to him and gave his news. Goebbels then telephoned Hitler and was authorized to occupy the Bendlerstrasse building. Schlee was ordered by Remer to do this and to arrest 'all generals', using the guard on the spot and certain additional forces.[39] Meanwhile word was received that a loyal company of armoured infantry was already in the Bendlerstrasse and so Schlee's departure was postponed pending agreement with this unit. Then it was found that it had either been withdrawn, or had never arrived in the first place.

Schlee hastened to leave with Second Lieutenants Arnds and Schady. They set up a chain of posts around the entire block and occupied the main entrance[40] where there was total confusion and several officers, armed with submachine-guns, were trying to give orders. Schlee had those unwilling to obey his orders arrested and locked them up in the porter's lodge. As a result of his determination and the general confusion at the entrance with officers running hither and thither, there was no shooting. Having occupied the entrance, Schlee despatched a party of twenty men to the signal centre, posted machine-guns at all exits and set about arresting the conspirators inside the building. He found, however, that 'loyal German officers had taken matters into their own hands', had released Colonel-General Fromm and arrested the five leading conspirators.[41] Lieutenant-Colonel Gehrke, who had meanwhile returned from his successful mission, arrived as Fromm was being freed and later, on hearing of the executions ordered by Fromm, Remer arrived as well. When he returned to the Hermann-Göring-Strasse about 1.0 a.m. he found Himmler, now his superior officer, there and briefed him. This was the end of the *putsch* as far as Remer and the Guard Battalion were concerned.[42]

About 8.0 p.m. Lieutenant-General von Hase with Lieutenant-Colonel Hermann Schöne, his operations officer, had gone to *Wehrkreis* HQ on the Hohenzollerndamm. Hase had been asked to come and he could do no more from his own office since he had totally lost control of the troops under his command.[43] In *Wehrkreis* HQ he found Major-General Herfurth, the Chief of Staff, and Lieutenant-General von Thüngen, whom the conspirators had just appointed *Wehrkreis* commander, both somewhat undecided. Thüngen said that all was calm; nowhere had there been bloodshed. In general, however, he was adopting a passive attitude; he had long ago heard that the assassination attempt had failed. Hase telephoned to Olbricht who said that the radio announcement was untrue; he then urged Thüngen to do something, saying that as commander he must issue some orders. But Thüngen thought the situation too obscure; no one knew, he said, whether Hitler was really alive or not. After 9.0 p.m., having talked on the telephone to Lieutenant-General Burgdorf and General Hoffmann, commander of Air Region III, Thüngen informed the staff of *Wehrkreis* HQ that he was carrying out no more orders from OKH. About 10.0 p.m. Thüngen, Herfurth and Lieutenant-Colonel Mitzkus, the operations officer, began cancelling the orders issued during the evening. About 10.30 p.m. Thüngen left *Wehrkreis* HQ and did not return.

Towards 9.0 p.m. Hase and Schöne returned to the Commandant's HQ, Hase having first telephoned Major Hayessen and learnt that Remer had gone over to Goebbels' side. They arrived soon after 9.0 p.m. About 9.15 p.m. General Reinecke, head of the General *Wehrmacht* Office (*Allgemeines Wehrmachtsamt*) called the Commandant's office from his official residence and, speaking on behalf of Field Marshal Keitel, demanded that all available troops be placed under his orders forthwith in order to occupy the Bendlerstrasse building. Reinecke had been visited by Lieutenant-General Thiele about 8.0 p.m. and so already knew what was going on in the Bendlerstrasse.[44] Keitel had called Reinecke about 9.10 p.m. and ordered him to take command of Hase's troops and occupy the Bendlerstrasse. Reinecke had thereupon called Hase who first quoted an order from Fromm but nevertheless promised to act on the orders now received from Reinecke. Hase was to report to Reinecke what troops he had available and where, but it never came to that.[45] Hase sent an officer to Remer ordering him to come to the Commandant's HQ.[46] Remer replied that he could not come since he was acting on direct orders from the *Führer*; he proposed that Hase, escorted by two sergeants of the Guard Battalion, come to Goebbels' house. Hase drove over, presumably to demonstrate that his conscience was clear.

On arrival at the house Hase was politely greeted by Goebbels; he told the Minister that he had to transmit to Remer an order from Reinecke to occupy the Bendlerstrasse building. Goebbels, however, said that this was no longer necessary since Remer had already received instructions direct from the *Führer*. Hase was requested to remain; he asked if he might have dinner, which was provided; he happily discussed with Goebbels whether he should drink hock or moselle with it.[47] Hase was later taken away by the *Gestapo*.

As regards the other troops called out by the conspirators the story was similar to that of the Guard Battalion and the units from the Pyrotechnical School and the Armoured School in Krampnitz.

The 'Valkyrie' units of the Armoured Replacement Brigade in Cottbus had advanced to the edge of Berlin and detachments occupied the transmitters in Herzberg and Königswusterhausen; this they had reported to their commander adding, however, that Hitler would speak over the radio that evening. The troops remained completely loyal and the occupation of the transmitters was of no value to the conspirators since Hitler and his regime were still in power and capable of functioning; no announcements by the conspirators were broadcast from the studios in the Masurenallee. Lieutenant-Colonel Stirius, the acting brigade commander, could obtain neither orders nor satisfactory information from *Wehrkreis* HQ; finally he learnt that 'Valkyrie' had been cancelled and that the troops were on the move back.[48]

In the Infantry School, Döberitz, Colonel Wolfgang Müller had contrived by 9.0 p.m. to set further detachments of the troops which had been alerted, on the move. He himself arrived in the Bendlerstrasse about 10.0 p.m. and proposed that General Olbricht give him written authority to take command of the school and direct operations, since the commander was away.[49] Müller told Colonel Mertz von Quirnheim, whom he found resolute but downcast, that he had had difficulty in enforcing the order for the occupation of the radio installations in Nauen and Tegel; he now proposed that, instead of occupying Oranienburg I and II concentration camps as originally ordered, the troops earmarked for this purpose be ordered to the Bendlerstrasse. Mertz agreed, dictated the necessary order, had it signed by General Olbricht and handed it to Müller. When Müller arrived back in the commanding officer's office in Döberitz about 11.0 p.m., however, his written orders were of no use to him; the officers would not obey him and indicated to him that the *putsch* had collapsed, as enquiries of Goebbels had shown. Müller was forced to admit that he could do no more and decided to beat a retreat; he called off the entire operation, went himself to Goebbels and placed himself at the Minister's disposal. He was not arrested until several days later when denounced by some of his brother-officers, but the whole affair had been so well camouflaged and covered up that he was never brought to trial.

A unit from the Infantry School, Döberitz, under Major Jakob did succeed without difficulty in occupying Broadcasting House on the Masurenallee; Jakob demanded that broadcasting be stopped. He understood nothing of radio, however, and could not therefore check whether what he was told was actually happening. The OKH signals officer who should have been present never arrived because no one in Hase's office gave him orders and Hase could not issue orders because he had no troops with which to carry them out. Hase never even knew that Jakob had been successful since, try as he would, Jakob never managed to report the fact. He was under orders, after occupying Broadcasting House, to call a certain telephone number in the Bendlerstrasse; he tried it but there was no reply. The Bendlerstrasse therefore never learnt that Broadcasting House had been occupied.[50]

Shortly after 6.0 p.m. it was reported to Major Jakob that a strong SS formation was on the move towards Broadcasting House. When it arrived an altercation took place with the commander of the SS men, an *SS-Obersturmbannführer* who said that he had orders to 'protect' the building. Jakob demanded that the SS unit be under his, Jakob's, orders since he had already taken the neccessary action. Neither the SS commander nor his men adopted a hostile attitude and eventually it was agreed to occupy Broadcasting House in concert.[51] By 7.0 p.m., therefore, the place was guarded by both Army and SS but under control of the existing regime.

After 7.0 p.m. Major Remer telephoned Jakob and arranged for him to speak to Goebbels. Jakob was suspicious; Goebbels might well be one of the traitors and he was willing to accept orders only from the Infantry School. When Goebbels requested him, however, to leave everything as it was, he could not object – those were precisely his orders.[52] Towards 9.0 p.m. the commander of the instructional group, Jakob's commanding officer, appeared and explained the situation. The SS withdrew on the morning of 21 July and Major Jakob's unit that afternoon.

Had the planned measures been taken – and one or two hours earlier this would probably have happened – there would have been no radio announcement of Hitler's survival. This of course presupposed effective, not merely external, control of Broadcasting House and the transmitter. This would not, however, necessarily have guaranteed the success of the *coup*. The struggle between the Bendlerstrasse and 'Wolfschanze' for the loyalty of the *Wehrkreis* commanders and execution or non-execution of the *putsch* measures would have been harder and more bitter. At the latest by 4.0 p.m., when communications were reopened on orders from the existing authorities, Hitler would have been able to telephone in person to *Wehrkreis* commanders and, even without a radio announcement, Hoepner, Olbricht, Beck and Stauffenberg would hardly have been able to cope with this. Nevertheless control and intelligent exploitation of the radio by the conspirators would have introduced a factor in developments, the effect of which would have been unpredictable but which *might* have been decisive.

The 'Valkyrie' units of the Army Ordnance School I in Treptow had been ready to move soon after receipt of the order from Berlin. Since the necessary vehicles had not arrived, however, the troops had had to move off towards Berlin on foot or by street-car.[53] The commander, Major-General Bruns, had gone to Berlin for the second time in the single motor-cycle and side-car available to the school. When he arrived about 9 p.m. he had some difficulty in getting through to the City Commandant's headquarters. He could not find Lieutenant-General von Hase, his immediate superior; it was said that he was with Goebbels. Finally he pushed his way laboriously through the road-blocks to the Hermann-Göring-Strasse looking for the general but could obtain no coherent information from the numerous officers, SS and Party officials whom he found there. Towards 10.0 p.m. he happened to glance through a door guarded by SS men and saw Hase sitting at dinner.

This being so, it seemed to Bruns that all was not well with the *coup*, if indeed all was not already lost; he wanted to get back to his battalion. On leaving the house he observed in the Tiergarten units of the Pyrotechnical School and of the Guard Battalion, both in full battle order and apparently facing each other menacingly.[54] Bruns tried to contact the troops of the Pyrotechnical School but men of the Guard Battalion forced him to remain within the barriers and return to the Commandant's office by the same route by which he had come. Tanks had arrived meanwhile at the Commandant's headquarters but at the Castle, where he expected to find his men, there was no one. He accordingly drove back towards Treptow to intercept the battalion but it had used short cuts to Berlin and Bruns missed it.

From Treptow Bruns called the Commandant's headquarters and about midnight contacted Lieutenant-Colonel Schöne, the operations officer. From him he learnt that No 1 Company of the school had reached the headquarters meanwhile but just short of the Castle had been diverted to the Bendlerstrasse by a staff officer; parts of it had arrived there about 9.45 p.m.[55] Soon afterwards Bruns received a report through a cyclist orderly of the battalion that Nos 2 and 3 Companies had reached their objective, the Castle; they had occupied it after a sharp altercation with an officer of the Guard Battalion and proposed to hold it. No 2 Company commander asked for mortars so that he might liberate the commander of No 1 Company and his escort who were now incarcerated in the Commandant's headquarters; Bruns saw no point in this, since they were in no danger. Instead Bruns managed to obtain the company commander's release by telephoning and he was back in barracks in Treptow by 6.0 a.m. Bruns could not have sent the mortars in any case, since the transport had still not arrived.[56]

About 2.0 a.m. on 21 July the senior platoon commander of No 1 Company reported back to his commander in barracks. He had hurried on to the Bendlerstrasse ahead of his company on a bicycle and there had been ordered by agitated officers of OKH to secure the entrances. Then, near the room where he was being briefed, he heard a shot and the words 'you swine'. In consternation he had dashed down the stairs and had come up against an apparently sensible captain of the Guard Battalion who told him that the attempted *coup d'état* had collapsed and advised him urgently not to 'make trouble' by any action such as 'securing' the entrances; the Bendlerstrasse building, he said, was now being occupied by the Guard Battalion and the SS who were in process of arriving. The platoon commander could see for himself that the prudent captain was right. He therefore stopped the men of the Ordnance School, who had not yet arrived, and led them back to Treptow.

Under these conditions no *coup d'état* was possible. It was not surprising, therefore, that as the evening wore on, the conspirators in the Bendlerstrasse became increasingly discouraged and finally abandoned their enterprise.

In the early stages, while the movement orders positioning units of the Replacement Army for the seizure of power were going out and in some cases were being executed, Stauffenberg, Olbricht and Mertz tried to gain control of the various agencies in the building and use them for the purposes of the *coup*. The most important were the OKH/AHA Signals Group and the staffs of C-in-C Replacement Army and of the AHA.

About 3.45 p.m. Colonel Hassel, head of the Signals Group, received a call in his office in Düppel camp from Lieutenant-Colonel von der Lancken, Olbricht's assistant, asking him to come to the Bendlerstrasse at once.[57] Hassel took with him Major Rufer from his staff and arrived in Olbricht's office about 4.15 p.m. Olbricht said that Hitler was dead – Stauffenberg had just reported the fact by telephone; 'Valkyrie' had been issued and would Hassel now please send to the City Commandant's headquarters the twenty signal officers earmarked – ten from Thiele's command and ten from Hassel's. Hassel issued the necessary orders to Düppel and then went to Thiele whose office was in the Bendlerstrasse. Thiele, however, said that this did not now apply since matters outside were not going as they should and the communications black-out of 'Wolfschanze' was not working (Thiele himself had given Major Degner a categoric order to lift it). At Olbricht's request Hassel therefore despatched a further ten officers from Düppel.

At about 4.30 p.m. Colonel-General Hoepner, in civilian clothes and suitcase in hand, arrived in Olbricht's office where Colonel-General Beck was sitting on the sofa. Olbricht decided to talk to Thiele but he was with Fromm and so Olbricht went into Fromm's room as well. As he emerged he called out: 'The *Führer* is alive! I must speak to Fellgiebel at once.'[58] Hassel made the call and said to Fellgiebel that Olbricht wished to speak to him. Fellgiebel said: 'All this is no good any more' and put down the receiver. Olbricht said: 'There's the first one to defect' but Hassel did not believe it. What Fellgiebel meant was that, whether Hitler were alive or not, this was a time for action, not talking. Thiele then called Walter Schellenberg, head of Section VI (SD Foreign Intelligence) in the RSHA and also of 'Amt Mil' (Military Section) since the incorporation of the *Abwehr* into the SS. Thiele asked what was really up and Schellenberg said that there seemed to be a *putsch*; Thiele said that he thought so too – no doubt hoping to cover himself. Soon afterwards Thiele drove off – to Schellenberg in the Berkaerstrasse.

Since the take-over of the radio by the conspirators was not happening, about 6.0 p.m. Hassel proposed to send Major Ludwig Kempe to the National Radio (*Deutschlandsender*) to take a grip of matters. Kempe, however, demanded orders in writing and Hassel, unwilling to risk himself further, said that there was no time for that. Kempe did not, therefore, go to the National Radio.[59] Hassel then went back to Thiele who said that it had all gone wrong and he must get out of here. From Thiele Hassel went to Stauffenberg who, when asked how matters stood, said: 'Well, the chap's not dead, but the outfit's under way; one can't say anything yet'. Someone must be sent to the telegraph offices and the National Radio, Stauffenberg said, since the latter was still functioning. Hassel could only tell him what had happened: he had sent his twenty officers to the City Commandant but the military occupation must be ordered from there. Hassel then collected passes for himself and Major Rufer and went home. He was afraid that he might not be a free agent in his office in Düppel. During the evening several of the conspirators present in the Bendlerstrasse, including Dr Gerstenmaier, offered to conduct a raid on the *Deutschlandsender* but there were never any troops available; the fact that Broadcasting House and the transmitters in Nauen and Tegel had been occupied successfully, though ineffectually, was not known.[60]

About 5.0 p.m. Mertz von Quirnheim, Chief of Staff AHA, ordered Lieutenant-Colonel Pridun, head of Group I in the operations section, and Major Harnack, one of his desk officers, to issue the 'Valkyrie' orders to the entire Replacement Army at once.[61] Harnack began to issue, or give orders for the issue of the orders by telephone and teleprint; Pridun meanwhile went to Lieutenant-Colonel Franz Herber, the supply officer, who was responsible for organizing transport and equipment for the units called out. In annexes to the orders units had to be told where to draw their vehicles, weapons and other equipment and this depended on their direction of movement and type of operation. Herber felt that he must have more information about the purpose of the operation, whereupon Pridun called Mertz and asked that the staff be briefed as was normal in exceptional situations.

Mertz thereupon summoned the senior officers of his staff to his office, where they assembled between 5.0 and 6.0 p.m. He told them that the *Führer* had been assassinated and that Party and SS circles were behind the plot; to maintain order and continue the battle at the front the *Wehrmacht* had assumed plenary powers; the police had placed themselves under Army orders; members of the staff were to continue in their posts and do their duty as before. All then returned to their offices.

Following Mertz' instructions Herber ordered Major Fliessbach, head of the supply group responsible for ammunition, to ensure that members of the AHA staff were armed – Mertz had said that disturbances were to be anticipated. Forseeing a long evening Herber then went to the mess on the Matthäi-Kirchplatz for dinner. He had difficulty in leaving the building and first had to obtain an official pass from Olbricht; he took the opportunity to tell him that he had ordered the staff to be armed. Olbricht approved and authorized Herber to leave the building temporarily. Apart from the double guards on the Bendlerstrasse Herber saw nothing unusual; at first nothing out of the ordinary happened to Pridun either.

The staff of C-in-C Replacement Army were briefed about the same time as that of the AHA. About 5.15 p.m. they were summoned to the commander and, on Haeften's instructions, assembled in the Chief of Staff's room (Stauffenberg's) on the first floor. After a time Colonel-General Hoepner came in in uniform but without Stauffenberg; he asked whether everyone was present and then said that: the *Führer* was dead; Colonel-General Beck had assumed leadership of the *Reich* and Field Marshal von Witzleben had taken command of the *Wehrmacht*; he, Hoepner, had been charged with the duties of C-in-C Replacement Army. Finally Hoepner stressed the necessity for loyal cooperation in this great hour and went out into the map room situated between the offices of Stauffenberg and Fromm.[62] Colonel von Roell, head of Group II, sent his officers, Major Ruhe, Captain Komp and Captain Waizenegger, back to their offices. He himself waited with Major-General Kennes, head of the supply group, in Stauffenberg's outer office to be told more, particularly about the position of Colonel-General Fromm. While they were waiting a telephone call came through from Field Marshal Keitel; it was not put through to the commander but transferred to the AHA.

About 6.0 p.m. or just before, Stauffenberg invited into his office the heads of the three staff groups – Major-General Kennes, Lieutenant-Colonel Joachim Sadrozinski and Colonel von Roell – together with Lieutenant-Colonel Franz Kleber and Colonel Rohowsky. He told them that Hitler was dead; Colonel-General Fromm had failed to rise to the occasion and had been arrested; plenary powers had been transferred to *Wehrkreis* commanders and the police were everywhere under their orders. Kennes asked for information on future cooperation between his group and the Ministry for Armaments and War Production but Stauffenberg was called into the adjoining map room by General Olbricht before he could answer. As Roell went back to his office he met in Stauffenberg's anteroom Berthold Graf Stauffenberg in naval uniform and Colonel Fritz Jäger.[63]

Colonel-Generals Beck and Hoepner could do little but await developments; meanwhile, Olbricht, Mertz and Stauffenberg were involved in feverish activity to ensure that orders were carried out; at this point they were the real leaders of the revolt. Between 5.0 and 6.0 p.m. copies of the long teleprinter message No 2 had to be made, additional executive instructions dictated by Mertz, passes to enter or leave the building prepared and signed, telephone calls answered; questions from the *Wehrkreise* and other recipients of the orders were arriving almost uninterruptedly; Mertz and Stauffenberg were continually confirming the validity of the orders and answering questions concerning the whereabouts of Colonel-General Fromm. During this period the other conspirators who had arrived in the Bendlerstrasse – Gisevius, Schulenburg and Yorck, for instance, but also many officers earmarked for specific duties during the *coup* – were little more than extras. They should have been in action long ago but the start of the *coup* had been much delayed and until the first two or three hours had passed, until troops were available and the first most important objectives occupied and secured, they could do nothing. Lieutenant von Kleist was the only one to be given orders: about 6.0 p.m. Olbricht despatched him to the government quarter to see how matters stood. Kleist was able to report that the Guard Battalion had set up the road blocks ordered and tanks had driven along the East-West Avenue; in the Hermann-Göring-Strasse he had seen small groups of SS men being disarmed by men of the Guard Battalion.[64] Later, about 9.30 p.m., Olbricht sent Kleist out once more, this time to Hase in the City Commandant's headquarters, to bring up reinforcements for the Bendlerstrasse. He could only report, however, that everything was in total confusion and disorder and that the Commandant's headquarters was 'a complete muddle'.

Soon after 6.0 p.m. Beck asked for Field Marshal von Witzleben. Gisevius replied that Witzleben was said to be on his way to Zossen to take over command of the *Wehrmacht*. At Zossen were to be found the greater part of the Army General Staff and General Eduard Wagner, the Deputy Chief of Staff representing Colonel-General Zeitzler, the Chief of Staff of the Army.[65] Beck considered that the C-in-C should not be in Zossen but in Berlin, in the Bendlerstrasse.[66] About 6.0 p.m. Witzleben had arrived in 'Maybach II' (Zossen) with his aide Graf Lynar and had gone to see General Wagner. Wagner's aide, Graf Kanitz who was on duty in the anteroom, remembers the impression Witzleben made on him on that day: old, broken, and far less spry and straight than in the earlier years of the war. Witzleben was in Wagner's office for only five minutes, while Kanitz chatted with his uncle Graf Lynar; then the Field Marshal and the General emerged, Wagner saw his visitor to the front door, and then Witzleben was on his way to Berlin – there was obviously no active centre of the conspiracy in Zossen.[67] Wagner, however, had his section chiefs convened by Kanitz and told them that the assassination attempt had miscarried, adding that they were to stay in their offices and await further developments.[68]

In Olbricht's anteroom secretaries were typing copies of the teleprinter messages; Lieutenant-Colonel Bernardis was in Fräulein Lerche's office checking them. At the window, grinding his teeth, stood Lieutenant-Colonel Bolko von der Heyde, Olbricht's operations officer; though refusing to cooperate, he had not been arrested; he gazed furiously into the offices and from time to time lamented to the secretaries about the death of the *Führer*; in any case, he said, having nothing to do, he would like to get something to eat.[69] When Stauffenberg heard of this he ordered the guards on the gate to block the exit and allow no one out without a valid pass.

Soon after this little scene *SS-Oberführer* Dr Achamer-Pifrader arrived from the RSHA in order to invite Stauffenberg to a conference with *SS-Gruppenführer* Heinrich Müller, head of the *Gestapo*.[70] Stauffenberg locked him and his escort up and handed them over to Colonel Jäger. Dr Otto John encountered the trio in the passage as he arrived in the Bendlerstrasse from the Lufthansa head office at Tempelhof.

The impression made on John by the activity of those now directing this *coup* was as unsatisfactory as that of Gisevius. He had always pictured 'the General Staff working with superior control and rationality' but this apparent hectic confusion was something quite different.[71] John did not know that valuable time had been lost in the early stages and that the conspirators were therefore swimming against the tide from the outset; they were pursuing an affair without any solid prospects of success and were therefore not operating in a General-Staff-like manner at all. Gisevius had grasped this situation and was urging action. When Stauffenberg reappeared he said: 'Don't you see what kind of duds you have around you here?' He suggested that, pending the arrival of the troops, assault parties of officers be formed to seize the RSHA in the Prinz-Albrecht-Strasse and the Propaganda Ministry and to shoot *Gestapo* Müller and Goebbels out of hand, adding: 'We've got to have some corpses now', then all this wavering would end and the conspirators would really feel compelled to see the thing through.[72] Stauffenberg was not averse to this and said that he would talk to Colonel Jäger about it. A little later Jäger was in fact despatched to the Commandant's headquarters with orders on these lines; he was to take command of the necessary raiding parties and carry out the action proposed. Before he arrived, however, the news of Hitler's survival had been broadcast and the intervention of Goebbels and Remer paralysed all action. Without troops Jäger could do no more.

Graf von Helldorf sent across his aide to ask Gisevius how things were going. Since he had nothing else to do, Gisevius drove back with the aide to Helldorf.[73] He reached police headquarters about 7.0 p.m. and listened to Helldorf's complaints.[74] The entire police machine had been frozen and in readiness for two hours, Helldorf said, but nothing was happening; no instructions had arrived; Lieutenant-General von Hase should have been in touch with him long ago asking for the criminal police officers earmarked to make the arrests; the Guard Battalion was not doing what it should; both the RSHA and Goebbels were quite happy, as telephone conversations with Müller and Goebbels had shown; SS troops were said to be on the move and an announcement that Hitler was unharmed had been broadcast.[75] Gisevius explained that these delays were inherent in the initial stage and had been anticipated; they were also due to the attitude of General von Kortzfleisch, commander of *Wehrkreis* III. These statements were undoubtedly correct but they could hardly dissipate anxiety about the outcome of the enterprise.

In fact the inevitable initial period was not the only reason for the lack of progress. Now that Hitler's survival began to seem probable and then certain, many of the conspirators became half-hearted. When confronted with the choice between pursuit of an enterprise almost certainly condemned to failure leading to torture or death and a feeble glimmer of hope of escape, by no means all possessed the steadfastness and courage of Stauffenberg, Mertz, Schulenburg, and others. When Gisevius – according to his account between 7.0 and 8.0 p.m. – returned to the Bendlerstrasse, Lieutenant-General von Thüngen was still there, apparently waiting for a car and in no particular hurry. Olbricht told Gisevius of the radio bulletin which had been broadcast meanwhile; there was no longer any doubt of Hitler's survival. Did Gisevius think, he asked, that one could retreat now? Gisevius did not.[76]

Dr John, in an effort to find out what the situation really was, had turned to Graf Schwerin earlier in the evening. Schwerin did not know either but said that Beck was determined to see the thing through, adding 'if only the occupation of the radio station had clicked';[77] moreover counter-orders had already been issued from the *Führer*'s headquarters and touch had been lost with the Commandant's headquarters on Unter den Linden.[78] Colonel Hansen, John's special contact, had not arrived and was not expected that evening; it seemed improbable that John would receive any instructions that day for his contacts with the Western Allies – Schwerin had said that, with all this activity, it was quite impossible for John to talk either to Beck or Olbricht on the subject;

there was therefore really nothing for John to do but go away.[79] He wanted to go to Popitz and find out about the meeting between Witzleben and Gereke. For the moment, however, he remained and watched officers running hither and thither, Berthold Graf Stauffenberg pacing thoughtfully up and down in his naval uniform, Olbricht and Stauffenberg telephoning feverishly and urging officers in *Wehrkreis* HQs to carry out orders received – all was in order – counter-orders from the *Führer*'s headquarters were to be anticipated but should not be obeyed since they were not authentic – Keitel was lying – Hitler was definitely dead – the *Reich* was in danger – the *Wehrmacht* had full powers – all signal centres to be occupied as top priority – and so forth. During this period between 6.0 and 7.0 p.m., the conversation between Beck and Kluge took place, the outcome of which was Kluge's refusal to participate in the *coup*.[80]

About 8.0 p.m. John called his brother as he had promised but was soon interrupted by the telephone operator since the line was needed. Generals were standing around waiting for a conference which had been summoned; a secretary brought in sandwiches; Field Marshal von Witzleben and his aide, Major Graf von Lynar, arrived at last; a secretary was unable to contact a *Wehrkreis* commander because he had gone to dinner; Haeften gave instructions for the detention of certain 'unreliable' officers who had been arrested.[81] John found this all most reassuring; there would be some clashes with Himmler's troops, he thought, but in general terms it seemed to him that all was going well; the Army was on the move.

Since he could not do anything, John decided to go. 'If you call early tomorrow, we shall know what's up.' Schwerin said to him.[82] In the passage he met Haeften and said that he was going but would telephone at 8.0 a.m. in the morning. 'Perhaps we shall all have been hanged by then,' Haeften said drily but then chuckled and said '*Auf Wiedersehen*'.[83] John escaped just before counter-measures began.

Meanwhile Gisevius had reported to Beck, Stauffenberg and Schulenburg the results of his excursion to police headquarters. Stauffenberg said that he had ordered Hase to contact Helldorf at once.[84] But it was now too late; by this time no troops were taking orders from Hase and he was on his way to *Wehrkreis* HQ. About 7.0 p.m. the question of simply dismissing and replacing Major Remer was discussed but this all remained in the air; Remer was no longer taking orders from the conspirators and they had neither resources nor authority.[85]

Beck continually reverted to the radio and the necessity to broadcast some proclamation from the leaders of the *coup*. General Fritz Lindemann, Director of Artillery in HQ Replacement Army, had been earmarked to read the first radio announcement.[86] Now, however, he could not be found; perhaps, people thought, he was waiting in the Commandant's headquarters or was trying to get there (actually between 7.0 and 8.0 p.m. he was on his way from Zossen to Berlin). Beck accordingly asked Gisevius whether he was prepared to read the necessary proclamation and to draft it first since Lindemann had the only copy with him. Beck said that he could not leave the Bendlerstrasse at this point, though he wished to speak on the radio himself later; when Hoepner told him of the radio bulletin about the assassination attempt and the possibility of a speech by Hitler, Beck said that he must speak first.[87] Beck's view was that the other side would maintain that Hitler was alive whether he were or not and that, if he was alive, he must under all circumstances be stopped speaking on the radio.

Gisevius therefore started to draft but in the general bustle could not put anything down. He could not help hearing Stauffenberg on the telephone, imploring, commanding and persuading officers in the *Wehrkreise*; he himself was continually being asked about the attitude of the police – and meanwhile Helldorf and Nebe were still waiting for instructions from Hase or *Wehrkreis* HQ.[88] Beck then said to Gisevius that he might find himself in front of the microphone at any moment. When Gisevius objected that the transmitters had not yet been occupied, Stauffenberg said that this would happen soon – as soon as the tanks were there – it would be done by 8.0 p.m. Beck accordingly discussed with Gisevius the main points in the proclamation: no matter what Goebbels' propaganda proclaimed, it said, a *Führer* in whose immediate entourage divergencies and doubts were such that one of his staff, assisted by a sizeable group of senior officers could make a bomb attack on him, was morally dead.[89] Gisevius noted down these ideas and also phrases tossed to him from time to time by Stauffenberg, Olbricht, Hoepner, Yorck, Schwerin and Schulenburg.

At about 7.55 p.m. Stauffenberg and Beck spoke on the telephone to the Chief of Staff, Army Group North, which was almost surrounded in Courland by the Red Army. Beck ordered an immediate withdrawal.[90] He then ordered that this instruction be recorded in the Bendlerstrasse; it would be of importance for future historians, he said; no one could tell what might happen in the next few hours; execution of the order might be prevented and result in a new Stalingrad.

As already mentioned, about 8.0 p.m. Field Marshal von Witzleben arrived in the Bendlerstrasse at last with his aide, Graf von Lynar; they came from General Wagner's office where they had heard that the assassination had been attempted but had failed.[91] Both looked furious and were obviously highly displeased with the course of events. At the Bendlerstrasse gate they had been stopped by Captain Cords because they did not have one of the orange identification cards signed by Stauffenberg that were now required, and Cords did not recognize the Field Marshal, had to ask him for his name and then check with Stauffenberg by telephone; naturally the famous Field Marshal was angry, and it was not difficult for him to make inferences concerning the competence and efficiency of the conspirators.[92] When Stauffenberg reported to Witzleben, he merely said: 'This is a fine mess.'[93] Witzleben then reported himself present to Beck who was his superior officer in the hierarchy of the *coup* and they both went into Fromm's room. Beck gave an account of what had happened so far – issue of the orders to the *Wehrkreise*, the counter-orders and the report that Hitler had survived the attack. The discussion became violent; after a short time Stauffenberg and Schwerin were called in and hauled over the coals by Witzleben, banging his fist on the table. Stauffenberg and Beck insisted that the report of Hitler's survival was a lie but Witzleben was not willing to believe that. No one could dispute the fact that neither the *Reich* capital nor the radio installations were in the conspirators' hands. The violent altercation lasted three-quarters of an hour and then Witzleben drove back to Zossen in a rage. On hearing the Field Marshal's story, General Wagner said to him: 'We're going home.'[94] No witnesses to the conversation between Beck and Witzleben are now alive and none of them gave a detailed account before they died, but the result was clear enough: Witzleben wished to have nothing to do with so badly conducted an affair – there were not even any troops available; he was not prepared to issue orders when he knew beforehand that they would not be carried out.

Meanwhile, somewhat earlier in the evening, Olbricht had called together the remaining heads of branches, most of whom had already left the building; they arrived gradually, among them Lieutenant-General Karl-Wilhelm Specht, Inspector-General of officer training, and General Walter Kuntze, Chief Education Officer of the Replacement Army, with his chief of staff and deputy, Major Rittmann.[95] Between 7.0 and 8.0 p.m. Stauffenberg took the generals in to Olbricht who told them that Hitler had been assassinated and that a new government had been formed under Witzleben and Beck.[96] Specht asked what people were supposed to believe; the radio, after all, had announced that Hitler was alive. To this Olbricht had no clear or satisfactory answer. Generals Kuntze, Specht and another general then rose to their feet and said that they had sworn an oath to the *Führer* and that this information meant nothing to them; they could not continue to work on this basis.[97] They then left the room and no one tried to stop them.

Such were the developments in Fromm's and Olbricht's offices. Meanwhile the attempted *coup* was collapsing, partly because the conditions for success – the death of Hitler, rapid action to forestall those in power – were not present and partly owing to lack of personal effort on the part of generals involved in the *coup* such as Hase, Thüngen and Thiele. At the same time an opposition movement began inside the staffs of C-in-C Replacement Army (Fromm) and the AHA (Olbricht).

After Fromm and his aide, Captain Bartram, had been arrested about 5.0 p.m., Bartram first briefed Fromm on the situation – he was one of the first non-conspirators in the building to realize that a *putsch* was in progress.[98] When Fromm had calmed down, the two considered what to do. Fromm said that troops must be summoned to deal with this clique; his thoughts turned to the Infantry School in Döberitz and Bartram's to the Guard Battalion of the 'Grossdeutschland' Armoured Corps, to which he himself belonged. The telephone in the room allotted to Bartram and Fromm had been cut off and fully armed double sentries were posted in the anteroom; Fromm had no weapon and Bartram only a dagger. The room, however, had another little-known exit giving on to a dark passage and a staircase leading to the upper storey, something easily overlooked in this rambling old building. This exit was unguarded. Bartram slipped out unobserved and went up the stairs to

Major-General Kennes. He told Kennes what had happened and passed on an order from Fromm to alert Döberitz. But Kennes did nothing.[99]

Later, after Kennes and the other heads of branches had been briefed by Stauffenberg, he realized that a *putsch* was taking place but did not dare use the telephone since he assumed that it would be tapped.[100] Kennes failed in an attempt to leave the building. He then summoned his staff and told them to leave the building as best they could and, on orders from Colonel-General Fromm, alert troops to expel the conspirators. All this led to nothing, however, since the troops had already received different orders and were on the move anyway; finally they were placed under command of Remer and, without any participation by Fromm, used for the purpose he wished.

After the briefing when Hitler's death and the assumption of plenary powers by the *Wehrmacht* had been announced, Roell had gone back to his office. While ruminating on what had happened he heard fragments of a radio bulletin telling of the assassination attempt and saying the *Führer* was in good health. He decided to telephone to Lieutenant-General Burgdorf, Deputy Chief of the Army Personnel Office, and put through a call to 'Mauerwald'. Meanwhile Colonel von Roell asked Major-General Kennes, Colonel Rohowsky and Lieutenant-Colonel Kleber (of Group III) to come to his office so that he could tell them at once what had emerged from his talk with Burgdorf. While they were waiting Bartram came in and reported what had happened to him and Fromm.

When the call to Burgdorf came through Roell told him 'that Colonel-General Hoepner had arrived as the new C-in-C Replacement Army'; he asked for instructions.[101] This was apparently the first time that Burgdorf had heard what was going on in Berlin; he gave Roell and the others strict orders to report at once to him[102] or to Major-General Maisel in Lübben. Roell informed the others and also Captains Komp and Waizenegger.

At first they failed in an attempt to leave the Bendlerstrasse because they had no passes. Colonel von Roell accordingly despatched Captain Komp to Olbricht's office to obtain passes in their names and, incredibly enough, he succeeded without difficulty. About 8.0 p.m., after the arrival of Field Marshal von Witzleben, they all departed in one of their staff cars via the Potsdamer Strasse towards Tempelhof and then on to Lübben. On the way they stopped at the Zossen training area on Lake Leber, where Colonel-General Fromm's house was, and told his wife that he would not be home that night. In Lübben Roell reported to Maisel and briefed him. In Roell's presence Maisel checked with Lieutenant-Colonel Weiss, assistant to the Chief of the Army Personnel Office, 'that all *Wehrkreise* had received the necessary counter-orders'.

Meanwhile Bartram was indefatigable in his efforts to set some counter action in motion; he informed members of the staff that Fromm had been arrested and a *putsch* was taking place; he kept an eye open for possibilities of escape. Each time that he returned from one of his excursions he reported the situation to his commander. They wondered whether Fromm should not try to escape through the unguarded exit but thought that a tall colonel-general in full uniform could hardly be expected to pass unobserved in the same way as could an innocent-looking one-legged captain whom hardly anyone knew. They proposed, therefore, to wait for darkness and then escape into the Tiergartenstrasse via an entrance for lorries which they thought would be unguarded and which was being used during construction of an air raid shelter in the courtyard; one of Kennes' staff ordered Fromm's driver to the Tiergartenstrasse.[103]

During one of his excursions Bartram met Kortzfleisch, who had not yet been arrested, and took him to Fromm; subsequently he succeeded in doing the same with General Kuntze and Lieutenant-General Specht. They exchanged information and Fromm ordered each of his visitors to mobilize troops and initiate counter-action. He showed Specht and Kuntze the secret exit and they succeeded in leaving the building; he turned down their proposal that he go with them, however. Specht and Kuntze reached Potsdam where local Army schools were alerted for operations against the conspiracy; this later proved superfluous. Meanwhile Fromm and Bartram heard the radio announcement that the assassination attempt had failed and that Hitler had survived. This at least showed them that the revolt was going badly in that the radio stations were evidently still in the hands of the previous rulers and being used for their purposes.[104]

But the counter-action so frequently ordered by Fromm was slow in coming; it was now dark and so, for better or worse, Fromm had to do something himself. He first sent Bartram to ask Hoepner that he be allowed to go to his apartment, volunteering to take no action and not even to telephone. This was about 9.0 p.m.[105] Fromm was given permission and an armed guard was posted at the door of his apartment. Fromm now had a telephone available but he did not use it, perhaps because of his promise (though he had no need to feel obligated in his situation), perhaps from fear of discovery or perhaps to avoid jeopardizing his planned escape, which he pursued so unenergetically. He discussed again with Bartram how they could evade their guards but it was really too late for this now since, for no good reason, Fromm had deprived himself of the advantage of the unguarded exit. About 10.0 p.m. he despatched Bartram into the room where they had first been held to fetch the radio set and on the way Bartram at last stumbled into the counter-action, now under way quite independently of Fromm.

The officers of the AHA staff who were neither in the secret nor involved in the attempted *coup d'état* became increasingly puzzled by the discrepancies between the statements of Olbricht, Hoepner and Stauffenberg on the one hand and the radio announcements on the other. Lieutenant-Colonels Herber, von der Heyde and Pridun together with Major Harnack discussed the situation and came to the conclusion that, here in the Bendlerstrasse, an attempt was being made to remove not only Hitler but the entire National-Socialist government.[106] The announcement broadcast at 9.0 p.m. that Himmler had been appointed C-in-C Replacement Army, increased their suspicions.[107] They decided to demand an explanation from General Olbricht, their official superior; Herber, as the senior officer, was to arrange this.

Thereupon all officers were ordered to Olbricht and they assembled around

9.0 p.m.[108] Olbricht did not explain as they hoped, however, but merely gave instructions for the protection of the building. The Guard Battalion sentries had been withdrawn, he said, and the building must now be defended; every staff officer must play his part; normal duty was temporarily suspended. Captain Cords had reported that Remer had ordered all guard troops (which were part of the Guard Battalion) to be withdrawn from the Bendlerstrasse building complex about 8.30 p.m. where they had manned entrances and breaches in the walls; only the guards at the main gate had stayed, probably in the hope of keeping the conspirators unsuspecting.[109] The troops of the Army Ordnance School had not yet arrived at that time. Olbricht ordered every General Staff officer to participate in guard duties; two to three groups were organized to protect the building in turns, the first one was to report to Cords at the main gate at once. As regards the situation Olbricht gave only vague indications of the necessity for all this and reacted evasively to all questions, referring to prevention of a threatened catastrophe which had led responsible men to seize the initiative.

The weapons ordered by Herber had not yet arrived. Not a single General Staff officer reported to Cords either. Somewhat later there arrived in the Bendlerstrasse a platoon from the Army Ordnance School and Cords managed to have it placed under his command for guard duty. He let Klausing know that finally 'we' (the conspirators) had 'our own troops', but when Cords went back to the main gate a few minutes afterwards, a strong detachment of the Guard Battalion was just arriving. It seemed pointless to Cords to have his Army Ordnance School men shoot at all these Guard Battalion soldiers to prevent them from entering the Bendlerstrasse complex. He merely ordered the main gate to be shut with the small pedestrians' entrance open, and he had the other entrances guarded as well as possible under the circumstances.

Herber, Heyde, Harnack and others were not satisfied. On leaving Olbricht they continued to discuss the situation in the passage and in Heyde's office. It seemed clear to them that a *putsch* was in progress, apparently against the existing government. They were not in the secret nor were they involved but they were subordinates of the conspirators who were now dragging them into it without taking them into their confidence, and all this at a moment when the *coup* was already collapsing. Admittedly, whatever their motives may have been, they had not initially opposed the *coup*, of which they had some inkling; admittedly too, when the conspirators' statements were contested by the radio, they had not come down in favour of either side. Consequently they saw all the less reason to help defend a failing conspiracy. On the contrary – feeling as little sympathy for the conspirators as they did for the regime, under the circumstances they saw no choice but to save their skins.[110]

Six staff officers were detailed by Olbricht as the first shift to guard the six exits to the building. Among them were Harnack, Herber, Heyde and Pridun. The *putsch* was now a certainty; equally certain was that it was collapsing. Anyone who wished to save his neck must act the loyal officer. As Lieutenant-Colonel Pridun remembers it: 'The gentlemen assembled in Lieutenant-Colonel von der Heyde's office, one of whom I was, stated clearly that in this situation they could not forswear their oath.' They decided first to demand more precise information from Olbricht, particularly on the object of their guard duty and whom they were defending the building against. Meanwhile the weapons had arrived and they seized a number of sub-machine guns, pistols and hand grenades.[111] Herber took a pistol and put a hand grenade into his trouser pocket. Then, as senior officer of the group, he became their spokesman once more.

Once more Olbricht answered Herber's representations and questions evasively; there was news of the *Führer*'s death, he said, but also news to the contrary.[112] Herber said that this was not enough and he must insist on information from Colonel-General Fromm. Olbricht then referred him to Hoepner, saying that he was ready to go too.

While this conversation was going on shots were heard in the passage, apparently fired from nervousness. Olbricht said: 'Now they have probably shot the good Stauffenberg who has been wounded before!'[113] It is not entirely clear who fired at whom. When, however, dozens of officers were suddenly running around armed, it was almost unavoidable that in the general excitement someone would fire, to lend weight to some threat or demand or to stop a fugitive. It seems clear, however, that Captain Klausing fired on Lieutenant-Colonel Herber as he came out of Olbricht's room and that Herber fired back. His driver remembers Stauffenberg clamping his service pistol to his side with the stump of his right arm, cocking it with the three fingers of his left hand and then firing at Lieutenant-Colonel Pridun. Mertz von Quirnheim's secretary and one of Fromm's secretaries remember a whole series of shots being fired and Stauffenberg being wounded in the left forearm or shoulder-blade. When Gerstenmaier was later led away, he had to step across a large pool of blood.[114] After he had been shot at, Stauffenberg asked Fromm's secretary to put through a call to Paris for him; in Paris there still seemed some hope of a breakthrough for the *coup*. But the call never went through.[115] Throughout the day Stauffenberg had worn his eyepatch over his empty left eye-socket. Now he took it off, a sign of weariness and irritation.[116]

Despite the shooting Olbricht and Herber succeeded in reaching Fromm's office unchallenged. They were received by Colonel-General Hoepner; Mertz joined them; Beck, Haeften and Stauffenberg were already there. Herber accused Hoepner of having interrupted supply to the front by his issue of the 'Valkyrie' order; anyway, he said, at last he wished to know what the game was and demanded to speak to Fromm. Hoepner said that he himself had no precise information and was awaiting orders from Witzleben. He referred Herber to Fromm, who was in his apartment. Haeften was burning papers on the floor. About this time Stauffenberg, with an indescribably sad expression on his face, said to Fromm's secretary: 'They've all left me in the lurch.'[117]

Fromm was in fact still in his apartment; Captain Freiherr von Leonrod was on guard outside; Bartram appeared in the passage leading to it. Asked what Fromm was doing Bartram replied that he wanted to listen to the latest news on the radio.[118] One of the staff officers, armed like the rest, had been present at the scene with Olbricht and during the shooting. He now rang

Fromm's doorbell, was admitted and reported the situation to the Colonel-General. After reflecting briefly Fromm went to his office. The guard on Fromm's apartment had now vanished.[119]

When Fromm entered his office, bent on reassuming his prerogatives, he found there Colonel Graf Stauffenberg, his Chief of Staff, who glowered at him, Colonel Mertz von Quirnheim, Lieutenant von Haeften, Colonel-General Beck, General Olbricht and Colonel-General Hoepner. All were being held at gunpoint by armed staff officers. It was about 10.0 p.m. or a little later. Fromm declared the conspirators under arrest, saying: 'Well, gentlemen, I am now going to do to you what you did to me this afternoon.'[120] He ordered them to relinquish their weapons, saying that they had been caught redhanded committing treason and would be tried by court martial. The *coup d'état* was at an end.

PART X/WRECK OF THE OPPOSITION

46 Summary Court Martial

Colonel-General Fromm first declared that the leaders of the attempted revolt – Colonel-General Beck, Colonel-General Hoepner, General Olbricht, Colonel Graf von Stauffenberg, Colonel Mertz von Quirnheim and Lieutenant von Haeften – were under arrest and demanded that they hand over their weapons. The others present he constituted as a court martial. Colonel-General Beck asked to be allowed to keep his pistol 'for private use' and Fromm allowed him this but told him to hurry.[1] Beck raised his gun and tried to say a few words to Fromm about their long years of military service together but Fromm interrupted him brusquely and again told him to hurry. Beck shot himself in the temple, staggered and was supported by Stauffenberg. Then he shot himself again and collapsed, but he was still alive.

After Beck's attempted suicide Fromm asked the arrested men whether they had any last wishes. Colonel-General Hoepner said that he had had nothing to do with the affair at all and wished to defend himself; Fromm reluctantly allowed him to write something down. Olbricht also asked for permission to write and was given it. The writing lasted nearly half an hour; Fromm was becoming impatient and was unwilling to postpone any longer the shooting of the leaders of the *coup*. When it was reported that a detachment of the 'Grossdeutschland' Guard Battalion had arrived, he announced: 'In the name of the *Führer* a court martial convened by me has pronounced sentence: Colonel von Mertz, General Olbricht, the Colonel whose name I will not mention, and Lieutenant von Haeften are condemned to death.'[2]

Stauffenberg, who had stood by in angry silence, now spoke. In a few short clipped sentences he assumed responsibility for everything. All the others, he said, had acted as soldiers and as his subordinates; they had merely carried out his orders.[3] Fromm, standing in the doorway, said nothing. Then he stepped aside; his meaning was clear. Stauffenberg, Mertz von Quirnheim, Olbricht and Haeften walked quietly past him, showing no emotion. An hour earlier Haeften had given Schweizer, Stauffenberg's driver, instructions for a possible escape, but he was quite calm now.[4] Hoepner should have been shot with the others and he now pleaded with Fromm, but Fromm shook his head. Then Hoepner asked for a private talk with Fromm and Fromm agreed; they both went into Stauffenberg's office. What was said there is not known but when Fromm emerged he ordered Hoepner to be kept under guard and said that he himself was going to Dr Goebbels.[5]

While Beck was trying to commit suicide Fromm had ordered his aide, Captain Bartram, to position a firing squad of ten men under an officer.[6] Bartram hurried down to the guardroom, on the way meeting Lieutenant-Colonel Gehrke and Lieutenant Schlee.[7] He passed Fromm's order for a firing squad on to Schlee, who detailed Second-Lieutenant Werner Schady and ten NCOs.[8] Schady reported to Fromm and was ordered to shoot the four condemned men and to escort Colonel-General Hoepner to the military prison in Lehrter Strasse. As Beck was still alive, Fromm ordered a staff officer to give him the *coup de grâce*. The officer ordered a member of the Guard Battalion to do it.[9]

As Haeften was going down the stairs the instinct of self-preservation asserted itself and he tried to tear himself free. But when the condemned men arrived in the courtyard where they were to be shot, he was calm and controlled again.[10]

One by one the officers were led in front of a heap of sandy earth excavated during construction work in the courtyard. Drivers of vehicles parked in the courtyard were instructed to position them so that their headlights would illuminate the scene. General Olbricht was shot first and then it was Stauffenberg's turn.[11] He shouted: 'Long live holy Germany.' The salvo rang out but Haeften had thrown himself in front of Stauffenberg and was shot first. Only the next salvo killed Stauffenberg. Then came Mertz von Quirnheim. It was about 12.30 a.m.[12]

Colonel-General Fromm then mounted a military vehicle and made a rousing speech to the soldiers, referring to the beloved *Führer* and to Providence. In conclusion he did not neglect to call for three thunderous 'Sieg Heils' to the *Führer*. Then he drove off to Goebbels.[13]

47 Arrests

At the same time as Beck, Hoepner, Stauffenberg, Olbricht, Mertz and Haeften a number of other officers and civilians were detained: Graf Yorck von Wartenburg, Graf von der Schulenburg, Graf Schwerin von Schwanenfeld, Berthold Graf von Stauffenberg, Lieutenant-Colonel Bernardis, Lieutenant-Colonel von der Lancken, Olbricht's aide (who was not in the secret and not involved) Captain Barnim von Ramin, and Dr Eugen Gerstenmaier.

Dr Otto John, without knowing it, narrowly escaped arrest and was able to disappear to Madrid on 24 July on a Lufthansa plane.[1] Major (*Luftwaffe*) Friedrich Georgi, Olbricht's son-in-law, was able to leave the building after it had been cordoned off by the Guard Battalion because he was sponsored by Olbricht and wore *Luftwaffe* uniform;[2] he was arrested later, however, as 'kith and kin'. Captain Klausing was equally able to escape sometime after 11.0 p.m. and before the arrival of the SD; so also was Lieutenant Ludwig Freiherr von Hammerstein who knew every nook and cranny of the building from childhood when his father was C-in-C of the Army and lived in the official apartment. Captain Hans Fritzsche attached himself to an elderly innocent-looking Austrian colonel of the *Wehrmacht* Propaganda Section, passed himself off as his aide and so got through.[3] Second-Lieutenant von Oppen got out by attaching himself to an SS officer whom he had treated very well while holding him under detention during the afternoon. Fritzsche and Oppen were nevertheless arrested later.[4] Second-Lieutenant Ewald Heinrich von Kleist, on the other hand, after returning to the Bendlerstrasse from his mission to the headquarters of the City Commandant and the police, made two unsuccessful attempts to escape, striking down an officer and then a soldier who was guarding him with fixed bayonet; searching for a window from which to jump, however, Kleist blundered into a room full of SS men.[5]

Gerstenmaier's impression was that those under arrest were to be shot immediately – and he was not alone in this.[6] A number of people – Yorck, Schulenburg, Schwerin, Berthold Graf Stauffenberg, Bernardis, Lancken and Gerstenmaier – were herded into Stauffenberg's office and held there at gunpoint; they had not, however, formally surrendered and they therefore burnt all available documents connected with the attempted *coup*. Some of them then attempted to break through the cordon into the passage but were finally taken prisoner. Dr Gerstenmaier was immediately handed over to an execution squad (at least this was his impression from the talk and orders he heard); at this moment, however, shortly after 12.30 a.m., an SS detachment moved into the building under command of *SS-Sturmbannführer* Otto Skorzeny (the man who had distinguished himself in September 1943 by the exploit of liberating Mussolini from captivity on the Gran Sasso).

When Remer's men had cordoned off the government quarter and the RSHA on orders from Lieutenant-General von Hase, the *Gestapo* had initiated defensive and counter-measures; these only really became effective, however, after 8.0 p.m. when government agencies in the city centre regained some freedom of movement with the change of allegiance by the Guard Battalion.

The RSHA had of course heard of the assassination attempt very early on and towards 2.0 p.m. a special detachment of the Sabotage Commission led by Kopkow, a criminal police counsellor (*Kriminalrat*) had been despatched to Rastenburg by air.[7] During the afternoon suspicion centred on Stauffenberg but, when Achamer-Pifrader was sent to the Bendlerstrasse, no one was yet thinking that a full-scale *putsch* was being organized there. Even though the truth must have been clear between 6.0 and 7.0 p.m. at the latest, some considerable time elapsed before energetic counter-measures were taken by the SS and RSHA. The SS units alerted by Jüttner remained at readiness and not until 6.45 p.m. did *SS-Gruppenführer* Müller order the RSHA to be prepared for defence; then a platoon of the RSHA Guard Company moved in together with a platoon from No 2 Tank Repair Company of the SS 'Leibstandarte Adolf Hitler' comprising fifty-one men.[8] It was between 10.0 and 11.0 p.m. before the troops available and their resources in weapons and ammunition could be considered adequate; one tank and one armoured scout car from the police only arrived after 1.0 a.m. on 21 July, when it no longer mattered. About 5.0 a.m. the majority of these precautions were rescinded by Himmler.[9] Whatever other motives may have played a part (and Himmler naturally would never have referred to them), the primary reasons for this dilatory action on the part of the SS were undoubtedly surprise and the fact that, with Remer's change of front, the *putsch* in Berlin had been suppressed by units from the Army itself. Himmler, of course, as the new C-in-C Replacement Army had command authority over both SS and Army units stationed in the *Reich*, and in a formal sense the issue of a confrontation between SS and Army could be seen as resolved by personal union. Undoubtedly also everyone wished to prevent fighting between SS and Army.[10]

SS-Brigadeführer Walter Schellenberg, head of Section VI (SD Foreign Intelligence Service) of the RSHA first heard of the events in Berlin late in the afternoon; he at once took Skorzeny off a train to Vienna. By 7.0 p.m. Skorzeny was back in the Berkaerstrasse and was given orders for countermeasures by Schellenberg.[11] He departed on fact-finding missions in Berlin, visiting both the SS 'Leibstandarte Adolf Hitler' and Student, the paratroop general. About midnight he was ordered to take an SS company to the Bendlerstrasse to reinforce Major Remer.[12]

Skorzeny turned into the Bendlerstrasse about 1.0 a.m. and there met *SS-Obergruppenführer* Kaltenbrunner, head of the RSHA and Colonel-General

Fromm; the latter was proposing to telephone to Hitler and, whatever happened, go to Goebbels, but he also said that he was now going home.[13] Major Remer was there and met Skorzeny at the outer gate. It was about half an hour after the executions when Skorzeny reached the first floor and was briefed by the leaders of the 'counter-movement'.[14]

For the moment there was no question of further executions; Skorzeny had neither authority nor cause to order them. He first had to take stock of the situation and he could not shoot people merely on some statement from some staff officer who might only have turned loyalist to cover himself. During his tour of inspection Skorzeny came across Kleist, handcuffed and waiting to be interrogated and removed. Skorzeny bowed slightly and introduced himself: 'Skorzeny.' Kleist rose, equally bowed slightly and said: 'Kleist.' Only then did Skorzeny notice the handcuffs; he murmured 'Oh' and turned away.[15] To add to the confusion Skorzeny had thought that the best method of reestablishing order in the place was to order everyone to return to their offices and resume the work interrupted during the afternoon. But the heads of the various departments were missing and in this situation no one was prepared to take responsibility of any kind. Skorzeny was therefore continually being asked for decisions on replacement and supply problems, of which he understood nothing.[16] Matters only began to calm down as Kaltenbrunner, General Reinecke, Lieutenant-General Thiele and finally *SS-Obergruppenführer* Jüttner, deputy to Himmler in his new capacity as C-in-C Replacement Army, arrived and gathered up the reins.

Meanwhile the bodies of the five dead leaders – Beck, Olbricht, Stauffenberg, Mertz and Haeften – were carried away on a truck and taken to the Matthäikirche cemetery in Schöneberg.[17] They were buried there that night, in their uniforms with full medals and decorations. The next day, however, Himmler had them exhumed, identified and cremated. The ashes were scattered in the open.[18]

Both despite and because of the general confusion in the Bendlerstrasse arrests were widespread; men who had nothing to do with the case were arrested and many of those involved remained undiscovered. A captain who had nothing to do with the affair at all was taken off to the *Gestapo* prison in the cellar of the RSHA building in the Prinz-Albrecht Strasse because he had telephoned to his wife during the night; there he met a number of the conspirators and present during some of the first interrogations. Not until four days later was he released with no reasons given; he returned to his office, where he was received with astonishment. When he was arrested his fellow-officers had studiously avoided his outstretched hand as he said goodbye.[19] In addition to those already mentioned the following were arrested that night or next day: Lieutenant-Colonel Sadrozinski, Fromm's Operations Officer, Major Freiherr von Leonrod and Captain Helmuth Cords.[20] Initially the interrogators hardly knew where to begin or to look, but as *SS-Obersturmbannführer* Georg Kiessel, head of the evaluation section in the special commission formed immediately after 20 July, said: 'The stalwart attitude of the idealists immediately shed some light on the matter . . . They did try to cover up for their comrades but for an experienced investigator it was easy to piece the story together.'[21] Prisons and concentration camps filled up.

In view of the large number of arrests connected with 20 July 1944 – Kiessel refers to 600 – it is not possible to give details even of the majority of names and circumstances. Moreover by no means all names of persons arrested or even those later executed are known. The purpose of this and the following chapter is therefore merely to give a survey of the consequences of the attempted *coup* for the resistance movement, of the extent and methods of its persecution.

Ironically Colonel-General Fromm, who had made up his mind to suppress the *coup* – after it had failed – was arrested almost simultaneously with the first conspirators. He had gone to Goebbels' house, where Lieutenant-General von Hase was already under detention, and was initially 'interned'.[22] Later Fromm was placed on trial for alleged cowardice.

In the City Commandant's headquarters at No 1 Unter den Linden Remer's men meanwhile tried simply to detain everybody present until the situation had been clarified; they were not invariably successful in face of the self-assured attitude of many of the officers.[23] Major Hayessen was arrested that night – and by one of his co-conspirators, Lieutenant-Colonel Schöne, who was arrested himself soon afterwards. Major Adolf-Friedrich Graf von Schack, one of the section heads, was also arrested; he had helped Hayessen burn papers under the eyes of Schöne who had made no effort to stop them.

In *Wehrkreis* headquarters on the Hohenzollerndamm the first to come under suspicion for complicity in the plot were Lieutenant-General von Thüngen and Major von Oertzen. Thüngen was able to leave without trouble that night; Major-General Herfurth, the Chief of Staff, too was not arrested at once. Oertzen, however, was detained and interrogated; he soon became involved in inconsistencies by trying to deny easily provable facts such as his posting to *Wehrkreis* III headquarters in the autumn of 1943.[24] He was first interrogated by General von Thüngen together with Colonel von Wiese, commander's assistant, on orders from General von Kortzfleisch who had returned to the headquarters about 11.0 p.m.; the results were submitted to Kortzfleisch who at first considered that Oertzen had only become involved in the *putsch* accidentally and unknowingly but that he must nevertheless be held in 'protective custody'. Colonel von Wiese told Oertzen that he was under arrest and removed his pistol. On the morning of 21 July Oertzen contrived, during a visit to the toilet, to burn and flush down certain incriminating documents; on the way back he hid two rifle grenades in a couple of sand buckets in the passage. About 10.0 a.m. Oertzen asked Second-Lieutenant Hentze, his escort, for permission to go to the toilet again and then to 'take a breath of fresh air' in the passage. Unnoticed he snatched up one of the grenades and detonated it close to his head; Hentze, who rushed up, was wounded. Oertzen himself collapsed severely wounded and was thought to be dead; a doctor was called and the area sealed off. Meanwhile Oertzen crawled the couple of yards to the next sand-bucket, took out the second grenade, placed it in his mouth and blew his head off. The officers standing around only just had time to take cover. Soon afterwards General von Kortzfleisch, the loyal Nazi, arrived. Major von Oertzen had died like a man, he said.

Field Marshal von Witzleben, after his second visit to General Wagner on the evening of 20 July, drove back to Seesen, Graf von Lynar's country house. He was arrested there on 21 July.[25]

At the same time arrests began of persons who had long been known as opponents of the regime even though there was still no proof that they were connected with concrete plans for a revolt. Among them were Dr Schacht, the ex-Minister of Economics, Colonel-General Halder, Popitz, Noske the ex-Minister, Major-General Oster and Admiral Canaris.[26] All were interrogated but initially without tangible result. At his first interrogation Witzleben denied all connection with the conspiracy.[27] He did not know how far it had already been given away by the action taken. No one should be reproached for attempting to save his own life and in this situation truthfulness might have imperilled not only himself but his co-conspirators. Witzleben was in fact far more realistic than many of the others. Later, and particularly before Freisler in the People's Court, he admitted quite frankly that he had been involved; he was composed and dignified despite the deliberately degrading external circumstances.

General Eduard Wagner soon realized that with the arrest of Witzleben, Fellgiebel, Stieff and others his turn would not be long in coming. He was highly incriminated, having been visited twice by Witzleben on 20 July and having provided Stauffenberg's aircraft. He shot himself in Zossen at 12.41 p.m. on 23 July.[28]

Equally during the first few days after the *coup* many arrests were made on the basis of the teleprinter messages appointing liaison officers and Political Representatives to the *Wehrkreise*. If not available in the Bendlerstrasse the messages could easily be discovered in the *Wehrkreis* HQs or other offices to which they had been directed either in error or by signal service personnel trying to sabotage the *coup*. Apart from these, however, no actual lists were found either in the Bendlerstrasse or elsewhere, as some stories have it; the *Gestapo* had to labour for weeks to reconstruct a government list, and even then it was incomplete. An important haul of documents from a safe in Zossen in September, including much material assembled by Hans von Dohnanyi, Hans Oster and Dietrich Bonhoeffer with details, among other things, of the 1938 preparations, did not assist the *Gestapo* much. Primarily this material only served to implicate further people who, according to Freisler's standards, were condemned already. The most compromising documents, reports on the soundings through the Vatican for instance, again were of little help since they had been dealt with through the *Abwehr* and were largely camouflaged as 'intelligence material'. In matters of espionage, where double agents are involved, it is in practice impossible to differentiate between actual treason and ostensible treason intended to deceive the enemy, unless it can subsequently be established what was actually 'betrayed' and this can very seldom be done since it postulates access to enemy records.[29] The 'intelligence material' available, however, could not possibly be used as evidence in court.

One of the first to be arrested in the *Führer*'s headquarters was General Erich Fellgiebel. As early as the afternoon of 20 July Högl, deputy head of the security service, had invited Fellgiebel to return from 'Mauerwald' to 'Wolfschanze'.[30] Stauffenberg was already under suspicion as the assassin and Fellgiebel's numerous contacts with Stauffenberg that day had been noticed. Fellgiebel had come to 'Wolfschanze' without any really valid reason; Lieutenant-Colonel Sander, the *Wehrmacht* signals officer there, had been extremely irritated because Fellgiebel had spent the entire morning in his office without wanting anything definite; Sander could not get on with his work and thought the behaviour of the General, who was usually so busy, to be most mysterious. During the evening the explanation became clear. After his second visit to 'Wolfschanze' in late afternoon Fellgiebel had returned to 'Mauerwald', but late in the evening he was summoned to 'Wolfschanze' once more, this time on orders from Field Marshal Keitel. The order was received by Sander who passed it on to Major Wolf, commander of the *Führer* Signals Detachment. Wolf called Hahn in 'Mauerwald' and asked to be connected with Fellgiebel, and Fellgiebel said: 'What's up, my friend?' When Wolf told him Keitel's order, Fellgiebel assured him: 'I'll be there in three quarters of an hour.'[31]

Fellgiebel now knew of course that he was under suspicion; this would have been the moment for him to escape, in one way or another, from the fearful fate which awaited him. Few of the conspirators, however, were prepared for Hitler's sadistic cruelty; it was generally assumed that those convicted of treason would at least be thought worthy of a bullet. Many could not conceive that a German government would allow senior officers and officials of the Army and the *Reich* to be barbarously tortured and finally hanged – their juniors knew better the depths to which the powers that be could fall. When Lieutenant Arntz, Fellgiebel's aide, asked 'his General' whether he had a pistol, Fellgiebel replied: 'One stands, one does not do that.'[32] He did not wish to miss the opportunity of telling his interrogators to their face – how could they be other than officers of a court martial – the truth that the *Reich* was led by criminals. So he went unresistingly back to 'Wolfschanze', where he was arrested. As he left he said to Arntz: 'If I believed in another world, I would say *"Auf Wiedersehen"*.'[33] Fellgiebel's driver came back to 'Mauerwald' alone and in tears.

The mere fact that Colonel Hahn, Fellgiebel's Chief of Staff in East Prussia, was not arrested until 12 August speaks volumes for the fortitude of the General. In the French resistance it was taken for granted that anyone caught by the Germans could not be expected to conceal the truth for more than twenty-four hours; they knew the *Gestapo*'s methods;[34] in twenty-four hours all tracks must have been covered and all compromised persons have vanished. Fellgiebel was terribly tortured but for at least three weeks he did not reveal the names of any of his co-conspirators, though he was perfectly truthful and frank about his own role. Naturally, whether he had lied or not, no one would have believed that he alone was responsible for all the measures connected with the communications blackout; clearly his immediate subordinates, Hahn, Thiele and Hassel, had not been acting as mere recipients of orders. By interrogating other conspirators, particularly Lieutenant-Colonel Bernhard Klamroth, the *Gestapo* tracked down the preparatory discussions. The scope of the signals preparations made began to emerge in hazy outline.[35]

Soon after 20 July Lieutenant-General Thiele came to 'Mauerwald' as Fellgiebel's successor. On assuming office he made a speech which most of his audience found repulsive, mendacious and undignified; General Fellgiebel, whom he had so much respected, he described as a blot on the German Army and the Signal Corps.[36] Most of his staff then shunned him; he was generally nervous, irritable and prone to outbursts of rage; he thought that he was generally suspected which must have contributed to his own detection. When arrested on 11 August, however, one day before Hahn, he seems to have regained his composure; many other conspirators in the Signal Corps – Burchardt, Degner, Arntz, Höpfner, Hassel, Köllner, to mention only the more important – remained relatively unmolested. Many of them – Lieutenant-Colonel Hassel for instance — were arrested, detained and ill-treated but none of them were brought to trial. General Albert Praun, Thiele's successor appointed on 12 August by Colonel-General Guderian, the new Chief of Staff of the Army, immediately remonstrated with Kaltenbrunner against further arrests and persecution of Signal Corps personnel; he could not work and keep communications functioning, he said, if members of his staff were continually being removed and accused. On 13 August, the day after Praun's appointment, Lieutenant-Colonel von der Osten, commander of the Signals Intelligence Centre in Lötzen, committed suicide.[37] Kaltenbrunner referred Praun to Müller, head of the *Gestapo*, who said that Osten's suicide was 'unnecessary' since there was no proof against him. There was no intention, Müller said, to investigate other members of Praun's staff.

A halt had to be called because the experts were required, but this was not the only reason, let it be emphasized. Many members of the staff owe their lives to Fellgiebel's prudent habit of telling people only the minimum they needed to know, to the fortitude of those under arrest and not least to the circumspection of other officers such as Lieutenant-Colonel Sander, Lieutenant-Colonel John von Freyend and Major von Szymonski.

Another arrested in East Prussia during the first few hours was Major-General Stieff, head of the Organization Section of the Army General Staff; he was detained in 'Mauerwald' around midnight.[38] Once again the *Gestapo* was assisted by the astonishing frankness with which senior officers in particular were prepared to make statements; as Guderian put it to General Praun, Fellgiebel's and Thiele's successor: 'As officers they were accustomed to giving evidence to courts of honour composed of men of their own profession, not *Gestapo* investigators.'[39] As early as 22 July Stieff's interrogation revealed that he had discussed the assassination of Hitler with Lieutenant-General Heusinger, General Wagner and General Lindemann.[40] Even so it was another six days, during which Stieff was certainly tortured, before he gave away details of the preparations. A *Gestapo* report to Bormann, dated 28 July, says: 'The confession eventually made by Major-General Stieff together with the interrogations of Schulenburg and various others [provide] *important information.*' In all this, however, Stieff implicated primarily only himself and others already dead.[41]

By 25 July the *Gestapo* was fairly well informed about procurement of the explosive and had evidence of the parts played by Stieff, Oertzen, Lieutenant Albrecht von Hagen, Lieutenant-Colonel Klamroth and Major Kuhn; all apart from Oertzen and Kuhn were already under arrest (Kuhn escaped by deserting to the Red Army).[42] The others involved now had to reckon with their arrest: Lieutenant-Colonel Werner Schrader committed suicide on 28 July in his quarters in Zossen, leaving a note on his table: 'I will not go to prison; I will not let them torture me.'[43] Colonel Wessel Freiherr von Freytag-Loringhoven, head of the Army Affairs Section in OKH, had already committed suicide on 23 July.[44] It was late July or early August, however, before the *Gestapo* could list any considerable number of fresh names; here they were helped by the discovery of Captain Hermann Kaiser's diary with its easily decipherable cover names; the suicides referred to above also provided clues.[45]

For weeks investigations were confined to a relatively restricted circle. Eventually, however, progress was made as a result of the intensive evaluation of information already available, hauls of documents and finally the statements of Dr Goerdeler who was arrested on 12 August having been on the run for weeks.[46] Under interrogation Goerdeler made 'extraordinarily *far-reaching statements*'. Gerhard Ritter, Goerdeler's biographer, is convinced that this was not done under torture or to save his own life or even to inundate the *Gestapo* with so much material that they would be overtaken by the end of the war before they could deal with it. Goerdeler's motive was simply to reveal the truth. He wanted the *Gestapo*, and through it the Nazi regime, to know precisely the nature and scope of the opposition. He was still hoping that Hitler could be persuaded to reverse his policy or that he himself might have an interview with Hitler or Himmler and so convince them. The accuracy of detail provided by Goerdeler nevertheless prevented the *Gestapo* realizing how much dust was being thrown in their eyes, in the same way as the detailed description of events in the Bendlerstrasse signal centre given in the Army Signals report in fact obscured the truth.[47] Many of Goerdeler's friends escaped the *Gestapo* altogether and for this he was partially responsible since he knew where they might be found and of course the extent to which they had been involved in the conspiracy. This was true in the cases of Jakob Kaiser, Dr Elfriede Nebgen, Hans Walz and Ernst Lemmer.

There was no direct connection between the 20 July investigations and the mass arrests of 22 August 1944 when some 5,000 ex-parliamentary deputies and officials of the old political parties (including Konrad Adenauer and Kurt Schumacher) were taken into custody in a synchronized operation throughout the *Reich* and thrown into concentration camps; this had been planned long before by the *Gestapo*.[48] It is worth mentioning, however, as an indirect sequel to 20 July both because of the size of the operation and because it later influenced estimates of the number of arrests made. It is also a sign of perplexity on the part of the *Gestapo*.

Even so prominent a fugitive as General Fritz Lindemann was only arrested in Berlin on 3 September after weeks of investigation. He tried to jump out of a third-floor window but was shot in the legs and stomach by the police. He was immediately operated on so that he might be brought to trial but died of his wounds on 21 September.[49] Five of those who had helped him while on the run or had kept him hidden at various times between 22 July and 3 September, however, were condemned to death by the People's Court on 27 November and 1 December respectively.[50] Two of them were 'Jewish half-castes first grade' and another the widow of a Jew, so in great danger anyway; all could be carted off to a death camp any day and in addition they had already hidden another fugitive. Now they lodged General Lindemann, passing him off as a retired major and journalist by the name of Exner. They were not in the least deterred when, in mid-August, a reward of 500,000 marks was offered for information leading to Lindemann's arrest.

Arthur Nebe, head of the *Reich* Criminal Police Office, succeeded in escaping his pursuers for a long time thanks to his policeman's expertise and the readiness of friends to help him.[51] At first he pretended to cooperate industriously in uncovering the conspiracy, but when Graf von Helldorf was arrested on 24 July, he had to take to his heels.[52] He then pretended suicide, leaving behind farewell notes and valuables such as food and passes which no living person could be assumed to have relinquished; he reappeared under a false name and with dyed hair and was sheltered by friends until his arrest on 16 January 1945. Dr Gisevius, who had gone to ground at the same time as Nebe, was able to escape into Switzerland on 23 January 1945, using forged papers.[53]

In the *Wehrkreise* and the occupied territories arrests remained at a comparatively low level bearing little relation to the actual scope of the conspiracy. In Vienna Schirach, the *Gauleiter*, personally tore the Golden Party Badge from the tunic of General Sinzinger, the City Commandant, because he had carried out the orders from Berlin and arrested members of the SS.[54] Colonel Kodré, Chief of Staff in *Wehrkreis* HQ, was several times arrested by the *Gestapo* and only liberated from Mauthausen concentration camp at the end of the war.[55] General von Esebeck suffered a similar fate and of course the Political Representatives and numerous Austrian nationalist politicians, who had long been suspect, were arrested. In other *Wehrkreise* too officers were arrested, whether in the secret or not, for attempting to carry out the orders from Berlin. Hardly one was executed, however.

Even in the staffs of the Military Commander Belgium and Northern France and the Military Commander France arrests and persecution were kept within comparatively restricted limits. General Freiherr von Falkenhausen was arrested on 29 July; his Chief of Staff, Colonel Bodo von Harbou committed suicide in his cell after arrest.[56] In Paris, on the collapse of the revolt, both its leaders and its SS and SD victims agreed to present the whole thing to the outside world as an exercise and internally as a misunderstanding. Oberg, the Senior SS and Police Commander, Knochen, head of the SD, and General Blumentritt, Chief of Staff to C-in-C West, agreed on a 'formula' for their reports to higher authority.[57] There was considerable community of interest – the officers had carried out Berlin's orders with enthusiasm, the SS men, who thought them 'genuine', had complied almost without resistance. Otherwise arrests in France would have been far more widespread.

General von Stülpnagel, the Military Commander France, who had been dismissed by Field Marshal von Kluge during the night 20–21 July, obviously could not be reinstated. He was far too compromised and formal investigation in his case was unavoidable. General Blumentritt attempted to cover Stülpnagel and justify his actions on 20 July but Kluge, who was only too eager to dissociate himself from the *coup*, had already reported on Stülpnagel to OKW. On the morning of 21 July Stülpnagel was ordered to report to Berlin. Meanwhile Lieutenant-Colonel von Hofacker, Dr Horst, Dr Teuchert and Dr Thierfelder destroyed all documentary evidence of the *coup* and warned others involved.[58]

Stülpnagel decided to go to Berlin by road. On the old Meuse battlefield north of Verdun he ordered his driver to stop and sent the car on. He walked down to the Meuse canal and shot himself through the head but without killing himself. Hearing the shot his escort turned back, found him floating in the canal and took him to a hospital in Verdun. He was operated on that night and, though his life was saved, he was blind. Those accompanying him first thought that he had been attacked by French partisans but it was soon clear that this was a suicide attempt; it could only be regarded as an admission of guilt and so the search for others involved began. Since Kluge's report to OKW no one believed the story of a 'misunderstanding' any more.[59]

One of Stülpnagel's drivers was interrogated for hours during the night 22–23 July and he admitted that in the Military Commander's headquarters the 'partisan attack' was thought to be attempted suicide; Colonel von Linstow had besought him to stick to the 'partisan attack' version, saying 'We owe that to our General.'[60] In view of his instructions from the RSHA and events since 20 July, Oberg could no longer remain inactive and pretend that there were no grounds for suspicion. On 23 July Linstow was interrogated, placed under house arrest and arrested on 27 July. Hofacker was arrested on 25 July. Others arrested were Colonel Finckh, the deputy chief of staff, Captain Dr Gotthard Freiherr von Falkenhausen of the economics staff, Dr Ernst Röchling of Military Administration, *Geheimrat* Kreuter and Freiherr von der Osten-Sacken.[61] Then the wave of arrests in France subsided. General Blumentritt remained and for a time Field Marshal von Kluge, although he was immediately under suspicion. Boineburg-Lengsfeld, the City Commandant, and Major-General Brehmer were posted away. Colonel von Kraewel was left in peace.[62]

The shadows of investigation were lengthening, however, and the battle in France, Kluge thought, seemed likely to cost him his reputation as a soldier. So on 15 August the Field Marshal drove into the Falaise pocket presumably to seek death. On the way he was held up for a long time by fighter-bomber attacks and he lost his radio truck; he was out of touch for several hours and could not be contacted from OKW; by the evening Hitler was convinced that he had deserted to the enemy. Without waiting further Hitler appointed Field Marshal Model to succeed Kluge as C-in-C West. Kluge returned to his command post but was not told of the change of command until an hour before Model's arrival on 17 August. On 19 August Kluge drove off in the direction of Germany but during a halt near the old World War I battlefields he took cyanide.[63]

Six months from the start of their investigations the *Gestapo* still had nothing like precise knowledge of the resistance movement, as the reports of the '20 July Special Commission' show.[64] The investigations were pursued with energy and only really lost momentum in the closing months of the war, partly owing to the disorganization resulting from air raids and moves of offices, partly because, with the end of the war approaching, many *Gestapo* men had no wish to compromise themselves further; this did not necessarily mean any relaxation of effort, however – rather the reverse since in the final days it became all the more necessary to eliminate people already in jails or under investigation who might have unpleasant stories to tell.

This lack of information and knowledge is all the more astounding in that Himmler's men employed every means to extract confessions. Their failure can only partially be ascribed to the limited intelligence of the *Gestapo* officials; it was largely due to the fortitude of their victims. Such prominent conspirators, for instance, as Captain Freiherr von dem Bussche, Captain von Breitenbuch, Major-General Freiherr von Gersdorff, General Lanz and Colonel Graf von Strachwitz were never arrested though many of those under arrest and later executed knew all about their part in the affair. Moreover all forms of torture were used without hesitation.

On the other hand many of the conspirators might have escaped with false papers, gone to ground or hidden with friends; many doors would have been open to them. The experiences of General Fritz Lindemann are an illustration; they also illustrate the fate of those who gave help. The majority of those on the run refused to imperil their friends. Many simply waited to be arrested; Ulrich von Hassell, for instance, wandered about the streets of Berlin for weeks and finally sat at his own desk waiting for the thugs to come.[65]

But this was not all. Under the devilish Nazi tyranny the system of 'kith and kin' arrest had been introduced and invested with the sanctity of ancient Germanic custom; inhuman though it was, at least it clarified the situation from the opposition's point of view. In a speech to *Gauleiter* on 3 August 1944 Himmler said: 'When they [the people's Germanic forbears] put a family under the ban and declared it outlawed or when there was a vendetta in the family, they were totally consistent about it. If the family was outlawed or banned, they said: "This man has committed treason; there is traitor blood there; it will be exterminated." And in a vendetta they exterminated the entire clan down to its last member. The Stauffenberg family will be exterminated down to its last member.'[66]

'Kith and kin' arrest was a method, not only of torture but of ideologically cloaked revenge. The entire 'Stauffenberg traitor clan' was to be 'rendered harmless'. Accordingly there were arrested: the wives of Claus and Berthold von Stauffenberg, their brother Professor Alexander Graf von Stauffenberg, cousins, uncles and aunts, even numerous relatives by marriage only, little children and old men – the eighty-five-year-old father of a cousin of Stauffenberg's, for instance, his mother, his mother-in-law Freifrau von Lerchenfeld and many other relatives and acquaintances.[67] Similarly all available members of the families of Goerdeler, Lehndorff, Schwerin von Schwanenfeld, Tresckow, Seydlitz, Hagen, Freytag-Loringhoven, Hase, Lindemann, Bernardis, Hansen, Hofacker, Finckh, Yorck von Wartenburg, Moltke, Hoepner, Oster, Dohnanyi, Bonhoeffer, Haushofer, Trott zu Solz, Leber, Leuschner, Jakob Kaiser, Hammerstein, Popitz, Harnack, Kleist, Haeften, Haubach and Schulenburg were arrested – to name only a few. There were no definite criteria for 'kith and kin' arrest; it was done on a 'case by case' basis, in other words arbitrarily; Himmler had explicitly refused to lay down any principles.[68]

The prisoners were carted, sometimes in cattle trucks, from prison to prison and concentration camp to concentration camp. Notorious camps such as Stutthof, Lauenburg, Buchenwald, Sachsenhausen and Dachau were among the stations on this unmerited *via dolorosa*. At the end of the war many of them were in the famous 'VIP column' which left Dachau for the Tyrol; as American troops approached they were all to be shot by the SS, but on orders from Colonel-General Heinrich von Vietinghoff, C-in-C South-West, men of the Army disarmed the SS guards and liberated the prisoners.[69]

Not only the perpetrator of the deed, whether accomplished or attempted, was therefore to be persecuted and punished, but also the spirit of the deed. The spirit of patriotism, humanity, peace and justice was to be rooted out at the same time. Not merely individuals, therefore, but their 'kith and kin', their families in which the spirit of freedom and resistance to injustice and arbitrary action had grown and been nurtured, were to be exterminated. To achieve this object even approximately, the regime would have had to destroy complete strata of society. So radical a social revolution had frequently been envisaged by Hitler but he had invariably postponed it in favour of shorter-term aims, in particular satisfaction of his desire for war; tugs and pulls within the Party had helped to stop it and finally total war made any such profound disruption of the structure of the state impossible. The Nazis found it impossible to be as consistent as they wished.

'Kith and kin' arrest was a particularly sophisticated form of torture. When interrogating suspects the *Gestapo* could, quite legally, threaten to ill-treat their wives, children, parents, brothers and sisters or other relatives. No one can appreciate the fortitude required under these conditions to refuse to give information or conceal knowledge. Not all those arrested managed to say just enough to make the *Gestapo* believe them and – perhaps – protect their families but not enough to betray or incriminate someone still alive about whom the *Gestapo* did not already know.

There were other kinds of torture too. They were entirely official and no amount of lying to post-war courts by *Gestapo* officials could alter that fact; they were known as 'intensified interrogation'. People felt somewhat shame-faced about it, however, and suffered from twinges of conscience. As early as 28 May 1936 Reinhard Heydrich, then head of the 'Prussian Secret State Police', wrote to all heads of offices to 'point out that application of intensified interrogation methods may in no case be officially recorded'.[70] Even in 1941 there was no wish to carry things too far; in a further circular to heads of offices Heydrich reminded his subordinates that certain regulations must be observed. Intensified interrogation might only be applied without special per-mission to 'communist or marxist functionaries, Jehovah's Witnesses and saboteurs'.[71] 'If an intensified interrogation should be justifiable and required [!] in other particularly important cases', Heydrich's specific permission had to be requested, though not for Poles or Russians. On 12 June 1942, however, Heinrich Müller, Chief of the Security Police and SD, 'for simplicity's sake' informed the relevant officials of a revision of a decree dated 1 July 1937 con-cerning intensified interrogation: intensified interrogation might only be employed if it had been established that the prisoner *could* give information about 'important facts concerning hostility to the state and nation' but was not *willing* to do so.[72] Even then persons to whom intensified interrogation might be applied without special permission were limited to 'communists, marxists, Jehovah's Witnesses, saboteurs, terrorists, members of resistance movements [in the occupied territories], parachute agents, anti-socials, Polish or Soviet Russian malingerers and lay-abouts'. Exceptions were allowed with special permission and the same applied as follows: 'Intensified interrogation may not be used to extract confessions of deeds done by the person concerned ... Exceptions require my previous permission.'

Müller's circular also gave some indication of methods to be employed: 'the most modest food (bread and water), hard bed, dark cell, deprivation of sleep, fatiguing exercises' could be terrible tortures. Imagine a man being forcibly deprived of sleep for days and nights at a stretch or compelled to stand motionless (fatiguing exercise). 'Administration of blows with a stick' was also included; for more than twenty strokes a doctor had to be summoned – but who was counting and who checked on the interrogators? The post-war concentration camp trials, moreover, showed what some doctors were prepared to do.

Once one knows these official regulations, many a peculiar phrase in the reports on interrogations and investigations made to Hitler and Bormann by the '20 July Special Commission' become comprehensible. When it says, for instance, that 'only after a pause of several days did Schlabrendorff reveal...' it is easy to guess what happened during the pause. In fact Fabian von Schlabrendorff was so severely tortured that he was ultimately forced to aban-don his initial policy of total silence and make statements implicating himself and others already dead. Only in this way, he thought, could he avoid tortures during which he might lose control of himself and his tongue. The *Gestapo* had discovered that there had been contacts between Schlabrendorff and Graf von Lehndorff, earmarked as liaison officer for *Wehrkreis* I; Lehndorff could not deny that Schlabrendorff and Tresckow, recognized as one of the leading conspirators in September 1944 (he had taken his own life on the eastern front on 21 July 1944) had cooperated closely and Schlabrendorff had been arrested on 17 August. Not until 18 September, however, could the Commission report that he had said anything.[73] Meanwhile Schlabrendorff had been tortured; on several occasions his fellow-prisoners in the Prinz-Albrecht-Strasse had seen him carried back to his cell unconscious after an 'interrogation'. The case of Fabian von Schlabrendorff provides a particularly good example because, even before the end of the Third *Reich*, the tortures to which he had been subjected had been documented in the People's Court and the *Gestapo* officials concerned could not deny them either at the time or later.[74]

In the first stage Schlabrendorff's hands were tied behind his back and his fingers encased in a contraption in which spikes penetrated into the finger-tips; with the turning of a screw they penetrated deeper. When this produced no answer the prisoner was strapped down on a sort of bedstead and his legs encased in tubes covered on the inside with sharp metal spikes; the tubes were slowly drawn tighter so that the spikes gradually penetrated deeper into the flesh. During this process his head was pushed into a sort of metal hood and covered with a blanket to muffle his screams. Meanwhile he was belaboured with bamboo canes and leather switches. In the third stage, using the same bedstead, his body was stretched either violently and in jerks or gradually. If he lost consciousness he was revived with douches of cold water. These tortures had still extracted no confession from Schlabrendorff and so another method was tried. He was trussed up, bent forwards so that he could move neither backwards nor sideways and was then beaten from behind with a heavy club; with each blow he fell forward on his face with his full weight. All these tortures were applied to Schlabrendorff on the same day but the only result was that he lost consciousness. The next day he had a heart attack and could not move for several days. As soon as he had recovered, however, the tortures were repeated. Finally Schlabrendorff decided to say something: he knew that Tresckow had frequently spoken of removing Hitler either with or without force and that he had been particularly busy just before 20 July; he had sent Major von Oertzen to Berlin but he, Schlabrendorff, knew no more than that. This seemed temporarily to satisfy the *Gestapo*; it was enough to prove complicity. Schlabrendorff was left in peace for a time.

Many others were equally beaten and tortured, the majority by notorious thugs such as *Kriminalkommissar* Stawizki of the '*Lange* Squad' attached to the '20 July Special Commission'. Admiral Canaris was bound hand and foot and tortured by brilliant permanently-lit lights with his cell door permanently open; General Fellgiebel, Dr Walter Bauer, Dr Carl Langbehn, Graf von Bismarck, Walter Cramer, Erwin Planck the ex-State Secretary, and Dr Eugen Gerstenmaier (to name only a few) were all severely beaten, ill-treated and tortured.[75] During Dr Walter Bauer's interrogations, *Gestapo* officials made sham telephone calls ordering the arrest of his wife, children, father, and of his brothers and sisters. When he was being beaten to a pulp by the *Gestapo* thugs, phonograph records with children's songs were played at full volume to drown out the screams of the tortured man. Finally, Dr Bauer was stretched over a chair and beaten with a rubber truncheon until he fell to the ground and agreed to sign a confession to the effect that he had been involved in the preparation of the *coup*. He revoked his confession after a few days, as soon as he had recovered a little. In at least one case – that of Adam von Trott zu Solz – execution of the death sentence was postponed in order to extract further information: 'Since Trott has undoubtedly withheld a great deal, the death sentence pronounced by the People's Court has not been carried out so that Trott may be available for further clarification'.[76]

In the light of such horrors and the number of persons arrested it is both astonishing and admirable that these prisoner patriots were able to save the lives of so many of those involved by their suffering, their silence and their deception of the *Gestapo*. The opposition had collapsed; no more could be done against the regime; the entire enterprise had been a failure. Under these circumstances their resistance can only be explained by reference to the sources from which resistance to Nazism and Hitler's government had drawn its strength from the outset – the sense of ethical obligation to fight injustice, crime and destruction even at the price of one's own life.

48 People's Court, Executions, Concentration Camps

The 'People's Court' was set up in 1934 to give practical expression to the 'sound sense of the people' (*gesundes Volksempfinden*) against enemies of 'the community' (*Volksgemeinschaft*).[1] In fact every aspect of it was dubious: the stated intention; the assumption that the sense of the people was indeed sound and that the court's sentences would reflect this 'sense'; the claim that those brought before it, even if found 'guilty', were in fact enemies of the 'community'. The truth was that from the outset the People's Court was intended as an instrument of political domination by the Nazi government, an instrument of 'National-Socialist law' which flew in the face of all humanist liberal principles and traditions of justice; it was an instrument of terror designed for suppression of any form of opposition. Long before 20 July 1944 the judgements of this court had frequently been shown to be arbitrary and contrary to existing statute law. In many cases sentences were decided before the trial had even begun; they could be quashed or commuted by the government as it saw fit.

On 11 August 1944 Dr Sonnenhol, a vice-consul, informed the head of 'Inland II' in the Foreign Ministry, in writing as follows: 'At today's meeting with *SS-Oberführer* Panzinger[2] the following emerged: 1. von Trott zu Solz will be condemned to death at the next session of the People's Court, probably on Tuesday or Wednesday of next week.'[3]

On 22 December 1942 *SS-Gruppenführer* Heinrich Müller, head of *Amt IV* (*Gestapo*) in the RSHA, wrote to Himmler to say that he had been informed by General Staff Judge Lehmann (*Generalstabsrichter*) in OKW, that the sentences passed on members of the Schulze-Boysen group ('Red Orchestra') had been confirmed by the *Führer* but that 'the *Führer* has not confirmed the sentences on Frau Harnack and Gräfin Brockdorff [six and ten years hard labour respectively]; the *Führer* has decided instead that both sentences be reviewed by another chamber'.[4] The two women were duly sentenced to death and hanged.

According to current procedure, moreover, from September 1939 criminal cases in which one or more persons subject to the 'general judiciary' (non-military courts) were involved together with one or more persons subject to

Wehrmacht jurisdiction, could be brought before courts of the 'general judiciary' and in current terminology this included the People's Court which in the framework of a constitutional state (*Rechtsstaat*) should have been classified as a special court.[5] The 20 July conspiracy naturally was subject to this provision. The relevant law explicitly laid down that criminal cases falling within the competence of the *Reich* Court Martial might, under such circumstances, 'be transferred to the People's Court by agreement between the Chief of OKW and the *Reich* Minister of Justice for consolidation [of the civil and military judiciary process]'. To make doubly sure the law also included the following: 'The *Führer* and Supreme Commander of the *Wehrmacht* can order a retrial even if a sentence has become legally final', that is *after* all possibilities for appeal had been exhausted. This was known as the '*Führer* principle'. In some mystic fashion the *Führer* personified the vital interests, the spirit and the legal system of the people, or so it was said. In fact this was sheer arbitrary rule with a superficial cloak of 'legal' regulations. In September 1944 the competence of the 'general judiciary' was extended to cover political misdemeanours committed by soldiers;[6] the purpose of this was to further, not the interests of justice but of closer control over the *Wehrmacht* which had hitherto preserved a certain independence.

Nevertheless the procedure was still complicated and a number of legal barriers had to be surmounted owing to the independent competence of the *Wehrmacht* courts, limited though that was; it was therefore thought preferable to transfer those of the 20 July suspects who were amenable to military justice, formally and individually to the jurisdiction of the 'general judiciary', in other words of the People's Court. For this purpose a 'court of honour' was constituted to propose to the *Führer* expulsion of the suspects from the *Wehrmacht* – without a hearing, without formal evidence, without a finding, merely on the basis of the *Gestapo*'s report on the results of their investigations. This seemed a practical solution seeing that proof of collusion with civilians could not invariably be brought and the first trials were required to take place very quickly to produce maximum propaganda effect. Members of the 'court of honour' were Field Marshal Keitel, Colonel-General Guderian and General Walter Schroth, later also General Karl-Wilhelm Specht and Lieutenant-General Heinrich Kirchheim representing Guderian, with Field Marshal von Rundstedt as President. Major-General Ernst Maisel and Lieutenant-General Wilhelm Burgdorf were also present at the sessions.[7]

The trial before the People's Court of the first group of conspirators took place on 7 and 8 August in the Great Hall of the Berlin Supreme Court with Dr Roland Freisler presiding. He wore a blood-red robe; great swastika flags hung down the walls; the carefully selected 'public' was mostly in the uniforms of the *Wehrmacht*, the SS, the SA or the police. This was to be a show trial to be used for Dr Goebbels' propaganda and to satisfy the *Führer*'s thirst for revenge. Behind the flags sound-track film cameras were concealed, set in motion on a signal from Freisler who conducted the proceedings almost single-handed. Whenever he gave the signal Freisler would start shouting and screaming at the accused in outrageous, frequently obscene language designed to break them down psychologically and present them as miserable, morally worthless criminals actuated by base motives.[8]

The propaganda purpose was not achieved and only excerpts from the films were later shown to the public. Even these selected extracts had the opposite effect to that intended. All the accused behaved like upright courageous men; their statements put the regime in the dock. Their quiet dignity, accentuated by their sufferings in captivity, merely underlined the contrast with their screaming, gesticulating, undignified judge.

The first trial was that of Field Marshal von Witzleben, Colonel-General Hoepner, Major-General Stieff, Lieutenant von Hagen, Lieutenant-General von Hase, Lieutenant-Colonel Bernardis, Captain Klausing and Lieutenant Graf Yorck von Wartenburg. Witzleben in particular answered Freisler fearlessly and was never at a loss but the others too showed themselves courageous and remained unimpressed by Freisler's bellowing. Witzleben's braces had been removed and Hoepner appeared in court in a cardigan. Even Freisler found this embarrassing and during the lunch-break he ordered that they be allowed to appear more decently dressed.[9] Despite strict security precautions, with so large an audience details of the proceedings inevitably leaked out; Freisler therefore on occasions attempted to ensure that only authorized persons were present.[10] It became known, however, that Witzleben had said to Freisler: 'You can hand us over to the executioner but in three months' time this outraged and suffering people will call you to account and drag you alive through the mud of the streets.'[11]

Freisler attempted, usually with success, to prevent the accused telling of their motives. Stieff made several efforts to do so but each time Freisler cut him short. Nevertheless many of those in the dock did contrive to say briefly why and to what purpose they had acted. Fritz-Dietlof Graf von der Schulenburg said: 'We have accepted the necessity to do our deed in order to save Germany from untold misery. I expect to be hanged for this, but I do not regret my action and I hope that someone else in luckier circumstances will succeed.'[12] Schwerin von Schwanenfeld had referred to 'the numerous murders in Poland' before Freisler could interrupt him.[13] Stieff said that he had acted 'for Germany'.[14] Yorck said: 'The vital point running through all these questions is the totalitarian claim of the state over the citizen to the exclusion of his religious and moral obligation towards God.'[15] Throughout the proceedings Yorck was particularly fearless and steadfast.[16] Hans-Bernd von Haeften said: 'My conception of the *Führer*'s role in world history is that he is a great perpetrator of evil.'[17]

Josef Wirmer the lawyer, who knew that he had no hope of saving his life, hurled at Freisler: 'If I am hanged, the fear will be yours, not mine' and when Freisler scoffed at him: 'You'll be in hell soon,' Wirmer shot back: 'It will be a pleasure if you follow me there quickly, Mr President.'[18] Ulrich von Hassell seemed to be the prosecutor rather than the accused when before the court; Hermann Maass, who had twice been interrupted by Freisler's shouting, demonstrated his contempt by refusing to plead; Fritz-Dietlof Graf von der Schulenburg poured all his sarcasm on Freisler and General Fellgiebel told him to hurry up with the hangings or he, Freisler, would hang before the accused.[19] Freisler's conduct of the proceedings became so undignified that even the official Nazi observers and Thierack, the Minister of Justice, complained to Bormann about him.[20]

The trials continued into the closing weeks of the war and at this period, when nothing could any longer conceal the collapse of the regime and its military defeat, Hitler's rage and arbitrariness knew no bounds. Only rarely and unpredictably did some court official dare to procrastinate with a case and so save someone's life – by placing the file at the bottom of the pile, for instance – and even this generally cost the life of someone else.[21]

Fabian von Schlabrendorff was brought before the People's Court with other defendants on 21 December 1944; the court was overloaded, however, and the cases of Dr Andreas Hermes, the ex-Minister, Dr Franz Kempner, the ex-State Secretary, Schlabrendorff and Colonel Wilhelm Staehle did not come up that day.[22] Schlabrendorff's trial was re-scheduled for 3 February 1945 but, as it was about to begin, the air raid sirens sounded; both the court and the accused took refuge in the cellars. During the air raid a direct hit was scored on the People's Court; the ceiling of the cellar fell in and a beam struck Freisler (he died in hospital). Schlabrendorff's defence counsel subsequently told him that Freisler still had the papers on the case in his hand.[23] A new date was set – 16 March 1945. Schlabrendorff succeeded in giving a detailed description of the tortures to which he had been subjected and in pointing out that Frederick the Great had abolished torture in Prussia two hundred years before; this was not contested by the *Gestapo* and so the court, under the presidency of Dr Crohne, acquitted him and released him from arrest. As he emerged he was again apprehended by the *Gestapo*. A few days later he was told that the decision of the People's Court was obviously wrong and he would now be shot instead of hanged; he had to give a signed acknowledgement of this information. After another few days he was taken, with other prisoners, to Flossenbürg where he was to be shot after Canaris, Dohnanyi, Oster, Bonhoeffer and others had been executed. His life was saved by the evacuation of the camp in face of the advancing Americans. He was taken with the other prisoners to Dachau and thence to South Tyrol where he was liberated.[24]

Colonel-General Fromm was not brought to trial until March 1945. He was accused of violating court martial regulations because he had had the leaders of the conspiracy shot during the night 20–21 July, but he was condemned for cowardice. Dr Hopf, the official observer, however, wrote to Bormann that, although the presiding judge had fortunately not stumbled over this question, the case against Fromm was in fact a very shaky one; it was not impossible that Fromm had remained inactive, not from cowardice but from sympathy with the conspirators and to ensure that he was on the right side should the rising succeed. If the court had accepted this, however, it would have had to condemn Fromm for treason.[25]

Hitler himself had prescribed hanging as the method of execution of the conspirators; until 1942 beheading had been the normal method and this was used again later in 1944 (before 20 July 1944 condemned soldiers were usually shot). Witzleben, Hoepner, Stieff, Hagen, Hase, Bernardis, Klausing and Yorck, the first eight defendants of 7 and 8 August, were hanged on the afternoon of 8 August in Plötzensee prison in the presence of Dr Hanssen, the Public Prosecutor. All went to their death with courage and without complaint, Stieff even laughing defiantly although death did not come easily to them all or to those who followed them. Execution by hanging is invariably cruel, as horrible photographs of war-time hangings and of the post-war executions in Nuremberg and elsewhere show. On Hitler's orders, however, the procedure in Plötzensee was particularly bestial. The guillotine was still there in the room; the executioner and his assistants were fortifying themselves with brandy; sound-track film cameras were mounted to record the death of his victims for Hitler's benefit (they were naked, their trousers having been removed after hanging). The film was taken to the *Führer*'s headquarters at once and shown there. Photographs of the hangings were still lying on Hitler's map table on 18 August. The prisoners were hanged with thin rope one by one from meat-hooks fastened to a girder fixed across the room just below the ceiling. The execution shed survived the bombs and shells of the war and has become a memorial and so, apart from the guillotine, these contrivances can still be seen today. Death by hanging can always be slow and painful, even if suffering is not intended. At least in the first instance, however, orders were to make death as protracted as possible. Once the noose has been fixed to the hook, if the prisoner is then raised by the executioner's assistants and then let fall with all his weight, he has a chance of breaking his neck or at least of losing consciousness; if, however, he is lowered carefully or a small stool is slowly withdrawn from under him, he will be slowly strangled. It is significant that, even if the first method is used, regulations generally prescribe that the prisoner be left hanging for twenty minutes.

After each execution a curtain was drawn in front of the last body before the next prisoner was brought in.[26] The actual process of execution was invariably short, lasting only a few seconds. Reports mostly refer to times between seven and twenty seconds during which the prisoner was brought in, seized by the executioners and hanged or beheaded.[27] Only in the case of decapitation, however, did execution certainly bring suffering to an end. In that case everything was much quicker; the prisoner was produced, seized by the executioner's assistants, strapped into the machine and beheaded. In late 1944 this method was resumed after fortnightly hangings had taken place for months.[28] In March 1945, however, came a reversion to hanging – in Nebe's case, obviously because it was considered a worse punishment.[29] Fromm on the other hand was shot – on 12 March 1945 in Brandenburg prison – clearly as a sign of clemency and as more appropriate and normal in the case of his crime (cowardice).[30]

Many of the convicted conspirators of 20 July were executed on the day they were sentenced. Since in many, if not the majority of, cases sentence had been decided upon beforehand, it is hardly surprising that the review procedure was not followed, even as a formality. In a couple of hours no one could absorb the record of a trial at which a man's life was at stake or make a conscientious check of all the circumstances. On the other hand, as already mentioned, in many cases execution was postponed, not to allow time for review but to extract more information about the conspiracy and their fellow-conspirators from those condemned to death. Major (res.) Hans-Georg Klamroth and Adam von Trott zu Solz were sentenced on 15 August 1944; sentence was confirmed the same day; they were not executed, however, until the 26th, in Trott's case because he had 'undoubtedly withheld a great deal'.[31] Fellgiebel, Hansen and Sadrozinski had to wait for death for a month; Leber was sentenced on 20 October 1944 and sentence was confirmed the same day but he was not executed until 5 January 1945.[32] Goerdeler had to wait for execution from 8 September 1944 to 2 February 1945.[33] All this was typical of the cruelty and inhumanity of the Nazi regime – but there were plenty of other instances.

Owing to conditions in France and the fortitude of those arrested the group of conspirators there emerged from the investigations with comparatively few casualties. Stülpnagel, Hofacker, Linstow and Finckh were condemned to death and executed on 30 August except for Hofacker who had to wait until 20 December.[34] Field Marshal von Kluge had already committed suicide but meanwhile the role played by Rommel had become increasingly clear. Hitler recoiled before putting this most popular general on trial and preferred to get rid of him unobtrusively (Rommel was still convalescing from his wounds). On 14 October 1944 Hitler despatched Major-General Maisel and Lieutenant-General Burgdorf to Herrlingen near Ulm, where Rommel lived, and they presented him with the choice between taking poison which they had brought with them, followed by a state funeral, or being arraigned before the People's Court – with all the consequences for his family. Apart from his concern for his family Rommel would probably have been glad to have the opportunity to appear as accuser before the People's Court. On the other hand he knew the procedure adopted there and was in any case convinced that he would not reach Berlin alive even if he agreed to stand trial. The only alternative was the poison. After an hour's discussion with Maisel and Burgdorf, during which time the village was surrounded by SS troops, Rommel took leave of his family, saying to his wife: 'I shall be dead in a quarter of an hour.' Then he got into a car with the two generals. On the road to Ulm a halt was made and Rommel took the poison. A state funeral was ordered in Ulm, an embolism resulting from his wounds being given as the cause of death.[35]

The official registration of executions by the Ministry of Justice and prison governors ceased in April 1945. The last twenty-eight executions in Brandenburg prison took place on 20 April 1945, the *Führer*'s birthday.[36] The total number of executions for 1945 is estimated at 800 which is certainly too low. Executions registered by the Ministry of Justice for 1944 totalled 5,764 and for 1943 5,684.[37] In any case nothing like all these executions were connected with 20 July, as might be supposed from a post-war British Admiralty report. The number of 20 July executions is estimated at about 200.[38]

While the official executions were taking place there were semi-official and unofficial ones which continued to the very end of the war. A particularly horrible instance of semi-official execution is the fate of the group centred on Canaris. It had obviously been too risky to put this group of ex-*Abwehr* officers on trial before the People's Court. Their defence was that the offences of which they were accused formed part of their espionage activities and this would have been difficult to disprove. In any case detailed discussion of their activities before a court would not have been expedient. Then in April Admiral Canaris' complete diary was discovered[39] and this enraged Hitler so much that he ordered the execution of the entire group. In fact it had never been intended to let them escape any more than the convoy of prisoners whose execution was postponed as the front approached and who eventually reached South Tyrol where they were liberated as already mentioned.

On 7 April *SS-Standartenführer* Walter Huppenkothen arrived in Flossenbürg with special instructions from Berlin for the execution of certain prisoners and the removal of others; the latter included Halder, Thomas, Schacht, Schuschnigg, Falkenhausen, Best (of the British Secret Service), Lieutenant Vassily Kokorin (a nephew of Molotov) and Colonel von Bonin; these were not to be executed straight away; on the contrary they were to be well treated.[40] On the way, on 6 April, Huppenkothen stopped off at Sachsenhausen concentration camp whither Dr Hans von Dohnanyi had been brought that morning; he had managed to contract a serious infection with the aid of some food smuggled in by his wife and had therefore been in the police hospital. Before his removal the doctor there had given him drugs to incapacitate him in the hope of saving his life. But such subterfuges were no longer of use. Though Dohnanyi was only semi-conscious and on a stretcher, he was 'tried' by Huppenkothen. As far as is known, he was executed on 9 April.[41] On 7 April Huppenkothen went on to Flossenbürg near Weiden. Dr Otto Thorbeck, an SS judge, had been ordered up from Nuremberg; he had to bicycle the last twelve miles from Weiden to Flossenbürg.

Here all had been made ready for a court martial on Canaris, Oster, Dr Sack, the Army Judge Advocate, Captains Strünck and Gehre and Dr Dietrich Bonhoeffer. During the trial Canaris, if not others, was severely beaten as he had been previously. On the morning of 9 April all were hanged in Flossenbürg camp.[42]

The same morning a contingent of other prisoners was moved from Flossenbürg to Dachau, joining up on the way with prisoners from Schönberg camp some 100 miles to the south. On 12 April, as the sound of battle neared Flossenbürg camp, the last prisoners were moved to Dachau. Ultimately over a hundred more or less prominent prisoners were assembled there, including Dr Josef Müller, Dr Franz Maria Liedig, Schlabrendorff, Schacht, Halder, Falkenhausen, Schuschnigg and his wife, Thomas, Bonin, Best, Kokorin, Dr Hermann Pünder, Frau Goerdeler and many others under 'kith and kin' arrest.[43] They were finally taken under American protection in South Tyrol and were released during the summer of 1945.

An instance of the unofficial method of execution is the death of the prisoners in Moabit prison in the Lehrter Strasse, Berlin. They included Dr Klaus Bonhoeffer and Dr Rüdiger Schleicher who had both been tortured, condemned to death and kept waiting for two months for execution.[44] Many others were awaiting their fate at the hands of the *Gestapo* including Dr Andreas Hermes, Dr Theodor Steltzer, Dr Hans John, Friedrich Justus Perels, Wilhelm zur Nieden, Carl Marks, Hans Ludwig Sierks,[45] all of whom had been condemned to death. On 21 April, when the prison was already under Russian artillery fire, eleven prisoners accused of less serious crimes or who had not (or not yet) been condemned to death, were released. They included Dr Walter Bauer[46] and Arnold Bistrick, the industrialists, Georg Stöhr, a businessman, Hermann Schilling, a treasury official, Dr Plewe, a magistrate, Lieutenant-Colonels Holm Erttel and Ferdinand Zeh, Dr Heinz Haushofer, brother of Professor Albrecht Haushofer, and Theodor Baensch. The next morning Dr Bauer went to Dr Eggensperger, a civil servant in the Ministry of Justice whom he knew, and besought him to order the release of all political prisoners in the Lehrter Strasse at once to prevent them being liquidated at the last moment or killed in the fighting.

Dr Thierack, the Minister of Justice, however, had apparently left Berlin during the night 20–21 April, leaving instructions that the reviewing official for cases dealt with by the People's Court should be the Public Prosecutor of that court; for other cases the reviewing officer was to be the Public Prosecutor of Berlin in his capacity as judicial representative of the *Reich* Defence Commissar – Dr Goebbels. While Berlin was being reduced to rubble by Russian gunfire, however, Goebbels was still in the Chancellery bunker with Hitler and it was common knowledge that, in these last ten days, people were being shot out of hand in Berlin for refusal to obey orders, acting contrary to orders or other offences now frequently committed; if one wished to remain alive, therefore, one could not give orders purely according to the dictates of humanity.

Nevertheless on the afternoon of 23 April Dr Eggensperger, who was trying his hardest, succeeded in persuading *Ministerialdirigent* Hesse, who represented the Minister of Justice, to drive with him to Moabit prison, where they proposed to insist on the immediate release of all political prisoners. From Moabit they tried to go to the Lehrter Strasse but could not get through because of tank barriers which had apparently been put up that day. They would in any case have been too late to stop the massacre which had meanwhile been decided upon and initiated. Perhaps it was because 22 April was a Sunday that nothing could be done to release the prisoners earlier.

Even had they not been too late, success would have been highly questionable. When Hanssen, the senior Public Prosecutor, heard from Dr Eggensperger on the evening of 23 April that the Moabit prisoners had been released, he said that Dr Goebbels, the *Reich* Defence Commissar, would not take such things as a joke and that whoever had opened the doors of Moabit was risking his neck. He, Hanssen, would ensure that such a 'mess' would not be repeated in the Lehrter Strasse. He had no need to worry, however.

On the evening of 22 April, before therefore Dr Bauer's intervention had led to Eggensperger's journey to Moabit with Hesse, the *Gestapo* had begun to remove the prisoners in the Lehrter Strasse. First twenty-one prisoners were released including Wilhelm Roloff, managing director of the 'Nordsee' trading concern, Hans Lukaschek, Kraft Freiherr von Palombini who had sheltered Goerdeler while on the run, Lothar Francke, head of a section in Lufthansa,[47] Hermann Freiherr von Lüninck and Otto Kunze. Then about 11.0 p.m., apparently on orders from the notorious *SS-Obersturmbannführer* Stawizki, sixteen other prisoners were paraded. They were told that they would be released from the RSHA in the Prinz-Albrecht-Strasse and so must be moved there.

About midnight the prisoners were divided into two groups and led out into the Lehrter Strasse where they had to give up all papers and valuables they had just received since they were to be released; their belongings were loaded on to a van which was standing ready and the prisoners were put in charge of some thirty SS men.[48] The first eight consisted of Dr Rüdiger Schleicher, Dr Klaus Bonhoeffer, Dr Hans John, Carl Marks, Friedrich Justus Perels, Wilhelm zur Nieden and Hans Ludwig Sierks, all of whom had been condemned to death, and Dr Richard Künzer, a foreign service officer who had not. While they were waiting in the prison courtyard before being led out, another eight prisoners were summoned and led out into the street where they were told that they would be taken to Potsdam Station. The first eight followed soon afterwards.

About 1.0 a.m. on 23 April all sixteen were conducted down the Lehrter Strasse and then across the Invaliden Strasse into the grounds of the Universal Exhibition Park (Ulap). There they were again divided into two groups. An SS man with loaded revolver or sub-machine gun walked behind each prisoner. On a word of command all the prisoners were shot from behind in the nape of the neck.

The second group included Colonel Wilhelm Staehle, Lieutenant-Colonel Ernst Munzinger, Major Hans Victor von Salviati, Professor Albrecht Haushofer, a Russian prisoner of war named Sergei Sossimov, a certain Carlos Moll and two communists, Max Jennewein and Herbert Kosney.[49] Kosney turned his head at the moment the SS man fired. The bullet went through his neck and cheek; he collapsed but remained conscious and pretended to be dead. When the SS had gone he bandaged himself as best he could and crawled to the dressing station of a militia unit. As a result of his report the bodies of the first group were found and, three weeks later, those of Kosney's group. When his brother found him, Albrecht Haushofer was still clutching a sheaf of sonnets written in Moabit prison.

For those remaining in the Lehrter Strasse the terrible uncertainty continued. On 23 April Johannes Albers, the former trade union leader who had been condemned to death on 20 April, was taken to Plötzensee for execution but was liberated there by the Red Army.[50] The same occurred in the case of Kurt Sorge, an engineer, Captain Paul van Husen and a certain Wilhelm Schmidt, who had equally been condemned to death. Certain others were released on 23 April, however: Dr Joachim Wrede, Hermann Moritz, Carl Bassen the architect, a certain Paul Herpich and a Swedish *SS-Untersturmführer*. On the evening of 23 April the *Gestapo* handed over the entire Lehrter Strasse prison to the judicial authorities but this boded no good since the *Gestapo* and SS considered that they could not subsequently be held responsible for the murder of prisoners who had been handed over to the judiciary. When the *Gestapo* departed that evening, the worst seemed to be over. About 1.0 a.m. on 24 April, however, the SS returned – for the last time – and took with them Albrecht Graf von Bernstorff, Karl Ludwig Freiherr von Guttenberg and Ernst Schneppenhorst, the trade union leader. They were murdered. Between 20 and 22 April an unknown number of *Gestapo* prisoners in the Prinz-Albrecht-Strasse suffered the same fate.[51]

On 25 April the remaining prisoners succeeded in convincing Berg, the prison governor, that they could and should be set free. Their most effective argument was that Berg would otherwise very likely be shot by the Red Army. At 6.0 p.m. therefore, the political prisoners were finally released; they included: Colonel Otto Armster, Eberhard Bethge, Captain Helmuth Cords, Justus Delbrück (ex-*Abwehr* staff), Professor Constantin von Dietze, Friedrich Ernst, Friedrich Erxleben, Dr Maximilian von Hagen, Colonel Kurt Hassel, Dr Andreas Hermes, Captain (Navy) Sydney Jessen, Professor Adolf Lampe, Friedrich Leon, Dr Fiszel Majnemer, Gustav Noske, the former *Reichswehr* Minister, Major Oskar Graf von Pilati, Jesco von Puttkamer-Nippoglense, Hans-Joachim von Reclam-Schlee, Professor Gerhard Ritter, Father Augustinus Rösch (Order of Jesuits), Colonel Hans-Joachim von Steinaecker, Dr Theodor Steltzer, Hans Detlof von Winterfeldt, Willi Wiegand, Berengar von Zastrow and Friedrich-Carl von Zitzewitz-Muttrin. They escaped, but the shadow of the dead remained with them for the rest of their lives.

The children arrested as 'kith and kin' had to wait longer for their freedom than these 'traitors' and 'enemies of the state'. They numbered about fifty, some of them babies. In autumn 1944 they were taken to Bad Sachsa where they were forbidden to use their own names. After a time the older children discovered from one of the kindergarten mistresses that the original intention had been to keep them in Bad Sachsa for two months while their parents and elder brothers and sisters were killed and then to distribute them, some to SS schools and some to SS families. This plan, however, had been abandoned.[52] In October some of the children were sent to schools and some allowed to go home. In February Dr Goerdeler's grand-children, Rainer aged 4 and Karl aged 9 months, arrived. Rainer was in tears and told Cäsar von Hofacker's daughter in Swabian that he wanted to go home. Bad Sachsa was occupied by the Americans on 12 April 1945 but there was no prospect of a return home until 4 May, when the new Burgomaster took charge of the children, telling them: 'Now you can use your real names again; you have no need to be ashamed of them or of your fathers, for they were heroes.'[53]

During the confusion of the first weeks after the war the surviving relatives of the conspirators were either unable to return home themselves or alternatively did not know where their children were. The mother of the two Stauffenbergs was released from *Gestapo* arrest in Balingen and allowed to go home to Lautlingen in the autumn of 1944, and Gräfin von Üxküll-

Gyllenband, one of their aunts, returned to Lautlingen after a short period under arrest. They had to remain there under *Gestapo* surveillance until liberated by French troops. Not until early June did Gräfin von Üxküll-Gyllenband succeed in bringing the children back from Bad Sachsa to Lautlingen. By great good fortune the local French commander had been well treated when a prisoner of war in Lautlingen and he made a military vehicle available – requests had been made to the American and French Military Governments and to the Red Cross but they had replied that they could not be troubled with German children. Before her death Melitta Gräfin von Stauffenberg, the well-known airwoman, wife of Alexander von Stauffenberg, had contrived to tell Gräfin von Üxküll where the children were. Only the bombing of Nordhausen station had prevented them being moved to Buchenwald concentration camp. On 6 June, therefore, in the French military vehicle Gräfin von Üxküll arrived in Nordhausen the day before the Russians were due to move in. On 7 June she drove west with the children. The heritage and lineage of the resistance to Hitler lives on, however, not only in the families of those who gave their lives, but wherever their sacrifices and sufferings are remembered.

Notes

[Translator's Note: Reference is made in these Notes to a number of German works of which an English translation exists, and an effort has been made to adapt the references to the English translation. This is not always possible, however, since in some cases a book has been abridged in translation (Gisevius: *Bis zum bittern Ende – To the Bitter End*, for instance) and in others the reference is to a later edition of the book than that from which the translation was made. In such cases an indication is given as to whether the reference applies to the German or English versions by using an abbreviated title, e.g. 'Gisevius (*Ende* Vol. I or Vol. II)' or 'Gisevius (*Bitter End*)'.]

NOTES/PART I/CHAPTER 1

1 Bruno Gebhardt: *Handbuch der deutschen Geschichte*, Vol. IV, pp. 346–7. See also Gerhard Ritter: *Carl Goerdeler und die deutsche Widerstandsbewegung*, pp. 99–102.
2 Paul Kluke: 'Der Fall Potempa' in *Vierteljahrshefte für Zeitgeschichte* (hereafter referred to as *VfZ*), 5 (1957), pp. 279–97.
3 Hans Rothfels: *Die deutsche Opposition gegen Hitler: Eine Würdigung*, p. 52.
4 Gebhardt, p. 352.
5 These cases are quoted from '100 Einzelfälle, Anlage zur Denkschrift über die Notlage der Arbeiterschaft vom Gesamtverband der christlichen Gewerkschaften vom 16.9.1932' in Helmut J. Schorr and Adam Stegerwald: *Gewerkschaftler und Politiker der ersten deutschen Republik. Ein Beitrag zur Geschichte der christlich-sozialen Bewegung in Deutschland*, p. 259.
6 Karl Dietrich Bracher, Wolfgang Sauer and Gerhard Schulz: *Die national-sozialistische Machtergreifung: Studien zur Errichtung des totalitären Herrschaftssystems in Deutschland 1933–34*, pp. 62–3, 246–7. A differing view is to be found in Ritter, *Goerdeler* pp. 100–1. (English translation – *The German Resistance*, pp. 44–5). Also: Thomas Weingartner, *Stalin und der Aufstieg Hitlers*, passim.
7 Bracher/Sauer/Schulz, p. 63; Hans Mommsen: 'Der Reichstagsbrand und seine politischen Folgen' in *VfZ* 12 (1964) pp. 384–8, 411–13.
8 Rothfels, p. 52; Bracher/Sauer/Schulz, pp. 63–4. See also the severe criticism of the attitude of his party by Dr Julius Leber, the Social-Democratic Party leader, quoted in Ritter, *Goerdeler*, p. 469, Note 7 (*Resistance* p. 43, Note 1).
9 Bracher/Sauer/Schulz, pp. 54–5 – also applicable below.
10 Mommsen, pp. 352–4, 382–96.
11 See Hermann Mau and Helmut Krausnick: *Deutsche Geschichte der jüngsten Vergangenheit 1933–1945*, pp. 26–7; Gebhardt, p. 191.
12 Mau and Krausnick, pp. 28–32; Gebhardt, p. 192; see also Max Domarus: *Hitler: Reden und Proklamationen 1932–1945*, two vols, pp. 1067–8.
13 Gebhardt, pp. 192–3, 196: Mau and Krausnick, pp. 28–32.

14 Gebhardt, p. 196.
15 Bracher /Sauer/Schulz, pp. 64–5 – also applicable below.
16 Gebhardt, p. 196.
17 Bracher/Sauer/Schulz, pp. 72–3 – also applicable below.
18 Ibid., pp. 136–8.
19 Ibid., pp. 139–44 – also applicable below.
20 Ritter, *Resistance*, p. 30.
21 Bracher/Sauer/Schulz, pp. 155–8 – also applicable below.
22 Ibid., pp. 163–8.
23 Ibid., pp. 178–86 – also applicable below.
24 Ibid., pp. 198–9.
25 Ibid., pp. 205–14.
26 Ibid., pp. 317–19.
27 Ibid., pp. 326–47; Friedrich Baumgärtel: *Wider die Kirchenkampf-Legenden*, pp. 32–3; list of specific measures against the Confessional Church (as at December 1939) in Groscurth papers, Federal Archives (Bundesarchiv; henceforth BA), Coblence, EAP 21–X–15/1; see also Ritter, *Resistance*, pp. 49–53 and Friedrich Zipfel: *Kirchenkampf in Deutschland 1933–1945*.
28 Bracher/Sauer/Schulz, pp. 341–7 – also applicable below.
29 See 'Official Abstract of Pope's Encyclical on Germany', *New York Times*, 23 March 1937, p. 5; Heinrich Portmann: *Kardinal von Galen – Ein Gottesmann seiner Zeit*.
30 Bracher/Sauer/Schulz, pp. 289–90; also the penetrating comments by Carl Friedrich von Weizsäcker in *Die Tragweite der Wissenschaft*, Vol. I, p. 12.
31 Bracher/Sauer/Schulz, pp. 290–307.
32 Ibid., p. 863.
33 Ibid., pp. 864–5, 871–3 – also applicable below.
34 Günther Weisenborn: *Der lautlose Aufstand: Bericht über die Widerstands-bewegung des deutschen Volkes 1933–1945*, p. 30.
35 Eric H. Boehm (editor): *We survived: The Stories of Fourteen of the Hidden and Hunted of Nazi Germany*, p. VIII; information is based on *Gestapo* documents, as is that of Gabriel A. Almond: 'The German Resistance Movement' in *Current History* 10 (1946), pp. 409–527.
36 Weisenborn, p. 30.
37 *Trial of the Major War Criminals before the International Military Tribunal, Nuremberg 14 November 1945 – 1 October 1946* (henceforth referred to as *Trial*), Vol. XXXVIII, pp. 362–5; Rothfels, p. 18 obviously overlooked the fact that the figures referred only to six specific camps when he says that, according to SS documents, there were '21,400 internees on the outbreak of war'. See also Martin Broszat: 'The Concentration Camps 1933–1945' in *Anatomy of the SS State*, pp. 503–4.
38 Weisenborn, pp. 31–2.
39 Nikolaus von Halem, for example, had to sign a statement in which he promised to keep silent about his experiences in the concentration camp, under penalty of death, when he was transferred to the custody of the People's Court in 1944 to stand trial; Dr Emil Mertens, diary on his experiences in Brandenburg/Havel penitentiary, excerpts in If Z ED 106 Archiv Walter Hammer Bd. 105.
40 Microfilm of the 'Mordregister' in BA EC 941 N; Rudolf Pechel: *Deutscher Widerstand*, pp. 326–38; Walter Hammer: *Hohes Haus in Henkers Hand: Rückschau auf die Hitlerzeit, auf Leidensweg und Opfergang Deutscher Parlamentarier*, p. 114.
41 Annedore Leber: *Das Gewissen entscheidet*, p. 21.
42 'Fuehrer Conferences on Naval Affairs, 1939–1945' in *Brassey's Naval Annual* 59 (1948), p. 405.
43 BA, EAP 173–a–10/64.

CHAPTER 2

1 Rudolf Pechel: *Deutscher Widerstand*, pp. 262–5; Friedrich Hossbach: *Zwischen Wehrmacht und Hitler 1934–1938*, p. 81; Gerhard Ritter: *Carl Goerdeler und die deutsche Widerstandsbewegung*, pp. 146–7 (English ed: *The German Resistance*, much abridged); Bruno Gebhardt: *Handbuch der deutschen Geschichte*, Vol. IV, pp. 224–5.

2 Thilo Vogelsang: 'Neue Dokumente zur Geschichte der Reichswehr 1930–1933' in *VfZ* 2 (1954), pp. 434–5.

3 Hossbach, pp. 83–5.

4 Pechel, pp. 262–6; see also Max Domarus: *Hitler: Reden und Proklamationen 1932–1945*, passim; Ian Colvin: *Vansittart in Office*, pp. 156–60; Louis P. Lochner: *Tycoons and Tyrant*, pp. 183–6.

5 On this subject and on the intensive efforts by certain members of the conservative opposition in Britain see Eugen Spier: *Focus: A Footnote to the History of the Thirties*, pp. 9–14, 122–9. The group called itself 'Focus in Defence of Freedom and Peace' and constituted a forum, in particular for Churchill when he was out of office in the thirties. It used to meet in a hotel and discuss how to bring influence to bear on the government and leading circles and how to organize some form of resistance to Hitler by the countries of Europe.

6 Ernst Niekisch: *Gewagtes Leben: Begegnungen und Begebnisse*, pp. 140–1, 145–50; Harry Pross: *Literatur und Politik: Geschichte und Programme der politisch-literarischen Zeitschriften im deutschen Sprachgebiet seit 1870*, pp. 274–7; Pechel, p. 73; Fabian von Schlabrendorff: *Revolt against Hitler*, p. 34; Günther Weisenborn (editor): *Der lautlose Aufstand*, pp. 184–5; Ritter, p. 476 Note 8; James Donohoe: *Hitler's Conservative Opponents in Bavaria 1930–1945: A Study of Catholic, Monarchist and Separatist Anti-Nazi Activities*, pp. 18–21; this is based on the files of the People's Court in the Berlin Document Centre (henceforth BDC).

7 Niekisch, pp. 250–1.

8 Pechel, p. 73; Schlabrendorff, p. 34.

9 Niekisch, pp. 246–7.

10 Pechel, pp. 74–5; Schlabrendorff, *Offiziere gegen Hitler* (Fischer Bücherei), p. 21.

11 Niekisch, pp. 246–8.

12 Ibid., pp. 247–8; Schlabrendorff, op. cit., pp. 20–1.

13 See Hans Rothfels: *The German Opposition to Hitler*, pp. 50–1.

14 Schlabrendorff, op. cit., pp. 22–4: Helmut Krausnick: 'Vorgeschichte und Beginn des militärischen Widerstandes gegen Hitler' in *Vollmacht des Gewissens I*, p. 223.

15 Rothfels, op. cit., pp. 15–16; on the situation as a whole see also Wilhelm Hoffmann: *Nach der Katastrophe*.

16 Kurt Kliem: 'Der sozialistische Widerstand gegen das Dritte Reich dargestellt an der Gruppe "Neu Beginnen"', Dissertation University of Marburg 1957 (typescript), pp. 5–7; see also Ritter, op. cit., p. 102; Hans J. Reichhardt: 'Möglichkeiten und Grenzen des Widerstandes der Arbeiterbewegung' in *Der deutsche Widerstand gegen Hitler: Vier historisch-kritische Studien*, edited by Walter Schmitthenner and Hans Buchheim, pp. 200–209; see also the summary of activities of similar groups by H[ans] R[othfels] in 'Die Roten Kämpfer: Zur Geschichte einer linken Widerstandsgruppe' in *VfZ* 7 (1959), pp. 438–60.

17 Kliem, pp. 35–40.

18 Ibid., pp. 45, 55–7.

19 Ibid., pp. 60–3; Erich Matthias: 'Der Untergang der Sozialdemokratie 1933' in *VfZ* 4 (1956), p. 199 Note 15.

20 Kliem, p. 66.

21 Ibid., pp. 67–75.

22 Ibid.; see also Rothfels, *German Opposition*, pp. 46–7.

23 Rothfels, op. cit., pp. 47–8.

24 Kliem, pp. 165–8, 236–48.

25 Emil Henk: 'Sozialdemokratischer Widerstand im Raum Mannheim' in *100 Jahre SPD in Mannheim: Eine Dokumentation*, issued by the Mannheim branch of the Social-Democrat Party, pp. 68–73.

26 See the comprehensive survey by Arnold Krammer 'Germans against Hitler: The Thaelmann Brigade' in *Journal of Contemporary History* 4 (1969), pp. 65–83.

27 Emil Henk: *Die Tragödie des 20. Juli 1944: Ein Beitrag zur politischen Vorgeschichte*, p. 8.

28 Weisenborn, pp. 157–8; Gertrud Glondajewski and Heinz Schumann: *Die Neubauer-Poser-Gruppe: Dokumente und Materalien des illegalen antifaschistischen Kampfes (Thüringen – 1939 bis 1945)*; Walter Hammer: *Hohes Haus in Henkers Hand: Rückschau auf die Hitlerzeit, auf Leidensweg und Opfergang Deutscher Parlamentarier*, p. 70.

29 See p. 33 below; People's Court case R. Mewes 1943, BDC.

30 Friedrich Schlotterbeck: *Je dunkler die Nacht, desto heller die Sterne: Erinnerungen eines deutschen Arbeiters 1933 bis 1945*; by the same author: . . . *Wegen Vorbereitung zum Hochverrat hingerichtet*.

31 Rothfels, *German Opposition*, p. 13.

32 [Kurt Gerstein]: 'Augenzeugenbericht zu den Massenvergasungen' in *VfZ* 1 (1953), pp. 177–94; reprinted in Helmut Franz: *Kurt Gerstein: Aussenseiter des Widerstandes der Kirche gegen Hitler*.

33 On this subject see Gebhardt, pp. 298–9 which includes sources and bibliography; also Max Bierbaum: *Nicht Lob, nicht Furcht: Das Leben des Kardinals von Galen nach unveröffentlichten Briefen und Dokumenten*, pp. 361–6; also *Evangelische Dokumente zur Ermordung der 'unheilbar Kranken' unter der nationalsozialistischen Herrschaft in den Jahren 1939–1945* edited by Hans Christoph von Hase. This also includes many source references.

34 Kunrat Freiherr von Hammerstein: *Spähtrupp*, pp. 39–43; see also Gebhardt, pp. 179–80 and sources there quoted, which include a report by Bussche (*Frankfurter Allgemeine Zeitung*, 5 Feb. 1952) accepted by Hammerstein and a report by Colonel-General von Hammerstein which his son has also used. Bussche gives the date of the interview with Hindenburg as 27 January; see also Ritter, *Goerdeler*, pp. 134–7 (*Resistance* pp. 66–7) and Krausnick, pp. 196–220.

35 Hammerstein, p. 40.

36 Ibid., pp. 44–9.

37 Ibid., pp. 11–94, in particular pp. 40, 46, 50–1, 54–61; Krausnick, p. 203; Schlabrendorff is therefore wrong when he says in *Offiziere*, p. 24 that Hammerstein had considered 'nipping Hitler's seizure of power in the bud with the aid of the *Reichswehr*', but had not been able to make up his mind to do so because it would have implied acting against Hindenburg. The statement is repeated in the new English edition of Schlabrendorff's book, *The Secret War against Hitler*, pp. 47–8, although disputed by a source as intimately concerned as Hammerstein's son. It is quite probable, however, that, as Schlabrendorff also says, Hammerstein *later* often wondered to himself and others whether it would not have been right to take forcible action against Hindenburg.

38 Hammerstein, pp. 64–5; Bracher/Sauer/Schulz: *Die nationalsozialistische Machtergreifung*, p. 733.

39 Krausnick, pp. 211, 214–15; Hammerstein, p. 66. There is still disagreement as to whether Colonel-General von Hammerstein was inert and negligent; see Hammerstein, pp. 79–94.

40 Bracher/Sauer/Schulz, p. 743; Wolfgang Keilig: *Das deutsche Heer 1939–1945*, pp. 211–91.

41 Krausnick, p. 227.
42 Ibid., Ritter, *Goerdeler*, pp. 127–8 (*Resistance*, p. 61).
43 Hammerstein, p. 68.
44 Graf Kielmansegg: *Der Fritschprozess 1938: Ablauf und Hintergründe*, p. 27.
45 See documentation by T[heodor] E[schenburg]; 'Zur Ermordung des Generals Schleicher' in *VfZ* 1 (1953), pp. 71–95; Hermann Mau: 'Die "Zweite Revolution" – der 30. Juni 1934' in *VfZ* 1 (1953), pp. 119–37; Hammerstein, pp. 68–79; also Klaus-Jürgen Müller: *Das Heer und Hitler: Armee und nazionalsozialistisches Regime 1933-40*, pp. 88–141.
46 Gebhardt, p. 197; Krausnick, p. 220; Bracher/Sauer/Schulz, p. 929.
47 Hammerstein, pp. 69–70.
48 Krausnick, pp. 224–6.
49 Ibid., pp. 224–9.
50 Mau, p. 133.
51 Hammerstein, p. 71; Krausnick, p. 229.
52 Krausnick, p. 230.
53 Ibid.
54 Ibid., pp. 226, 233.
55 Ibid., p. 234.
56 Ibid., p. 218; Ritter, *Goerdeler*, pp. 128, 174.
57 Gebhardt, p. 198.
58 Quoted in Krausnick, p. 236 Note 161; reproduced *in extenso* in Walther Hofer: *Der Nationalsozialismus: Dokumente 1933–1945*, pp. 63–4.
59 Quoted in Krausnick, p. 237.
60 Reproduced in Hofer, p. 71 and Krausnick, p. 237; see also Edgar Röhricht: *Pflicht und Gewissen: Erinnerungen eines deutschen Generals 1932 bis 1944*, pp. 76–9.
61 Domarus, p. 447. A year earlier, in July 1933, Hitler had already declared the revolution at an end; at that time, however, he clearly *could not* check the indiscipline of the SA. See Mau, p. 120 and Domarus, p. 286.
62 Rothfels, *German Opposition*, p. 49; Ritter, op. cit., pp. 127–8 (*Resistance*, pp. 60–1).
63 Pechel pp. 76–7; Edmund Forschbach: 'Edgar Jung und der Widerstand gegen Hitler' in *Civis* 6 (1959), pp. 84–5.
64 Krausnick, p. 227. Rothfels (*German Opposition* p. 49) gives Jung as the instigator but not the author of the speech; Pechel (*Widerstand* p. 77) gives Jung as the sole author as does Hans-Bernd Gisevius in *To the Bitter End*, p. 127.
Forschbach (pp. 87–8) explicitly emphasizes the fact that Jung was the author and says that he himself was present at a discussion, mentioned with certain inaccurate details by Gisevius, of the contents of the speech in a Berlin restaurant.
65 An extract from the speech is given in Hofer, pp. 66–8.
66 Forschbach, p. 88; Krausnick, pp. 227–8.
67 Mau, pp. 126–30, 135–7.
68 Gisevius, op. cit., pp. 157–8 and *Bis zum Bitteren Ende*, Vol. I, pp. 231, 290–1.
69 Pechel, p. 77.
70 Forschbach, p. 88.
71 Pechel, p. 78; Gisevius, *Ende*, Vol. I, pp. 290–1.
72 Ernst Wiechert: 'Der Dichter und seine Zeit' in *Deutsche Blätter* 1 (1943), No 6, pp. 4–8.
73 Wolfgang Abendroth: 'Das Problem der Widerstandstätigkeit der "Schwarzen Front"' in *VfZ* 8 (1960), pp. 181–7; Donohoe, pp. 15–18.
74 Pechel, pp. 80–1.
75 Ibid., pp. 81–4; Niekisch, p. 155; Schlabrendorff, *Offiziere*, pp. 76–7, 141; Ernst Röhm: *Die Geschichte eines Hochverräters*, pp. 115, 137–8.

76 Rudolf Pechel: 'Tatsachen' in *Deutsche Rundschau* 69 (1946), p. 179 and *Widerstand*, pp. 82–3.

77 Pechel: 'Tatsachen', p. 179; in *Widerstand*, pp. 82–3 no date is given for Römer's release from Dachau but the impression that it was very soon after his arrest in 1934 is probably wrong.

78 Pechel gives 19 June in 'Tatsachen', p. 179 and 25 September in *Widerstand*, p. 84; Harald Pölchau: *Die letzten Stunden: Erinnerungen eines Gefängnispfarrers aufgezeichnet von Graf Alexander Stenbock-Fermor* pp. 96–9, also gives 25 September.

79 Pechel: 'Tatsachen', p. 179.

80 'Anklageschrift des Oberreichsanwalts beim Volksgerichtshof vom 15. Feb. 1944 gegen Robert Uhrig, Walter Budeus, Kurt Lehmann, Willy Sachse, Fritz Riedel, Karl Frank, Leopold Tomschik, Franz Mett, Rudolf Grieb, Erich Kurz, Paul Gesche, Otto Klippenstein', in BDC; Pölchau, pp. 97–8; Weisenborn, pp. 158–60; Änne Saefkow: 'Helden des anti-faschistischen Widerstandes', *Neues Deutschland*, 18 September 1947; Pechel, *Widerstand*, p. 84; Reichhardt, pp. 197–9.

81 Anklageschrift.

82 Ibid.

83 Ibid.

84 Pechel, *Widerstand*, pp. 82–4 and Weisenborn, p. 99 – also applicable below; see also statements by Otto Aster, a member of the Römer group, in 'Protokoll aus der Verhandlung Halder [vor der] Spruchkammer X München [15–21 Sept. 1948]' mimeographed Protokoll B der Anklagebehörde der Spruchkammer München X, Az. BY 11/47, pp. 126–7; see also Rothfels, *German Opposition*, pp. 51–2.

85 Schlabrendorff, *Revolt*, p. 116 (*Secret War*, pp. 58–9); Niekisch, p. 249; Annedore Leber: *Das Gewissen entscheidet*, pp. 221–4. Below: Dr H. Mylius and A. Bistrick, verbal information 22 May and 3 June 1971, resp.

86 Leber, op. cit., pp. 221–2. See also Weisenborn, p. 92; Donohoe, pp. 105–13, 256–67; Ger van Roon: *Neuordnung im Widerstand: Der Kreisauer Kreis innerhalb der deutschen Widerstandsbewegung*, p. 222. Guttenberg was clearly involved in the Halem-Römer plot for an assassination – Franz Sonderegger to President of Provincial Court I, Munich, 14 January 1951 – in IfZ (ZS).

87 Schlabrendorff, *Revolt*, p. 112; Pechel, *Widerstand*, p. 83. It is not clear whether the contacts and the plan were betrayed by Römer after his arrest or by one of the others involved; Pechel says that 'there was a blackguard in Römer's immediate circle who denounced him'. According to Niekisch (pp. 249–50) Halem had 'discovered a man' prepared to attack Hitler, had obtained 'a sinecure office with Graf Schaffgotsch' for him but he then 'lifted not a finger'. According to Schlabrendorff (*Revolt*, p. 117) Halem found the preparatory period demanded by Römer to be too long and the cover post which he had obtained for Römer was no longer maintained – with disastrous results, for apart from one or two minor figures the entire circle was arrested; Römer confessed everything and was executed with many accomplices in 1944 (Schlabrendorff, *Offiziere*, p. 141).

88 Pechel, *Widerstand*, p. 84; see also Hammerstein, pp. 200–205.

89 Pechel, op. cit., p. 83; Heinrich von Brentano: *Gedenkrede des Bundesministers Dr von Brentano bei der Enthüllung der Ehrentafel für die Opfer des 20. Juli im Auswärtigen Amt am 20. Juli 1961* (unpaginated), passim.

90 Brentano, passim; Gräfin von Reventlow (editor): *Albrecht Bernstorff zum Gedächtnis*, passim.

91 Reventlow, pp. 42, 53–6, 64, 68, 74; see also Kurt von Stutterheim: *Die Majestät des Gewissens: In Memoriam Albrecht Bernstorff*.

92 The 'tea party' was a birthday celebration – see Lagi Countess Ballestrem-Solf: 'Tea Party' in Eric H. Boehm (editor): *We Survived: The Stories of Fourteen of*

the Hidden and Hunted of Nazi Germany, pp. 135–49; Brentano; Pechel, *Widerstand*, pp. 88–93; Führerinformation 1944 No 181 from *Reich* Minister of Justice dated 18 July 1944, State Archives Nuremberg, NG 1249. See also Schlabrendorff, *Offiziere*, pp. 30–1.

93 See Peter Paret: 'An Aftermath of the Plot against Hitler: the Lehrterstrasse Prison in Berlin, 1944–5' in *Bulletin of the Institute of Historical Research* 32 (1959), pp. 88–102.

94 Ballestrem-Solf, pp. 135–49; Führerinformation; according to a statement by Kriminalkommissar Franz Sonderegger, a *Gestapo* official who interrogated many members of the resistance, Reckzeh had 'given information spontaneously' after having entered the circle by accident – Sonderegger calls it the 'Thadden circle'; this statement is contained in the record of interviews held on 12 October 1952 by Freiherr von Siegler and Dr Helmut Krausnick and subsequently Dr Hermann Mau with Franz Xaver Sonderegger (record available in IfZ, Munich, typescript, ref. ZS 303/1). According to the account by Lagi Gräfin von Ballestrem-Solf, Dr Wilhelm Solf's daughter, very shortly after the tea party in September 1943 the circle was warned by Graf von Moltke that Dr Reckzeh was a *Gestapo* agent (Ballestrem-Solf, p. 135). As far as the identity of Dr Reckzeh is concerned, it has been established that at the time there were two of that name in Berlin: Dr Paul Reckzeh, doctor, 20a Seebergsteig, Berlin-Grunewald and Professor Paul Reckzeh, head doctor, 13 Bleibtreustrasse, Berlin-Charlottenburg. The Professor is dead; the other, his son, presumably moved to East Berlin and no information on him is obtainable. Detailed investigations are recorded in Irmgard von Lühe: *Elisabeth von Thadden: Ein Schicksal unserer Zeit*, pp. 192–216, 224–7. Irmgard von Lühe gives a detailed account of the penetration of the circle by Dr Reckzeh (whom she merely calls 'Reck' to protect his relatives) and his informer activities on behalf of the *Gestapo*, also of the arrests of members of the circle. Reckzeh is also described as the Professor's son in Hammerstein, p. 230.

95 Führerinformation; Annedore Leber (editor): *Conscience in Revolt*, pp. 159–62.

96 See E. A. Bayne: 'Resistance in the German Foreign Office' in *Human Events III* (1946) No 14, p. 1.

97 See the comprehensive work by Ger van Roon: *Neuordnung im Widerstand*, passim; also Eugen Gerstenmaier: 'Der Kreisauer Kreis: Zu dem Buch Gerrit van Roons "Neuordnung im Widerstand" ' in *VfZ* 15 (1967), pp. 221–46.

98 Cf. pp. 205–11 below.

99 On this subject see Rainer Hildebrandt: *Wir sind die Letzten: Aus dem Leben des Widerstandskämpfers Albrecht Haushofer und seiner Freunde*, pp. 138–60; David J. Dallin: *Soviet Espionage*, pp. 234–62; Paul Leverkuehn: *Der geheime Nachrichtendienst der deutschen Wehrmacht im Kriege*, pp. 86–90; W. F. Flicke: *Spionagegruppe Rote Kapelle*, passim; Schlabrendorff, *Secret War*, pp. 195 et seq.; Axel von Harnack: 'Arvid und Mildred Harnack: Erinnerungen an ihren Prozess 1942/43' in *Die Gegenwart* 2 (1947) No 1/2, pp. 15–18. See also Seventh Army Interrogation Centre APO 758 Consolidated Interrogation Report: The Espionage Case 'Rote Kapelle' and the Seydlitz Affair, 5 Oct. 1945, Ref No SAIC/CIR/18, National Archives, Washington (henceforth: NA) Record Group 165.

100 Joachim G. Leithäuser: *Wilhelm Leuschner*, pp. 107–56; *Gestapo* instruction on telephone-tapping for Wilhelm Leuschner, Berlin 8 June 1938, typed copy, BA, II A 2/38g; Walter Theimer: 'Wilhelm Leuschner: "Einigkeit" ' in *Das Parlament*, 20 July 1952, p. 3; Elfriede Nebgen: *Jakob Kaiser: Der Widerstandskämpfer*, pp. 39–48, 54–9, 99–106, 114–15.

101 Roon, pp. 129–30; Leber: *Conscience in Revolt*, pp. 238–42.

102 Leber, op. cit., pp. 243–6; Otto John: 'Männer im Kampf gegen Hitler (VI): Carl Mierendorff, Theodor Haubach, Adolf Reichwein' in *Blick in die Welt*, 2 (1947)

No 11, pp. 14–15; Roon, pp. 186–7; see Haubach's letters in BA, papers of Alma de l'Aigle, No 14 and Alma de l'Aigle: *Meine Briefe von Theo Haubach*, passim.

103 Eberhard Zeller: *The Flame of Freedom*, pp. 86–90; Roon, p. 207.

104 Pechel, *Widerstand*, pp. 84–6.

105 Law against traitorous attacks on State and Party and for the protection of the Party uniform, 20 December 1934, *Reichsgesetzblatt 1934 Teil I*, p. 1269.

CHAPTER 3

1 Hugh Trevor-Roper: 'Hitlers Kriegsziele' in *VfZ* 8 (1960), pp. 121–33; Gerhard Ritter: *Carl Goerdeler und die deutsche Widerstandsbewegung*, p. 245. See also a remark by Hitler in 1936 (sic) which took war with Russia for granted– in files of the so-called 'Wilhelmstrasse Trial', volume of prosecution documents 118a, identical with Schacht Exhibit No 48 in Defence Documents Book, Supplement: Nuremberg Document 4955 NI, quoted in Ritter, *Goerdeler*, p. 83.

2 Friedrich Hossbach: *Zwischen Wehrmacht und Hitler*, pp. 13–14, 181–92. The document is known as the Hossbach Minutes, although it was not really a record nor intended as such; it has been reproduced and published on many occasions, e.g. in *Trial of the Major War Criminals before the International Military Tribunal: Nuremberg 14 November 1945 – 1 October 1946* (hereafter referred to as *Trial*), Vol. XXV, pp. 403–13; and in Hossbach, pp. 181–9.

3 Hossbach, pp. 20, 39, 45, 96–7.

4 Ibid., p. 191.

5 On this subject see Graf Kielmansegg: *Der Fritschprozess 1938*, pp. 32–3.

6 Walther Hofer: *Die Entfesselung des Zweiten Weltkrieges*, pp. 61–71; on the second conference see also [Franz] Halder: *Kriegstagebuch*, Vol. I, pp. 23–6. The minutes of the meeting of 23 May were initially reproduced in *Trial*, Vol. XXXVII, pp. 546–56, also in *Documents on German Foreign Policy 1918–1945* (hereafter referred to as *DGFP*), Series D, Vol. VI, No 433 (pp. 574–80); apart from the typewritten list of those present and the usual indications such as 'Top Secret', the entire document is in the handwriting of Schmundt, Hitler's Chief Aide and a General Staff Lieutenant-Colonel at the time. The minutes of the second meeting are to be found in *DGFP* Series D, Vol. VII, documents 192 and 193 (pp. 200–206), in *Documents on British Foreign Policy 1919–1939* (hereafter referred to as *DBFP*) Third Series, Vol. VII, No 314 (pp. 257–60) and in *Trial*, Vol. XXVI, pp. 338–44, and Vol. XLI, pp. 16–25.

7 Hossbach, pp. 190–2; see also Ernst von Weizsäcker: *Erinnerungen*, p. 147.

8 Wolfgang Foerster: *Generaloberst Ludwig Beck: Sein Kampf gegen den Krieg*, pp. 80–2 – also applicable below.

9 Ibid., p. 58.

10 Hossbach, p. 119.

11 Reproduced in Hossbach, pp. 59–62.

12 Ibid., pp. 120–1.

13 This is what Kielmansegg says (p. 5), but unfortunately without citing evidence. Hitler's speech in February 1939 to generals is referred to by Harold C. Deutsch: *Hitler and His Generals: The Hidden Crisis, January–June 1938*, pp. 263–4, on the basis of notes by some of those present.

14 Hitler frequently expressed himself on these lines to Göring, to Engel, his aide, and to others; see Helmut Krausnick: 'Vorgeschichte und Beginn des militärischen Widerstandes gegen Hitler' in *Vollmacht des Gewissens I*, p. 283 and Kielmansegg, p. 104.

15 On the Blomberg scandal and the Fritsch crisis see Jodl's diary, extracts from which are reproduced in *Trial*, Vol. XXVIII, pp. 345–90 (on p. 356 Jodl gives the day on which Hitler gave permission for Blomberg's marriage as 23 December

1937); Hossbach, pp. 105–6, 164–71; Hermann Foertsch: *Schuld und Verhängnis*, passim; Kielmansegg, passim; Fabian von Schlabrendorff: *The Secret War against Hitler*, pp. 373–416 where the judgement in the Fritsch case is reproduced; Edgar Röhricht: *Pflicht und Gewissen*, pp. 111–18; Hans Bernd Gisevius: *Bis zum bittern Ende*, Vol. I, pp. 383–459 (*To the Bitter End*, p. 224–67); Gisevius: *Wo ist Nebe?*, pp. 271–88; Hermann Bösch: *Heeresrichter Dr Karl Sack im Widerstand* (biography of Sack) – in particular Chap. 3; Fritz Wiedemann: *Der Mann der Feldherr werden wollte*, pp. 109–20; Rudolf Pechel: *Deutscher Widerstand*, pp. 140–50; Friedrich Wilhelm Heinz: 'Von Wilhelm Canaris zur NKWD', typescript (about 1949), NA microfilm R 60.67, pp. 73 et seq; John W. Wheeler-Bennett: *The Nemesis of Power*, pp. 353–82; Alan Bullock: *Hitler: A Study in Tyranny*, pp. 415–19 (there are errors and inaccuracies which have not been altogether eliminated in the new edition); Krausnick, pp. 282–305; Bruno Gebhardt: *Handbuch der deutschen Geschichte*, Vol. IV, pp. 228–31; recently – Klaus-Jürgen Müller: *Das Heer und Hitler*, pp. 255–99, where, however, nothing new is produced on the background to Fritsch's removal and no mention is made of the connection between Brauchitsch's appointment and his divorce case; the complex of intrigues and scandals is dealt with extensively in Deutsch, passim.

16 Hossbach, pp. 120–1.
17 Ibid., p. 121.
18 Himmler to Göring 29 July 1942, BA EAP 104/3. Schmidt was therefore shot much later than (e.g.) Ritter (p. 151) assumes, presumably on the basis of Hitler's speech in Barth on 13 June 1938 (no reference is given).
19 Kielmansegg, pp. 98–9; Krausnick, pp. 286–7; Funk Gisevius, *Bitter End*, p. 245.
20 Hossbach, p. 119.
21 On this and below see: Gebhardt, pp. 228–31; Hossbach, p. 124; Wolf Keilig: *Das deutsche Heer 1939–1945*, pp. 211/43, 91, 160; Max Domarus: *Hitler: Reden und Proklamationen 1932–1945*, pp. 782–5.
22 Domarus, p. 783; Bullock, p. 418 mentions 16 generals. Deutsch, pp. 260–5, is vague on details and numbers.
23 Hossbach, p. 125.
24 Keilig, p. 203/16–22; cf. Hossbach, p. 125.
25 Hossbach, p. 125.
26 Cf. Röhricht, pp. 111–18.
27 Hossbach, pp. 121–3; see also Foerster, pp. 92–3.
28 Krausnick, p. 289.
29 Hossbach, p. 122.
30 Krausnick, pp. 301–3; Foerster, pp. 94–6; Müller, p. 270; not in Domarus.
31 Keilig, p. 211/91.
32 Gebhardt, p. 230; see report by ADC, Lt. (res.) Rosenhagen in BA EAP 21–x–15/1; Gerd Bausch: 'Der Tod des Generalobersten Werner Freiherr von Fritsch', *Militärgeschichtliche Mitteilungen* 1970 No. 1, pp. 95–112.
33 Krausnick, pp. 289–90; Hossbach, pp. 122–3.
34 Krausnick, pp. 300–303 and in particular Notes 247 and 254; Gisevius, *Bis zum bitteren Ende* (special edition), p. 330 (not in original nor in 1954 edition).
35 Here and below see: Röhricht, pp. 109–18; Ritter, *Goerdeler*, pp. 169–70 (*Resistance*, pp. 78–9) and in particular Note 23; Krausnick, pp. 292–6, 305–10; *Spiegelbild einer Verschwörung*, pp. 430–1; Gisevius, *Ende*, Vol. I, pp. 407–50. (*Bitter End*, pp. 241–67). In notes made while under arrest in autumn 1944 Goerdeler recorded the various initiatives taken during the Fritsch crisis with which he was connected – representations to Gürtner, the Minister of Justice, Schwerin von Krosigk, the Finance Minister, Schacht, General Walter Heitz, President of the *Reich* Court Martial, General Wilhelm List in Dresden, C-in-C

of Group Headquarters 2 from 4 February 1938 and of Group Headquarters 5 from 1 April 1938 (Keilig, pp. 211/201) and Colonel Hermann Hoegner, Chief of Staff to General von Rundstedt, C-in-C of Group Headquarters 1 (Keilig, pp. 211/81).

36 Krausnick, p. 294 Note 216. Under interrogation by the *Gestapo* in autumn 1944 Oster confirmed the existence of this 'plan' for the period of the Fritsch crisis; *Spiegelbild*, p. 430.

37 Röhricht, p. 112; verbally to the author on 30 August 1966 from Alix von Winterfeldt, secretary to Colonel-General Fromm, C-in-C Replacement Army.

38 Gisevius, *Ende*, Vol. I, p. 410. Despite the hopelessness of the situation, in March or April Goerdeler made a statement to the effect that a *coup* against Hitler would take place shortly; this filtered through to Brauchitsch and gave rise to serious difficulties; Ritter, *Goerdeler*, pp. 171–2.

39 Röhricht, pp. 112–14.

40 Ibid., pp. 116–18.

41 Gisevius, *Ende*, Vol. I, pp. 407–9 (*Bitter End*, pp. 240–1); Jodl's diary, *Trial*, Vol. XXVIII, p. 365; *Spiegelbild*, p. 430; Krausnick, pp. 308–9. On 30 November 1944 Himmler wrote to *SS-Obergruppenführer* Herff, Chief of the SS Main Personnel Office, explaining the reduction in rank of Nebe to SS enlisted man and his simultaneous expulsion from the SS: 'As written notes discovered and the investigations of the *Gestapo* show, Nebe has been in the closest contact for years with persons who played leading roles in the 20th July putsch.'

42 Gisevius, *Bitter End*, pp. 257–61 confirmed by Frau Elisabeth Gärtner-Strünck, wife of Captain Strünck late of the *Abwehr* formerly an insurance director – IfZ, ZS 1811.

43 Gisevius, *Ende*, Vol. I, pp. 410–12; *Ende* (1954 ed.), p. 273.

44 [Walter] Huppenkothen: 'Der 20. Juli 1944', typescript, [1953] IfZ ZS 249/II, quoted in Krausnick, p. 309; according to him Major-General Graf von Brockdorff-Ahlefeldt, commanding the Potsdam Division, was involved in these plans; Witzleben was ready to participate but was prevented from doing so by illness.

45 *Spiegelbild*, p. 430.

46 Georg Thomas: 'Gedanken und Ereignisse' in *Schweizer Monatshefte* 25 (1945), p. 541; letter of 8 March 1964 to the author from Frau von Hase, widow of the former *Wehrmacht* Commandant of Berlin; cf. Krausnick, p. 309; Albert Krebs: *Fritz-Dietlof Graf von der Schulenburg*, p. 164.

47 Information from Frau von Hase, 8 March 1964; Krebs, p. 164; cf. Krausnick, p. 309.

48 Gisevius, *Ende*, Vol. I, pp. 419–20, 427, 429–30.

49 Gisevius, *Ende*, Vol. I, pp. 417–20.

50 Gisevius, *Ende*, Vol. I, pp. 450, 457–8; Hossbach, p. 172; Heinz, p. 75; Ritter, *Goerdeler*, p. 150 (*Resistance*, pp. 77, 152).

51 Jodl's diary, *Trial*, Vol. XXVIII, pp. 361–2; Krausnick, pp. 297–300.

52 Ibid. Diary of Captain (res.) Hermann Kaiser, 12 May 1943 (photocopy in possession of author); cf. Ludwig Kaiser, 'Ein Beitrag zur Geschichte der Staatsumwälzung vom 20. Juli 1944 (Goerdeler-Bewegung), Teilbericht', NA Record Group 338 MS no. B-285.

53 For this and below see Hossbach, pp. 113–26; Foerster, pp. 87–99; Gisevius, *Ende*, Vol. I, pp. 396–9, 456; Krausnick, pp. 295–305.

54 Foerster, p. 87 quoting a note by Beck which Foerster read after Beck's resignation but was lost during the war.

55 Foerster, p. 87; Peter Bor: *Gespräche mit Halder*, pp. 112–13; Hossbach, p. 113 says that on the next morning, 27 January, he succeeded in removing Beck's doubts about the nature of the intrigue.

56 Krausnick, pp. 306–7; Eberhard Zeller in *The Flame of Freedom*, pp. 3–19 gives

an excellent short biography of Beck at the beginning of the book but in this chapter (not in the book as a whole) fails to give the background. The impression is thus given that Beck was the first man in an influential position to give thought to a *coup*.

57 'Protokoll aus der Verhandlung Halder [vor der] Spruchkammer X München [15.–21. Sept. 1948],' mimeographed Protokoll B der Anklagebehörde der Spruchkammer München X, Az. BY 11/47, p. 67, IfZ; Bor, pp. 112–13.

58 'Protokoll . . . Halder', p. 67.

NOTES/PART II/CHAPTER 4

1 Bruno Gebhardt: *Handbuch der deutschen Geschichte*, Vol. IV, pp. 231–6, also applicable below; Ernst von Weizsäcker: *Erinnerungen*, pp. 148–51.

2 See the account by Fritz Wiedemann in *Der Mann der Feldherr werden wollte*, pp. 121–2. According to this Göring telephoned through the text of the 'call for assistance' from Berlin to Seyss-Inquart, ending with the words: 'So – I have now received your telegram!'

3 On this point and below see Gebhardt, pp. 237–44; Weizsäcker, pp. 162–90.

4 See Max Domarus: *Hitler: Reden und Proklamationen 1932–1945*, pp. 837–8.

5 *Trial of the Major War Criminals before the International Military Tribunal*, Vol. XXV, pp. 414–27 and Vol. XXVIII pp. 372–3; see also Helmut Krausnick: 'Vorgeschichte und Beginn des militärischen Widerstandes gegen Hitler' in *Vollmacht des Gewissens*, Vol. I, pp. 310–12; Gebhardt, p. 239 does not mention these documents so that the impression might be given that military measures were only initiated on the German side after 20 May. For proceedings within the higher levels of the German military see Klaus-Jurgen Müller: *Das Heer und Hitler*, pp. 300–44.

6 *Trial*, Vol. XXV, pp. 433–8, 445–7. On 28 May Hitler held a conference in the *Reich* Chancellery with Göring, Keitel, Brauchitsch, Raeder, Beck, Ribbentrop and Neurath, when he explained his intentions verbally. In at least two public speeches, on 12 September 1938 and 30 January 1939, Hitler himself stated that on 28 May he had ordered preparation of military measures against Czechoslovakia; on 30 January he even referred to an 'order for preparation of military intervention against this State with a date of 2 October'; see Domarus, pp. 868–9.

7 Domarus, p. 875.

8 Krausnick, pp. 312–13.

9 Jodl's diary in *Trial*, Vol. XXVIII, pp. 373–4.

10 Ibid.

11 Ibid., pp. 374–5; Erich Kordt: *Nicht aus den Akten*, pp. 238–9.

12 *Trial*, Vol. XXV, pp. 460–2; Domarus, pp. 880, 883.

13 *Trial*, Vol. XXV, pp. 460–2. Italics represent underlining in original.

14 Ibid., pp. 462–9.

15 Ibid., pp. 469–75; also Jodl's diary in *Trial*, Vol. XXVIII pp. 381–2 and in general pp. 372–89.

16 Domarus, pp. 889–906.

17 Ibid., pp. 922–33.

18 On this point and below see Gebhardt, pp. 240–4.

19 Ibid., p. 242.

CHAPTER 5

1 See Gerhard Ritter: *Carl Goerdeler und die deutsche Widerstandsbewegung*, p. 174 (*The German Resistance*, p. 101).

2 On this point and below see Ritter, *Goerdeler*, pp. 21, 26–7, 47, 50, 59 (*Resistance*, pp. 18–19, 25–7).

3 Ritter, *Goerdeler*, p. 68 (*Resistance*, p. 30). See also documentation in 'H Kr' (Helmut Krausnick): 'Goerdeler und die Deportation der Leipziger Juden' in *VfZ* 13 (1965), pp. 338–9.

4 Ritter, *Goerdeler*, p. 71; Elfriede Nebgen: *Jakob Kaiser*, p. 132.

5 Ritter, *Goerdeler*, pp. 71–6 (*Resistance*, pp. 31–3).

6 Ritter, *Goerdeler*, pp. 76–8 (*Resistance*, p. 33).

7 Ritter, *Goerdeler*, p. 86 (*Resistance*, pp. 35–6).

8 Ibid.; even in the spring of 1936 Goerdeler had said privately that his continuance in office depended on the fate of the Mendelssohn memorial; see Harold C. Deutsch: *The Conspiracy against Hitler in the Twilight War*, pp. 11–12.

9 On this point and below see Ritter, *Goerdeler*, pp. 157–161 (*Resistance*, pp. 80–3); Otto Kopp: 'Die Niederschrift von Hans Walz "Meine Mitwirkung an der Aktion Goerdeler" ' in Otto Kopp (editor): *Widerstand und Erneuerung*, pp. 98–120.

10 Goerdeler gave detailed reports in writing on all his journeys to Krupp, Bosch, Göring, Schacht, Fritsch, Beck, Halder and Thomas and initially also to the *Reich* Chancellery. The reports have been preserved and are dealt with by Gerhard Ritter in his biography of Goerdeler.

11 Ritter, *Goerdeler*, pp. 166–7.

12 Verbally to the author from Pierre Bertaux on 9 June 1965, also extracts from his diary of 1938 sent with a letter dated 10 May 1967; Ritter (op. cit., pp. 167–73) did not know the details of these contacts.

13 Bertaux cannot remember with complete certainty whether Goerdeler and Schairer came together; there is also an entry in his diary only four weeks later referring to a conversation 'some months ago'; the meeting may therefore have taken place somewhat earlier, perhaps even in August 1937 but Bertaux himself does not think this likely. The information given by Ritter (op. cit., p. 170 and p. 484 Note 25) showing that Goerdeler was in London from 15 March to 14 April 1938, is therefore incomplete; see also Ritter, op. cit., p. 160, and A. P. Young: *The 'X' Documents*, passim.

14 Ian Colvin: *Vansittart in Office*, pp. 150, 153–5. Colvin's book is not a work of scholarship (this is even more applicable to the work quoted below); far too frequently he fails to give sources, giving the erroneous impression that the book reproduced certain documents for the first time. Nevertheless it does give a valuable account of Vansittart's work and career and in some cases produces hitherto unknown material, some of it from Vansittart's papers. According to Ian Colvin in *Master Spy (Chief of Intelligence)*, pp. 70–1, Vansittart said much the same about Kleist-Schmenzin: ' "Of all the Germans I saw", Lord Vansittart told me afterwards, "Kleist had the stuff in him for a revolution against Hitler. But he wanted the Polish Corridor, wanted to make a deal".' Colvin does add, however, that there is no other evidence of Kleist having spoken about Poland. On Kleist's mission see pp. 60–3 below.

15 Ritter, op. cit., pp. 170–1 (*Resistance*, pp. 83–4) explicitly emphasizes this; Hermann Graml in 'Die aussenpolitischen Vorstellungen des deutschen Widerstandes' in Walter Schmitthenner and Hans Buchheim (editors): *Der deutsche Widerstand gegen Hitler*, p. 29 (*The German Resistance to Hitler*, pp. 13–14), says nothing new on this point.

16 Bernd-Jürgen Wendt: *München 1938*, p. 13; Graml, pp. 15–29. Both these books attempt, with some success, to give an unprejudiced account of the foreign policy ideas of the German opposition; as already mentioned, this produces little that is new but emphasizes another angle from that of Ritter and Rothfels who dealt primarily with the wishes of the opposition rather than circumstances on the other side. On the mistrust aroused by Goerdeler see Eugen Spier: *Focus: A Footnote to the History of the Thirties*, pp. 133–4.

17 Wendt, pp. 17–28 – also applicable below; Graml, pp. 15–29. On British, French

and general European policy during the Sudeten crisis (March-October 1938) see *Documents on British Foreign Policy 1919–1939*, (hereafter referred to as *DBFP*), Third Series, Vols. I and II; *Documents on German Foreign Policy 1918–1945* (hereafter referred to as *DGFP*), Series D, Vol. II; Keith Feiling: *The Life of Neville Chamberlain*, pp. 363–82; Boris Celovsky: *Das Münchner Abkommen 1938*; Helmuth K. G. Rönnefarth: *Die Sudetenkrise in der internationalen Politik* (includes some passages on the activity of the opposition which cannot be regarded as definitive despite a broad basis of sources); Hans Rothfels: *The German Opposition to Hitler*, pp. 56–63; Ritter, *Goerdeler*, pp. 183–203.

18 Wendt, pp. 29–35, 45–51, 64; Graml, p. 29.

19 See Chamberlain's statements in his radio broadcast of 26 November 1939 in *Keesing's Contemporary Archives*, Vol. III, 1937–1940, pp. 3819–20.

20 On this point and below see Wendt, pp. 36–45. Trott argued for what he called an honourable conspiracy in 1939 to prevent or shorten war, and to overthrow Hitler, when he tried to get England and America to support the opposition; it was nothing new, he said, and it had been an instrument of European policy many times before the 19th century, particularly in wars of religion. See David Astor, 'Why the Revolt against Hitler Was Ignored: On the British Reluctance to Deal with German Anti-Nazis', *Encounter* 32 (1969) No 6, p. 9.

21 Kopp, p. 106.

22 Chamberlain to Halifax, 19 August 1938, *DBFP* II, p. 686.

23 Graml, p. 29; Colvin, *Vansittart*, p. 310.

24 Ritter, *Resistance*, p. 114.

25 Colvin, op. cit., pp. 152–5 and passim.

26 Ibid., p. 154.

27 Ibid., pp. 201–2, 206.

28 Ibid., p. 199.

29 The arguments adduced by Sir John W. Wheeler-Bennett in *The Nemesis of Power*, p. 415, to explain the British attitude are tendentious and miss the point. It is simply not true that the majority of those who demanded that Britain and France stand firm, were enthusiastic supporters of Hitler and only changed their tune when they realized that Hitler could obtain no more for Germany without endangering what had already been won. The truth is the opposite. The majority of these men fought Hitler from the outset in so far as they could. See Rothfels op. cit. and Ritter, *Goerdeler*, both of whom, in their notes, dispute Wheeler-Bennett's distortions.

30 Colvin, op. cit., pp. 216–17; Ritter, *Goerdeler*, pp. 186–7 (*Resistance*, pp. 96–7); Rothfels, *Die deutsche Opposition gegen Hitler*, pp. 63–70, 137–9; Rothfels: 'Trott und die Aussenpolitik des Widerstandes' in *VfZ* 12 (1964), pp. 300–305.

31 On the Wiedemann mission see Wiedemann: *Der Mann der Feldherr werden wollte*, pp. 158–67; Winston S. Churchill: *The Second World War*, Vol. 1, p. 290; *DBFP* Vol. I, Nos 510, 511; Kordt: *Nicht aus den Akten*, p. 234; Rönnefarth, Part I, pp. 362–6. The report on his conversation with Lord Halifax (*DBFP* I, No 510) repeats Wiedemann's statement that Hitler's patience was not inexhaustible and that a serious incident might lead to German intervention; according to this report, however, at the same time Wiedemann gave an assurance that a solution by force was not envisaged in the foreseeable future. It is conceivable that Wiedemann did mention the date of March 1939 but asked Halifax not to record it in writing. See Rönnefarth, pp. 364–5.

32 See Rudi Strauch: *Sir Nevile Henderson*, pp. 134–8, quoted in Wendt, pp. 13–14.

33 *DBFP* II, No 595, quoted in Wendt, p. 14.

34 Wendt, p. 14.

35 Colvin, op. cit., pp. 210–11; this gives the timing of the meeting with Kleist as

'just after the fall of Austria'. In Colvin's book on Canaris (*Master Spy* or *Chief of Intelligence*), which is far less carefully documented than his biography of Vansittart, the date of his first meeting with Kleist is given as February 1938 (p. 5), that of discussions of the type mentioned here as April 1938 (p. 57) and early May 1938 (pp. 58–60). In his book on Vansittart more emphasis is laid on the transmission of the results to Ogilvie-Forbes, though he points out that there is no written proof that Ogilvie-Forbes passed them on to London in his turn. Schlabrendorff makes no mention of the matter in *Revolt against Hitler* and only a passing reference to it in *Secret War* (p. 91). Kleist's other activities and Schlabrendorff's estimate of Colvin ('intelligent, cautious, daring and discreet') give credibility to his account. Rothfels, *German Opposition*, pp. 58–9 and Ritter, *Goerdeler*, p. 184 (*Resistance*, p. 95) do not mention this initiative on the part of the opposition; Ritter, like Rothfels, thinks that the first warning to the British government came from Kleist, but not until August 1938. On events connected with Kleist's journey see also Wendt, pp. 14–16 and Rönnefarth, pp. 402–4.

36 Colvin, *Vansittart*, p. 218.

37 Ibid., pp. 206, 216, 218–21.

38 Ibid., pp. 221–9; Schlabrendorff: *Offiziere gegen Hitler*, pp. 41–2 and *Secret War against Hitler*, pp. 91–5. On points below see also Ritter, *Goerdeler*, pp. 184–7 (*Resistance*, 95–6) and Rothfels, *German Opposition*, p. 59; both these two doubt the major role played by Colvin in preparing Kleist's mission; see also Hans Rothfels: 'The German Resistance in Its International Aspects' in *International Affairs* 34 (1958), pp. 479–80; also the account in Wheeler-Bennett, pp. 409–13. According to information given to Dr Helmut Krausnick ('Vorgeschichte und Beginn des militärischen Widerstandes gegen Hitler' in *Vollmacht des Gewissens* I, p. 330) by Kleist's son, Ewald-Heinrich von Kleist, the *initiative* for the journey came from Kleist himself. According to his account of the origin of the mission the part played by Colvin consisted in notifying and recommending Kleist to his friend Lord Lloyd; Colvin also says that, when asked by British passport officials and the Military Attaché, he had told them that Kleist possessed letters of introduction to Winston Churchill and Lord Lloyd and was one of the secret opponents of Hitler – Colvin, op. cit., pp. 221–3. On Colvin's activity as an intermediary see also Schlabrendorff, *Offiziere*, p. 41 and *Secret War*, p. 91; also the doubts of Ritter (*Goerdeler*, p. 488 Note 49) and Rothfels (*Die deutsche Opposition gegen Hitler*, p. 190, Note 46).

39 Colvin, op. cit., p. 223. This letter is not repoduced in *DBFP* II but is mentioned in a special annex on 'unofficial German contacts' in August and September 1938 (p. 683).

40 Colvin, *Vansittart*, p. 223 and *Master Spy* or *Chief of Intelligence*, p. 67.

41 Colvin, *Master Spy* or *Chief of Intelligence*, pp. 69–70 and *Vansittart*, p. 223 says that Kleist arrived in London on 17 August; all other contemporary reports give the date as the 18th – see *DBFP* II pp. 683–96; on the Kleist mission see also Krausnick, op. cit., pp. 330–3.

42 See Vansittart's report to Lord Halifax quoted by Colvin in *Vansittart*, pp. 223–7; he does not mention that it had already been published in DBFP II, pp. 683–6.

43 In fact, on the day of Kleist's arrival, the British government was informed by Colonel Mason-Macfarlane, its Military Attaché in Berlin, that the planned date of attack was end September – Ritter, *Goerdeler*, p. 186 (*Resistance*, p. 96) based on *DBFP* II, No. 658.

44 This message to Lord Lloyd may have originated from Colvin but he was, no doubt, not Lloyd's only contact in Germany.

45 *DBFP* II, No 658 and p. 685; see also Colvin, op. cit., p. 230.

46 Chamberlain's letter to Halifax – *DBFP* I, pp. 686–7, reproduced in Colvin, op.

cit., pp. 227–8.

47 Schlabrendorff, *Offiziere*, pp. 43–4 and *Secret War*, pp. 93–4.

48 *DBFP* II, No 648.

49 Ibid.

50 Weizsäcker Exhibit 38, W. Doc. 38, W.-Doc.-Book 1c, Case 11 quoted in plea by defence counsels Warren E. Magee and Hellmut Becker on 28 April 1949 for revision of sentence and release from arrest for Ernst Freiherr von Weizsäcker – roneoed. The files, or copies thereof, are to be found in State Archives (henceforth: StA) Nuremberg and National Archives, Washington (henceforth: NA).

51 Record of Churchill's conversation with Kleist in *DBFP* II, pp. 687–8. For security reasons Churchill's letter (see Colvin, op. cit., p. 229) was transmitted to Colvin via a British diplomat in Berlin and passed on to Kleist by Colvin. Schlabrendorff (*Offiziere*, p. 42 and *Secret War*, p. 95) says that the letter was sent to Berlin by the British diplomatic bag, fetched by him (Schlabrendorff) from the British Embassy and then passed on to Kleist. The text of the letter is to be found in *DBFP* II, pp. 688–9 and extracts therefrom in a summary prepared by the German Foreign Ministry on foreign reactions to the Sudeten crisis and the possibility of war – *DGFP* II, No 436.

52 Extract in *DBFP* II, pp. 172–5.

53 Colvin, op. cit., p. 234.

54 Colvin, *Master Spy* or *Chief of Intelligence*, p. 72. In his report of 18 August Vansittart says that Kleist would return to Germany on 'Tuesday' which would be 23 August; see also Colvin, *Vansittart*, p. 226.

55 Schlabrendorff, *Offiziere*, p. 42 and *Secret War*, p. 95; Ritter, *Goerdeler*, p. 488, Note 49; *DGFP* II, No 436. Colvin in *Vansittart*, pp. 233–4, quotes his letter to Lord Lloyd of 30 August 1938, in which he gives Kleist's impression of the effect on Berlin made by his mission.

56 Krausnick, pp. 333–4; for details see pp. 78–80 below.

57 Böhm-Tettelbach's evidence in 'Protokoll aus der Verhandlung Halder [vor der] Spruchkammer X München'. pp. 3, 69–70, 87, IfZ; Peter Bor's account in *Gespräche mit Halder*, p. 121, is based on this source; Hans Böhm-Tettelbach, 'Ein Mann hat gesprochen' in *Rheinische Post*, 10 July 1948, p. 2; Wheeler-Bennett, pp. 413–14; see also Ritter's correction (*Goerdeler*, p. 489, Note 55); Krausnick, op. cit., pp. 339–40 cites further evidence by Halder and Böhm-Tettelbach; also Hans-Bernd Gisevius: *Bis zum bittern Ende*, Vol. II, p. 66 (not in English translation); Kordt, p. 258. From almost all sides people were trying to bring pressure to bear on Hitler, even from the German Embassy in Moscow; on 20 August the private secretary to Graf Friedrich Werner von der Schulenburg, the German Ambassador, told a British colleague that only a completely categorical declaration by Britain would convince Hitler that Britain would intervene in the event of a German attack on Czechoslovakia; he would never believe the reports of German diplomats. Krausnick, op. cit., p. 353, quotes *DBFP* II, No 673.

58 Krausnick, op. cit., pp. 339–41.

59 Ibid., p. 340 (implied); Wheeler-Bennett, p. 414.

60 Krausnick, op. cit., p. 340.

61 Ibid.; Kordt, p. 244.

62 Wheeler-Bennett, pp. 416–17 states that the first time Weizsäcker declared himself to be a member of the resistance movement was at his trial before the International Military Tribunal, Nuremberg, and that he had made no mention of this when previously confidentially interrogated by the Allies; he was not opposed to war, Wheeler-Bennett says, provided that it did not jeopardize the existence of the German *Reich*; he had never made any real protest against Hitler's war policy. In point of fact, Weizsäcker had to choose between frank out-

spoken protest such as that of Beck, leading inevitably to resignation or dismissal, and an attempt to sabotage Hitler's policy when it was leading to war. From outside, after having left the foreign service, Weizsäcker could have presented himself as an honest and upright man, but he could have achieved nothing. Working from inside, he could at least try to stop, avert or contain the evil. Evidence exists that this was what he did, in full knowledge that he was likely to be misunderstood, and this evidence is more convincing than Wheeler-Bennett and the documents which he quotes as proof, in which Weizsäcker naturally had to speak the language of the regime. See Carl J. Burckhardt: *Meine Danziger Mission 1937–1939*, pp. 67–8, 145, 181–3; statements by the Norwegian Bishop Berggrav and the Bishop of Chichester to the International Military Tribunal at the Weizsäcker trial and extracts from statements by Sir Nevile Henderson, François-Poncet, Lord Halifax and Churchill in *Trials of War Criminals before the Nuernberg Military Tribunals under Control Council Law No 10,* Vol. XIV (The Ministries Case), pp. 98, 104–5, 109, 112, 125; Hellmut Becker: 'Plaidoyer für Ernst von Weizsäcker', roneoed, Nuremberg 1948 – in State Archives – and the plea for release from arrest (Note 50 above).

63 Kordt, pp. 177–83; Ritter, *Goerdeler,* p. 191 (*Resistance,* p. 100).

64 Ernst von Weizsäcker: *Erinnerungen,* pp. 173–7; Burckhardt, p. 182.

65 On this point and below see Kordt, pp. 241–4.

66 Burckhardt, pp. 181–3; Weizsäcker, p. 179. Weizsäcker gives the timing as 'end August' but Burckhardt, based on his notes, says that he arrived in Berne on the following day, on 2 September.

67 Burckhardt, pp. 183–7. Here the letter is given in German; the English original is in *DBFP* II, pp. 689–92. Oddly a telegram from Sir George Warner to Lord Halifax is dated late afternoon of 5 September (*DBFP* II, No 775), although Stevenson's letter shows that Burckhardt's talk with Weizsäcker took place on 1 September and Burckhardt must have been in Berne next day.

68 The original shows 'Prime Minister'. Burckhardt, p. 185 wrongly translates 'Foreign Minister'.

69 Kordt, pp. 246–9; Weizsäcker, pp. 177–9; Krausnick, op. cit., pp. 340–2; Wheeler-Bennett, pp. 417–19; Rothfels, *German Opposition,* pp. 57–60 and 'German Resistance'; pp. 480–1; Ritter, *Goerdeler,* pp. 191–2 (*Resistance,* pp. 100–101). All these accounts are based almost exclusively on information from the Kordt brothers. Affidavits lodged by Vansittart for the Nuremberg trial on 12 and 31 August 1948 are worth noting – StA, Nuremberg, NG 5786 and NG 5786A are German translations of the English originals; the quotation is here retranslated. Vansittart describes the Kordt brothers as opportunists who never offered any real resistance, as proved by the fact that they served Hitler to the end and never seized an opportunity to defect. Rothfels (*deutsche Opposition,* pp. 190–1 Note 47) gives a possible explanation for Vansittart's remarkable lapse of memory – the sentence in the second affidavit: 'The whole basis of my attitude to Germany was the conviction that there neither was nor could be any effective opposition there.' It is hardly possible to ignore the undertone of hatred in Vansittart's further statements. Colvin, Vansittart's biographer, goes even further (*Vansittart,* p. 325) and refers to 'the vehement disillusion and rejection of all things German that characterized Vansittart in the war years and after' and in the next sentence: 'That he was emphatically warned by Kordt on or about 16 June [1939] of the German–Russian negotiations there is no reason to doubt.'

70 In his diary Jodl mentions only 5 active and 14 *Landwehr* divisions – *Trial of the Major War Criminals before the International Military Tribunal,* Vol. XXVIII, p. 388.

71 Kordt, pp. 249–52.

72 Ibid., p. 279; *DGFP* II, No 382; Wendt, p. 136, Note 17. Wendt explains the contradiction between Theo Kordt's official report (*DGFP* II, No 382) and that to

his brother Erich Kordt (Kordt, p. 279), not by the necessity for camouflage and use of the regime's terminology, but by the fact that Weizsäcker and the Kordt brothers were pursuing the same aim as Hitler – annexation of the Sudetenland – and were opposed only to Hitler's methods. This is unconvincing; obviously, in his official report, Theo Kordt could not say that he had told Wilson that he was a member of the opposition.

73 Wheeler-Bennett, p. 418.
74 Kordt, p. 279.
75 Ibid., pp. 250–2, 279–81 – also applicable below.
76 Wendt, pp. 68–71 points out the divergence between Kordt's statements and Weizsäcker's attitude as described in his memoirs. He says that either Weizsäcker had forgotten that he had given Kordt much stricter instructions than merely to obtain the clearest, most discreet and, for Hitler, most inoffensive warning possible; alternatively that, in agreement with the more revolutionary Oster, the Kordt brothers had gone further than Weizsäcker intended.
77 Rothfels, *deutsche Opposition*, p. 68, where no source is given; Rönnefarth, Part I, p. 506 and Part II, p. 247, Note 41, based on evidence by Theo Kordt in the Wilhelmstrasse Trial, 14 July 1948, Minute 12029. Halifax's phrase translated back from the German.
78 Ritter, *Goerdeler*, pp. 489–90, Note 57.
79 *DBFP* II, Nos 811, 815; see also Krausnick, op. cit., pp. 354–5.
80 *DBFP* II, Nos 819, 823, also pp. 646–55 in same volume.
81 Ibid., No 825.
82 Ibid., No 837, Note 1.
83 Ibid., pp. 680–2.
84 Kordt, pp. 256–7.
85 Max Domarus: *Hitler: Reden und Proklamationen 1932–1945*, pp. 897–906.

CHAPTER 6

1 Friedrich Hossbach: *Zwischen Wehrmacht und Hitler 1934–1938*, p. 193; Wolfgang Foerster: *Generaloberst Ludwig Beck: Sein Kampf gegen den Krieg*, pp. 84, 141–2; Schlabrendorff in *Offiziere gegen Hitler*, pp. 37–8 (not in *The Secret War against Hitler*) tells of a 'conversation' between Beck and Hitler but there was not, in fact, ever any such thing. Rudolf Pechel in *Deutscher Widerstand*, p. 152, is also wrong when he says that during a conversation with Hitler in the autumn of 1938 Beck demanded guarantees against military adventure and resigned when these were refused. There were many stories about this alleged conversation; people could not believe that the Chief of the General Staff of the Army had never been able to speak personally to Hitler, the Supreme Commander of the *Wehrmacht*. Even Otto John in 'Männer im Kampf gegen Hitler (IV) – Wilhelm Leuschner', *Blick in die Welt* 2 (1947) No 9, p. 20, mentions this 'conversation' despite the fact that he was himself close to these events.
2 Hossbach, p. 136.
3 Rudolf Beck: 'Beiträge zur Lebensgeschichte und Charakteristik des Generaloberst Ludwig Beck', typescript unsigned and undated (presumably before 1952), p. 2; Foerster, pp. 90–1; see also Max Domarus: *Hitler: Reden und Proklamationen 1932–1945*, pp. 1047–67 which gives Hitler's speech of 30 January 1939, when he admitted in public that on 28 May 1938 he had issued the order 'for preparation of military action against this state [Czechoslovakia] with the target date of 2 October [1938]'.
4 Verbally to the author on 30 August 1966 from Alix von Winterfeldt who was at the time secretary to Colonel-General Fromm, C-in-C of the Replacement Army; Heinz Guderian: *Panzer Leader*, pp. 32–3; Foerster, pp. 137–8. Ulrich von Hassell: *The von Hassell Diaries*, pp. 242–3; Eduard Spranger: 'Generaloberst

Beck in der Mittwochsgesellschaft: Zu dem Buch: Ludwig Beck "Studien" ' in *Universitas* 11 (1956), p. 192 ('There was a knowing serenity about Ludwig Beck ...'); Gerhard Ritter: *Carl Goerdeler und die deutsche Widerstandsbewegung*, p. 147 (*The German Resistance*, 75–6); Günther Blumentritt: 'Stellungnahme zu dem Buch "Offiziere gegen Hitler: Nach einem Erlebnisbericht von Fabian v. Schlabrendorff ... 1946"', typescript, 1946, in Otto John's papers Folio 2, p. 20; Gert Bucheit in *Ludwig Beck: Ein preussischer General* relies primarily on sources already mentioned here.

5 Foerster, p. 90; Spranger, p. 192.

6 Ritter, *Goerdeler*, p. 177 (*Resistance*, pp. 89–90); for Brauchitsch see character description based on statements by Halder in Harold C. Deutsch: *The Conspiracy against Hitler in the Twilight War*, pp. 34–5.

7 Jodl's diary in *Trial of the Major War Criminals before the International Tribunal*, Vol. XXVIII, p. 360.

8 *Trial*, Vol. XX, p. 624; Ritter, *Goerdeler*, p. 181.

9 Ritter, *Goerdeler*, pp. 177–83 (*Resistance*, pp. 90–2); also applicable below; Edgar Röhricht: *Pflicht und Gewissen*, pp. 131–6.

10 Ritter, *Goerdeler*, p. 179 (*Resistance*, pp. 92–3).

11 Copy of the memorandum from Beck's papers in Foerster, pp. 100–105; signed typed draft in BA – MAH 08-28/4; Klaus-Jürgen Müller: *Das Heer und Hitler*, p. 301.

12 Müller, p. 305.

13 Foerster, p. 107; *Trial*, Vol. XXV, p. 434.

14 Reproduced in Foerster, pp. 109–13, see also pp. 106–9; Helmut Krausnick: 'Vorgeschichte und Beginn des militärischen Widerstandes gegen Hitler' in *Vollmacht des Gewissens I*, pp. 310–12.

15 Foerster, p. 98; manuscript draft by Beck in BA – MA H 08-28/3; Müller, pp. 309–13, 318. Basing himself on his general knowledge of Beck's thinking, Müller maintains that Beck's agreement with Hitler's aims (*Lebensraum*, destruction of Czechoslovakia by force) was not a tactical manoeuvre but represented Beck's convictions at the time. According to Müller Beck also thought that the probability of success should be the criterion for or against military action against Czechoslovakia. See also Ritter, *Goerdeler*, pp. 174–5 (*Resistance*, pp. 86–7); Ernst von Weizsäcker: *Erinnerungen*, p. 174; Spranger, pp. 185–6, 193.

16 Foerster, p. 109.

17 *Trial*, Vol. XXV, pp. 434–9 and Jodl's diary in Vol. XXVIII, p. 373.

18 Foerster, pp. 114–16; BA – MA H 08–28/3; Müller, pp. 651–4.

19 The date of the war game is not given either by Foerster or by Röhricht or by Müller.

20 Beck said something on these lines to Ritter in 1943 (*Goerdeler*, p. 492, Note 200): in the view of the General Staff a French attack could not have been halted until it had reached Gotha.

21 Foerster, p. 115; Röhricht, p. 120.

22 Röhricht, pp. 120–1.

23 Ibid., pp. 121–3.

24 Foerster, pp. 116–21 (extracts); typescript signed by Beck in BA–MA H 08–28/4; Müller, pp. 317–26.

25 Foerster, p. 120.

26 Müller, pp. 317–26 has missed this convincing argument.

27 Foerster, pp. 121–4; on Beck's memoranda and lectures see Krausnick, op. cit., pp. 317–27; Ritter, *Goerdeler*, pp. 174–83 (*Resistance*, pp. 86–91).

28 Foerster, p. 122; BA–MA H 08–28/4; Müller, pp. 321–6.

29 Müller, p. 324 reads into the remark about a 'clarifying showdown between *Wehrmacht* and SS' a desire on Beck's part to eliminate Hitler's extremist advisers, whom Beck (according to Müller) regarded as the originators of Hitler's

war policy, and to reestablish the customary influence of the Army leaders on those of the state. Whereas Müller is usually meticulous in his interpretation of Beck's notes, in this case he does not deal with the question why Beck did not write what he meant; supposing that Beck did mean what he wrote, Müller does not explain why these extremist advisers should have been found only in the SS and not in the Foreign Ministry and the Party as well.

30 Foerster, pp. 124–5 (extract); BA–MA H 08–28/4; Müller, pp. 326–8.

31 Foerster, p. 124; see also Ritter, *Goerdeler*, pp. 130–53 (*Resistance*, pp. 74–9).

32 Foerster, p. 125.

33 Erich Kosthorst in *Die deutsche Opposition gegen Hitler zwischen Polen- und Frankreichfeldzug*, p. 54, takes the view that, while in office, Beck was not prepared to initiate a *coup*: Müller, pp. 329–32 says that Beck thought 'solely of a reform programme', not of overthrowing the regime, and that he did not realize that reform was impossible without overthrowing it – despite 30 June 1934, 5 November 1937, the occupation of Austria and the despicable treatment of Fritsch by Hitler. Müller's arguments (pp. 330–1) against any intention on Beck's part to initiate a *coup* are not cogent. He says, for instance, that to try to restrict the internal upheaval to Berlin was 'illusory and unrealistic' – but this would be equally applicable to any hope of initiating reform without overthrowing the regime, as Müller himself later says (p. 332); he says that Beck thought it possible to deal with the SS leaders 'somewhat in the way the SA leaders were dealt with on 30 June 1934' without a *coup d'état* against the Hitler regime – this must be described as equally illusory; finally on his p. 341 Müller quotes statements by Beck of August and November 1938 (he had refused to approve 'any sort of Nazi adventure. An ultimate German victory is an impossibility' – he could 'not remain inactive while this gang of criminals plunged into war') which clearly disprove his own theory that Beck was suffering from illusions about the nature of the regime and the possibility of reforming it. Whether Beck had the strength of character to carry out a *coup d'état* is an unanswerable question; the fact that he made no attempt to do so is completely explicable on other grounds, primarily Brauchitsch's refusal to participate; alone and as Chief of Staff with no troops under his command, Beck could do nothing.

34 From files of OKM [Naval High Command], Section 1, dealing with 'Operation Green'; extracts are in Krausnick, pp. 314–15 and Walter Baum: 'Marine, Nationalsozialismus und Widerstand' in *VfZ* 11 (1963), pp. 22–3; see also Müller, pp. 316–17.

35 Extracts from the same source as Guse's notes in Krausnick, pp. 316–17.

36 See p. 59 above. In the light of the manifold origins of the plans it seems premature, or at least an over-simplification, to describe this turning point as 'the starting point for the planning of the *coup d'état*' as do Rothfels in *German Opposition*, p. 57 and Max Braubach in *Der Weg zum 20. Juli 1944*, p. 16 referred to by Rothfels on his p. 190 Note 41; emphasis on the fact that this was the moment when Beck became ready for a coup, however, is correct.

37 Foerster, pp. 125–8 – extract from Beck's notes for an address dated 29 July.

38 Ibid.

39 Beck originally wished to act immediately after receipt of the French and British protest notes, anticipated for the end of August; Foerster, pp. 124, 127.

40 Lutz Graf Schwerin von Krosigk: *Es geschah in Deutschland*, pp. 191–2.

41 Foerster, pp. 126–7, 136–7 – also applicable below; Krausnick, p. 329.

42 Hossbach quoted by Foerster, pp. 127–8 and p. 170 Note 83; Gisevius: *Bis zum bittern Ende*, Vol. II, p. 20 and *Bis zum bittern Ende* (special edition, 1964), pp. 336–9 (not in English translation); see also Krausnick, pp. 320–1; in contrast see Müller, pp. 326–32.

43 Extracts in Foerster, pp. 128–37.

44 Ibid., p. 145. According to the Chief of the General Staff of Group Command IV,

Major-General Curt Bernard, the Chiefs of the General Staff of Army Groups 'received a secret written communication from the Chief of the General Staff of the Army, General Beck, in which he asked us to represent and support his political and military opinions with which we were familiar *vis-à-vis* Hitler. It was then general knowledge in the General Staff that the Commander-in-Chief of the Army, Colonel-General von Brauchitsch, shortly before this was supposed to have handed Hitler a memorandum prepared by Beck in which urgent warnings were submitted against the continuation of a policy that must lead to a two-front war which could not be carried on by Germany in the long term.' [Curt] Bernard, account dated 28 May 1945, typescript, IfZ, ED 106 Archiv Walter Hammer, Vol. 90.

45 Foerster, pp. 138–42; Krausnick, pp. 322–4. These two both rely primarily on the account of Colonel-General (then General) Wilhelm Adam, Krausnick also on that of the later Field Marshal Freiherr von Weichs. See also Ferdinand Sauerbruch: *Das war mein Leben*, pp. 530–4 (Beck told him of all this in 1939); Wilhelm Adam: 'Eidesstattliche Erklärung Nr. 2: betrifft: Stimmung unter den höheren Generalstabsoffizieren bald nach der "Machtergreifung" ', typescript, undated, in IfZ ZS 6 and 'Colonel-General Wilhelm Adam', typescript, undated, in John's papers, folio 3; for details see Müller, pp. 334–7.

46 Foerster, pp. 138–42; Krausnick, pp. 322–4; according to Adam by Beck, according to Weichs by Brauchitsch.

47 Adam did this at the end of August when Hitler made a tour of inspection along the Siegfried Line; see 'Colonel-General Wilhelm Adam', p. 3; confirmation by Lieutenant-General (retd) Gerhard Engel in 'Protokoll aus der Verhandlung Halder [vor der] Spruchkammer X München', p. 81. IfZ.

48 Jodl's diary, *Trial*, Vol. XXVIII, p. 378, quoted by Krausnick, p. 327.

49 Hossbach, pp. 129, 171–3.

50 Jodl's diary, *Trial*, Vol. XXVIII, pp. 373–4 reads: '10 August. The Army Chiefs and the Chiefs of Air Force Groups, Lieutenant-Colonel Jeschonnek and I are ordered to come to the "Berghof". After the meal, the *Führer* gives a speech of nearly three hours in which he sets forth his political thought. Afterwards, attempts by individual generals to point out to the *Führer* our lack of preparedness fail pitifully, especially the remark by General von Wietersheim which he attributes to General Adam that the western defences could be held for three weeks at the most. The *Führer* becomes very angry and blows up with the words, then the entire Army was worthless; "I tell you, General, the position will be held not three weeks but three years".' Cf. Domarus, p. 880; Bernard, also applicable below.

51 Foerster, pp. 142–3.

52 Ibid., p. 145; see also Krausnick, pp. 333–5; Ritter, *Goerdeler*, p. 486, Note 44.

53 *Trial*, Vol. XXV, p. 477; Foerster, pp. 151–2; Hossbach, p. 193.

54 Ludwig Beck: *Studien*, p. 53; see also Foerster, pp. 148–50.

55 Beck, op. cit., pp. 60–4.

56 These thoughts appear in Beck's addresses to the 'Wednesday Society' on 24 April 1940 and in June 1942 – 'Thoughts on war' (*Studien*, pp. 118–20) and 'The Doctrine of total war' (*Studien*, pp. 251–8). On the 'Wednesday Society', a circle of intellectuals who met every fortnight, see Eberhard Zeller: *The Flame of Freedom*, p. 404 note 33.

57 Beck, op. cit., p. 257.

58 Ibid., p. 258.

CHAPTER 7

1 Waldemar Erfurth: 'Generaloberst a.D. Halder zum 70. Geburtstag (30.6.1954)' in *Wehrwissenschaftliche Rundschau* 4 (1954), pp. 242–3; Ernst von Weiz-

säcker: *Erinnerungen*, p. 174; Helmut Krausnick in 'Vorgeschichte und Beginn des militärischen Widerstandes gegen Hitler', in *Vollmacht des Gewissens*, Vol. I, pp. 335–9, relies on the very comprehensive material in the archives of the IfZ; see also Kurt Sendtner: 'Die deutsche Militäropposition im ersten Kriegsjahr' in *Vollmacht des Gewissens*, Vol. I, pp. 397–405, 486–90.

2 Hans Bernd Gisevius: *Bis zum bittern Ende*, Vol. II, pp. 23, 26 (*To the Bitter End*, pp. 283–5); Weizsäcker, p. 174; Halder's evidence in 'Protokoll aus der Verhandlung Halder [vor der] Spruchkammer X München', p. 68, IfZ; Krausnick, p. 339; Erfurth, p. 243; *Trials of War Criminals before the Nuernberg Military Tribunals under Control Council Law No 10*, Vol. X (The High Command Case), p. 543.

3 See Adolf Heusinger in hearing on Halder (Note 2 above), p. 100; Hans Rothfels: *The German Opposition to Hitler*, pp. 61–2, 74–5.

4 [Franz] Halder: *Kriegstagebuch*, Vol. I, pp. 362, 374–5; Hermann Graml: 'Die deutsche Militäropposition vom Sommer 1940 bis zum Frühjahr 1943' in *Vollmacht des Gewissens*, Vol. II, pp. 421–5; Harold C. Deutsch: *The Conspiracy against Hitler in the Twilight War*, pp. 182–3.

5 Halder was not altogether aware of these conflicting considerations but they nevertheless give rise to certain reservations concerning him. Erich Kosthorst in *Die deutsche Opposition gegen Hitler zwischen Polen- und Frankreichfeldzug*, pp. 51–61 allows Halder 'a high degree of credibility' and gives an explicit warning against unjustified attacks on him; his proof that in 1938 Halder was determined to act, however, is the following: 'A high degree of involvement is indicated if Halder was prepared to issue the order for a *coup d'état* planned in detail by others; this would have been a revolutionary step unheard-of in the history of his office.' This was not very meaningful when applied to someone who always said himself that he had no command authority – see Protokoll . . . Halder, passim and *Trial of the Major War Criminals before the International Military Tribunal*, Vol. XX, p. 596. Together with Gisevius Otto John is one of the best known critics of Halder among the men of the resistance; he has stressed Halder's inactivity on several occasions, for instance in his unpublished manuscript 'Some Facts and Aspects of the Plot against Hitler', typescript, London 1948, pp. 23–4; in 'Der 20. Juli 1944', typescript, London, undated, p. 4; in 'Zum Jahrestag der Verschwörung gegen Hitler – 20. Juli 1944' in *Wochenpost*, No 138, 18 July 1947, p. 4. John's criticism that the attempted *coup* of 1938 failed because of Halder's vacillation, however, is too flat-footed and is based more on the accounts of third parties than his own experiences. Colonel Friedrich Wilhelm Heinz, who was intimately involved in the 1938 plans (see pp. 91–3 below) accuses Halder of lack of backbone and resolution, saying that he was always demanding the murder of Hitler from Canaris and Oster but did nothing himself – see Friedrich Wilhelm Heinz: 'Von Wilhelm Canaris zur NKWD', typescript, undated (about 1949), pp. 82–3, 119–20, NA, microfilm R 60.67. Equally Gisevius in *To the Bitter End*, pp. 286–8 says that Halder always took the first step but never dared take the second. On the other hand Halder says that he was always being urged to act by Canaris. His reply to the accusation that he did not pursue the *coup* with sufficient energy is that he always had in mind the danger of civil war, for which he might have been saddled with responsibility – see Halder's evidence in the High Command Case, *Trials of War Criminals*, Vol. X, p. 545 and in Hearing before Spruchkammer X, p. 62, also Peter Bor: *Gespräche mit Halder*, p. 120 and Halder's statement given in Hjalmar Schacht *Account Settled*, pp. 120–2.

6 Halder – statements in 'Protokoll . . . Halder', p. 69; Krausnick, p. 341.

7 Krausnick, pp. 341–2; Halder: *Kriegstagebuch*, Vol. III, p. 534; Wolf Keilig in *Das deutsche Heer 1939–1945*, p. 211/117 shows Halder erroneously as Chief of Staff of 6 Division which was in Bielefeld.

8 Gisevius, *Bitter End*, p. 324. Krausnick, p. 342; Hermann Graml: 'Der Fall Oster' in *VfZ* 14 (1966), pp. 26–39; Annedore Leber: *Conscience in Revolt*, pp. 173–7.

9 At the end of 1937 Schacht was no longer Minister of Economics but Minister without Portfolio. He was 'deprived of his position' temporarily on 22 January 1943 and finally on 23 July 1943 – see Bertold Spuler: *Regenten und Regierungen der Welt: Minister-Ploetz*, Part II, Vol. 4, p. 151. On Schacht's connections with the conspiracy see Lutz Graf Schwerin von Krosigk: *Es geschah in Deutschland*, pp. 182–3; Schacht's evidence in 'Protokoll . . . Halder', where in effect he confirms Gisevius' account and Schacht, op. cit. pp. 120–2; evidence for and against Schacht in his own hearing before a denazification court: 'Der "Mann der Vernunft": Starke Entlastungsaussagen im Schact-Prozess' in *Die Welt*, 24 April 1947; 'Ersing belastet Schacht' in *Der Tagesspiegel*, 24 April 1947; 'Entlastungszeugen im Schacht-Verfahren' in Der *Tagesspiegel*, 25 April 1947; 'Für und wider Schacht: CDU-Vorsitzende Kaiser und Müller als Zeugen geladen' in *Die Welt*, 26 April 1947; 'Dokumente im Schacht-Verfahren' in *Der Tagesspiegel*, 26 April 1947; 'Schacht und der 20. Juli: Widersprüchliche Zeugenaussagen in Stuttgart' in *Die Neue Zeitung*, 28 April 1947; 'Kaiser über Schacht: Kein aufrichtiger Gefolgsmann Hitlers, aber umstrittene Rolle' in *Die Welt*, 29 April 1947; 'Für und wider Schacht: Beteiligung in der Widerstandsbewegung umstritten' in *Die Welt*, 30 April 1947; Krausnick, p. 343; Gerhard Ritter, *Carl Goerdeler und die deutsche Widerstandsbewegung*, p. 490, Note 59.

It is difficult today to reconstruct a precise picture of the preparations for a *coup* in 1938; even in 1945 the few survivors among the main participants were not agreed on numerous details – a common occurrence. A fairly reliable reconstruction is possible, however, since the principal sources are independent of each other and adequately detailed – Gisevius, *Bitter End* (also the various German editions); 'Protokoll . . . Halder' including his own statements and those of other witnesses; Heinz: 'Canaris'; *Spiegelbild einer Verschwörung*, pp. 430–1; [Walter] Huppenkothen: 'Der 20. Juli 1944', typescript, undated [1953], IfZ ZS 249/II; Krausnick, passim, where much unpublished evidence is used.

10 Gisevius, *Bitter End*, pp. 281–3.

11 Schacht – evidence in 'Protokoll . . . Halder', p. 121; Gisevius, *Bitter End*, p. 287.

12 Gisevius, loc. cit.

13 Gisevius, *Bitter End*, p. 288; Gisevius' evidence in *Trial*, Vol. XII, p. 212; Schacht, *Account*, p. 122; see also Eduard Wagner: *Der Generalquartiermeister: Briefe und Tagebuchaufzeichnungen*, pp. 62–3.

14 As far as Schacht remembers the day was 'a Sunday' – Schacht's evidence in 'Protokoll . . . Halder', p. 122. This can only have been 28 August or 4 September; it seems unlikely that Halder would have spoken to Oster on 27 August and to Schacht on the very next day, before he was really installed in his new office. According to Krausnick (p. 343 Note 403) Schacht gave 'a Sunday early in September as the date of this visit' [by Halder] but this does not tally with the passage cited by Krausnick (Schacht, *Account*, p. 121) where the date is merely given as 'summer 1938'. According to a statement by Halder made to Schacht's defence counsel at the Nuremberg Trial Schacht had been 'introduced by General Oster' and had come to Halder 'shortly after my assumption of office in September 1938' together with Oster and Gisevius (Schacht, op. cit., p. 121). In this terse statement, which Schacht describes as 'incomplete', Halder was referring to their second meeting; he only implicitly refers to the first meeting, saying that before the second meeting he had only met Schacht 'officially'. He might, however, have been referring to their meeting in the winter 1937–38; but this would mean that he was suppressing all mention of his visit to Schacht and, apart from Halder's incomplete and imprecise account, there is nothing to throw

doubt on it – see Schacht, op. cit., pp. 120–1. According to *Trial*, Vol. XII, pp. 211–12 Gisevius stated that a few days after Halder's assumption of office he had, on his own initiative, spoken to Oster who had recommended Schacht as someone to talk to on political matters; Halder had thereupon asked Oster to introduce them and had been taken to Schacht by Gisevius; Halder had therefore visited Schacht at the end of July 1938, Gisevius said. The record of the Nuremberg Trial contains many misunderstandings and omissions. In the light of confirmation from other sources the statement 'shortly after my assumption of office' seems to be correct. This therefore brings us to 4 September as the Sunday in question.

15 Gisevius, *Bitter End*, pp. 286–8. Here the wording is 'take over the administration' and in his evidence at the Nuremberg Trial (*Trial*, Vol. XII, p. 212) Gisevius referred to a 'leading position' for Schacht. Schacht himself said in proceedings in 1948 ('Protokoll ... Halder', p. 122) that Halder had asked him whether he would be available 'for foreign affairs'.

16 Schact in 'Protokoll ... Halder', p. 122.

17 Gisevius, *Bitter End*, pp. 286–8, *Trial*, Vol. XII, pp. 212, 288–90; Heinz, 'Canaris', p. 98.

18 According to Gisevius' evidence at Nuremberg (*Trial*, Vol. XII, p. 212) this may have taken place on 5 September; it was in any case very shortly after Halder's talk with Schacht and on the very next morning Halder asked Oster for an expert on police questions. According to Gisevius, *Bis zum bitteren Ende* (special edition, p. 348; not in first edition, Vol. II, p. 31) the talk took place 'one evening in the first week of September'; see also *Bitter End*, pp. 287–96.

19 Gisevius, *Bitter End*, pp. 290–2; *Trial*, Vol. XII, p. 212.

20 Gisevius, *Bitter End*, pp. 299–300, 305–6; *Trial*, Vol. XII, p. 212.

21 Gisevius, *Bitter End*, pp. 293–7; *Trial*, Vol. XII, p. 213.

22 Schacht, *Account* 121; Gisevius, *Bitter End*, pp. 288–9, 293–7 (*Ende*, Vol. II, pp. 30, 35–9).

23 Gisevius, *Bitter End*, pp. 293–5; see also Wolfgang Foerster: *Generaloberst Ludwig Beck*, pp. 115–16; Edgar Röhricht: *Pflicht und Gewissen*, p. 119; Ritter, op. cit., p. 492, Note 73.

24 Gisevius, *Bitter End*, pp. 289, 300–1; Schacht in 'Protokoll ... Halder', p. 122; see also Ritter, op. cit., p. 490, Note 59.

25 Gisevius, *Bitter End*, p. 291.

26 Ibid.

27 Ibid., p. 296; Gisevius' evidence in *Trial*, Vol. XII, p. 213.

28 Sendtner, p. 401: see also pp. 90, 129 below.

29 Gisevius, *Bitter End*, p. 297.

30 Ibid., pp. 320–1; Max Domarus: *Hitler: Reden und Proklamationen 1932–1945*, pp. 888–9.

31 Domarus, pp. 900–5.

32 Gisevius said in Nuremberg that nothing more was heard from Halder 'for some weeks'; as the diplomatic tension became worse, they became impatient – see *Trial*, Vol. XII, p. 213 and Gisevius, *Bitter End*, p. 299; in Gisevius' special edition, p. 355, the timing of Schacht's visit to Halder is given as mid-September. This further confirms the assumption that the first talk between Schacht and Halder took place on 4 September.

33 Gisevius, loc. cit.

34 Fabian von Schlabrendorff: *Revolt against Hitler*, p. 42.

35 Gisevius, *Bitter End*, p. 299–300 (special edition, p. 355). This discussion certainly took place later than 12 September and not before the evening of 13 September if the details given in Gisevius, *Bitter End*, pp. 318–27 (*Ende*, Vol. II, pp. 64–76) are correct.

36 Gisevius, *Bitter End*, p. 300; Gisevius' evidence in *Trial*, Vol. XII, p. 213.

37 Ibid. Halder would know with certainty forty-eight hours beforehand.

38 Ibid.

39 Jodl's diary in *Trial*, Vol. XXVIII, p. 376.

40 Ibid., pp. 376–9. See also record of the discussion in *Trial*, Vol. XXV, pp. 464–9, 485–6 – also applicable below.

41 Gisevius, *Bitter End*, p. 300–1; Gisevius' evidence in *Trial*, Vol. XII, p. 214.

42 Gisevius, *Bitter End*, pp. 301, 305 and Gisevius' evidence in *Trial*, Vol. XII, p. 214, where he either implies or states that Oster had *at last* been persuaded to recruit Witzleben; this does not appear in Gisevius' 1954 edition, p. 338, nor in special edition, p. 360. In the special edition Gisevius also no longer states that Witzleben did not learn of the background to the Fritsch crisis for the first time at this stage but in June, at which time he also learnt that war was being planned against Czechoslovakia (these points are still given, however, in the 1954 edition, p. 338). If my previous time calculations and the sequence of events from beginning to end of September given in Gisevius' chronology (*bittern Ende*, Vol. II, pp. 64–76 with special reference to pp. 67–8 and special edition pp. 369–78 with special reference to pp. 370–1; *Bitter End*, pp. 318–27) are correct, Witzleben must have been drawn into the inner circle of conspirators before this talk with Halder. Other sources confirm this. According to Heinz ('Canaris', pp. 96–98) Oster in whose house the vital discussions took place, was primarily responsible for winning Witzleben over; Beck and Goerdeler were also involved.

Schacht maintains that *he* recruited Witzleben and as early as spring 1938 – Schacht's evidence in 'Protokoll ... Halder', p. 121. This is confirmed by Lieutenant-Colonel Dr Reinhard Brink who was on Witzleben's staff in 1940–1942 – see Schacht, *Account*, pp. 254–5 and Gisevius' evidence in *Trial*, Vol. XII, p. 214.

The conflict between Schacht's, Brink's and Gisevius' evidence at Nuremberg on the one hand and Gisevius in *Bitter End*, pp. 305–6, on the other must lie in the fact that Witzleben had long been prepared to participate in principle but only as a result of the talk with Schacht arranged by Oster was he committed to participate in a concrete plan – which had only just emerged at this point. This must be maintained against Ritter, op. cit., p. 490 Note 61, which states that Oster recruited Witzleben, quoting Gisevius, *Bitter End*, p. 305; this is clearly a misunderstanding since on p. 306 Gisevius indicates that the decisive factor was Schacht's exposé to Witzleben and Brockdorff-Ahlefeldt.

43 Gisevius, *Bitter End*, p. 305; Wolf Keilig: *Das deutsche Heer 1939–1945*, p. 211/368.

44 Gisevius, loc. cit., Schacht, op. cit., p. 120; Schacht's evidence in 'Protokoll ... Halder', p. 121; see also *Trial*, Vol. XXXIII, p. 354.

45 Gisevius, *Bitter End*, pp. 305–6; Gisevius' evidence in *Trial*, Vol. XII, p. 214.

46 Gisevius, *Bitter End*, p. 306; Krausnick, p. 344.

47 This is the sequence of events given in Gisevius, *Bitter End*, pp. 319–24, although in Gisevius, *Bitter End*, pp. 300–7 the impression is given, supported by Gisevius' evidence in *Trial*, Vol. XII, p. 214, that the second meeting between Schacht and Halder took place first and that this was followed by Witzleben's visit to Schacht. In 1948 Schacht also recalled that he was visited first by Halder and then by Witzleben and that he then went to Halder – see Schacht, *Account*, pp. 255–6 and his evidence in 'Protokoll ... Halder', p. 122, also p. 121 where he refers to continuous cooperation with Witzleben during the summer of 1938 followed by a laborious process of winning over Halder.

48 Gisevius, *Bitter End*, p. 306–7 (special edition, p. 361); Gisevius in *Trial*, Vol. XII, p. 214.

49 Gisevius, p. 307, 315–16.

50 Bor, p. 122.

51 Halder, evidence in 'Protokoll ... Halder', p. 62.

52 Gisevius, *Bitter End*, p. 307; Bor, p. 121; Schacht, *Account*, pp. 120, 255.
53 Schacht, op. cit., p. 255.
54 Gisevius, *Bitter End*, pp. 307–10.
55 Ibid., p. 310.
56 Ibid., p. 312.
57 Evidence by General Burkhart Müller-Hillebrand 'Protokoll . . . Halder', p. 88; Gisevius, *Bitter End*, pp. 314–15. In Gisevius' first edition (*Bittern Ende*, Vol. II, pp. 38–9; *Bitter End*, p. 296) he stated wrongly that Halder had 'command authority over the troops'; this was still in the 1954 edition, p. 329, but it has been dropped in the special edition (p. 352). In 1939 a new handbook for General Staff duties in wartime laid down that General Staff officers were merely assistants and played no responsible part in the decisions of their commander (Krausnick, p. 372). See also Manstein's evidence in *Trial*, Vol. XX, p. 596.
58 Gisevius, *Bitter End*, p. 314.
59 Gisevius, *Bitter End*, pp. 314–16.
60 Ibid., pp. 316–17.
61 Halder in 'Protokoll . . . Halder', p. 69; Krausnick, pp. 344, 346.
62 Gisevius, op. cit., pp. 316–17; Schacht, op. cit., p. 122 (Halder's account).
63 For a character study of Brauchitsch see Hermann Foertsch: *Schuld und Verhängnis*, p. 203; Ritter, *Resistance*, pp. 151–2; Deutsch, pp. 34–5.
64 Halder's evidence in 'Protokoll . . . Halder', p. 69; Bor, p. 121. Ritter is therefore wrong when he says about Halder's intentions without reference to source: 'Brauchitsch, the generalissimo, was to initiate the *putsch* . . .' (Ritter, *Resistance*, p. 101).
65 Bor, p. 121.
66 See p. 95 below.
67 Gisevius, *Bitter End*, p. 317; Schacht, op. cit., pp. 122–5, 254–6. See also account of the plan for a *coup* given by Beck to Sauerbruch in 1939 – Ferdinand Sauerbruch: *Das war mein Leben*, pp. 533–4. Also see Halder's evidence in the OKW Trial, *Trials of War Criminals*, Vol. X, pp. 543–4.
68 Gisevius, *Bitter End*, p. 317; Heinz, 'Canaris', p. 98. In *Ende*, Vol. II, p. 63 Gisevius says that he spent 'the next fortnight' in this way (not in English translation, p. 317); he must therefore have begun work about 5 or 6 September. In the special edition (p. 365), however, he merely refers vaguely to 'those dramatic weeks'.
69 Gisevius, *Bitter End*, pp. 316–17.
70 This is according to information given verbally to the author on 27 February 1965 by Major Josef Wolf. During the later war years he was head of the '*Führer* Signal Detachment' in the *Führer*'s headquarters. This was responsible for maintenance of communications from and to the top-level leadership of the Reich and the *Wehrmacht*.
71 Gisevius, *Bitter End*, pp. 316–17; Bor, p. 121.
72 Ibid., p. 316.
73 Gisevius, *Ende*, Vol. II, pp. 63–4.
74 Halder's evidence in 'Protokoll . . . Halder', pp. 6, 69, 71; see also Krausnick, p. 345.
75 Joachim Kramarz: *Stauffenberg: The Life and Death of an Officer*, pp. 60–1, 70.
76 Ibid.; Gisevius, *Ende*, Vol. II, p. 71; Krausnick, p. 346; Sauerbruch, pp. 533–4.
77 Halder's evidence in 'Protokoll . . . Halder', p. 69; Krausnick, p. 345.
78 Halder in 'Protokol . . . Halder', p. 70, Krausnick, pp. 358–9; list of appointments in *Trial*, Vol. XXV, p. 477.
79 According to Krausnick (p. 345) at latest by August 1938 General Adam had told Halder that he was prepared actively to participate in a *putsch*.
80 Information to the author from Margarethe von Hase on 3, 8 and 31 March 1964; Krausnick, pp. 309, 344 Note 407a.

81 Gisevius, *Bitter End*, p. 320; Elisabeth Gärtner-Strünck, typed note, 20 April 1964; Rhona Churchill: 'Widow Strunk [sic] goes to Nuremberg' in *Daily Mail*, 28 March 1946; Krausnick, p. 346.

82 Friedrich Hossbach: *Zwischen Wehrmacht und Hitler 1934–1938*, p. 136.

83 Albert Krebs: *Fritz-Dietlof Graf von der Schulenburg*, pp. 137, 154.

84 Ibid., pp. 84–6, 89, 111–13, 132–5.

85 Ibid., p. 163.

86 Ibid., pp. 95, 158, 164; Albrecht von Kessel: 'Verborgene Saat', typescript, pp. 76, 105.

87 According to Halder's evidence in 'Protokoll . . . Halder', (p. 69) active use of the police had been promised. Gisevius (*Bitter End*, pp. 319–20) says that Helldorf had been frankly asked to participate and had agreed; on the other hand, Gisevius says (*Bitter End*, p. 320) that Helldorf had been let into the secret with caution and apparently not completely. Paul Kanstein, then head of the Berlin Political Police, says that at a meeting at which General von Kamptz, Commandant of the Regular Police [*Schutzpolizei*] was present, it was decided that the Berlin Police should merely be neutral – see Krebs, p. 170 and Krausnick, p. 345. Schulenburg himself seems to have been convinced that there would be fighting in Berlin; on 22 September he hurriedly sent his wife and children to the country 'because of the uncertainty of the situation in Berlin'; on 28 September he telephoned to say that they could return (Krebs, p. 170). His anxiety may, of course, have been due to the threat of war and of possible air raids.

88 Gisevius, *Bitter End*, pp. 309–11.

89 Ibid., pp. 296–7.

90 Ibid. After the war Halder said that he had always opposed assassination as the first step towards the aim for which the resistance movement was striving, though he understood the 'hot-blooded youth'. At that time (1948) he was, of course, trying to explain why he had not killed Hitler himself on one of the many opportunities he had. See Halder's evidence in 'Protokoll . . . Halder', pp. 78a, 78c and also that of Dr Hermann Pünder (ibid., pp. 104–5) who said that in 1934 and 1935 Halder had spoken against the use of force and murder, clearly for the reasons recorded by Gisevius; see Sendtner, p. 401 and pp. 129, 136, 138 below.

91 Otto John: 'Männer im Kampf gegen Hitler (VII): Hans von Dohnanyi' in *Blick in die Welt* 2 (1947), No 12, pp. 16–17 and 'Am achten Jahrestag der Verschwörung' in *Das Parlament*, 20 July 1952, p. 2; now also in Otto John's autobiography *Twice through the Lines*, pp. 32–3. Pechel: *Deutscher Widerstand*, p. 151, says Hitler was not to be murdered but was to be brought to justice. See also Rainer Hildesbrandt: *Wir sind die Letzten*, p. 93; Gisevius, *Bitter End*, p. 311 (in greater detail in special edition, p. 341). Gisevius is not quite fair in his scorn for this idea; he himself had held the view that the regime could be dealt with without arresting or killing Hitler *immediately* (*Bitter End*, p. 311). This is confirmed by a letter from Heinz to the author dated 22 March 1966.

92 See Ritter, *Goerdeler*, pp. 195–6, 491 Note 64 (*Resistance*, pp. 104, 148 Note 2) where he refers to letters from Heinz and confirmation by third parties; letters from Heinz to the author; Heinz, 'Canaris', pp. 98–100; statements by Heinz quoted in Sendtner, pp. 436–9; Gert Buchheit in *Der deutsche Geheimdienst*, pp. 146–9 does not mention these last two sources but relies on personal information from Heinz. See also Hildebrandt, p. 93.

93 See statements by Commander (Navy) Franz Maria Liedig in Headquarters United States Forces European Theatre, Military Intelligence Service Centre, Special Interrogation Report (CSIR) No 6: 'Events of 20 July 44', Hoover Library Ts Germany, USA 7 F 697 – now also available in NA; Heinz, 'Canaris', p. 101; Ritter, *Goerdeler*, pp. 168–9, 491 Note 64; Part IV of this book. In a draft of a constitution Professor SchmidNoerr goes much further in rejecting all 'party divisions' – Friedrich Alfred SchmidNoerr: 'Dokument des Widerstandes:

Entwurf einer deutschen Reichsverfassung', *Voran und beharrlich*, No 33/34 (1961), passim.

94 John Wheeler-Bennett: *The Nemesis of Power*, p. 386, Note 2.

95 Heinz, 'Canaris', pp. 102–4; Ritter, op. cit., pp. 296–9; Krausnick, pp. 348–9 – also applicable below. In confirmation of Heinz's statements Ritter (op. cit., pp. 195–6, 491 Note 64; *Resistance*, p. 104 Note 1) cites Her Royal Highness Princess Wilhelm of Prussia who remembers that 'before mid-August' a constitutional memorandum was discussed with Prince Wilhelm for a whole day in Klein-Obisch; it had been drafted by the Oster-Schulenburg-Heinz group. Krebs, Schulenburg's biographer, says nothing on this subject; on the other hand (p. 176) he quotes Ulrich von Hassell (*The von Hassell Diaries*, pp. 209–10) as proof that Schulenburg personally was fiercely opposed to the return of the Crown Prince.

96 Heinz, 'Canaris', pp. 103–4; Ritter, *Goerdeler*, pp. 296–9 (*Resistance*, p. 191).

97 Ritter, *Goerdeler*, p. 195 (*Resistance*, p. 104); Krausnick, p. 347; Heinz, 'Canaris', p. 99; letter from Heinz to the author 8 March 1966. Goerdeler's presence is mentioned only by Heinz ('Canaris', p. 99). According to Ritter, (*Goerdeler*, p. 160, *Resistance*, p. 83) Goerdeler could not have been there. Buchheit (p. 147), based on Heinz's account, also does not mention him but says that Major Groscurth and Dohnanyi were present.

98 Heinz, 'Canaris', p. 99; Krausnick, p. 347.

99 Heinz, op. cit., pp. 78, 96, 98; Ritter, *Goerdeler*, pp. 195–6 (*Resistance*, p. 104); Heinz to the author 8 March 1966; Joachim G. Leithäuser: *Wilhelm Leuschner*, p. 179. Hermann Maass later campaigned actively for the assassination of Hitler – letter from Gotthold Müller to the author 18 November 1966. Liedig in CSIR No 6 mentions a 'plan for arrest', but only in 1939.

100 Leithäuser, p. 182; John, 'Männer im Kampf (IV)'.

101 Heinz, 'Canaris', pp. 123–4, 133; see also statements by Lahousen referred to in Gisevius, special edition, p. 407. Based on personal information from Heinz, Buchheit (p. 148) mentions as members of the raiding party Konrad Graf von Finkenstein, Albrecht Erich Günther, Hans-Jürgen Graf von Blumenthal (executed after 20 July 1944), Haubold Graf von Einsiedel, Captain Freiherr Treusch von Buttlar-Brandenfels, Graf von der Recke, Lieutenant Bistrick (later in the training depot of the Brandenburg Regiment) and the student leaders Junker and Hoffmann. See also Halder, *Kriegstagebuch*, Vol. I, p. 32.

102 Heinz, 'Canaris', p. 98; Krausnick, p. 347; Buchheit, p. 148.

103 Heinz, op. cit., p. 99. Hildebrandt (p. 93) refers to Heinz's group as 'Social Revolutionaries'.

104 [Erwin Lahousen] (at the time Lieutenant-Colonel on the General Staff serving in the *Abwehr*): 'Sidelights on the Development of the "20 July" in the Foreign Countries/Intelligence Service (Amt Ausland/Abwehr) for the Period of Time from the End of 1939 to the Middle of 1943', typescript, undated (probably August 1945), p. 2, NA Record Group 238.

105 Heinz, op. cit., pp. 99–100; Heinz to the author 8 March 1966; Krausnick (p. 348) quotes on this subject Hildebrandt, p. 93; Buchheit, p. 148.

106 Heinz, 'Canaris', p. 104; Lahousen, p. 2.

107 Halder's evidence in 'Protokoll . . . Halder', p. 69; Krausnick, pp. 342–3.

108 Erich Kordt: *Nicht aus den Akten*, pp. 258–9.

109 See pp. 54–68 above.

110 Kordt, p. 262. Wheeler-Bennett's statement (p. 423) that the conspirators finally abandoned their plans at the time of Chamberlain's visit on 15 September is incorrect; see also Ritter, *Goerdeler*, p. 491 Note 66 (*Resistance*, p. 105 Note 2).

111 Ritter, *Goerdeler*, pp. 196–7 (*Resistance*, pp. 105–6); Krausnick, p. 362.

112 Kordt, p. 259.

113 Ritter, *Goerdeler*, p. 199 (*Resistance*, p. 106); Krausnick, pp. 362–3.

114 Bruno Gebhardt: *Handbuch der deutschen Geschichte*, Vol. IV, p. 240.
115 *Documents on British Foreign Policy, (DBFP)* Third Series, Vol. II, No 1111.
Otto John in *Twice through the lines*, pp. 26–7 says that Dohnanyi and Klaus
Bonhoeffer were firmly convinced that Halifax and Chamberlain had been determined ever since November 1937 to oppose Hitler by force should he pursue his
eastward expansion but that this proved to be an illusion.
116 Jodl's diary in *Trial*, Vol. XXVIII, p. 388, quoted in Krausnick, p. 365; Ritter,
Goerdeler, p. 201 (*Resistance*, p. 109); Domarus, p. 937; Gisevius' evidence in
Trial, Vol. XII, pp. 218–19; Gisevius, *Bitter End*, pp. 324–5; Colvin, *Vansittart*,
p. 263; William L. Shirer: *Berlin Diary*, pp. 142–3; Fritz Wiedemann: *Der
Mann der Feldherr werden wollte*, pp. 176–7; Kordt, pp. 259–60, 265–8; Ernst
von Weizsäcker: *Erinnerungen*, p. 188.
117 *DBFP*, Vol. II, No 1127, referred to in Ritter, *Goerdeler*, p. 200 (*Resistance*, p.
108); *DBFP*, Vol. III, No 1129; see also Kordt, p. 270.
118 Krausnick, p. 365.
119 Ibid.
120 Ibid., pp. 325–6.
121 *Documents on German Foreign Policy (DGFP)*, Series D, Vol. VII, Nos 192, 193;
DBFP Vol. VII, No 314; *Trial*, Vol. XXVI, pp. 338–44 and Vol. XLI, pp. 16–25.
See also pp. 109–12 below.
122 Jodl's diary in *Trial*, Vol. XXVIII, p. 387.
123 Gisevius' evidence in *Trial*, Vol. XII, p. 218.
124 Jodl's diary in *Trial*, Vol. XXVIII, p. 387.
125 Ibid., p. 388.
126 Weizsäcker, p. 187; Krausnick, p. 367.
127 Nebgen, p. 107 on the basis of a statement by Hammerstein's son Ludwig in
1965.
128 Gisevius, *Bitter End*, p. 325; Gisevius' evidence in *Trial*, Vol. XIII, p. 219; according to Kordt (pp. 268–9) he did not give the papers to Oster until the morning of the 28th; see also Ritter, *Goerdeler*, pp. 200–1 (*Resistance*, pp. 109–110).
129 Gisevius' evidence in *Trial*, Vol. XII, p. 219; Kordt, pp. 269, 278; Krausnick, p.
367.
130 Jodl's diary, in *Trial*, Vol. XXVIII, p. 388; Krausnick, p. 367.
131 According to Otto John in *Twice through the Lines*, p. 33, when in the British
POW camp at Bridgend in 1947, Brauchitsch told him that 'at the time nobody
had approached him with any plan to overthrow Hitler', that nothing was further
from his thoughts than issue of an order for a rising against Hitler and that, even
subsequently he had no intention of allowing himself to become a tool of an anti-
Hitler conspiracy; at the time the German people was extremely content with
Hitler and his successes and those who thought they knew better should have
done away with Hitler themselves.
132 Gisevius' evidence in *Trial*, Vol. XII, p. 219; Gisevius, *Bitter End*, p. 325.
133 Kordt, p. 270.
134 Ibid., pp. 263, 270.
135 Gisevius, *Bitter End*, p. 325.
136 Kordt, p. 271; Bor (p. 122) gives 14 September as the date for the triggering of
the *putsch*, cancelled at the last minute, saying: 'On 14 September Halder issued
the codeword for the start of the *coup d'état* as arranged.' This is certainly incorrect although in mid-September everyone was reckoning on the outbreak of
war – see Gisevius, *Bitter End*, p. 321 and Kordt, p. 258; Weizsäcker (p. 193)
also says that concrete plans for 14 September existed; according to Pechel (p.
151) 'the date . . . was fixed for early September, as soon as Hitler should return
to Berlin from Berchtesgaden'.
　　The case against 14 September as one of the proposed dates is as follows: 1. It
is mentioned only by Halder in Bor, p. 122 and Weizsäcker, p. 193. Pechel, p. 151

gives 'early September'. Nowhere does Halder mention more than *one* date on which the rising was to be or had been ordered and, except in the passage in Bor, he invariably implies the end of September; 2. Halder did not wish to initiate the *coup* until Hitler had given orders for invasion and therefore for war; in no case could this have been before 30 September or 1 October (the original date), as Halder knew very well.

Halder's evidence at his own hearing ('Protokoll . . . Halder', p. 70) that Hitler returned unexpectedly from Berchtesgaden and that he (Halder) thereupon summoned Witzleben, is certainly incorrect. Hitler was probably back in Berlin by 24 September (Kordt, p. 262) and certainly by the 26th on which day he made a major speech in the Sports Palace (Domarus, pp. 921–33). Halder's account reproduced by Schacht (op. cit., p. 122) is similarly inaccurate. In view of Halder's inaccuracy (he frequently links different events which occurred at differing times), Gisevius' account (cf. *Bitter End*, pp. 321–5) is to be preferred. Halder, for instance, has a dramatic story that General von Witzleben was present in his office and he was about to issue the order for the *coup* when his Aide Captain Hauser came in with the news of the summoning of the Munich Conference. This is not very probable; Witzleben can hardly have waited for hours in Halder's office. See Halder's evidence in 'Protokoll . . . Halder,' pp. 3, 70; Kurt Assmann: *Deutsche Schicksalsjahre*, pp. 471–2; Schacht, op. cit., p. 122; according to Kordt, p. 278 Halder had already issued orders to move to 'units in Potsdam and Hof' when news of the summoning of the Munich Conference arrived.

137 See Hitler's own directive in *Trial*, Vol. XXV, p. 475.

138 *DBFP*, Vol. II, No 615; Eugen Spier: *Focus*, p. 127.

139 Bernd-Jürgen Wendt in *München 1938*, p. 7 and passim, defends the British and French governments against this accusation by Kordt, Schacht, Gisevius, Rothfels, Ritter and Krausnick. However understandable the feeling of the opposition that it had been left in the lurch, there must be some sympathy for the attitude of the Western governments, particularly in the light of the opposition's publicly proclaimed aims on foreign policy – see pp. 54–68 above. The argument implicit in these strictures on Britain and France is that Hitler's regime was basically evil and should therefore have been resisted by all available means; this presupposes a crusading spirit leading other peoples to adopt an ethically 'right' attitude.

NOTES/PART III/CHAPTER 8

1 Bruno Gebhardt: *Handbuch der deutschen Geschichte*, Vol. IV, p. 242 – also applicable below.

2 Ibid., pp. 244–9 – also applicable below. See also Walther Hofer: *Die Entfesselung des Zweiten Weltkrieges*, passim.

3 See Erich Kordt: *Nicht aus den Akten*, p. 290; Helmut Krausnick: 'The Persecution of the Jews' in *Anatomy of the SS State*, pp. 1–24.

4 Helmut Krausnick: 'Vorgeschichte und Beginn des militärischen Widerstandes gegen Hitler' in *Vollmacht des Gewissens*, Vol. I, pp. 368–71.

5 Ibid., p. 373.

6 Ibid., p. 376; Wolf Keilig: *Das deutsche Heer 1939–1945*, p. 211/368.

7 [Georg] von Sodenstern, 'Zur Vorgeschichte des 20. Juli 1944', typescript 1947, NA, Record Group 338 MS No B-499; also applicable below.

8 Gisevius went there on 20 August; Hans Bernd Gisevius: *Bis zum bittern Ende*, Vol. II, pp. 117–19; *To the Bitter End*, pp. 358–9.

9 Krausnick, op. cit., p. 376.

10 Sir John W. Wheeler-Bennett: *The Nemesis of Power*, p. 427 – based on a statement by Halder in February 1946.
11 Krausnick: 'Vorgeschichte', p. 376.
12 Gisevius, *Bitter End*, pp. 335–6; on Halder's attitude during these months see also Klaus-Jürgen Müller: *Das Heer und Hitler*, pp. 378–421.
13 *Trial of the Major War Criminals before the International Military Tribunal*, Vol. XII, p. 221.
14 Gisevius, *Bitter End*, p. 335–6.
15 Krausnick, 'Vorgeschichte', p. 376; Halder's evidence in 'Protokoll aus der Verhandlung Halder [vor der] Spruchkammer X München', IfZ; Peter Bor: *Gespräche mit Halder*, p. 124.
16 Walter Warlimont: *Inside Hitler's Headquarters*, pp. 24–5, 590 Note 34. According to Warlimont these timetables were not introduced until 1939 (?summer). Accordingly, as Warlimont says, Halder is wrong when he says that Hitler introduced these tables because he was suspicious of OKH and wished to be able to know at any time where every army division was and what it was doing. Hitler was undoubtedly suspicious, but it does not necessarily follow that this was the reason for his action.
17 Bor, p. 125; Halder's evidence in 'Protokoll . . . Halder,' pp. 6–7.
18 See Part VII, Chap. 34 below.
19 Information from Rear-Admiral Karl-Jesko von Puttkamer to Dr Heinrich Uhlig in IfZ ZS 285.
20 [Franz] Halder: *Kriegstagebuch*, Vol. I, pp. 30–4; Halder's evidence in 'Protokoll . . . Halder', pp. 6–7; Bor, p. 125. Halder's account of a repetition of this procedure on 30 August does not appear in his diary (Vol. I, pp. 44–6); there he refers to the actual date of attack, 1 September.
21 Otto John: 'Männer im Kampf gegen Hitler (IV): Wilhelm Leuschner' in *Blick in die Welt* 2 (1947), No 9, p. 20; Joachim G. Leithäuser: *Wilhelm Leuschner*, p. 182; Eberhard Zeller: *The Flame of Freedom*, p. 82; Elfriede Nebgen: *Jakob Kaiser*, pp. 114–15.
22 Here and below see Albrecht von Kessel: 'Verborgene Saat', typescript, Vatican City 1944–5, pp. 139–40. Kessel, letter to author dated 15 July 1970.
23 Otto Kopp: 'Die Niederschrift von Hans Walz "Meine Mitwirkung an der Aktion Goerdeler" ' in Otto Kopp (editor): *Widerstand und Erneuerung*, pp. 107–8.
24 Ibid., pp. 109–10.
25 Gerhard Ritter: *Carl Goerdeler und die deutsche Widerstandsbewegung*, pp. 204–13 (*The German Resistance*, pp. 115–16).
26 Ritter, *Goerdeler*, pp. 216–19 (*Resistance*, pp. 119–20) – also applicable below.
27 Ritter, *Goerdeler*, pp. 219–22 (*Resistance*, p. 119).
28 Ritter, *Goerdeler*, pp. 219–22 (*Resistance*, pp. 121, 124). Gisevius holds much the same view – see *Trial*, Vol. XII, p. 221.
29 Ritter, *Goerdeler*, pp. 222–3 (*Resistance*, pp. 124–6).
30 Ritter, *Goerdeler*, pp. 223–5 (*Resistance*, ibid.). Hermann Graml in 'Die aussenpolitischen Vorstellungen des deutschen Widerstandes' in *Der deutsche Widerstand gegen Hitler* edited by Walter Schmitthenner and Hans Buchheim undoubtedly does Goerdeler an injustice when he says (pp. 27–9): 'Goerdeler's revisionist policy gradually turned into power politics with an admixture of Central European imperialist thinking designed to be both provident and patriarchal but in its scope and formulation it was closely related to national-liberal, pan-German and Prussian nationalist thought'. It is, however, correct to say that Goerdeler's policy could, and indeed inevitably did, give rise to such an *impression* abroad.
31 Ritter, *Goerdeler*, p. 225 (*Resistance*, p. 126).
32 Ibid.
33 Ritter, *Goerdeler*, p. 496 Note 30 (*Resistance*, p. 127 Note 1) where Ritter

examines the question whether, as Gisevius maintains (*Bitter End*, pp. 346–7 – omitted in special edition), Schairer made known Goerdeler's forecasts of Germany's internal weaknesses both in London and Paris and discussed them with Daladier; Ritter quotes a letter he received from Schairer in which both these questions were answered in the negative.

34 Gisevius in *Trial*, Vol. XII, p. 221; Ritter, *Goerdeler*, p. 224 (*Resistance*, p. 126).

35 Gisevius, loc. cit.

36 Ibid., p. 222.

37 Ibid.

38 Ibid.; Ritter, *Goerdeler*, p. 225.

39 Ritter (op. cit., p. 225) expresses certain doubts as to whether this last part of the message was passed on with Goerdeler's knowledge and agreement, if at all – as Gisevius stated in Nuremberg (*Trial*, Vol. XII, p. 222). Possibly Goerdeler, the optimist, thought that Hitler would be satisfied with Danzig and the Corridor if he got them. Since Prague, however, the Western governments must have been quite clear that Hitler never merely wanted what he asked for.

40 Ritter, op. cit., pp. 229–30; see also Wheeler-Bennett, pp. 440–1 (inaccurate in this passage).

41 According to Wheeler-Bennett (p. 437) on 29 March 1939 the British journalist Ian Colvin, among other people, passed to the British government messages from the German opposition and so contributed materially to a stiffening of the British attitude. Colvin himself says nothing on the subject (*Master Spy* or *Chief of Intelligence*, p. 87); see Ritter, op. cit., pp. 229, 497 Note 36 (*Resistance*, p. 131 Note 2).

42 Here and below see *Documents on German Foreign Policy* (*DGFP*), Series D, Vol. VI, No 497; David Astor: 'The Mission of Adam von Trott' in *The Manchester Guardian Weekly*, 7 June 1956, p. 7; David Astor, 'Why the Revolt against Hitler Was Ignored: On the British Reluctance to Deal with German Anti-Nazis', *Encounter* XXXII (1969) No 6, pp. 6–8; cf. Christopher Sykes: *Troubled Loyalty: A biography of Adam von Trott zu Solz*, p. 214; Hans Rothfels: *The German Opposition to Hitler* pp. 130–2; Hans Rothfels: 'Trott und die Aussenpolitik des Widerstandes' in *VfZ* 12 (1964), pp. 300–3; Hans Rothfels: 'The German Resistance in Its International Aspects', *International Affairs* 34 (1958), pp. 482–3; Wheeler-Bennett, pp. 441–3 (he himself spoke to Trott at this time).

43 Fabian von Schlabrendorff: *The Revolt against Hitler*, p. 46; Hans Rothfels, *Die deutsche Opposition gegen Hitler*, p. 138 (not in English ed.); Wheeler-Bennett, pp. 441–3.

44 Eugen Spier: *Focus*, p. 127.

45 Although Schlabrendorff does not explicitly say so, the proviso was obviously implied that external political conditions were those which the opposition considered necessary.

46 Wheeler-Bennett, p. 441.

47 Rudolf Pechel: *Deutscher Widerstand*, pp. 153, 292–3; Müller, op. cit. p. 407; Fritz Rieter: 'Zwanzig Jahre nach dem Attentat auf Hitler' in *Schweizer Monatshefte* 44 (1964), p. 313; Ulrich von Hassell: 'Das Ringen um den Staat der Zukunft' in *Schweizer Monatshefte* 44 (1964), pp. 314–27; Astor 'Why the Revolt . . .', p. 7.

48 Kordt, pp. 310–19; Ernst von Weizsäcker: *Erinnerungen*, pp. 234–5, 244–62.

49 Kordt, p. 336.

50 Ibid., p. 337.

51 Ritter, *Goerdeler*, p. 235 (*Resistance*, p. 135).

52 Ritter, *Goerdeler*, p. 236 (*Resistance*, p. 135).

53 Müller, op. cit., pp. 399–403. Müller's assertion that at this time 'the rest of the opposition was inactive and paralysed' is therefore incorrect.

54 Friedrich Wilhelm Heinz: 'Von Wilhelm Canaris zur NKWD', typescript on microfilm (about 1949), p. 110 – NA, R 60.67; Kessel (p. 138) gives general confirmation to these views.

55 Leithäuser, p. 184.

56 'Testimony of Mr Louis P. Lochner taken at Berlin, Germany, on 25 July 1945, by Colonel John H. Amen', IGD, NA, Record Group 238; Louis P. Lochner: *What About Germany?* (includes extracts from the memorandum), pp. 1–5; letter from Lochner to the author, 12 January 1967; *Documents on British Foreign Policy (DBFP)*, Third Series, Vol. VII, No 314; Halder: *Kriegstagebuch*, Vol. I, pp. 23–6; Ulrich von Hassell: *Vom andern Deutschland*, p. 66 (not in English translation); Gisevius, *Bitter End*, p. 360; Ritter, *Goerdeler*, pp. 498–500 Note 55 (*Resistance*, p. 137 Note 1) which contains some critical statements on sources; also Winfried Baumgart: 'Zur Ansprache Hitlers vor den Führern der Wehrmacht am 22 August 1939', *VfZ* 16 (1968), pp. 120–49 – the point has escaped him, however, that the first occasion on which Lochner stated that he received the memorandum from Maass was not 25 July 1949 during the Manstein trial but 25 July 1945 while being questioned in Nuremberg.

57 Kordt, pp. 322–9; Weizsäcker, pp. 244–62.

58 Jodl's diary in *Trial*, Vol. XXVIII, p. 390; Kordt, pp. 328–9.

59 Kordt, pp. 337–8.

60 Here and below see Keilig, pp. 40/1939/4, 41/1; Gisevius, *Ende*, Vol. II, pp. 109–16 (*Bitter End*, pp. 352–58); Gisevius in *Trial*, Vol. XII, p. 224; Georg Thomas: 'Gedanken und Ereignisse' in *Schweizer Monatshefte* 25 (1945), pp. 542–3 (this gives Thomas's recollections – the majority of authors who have written on the opposition have seen them only in mimeographed form and have therefore described them as unpublished); Schlabrendorff: *Revolt*, pp. 46–7 and *Secret War*, pp. 110–11.

61 Schlabrendorff in *Revolt*, p. 48, mentions the same people except for Wittke and Gisevius.

62 Thomas, pp. 542–3. Gisevius in *Trial*, Vol. XII pp. 224–5 gives a slightly different version in that he situates discussion, distribution and rejection of *both* aide-memoires as earlier than 25 August. In fact both the timing and content of the second aide-memoire – Gisevius calls it a memorandum but can only be referring to the tables and graphs mentioned by Thomas – seems to have been inseparably bound up with the more or less hectic efforts made in those days to preserve peace. Gisevius in *Bitter End*, pp. 352 and 355–6, and in *Ende*, Vol. II, pp. 112–14 adopts Thomas's account. Schlabrendorff in *Revolt*, p. 48, and *Secret War*, p. 111 seems to be under the impression that the second of Thomas's aide-memoires never got beyond Keitel either.

63 Gisevius in *Trial*, Vol. XII, p. 224; *Ende*, Vol. II, pp. 112–14 (*Bitter End*, pp. 355–8).

64 Gisevius, *Bitter End*, p. 368.

65 Gisevius, *Bitter End*, pp. 368–70; Gisevius in *Trial*, Vol. XII, pp. 224–5; Schacht's evidence in 'Protokoll . . . Halder,' p. 123.

66 Gisevius in *Trial*, Vol. XII, p. 225, *Bitter End*, pp. 369–70.

67 Kordt, p. 329; Weizsäcker, p. 257; Gisevius, *Bitter End*, p. 370 and special edition, p. 408 where he reports Lahousen's confirmation of Canaris's attitude but without throwing light on Canaris's somewhat obscure remark that 'everything would now take the desired course'. It is not clear whether he was referring to the rising, to a refusal to conform by the military leaders or the collapse of the Nazi dictatorship.

68 Gisevius, *Bitter End*, p. 373; Gisevius in *Trial*, Vol. XII, p. 225.

CHAPTER 9

1 Ulrich von Hassell: *The von Hassell Diaries*, pp. 67–70; Ernst von Weizsäcker: *Erinnerungen*, pp. 260–1. John W. Wheeler Bennett in *The Nemesis of Power*, p. 453 Note 3, wonders what the purpose of this could have been and comments that it could only have resulted in capitulation either by Poland or by Hitler, both highly improbable. On the question of Polish readiness for some sort of compromise after the conclusion of the Assistance Pact with Britain Wheeler-Bennett merely comments that the opposition in the German Foreign Office regarded the pact as provocative. It can only be assumed, Wheeler-Bennett says, that the opposition wished to see Germany's demands on Poland met, but by peaceful means. He adds the warning that 'it must never be forgotten that these men, though genuine in their hostility to Hitler and in their desire to preserve peace, were also good German patriots'.

2 Fabian von Schlabrendorff: *Revolt against Hitler*, p. 50 and *The Secret War against Hitler*, pp. 105–6.

3 Ibid.; Rudolf Pechel: *Deutscher Widerstand*, p. 153; [Franz] Halder: *Kriegstagebuch*, Vol. I, p. 61 Note 4; Kunrat Freiherr von Hammerstein: *Spähtrupp*, p. 79; Hans-Adolf Jacobsen: *Fall Gelb*, p. 4. Hammerstein (Kunrat's father) was C-in-C of Army Detachment A from 9 September to 10 October 1939, see Detachment's War Diary: 'Kriegstagebuch Nr. 1 der Armee-Abteilung A', BA, W 2h and NA Microcopy T-312 roll 1612. Wolf Keilig in *Das deutsche Heer 1939–1945*, pp. 211–18, is incorrect when he gives the dates as 10–21 September. Erich Kosthorst in *Die deutsche Opposition gegen Hitler zwischen Polen- und Frankreichfeldzug*, p. 21, dismisses Hammerstein's plan as utopian, clearly assuming that the detailed plans and preparations, which were not disclosed, never existed. Or does he imply that an attempt to arrange a visit by Hitler was utopian? See also Allen Welsh Dulles: *Germany's Underground*, p. 53 where, as in other places, eyewitness accounts (Schlabrendorff's in this case) are superficially and inaccurately recorded (or translated).

4 Sir George Ogilvie-Forbes confirmed this in writing to Wheeler-Bennett after the war – Wheeler-Bennett, p. 458 Note 4.

5 Ibid., p. 459; see also Otto A. W. John: 'Am achten Jahrestag der Verschwörung' in *Das Parlament*, 20 July 1952, p. 2 where he says that Hitler was to be made 'harmless' without judicial proceedings.

6 Pechel, p. 154; Hassell: *Vom andern Deutschland*, p. 78 (not in English translation); Dulles (p. 66) gives an almost identical pronouncement by Beck but timed at the end of 1942 or early 1943; Hans Rothfels in *The German Opposition to Hitler*, p. 70, quotes Beck from Dulles's book but connects this with autumn 1939; Wheeler-Bennett (p. 459) confuses the two statements and says that Dulles has wrongly ascribed to Beck the remark which Pechel says was made by Hammerstein.

7 Halder, op. cit., p. 84; Max Domarus: *Hitler: Reden und Proklamationen 1932–1945*, pp. 1347–54, 1366–8, 1376, 1434; Hans Baur: *Hitler's Pilot*, p. 101; Walther Hubatsch; 'Das dienstliche Tagebuch des Chefs des Wehrmacht-führungsamtes im Oberkommando der Wehrmacht, Generalmajor Jodl, für die Zeit vom 13. Okt. 1939 bis zum 30. Jan. 1940' in *Die Welt als Geschichte* 13 (1953), p. 64.

8 Gerhard Ritter: *Carl Goerdeler und die deutsche Widerstandsbewegung*, p. 239; Klaus-Jürgen Müller in *Das Heer und Hitler*, pp. 471–573, gives a detailed account of the various deliberations in opposition circles about what *could* be done; unless they led to some action I have, in most cases, omitted them.

9 See entry for 23 September 1939 in the diary of Groscurth, the *Abwehr* liaison officer: 'Admiral Canaris says that the actions of the murder squads [Einsatzkommandos] in Fourteenth Army area (Woyrsch) are downright ghastly.

Intervention necessary.' – [Helmuth Groscurth]: 'Tagebuch [der] Verb. Gruppe OKW Ausl./Abw. zu OKH ab 1.9.39–26.9.39', BA EAP 21-X-15/1. The diaries and connected documents have now been published as *Tagebücher eines Abwehroffiziers 1938–1940*, edited by Helmut Krausnick, Harold C. Deutsch and Hildegard von Kotze.

10 On this point and below see Hans Rothfels: *The German Opposition to Hitler*, pp. 130–2; Rothfels: 'The German Resistance in Its International Aspects' in *International Affairs* 34 (1958), pp. 483–4; Rothfels: 'Adam von Trott und das State Department' in *VfZ* 7 (1959), pp. 318–32, which includes the memorandum and other documents; Rothfels: 'Trott und die Aussenpolitik des Widerstandes' in *VfZ* 12 (1964), pp. 300–18 where certain of Trott's papers are also reproduced; Margret Boveri: *Wir lügen alle*, pp. 636–41; Alexander B. Maley: 'The Epic of the German Underground' in *Human Events* 3 (1946) No 9, 27 February 1946, pp. 4–5. Wheeler-Bennett's account (pp. 486–8) says nothing of his own connections with Trott during the latter's mission in late 1939 and is supported by no reference to sources.

11 Boveri, p. 638.

12 Scheffer, it must be remembered, was recounting this difference of opinion almost twenty years later. If his memory is correct – that Trott wished to delete the sentence concerned and did in fact expunge it – there can have been a misunderstanding or, still more probably, a question of tact and tactics. In fact Trott thought the same way but it might have been too compromising to set the thought down in writing and explicitly attribute it to the opposition – see Boveri, p. 639 and Rothfels in 'Adam von Trott', pp. 321, 329, 332. It is also conceivable that the opposition's preference for a German defeat did not appear in the draft but that Trott unsuccessfully urged the inclusion of such a passage and then, as the available documents clearly show, put the idea forward verbally; Rothfels in 'Adam von Trott', pp. 318–19 indicates as much when he comments that Trott disagreed with the memorandum on one highly characteristic point.

13 Boveri, pp. 639–40; Rothfels, 'Adam von Trott', p. 321; Rothfels, 'Trott und die Aussenpolitik', p. 306; Ritter, *Goerdeler*, p. 257 (*Resistance*, p. 157).

14 Rothfels, 'Adam von Trott', pp. 321–2.

15 Boveri, p. 640; Mother Mary Alice Gallin: *Ethical and Religious Factors in the German Resistance to Hitler*, pp. 110–11.

16 Rothfels, 'Adam von Trott', pp. 322–9 – also applicable below.

17 Gallin, pp. 110–11, 205.

18 Ibid., pp. 111, 205.

19 Ibid., p. 205.

20 Christopher Sykes: *Troubled Loyalty*, pp. 303–4.

21 See Hans Rothfels: 'Zwei aussenpolitische Memoranden der deutschen Opposition (Frühjahr 1942)', *VfZ* 5 (1957), pp. 390–1. Sykes, p. 303; David Astor: 'Why the Revolt against Hitler Was Ignored: On the British Reluctance to Deal with German Anti-Nazis', *Encounter* XXXII (1969) No 6, p. 6.

22 Hans Mommsen: 'Gesellschaftsbild und Verfassungspläne des deutschen Widerstandes' in *Der deutsche Widerstand gegen Hitler*, edited by Walter Schmitthenner and Hans Buchheim, pp. 94–5 (*The German Resistance to Hitler*, pp. 76–9).

23 Astor, 'Why the Revolt . . .', p. 6; Sykes, p. 214.

24 Maley, p. 5.

25 Rothfels, 'Trott und die Aussenpolitik', pp. 305, 313–15.

26 Ibid., pp. 306, 316–18. Wheeler-Bennett made no mention of this in his book, *The Nemesis of Power*, in which he describes many of the efforts of the German opposition to overthrow Hitler's regime and to enlist Allied support. The reasons why he fails to mention his intimacy with Trott are not clear. Wheeler-Bennett did not – contrary to his promise to Trott – contact David Astor to coordinate

efforts at establishing more useful contacts between the British Government and the German opposition, but on the contrary 'advised *against* offering specific encouragement to the German opposition and supported the "Unconditional Surrender" policy'; Astor, 'Why the Revolt . . .', pp. 8, 10, 11.

27 Rothfels, 'Adam von Trott', p. 332. After completion of the original manuscript of this book a special study of opposition activity from end September 1939 to early May 1940 appeared by Harold C. Deutsch: *The Conspiracy against Hitler in the Twilight War*. Where Deutsch has reached different or fuller conclusions than my own, I have quoted him. As regards the success of Trott's mission Deutsch suspects (p. 157) that it assisted the tendency in London to give a positive answer to Müller's soundings (see pp. 158–65 below).

28 Sykes (pp. 303–23) traced the various sources of the suspicion, as well as Trott's contacts, in great detail, though usually with a lack of precise dates.

29 Henry Morgenthau Jr, Diary, Vol. 238, pp. 87–90, Franklin D. Roosevelt Library, Hyde Park, New York.

30 Sykes, p. 320.

31 Morgenthau's Diary, also applicable below.

32 Trott was shadowed by F.B.I. agents until he left the United States from San Francisco; Sykes, pp. 303–23.

33 Kordt, pp. 339–40; Weizsäcker, p. 273.

34 Kordt, p. 367. According to Otto John in *Twice through the Lines*, p. 58, Conwell Evans was already working for the British Secret Service at this time and was to pump Theo Kordt.

35 *New York Times*, 5 September 1939, p. 6.

36 Domarus, pp. 1389–92; Weizsäcker, pp. 267–8.

37 *Trial of the Major War Criminals before the International Military Tribunal*, Vol. XXXVII, pp. 466–86; Walther Hubatsch: *Hitler's War Directives*, pp. 13–14; see also Kosthorst, p. 33.

38 Halder, *Kriegstagebuch*, Vol. I, pp. 84–90; Jacobsen, op. cit., p. 8. Deutsch (pp. 69–70) lists Keitel, Warlimont, Raeder and Göring as also present at the meeting on 27 September 1939 but this is not supported by his reference (Halder, op. cit., pp. 86–90).

39 A comprehensive report on these discussions provided by Colonel Oster is to be found in the papers of the Special Duties Section of *OKW Ausland/Abwehr*, the *Abwehr*'s liaison group at OKH – [Helmuth Groscurth]: 'Kriegstagebuch der Abt z.b.V 27.9 – 14.11.39', 25 Oct and Annex 13 in BA, EAP 21-X-15/1 (cf. Groscurth, *Tagebücher*, pp. 300–1).

40 Domarus, pp. 1395–9; Wheeler-Bennett, pp. 463–6; Kosthorst, p. 27.

41 Halder, op. cit., p. 114; Wheeler-Bennett, pp. 464–6.

42 Kordt, pp. 355–6.

43 *The Parliamentary Debates, Official Report* (Hansard), 5th Series, House of Commons, Vol. 352, 12 October 1939, cols 565–6.

44 Kordt, pp. 367–8, 442–3; concerning this misunderstanding see Rothfels: *Die deutsche Opposition*, pp. 139, 202 Note 7; Wheeler-Bennett, pp. 467–9.

45 Kosthorst (pp. 82–3) quotes unpublished documents from the Weizsäcker trial. These show that discussions between Theo Kordt and Conwell Evans took place in Berne on 25, 27 and 29 October. See also Deutsch, pp. 160–3. For continuation of these contacts see pp. 154–5 below.

46 On this and below see S. Payne Best: *The Venlo Incident*, pp. 7–46; Wheeler-Bennett, pp. 476–9. Wheeler-Bennett used Dutch sources and the files of the Nuremberg trial, in particular a report dated 29 March 1940 signed by Frick, the Minister of the Interior, and Himmler, the *Reichsführer-SS* and Chief of the German Police, also a report from the *Gestapo* Office, Düsseldorf dated 9 November 1939 – both in StA, Nuremburg, NG 4672. Kurt Sendtner in 'Die deutsche Militäropposition im ersten Kriegsjahr' in *Vollmacht des Gewissens*,

Vol. I, pp. 456–7 Note 76 gives a report by Stevens. See also Walter Schellenberg: *The Schellenberg Memoirs*, pp. 82–98. Evidence of British suspicions based on the Venlo incident: D. G. Osborne to Halifax 12 Jan. 1940 in Peter Ludlow: 'Papst Pius XII, die britische Regierung und die deutsche Opposition im Winter 1939/40' in VfZ 22 (1974), p. 331.

47 Hassell, *Diaries*, pp. 71–5.

48 Oster arranged for the Swede to report to him on his talks with Göring and informed the Chief of the General Staff through the *Abwehr* liaison group with OKH – Groscurth's diary for 27 October 1939 and Annex 15 in BA, EAP 21 X 15 /1 (cf. Groscurth, *Tagebücher*, pp. 301–2).

49 Hassell, op. cit., pp. 77–82.

50 Hassell, *Deutschland*, p. 84 (not in English translation).

51 Hassell, *Diaries*, p. 84.

52 Gisevius, *Bitter End*, p. 380.

53 Here and below see: Christine von Dohnanyi: 'Aufzeichnungen', typescript undated, in IfZ, ZS 603; Otto John: 'Männer im Kampf gegen Hitler (IV): Wilhelm Leuschner' in *Blick in die Welt* 2 (1947) No 9, p. 20; Hassell, *Deutschland*, p. 84; Elfriede Nebgen: *Jakob Kaiser*, pp. 114–15; Emil Henk: *Die Tragödie des 20 Juli 1944*, pp. 10–15 where eyewitness stories are given but without precision. Deutsch (pp. 88–91) gives a good survey of Dohnanyi's career.

54 Heinz Boberach (editor): *Meldungen aus dem Reich*, pp. 8, 9 and Note 1.

55 Dohnanyi; Otto John: 'Männer im Kampf [I], *Blick in die Welt* 2 (1947), No 6, 'Männer ... (IV)', 'Some Facts and Aspects of the Plot against Hitler', p. 28; Kosthorst, p. 19. Leuschner did not therefore meet Beck for the first time in the second half of 1941 as did Jakob Kaiser and Habermann and as Nebgen (pp. 124–7) assumes.

56 Dohnanyi; see also Henk, p. 9.

57 Dohnanyi. See also notes by Frau Christine von Dohnanyi of 1945 on the papers discovered in Zossen by the Gestapo after 20 July 1944; they included Dohnanyi's 'chronicle'; the notes are reproduced in Eberhard Bethge: *Dietrich Bonhoeffer*, pp. 1096–1101; cf. Deutsch, pp. 89–90; Ritter, *Goerdeler*, p. 501 Note 10 quotes a statement by Huppenkothen before the Munich Court of Assize in February 1951 to the effect that the papers found in Zossen were destroyed by the *Gestapo*; see also [Walter] Huppenkothen: 'Der 20. Juli 1944', typescript [1953] p. 2, IfZ ZS 249–II; Franz Sonderegger: letter to President of Provincial Court I in Munich dated 14 January 1951 – copy in IfZ.

58 Kordt, p. 355; Ritter, op. cit., pp. 243–5 (*Resistance*, pp. 143–4).

59 Kosthorst, p. 32.

60 A copy is to be found in the Groscurth papers in BA, EAP 21-X-15/2 (printed in Groscurth, *Tagebücher*, pp. 479–83); at least one further copy would have been among the papers found by the *Gestapo* on 22 September 1944 in a safe in Zossen – letter from Franz Sonderegger (Note 57 above), pp. 2–3. It is impossible to determine who read this memorandum but it was undoubtedly submitted to Brauchitsch or at least Halder and was in any case used by Groscurth in his interviews with Halder. See Groscurth diary, passim; Sendtner, p. 412. The copy of the memorandum in the Groscurth papers includes a number of critical, even acid and unfriendly marginal comments; since Groscurth knew perfectly well who the author of the document was, these must have been camouflage for the retention of anything so defeatist.

61 BA, EAP 21-X-15/2.

62 Hassell, *Diaries*, p. 104; Keilig, pp. 32/6, 211/193–4; Halder, op. cit., p. 20; Jacobsen, op. cit., pp. 2–3. Prior to 1 September Army Group C was known as 'Army Group 2'.

63 Hans-Adolf Jacobsen: 'Das "Halder-Tagebuch" als historische Quelle' in *Festschrift Percy Ernst Schramm zu seinem siebzigsten Geburtstag von seinen*

Schülern und Freunden zugeeignet, edited by Peter Classen and Peter Scheibert, Vol. II, pp. 259–60. The memorandum with its covering letter to Brauchitsch is reproduced in Kosthorst, pp. 159–66; see also Halder, op. cit., p. 104. On his p. 44 Kosthorst maintains that Colonel-General von Bock, C-in-C of Army Group B, also received a copy but adduces no proof therefor. The distribution in the covering letter to Brauchitsch shows only four copies: No 1 for Brauchitsch, No 2 for Halder, No 3 for Leeb himself and No 4 which was the draft for Colonel Vincenz Müller, Leeb's Operations Officer. Dr Laternser, Leeb's defence counsel at the Nuremberg trial, however, stated as a proven fact that the document was forwarded to Bock – [Hans] Laternser: *Verteidigung deutscher Soldaten*, p. 298. See also Jacobsen, *Fall Gelb*, pp. 44–5.

64 The letter is reproduced in Kosthorst, pp. 167–8; see also Jacobsen, op. cit., p. 45.

65 Kosthorst, pp. 47–8; Laternser, p. 298; Jacobsen (op. cit., pp. 15, 44–5) only refers indirectly to Bock's memorandum.

66 Halder, op. cit., p. 99; probably such a meeting, at which Leeb was also present, took place on 4 October but the indication in Halder, op. cit., p. 97 is not enough to establish this.

67 Rundstedt's memorandum to Brauchitsch is reproduced in Kosthorst, pp. 169–73; see also Halder, op. cit., p. 117; Jacobsen, op. cit., p. 45.

68 See Halder, op. cit., pp. 84 and 98 giving reports on the Polish campaign from Bock and Major-General Friedrich-Wilhelm von Chappuis (then Chief of Staff of XIV Corps) showing that the infantry had 'nothing approaching' the combat efficiency of the troops of 1914.

69 Halder, op. cit., p. 105. Until research had been done on the original of the diary by Kosthorst and Hans-Adolf Jacobsen an erroneous version due to a typing error was in circulation which did not fit the context. This showed: 'C-in-C three possibilities: Await attack, fundamental changes.' One of the 'three possibilities' was therefore missing. On this point see Kosthorst, p. 40 Note 46a and Halder, op. cit., p. 105 Note 1. 'C-in-C' in this connection could mean Cs-in-C of Armies, Corps or Army Groups. In Halder's diary Brauchitsch is usually referred to as 'Army C-in-C' [ObdH], though in many cases Halder uses only 'OB' and the abbreviation does not always, or does not unequivocally, refer to the C-in-C of the Army. See Jacobsen, *Fall Gelb*, p. 26.

70 Halder's evidence in OKW Trial (The High Command case) in *Trials of War Criminals before the Nuernberg Military Tribunals under Control Council Law No 10*, Vol. X, p. 545; Dohnanyi, p. 6; cf. Kosthorst, p. 41. Jodl in Walther Hubatsch: 'Das dienstliche Tagebuch des Chefs des Wehrmachtführungsamtes im Oberkommando der Wehrmacht, Generalmajor Jodl, für die Zeit vom 13. Okt. 1939 bis 30. Jan. 1940' in *Die Welt als Geschichte* 12 (1952), p. 280; Hassell, op. cit., p. 88.

71 Jodl in Hubatsch, op. cit., p. 280.

72 Keilig, pp. 80/10, 211/264.

73 Halder, *Kriegstagebuch*, p. 106; Deutsch, pp. 72–4.

74 Here and below see Deutsch, pp. 72–3 (clearly in error, he gives the date of the meeting as 30 October, not 25 October); Halder, op. cit., pp. 113–17.

75 Deutsch, pp. 74–7; for details see p. 170 below. Müller, p. 411 reports without reference to a source the following remark of General von Reichenau on 22 August 1939: 'The man is greatly mistaken if he thinks this war will be over in a few weeks. This will not be a six-weeks war, this will be a six-year war.'

CHAPTER 10

1 [Helmuth Groscurth], Kriegstagebuch Abt.z.b.V. 27.9.–14.11.39, entry 20 Oct. 1939, EAP 21-X-15/1; printed in Helmuth Groscurth, *Tagebücher eines Abwehroffiziers 1938–1940*, p. 299.

2 Kurt Sendtner: 'Die deutsche Militäropposition im ersten Kriegsjahr' in *Vollmacht des Gewissens*, Vol. I, p. 405 – based on Halder's evidence before the *Spruchkammer*.

3 Otto John: 'Männer im Kampf gegen Hitler (IV): Wilhelm Leuschner' in *Blick in die Welt* 2 (1947); Harold C. Deutsch: *The Conspiracy against Hitler in the Twilight War*, p. 47.

4 Here and below see Groscurth, *Tagebücher*, pp. 211–15, 302–5; Deutsch, pp. 196–7, 217–18, 288. Deutsch merely refers to 'Halder's half-intention to kill Hitler personally'.

5 Verbally to the author by Dr Hasso von Etzdorf on 24 August 1972.

6 Erich Kordt: *Nicht aus den Akten*, pp. 356–7; Hasso von Etzdorf in 'Protokoll aus der Verhandlung Halder [vor der] Spruchkammer X München', p. 139; conversation on 26 September 1953 between Dr von Etzdorf, and Dr H. Krausnick of Institut für Zeitgeschichte, typescript dated 12 June 1958, IfZ ZS 322; Gerhard Ritter, *Carl Goerdeler und die deutsche Widerstandsbewegung*, p. 246 (*The German Resistance*, p. 146); Erich Kosthorst: *Die deutsche Opposition gegen Hitler zwischen Polen- und Frankreichfeldzug*, p. 57, based on Halder's recollections and information; cf. Sendtner, p. 405; [Walter] Huppenkothen: 'Der 20. Juli 1944', p. 3; Franz Sonderegger: Letter to Provincial Court, p. 2; Christine von Dohnanyi: 'Aufzeichnungen', p. 7; Sendtner, p. 413 Note 33 based on evidence from Dr Josef Müller; Deutsch, pp. 201, 204. According to Halder's evidence (frequently somewhat vague in other cases as well) before the court – 'Protokoll . . . Halder', p. 32 – he did no more than consider the matter; this may well be so as far as Halder was concerned; the other conspirators were more resolute. Ritter (*Goerdeler*, p. 503 Note 23) considers that Huppenkothen's statements include inaccuracies but 'much inherent probability'. Deutsch (p. 199) also quotes information from Groscurth's secretary; in his well-founded opinion Huppenkothen's statements are reliable (Deutsch, pp. 118–19, 200). Klaus-Jürgen Müller in *Das Heer und Hitler*, pp. 491, 494, 496, 498–505, 511–14 attempts to prove, not entirely conclusively but with ample evidence, that Halder could not have issued such an instruction before 31 October. He does, however, show conclusively that, as was to some extent known, Halder and Stülpnagel did issue instructions to Groscurth on 31 October and on 2 or 3 November – see Groscurth, *Tagebücher*, pp. 222–4.

7 Hoepner was commanding XVI Corps which included 1 Panzer Division located in Thuringia from 23 September – Wolf Keilig: *Das deutsche Heer 1939–1945*, pp. 103/2, 211/159.

8 Alexander [Freiherr] von Falkenhausen, ['Bericht über meine Stellung zur N.S.D.A.P. und ihrem Regime'], typescript, 1946, NA, Record Group, 338 MS No B–289.

9 Keilig, pp. 211/111, 90/4; 2 Panzer Division was in XIX Corps – Keilig, pp. 90/4, 103 I/1; Dohnanyi, p. 7.

10 Kosthorst, p. 57. These divisions must have been part of the field army and would therefore not have been under General Fromm as C-in-C of the Replacement Army.

11 Both this study and the plan of action drafted by Groscurth have been lost. The study was found by the *Gestapo* in 1944 but probably burnt in 1945. Groscurth's plan or at any rate all plans in the possession of Halder must have been destroyed in November 1939 – see Notes 15 and 16 below.

12 Sonderegger's letter to Provincial Court, p. 2; Huppenkothen, p. 3. See also Sendtner, p. 413 Note 33; based on information from Dr Josef Müller he describes Oster's papers as 'sketches' 'setting out a form of programme for measures to be taken in connection with a *coup*'; he does not regard them as a programme for action comparable either in detail or utility with that of 1938. Ritter (*Goerdeler*, p. 502 Note 13; *Resistance*, p. 146 Note 2) says that

Groscurth's preparations as ordered by Halder must initially — until about 2 November — have been carried on independently of and without the knowledge of the Beck-Oster-Gisevius group; he also says, on the other hand, that they were known to Etzdorf and other members of the Foreign Ministry and that Goerdeler 'must have learnt something of them before 29 October when he asked Hassell to come to Berlin'. If all these people knew something, it seems unlikely, without conclusive proof or evidence to the contrary, that Oster knew nothing. According to Hans Bernd Gisevius (*To the Bitter End*, p. 382) he heard on 1 November of an 'important action' being planned by a group in OKH and this must have come from Oster or Groscurth. Halder may have tried to stop the continuous passage of information to Oster but Groscurth can hardly have conformed to an order of this nature.

13 Huppenkothen, p. 3; Dohnanyi, p. 7; Sendtner, p. 413 Note 33. Deutsch (p. 201) assumes that Hitler, Göring, Goebbels, Ribbentrop, Himmler, Heydrich and 'Dietrich' were to be killed.

14 Huppenkothen, pp. 3–4; Groscurth's diary 15 November 1939 (*Tagebücher*, p. 310); Sendtner (p. 413 Note 33) based on information from Dr Müller mentions the Stargard Panzer Regiment; see also Kosthorst, pp. 62, 94. Geyr von Schweppenburg in *The Critical Years*, pp. 203–4, says that he refused a proposal by General Karl-Heinrich von Stülpnagel, then Deputy Chief of Staff I, to participate in a *coup* thinking it impossible since, after the victory over Poland, the majority of officers were far too attached to Hitler and, moreover, the troops would not have obeyed them.

15 Some of them at least were discovered by the *Gestapo* in 1944; they are described as Huppenkothen and Sonderegger remember them — Huppenkothen, pp. 3–4 and Sonderegger's letter to Provincial Court, p. 2. See also Deutsch, pp. 202–3 — also applicable below.

16 Huppenkothen, p. 4; on Canaris's diary see Deutsch, p. 305 Note 155.

17 Ritter, *Goerdeler*, p. 246 and Note 13.

18 Otto John: *Twice through the Lines*, p. 59 — also applicable below.

19 Kordt, pp. 358–66 where such fragments as remain are reproduced — also in BA, EAP 21-X-15/2 (printed in Groscurth, *Tagebücher*, pp. 498–503). See also Müller, pp. 503–5.

20 The 'revolution from above' inevitably stressed the authoritarian aspect; this and the various statements to the effect that the 'popular mood' was either sufficiently favourable to the *coup* or was of no great importance have on occasions led to serious misunderstanding of the opposition's political intentions. Admittedly *some* constitutional ideas current in resistance circles evidenced great aversion to the democractic and parliamentary political practices which had apparently been discredited by the Weimar 'system' but it is not right to quote, out of context and as evidence of this tendency, arguments about public opinion put forward *ad hominem*, in others words for the benefit of Halder and Brauchitsch. See Hans Mommsen; 'Gesellschaftsbild und Verfassungspläne des deutschen Widerstandes' Walter Schmitthenner and Hans Buchheim (editors): *Der deutsche Widerstand gegen Hitler*, pp. 123–6 (*The German Resistance to Hitler*, pp. 105–108), and pp. 140, 148, 150, 165, 291–2, 295 below.

21 The parts of the memorandum dealing with the later stages and a section on the future German constitution have been lost — Kordt, p. 366. The copy in BA, EAP 21-X-15/2, pp. 13–15 (now printed in Groscurth, *Tagebücher*, pp. 498–503) includes guidelines for a public pronouncement which are not to be found in Kordt's book.

22 Letter from Groscurth to Witzleben 31 October 1939, BA, EAP 21-X-15/2 (*Tagebücher*, p. 391); Deutsch, p. 207.

23 [Franz] Halder: *Kriegstagebuch* Vol. I, p. 111; Hans-Adolf Jacobsen: *Fall Gelb*, p. 39.

24 Halder, op. cit., p. 112.

25 Groscurth's diaries 25 October 1939 (*Tagebücher*, pp. 220–1, 300–1).

26 Halder, op. cit., p. 113; Walther Hubatsch: 'Das dienstliche Tagebuch des Chefs des Wehrmachtsführungsamtes im Oberkommando der Wehrmacht, Generalmajor Jodl, für die Zeit vom 13. Okt. 1939 bis zum 30. Jan. 1940', in *Die Welt als Geschichte* 12 (1952), p. 280; Jacobsen, p. 39. As regards the venue for the conference – on 24 and 26 October Hitler was in the *Reich* Chancellery; 25 October was a Wednesday – see Max Domarus: *Hitler: Reden und Proklamationen 1932–1945*, pp. 1402–3. It is improbable that Hitler would have gone to Berchtesgaden for so short a time and the fact would have been noted by Domarus or Halder.

27 Halder, op. cit., p. 114; Hubatsch, p. 282; Jacobsen, pp. 40–1; Domarus, p. 1403.

28 Halder, op. cit., pp. 114–15.

29 Ibid., p. 115; Hubatsch, p. 282.

30 Halder, op. cit., pp. 115–16; Kosthorst, pp. 60–2; Jacobsen, p. 45; Sendtner, pp. 406–11; Groscurth, *Tagebücher*, pp. 221–2 and note 575. Stülpnagel did not undertake tours of the front lasting for weeks, as might be implied by Halder's evidence before the Court ('Protokoll ... Halder', pp. 31–2); Sendtner also questioned this, and Halder's and Groscurth's diaries rule it out. Stülpnagel may, however, well have gone to the front on several occasions during these weeks. According to Halder's evidence in *Trials of War Criminals before the Nuernberg Military Tribunals under Control Council Law No. 10*, Vol. X, p. 858 Stülpnagel's tours only took place after 23 November and this is also maintained by Ritter, *Goerdeler*, p. 505 Note 38. Halder's reference must therefore be to *further* tours by Stülpnagel. See Deutsch, p. 208.

31 Halder's evidence in 'Protokoll ... Halder', p. 31; see also Müller, pp. 508–10.

32 Halder, *Kriegstagebuch*, Vol. I, pp. 115–16; Groscurth, *Tagebücher*, pp. 221–5. Deutsch (pp. 208–9) thinks it inconceivable that Halder's one really firm decision in favour of the *coup* could have resulted from so negative an outcome to Stülpnagel's tour; he therefore concludes that the tour by Stülpnagel which produced this negative result must have taken place later. It is of course possible that the most negative report given by Stülpnagel to Halder concerning the readiness to revolt of the generals to whom he had spoken was produced at the end of November, as Halder himself said in *Trials of War Criminals*, Vol. X, p. 858, when these events were fresher in his memory than in his talks with Kosthorst and Deutsch later. The argument is not conclusive, however, because Halder here gives the timing of *all* Stülpnagel's tours (inaccurately) as the end of November or later; if Deutsch's reasoning is pursued to its logical conclusion, the other serious rebuffs suffered by Halder shortly before 5 November must be situated in a later period; see also further discrepancies in Deutsch, pp. 212–15. Moreover Halder had long known the attitude of generals such as Bock, Rundstedt and Manstein, as Deutsch himself says on his p. 211; he also knew that generals like Leeb and Witzleben thought differently. At the same time as Stülpnagel's report (which is not altogether confirmed) Halder received the memoranda from Leeb, Bock and Rundstedt (see pp. 124–7 above); of these only Leeb's gave an indication of readiness to participate in a *coup*. Perhaps the most uncertain factor in Deutsch's calculation is Halder's degree of determination at any particular time; on this one can still only speculate since Halder never managed a 'breakthrough to action'.

33 'Protokoll ... Halder', pp. 31–2; Kosthorst, pp. 60–2. Halder's evidence to the Court was understandably somewhat dramatized but in general it was accurate apart from the fact that it does not mention Leeb.

34 Kosthorst, p. 61.

35 Ibid., p. 62; Jacobsen, p. 45; see also Ulrich von Hassell: *Vom andern Deutschland*, p. 108 (not in English translation) and Sendtner, p. 410 Note 28.

36 Deutsch (p. 212 Note 99) identifies this date with almost complete certainty; Sendtner (p. 419) and Kosthorst (p. 62) incline towards the first few days of November.

37 Sendtner, pp. 424–5 on information from Haseloff. Kosthorst, p. 62 is based on information from Edgar Röhricht who does not, however, repeat it in his own book (*Pflicht und Gewissen*, pp. 153–9); there Röhricht merely refers indirectly and in general terms to the period around 23 November.

38 Sendtner, p. 425.

39 Kosthorst, pp. 62–3.

40 See pp. 158–64 below.

41 Kosthorst, p. 93.

42 BA, EAP 21-X-15/2 (printed in Groscurth, *Tagebücher*, pp. 483–6).

43 It is not possible to say whether a note in Groscurth's diary for 6.0 p.m. 31 October (*Tagebücher*, p. 303) 'Discussion by Section Head [himself] with General Halder on internal political situation' can be taken as an indication of this.

44 *United States of America Congressional Record: Proceedings and Debates of the 76th Congress, Second Session*, Vol. 85, Part 1, pp. 1024–7.

45 *Keesing's Contemporary Archives*, Vol. III 1937–1940, p. 3772.

46 Halder, *Kriegstagebuch*, Vol. I, p. 117; Jacobsen, pp. 45–6.

47 Halder, op. cit., pp. 117–18.

48 Ibid., p. 119.

49 Ibid., Gisevius, *Bitter End*, pp. 381–5; Ritter, *Goerdeler*, pp. 247–8 (*Resistance*, pp. 147–8); Sendtner, pp. 475–6. Ritter, op. cit., p. 503 Note 21 quotes Gisevius (*Bis zum bittern Ende*, p. 154; *Bitter End*, p. 383) where the talk between Thomas and Halder is said to have taken place on 2 November; this is almost certainly incorrect. In *Bis zum bitteren Ende*, revised special edition (ca. 1964), p. 416 Gisevius gives the date as 4 November which checks with Halder's statement; it is not clear whether Gisevius corrected an error in his earlier editions or amended his contemporary notes.

50 On this point and below see Sendtner, pp. 413–14; Kosthorst, p. 95; Albrecht von Kessel: 'Verborgene Saat', p. 179; Gisevius, special edition, pp. 415–17 (cf. *Bitter End*, pp. 382–5); Deutsch, pp. 215–18; Ritter, *Goerdeler*, pp. 248, 504 Note 25 (*Resistance*, p. 149); Müller, pp. 511–16. Goerdeler was in Stockholm and returned on 4 November. In contrast to Sendtner, Kosthorst and Ritter, Deutsch relies on the private diary and a letter of Groscurth (both now printed in Groscurth, *Tagebücher*, pp. 222–4 and notes 581 and 584), and has established convincingly that Halder must have issued the 'codeword' on 31 October, before his tour of the front. If Halder wished to strike on 5 November (should Hitler issue the final order for the offensive which had to go out seven days before the attack), he could not have issued the 'codeword' for the revival of the old 1938 plans and other preparations for the *coup* on his return on 3 November. This does not accord, however, with Deutsch, p. 220; in any case Deutsch notes that the dates given by Gisevius (on which he relies in this case) are frequently unreliable.

51 Etzdorf verbally to author 24 August 1972.

52 Kessel, p. 179. This agrees with Deutsch, pp. 222–3 where he says that through Etzdorf and Groscurth Dr Werner Haag of the Foreign Ministry offered himself to the conspirators with a plan to kill Hitler on some ceremonial occasion such as a wreath-laying by concealing explosive in the flowers. The offer was refused as too unlikely to succeed. It was assumed that the flowers and wreaths would be examined before being handed to Hitler for laying. This subterfuge was too well known.

53 Kordt, pp. 369–76; Gisevius, special edition, p. 463; Hasso von Etzdorf: record of conversation with Dr Krausnick, p. 4; Kosthorst, pp. 87–8; Sendtner, p. 412. For details of these two attempts at assassination see Chap. 30 below. Halder's

attitude was contradictory; he was opposed to an attempt which could be laid at the door of himself or the Army and which might be reminiscent of unhappy occurrences like the Kapp *putsch*; he proclaimed his sympathy, however, in the eventuality that what he called 'hot-headed youth' might nerve themselves to do something of the sort; apparently also he himself spontaneously referred to an attempt at assassination. See Halder's evidence in 'Protokoll . . . Halder', pp. 78a, 78c; Ritter, *Goerdeler*, pp. 249–50. See also Halder's statements recorded on pp. 84, 129 above.

54 Jacobsen, pp. 46, 141.

55 On this point and below see Halder, *Kriegstagebuch*, Vol. I, pp. 119–20; Halder's evidence in 'Protokoll . . . Halder', pp. 15–16; Brauchitsch's statements in *Trial of the Major War Criminals before the International Military Tribunal*, Vol. XX pp. 575–6; Groscurth's diary, 5 November 1939 (*Tagebücher*, pp. 224–5, 305); Helmuth Greiner: *Die Oberste Wehrmachtführung 1939–1943*, pp. 66–9; Kordt, p. 372; John W. Wheeler-Bennett: *The Nemesis of Power*, pp. 470–1 (corrections in Deutsch, p. 227 Note 140); Kosthorst, pp. 98–9; Jacobsen, pp. 46–7; Deutsch, pp. 226–9.

56 Halder, *Kriegstagebuch*, Vol. I, p. 120; Jacobsen, pp. 46–9; Deutsch, p. 229. In his evidence before the *Spruchkammer* ('Protokoll . . . Halder', p. 16) Halder said that he had 'only heard fragments of the contents of the discussion much later from this very reserved man [Brauchitsch]'. This is contrary to Halder's diary. The discrepancy is characteristic of Halder's tendency to prevaricate when recalling this period, even when proof to the contrary was easy to produce. Similarly Halder stated that Brauchitsch had no interview with Hitler between 5 and 22 November whereas according to his diary (*Kriegstagebuch*, Vol. I, pp. 120–31) Brauchitsch saw Hitler at least three times during this period. On this subject and below see Müller, pp. 520–7.

57 Wheeler-Bennett, p. 471; Eberhard Zeller: *The Flame of Freedom*, p. 39 (without evidence); Sendtner (p. 414) clearly follows Zeller; Ritter (*Goerdeler*, p. 249 and 504 Note 27 – *Resistance*, p. 149 and Note 2) refers to Wheeler-Bennett, p. 471 who bases his account on statements by Brauchitsch and Halder; Kosthorst, p. 99 (without evidence and apparently based on Halder); Deutsch, pp. 228–9. In his evidence before the denazification court Halder confused the 5 November and 23 November meetings in some respects; his timetable of events leading up to these conferences is therefore not altogether reliable ('Protokoll . . . Halder', pp. 15–17).

58 Jacobsen, p. 49.

59 Gisevius, *Bitter End*, p. 386 (according to this, Stülpnagel gave the order to destroy the papers, apparently at Halder's instigation) Kosthorst, pp. 99–100; Sendtner, p. 415 (without evidence). On 4 November Groscurth noted in his diary: '8.0 p.m. Head of Section [himself] discussed with Deputy Chief of Staff I [Stülpnagel] necessity of headquarters protection. Nothing to be done.' See Deutsch, p. 219. Was security regarded as adequate or were they relying on troops whom it was intended to summon? Zossen camp was under OKW and with the agreement of that office the *Gestapo* could well have penetrated into OKH if no specially reliable units were available to defend it.

There are numerous accounts of an incident said to have occurred on the same day – Zeller, p. 403 Note 24 quoting Kessel as the source; Allen Dulles: *Verschwörung in Deutschland*, pp. 76–7 (not in English edition), probably also based on Kessel; Sendtner, p. 415 who expresses grave doubts as to the authenticity of the incident; according to Rainer Hildebrandt in *Wir sind die Letzten*, p. 78, Albrecht Haushofer told him of the incident in autumn 1940. The relevant passage in Kessel (pp. 179–80) reads as follows: 'On 5 November the general who held all the strings in his hand – I never heard his name and did not ask subsequently – had his customary interview with Hitler. At the end Hitler suddenly asked him what he was up to. Not yet being suspicious the general calmly told him of a whole series of things which he was doing in the course of business. To which Hitler replied: "No, I don't mean that; I can see it on your face that you are planning something else." The general, who had difficulty in keeping control of himself, pretended to be astonished and not to understand; he was allowed to go, apparently still in Hitler's good graces. He rushed back to the General Staff and said that the whole affair must have been betrayed. All involved showed the utmost consternation; measures were taken at once to erase all trace of the plan and the troops were ordered back to the western front. A few days later it emerged that there had been no betrayal and Hitler could have known nothing.' According to Gisevius (special edition p. 418) 'the general' was Brauchitsch. Apart from the actual course of the discussion the incident would fit Brauchitsch's interview of 5 November. The vital part of the story, however, (Hitler's remark implying that he had some definite suspicion) must be written off as a cover-up story which found its way into the Foreign Ministry and so to Kessel. See also the incident recorded in Deutsch, p. 204 based on recollections by Theo Kordt.

60 Ritter, *Goerdeler*, p. 502 Note 19 based on evidence of witnesses in the Huppenkothen trial; Deutsch, p. 232. Later, after his arrest, Dohnanyi urged that the papers be destroyed but Beck wished to preserve them as evidence of the desires, spirit and long history of the opposition. They were found by the *Gestapo* in Zossen on 22 September 1944.

61 Halder, *Kriegstagebuch*, Vol. I, pp. 120–2; Groscurth's diary 5–9 November 1939 (*Tagebücher*, pp. 224–7, 305–7).

62 Groscurth's diary 5 November 1939 (*Tagebücher*, pp. 224–5, 305); Deutsch, pp. 213–32; Müller, p. 524. In his pages 518–20 Müller emphasizes that Halder had not agreed to initiate the *putsch* as the automatic sequel to some other occurrence; he does not, however, say what Halder's criteria for initiation were if they were not issue of the order to attack by Hitler and Brauchitsch's participation in or toleration of a *putsch*.

63 Gisevius, *Bitter End*, p. 386; Müller (pp. 525–9) accepts as correct this statement by Gisevius and maintains that it is confirmed by Groscurth's private diary for 5 November (*Tagebücher*, pp. 224–5). Müller then deals with the situation in his usual detail including Halder's possible attitude of mind and motives; in the process, however, he becomes involved in wrong conclusions and contradictions without explaining the failure to exploit this favourable opportunity. Otto John in *Twice through the Lines*, pp. 33, 63–4, records what Brauchitsch told him in Bridgend POW camp in 1947: he could not have been persuaded into a *coup d'état* between the Polish and French campaigns any more than in 1938. This does not, however, affect the possibility that he might have tolerated a *coup*.

64 Deutsch (pp. 235–6) assumes that Halder's nerve failed. The example of 1938, however, and other instances show that this 'failure' was nothing unique but was in fact the rule.

65 Gisevius, who witnessed these events, *Bitter End*, pp. 386–7; Deutsch, p. 233 Note 151; confirmation in Groscurth's private diary for 5 November 1939 (*Tagebücher*, pp. 224–5); Müller, pp. 526–7.

66 Gisevius, *Bitter End*, p. 387; Deutsch, p. 234.

67 Friedrich-Wilhelm Heinz: 'Von Wilhelm Canaris zur NKWD', p. 151; Karl Heinz Abshagen: *Canaris*, pp. 118, 122; Gisevius, *Bitter End*, p. 387.

68 Gisevius, *Bitter End*, p. 387.

69 Groscurth's diary, 6 November 1939 (*Tagebücher*, p. 305); his private diary (*Tagebücher*, p. 225) confirms Gisevius, special edition, pp. 420–2.

70 Gisevius, *Bitter End*, p. 388.

71 Ibid., Groscurth's diary 6 November 1939 (*Tagebücher*, pp. 225, 305). Details given by Gisevius and Groscurth tally almost exactly. Gisevius of course, could

not have had access to Groscurth's diary when writing his book. Further confirmation from Dutch sources is to be found in Deutsch, p. 96.

72 Groscurth's diary, 6 November 1939 (*Tagebücher*, pp. 225, 305); according to Gisevius, *Bis zum bittern Ende*, Vol. II, p. 162), Witzleben telephoned Canaris himself the following morning.

73 Gisevius, *Ende*, Vol. II, p. 162; see also Kosthorst, p. 107, which is based on Gisevius, *Ende*, Vol. II, pp. 162–5 and Halder, *Kriegstagebuch*, Vol. I, p. 126. Keitel's minute to Headquarters of the three Services that the attack had been 'postponed by three days at the moment' is dated 7 November 1939; *Trial*, Vol. XXXIV, Document 072–C, p. 284; Jacobsen, p. 49; Groscurth's diary, 7 and 8 November 1939 (*Tagebücher*, pp. 226, 305–6).

74 Gisevius, special edition, p. 422; Deutsch, p. 96. For details on the passage of information to Sas by Oster see pages 169–70 below.

75 Gisevius, *Ende*, Vol. II, p. 163.

76 Ibid., Deutsch, pp. 238–9 based on notes made at the time by Müller and given in Vincenz Müller: *Ich fand das wahre Vaterland*, p. 369; Klaus-Jürgen Müller in *Heer*, p. 532 accepts Kosthorst's date, which is wrong.

77 Gisevius, *Bitter End*, p. 389. This was therefore two or three days before Halder's alleged decision in favour of a *coup*.

78 Ibid. Halder continually put forward this viewpoint – see *Trials of War Criminals*, Vol. X, pp. 546, 858. On 14 November 1939 Stülpnagel told Oster: 'Generals, including Witzleben, think they cannot do anything because their troops would not stand united behind them for an action [*coup*].' Groscurth, *Tagebücher*, pp. 230–1 and Note 618.

79 Gisevius, *Bitter End*, p. 390; Halder, *Kriegstagebuch*, Vol. I, p. 126; Deutsch, 249–52; Müller, *Heer*, pp. 543–6, also applicable below.

80 Groscurth, *Tagebücher*, 10 December 1939, p. 236; Hassell, *Vom andern Deutschland*, pp. 87–9 (only partly in English translation).

81 Halder, op. cit., pp. 121–2; Groscurth's diary, 7 and 8 November 1939 (*Tagebücher*, pp. 226, 305–6); Jodl in Hubatsch, p. 285; Hans Baur: *Hitler's Pilot*, pp. 104–5; Ritter, op. cit., p. 250 (*Resistance*, p. 150).

82 Halder, op. cit., p. 122; Groscurth's diary 8 November 1939 (*Tagebücher*, pp. 226, 306); Jacobsen, pp. 49, 277 Note 25; Deutsch, pp. 72–9, 243–4, where he follows Rothfels: *The German Opposition to Hitler*, pp. 81–2. According to Deutsch (p. 244) the warnings to Belgium resulted in King Leopold driving from Brussels to The Hague by car and agreeing on the peace mediation offer with Queen Wilhelmina.

83 Groscurth's diary, 8 November 1939 (*Tagebücher*, pp. 226, 306). Groscurth's timing is slightly incorrect; see Peter Hoffmann: *Die Sicherheit des Diktators*, p. 123.

84 Ibid.

85 Ibid., 9 November 1939 (*Tagebücher*, pp. 227, 306–7). Heinz (pp. 117–19) says that Canaris forecast the assassination attempt on 8 November but that Hitler only called off the offensive during the night 8–9 November. Both statements are incorrect. Ritter (*Goerdeler*, p. 250, *Resistance*, p. 150) considers that it can 'hardly be doubted' that the attempt was a propaganda trick. Anton Hoch in 'Das Attentat auf Hitler im Münchner Bürgerbräukeller 1939' in *VfZ* 17 (1969), pp. 383–413, concludes that Elser was in fact a lone wolf. See Chapter 30 below.

86 Groscurth's diary, 10 November 1939 (*Tagebücher*, pp. 228, 307); Gisevius, *Bitter End*, pp. 390–5.

87 Jacobsen, p. 49.

88 On this point and below see Gisevius, *Bitter End*, pp. 393–4; Deutsch, p. 256; Müller, op. cit., pp. 535–6.

89 Groscurth, Private Diary 12 November 1939 (*Tagebücher*, p. 229).

90 On this point and below see Gisevius, *Bitter End*, pp. 394–5; Groscurth's private

diary 10 and 11 November 1939 (*Tagebücher*, pp. 228–9); Deutsch, pp. 241–2.

91 Kosthorst, p. 49; the date given by Kosthorst (10 November) is corrected by Jacobsen, p. 50, 277 Note 28; [Hans] Laternser: *Verteidigung deutscher Soldaten*, pp. 298–9; Groscurth's diary, 9 November 1939 (*Tagebücher*, pp. 227, 306–7).

92 Laternser, p. 299.

93 Ibid., Kosthorst, pp. 49, 106–7; cf. Groscurth's private diary 13 November 1939 (*Tagebücher*, p. 230).

94 On this point and below see Halder, op. cit., pp. 121–3; Jodl in Hubatsch, pp. 285–7; Jacobsen, pp. 49–51.

95 Halder, op. cit., pp. 131–2; Jodl in Hubatsch, p. 59; Halder's evidence in 'Protokoll . . . Halder', pp. 16–17; Halder's evidence at OKW Trial in *Trials of War Criminals*, Vol. X, pp. 545–8; Groscurth's diary 23 November 1939 and private diary 10 December 1939 (*Tagebücher*, pp. 234–5, 313; Röhricht, pp. 149–52; Kordt, pp. 376–7; Sendtner, pp. 418–23. Wheeler-Bennett's account (p. 474) is only partially correct; he is wrong, for instance, in saying that after his main speech Hitler kept Brauchitsch back for a personal lecture on the 'spirit of Zossen'.

96 Jodl in Hubatsch, p. 59; Halder, op. cit., p. 131; Kosthorst, pp. 108–9; Jacobsen, op. cit., pp. 59–63. Three unofficial versions of the speech are extant: *Trial*, Vol. XXVI, pp. 327–36; Hans-Adolf Jacobsen: *1939–1945: Der Zweite Weltkrieg in Chronik und Dokumenten*, pp. 133–9; Domarus, pp. 1421–7; *Documents on German Foreign Policy*, Series D, Vol. VIII, No 384. A footnote to the latter says that the record, authorship of which is unknown, was found in the OKW files in Flensburg in 1945. Halder gave the content from memory in *Trials of War Criminals*, Vol. X, pp. 548, 856–9. His evidence at this trial generally agrees with that before the denazification court and with the versions referred to above. For details on this subject see Jacobsen, *Fall Gelb*, p. 60 where the other versions and accounts are referred to.

97 *Trial*, Vol. XXVI, p. 330.

98 Halder, *Kriegstagebuch*, Vol. I, p. 131; Jodl in Hubatsch, p. 59. Halder gives the time as 2.30 p.m., Jodl as 1.30 p.m. Jacobsen (*Fall Gelb*, pp. 63–4, 281 Note 39) accepts Halder's timing. See above sources for content of Hitler's statements.

99 On this point and below see Brauchitsch's evidence in *Trial*, Vol. XX, p. 575; Halder's evidence in *Trials of War Criminals*, Vol. X, p. 857; Halder's evidence in 'Protokoll . . . Halder', pp. 16–17; Halder, *Kriegstagebuch*, Vol. I, p. 132; Jacobsen, op. cit., p. 64; Ritter, *Goerdeler*, p. 255 (*Resistance*, p. 154).

100 He himself subsequently said that Hitler had made this accusation – 'Protokoll . . . Halder', pp. 16–17.

101 Kosthorst, pp. 50, 105.

102 Halder's evidence in *Trials of War Criminals*, Vol. X, pp. 545–6, 858.

103 On this point and below see Georg Thomas 'Gedanken und Ereignisse' in *Schweizer Monatshefte* 25 (1945), pp. 543, 546–8; Halder, *Kriegstagebuch*, Vol. I, p. 133; Huppenkothen, p. 4; Ulrich von Hassell: *The von Hassell Diaries*, pp. 89–90.

104 Gisevius, *Bitter End*, pp. 397–8. The entry in Halder's diary on his talk with Thomas reads: 'Popitz. Schacht-Thomas [Note] C-in-C.' There is no record of anyone else having been there when Thomas saw Halder; the entry must therefore mean that Thomas referred to Popitz and Schacht in order to give his views greater weight; Thomas (p. 548) refers to Goerdeler, Beck and Oster but not to Schacht. Kosthorst (p. 111 Note 53) explains this by saying that Thomas only mentioned to Halder the names which he thought most effective. See Deutsch, pp. 266–8.

105 Peter Bor: *Gespräche mit Halder*, p. 125. On 26 December 1939 Halder told Dr Walter Conrad (an official in the Ministry of the Interior, Church Affairs section)

who lived in the same house with Halder: he, Halder, doubted that a *coup* to remove the Hitler regime could be initiated during the war; after the war, yes, but first it was necessary to bring the war to a good conclusion. Upon Conrad's reply: a victorious Hitler could never be overthrown, and in any case Hitler was not capable of bringing the war to a good end, Halder said: he agreed in principle with these thoughts, but in the current conditions no progress could be made because the stab-in-the-back legend was too deeply rooted in the consciousness of the soldiers. Dr Walter Conrad, 'Meine Besprechungen mit Generaloberst Halder über die Beseitigung Hitlers', typescript, undated, BA-MA N 124/28.

106 Hassell, op. cit., p. 90; Huppenkothen, p. 4.

CHAPTER 11

1 'Eine Wendung im bisherigen Krieg?', typescript 20 November 1939, BA, EAP 21-X-15/2 (printed in Helmuth Groscurth, *Tagebücher eines Abwehroffiziers 1938–1940*, pp. 486–90).

2 At the reopening ceremony of the Staff College in Berlin, 15 October 1935.

3 'Betrachtung über die deutsche Lage um die Jahreswende 1939/40', BA, EAP 21-X-15/2 (printed in Groscurth, *Tagebücher*, pp. 493–7).

4 BA, EAP 21-X-15/2 (printed in Groscurth, *Tagebücher*, pp. 509–14). See also analysis by Hans Mommsen: 'Gesellschaftsbild und Verfassungspläne des deutschen Widerstandes' in Walter Schmitthenner and Hans Buchheim (editors): *Der deutsche Widerstand gegen Hitler*, pp. 90–1 (*The German Resistance to Hitler*, pp. 73–4).

5 [Helmuth Groscurth]: 'Kriegstagebuch Abt. z.b.V. 15. November 1939 [– 1. Feb. 1940]', BA, EAP 21-X-15/1; 18, 19, 20, 21 December 1939 (*Tagebücher*, pp. 312–13); Harold C. Deutsch, *The Conspiracy against Hitler in the Twilight War*, pp. 281–3.

6 [Franz] Halder: *Kriegstagebuch*, Vol. 1, p. 145 and Note 1–22. 12.39; see also Ulrich von Hassell: *Vom andern Deutschland* (not in English translation), p. 108.

7 Halder, p. 160.

8 Groscurth's diary 5 January 1940 and private diary 21 December 1939 (*Tagebücher*, pp. 238, 318); copy of a letter from Groscurth to Ulrich Graf Schwerin von Schwanenfeld (aide to Witzleben at the time) dated 17 February 1940, BA EAP 21-X-15/2 (*Tagebücher*, p. 472). According to Halder, p. 160 and Note 1 there was a memorandum from Blaskowitz dated 6 February 1940. Canaris spoke to Halder about Blaskowitz's reports and conditions in Poland on 18 January 1940. Groscurth rightly suspected that his use of Blaskowitz's secret report during his tour of the West had contributed to his 'fall' as Head of the Special *Abwehr* Section attached to OKH. He was relieved of his office, however, on 1 February 1940, so Blaskowitz's later memorandum can have had nothing to do with the case. See Groscurth's diary 1 February 1940 (*Tagebücher*, pp. 245, 323) and Deutsch, op. cit., p. 180.

9 BA, EAP 21-X-15/2 (printed in Groscurth, *Tagebücher*, pp. 514–18).

10 See Chap. 10 Note 20 above.

11 Halder, pp. 152–3; see also Chapter 12 below.

12 See Chap. 10 Note 20 above.

13 Ulrich von Hassell: *The von Hassell Diaries*, p. 96.

14 Ibid., pp. 96, 102; Erich Kosthorst: *Die deutsche Opposition gegen Hitler zwischen Polen- und Frankreichfeldzug*, pp. 117–18. These ideas reflect Oster's and Gisevius' efforts to galvanize Witzleben into some opposition activity.

15 Hassell, op. cit., p. 98.

16 Ibid., p. 102; Jodl in Walther Hubatsch: 'Das dienstliche Tagebuch des Chefs des Wehrmachtsführungsamtes im Oberkommando der Wehrmacht, Generalmajor Jodl, für die Zeit vom 13. Okt. 1939 bis zum 30. Jan. 1940', in *Die*

Welt als Geschichte 12 (1952), pp. 61–9 where the various postponements are noted in each case; Halder, op. cit., pp. 137–237; Hans-Adolf Jacobsen: *1939–1945: Der Zweite Weltkrieg in Chronik und Dokumenten*, p. 23; Hans-Adolf Jacobsen: *Fall Gelb*, pp. 90–3, 141 (which gives a table of the various dates for the offensive and the postponements).

17 Halder, p. 159; Walter Huppenkothen: 'Der 20. Juli 1944', p. 4 – based on interrogations conducted after 20 July 1944 and a note by Beck which fell into the hands of the *Gestapo*; Fabian von Schlabrendorff: *Revolt against Hitler*, p. 107; Kosthorst (p. 118) would like to accept an earlier date but does not know which and has no evidence apart from a vague recollection by Halder and the comment that '16 January would leave it in the air'. Further details of the conversations are to be found in Kosthorst, pp. 118–20 but they lack evidence and are apparently based on information from Halder. See also Deutsch, pp. 275–6.

18 Halder, p. 159 Note 4; Kosthorst, p. 118.

19 Huppenkothen, p. 4; Schlabrendorff, p. 107; Kosthorst, pp. 118–19.

20 Kosthorst, p. 119 – also applicable below.

21 According to Schlabrendorff (p. 107) at this time Halder based his refusal on the fact that Brauchitsch thought differently and did not think that the Army would carry out a *coup d'état*, also that Britain was fighting not merely Hitler but the German people. This is confirmed by what Halder told Groscurth on 13 January 1940; see Groscurth's private diary (*Tagebücher*, p. 241). According to a much later account by Halder given by Kosthorst (p. 119) Halder had said to Beck that he did not take Brauchitsch's unwillingness too seriously; he could always drag him along. The project could only succeed, however, if supported by a broad front of people in Germany determined to carry it through. This did not exist and the *coup* would be a sort of Kapp *putsch*; he could not risk the good name of the Commander-in-Chief of the German Army for a *coup* with such small prospects of success.

22 Halder, p. 195.

23 See pp. 167–8 below.

24 The report was given orally to Groscurth who took notes on 5 January 1940: BA, EAP 21-X-15/2; Groscurth's diaries 13 Jan. 1940, BA, EAP 21-X-15/1; another unsigned and undated report may also have come from Helldorf, this and all the above are printed in Groscurth, *Tagebücher*, pp. 241, 319, 466–8, 504–5.

25 Groscurth's diary, 5 Jan. 1940 (*Tagebücher*, pp. 239, 318).

26 On this point and below see copy of decree in Jacobsen, *1939–1945*, pp. 569–70; [Theodor] Groppe, 'Erlebnisse eines alten Soldaten während der Nazi-Zeit 1933–1945', typescript 9 November 1945, NA, Record Group 338 MS. No B-397, pp. 7–18, including text of decree and ensuing correspondence; Theodor Groppe: *Ein Kampf um Recht und Sitte*, passim; Halder, op. cit., November 1939-January 1940, passim; Groscurth's diaries, November 1939-January 1940, passim (*Tagebücher*, pp. 222–45, 303–23); Groscurth to Schwerin von Schwanenfeld 17 February 1940, BA, EAP 21-X-15/2 (*Tagebücher*, p. 472).

27 Halder, p. 160; on this point and on Brauchitsch's inactivity see also Deutsch, pp. 180–9.

28 Halder, pp. 170–1.

29 Groscurth's diaries, 26, 27, 29, 31 Jan. 1940 (*Tagebücher*, pp. 244–5, 322–3).

30 Groscurth's papers in BA, EAP 21-X-15/2 (*Tagebücher*, p. 472). On Groscurth's posting see also Etzdorf – record of conversation with Krausnick. According to the Order of Battle of 10 May 1940 75 Div. was in Witzleben's First Army which in turn belonged to Leeb's Army Group C – see Halder, attached map headed 'Situation in the West 10 May 1940'.

31 Groscurth's diaries, 1 Feb. 1940 (*Tagebücher*, pp. 245, 323), Halder, pp. 200–3; Deutsch, pp. 284–7.

32 Hassell, pp. 88–9.

CHAPTER 12

1 Report dated 5 January 1940 by Richert, the Swedish Minister, reproduced in translation in ' "Widerstand ist vaterländische Pflicht": Aus den akten des Schwedischen Ministerium des Äusseren' in *Politische Studien* 10 (1959), pp. 435–9.

2 Erich Kosthorst: *Die deutsche Opposition gegen Hitler zwischen Polen- und Frankreichfeldzug*, pp. 126–9.

3 Gerhard Ritter: *Carl Goerdeler und die deutsche Widerstandsbewegung*, p. 258; (*Resistance*, pp. 157–8); Sumner Welles: *The Time for Decision*, pp. 90, 120–1 (Welles was in Berlin from 1 to 5 March); Otto Kopp: 'Die Niederschrift von Hans Walz' in *Widerstand und Erneuerung*, p. 111.

4 Ibid.

5 Ritter, op. cit., p. 258 (*The German Resistance*, pp. 157–8).

6 Ibid.

7 Ritter, *Goerdeler*, pp. 258–9. Ritter does not give the names of the two representatives or of the person accompanying Wirth.

8 Ibid., p. 259 (*Resistance*, p. 158).

9 Ibid., pp. 259–60 (*Resistance*, p. 159).

10 Ibid.

11 See pp. 54–68 above.

12 This seems to have been a failure on the part of Gessler, the former *Reichswehr* Minister but he denies having had anything whatsoever to do with the affair. Hassell on the other hand (*The von Hassell Diaries*, pp. 120, 122 – entries for 22 March and 6 April) says that Gessler spoke to him personally on the subject. See also Ritter, *Goerdeler* pp. 260, 507 Note 49 (*Resistance*, p. 159 and Note 1); on Wirth see also Harold C. Deutsch: *Conspiracy against Hitler in the Twilight War*, p. 132 Note 91.

13 On this point and below see Erich Kordt: *Nicht aus den Akten*, pp. 379–83; Ritter, *Goerdeler*, pp. 260–1 (*Resistance*, pp. 159–60); Deutsch, pp. 158–66; see also pp. 108–9, 119–20 above.

14 Groscurth's diary, 15 November 1939, BA, EAP 21-X-15/2 (Helmuth Groscurth, *Tagebücher eines Abwehroffiziers 1938–1940*, p. 311).

15 Kosthorst, p. 90.

16 Kordt, p. 381 where the letter is given *in extenso*.

17 Ritter, *Goerdeler*, p. 261.

18 On this point and below see Hassell, op. cit., pp. 108–11; J. Lonsdale Bryans ('Mr X' in Hassell's diary): *Blind Victory*, pp. 36–81 and 'Zur amtlichen britischen Haltung gegenüber der deutschen Widerstandsbewegung' in *VfZ* 1 (1953), pp. 348–50; Ritter, op. cit., pp. 261–3 (*Resistance*, pp. 160–2); Sir John Wheeler-Bennett: *The Nemesis of Power*, pp. 488–90; Kurt Sendtner: 'Die deutsche Militäropposition im ersten Kriegsjahr' in *Vollmacht des Gewissens*, Vol. I, pp. 472–3.

19 Lonsdale Bryans in 'Zur amtlichen britischen Haltung' (p. 348) says that Halifax at once granted him full diplomatic status, which is certainly exaggerated. He was not even given a written instruction legitimizing him in Hassell's eyes.

20 According to Ritter (*Goerdeler*, p. 261 – *Resistance*, p. 160) this was what the opposition wanted; Hassell, however, (op. cit., p. 109) states explicitly that this was 'X's aim'.

21 Given in Hassell, op. cit., pp. 110–11.

22 Hermann Graml: 'Die aussenpolitischen Vorstellungen des deutschen Widerstandes' in Schmitthenner and Buchheim, *Der deutsche Widerstand gegen Hitler*, p. 33 (*The German Resistance to Hitler*, pp. 17–18); Elfriede Nebgen: *Jakob Kaiser*, p. 120.

23 Graml, 'Vorstellungen', pp. 33–34.

24 Ibid., p. 34; Wheeler-Bennett (p. 489) has overlooked this point.

25 Ritter, *Goerdeler*, p. 262.

26 Lonsdale Bryans 'Zur amtlichen britischen Haltung', pp. 349–50 – also applicable below; see also Ritter, op. cit., p. 263 (*Resistance*, p. 161).

27 Dr Müller's mission see pp. 158–64; Ritter (*Goerdeler*, p. 263; *Resistance*, p. 161) assumes that Dr Wirth's message is referred to. Hassell, however, (op. cit., p. 124) says that he told Lonsdale Bryans that he thought he knew which this other channel was, that it had to do with a 'serious action' and 'on our side had reached the same group with which I was in contact'. If this is so, it cannot be Dr Wirth's message since this never reached the conspirators in Germany. Wheeler-Bennett (p. 490) assumes without further ado that this refers to the Vatican talks. Sendtner (p. 472 Note 88) considers this most unlikely since he assumes (erroneously) that the Vatican talks had been concluded in January which means that 'a week before' cannot be right. Deutsch (p. 170) assumes that Cadogan made a slip of the tongue and said 'week' instead of 'month' and that he was referring to the confirmation of the British attitude which reached Dr Müller in March. Equally Lonsdale Bryans may have misheard or suffered from lapse of memory.

28 Hassell, op. cit., p. 114; Ritter, *Goerdeler*, p. 263 (*Resistance*, p. 161) gives 15 April (incorrectly).

29 Ritter, *Goerdeler*, p. 263 (*Resistance*, p. 161).

30 Hassell, op. cit., pp. 124–5. Hassell's comment quoted by Deutsch (p. 170) to the effect that this was not what the opposition required, is not to be found in the passage referred to by Deutsch.

31 See Ritter, *Goerdeler*, p. 265 where he says that the story of the opposition being left in the lurch is a fairy-tale.

32 On this point and below the main sources are: Report by Dr Müller on his talks in the Vatican between 6 and 12 November 1939 in BA, EAP 21-X-15/2 (the Groscurth papers) printed in abbreviated form in Groscurth, *Tagebücher*, pp. 506–9; the so-called 'X Report' drafted by Dohnanyi and submitted to Halder and Brauchitsch in the spring of 1940; it was apparently found on 22 September 1944 by the *Gestapo* in the Zossen files; Halder looked at it on several occasions while under arrest but it then apparently disappeared and was probably burnt in 1945 with other *Gestapo* files. See also Ritter, *Goerdeler*, p. 264 (*Resistance*, p. 162); Müller's evidence at the Huppenkothen trial – 'Für das anständige Deutschland' in *Telegraf*, 15 October 1952; Sendtner, pp. 464–9; Hassell, op. cit., pp. 117, 122–3; Halder's evidence at hearing before denazification court – 'Protokoll aus der Verhandlung Halder [vor der] Spruchkammer X München', pp. 32–4, 75; Georg Thomas: 'Gedanken und Ereignisse', *Schweizer Monatshefte* 25 (1945), pp. 546–7; *Spiegelbild einer Verschwörung*, p. 509; Gisevius's evidence in *Trial of the Major War Criminals before the International Military Tribunal*, Vol. XII, pp. 229–31; Robert Leiber: 'Pius XII.†' in *Stimmen der Zeit*, 163 (1958), pp. 98–9; Otto John: 'Some Facts and Aspects of the Plot against Hitler', pp. 29–31; [Walter] Huppenkothen 'Der 20 Juli, 1944', pp. 4–5; Franz Sonderegger – letter to Provincial Court I, Munich, pp. 2–4; Sonderegger's statements to Arbeitskreis Europäische Publikation e.V. 15 October 1952 in IfZ, ZS 303/2; Christine von Dohnanyi: 'Aufzeichnungen', pp. 7–8; official confirmation of the mediation activities of the Holy See in *Osservatore Romano* No 36 of 11 February 1946 referred to in Sendtner, pp. 460–2 and Kosthorst, p. 133. Further sources now evaluated by Deutsch (pp. 111–48). Other accounts are to be found in Ritter, *Goerdeler*, pp. 248, 502–3 Note 20, 263–6 (*Resistance*, pp. 148 and Note 2, 161–4); Sendtner, pp. 442–506; Kosthorst, pp. 130–46; Gert Buchheit: *Der deutsche Geheimdienst*, pp. 294–6. A recent contribution by John S. Conway ('The Vatican, Great Britain, and

Relations with Germany, 1938–1940', in *The Historical Journal* XVI (1973), pp. 147–67) based on records of the British Foreign Office and Cabinet Papers.

33 Ritter, *Goerdeler*, pp. 120, 248 (*Resistance*, p. 147); Wheeler-Bennett, p. 492; Deutsch, pp. 111–14.

34 Sendtner (p. 450) says that this only happened early in November after it had been established that the British were ready to negotiate. Buchheit (p. 294) says the same but without giving sources.

35 Ritter, *Goerdeler*, p. 248 (*Resistance*, p. 147); Sendtner, p. 445; Kosthorst, p. 131.

36 *Spiegelbild*, p. 509; Deutsch, p. 114.

37 BA, EAP 21-X-15/2 (partly printed in Groscurth, *Tagebücher*, pp. 506–9). Mention is made of the goodwill anticipated from the Western Powers in the event of a change of regime in Germany; this would not have been so easy to explain.

38 Sendtner, p. 445; Kosthorst (p. 131) is merely sure that it happened before November 1939; see Buchheit, pp. 293–4 and Deutsch, pp. 117–19.

39 Kosthorst, p. 133.

40 Ibid., pp. 132–3; Sendtner, p. 446.

41 Sendtner, p. 446. So far it has not been possible to establish the precise dates of Dr Müller's journeys to Rome; not even Deutsch could do so since Müller could no longer remember them – see Sendtner, p. 445 and Deutsch, pp. 117–19. There is no real doubt on the material points; Father Leiber informed Allied agents in July 1944, at the latest, of the opposition's attempts to engineer a *coup* (Office of Strategic Services, Research and Analysis Branch Summaries Index File 88111S, NA, Record Group 226). According to Müller, the Vatican contacts began in September 1939, according to Leiber in October (Deutsch, pp. 117–19). Conway (p. 160) has not found any evidence in the British Foreign Office files to suggest that the contact of the German opposition with the Vatican had been linked up with the Foreign Office before 1 December 1939. The absence of evidence there does not exclude the possibility of contacts, either undocumented, or documented elsewhere. The Vatican files might clear up the discrepancies between Müller's and Leiber's versions, also between them and the apparent absence of any written report from Osborne, the British Minister to the Vatican, to the British Foreign Office, before his report on talks with Mgr Kaas dated 1 December 1939 (quoted by Conway, pp. 160–1). Since the evidence produced by Conway so far only fails to *confirm* Müller's and Leiber's versions, and since it is not entirely conclusive as regards the timing, I do not propose to change my account on this point until more evidence disproving or correcting Müller's and Leiber's version is available. See also the office minute of 18 October referred to by Huppenkothen at his trial in 1952 noting that Dr Müller had just returned from Rome – Ritter, *Goerdeler*, p. 502 Note 20.

42 Sendtner, p. 446; Deutsch, p. 111.

43 According to Deutsch (p. 119) this was after 5 and before 18 October when Müller returned from his second journey to Rome.

44 Kosthorst, p. 132; Deutsch, p. 120 Note 50, 121–2 Note 56; Sendtner (p. 448) considers it probable that the answer to this question too was available shortly after mid-October – confirmed by Deutsch, p. 119.

45 Kosthorst, pp. 132–3; Sendtner, p. 448. The timing of the Vatican inquiry in London through Osborne is disputed in favour of a date no earlier than 1 December by Conway (p. 160) on the strength of what he found in the British Foreign Office files: Osborne reported to the Foreign Office in a telegram dated 1 December 1939 on a conversation with Mgr Kaas in which Kaas relayed the information that German military opposition circles were ready to take over control of Germany if they could be assured of what they regarded as a fair and honourable peace. Osborne's reply, subsequently approved by the Foreign Office, was that before any useful discussions could take place there would have to be

'assurance of the definite abandonment of the present German policy of rape on the instalment system and contempt for treaty undertakings; that is to say there must be guarantees for the future as well as reparation for the past'. It may be suggested again, as in note 41, that there may have been other channels and communications. Before one is ready to declare Dr Müller a witness who is not to be believed, the contemporary evidence cited below must be allowed to stand.

46 Ibid.; Groscurth's diary 20 October 1939 (*Tagebücher*, p. 299); Deutsch, p. 119 based on statements by Huppenkothen who knew Dohnanyi's notes and in Deutsch's opinion has a remarkable memory. When visiting Halder on 4 November Thomas made use of some of the results of Müller's mission; see [Franz] Halder, *Kriegstagebuch*, Vol. I, p. 119; and above, p. 136. As far as dates are concerned I have followed Deutsch, p. 119.

47 Sendtner, p. 449; Kosthorst, p. 133; Deutsch, pp. 124–6. Others whom Müller talked to in Rome were Mgr Ludwig Kaas, the former Centre Party leader, who had emigrated in 1934, Mgr Johann Schönhöffer of the Propaganda Fides, Father Ivo Zeiger of the Order of Jesuits, Rector of the Collegium Germanicum in Rome. In Müller's reports they are all given 'cover-names' – Kaas is 'Uncle Ludwig', Schönhöffer is 'Giovanni' etc. According to Huppenkothen's evidence those of Father Leiber's missives which Müller kept did not fall into the hands of the *Gestapo*. See also Deutsch, pp. 147–8; Ritter, *Goerdeler*, p. 264 (*Resistance*, p. 162); Sendtner, pp. 453–4; Kosthorst, p. 134 follows Müller's radio broadcast given in Günther Weisenborn: *Der lautlose Aufstand*, p. 241–2.

48 Sendtner, pp. 449–50; see also report by Müller on 'discussions in Rome with the Vatican' (as Groscurth titled his copy in his own hand), BA, EAP 21-X-15/2 (partly printed in Groscurth, *Tagebücher*, pp. 506–9). The substance of these preliminary exchanges is confirmed by Osborne's report of 1 December (see note 45 above).

49 Sendtner, pp. 456–8; Müller – 'discussions'; Deutsch, pp. 136–7, 157, 173–4.

50 Conway, pp. 162–4, also applicable below. Conway cites communications from Osborne to Halifax of 12 January and 7 February 1940, from Halifax to Osborne of 17 February 1940, and p. 159 of Cabinet Papers 1940, 65/11.

51 See above, p. 151.

52 See note 50 above, also applicable below.

53 Conway, p. 164.

54 Conway, p. 165 based on Osborne's reports to Halifax dated 16 and 19 March 1940.

55 Conway, p. 166 based on Osborne's report to Halifax dated 3 April 1940.

56 Kosthorst, p. 134; Sendtner, pp. 455, 460; Groscurth's diary 2 January 1940 (*Tagebücher*, p. 318), Ritter, *Goerdeler* (*Resistance*, p. 162) p. 264; Deutsch, pp. 289–315. Conway, pp. 162–5.

57 Müller's evidence at the Huppenkothen trial in *Telegraf*, 15 October 1952; Sendtner, pp. 448, 460–2; Deutsch, pp. 137–9, 297.

58 Müller: 'discussions'.

59 Ibid.

60 Sendtner, pp. 462–3.

61 Ibid., pp. 468–9; Kosthorst (pp. 136–7) quotes Halder 'whose memory had repeatedly proved sound'; his recollection of the papers he saw about Dr Müller's soundings was that not only all eastern questions (the Corridor, reestablishment of a Czech state but as a German sphere of influence) and the fate of Austria were settled 'entirely according to German ideas', but also that 'the German western frontier of 1914 was to be reestablished', in other words Alsace and Lorraine would be taken from France! Since in the first place no one else remembers such a concession (which Kosthorst also thinks ludicrous) but secondly Halder's memory is so good, Kosthorst concludes that this point should be 'left out of account for the moment'. He found no solution to this conflict of evidence later. In

his 'Pius XII', pp. 98–9 Father Leiber describes the Pope's alleged agreement to reestablishment of the German 1914 frontier with Poland as 'a complete invention. The Pope would never have lent his hand to any dismemberment or partition of Poland'. This must have been a forgery, Father Leiber concludes.

Dr Otto John probably knew of the terms from Müller's reports, perhaps via Oster or Dohnanyi, in any case not only from the X Report; in *Some Facts*, p. 29 he says nothing about the western frontier, merely referring in general terms to the Western Powers' offer to reestablish the position as at the conclusion of the Munich Agreement. See Ritter, *Goerdeler*, p. 264.

62 Ritter, *Goerdeler*, p. 264 (*Resistance*, p. 162); Kosthorst, p. 135; Sendtner p. 464; Klaus-Jürgen Müller: *Das Heer und Hitler*, pp. 558–66.

63 Kosthorst, pp. 134–5; Halder in 'Protokoll . . . Halder', p. 33.

64 Ulrich von Hassell: *Vom andern Deutschland* p. 124; Sendtner, pp. 464–7; Thomas, p. 546.

65 Thomas, pp. 546–8. Thomas never referred to an 'X Report' but invariably to the 'Report from Rome'. In April 1940 he transmitted a report to Halder but did not read it himself; see Kosthorst, pp. 135–6. According to his own account Thomas only knew of a 'minute' by Dohnanyi shown him by Huppenkothen while he was being interrogated; this *might* be the same as the X Report but Thomas could not tell since he had not read the report which he handed to Halder in April 1940. Sendtner (p. 467) assumes, but without evidence therefor, that Thomas did know the X Report. It is worth mentioning that the entry in Hassell's diary for 19 March 1940 (*Diaries*, p. 117) refers to 'extraordinarily interesting documents covering the conversations of a Catholic intermediary with the Pope', shown him by Dohnanyi and Oster that day; he does not refer to a definite 'report', however, or similar comprehensive document. Kosthorst (pp. 134–5) and Sendtner (p. 469) assume, without evidence, that Hassell had seen the X Report. Moreover Frau von Dohnanyi's account (p. 8) mentions 'a memorandum for the generals submitted to them at the same time as the results of the peace feelers – the so-called X Report', in which Dohnanyi had set out his anxiety about a new stab-in-the-back legend; this may have been the minute referred to by Thomas.

66 Kosthorst (p. 136) based on Halder's recollections refers to 'Czecho'; Halder in 'Protokoll . . . Halder', p. 33 says 'Czechoslovakia'.

67 Kosthorst (pp. 134–46) deals with the X Report in detail based on verbal information from Halder; he becomes involved in contradictions because he sometimes considers Halder reliable and at other times not. See also Sendtner, pp. 464–71; Leiber, p. 98; Deutsch, pp. 300–2. In 'Protokoll . . . Halder', p. 33, Halder says: 'While being interrogated by the *Gestapo* I had this report lying before me for hours and read it through several times. My memory of it is consequently very clear.' Kosthorst (pp. 134–5) says that Halder thought that the X Report had been shown to him during his interrogation (he must have known it since he had read it thoroughly in April 1940 – see p. 167 below); Kosthorst then says that this is improbable since Halder had never actually had the document and the paper shown to him in 1940 was 'clearly a heavily amended text'. This is not very convincing. The vital question is whether what Halder was shown in 1940 and while under interrogation were one and the same thing. A little later (pp. 137–8) Kosthorst again insists on the reliability of Halder's memory.

Halder's tendency was to stress the improbability and unreliability of the X Report and this could only be refuted if the Report were available. He criticized it because it had neither heading nor signature and included fantastic concessions, some of which were of no interest 'to us soldiers' and others, such as Alsace-Lorraine, which even the politically uninitiated would realize were totally unrealistic. There must therefore be serious doubts about the accuracy of Halder's explanation why the X Report could not lead to a *coup* on the part of the Army.

Deutsch (pp. 300–2) inclines to the view that the version of the X Report shown to Halder on 4 April 1940 did not contain the incredible provisions about Alsace-Lorraine; he thinks that in his post-war accounts Halder, perhaps unconsciously, gave way to the tendency to decry the X Report because it had led to his final refusal to cooperate with the opposition. See also the summary of statements about the contents of the X Report in Deutsch, p. 302.

Halder's account of the contents of the Report is also invalidated if Hassell knew what the Report contained and was ready to take it to Halder and finally – an important point missed by Deutsch but appearing in all Halder's accounts – by the fact that Halder passed the document on to Brauchitsch recommending him to read it. This one would hardly have expected of him if the Report was as Halder described it after the war.

68 Leiber, p. 98. The author follows the timing that is cogently suggested by the British Foreign Office and Cabinet files, as cited by Conway, pp. 162–4.

69 Sendtner, p. 474; Kosthorst, p. 136; Huppenkothen, p. 5; Halder, *Kriegstagebuch*, Vol. I, p. 245.

70 Such suppositions appear in Kosthorst, pp. 139–41 and Sendtner, pp. 483–6, 489. Deutsch (pp. 303–4), though without concrete evidence, gives as a possible explanation, apart from the Sumner Welles mission, the desire which he suspects existed, to make a further assault on the generals after the anticipated failure of the Norwegian expedition. Otto John in *Twice through the Lines*, p. 63, says that the report was withheld so long because the opposition thought that the continuous postponements of the date of the offensive meant that Brauchitsch was beginning to realize that he would have to act. Logically, however, this should have hastened the submission of the Report.

71 Groscurth's diary, 16 November 1939, 2, 12, 19 January, 1 February 1940 (*Tagebücher*, pp. 312, 317, 319, 323); Hassell, *Diaries*, pp. 108, 116.

72 Hassell: *Diaries*, p. 106.

73 Ibid., pp. 106–7.

74 Ibid., pp. 107–11.

75 Ibid., pp. 106–13, 117; Welles, pp. 90, 120–1; *Keesing's Contemporary Archives 1937–1940*, p. 3963.

76 Hassell, op. cit., p. 114.

77 Ibid., pp. 111, 115.

78 Ibid., p. 116.

79 Ritter, *Goerdeler*, pp. 265–7 (*Resistance*, pp. 164–5).

80 Deutsch gives no evidence for his statement (p. 307) that the Beck-Oster group knew nothing of Goerdeler's visits to Halder.

81 Hassell, op. cit., p. 117.

82 Ibid.

83 Ibid., pp. 118–19; the entry in Halder's diary (op. cit., p. 231) 'discussion with Dr' must refer to Goerdeler.

84 Halder, op. cit., p. 231.

85 Hassell, op. cit., pp. 118–19.

86 Kosthorst, p. 143.

87 Hassell, op. cit., p. 119.

88 Ibid.

89 The letter is not extant and its date is not known but there are many references to it. See Ritter, *Goerdeler*, p. 266 and Note 62 (*Resistance*, p. 164 and Note 2); Fabian von Schlabrendorff: *Offiziere gegen Hitler*, p. 50; Huppenkothen, p. 4, where the date is given as 'Easter 1940', which would make it 24 or 25 March; Hjalmar Schacht: *Abrechnung mit Hitler*, p. 162 (not in translation) which gives 'April 1940'; Thomas, p. 546; Hassell, op. cit., p. 121. There is only inconclusive evidence for a third visit by Goerdeler to Halder which Deutsch (p. 306–7) accepts as having taken place on 1 April. An indication that it did take place may

be Hassell's remark (op. cit., p. 121) that Goerdeler had told him that Halder had wept when he referred to his enormous responsibility. Kosthorst (p. 141) says that Halder mentioned to him three visits by Goerdeler.

90 Kosthorst (p. 144), describing Goerdeler's and Hassell's contacts with Halder, adds the comment that the ground had not been well prepared for Halder's reception of the X Report and so, undoubtedly unintentionally, gives the impression that the ground would have been better prepared without these contacts. No one who knows the events of 5 November 1939 can believe this unless he is guilty of self-deception.

91 Halder: *Kriegstagebuch*, Vol. I, December 1939 – March 1940, passim and p. 237; Oster and Dohnanyi told Hassell of this on 3 April – Hassell, op. cit., pp. 121–2.

92 Halder, op. cit., p. 227.

93 Ibid., pp. 230–1.

94 Ibid., p. 231.

95 Ibid., pp. 240–4.

96 Ibid., p. 245; Halder in 'Protokoll . . . Halder', pp. 32–3; Hassell: *Vom andern Deutschland*, p. 129; Huppenkothen, p. 5; Sendtner, pp. 474–7; Kosthorst, p. 136; Wheeler-Bennett (p. 493, Note 1) is wrong when he says that the date of transmission of the X Report is not known.

97 Hassell: *Diaries*, p. 127.

98 Halder in 'Protokoll . . . Halder', p. 33; Wheeler-Bennett, p. 492; on what follows below see John, *Twice Through the Lines*, pp. 63–4; in 1947 Brauchitsch confirmed that Halder's reply had been that he (Brauchitsch) had better have him arrested. Brauchitsch did not realize that men can comprehend and support an ideology and therefore can also be argued out of it; he also did not realize that in this case the ideology was not that of 'a people numbering millions' but of Hitler – see pp. 36–7 above. As regards the '1914 western frontier', from about June 1940 to June 1943 even men like Jakob Kaiser thought that, if Germany liberated herself she could retain Strasburg and Alsace – see Nebgen, pp. 159–60.

99 Halder, op. cit., p. 248. Shortly after the war Halder gave the following reasons for his refusal to be further associated with the *coup*: he had no confidence in Goerdeler who was a glib gambler; the attitude of Britain was uncertain; the army would have been merely the servant of the revolution without further influence after the *coup*; he did not know who, apart from the Beck group, was behind the plan; the Norwegian operation had changed the situation. CSDIC (UK), GG Report – Report on information obtained from Senior Officer PW on 8–13 Aug. 45; GRGG 344, typescript, 21 Aug. 1945.

100 See above, p. 161.

101 Huppenkothen, p. 5.

102 Halder, op. cit., p. 259.

103 Ibid., p. 268.

104 Fabian von Schlabrendorff: *The Secret War against Hitler*, p. 108; see also Wheeler-Bennett, p. 493.

105 Hassell, *Diaries*, pp. 122–3, 126–7; Ritter, *Goerdeler*, pp. 268, 510 Note 67 (*Resistance*, p. 166 and Note 2). An editor's note in Hassell, *Vom andern Deutschland*, p. 129 says that Groscurth had been selected for this tour; since he had been posted, this seems unlikely and there is probably confusion with his tour of December 1939.

106 Probably on 29 or 30 April; Sendtner, pp. 498–505; Sonderegger, letter to court, p. 8; Deutsch, pp. 336, 341. Kosthorst (p. 145) gives '1 or 2 May' without evidence or explanation why he differs from Sendtner.

107 Sendtner, pp. 492–506. Details of further warnings and contacts by Dr Müller are in Deutsch, pp. 331–49. On the sources from which the planned date became known to the enemy see Sendtner, pp. 495–506, 518–31; also report dated 5

January 1940 from Richert, the Swedish Minister in Berlin, on revelations by Ewald von Kleist-Schmenzin in 'Widerstand ist vaterländische Pflicht', pp. 435–9.

108 'Deutsche Gespräche über das Recht zum Widerstand' in *Vollmacht des Gewissens*, Vol. I, pp. 31–42.

109 On Oster's resistance activity see the detailed study by Hermann Graml, 'Der Fall Oster', *VfZ* 14 (1966), pp. 26–39; also Allen Dulles: *Germany's Underground*, pp. 51–61; Buchheit, pp. 286–9, 296–307; Sendtner, pp. 507–17; Deutsch, pp. 51–5, 92–101, also on the basis of Belgian and Dutch sources.

110 Deutsch, pp. 74–7, 143–5 – also applicable below.

111 Ibid., pp. 96–7 based on Dutch and Belgian sources.

112 Halder, op. cit., pp. 151, 161–2, 165, 281–2.

113 Deutsch, pp. 319–23.

114 Halder, op. cit., p. 283.

115 Sendtner, p. 510; Graml, p. 36.

116 Sendtner, pp. 510–11.

117 Ibid., p. 511; Halder, p. 286; Graml, pp. 37–9.

118 On this point and below see: Sendtner, pp. 511–15; Graml, pp. 37–9. Deutsch (p. 326) assumes, but without evidence, that Beck was not told of the contacts between Oster and Sas.

119 Graml maintains that the object was to prolong the period available to the generals to revolt by betraying the offensive so that it might be called off as too risky. This is not convincing, however, except as applied to the few weeks between mid-October and 7 November, on which day Oster told Sas that he was no longer counting on an attempted *coup* by the generals – Graml, p. 38.

120 Sendtner, pp. 516–17.

121 Graml, p. 39.

122 Ibid.

Notes

1 Friedrich Albert SchmidNoerr: 'Dokument des Widerstandes: Entwurf einer Deutschen Reichsverfassung' in *Voran und beharrlich*, Nos 33/4 of 1961, pp. 1–12.
2 Hans Mommsen: 'Gesellschaftsbild und Verfassungspläne des deutschen Widerstandes' in Walter Schmitthenner and Hans Buchheim (editors): *Der deutsche Widerstand gegen Hitler*, pp. 162–3 (*The German Resistance to Hitler*, pp. 143–4).

CHAPTER 14

1 See Ulrich von Hassell: *The von Hassell Diaries*, pp. 333–7 and *Vom andern Deutschland*, pp. 336–44 – 'Gesetz über die Wiederherstellung geordneter Verhältnisse im Staats- und Rechtsleben' primarily written by Popitz, also *Deutschland*, pp. 345–8 – 'Richtlinien zur Handhabung des Gesetzes über den Belagerungszustand', also mainly by Popitz (the law itself has been lost). See also Hans Rothfels: *The German Opposition to Hitler*, pp. 99–101; Gerhard Ritter: *Carl Goerdeler und die deutsche Widerstandsbewegung*, pp. 315–17 (not in English translation); Hans Mommsen: 'Gesellschaftsbild und Verfassungspläne des deutschen Widerstandes' in Walter Schmitthenner and Hans Buchheim (editors) *Der deutsche Widerstand gegen Hitler*, pp. 126–32 (*The German Resistance to Hitler*, pp. 108–14.)
2 Mommsen, p. 128 (110).

CHAPTER 15

1 Ulrich von Hassell: *Vom andern Deutschland*, pp. 336–44; Hans Mommsen: 'Gesellschaftsbild und Verfassungspläne des deutschen Widerstandes', by Walter Schmitthenner and Hans Buchheim in *Der deutsche Widerstand gegen Hitler*, pp. 128–32 (*The German Resistance to Hitler*, pp. 110–14).
2 Otto John: *Twice through the Lines*, pp. 45–6, 56–7, 69–70, 72–3.
3 Gerhard Ritter: *Carl Goerdeler und die deutsche Widerstandsbewegung*, pp. 315–17 (*The German Resistance*, pp. 208–10).
4 See Popitz's statements during interrogation by the *Gestapo* (when he may have portrayed himself as somewhat more of an anti-Semite than he really was) in *Spiegelbild*, p. 449: 'As one thoroughly familiar with conditions during the Weimar Republic, I was quite persuaded that the Jews must disappear from public and economic life. Regarding the method, I recommended repeatedly a more gradual approach, particularly for foreign policy considerations.'
5 The guidelines are given in Hassell, *Deutschland*, pp. 345–8.

CHAPTER 16

1 See Appendix to Gerhard Ritter: *Carl Goerdeler und die deutsche Widerstandsbewegung* – 'Gedanken eines zum Tode Verurteilten – September 1944 im Gefängnis', pp. 569–76, extract from 'Das Ziel', pp. 577–8, 'Friedensplan', p. 585, 'Friedensplan' (probably late summer 1943), pp. 586–92, 'Geheime Denkschrift für die Generale', March 1943, pp. 593–611, draft of letter to Field Marshal von Kluge, 25 July 1943, pp. 612–16; see also Gerhard Ritter: *The German Resistance*, pp. 178–97. See also Wilhelm Ritter von Schramm: *Beck und Goerdeler*, 'Das Ziel', pp. 81–166 – on Goerdeler's authorship, in contrast to Schramm's theory, see Hans Mommsen: 'Gesellschaftsbild und Verfassungspläne des deutschen Widerstandes', in Walter Schmitthenner and Hans Buchheim (editors): *Der deutsche Widerstand gegen Hitler*, pp. 266–7 Note 68 and on the date pp. 269–70 Note 109 in contrast to Ritter and Schramm (*The*

German Resistance to Hitler, pp. 248–9, 252–3). See also a memorandum which Schramm calls 'Der Weg' (pp. 167–232) but to which he cannot attach a date, 'Regierungserklärung' (pp. 233–46) – already published by Ritter as 'Das Regierungsprogramm vom 20. Juli 1944' in *Die Gegenwart* I (1946) nos 12/13, pp. 11–14; radio address, pp. 247–53; Goerdeler's peace plan entitled here as 'Ausarbeitung Goerdelers', pp. 255–64. An extract from 'Das Ziel' is given in *Spiegelbild einer Verschwörung*, pp. 119–23; Goerdeler's peace plan (without title) on pp. 249–55; 'Das Regierungsprogramm' referred to as 'Regierungserklärung' on pp. 147–56 and radio address entitled 'Rundfunk' on pp. 213–17. Many unpublished memoranda and documents from Goerdeler's papers are to be found in the BA, Koblenz.

2 On this point and below see Ritter, *Goerdeler*, pp. 280–8 (*Resistance*, pp. 197–201); Mommsen, pp. 132–46 (114–27); Constantin von Dietze: 'Die Universität Freiburg im Dritten Reich' in *Mitteilungen der List Gesellschaft*, Folio 3 (1960/61) No 3, pp. 95–105; Elfriede Nebgen: *Jakob Kaiser*, p. 128.

3 Schramm, pp. 81–166; Ritter, *Goerdeler*, pp. 569–76 (*Resistance*, pp. 182–90); the account below is also based on these two sources.

4 Nebgen, pp. 90–1, 95.

5 See information extracted by the *Gestapo* on the planned organization of a united trade union in BA, EAP 105/26 following p. 113 (not in *Spiegelbild*); Nebgen, pp. 90–1, 95, 122, 128, 149–50; Ritter, *Goerdeler*, p. 292 (*Resistance*, pp. 186–7). Nebgen (p. 122) says that Leuschner's statements to the Gestapo as given in *Spiegelbild*, pp. 383 et seq. are correct at least in so far as the planned united trade union is concerned. Nebgen (pp. 90–1) objects to an alleged statement by Mommsen, p. 162 (p. 143 in the English translation) that Kaiser, Leuschner and Habermann were aiming at a sort of democratic corporate state, but Mommsen does not say this on the page referred to.

6 Nebgen, pp. 64–5. See also [Hans] Walz: 'Gedanken zur politischen Zielsetzung von Carl Goerdeler', typescript, May 1968; *Spiegelbild*, p. 501.

7 Nebgen, pp. 151–5; Otto John: *Twice through the Lines*, pp. 45–6, 56–7, 69–70, 72–3, also applicable below.

8 Schramm, pp. 105–7.

9 Schramm (p. 275 note 20) offers the apologetic comment regarding the remarks on the Jews that the worst excesses had not yet occurred at the time, and that later on such proposals as those of Goerdeler had lost currency (among the opposition). Concerning the first 'explanation', it may be pointed out that Goerdeler's memorandum is dated end 1941 by Mommsen (pp. 269–70 note 109, pp. 252–3 in English translation); therefore Goerdeler may be presumed to have known of the excesses perpetrated in Poland, and even those of more recent date in Russia. Moreover, he himself refers to 'destruction etc. of Jewish possessions and lives' which cannot be defended before one's conscience or before history. Consequently the claim that the worst excesses had not yet occurred cannot explain what amounts to a proposal by Goerdeler for special discriminatory legislation directed against Jews who came to Germany after 1914 and their descendants. Concerning the second 'explanation', it may be pointed out that Goerdeler himself in any case had not abandoned his ideas on the subject, but still advanced them after having been sentenced to death in 'Gedanken eines zum Tode Verurteilten – September 1944 im Gefängnis'; cf. Mommsen, p. 270 Note 109 (pp. 252–3 in English translation). Ritter, *Goerdeler*, pp. 569–76 did not reproduce the appropriate passage in his excerpt. Since Goerdeler did not attempt to write or say on most other occasions what he thought might produce a more benevolent disposition of his interrogators, and in view of the total body of evidence on Goerdeler's thought it must be assumed that he meant what he said.

10 Mommsen, pp. 138–9 (120–1 in English translation).

11 Ritter, *Goerdeler*, p. 299.

Notes

1 There is now a fundamental work on the Kreisau Circle – *Neuordnung im Widerstand* by Ger van Roon. (The English translation, *German Resistance to Hitler*, is greatly abridged.) Eugen Gerstenmaier in 'Der Kreisauer Kreis zu dem Buch Gerrit van Roons "Neuordnung im Widerstand" ', *VfZ* 15 (1967), pp. 221–46, has certain important comments and corrections to make on Roon's book. Gerstenmaier also gave certain verbal information to the author on 17 August 1965. On meetings of the Kreisau Circle see Roon, *Neuordnung*, pp. 248–56.

2 Dr Eugen Gerstenmaier, who was one of those who took a most active part in the discussions, emphatically denies that the Kreisau programmes were decided by majority vote; in so far as decisions were taken at all, he says, they resulted from voluntary agreement – Gerstenmaier 'Kreisauer Kreis', p. 227. The final drafts of summer 1944 were prepared by Drs Haubach and Gerstenmaier but without the assistance of Dr Mierendorff, who had been killed in an air raid on Leipzig in December 1943, and Graf von Moltke, who had been arrested in January 1944. Gerstenmaier, verbal information.

3 Hans Mommsen: 'Gesellschaftsbild und Verfassungspläne des deutschen Widerstandes' in Walter Schmitthenner and Hans Buchheim (editors): *Der deutsche Widerstand gegen Hitler*, pp. 132–46 (*The German Resistance to Hitler*, pp. 114–27). On 'Principles for reorganization' and 'Reich structure' see Theodor Steltzer: *Sechzig Jahre Zeitgenosse*, pp. 298–303. See also Gerstenmaier, 'Kreisauer Kreis', pp. 239–41.

4 See somewhat unreliable information given by Werner Münchheimer in 'Die Verfassungs- und Verwaltungsreformpläne der deutschen Opposition gegen Hitler zum 20. Juli 1944' in *Europa-Archiv* 5 (1950), pp. 3188–95; Albert Krebs: *Fritz-Dietlof Graf von der Schulenburg*, pp. 269–85; Mommsen, pp. 101–4 (pp. 83–6 in English translation) with certain critical comments; Roon (pp. 394–6) refers to a draft map discussed by the Kreisau Circle showing the distribution of the *Länder*; Dr Paulus van Husen and Gräfin Yorck von Wartenburg each still have a copy; Gerstenmaier in 'Kreisauer Kreis', p. 228, confirms that it originated from Schulenburg.

5 Mommsen, pp. 145–6 (126–7 in English translation). Roon (pp. 407–8), who has the best collection of source material on the Kreisau Circle, unfortunately does not deal with these questions.

6 Roon (p. 408) says: 'The composition of the Reich Council was clearly designed to accommodate the federalists', but it is incomprehensible how he reaches this conclusion. The tendency to centralism is clear. Mommsen (p. 146, 126–7 in English translation) even says that 'The National-Socialist *Gleichschaltung* of the *Länder* was regarded as a *fait accompli*'. Gerhard Ritter in *Carl Goerdeler und die deutsche Widerstandsbewegung*, p. 308 (*The German Resistance*, p. 202), like Roon, overlooks the centralism inherent in the Kreisau draft, saying: 'The future Reichstag, like the Upper House, would be entirely controlled by representatives of provincial particularism.'

7 Mommsen, pp. 139–40 (120–1 in English translation).

8 On this point and below see Gerstenmaier, 'Kreisauer Kreis', pp. 239–41. Verbal information from Gerstenmaier.

9 Gerstenmaier, 'Kreisauer Kreis', p. 240.

10 Ibid., pp. 240–1.

11 Roon (pp. 428–9) seems to have missed the illiberal implications.

12 The Kreisau draft of 9 August 1943 contains this: 'Key firms in the mining, iron and steel, chemical and energy-producing industries will be taken over and become public property.' See Roon, p. 566 and Steltzer, *Sechzig Jahre*, p. 304. Gerstenmaier (op. cit., p. 229), on the other hand, says that 'taken as a whole' the 'men of Kreisau' would not have agreed with the draft proclamation of 14 June

1943 in which 'Mierendorff announced "the expropriation of key concerns in heavy industry . . . as fundamental to a socialist economic order".' According to Gerstenmaier, therefore, the draft of August 1943 would also not have been representative of the views of the 'men of Kreisau'. In fact there were no such documents. According to Gerstenmaier's account already mentioned, the Circle should not be regarded as a group united in its views but one of people with their own convictions who worked voluntarily together, where many ideas were discussed apart from the necessity for a *coup*, but which took no *decisions* on national or constitutional matters. There can therefore be no answer to the question what would have happened after a *coup*; it is only possible to indicate the ideas emerging from the various groups.

13 Mommsen, p. 137 (119 in English translation).
14 Ibid., pp. 117, 142 (99, 123–4 in English translation).
15 Ibid., p. 157 (138 in English translation); see also Chapter 39 below. Peter Hoffmann: 'Claus Stauffenberg und Stefan George: Der Weg zur Tat' in *Jahrbuch der Deutschen Schillergesellschaft* 12 (1968), pp. 520–42. Unfortunately Kramarz, in his book on Stauffenberg, says little or nothing on these questions.

CHAPTER 18

1 On this point and below see Franz Josef Furtwängler: *Männer, die ich sah und kannte*, pp. 215–16; Otto John: 'Männer im Kampf gegen Hitler (II)' in *Blick in die Welt* 2 (1947) No 7; Otto John: 'Männer im Kampf gegen Hitler (IV): Wilhelm Leuschner' in *Blick in die Welt* 2 (1947) No 9, p. 20; [Julius Leber]: *Ein Mann geht seinen Weg*, pp. 280–1.
2 Wolfgang Treue: *Deutsche Parteiprogramme seit 1861*, p. 116.
3 *Spiegelbild einer Verschwörung*, pp. 206, 212, 235; Theo Haubach, handwritten notes for his defence, 1944–5, IfZ ED 106 Archiv Walter Hammer Bd. 48.
4 *Spiegelbild*, p. 501; evidence by Haubach before the People's Court in *Volksgerichtshof-Prozesse zum 20. Juli 1944*, pp. 99–100. Christian Müller in *Oberst i.G. Stauffenberg* (p. 406) appears to be mistaken when he assumes that a popular movement was conceived according to Leber's ideas; the terminology which includes 'estates', 'strata' and 'regions' is wholly foreign to Leber's way of thinking.
5 *Spiegelbild*, p. 501.
6 Ibid.; Haubach.
7 Cf. Treue, pp. 117–18.
8 Treue, p. 119; *Spiegelbild*, p. 316.
9 *Spiegelbild*, pp. 211, 234, 316–17.
10 Treue, p. 119; *Spiegelbild*, p. 316.
11 *Spiegelbild*, pp. 234, 317.
12 Treue, p. 118; *Spiegelbild*, p. 316.
13 *Spiegelbild*, p. 317.
14 *Spiegelbild*, p. 317; cf. John, *Twice*, p. 57.
15 *Spiegelbild*, p. 468.
16 *Spiegelbild*, pp. 233–34.
17 *Spiegelbild*, p. 315.
18 *Spiegelbild*, p. 499. In the *Gestapo* report of 19 August 1944 (*Spiegelbild*, p. 264) Leuschner is said to have been caused by Goerdeler to give up his earlier-held opinion that the *Deutsche Gewerkschaft* (United Labour Union) should be organized after the war was lost and the regime had therefore changed. This is misleading, since the next sentence is: 'In the end [Leuschner] together with the labour union clique clearly hitched up with the assassination and *coup* plans.' This means that, contrary to the first statement, Leuschner was caused by Goerdeler to give up waiting for the collapse.

19 Joachim G. Leithäuser: *Wilhelm Leuschner*, p. 248.
20 See below, pp. 367–70.
21 See John, op. cit., p. 104; Haubach; *Foreign Relations of the United States. Diplomatic Papers: 1944*, Vol. I, p. 511.
22 John, op. cit., pp. 138–9.
23 *Spiegelbild*, pp. 415, 499–500; *Volksgerichtshof-Prozesse*, p. 114.
24 *Spiegelbild*, pp. 499–500.
25 Ibid.; cf. *Spiegelbild*, p. 364 where Strünck is quoted as stating that Gisevius had explained his opposition to including the labour unions on 15 July 1944 by maintaining they had given proof of their political incompetence before 1933; also *Spiegelbild*, p. 500.
26 Leber, pp. 290–1.

NOTES/PART V/CHAPTER 19

1 Ger van Roon: *Neuordnung im Widerstand*, pp. 301–2.
2 Ibid., pp. 305–6.
3 Walter Stubbe: 'In memoriam Albrecht Haushofer' in *VfZ* 8 (1960), p. 237 (Stubbe was an assistant to Albrecht Haushofer). See also Rainer Hildebrandt: *Wir sind die Letzten*; Edmund A. Walsh: 'Die Tragödie Karl Haushofers' in *Neue Auslese* 2 (1947), No 3, pp. 27–8, also *Total Power*, pp. 52–9; Ursula Michel: *Albrecht Haushofer und der Nationalsozialismus*, dissertation, Kiel 1964; *In memoriam Albrecht Haushofer*, edited by Rolf Italiaander; Rolf Italiaander: *Besiegeltes Leben*, pp. 11–53.
4 Hildebrandt, pp. 34–9; Stubbe, pp. 238–9.
5 Hildebrandt, pp. 51–3 and Stubbe, p. 239. See also later on this page.
6 Michel, pp. 49–53, 64–6, 119–27, 154, 161, 206, 214.
7 Ibid., p. 233 and Annex p. 53.
8 Hildebrandt, p. 130.
9 Given in Stubbe, p. 240.
10 Ibid., p. 241.
11 Ibid., pp. 243–4.
12 Italiaander, *Leben*, p. 29; Stubbe, p. 250; Michel, pp. 244–62.
13 *Documents on German Foreign Policy (DGFP)*, Series D, Vol. XI, No 12.
14 Hess to Karl Haushofer 10 September 1940, *DGFP*, Vol. XI, No 46; [Albrecht Haushofer]: 'Gibt es noch Möglichkeiten eines deutsch-englischen Friedens', typescript 8 September 1940, BA, Haushofer Papers HC 833; reproduced in Stubbe, pp. 246–8; Michel, p. 244.
15 Michel, p. 244; printed in Stubbe, pp. 246–8; *DGFP* Vol. XI, Nos 61, 76.
16 *DGFP* Vol. XI, No 46.
17 *DGFP* Vol. XI, No 76; reproduced in Stubbe, pp. 248–9.
18 *DGFP* Vol. XI, No 76, Enclosure 2 and Note 7, No 93, No 94. According to this Stubbe is in error when he says (p. 250) that the letter never reached the Duke of Hamilton; see also *Trials of the Major War Criminals before the International Military Tribunal* Vol. XXXVIII, p. 175; Michel, pp. 251–4.
19 Stubbe, p. 250; Hildebrandt, pp. 109–10 (frequently uncertain and tentative).
20 *DGFP* Vol. XI, No 76 Enclosure 2 Note 7; *Trial*, Vol. XXXVIII, p. 175 (Document 116-M) – Report by Wing Commander the Duke of Hamilton on his talk with Hess on 11 May 1941.
21 Stubbe, pp. 250–1 says, without giving further details, that after November 1940, Haushofer was successful in gaining contact with Britain acting as an unofficial emissary with official cover and at the same time as a representative of the opposition.
22 Report by Albrecht Haushofer to Hitler on his activities on behalf of Hess

written in the Obersalzberg on 12 May 1941, BA, Haushofer Papers HC 833; given also in *DGFP* Vol. XII No 500 and Stubbe, pp. 252–5. See also corrections by Professor Burckhardt in Stubbe, 251–3 Note 25. When writing his report shortly after Hess's flight to Britain Haushofer was under arrest and in danger of his life. He had to justify himself to Hitler and also prove that he was in no way responsible for Hess's flight. This largely explains the discrepancies in his report.

23 Ulrich von Hassell: *The von Hassell Diaries*, p. 156; Hildebrandt, p. 110. Burckhardt possibly sent his greetings to Haushofer through Hassell or his wife – see Stubbe, pp. 251–2 and Hassell, pp. 176–7.

24 Hassell, pp. 159–60.

25 Stubbe, p. 251.

26 According to Hildebrandt (p. 111) he commissioned Heinrich Stahmer, his former student working in the Foreign Ministry, to obtain this invitation for him. According to *DGFP*, Vol. XI p. 1260 Stahmer had been Minister at the German Embassy in Tokyo since September 1940. See also Stubbe, p. 251 which says that Stahmer was Secretary in the Foreign Service [*Legationssekretär*] and was willing to arrange the lecture.

27 Stubbe, p. 251.

28 James Leasor: *The Uninvited Envoy*, passim; Max Domarus: *Hitler: Reden und Proklamationen 1932–1945*, pp. 1709–18; Hildebrandt, pp. 112–15.

29 Stubbe, p. 251; Hassell, p. 177.

30 A[lbrecht] H[aushofer]: 'Englische Beziehungen und die Möglichkeit ihres Einsatzes', typescript, Obersalzberg 12 May 1941, BA, Haushofer Papers HC 833.

31 Hassell, p. 177; Stubbe, p. 253 Note 25.

32 Hildebrandt, p. 113.

CHAPTER 20

1 Ulrich von Hassell: *The von Hassell Diaries*, pp. 186, 189.

2 The Atlantic Charter in Hans-Adolf Jacobsen: *1939–1945: Der zweite Weltkrieg in Chronik und Dokumenten*, pp. 264–5.

3 Hans Rothfels: *Die deutsche Opposition gegen Hitler*, p. 155 (not in English translation).

4 Hassell, pp. 189–90.

5 Ibid., pp. 217–18.

6 Ibid.

7 Ibid., pp. 173–4, 184, 193–4, 197–8; correspondence between the RSHA and/or Himmler's Personal Staff and the Foreign Ministry with Enclosures, 6 November 1941–15 January 1942, BA, NS 19/414; Mother Mary Alice Gallin: *Ethical and Religious Factors in the German Resistance to Hitler*, pp. 123–4, 204; see also Rothfels: *Deutsche Opposition*, pp. 151, 204–5, Note 29.

8 Colonel William J. Donovan (then Coordinator of Information in the Office of Strategic Services, later Chief of OSS) to President Franklin D. Roosevelt [1 October 1941]; W. D. Whitney to Donovan 1 October 1941; Franklin D. Roosevelt Library, Hyde Park, N.Y., PSF Safe/Germany, also applicable below.

9 Rothfels (*Deutsche Opposition*, pp. 204–5 Note 29; less detailed in English ed.) considers that the 'proposition' had something to do with a monarchical restoration; he bases this on the report of a member of the American Naval Intelligence Service (Alexander B. Maley: 'The Epic of the German Underground' in *Human Events* (Washington) III (1946), No 9 of 27 February 1946, p. 6). According to this Stallforth did not arrive in Washington until 1 December and did not speak to Roosevelt until 7 December. In fact Stallforth reported on his contacts in Germany to Colonel Donovan and W. D. Whitney in Washington as early as 30 September (see evidence cited in note 8). Based on

Maley's report in 'The Epic . . .', Rothfels (*Deutsche Opposition*, pp. 204–5 note 29) relates a version of the 'proposition' that contains further details: Evacuation by Germany of all territories occupied since 1933 except the Saar, Austria and Danzig; exchange of the Polish Corridor for East Prussia (as at 1933); no reparations.

CHAPTER 21

1 On this point and generally see: Louis P. Lochner: *Stets das Unerwartete*, pp. 355–7 (not in English version); Otto John: *Twice through the Lines*, pp 69–74; Hans Rothfels: *The German Opposition to Hitler*, pp. 133–4; Mother Mary Alice Gallin: *Ethical and Religious Factors in the German Resistance to Hitler*, pp. 124, 145–7; Lochner to Mr Lauchlin Currie, 19 June 1942, Franklin Roosevelt Library, Hyde Park, N.Y., 198-a.
2 Allen W. Dulles: *Germany's Underground*, passim; Gallin, bibliography, pp. 203–7. See also the chapter on Gisevius' foreign contacts, below pp. 235–9.
3 *Foreign Relations of the United States. Diplomatic Papers: The Conferences at Malta and Yalta 1945*, pp. 361–84, 389–400, 593–4, 698, 759, 768–9, 836, 894–7.

CHAPTER 22

1 On these contacts in general see: Ger van Roon: *Neuordnung im Widerstand*, pp. 295–322 (*German Resistance to Hitler*, pp. 177–200); Eberhard Bethge: *Dietrich Bonhoeffer* (English translation), pp. 626–702. Roon produces much detail but not a coherent account of connected developments.
2 Reproduced with a foreword by Hans Rothfels in 'Zwei aussenpolitische Memoranden der deutschen Opposition (Frühjahr 1942)' in *VfZ* 5 (1957), pp. 388–95. See also Willem A. Visser't Hooft: *Die Welt war meine Gemeinde*, pp. 182–200. The memorandum may have originated from the same circle that had been behind Lochner's mission. Indications are to be found in various documents of some connection between the Lochner mission, the Trott/Kreisau memorandum and Schönfeld's and Bonhoeffer's meeting with the Bishop of Chichester; there are repeated references to the opposition having 'crystallized' in the autumn 1941, for instance, in Trott's memorandum (Rothfels, op. cit., p. 394) and in the Bishop's report (Dietrich Bonhoeffer: *Gesammelte Schriften*, Vol. I, p. 373).

    According to Eugen Gerstenmaier in 'Der Kreisauer Kreis. zu dem Buch Gerrit van Roons "Neuordnung im Widerstand".' *VfZ* 15 (1967), pp. 236–7, the originator of the memorandum was Schönfeld. In the winter 1941–2 Gerstenmaier himself wrote a draft which he gave to Trott and Haeften, asking them to revise it. They and Schönfeld spent many evenings over it together and Schönfeld finally took it to Geneva where he and Albrecht von Kessel, then German Consul there, possibly revised it yet again. In contrast to Ger van Roon: *Neuordnung im Widerstand*, p. 302 who refers to it as 'a Kreisau product', Gerstenmaier emphasizes that the memorandum did not originate from 'the Kreisau Circle' but from individuals who belonged to it and that it had a bearing on foreign policy discussions within the Circle.
3 George K. A. Bell: 'Die Ökumene und die innerdeutsche Opposition', *VfZ* 5 (1957), p. 369.
4 *Keesing's Contemporary Archives*, Vol. III 1937–1940, p. 3700.
5 Cf. Gerstenmaier, 'Kreisauer Kreis', p. 237.

6 For details on this point and the exchange of letters with Eden see: Bell, op. cit., pp. 362–78; Schönfeld's memorandum and foreword in Rothfels, op. cit., pp. 388–97; the Bishop's memorandum to Eden, Schönfeld's memorandum to the Bishop, letters from Bonhoeffer to the Bishop and the exchange of correspondence between Eden and the Bishop in Bonhoeffer, op. cit., pp. 372–89, 488–503. See also Alexander B. Maley: 'The Epic of the German Underground' in *Human Events* III (1946), No 9, p. 6; Hans Rothfels: *The German Opposition to Hitler*, pp. 134–6; Roon, op. cit., pp. 308–14; Bethge, pp. 656–76.

7 Bethge, pp. 839–41.

8 For details of Bonhoeffer's contacts see Bethge, pp. 629–34.

9 Ibid., pp. 638–49.

10 Ibid., pp. 660–1.

11 Gerhard Ritter in *Carl Goerdeler und die deutsche Widerstandsbewegung*, p. 328 (*The German Resistance*, p. 217) says that Goerdeler was behind Schönfeld's attempt to contact Bell but Rothfels in *Deutsche Opposition*, p. 204 Note 22 considers this unlikely. See also Elfriede Nebgen: *Jakob Kaiser*, p. 134.

12 Ulrich von Hassell: *The von Hassell Diaries*, p. 275.

13 Ibid., p. 224.

14 Bethge, pp. 661–76.

15 Ibid., p. 648.

16 Bell, p. 369.

17 *Foreign Relations of the United States; Diplomatic Papers, 1944*, Vol. I, pp. 484–579.

18 Winston S. Churchill: *Blood, Sweat and Tears: Speeches*, p. 328.

19 Hans Bernd Gisevius: *Wo ist Nebe?*, p. 221.

20 Henrik Lindgren: 'Adam von Trotts Reisen nach Schweden 1942–1944' in *VfZ* 18 (1970), pp. 274–277, also applicable below.

21 Lindgren, pp. 274–277.

CHAPTER 23

1 Allen Dulles: *Germany's Underground*, pp. 131–2 which gives Trott's views *in extenso* – also applicable below; Ger van Roon: *Neuordnung im Widerstand*, pp. 311–12, based on information from Schulze-Gaevernitz. Regarding alleged 'eastward leanings' see below, pp. 232–4 and 601 Note 7.

2 Ulrich von Hassell: *The von Hassell Diaries*, p. 283. On further attempts to make contact connected with Himmler see *Foreign Relations of the United States Diplomatic Papers, 1944*, Vol. I, pp. 484–579.

3 Dulles, pp. 22–3.

4 Roon, pp. 317–22. Much of this is still obscure; Roon says: 'By no means all the conversations which Trott held are so far known.'

5 Ibid.

6 Cf. Wilhelm Wengler: 'Vorkämpfer der Völkerverständigung und Völkerrechtsgelehrte als Opfer des Nationalsozialismus: 9. Graf von Moltke (1906–1945)' in *Die Friedens-Warte* 48 (1948), pp. 297–305. Wengler was at this time scientific assistant in the *Abwehr* and went to Istanbul with Moltke; see Roon, p. 318.

7 See Moltke's letter to Professor Lionel Curtis in Oxford in 1942, in which he said: 'We hope that you will realize that we are ready to help you win both the war and the peace' – Count Helmuth James von Moltke: *A German of the Resistance: The Last Letters*, p. 29, reprinted in Michael Balfour and Julian Frisby: *Helmuth von Moltke: A Leader against Hitler*, pp. 184–6. With such phraseology the danger of misunderstanding is great. Moltke had no intention of making his contribution by the betrayal of military secrets. He wished instead to overcome the human problems besetting both sides by a concerted effort and he

was thinking of the contribution which could be made from within and by Germans to the overthrow of the Hitler regime. In any case he was not thinking of strategic, territorial, economic or political advantages to be gained for Germany by military effort, since under the circumstances he regarded these as unjustified. In Moltke's defence on the subject of this misunderstanding see Eugen Gerstenmaier: 'Der Kreisauer Kreis: zu dem Buch Gerrit van Roons "Neuordnung im Widerstand" ', *VfZ* 15 (1967), pp. 238–9.

8 On this point and below I have followed Karl Brandt: 'Gedenkrede zum Gedächtnis der Toten des 20. Juli 1944' delivered at the ceremony in Berlin on 20 July 1965, roneoed, p. 9; letters from Brandt to the author, 11 May and 6 August 1968. Gert Buchheit: *Der deutsche Geheimdienst*, p. 427 follows Albert C. Wedemeyer in *Der verwaltete Krieg*, pp. 470–1 and Franz von Papen: *Memoirs*, pp. 499–500 in saying that Admiral Canaris together with Ambassador von Papen, approached George H. Earle, the US Naval Attaché in Ankara, with a proposal to submit an offer of capitulation following an imminent *coup d'état*. President Roosevelt is said to have sent word in reply that all such requests should be addressed to General Eisenhower. Evidence so far available (the point could easily be cleared up by documents still held secret in Washington) does not enable one to conclude that the attempt at contact reported by Brandt is the same as that referred to by Wedemeyer and Papen.

9 In his letter to the author of 11 May 1968 Brandt says that this was to take place at a cabinet meeting.

10 Reproduced in Roon, pp. 591–3. According to Gerstenmaier in 'Kreisauer Kreis', p. 243 and in contrast to Roon, Moltke had not *counted* on being arrested so soon. This does not mean, however, that Moltke was not afraid that this might happen as Bonhoeffer and Dohnanyi had been in the hands of the *Gestapo* for months, as had Dutch and Danish members of the resistance movements with whom Moltke had been in contact.

11 Roon, pp. 321–2.

CHAPTER 24

1 Ulrich von Hassell: *Vom andern Deutschland*, p. 271; Ger van Roon: *Neuordnung im Widerstand*, pp. 313, 316–17; report dated 12 September 1944 to Cordell Hull, the Secretary of State, by Johnson, American Minister in Stockholm, *Foreign Relations of the United States: Diplomatic Papers, 1944*, Vol. I, pp. 550–1. On Trott see also the biography by Christopher Sykes: *Troubled Loyalty*; Henrik Lindgren: 'Adam von Trotts Reisen nach Schweden 1942–1944' in *VfZ* 18 (1970), pp. 278–9.

2 Hassell gave similar hints about the danger of Russian hegemony in Europe (*The von Hassell Diaries*, p. 293) and both Hassell and Friedrich Werner Graf von der Schulenburg, who had been Ambassador in Moscow, considered the possibility of hinting at a separate peace in the East.

3 See Bertold Spuler: *Regenten und Regierungen der Welt: Minister-Ploetz*, Part II, Vol. 4, p. 510; Roon (p. 313) refers to 'John Günther'.

4 Roon (p. 316) refers to him as 'a Minister in the Churchill government'; he is not listed as a member of the Churchill cabinet of 1940–45 in Spuler, pp. 267–71; see also *Who's Who*, 1961, which shows that Walter Turner Monckton was created 1st Viscount Monckton of Brenchley in 1957, Deputy Under-Secretary of State for Foreign Affairs 1940, Director-General of British Propaganda and Information Services in Cairo 1941–2. See also Hans Rothfels: 'Trott und die Aussenpolitik des Widerstandes' in *VfZ* 12 (1964), p. 309.

5 The lady was apparently Frau Inga Kempe, née Carlgren; in February 1958 she wrote to Frau Clarita von Trott zu Solz about Trott's Swedish contacts. See

Rothfels, op. cit., p. 309 and Johnson to Hull, 12 September 1944 (Note 1 above).

6 A new account of Trott's foreign contacts is now available in Sykes, op. cit. – see in particular pp. 399–406. Nevertheless Sykes has not used the valuable sources published in *Foreign Relations of the United States* and, on matters not directly concerning Trott, his book contains far too many inaccuracies.

7 Given in Rothfels, op. cit., pp. 318–22, also comments on pp. 308–9. See also Roon (p. 309) who emphasizes that the first person plural 'we' is used in this document and that it was certainly not drafted by Trott alone. See also Eugen Gerstenmaier: 'Der Kreisauer Kreis: zu dem Buch Gerrit van Roons "Neuordnung im Widerstand" ' in *VfZ* 15 (1967), p. 237.

8 Rothfels, op. cit., p. 309. As far as Dr Wilhelm Hoffmann remembers Trott was in Stuttgart on 25 June. As regards these last contacts Roon (pp. 307–8) gives only vague information. Rothfels was able to be more definite as early as 1964 but even he was compelled to say that much still remained obscure as regards Trott's foreign contacts after October 1943. Meanwhile the United States government has published numerous documents which throw some light on the subject – see *Foreign Relations*, pp. 484–579.

9 See below, p. 231.

10 Memoranda by Roosevelt dated 17 January and 1 April 1944 commenting on the demand for unconditional surrender – *Foreign Relations*, pp. 493–4, 501–2.

11 Ibid., pp. 513–14.

12 Churchill to Roosevelt 25 May 1944, ibid., pp. 517–18.

13 Stalin to Roosevelt 26 May 1944, ibid., p. 519.

14 Cf. below, pp. 233–4, 362–4.

15 See Notes 12 and 13 above.

16 On the March visit see the following which agree on all important points: Johnson to Cordell Hull, 12 and 14 September 1944, *Foreign Relations*, pp. 550–3; article by Willy Brandt in the Stockholm *Dagens Nyheter* 12 September 1944, contents of which are also to be found in the files of the Foreign Ministry in Bonn (Inland IIg 59); report on conversations in Rome between Albrecht von Kessel, First Secretary of the German Embassy to the Vatican, and W. H. C. Frend of the (British) Psychological Warfare Branch of Allied Forces Headquarters, 22 July – 2 August 1944, in *Foreign Relations*, pp. 532–7; Albrecht von Kessel: 'Verborgene Saat', typescript, Vatican City, 1944–5, p. 257; copy of extract from the Ms. in Rothfels, op. cit., pp. 322–3. According to Kessel Trott told him in person only about his March visit and this took place in Venice in the second half of May 1944 after an earlier meeting in Geneva had not materialized. Kessel's information therefore can refer only to the March visit. cf. Lindgren, pp. 280–1.

17 Concerning the circle around Stauffenberg see participants of the conference in Wannsee on 16 July 1944 in *Spiegelbild einer Verschwörung*, pp. 91–2, 101, 136, 175: Hansen, Hofacker, Mertz, Schwerin von Schwanenfeld, F. D. Graf von der Schulenburg, Berthold and Claus Graf von Stauffenberg, Trott. On 16 June 1944 Stauffenberg had conferred with Leber, Leuschner, Wirmer, Letterhaus, J. Kaiser, F. D. Graf von der Schulenburg; ibid., pp. 118, 179. The conference in Wannsee was not held on 17 July 1944 as Rothfels says (op. cit., p. 309). It appears from Roon, p. 317 that the Kreisau Circle was included although Roon does not mention the March visit. Rothfels (op. cit., pp. 309–10) does not consider the question of who supported the effort. Lindgren (p. 280) refers to an 'instruction' to which Trott had adhered and bases this on Kessel as quoted by Rothfels (op. cit., p. 322); but here Kessel only says: 'As had been agreed beforehand, he [Trott] had not requested any declarations or promises ...'

18 See below, pp. 233–4.

19 See pp. 375–6 below.

20 After Trott's execution had been postponed in order to 'obtain further clarifica-

tion' from him, he told the *Gestapo* of this alleged view of Stauffenberg's which clearly applied to the pre-invasion period – *Spiegelbild*, pp. 249, 367, 505, 507. There is no doubt that Trott was tortured. There are other reasons, however, why *Gestapo* reports should be regarded with suspicion. Trott may have said something incriminating to no one still alive but still not true. It may also have suited the book of the *Gestapo* reporters to lay emphasis on possible collaboration with the West against Russia and psychologically Trott's derogatory comments on Stauffenberg's views may have seemed a good way of doing this. The question cannot be decided without more reliable evidence of Stauffenberg's views.

21 See reports on Himmler's and Ribbentrop's contacts with the Allies in *Foreign Relations*, pp. 484–579. Dulles's reports from Berne named at least a few of the members of the opposition, but only those who could be presumed to belong to a *fronde* without any hard inside information. Cf. Appendix, p. 747.

22 Ibid., pp. 497–8, 506–7.

23 For evidence of this and the following three paragraphs see Schulze-Gaevernitz's report to Dulles in *Germany's Underground*, pp. 137–8 and reports by Dulles to OSS, Washington, of March and May 1944 in *Foreign Relations*, pp. 505–7, 510–13.

24 Johnson to Secretary of State, 26 June and 14 September 1944 in *Foreign Relations*, pp. 523–5, 552–3; Rothfels, op. cit., pp. 309–10; Roon, pp. 316–17; Lindgren, pp. 281–2. The assertion by Christian Müller (*Oberst i.G. Stauffenberg*, p. 415) that 'practically nothing can be learned any more about this trip' was based on Sykes (pp. 425–6) who had first made this incorrect assertion which is now disproved by Lindgren's article. According to a report by Schulze-Gaevernitz to Roon, (pp. 311–12 Note 29) Trott came to Switzerland again in June and met Gaevernitz but this is reported nowhere else.

25 See Lindgren, p. 281.

26 Trott's memorandum in Lindgren, pp. 290–1. Since 'these men' *cooperated* with the other groups listed, they cannot have been identical with them; Trott must have been referring to the Kreisau Circle or to the Beck-Goerdeler group. The 'militant type of opposition in Germany' that hoped to gain effective control in Germany and 'on whose behalf this statement has been written' by Trott relied 'on the unreserved cooperation of certain senior personalities in the *Oberkommando*, certain leading elements in the uncorrupted sections of the *Ordnungspolizei* and the municipal police authorities of several of the larger cities, and certain militant groups formerly belonging to the Social Democratic Party, Reichbanner [sic], Trade Union movement etc.'.

27 Roon (p. 317) seems to have no knowledge of these contacts, Rothfels (p. 309) mentions them quoting source. See also Theodor Steltzer: *Sechzig Jahre Zeitgenosse*, p. 158.

28 Cf. *Foreign Relations*, pp. 510 Note 90, 537–40, 571–2.

29 Ibid., pp. 510–11; cf. above, p. 230; Rothfels, op. cit., p. 309; Lindgren, p. 282. Trott told the *Gestapo* and the People's Court that his report to Stauffenberg had been that the Western Powers would not think of negotiations now that victory was near; military retreat, Trott said he stated, was not a good basis for peace negotiations, rather, 'the precondition for any peace was the convincing stabilization of our military resistance', *Spiegelbild*, p. 111; Urteil des Volksgerichtshofes vom 15. August 1944 gegen B. Klamroth [et al.], NA, microcopy T-120 roll 1038. It seems clear that Trott tried to defend himself with these statements, especially since he emphasizes that contrary to himself, Stauffenberg was in a constant last-minute-panic mood. See also *Spiegelbild*, p. 101 where Hansen seems to have given Trott's statement correctly: 'that there was willingness to negotiate on the enemy's side as soon as the precondition was created, namely a complete change of regime [in Germany]'. In a later interroga-

tion ('Trott now admits ...', *Spiegelbild,* p. 175) Trott reported that Stauffenberg had recommended common action by Germany and the Western Powers against the Soviet Union. For speculation on Russian peace feelers including a vague hint that contacts between the underground Communist Party in Germany and the conspiracy may have been connected with the peace feelers, see Vojtech Mastny: 'Stalin and the Prospects of a Separate Peace in World War II', *AHR* 77 (1972), pp. 1365–88, esp. 1382.

30 Gerhard Ritter: 'Lessons of the German Resistance' in *Wiener Library Bulletin* 9 (1955) Nos 1–2, p. 4; Mother Mary Alice Gallin: *Ethical and Religious Factors in the German Resistance to Hitler,* p. 132. Roon, op. cit., pp. 149, 317; Eberhard Zeller: *The Flame of Freedom,* p. 112.

CHAPTER 25

1 Hans Bernd Gisevius: *To the Bitter End,* pp. 377–8. Not 'Frazer' as in Gisevius; not 'Frazer, George', as in Gerhard Ritter: *Carl Goerdeler und die deutsche Widerstandsbewegung,* p. 242; see *Who's Who in America,* Vol. 18, 1934–1935.

2 Gisevius: *Bis zum bittern Ende* (1954 ed. in one vol.) p. 474; Gisevius verbally to the author 8 September 1972.

3 Gisevius, *Bitter End,* pp. 451–34; cf. *Spiegelbild einer Verschwörung,* p. 503. Willem A. Visser't Hooft: *Die Welt war meine Gemeinde,* pp. 195, 228–233.

4 Gisevius, *Ende* (1954 ed.), pp. 489–90; Allen Welsh Dulles: *Germany's Underground,* p. 128; cf. *Spiegelbild,* pp. 248, 364, 503–4, 506.

5 Gisevius, op. cit., p. 490.

6 Gisevius, op. cit., p. 689; Dulles, p. 136. Shortly before his death in January 1974 Gisevius wrote to the author (the letter was mailed on 4 March 1974 by Gisevius' son) denying emphatically that he said some of the things Dulles reported he had said; the revolution Gisevius referred to, he said in his letter, was meant to be along the lines developed by Rauschning in his books, *not* a Bolshevik revolution; he had not advocated, Gisevius said further, a continuation of the war in the east.

7 Gisevius, op. cit., p. 535. Dulles (p. 133) states: 'Gisevius often took the same general line as Trott, but he was also realistic enough to accept my word for it that there could be no question of Germany surrendering to the West alone. Once convinced, he used his influence with his friends in Berlin to persuade them that it was 'one' war and that there would be 'one' peace – with the West *and* East.' Gisevius (op. cit., pp. 523–5) does not contradict this, but he does not express his recollections as directly as Dulles; nor did he act entirely as his conviction would have dictated. Although Gisevius did, as Dulles reports, often take the same general line as Trott, Gisevius (op. cit., p. 535) describes Trott as 'eastward-oriented' because Trott pointed out to Dulles the danger of a German tendency to ally with the East if there were no positive reaction from the West to overtures from the opposition.

8 Dulles, p. 133; *Foreign Relations of the United States: Diplomatic Papers, 1944,* Vol. I, pp. 510–13.

9 Gisevius, op. cit., pp. 523–5; Dulles, pp. 135–6.

10 Dulles, p. 133; Ulrich von Hassell, *The von Hassell Diaries,* p. 253.

11 See below, pp. 237–8.

12 Gisevius' polemics against John in Gisevius, op. cit., pp. 529–31. Dulles (p. 133) says Gisevius, 'once convinced', used his influence with his friends in Berlin to persuade them of the Allied position. But Dulles and Gisevius both report that Gisevius and Waetjen advanced the idea of German surrender to the West alone as late as April 1944: Dulles, pp. 135–6; Gisevius, op. cit., p. 524 where Gisevius (*To the Bitter End,* p. 482) expressly differentiates between Waetjen and himself on the one hand and his friends in Berlin on the other: 'To a large extent Anglo-American policy was governed by the fear that any unilateral conversations with

the German Opposition might ultimately lead, through maladroitness, indiscretion, or deliberate intent, to an agreement between the Nazis and the Bolshevists. From our conversations with Dulles, Waetjen and I were more aware of this than were our friends in Berlin. Consequently, we decided to lay our cards on the table.

'We informed the Allied representative that the German *fronde* was now going to attempt assassination, and we gave him details about the generals and civilians who were ready to strike at the Nazis. We also discussed earnestly the demand, raised by so many Allied statesmen, that this time all Germany must be occupied by the Allied Powers.' The next sentences in the English edition only imply that Gisevius and Waetjen tried to argue for an armistice to be negotiated with the opposition; in the German edition (1954 ed., p. 524), the sentence following the second but last one quoted verbatim above reads as follows (my translation): 'Moreover, we tried to advance the thought how under certain circumstances a surrender in the East could be avoided at least during the stage of preliminary talks [between the Western Allies and the opposition].' This is confirmed in detail by Dulles's reports to his superiors, printed in *Underground*, pp. 135–66, and in *Foreign Relations*, pp. 510–13; see also the reports cited in note 20, below. Thus it is clear that Gisevius himself pursued ideas down to the eve of the revolt that he later denounced as illusory when he attributed them to others.

13 Gisevius, verbally to the author 8 September 1972; Hassell, op. cit., pp. 223–4. See below, pp. 295–6. Dulles (*Underground*, p. 148) states: 'I first had the story of Langbehn's encounters with the Gestapo from Marie-Louise Sarre, daughter of a well-known German art historian and museum director and herself a sculptress.' And (p. 162): 'Langbehn's arrest, which ended the conversations with Himmler, came about in a curious way. In September 1943, he went to Switzerland, to sound out his Allied contacts on the idea of using Himmler to unhorse Hitler. A coded message sent by some Allied agency, neither American nor British, was deciphered by the Gestapo ...' (The term 'Gestapo' is used by Dulles to mean not only the secret political police but also the SD and other organizations subordinate to Himmler.) Schulze-Gaevernitz, Dulles's assistant, stated on 1 September 1964 during the trial of *SS-Obergruppenführer* Karl Wolff that Langbehn had informed him in 1943 of his contacts with Himmler; Bernt Richter, 'In der Götzendämmerung', typescript of radio broadcast, pp. 17–19. See also Walter Schellenberg, *The Schellenberg Memoirs*, p. 428, and *Foreign Relations*, pp. 485–6, 489 on Himmler's contacts in Stockholm in December 1943 'to clarify what was meant by the term "unconditional surrender".'

14 See H[ans] R[othfels]: 'Zwei aussenpolitische Memoranden der deutschen Opposition (Frühjahr 1942)' in *VfZ* 5 (1957), pp. 388–95.

15 See above, p. 219.

16 Henrik Lindgren: 'Adam von Trotts Reisen nach Schweden 1942–1944: Ein Beitrag zur Frage der Auslandsverbindungen des deutschen Widerstandes' in *VfZ* 18 (1970), p. 291.

17 *Spiegelbild*, pp. 364, 415, 499–500.

18 Gisevius, *Bitter End*, pp. 471–4; Hassell, op. cit., p. 285.

19 Gisevius, verbally to the author 8 September 1972, and Gisevius' pocket diary of 1944; cf. *Spiegelbild*, pp. 503–4; Hans Rothfels: *Die deutsche Opposition gegen Hitler*, p. 156; Ger van Roon: *Neuordnung im Widerstand*, pp. 308, 311–12; Mother Mary Alice Gallin: *Ethical and Religious Factors in the German Resistance to Hitler*, p. 129; Eugen Gerstenmaier: 'Der Kreisauer Kreis: zu dem Buch Gerrit van Roons "Neuordnung im Widerstand" ' in *VfZ* 15 (1967), p. 245; *Foreign Relations*, pp. 497–8.

20 *Foreign Relations*, pp. 505–7, 510–13; OSS Research and Analysis Branch Summary L 39970 of 18 July 1944 and L 39971 of 22 July 1944, NA, Record Group 226 (these reports repeat information given in an earlier report dated 12 April 1944

and specifically referred to); Dulles, op. cit., p. 135–6; Gisevius, *Bitter End*, pp. 477–8. According to Dulles, Gisevius and Waetjen handed over a written declaration.

21 OSS R & A Branch Summary L 39971 of 22 July 1944 (reporting contents of report dated 12 April 1944). In *Spiegelbild,* p. 248 one finds the claim (by Strünck, Hansen or Goerdeler?) that 'all soundings in Switzerland had indicated that negotiations with Britain were possible'. Gisevius can hardly have maintained this (so that Strünck, Hansen, Goerdeler or someone else might have repeated it); it appears to be one of the many statements made in order to suggest that a negotiated end of the war was still possible – perhaps with the help of the conspirators.

22 *Foreign Relations*, p. 512; OSS R and A Branch Summary L 39971 of 22 July 1944 (reproducing contents of report dated 16 May 1944); Dulles, p. 139; Gisevius, *Ende* (1954 ed.), p. 527. According to [Julius Leber]: *Ein Mann geht seinen Weg*, p. 286, Stauffenberg and Leber were discussing at this time a plan to lead the military forces of the Western Allies through the minefields in order to avoid German collapse in the east, but gave up this plan as unrealistic.

23 Preparations appear in fact to have been made; Bruno Grosser to author 18 July 1964.

24 See note 22.

25 Gisevius, op. cit., p. 547.

26 Ibid.; *Foreign Relations*, p. 513; Dulles, p. 139. Christian Müller in his *Oberst i.G. Stauffenberg*, pp. 435, 439, seems to give more credence to the *Gestapo* reports than to those of Gisevius and Dulles. Only *Spiegelbild*, pp. 248, 364 (based on Strünck's and Hansen's testimony) contains any evidence that, as Müller alleges, Gisevius gave Beck hopes for negotiations; but Müller does not discuss the possibility that certain prisoners of the *Gestapo* may have suggested a liquidation of the war in the west, perhaps with their help, partly to save their own lives by indicating that they might be instrumental in the negotiations.

27 Gisevius, op. cit., p. 547; *Foreign Relations*, p. 513; Dulles, p. 139.

28 OSS R and A Branch Summary L 39971 of 22 July 1944 (reproducing contents of reports dated 12 and 18 July 1944), and OSS R and A Branch Summary L 39970 of 18 July 1944 (based on Dulles's cables from Berne dated 13 and 15 July 1944 – 'Breakers Cables Nos 4110–4114 and 4111–12'), NA, Record Group 226; Dulles, *Underground*, pp. 139–40; Gisevius, op. cit., p. 547.

29 Thus, the idea of cooperation with the Western Allies against the Russians seems to have been abandoned – contrary to C. Müller, p. 451 who this time prefers Trott's statements (which must be considered in the same light as those of Strünck and Hansen; cf. note 26) to the *Gestapo* to those of Gisevius and Dulles.

CHAPTER 26

1 Theodor Steltzer: *Von deutscher Politik*, pp. 80–1 with a reproduction of the memorandum on pp. 81–96; it is also to be found in Steltzer: *Sechzig Jahre*, pp. 285–97; see also Ger van Roon: *Neuordnung im Widerstand*, pp. 328–9. During the war Steltzer was Transport Officer at the headquarters of C-in-C Norway in Oslo – see *Sechzig Jahre*, pp. 120–48 and Roon, pp. 139, 324.

2 Ulrich von Hassell: *The von Hassell Diaries*, p. 295; Gerhard Ritter: *Carl Goerdeler und die deutsche Widerstandsbewegung*, pp. 337–8 (*The German Resistance*, p. 225).

3 William J. Donovan to President Roosevelt 20 March 1944, Franklin D. Roosevelt Library, PSF Safe File Box 4.

4 Walter Baum: 'Marine, Nationalsozialismus und Widerstand', *VfZ* 11 (1963), p. 30; Ritter (pp. 396, 550 Note 104) says 'There are reasons to suppose . . .' that

Captain Hermann Kaiser told the *Gestapo* that Stauffenberg had two contacts to the Allies – *Spiegelbild einer Verschwörung*, p. 126.
5 *Spiegelbild*, p. 175 – there printed in italics.
6 Probably Gottfried Graf von Bismarck-Schönhausen, Government Representative [*Regierungspräsident*] in Potsdam, as Ritter thinks (p. 550 Note 104); see also *Spiegelbild*, pp. 247–8 and index.
7 It is incomprehensible why Goerdeler should have accused Bismarck of this. Bismarck was still alive and was later released – see *Volksgerichtshof-Prozesse zum 20 Juli 1944*, pp. 104–5. Graf Bismarck-Schönhausen died in 1955; Ritter apparently had not questioned him. Fabian von Schlabrendorff, who is related to the Bismarck family by marriage, thinks the whole affair improbable – letter to the author 30 May 1968. See also account by Lieutenant-General Speidel of a possible contact with Eisenhower's headquarters in the summer of 1944 through Colonel J. E. Smart, a prisoner of war who had been on Eisenhower's staff – Hans Speidel: *We defended Normandy*, p. 87 (in a letter to the author of 22 January 1969 Smart disputes Speidel's story). Frau Elisabeth Wagner, widow of the General and Deputy Chief of Staff, says that about a week before 20 July 1944 her husband said that 'they could now wait no longer for the outcome of negotiations with Eisenhower via the Sorbonne since it was high time to act' – Eduard Wagner: *Der Generalquartiermeister*, pp. 235–6; cf. Otto John: *Twice through the Lines*, pp. 138–9. Eberhard Zeller in *The Flame of Freedom*, pp. 269–70 refers, like Ritter, to Stauffenberg's alleged but unexplained contacts to Churchill and Eisenhower; cf. *Spiegelbild*, pp. 247–8, 506–7. Kramarz, Stauffenberg's biographer, contributes nothing on this important question and does not even refer to Ritter who had dealt with it in detail – see Joachim Kramarz: *Stauffenberg* (English translation), Chap. 19. Christian Müller in *Oberst i.G. Stauffenberg*, pp. 413–16 has equally failed to clear up this point and only considers a part of the sources cited above. The dubious quality of Trott's testimony before the *Gestapo* (cf. *Spiegelbild*, p. 507) must be pointed out again; it was the tenor of Trott's testimony to suggest to his interrogators ways of ending the war in the west while continuing it in the east. If it had been recognized that Trott might hold the key to such an arrangement, this might have saved his life.
8 Roon, *Neuordnung*, pp. 323–44, 'Oberst Wilhelm Staehle' in *VfZ* 14 (1966), pp. 209–23 and *Wilhelm Staehle*, passim; Albrecht Kessel's report of July 1944 in *Foreign Relations of the United States. Diplomatic Papers, 1944*, Vol. I, p. 536.
9 Roon, *Neuordnung*, pp. 323–4.
10 Ibid., pp. 326–7.
11 Ibid., pp. 338–9, based on the account of one of Moltke's Danish contacts written in 1962; Alfred Joachim Fischer: 'Retter der dänischen Juden: Einen Massenmord auf Führerbefehl verhindert' *Stuttgarter Zeitung*, 20 April 1970, p. 3; Leni Yahil: *The Rescue of Danish Jewry*, esp. pp. 187, 239.
12 Roon, op. cit., pp. 329–34.
13 Roon, 'Staehle', pp. 209–23.
14 *Spiegelbild*, p. 363; verbally from Hermann Reinecke to the author, 30 April 1965.

CHAPTER 27

1 Gerhard Ritter: *Carl Goerdeler und die deutsche Widerstandsbewegung*, p. 376 (*The German Resistance*, p. 257).
2 Ibid., p. 379 (260). See also *Foreign Relations of the United States: Diplomatic Papers, The Conferences at Malta and Yalta 1945*.
3 Cf. above, pp. 235–9 and below, pp. 362–4.

4 Ibid., p. 381 based on Hans Bernd Gisevius: *To the bitter End*, pp. 478–84 and *Bis zum bittern Ende*, edition, pp. 446–8, 457–64; also on Allen Dulles: *Germany's Underground*, pp. 81 et seq., 169–70 (the latter largely based on reports from Gisevius). See also certain more or less fanciful stories such as Karl Michel: 'Stauffenberg: Der neue Dynamismus' in *Die Tat* (Zurich), 25 November 1946 and *Ost und West*. More recently there appeared Kurt Finker: *Stauffenberg und der 20. Juli 1944* – see in particular pp. 184–218. (second ed. pp. 189–90, 198). Quoting statements by Goerdeler, Gisevius and Dulles, Finker tries to prove that Stauffenberg: (a) was politically inclined towards the Left and the East and (b) tried to contact the National Free Germany Committee and did establish an indirect contact. Finker's evidence, however, is questionable and inconclusive. Stauffenberg's alleged friendship with Moltke for instance, and with Yorck, Trott, F. D. Graf von der Schulenberg, Leber, Leuschner, Maass and Reichwein reveals little about Stauffenberg's political concepts. The famous 'oath' (see Finker, 2nd ed., p. 219, and below, p. 321 in no way leads to conclusion that Stauffenberg had left-wing and socialistic leanings of any sort. Gisevius, who makes no secret of his own conservatism, considers Stauffenberg as having moved far to the left (Hans Bernd Gisevius: *To the Bitter End*, pp. 497–8); his evidence is not conclusive, and he can hardly be considered objective and impartial in his judgement of Stauffenberg, yet Finker relies on him heavily. There are certain contradictions in Gisevius' portrayal of Stauffenberg as 'eastward leaning', see below, p. 606. What is to Finker's mind (second ed., pp. 220–1) proof 'that Stauffenberg and his friends, in sharp contrast with Goerdeler and Beck, favoured an immediate end of the war on *all* fronts' (italics mine) emerges as equally inconclusive under scrutiny; the *Gestapo* report cited by Finker (*Spiegelbild einer Verschwörung*, pp. 101–2), giving results of an interrogation of Colonel Hansen, never mentions any opinion by Stauffenberg on the issue, but only that Trott had advocated negotiations with both sides (east and west). This does not invalidate the idea which Finker seeks to exclude from what must be considered Stauffenberg's concepts, i.e. to open the front in the west but to defend it in the east. At the beginning of 1944 Stauffenberg told his friend Colonel Peter Sauerbruch that he was in favour of throwing reserves into the eastern front (*Spiegelbild*, p. 402); this is confirmed as Stauffenberg's position for a time somewhat later but still before the invasion of Normandy by Allied forces, in [Julius Leber]: *Ein Mann geht seinen Weg*, p. 286: 'As a matter of fact it was Stauffenberg particularly who shortly before the Western Allied invasion [of Normandy] raised with Leber the question whether it would not serve German interests to enable the Western Allies to pass through the German minefields in order thus to prevent the collapse of the eastern front. Both agreed, however, that this idea was unrealistic, and it was not pursued thereafter.' On the other hand, a good deal of scepticism is appropriate in evaluating Trott's statement to the *Gestapo* that Stauffenberg had believed it possible to march against the Soviet Union together with Britain (*Spiegelbild*, pp. 175, 367, 402; cf. above, p. 599, Note 20). According to Hansen, Trott favoured negotiations with both East and West, *Spiegelbild*, p. 101.

Finker's tortuous attempts to prove Stauffenberg's alleged tendency towards contacts with the National Free Germany Committee (second ed., pp. 237–8) are equally unconvincing. Finker justifiably terms a certain *Gestapo* report a dubious source, but then he cites a propaganda directive of the NSDAP as an indication that Stauffenberg could have contacts with the NKFD, and he declares it a fact that Stauffenberg's widow, Nina Gräfin von Stauffenberg, had stated that 'the people in the resistance viewed this group (the NKFD – K.F.) with interest.' He further cites Nina Gräfin von Stauffenberg's statement to him that Stauffenberg 'on one of his visits brought with him to Bamberg a few issues of the paper *Freies Deutschland*' (the organ of the NKFD, produced in Russia).

Nina Gräfin von Stauffenberg did not tell Finker *verbatim* what she told the author on 23 August 1969, confirmed on 14 May 1970 and a letter to the author of 19 January 1973: That Stauffenberg expressly rejected the idea of cooperation with the NKFD; and that, when he brought home those issues of *Freies Deutschland*, his comment had been: 'What I am doing is high treason [Hochverrat]. But what these are doing, that is treason [Landesverrat].' Gräfin Stauffenberg added, however, that she left no room for doubt in her conversation with Finker that Stauffenberg did not want to cooperate with the NKFD; letter to the author 19 January 1973. See also Stauffenberg's remark that he did not think much of proclamations from behind barbed wire (*Spiegelbild*, p. 507). The proclamations of the NKFD, of course, were made from POW camps in Soviet Russia (cf. Bodo Scheurig, *Free Germany*, passim.). Finker's assertions about Stauffenberg's political leanings are thus clearly untenable. His case is not helped, it might be added, by his personal attacks on western fellow historians.

Christian Müller says in *Oberst i.G. Stauffenberg* (p. 451) that Stauffenberg had proposed on 16 July 1944 a military 'western solution' and a common front with the Western Allies against the Soviet Union, but Müller half retracts this again at the same time and does not decide for himself whether Stauffenberg actually wanted this sort of arrangement or not. Müller cites *Spiegelbild*, pp. 56–7, 91–2, 101–2, 136, 175, but only pp. 101 and 175 are relevant to the issue under examination. On p. 101, Hansen is quoted as having said that in the discussion someone whom he does not name had advocated negotiations with the enemies in the west as well as with those in the east; on p. 175 Trott is quoted as having said that Stauffenberg had believed, in contrast with his, Trott's, opinion, that the Western Powers would negotiate with the opposition and possibly combine forces with Germany against the East in order to prevent a further advance of the Soviet Union in Europe. The alleged hope of combined military operations against the Soviet Union is thus based only on Trott's statements, whose possible motivation has been pointed out on p. 604 Note 7. Trott incidentally took the position on other occasions during his interrogations that military efforts should be intensified, and that the fighting in the west should be ended in order to bring the struggle in the east to a successful conclusion (*Spiegelbild*, p. 111); again, it cannot be ruled out that Trott hoped to show to his interrogators, ultimately Himmler, a way out of the war that they might take – with the help of the opposition, and after a change of regime involving at least the removal of Hitler. Müller fails to discuss or resolve these points or the contradictions in Trott's testimony; nor does Müller consider a remark attributed to Stauffenberg in *Spiegelbild*, p. 266 that, if things did not change in the east, the war was lost and it was necessary to try and start negotiations with the Russians. Of course, all of these statements are of doubtful reliability not only because they contain special pleading by the accused who were trying to save their lives and, in many cases, their cause, but also because certain *Gestapo* officials may have agreed with the accused and coloured their reports accordingly. The other principal source on Stauffenberg's position is Gisevius (*Bitter End*, pp. 503–4); but Gisevius is not conclusive either, simply because in his conversation with Stauffenberg on the subject, on 12 July 1944, Stauffenberg refused to take an unequivocal stand. Gisevius wrote his account only a few months after the events, still before the end of the war; his reliability in reporting events he witnessed is frequently impressive (although innuendoes often unmistakably indicate what he likes and dislikes) and he admits candidly that he was unable to elicit from Stauffenberg an unequivocal statement. According to Gisevius' report Stauffenberg said that the decision in the East had already been reached and all political activity had to be directed toward the East; it was too late for the West, and Gisevius was a hopeless 'Westerner'. But after his statements, Stauffenberg kept saying that he had really not decided the point in question in his own mind and was playing the role of an *advocatus diaboli*. Gisevius, however, professes to have been convinced even then that Stauffenberg had in fact made up his mind, and that his choice was to try and cooperate with the East; this conclusion by Gisevius is admittedly not confirmed by any clear statement from Stauffenberg, but based on impression and intuition.

5 For details on this point and on Russian volunteers fighting on the German side in so far as Stauffenberg was concerned with them see Joachim Kramarz: *Stauffenberg* (English translation), Chapter X.

6 Verbally from Nina Gräfin von Stauffenberg to the author, 23 August 1969.

7 See p. 234 above.

8 Ritter, *Goerdeler*, pp. 382, 546 Note 74 (*Resistance*, p. 265 and Note 1).

9 Hans Rothfels: *The German Opposition*, pp. 146–9.

10 Gisevius, *Bitter End*, p. 481 (incorrectly giving 'April 1943' instead of 'April 1944') and *Bis zum bittern Ende*, Vol. II, p. 278.

11 Ritter, *Goerdeler*, p. 547 Note 76.

12 Ibid., pp. 385–6 (*Resistance*, p. 266).

13 Ulrich von Hassell: *The von Hassell Diaries*, p. 283.

14 See p. 233 above.

15 *Spiegelbild*, p. 308.

16 Ibid.; Ritter, *Goerdeler*, pp. 386–8 (*Resistance*, p. 267); confirmation in Edgar Röhricht: *Pflicht und Gewissen*, pp. 206–7 – reporting a conversation with Tresckow in January 1944 when he pleaded for serious consideration of an understanding with the East since clearly nothing could be expected from the West and Russia was obviously going to be the victor of the war on the continent.

17 Otto John: *Twice through the Lines*, p. 139.

18 Ritter, *Goerdeler*, pp. 386–9 (*Resistance*, pp. 259–63) on this point and below; see Peter Kleist: *Zwischen Hitler und Stalin 1939 bis 1945*, pp. 239–80.

19 William J. Donovan to President Roosevelt 20 March 1944, FDR Library, Hyde Park, N.Y. Safe File Box 4.

20 The *Gestapo* also reached this conclusion – *Spiegelbild*, pp. 492–5, 502–8.

CHAPTER 28

1 Annedore Leber: *Conscience in Revolt*, pp. 149–51; generally below see: Otto John: 'Some Facts and Aspects of the Plot against Hitler', typescript, London 1948, pp. 41–7 and 'Zum Jahrestag der Verschwörung gegen Hitler – 20 Juli 1944' in *Wochenpost* (newssheet for prisoners of war in Britain) No 138 of 18 July 1947, pp. 4–6; John's reports on his trips to Spain in February and March 1944 – copies in papers of Dr Walter Bauer of Fulda (partly printed in Otto John, *Twice through the Lines*, pp. 317–20) report by Allen Dulles from Berne, end January, in *Foreign Relations of the United States: Diplomatic Papers, 1944*, Vol. I, pp. 496–8; Anklageschrift (case for prosecution) of 20 December 1944 against Dr Klaus Bonhoeffer, Dr Rüdiger Schleicher, Dr Hans John, Friedrich Justus Perels and Dr Hans Kloss – copy in possession of Stiftung 'Hilfswerk 20. Juli 1944'. See also Gert Buchheit: *Der deutsche Geheimdienst*, pp. 427–37.

2 On this point and below see Otto John: *Twice*, pp. 79–83, 95–100.

3 Ibid., pp. 317–21 (for reports); see also p. 141.

4 Dulles' Report in *Foreign Relations*, p. 498; John, 'Facts', pp. 44–5 and 'Zum Jahrestag', p. 5.

5 Buchheit, p. 427 based on Albert Wedemeyer: *Der verwaltete Krieg*, pp. 470–1 and Franz von Papen: *Memoirs*, pp. 499–500. See also p. 598, note 8 above.

6 On this point and below see: John 'Zum Jahrestag', p. 5, 'Facts', pp. 41–7, 'Am achten Jahrestag der Verschwörung' in *Das Parlament*, '20 July' special edition, 1952. A somewhat different version of John's report on 20 July is given in

Heinrich Fraenkel and Roger Manvell: *Der 20. Juli*, pp. 227–30 (not in English version); see also John, *Twice*, pp. 142–3; Joachim Kramarz: *Stauffenberg* (English translation), pp. 164–6. Kramarz refers to Stauffenberg's optimism about the possibilities of negotiation following a *coup* and to the contact which he believed he had established to Eisenhower's headquarters but he does not say through whom this contact was made. See also *Spiegelbild einer Verschwörung*, pp. 126–7, 249, 367, 505, 507.

7 In addition to the sources referred to in Note 6 above see also Gerhard Ritter: *Carl Goerdeler und die deutsche Widerstandsbewegung*, pp. 395–6 (*Resistance*, p. 274) who follows John W. Wheeler-Bennett in *The Nemesis of Power*, p. 626 who equally has his information from John.

8 Eberhard Zeller, *The Flame of Freedom*, pp. 287–8.

9 John: *Twice*, p. 144; see also p. 248 below.

10 In John's account in 'Zum Jahrestag', p. 5, these views are attributed to Hansen who however was apparently recounting them as those of Stauffenberg; in John's account as given in Fraenkel and Manvell, *The July Plot*, pp. 253–8, they are attributed to Stauffenberg, as they are by John himself in *Twice*, p. 144.

11 John: *Twice*, pp. 143–4, Kramarz (p. 169) says that Stauffenberg discussed with Leber whether, to avoid enormous casualties, it would not be best to lead the Allies through the German minefields after their landing and so postpone the collapse of the eastern front. Kramarz does not say that Leber and Stauffenberg themselves reached the conclusion that the idea was unrealistic – see [Julius Leber]: *Ein Mann geht seinen Weg*, p. 286.

According to Kramarz (pp. 166–7, 174) towards the end of May Stauffenberg commissioned Captain Kaiser, his liaison officer to Goerdeler and War Diary Officer on the staff of C-in-C Replacement Army, to draft a list of German requirements for negotiations with the Allied Supreme Command. Ritter, *Goerdeler*, pp. 550–1 Note 104 and Zeller, pp. 340–1 also ascribe the programme to Stauffenberg and this is repeated by the editors of *20. Juli 1944* (Bonn 1961), pp. 94–5. Kramarz, however, did not make a critical examination of the origin or content of the list; he did not use the source material in reports of legal proceedings and opinions kept in the Bundesarchiv but not printed in *Spiegelbild*. Christian Müller (*Oberst i.G. Stauffenberg*, p. 582 note 108) cites the first edition of the author's present work, published in 1969 and says that 'in the literature that appeared so far this negotiation plan of Goerdeler has been attributed to Stauffenberg throughout'. This is not so although in the first edition of the present work the author pointed out that the programme cannot have been Stauffenberg's but can only have been Goerdeler's. See below.

The following text is taken from the judgement of the People's Court at the trial of Kaiser on 17 January 1945 to be found in BA, EAP 105/30 (significant divergencies from that given in Spiegelbild, pp. 126–7, which Kramarz used as his source, are given in square brackets):

'1 Immediate cessation of air warfare.

2 Abandonment of enemy plans for invasion [the word 'enemy' is missing in *Spiegelbild*].

3 Avoidance of further bloodshed.

4 Preservation of a continuing defensive capability in the East after [the word 'after' does not appear in *Spiegelbild* – there is a comma instead] evacuation of all occupied territories in the North, West and South [*Spiegelbild* only gives 'West and South'].

5 No occupation of Germany.

6 A free government with its own self-chosen constitution [*Spiegelbild* says 'a free government, an independent self-chosen constitution'].

7 Complete cooperation in drawing up [*Spiegelbild* – 'in fulfilling'] the armistice conditions and [*Spiegelbild* has a comma instead of 'and'] in the

preparation and [*Spiegelbild* has 'of the' instead of 'and'] fashioning of the peace.

8 Guarantee of the 1914 *Reich* frontiers in the East; preservation of the Alps, Danube and Sudeten Regions [*Gaue*] and autonomy for Alsace-Lorraine [*Spiegelbild* says 'the 1914 Reich frontiers in the East, maintenance of Austria and the Sudetenland within the *Reich*, autonomy for Alsace-Lorraine, acquisition of the Tyrol as far as Bolzano, Merano'].

9 Energetic reconstruction and German collaboration in the reconstruction of Europe.

10 Germany herself to deal with German criminals.

11 Re-establishment of German honour, self-respect and standing in the world.'

According to the *Gestapo* report in *Spiegelbild*, pp. 126–7 in which this programme is reproduced it was an aide-memoire drafted by Kaiser on 25 May 1944 'for Stauffenberg'. 'For Stauffenberg' does not necessarily mean 'at Stauffenberg's request' and the *Gestapo* report is dated 2 August when Goerdeler had not yet been arrested and interrogated. According to Freisler's detailed statement in passing sentence on Kaiser on 17 January 1945, however, Kaiser copied the programme into his diary on 25 May (a typing error '25.1.' is corrected later in the record of sentence) as 'a comparison of those points which, according to his traitorous ideas, favoured Stauffenberg's plan and had the temerity to present these as advantages stemming from this treachery . . .' (the programme is reproduced at this point in the judgement of the People's Court).

Stauffenberg's plan referred to was that for the *coup*, not this list of demands. There is nothing in it that necessarily or even probably leads to the conclusion that the points listed by Kaiser 'for Stauffenberg' represented Stauffenberg's own views; in the light of Kaiser's evidence at his trial this cannot be so; he said that 'all this was merely a copy of the contents of a letter which he had handed to Graf von Stauffenberg on behalf of Goerdeler'. At the time Goerdeler was still alive, though perhaps Kaiser did not know this for sure, but why should he incriminate Goerdeler instead of Stauffenberg who was certainly dead? Conversely the *Gestapo* can hardly have been interested in incriminating material against Goerdeler who had long since admitted everything and had been sentenced. They would not, therefore, have exerted any pressure on Kaiser *for this reason*. In fact at the time the list was intended to urge Stauffenberg to action. On 26 May 1944, the day after the entry in Kaiser's diary, a meeting took place in his office between Goerdeler and Stauffenberg, after which Goerdeler said to Kaiser that there was no need to hustle Stauffenberg; he had given his word of honour to act (sentence on Kaiser). Goerdeler's optimism is confirmed by Hans Bernd Gisevius (*To the Bitter End*, p. 499); as late as 12 July 1944 Goerdeler still thought that the Allies would not insist on unconditional surrender after an internal *coup*. According to a *Gestapo* report (*Spiegelbild*, p. 118) Leber declared himself in favour of giving up East Prussia, Alsace-Lorraine, the Sudeten area 'etc.' on 16 June 1944 in the Berlin hotel *Esplanade*; the 'other participants' in the conversation are said to have protested vigorously.

12 Hans Speidel: *We defended Normandy*, pp. 82–91.

13 In his note 'An Eyewitness's Account of the 20th July 1944 Plot Against Hitler That Failed', typescript, London 1946, pp. 1, 2, 10 John says: 'I had repeatedly tried to convince them [Stauffenberg and Hansen] that they must be prepared for 'Unconditional Surrender' in order to put an end to the war. They seemed to be unable to envisage it.' On the other hand in a note, probably written later, entitled 'Der 20. Juli 1944' (typescript, London undated [before 1952] p. 11) referring to the fact that he reproached himself after 20 July, he says: 'The fact remains that, consciously and deliberately, against my better judgement, I not only failed to destroy the illusions about the possibilities of a negotiated peace but actually kept them alive.' The contradiction is only partially explained if it is

assumed that this refers primarily to 'the generals' and that John thought that by describing contacts with the Western Powers as possible (he had after all established one) he was 'keeping alive' these illusions.

14 John, 'Account', p. 1 and *Twice*, p. 145.

15 Statements by Peter Graf Yorck von Wartenburg to the *Gestapo* and the People's Court in *Trial of the Major War Criminals before the International Military Tribunal*, Vol. XXXIII, p. 423. Cf. above, pp. 605–7, note 4.

16 Gisevius (pp. 502–3, 510–12). Hansen was clearly reading into Stauffenberg's question a far more far-reaching programme when he said to Gisevius on 13 July 1944 that Stauffenberg 'was imagining a joint victorious march of the German and Red armies against the plutocracies' – Gisevius, p. 510. On subsequent points see John, 'Account' and *Twice*, pp. 145–6.

NOTES/PART VI/CHAPTER 29

1 See above, ch. 6, 7, 10, and below, pp. 300, 366, 370–2 (Goerdeler and Moltke opposed to assassination). On the importance of the oath see also statements by *Heeresoberpfarrer* Lieut. Col. Chaplain Rudolf Damrath as a prisoner of war on 17 March 1945, NA, Record Group 226 (OSS records), OSS R and A Branch Summaries XL 8003. Damrath had been stationed in Paris and well acquainted with the major conspirators there.

2 Secret report dated 1 June 1933 from the *Reich* Public Prosecutor to the Minister of Justice and correspondence thereon between the Ministry of Justice and the *Reich* Chancellery – BA, R 43 II/1519; see also Max Domarus: *Hitler, Reden und Proklamationen 1932–1945*, pp. 216–17.

3 Dr Helmuth Mylius, written statement of 21 January 1969; cf. above, p. 31.

4 On this point and below see Günther Weisenborn: *Der lautlose Aufstand*, pp. 301–2 Note 4; Wolfgang Abendroth: 'Das Problem der Widerstandstätigkeit der "Schwarzen Front" ' in *VfZ* 8 (1960), p. 186; cf. Adolf Hitler: *Hitler's Table Talk*, p. 451; 'Helmut Hirsch' in *Schriften des Bundes deutscher Jungenschaften* 31, Bad Godesberg [1967], pp. 3–4, 8–9, 15–21, 26–9, 36–50, including comprehensive extracts from the judgement of the People's Court; [William E. Dodd]: *Ambassador Dodd's Diary 1933–1938*, pp. 402–4, 410–12, 414. Otto Dietrich in *The Hitler I Knew*, p. 168, says explicitly that only two attacks on Hitler were made, those of 8 November 1939 and 20 July 1944. Dietrich was Hitler's Chief Press Officer from 1933 to 1945. He is right in so far as only on these two occasions did explosions actually take place. Hitler, however, knew of other serious *attempts* – see Hitler, op. cit., p. 451.

5 Weisenborn, pp. 301–2; sentence of People's Court of 2 July 1940 against Karl Hoffmann, Erich Schulz, Willi Tosch and Alfred Jurzik, BDC; also files of People's Court and of Plötzensee Penitentiary with notation of executions in BDC.

6 Henry Picker: *Hitlers Tischgespräche im Führerhauptquartier 1941–1942*, p. 211 (not in English edition); Abendroth, p. 186; BA to the author 25 February 1969.

7 *Gestapo* Office in Oppeln to *Gestapo* headquarters (the *Gestapa*), Berlin, 5 March 1937 – copy in BA RG 1010/3183.

8 *Gestapo* Head Office Koblenz to district magistrates (among others), 5 April, 13 May, 3 June, 1 and 14 July 1938; SD Office Koblenz to out-stations 28 April 1938, BA, NS 29/vorl. 435.

9 SD Sub-Region Koblenz to out-stations, 1 September 1938 – BA, NS 29/vorl. 435.

10 *Der Spiegel* No 32, 4 August 1969, p. 18; Ewen Butler: 'I talked of plan to kill

Hitler', *The Times* 6 August 1969, p. 1. See also Peter Hoffmann: *Die Sicherheit des Diktators*, pp. 113–14.

11 Alhard Gelpke: 'Exposé Nr 2', typescript, May 1956, Hoover Library Ts Germany G 321; *The Times*, 5 February 1936, p. 12, 6 February 1936 p. 14, 7 February 1936 p. 13, 13 February 1936 p. 12, 10 December 1936 p. 13, 15 December 1936 p. 15. See also Emil Ludwig: *Der Mord in Davos*; Domarus, pp. 572–5.

12 Gelpke, op. cit.

13 Ibid.; 'Bericht Nr. 28' (on a table talk by Hitler on 6 September 1941), typescript, Führer's headquarters 7 September 1941, from Rosenberg's liaison officer with Hitler (not published) – BA R 6 o.Nr.; 'Führerinformation' from *Reich* Minister of Justice 7 September 1942 and 'Führerinformation' No 131 14 October 1942 – BA R 22/4089; report by Public Prosecutor of People's Court to *Reich* Minister of Justice, 3 October 1942 – BA R 22/3090; Dr Heinz Boberach (of BA) to the author 25 November 1968. Perhaps in his table talk of 3 May 1943 (Hitler, *Table Talk*, p. 451) Hitler was referring to Bavaud when he talked of a Swiss who had followed him around on the Berghof for three months and had ultimately been arrested owing to the alertness of a railway official. For details of Bavaud's efforts see Peter Hoffmann: 'Maurice Bavaud's Attempt to Assassinate Hitler in 1938' in *Police Forces in History*, ed. by George L. Mosse, pp.173–204.

14 See pp. 30–4 above.

15 Franz Sonderegger to President of District Court I, Munich, 14 January 1951, copy in IfZ; Rudolf Pechel: *Deutscher Widerstand*, pp. 82 4; Ernst Niekisch: *Gewagtes Leben*, pp. 155, 249–50; Fabian von Schlabrendorff: *Revolt against Hitler*, pp. 116–20; Eberhard Zeller: *The Flame of Freedom*, pp. 134–5; Weisenborn, pp. 99, 158–60; Harald Poelchau: *Die letzten Stunden*, pp. 96–9.

16 This passage and below are based primarily on Botho von Wussow: 'Einige Sätze zu dem SS-Bericht über den 20. Juli 1944 . . .' typed copy, 1947.

17 Albert Zoller: *Hitler privat*, p. 177; *Trial of the Major War Criminals before the International Military Tribunal*, Vol. XXVI, p. 339.

18 *Trial*, XXVI, p. 332.

19 Hitler, *Table Talk*, p. 452.

20 Ibid., p. 512.

21 Picker, *Tischgespräche*, p. 258.

22 Hitler, *Table Talk*, p. 453.

23 Picker, *Tischgespräche*, p. 258.

24 See the author's *Sicherheit*, passim, for an extensive treatment of this question.

CHAPTER 30

1 See pp. 91, 560–1, and Notes 92, 99, 101. It is not known whether or to what extent Nikolaus von Halem was involved in this attempt.

2 Hans-Adolf Jacobsen: *Fall Gelb*, p. 279 Note 4.

3 See pp. 93–6 above.

4 On this point and below see Erich Kordt: *Nicht aus den Akten*, pp. 370–6; Hans Bernd Gisevius: *To the Bitter End*, p. 429; record of conversation in Bonn on 26 September 1953 between Dr von Etzdorf and Dr H. Krausnick, IfZ ZS 322; Dr Hasso von Etzdorf verbally to the author on 24 August 1972; Consul Susanne Simonis to the author 8 March 1971; Friedrich Wilhelm Heinz to the author 8 March 1966; Erich Kosthorst: *Die deutsche Opposition gegen Hitler zwischen Polen- und Frankreichfeldzug*, pp. 87–8; Kurt Sendtner: 'Die deutsche Militäropposition im ersten Kriegsjahr' in *Vollmacht des Gewissens*, Vol. I, p. 412; Erwin Lahousen: 'Zur Vorgeschichte des Anschlages vom 20. Juli 1944', IfZ ZS 658.

5 Kordt, p. 371. On 11 November the attempt would probably have been rightly timed and not premature; had the order for the offensive on 12 November been issued, it could hardly have been cancelled.

6 Gisevius, pp. 383–4; Harold C. Deutsch: *The Conspiracy against Hitler in the Twilight War*, p. 225 – also applicable below.

7 Lahousen.

8 Kordt (p. 373) says that in conversation Oster hinted at the following possible sources of the explosive used by Elser: The *Abwehr* laboratory on the Quenz estate near Brandenburg run by Major Marguerre, Göring's 'research drug-store', the 'Himmler-Heydrich firm'. Lahousen also mentions a laboratory belonging to Section II of the *Abwehr* at Tegel.

9 [Erwin] Lahousen – 'Tagebuch (OKW-Abwehr Aug. 1939–[3 Aug. 1943])', NA microfilm OKW 2280, copy in IfZ (No 154/59), pp. 26–7. One can only speculate whether Lahousen was trying to cover himself by the entry in his diary or whether, given the circumstances, he issued this instruction on his own initiative and without his tongue in his cheek. In a sworn affidavit dated Seefeld/Tirol 1 July 1947 (copy provided by Mrs Lore Kordt) Lahousen wrote: 'Major Marguerre who was not in our [conspiratorial] group followed these regulations most accurately. It was therefore at the time not possible for me to carry out my mission without causing unwelcome attention whereby the undertaking would have been endangered.'

10 See Paul Leverkuehn: *Der geheime Nachrichtendienst der deutschen Wehrmacht im Kriege*, p. 32, where it is stated that, shortly after 8 November, Himmler in person accompanied by an aide paid an unexpected visit to the *Abewhr* laboratory in Tegel. Etzdorf told the author on 24 August 1972 that Oster, Canaris and Groscurth really did not want to go through with it any more and that Oster's and Groscurth's efforts to procure the explosives were not entirely serious. Perhaps they considered the chances of success small ('Kordt is not a Macedonian', as one of them put it), and perhaps they did not wish to endanger themselves and the cause for the sake of a rather unpromising effort.

11 See Johann Georg Elser: *Autobiographie eines Attentäters*. For further details based on wide-ranging research see Anton Hoch: 'Das Attentat auf Hitler im Münchner Bürgerbräukeller 1939' in *VfZ* 17 (1969), pp. 383–413; Peter Hoffmann: *Die Sicherheit des Diktators*, pp. 118–32. The following short account is also based on: files of the Munich *Gestapo*, BA RG 1010/3035; Franz Xaver Rieger and Waldemar Zipperer: 'Schilderung des Aufgriffs des Georg Elser . . .', 15 December 1939, in MFA W 01–6/301 (OKW 788); [Kurt Geissler]: 'Befragung über das Bürgerbräu-Attentat 1939' 19 December 1939, BA NS 20/65; *Völkischer Beobachter*, 7, 8, 9, 10 November 1939; Helmuth Groscurth: *Tagebücher eines Abwehroffiziers 1938–1940*, pp. 306–9; 'Bericht Nr. 28' by Rosenberg's liaison officer to the *Führer*'s headquarters for 6 September 1941, typescript, *Führer*'s headquarters 7 September 1941, BA R 6 Nr.; Friedrich Wilhelm Heinz: 'Von Wilhelm Canaris zur NKWD', typescript, (about 1949), NA Reel No R 60.67, pp. 117–19; Hans Baur: *Hitler's Pilot* pp. 104–7; Leverkuehn, p. 32; Walter Schellenberg: *The Schellenberg Memoirs*, pp. 90–5; Henry Picker: *Hitlers Tischgespräche, im Führerhauptquartier 1941–1942*, pp. 210, 306; Max Domarus: *Hitler: Reden und Proklamationen 1932–1945*, pp. 1404–16; Hans Bernd Gisevius: *Wo ist Nebe?*, pp. 195–200, 209–12, 214–15, based on information from Nebe; S. Payne Best: *The Venlo Incident* – reproduces between pp. 208 and 209 a letter from Heinrich Müller (head of Section IV (*Gestapo*) in the RSHA) to Commandant of Dachau concentration camp dated 5 April 1945; Nerin E. Gun: *The Day of the Americans*, pp. 113–15, 147–53; Hans Langemann: *Das Attentat*, pp. 292–6, based on a report by Kriminalrat Hans Lobbes who was then head of a group in the *Reichskriminalpolizeiamt*; verbal information to the author on 30 July 1968

from Dr Albert Widmann, a chemist of the RKPA Technical Institute who was involved in the investigation at the time.

12 Hoch, pp. 396–8, 404–5, 412; Oswald Bumke: *Erinnerungen und Betrachtungen*, p. 181; Heinz (Canaris, p. 118) says that Canaris told him and Oster on the afternoon of 8 November that the western offensive had definitely been ordered for the 12th and to raise popular enthusiasm, hitherto lacking, an assassination attempt (a train derailment or such like) had been planned. Hitler only decided to call off the offensive during the return journey to Berlin on the night 8/9 November. The date had already been postponed, however, on 7 November – see Chapter 10, p. 141. Hitler himself was still saying in 1942 that Otto Strasser was primarily responsible for the attack (Picker, pp. 210–11).

13 *Völkischer Beobachter*, 7 November 1939.

14 Ibid., 7, 8, 9, 10 November 1939.

15 Baur, pp. 104–5 'Bericht Nr 28' by Rosenberg's liaison officer (see Note 11 above); in this Hitler says that his escape was due 'solely to the fact that, owing to bad weather at the last moment, he refrained from using his aircraft and had left earlier by special train'. Baur's recollection is similar but he does not dramatise 'the last moment' and does not mention the special train. See *Kursbuch der Deutschen Reichsbahn* (German National Railway timetable), summer schedule 1939 (valid to 30 November that year), pp. 5, 7; railway head office Nuremberg to the author, 11 June 1970; Hoch, pp. 410–11 and Hoch to the author 8 June 1970 confirm that a special train was used. This still does not explain the abrupt ending of a normally long speech. According to Heinrich Hoffmann: *Hitler was my Friend*, p. 119, Hitler felt uneasy and left early for that reason.

16 According to Allen Dulles: *Germany's Underground*, p. 55, photographs of the ceremony show a *Gestapo* officer near Hitler with a watch in his hand. The simple explanation of this would be that Hitler did not wish to miss his special train, the departure time of which could not be altered at short notice owing to other traffic.

17 Rieger; Zipperer.

18 Best, reproduction between pp. 208 and 209; Hoch, p. 413.

19 [Georg] von Sodenstern: 'Zur Vorgeschichte des 20. Juli 1944', typescript 1947, NA Record Group 338 MS No B-499.

20 Eugen Gerstenmaier verbally to the author 17 August 1965 and 'Der Kreisauer Kreis: zu dem Buch Gerrit van Roons "Neuordnung im Widerstand" ' *VfZ* 15 (1967), p. 233 (in this Gerstenmaier dates the plan as 1942 whereas according to his verbal information it had been pursued ever since 1940 and was abandoned in 1942); Fabian von Schlabrendorff (ed.): *Eugen Gerstenmaier im Dritten Reich*, pp. 27, 31; Ger van Roon: *Neuordnung im Widerstand*, pp. 189–93; Albert Krebs: *Fritz-Dietlof Graf von der Schulenburg*, pp. 191–202.

21 Baur, pp. 114–15; Albert Speer: *Inside the Third Reich*, pp. 170–2; Domarus, p. 1534; *Kriegstagebuch des Oberkommandos der Wehrmacht (Wehrmacht-führungsstab), 1940–45*, Vol. IV, p. 1869; Picker, pp. 134, 480; [Franz] Halder: *Kriegstagebuch*, Vol. II, pp. 22, 24, 28. 'Kriegstagebuch' No 3: Führer-Hauptquartier 15. Feb. 1940 – 31. Juli 1940 (OKW/162, microcopy T-78 roll 351);Hoffmann, *Sicherheit*, pp. 157–8.

22 Schacht's evidence at hearing on Halder before Denazification Court in 'Protokoll aus der Verhandlung Halder [vor der] Spruchkammer X München', p. 124.

23 Graf von Waldersee to the author, 21 and 30 July 1965; Marianne Gräfin Schwerin von Schwanenfeld: 'Ulrich-Wilhelm Graf Schwerin von Schwanenfeld', typescript, undated; see also Rudolf Pechel: *Deutscher Widerstand*, p. 156.

24 Ulrich von Hassell: *The von Hassell Diaries*, pp. 153–4; Wolf Keilig: *Das deutsche Heer 1939–1945*, p. 211/333.

Notes

25 Gerhard Ritter: *Carl Goerdeler und die deutsche Widerstandsbewegung*, p. 274.
26 Graf von Waldersee thinks it possible that the troops were already on the move –
'K.T.B. 1.1.41–30.6.41, H.Gru.Kdo. D Ia' NA microcopy T-311, roll 12; see also
Halder, *Kriegstagebuch*, Vol. II, p. 389.
27 Waldersee and Schwerin (Note 23 above).
28 Achim Oster verbally to the author 26 May 1964; RSHA (Amt IV A 4a) express
letter, Berlin, 3 March 1942, EAP 173-e-10-12/90a, NA microcopy T-175 roll
490.
29 *SS-Gruppenführer* Heinrich Müller to *SS-Oberführer* Johann Rattenhuber and
Reichsführer-SS Heinrich Himmler, teleprint 7 May 1942, BA NS 19/421.

NOTES/PART VII/CHAPTER 31

1 Hermann Graml: 'Die deutsche Militäropposition vom Sommer 1940 bis zum
Frühjahr 1943' in *Vollmacht des Gewissens*, Vol. II, pp. 421–5; see pp. 147, 151
above.
2 See Heinrich Uhlig: 'Der verbrecherische Befehl' in *Vollmacht des Gewissens*,
Vol. II, pp. 287–410 and in particular pp. 304–5.
3 Copy of the Commissar Order in Hans-Adolf Jacobsen: 'The *Kommissarbefehl*
and Mass Executions of Soviet Russian Prisoners of War' in *Anatomy of the SS
State*, pp. 507–35 and in particular pp. 532–3.
4 Graml, op. cit., pp. 430–1; Uhlig, pp. 391–2.
5 Graml, op. cit., pp. 427, 429–31, 447; H[ans] R[othfels]: 'Ausgewählte Briefe von
Generalmajor Helmuth Stieff', *VfZ* 2 (1954), pp. 291–305.
6 *Guides to German Records Microfilmed in Alexandria, Va., No 52, Records of
German Field Commands: Army Groups (Part II)*, p. 45.
7 Not 'Chief of Staff, Army Group Centre' as, for instance, Joachim Kramarz calls
him in *Stauffenberg*, p. 133.
8 Eberhard Zeller: *The Flame of Freedom*, pp. 146–7; Bodo Scheurig: *Henning
von Tresckow*, pp. 16–26, 50–56 with some corrections of dates.
9 'Handliste der Generalstabsoffiziere 1943' (roll of General Staff officers 1943),
OKH/HPA Amtsgr. P 3, NA microcopy T-78 roll R 57. Zeller, pp. 147–8 gives
similar estimates.
10 Fabian von Schlabrendorff: *Revolt against Hitler*, p. 47.
11 Hitler's directive to Army Group Centre 20 December 1941 in Hans-Adolf
Jacobsen: *1939–1945*, pp. 286–7; cf. *Spiegelbild einer Verschwörung*, pp. 349,
378.
12 On this point and below see: Wolfgang Foerster: *Generaloberst Ludwig Beck*, p.
171 Note 96; Friedrich Hossbach: *Zwischen Wehrmacht und Hitler*, p. 195;
Schlabrendorff, op. cit., p. 58; 'Handliste' lists of General Staff officers arrested,
released and sentenced (1944–1945), OKH/HPA Ag P 3, BA EAP 105/2;
Spiegelbild, pp. 378–9; R. Chr. Frhr. v. Gersdorff; 'Bericht über meine
Beteiligung am aktiven Widerstand gegen Nationalsozialismus' typescript, 1963
[Erich] v. Manstein: 'Richtigstellung zur Darstellung der Haltung des Feld-
marschalls v. Manstein im Buch "Offiziere gegen Hitler"', typescript (about
1950), Otto John's papers, folio 4; information from the Foundation 'Hilfswerk
20. Juli 1944'; Philipp Freiherr von Boeselager verbally to the author 19
November 1964; Colonel Berndt von Kleist to the author 26 February 1965;
Zeller, pp. 150–5; Mrs Gisela von Voss (widow of Col. von Voss) to the author 22
January 1975. See also the author's 'The Attempt to Assassinate Hitler on March
21, 1943' in *Canadian Journal of History/Annales Canadiennes d'Histoire* II
(1967), pp. 67–83.
13 See '*Amt V* [of RSHA], Betrifft: Selbstmord des Majors Ulrich von Oertzen
. . .', typescript, Berlin 22 July 1944, BA R 58/1051; *Kriminaltechnisches Institut*

der *Sicherheitspolizei, Abteilung Chemie* 'Selbstmord des Majors Ulrich von Oertzen', typed copy, 23 July 1944, BA R 58/1051.

14 'Handliste'; Erich Herrlitz verbally to the author 14 January 1965; Johann Sinnhuber (commanding LXXXII Corps in 1944) to the author 27 January 1964.

15 Eberhard von Breitenbuch verbally to the author 8 September 1966.

16 Schlabrendorff, op. cit., p. 57.

17 Graml, op. cit., pp. 432–7.

18 Ibid., p. 432 which wrongly gives May; this is applicable only to issue of the order restricting powers under military law. See copy of the Commissar Order in *Anatomy of the SS State*, pp. 532–3.

19 Copy in Uhlig, pp. 388–91.

20 Rudolf-Christoph Freiherr von Gersdorff: Evidence to Military Court V in Case XII (United States versus Leeb and others), 16 April 1948, record pp. 2120–78, StA Nuremberg. Graml, op. cit., pp. 432 et seq. apparently quotes this evidence but without giving source and refers to another 'report' by Gersdorff. See also Gersdorff: 'Beitrag zur Geschichte des 20. Juli 1944', typescript, Oberursel 1946.

21 Graml, op. cit., p. 433.

22 Ibid., pp. 433–4; Gersdorff's evidence (Note 20 above), p. 2130.

23 Graml, op. cit., p. 434.

24 Gersdorff's evidence, pp. 2134–5; Hans Bernd Gisevius: *Wo ist Nebe?* pp. 240–6 based on information from Nebe who was head of an *Einsatzgruppe* for a time.

25 Graml, op. cit., p. 435.

26 Ibid., pp. 441–2; Gersdorff's evidence, pp. 2158–9; Gisevius, op. cit., pp. 240–6; Harold C. Deutsch: *The Conspiracy against Hitler in the Twilight War*, p. 123.

27 Gersdorff's evidence, pp. 2133–4.

28 Ibid., p. 2167; Schlabrendorff, op. cit., p. 64; Herrlitz; Graml, op. cit., pp. 441–2.

29 'Kriegstagebuch Nr. 1 (Band Dezember 1941) des Oberkommandos der Heeresgruppe Mitte' kept by Captain (Res) Petersen, Annex to p. 1943, report by Major Freiherr von Gersdorff 9 December 1941, copy in IfZ.

30 Graml, op. cit., p. 443.

31 Georg Thomas: 'Gedanken und Ereignisse' in *Schweizer Monatshefte* 25 (1945), pp. 543–4; Ulrich von Hassell: *The von Hassell Diaries*, p. 195; Graml, op. cit., p. 451 which indicates that, contrary to Schlabrendorff in *Offiziere gegen Hitler*, p. 67, Thomas did not discuss with General von Sodenstern, Chief of Staff, Army Group South.

32 Hassell, pp. 181, 184.

33 Lieutenant Oster to the *Gestapo, Spiegelbild*, p. 431; quoted in Graml, op. cit., p. 449.

34 Schlabrendorff, *Revolt*, p. 67.

35 Ibid. See Rudolf Pechel: *Deutscher Widerstand*, p. 155 who gives the date of these talks as end December 1941; according to Schlabrendorff, op. cit., p. 67 and Hassell, p. 199 it must have been mid-October. Schlabrendorff cannot at this time have received his instructions from Kluge as the editor of Hassell's diary thinks, but only from Tresckow.

36 [Franz] Halder: *Kriegstagebuch*, Vol. III, p. 390; Schlabrendorff, op. cit., p. 67; Hassell, p. 217.

37 Schlabrendorff, op. cit., p. 67.

38 Hassell, p. 199.

39 Ibid.

40 Ibid., pp. 200–1, 206–7.

41 Ibid., pp. 211–12; Halder, op. cit., pp. 354–6.

42 Hassell, pp. 214–17.

43 Ibid., p. 218.

44 Ibid., pp. 219–24; Wolf Keilig: *Das deutsche Heer 1939–1945*, p. 211/368; Halder, op. cit., p. 422.

45 Hassell, p. 223; Schlabrendorff, *Revolt*, pp. 68, 70.
46 Schlabrendorff, op. cit., p. 62.
47 Cf. Keilig, p. 211/168.
48 Schlabrendorff, op. cit., p. 65.
49 Ibid., p. 66; Hermann Kaiser (War Diary Officer on staff of C-in-C Replacement Army), diary 6 April 1943 in 'Generäle: Neue Mitteilungen zur Vorgeschichte des 20. Juli' in *Die Wandlung* I (1945/6), pp. 528–37; cf. Helmut Heiber (ed.): *Hitlers Lagebesprechungen*, p. 618; expenditure records, authorizations and correspondence regarding tax-free status with respect to gratuities for Kluge and other high-ranking personalities in BA R 43 II/985c (files of *Führer*'s Adjutant's Office).
50 Schlabrendorff, op. cit., p. 66.
51 Ibid., pp. 68–9; Gersdorff, 'Beitrag'.
52 Ibid., p. 72; Hassell, pp. 240–1, 247. Graml, op. cit., p. 464 gives the date as 'probably in October'.
53 Hassell, pp. 246–7; Gerhard Ritter: *Carl Goerdeler und die deutsche Widerstandsbewegung*, p. 358 (*The German Resistance*, p. 233).
54 Schlabrendorff, op. cit., p. 72.
55 Ludwig Kaiser: 'Ein Beitrag zur Geschichte der Staatsumwälzung vom 20. Juli 1944 (Goerdeler-Bewegung), Teilbericht', typescript, NA Record Group 338 MS No B-285; transcript of Hermann Kaiser's diary, prepared by Ludwig Kaiser, entry for 21 January 1943.
56 Schlabrendorff, op. cit., pp. 72, 90; H. Kaiser, diary 25 January 1943.
57 H. Kaiser, diary 6 and 19 February 1943.
58 Ibid.
59 Schlabrendorff, op. cit., p. 72.
60 The division of responsibilities between 'the field' and the centre under Oster was not so precise or clear as Schlabrendorff describes in *Offiziere gegen Hitler*, pp. 89–92.
61 Schlabrendorff, *Revolt*, pp. 75–6.
62 Gersdorff, 'Beitrag'.
63 See Stauffenberg's comments in Kramarz, p. 185 and those of Tresckow in Schlabrendorff, op. cit., p. 145; also Gersdorff to the author 23 January 1966 and Axel Freiherr von dem Bussche to the author 9 February 1966.
64 Bussche 9 February 1966.
65 Gersdorff, 'Beitrag', 'Bericht' and verbally to the author 25 May 1964 (henceforth referred to as 'Gersdorff 1').
66 On this point and below see: Gersdorff, 'Beitrag', 'Bericht', Gersdorff 1; verbally to the author 16 November 1964 (henceforth referred to as Gersdorff 2); Herrlitz; Lieutenant-Colonel Wilhelm Hotzel to the author August 1965; Schlabrendorff, op. cit., p. 80. The duties of these *Abwehr* detachments corresponded to those of the sections in the *Abwehr* office: *Abwehr I* was responsible for offensive espionage and was in charge of 'Front-line Reconnaissance Detachment' 103 (Enemy Intelligence) under Lieutenant-Colonel Erich Herrlitz; *Abwehr II* was responsible for Detachment 203 (Sabotage and Subversion) under Lieutenant-Colonel Wilhelm Hotzel and *Abwehr III* for Detachment 303 (Counter-espionage) under Lieutenant-Colonel Tarbuck. Apart from a short period when all three were concentrated under Colonel Dr Steffan, Lieutenant-Colonal Herrlitz, as the senior, reported for all three units to the Army Group Intelligence Officer.
67 Gersdorff, 'Beitrag'; *Spiegelbild*, p. 128. The source for some of the information about this explosive cannot be given as my informant is still working on secrecy-classified matters. For the most part I have been allowed to use and quote from official publications by the British Ministry of Defence (letter of 23 November 1964). Many details are to be found in *Field Engineering and Mine Warfare Pamphlet No 7 – Booby Traps*, London 1952, pp. 26–8.

68 See sketch in Appendix p. 741.
69 See *German Explosive Ordnance (Bombs, Fuses, Rockets, Land Mines, Grenades and Igniters)*, passim. Other types of explosives and igniters might have been used, however; there were standard explosive charges available weighing 100 and 200 grams, and they could be fitted with igniters for a delay of 4.5 seconds or for simultaneous ignition; if exploded near the chest, back, head or throat, they could be fatal. Information received from Colonel Witzig, Head of Special Staff ATV of Pioneer School of the [Federal] Army, letter to the author April 1973.
70 See sketch in Appendix p. 741.
71 Alexander von Pfuhlstein: 'Meine Tätigkeit als Mitglied der Berliner Verschwörerzentrale . . .', roneoed, Kreuzwertheim 1946 and '12 Abhandlungen über persönliche Erlebnisse', typescript, Kreuzwertheim 1946, IfZ ZS 592 [Erwin Lahousen]: 'Sidelights on the Development of the "20 July",' typescript (probably August 1945), NA Record Group 238, and 'Zur Vorgeschichte des Anschlages vom 20. Juli 1944', typescript, Munich 1953, IfZ ZS 652 and 'Tagebuch OKW-Abwehr Aug. 1939−[3 Aug. 1943]', NA OKW 2280; Friedrich Wilhelm Heinz: 'Von Wilhelm Canaris zur NKWD', (about 1949), NA microfilm reel No R 60.67; Paul Leverkuehn: *Der geheime Nachrichtendienst der deutschen Wehrmacht im Kriege*; Dr Johannes Erasmus (Operations Officer of the 'Brandenburg' Division in 1944) to the author 29 August 1965; *Spiegelbild*, pp. 370−1, 405−6; Gert Buchheit: *Der deutsche Geheimdienst*, pp. 307−29. On pp. 307−8 Buchheit considers that use of the 'Brandenburg' Division as a mobile force for the *coup* was impossible 'from the outset' and bases this opinion solely on Karl Heinz Abshagen: *Canaris*, p. 237 (not in English translation) who equally adduces no evidence. From 23 November 1942 to 17 February 1943 Hitler was at 'Wolfschanze' near Rastenburg, from 19 February to 13 March in 'Wehrwolf' near Vinnitsa, then in Berlin for a short time and then back in 'Wolfschanze' − *Kriegstagebuch des Oberkommandos der Wehrmacht (Wehrmachtführungsstab) 1940−1945*, Vol. III, pp. 136, 207; Heiber, pp. 143, 181, 498; Max Domarus: *Hitler: Reden und Proklamationen 1932−1945*, p. 2314; Hans Baur: *Hitler's Pilot*, pp. 136−7.
72 List of General Staff officers arrested, released and sentenced, BA EAP 105/2; Marianne Gräfin Schwerin von Schwanenfeld: 'Ulrich-Wilhelm Graf Schwerin von Schwanenfeld,' typescript, undated; Pfuhlstein, 'Tätigkeit'; Heinz, 'Canaris', pp. 149−151; Heinz to the author 8 March 1966; Heinz was serving in Serbia in April 1943, commanding IV Regiment, 'Brandenburg' Division.
73 Keilig, p. 211/250.
74 Heinz in 'Canaris', pp. 149−51, accuses Pfuhlstein of having 'betrayed' the division to Jodl and Warlimont and intrigued with them against Canaris. Heinz describes Pfuhlstein as highly ambitious. According to Heinz he gave preference to Nazis as his aides and appointed a fulltime Nazi functionary as Commander of No I Regiment. This is contradicted by Canaris who, on 1 November 1943, described Pfuhlstein as tireless in increasing the efficiency of his division and in conclusion requested that he be left in his appointment for the moment − 'Handliste' of Army Personnel Office for 1943, Group P 3.
75 Lahousen, 'Sidelights', p. 3; according to Lahousen Canaris had always thought that the unit could be used but Oster did not; Heinz to the author 8 March 1966. In their statements to the *Gestapo* neither Pfuhlstein nor Heinz referred to this point. They were of course saying as little as possible; they stressed the pessimism of Canaris and Oster and their conviction that a 'change' of leadership was necessary if there was to be a return to sensible military command arrangements; they said nothing, however, of a really incriminating nature about the activities of their superiors. *Spiegelbild*, pp. 370−1, 405−7.
76 On this point and below: Major Philipp Freiherr von Boeselager, verbal informa-

tion to the author 19 November 1964; files on formation of the 'Boeselager' Cavalry Regiment in the Boeselager family papers, Schloss Kreuzberg; Cord v. Hobe, Walter Görlitz: *Georg von Boeselager: Ein Reiterleben*, pp. 96–101; Schlabrendorff, op. cit., p. 79; Gersdorff, 'Beitrag'; Herrlitz.

77 Boeselager papers, file 10a; Ulrich Gigas (Lieutenant – Supply Officer to 'Cavalry Regiment Centre') to Philipp Frh. von Boeselager, 28 October 1969; Boeselager to the author 28 August 1969.

CHAPTER 32

1 See Hermann Kaiser, diary Jan.–Feb. 1943, passim.

2 Gerhard Ritter: *Carl Goerdeler und die deutsche Widerstandsbewegung*, p. 350; (*The German Resistance*, pp. 235–6).

3 Verbally from Major Philipp Freiherr von Boeselager to the author, 19 November 1964; Cord Hobe and Walter Görlitz: *Georg von Boeselager*, pp. 97–8; Fabian von Schlabrendorff: *Revolt Against Hitler*, p. 124; Colonel Berndt von Kleist to the author 26 February 1965; Walther Schmidt-Salzmann to the author 14 February 1966; Rudolf-Christoph Freiherr von Gersdorff: 'Beitrag zur Geschichte des 20. Juli 1944' and verbally to the author on 25 May 1964 (henceforth referred to as 'Gersdorff I'). According to Schlabrendorff, loc. cit., and letter to the author of 22 October 1966 the plan to shoot Hitler only originated after 13 March; sources in touch with Boeselager, however, state explicitly that the plan was considered before this date. Breitenbuch also says that the plan for a group attack was considered both in 1943 and 1944.

4 See Konrad Lorenz: *On Aggression*, p. 226; Dieter Ehlers: *Technik und Moral einer Verschwörung*, pp. 118–24.

5 R.Chr.Frh.v. Gersdorff verbally to the author 25 May 1964. Members of Hitler's immediate entourage deny that he protected himself in this way, most notably his valet, Heinz Linge, in a letter to the author of 15 April 1969, also Otto Günsche 5 November 1972. On the one hand this is understandable since it would spoil the image of their master. On the other hand it is of no importance because the conspirators believed it to be so and their conviction governed developments. For details of Hitler's personal security see Peter Hoffmann: *Die Sicherheit des Diktators*.

6 Here and below see: 'Ein "Plan Lanz" war Rommel bekannt', *Passauer Neue Presse*, 21 July 1949, p. 3; Hubert Lanz; 'Ein Attentatsplan auf Hitler im Februar 1943' typescript, Munich 1965; Christine von Dohnanyi: 'Aufzeichnungen', p. 9 in IfZ ZS 603; Hyazinth Graf Strachwitz: 'Ein Beitrag zur Geschichte des deutschen Widerstandes gegen das nationalsozialistische Regime', typescript, Allendorf 1947, NA Record Group 338 MS No B-340; Hyazinth Graf von Strachwitz to the author 8 January 1965 and 20 January 1966, also 'Aufzeichnung für die Personalakten', typescript, Garmisch 1945; Major-General Paul W. Loehning (commandant of Kharkov at the time), sworn statement Neu-Ulm 26 August 1946; Hans Speidel, statement, Freudenstadt 19 May 1946 and letter to the author 10 July 1965; Hans Baur: *Hitler's Pilot*, p. 149; *Kriegstagebuch des Oberkommandos der Wehrmacht (Wehrmachtführungsstab) 1940–1945*, Vol. III, p. 136–7; Max Domarus: *Hitler: Reden und Proklamationen 1932–1945*, p. 1988. Wilhelm von Schramm in *Aufstand der Generale: der 20. Juli in Paris*, p. 23 (not in English translation) is not therefore fully informed about Speidel's resistance activity when he says that until April 1944 Speidel was 'neither more nor less "oppositionist" than the majority of senior Army General Staff officers'.

7 On this point and below see Baur, p. 149–50; Hermann Teske: *Die silbernen Spiegel*, p. 173.
8 Schlabrendorff, op. cit., p. 77; Kaiser, diary 19 Feb. 1943.
9 Kaiser, diary 19 February 1943.
10 Hans Bernd Gisevius: *To the Bitter End*, pp. 459–61.
11 Schlabrendorff, op. cit., p. 77; much of Schlabrendorff's information was confirmed and supplemented by extracts from the diary of Captain (Res.) Hermann Kaiser.
12 *Spiegelbild einer Verschwörung*, p. 329; Josef Wolf (commander of the '*Führer* Signal Detachment') verbally to the author on 27 February 1965.
13 Schlabrendorff, op. cit., p. 77; Erwin Lahousen: 'Zur Vorgeschichte des Anschlages vom 20. Juli 1944', typescript, Munich 1953, IfZ ZS 652.
14 Possibly Tresckow only now hit upon the 'clam'. At about this time thoughts turned against a group attack. Lahousen does not think that the explosive brought by Canaris was used in the 'Schlabrendorff attempt' but he is hardly in a position to judge unless his statement is based on information from those involved or subsequent investigations of other attempts which became known to the *Gestapo*. Those of 13 and 21 March were not known, however, and the 'clam' was never used later. Those involved told their friends as little as possible. See Dohnanyi, pp. 9–10.
15 Helmuth Greiner: *Die Oberste Wehrmachtführung 1939–1943*, p. 441. It is not clear what part Schmundt, and through him Tresckow, played in persuading Hitler. According to Schlabrendorff, op. cit., pp. 78–9, Tresckow and Schmundt were mainly instrumental in bringing about Hitler's journey to the front.
16 See *Kriegstagebuch*, Vol. III, p. 207; Teske, pp. 172–3; Schlabrendorff, op. cit., pp. 81 et seq.; Gersdorff I; Erich Kempka verbally to the author 19 August 1965.
17 They were not quite so thick on the ground as Teske remembers, however, as is shown by photographs in the possession of Philipp Freiherr von Boeselager; see also Hoffmann, *Sicherheit*, pp. 162–6.
18 Major (Cav. Res.) Gustav Friedrich (then in Cav. Reg. 'Centre') to the author 19 May and 24 June 1971, also applicable below.
19 Baur, p. 52; Henry Picker (ed.): *Hitlers Tischgespräche im Führerhauptquartier 1941–1942*, pp. 244, 307, 386–7.
20 It is no longer possible to establish whether, on this day or on some other occasion, Tresckow tried to conceal a bomb in the side-pocket of Hitler's car. According to Schlabrendorff (*Offiziere gegen Hitler*, p. 95) this method was not tried on 13 March 1943 whereas Gersdorff in 'Gersdorff I' said that it was. Lieutenant Walter Frentz, who was then a *Luftwaffe* film reporter in Hitler's personal entourage told the author on 1 June 1965 of a visit to the front by Hitler early in 1943, he thought to Minsk; on this occasion a package was handed to Professor Karl Brandt, one of Hitler's doctors, and he put it into the internal postal service in 'Wolfschanze'; it was opened and checked by the SD and a time bomb was found. No one else of Hitler's entourage who gave information to the author remembers the incident which was certainly not an everyday one. On Gehre's role see Otto John: *Twice through the Lines*, pp. 106–7.
21 See *Kriegstagebuch*, Vol. III, p. 207.
22 Schlabrendorff, *Revolt*, pp. 83, 85 refers in both cases to bottles of brandy but in later editions to Cointreau – in *The Secret War against Hitler*, p. 233 for instance, where specific reference is made to the fact that Cointreau bottles are square and the only ones of the same shape as the clams in their package. This was confirmed by Gersdorff to the author on 15 Jan. 1965 and Schlabrendorff verbally to the author on 6 August 1968.
23 Hans Baur (Hitler's pilot) to the author on 10 January 1969: the heating system in the cabin sometimes failed; there was no heating in the cockpit or luggage hold.

24 On this point and below see: *Völkischer Beobachter* (Munich edition), 11 March
   1940, 17 March 1941, 16 March 1942, 22 March 1943; *Reichsgesetzblatt: Teil I,
   1943*, p. 137: 'Führer's Decree on Heroes Memorial Day 1943. Date: 12 March
   1943. This year Heroes Memorial Day is 21 March. Führer's Headquarters, 12
   March 1943. The Führer, Adolf Hitler. Dr Lammers, Minister and Head of
   Reich Chancellery.' Schlabrendorff, *Revolt*, p. 86; Gersdorff, 'Beitrag' and
   'Bericht über meine Beteiligung am aktiven Widerstand', Gersdorff I and verbally to the author on 16 November 1964 (henceforth referred to as 'Gersdorff II');
   minute-by-minute programme for Memorial Day ceremony 1940 (BA NS
   10/126) and 1941 (Militärgeschichtliches Forschungs amt W 01–6/321) – those
   for 1942 and 1943 have not so far been found; *Deutsche Wochenschau* No 655 of
   1943 (14/1943), BA, film section; 'Daily Digest of World Broadcasts (From Germany and German-occupied territory)', Part I No 1343 for the period 0001 Sunday 21 March to 0001 Monday 22 March 1943 (GMT), BBC, London 22 March
   1943; BBC Monitoring Service to the author 8 December 1965; Lieutenant-
   Colonel Ernst John von Freyend (Keitel's aide) verbally to the author 14 May
   1964 and letter 31 May 1965; Rear-Admiral Karl Jesko von Puttkamer (Naval
   Aide to Hitler) verbally to the author 5 March 1964; Major Gerhard von
   Szymonski (*Luftwaffe* Aide to Keitel) verbally to the author 2 July 1964; Robert
   Bergschmidt (desk officer for major ceremonies in the Ministry of Propaganda) to
   the author 9 February 1965; Grand Admiral Karl Dönitz to the author 5
   December 1964; Captain Freiwald (former Aide to Dönitz) to the author 7
   January 1965; Frentz; Lieutenant-Colonel Walter Froneberg (then Desk IIc,
   General Section OKW) to the author 3 May 1965; General Hermann Reinecke
   (then Head of the General *Wehrmacht* Office) to the author 16 December 1964,
   19 April 1965, 20 December 1965 and verbally on 30 April 1965; Frau Charlotte
   de Blanc (sister to secretary to Colonel Hans Friede, head of OKW General Section) to General Reinecke 15 July 1965; Colonel Alfred von Reumont (in General
   Wehrmacht Office 1941–2 and again from end 1943) to the author 14 March
   1965; Schlabrendorff to the author 22 October 1966 and verbally on 19 July
   1964; *Kriegstagebuch*, Vol. III, p. 232; *German Explosive Ordnance* passim;
   Peter Hoffmann: 'The Attempt to Assassinate Hitler on March 21, 1943', *Canadian Journal of History/Annales Canadiennes d'Histoire* II (1967), pp. 67–83.
25 *German Explosive Ordnance*, pp. 283–327; *Field Engineering and Mine Warfare Pamphlet No 7: Booby Traps*, pp. 19–23, 26–8; Colonel Witzig (German
   Army Pioneer School) to author April 1973.
26 On precise time of the start see: *Daily Digest of World Broadcasts*, No 1343 and
   BBC Monitoring Service to the author 8 December 1965. 1300 hrs British
   Summer Time = 1200 hrs GMT. 1200 GMT = 1300 Central European Time. In
   Germany summer time was not in force until April (*Reichsgesetzblatt: Teil I,
   1940* pp. 232–3., *1942* pp. 593–4, *1943* p. 542, *1944* p. 198). 1300 British Summer
   Time therefore = 1300 Central European Time in Berlin.
27 According to accounts by Szymonski and John von Freyend, aides to Keitel, they
   had already met Gersdorff at the main entrance to the museum and stayed
   talking to him there until Hitler's arrival. Gersdorff does not remember this nor is
   it to be seen on the news film.
28 Gersdorff in 'Gersdorff I and II' said that he was a sort of museum officer
   belonging to the *Abwehr* in Army Group Centre.
29 Gersdorff II; Strachwitz to the author 20 Jan. 1966.
30 *Daily Digest*.
31 According to Gersdorff's account, during this unscheduled pause Hitler inspected some captured Russian tanks drawn up on the west side of the museum
   between the museum and the memorial. Earlier Gersdorff gave reasons additional to those recorded here for the failure of the attempt: 1. (in 'Beitrag') at
   the start of the visit to the exhibition Schmundt told him that only a maximum of

8–10 minutes was available for it. If this happened, perhaps in answer to an understandably anxious question from Gersdorff, it must have been after Hitler had entered the exhibition rooms, therefore after Gersdorff had pressed his fuse. Schmundt's remark was not, therefore, the cause of the failure. 2. Schlabrendorff in his later editions (for instance *Secret War*, p. 239) says: 'It was most difficult to find a suitable fuse at such short notice but Gersdorff finally figured out a way to trigger the bomb and went off to the ceremony with the explosive in his coat pocket. However he never got a chance to use it, for Hitler appeared only briefly and left after a few minutes.' The inaccuracy of this report is not the only one in Schlabrendorff's book. All reports by those present and the Monitoring Service of the BBC which recorded the broadcast made at the time, agree with Gersdorff's account as it is given here, although only a few of those involved noticed that the visit to the exhibition had gone wrong. In his first account ('Beitrag') Gersdorff said nothing about the search for fuses, but then Schlabrendorff's book appeared, the early editions of which placed the blame for failure on non-availability of fuses; this was correct to the extent that no instantaneous fuses could be found (*Revolt Against Hitler*, p. 86; *They almost killed Hitler*, p. 61). From then on Gersdorff referred to the fuse problem and Schlabrendorff changed to saying that Gersdorff 'figured out a way'. Schlabrendorff in any case was only given a short account of what happened. Being a modest man, Gersdorff was unwilling to talk about the affair and it would have been tactless of others to enquire about details, quite apart from the fact that people had many other worries and further attempts were already being planned. 3. Talking to John von Freyend and Szymonski in the latter's house in Cologne (he was a distant cousin of Gersdorff) early in the 1950s, Gersdorff said that he had never activated the fuse. This he did, as also in his report of 1 January 1946 ('Beitrag') out of consideration for those still alive who had been present when the attempt was to be made, in particular Graf von Hardenberg and Szymonski. The affair having misfired and being still alive himself, he did not wish to appear as someone prepared to sacrifice his friends in order to do away with a criminal like Hitler and his entourage – although at least Graf von Hardenberg would have been prepared to sacrifice himself (Gersdorff to the author 22 March 1966). After the war things looked very different; sympathy for assassins and conspirators and comprehension of the situation at the time waned rapidly. None of this, however, affects the truthfulness of Freiherr von Gersdorff, as I have been able to confirm many times. On all important points, including some he could never hope to prove (the details of the clams and the unscheduled curtailment of the visit to the exhibition for instance) Freiherr von Gersdorff's account can be proved to be completely genuine.

32 Dr E. K. Freiherr von Gersdorff to the author, 2 and 10 December 1964.

CHAPTER 33

1 *Guides to German Records Microfilmed at Alexandria, Va*, No 54, p. 94.

2 [Erich] v. Manstein: 'Richtigstellung zur Darstellung der Haltung des Feldmarschalls v. Manstein . . .', typescript, undated.

3 *Trial of the Major War Criminals before the International Military Tribunal*, Vol. XX, p. 625, Vol. XII, pp. 240–1; Hermann Kaiser, diary 6 April 1943 in 'Generäle: Neue Mitteilungen zur Vorgeschichte des 20. Juli', in *Die Wandlung* 1(1945/46), pp. 531–2, and in Ludwig Kaiser: 'Ein Beitrag zur Geschichte der Staatsumwälzung vom 20. Juli 1944 (Goerdeler-Bewegung), Teilbericht', with transcript of Hermann Kaiser's diary (including parts not published in 'Generäle').

4 Rudolf Christoph Freiherr von Gersdorff: 'Beitrag zur Geschichte des 20. Juli 1944', typescript, 1 Jan. 1946; Gersdorff to Krausnick 19 Oct. 1956, IfZ ZS

47/II; Gersdorff to the author 25 May 1964 (henceforth referred to as 'Gersdorff I'); Gersdorff: 'Bericht über meine Beteiligung am aktiven Widerstand ...', typescript, Munich 1963; Fabian von Schlabrendorff: *Offiziere gegen Hitler*, pp. 126–7; Manstein, 'Richtigstellung'; Manstein: 'Persönliche Notizen', typescript, Bridgend 1947; *Trial*, Vol. XX, p. 625.

5 This remark only makes sense if Manstein was prepared in advance to recognize an opposition government as legal but what Manstein probably meant was 'effective' rather than 'legal'.

6 Manstein, 'Notizen'; Schlabrendorff: *Secret War against Hitler*, pp. 187–8.

7 Statement by Gersdorff in Hermann Graml: 'Die deutsche Militäropposition vom Sommer 1940 bis zum Frühjahr 1943' in *Vollmacht des Gewissens*, Vol. II, pp. 473–4.

8 Hermann Kaiser, diary, 6 April 1943 in 'Generäle' pp. 531–2; Joachim Kramarz in *Stauffenberg* (English translation), p. 132, much oversimplifies when he says, based solely on a statement to the *Gestapo* by Goerdeler, that Kluge had been won over in September 1943; thus formulated, this is incorrect.

9 See Kaiser's diary, passim.

10 Fabian von Schlabrendorff: *Revolt Against Hitler*, p. 88; Gerhard Ritter: *Carl Goerdeler und die deutsche Widerstandsbewegung*, pp. 365, 540 Note 43, based on information from Frau von Tresckow. Also Frau Eta von Tresckow to the author 26 July 1971.

11 'Handliste der Generalstabsoffiziere ...' (roll of General Staff officers 1943), NA T-78 Roll R 57; the dates given by Wolf Keilig in *Das deutsche Heer 1939–1945*, p. 211/342 differ by a few days.

12 Kaiser's diary, 6 April 1943 in 'Generäle', pp. 531–2.

13 Heinz Guderian: *Panzer Leader*, pp. 300–2.

14 Kaiser's diary 15, 20 and 22 Feb. 1943, in transcript.

15 Ritter, op. cit., pp. 353–8 (*The German Resistance*, pp. 239–41).

16 Ibid., facsimile reproduction between pp. 352 and 353, p. 358 (*Resistance*, pp. 241–2).

17 Kaiser, diary (transcript) 17 and 19 May 1943, and Kaiser's evidence in *Spiegelbild einer Verschwörung*, pp. 100–1.

18 Ferdinand Sauerbruch: *Das war mein Leben*, p. 550; Ulrich von Hassell: *The von Hassell Diaries*, p. 269; according to Kunrat Freiherr von Hammerstein in *Spähtrupp*, p. 211, Beck was operated on on 8 March 1943.

19 Kaiser's diary 6 April 1943 in 'Generäle', p. 532.

20 Helmut von Gottberg (at that time Lieutenant and Adjutant in 9 Infantry Reserve Battalion, Potsdam) to the author 16 June 1966; Hassell, p. 269.

21 Albert Krebs: *Fritz-Dietlof Graf von der Schulenburg*, pp. 237, 245.

22 Hassell, pp. 269, 273, 277, 285; Ludwig Freiherr von Hammerstein-Equord in notes prepared for Dr H. Pigge on 6 April 1970 says that Schulenburg had asked him on 25 February 1943, at a farewell party for Ferdinand Freiherr von Lüninck in the officers' mess of 9 Infantry Rgt in Potsdam, whether he would be available for a *coup* against Hitler; when Hammerstein consented, Lüninck told him 'to recruit more such good people'. Schlabrendorff, *Revolt*, p. 89; Hans Bernd Gisevius: *To the Bitter End*, pp. 473–8; Ritter, *Goerdeler*, p. 352 (*Resistance*, pp. 236–7); Kaiser's diary 6 April 1943 in 'Generäle', p. 532; Ger van Roon: *Neuordnung im Widerstand*, pp. 74, 287; Franz Sonderegger (ex-*Gestapo* official) to President of District Court I, Munich, 14 Jan. 1951, p. 8, copy in IfZ; Gert Buchheit; *Der deutsche Geheimdienst*, pp. 418–33; Eberhard Bethge: *Dietrich Bonhoeffer* (English translation), pp. 643–7, 698–700.

23 Edgar Salin in 'Über Artur Sommer, den Menschen und List-Forscher' in *Mitteilungen der List Gesellschaft*, folio 6 (1967), pp. 81–90, records similar activity by Dr A. Sommer who was then working in the *Ausland/Abwehr*.

24 M. Bormann to *Reich* Treasurer of NSDAP, 17 Jan. 1939, BDC.

25 Bethge, 686–92.

26 Keitel to Oster 16 Dec. 1943, MFA OKW 149.

27 Hans Bernd Gisevius: *Wo ist Nebe?*, pp. 230–3, 221.

28 Schlabrendorff, *Offiziere*, p. 101; Alexander von Pfuhlstein: 'Meine Tätigkeit als Mitglied der Berliner Verschwörerzentrale', roneoed, Kreuzwertheim, May 1946, p. 6; Hermann Bösch: *Heeresrichter Dr. Karl Sack im Widerstand*, pp. 85–8; Gisevius, *Nebe*, pp. 263–5; 'Fehlschlag' in *Der Spiegel* No 27, 30 June 1969, p. 105.

29 Sack had been in this post in OKH since 1 Oct. 1942 and until 21 Dec. 1942 was entitled 'Senior Army Judge'; he was then promoted to senior civil servant [*Ministerialdirektor*]. From 1 May 1944 his title was 'General Staff Judge' (Bösch, pp. 61–2). Until November 1939 Sack had been with the *Reich* Court Martial and then, at his own request, had been sent to the front as Legal Adviser to Army Group A (Rundstedt), where he met Tresckow; at the end of August 1941 he was appointed Section Head in the Legal Department of OKW (Bösch, pp. 61–4).

30 See Heinz Höhne: *The Order of the Death's Head* and in particular Chap. 18.

31 Albert Speer in *Inside the Third Reich*, p. 380, says that he was himself present when Himmler asked for Hitler's authorization but gives the date as late autumn 1943.

32 On this point and below see: Ritter, *Goerdeler*, pp. 360–2 (main sources are given on p. 539 Note 40); *Resistance*, pp. 244–5; Allen Dulles: *Germany's Underground*, pp. 147 et seq. where the indictment against Popitz and Langbehn is reproduced; sentence on Popitz and Langbehn of 3 Oct. 1944, copy in possession of Dr H. von zur Mühlen; Walter Schellenberg, 'Testimony', 13 November 1945, pp. 13–19, State Archives, Nuremberg, NG 4718; *Spiegelbild*, p. 351; Hassell, p. 275. T[heodor] E[schenburg]: 'Die Rede Himmlers vor den Gauleitern am 3. August 1944' in *VfZ* 1 (1953), pp. 375–6. Goerdeler hinted at this possibility in the draft of his letter to Kluge of 25 July. For the date see Himmler's engagement diary 26 August 1943, BA EAP 21-b/1-5 (NA microcopy T-84 roll R 25). The American Intelligence Service was informed about Himmler's contacts at the latest from 23 August 1943 although with some inaccurate details (there was reference to Himmler-Manstein negotiations, for example); OSS Research and Analysis Branch Summaries No 41507S, NA Record Group 226.

33 Dulles, pp. 148–9.

34 See Kaiser's diary 20 Feb., 7 June, 19 July 1943 in 'Generäle', p. 531: according to Schulenburg and Olbricht Fromm was 'lazy, without courage, went out shooting and was always allowing himself to be elbowed out of his prerogatives'. In July 1943 Field Marshal von Bock warned against Fromm saying that he was not reliable; Dulles, p. 149. Hassell (pp. 248, 256–7) refers to Fromm as 'blustering', a 'weather vane trumpeting brave opinions' and an opportunist because he thought that in spring 1943, when the situation on the eastern front had improved, 'it' in other words the *coup*, was no longer necessary. At latest by 1942 Fromm knew that the war could not be won – Hammerstein, p. 209 and Alix von Winterfeldt (former secretary to Fromm) verbally to the author 30 August 1966. Lieutenant-General (later General) Günther Blumentritt referred to Fromm in his comments on Schlabrendorff's book *Offiziere* ('Stellungnahme zu dem Buch "Offiziere gegen Hitler" '): 'I mourn all those involved in 20 July. As regards Fromm, however, I must remark that long before the war he was always saying: "We are invariably on the right side." He was a strong ambitious man who played politics ... Fromm could never have enough "offices".' Ritter (*Goerdeler*, pp. 358–9 – *Resistance*, p. 242) calls Fromm a 'climber and opportunist'. Fromm is almost invariably given credit only for intelligence and diplomatic ability.

35 Hassell, p. 263. Hammerstein, who was mortally ill, warned against inadequate preparation and organization of the *coup*. On the almost automatic connection between office and position, on which exaggerated emphasis was placed in Germany, see Dieter Ehlers: *Technik und Moral einer Verschwörung*, pp. 36–7.

36 Hammerstein, p. 199.

37 Kaiser's diary, passim.

38 Kaiser's diary, 28 May 1943 in L. Kaiser, 'Beitrag'.

39 *Spiegelbild*, pp. 398–402.

40 Kaiser's diary, 2 June 1943 in L. Kaiser, 'Beitrag'.

41 Kaiser's diary, 9 June 1943 in L. Kaiser, 'Beitrag'.

42 Kaiser's diary, 14 July 1943 in L. Kaiser, 'Beitrag'.

43 Hassell, p. 283; Ritter, *Goerdeler*, pp. 333–6 (*Resistance*, pp. 243–4).

44 Ritter, *Goerdeler*, pp. 359–60, 616–616 (copy) – *Resistance*, pp. 242–3; extracts from the letter are also given in 'Generäle', pp. 535–7.

45 Schlabrendorff, *Secret War*, pp. 164–5 (he does not mention this in the corresponding passage in *Offiziere*, (p. 75); Ritter, *Goerdeler*, p. 360 (*Resistance*, p. 244).

46 Kaiser's diary 20 Feb. 1943 in 'Generäle', p. 531.

47 Schlabrendorff, *Offiziere*, p. 101.

48 Kaiser's diary 6 April 1943 in 'Generäle', p. 531.

49 See pp. 296–7 above.

50 Ritter, *Goerdeler*, pp. 336, 363.

51 Schlabrendorff, *Revolt*, pp. 88–95.

52 Ritter, op. cit., p. 365 (*Resistance*, pp. 246–7).

53 *Spiegelbild*, p. 88 – evidence by Stieff and Schulenburg.

54 From 'Falko' – according to Kaiser's diary a member of HQ Replacement Army.

55 See below, this page; *Spiegelbild*, p. 88; H[ans] R[othfels]: 'Ausgewählte Briefe von Generalmajor Helmuth Stieff (hingerichtet am 8. August 1944)' in *VfZ* 2 (1954), p. 305. 'Orgieff' must have referred to Stieff, making up his 'cover' name from a combination of part of his own name and the common abbreviation for the Organization Section in the General Staff that he headed; cf. Christian Müller: *Oberst i. G. Stauffenberg*, p. 565 note 5.

56 Ritter, *Goerdeler*, p. 363 (*Resistance*, p. 246).

57 Ibid.

58 Rothfels, 'Briefe' pp. 291–305; Annedore Leber: *Das Gewissen entscheidet*, pp. 247–50 (also primarily extracts from Stieff's letters).

59 Rothfels, 'Briefe', p. 305 Note 18 based on a letter from Stieff to his wife dated 28 Feb. 1943 in which he said that he had been approached with a request to participate in an attempt to assassinate Hitler; Stieff's evidence to the *Gestapo* in *Spiegelbild*, pp. 87–8 and before the People's Court in *Trial*, Vol. XXXIII, pp. 307–8.

60 *Spiegelbild*, p. 88; Rothfels, 'Briefe', p. 305; Stieff's evidence in *Trial*, Vol. XXXIII, p. 308.

61 Rothfels, 'Briefe', p. 305. It is a fair question which cannot definitely be answered whether into these words can be read a decision to participate but equally a decision not to make the attempt himself.

62 *Spiegelbild*, p. 88.

63 Ibid.; Ritter, *Goerdeler*, p. 363 (*Resistance*, p. 246). Ritter suggests that Kluge had not yet quite made up his mind and that, in his evidence, Stieff did not wish to incriminate Kluge who was still alive. Both suggestions may be correct, the first particularly because Kluge was always wavering and never quite made up his mind. Nevertheless Stieff's confidence expressed in a letter dated 21 August implies that there was more to it; Leber, p. 250.

64 Ritter, *Goerdeler*, p. 363 (*Resistance*, pp. 246–7); *Spiegelbild*, pp. 410–12 includes a detailed account of this meeting by Goerdeler; Schlabrendorff, *Offiziere*, p. 126.

65 In 1943 this was undoubtedly utopian and hardly explicable by sheer optimism. In his evidence to the *Gestapo* describing this programme Goerdeler said that he had told Kluge in September 1943 that it was practicable and a month later Jakob Wallenberg had told him that this was the British view – *Spiegelbild*, p. 411, Ritter, *Goerdeler*, pp. 363–4 (*Resistance*, pp. 246–7). It seems likely that Goerdeler: (a) painted a rosier picture to Kluge than he knew was justified; (b) painted an even rosier picture to the *Gestapo* in the hope (which he explicitly recorded) that even in September 1944 he could still be of use as a peace intermediary – see Ritter, *Goerdeler*, pp. 426–45. Goerdeler was sentenced to death on 8 September 1944; he hoped that he might be kept alive as an important source of contacts, information and expert advice until liberation by the Allies and this no doubt had some influence on his attitude and evidence. Kluge had meanwhile committed suicide (18 August 1944); Goerdeler was giving his evidence on 21 September and could therefore well incriminate Kluge – see Hans Speidel: *We defended Normandy*, pp. 144–5.

66 Ritter, *Goerdeler*, p. 337 (*Resistance*, p. 246); Hammerstein, p. 219.

67 Ritter, *Goerdeler*, p. 365 lays a little too much stress on the defection of Kluge as the reason for the absence of a *coup* in autumn 1943. Roon, p. 284, based on information from Dr Hans Lukaschek, tells of a plan to arrest Hitler in his headquarters in 'Wolfschanze' on 13 August 1943; the plan is said to have misfired because Hitler did not arrive. Roon gives no details or other evidence for this story. Eugen Gerstenmaier in 'Der Kreisauer Kreis: Zu dem Buch Gerritt van Roons "Neuordnung im Widerstand" ', *VfZ* 15 (1967), p. 231 repeats Lukaschek's story as 'reliable, I think'. Professor Rothfels was good enough to make available to me an extract from Lukaschek's account which also refers to this attack planned for 13 August. According to this Lukaschek had the story from Moltke; he says: 'He [Moltke] reported that on 13 August Hitler was due to come to Wolfschanze the headquarters in East Prussia, with Göring and Himmler. The Panzer division doing guard duty was firmly under control of men resolved to carry out the *coup*. Hitler and the others were to be made prisoner and then brought to trial . . . He [Moltke] handed me a commission appointing me *Reich* Commissar for the Eastern Provinces . . . . But – Hitler did not come to Wolfschanze on 13 August and the Panzer division concerned was, as usual, moved.'

In fact, except for the 27th, Hitler spent the whole of August in 'Wolfschanze' – see Heinz Linge: 'Record of Hitler's activities 11 August 1943–30 December 1943', NA Record Group 242 Miscellaneous Box 13 EAP 105/19; Gerhard Wagner (editor): *Lagevorträge des Oberbefehlshabers der Kriegsmarine vor Hitler 1939–1945*; David Irving: *Hitler und seine Feldherren*, pp. 501–14, esp. 504, 507, 508. The story is not, therefore, based on fact. Who was commanding the panzer division? It must have been the 'Grossdeutschland' Division. It is incredible that neither Roon nor Gerstenmaier question the handing over of the 'commission'; there should be some explanation for so curious and foolish a procedure. Apparently no one else received such a document. It is also curious that Moltke seems to have told no one other than Lukaschek about this plan and there is no evidence for it anywhere else. If there was some secret agreement between Moltke and this reliable commander of the panzer division, then both were incredibly badly informed about Hitler's whereabouts. Even this does not explain why Moltke is supposed to have made just this single 'appointment'.

Lukaschek is unreliable on other matters. Roon, for instance, (p. 288) quotes Lukaschek for his information about meetings of the Kreisau Circle in April 1944 when Yorck is supposed to have said to Lukaschek that Stauffenberg had been made 'Chief of Staff of the Replacement Army', which did not actually take place until 1 July – see p. 323 below.

68 Professor Rudolf Fahrner to Professor Walter Baum 25 July 1962, IfZ, ZS 1790.

Notes

CHAPTER 34

1 Hermann Kaiser's diary 1943, passim, in 'Generäle: Neue Mitteilungen zur Vorgeschichte des 20. Juli' in *Die Wandlung* 1 (1945/46), pp. 528–37, and in Ludwig Kaiser: 'Ein Beitrag zur Geschichte der Staatsumwälzung vom 20. Juli 1944 (Goerdeler-Bewegung), Teilbericht', with transcript of Hermann Kaiser's diary including parts not published in 'Generäle'.

2 General (retd) Rudolf Koch-Erpach to the author, 9 May 1964; see also diagram in Appendix p. 739.

3 [Franz] Halder: *Kriegstagebuch*, Vol. III, p. 345.

4 Ibid., pp. 347–8.

5 Order by Chef H Rüst u BdE concerning 'Walküre II', AHA Ia VII Nr. 1720/42 g Kdos vom 26. Mai 1942, signed by Olbricht, BA – MA RH 15/v. 175; partial organization and call-ups were prepared in 1942 under codewords 'Brunhilde' and 'Kriemhilde'; 'Verwendungsbereitschaft des Ersatzheeres', order by Chef H Rüst u BdE, AHA Ia (I) Nr. 4810/42 g. Kdos. vom 13. Oktober 1942, BA – MA RH 15/v. 174; Major-General (retd) Ludwig Freiherr Rüdt von Collenberg (Chief of Staff *Wehrkreis* VIII from Dec. 1942 to Sept. 1944) to the author 3 Feb. 1964; Major-General Hellmuth Reinhardt (at the time Colonel, Chief of Staff to General Olbricht in the AHA) to the author 12 Nov. 1967 and 2 July 1972.

6 Copy No 83 referred to is in BA – MA, Freiburg, and carries the file no 'WK XVII/99'. Copy No 218 is reproduced in *Spiegelbild einer Verschwörung*, pp. 160–6; according to the distribution list this was an AHA file copy to which was attached instruction by Stauffenberg dated 11 Feb. 1944 which is not in the BA–MA files. The reproduction, however, is from copies passed for safe keeping to the Nazi Party archives in Munich together with file copies of the so-called Kaltenbrunner Reports; the reproduction does not show that it was made from these copies. These same copies are used for the reproduction on pp. 80–7 of *20. Juli 1944*, 1st and 2nd editions edited by Hans Royce, fuller revised edition by Erich Zimmermann and Hans-Adolf Jacobsen, Bonn 1961. Joachim Kramarz in *Stauffenberg* (English translation) pp. 134–9 barely deals with the 'Valkyrie' orders or the many important questions connected with them; not only does he give no account of their origin (evidence is lacking for one or two highly over-simplified comments on pp. 134–5) but he draws no conclusion about Stauffenberg's part in their redrafting.

7 Reinhardt verbally to the author on 1 July 1972.

8 Eberhard Zeller in *The Flame of Freedom*, pp. 236–7 gives statistics for these foreigners taken from a publication by the German Institute for Economic Research, Berlin, of 1954; in 1942 there were over four million and in 1944 some eight million.

9 See pp. 306–9 below.

10 Koch-Erpach (see Note 2 above).

11 Albert Speer: *Inside the Third Reich*, p. 378–9; see Walther Hubatsch: *Hitler's War Directives*, pp. 167–73; also pp. 380–1 below.

12 See Chap. 42 below.

13 *Spiegelbild*, pp. 26–8, 50–3, 76–82 gives lists or posting orders. On duties of the liaison officers see *Spiegelbild*, pp. 145, 334. Kramarz (p. 153) mentions only the second category of liaison officer. See also Chap. 39 below and lists of General Staff officers arrested, released and sentenced.

14 Nothing can be discovered about the attitude of Colonel Wolfgang Hassenstein, the Chief of Staff. He was executed on 30 Jan. 1945 – see appointments card index of Army Personnel Section P 3, NA microcopy T-78, roll R 55.

15 See in general Chaps. 39, 43 and 44 below.

16 *Spiegelbild*, pp. 145, 334; names of liaison officers on pp. 26–8, 50–3, 76–82.

17 On this point and below see: Heinz-Günther Albrecht: 'Die militärischen

Vorbereitungen der damaligen Führungsstelle der Widerstandsbewegung im Generalkommando Berlin im Hinblick auf den geplanten Regierungssturz', typescript 1946/7; Albrecht to the author 27 Aug., 1967; Ehrengard Gräfin von Rantzau (née Gräfin von der Schulenburg): 'Erinnerungen an die Vorbereitungen zum 20. Juli 1944', typescript, undated; Bruno Mitzkus: 'Um den 20. Juli und das Ende im Wehrkreiskommando III Berlin', typescript, Bad Homburg 1947; Frau Margarete von Hase verbally to the author 31 March 1964; Helmut von Gottberg (at the time Personnel Officer of 9 Infantry Reserve Battalion in Potsdam) to the author 22 April 1966; Helmuth Schwierz: 'Bericht über meine Tätigkeit am 20 Juli 1944 . . .', typescript, Siegen, undated, and letter to the author 25 March 1965; Carl-Hans Graf von Hardenberg-Neuhardenberg, statement on oath concerning Major-General von Rost, Kempfeld/Hochwald, 12 August 1946; Amt V [of RSHA] minute 'Betrifft: Selbstmord des Majors Ulrich von Oertzen, vom 22. Juli 1944', BA R 58/1051; Wolfgang Müller: 'Was geschah am 20. Juli 1944?' in *Das freie Wort* 3 (1952) no 29 of 19 July 1952.

18 For Stauffenberg's career see Chap. 35 below.

19 Zeller (pp. 195–7, 203–5, 209) was the first to attempt to summarize the available sources. Kramarz (pp. 134–41) supplies a few additional details. See also Kunrat Freiherr von Hammerstein: *Spähtrupp*, p. 267; Fabian von Schlabrendorff: *Revolt Against Hitler*, pp. 89–95; Albert Krebs: *Fritz-Dietlof Graf von der Schulenburg*, pp. 259–68.

20 Schlabrendorff, pp. 91–2; Nina Gräfin von Stauffenberg to the author 30 July and 13 August 1968. Zeller (p. 197) says that Stauffenberg postponed his operation and probably decided to go to Berlin at short notice because he had heard that Tresckow would still be there for a few weeks. Kramarz (p. 125) accepts this supposition and turns it into a positive statement but does not give source. Unfortunately no new information could be obtained from Frau von Tresckow. According to Schlabrendorff (p. 88) before taking over his regiment Tresckow spent 'fully ten weeks' (so, from the beginning of August) in Neubabelsberg, a suburb of Potsdam where his sister lived. Neither Zeller nor Kramarz take account of this.

21 Gerhard Ritter in *Carl Goerdeler und die deutsche Widerstandsbewegung*, pp. 367 and 541 Note 48 (*The German Resistance*, pp. 249, 250 and Note 2), based on information from Frau von Tresckow, stresses Tresckow's preparatory work; Stauffenberg he says, *took over* the orders, mobilization timetable, occupation plans, proclamations and 'Secret operational instructions' prepared by Tresckow in August and September 1943. This is undoubtedly correct but applies only to the 'Valkyrie' orders as they were in September 1943; it does not apply to the changes or to the later versions of the proclamations which were drafted by the Stauffenberg brothers with Professor Fahrner (see Chap. 39 below); nor does it apply to the organization of the network of Political Representatives and OKH Liaison Officers to the *Wehrkreis*.

22 This may be inferred from Schlabrendorff, p. 96; it is confirmed by Hammerstein, p. 267 based on a report by Bussche received by Hammerstein in late 1943 or early 1944. When Bussche went to East Prussia in November 1943 for the first presentation of uniforms (see Chap. 36 below) at which it was intended that he should kill both himself and Hitler, he took the liberty of opening an envelope given him by Stauffenberg and addressed to a senior officer in the *Führer*'s headquarters; it contained a proclamation to be broadcast to the people and the *Wehrmacht* saying that the SS had killed Hitler. For a long time Bussche did not realize that this story was intended merely to keep the fronts intact, in other words to ensure the smooth development of the *coup*.

23 Ritter, *Goerdeler*, p. 373.

24 Zeller, pp. 203–5. Kramarz (p. 136) refers to these drafts as 'supplementary orders', failing to recognize their real significance. From time to time cases of

documents from the *Gestapo* and other Nazi agencies appear – see Simon Wiesenthal: *The Murderers among Us*, Chap. 5. There is a remote possibility that certain files fell into the hands of the Red Army and are now under lock and key either in Russia, Poland or East Germany.

25 As far as Professor Fahrner recalls (see Kramarz, pp. 138–9) the content of these orders was identical with that of the orders and proclamations drafted by him with the Stauffenberg brothers in the autumn of 1943; he added, however, that they included 'a short legal justification and explanation of their purpose'. Kramarz does not mention the proclamations outlined by Zeller (pp. 258–9) although Fahrner was the source for these too.

26 Professor Fahrner's account to Zeller (pp. 258–9) of the drafts on which he worked with Claus and Berthold von Stauffenberg was based on notes made in prison in 1945. They are very similar to the 'Proclamation to the *Wehrmacht*' found by the *Gestapo* among Goerdeler's papers and reproduced in *Spiegelbild*, pp. 199–203. Naturally the majority of drafts stemming from the Goerdeler-Beck-Stauffenberg circle were similar in content. See Wilhelm Ritter von Schramm (editor): *Beck und Goerdeler*, pp. 233–53.

27 Schlabrendorff, p. 95; Hammerstein, p. 267; Rantzau; Kramarz, pp. 135–6; Nina Gräfin von Stauffenberg to the author 30 July 1968.

28 On this point and below see: account by Gräfin von Hardenberg in Kramarz, p. 136; more briefly Hammerstein, p. 267; Gräfin von Stauffenberg to the author 30 July 1968.

29 Schlabrendorff, p. 95.

NOTES/PART VIII/CHAPTER 35

1 Joachim Kramarz: *Stauffenberg*, pp. 21–4.
2 Eberhard Zeller: *The Flame of Freedom*, pp. 191–5.
3 Walter Baum: 'Marine, Nationalsozialismus und Widerstand', *VfZ* 11 (1963), p. 25.
4 'Handliste der Generalstabsoffiziere 1943' (roll of General Staff officers 1943), OKH Personnel Section, Amtsgr. P 3, NA microcopy T-78 roll R 57; Nina Gräfin von Stauffenberg to the author 30 July 1968.
5 Theodor Pfizer: 'Die Brüder Stauffenberg' in *Robert Boehringer: Eine Freundesgabe*, edited by Erich Boehringer and Wilhelm Hoffmann, pp. 487–509, also Ludwig Thormaehlen: 'Die Grafen Stauffenberg, Freunde von Stefan George', *Boehringer*, pp. 685–96; Zeller, pp. 173–97; Kramarz, passim; Max Rehm: 'Claus Schenk Graf von Stauffenberg: Generalstabsoffizier, Widerstandskämpfer gegen Hitler 1907–1944' in *Lebensbilder aus Schwaben und Franken*, Vol. 9, pp. 412–23. See also the author's 'Claus Graf Stauffenberg und Stefan George: Der Weg zur Tat' in *Jahrbuch der Deutschen Schillergesellschaft* 12 (1968), pp. 520–42. Bodo Scheurig's account in *Claus Graf Schenk von Stauffenberg* is inadequate. There is now a book on Stauffenberg by an East German historian – Kurt Finker: *Stauffenberg und der 20. Juli 1944*. Finker treats the anti-Hitler opposition as a whole somewhat more leniently than previous East German authors. He attempts to show that Stauffenberg and his immediate associates were sympathetic to Communism, the 'Free Germany National Committee' and above all the Soviet Union, but he does not make his case (see pp. 605–7 above). Apart from a few minor details Finker produces nothing new on Stauffenberg's biography nor on the course of events in the attempted assassination and *coup* – the culmination of his hero's career. In general Finker bases himself on Zeller and on Kramarz's very cursory account; he ignores the results of a good deal of recent research.

Much new information has been assembled by Christian Müller, *Oberst i.G. Stauffenberg*, by interviewing witnesses, by new interpretations of known sources, and partly also on the basis of newly discovered primary sources such as letters to Max Kommerell and to Nina Gräfin von Stauffenberg which had not been made available to Scheurig, Kramarz or Finker. Of course Müller repeats Kramarz, Zeller and other authors in long passages of his book. Moreover, his book is strewn throughout with dubious statements and innumerable attacks upon other authors in addition to what Müller doubtless regards as scholarly polemics. Müller's findings have been taken into account and wherever they have caused the present author to modify his own account this is stated in the notes.

6 This is what, for instance, Major-General Dietrich Beelitz says in a letter to the author of 28 April 1964; see also a similar view in Kramarz, p. 39. Hans Bernd Gisevius in *Bis zum bitteren Ende* (special edition) pp. 458, 481, says flatly that Stauffenberg had 'long been an ardent supporter of the National-Socialist movement' and that on 13 July 1944 Colonel Hansen had said that at an earlier stage 'in the headquarters', in other words in 1941 and 1942, it was no good talking to Stauffenberg since he was 'a convinced national-Socialist' – see p. 319 below. Gisevius only met Stauffenberg, whom he judges so severely, during the night 12/13 July 1944. The situation and the background of the two groups – Stauffenberg and his friends on the one side, Gisevius, Helldorf and Nebe on the other – is quite enough to explain these antagonisms. In addition there was Gisevius' understandable mistrust of Stauffenberg's indefinite, though lofty, political and social ideas. His background, views and personality clearly made Gisevius unsuitable to deal with Stauffenberg – see Gisevius, special edition, pp. 474–9 and *To the bitter End*, pp. 501–10.

7 Beelitz verbally to the author 21 April 1964; Karl Dietrich Bracher, Wolfgang Sauer and Gerhard Schulz: *Die nationalsozialistische Machtergreifung*, p. 739; also Carl Zuckmayer: *Als wär's ein Stück von mir*, p. 452. On Mertz von Quirnheim also Colonel Hans Linemann to the author 9 January 1971 and Lieutenant-Colonel Hellmuth Meyer to the author 12 June 1970 (both Linemann and Meyer served with Mertz in No 8 Inf. Rgt in the early 1930s); Frau Hilde Mertz von Quirnheim, diaries for 1944 and 1945, and memoir 'Albrecht Ritter Mertz von Quirnheim, Oberst i.G.' typescript, undated.

8 *Spiegelbild einer Verschwörung*, pp. 447–50. C. Müller particularly has opened the way for a more critical and differentiated examination of this phenomenon than seems to have been possible in the first twenty-five years after the Second World War. The topic is one of great significance and has not by any means been exhausted by C. Müller or any other author thus far, largely because the family and friends of Claus Graf Stauffenberg are still being highly selective in what they tell or show researchers.

9 Zeller, p. 423 Note 19; Hermann Foertsch: *Schuld und Verhängnis*, p. 22.

10 Kramarz, pp. 44–7.

11 Kramarz (pp. 45–9) has made a study of this incident; on the misleading information in Scheurig op. cit., see Kramarz, p. 221 Note 5.

12 According to Kramarz (p. 221 Note 9) the date of this incident is uncertain and it might have been much later – 6 March 1933. The swastika was only raised to the status of national emblem by a 'decree' (illegal) from the *Reich* President dated 12 March 1933 (Bracher/Sauer/Schulz, p. 147); a law was finally passed on 15 Sept. 1935 – *Reichsgesetzblatt Teil I, 1935* No 100 – cited by Kramarz, p. 47. As far as Max Theodor Freiherr von Süsskind-Schwendi, who was then on the staff of 17 Cavalry Regiment, remembers, the incident took place in February – Süsskind-Schwendi to the author 22 Jan. 1966.

13 In the German edition of the present work the author stated, based on a letter from M. Frh. von Süsskind-Schwendi, that none of the officers of No 17 Cavalry Regiment were enthusiastic about Hitler's assumption of power. In the light of

C. Müller's new findings, and of the results of the author's own more detailed research of this issue, Süsskind-Schwendi's information must be relegated to the great body of post-war apologetic statements.

14 Nina Gräfin von Stauffenberg verbally to the author 7 Aug. 1972; Gisevius, *Bitter End*, pp. 503–4.

15 From Süsskind-Schwendi. The cockade on army hats and caps was not replaced by the eagle over the swastika until February 1934; then this was done by order of Blomberg with the purpose of giving the Chancellor a stronger position vis-à-vis the SA. See Bracher, Sauer, Schulz, p. 917; Klaus-Jürgen Müller: *Das Heer und Hitler*, p. 68. On 14 March 1933 a decree laid down that members of the armed forces were to wear the *Reich* cockade with the colours of the *Reich*'s war flag, black-white-red, and surrounded by the oak-leaf wreath. See *Reichsgesetzblatt Teil I 1933*, p. 133. Süsskind-Schwendi is therefore in error either concerning the year or the incident.

16 See Zeller, pp. 184–6 based on information from Professor Rudolf Fahrner who had been a friend of the Stauffenberg brothers since about 1934–5.

17 Hoffmann, 'Stauffenberg', pp. 525–6.

18 Pfizer, p. 487 based on Rainer Maria Rilke: *Briefe*, Vol. 2, pp. 125–6.

19 Kramarz, p. 30.

20 Kramarz, pp. 27–31; Pfizer, p. 490.

21 Kramarz (p. 35) mentions twelve friends with whom the Stauffenberg brothers kept watch at George's deathbed; he does not give his source, however – it was probably Pfizer, p. 490. See however Robert Boehringer: *Mein Bild von Stefan George*, pp. 188–91 – Boehringer was present himself.

22 See note 13; *Spiegelbild*, pp. 448–50. Naturally the statements made to the *Gestapo* must be treated with caution, but there seems to be no reason to assume that Berthold Graf Stauffenberg or Nikolaus Graf Üxküll tried to any considerable extent to tell the *Gestapo* things that might cause them to appear in a 'better' light.

23 *Spiegelbild*, p. 448.

24 Kramarz, p. 50; Nina Gräfin von Stauffenberg to the author 13 Aug. 1968.

25 Information from a bookseller in Wuppertal from whom Stauffenberg used to buy – Kurt Nettesheim to the author 22 Aug. 1968; see also the author's 'Stauffenberg' (Note 5 above), pp. 533–5.

26 From Nettesheim.

27 Nina Gräfin von Stauffenberg to the author 11 Sept. 1968.

28 From Nettesheim. Similarly in Zeller, pp. 186–8.

29 Zeller, pp. 186–8 – also applicable below.

30 Kramarz, pp. 68, 105–7; Finker, p. 64.

31 Heinz Danko Herre (formerly in OKH/*Fremde Heere Ost*) verbally to the author on 9 Sept. 1972.

32 Zeller, p. 187.

33 Ger van Roon: *Neuordnung im Widerstand*, p. 286 (*German Resistance to Hitler*, p. 269) – also applicable below, Hans-Christoph Freiherr von Stauffenberg verbally to the author on 28 July 1971 and 5 July 1972, and address delivered at Bad Boll on 2 August 1963, roneoed. Cf. above, p. 247 and below, p. 376.

34 Zeller, pp. 188–91. Professor Julius Speer (from Jan. 1941 in the Organization Section of OKH under Major Finckh) to the author 22 Feb. 1966. Göring boasted, for instance, that he could supply Stalingrad from the air until it was relieved; see also Ferdinand Prinz von der Leyen: *Rückblick zum Mauerwald*, p. 86.

35 Speer says that Stauffenberg himself applied to go to the front; see also a similar remark by Manstein in Kramarz, p. 109.

36 Zeller, p. 188.

37 Kramarz, p. 107.

38 Ibid., pp. 106–7.

39 Ibid., pp. 108–10; Hammerstein, p. 191.

40 On this point and below: Nina Gräfin von Stauffenberg to the author 30 July, 13 Aug. 1968, 19 Jan. 1969; Dr J. Rohwer to the author 7 Jan. 1969; Wolf Keilig: *Das deutsche Heer 1939–1945*, p. 36/17; Kramarz, pp. 113–19, 121–5. On pp. 121–5 Kramarz confuses the order in which Stauffenberg stayed in these various places in the summer of 1943.

41 On this point and below: Ludolf Gerhard Sander (Lieutenant-Colonel, *Wehrmacht* Signals Officer in the *Führer*'s headquarters and a cavalryman like Stauffenberg) verbally to the author 24, 25 April 1964. Gisevius, special edition, p. 481 and *Bitter End*, pp. 503–5; Ferdinand Sauerbruch in *Das war mein Leben*, pp. 430–3, says that until death Stauffenberg had a bullet in his head which had gone in through his eye. Nina Gräfin von Stauffenberg in a letter to the author dated 11 Sept. 1968 doubts this.

42 Kramarz, p. 122; cf. *Spiegelbild*, p. 402; the author's 'Stauffenberg', passim; Gerhard Ritter: *Carl Goerdeler und die deutsche Widerstandsbewegung*, p. 367 – also applicable below (*The German Resistance*, pp. 248–9).

43 Zeller, p. 395 without quoting source: confirmed by Professor Fahrner in Kramarz, p. 185. The sense and in some cases the wording of the 'oath' is to be found in the poem 'Vorabend: Berthold-Claus' in Alexander Schenk Graf von Stauffenberg: *Denkmal*, p. 21–5; the translation in Zeller, p. 395 is given here with revisions by the author.

44 The phrase used by H. Maass to the *Gestapo* may be considered exaggerated: Stauffenberg's memorandum containing his concept of a social order after the *coup* was 'an attempt to protect the interests of the nobility even under a trade union regime'; *Spiegelbild*, p. 465. Klausing's statement that 'Stauffenberg lacked entirely an integrated and comprehensive political concept' is also inaccurate in this formulation; *Spiegelbild*, p. 367.

45 This according to statements by Maass and Brücklmeier in *Spiegelbild*, pp. 465 and 500 respectively.

46 *Spiegelbild*, p. 331. Sperr favoured a far less centralist structure of the German state than that which existed.

CHAPTER 36

1 Eberhard Zeller: *The Flame of Freedom*, p. 174; Joachim Kramarz: *Stauffenberg: The Life and Death of an Officer*, pp. 201–3, gives extracts from this document taken from the published version in *Wissen und Wehr* 19 (1938), pp. 459–76.

2 Zeller, pp. 260 and 429 Note 1.

3 Kramarz, p. 142.

4 Ibid., p. 143 where it is stated without evidence that Stieff had regular access to the briefing conferences. This is probably based on Stieff's evidence to the *Gestapo* that he had no *wish* to carry out the attack, alternatively on his statement to the other conspirators that it was not possible to carry a bomb into the conference room unobserved – see *Spiegelbild einer Verschwörung*, pp. 89–90 and Fabian von Schlabrendorff: *Revolt Against Hitler*, p. 126. Helmut Heiber (editor) in *Hitlers Lagebesprechungen*, pp. 13, 35–47 does not list Stieff as one of those regularly present at the briefing conferences. However, two photographs from the year 1944 show Stieff immediately next to Hitler at demonstrations of new uniforms and weapons: Henry Picker [and] Heinrich Hoffmann: *Hitlers Tischgespräche im Bild*, pp. 50–1; Roger Manvell and Heinrich Fraenkel: 'The Bomb Plot' in *History of the Second World War*, p. 1965.

5 *Trial of the Major War Criminals before the International Military Tribunal*, Vol. XXXIII, pp. 310–12; *Spiegelbild*, pp. 89–90; H[ans] R[othfels]: 'Ausgewählte Briefe von Generalmajor Helmuth Stieff', *VfZ* 2 (1954), pp. 291–305. In a letter dated 25 July 1952 to Professor Walter Baum and available in the IfZ (ZS 1790) Professor Rudolf Fahrner says that when he was asked to go to Berlin by the Stauffenberg brothers in October 1943, the assassination attempt was imminent; Stieff had declared himself ready to do it. The idea that Stieff could and would make the attempt, however, was apparently widespread in opposition circles; Erich Weniger says that General Karl Heinrich von Stülpnagel's entourage in Paris thought so – 'Zur Vorgeschichte des 20. VII. 1944: Heinrich von Stülpnagel' in *Die Sammlung* 4 (1949), p. 490.

6 Theodor von Dufring (brother-in-law of Meichssner) to the author 10 August and 29 September 1971.

7 *Spiegelbild*, p. 89, and Kramarz, pp. 150–1 statement by Captain Paulus van Husen who was a member of the OKW Operations Staff (WFSt) Berlin detachment, headed by Meichssner. From the context this conversation must have taken place before the Normandy invasion and after the end of February because the *Führer*'s headquarters was in Berchtesgaden at the time and the talk took place in the train on the way there.

8 Helmut von Gottberg to the author 22 April 1966; see also Albert Krebs: *Fritz-Dietlof Graf von der Schulenburg*, p. 289.

9 Kunrat Freiherr von Hammerstein: *Spähtrupp*, pp. 234–5; Krebs, p. 289.

10 See p. 292 above.

11 On this point and below see: Axel von dem Bussche: 'Eid und Schuld' in *Göttinger Universitätszeitung*, 7 March 1947, pp. 1–4; Bussche's evidence at the OKW Trial in Nuremberg – 'Freiheitskämpfer gegen Hitler' in *Die Zeit*, 22 July 1948, p. 3; Bussche – Interview with Daniel Schorr, CBS television programme 'The Twentieth Century', Part II, 1 Dec. 1964; Bussche – report on gramophone record 'Der stille Befehl', 'Harmonia Mundi' record Society, No PL 50115, Münster undated; Bussche to the author 9, 10 Feb., 1 Mar. 1966, 18 Sept. 1967, 22 April 1970; Dr Richard Freiherr von Weizsäcker (Regimental Adjutant of 9 Infantry Regiment) to the author, May 1970; Allen Welsh Dulles: *Verschwörung in Deutschland*, p. 93 (not in English version); Krebs, p. 215; Heinz-Günther Albrecht, 'Die militärischen Vorbereitungen der damaligen Führungsstelle der Widerstandsbewegung . . .', typed copy of a memorandum of 1946/7; Gottberg to the author 22 April 1966; *Trial*, Vol. XXXI, pp. 446 et seq. For the ban on chivalrous behaviour see Werner Kienitz: 'Der Wehrkreis II vor dem Zusammenbruch des Reiches', typescript, Hamburg 1953, BA Ost-Dok. 8 Po 22; Max Domarus: *Hitler: Reden und Proklamationen 1932–1945*, p. 2045.

12 Hammerstein, p. 235; see also Note 11 above.

13 T[heodor] E[schenburg]: 'Die Rede Himmlers vor den Gauleitern am 3. August 1944', *VfZ* 1 (1953), pp. 357–94; *Trial*, Vol. XXXIII, p. 313. See also Hans W. Hagen: *Zwischen Eid und Befehl* (rather unreliable except when telling of his own experiences), p. 44.

14 Further details on procurement of explosive in following chapter.

15 See Knaak's evidence to the *Gestapo* shortly before 30 Aug. 1944 in *Spiegelbild*, pp. 318–19 – see also pp. 88–9, 128–9; *Kriegstagebuch des Oberkommandos der Wehrmacht (Wehrmachtführungstab) 1940–1945*, Vol. IV, pp. 856–7; Albert Praun: *Soldat in der Telegraphen- und Nachrichtentruppe*, map supplement, p. 24. When interrogated, Knaak and Lieutenant (res.) von Hagen who was sent to Knaak by Kuhn said as little as possible and covered up much. Neither the *Gestapo* reports, therefore, which are apparently so accurate, nor the shorthand record of the trial before the People's Court on 7 and 8 Aug. 1944 are entirely reliable – see *Trial*, Vol. XXXIII, pp. 299–530 and in particular 305–42.

16 According to his evidence before the People's Court in *Trial*, Vol. XXXIII, pp.

329–34 Hagen flew to Army Group Centre; this was in Minsk; Orscha was further east, only 2–3 miles behind the front line. Bussche thinks that Hagen flew to a pioneer depot near Smolensk but Smolensk was then once more in Russian hands.

17 Bussche to the author 9 Feb. 1966 and 18 Sept. 1967.

18 Zeller (pp. 264–6) accepts Knaak's and Stieff's evidence to the *Gestapo* in *Spiegelbild*, pp. 89, 318–19; according to this new equipment had had to be obtained because the previous $4\frac{1}{2}$-second fuse which made a noise, had proved unsuitable; but this is not accurate. Bussche had asked for precisely this material for his attempt and had obtained it specially. The other conspirators may have thought it unsuitable but Stieff's statement was made in self-defence – he wished to imply that he had obtained only unsuitable material.

19 Albrecht, 'Vorbereitungen'.

20 'Das Spiel ist aus – Arthur Nebe . . .', *Der Spiegel*, 23 Mar. 1950, p. 31.

21 Zeller, pp. 263–4 based on a statement by Bussche.

22 From three sources comes the report that an assassination attempt failed in December 1943 because Hitler did not appear or some function was cancelled. In the second half of May 1944 while in Venice Trott told Kessel that attempts made in December 1943 and February 1944 had failed because of Hitler's nonappearance; Hans Rothfels: 'Trott und die Aussenpolitik des Widerstandes', *VfZ* 12 (1964), p. 322 (based on memo by Kessel written in the German Embassy to the Vatican in 1944 and 1945). Kessel also seems to have been the source used by Dulles in *Germany's Underground*, p. 95, when he says that Stauffenberg tried to murder Hitler on 26 Dec. 1943. See also Ulrich von Hassell: *The von Hassell Diaries*, pp. 297–8; Gerhard Ritter: *Carl Goerdeler und die deutsche Widerstandsbewegung*, pp. 375, 540 Note 44 (*The German Resistance*, p. 270). Major Freiherr von Leonrod admitted to the *Gestapo* that in December Stauffenberg had recruited him into the conspiracy as OKH liaison officer to *Wehrkreis* VII and had said to him that he might be wanted before Christmas – *Spiegelbild*, pp. 54, 258, 262; Kramarz, p. 144. Finally the judgement of the People's Court on Goerdeler stated that he had been 'alerted' for 25–27 December 1943 – *Spiegelbild*, p. 533; *Volksgerichtshof-Prozesse zum 20. Juli 1944*, p. 113. According to Zeller (p. 265) based on Dulles (op. cit., p. 69) and *Spiegelbild*, p. 90 (which in fact has nothing on the subject) Stauffenberg was to represent Olbricht at a conference in Hitler's headquarters late in December but it was called off because Hitler had already left for Berchtesgaden. According to Heinz Linge, however, ('Record of Hitler's Activities 11 August 1943 – 30 December 1943', transcripts, 1952, NA Record Group 242 Misc. Box 13) Hitler spent the whole of December in 'Wolfschanze'. See also Note 11 above.

23 Ewald Heinrich von Kleist verbally to the author 19 July 1964 and letters 15 Sept. 1964, 14 Sept. 1967; Gotthold Müller: 'Meine Beziehungen zum Grafen Fritz von der Schulenburg', typescript, Stuttgart 1961; Zeller, pp. 265–6 apparently based on a statement by Kleist not found elsewhere; Krebs, p. 289; Hammerstein, pp. 234–5.

24 Albrecht, 'Vorbereitungen' – also applicable below; see also Note 23 above.

25 Speer raised the question of a uniform demonstration in conferences with Hitler during the days 19–22 June 1944 after General Zeitzler had informed him that he was trying to bring about such a demonstration (possibly at the instigation of General Wagner or Major-General Stieff?); Hitler consented to having 'the new proposals for Army clothing shown' to him. See Willi A. Boelcke (editor): *Deutschlands Rüstung im Zweiten Weltkrieg: Hitlers Konferenzen mit Albert Speer 1942–1945*, p. 385; evidence to the People's Court by an unidentified person that repeated attempts had been made 'to lay on such inspections' until the *Führer*'s headquarters moved to Berchtesgaden – *Volksgerichtshof-Prozesse*, pp. 122–3. In a letter to the author of 11 October 1965 Dr Hans Karl von Hasselbach

(one of Hitler's doctors) says that another demonstration (tanks and new uniforms) was held on the autobahn on 20 April 1944 near Klessheim Castle, Salzburg, and that on this occasion Hitler had shaken soldiers by the hand. An assassination attempt had been planned.

Yet another plan is recorded by Heinz Burchardt (at the time a Major in the office of Chief Signal Officer of OKH) in 'Zugehörigheit zur Widerstandsbewegung vom 20. Juli 1944', typescript, Munich 1946, in the possession of Friedrich Degner and 'Kurze Darstellung der Ereignisse', typescript, Bonn-Dottendorf 1966; also Friedrich Degner verbally to the author 24, 25 Aug. 1965; these are based on statements by Colonel Hahn (then Chief of Staff to Fellgiebel) to the effect that Hitler's aircraft was to be shot down while flying from Berchtesgaden to Rastenburg. Nothing more precise can be discovered.

Finally Rudolf Pechel in *Deutscher Widerstand*, pp. 164–6 records an attempt made to kill Hitler at a demonstration of uniforms on 20 February 1944 by a certain Lieutenant Johann Hofmann and his father Colonel Josef Hofmann; the demonstration was suddenly put forward by two hours and the 'infernal machine' was set for 11.05 on the assumption that the demonstration would begin at 11.00. The 'assault pack' containing it was returned and exploded in the courtyard of the *Reich* Chancellery. Both father and son were sentenced to death and imprisonment respectively. The same story appears, but without quoting source in Georges Blond: *The Death of Hitler's Germany*, p. 13.

26 *Spiegelbild*, p. 90; Domarus, p. 2117; cf. photographs of 1944 showing Stieff at uniform and weapons demonstrations in the presence of Hitler, in Picker and Hoffmann, pp. 50–1, and Manvell and Fraenkel, 'The Bomb Plot', p. 1965.

27 Schlabrendorff, *Revolt*, p. 125.

28 Ibid.; Adolf Heusinger verbally to the author 6 Aug. 1964 on which occasion he confirmed that he had been approached by the conspirators and had been initiated into the plans.

29 *Spiegelbild*, p. 90; Schlabrendorff, *Offiziere gegen Hitler*, p. 132 (not in Engl. ed.); Ger van Roon: *Neuordnung im Widerstand*, pp. 157–8 but without details of source. Ruth Müller, who had known Werner von Haeften, wrote to Ricarda Huch on 4 April 1947: 'Since [Werner von] Haeften's participation in the preparation of the 20 July, the picture of him was somewhat dimmed for those who knew him closely. He did not belong to those who were able to use unethical means to ethically desirable ends. He was not – and here may lie the key for the failure of 20 July – an assassin, and he suffered greatly under the inevitability (as he saw it) of having to be one. Shortly before the end he told me (approximately): "And if one removes Hitler, then one cannot deny being a murderer nor refuse to bear this guilt and accept it with all its consequences".'

30 Eberhard von Breitenbuch verbally to the author 8 Sept. 1966 and letter 8 Nov. 1966; Schlabrendorff, *Revolt*, p. 127; Zeller, pp. 266–7, based on a statement by Breitenbuch.

31 See p. 300 above.

32 Not therefore 'for' 9 March as Zeller (p. 267) says, apparently based on an inaccurate statement by Breitenbuch.

33 Breitenbuch's description from memory does not allow precise identification of the equipment. The German Army had a number of similar grenades but none of them had to be procured from Switzerland. Tresckow perhaps made a point of this because of the failure of the acid fuse to function on 13 March 1943; Breitenbuch knew nothing of this but it was very much on Tresckow's mind. Perhaps the fuse came from Switzerland. The Germans may not have had stocks of the type of fuse described by Breitenbuch – with settings for 1 second, 3 seconds and 3 minutes – see *German Explosive Ordnance*, pp. 283–317. On the other hand there are many indications that the bomb which Tresckow and Oertzen brought

with them and offered to Breitenbuch was a German rifle grenade – the measurements agree more or less with Breitenbuch's description and it could be fitted with either a chemical or electrical fuse (see *German Explosive Ordnance*, pp. 332–4, 309–12). After his arrest on 22 July 1944 Oertzen committed suicide with a German rifle grenade and the assumption is not too far-fetched that it was the same which he had offered to Breitenbuch five months before. On this subject see: 'Report by the Security Police Technical Institute of Criminology, Chemical Section, "Selbstmord des Majors Ulrich von Oertzen",' typed copy, 23 July 1944, BA R 58/1051. Tresckow also committed suicide with a rifle grenade – Schlabrendorff, *Offiziere*, p. 154.

34 Breitenbuch could not be certain whether the fuse made a noise because no trial models were available.
35 Information from Breitenbuch.
36 Ibid.

CHAPTER 37

1 Ferdinand Sauerbruch in *Das war mein Leben*, pp. 432–3, says he told Stauffenberg early in July 1944 that the exertions entailed by the attempted *coup* were overtaxing his health and affecting both his judgement and his energy.
2 See Chapter 32 above.
3 Dr E. K. Freiherr von Gersdorff to the author 2 and 10 Dec. 1964; Rudolf-Christoph Freiherr von Gersdorff verbally to the author 16 Nov. 1964.
4 On this point and below see: *Spiegelbild einer Verschwörung*, pp. 54–5, 84, 89–91, 93, 128–30, 170, 194, 318–19; *Trial of the Major War Criminals before the International Military Tribunal*, Vol. XXXIII, pp. 311–12, 330–5, 339–41 – largely based on the *Gestapo* reports but partly on evidence at the trial; Philipp Freiherr von Boeselager verbally to the author 19 Nov. 1964; Bussche to the author 9 Feb. and 1 Mar. 1966, 18 Sept. 1967, partially repeating what Major Kuhn had told him; [Rudolf-Christoph] Frh. v. Gersdorff: 'Beitrag zur Geschichte des 20. Juli 1944', typescript, Oberursel 1946 and verbally to the author 25 May and 16 Nov. 1964; reproductions and photographs of the fragments of fuse discovered and of the fuse in the package thrown away by Haeften, NA EAP 105/14, Record Group 242; comments thereon to the author on 5 Aug. 1964 by an expert who wishes to remain anonymous. See also reproductions in the German ed. of the present work. Eberhard Zeller in *The Flame of Freedom*, p. 264 gives solely the *Gestapo* reports; Joachim Kramarz in *Stauffenberg* pp. 148–9, 170 deals with the explosives problem only *en passant*.
5 The *Gestapo* reports usually refer to it as Camp 'Fritz', name of a section of 'Mauerwald'; see *Kriegstagebuch des Oberkommandos der Wehrmacht (Wehrmachtführungsstab) 1940–1945*, Vol. IV, p. 1869.
6 Fabian von Schlabrendorff in *Revolt Against Hitler*, p. 122, reporting second-hand, says that the security services were alerted because the explosive went off spontaneously, but this is not confirmed by any other source. Bussche's account originates direct from Kuhn. Lieutenant-Colonel B. Klamroth described the events to the *Gestapo* and to the People's Court: Sentence of People's Court 15 August 1944 against B. Klamroth and others, NA microcopy T-120 roll 1038.
7 According to a statement by Schrader quoted in the *Gestapo* report of 3 Aug. 1944 (*Spiegelbild*, p. 129) Freytag-Loringhoven threw it into the Mauersee; the *Gestapo* did not believe this and thought instead that this was the explosive used in the actual attack. According to Gersdorff in 'Beitrag' the explosive and fuse obtained by Freytag-Loringhoven were of the same type as that which he had procured for Tresckow in Smolensk.

8 From an interrogation report (not one of the so-called Kaltenbrunner reports) quoted textually by Freisler during Stieff's trial on 7 Aug. 1944; *Trial*, Vol. XXXIII, p. 311. According to Knaak's evidence in *Spiegelbild*, pp. 318–19 it consisted of 'three charges with ignition fuses'. Stieff made many admissions to the Gestapo which he then tried to water down in court. In fact he gave away so much that one must suspect torture, particularly since he remained quite firm facing Freisler. See also p. 526 below. Equally it was in Knaak's interest to play down the importance of the material. According to Bussche it was a standard charge for bridge demolition. All these various descriptions agree in differentiating it from plastic.

9 According to *Trial*, Vol. XXXIII, p. 339 this was about 25 May. B. Klamroth himself confirmed in his trial that he supplied the explosive at the instigation of Stieff (sentence against Klamroth).

10 In interrogation before the People's Court on 7 Aug. 1944 Hagen said that in late November 1943 he and Kuhn had hidden *two* packages of explosive near the wooden watch-tower in 'Mauerwald' camp; this is confirmed by Bussche based on a statement by Kuhn. Both packages ended in the Army Affairs section (*Heereswesen-Abteilung*) where one remained temporarily; the other was given straight back to Kuhn. What happened to the first one is unclear but it must have made its way back to the conspirators. A further package of British plastic – 'British hexogen in its original wrapping with all necessary accessories' – was obtained by Tresckow in 1943 on the eastern front – *Spiegelbild*, p. 128; cf. ibid., p. 55. This may have been one of the two packages referred to. The other is probably the one which Georg Freiherr von Boeselager sent via his brother, Philipp Freiherr von Boeselager, in a suitcase to Major-General Stieff. When Stieff went on leave in November he gave the suitcase for safe keeping to a foreign service officer, H. H. von Herwarth, who in turn placed it for a time with General Ernst August Köstring, ex-Military Attaché in Moscow – Boeselager and information from Herwarth to the author 28 Oct. 1969. The explosive which Freiherr von Gersdorff kept in his brother's house in Breslau may also have some connection with that used by Stauffenberg; it was also plastic. Gersdorff fetched it from his brother in January 1944 and took it with him to a meeting with Stauffenberg, Tresckow, Schlabrendorff and Freytag-Loringhoven – Kramarz, pp. 148–9 based on information from Gersdorff. Kuhn has so far refused to supply any further information. Christian Müller in *Oberst i.G. Stauffenberg*, p. 583 note 118 says that the explosive can only have been the one procured by Knaak, and that this is clear if one took into account all the sources, yet he only bases himself on *Spiegelbild*, p. 55. Here, one detects a contradiction between the finding of the criminal police that, contrary to what Klamroth said, it was a special German imitation of British explosive, but not regular Germany army ordnance, and the expression 'handing over of these [explosive] charges'. If Stauffenberg, as the *Gestapo* report then assumes, had already had in his possession some of the special German imitation, the contradiction is unresolved. The *Gestapo* report states: 'According to Klamroth [what reached Stauffenberg via Oertzen-Hagen-Stieff-Klamroth] was regular army ordnance explosive, while the criminal police examination of the package of explosive picked up after the attempt showed that it was a special type of explosive (hexonite).' There are other contradictions in the *Gestapo* reports, e.g. *Spiegelbild*, pp. 55 vs. pp. 128–9 where the *Gestapo* report claims the earlier report (p. 55) had cleared up the procurement of the German explosives completely. See also Hagen's evidence in *Volksgerichtshof-Prozesse zum 20. Juli 1944*, p. 18: Kuhn had described the explosive buried in 'Mauerwald' as being of non-German origin.

11 Arnold von Tresckow verbally to the author 5 Aug. 1968.

12 *Spiegelbild*, pp. 129–130, 194. The report of the commisssion investigating the scene of the attempt lists the remnants of *two* British igniters found in the hut-

ment, to wit, 'two pressure springs from British chemical-mechanical time-delay-fuse sticks', and: 'fuse parts found at the scene of the attempt originating from two igniters of the same type as that [singular!] found along the road'. The report further states that the package of explosive thrown out by Stauffenberg and Haeften had contained two 'initial-ignition bodies' (correctly: two tetryl detonating charges) and *one* British chemical-mechanical time-delay-fuse stick for 30-minutes' delay; *Spiegelbild*, p. 84. If all these statements are taken literally, one would have to conclude that Stauffenberg used two 30-minute fuses.

13 On this point and below see: WASAG Chemicals Ltd to the author, 4 Dec. 1969, 17 Feb., 17 Mar. 1970; Dr Walter Sauermilch (then head of the explosives laboratory in the Reinsdorf factory) to the author 6 May, 13 May, 30 May 1970; Arnold von Tresckow to the author 17 Aug. 1968; verbal information to the author on 30 July 1968 by Dr Albert Widmann, a chemist involved in the investigations after 20 July 1944.

14 See photograph in German edition of the present work, from NA EAP 105/16. Appendix. The fragility of the bomb may have been due to the fact that the British tubular tetryl detonating charges had been forced into it without first making a cavity for them. The fuse was then inserted into the detonating charge. In fact with so volatile an explosive a detonating charge was unnecessary but everyone wished to be as certain as possible and avoid a repetition of the mishap of 13 March 1943. Moreover the explosive pack used in the attack contained two time fuses which inevitably increased the certainty of success if both were set off.

15 WASAG Chemicals Ltd to the author 17 Mar. 1970.

16 See pp. 402–4 below.

CHAPTER 38

1 For a character sketch of Fellgiebel see sources given in Note 4 below.

2 Albert Praun: *Soldat in der Telegraphen- und Nachrichtentruppe*, p. 225.

3 The greater part of OKH moved at this time and many sections had already done so, including some of Fellgiebel's. Members of the sections concerned agree on this – Arntz, Beichele, Burchardt, Degner, Jalass (see Note 4 below); also 'Militärischer Bericht Nr. 1217' dated 16 July 1944 from Hansamann of the Swiss secret service, made available by Peter Dietz of Schaffhausen. This said that the HQ in the Rastenburg area was apparently being dismantled; anti-aircraft formations previously located near Rastenburg were moving westwards. Fellgiebel had his men in both headquarters but the transfer process may, on occasions, have been difficult and disruptive. It is conceivable that, had all the above officers been present in 'Mauerwald' on 20 July, the measures taken there, particularly the cut-out of the repeater stations, would have been more effective. This may be the background to an ejaculation by Hahn recorded by Johann A. Graf Kielmansegg in ' "Any day other than today" Am 20. Juli 1944 im Hauptquartier', *Die Zeit*, 21 July 1949; just after 3 p.m. on 20 July Hahn lamented that of all days this was the worst since all communications were due to be switched over to 'Zeppelin' near Zossen. The above will also correct the view, based on limited source material, taken by the author in 'Zu dem Attentat im Führerhauptquartier "Wolfsschanze" am 20. Juli 1944', *VfZ* 12(1964), pp. 279–80 Note 124.

4 On the whole question of signals in connection with the *coup d'état* I have used the following sources: verbal information to the author – Hellmuth Arntz 21 Nov. 1964, Heinz Burchardt 13 July 1965, Friedrich Degner 24, 25 Aug. 1965, Kurt Hassel 11 Dec. 1964, Hans Hornbogen (at the time 2nd Lieutenant in charge of signals traffic in the *Führer* Signal Detachment, 'Wolfschanze') 14 Jan. 1965 and

letter 4 April 1965, Major Erich Jalass (then Lieutenant on Fellgiebel's staff in 'Mauerwald') 24 June 1965, Josef Wolf (at the time Major commanding the *Führer* Signal Detachment in 'Wolfschanze') 27 Feb. 1965, General Heusinger 6 Aug. 1964, Colonel Sander 24, 25 April 1964; letters to the author – Albert Beichele (Police Inspector – at the time Lieutenant-Colonel in charge of Group III (Line Communications) under the Army Chief Signals Officer) 18 June 1965, 14 Jan. 1966, 31 Dec. 1967; General Heinz Burchardt ('Kurze Darstellung der Ereignisse') 9 Feb. 1966; Gerhart Goebel of the Central Longdistance Bureau of the German Post Office, 21 Jan. 1966; Christian Hofmann (civil servant — at the time in charge of radio stores) in Group III (Equipment) under Army Chief Signals Officer) 16 Jan. 1965; Werner Jesek (Post Office official – at the time on secondment from the Post Office as an NCO in the *Führer* Signal Detachment) 24 May 1965; Major-General Erich Kohlhauer (at the time Colonel, Signal Commander in Army Group Centre but previously in OKW Signals Directorate) 7 March 1965; Karl Kuhnert (senior Post Office official – at the time technical supervisor in the Army Signals Traffic Directorate) 1 Dec. 1964, 17 Jan. 1965; Brigadier-General Herbert Maultzsch (until 10 July 1944 Lieutenant-Colonel in Army Chief Signals Officer's office) 10 May 1965; Emil Pestinger (ex-Post Office official – at the time technical official in OKH Signals) 20, 31 Dec. 1964, 19 Jan. 1965; Lieutenant-Colonel Alfons Waberseck (at the time Major, Desk Officer for Line Communications under Army Chief Signals Officer) 4 Feb. 1965; [Senor] Wille (at the time Post Office telegraph supervisor in Zossen) – 'Niederschrift über die Vorgänge beim Postamt Zossen 10 am. 20.7. 1944', typescript, Zossen 1944; Wolf to the author 18 Dec. 1968; extract from OKH telephone directory as at 1 March 1944, pp. 41–2, provided by Beichele. See also Rolf Göhring: 'General Fellgiebel: Leben, Wirken und Tod eines genialen Vorkämpfers der Nachrichtentruppe', *Impulse*, June 1960, pp. 8–10; Praun, passim; Fabian von Schlabrendorff: *Offiziere gegen Hitler*, pp. 125–6; evidence by Major-General Stieff in *Trial of the Major War Criminals before the International Military Tribunal*, Vol. XXXIII, pp. 318–19; *Spiegelbild einer Verschwörung*, pp. 98–9, 146, 225–6, 329–30, 376–8, 407; Eberhard Zeller: *The Flame of Freedom*, pp. 218, 243–5. See also diagrams at Appendix, pp. 736–8 below.

5 German long-distance cable network (outline map) from OKW Operations Staff, Signal Directorate, in Major Wolf's papers and sketch of carrier frequencies from *Luftwaffe* headquarters Section II; also line diagram of communications Wolfschanze-Berlin as at 9 Aug. 1943 (which according to Wolf remained unchanged until 20 July 1944) – see Appendix p. 738 below.

6 Praun, p. 222.

7 This is the view of well-known survivors such as Schlabrendorff (op. cit. p. 125) and Hans Bernd Gisevius (*To the Bitter End*, pp. 531–2, 538); also John W. Wheeler-Bennett in *The Nemesis of Power*, p. 642; Ludwig Jedlicka: *Der 20. Juli 1944 in Österreich*, p. 59; Jürgen von Kempski: 'Betrachtungen zum 20. Juli, in *Merkur* 3 (1949), pp. 807–16; Alexander Graf Stauffenberg: 'Die deutsche Widerstandsbewegung und ihre geistige Bedeutung in der Gegenwart', speech in Amerika-Haus, Erlangen 20 June [sic] 1951, roneoed; Emil Henk, speech on 20 July 1960 at commemorative ceremony for 20 July 1944, roneoed, Frankfurt 1961; Kunrat Freiherr von Hammerstein: *Flucht*, p. 116; Kurt Finker: *Stauffenberg und der 20. Juli 1944*, p. 376 Note 31. See also Zeller, pp. 439–40 Note 53 and the author's 'Attentat', p. 279 Note 124.

8 *Spiegelbild*, p. 329.

9 Beichele in a letter to the author dated 31 Dec. 1967 says that the exchange known as 'Alarich' in Zossen, which existed but was never used, had been specially installed as a secret exchange for the conspirators; it was to be taken into use on the day of the *coup* when the other exchanges were to be switched off. This is nowhere confirmed by any knowledgeable person. Attempts to initiate

signals officers into the plot were confirmed by Ulrich Poppe verbally to the author 4 June 1971.

10 Jesek on routing of cables; also technical drawings by Jesek in Major Wolf's papers.

11 Diagram of Wolfschanze's telephone communications as at 21 Jan. 1943 ('T-Verbindungen Wolfschanze, Stand vom 21.1.43') – from Wolf's papers (see Appendix).

12 Lieutenant [Karl-Friedrich] Albrecht: 'Auswertung der Aufbauübung der Vermittlung 'Zeltstadt', am 1. u. 2.10.43' typescript, [Wolfschanze] 2 Oct. 1943; notes on orders for vehicles, cable connections and switching plan, in Wolf's papers; information from Wolf.

13 Beichele to the author 18 June 1965; Kuhnert to the author 1 Dec. 1964. On 5 July 1944 Kuhnert was recalled by telegram from Army Group North to OKH Signals; when he arrived in Zossen he was surprised to find there 'most of the former members of Fellgiebel's office, including Lieutenant-Colonel von der Osten-Sacken (who shot himself after 20 July in Zossen [in fact it was in Lötzen]), Major Binder, Major Waberseck and many others'. The majority only realized later that Fellgiebel had been trying to assemble his old associates round him. The dictates of secrecy and the custom of imparting only partial knowledge meant that very few knew what the real object was and that even these few did not know many others in the conspiracy.

14 *Spiegelbild*, p. 329 – Hahn's evidence.

15 From Degner.

16 German long-distance cable network; *Spiegelbild*, p. 146; Hellmuth Arntz: 'Account of the Twentieth of July Putsch by one of the Minor Conspirators', CSDIC (UK), SIR 1610, typescript, 11 Apr. [sic] 1945 – also applicable below.

17 Wolf to the author 18 Dec. 1968.

18 Hans Bernd Gisevius, *Bis zum bittern Ende*, Vol. II, p. 329. Zeller, p. 286.

19 Dr Sydney Jessen to Professor Walter Baum 20 Sept. 1957, IfZ ZS 1484; Walter Baum: 'Marine, Nationalsozialismus und Widerstand', *VfZ* 11 (1963), pp. 26–8.

20 This is what Degner says: he is supported by Burchardt in 'Zugehörigkeit zur Widerstandsbewegung' and his 'Darstellung'; there he says that he was only told of this plan on 13 or 14 June. So far there is no other confirmation of this train journey. On procurement of explosive for an 'attack on Stalin' see p. 336 above.

21 Burchardt gives 13 or 14 June; judging from the accounts of the move from 'Mauerwald' to 'Zeppelin', however, it must have been July – see Note 3 above.

22 Burchardt to the author 9 Feb. 1966; information from Degner. Hans Hornbogen, who was in charge of the 'Wolfschanze' Area I exchange on 20 July, reports that, when Fellgiebel telephoned from there to Berlin and 'Mauerwald', he spoke in a 'totally unintelligible code', so that he, Hornbogen, could gather nothing of the conversation.

23 The tension between Hassel and Hahn seems to be reflected in the accounts of many ex-signals officers which betray an occasional tone of mistrust.

24 Wolf Keilig: *Das deutsche Heer 1939–1945*, pp. 56, I/2–3; Praun, pp. 221, 227.

25 Keilig, p. 45/5; Praun, p. 226.

26 Keilig, 55/7; Praun, p. 227. Where these two diverge preference should be given to Praun in view of Keilig's numerous inaccuracies. The various titles were repeatedly changed during the war.

27 It was not in a cellar. Wolfram Röhrig (in summer 1944 Second Lieutenant in charge of signals traffic in the Bendlerstrasse) verbally to the author 29/30 June 1965.

28 Here and below I have followed primarily Hassel's account. In many cases he is the only witness still alive and in his report to the *Gestapo*, of course, he gave away as little as possible – *Spiegelbild*, pp. 376–8.

29 As far as Hassel remembers he asked General Olbricht at the time whether there was not some other purpose behind this and Olbricht told him in general terms, saying 'after all we know each other'; Olbricht advised him to talk to Oertzen or Stauffenberg. This makes it look as if the time was about November 1943. In the autumn of 1942 Stauffenberg and Olbricht were not working as closely together as Hassel's account would postulate. It is conceivable that in January or February 1943 Hassel had an opportunity of talking to Stauffenberg and Oertzen – see Joachim Kramarz: *Stauffenberg: The Life and Death of an Officer*, pp. 113–14.

30 *Spiegelbild*, pp. 376–7.

31 From Hassel; Ludwig Kempe to the author 2 Jan. 1970. Further details in Chaps 42 and 45 below. *Spiegelbild*, p. 377 states that Olbricht informed Hassel and the latter 'as usual' passed it on to Thiele. When Hassel made this statement to the *Gestapo* he knew that Olbricht was no longer alive since he had been shot on the evening of 20 July; he did not know, or could not be sure, whether Thiele was still alive. Hassel probably made this statement before 4 September when Fellgiebel, Thiele and Hahn were executed. The report in *Spiegelbild*, pp. 376–8 is dated 11 September.

CHAPTER 39

1 Professor Rudolf Fahrner to Professor Walter Baum 25 July 1962, IfZ ZS 1790.

2 On this whole subject see: Walter Baum: 'Marine, Nationalsozialismus und Widerstand' in *VfZ* 11 (1963), pp. 33–9; also Gerhard Ritter: *Carl Goerdeler und die deutsche Widerstandsbewegung*, p. 406 (*The German Resistance*, p. 255).

3 Werner Kienitz: 'Der Wehrkreis II vor dem Zusammenbruch des Reiches', typescript, Hamburg 1953, p. 6; Major-General Anton Glasl (then Chief of Staff, *Wehrkreis* XVIII) verbally to the author 4 Dec. 1964; Major-General Max Ulich (then Chief of Staff *Wehrkreis* VII) to the author 6 April 1964; see also the author's 'Der 20. Juli im Wehrkreis II (Stettin)' in *Aus Politik und Zeitgeschichte*, 14 July 1965, p. 26.

4 Jakob Kaiser: 'Deutschlands Teilung war vermeidbar' in *Das Parlament*, 20 July 1954; cf. Elfriede Nebgen: *Jakob Kaiser*, pp. 165, 177. According to Ritter, *Goerdeler*, p. 543 Note 61 recruiting for Political Representatives had been going on at Stauffenberg's insistence since the autumn of 1943, but the initiative undoubtedly came from Beck; this is confirmed by Nebgen, p. 177 who adds that Fritz-Dietlof Graf von der Schulenburg was the driving force. Ritter (*Goerdeler*, pp. 374–5 and 545 Note 68) doubts both the solidity and scope of the 'organization' which Emil Henk says that he built up in *Die Tragödie des 20. Juli 1944*, pp. 46–51 ('a thousand reliable men' in the area between Kassel and Heidelberg). See also Kurt Finker: *Stauffenberg und der 20. Juli 1944*, pp. 171–2, on the existence of one or more organizations of agents who were to assist in initiating a mass movement at the right time. Below see also Nebgen, pp. 180–1.

5 Issue of orders by telephone would have been slower rather than quicker and the official teleprinter gave a greater air of authority from the point of view of officers in the *Wehrkreis*, who in many cases had to persuade far more senior officers. The idea that these lists fell into the hands of the *Gestapo* unnecessarily is nonsensical since appropriate teleprints were received by all *Wehrkreis* and other agencies, and 'Wolfschanze' received all of them, too.

6 *Spiegelbild einer Verschwörung*, pp. 26–8, 50–3, 76–82, 145, 256–61, 333–4 and many other places (see index); lists of General Staff officers arrested, released and sentenced (1944–5), OKH Personnel Section P3, BA EAP 105/2; Ritter, op. cit., pp. 372–3, 620–1; Eberhard Zeller: *The Flame of Freedom*, pp. 212–25. See also detailed references below.

7 Amt V (of RSHA): 'Betrifft Selbstmord des Majors Ulrich von Oertzen', typescript, Berlin 22 July 1944, BA R 58/1051; Zeller, p. 305.

8 F. Zimmermann: *Ludwig Freiherr von Leonrod*, pp. 18–21.

9 *Spiegelbild*, pp. 259, 296.

10 Ibid., p. 312.

11 Augusta Freifrau von Sell to the author 6 January 1971; the information in *Spiegelbild*, p. 51 according to which Sell was an aide to Field Marshal von Mackensen is incorrect.

12 Ibid., pp. 312–13; personnel files of Stiftung 'Hilfswerk 20. Juli 1944'.

13 Ludwig Jedlicka: *Der 20. Juli 1944 in Österreich*, p. 115.

14 See Günther Weisenborn: *Der lautlose Aufstand*, p. 308 Note 21, where he indictates that a trade union secretary named Georg Conrad Kissling committed suicide in 1936 after severe maltreatment by the *Gestapo*.

15 Alfred Späth: 'Zum Andenken an Nikolaus Graf von Üxküll', *VfZ* 8 (1960), pp. 188–92.

16 *Spiegelbild*, p. 395.

17 Philipp Freiherr von Boeselager verbally to the author 19 Nov. 1964.

18 The most comprehensive description so far of events in France was published in 1953 by Wilhelm von Schramm entitled *Aufstand der Generale*; a revised and expanded edition appeared in 1964. [Translator's note: the English translation, *Conspiracy among Generals*, was made from the 1953 edition and many of the references given here are not to be found in it]. For details of Schulenburg's activities in Paris see Albert Krebs: *Fritz-Dietlof Graf von der Schulenburg*, pp. 249–58; see also Ritter, op. cit., pp. 397–8.

19 Hans Freiherr von Boineburg-Lengsfeld to Dr Helmut Pigge, 1970.

20 Schramm, *Conspiracy*, pp. 13–14.

21 Schramm, *Aufstand*, p. 14.

22 Schramm, *Aufstand*, p. 15.

23 OSS Research and Analysis Branch Summary L39971 of 22 July 1944, NA Record Group 226.

24 Hans Speidel: 'Zur Vorgeschichte des 20. Juli 1944', typescript, Freudenstadt 16 June 1947, NA Record Group 338 MS no B-721.

25 Schramm, *Aufstand*, pp. 19–23; see also pp. 279–80 above. On his p. 23 Schramm clearly does not know of Speidel's earlier activity and says that he only became active in the opposition in April 1944.

26 Schramm, *Aufstand*, p. 32; interrogation of Alexander von Falkenhausen by Mr Ortmann on instructions from Mr Dobbs, SS Section, 6 Nov. 1946, 1330–1530, Interrogation No 175, typescript (photostat), Nuremberg 1946, IfZ ZS 888. Alexander von Falkenhausen: 'Bericht über meine Stellung zur N.S.D.A.P. und ihrem Regime', typescript, 15 November 1946, NA Record Group 338 MS no B-289.

27 Friedrich Wilhelm Heinz: 'Von Wilhelm Canaris zur NKWD', typescript (about 1949), NA microfilm R 60.67; Wolf Jobst Siedler: *Behauptungen*, pp. 60–1 – no sources given.

28 Schramm, *Conspiracy*, p. 14; Hans Speidel 'Vorgeschichte', and *We defended Normandy*, p. 84.

29 Speidel, *Normandy*, pp. 84–5; Schramm, *Aufstand*, p. 30.

30 Speidel, op. cit., p. 86; Karl Kaufmann verbally to the author 15 Jan. 1965; Schramm, *Aufstand*, p. 32.

31 Speidel, 'Vorgeschichte', also applicable below.

32 Speidel, *Normandy*, pp. 82–91.

33 Ibid., pp. 92, 105 et seq.; Max Domarus: *Hitler: Reden und Proklamationen 1932–1945*, pp. 2106–7; Peter Hoffmann: *Die Sicherheit des Diktators*, pp. 212, 302–3.

34 Speidel, op. cit., pp. 105–6.

35 Ibid., pp. 106–9.

36 Ibid., p. 110.

37 Schramm, *Aufstand*, pp. 35, 37 assumes, without evidence, that Rommel intended to have Hitler arrested.

38 Ibid., p. 38; *Spiegelbild*, p. 46.

39 Schramm, op. cit., p. 38; Wolf Keilig: *Das deutsche Heer 1939–1945*, p. 211/206.

40 Schramm, op. cit., p. 38.

41 Speidel, op. cit., pp. 122–3. After his talk with Rommel Hofacker was able to report to his co-conspirators in Paris that the Field Marshal was totally prepared to act; it had hardly been possible to restrain him and he would have liked to have struck straight away. Schramm, op. cit., p. 47.

42 Speidel, op. cit., p. 124.

43 Ibid., pp. 125–6.

44 Schramm, op. cit., pp. 185–6; Falkenhausen, 'Bericht'.

45 Speidel, op. cit., p. 124; Schramm, *Conspiracy*, pp. 29–31.

46 Cord v. Hobe and Walter Görlitz: *Georg von Boeselager*, pp. 99–100; Philipp Freiherr von Boeselager to the author 15 Jan. 1965; Ritter, *Goerdeler*, pp. 400–1 (*Resistance*, p. 278).

47 Speidel, op. cit., p. 121.

48 Jedlicka, p. 12.

49 Adolf Schärf: *Erinnerungen aus meinem Leben*, pp. 166–8; *Keesing's Contemporary Archives*, Vol. V 1943–1945, p. 6074.

50 Schärf, p. 167; Nebgen, pp. 147–9.

51 Jedlicka (pp. 23–9) relies on Adolf Schärf in *Österreichs Erneuerung 1945 bis 1955*, pp. 19 et seq. (the information is also in Schärf, *Erinnerungen*, pp. 166–8), also on Otto Molden: *Der Ruf des Gewissens*, pp. 148–51. See also Lois Weinberger: *Tatsachen, Begegnungen und Gespräche*, pp. 124–43; Nebgen, pp. 35–9, 82–93, 120–1, 140–1, 143–4, 147–9, 157–8 – also applicable below.

52 Jedlicka, p. 31, based on Weinberger, p. 144 and *Spiegelbild*, pp. 358–9; see also pp. 357–8 below.

53 Karl Szokoll: 'Der 20. Juli 1944 in Wien' in *Die Presse*, 31 Jan. 7 Feb. 1948, reprinted in Jedlicka, pp. 136–40 (dates given as 1 and 7 Feb.). Confirmed in a letter dated 22 Sept. 1964 to the author from Colonel Heinrich Kodré, then Chief of Staff in Vienna.

54 Jedlicka, pp. 33–45; *Trial of the Major War Criminals before the International Military Tribunal*, Vol. XXXIII, pp. 434–8; Szokoll; Kodré to the author 22 Sept. 1964.

55 Kodré in Jedlicka, p. 123.

56 Ibid., pp. 43–4.

57 Ritter, *Goerdeler*, pp. 372–3.

58 *Spiegelbild*, p. 256.

59 Main sources are *Spiegelbild*, pp. 26–8, 50–3, 76–82, 256–61 and passim, also trial proceedings and judgements which will be referred to individually with further notes; Nebgen, pp. 177–81.

60 He is consequently usually referred to as Dohna-Tolksdorf. See also the 'murder list' in *20. Juli 1944* published by the Bundeszentrale für Heimatdienst, pp. 210–11; *Spiegelbild*, p. 518; 'Handliste der Generalstabsoffiziere 1943' OKH Personnel Section P3 NA microcopy T-78 roll R 57; Keilig, p. 211/67; Annedore Leber: *Das Gewissen entscheidet*, pp. 238–41; Hans Rothfels: *The German Opposition to Hitler*, p. 88.

61 Willisen to IfZ 1 Sept. 1965.

62 Willisen; Annedore Leber: *Conscience in Revolt*, pp. 166–9. 'Vorlage an den Reichsleiter. Betrifft: Verhandlung vor dem Volksgerichtshof gegen weitere Verräter des 20. Juli 1944', typed copy, Berlin 23 Feb. 1945, BA EAP 105/30. See also Bodo Scheurig: *Ewald von Kleist-Schmenzin*, pp. 185–6, 235 Note 62.

63 Leber, *Gewissen entscheidet*, pp. 208–10; report on proceedings in *Spiegelbild*, pp. 558–9.

64 Albrecht Fischer: 'Erlebnisse vom 20. Juli 1944 bis 8 April 1945' in Otto Kopp (editor): *Widerstand und Erneuerung*, pp. 121–30; report on proceedings and judgement in BA EAP 105/31.

65 Fischer, pp. 149–52; report on proceedings as above.

66 Report on proceedings in *Spiegelbild*, pp. 545–6; Walter Hammer: *Hohes Haus in Henkers Hand*, p. 63; see also Hejo Schmitt: 'Bernhard Letterhaus' in *Deutsche Rundschau* 83 (1957), pp. 155–8; Nebgen, p. 178.

67 Hammer, pp. 43–4.

68 Cf. Ger van Roon: *Neuordnung im Widerstand*, pp. 116–22 and passim.

69 Leber, op. cit., pp. 70–2; Hammer, pp. 96–7; Nebgen, p. 179.

70 Nebgen, p. 178; Ritter, op. cit., p. 620.

71 Report on proceedings in BA EAP 105/31; Hammer, pp. 70–1; Nebgen, p. 180.

72 Bertold Spuler: *Regenten und Regierungen der Welt*, Vol. 4, pp. 558–63; Nebgen, p. 180.

73 Hammer, pp. 34–5; Nebgen, p. 180.

74 Spuler, pp. 406, 419; Hammer, pp. 92–3; Nebgen, p. 178.

75 Report on proceedings and judgement in BA EAP 105/30.

76 Ibid., EAP 105/30–31; Hammer, p. 65; Nebgen, p. 180.

77 Cf. report on proceedings in BA EAP 105/31; Hammer, p. 85; Leber, op. cit., pp. 67–8; Nebgen, p. 180.

78 Cf. report on proceedings and judgement in BA EAP 105/30–1; Nebgen (pp. 178–9) says that the account of Kossmann's commitment in *Spiegelbild*, p. 381 is correct.

79 Jedlicka, pp. 76–7, 115; Nebgen, pp. 178–9; Seitz's nomination does not seem to have been entirely agreed with him at this point.

80 Jedlicka, pp. 77–9, 115; Nebgen, pp. 178–9.

81 Jedlicka, pp. 78–9.

82 Ibid., pp. 79–81.

83 Report on proceedings in *Spiegelbild*, p. 545 and BA EAP 105/31.

84 *Spiegelbild*, p. 28.

85 Ritter, op. cit., p. 367 (*Resistance*, p. 249).

86 Ritter, *Goerdeler*, p. 368 (*Resistance*, p. 250).

87 Franz Sonderegger (ex-*Gestapo* official) in his letter of 14 Jan. 1951 to President of Provincial Court I, Munich (copy in IfZ) says that, when asked the purpose of the collection of documents found in Zossen, Dohnanyi replied that, in the event of a successful *coup*, proof of the work of the non-military must be available; otherwise the generals would take all the credit – and power. Hans Bernd Gisevius in *Bis zum bittern Ende*, Vol. II, passim and Wolfgang Foerster in *Generaloberst Ludwig Beck*, passim, refer to Beck's constant efforts to record all developments connected with the opposition.

88 Krebs, p. 239; Eugen Gerstenmaier: 'Der Kreisauer Kreis: Zu dem Buch Gerrit van Roons "Neuordnung im Widerstand" ' in *VfZ* 15 (1967), p. 224; Gisevius, op. cit., pp. 333–4.

89 Fabian von Schlabrendorff: *Revolt Against Hitler*, p. 145; Ulrich von Hassell: *Vom andern Deutschland*, p. 293.

90 On this point and below: Ritter, *Goerdeler*, p. 369 (*Resistance*, pp. 251–3) based on judgement on Goerdeler given in *Spiegelbild*, pp. 530–42; Ritter, *Goerdeler*, p. 618; Nebgen, p. 165.

91 Ulrich von Hassell: *The von Hassell Diaries*, pp. 353–4 and *Deutschland*, pp. 331–2 (letter of 25 June 1946 from Dr Eugen Gerstenmaier to Wolfgang Ulrich von Hassell, Hassell's eldest son); Gerstenmaier, 'Kreisauer Kreis', p. 245; Roon, pp. 270–1, 277; Gisevius' evidence in *Trial*, Vol. XII, pp. 240–2; Gisevius, op. cit., pp. 255–6. Roon does mention Schulenburg as being present but Hassell

(*Deutschland*, pp. 260) and Gerstenmaier in his letter to Hassell's son (p. 331) do so.

92 Nebgen, pp. 136–8 – also applicable below; Note 91 above; *Spiegelbild*, pp. 393–4.

93 See Part IV above and Hans Mommsen: 'Gesellschaftsbild und Verfassungspläne des deutschen Widerstandes' in *Der deutsche Widerstand gegen Hitler*, edited by Walter Schmitthenner and Hans Buchheim, pp. 73–167.

94 Gerstenmaier, op. cit., p. 245.

95 Roon, p. 277; Ursula von Kardorff: *Berliner Aufzeichnungen aus den Jahren 1942 bis 1945*, p. 161.

96 Roon, p. 281.

97 Ibid., pp. 283–4.

98 Cf. *Spiegelbild*, pp. 234, 264, 300; Henrik Lindgren: 'Adam von Trotts Reisen nach Schweden 1942–1944: Ein Beitrag zur Frage der Auslandsverbindungen des deutschen Widerstandes', *VfZ* 18 (1970), pp. 289–291; H[ans] R[othfels]: 'Adam von Trott und das State Department', *VfZ* 7 (1959), p. 309; Roon, p. 317. Cf. above, pp. 232–3.

99 Gerstenmaier, op. cit., p. 231.

100 See pp. 357–8 above. The following could be mentioned: Lehndorff, Leonrod, Uxküll, Dohna, Lukaschek, Dahrendorf.

101 Roon tries to maintain that the connection was not close (p. 286); Gerstenmaier, op. cit., p. 236. See Roon, p. 288 on a visit by Delp to Stauffenberg early in 1944. Roon, p. 286 Note 54 considers that Joachim Kramarz in *Stauffenberg: The Life and Death of an Officer*, pp. 129–30 overemphasizes the significance of this contact but he misses the point since Kramarz does not evaluate its significance in this passage. If Roon maintains that the connection was not so close, this means that he rejects the evidence quoted by Kramarz from Olga von Saucken, one of Graf Üxküll's daughters, Gräfin Yorck von Wartenburg, Yorck's widow, and Dr Paulus van Husen whom Roon frequently quotes as an authority.

102 Gerstenmaier (op. cit., pp. 230–1) argues that Moltke drafted his letter so that it would not upset the line of defence that the Kreisau Circle had agreed to follow before the People's Court – to present the circle as an innocent debating society, but this is not convincing. In his letter of 10 January 1945 Moltke refers explicitly to the 'submissions we all made in our defence, that the police knew that the whole thing arose out of official business, that Eugen didn't catch on, that Delp was never actually present'. Freisler had rightly disregarded this (Moltke concluded). See Count Helmuth James von Moltke: *A German of the Resistance*, p. 40; Roon, p. 139. If this fell into the hands of the *Gestapo*, how could it do other than make everything which Moltke and other members of the Kreisau Circle said totally untrustworthy? In his letter Moltke had abandoned the line which he had adopted in his own defence and on which Gerstenmaier insists. In his letter, moreover, Moltke does not emphasize that he had done nothing but think, though he does say that he is to be executed for his thoughts and that he would prefer to die for this 'crime' rather than any other. Moltke was not writing for the benefit of the *Gestapo* but equally he was not giving an accurate description of what he had done; he was explaining what he had done and why he was to be executed according to the results of the investigations and his trial.

103 Roon, pp. 271, 274–5 – also applicable below; see also Hans Mommsen: 'Pläne und Träume zum Tag X' in *Der Spiegel*, No 36 of 28 August 1967, pp. 94–7 (review of Roon's book); Nebgen, pp. 175–6 – also applicable below.

104 Roon, p. 274. On the history of the 'National Committee' see Bodo Scheurig: *Free Germany*; Finker, pp. 203–18.

105 *Foreign Relations of the United States: Diplomatic Papers, 1944*, Vol. I, pp. 510–11. Cf. above, pp. 243–5.

106 Anton Ackermann: 'Legende und Wahrheit über den 20. Juli 1944' in *Einheit* 2

(1947), pp. 1172–82; this denies the infiltration of a *Gestapo* informer; also Albert Norden: 'Die Bedeutung des 20. Juli' in *Die Weltbühne* 2 (1947), pp. 553–60; Werner Plesse: 'Zum antifaschistischen Widerstand in Mitteldeutschland 1939–1945' in *Zeitschrift für Geschichtswissenschaft* 2 (1954), pp. 813–43; recently also the *very* short account by Finker (p. 176; p. 230 in his second edition) where he does not say *why* 'all those involved were arrested early in July'. For an eyewitness account see Rudolf Schmid: 'Die Ereignisse des 22. Juni 1944: Wer kennt den Gestapospitzel Heim?' in *Telegraf*, 3 Jan. 1947; verbal information from Schmid to Ritter (*Goerdeler*, pp. 109, 471 Note 19 – *Resistance*, p. 48 and Note 4); verbal information from Frau Rosemarie Reichwein to Ritter (ibid.); Annedore Leber: 'Dr Leber und Stauffenberg' in *Telegraf*, 16 June 1946 and *Den toten, immer lebendigen Freunden*, pp. 11–12; Ewald Thomas (brother of Ferdinand Thomas) to the author 16 August 1972; Mordregister, BA EC 941 N (containing personal data, the date of execution, and the reason – 'The convicted has, in the fifth year of the war, established contact between a group of Marxist intellectuals and a Communist organization'). From those intimately connected with events surrounding the contact: Otto John: 'Männer im Kampf gegen Hitler (VI)' in *Blick in die Welt*, 2 (1947) No 11, pp. 14–15; Gustav Dahrendorf: 'Irrungen um Thomas', *Hamburger Echo*, 4 Sept, 1946 and 'Dr Julius Leber' in *Telegraf*, 7 Jan. 1947. Based on statements and documents: Franklin L. Ford: 'The Twentieth of July in the History of the German Resistance' in *American Historical Review* 51 (1946), pp. 609–26; cf. James L. Henderson: *Adolf Reichwein*, pp. 159–64; unfounded suppositions in Michal [sic] Vyvyan: 'The German "Opposition" and Nazi Morale' in *The Cambridge Journal* 2 (1948/9), pp. 148/68. It has been variously said that Ferdinand Thomas was the *Gestapo* informer; this apparently originated from a report by Dahrendorf. In his article 'Irrungen um Thomas' in the *Hamburger Echo* of 4 Sept. 1946, however, Dahrendorf has corrected this, saying that Thomas was not the informer; he was some unknown person who had occasionally masqueraded under the name of Thomas. See Roon, pp. 120, 198, 208, 274–5 and in more detail pp. 288–9. See also Hedwig Maier's suppositions in 'Die SS und der 20. Juli 1944' *VfZ* 14 (1966), p. 305 where 'It may be supposed' that 'at this meeting, held shortly before Stauffenberg's assassination attempt, the subject of the vital "initial flash" was raised'; according to Maier, Leber must certainly have told the Communists, and therefore the *Gestapo* informer, that an assassination attempt was imminent. Maier gives no evidence for this highly speculative statement; she does not mention the testimony to the contrary.

107 Leber, 'Dr Leber und Stauffenberg'; confirmed in Schmid, 'Ereignisse'.

108 Ritter, *Goerdeler*, p. 371.

109 On this point and below: Dr Heinrich von zur Mühlen to Dr Otto John 28 May 1948 and John to zur Mühlen 11 June 1948, in John's papers Folio 4; Ritter, op. cit., pp. 369–70, 541–2 Note 54, 391, 549 Note 96 based partially on the case for prosecution against Goerdeler and partly on information from Dr Otto John and Dr Günter Gereke [sic]; Otto John: *Twice through the Lines*, pp. 120–2, 137–8; Nebgen, pp. 132–3; cf. John W. Wheeler-Bennett: *The Nemesis of Power*, p. 603.

110 *Trial*, Vol. XXXIII, p. 358.

111 Gereke told zur Mühlen that the decisive meeting between him and Witzleben took place on 19 July; there had been others earlier.

112 Ludwig Bergsträsser: 'Erinnerungen an Wilhelm Leuschner' in *Das Parlament*, 20 July 1954, p. 8; sentence on Goerdeler, Leuschner, Josef Wirmer, Hassell and Lejeune-Jung on 8 Sept. 1944 in *Spiegelbild*, pp. 530–42.

113 Ritter, op. cit., p. 374 (*Resistance*, pp. 255–6); Nebgen, p. 128 – Goerdeler's collaboration with Kaiser, Leuschner and Habermann from end 1941.

114 Leuschner's mistrust of the military is understandable and, from his point of view justified. Nothing had happened for years and he was told little about the

preparations. Nebgen (p. 184) confirms that early in 1944 many were 'discontented' at the continuous postponements of the *coup*. This is much exaggerated in the *Gestapo* interrogation reports, however, so that it appears as Leber's only contribution to the discussion. *Spiegelbild*, pp. 179, 211–12; Ritter, *Goerdeler*, pp. 390–1, 549 Note 96 (*Resistance*, p. 270).

115 See p. 240 above. Findings of People's Court on Kaiser, 17 Jan. 1945, in BA EAP 105/30, including extracts from Kaiser's diary; *Spiegelbild*, p. 118.

116 Schlabrendorff, *Revolt*, pp. 106–7; Nebgen, p. 140; Gisevius, *Bitter End*, pp. 497–8, 512. Based on what Goerdeler and Hansen told him Gisevius then presents a one-sided view of Stauffenberg which at times degenerates into sheer polemics, although it does contain a great deal of information that would be more useful if it were balanced (Gisevius, op. cit., pp. 497–506; some variations see *Bis zum bittern Ende*, Vol. II, pp. 301–13 and the 1954 edition of the same title, pp. 559–67). Goerdeler himself told Gisevius on 12 July, the day on which Gisevius met Stauffenberg for the first time, that he (Goerdeler) 'had seen Stauffenberg no more than two or three times' (Gisevius, *Bitter End*, p. 496), so that much of Gisevius' account must be considered hearsay. A statement such as that Stauffenberg 'had shifted to the rebel side only after Stalingrad' (*Bitter End*, p. 506) is certainly a gross simplification; to say that Stauffenberg left the scene of the attack on Hitler on 20 July 1944 because he had the ambition to play a role afterwards (Gisevius, *Bis zum bitteren Ende*, special edition, pp. 462–4; not in earlier editions, nor in English edition) is speculative at best. Gisevius overlooks the fact that Stauffenberg was indispensable for the *coup* in Berlin, as the events clearly proved; and his credibility as a source is impaired by the tendentious form of the presentation. Christian Müller (*Oberst i.G. Stauffenberg*, pp. 577–8) omits a careful analysis of Gisevius' material.

117 Ritter, *Goerdeler*, pp. 366–7, 396 (*Resistance*, pp. 270–1).

118 Ritter, *Goerdeler*, pp. 540–1 Note 46 (*Resistance*, p. 249 Note 2); John, *Twice*, pp. 102, 133.

119 Ritter, *Goerdeler*, pp. 540–1 Note 46.

120 Ibid., pp. 372, 541 Note 52; cf. Kramarz, p. 161; Fritz-Dietlof Graf von der Schulenburg's and Cäsar von Hofacker's evidence in *Spiegelbild*, pp. 521–2. Below see Nebgen, pp. 139, 164, 174, 184.

121 Finding on Hermann Kaiser in BA EAP 105/30, based on H. Kaiser's diary. Gisevius (*Ende*, Vol. II, p. 305; not in English edition) says the opposite – that Goerdeler was not informed by Stauffenberg, apparently reproducing Goerdeler's complaints. A certain amount of scepticism is usually advisable when Gisevius reports negatively on Stauffenberg, despite Gisevius' reliability as a witness when he relates his own experiences.

122 Ritter, *Goerdeler*, p. 408 (*Resistance*, p. 286); *Spiegelbild*, pp. 177, 217. Cf. below, pp. 390–1.

123 Roon, p. 288.

124 *Spiegelbild*, pp. 118, 211–12; Ritter, *Goerdeler*, pp. 390–1, 549 Note 96 (*Resistance*, p. 271).

125 Roon, p. 289 based on statements by Lukaschek and also Husen that 'all were finally agreed on this step'; Roon only records this in a footnote leaving his text to give the impression that everyone was against the proposal. Since this is based on Lukaschek's statement, it is doubtful. Leuschner was opposed to contact with the Communists because of his experience of them in a concentration camp; Nebgen, pp. 175–6; below see pp. 173–4.

126 In this I have followed primarily Ritter, *Goerdeler*, pp. 368–71 and 617–19 (*Resistance*, pp. 251–3). In *20. Juli 1944*, p. 39 appears a table ostensibly compiled from 'Ritter, *Goerdeler*, pp. 617 et seq. and the Kaltenbrunner reports of July and August 1944'; it is inaccurate and unreliable but is reproduced by Hans-Adolf Jacobsen in his *1939–1945*, p. 727. The 'Government of 20 July 1944' in

Spuler, pp. 155–6 is totally inadequate.

The list as at January 1943 is based primarily on one submitted by Goerdeler to Dr Otto Schniewind, that of August 1943 on a table taken by Friedrich Freiherr von Teuchert from Berlin to Paris, where he was serving in the military administration; see also Roon, p. 271 – for Leber as Minister of Interior. The list as at January 1944 is based on information from Josef Ersing, the former Christian trade union leader, to Professor Ritter and Josef Wirmer's evidence to the *Gestapo*.

The lists given in the reports dated 27 July 1944 (*Spiegelbild*, pp. 59–61), 14 August 1944 (*Spiegelbild*, p. 210) and annex to *Gestapo* report of 6 September 1944 (BA EAP 105/25) are based exclusively on the *Gestapo*'s investigations which did not take into account the timings at which the various proposed appointments were valid. The annex to the report of 6 Sept. is a diagrammatic layout which does not appear in *Spiegelbild*, p. 361 – see copy in John J. McCloy: *Die Verschwörung gegen Hitler*, p. 131; Ritter (*Goerdeler*, pp. 617–19 Note 1) wrongly describes this as an annex to the *Gestapo* report of 29 Sept. 1944; the reason is that when Ritter was working on these papers in Alexandria, Va. he followed the order in which they were stored there and which was perpetuated in the microfilm made before their return to the Federal Republic; the annex concerned followed the report of 29 September and the annexes referred to therein but in fact it did not belong there.

The list as at July 1944 is based on information from Jakob Kaiser to Ritter; Gisevius, *Bitter End*, pp. 499–500, and *Ende*, Vol. II, pp. 335–6; Paul Löbe (answering an article by Horst Lommer) in *Der Tagesspiegel*, 30 April 1947; Nebgen, pp. 166–71; see also *Foreign Relations*, p. 511.

127 Ritter, *Goerdeler*, pp. 389–90, 404 (*Resistance*, pp. 269–70); Kramarz, pp. 169–70, but see p. 160; *Spiegelbild*, p. 112; Nebgen, p. 198.

128 Schlabrendorff, *Offiziere*, p. 88; Nebgen, pp. 164, 184.

129 *Spiegelbild*, p. 436.

130 Gisevius, *Bitter End*, pp. 463–4.

131 Gerstenmaier, 'Kreisauer Kreis', p. 235; see pp. 362–3 above.

132 Gerstenmaier, 'Kreisauer Kreis', pp. 228–36; Roon, pp. 157–8, 278–89.

133 Roon, pp. 157–8; *Spiegelbild*, p. 90.

134 Kramarz, p. 151 based on information from Colonel Peter Sauerbruch; Schlabrendorff, *Offiziere*, p. 132.

135 Eugen Gerstenmaier verbally to the author 17 Aug. 1965 and 'Kreisauer Kreis', pp. 232–3.

136 Roon, p. 139.

137 Gerstenmaier as in Note 135 above; Eberhard Bethge: *Dietrich Bonhoeffer* (English translation), p. 659.

138 Gerstenmaier as in Note 135 above. Ritter (*Goerdeler*, pp. 305, 321) refers to the 'Moltke circle'. Rothfels in *The German Opposition to Hitler*, pp. 121–2, follows Moltke's letter of January 1945 from Tegel prison and comments on it given him by Gräfin von Moltke; he emphasizes, however, that Moltke was prepared to participate in the *coup*, as evidenced by his presence at the meeting of 8 January 1943. In addition Rothfels, based on Moltke's own statements and the attitude of the other members of the Circle after January 1944 when Moltke was arrested, thinks that, had he remained at liberty, Moltke would probably have played an active part in the preparations for the *coup*. C. Müller (p. 576 note 12) fails to offer evidence on which he might base his contrary opinion. Countess von Moltke, however, has confirmed the author's view in a letter dated 3 February 1969. Recently, Michael Balfour and Julian Frisby came to the same or similar conclusions in their *Helmuth von Moltke* (pp. 157, 165, 209–10, 213, 264, 270, 291–2, 303–6).

139 Gerstenmaier as in Note 135 above; Schramm, *Aufstand*, p. 20.

Notes

140 From Gerstenmaier.
141 Roon, p. 336. This remark by Moltke and his views on the subject are not picked up by Roon in his index and apparently also escaped Gerstenmaier in 'Kreisauer Kreis', pp. 230–6. Roon says nothing about the glaring discrepancy between this remark and his statement on p. 285 that 'at this point it must clearly be stated that, like Goerdeler, Moltke was always opposed to assassination'. In his footnote 44 on this sentence Roon does admit that Moltke merely 'opposed assassination as "impermissible" ' (or does Roon merely refer, as he says, to the question itself?) See Gerstenmaier, 'Kreisauer Kreis', p. 233. Balfour and Frisby (pp. 210, 213, 264, 270, 291–2, 303–6) do not finally take a stand on whether or not Moltke either did approve of or might have approved of the assassination of Hitler; reporting a number of contradictory statements by Moltke and most of the salient evidence available besides Moltke's own words, they incline towards the view that he did oppose and (if he had remained at iberty) would have opposed an assassination throughout, but they lack conclusive proof, and they are unable to explain Moltke's statements to the contrary (especially pp. 213 and 264).
142 Moltke, pp. 39–40.
143 Ibid., p. 54; see pp. 362–3 above.
144 Gerstenmaier, 'Kreisauer Kreis', p. 234. Roon's account of this final talk (p. 290) is based on information from Gerstenmaier; he concludes that Moltke finally agreed with Gerstenmaier that assassination was permissible, if not necessary (Roon does not say this precisely). Incomprehensibly Roon then adds: 'It should not be concluded from this that he had finally given his agreement.' What do we conclude therefore? See also Gerstenmaier, p. 233.

On his p. 289 Roon also makes the untenable supposition that, after their arrest on 4 and 5 July 1944 respectively, Reichwein and Leber were severely tortured, that their friends feared action by the *Gestapo* as a result of the statements extorted from them and 'consequently urged the military to take action soon'. Equally unacceptable is his statement in the same paragraph: 'Assassination now seemed to them the only possible way out, although they did not abandon their basic aversion to it.' This was not the way things were. Action was taken, as Gerstenmaier says in 'Kreisauer Kreis', p. 232, not only 'when they were at our throats' but when war, murder and crime had reached such monstrous proportions that passive resistance no longer seemed a responsible attitude. This situation had been reached well before the summer of 1944 and by that time, apart from one or two isolated exceptions like Steltzer, the advocates of non-violent methods had ceased to oppose either the *coup* or assassination.

CHAPTER 40

1 Eberhard Zeller in *The Flame of Freedom*, pp. 187–8, gives an account by Professor Julius Speer; see also pp. 318–20 above.
2 For Stauffenberg's assurances that he was prepared to do it see Ferdinand Sauerbruch: *Das war mein Leben*, p. 431; Alix von Winterfeldt (secretary to Gen. Fromm) verbally to the author 30 Aug. 1966; Joachim Kramarz: *Stauffenberg: The Life and Death of an Officer*, pp. 170, 175.
3 Fabian von Schlabrendorff: *Revolt Against Hitler*, pp. 131–2; see also p. 354 above.
4 Helmuth Spaeter: *Die Geschichte des Panzerkorps Grossdeutschland*, Vol. II, p. 548; *The Bormann Letters*, pp. 56–8.
5 Zeller, p. 289 gives Fahrner's account.
6 Delia Ziegler (Stauffenberg's secretary at the time): 'Bericht über den 20.7.1944',

typescript, undated (probably 1946), p. 2; Erwin Topf: 'Klaus Graf Stauffenberg' in *Die Zeit*, 18 July 1946, gives a similar account.

7 Zeller, pp. 285–7.

8 Annedore Leber: *Das Gewissen steht auf*, p. 126.

9 Kramarz, p. 185 – account by Bernd von Pezold.

10 Nina Gräfin von Stauffenberg in a letter to the author dated 30 July 1968 says that the right hand and fifth and fourth fingers of the left hand were missing. Karl Schweizer (Stauffenberg's driver), verbally to the author 18 June 1965 said: right hand, first and probably middle finger of left hand. Sauerbruch, p. 430 says right arm and three fingers of left hand.

11 Sauerbruch, p. 431.

12 Kramarz, pp. 150–1, based on account by Captain Paulus van Husen. Since the conversation to which van Husen listened took place in the Berchtesgaden train on the way to the headquarters and the HQ was there, apart from short breaks, from February to early July, it may have occurred at any time between late February and early July. Husen can no longer remember exactly when it was – Husen to the author 16 Jan. 1968.

13 'Handliste der Generalstabsoffiziere 1943', OKH Army Personnel Ag P 3, NA microcopy T-78 roll R 57.

14 Sentence of People's Court against Bernhard Klamroth et al. of 15 August 1944, NA microcopy T-120 roll 1038; *Spiegelbild einer Verschwörung*, p. 94; *Trial of the Major War Criminals before the International Military Tribunal*, Vol. XXXIII, pp. 334–5; Zeller, p. 273; see p. 335 above.

15 *Spiegelbild*, pp. 90–1; *Trial*, Vol. XXXIII, pp. 316–20; Kramarz p. 173 accepts Zeller's unsupported statement (p. 282) that Colonel Finckh told Rommel on 25 June that Stauffenberg was planning a *coup* in Berlin.

16 *Spiegelbild*, p. 19.

17 Yorck's evidence before the People's Court in *Trial*, Vol. XXXIII, p. 426. Hagen told the *Gestapo* that Stauffenberg had said to him on 25 May that he would be using the explosive which he (Hagen) had brought for an attack which he was planning on Hitler – ibid., p. 339. Both the context and wording in this case indicate that Stauffenberg was *planning* an attack, but not necessarily that he had decided to do it himself.

18 Kramarz, p. 175.

19 Quoted from Kaiser's diary in sentence on Kaiser 17 Jan. 1945 – BA EAP 105/30. Cf. *Spiegelbild*, pp. 307, 395, 402, 404. The objection raised by Christian Müller (*Oberst i.G. Stauffenberg*, p. 588 note 58) misses the point since only an *approximate* date of 24 June is mentioned here.

20 Schlabrendorff, op. cit., p. 131 – also applicable below; Cord von Hobe and Walter Görlitz: *Georg von Boeselager*, pp. 98–101; information from Boeselager 19 November 1964.

21 Boeselager to the author 28 Aug. 1969; Ulrich Gigas (Lieutenant, Supply officer in Cavalry Regiment 'Centre') to the author 28 Oct. 1969. Gigas was summoned by Lt.-Col. Georg Freiherr von Boeselager during the evening of 20 July to be told by Boeselager that all preparations were to be rescinded immediately.

22 Elfriede Nebgen: *Jakob Kaiser*, p. 193 – also applicable below.

23 Zeller, pp. 289–90.

24 Kramarz (p. 180) gives a story by Dr Paulus van Husen of a meeting in his house between him, Stauffenberg, Yorck and Lukaschek: 'When Stauffenberg left for the overnight train, his last remark was: "So there's nothing for it but to kill him." I believe that it was this conversation in which Stauffenberg finally confirmed himself in his decision to do it himself.' The date of this conversation can only be inferred from one of Kramarz's notes as being 14 July. In a letter to the author of 16 Jan. 1968 Husen gives it as 14 July but it is highly probable that he is wrong, as Kramarz suspects. It may have been on the evening before another

visit by Stauffenberg to the headquarters, that of 6 or 10 July, for instance. See
pp. 380–2 below.

25 Cf. above, p. 329; *Spiegelbild*, p. 90; according to Horst Kopkow-Cordes,
head of the on-the-spot commission of the 'Special Commission 20 July 1944' in
'Account of the Plot of 20 July 44', typescript, 9 April 1946, Stieff was due to
make the attempt on '10 July' but, as he admitted to Kopkow-Cordes, had not the
courage.

26 *Spiegelbild*, p. 130.

27 Zeller, pp. 292–3. According to *Spiegelbild*, p. 90, the demonstration of equipment was held in Klessheim (near Salzburg) on 7 July 1944; Stieff said on 7
August 1944 before the People's Court that he had prevented the attack planned
for such a demonstration (*Trial*, Vol. XXXIII, p. 313).

28 Sauerbruch, p. 432; Stauffenberg's driver remembers Stauffenberg visiting
Sauerbruch some six weeks before 20 July – information from Schweizer 18 June
1965.

29 Schlabrendorff, op. cit., p. 132; Kramarz, p. 171.

30 'SS-Bericht über den 20. Juli: Aus den Papieren des SS-Obersturmbannführers
Dr Georg Kiesel' in *Nordwestdeutsche Hefte* 2 (1947), No 1/2, p. 17; this much-
quoted account, said to be from an interrogation, is an anonymous revision of an
account by Kiessel (this is the correct spelling which he uses himself) which he
had drafted and signed and which is referred to here – Dr Georg Kiessel: 'Das
Attentat des 20. Juli 1944 und seine Hintergründe', typescript, Sandbostel, 6
Aug. 1946, p. 14; see also 'Aussage Huppenkothen: Personelle Zusammensetzung und Aufgabenverteilung der Sonderkommission 20. Juli 1944', typescript,
undated (earlier than March 1953), IfZ ZS 249/III; see also p. 320 above.

31 Hans Bernd Gisevius in *To the Bitter End* describes Fromm as informed and initiated (p. 508) though not finally committed to the conspirators' cause (p. 513);
Fromm's remark about Keitel is given only in the German editions – see *Bis zum
bittern Ende*, Vol. II, p. 331. In a letter dated 10 March 1947 to Frau Annemarie
Koch, widow of Dr Hans Koch who was earmarked by the opposition for President of the *Reich* Court, Dr Clemens Plassmann gives Fromm's remark as
follows: 'If you make your ridiculous *coup*, don't forget my friend Wilhelm
Keitel!' (Personal reports in possession of 'Hilfswerk 20. Juli 1944' Foundation).
In spite of such evidence and the considerations given below others who knew
Fromm well believe that he did not know of the preparations for the *coup* (Captain Heinz-Ludwig Bartram, his personal Aide, for instance, in '20. Juli 1944',
typescript, [1954], BA H 90-3/4, p. 7). These people did not know how much
Fromm knew; he did not, of course, know the details of the plot and undoubtedly
did not wish to.

32 Frau Alix von Winterfeldt verbally to the author 30 Aug. 1966.

33 [Günther] Blumentritt: 'Stellungnahme zu dem Buch "Offiziere gegen Hitler"
...' typescript, Nov. 1946, p. 19, in Otto John's papers, folio 2; see also pp. 297,
623 Note 34 above.

34 Ulrich von Hassell: *The von Hassell Diaries*: pp. 256, 257.

35 'Generäle: Neue Mitteilungen zur Vorgeschichte des 20. Juli' in *Die Wandlung* 1
(1945/46), p. 531.

36 Allen Dulles reported thus to Washington: OSS Research and Analysis Branch
Summary L39970 of 18 July 1944, NA Record Group 226.

37 Kunrat Freiherr von Hammerstein: *Spähtrupp*, p. 209.

38 Botho von Wussow: 'Einige Sätze zu dem SS-Bericht über den 20. Juli 1944...',
typescript, original in possession of Gräfin Schwerin von Schwanenfeld; see also
Trial, Vol. XXXIII, p. 397.

39 OSS Research and Analysis Branch Summary L39970 of 18 July 1944 based on
Dulles's reports from Berne dated 13 and 15 July 1944 ('Breakers Cables nos.
4110–4114 and 4111–12', as they are termed in the summary; cf. Allen Welsh

Dulles: *Germany's Underground*, p. 134), NA Record Group 226.

40 Sentence on Kaiser, BA EAP 105/30; Kramarz, p. 171; Alix von Winterfeldt.

41 Dr Hopf's report to Bormann on trial proceedings on 7 or 8 March 1945, BA EAP 105/30. This may, of course, have been a polite way of expressing something much more violent.

42 *Trial*, Vol. XXXIII, p. 416.

43 Gisevius in *Trial*, Vol. XII, pp. 259–60; Gisevius *Bitter End*, p. 524; Gerhard Ritter: *Carl Goerdeler und die deutsche Widerstandsbewegung*, p. 408.

44 Annedore Leber: *Den toten immer lebendigen Freunden*, pp. 11–12; [Julius Leber]: *Ein Mann geht seinen Weg*, p. 292.

45 Hedwig Maier in 'Die SS und der 20. Juli 1944', *VfZ* 14 (1966), pp. 299–316, has attempted to summarize the indications but on closer inspection they prove to be mere suppositions by post-war authors unsupported by any basic study of sources; but there also exist some more tangible indications as outlined below.

46 Harold C. Deutsch: *The Conspiracy against Hitler in the Twilight War*, pp. 129–36; Heydrich to Ribbentrop 6 Nov. 1941, typed copy with annexes BA NS 19/414; see also pp. 211–3 above.

47 Hassell, op. cit., pp. 232, 265, 269–70, 277, 287–8; Eberhard Bethge: *Dietrich Bonhoeffer* (English translation), pp. 686–91; Maier, (pp. 302, 308) states without evidence that Dohnanyi was released again after a few months but there is no other support for this; case for prosecution against Langbehn and Popitz is given in Dulles *Underground*, pp. 151 et seq.; Lagi Countess Ballestrem Solf: 'Tea Party' in Eric H. Boehm: *We survived*, pp. 135–6; Ritter, op. cit., p. 371; statements by Franz Sonderegger (ex-*Gestapo* official) to representatives of 'Europäische Publikation', Munich 15 Oct. 1952, IfZ ZS 303 II, pp. 12–14; see also T[heodor] E[schenburg]: 'Die Rede Himmlers vor den Gauleitern am 3. August 1944', *VfZ* 1 (1953), pp. 375–6.

48 *Spiegelbild*, p. 363; Hermann Reinecke verbally to the author 30 April 1965; on Reichwein and Leber see pp. 362–3 above; Maier (p. 311) gives 9 June 1944 as the date of Leber's arrest but this is wrong and unsupported.

49 *Spiegelbild*, p. 363.

50 Himmler's contact with Popitz is not so obscure as Hedwig Maier thinks (p. 304) – see p. 296 above. Though she is Director of a *Land* Court, Hedwig Maier is ill-informed when she says (p. 310) that 'no one of Himmler's immediate entourage is still alive'. When her article was written a German court was dealing with the former *SS-Obergruppenführer* Karl Wolff, and the former *SS-Obergruppenführer* Gottlob Berger was still alive. Hedwig Maier pays no attention to the case for the prosecution on Popitz and Langbehn given in Dulles, op. cit., pp. 151 et seq. where the contact is described in detail.

51 Sentence of People's Court on Nebe 2 March 1945, BA EAP 105/30; Gisevius, op. cit., p. 524; Ritter, op. cit., p. 408 (*The German Resistance*, p. 286); Nebgen, pp. 192–3. Goerdeler himself heard of it on 18 July.

52 This is Hedwig Maier's main theme and is not disputed, though it is not new; basic research might perhaps have produced more evidence for it. *SS-Standartenführer* Joachim Ruoff who was at the time Ia officer of the *SS-Führungshauptamt* under *SS-Obergruppenführer* (Lt. Gen.) Jüttner told the author on 3 June 1971: Jüttner knew Fromm, Warlimont, Himmler and others well through his official duties; on the afternoon of 20 July 1944, when he learned of the assassination attempt, he had said immediately: this was the Bendlerstrasse! Ruoff then proposed giving out the codeword 'Scharnhorst' to alert all SS units; this was done, with the proviso that the SS units were to follow only orders from Himmler or Jüttner. Ruoff believes, relying on his memory, that this was no later than 15.30 hours. Towards evening, Himmler arrived at Tempelhof airfield, coming from 'Wolfschanze'; Jüttner and Ruoff had met him there and drove with him to the SS offices in Sarow on Scharmützelsee. Here

they all remained for at least two hours, until Kaltenbrunner telephoned to say there was shooting in the Bendlerstrasse; this was about 2200 hours. Thus Himmler must have arrived in Tempelhof between 1900 and 2000 hours. Besides the alert already mentioned, the SS leadership did nothing beyond detailing a reinforced escort for Himmler's arrival at Tempelhof. More was unnecessary since the units in Lichterfelde had been alerted and could be deployed at a moment's notice, according to Ruoff. On probable reasons for SS inactivity see below, Chap. 42, Note 74.

53 Cf. below, pp. 425, 481, 685, Note 74. Schellenberg testified in Nuremberg in November 1945 that it was his view that 'Himmler had something to do with the conspiracy', and that Himmler's possible foreknowledge or even complicity had been mentioned in interrogations following 20 July 1944; thereupon Kaltenbrunner and Fegelein had begun to undermine Himmler's position. See 'Testimony of Walter Schellenberg taken at Nurnberg [*sic*], Germany, on 13 November 1945', NA Record Group 238 Box 6. In the case of the Popitz-Langbehn connection, Himmler's knowledge, of course, is a matter of record and not unknown at least to Hitler and Wolff. Cf. pp. 296, 623 Note 32 above.

54 Transmitted to the author by Herr Peter Dietz of Schaffhausen. Extracts from the reports of another Swiss intelligence service have now been published and they are in some cases accurate on the German opposition – Kurt Emmenegger: *Qn wusste Bescheid*, pp. 44–51.

55 Conversation in July 1966 between Herr Peter Dietz and Burckhardt, formerly Swiss Military Attaché in Berlin, now Director in the Bührle machine-tool factory in Zurich-Oerlikon.

56 Zeller (*Flame*, p. 271) mentions, without giving evidence, an alleged Reuter report of about mid-June 1944 to the effect that the German General Staff officer who was to kill Hitler had already been earmarked. A search through *The Times* of June 1944 shows nothing on the subject. Hans Baur: *Hitler's Pilot*, p. 164, mentions a similar report of spring 1944; Nicolaus von Below: 'Hitlers Adjutant über den 20. Juli im FHQ' in *Echo der Woche* 15 July 1949, p. 5, says that in February 1944 Hitler showed him a foreign press report saying that a General Staff officer had already been designated assassin. This may be Zeller's source. A search of *The Times* of February 1944 produced no confirmation.

57 Gisevius, op. cit., pp. 485–6.

58 See pp. 392–3 below.

59 Critics of the preparations (for instance Gisevius in his 1954 German edition of *Ende*, p. 542 and *Bitter End*, pp. 506–10) tend to overlook the conditions of obscurity and incalculability in which the *coup* was prepared and conducted and the clashes of personality which affected these conspiratorial manoeuvres.

60 [Kurt] Peschel, typed notes, Wolfschanze 22 July 1944, BA EAP 105/34; Colonel Franz Herber to the author 25 Jan. 1966; *Spiegelbild*, p. 91; Albert Speer: *Inside the Third Reich*, p. 378; Kramarz, pp. 171–2, 176 does not refer to Peschel's notes nor the passage in *Spiegelbild*; he relies entirely on Nina Gräfin von Stauffenberg and Annedore Leber; yet Ritter (*Goerdeler*, p. 553 Note 120) had already reproduced Peschel's report in full; Zeller (pp. 274, 277) mentions this visit of Stauffenberg's to the headquarters but without giving evidence.

61 Bartram, pp. 7–8.

62 Peschel; *Spiegelbild*, p. 130; Speer, pp. 378–9.

63 Schlabrendorff (op. cit., pp. 122–3) paid two visits to 'Wolfschanze' in 1944 and also obtained information from Lieutenant-Colonel Dietrich von Bose, an officer of Jodl's staff; Schlabrendorff verbally to the author 6 Aug. 1968. Below see Nina Gräfin von Stauffenberg to the author 11 Sept. 1968.

64 *Spiegelbild*, p. 91; *Trial*, Vol. XXXIII, pp. 317–19.

65 Peschel; *Spiegelbild*, p.130; Speer, p. 378–9. [Rudolf Schmundt:] 'Tätigkeitsbericht des Chefs des Heerespersonalamts General der Infanterie

Schmundt begonnen: 1. 10. 1942 [fortgeführt bis 29. 10. 1944]', NA T-78 roll 39, 7 and 13 July 1944; Willi A. Boelcke (editor): *Deutschlands Rüstung im Zweiten Weltkrieg: Hitlers Konferenzen mit Albert Speer 1942–1945*, p. 390; Heinrich Himmler: *Geheimreden 1933 bis. 1945 und andere Ansprachen*, p. 215; David Irving: *Hitler und seine Feldherren*, pp. 604–605; further documentation of Himmler's presence is cited in Mr. Irving's English draft ms. which he had kindly made available to the author.

66 Speer (pp. 378–9) remembers that Stauffenberg's briefcase looked remarkably plump.

67 Diary of Col. Mertz's wife, Hilde Mertz von Quirnheim, entry of 15 July 1945. Frau Mertz made diary entries throughout July 1944, but in cautious and short form only; a year later, she put down the details for each of the fateful July days in a second diary.

68 See p. 376 above. Zeller (p. 292) records statements by Stauffenberg to the effect that he had *now* finally decided to make the attempt himself and then direct the *coup* in Berlin; he thought that he could be back in Berlin in two hours. Unforunately Zeller's evidence proves to be too thin – Sebastian Haffner in ' "Beinahe": Die Geschichte des 20. Juli 1944' *Neue Auslese* 2 (1947), No 8 pp. 1–12, who does not give his sources. There is a somewhat more reliable indication of the time of Stauffenberg's decision in Zeller, p. 293 – a remark by Urban Thiersch referring to 8 July: 'Stauffenberg will do it himself. He [? Thiersch] should inform his superior officer, Colonel Hansen.'

69 On this point and below see: *Trial*, Vol. XXXIII, pp. 319–20, 358–9, 384–94, 427, 432, 437; *Spiegelbild*, pp. 44, 49, 91, 125, 130, 146; sentence on Captain Kaiser; instruction suspending proceedings against Ewald Heinrich von Kleist and others, BA EAP 105/30; Peschel; Giesvius, *Bitter End*, pp. 491–3; Kramarz (p. 177) produces only the data from *Spiegelbild* and *Trial*, Vol. XXXIII together with personal information from Professor Percy Ernst Schramm which, however, had already appeared in essence in *Kriegstagebuch des Oberkommandos der Wehrmacht (Wehrmachtführungsstab) 1940–1945*, Vol. IV, p. 1754 Note 1; Zeller's account (p. 293) is short and based on *Spiegelbild*. Two references in *Spiegelbild*, pp. 125 and 146, leave open the date of the meeting between Klamroth, Stieff, Fellgiebel and Stauffenberg – 'about 10 July 1944' and 'on 10 or 11 July 1944'; This stems from uncertainty on the part either of those interrogated or the interrogators. Working on other sources there can be no question of any date for this meeting other than 11 July; there is nothing elsewhere to indicate that Stauffenberg made the journey from Berlin to Berchtesgaden and back twice, on 10 and 11 July.

70 Olbricht, Yorck von Wartenburg and Klausing all agree on this point; they all heard it from Stauffenberg (see Note 69 above); the same account was given by Ludwig Freiherr von Hammerstein-Equord in notes sent to Dr Helmut Pigge on 6 April 1970; Irving, p. 606 (without documentation); *Spiegelbild*, pp. 17, 21, 44, 49.

71 Gisevius, *Ende*, Vol. II, p. 321. Cf. *Spiegelbild*, pp. 17, 21, 44, 49.

72 *Spiegelbild*, p. 130; Gisevius, *Ende*, Vol. II, p. 321. Gisevius, *Bitter End*, pp. 491–3. The supposition that Stauffenberg knew before the conference began that Himmler would not be there is confirmed by a remark made by Olbricht to Hoepner in Berlin on 11 July as given by Hoepner to the *Gestapo* (*Spiegelbild*, pp. 44–9): 'One could suddenly be faced with a new situation and therefore he [Olbricht] had asked him – Hoepner – to come to Berlin that day. However he had then received information that the scheduled conference in the *Führer*'s headquarters was not taking place because the *Reichsführer-SS* had not arrived.'

73 There is considerable obscurity about Himmler's and Göring's habits, particularly as regards attendance at Hitler's situation conferences. Below, one of the aides, said (in 'Adjutant') that in 1944 it was almost exceptional if Himmler

and Göring were not at Hitler's briefing conferences. Hedwig Maier (p. 305) assumes that Himmler was 'usually' present; her source here is Helmut Heiber: *Hitlers Lagebesprechungen*, p. 13, which does not say this; Heiber merely says that Göring, Dönitz and Himmler 'also took part in the conferences' somewhat like any commanders summoned from the front, 'when they happened to be in the *Führer*'s headquarters'. Göring, Dönitz and Himmler had their own headquarters some distance from the 'Berghof' or 'Wolfschanze', alternatively in Berlin. Hedwig Maier's date for Stauffenberg's attempt – 12 July – is also wrong. On Himmler's and Göring's habits see Heinz Linge: 'Record of Hitler's Activities'; Himmler's telephone diary 21 Aug.–22 Nov. 1943, BA EAP 21-b/1-5, engagement diary 2 Jan.–16 Dec. 1943, 3 Jan.–31 May 1944 ibid., notes on meetings with Hitler May 1934–Dec. 1944, BA NS 19/275, 19/331; General Adolf Heusinger to the author 9 Sept. 1967; Rear-Admiral Karl Jesko von Puttkamer to the author 10 Sept. 1967.

74 According to *Spiegelbild*, p. 125 it was in the 'Berchtesgadener Hof' hotel, but see Schramm in *Kriegstagebuch des OKW*, Vol. IV, p. 1754 Note 1 and Kramarz p. 177; also Otto Reheuser (then telegraph construction officer in regional post office, Munich) verbally to the author 7 Aug. 1968.

75 Sentence on Kaiser; Gisevius, *Ende*, Vol. II, p. 305 says that Goerdeler was not informed beforehand.

76 *Trial*, Vol. XXXIII, pp. 350, 358–9.

77 'Das Spiel ist aus', *Der Spiegel* 23 March 1950, p. 23; *Volksgerichtshof-Prozesse zum 20. Juli 1944*, p. 51; Gisevius, *Bis zum bitteren Ende* (special edition), p. 507.

78 Suspension order (Note 69 above); Hammerstein, *Spähtrupp*, p. 263.

79 *Trial*, Vol. XXXIII, p. 433. Before the People's Court Hoepner referred to a telephone conversation with Olbricht on the evening of Friday, 14 July when Olbricht said: 'Stauffenberg went there today.' *Trial*, Vol. XXXIII, p. 394. According to this Stauffenberg left for the *Führer*'s headquarters on 14 July, presumably travelling by train; his driver remembers in complete detail that he took Stauffenberg to the Schlesische station on the evening of the 14th – verbally from Karl Schweizer 18 June 1965 and letter of 2 November 1967 giving 15th as the date; Husen gives 14th. General Reinecke remembers coming back to Berlin in the courier train with Stauffenberg on the night 15th/16th – Reinecke to the author 31 May 1964 and 7 Nov. 1967; Hoepner's statement that Olbricht had said that Stauffenberg was off to 'Wolfschanze' 'today' tallies with the 14th. It is at least possible, however, that Hoepner was referring to two different telephone calls; during the People's Court proceedings misleading expressions were frequently used and mistakes frequently occurred – questions and answers were flying back and forth quickly, Freisler was always interrupting and screaming at the accused and the shorthand writer did not always note everything correctly. This source must not be judged by the standards of a mediaeval manuscript quite apart from the fact that the object of the proceedings was not to discover the truth but to break the accused down. Hoepner said: 'He [Olbricht] said: "Stauffenberg went there today".' This, Hoepner said, was the expression used during a telephone conversation on 14 July but it was also in answer to an assertion by Freisler that Olbricht had telephoned Hoepner and said or hinted that 'It may happen today'. The interrogation report in *Spiegelbild*, p. 44, says that on his arrival in Berlin on 15 July Hoepner heard from Olbricht that Fromm and Stauffenberg had flown to the *Führer*'s headquarters that day. Hoepner had arrived having been summoned by Olbricht the previous evening. There must therefore be some confusion between the alleged telephone conversation on 14 July from which the quotation above is supposed to have come, and another on 15 July. A few sentences later in Hoepner's cross-examination before the People's Court Freisler quoted as follows from the *Gestapo* report on Hoepner's in-

terrogation (only indirectly given in *Spiegelbild*, p. 44): 'Olbricht told me that Fromm and Stauffenberg had flown to the Führer's headquarters; if something fresh should happen, he would rather that I was with him so that he could tell me at once' – *Trial*, Vol. XXXIII, p. 394. Hoepner's reply was: 'That's right.'

Apart, therefore, from Hoepner's inaccurate and misleading statement before the People's Court, the only evidence that Stauffenberg went *to* 'Wolfschanze' by train on the 14th comes from Husen and Schweizer, the driver, both of whom remember the details but are not totally certain of the date. What they remember may well have taken place on another day. Franz Herber (then a staff officer in the AHA) in 'Was ich am 20.7.44 in der Bendlerstrasse erlebte' (typescript, un-dated – probably 1948 – BA H 90-3/4) says that 'a few days before the assassination attempt' he 'travelled to the headquarters in the same sleeper' as Stauffenberg. Asked for details Herber replied in a letter to the author dated 25 Jan. 1966: '1. I did not travel with Graf Stauffenberg during the *first weeks of July 1944*. I had previously met him once in HQ OKH and a second time, according to my diary, "in the Reich Chancellery" and in "Frankenstrupp" – as far as I remember this was the codename of OKH headquarters [near Berchtesgaden]. 2. On the first journey we left Berlin on the evening of 29 May returning at midday on 31 May; the second time we left on the evening of 9 June returning on the morning of 12 June. 3. On both occasions we travelled in the same sleeper on the night train from Berlin ... 8. On both occasions I travelled back in the same sleeper with St[auffenberg].'

Other sources refer to a flight to 'Wolfschanze' – *Spiegelbild*, p. 130; Klausing in *Trial*, Vol. XXXIII, pp. 394, 397, 427. Here again inaccurate expressions might have been used and memories might be at fault. Finally, however, a written report dated 23 July 1944 from Lieutenant Geisberg of the *Führer's* headquarters Camp Commandant's staff says that he fetched Fromm, Stauffenberg and Klausing from Rastenburg airfield on 15 July – BA EAP 105/34 and NA, microcopy T-84 roll 21 – also applicable below; this is confirmed by a report from Streve, the Commandant, also dated 23 July 1944, ibid. These must be regarded as establishing the date and method of travel for Stauffenberg's journey to the headquarters. On Stauffenberg's return, see Note 110 below.

80 See pp. 338, 345 above. Walter Warlimont in his *Inside Hitler's Headquarters 1939–1945* (pp. 438–9) and in a letter to the author of 30 March 1964 says that the headquarters was moved to East Prussia definitively as early as 9 July 1944; cf. the author's 'Zu dem Attentat im Führerhauptquartier "Wolfsschanze" am 20. Juli 1944', *VfZ* 12 (1964), pp. 257–8. General Jodl noted in his pocket diary for 8 July 1944 'flight to Wolfschanze', and for 9 July 1944 'return flight to Berchtesgaden', for 14 July 1944 again 'flight to Wolfschanze'; NA microcopy T-84 roll R 149. In 1945 Warlimont himself remembered the events more accurately when he wrote that the headquarters was moved back to 'Wolfschanze' on 14 July 1944; Walter Warlimont: 'Circumstances of the Attempt of 20 July 1944', typescript 3 August 1945, NA Record Group 238 ETHINT-5.

81 See plans at Appendix.

82 See plan at Appendix. Many post-1945 accounts of 20 July and previous attempts maintain that the briefing conference was normally held in a bunker and that on *20 July only* it was held in a flimsy hut owing to the heat (or for other reasons). This story appears, for instance, in Walter Theimer: 'Die Verschwörung des 20 Juli' in *Die Welt* of 19 July 1947, p. 3; Dulles, *Underground*, p. 6; Hans Rothfels: *The German Opposition to Hitler*, p. 78 (revised in a new German edition – *Die deutsche Opposition gegen Hitler*, p. 87); Hans Hagen: *Zwischen Eid und Befehl*, pp. 49, 58. Chester Wilmot in *The Struggle for Europe*, p. 370, says explicitly that the 15 July conference took place 'in the bunker'. Adolf Heusinger in *Befehl im Widerstreit*, p. 352, says that the 20 July conference was held in an annex to Hitler's own bunker in 'Wolfschanze' (which was in fact used until the

headquarters moved to Berchtesgaden in February 1944), thereby contributing considerably to the general confusion. The account in Wheeler-Bennett, p. 637 is equally misleading. Berthold von Stauffenberg's twin brother Alexander has also helped to spread the story that the conference of 20 July was not held in the usual place; he produces a remarkable and quite unconfirmed variation – that the conspirators had carefully constructed a model concrete bunker and tested bombs in it 'with marked success' but instead of a bunker the conference took place in the 'tea house', a flimsy hut – Alexander Graf Stauffenberg: 'Der zwanzigste Juli 1944', typescript, 1946, in the possession of Gräfin Schwerin von Schwanenfeld. Of course, Alexander Graf Stauffenberg was neither a witness nor a participant to the preparations, nor even informed by his brothers. Marlene Gräfin von Stauffenberg verbally to the author 23 Aug. 1972. Walter Baum in 'Marine, Nationalsozialismus und Widerstand', *VfZ* 11 (1963), p. 31, still repeated the story that the conference was moved to a hut because of the heat. In fact from 15 to 20 July, both inclusive, all 'morning briefing conferences' took place in the hut near the bunker in which Hitler was living; the evening conferences were held in the bunker. See the author's 'Zu dem Attentat . . .', p. 257 and *Die Sicherheit des Diktators*, pp. 217–18, 231.

83 Geisberg; photograph by Heinrich Hoffmann (NA 242-HL-7233) and in Appendix of the German original edition of the present work.

84 Peschel.

85 Sources are not clear on this important point and so one must rely on indications. Events on 20 July make this supposition seem highly probable: see pp. 398–9 below.

86 See below, pp. 398–9.

87 Peschel.

88 *Spiegelbild*, p. 21, giving evidence by Berthold Graf Stauffenberg to whom his brother had shown the briefcase with the explosive and the shirt over it shortly before 20 July 1944. On 20 July 1944, Claus Graf Stauffenberg said shortly before the midday conference that he wished to change his shirt; see below, p. 398.

89 It is unlikely that Klausing helped if he was to wait for Stauffenberg at the car so that they could leave at once after the attack. See *Spiegelbild*, p. 130. On the role of Stieff see below, pp. 384–5. There must have been two briefcases.

90 Heinrich Himmler: manuscript notes on meetings with Hitler et al., May 1934–December 1944, BA NS 19/275 and 331 (NA T–175 roll 94).

A chart in which the *Gestapo* attempted to show the origin and travels of the explosive used by Stauffenberg on 20 July 1944 (*Spiegelbild*, p. 194) would indicate that Stauffenberg or Klausing or both had taken the explosive from 'Wolfschanze' on to 'Hochwald' (Himmler's headquarters near Grossgarten, a few miles east of 'Wolfschanze') on 15 July, before they returned to Berlin; in *Spiegelbild*, p. 49, a planned meeting between Stauffenberg and Himmler is mentioned. There is no evidence other than the chart to indicate that the conference did take place, and both Geisberg and Klausing gave evidence indicating that it did not take place. C. Müller (pp. 448 and 593 note 136) assumes that the conference did take place in 'Hochwald', accepting the information in the chart. This information may be the result of misunderstanding of the information reproduced in *Spiegelbild*, p. 49 where there is a reference to a *planned* conference; nowhere, however, is there any mention of such a conference as having taken place. If it had occurred, why should it be referred to as merely planned? On the other hand, the report in *Spiegelbild*, p. 49 does state that Himmler 'was not there': 'During his interrogation Klausing stated that the attack had not been carried out on 11 July mainly because the *Reichsführer-SS* had not been present, and [that] also on 15 July Stauffenberg had learned after the first conference, on the way to a planned further conference with the *Reichsführer-SS*, that the latter was not there.' From Dr Peschel's notes it must be concluded that the last conference at which the Stenographic Service took notes (thus, the last one at which Hitler was present) and in which Stauffenberg participated ended at 1425 hours. One may further conclude from Geisberg's report that Keitel's special train 'Braunschweig' had left the Moysee halt after Stauffenberg had boarded the train at about 1500 hours. Geisberg: 'After a good half hour Colonel-General Fromm left the main dining car and we hurried to the car.' The train must have stopped, but the report does not mention where. Fromm now wished to be driven to 'Mauerwald'; since this OKH headquarters was located immediately next to the railroad, the train may have stopped somewhere else. The camp was sprawling, however, and possibly Fromm and his company wished to be driven from the train stop to a distant building. Geisberg was ordered to redirect the 'Ju 52' aeroplane that Fromm and Stauffenberg wished to use for their return to Berlin to Lötzen airfield. At any rate, Stauffenberg appears to have come no closer to Himmler's headquarters 'Hochwald' and to the conference with Himmler than a train stop somewhere in the area. Now Geisberg, still according to his own report, had to take five gentlemen including Fromm, Lieutenant-General Buhle, and – as one must conclude from the context – Keitel, Stauffenberg and Klausing to 'Mauerwald'. Müller's assumption that Stauffenberg had a conference with Himmler on 15 July 1944 must be regarded as unconfirmed in the light of the other evidence.

91 Gisevius (*Bitter End*, p. 519), *Spiegelbild* (pp. 44, 49, 330) and *Trial* (Vol. XXXIII, p. 427 – statement by Yorck – and p. 433 – statement by Klausing) all indicate that it was Himmler's absence at the briefing conference on 15 July which caused Stauffenberg not to try to detonate his explosive immediately. The author had tended to discount these stories, finding it difficult to believe that the conspirators not only seriously tried to kill Hitler, Himmler and possibly Göring all at the same time (they must have known how rarely both Himmler and Göring attended the situation conferences, and the odds were even more against a combination Hitler-Himmler-Göring-Stauffenberg), but that they had not made any arrangements in case Stauffenberg had a chance to kill Hitler but not Himmler or Göring; after all, the advance alert for troops around Berlin given on 15 July could not be repeated. The emergence of another source, the diaries of Colonel Mertz's wife, have finally forced the author to accept what does not seem logical.

92 Frau Mertz von Quirnheim noted in her diary for 15 July 1944 on 15 July 1945: 'Early at 7 [a.m.] Albrecht telephoned the duty officer at Bendlerstrasse – after he had first called Stauffenberg and had learned that he had left – and told him to give out alert readiness orders according to a list from which he read, alerting the various officer and non-commissioned officer schools etc. in Berlin, Potsdam, Krampnitz and environs.' If Frau Mertz may be taken literally, this was not yet the actual call-up, but a preliminary alert. See also below, p. 677 Note 15.

93 For details see pp. 387–8 below. Kramarz (p. 244 Note 23) says, without evidence, that Beck had explicitly demanded that the attempt be made under all circumstances.

94 *Spiegelbild*, p. 330. According to Geisberg's report Stauffenberg telephoned Stieff and Fellgiebel via Amt 'Anna' immediately after his arrival in the Kurhaus mess in Area II of 'Wolfschanze'.

95 *Spiegelbild*, p. 49; Gisevius (*Ende*, Vol. II, pp. 339–42; see also *Bitter End*, pp. 517–20), after recounting the course of events, asks why Stauffenberg telephoned yet once more and concludes that he had 'lost his head' and was suffering from 'psychological inhibitions'. Cf. below, pp. 384–5. See also *Spiegelbild*, p. 44; *Trial*, Vol. XXXIII, pp. 427, 433; Gisevius, *Bitter End*, p. 519; diary of Frau Mertz von Quirnheim. Only Gisevius mentions Göring in this context.

Kramarz, p. 244 Note 23 says: 'In all earlier accounts the statement appears that Stauffenberg did not set off the bomb on 15 July because neither Himmler nor Göring were present. This statement stems from Gisevius (p. 352).' This is not correct. Schlabrendorff, for instance, (op. cit., pp. 135–6) says that the reason was that Hitler left the conference room unexpectedly and did not return and that Himmler and Göring were present. Zeller (pp. 295–6) is vague on the subject and even Ritter (*Goerdeler*, p. 405) *questions* whether Himmler's absence was the reason and adds that, according to the 'only available first-hand witness' (he must mean Helldorf via Gisevius, though he does not say so) the answer must be 'yes'. Zeller (p. 295) mentions some unidentified Colonel who perhaps would have thrown a second bomb, perhaps at Himmler, 'if one can believe an isolated unconfirmed report'. Zeller does not document this at all.

96 *Spiegelbild*, p. 45; Gisevius, *Bitter End*, p. 519; according to Yorck before the People's Court 'it was said' that Stauffenberg had had to telephone and when he got back the meeting had ended – *Trial*, Vol. XXXIII, p. 427.

97 Gisevius, *Ende*, Vol. II, pp. 345, 353–4 and *Bitter End*, p. 525. Gisevius suggests (*Bitter End*, p. 520; *Ende*, Vol. II, pp. 342, 353–4) that Stauffenberg was so nervous that he 'shied away before the jump' at the last moment, and that he was not prevented by external circumstances from setting off his bomb.

98 *Spiegelbild*, pp. 130–1; *Trial*, Vol. XXXIII, pp. 319–20. Stauffenberg had already considered 'acting' on 11 July 1944 whether Himmler was there or not; *Spiegelbild*, p. 130. Stieff also claimed that he had prevented the assassination attempt at the uniform demonstration; *Spiegelbild*, p. 90; *Trial*, Vol. XXXIII, p. 313.

99 Gisevius, *Bitter End*, p. 525. Apparently Stieff made no such claim after 20 July; this might have destroyed his original line of defence (although he was unable to maintain it during his trial, as it developed) that he had done his best to talk Stauffenberg out of the plan and then believed he had succeeded and therefore had not reported his knowledge of Stauffenberg's plan. Had Stieff admitted that he had had to resort to removing the briefcase from the conference room on 15 July, he could hardly have maintained that Stauffenberg had apparently given up his plan as a result of Stieff's intervention; Stieff would then further have had to admit that he knew that Stauffenberg was making another attempt on that day which he had again not reported. Cf. *Spiegelbild*, p. 33. C. Müller (p. 593 note 137) uses an obvious printing error in Gisevius' 1954 edition of *Bis zum bittern Ende* (p. 596) to help 'prove' Gisevius' alleged unreliability: Gisevius here says 'Sonntagabend' ('Sunday evening') instead of 'Sonnabend' ('Saturday evening') – as he does correctly a few pages later in the same edition (p. 599), and in *Ende*, Vol. II, p. 350 and *Bitter End*, p. 525.

100 Frau Mertz von Quirnheim's diary, 15 July 1944 and 1945.

101 Cf. above, pp. 380–1 and Note 67 above. Siebeck: Dr Eberhard Siebeck, then a captain and instructor at the War Academy in Hirschberg, was called to Berlin by his friend Mertz in the hope that he would join the conspiracy; Siebeck spent the weekend of 15–16 July 1944 with Mertz. Siebeck to the author 1 October 1971.

Gisevius, *Bitter End*, p. 519, based on information from Helldorf, reports that Haeften took the [first] telephone call from Stauffenberg and gave 'instructions' that Stauffenberg was to set off the bomb even in the absence of Himmler and Göring; Helldorf, Olbricht and Hoepner, who were standing by the telephone, were 'indignant' although basically in agreement with what Haeften said; about fifteen minutes later, Stauffenberg had called again: the conference had just ended as he had returned to it. This version obviously differs considerably from the one recorded by Frau Mertz von Quirnheim. See also Hoepner's statements to the *Gestapo* in *Spiegelbild*, pp. 44–5: from a telephone call between Mertz and Olbricht Hoepner had gathered 'that Mertz had just telephoned Stauffenberg and learned that the conference, which Stauffenberg had left for a moment, had ended prematurely'. In verbal information given the author on 8 September 1972 Gisevius allowed that Helldorf may have given him an incomplete version of the episode, that it seemed likely that Haeften had transferred Stauffenberg's call to Mertz (whether because there were too many others in the room for Haeften to speak freely, or because Stauffenberg wanted to talk to Mertz – the more plausible explanation), and that Stauffenberg was not likely to have asked Haeften rather than Mertz or one of the other leaders whether he should set off the bomb or not. The decision-making by Stauffenberg and Mertz to the exclusion of Beck, Olbricht and others, Gisevius further pointed out, jibed with Olbricht's impression on 20 July 1944 that he had been 'rail-roaded' by Mertz (Gisevius, *Bitter End*, pp. 540–1 and verbally to the author 8 September 1972), and it was characteristic of this amateurish conspiracy, and of the conspiracy of colonels within the conspiracy.

102 *Spiegelbild*, pp. 21, 45; confirmed by Gisevius, *Bitter End*, p. 519; Yorck's evidence before the People's Court in *Trial*, Vol. XXXIII, p. 427; Frau Mertz von Quirnheim, diary 15 July 1944 and 1945.

103 Gisevius, *Ende*, Vol. II, pp. 345, 351 and verbally to the author 8 September 1972; Frau Mertz von Quirnheim, diary for 16 July 1944 (with a dating error in the 1945 entry – 'Sunday, 17' – but given correctly in the contemporary entry).

104 Gisevius, *Ende*, Vol. II, pp. 350, 353.

105 Geisberg says that 'after the briefing' Fromm went off with certain others. Since he was waiting outside, he did not know that in the meanwhile not only the 'morning briefing' but also two 'special conferences' had taken place.

106 In his report Geisberg says that the 'Braunschweig' special train was standing at the Moysee halt. This was Keitel's train – see p. 339 above. Hitler's train was called 'Brandenburg'. There were also special trains for the OKW Operations Staff, 'Franken I' and 'Franken II' (Wolf papers); Hoffmann, *Sicherheit*, p. 84.

107 Geisberg; *Spiegelbild*, pp. 130–1.

108 This earlier time is in fact much more likely, as C. Müller, p. 593 note 135 points out, than 'towards 16.0 hours' (German edition of the present work, p. 456).

109 *Spiegelbild*, p. 130–1; Geisberg says: 'Shortly before departure of the "Braunschweig" special train Colonel Graf Stauffenberg made a telephone call to Berlin. The three of us, Colonel Graf Stauffenberg, Captain Klausing and I, then drove to the Field Marshal's train, I took them to the dining car and handed them over to Captain Starke.'

110 Reinecke to the author 30 May 1964, 7 Nov. 1967. Stauffenberg's return to Berlin only on 16 July is confirmed by Frau Mertz von Quirnheim's diary, 15 and 16 July 1944, and by Gisevius, *Ende*, Vol. II, p. 345; cf. above, note 79.

111 Sentence on Captain Kaiser, BA EAP 105/30; Ritter, *Goerdeler*, pp. 404–5 (*Resistance*, p. 283); Gisevius, *Bitter End*, pp. 517–18. Kramarz (p. 182) takes no account of these sources and accepts the highly disparaging *Gestapo* report in *Spiegelbild*, p. 362 according to which on 15 July Goerdeler was sitting, very vexed, with Strünck (Captain and member of the *Abwehr*) and was told nothing. In fact neither Beck, Gisevius nor Strünck were told that the attempt had not been made, either because no one dared to, as Gisevius hints (*Ende*, Vol. II, p. 345), or because Olbricht was too preoccupied cancelling the alert.

112 Report on proceedings from Dr Lorenzen to Bormann, 2 March 1945 on Nebe's trial, BA EAP 105/30; 'Das Spiel ist aus', pp. 23–6; cf. Gisevius, *Bitter End*, p. 492.

113 Sentence of People's Court of 15 August 1944 on B. Klamroth et al., NA microcopy T-120 roll 1038.

114 See note 112; Hammerstein, *Spähtrupp*, p. 263, and letter to Dr Helmut Pigge 6 April 1970.

115 Hagen, pp. 14–15; Ritter, *Goerdeler*, pp. 405, 554 Note 125 where he says (wrongly): 'Olbricht had deliberately issued the alert two hours before the arrival of news from the Obersalzberg [sic] to forestall any counter-measures by the SS.' Zeller (p. 295) says the same without giving his source (probably Ritter). Confirmation that the alert was issued at 11 a.m. in Gisevius, *Bitter End*, p. 517. *Spiegelbild*, p. 45; *Trial*, Vol. XXXIII, p. 394. According to Frau Mertz von

Quirnheim's diary (15 July 1944 and 1945), Mertz issued an alert very early in the morning, though perhaps a preliminary one. Albert Bollmann, then a captain and chief of artillery inspection in Training Group II with Training Staff 1 (gunnery school) of Infantry School Döbertiz, wrote to the author on 29 August 1971: codeword 'Valkyrie' was received there 'about 13.50 hours' on 15 July 1944; the alert was regarded as a practice alert, but it was fully complied with and carried out. Dr Friedrich Georgi, son-in-law of General Olbricht, maintains (verbally to the author 21 May 1973) that Olbricht did not issue the alert until after Stauffenberg's first telephone call from 'Wolfschanze'; this would agree with the timing given by Bollmann, and it would also fit into the time-frame given in Dr Peschel's notes (according to them, the first part of the 'morning briefing' on 15 July 1944 lasted from 13.10 to 13.40, and a subsequent 'special conference' from 13.40 to 14.20 hours). But it contradicts the evidence in Frau Mertz von Quirnheim's diary according to which Olbricht did not want Stauffenberg to go ahead at all; this leaves open the possibility that it was Mertz who not only told Stauffenberg to proceed with the attack but also alerted the schools without Olbricht's authorization. On the other hand, there are reasons to doubt that Georgi was informed about these details: he revised his story about the time that Olbricht received Fellgiebel's message on 20 July 1944 (see below, p. 674 Note 4); and an account written by Georgi during the night of 20/21 July 1944 appears to indicate that Georgi was informed about the plot for the first time an hour or two before Olbricht's death (Georgi, memo, ms. Bernau 21 July 1944), at which time Olbricht is not likely to have told Georgi the minutiae of 15 July.

116 On this point and below see: Bruno Mitzkus (ex-Operations officer in *Wehrkreis* III): 'Um den 20. Juli und das Ende im Wehrkreiskommando III' typescript, Bad Homburg 1947; Wolfgang Müller: 'Was geschah am 20. Juli 1944?' in *Das freie Wort* No 29, 19 July 1952; report by Amt V of the RSHA on suicide of Major Ulrich von Oertzen; Fritz Harnack verbally to the author 29 Aug. 1966; *Trial*, Vol. XXXIII, p. 394; Gisevius, *Bitter End*, p. 517; *Spiegelbild*, pp. 45, 91, 158; Otto Hitzfeld (then Lieutenant-General commanding the Infantry School, Döberitz), letter to Gert Buchheit 5 July 1966, signed copy in IfZ ZS 1858.

117 Gisevius, *Bitter End*, p. 519; Frau Mertz von Quirnheim, diary 15 July 1944 and 1945.

118 Bollmann, also applicable below.

119 Gisevius, *Ende*, Vol. II, pp. 345, 350 (*Bitter End*, p. 521–2) is the only author who received a first-hand account of this interview. Zeller (pp. 296–7) says without quoting a source that Stauffenberg and Beck discussed the 'deficiencies' of 15 July and Stauffenberg gave Beck his word that he would act next time whatever happened. Kramarz's account (pp. 182–3) is similar but based on Wheeler-Bennett, p. 634 and Wheeler-Bennett has no evidence for his statement. Hammerstein says (*Spähtrupp*, p. 269) that Beck *ordered* Stauffenberg not to make the attempt unless he could survive himself since, with his energy and position, he was essential for the conduct of the *coup* in Berlin.

120 Gisevius, *Ende*, Vol. II, pp. 350, 353–4.

121 *Spiegelbild*, pp. 91–2, 101–2, 111, 175; Ritter, *Goerdeler*, pp. 408–9 (*Resistance*, p. 286), based on parts of the interrogation reports given in *Spiegelbild*, mentions only the Stauffenberg brothers, Trott, Schulenburg and Hofacker; Zeller's account (pp. 296–7) is more complete; also Kramarz, p. 183 which is also based on the *Gestapo* reports. See also People's Court sentence on B. Klamroth et al., of 15 August 1944, NA microcopy T-120 roll 1038; Mertz and Hansen are not mentioned here. C. Müller, p. 451 has Mertz living in Stauffenberg's flat; actually Mertz had moved into Harnack-Hause with his new wife early in July (Frau Mertz von Quirnheim's diary, 4 July 1944 et seq.).

122 *Spiegelbild*, pp. 91–2, 101; Gisevius, *Ende*, Vol. II, pp. 342–5, 353, (*Bitter End*, pp. 521–7); Hammerstein, *Spähtrupp*, p. 264.

123 Hans Speidel: *We defended Normandy*, pp. 82–91, 118–25.
124 *Spiegelbild*, p. 136; see p. 354 above.
125 *Spiegelbild*, p. 101 (in italics). Cf. above, pp. 238–9.
126 The quotation is from sentence on B. Klamroth et al.; cf. the proposals transmitted to Washington by Allen Dulles, above, pp. 238–9.
127 See pp.337–47 above.
128 Speidel, pp. 91, 126–7.
129 Gisevius, *Ende*, Vol. II, pp. 342–5, 353 (*Bitter End*, pp. 521–7); Nebgen, pp. 192–3.
130 Leber, *Das Gewissen steht auf*, p. 126; Albert Krebs: *Fritz-Dietlof Graf von der Schulenburg*, p. 297; Gisevius, *Ende*, p. 351 (*Bitter End*, p. 526); Frau Margarete Hase verbally to the author 31 March 1964; Hammerstein, *Spähtrupp*, p. 266.
131 For instance, Baum, p. 31.
132 'Kriegstagebuch des Oberbefehlshabers West', BA – MA H 11-10–39A; Speidel, pp. 128–9. Rommel's car was shot at from the air and had an accident in which Rommel suffered a skull-fracture and other injuries.
133 Gisevius in *Trial*, Vol. XII, pp. 259–60 and *Ende*, Vol. II, pp. 348–9 (*Bitter End*, p. 524). Confirmed by Willy Litzenberg, a member of the '20 July Special Commission' in 'Der 20. Juli 1944', typescript, Nuremberg, 4 June 1946. According to this *Gestapo* Müller proposed to Himmler that Goerdeler and Beck be arrested; Himmler's refusal arrived a few days after 20 July. Nebe admitted to the People's Court that on 17 or 18 July he had told Gisevius of the proposed arrest of Goerdeler – sentence on Nebe. See also Hammerstein, *Spähtrupp*, pp. 270–1; *Spiegelbild*, p. 363. Gisevius (*Ende*, Vol. II, p. 348; *Bitter End*, p. 524) mentions a 'Colonel St.' who admitted under torture that Goerdeler was a candidate to succeed Hitler; Gisevius describes him as garrulous which is hardly fair if he made the statement under torture. The colonel was Colonel Staehle; Gisevius verbally to the author 4 August 1971. Ritter (*Goerdeler*, p. 411) does not deal with the question of the identity of the man who is supposed to have provided evidence for the arrest of Goerdeler. Ger van Roon in *Wilhelm Staehle*, p. 63, gives some details without fully clearing up the matter, and also without reference to Gisevius.
134 Gisevius, *Ende*, Vol. II, pp. 345–6.
135 If Helldorf was really so badly informed, it must be admitted that his past did not inspire much confidence. Gisevius (*Bitter End*, pp. 528–9) gives Helldorf's own view: 'Helldorf realized that his long term of office under the Nazis had compromised him too thoroughly. Within a few days after the *putsch* he would have to resign.' On the other hand Gisevius exaggerates this alleged lack of information given to Helldorf and others so much as to give the impression that he is putting into the mouth of men like Helldorf, Nebe, Hansen and even Beck his own annoyance at the fact that he was no longer in the conspiracy's inner circle and, owing to his long absence, no longer so completely informed.
136 Gisevius, *Bitter End*, pp. 525–6.
137 Gisevius, *Ende*, Vol. II, pp. 353–4.
138 Gisevius, *Bitter End*, pp. 525–6.
139 F. W. Heinz: 'Offener Brief an Herrn Remer', *Deutsche Wirklichkeit* no 18, 1 September 1949, pp. 8–9.
140 From Frau von Hase; Heinz, 'Offener Brief'.
141 Ibid; [Alexander von Hase]: 'Zur Sache Remer' (evidence for Oldenburg State Attorney), typescript, [1950]; Müller, 'Was geschah'; Gisevius, special edition, pp. 480–1; also *Ende*, Vol. II, p. 317 and *Bitter End*, p. 509.
142 Heinz Burchardt: 'Zugehörigkeit zur Widerstandsbewegung.'
143 *Spiegelbild*, p. 158.
144 Colonel (retd) Hans-Werner Stirius to the author 2 Feb. 1967.
145 Ritter, *Goerdeler*, p. 408 (*Resistance*, p. 286); *Spiegelbild*, p. 524; Nebgen, pp.

192–3 – also applicable below.

146 *Spiegelbild*, pp. 21, 92, 110, 146; *Trial*, Vol. XXXIII, pp. 429, 437; Hammerstein to Dr Pigge; Zeller referring to *Spiegelbild*, p. 21 (which does not say so) maintains that a 'summons' to Stauffenberg arrived in Berlin on the afternoon of 18 July ordering him to appear for a briefing in the headquarters on the 20th; in a note, however, (p. 433 Note 42) Zeller quotes Adolf Heusinger (*Befehl im Widerstreit*, pp. 350–2); this says that at the briefing conference of 19 July Keitel proposed to get Stauffenberg to come once more so that they could hear his views on release of further forces for the eastern front. Zeller does not comment on this discrepancy, although he could have said with some justification that Heusinger's memory frequently failed him. Ernst John von Freyend (Keitel's Aide) told the author on 14 May 1964 that Stauffenberg was summoned on the 19th to appear in 'Wolfschanze' on the 20th. This, however, like Heusinger's account, leaves open the possibility that Stauffenberg was summoned on the 18th, though perhaps not in such definite terms.

147 Philippa Gräfin von Thun-Hohenstein, née Bredow, to the author 24 Feb. and 25 May 1970; see also evidence by Graf von Welsburg in the 'Kaltenbrunner Report' of 30 Aug. 1944, BA EAP 105/24, pp. 55–9 (not in *Spiegelbild*, p. 319 since it contains details on persons still alive). Baum, pp. 31–2. Baum accepts Jessen's account in saying that the attempt was made on 20 July, when neither Himmler nor Göring were present and the briefing conference took place in a hut instead of a bunker, because of this rumour and that this, therefore, was responsible for the failure of Stauffenberg's attempt. I have available a report by Jessen (typescript entitled 'Aufzeichnung', 1946) which is to all intents and purposes identical with that used by Baum which is in IfZ, Munich. In the light of the description of events between 1 and 18 July as given here, it is clear that Jessen's conclusion is incorrect.

148 As already mentioned, the rumour did not in fact go further than the circle in which it originated. The *Gestapo* only got wind of it on 30 August 1944 – report of that date in BA EAP 105/24 (not in *Spiegelbild*, pp. 318–20). The report demolishes Hitler's statement about 'a very small clique of ambitious, unscrupulous, criminal and stupid officers' in that, referring merely to the circle in which Haeften and Jessen moved, it mentions a 'widespread and variegated' circle of people. See Hitler's broadcast in Max Domarus: *Hitler: Reden und Proklamationen 1932–1945*, pp. 2127–9; *20. Juli 1944*, pp. 185–6.

149 *Spiegelbild*, pp. 55, 117.

150 This is confirmed if, as it appears, Kranzfelder's warning preceded the decision on or forecast of the date for Stauffenberg's briefing. The 'fixture' was known about 5 p.m. and equally about 5 p.m. Kranzfelder arrived back in 'Koralle'. On this point, therefore Jessen is right, as will be seen below.

151 *Spiegelbild*, p. 117 – underlined in the original, in italics in print.

152 Jessen, 'Aufzeichnung'.

153 Stirius to the author 2 Feb. 1967 – also applicable below. Zeller (pp. 298–9) and Kramarz (p. 184) say that 19 July passed like any other day.

154 Heinz Pieper verbally to the author, 24 July 1965.

155 Lt.-Gen. Wolfgang Thomale to the author 11 August 1971.

156 Report by 'G.A.', an eyewitness, in 'Letzte Begegnung mit Graf Stauffenberg', *Stuttgarter Zeitung* 20 July 1950, quoted by Zeller (pp. 299, 433 note 43).

157 *Trial*, Vol. XXXIII, p. 359; F. Zimmermann: *Ludwig Freiherr von Leonrod*, p. 21.

158 *Trial*, Vol. XXXIII, pp. 395–6.

159 Ibid., pp. 485–6 (Hase's evidence).

160 From Schweizer; *Spiegelbild*, pp. 170, 194.

161 On this and below: Rainer Graf von Kanitz (Gen. Wagner's former aide) to Frau Elisabeth Wagner 23 March 1964 and verbally to the author 28 August 1972. C.

Müller (p. 596 notes 160, 161) doubts that Stauffenberg visited Wagner on 19 July, but says (based on information from Prof. Dr Julius Speer) that Stauffenberg had gone to see Wagner in Zossen twice before [presumably: not long before] 20 July 1944, so that the interviews might well have taken place on 18 and 19 July.
162 Kramarz, p. 185.
163 Zeller, p. 300 clearly based on information from Schweizer which Zeller obtained from Schweizer's sister in 1948; he refers to a church in Dahlem. In 1965 Schweizer thought that he could remember having to drive Stauffenberg to a church in Steglitz.
164 Zeller, p. 300; Kramarz, p. 185 – both without giving source. This is confirmed by Berthold Graf Stauffenberg's evidence on 22 July; on the evening of 19 July, he said, his brother had shown him the briefcase containing the bomb and he had accompanied his brother to the airport next morning – *Spiegelbild*, p. 21.

NOTES/PART IX/CHAPTER 41

1 Karl Schweizer verbally to the author 18 June 1965; *Spiegelbild einer Verschwörung*, p. 21; Frau Mertz von Quirnheim, diary 20 July 1944 and 1945.
2 From Schweizer. At the conclusion of a report on the interrogations of Yorck, Trott and Hermann Kaiser *Spiegelbild*, p. 112 suddenly produces an extract from the on-the-spot report of the RSHA 'Special Commission 20 July 1944' dated 26 July; this belongs to p. 86.
3 This may be inferred from *Spiegelbild*, pp. 86, 112. Herr Max Müller, who was serving on Rastenburg airfield in 1942, has made certain calculations which he made available to the author on 26 Nov. 1967; he also gave information on 31 Oct. 1967 to the 'Hilfswerk 20. Juli 1944' Foundation. He worked on a take-off time of 7 a.m., which is also given in *Spiegelbild*, pp. 22, 84, 86. The 'Ju 52' was slow (top speed 180 m.p.h.); at an average speed of 110 m.p.h., therefore, it would have taken some three hours to cover the 350 miles. According to Schweizer take-off was delayed until about 8 a.m., in which case the 'Ju 52' must have flown nearly at top speed. Based on information from Colonel (*Luftwaffe*) Aldinger, Colonel Meichssner told Professor Schramm, the OKW Operations Staff War Diary Officer, that Stauffenberg had used General Wagner's aircraft for both the outward *and* return journeys – [Percy Ernst Schramm]: 'Mitteilungen des Oberst d.G. Meichsner [sic] ... 23.7., 9 Uhr', State Archives Nuremberg PS 1808, also given in Herbert Kraus: *Die im Braunschweiger Remerprozess ... Gutachten nebst Urteil*, pp. 148–50. The 'He 111' may therefore have been used both ways. Since even in 1940 this aircraft had a top speed of 310 m.p.h. Stauffenberg and Haeften can have been back in Berlin about 2.45 p.m. See pp. 416–7 and 675 Note 14 below.
4 On the areas and enclosures and confusion about their nomenclature see diagram at Appendix and Peter Hoffmann: *Die Sicherheit des Diktators*, pp. 213–36. Heinz Pieper told the author on 24 July 1965 that he had sent a pool driver, Second Lieutenant Erich Kretz, to the airfield; Kretz himself (a courier driver) however, only remembers being allotted to Stauffenberg and Haeften at *midday* and taking them *back* to the airfield – Kretz verbally to the author on 29 Aug. 1965 and 31 Aug. 1966 (henceforth referred to as 'Kretz I' and 'Kretz II'). See also Helmuth Spaeter: *Die Geschichte des Panzerkorps Grossdeutschland*, Vol. II, p. 564. On the whole course of events in the *Führer*'s headquarters on 20 July see the author's 'Zu dem Attentat im Führerhauptquartier "Wolfschanze" am 20. Juli 1944' in *VfZ* 12 (1964), pp. 266–84. Considerably more is now known from fresh sources. On time of landing see *Spiegelbild*, p. 84. Lieutenant-Colonel Ernst John von Freyend (then Major and aide to Keitel) verbally to the author on 14 May 1965 maintained quite definitely that Stauffenberg

landed in Rastenburg about 9 a.m. or somewhat earlier; he only heard of Stauffenberg's arrival over the telephone, however, when he had reached the Area II mess; Lieutenant-Colonel Otto Lechler, then desk officer for organization in General Buhle's office, told the author the same thing on 5 June 1964 and Major Eduard Ackermann (also in Buhle's office at the time) said the same on 20 Nov. 1964. John von Freyend, Lechler and Ackermann (the latter perhaps independently of Lechler) are the only people to mention the earlier arrival time and they in fact had no touch with Stauffenberg until about 11 a.m. Other indications show that, if Stauffenberg really did arrive at 9 a.m. or earlier, he must have spent an hour and a half or more over breakfast. In 1950, however, Dr Bernd Wehner (in 1944 with the *Gestapo*'s on-the-spot commission), based on the commission's report of 26 July 1944, his own recollections and enquiries of his ex-colleagues, put the arrival time at 10.15 a.m. – *Spiegelbild*, p. 84; [Bernd Wehner]: 'Das Spiel ist aus' in *Der Spiegel*, No 12, 23 March 1950, p. 31. Wehner and his commission had of course questioned not only members of the *Führer*'s headquarters but also the airfield personnel. The 'Bericht zum Attentat auf den Führer am 20. Juli 1944' given in *Spiegelbild*, pp. 84–6 and 112–13 did *not* originate from Dr Wehner directly but evaluated the results of his investigations – Wehner to the author 27 Oct. 1965, 4 Dec. 1967. Dr Wehner does not know what happened to his own report after he handed it in but thinks it possible that inaccurate extracts were made, which would explain many of the obscurities and gaps. Information also from Pieper; Dr Wilhelm Tobias Wagner, senior dental officer to the *Führer*'s headquarters who was present at the breakfast, verbally to the author 29 July 1965; Dr Erich Walker, medical officer on the Camp Commandant's staff and also present at breakfast, verbally to the author 25 July 1965. The probable flying time of $1\frac{1}{2}$–2 hours and Schweizer's information about the delay in take-off make it look as if 9 a.m. was the normal *scheduled* time of arrival of the courier aircraft and this is the time remembered by those who had to arrange Stauffenberg's meetings with Keitel and Buhle. For many of the events of 20 July a number of those questioned give timings earlier than was in fact the case – see, for instance, Note 11 below on time of start of the briefing conference.

5 The commission of inquiry's report given in *Spiegelbild*, p. 84 says: 'Major-General Stieff, head of the OKH Organization Section, and Lieutenant von Haeften, aide to Stauffenberg, arrived at the same time [at the airfield].' Colonel Meichssner in Berlin gathered further details of Stauffenberg's flight from a briefing by Colonel (*Luftwaffe*) Aldinger – 'that Stauffenberg had used the Deputy Chief of Staff's aircraft and that General Stieff and Major Rall had also been in it' – Schramm 'Mitteilungen Meichssner'. There is no other evidence that Stieff was on the flight from Berlin.

6 From Pieper; Spaeter, p. 564; Wagner; Walker; Colonel Herbert Kandt (personnel officer in headquarters *Wehrkreis* I) to the author 11 Feb. and 13 Mar. 1964; Thadden died in 1945. Walker and *Spiegelbild*, pp. 84–5, both include Lieutenant-Colonel Streve, the Camp Commandant, but must be wrong; Spaeter also includes Haeften, obviously wrongly, and does not mention Wagner and Walker.

7 The early arrival of Thadden and his officer and the fact that they had to wait is another indication that Stauffenberg was delayed and that his *scheduled* time of arrival was earlier. On the purpose of the conference see [Rudolf Schmundt:] 'Tätigkeitsbericht des Chefs des Heerespersonalamts General der Infanterie Schmundt begonnen: 1.10.42 [fortgeführt bis 29.10.1944]', NA T–78 roll 39, 19 and 20 July 1944.

8 Lechler; Wagner; Walker. Pieper and Spaeter, p. 564 (the latter obviously based on Pieper) say that Stauffenberg went in the pool car which had waited at the mess; Pieper remarked that the briefcase was very heavy whereupon Stauffenberg said that it contained specimens from the Armaments Office. Ac-

cording to Dr Walker the remark was made by Jansen. No one says that *at this point* Stauffenberg had two briefcases. When he went to his meetings Haeften, who must have had the other case, was not with him; Stauffenberg could therefore hardly have had the case containing the bomb; it must have contained the papers he needed for his meetings. Independently of Pieper and more reliably, Walker and others say that Stauffenberg went off on foot with Jansen; Walker adds that Jansen made the comment about the weight of the case and Stauffenberg replied that that was so – there was a lot to talk about today. Wehner in 'Das Spiel ist aus', p. 31, is the only one to report that Stauffenberg met Fellgiebel on the way from the mess to Keitel's hut (see plan at Appendix); Jansen could not be found before his death in 1966 and so there is no other evidence. Lieutenant-Colonel Ludolf Gerhard Sander, the *Wehrmacht* Signals Officer, told the author verbally on 24 and 25 April 1964 that Fellgiebel arrived in his office in 'Wolfschanze' noticeably early that day, about 8 a.m.; he knows nothing, however, of the meeting between Stauffenberg and Fellgiebel mentioned by Wehner.

9 *Spiegelbild*, p. 85; letters to the author 11 Feb. and 13 Mar. 1964 from Colonel Kandt who was accompanying Thadden.

10 Not, therefore, in the same complex of buildings as is said in the author's 'Attentat', p. 267, which was based on less complete source material. *Spiegelbild*, p. 85; John von Freyend; Lechler; Sander; Wehner.

11 On the timing of the conference: Nicolaus von Below (at the time *Luftwaffe* aide to Hitler) verbally to the author 15 May 1964, also interrogation report 032/Case No 0279, typescript, 23 Jan. 1946 and 'Hitlers Adjutant über den 20. Juli im FHQu' in *Echo der Woche*, 15 July 1949; Heinz Buchholz (shorthand writer): 'Das Attentat auf Adolf Hitler am 20. Juli 1944', typescript, Berchtesgaden, 14 July 1945, University of Pennsylvania Library 46 M-25; Buchholz quoted in Percy Knauth: 'The Hitler Bomb Plot' in *Life*, 28 May 1945, pp. 17–18, 20, 23 and *Germany in Defeat*, pp. 175–82; Herbert Büchs (at the time Major in the OKW Operations Staff) verbally to the author 1 July 1964; John von Freyend; Rear-Admiral Karl Jesko von Puttkamer (at the time Naval Aide to Hitler) verbally to the author 5 Mar. 1964; [Percy Ernst Schramm]: 'Mitteilungen des Stellv. Chefs WFSt [General Warlimont] 21.7.44 20 Uhr' in Ops Staff War Diary, 22 July 1944, StA Nuremberg PS 1808, reproduced in Kraus, pp. 142–5 (henceforth referred to as 'Schramm (Warlimont)'; Heinz Waizenegger (at the time Lieutenant-Colonel and senior staff officer OKW Operations Staff) verbally to the author 9 Sept. 1963; Wehner. All these agree that the briefing conference had been put forward from its normal time of 1 p.m. to 12.30. General (*Luftwaffe*) Karl Heinrich Bodenschatz (then Göring's Permanent Liaison Officer to Hitler) gave accounts after the war that differ in details. When he was interrogated by an RAF officer on 15 May 1945, ten days after his capture, Bodenschatz gave 12.30 as the time of the start of the conference; Bodenschatz in C.S.D.I.C. (U.K.) G.G. Report 15 May 1945, S.R.G.G. 1219 (C), typescript. In another interrogation he gave 12.45; Dr Otto John's papers, folio 5, Adolf Heusinger in *Befehl im Widerstreit*, p. 352, gives 12 noon; Heinz Assmann (then Captain, naval officer in the OKW Operations Staff) in Kurt Assmann: *Deutsche Schicksalsjahre*, pp. 453–60 says that the conference was put forward from 12.30 to 12 noon; also [Alfred Jodl] in 'Der 20. Juli 1944 im Führerhauptquartier' typescript [1946], p. 2. Bodenschatz, Heusinger and Assmann are not very reliable on other matters.

12 On the following see Werner Vogel: 'Betr.: 20.7.1944 – eigene Erlebnisse', typescript, 26 June 1970 (see reproduction in Appendix) and verbally to the author 1 July 1971; according to John von Freyend Haeften did not reappear until he came into John von Freyend's office between 11 and 12 a.m.; John installed him in the waiting room. According to Lechler he came to Buhle's office with Stauffenberg but Lechler may be confusing Haeften and Jansen in his mind.

13 John von Freyend; Lechler; Vogel; similar accounts but without further detail in *Spiegelbild*, p. 85 and Wehner, 'Spiel', p. 31 – also applicable below. Two days later Berthold Graf Stauffenberg told the *Gestapo* that there was also a shirt in the briefcase with the bomb – *Spiegelbild*, p. 21.

14 This comes from John von Freyend in 1964; Vogel does not mention the point.

15 See pp. 382–3 above and pp. 405–6 below.

Christian Müller in *Oberst i.G. Stauffenberg*, pp. 614–15 offers unconvincing considerations on the issue of the second 'bomb'. His assertion that the second package of explosive was fitted with two fuses for thirty minutes delay is only a supposition; he himself notes that only *one* such fuse was found with the explosive, all wrapped in paper; see *Spiegelbild*, p. 84. All available information on the starting-time of the fuse, the time of the explosion, and the time elapsed between the two events forces one to assume that the fuse that was used had a ten-minute delay; see Note 44 below. The second fuse in the explosive Stauffenberg detonated may have been one for ten or thirty minutes delay, and it may have been started or not started – there is no evidence on these two points in the sources. Further: the fact that Stauffenberg did not put the second package into his briefcase during the interruption by Vogel causes Müller to infer that only one package fitted into the briefcase; Müller does not consider the interruption a factor of importance. While it is true that the effect of the interruption can only be inferred, and that Stauffenberg and Haeften – could they have been questioned – might not have been unimpeachable witnesses on this point, the author nevertheless considers it plausible and likely that Vogel's interruption caused Stauffenberg to use only one package. However, the question of what was the meaning and intended function of the thirty-minute fuse is justifiable – and still unanswered.

16 Below 'Adjutant'; John von Freyend; Lechler; Vogel; Puttkamer; Sander; [Percy Ernst Schramm]: 'Vorgänge im FHQu am 20.7.44 (Attentat auf den Führer)', StA Nuremberg PS 1808, copy in Kraus, pp. 139–41; Schramm (Warlimont).

17 Albert Bormann to the author 15 Nov. 1964.

18 John von Freyend.

19 On the weather: Assmann, p. 454; Below, 'Adjutant'; Büchs; John von Freyend; Sander; Vice-Admiral Hans-Erich Voss (at the time Rear-Admiral, Permanent Representative of the Naval C-in-C at the *Führer*'s headquarters) to the author 17 Mar. 1964. All agree that it was a hot day with a temperature of at least 20–25° C. On the fuse delay see p. 274 above.

20 Below, 'Adjutant'; Schramm (Warlimont).

21 Schramm (Warlimont); H[einz] W[aizenegger]: 'Der 20. Juli 1944 im Führerhauptquartier', *Stuttgarter Zeitung* 20 July 1949, p. 3; Below 'Adjutant' (also on Göring's and Himmler's absence).

22 Some sources say that Stauffenberg was there at the start of the conference and did not come late – Assmann, p. 455; Below, 'Adjutant'; Schramm 'Vorgänge'; Waizenegger verbal information. All others agree that Keitel and Stauffenberg together with Buhle (not mentioned by everybody) arrived a little late – Buchholz, 'Attentat'; Buchholz in Knauth, p. 177; Heusinger, op. cit., p. 353; John von Freyend; Puttkamer; Schramm (Warlimont). Dr Franz von Sonnleithner (Foreign Minister's permanent representative with the *Führer*), verbally to the author on 16 Jan. 1964 varied the story slightly, saying that Stauffenberg came by himself; Voss to the author 17 Mar. 1964. Estimates vary between five and ten minutes late.

23 Assmann, p. 455; Buchholz, 'Attentat'; Puttkamer; Sonnleithner; Schramm (Warlimont).

24 See photograph in German orig. ed. where Göring and others are inspecting the smashed table; John von Freyend. Voss in a letter to the author of 17 Mar. 1964 mentions this incident but without referring to John von Freyend; he thinks he

can remember standing between Heusinger and Brandt before making room for Stauffenberg. This is improbable since Brandt had to produce the maps for Heusinger during his briefing and would therefore hardly have allowed Stauffenberg to come between them. As far as Voss remembers there were many more people than could find room along that side of the table.

25 Adolf Heusinger verbally to the author 6 Aug. 1964. John von Freyend's statement that he 'placed' Stauffenberg between Heusinger and Brandt can therefore only apply to the first few moments after Stauffenberg's arrival; John von Freyend says that it was not Stauffenberg's final position. *Contemporary* accounts give no indication that the briefcase was moved from the inside to the outside of the table leg – information to the author 30 July 1968 from Dr Widmann of the Technical Criminal Institute in *Reich* Criminal Police Office. In addition to the information in *Spiegelbild*, pp. 83–6 and 112–13 there exists a note by ex-members of the on-the-spot commission, including Dr Wehner, showing the positions of those present and of the briefcase – Alexander Harder: *Kriminalzentrale Werderscher Markt: Die Geschichte des 'Deutschen Scotland Yard'*, facing p. 352. This plan was made later, however, probably for Wehner's 'Das Spiel ist aus', which appeared in 1950; no one at the time would have used 'Adolf Hitler' instead of *'Führer'*; Wehner to the author 4 Dec. 1967. There was also a plan prepared after conclusion of the on-the-spot investigations; it was on the judges' table of the People's Court on 7 Aug. 1944 during cross-examination of Major-General Stieff and it was included in the film of the trial: 'Der 20. Juli 1944 vor dem Volksgerichtshof', BA film No 3023–2; see also *Trial of the Major War Criminals before International Military Tribunal*, Vol. XXXIII, pp. 322–4 where Freisler describes in detail the photographs and plans in front of him. Also: Assmann, p. 455; Below, 'Adjutant'; Heusinger, *Befehl*, p. 353; Heusinger, verbal information; Puttkamer; Sonnleithner; Voss to the author 17 Mar. 1964; Waizenegger, '20. Juli' and verbal information; 'Das Spiel ist aus', p. 32. On 13 Feb. 1959 Voss wrote to Hans W. Hagen (the officer who had such an influence on Major Remer in Berlin on 20 July) saying that *he* had moved Stauffenberg's briefcase further under the table and closer to the table-leg – Hans W. Hagen: *Zwischen Eid und Befehl* p. 68 Note 5a. On 11 Oct. 1965 Professor Hans Karl von Hasselbach wrote to the author saying that in 1965 Voss had told him that *he himself* had moved Stauffenberg's briefcase and *then* gone to the other side of the table; on 17 Mar. 1964 in a letter to the author Voss said that he had gone to the other side of the table in order to be able to read the name of some place more easily. Voss's account to Hasselbach must be based on some misunderstanding; both he in his letter to the author and John von Freyend agree that Voss had had nothing to do with the briefcase before going to the other side of the table. Buchholz in 'Attentat' and Knauth, p. 178 is the only eye-witness to say that the briefcase was first placed on the inside of the table-leg and only moved to the outside by Colonel Brandt after Stauffenberg's departure. It is possible that he was the only one to see this but he was busy with his shorthand and was sitting at the opposite corner of the table. Brandt himself is dead, but he told Heusinger immediately before he died that Stauffenberg deposited the briefcase at the spot under the table where it subsequently exploded; Heusinger, interview with Joachim Fest 17 September 1970. Heusinger added that it was conceivable that the briefcase may have been in Brandt's way and that he pushed it a little further under the table with his foot. Walter Warlimont in 'Circumstances of the Attempt of 20 July 1944', typescript, 3 August 1945, NA Record Group 238 ETHINT-5 confirms that the briefcase was deposited at the outside of the table-leg to begin with. At any rate, the question whether the briefcase was moved is not of importance as regards Stauffenberg's method of making the attempt. Success could not be dependent upon a precise prearranged position for the briefcase. The plan was to kill all those present in addition at least to Hitler and, if they were there,

Himmler and Göring. Since no one could tell where they would be standing the explosion had to be powerful enough to kill everybody. Of the six to eight people standing as near to the briefcase as Hitler would have been had it been on the inside of the table-leg, only four died and only two of them within forty-eight hours (see pp. 404–5 below).

The position of the briefcase relative to Hitler and possibly Himmler and Göring was therefore a matter of chance but this does *not* apply to the *quantity* of explosive used. Here deliberate action by Stauffenberg clearly played a greater part – failure to use half the explosive he had with him. On the probable effect on the double quantity see: Hans Langemann: *Das Attentat*, pp. 348–9 and Note 57; Dr Albert Widmann (at the time explosives expert in the Criminal Technical Institute of *Reich* Criminal Police Office) in 'Das Spiel', pp. 30–1.

26 John von Freyend; Sonnleithner; Below, 'Adjutant'; 'Das Spiel', p. 32 which records Stauffenberg as saying to the telephone operator on duty that he was *expecting* a call from Berlin. According to Puttkamer Adam told him later that Stauffenberg did not ask for a call; Sander, who talked to Adam shortly after the explosion and listened to his report, does not say that Stauffenberg *asked* for a call; he says that on Fellgiebel's instructions he called the briefing hut and left a message for Stauffenberg asking him to come to his (Sander's) office after the briefing – which was how Stauffenberg knew where to find Fellgiebel, Haeften and the car. Major Josef Wolf, then commanding the *Führer* Signal Detachment, told the author on 27 February 1965 that the sergeant on duty at the telephone, Adam, had reported to him his surprise when he saw that Stauffenberg merely put the receiver to his head, put it down again and walked out; cf. below, p. 410. The only reports of Stauffenberg being called out are the less reliable ones in Buchholz, 'Attentat' and Knauth, p. 178 and Voss to the author 17 Mar. 1964. According to verbal information from Heusinger, he whispered something to Brandt and then went out; in *Befehl*, p. 353 Heusinger says that Stauffenberg whispered to Keitel: 'Field Marshal, I am going to make one quick call and come straight back. Keitel nodded and Stauffenberg whispered to Brandt: I'll leave my case here. I have a quick call to make.' This agrees exactly with John von Freyend's account. Adam, the telephone sergeant, noticed that Stauffenberg left without hat and briefcase and found it strange enough to report it immediately after the explosion to his commanding officer, Wolf. The point is that Stauffenberg's departure was in some way unusual enough to be noticed. One cannot, of course, conclude from the photograph taken on 15 July 1944 (in orig. German edition of the present work, and NA 242-HL-7233) that Stauffenberg came to the conference on either 15 or 20 July without a hat (cf. C. Müller, p. 602 note 8); it seems more likely that Stauffenberg, having arrived at the hut some time before Hitler on 15 July, had gone inside, deposited his hat and briefcase, and then had stood outside waiting.

27 From Hasselbach.

28 Sander; Hasselbach; Fellgiebel's evidence at his trial transmitted by General Hermann Reinecke (then one of the assisting judges at the People's Court) – letter to the author 31 May 1964.

29 *Spiegelbild*, p. 85; Sander.

30 *Spiegelbild*, p. 85; Sander. See also 'Das Spiel', p. 32.

31 *Spiegelbild*, p. 85; Sander.

32 This follows Sander's account to the on-the-spot commission (*Spiegelbild*, pp. 85–6) and to the author; also Schramm (Warlimont). The investigation did not entirely clarify the question of procurement of the car; those involved naturally concealed much and everyone wished to be as little involved as possible in Stauffenberg's escape. Moreover the original report of the on-the-spot commission was amended and abridged in subsequent *Gestapo* reports. It is certain that Sander made efforts to obtain a car and this emerges from other direct and in-

direct accounts by members of the headquarters; see diary continued by Schmundt's successor, 'Tätigkeitsbericht des Chefs des Heerespersonalamts...' NA microcopy T-78 roll 39, extracts in Hans-Adolf Jacobsen: *1939–1945*, pp. 475–8, where Fellgiebel is said to have obtained the car; according to Schramm (Warlimont) Sander did so; equally 'it was generally said' at the time that Sander obtained it – according to Erich Schüler (at the time cipher officer in the *Führer* Signal Detachment) verbally to the author 16 July 1965. Erich Kretz, the courier driver, says that he was despatched to Area I between 12 noon and 1 p.m., reported to Stauffenberg and fetched him direct from the briefing hut – Kretz II (1966). This would explain why Stauffenberg said that he already had a car and why Haeften had been unable to find it. On the other hand, when asked whether he fetched Stauffenberg from the briefing hut or Sander's office, Kretz said the briefing hut but then described a position for the hut which was that of the aides and adjutants' building – thus both to the author in Kretz I and to Herr Peter Dietz in a telephone conversation on 27 Feb. 1966 – record in the author's possession. When I showed him a plan he indicated the briefing hut. Kretz does not remember Stauffenberg talking to Fellgiebel between leaving the briefing hut and leaving the Area. He need not have seen this, however, while waiting in his car. After Stauffenberg got in, he does not remember stopping anywhere except at the guard post. On the other hand at two interviews he told the author that Haeften arrived at the car first, followed by Stauffenberg. Except that Kretz indicated the briefing hut when shown a plan, therefore, everything indicates that he collected Stauffenberg and Haeften at Sander's office, not at the briefing hut, and that he thought the office was the briefing hut. Kretz *must* have had a lapse of memory if one accepts firstly the description of his journeys for Stauffenberg as given by him and Pieper and secondly that Stauffenberg was with Fellgiebel and Sander as many accounts and reports agree – *Spiegelbild*, pp. 85–6; Assmann, p. 459; Buchholz, 'Attentat'; Hasselbach; Sander; Wilhelm Scheidt: 'Wahrheit gegen Karikatur' in *Neue Politik* No 11, 27 May 1948, pp. 1–2; Schmundt; Schramm (Warlimont); 'Das Spiel', p. 32; Otto Dietrich: *The Hitler I Knew*, p. 254 which says that the car used by Stauffenberg to go to the airfield was parked 150 yards from the briefing hut; Dietrich's press hut was in Area I about 100 yards from the briefing hut. Loose use of the term 'briefing house' may also have contributed to the confusion; the circular from [Albert] Bormann and Schmundt, for instance, dated 20 Sept. 1943 on creation of an 'Enclosure A' inside Area I lists among buildings to be included in the enclosure '8. Führer's Personal Aides' Office ... 13. *Führer's Wehrmacht* aides ... 813. Army Personnel Office etc. – Briefing house' – BA EAP 105/33. The Special Commission's report (*Spiegelbild*, p. 85) invariably refers to 'Bunker 88' which according to Sander, means the *Führer*'s Personal Aides' building. All these buildings were constructed together in one complex. Until March 1944 the briefing conferences were held in Hitler's own bunker, not in the visitors' bunker which he occupied in July 1944; at times they were held in the OKW building. In July 1944, but only from the 15th, they were held in the 'briefing hut'. The confusion is understandable and should not throw doubt on the credibility of the various witnesses. See the author's 'Attentat', p. 275 Note 101.

33 *Spiegelbild*, p. 86; Sander; Sander quoted in Annedore Leber and Freya Gräfin von Moltke: *Für und wider*, p. 205; Kretz II; Albert Praun: *Soldat in der Telegraphen- und Nachrichtentruppe*, p. 220, based on a statement by Sander of August 1944; Reinecke to the author 31 May 1964 giving Fellgiebel's evidence at his trial.

34 Stauffenberg's report as given by Hoepner – presumably not word for word – in *Trial*, Vol. XXXIII, p. 402; Dietrich, pp. 253–4; Eberhard Zeller: *The Flame of Freedom*, pp. 345–6.

35 *Spiegelbild*, p. 86; Kretz I and II.

36 *Spiegelbild*, p. 86; Kretz, I and II; 'Das Spiel' p. 32, gives a similar account but here Guard Post South is referred to as 'Gate III'; Pieper. Kretz knows nothing of the chevaux-de-frise referred to by Wehner in 'Das Spiel'. See plan of the headquarters at Appendix.

37 *Spiegelbild*, p. 86; Kretz I and II; 'Das Spiel', p. 32.

38 Kretz I and II; Dietz.

39 *Spiegelbild*, p. 84; Kretz I and II; Dr Widmann; sketches in Appendix.

40 Kretz I and II.

41 *Spiegelbild*, p. 86; Schramm, 'Mitteilungen Meichssner', is even more precise – '13.13'.

42 Büchs.

43 Assmann, p. 455 does not specify Buhle but does not give any other name; Puttkamer is not sure whether Buhle or Heusinger asked after Stauffenberg; Below in 'Adjutant' says that Keitel missed Stauffenberg and looked for him; Sander says that Buhle asked Adam three times about Stauffenberg.

44 This is the time given by all contemporary sources – *Spiegelbild*, p. 83 ('towards 12.50'); Schramm (Warlimont); Schramm, 'Vorgänge'; Schmundt. Subsequent reports generally, though not always, give an earlier time – Buchholz in Knauth, *Germany*, p. 178 ('exactly 12.45'); Buchholz, 'Attentat' ('about 12.45'); Below, 'Adjutant' ('12.40'); Spaeter, p. 563 ('precisely 12.42 German time'); Waizenegger, '20. Juli' ('12.40'); Waizenegger, verbal information ('12.40'); Dietrich, p. 252 ('about 12.50'). Warlimont in 'Circumstances' gave 'about 12.50'. The time given by the Special Commission ('towards 12.50'; *Spiegelbild*, p. 83) must be accepted, especially since it hardly differs from the times given by witnesses a year or more later – witnesses who must have been interviewed by the commission. If one takes into account what is known about the time for the start of the conference and about Keitel's and Stauffenberg's late arrival, one will see that there was a maximum of fifteen and a minimum of ten minutes during which the fuse may have been going. Fifteen minutes are unlikely on a warm day, but on the other hand not enough for a thirty-minute fuse even on a warm day.

45 Of the twenty-four people present only twelve are still alive and of these one does not wish to give information. One of those now dead left a detailed report and another a fairly detailed one. The only contemporary source is the final plan prepared by the investigating authorities; this was submitted to the People's Court and appears in the film of Stieff's trial – 'Der 20. Juli 1944 vor dem Volksgerichtshof', BA Film No 3023–2; see also *Trial*, Vol. XXXIII, p. 322–4. Buchholz's and Bodenschatz's accounts were prepared very soon after the event; but the others (Assmann, Below, Heusinger, Puttkamer, Sonnleithner, Voss, Waizenegger, to mention only the most important) some years later. 'Das Spiel', p. 28, shows Haagen instead of Buchholz as the second shorthand writer but this account contains other errors – for instance Waizenegger is shown on the opposite side of the room, in his usual place near Jodl, but he was not there at the moment of the explosion (see below); 'Buhl' is shown opposite Hitler instead of at the eastern end of the room, Berger is shown as 'Bergert', Günsche as 'Günther' etc. See the author's 'Attentat', pp. 271–2 and plan at Appendix.

46 Heusinger had previously been approached by Tresckow to take part in the conspiracy but he was not prepared to play an active role, although he did not show himself totally opposed. He was supposed to be warned before the attempt was made and imagines that this did not happen because Tresckow himself had not been warned, or not in time – Heusinger, verbal information.

47 In 'Das Spiel', p. 30, for instance.

48 Albert Speer, *Inside the Third Reich*, p. 389, says that on 21 July Hitler told him and others that Keitel had rushed to him shouting 'My Führer, you're alive, you're alive' and had embraced him.

49 Hasselbach; consultation notes taken by Hitler's physician Prof. von Eicken on

23 July 1944, NA ML 125, 125a and 131; Jodl op. cit., p. 2; [Heinz] Linge: 'Kronzeuge Linge berichtet' in *Revue*, No 12, 24 Mar. 1956, pp. 26–30; Albert Zoller: *Hitler privat*, p. 184; Kurt Haase (then warrant officer, medical corps, in the *Führer*'s headquarters) verbally to the author 9 Aug. 1965; interrogation of Julius Schaub by Dr Kempner, 1530–1600 12.3.47, IfZ ZS 137.

50 Dr Widmann in 'Das Spiel' pp. 29–31; Langemann, p. 349 Note 57; Dr Widmann verbally to the author 30 July 1968; Hans Bernd Gisevius: *Wo ist Nebe?*, p. 173, based on a statement by Nebe on 27 July giving the findings of the on-the-spot commission.

51 Hasselbach; Haase; Jodl, p. 4.

52 Hasselbach; Zoller, pp. 184–6; Bodenschatz, S.R.G.G. 1219 (C).

53 Haase; Linge; Bodenschatz; Rudolf Semmler: *Goebbels – the man next to Hitler*, p. 141.

54 Schmundt, pp. 172, 274.

55 Schmundt; *Spiegelbild*, p. 83; the author's 'Attentat', p. 273.

56 *Spiegelbild*, p. 84; 'Das Spiel', p. 31, gives 10 minutes as the time-delay for the fuse; Kretz I and II; experts.

57 *Spiegelbild*, p. 50; Wehner to the author 27 Oct. 1965; the idea that the communications bunker was to be blown up was publicized primarily by Hans Bernd Gisevius in *To the Bitter End*, pp. 531–2.

58 See pp. 338–43 above.

59 Explosives expert; reproductions in NA Record Group 242; Lieutenant-Colonel Faber (*Bundeswehr* Procurement Office, Koblenz) verbally to the author 2 July 1964.

60 See Sergeant-Major Vogel's report in Appendix.

Zeller (*Geist der Freiheit*, 3rd edition, p. 284) surmises that a certain officer of the headquarters was supposed to bring the second bomb to the briefing conference but he had been suddenly posted just before 20 July and this was therefore perhaps the reason for the failure of the attempt. In Zeller's 4th and 5th (German) editions (1963 and 1965) Zeller does not repeat this surmise. As far as I have been able to establish the officer in question was *SS-Obersturmbannführer* Friedrich Darges, one of the personal aides who was suddenly posted, having fallen out of favour in the headquarters for various reasons. Hitler's wrath descended on him at the 'morning briefing' of 18 July when he was being inattentive and talking to other officers during a briefing – see *The Bormann Letters*, p. 58. He was also said to have spent his time catching flies and, according to another story, had laughed when Hitler swiped at a fly and missed. According to a story vouched for by Büchs Darges' job was to deal with flies with a swotter but he had been unable to stop a certain fly continually buzzing round Hitler. Hitler had looked furiously at him and he had not quite been able to conceal a grin. Hitler's former SS Aide Otto Günsche told the author on 6 November 1972 that on or about 18 July 1944, during the midday briefing, a fly kept crawling around on the situation map where Hitler's hand happened to be, and when Hitler looked up at one point he saw the grinning face of Darges; Hitler had taken him aside immediately and had told him firmly though softly to report to the front at once. Darges was in fact posted to the front. In general terms all reports I have seen agree – Below, Büchs, John von Freyend, Puttkamer, Sonnleithner, Waizenegger; see also the author's 'Attentat', p. 284. In a letter to the author of 10 Mar. 1965 Darges himself did not answer the question but in conclusion he said: 'In contrast to other members of the Private Office I succeeded repeatedly in returning to the front-line unit to which I had belonged in 1942, the "Viking" Panzer Division.' See also Helmut Heiber: *Hitlers Lagebesprechungen*, p. 36. Waizenegger in '20. Juli' was probably the source of Zeller's surmise; this refers to the (unnamed) officer's posting and to the fact that after the attempt both he and the Todt Organization workers were under suspicion.

61 Speer, p. 381.

62 On this point and below: Professor Hellmuth Arntz (from 1943 Lieutenant and aide to General Fellgiebel) verbally to the author 21 Nov. 1964; Below, 'Adjutant' and verbal information; 'Fuehrer Conferences on Naval Affairs, 1939–1945', *Brassey's Naval Annual* 59 (1948), p. 407; Hans Hornbogen verbally to the author 14 Jan. 1965 and letter 4 Apr. 1965; Werner Jesek (Post Office official in the *Führer* Signals Detachment and at the time in the exchange bunker in Area I) letter to the author 24 May 1965; Sander, verbal information and Leber and Moltke, pp. 205–6; Schaub; Vice-Admiral Hans-Erich Voss to Professor Walter Baum 4 Apr. 1957, IfZ ZS 1786; Rear-Admiral Eduard Wagner to the author 17 Nov. 1964; Major Josef Wolf verbally to the author 27 Feb. 1965; Colonel Wolfgang Müller: 'Erich Fellgiebel', typescript, undated, in Walther-Peer Fellgiebel's papers (Müller was not on Fellgiebel's staff as is said in the author's 'Attentat', p. 279 Note 124 but in OKH Inf 2; his office was in Döberitz); [Arntz]: memoir of General Fellgiebel, typescript, undated, in Walther-Peer Fellgiebel's papers.

63 Heinz Burchardt: 'Zugehörigkeit zur Widerstandsbewegung vom 20. Juli 1944' typescript, Munich 1946, in F. Degner's papers and 'Kurze Darstellung der Ereignisse', typescript, Bonn-Dottendorf, 9 Feb. 1966.

64 Friedrich Degner verbally to the author 24, 25 Aug. 1965 and letter 1 Oct. 1968.

65 *Spiegelbild*, p. 330, gives the timing of Fellgiebel's first call to Hahn as 1 p.m.; Burchardt says: 'We hoped to conceal the fact that it [the communications blackout] had been imposed for other reasons and before the order [from Hitler or his staff]; the difference in timing was not too great.' Confirmation that the alert was issued before 12 noon in Kurt Albrecht (then Second Lieutenant in 'Zeppelin') to the author 30 Jan. 1969, also Hermann Graske (then Captain in 'Zeppelin') to Colonel Gottfried Kecker Jan. 1969 and Kecker to the author 9 and 27 Jan. 1969.

66 Praun, pp. 219–22.

67 From Wolf.

68 Arntz; Sander, verbal information.

69 Sander, ibid.

70 Ibid.; Wolf, verbally to the author 3 July 1971 (Wolf II); Jodl, p. 3 – also applicable below. Wolf says that it was impossible to contact Himmler but this refers to a period about 15 minutes later, in other words to another call.

71 Sander, verbal information; Wolf I; below see Colonel Kandt to the author 11 Feb., 13 Mar. 1964.

72 This from Rear-Admiral Wagner, 'Fuehrer Conferences', p. 407, and 'Lagevorträge des Oberbefehlshabers der Kriegsmarine vor Hitler 1939–1945', pp. 601–3; also Sander verbal information – also applicable below. In a letter to Professor Baum of 4 Apr. 1957 Voss merely says that he asked Below to pass the news on, which leaves open the question whether Below did so himself or through someone else.

73 Hornbogen. Sander knows nothing of this particular conversation but he was not in the exchange all the time. As far as the course of events is concerned it is of minor importance whether Thiele received the news personally from Fellgiebel or through one of his secretaries. Based on the recollections of Arntz, Hornbogen and Sander it seems certain that Thiele got the news. Thiele's two secretaries, Fräulein Ansorge (verbally to the author 26 February 1965 and letter 22 August 1971) and Fräulein Meier, (verbally to the author on 21 June 1965) in unison informed the author: they remember nothing; they do not know when Thiele was in his office between the times in question (12 noon and 4 p.m.) and when he was not; they know nothing of telephone conversations with 'Wolfschanze'; they observed nothing of importance at the critical time. This is what they had previously said to Frau Annedore Leber and other enquirers (Sander, verbal in-

formation; Zeller, pp. 347–8). For further evidence from the Berlin end see next chapter.

74 [Hellmuth] Arntz: 'Account of the Twentieth of July Putsch by One of the Minor Conspirators', CSDIC (UK), S.I.R. 1610, typescript, 11 April 1945. In a letter to the author of 24 Nov. 1964 Arntz gives a somewhat different story, saying that *this* was Fellgiebel's first conversation with Hahn since the explosion and that he (Arntz) must have been looking for Captain Jahnke in the mess during Fellgiebel's second conversation with Hahn; it was probably the other way round. Sander (verbal information) does not mention Fellgiebel's conversations with Hahn; he cannot have been in the exchange. The account in *Spiegelbild*, p. 330, based on Hahn's evidence, is, as already mentioned, obscure and unreliable. Both Arntz and Beichele (see Note 83 below), who had personal experience of Fellgiebel's methods of expression, are definite that there should be neither comma, full stop nor semi-colon after the words: 'Something fearful has happened.'

75 Sander, verbal information; Wolf I.

76 From Arntz.

77 Sander; *Spiegelbild*, p. 85; Hornbogen; Pieper; Wolf I.

78 Sander; Wolf to the author 18 Dec. 1968. Wolf says that characteristically and on his own initiative Adam went straight from him to Martin Bormann, although the correct channel was via Sander.

79 Sander says 20,000 marks and a house, Wolf I 30,000 marks, a house and promotion, Semmler (p. 143) 15,000 marks.

80 *Spiegelbild*, p. 86.

81 This is according to Below, verbal information, Wolf and Hornbogen – contrary to the earlier statement in the author's 'Attentat' p. 278 that only Sander and Fellgiebel could telephone outside the headquarters; this was based solely on Sander's account.

82 See pp. 338–43 above.

83 Arntz, verbal information; Praun, p. 222. In his CSDIC 'Account' Arntz said that he had ordered stations 'Anna' and 'Leopold' to be switched off; according to Albert Beichele (at the time Lieutenant-Colonel, head of the Line Communications Group in Army Chief Signals Officer's office in Zossen) in letters to the author 31 Dec. 1967 and 24 Apr. 1968, 'Leopold' was the peacetime designation of the garrison exchange in Lötzen; during the war this became part of the larger station 'Emma'. For timings I have given preference to Arntz's earlier account (11 Apr. 1945); those given in his later report differ somewhat.

84 Praun, p. 222.

85 See next chapter.

CHAPTER 42

1 The author's earlier inference from Olbricht's lack of activity and from a number of indications and hints that came up during Hoepner's trial (see *Trial of the Major War Criminals before the International Military Tribunal*, Vol. XXXIII, pp. 399–402) has proved untenable in the light of verbal information received from Dr Hans Bernd Gisevius on 8 September 1972. Gisevius' accounts, based on what Olbricht told him during the afternoon, vary slightly between earlier editions of his book and later ones. Fellgiebel telephoned Olbricht direct according to Gisevius: *Bis zum bittern Ende*, Vol. II, p. 372 and *To the Bitter End*, pp. 537–8. But Fellgiebel spoke to Thiele and Thiele immediately told Olbricht according to *Bis zum bittern Ende*, 1954 edition, pp. 613–14 and *Bis zum bitteren Ende*, special edition, pp. 516–17. There are some further, minor variations, particularly in the timing of Fellgiebel's telephone call and Olbricht's receipt of the information.

Without Gisevius' recent verbal information, the variations and uncertainty had seemed sufficient to the author to support the assumption that Thiele had in fact received Fellgiebel's message about 13.00 hours, but had not passed it on to Olbricht until about 15.00; this also emerged from Hoepner's testimony before the People's Court (*Trial*, Vol. XXXIII, pp. 399–402). Dr H. C. Friedrich Georgi, Olbricht's son-in-law and at the time a *Luftwaffe* Major, had appeared in the evening in the Bendlerstrasse, and Olbricht had briefed him on the day's events, only about three hours before he was shot. In a conversation with the author on 21 May 1973 Georgi insisted that Olbricht had not received Fellgiebel's message before about 15.00 hours, but conceded that he based his opinion not on details received from Olbricht on 20 July 1944, but on post-war publications. When it was pointed out to Georgi that Fellgiebel's words – 'Something fearful has happened: the Führer is alive' – did not necessarily mean that the bomb had exploded (see below), Georgi no longer insisted that Olbricht could not have received Fellgiebel's message about 13.00 hours. To sum up: it appears safe to accept Gisevius' assertion that not only Thiele but also Olbricht received Fellgiebel's message a few minutes after the explosion, that is, very shortly before or after 13.00 hours.

2 See above, p. 409.

3 See above, pp. 383–4, 387–8.

4 From Gisevius 8 September 1972; Hellmuth Arntz; Albert Beichele to the author 18 June 1965, 14 Jan. 1966; 'Entscheidende Minuten am 20. Juli', *Hamburger Allgemeine Zeitung*, 20 July 1949, pp. 1–2; Major-General Kurt Hassel (head of OKH Signals Group under Olbricht) verbally to the author 11 Dec. 1964; Emil Pestinger (at the time Post Office official in the Bendlerstrasse) to the author 31 Dec. 1964; Albert Praun: *Soldat in der Telegraphen- und Nachrichtentruppe*, pp. 218–19; Lieutenant-Colonel Ludolf Gerhard Sander verbally to the author 24–25 Apr. 1964. Joachim Kramarz in *Stauffenberg The Life and Death of an Officer*, pp. 189–90, gives no evidence for his statement that Thiele did not pass on Fellgiebel's message because it 'seemed to him a very vague piece of news'. Thiele's former secretaries (Charlotte Ansorge verbally to the author 26 February 1965 and letter 22 August 1971; Ilse-Dörte Meyer verbally to the author 21 June 1965) maintain that they do not know where Thiele was during those critical hours nor when he left his office and when he returned to it. The accounts by Arntz, Gisevius (verbally 8 September 1972), Hassel and Sander make it clear, however, that Thiele was at any rate not in his office. Arntz learned that Thiele had left the building in his car towards 14.00 hours and had not been seen in the building during the afternoon; Gisevius says that according to what he knows from his conversations with Olbricht that afternoon, both Olbricht and Thiele had gone to lunch; Hassel was unable to reach Thiele by telephone from about 12.00 hours to 15.00, but found him in his office about 16.00 where he refused to play his role by detailing signals officers for purposes of the *coup*; Sander says Thiele told him a few days later in response to a question he had been so nervous that he had had to take a walk.

5 Arntz verbally to the author 21 Nov. 1964.

6 Heinz Burchardt: 'Zugehörigkeit zur Widerstandsbewegung', typescript, Munich 1946 and 'Kurze Darstellung der Ereignisse', typescript, Bonn-Dottendorf 1966; Friedrich Degner verbally to the author 24–25 Aug. 1965; confirmation from Herr Gerhart Goebel of Long-distance Technical Office of German Post Office – letter to the author 21 Jan. 1966. Herr Goebel, a senior Post Office inspector, has made available to me important documents and information throwing light on events in Berlin and Zossen and I am particularly grateful to him. Thanks to Herr Goebel I have been able to base the account that follows on a report 'Niederschrift über die Vorgänge beim Postamt Zossen 10 am 20.7.1944' (typescript, Zossen 9 Aug. 1944) originating from Senor Wille, a telegraph in-

spector who was at the time senior Post Office traffic official in Zossen. 'Post Office Zossen 10' was the designation given by the Post Office to the Army post in Zossen. At the time Professor Kurt Timm, head of the Post Office directorate in Berlin, did not forward on Wille's report to avoid incriminating persons not already involved, to prevent further disturbance to signals traffic and to cover up certain errors on the part of Post Office officials.

7 This is confirmed by Lieutenant-Colonel (retd) Beichele, who was not a member of the conspiracy (see Chap. 41 Note 83 and Note 8 below). Eberhard Zeller in *The Flame of Freedom*, pp. 348–9, reaches the same conclusion based on information from Professor Arntz, i.e. that on the afternoon of 20 July, even after the black-out had been lifted in 'Wolfschanze', Fellgiebel permitted communications to be used 'only by his own reliable people'; this applied both to 'Mauerwald' and 'Zeppelin'. Zeller's supposition (p. 349) that lines between Berlin and East Prussia were temporarily blocked even for Fellgiebel and others is disproved by the statements of Burchardt, Degner (see also below) and Beichele; see also Note 9 below. Zeller (pp. 350–1) is entirely right in his assumption, however, that the codeword had been passed to Berlin as planned and also that Wagner passed information to Paris.

8 On this point and below: Beichele to the author 14 Jan. 1966, 31 Dec. 1967; Wille's report; Beichele remembers clearly that the special secret exchange prepared for the *coup* was named 'Alarich' – see p. 338 above. 'Anna-Bu', 'Emma-Bu' etc. meant 'Anna-Bunker', in other words 'Anna-Zossen'; 'Emma-Bunker' = 'Emma-Zossen' etc. The entire headquarters was due to move early in July and a start had already been made; as part of the preparations exchanges and switchboards identical to those in East Prussia were set up in Zossen where the headquarters was due to go.

9 On this point and below: [Eduard] Wagner: 'Der Verlauf des 20. Juli (aus dem Gedächtnis)', typescript, [Zossen] 21 July 1944 – photostat copy in IfZ ED 95; *Spiegelbild einer Verschwörung*, p. 330; Wille; Professor Kurt Timm verbally to the author 7 Aug. 1968; Kurt Albrecht to the author 30 Jan. 1969; Beichele to the author 14 Jan. 1966, 31 Dec. 1967; see also p. 470. General Wagner probably telephoned the Bendlerstrasse, perhaps Olbricht, about 2 pm. The news of the failure of the attempt and the survival of Hitler reached Berlin through other channels before 2 p.m. either before the black-out was imposed or by methods unaffected by it – for instance, between 1 and 2 p.m. a Signals Traffic Officer in the Berlin area (presumably Potsdam) called Lieutenant Hornbogen, the Signals Traffic Officer in 'Wolfschanze' and asked whether it was true that Hitler was dead, to which Hornbogen replied that he was alive – information from Hornbogen. Hornbogen remembers that Colonel Meichssner's office (the OKW Operations Staff's Organization Section in Potsdam) was connected to the exchange from which this call was made and that the caller was a Captain Gehre. This can hardly have been Captain Ludwig Gehre, a member of the *Abwehr* and one of the conspirators, since he had been on the run ever since the arrest of Kiep, Moltke and others – *Spiegelbild*, p. 225; Zeller, p. 219.

10 See Note 9 above – also applicable below.

11 Burchardt, 'Zugehörigkeit' and 'Darstellung'.

12 Beichele to the author 10 Sept. 1965, 31 Dec. 1967.

13 Beichele to the author 14 Jan. 1966.

14 Rainer Graf von Kanitz, former aide to General Eduard Wagner, letter to Frau Elisabeth Wagner 14 July 1972: 'Flying time Berlin-Rastenburg: "Ju 52" depending on wind conditions $2\frac{1}{2}$–3 hours. "He 111" depending on wind conditions $1\frac{1}{2}$–2 hours.' 'Fuehrer Conferences on Naval Affairs, 1939–1945', *Brassey's Naval Annual* 59 (1948), p. 407, gives Dönitz's flying time from Berlin to Rastenburg on 20 July 1944 as about two hours. This was also the time taken by the members of the *Gestapo* and Criminal Police, Kaltenbrunner, Wehner,

Kopkow and others from Tempelhof to Rastenburg; just after lunch, at the earliest about 1.15 p.m. (the news had to come from Himmler who did not receive it himself until five or ten minutes after the explosion), Dr Wehner was ordered by telephone to prepare to fly to Rastenburg at once. He drove from Weissensee to his apartment, from there to Nebe on the Werderscher Markt and thence to Tempelhof. Only a bare twenty minutes elapsed between departure from the Werderscher Markt and take-off, which must therefore have been about 2 p.m. Confirmed by verbal information from Dr Widmann, member of the commission to the author 30 July 1968. According to Gisevius, *Bitter End*, pp. 531–2, take-off was scheduled for 2.30 p.m. The aircraft used was a 'Ju 52' which was slower than the 'He 111'; they landed in Rastenburg about 4.30 – 'Das Spiel ist aus', p. 27. Heinz Höhne's statement in *The Order of the Death's Head*, p. 537, that Himmler had arrived in Berlin by 4.30 is of no value; Himmler was still in 'Wolfschanze' when Kaltenbrunner and the others arrived ('Das Spiel', p. 27); Höhne quotes 'Zeller op. cit., p. 249', clearly the 3rd (1956) edition; elsewhere he has used the 5th (1965) edition, though without differentiating between the various editions; neither of the passages in question refers to a flight to Berlin by Himmler. Zeller (pp. 304–5) though without evidence, gives Stauffenberg's flying time as two and a half hours – take-off 13.15 and landing 15.45 'according to one account' (Zeller does not specify but he probably means the *Gestapo* report in *Spiegelbild*, p. 22) and 16.05 according to another. This other account, which does not specify 16.05 but merely says 'about 16.00' is to be found in Annedore Leber and Freya Gräfin von Moltke: *Für und Wider*, pp. 114–15; it originates from Georgi, who was in the Bendlerstrasse only late in the evening of 20 July and was therefore no better informed than anyone else. His statement that Olbricht ordered the start of 'Valkyrie' on his own initiative and before Stauffenberg's report that the attempt had been successful, is contradicted by other important sources, as will be shown below. Kramarz (p. 189), based on a story by Georgi, says that between 2 and 3 p.m. that afternoon, perhaps later, an order was lying on Georgi's desk that Stauffenberg's aircraft was to be shot down to prevent him escaping abroad, but Georgi did not pass the order on.

It may be taken as certain that Stauffenberg landed shortly before 3 p.m. at the earliest. By all accounts a flying time noticeably shorter than $1\frac{1}{2}$ hours seems improbable. If the 'He 111' had flown as fast as possible, practicable and permissible, in others words between 220 and 250 m.p.h. depending on wind conditions, a flying time of $1\frac{1}{2}$ hours is plausible and it would have landed at 14.45, take-off at 13.15 being established. A *Gestapo* report dated 24 July 1944 (*Spiegelbild*, p. 22), however, says that Stauffenberg and Haeften landed 'about 15.45'. Stauffenberg's time of arrival in the Bendlerstrasse is equally established – about 4.30 p.m. (see p. 422 below).

If the timings 3.0 p.m./4.30 p.m. are accurate the fact that Stauffenberg apparently took from 3 p.m. to 4.30 to get to the Bendlerstrasse may be explained by the following: Fräulein Delia Ziegler, Olbricht's secretary, remembers Haeften calling from the airport between 2 and 3 p.m. asking that Schweizer, the driver, be sent to fetch them; he was therefore not ready waiting, which would indicate that landing took place at an airfield other than Rangsdorf (Delia Ziegler to the author 8 Jan. 1968). Fräulein Ziegler, however, says specifically that she cannot guarantee the accuracy of her timing. Colonel Meichssner, head of the OKW Organization Section in Potsdam, similarly reported that, according to a briefing on 20 July by Colonel (*Luftwaffe*) Aldinger, on landing in Berlin Stauffenberg found no car waiting; he had obtained a *Luftwaffe* car and driven to the Schellhaus, where he found an escort of several officers waiting – Percy Ernst Schramm, 'Mitteilungen des Oberst Meichssner' StA Nuremberg PS 1808. Major Remer, commander of the Berlin Guard Battalion, said while a prisoner of

war in 1946: 'How little Tommy ran a revolution! Stauffenberg kept waiting for
$1\frac{1}{2}$ hours at the airport without petrol for his car!'– [Wilhelm Grenzendörfer]:
'Notizen von der Schilderung des Generalmajors Remer . . .' prepared 24 June
1946 in the British internment camp 2221/Q in Belgium. All this may be correct
and may explain why Stauffenberg did not reach the Bendlerstrasse until about
4.30; it does not explain why he did not ring until about 4 p.m. – unless he was
prevented by the communications blackout. So far full information on this point
is lacking.

15 The conspirators' plans for D Day provided for Stauffenberg and Fromm to be
fetched from *Tempelhof* airport in an armoured car – *Spiegelbild*, p. 40; BA EAP
105/20. It was apparently assumed that both of them would fly to Hitler's
headquarters whenever Stauffenberg had to go there. Rangsdorf is given as the
place of landing by: the *Gestapo* (after investigation in Rastenburg) in
Spiegelbild, pp. 22, 86; Freisler in proceedings of People's Court 7 Aug. 1944,
confirmed by Yorck von Wartenburg and Hoepner's evidence on the same day,
Trial, Vol. XXXIII, p. 429, 401; Nicolaus von Below in 'Hitlers Adjutant über
den 20. Juli im FHQu', *Echo der Woche* 15 July 1949; [Rudolf Schmundt:]
'Tätigkeitsbericht des Chefs des Heerespersonalamts', typescript, NA
microcopy T-84 roll 39; an account (no sources given) by a certain von
Wülckenitz: 'Was am 20. Juli 1944 wirklich geschah' in *Der Tagesspiegel*, 20 July
1946. Recently received information tends to tip the scales in favour of
Rangsdorf; Dr Franz Bäke wrote to the author on 9 August 1972: 'On 20 July
1944 I visited the late Dr Eckel, then airfield commandant at Rangsdorf airfield
near Berlin. Towards 16.00 a plane landed, I think "He 111". Major Eckel was
surprised because the aircraft had not been signalled and he went out to check.
After about ten minutes he came back and told me Colonel Graf Stauffenberg had
landed, he was just going to see the General of Fighter Command to obtain a car
to take him into Berlin. Since I knew Stauffenberg well but had not seen him for a
long time, I said he could ride into Berlin with me and I went out to the airfield to
tell him. At this moment he was going by in a car, some fifty metres away. I called
to him but he did not seem to see me, which I understood later on, and he passed
behind a hedge that lined the road.'

Yorck and Hoepner had their information from third or fourth hand; they did
not personally answer the telephone when Haeften called; they are therefore at
best secondary sources. The others, except Bäke and Schweizer, have their information from East Prussia where only the alleged destination was known; if
anyone there knew where the actual landing took place, this has as yet not come
to light. The only primary sources known so far – Bäke and Schweizer – contradict each other; Schweizer says he waited in vain at Rangsdorf airfield until
late in the afternoon when an officer told him that Stauffenberg was already in
the Bendlerstrasse and Schweizer was to go there too. C. Müller's polemic
(*Oberst i.G. Stauffenberg*, p. 605 note 2) misses the point: Müller suppresses the
words 'or secondary', considers Rangsdorf likely, and seeks to invalidate
Schweizer's evidence by a consideration whose consequences he does not accept.
If Schweizer was expecting Stauffenberg's arrival only considerably later, as C.
Müller supposes, this means that either Schweizer was unreliable (for which
there is otherwise no evidence) or failed to understand Stauffenberg's instructions (unlikely), or that Stauffenberg had not told his driver when to expect him,
which would be a carelessness on Stauffenberg's part that C. Müller does not
appear to be considering. On a day such as this, Stauffenberg had to be
sure he was not without transportation when he arrived back in Berlin; there was
no telling whether the conference would be held earlier or whether another
'special conference' would suddenly give him the opportunity for his attack, so in
order to be certain, Schweizer had to be waiting from about 1 p.m. Although it
would have seemed wise to try to shake off any pursuers and to land somewhere

else than at the destination given or assumed, there is no evidence to indicate that this was done.

Rudolf Semmler in *Goebbels – the man next to Hitler*, pp. 135, 143 gives Tempelhof as the landing site; Wilhelm von Schramm in *Aufstand der Generale*, p. 68, without documentation, gives Staaken; Eugen Gerstenmaier in 'The Church Conspiratorial' in Eric H. Boehm: *We Survived*, p. 185, gives Berlin-Adlershof (Adlershof-Johannisthal was the name of an airfield near Treptow); no one seems to have thought of Gatow.

16 Georgi in Leber and Moltke, p. 114; to judge by its contents Georgi's account is not based on fresh research, as Zeller says (pp. 304–5 and 434 note 7) but primarily on the record of proceedings before the People's Court on 7 and 8 Aug. 1944 and on *Gestapo* reports.

17 *Spiegelbild*, p. 97 based on statements by Schulenburg; Gisevius verbally to author 8 September 1972.

18 *Trial*, Vol. XXXIII, pp. 401–2; Georgi in Leber and Moltke, p. 115.

19 On this point and below: Hoepner's evidence before the People's Court, *Trial*, Vol. XXXIII, p. 399; Note 9 above; Georgi in Leber and Moltke, p. 114; see also note 1 above.

20 See note 28 below.

21 *Spiegelbild*, p. 97 based on statements by Schulenburg; Schulenburg gave the same account to Gisevius on 20 July 1944 – Gisevius verbally to the author 8 September 1972. See the orders reproduced in the Appendix: the first two of them bear Mertz's short signature.

22 Gisevius verbally to the author 4 August 1971.

23 *Spiegelbild*, p. 97.

24 Gisevius, *Bitter End*, p. 547.

25 *Trial*, Vol. XXXIII, p. 400; Gisevius, *Bitter End*, pp. 538–9. On the rooms in the Bendlerstrasse see the sketch in the Appendix, based on sketches provided by Lt. Col. Kleber and by *Landeszentrale für politische Bildung* in Berlin.

26 The exact sequence of these events can no longer be determined. A principal source for them is the interrogation of Hoepner by Freisler (*Trial*, Vol. XXXIII, p. 400), but Hoepner here says he cannot remember the timing etc. precisely, and Freisler relies on the results of the preliminary investigation which in turn may not be entirely accurate. See also note 28 below.

27 *Trial*, Vol. XXXIII, pp. 400–1; *Spiegelbild*, p. 97.

28 *Trial*, Vol. XXXIII, p. 400. Copies of the orders (with certain inaccuracies) in *Spiegelbild*, pp. 28–30, 37–40; these were in turn taken from copies attached to *Gestapo* reports to be found in BA EAP 105/21.

With one or two exceptions all available sources are agreed on the time of launching of 'Valkyrie' for Berlin and adjacent schools and on issue of the teleprinter messages announcing Hitler's death to *Wehrkreis* commanders. Lieutenant-General Karl Freiherr von Thüngen, Inspector of Recruiting in *Wehrkreis* III at the time, told the *Gestapo* that Graf von Helldorf, the Police President, had been summoned to the Bendlerstrasse and had arrived in Olbricht's office about 4.15 p.m. – *Spiegelbild*, p. 57. Gisevius, *To the Bitter End*, pp. 533–4 says about 4.30. The first telephone call from Olbricht that things were on the move, however, was received by Helldorf between 3.45 and 4 p.m. (ibid.). One of General Fromm's secretaries remembers that Olbricht's activity in connection with the *coup* started about 3.30 p.m. that afternoon – Alix von Winterfeldt verbally to the author 30 Aug. 1966. The first news and instructions reached the City Commandant's office about 4 p.m., some say 'after 3' – Bernardis and Hase to the People's Court, *Trial*, Vol. XXXIII, pp. 438, 487; Frau Margarethe von Hase, letters to the author 3 and 8 March 1964. This is confirmed by the time at which orders from the Commandant reached the Guard Battalion – at 4.10 p.m. according to [Otto Ernst Remer:] 'Der Ablauf der

Ereignisse am 20.7.1944 . . .' (Berlin, 22 July 1944 – in BA EAP 105/32), reproduced in *20. Juli 1944*, published by *Bundeszentrale für Heimatdienst* in 1961, pp. 145–52; at 4.15 according to Rudolf Schlee, commanding No 4 Company of the Guard Battalion, in his 'Bericht' dated 23 July 1944 (BA EAP 105/32), also reproduced in *20. Juli 1944*, pp. 152–5; shortly after 4.10 according to [Hans W.] Hagen: 'Tatbericht über meine Tätigkeit als Verbindungsoffizier des Wachbataillons . . .' (Berlin – earlier than 25 July 1944) in *Spiegelbild*, pp. 12–15 and *20. Juli 1944*, pp. 155–9; information from Hagen in article by Volkmar Hoffmann in *Frankfurter Rundschau* 18 July 1964, p. 3 – 'Nie wieder bin ich solch einem Menschen begegnet . . .'

After the war Remer gave varying accounts. On 15 August 1945, while a prisoner of war, he told an American interrogation officer that he had received codeword 'Gneisenau' [sic] about 3 p.m. on 20 July 1944 from Lt. Gen. Hase's office, and that he had gone to Hase immediately as ordered; Otto Remer: 'The 20 Jul. 44 Plot (Interview)', PW Camp No 26, Third U.S. Army, typescript, NA Record Group 338 ETHINT 63. This report contains other inaccuracies, too, which – like the term 'Gneisenau' – cannot be explained as translation errors. On 24 June 1946, while still a prisoner of war, Remer described the events of 20 July before an audience of fellow-prisoners and Grenzendörfer, one of them, took notes. Here Remer says that the Commandant's order reached him at 2.30 p.m. and he went at once to the headquarters. At his trial in 1949 Remer also said that the 'Valkyrie' codeword reached him from the Commandant's office at 2.30 and that he reported to Hase at about 3 p.m. (Public Prosecutor of Provincial Court, Oldenburg – 9 Js 164/49, annex to hearing); in his book *20. Juli 1944*, p. 8, Remer says 'early afternoon'. Shortly after the war Hagen also (indirectly) gave a different time – about 3 p.m.; he ended his lecture about this time, he says, and Remer returned from reporting to the Commandant at 4 p.m. – Hans W. Hagen: 'Grössere und kleinere Fehler beim Bericht . . . von Otto John', undated (after 1949), in possession of the 'Hilfswerk 20. Juli 1944' Foundation. Otto John in 'Remer und der 20. Juli 1944' (undated – BA H 91–1/2) clearly accepted the timing in Hagen's report ('Tatbericht') after a cursory examination. Giving information to Volkmar Hoffmann in 1964 Hagen said that the 'Valkyrie' order reached the Guard Battalion shortly after 4 p.m.

Major Fritz Harnack, a member of Olbricht's staff, remembers quite definitely that about 2 p.m. he received the order to launch 'Valkyrie' from Mertz, Chief of Staff, AHA – 'Bericht über die Vorgänge des 20.7.44 in der Bendlerstrasse', typescript, Braunschweig 20 July 1948 and verbally to the author 29 August 1966. Major Werner Rode, then commanding the Armoured Infantry Training Group at Armoured School Krampnitz, wrote to Dr Helmut Pigge on 24 July 1971 and to the author on 14 August 1971: the School was ordered to form battle groups towards 4 p.m., but he, Rode, had taken a reconnaissance drive directed against the SS barracks in Lichterfelde on orders of Colonel Glaesemer as early as about 2 p.m. Lt. Col. Herbert Schobess, then commander of the Heavy Weapons Company in the combat battalion of Infantry School Döberitz, wrote to the author on 9 December 1971 that the alert was received there about 2 p.m. In a letter to the author dated 16 Dec. 1968 Gerhart Goebel passed on a report from Rudolf Jakob, an engineer, to the effect that Broadcasting House in the Masurenalle had been occupied by the conspirators' troops by 3.15, the order for which must have been given earlier – also Jakob to the author 28 Jan. 1969. All reports giving these earlier timings originate from the post-war period.

As regards other sources the differences between timings given after the event and after the war can be explained partially by lapses of memory and partly by the fact that they are referring to preliminary warnings, conversations or measures. False statements would not have been tenable during the period immediately after 20 July 1944 since they could easily have been exposed by questioning other witnesses; there seems to be no plausible motive for making false statements after the war.

In *Wehrkreis* III headquarters on the Hohenzollerndamm it was known between 3 and 4 p.m. that an assassination attempt on Hitler had been made and the rumour began to circulate that 'Valkyrie' had been launched – Bruno Mitzkus (Operations Officer): 'Um den 20. Juli und das Ende im Wehrkreiskommando III', typescript, Bad Homburg 1947; Dr Martin Sobczyk, Lieutenant-Colonel and head of the *Abwehr* office in *Wehrkreis* III, verbally to the author 27 Aug. 1965. The 'Valkyrie' order reached the Pyrotechnical School about 4 a.m. – Alexander Maître (captain and artillery instructor at the time) to the author 19 Feb. 1965; it reached the Armoured School in Krampnitz about the same time through Major von Oertzen or Lieutenant-Colonel Bernardis – Wolfgang Müller: 'Was geschah am 20. Juli 1944?' in *Das freie Wort*, 19 July 1952. In Cottbus the order reached the 'Grossdeutschland' Reserve Brigade before 4.25 p.m. – Hans Werner Stirius (at the time Lieutenant-Colonel commanding the Armoured Infantry Reserve and Training Regiment and Deputy Brigade Commander) to the author 2 Feb. 1967.

29 Harnack, 'Bericht' and verbal information. Shortly after the war Remer and Hagen said the same but just after 20 July 1944 they reported differently so that they do not support Harnack's account. Other reports indicate that this meeting took place about 4 p.m. or shortly thereafter – Franz Herber (at the time Lieutenant-Colonel – Supply – on the staff of AHA): 'Was ich am 20.7.44 in der Bendlerstrasse erlebte', typescript, undated (probably 1948), BA H 90–3/4; Herber says that 'shortly after 5 p.m.', having received his orders from Mertz, Harnack came to him and asked him to assist in issuing the orders for 'Valkyrie'; since, however, the orders had reached various of the addressees soon after 4 p.m. at the latest, Herber must be wrong by about an hour. See also: Delia Ziegler in Volkmar Hoffmann's article; Bernardis to the People's Court, *Trial*, Vol. XXXIII, pp. 438–9; Karl Pridun (at the time Lieutenant-Colonel in AHA Operations Section), note 'Betrifft: 20. Juli 1944 Stellungnahme' typescript, Bregenz 1953 IfZ ZS 1769.

30 Report by Amt V of the RSHA, 'Betrifft: Selbstmord des Majors Ulrich von Oertzen', typescript, Berlin 22 July 1944, BA R 58/1051; Bruno Mitzkus: 'Bericht über die Ereignisse . . . am 20. Juli 1944', typescript, 9 Aug. 1945; Bernardis to People's Court, *Trial*, Vol. XXXIII, p. 438; copies of orders in *Spiegelbild*, pp. 28–30, 37–41.

31 Hase to the People's Court, *Trial*, Vol. XXXIII, p. 487; Hagen in *Spiegelbild*, pp. 12, 38–40; Hans W. Hagen: *Zwischen Eid und Befehl*, p. 17; Hans Siebert (Remer's adjutant at the time) to the author 27 Oct. 1969; Remer, 'Ablauf'; Schlee. According to Gisevius in *Wo ist Nebe?*, pp. 155–8, Hayessen had been inadequately prepared and briefed and so did not really know what to do.

32 Hoepner to the People's court, *Trial*, Vol. XXXIII, p. 401; report to Martin Bormann by Dr Hopf on trial of Fromm before the People's Court, 7 Mar. 1945, BA EAP 105/30; Heinz-Ludwig Bartram (at the time captain and aide to Fromm): '20. Juli 1944', typescript 1954, BA H 90–3/4; Fabian von Schlabrendorff: *Revolt Against Hitler*, pp. 138–9, giving partly information imparted to him by Fromm while in prison and partly the case for the prosecution against Fromm.

33 *Trial*, Vol. XXXIII, p. 402.

34 In the report on Fromm's trial and Hoepner's evidence appears 'towards 4 p.m.' Bartram gives a time later than 4.15 but a few lines below says that Olbricht asked for an interview with Fromm 'towards 4 p.m.'

35 It is possible, though improbable, that during this conversation with Fromm Keitel discovered that Witzleben and Hoepner were leaders in the plot. As will be shown below when describing the counter-measures, Keitel knew at the latest by 4.15 that Fromm's, Witzleben's and Hoepner's names had been used in the issue

of the 'Valkyrie' orders. He may have learnt of this through calls from commanders or through the extensive monitoring of all communications which had been introduced meanwhile – verbal information from Sander, Waizenegger, Wolf. See also Kramarz, p. 194 where certain details of the transmission of information from the Bendlerstrasse are given based on a report by Colonel Rudolf Langhaeuser.

According to Bartram, Fromm's aide, Olbricht told his commander, after his talk with Keitel, that a new government to take over from the previous regime and consisting of responsible persons, was being formed; he asked whether Fromm would wish to participate as C-in-C Home Army. Bartram also says that Fromm asked Keitel whether any action was to be taken by the Replacement Army. Bartram then goes on, however, without mention of intervening events, to record happenings which in fact took place much later, towards 5 p.m. For the course of events, therefore, it is better to rely on Fromm's and Hoepner's accounts, given when memories were fresher, except in cases where some indication that they were defending themselves can be detected.

36 *Trial*, Vol. XXXIII, p. 404.
37 *Trial*, Vol. XXXIII, pp. 401–2.
38 On this point and below: report by Army Signals Department dated 22 June 1944 in *Spiegelbild*, pp. 63–5; Klausing's evidence to the People's Court in *Trial*, Vol. XXXIII, p. 433; Helmuth Cords to the author 11 April 1971 (Klausing had been sick for a few days before 20 July); Wolfram Röhrig verbally to the author 29/30 June 1965; Emil Pestinger (Post Office official working the Bendlerstrasse signals section) to the author 20 Dec. 1964. Kramarz (p. 194) records information from Major-General Rudolf Langhaeuser, predecessor of Lieutenant-Colonel Sadrozinski as head of Group I on the staff of C-in-C Replacement Army (also Langhaeuser verbally to the author 22 Aug. 1969): on 20 July Langhaeuser visited the Bendlerstrasse to collect a railway ticket and went to see his successor, Sadrozinski who was having a heart attack and putting on compresses. Sadrozinski asked Langhaeuser to take along a pile of teleprinter messages which had been returned unprocessed from the Signal Traffic officer. The traffic officer told Langhaeuser that he had been ordered from 'Wolfschanze' not to despatch the messages. Langhaeuser then read one of the messages; from his description of its contents it was the second (see p. 420 below). This may be one of the episodes 'forgotten' in other accounts. The impression may be given by the passages cited in *Trial*, Vol. XXXIII, *Spiegelbild*, p. 182, and Klausing's farewell letter in BA NS 6/50 that Klausing simply carried out orders and was being made use of by the other conspirators. This would be a wrong impression. Axel von dem Bussche in 'Eid und Schuld', *Göttinger Universitätszeitung*, 7 Mar. 1947 p. 4, confirms that Klausing was consciously and actively involved.
39 Two erroneous statements are made in the Army Signals Department's report up to this point (see *Spiegelbild*, pp. 63–5, 197):
    1. The first sentence of the first message – 'The Führer Adolf Hitler is dead' – was not crossed out but was despatched with the remainder of the text and received by the addressees. The statement in the report that, after some ten minutes, Klausing brought the message back again with the first sentence crossed out and that Röhrig then crossed it out again so completely that it was no longer legible, was made, as far as Röhrig remembers, to conceal the willingness with which he, his subordinates and in some cases his superiors set about despatch of the messages. It is, of course conceivable that one of the conspirators – ? Olbricht, Hoepner or Beck – in view of the tenor of the news from the *Führer*'s headquarters cut the sentence out before Stauffenberg's return and had it reinserted later. This possibility is invalidated by the reports from *Wehrkreis* headquarters, as will be seen in the next chapter. So far no originals of the *first* version have been found. All available copies are later versions or copies of

what was received in *Wehrkreis* HQs. The copy in *Mitteilungsblatt der Arbeitsgemeinschaft ehemaliger Offiziere*, No 12 of 1968 and Nos 1–2 of 1969 merely reproduces earlier publications *without* the *first* version. See copy of the message in Appendix, *Spiegelbild*, p. 65.

During the proceedings of the People's Court on 7 Aug. 1944 Freisler explicitly quoted the sentence as the first of the order in question – *Trial*, Vol. XXXIII, p. 362. See also the copy (source unknown) in Gerhart Binder: *Epoche der Entscheidungen*, p. 433. The Signals report then says, but does not explain, that about 6.30 p.m. the message was brought to Röhrig *yet again*, in other words for the third time, and that he despatched it, though with some hesitation, to the headquarters of the Navy and *Luftwaffe*. In this message the sentence 'The Führer Adolf Hitler is dead' was not crossed out and it was so received at 7.28 p.m. by the Chief of Staff, Naval Headquarters – MFA files of Naval Headquarters II M 1005/11. The only reason for the inclusion of this story would be to lend colour to the theory that Röhrig was a good loyal soldier who, as soon as he saw that the orders of his superiors were directed against the regime, did his best to stop them, that he was sluggish in the despatch of the suspect messages and sent the most dangerous one with the fatal sentence about Hitler's death 'only to the Navy and *Luftwaffe*' who could not execute the orders contained in them and that he had later informed the Navy and *Luftwaffe* 'of the doubts current here [in the Bendlerstrasse]'.

2. The other incorrect statement, which must be regarded as a defensive measure, is that the first message was not despatched until between 17.35 and 21.03; processing in fact started at once. The mere despatch stamp '1645' on the first message attached to the Army Signals report invalidates the statement that it was not sent until an hour after delivery to Röhrig (*Spiegelbild*, p. 65). Addressees' stamps also show time of despatch in addition to time of receipt – in Prague, for instance, the first message carries a despatch time of 16.45 and the second of 18.00 – Ferdinand Schaal: 'Der 20. Juli in Prag' in *Schwäbische Zeitung* (Überlingen), 26 July 1952.

The additional statement that the second message was not processed 'with the same urgency as the first' is contradicted in the next sentence of the same report and by the despatch stamp on the copy of the message. The report says that despatch of the second message took from 18.30 to 21.22, in other words less than three hours, whereas despatch of the first of about similar length took more than $3\frac{1}{2}$ hours. Despatch of the third message was allegedly delayed because the lines were engaged with transmission of the first two messages; oddly enough, however, no delay in despatch of the second message seems to have been occasioned by transmission of the first, since – again according to the Army Signals report – this was completed more quickly. Despatch did not in fact begin at 18.30 but at 18.00 according to the stamp on the message attached to the report. Provided that this was the actual despatch copy, the timing given thereon was the time of actual start of despatch (Wolf). Klaus Haetzel in 'Die längste Schicht am Fernschreiber' in *Telegraf*, 19 July 1964, p. 8, records a statement by Vera Noack, one of the operators, that despatch of a message addressed 'to all *Wehrmacht* agencies' was held up between 20.30 and 21.30; this, however, said that the *Führer* was alive and so forth. The fact that it was held up at this late stage, which was to the advantage of the conspirators, is noteworthy. Even according to the doctored report by Army Signals (*Spiegelbild*, pp. 63–5) there was no interruption in despatch of the initial order until after 9 p.m. The alleged intervention by Colonel Köllner came at a time when the *coup* was long since over and is in line with the report's general tendency to exculpate those involved.

Discrepancies are therefore innumerable and obviously an attempt was made to throw dust in the *Gestapo*'s eyes by producing a mass of timings, dates and details. The *Gestapo*, on the other hand, was less interested in establishing details of what happened than in annihilating the opposition and the main dangerous 'enemies of the state'.

In my previous accounts I worked on the assumption that the timings given in the Army Signals report were established, undoctorable and undoctored and that discrepancies occurring in the timings on copies of the messages were due to clerical errors – see my 'Zum Ablauf des Staatsstreichversuches des 20. Juli 1944 in den Wehrkreisen' in *Wehrwissenschaftliche Rundschau* 14 (1964), pp. 377–97, and 'Der 20. Juli im Wehrkreis II (Stettin)...' In *Aus Politik und Zeitgeschichte*, 14 July 1965, pp. 25–37. As regards times of despatch and the question of the first sentence of the first message ('The Führer Adolf Hitler is dead') these accounts should be regarded as outdated.

40 Anni Lerche to Dr Hans Bernd Gisevius 30 June 1946, intercepted and translated by British Censorship Office IRS 3 D.C.S., typescript, 17 July 1946.

41 From Degner; Claus-Peter Goetzke (at the time Lieutenant and technical head of the Bendlerstrasse Signal Centre) to the author 14 July 1964.

42 See copy in *Spiegelbild*, pp. 65–6.

43 Ibid., pp. 63–4.

44 On Röhrig's activities Zeller (p. 352) obviously followed the Army Signals report, as I did in my earlier accounts until in an interview with Röhrig I discovered the discrepancies. The alleged deliberate sluggishness during the period up to 9 p.m. was an invention for the benefit of the *Gestapo*. Awards of decorations and promotions, in so far as they took place, prove nothing except that the story had its effect.

45 See note 38 above; copy in *Spiegelbild*, pp. 66–7.

46 Copy of the list of appointments, including those of Political Representatives in *Spiegelbild*, pp. 76–82.

47 Copy of this order in *Spiegelbild*, p. 68.

48 Ibid., pp. 70–5.

49 From Röhrig.

50 Ibid.; Dr Georg Röhrig (Foreign Service Counsellor) to the author 15 Mar. 1966.

51 An article appeared in 1965 in a publication not normally devoted to serious news and consisting of facts, stories and garbled statements; according to this Röhrig had told a reporter that he had deliberately delayed transmission of the conspirators' teleprinter messages – Peter G. Eder: 'Deutschland, deine Helden', in *Zeitung*, 19 July 1965, pp. 17–21. This was the result of a telephone interview which Röhrig had granted to a reporter and which the latter then published in garbled form. In its issue of 16 Aug. 1965 (its last incidentally) the paper had to publish a correction – Wolfram Röhrig: 'Keine bewusste Initiative', *Zeitung* 16 Aug. 1965, p. 57.

52 With presently available sources the timing cannot be established more precisely. On this point and below see: Hoepner's evidence to the People's Court, *Trial*, Vol. XXXIII, pp. 402–4; Gisevius, *Bitter End*, pp. 547–9; Bartram; Schlabrendorff, op. cit., pp. 138–41, giving Fromm's account, generally confirmed by Dr Hopf's report to Bormann on Fromm's trial before the People's Court, BA EAP 105/30.

53 Hans Karl Fritzsche verbally to the author 14 July 1972; Fritzsche thinks he remembers (but is probably mistaken) that Gerstenmaier had already arrived at this time. Cf. below, pp. 424–6.

54 Fritzsche.

55 *Trial*, Vol. XXXIII, p. 402. See Lieutenant-General von Thüngen's evidence at his trial before the People's Court to the effect that word had gone round that Hitler had been carried out on a stretcher – *Volksgerichtshof-Prozesse zum 20. Juli 1944*, p. 77. An unknown witness repeated before the People's Court what he had heard Stauffenberg himself saying during his argument with Fromm: '... in any case, however, the Colonel-General [Fromm] asked: were you there? ... to

which Stauffenberg replied that he was in the adjoining room, had heard the explosion – I do not know whether these were the exact words but it must have been the sense of them – had heard a doctor being called – I can still remember that sentence – . . . and had seen the Führer being carried out . . . and then came a sentence to the effect that there was no more hope or it was all over . . . F[reisler]: He therefore asserted that the Führer was dead as he had seen with his own eyes. [Witness:] Yes.' A few sentences later in the same cross-examination the witness said: 'Stauffenberg said with quite colossal assurance that the Führer was dead' – ibid., pp. 80–1. See also Fromm's account of Stauffenberg's statements in Schlabrendorff, op. cit., pp. 140–1.

56 Schlabrendorff, op. cit., p. 140; *Volksgerichtshof-Prozesse*, pp. 80, 85 et seq. C. Müller errs in his assertion (p. 607 note 10) that Gisevius drew his knowledge of these events from Schlabrendorff's book, which had been published before Gisevius' work. In fact Gisevius' manuscript was finished and in Allen Dulles's hands before the end of the war – which is how Gero von Schulze-Gaevernitz, the real author of Schlabrendorff's book and an assistant of Dulles, got the material into Schlabrendorff's book; Gisevius verbally to the author 8 September 1972. Probably Fromm telephoned once more to Keitel between his two conversations with Stauffenberg and then ended with the words: 'Field Marshal, I can therefore rely on the Führer being alive' – Ewald Heinrich von Kleist to the author 2 Oct. 1968. According to Gisevius, *Ende*, Vol. II, pp. 369–70, Olbricht tried to get Beck, who had already arrived, to make one more attempt to persuade Fromm to participate but Beck refused, saying that it smacked too much of forcing his hand.

57 Schlabrendorff, op. cit., p. 140; Bartram says basically the same though with certain differences; confirmation in Gisevius, *Bitter End*, pp. 539–40.

58 Schlabrendorff, op. cit., p. 141; report on Fromm's trial, BA EAP 105/30. According to Ewald Heinrich von Kleist speaking to Volkmar Hoffmann, after his (second) telephone conversation with Keitel Fromm said to Olbricht and Stauffenberg, Haeften and Kleist being present: 'Hitler is not dead. Under these circumstances I regard myself as in baulk as a co-conspirator.' This is not correct – Kleist to the author 2 Oct. 1968, also applicable below.

59 Gisevius, *Ende*, Vol. II, p. 377. According to Wagner, 'Verlauf', Beck was at the Bendlerstrasse as early as 4 p.m. Ludwig Freiherr von Hammerstein-Equord wrote to Dr Helmut Pigge on 6 April 1970 that Oppen had received the telephone message from Klausing in the hotel 'Esplanade' at 4.15 p.m., as it had been agreed in advance; then Hammerstein, Oppen, Fritzsche and Kleist had hurried over to Bendlerstrasse, apparently on foot; in the Bendlerstrasse they were passed by Graf Schwerin and Beck in a car, Schwerin motioning to them to hurry. Fritzsche (verbal information) received the order to put a uniform tunic on Beck; the uniform was hanging in a locker. But Fritzsche did not know Beck and helped Hoepner into the tunic by mistake.

60 *Trial*, Vol. XXXIII, pp. 403–4; Schlabrendorff op. cit., p. 142.

61 Wagner, 'Verlauf' – also applicable below.

62 We shall probably never know whether Wagner really refused to cooperate further because of the failure of the attempt, unless further evidence from those who knew him can be discovered. In the light of the following, presumably accurate, statement it must be assumed that he did so refuse – Burchardt, 'Zugehörigkeit' and 'Darstellung': 'Höpfner came back from Wagner, who must meanwhile have heard of the failure of the attempt, empty-handed and without instructions concerning the *coup*.'

63 Gisevius, *Bitter End*, pp. 532–6; *Volksgerichtshof-Prozesse*, pp. 47–51.

64 Gisevius, *Bitter End*, pp. 534–7.

65 *Volksgerichtshof-Prozesse*, pp. 49–51.

66 Ibid., pp. 48, 51. Dr Peter Boysen wrote to the author on 23 June and 6 July 1970 that Helldorf was at the Bendlerstrasse at about 11 a.m.; Boysen, Lt. Col. and

section chief for army clothing in AHA, was just briefing Olbricht on new uniforms and had to interrupt his presentation because Helldorf wanted to see Olbricht.

67 Decision by Public Prosecutor of People's Court to suspend investigation proceedings in cases against Ewald Heinrich von Kleist, Georg Sigismund von Oppen and Hans Fritzsche for high treason and treason, 12 Dec. 1944, Az O J 41/44 gRs, BA EAP 105/30; Lerche; Kunrat Freiherr von Hammerstein: *Spähtrupp*, pp. 270–1, 279 giving account by his brother Ludwig; here the time of the telephone call is given first as 4.30 p.m. and then as 4.15. Ludwig Freiherr von Hammerstein-Equord to Dr Pigge also gave 4.15 p.m. as the time of Klausing's telephone call; see also Volkmar Hoffmann.

68 From Fritzsche.

69 Gisevius, *Ende*, Vol. II, p. 370; Hammerstein, *Spähtrupp*, p. 270. According to Elfriede Nebgen in *Jakob Kaiser*, pp. 192–4, the Bendlerstrasse must have known precisely where Goerdeler was on 20 July.

70 Gisevius, *Ende*, Vol. II, p. 377.

71 Otto John: 'Der 20. Juli 1944', typescript, London undated, p. 13; also with slight differences John's other accounts: 'An Eye Witness's Account of the 20th July 1944 Plot against Hitler that Failed', typescript, [London] 1946; 'Zum Jahrestag der Verschwörung gegen Hitler' in *Wochenpost* 18 July 1947, pp. 4–6; 'Some Facts and Aspects of the Plot against Hitler', typescript, London 1948, p. 61; *Twice through the Lines,* pp. 146–52. Gisevius in *Nebe,* pp. 158–60 and *Bitter End,* pp. 501–6 and *Ende,* Vol. II, p. 353 says that Hansen wished to have no more to do with so badly prepared a *putsch* and 'ostentatiously went on leave'.

72 John, *Twice,* p. 147.

73 John, 'Zum Jahrestag' and 'Some Facts'; Hammerstein, op. cit., pp. 279 et seq.; Cords. Dr Achamer-Pifrader's name about which C. Müller (p. 608 note 13) marvels is confirmed in 'Liste der SS-Obergruppenführer bis SS-Standartenführer des Reichssicherheitshauptamtes ...', NA microcopy T-175 roll 241. The evidence indicating it was indeed Dr Achamer-Pifrader and not Buchner appears conclusive and is not doubted by C. Müller but C. Müller is right in pointing out that the evidence in *Spiegelbild,* p. 22 and John's own timings make it seem more likely that John met Colonel Jäger and *Waffen-SS-Untersturmführer* Buchner rather than Achamer-Pifrader, who had come to Bendlerstrasse before 5 p.m. and had probably been arrested at once, while Buchner only came towards 6 p.m.

74 Joachim Ruoff (*SS-Standartenführer* and Jüttner's operations officer) to the author 23 Nov. 1969. That same night Himmler said that he had deliberately refrained from using the SS so that the army itself might liquidate this little clique within its own ranks; Goebbels agreed with him – Balzer (OKW liaison officer to Ministry of Propaganda), 'Aktennotiz für Chef OKW/WPr persönlich', typed copy, Berlin 21 June [correctly: July] 1944, BA NS 6/31. Himmler said the same in his speech to officers of a grenadier division at Bitsch training grounds on 26 July 1944; Heinrich Himmler: *Geheimreden 1933 bis 1945 und andere Ansprachen,* p. 218.

75 On this point and below: Eugen Gerstenmaier verbally to the author 17 Aug. 1965 and 'Zur Geschichte des Umsturzversuches vom 20. Juli 1944' in *Neue Zürcher Zeitung,* 23, 24 June 1945; also numerous accounts including those entitled 'Entscheidende Stunden in der Bendlerstrasse' in *Die Welt,* 19 July 1946 and 'Der 20. Juli 1944' in *Schriften des Südkurier* No 1, Constance, undated; Gerstenmaier in 'Church Conspiratorial', pp. 183–9 confirms 5 p.m. as the time of the radio announcement. See also Eugen Gerstenmaier: 'Die Kreisauer und der 20. Juli' in his *Reden und Aufsätze,* Vol. II, pp. 238–43; Lerche; Fabian von Schlabrendorff: *Eugen Gerstenmaier im Dritten Reich,* p. 23.

76 Hammerstein, op. cit., p. 279; *Spiegelbild*, p. 377; Wilhelm von Schramm: *Conspiracy among Generals*, pp. 23–5. See also Chapter 44 below.

77 From Lerche.

78 Hammerstein, op. cit., p. 281; Mitzkus, 'Bericht'; *Trial*, Vol. XXXIII, p. 409; Gisevius, *Ende*, Vol. II, pp. 382–3, 386 (*Bitter End*, pp. 543, 545).

79 Yorck von Wartenburg's evidence, *Trial*, Vol. XXXIII, p. 430; von Thüngen's evidence, *Volksgerichtshof-Prozesse*, pp. 74–6; judgement of People's Court on Thüngen 5 Oct. 1944, BA EAP 105/30. Mitzkus in 'Bericht' says that Thüngen met Hase 'about 7 p.m.'; but Hase had not arrived 'shortly after 7 p.m.' (see Chap. 45 below). See also Gisevius, *Ende*, Vol. II, pp. 383–9.

80 On this point and below: Mitzkus, 'Bericht'; Joachim von Wiese und Kaiserswaldau (then in *Wehrkreis* III personnel section with his office in the Uhlan Barracks, Fürstenwalde) to the author 10 Aug. 1964; Harnack; report by Amt V of RSHA on Oertzen's suicide, 22 July 1944, BA R 58/1051.

81 Copy of list in *Spiegelbild*, pp. 28–30, is inaccurate; see copy in BA EAP 105/30.

82 Here and below according to Mitzkus; on Herfurth's hesitancy see *Spiegelbild*, p. 196.

83 Also, for instance, in the Potsdam garrison – Schramm, information from Meichssner.

84 Stirius.

85 In his *Aufstand der Generale*, pp. 7 and 94, (*Conspiracy among Generals*, p. 71) Wilhelm Ritter von Schramm, for instance, has pointed out that the *coup* in Berlin was run 'far too much from office stools'.

86 Timetable and orders in *Spiegelbild*, pp. 37–41 (with some errors); see copy in BA EAP 105/20. Sentence of People's Court of 15 August 1944 on B. Klamroth et al., NA microcopy T-120 roll 1038.

87 From 11 a.m. to 1 p.m. Albert Speer, the Minister of Armaments, was addressing all ministers, state secretaries and other senior officials present in Berlin, some 200 persons in all, on the war effort – Albert Speer: *Inside the Third Reich*, pp. 380–1; see also p. 481 below. Had the conspirators not had to exercise special caution owing to the false start of 15 July, they might have been able to arrest most of the regime's functionaries at one blow.

88 Sentence of People's Court on B. Klamroth et al.

89 Hase's evidence, *Trial*, Vol. XXXIII, pp. 487–8.

90 From Hassel; see also *Spiegelbild*, pp. 377–8.

91 On this point and below: Hase's evidence, *Trial*, Vol. XXXIII, pp. 487–8; information from Frau von Hase; Remer, 'Ablauf'; Hagen, 'Tatbericht' and *Zwischen Eid und Befehl*, pp. 17–37; Siebert; Schlee; Holm Erttel: 'Meine Herren, es ist so weit!' in *Das freie Wort*, 19 July 1952; Hammerstein, op. cit., p. 201; note for Bormann by Dr Hopf 24 Oct. 1944 and Kaltenbrunner to Party Chancellery, Munich 27 Oct. 1944, BA EAP 105/32. The Guard Battalion was stationed in Moabit, not in Döberitz as John W. Wheeler-Bennett says in *The Nemesis of Power*, p. 655 and Heinrich Fraenkel and Roger Manvell in their somewhat superficial account, *The July Plot*, p. 127.

92 Wolter apparently was also supposed to observe Remer – this was Remer's own impression, too; Remer, 'Ablauf'; Major Karl Lüthje (then in OKH/In 8 with Wolter) to the author 15 March 1971.

93 Remer, 'Ablauf'; confirmed by Schöne at his trial on 10 Oct. 1944 – note for Bormann by Dr Hopf 24 Oct. 1944, BA EAP 105/32.

94 Hagen may have heard the first radio announcement between 5 and 6 p.m. – see p. 439 below. For his activity reference should be made to his own, Remer's and Goebbels' reports (broadcast of 26 July 1944, *Völkischer Beobachter*, Berlin edition, 27 July, p. 1; also Semmler, pp. 132–8); these may be angled in certain respects, for instance the time at which doubts are said to have arisen is earlier than was in fact the case; they can hardly be angled as regards their other

statements, however, since these could have been checked at the time and any falsification could have had serious consequences for Remer and Hagen. Any collusion between Remer and Hagen can only have been in very general terms since they differ on various important points, particularly timings.

95 Hagen's report says 'to my Minister Goebbels or to the SD'. It is doubtful whether he would have mentioned the SD at this point but later reference to it would have been a wise precaution since it had become more powerful than ever. Hagen still insists that he did see Field Marshal von Brauchitsch driving through the city in full uniform; there is no possibility of error, he says; it could not have been Witzleben, for instance – Hagen, 'Grössere und kleinere Fehler'. At about the time in question (2.15 p.m.) Witzleben was on the way to Zossen. Where was Brauchitsch? The *Gestapo* reports say nothing on the subject. For the timing of Hagen's appearance in Goebbels' apartment see Speer, p. 385.

96 On this point and below: Kurt Delius to the author 28 July 1965; Stirius; Major-General (retd) Hermann Schulte-Heuthaus to the author 20 Sept. 1965.

97 According to Kurt Finker in *Stauffenberg und der 20. Juli 1944*, pp. 266–8 a scout car company in Potsdam-Nedlitz also received the same order and actually executed it. Delius remembers that 'meanwhile', about 6 p.m. therefore, Colonel Schulte-Heuthaus, the Brigade Commander, returned. Schulte-Heuthaus merely remembers being on the road all day and that Stirius carried out the 'Valkyrie' order. Stirius says nothing about the brigade commander's return but emphasizes that his memory is not complete or infallible. I have followed Delius' account since on all important points it tallies with that of Stirius.

98 On the events at the Infantry School see Wolfgang Müller: *Gegen eine neue Dolchstosslüge*, pp. 42–3; *Spiegelbild*, pp. 459–60; Dr Georg Röhrig to the author, 15 Mar. 1966, 6 Feb. 1969. Müller says that Hitzfeld was privy to the conspiracy but Hitzfeld emphatically denies this. On this point: Otto Hitzfeld to Gert Buchheit 5 July 1966 and to Institut für Zeitgeschichte, Munich, 25 Sept. 1966; Wolfgang Müller to Hitzfeld 15 Oct. 1966; Hitzfeld to Müller 18 Oct. 1966 – all in IfZ ZS 1858. Müller seems simply to have been victim of a misunderstanding: in reply to a query over the telephone on 20 July 1944 Hitzfeld said that OKH's orders should be carried out (even against the SS); Müller accordingly thought that Hitzfeld was on the conspirators' side and knew of their plans. Events in Döberitz were confirmed in detail from notes made at the time by Lieutenant-Colonel H. Hüttner, tactics instructor in Döberitz, in a letter to the author dated 25 Jan. 1969; they are also confirmed by Capt. (retd) Rolf Sturm to the author 1 August 1971; by Albert Bollmann to the author 29 August 1971; and by Wilhelm Gaede (then Lieutenant and Inspection Chief with Training Group III of the gunnery school in the Infantry School) to the author 7 June 1971. Karl Schober: 'Eine Chance blieb ungenutzt' in *Darauf kam die Gestapo nicht*, pp. 54–5, says that the 'Valkyrie' alert reached Döberitz before 2 p.m. This is based on a report by Lieutenant-Colonel Friedrich Jakob and confirmed by: Jakob to the author 3 June 1969; Rudolf Jakob (engineer, then in Broadcasting House) to the author 28 Jan. 1969; Goebel to the author 16 Dec. 1968; Oskar Haaf (in charge of broadcasts and deputy to the *Reich* Broadcasting Director, Dr Glasmeier); H. J. Pantenius (then in Döberitz on the regimental commanders course under Colonel Ringler) to the author 5 Mar. 1970. It is not clear whether two alerts were received, one about 2 p.m. and the other about 4 p.m. or whether half of those reporting are suffering from a lapse of memory and the other half are not. See also Finker, p. 378 Note 39; Harnack. Bollmann says that codeword 'Valkyrie' arrived at Döberitz by telephone order as early as 'towards 3.30 p.m.'; the commanding officers were ordered to go to the staff headquarters of the Infantry School at Elstal in the Olympic Village, some 4 kilometres from (Bollmann's) Training Staff 1 in the old camp of Dalow-Döberitz.

99 Bollmann.

100 On this point and below: Otto Freundorfer (at this period section head in the National broadcasting programme) verbally to the author 18 Feb. 1965; Paul Gnuva (also in Broadcasting House) to the author 6 Apr. 1965; report by Major Jakob to Major-General Ferdinand Brühl, later his divisional commander, and recorded by the latter on 25 Apr. 1947 in Bridgend POW camp in Britain – Otto John's papers, folio 5; Schober, pp. 54–5; Utz Utermann (also in Broadcasting House) to the author March 1965; Finker, pp. 268–9; Müller in *Dolchstosslüge* pp. 42–7 does not mention Jakob's action and so apparently knew no details of it. Wheeler-Bennett (pp. 654–6) gives Jakob's account as recorded by Brühl; in general Wheeler-Bennett is not very clear about what happened.

101 Data on time of arrival at Broadcasting House vary. Most witnesses give times between 5 and 6 p.m.; thus Erich Zielke to the author 20 July 1970; cf. note 100 above. See Finker, p. 378 Note 39. Schober says that an entire battalion of some 400 men arrived; members of the broadcasting staff, however, refer only to 80–100 men.

102 The machine guns and mortars remained there until the next day; Günter Bergeré to the author 15 September 1971.

103 From Hassel; *Spiegelbild*, p. 377.

104 This is what Hassel remembers. The leader of the group sent out by In 7, Lt. Col. (retd) Friedrich Redlich told the author on 3 July 1971 that he recalls having led a group of only ten officers.

105 Redlich.

106 See Kramarz, p. 193 who gives a report by a certain Colonel 'R.K.'; he was supposed to occupy the National Radio transmitter and that at Nauen with a group of radio operators and members of the Propaganda Section (? the *Wehrmacht* Propaganda Section of OKW). Colonel R. K. reported to Stauffenberg and Olbricht apparently about 5 p.m. but was given no orders on the grounds that it was still too early. Evidently Colonel R.K. did not say whether or why he still received no orders later.

107 Pantenius, also applicable below; also Fritz Adam (then a captain and company commander of the cadre company of Training Group I with Training Staff 1 at Infantry School Döberitz) wrote to the author on 21 August 1971 that it was almost night by the time the trucks left for Tegel. Bollmann remembers that the Tegel transmitter was to be occupied by the unit from the Anti-Tank Inspectorate.

108 Hassel; Wagner, 'Verlauf'; report signed by an officer named Scheffler [?] in the office of the Artillery General, 'Bericht über die Angelegenheit Gen.d.Art. Lindemann', typescript, 26 July 1944, NA microcopy T-78 roll 269.

109 Fritz Theil to Marion Gräfin von Dönhoff 28 May 1948, typed copy and signed typed report, Godesberg, undated (probably 1956) – both in possession of 'Hilfswerk' Foundation.

110 Wagner, 'Verlauf'; *Spiegelbild*, p. 146; Scheffler [?] reports that Lindemann did not leave for Berlin until 'about 8 p.m.'.

111 See Chap. 45 below. Hüttner (Note 98) confirms Müller's statements in complete detail.

112 According to Müller in 'Was geschah' Gorn was still in the school.

113 Several of those who were witnesses or participants in the events give earlier timings: Werner Rode (then a major and commander of Armoured Troops Training Group at Krampnitz) to Dr Helmut Pigge 24 July 1971; Heinrich V. Prinz Reuss (then a lieutenant in In 6) to the author 15 May 1972, although with the variation that the order received between 1 and 3 p.m. was revoked almost immediately, then declared valid half an hour later. So long as reliable contemporary documents are lacking it will not be possible to solve the question of timing definitively.

114 Copy of the order at Annex to *Gestapo* reports in BA EAP 105/20, also in

Spiegelbild, p. 40; the general sense is also to be found in Wolfgang Müller: 'Die Wehrmacht am 20 Juli' in *Main-Post*, 21 July 1949 which refers to a report by Colonel Glaesemer dated 23 Oct. 1945; Müller, 'Was geschah'. See also Schramm, information from Meichssner. Confirmed by Frau Elli Tschöckell neé Ehlers (then secretary at In 6 with Colonel Bolbrinker) to the author 18 October 1971; Colonel Werner Mildebrath (then section chief for tanks at In 6): '20. Juli in Berlin', typescript, Hannover [1971]; Heinrich V. Prinz Reuss.

115 See Note 114 above.

116 Harald Momm verbally to the author 19 Aug. 1968; information from Dr Wilhelm Tobias Wagner. Momm later told the *Gestapo* that the word he used was 'sow' which was a sporting term; Momm was demoted and posted to the 'Dirlewanger' unit but eventually regained his old rank.

117 Rode, also applicable below.

118 John von Freyend; Momm. On hearing this Momm said: 'Well, it's clear, horses back in, saddles off!' John von Freyend says that this must have been between 5 and 6 p.m. Momm has only a vague recollection of these details.

119 On Bolbrinker's appointment see Wolf Keilig: *Das deutsche Heer 1939–1945*, p. 211/38.

120 Heinz Guderian: *Panzer Leader*, pp. 338–9. Guderian says that he himself took no action and there are no other indications that he did. His Chief of Staff, Major-General Thomale, was at 'Mauerwald' on 20 July 1944 and telephoned Bolbrinker after 7 p.m. to tell him that Hitler was alive and what had happened; Thomale to the author 11 August 1971. Otto Skorzeny in *Skorzeny's Special Missions*, pp. 114–15, says that during the evening he met 'Tank General B', presumably Bolbrinker, who told him that all armoured forces from Wünsdorf had moved on Berlin and were concentrated near the Fehrbelliner Platz where he had them well under control. He, B, had been ordered to use his tanks for armed reconnaissance of *Waffen-SS* barracks in Berlin. Skorzeny advised against this and said that civil war should be avoided.

121 Müller, 'Was geschah'; Tzschöckell; Mildebrath; Prinz Reuss; also applicable below.

122 Tzschöckell.

123 Walter Bruns: 'Vor, am und nach dem 20. Juli 1944', typescript, undated (between 1945 and 1948), John's papers, folio 5 – also applicable below.

124 From what he says he left at 7.30 p.m. but if, as he says later, he went immediately afterwards to the Hermann-Göring-Strasse and found Hase there, he must have left the school in Treptow later than 7.30. See Finker, pp. 281, 379 Note 48, also Chap. 45 below, pp. 489–90.

125 Zeller's unsupported statement (p. 310) that the first detachments of the Ordnance School and the Pyrotechnical School occupied their positions at the Castle and the Arsenal 'by 7 p.m.' is therefore not correct – see Müller, *Dolchstosslüge*, p. 46. Cords remembers having seen only a platoon of about thirty to forty men enter the courtyard, and that they came somewhat later than 9.45 p.m.

126 Cords. Cf. below, p. 501.

127 On this point and below: Helmuth Schwierz: 'Bericht über meine Tätigkeit am 20 Juli 1944 . . .', typescript, Siegen, undated (probably 1963); Schwierz to the author 15, 25 Mar. 1965; Martin Korff (then Major commanding cadets course at the Pyrotechnical School) verbally to the author 25 Feb. 1965; Maître to the author 19 Feb., 15 Mar. 1965; extracts from personal files provided by Central Information Bureau of BA 29 June 1965; Wilhelm Küpper (then Colonel, instructor at Pyrotechnical School) to the author 28 Apr. 1965; certificate from *Gestapo* to Berlin Police District 16 Sept. 1944 for submission to Economics Office – subject: period spent under arrest by Schwierz; [Wilhelm] Burgdorf to HQ *Wehrkreis* IX, 3 Oct. 1944, typed copy concerning probationary posting to the front for Schwierz.

128 Maître mentions fourteen parties; the recommendation for promotion for Major Korff submitted by the Pyrotechnical School on 12 Sept. 1944 (BA – personnel files) for distinguished services in connection with the suppression of the *putsch* refers to ten parties.

129 According to Korff his name was Hoffmann but there is no confirmation of this elsewhere. In the lists of General Staff officers arrested, released or sentenced (BA EAP 105/2) appears a Lieutenant-Colonel Walter Horstmann, born 18.1.1900 (appointment not given), who was arrested in connection with 20 July.

130 From Korff; Maître says that he was in the ministry guest-house.

131 This must have been about 6.45 p.m. Maître himself therefore does not seem to have penetrated as far as Goebbels but possibly said that his duty was to arrest Goebbels. This is what Semmler says (p. 133) but his information is not first-hand and some of it is wrong.

132 Korff's and Maître's accounts are somewhat different; they were not together.

133 This is Zeller's version (pp. 311, 435 Note 17) based on a report by Major Klapper, one of the two raiding party commanders under Colonel Jäger; the other one, Captain Johannes Dangschat, told the author on 18 July 1971: the raiding party was waiting in the Wilhelmstrasse for Colonel Jäger; after a while Dangschat sent a motorcycle courier to look for Jäger at the Commandant's HQ, but the courier could not find him; then the raiding party proceeded to the Commandant's HQ where in the meantime elements of the Guard Battalion had assumed control and had set up machine guns; when the leaders of the raiding party asked for Colonel Jäger, they were told to put themselves at the disposal of Major Remer; this they finally did, finding the situation too unclear for any further action; as Dangschat put it: 'To us, the thing seemed to have gone sour.' See also Hase's evidence to the People's Court, *Trial*, Vol. XXXIII, pp. 488–93; *Spiegelbild*, p. 45; Remer, 'Ablauf'.

134 Original in Major Wolf's papers. See also Schramm (information from Warlimont): 'The first [news about the attitude of the Berlin headquarters] came just before 5.0 p.m. when General Fromm called – so far [21 July] it is still not clear where he stands. He told the Chief of OKW that various rumours were going round in Berlin and asked whether he should proclaim a state of emergency. [Keitel] replied that there was no cause to do so. Asked whether Stauffenberg was in Berlin, Fromm replied that he was still in the Führer's headquarters.' This must have been earlier than 4.30, about 4 p.m. judging by other indications (cf. p. 421 above). General Wagner wrote in his report ('Verlauf') to Colonel-General Zeitzler: 'About 4 p.m. telephone call from Berlin (Stauffenberg) ... Soon afterwards telephone call from Colonel von Mertz ... Shortly afterwards telephone call General Stieff: "Just heard from C-in-C Replacement Army that executive power proclaimed over signature of Fromm. Complete madness. Do you know details, General?" Therefore Warlimont's timing 'shortly before 5 p.m.' seems somewhat too late. See also pp. 421–3 above. On the timing of Himmler's appointment as C-in-C Replacement Army see Schramm (information from Warlimont), p. 9 who says 'as early as afternoon of 20 July'.

135 This according to Schramm on information from Warlimont and Meichssner; he specifically refers to the 6.30 announcement as a repetition; also Röhrig verbally to the author; Bernardis in *Trial*, Vol. XXXIII, p. 439. Skorzeny (p. 113) says: before 6 p.m. as does Franklin L. Ford in 'The Twentieth of July in the History of German Resistance', *American Historical Review LI* (1945/46), pp. 609–26.

136 17.42 British double summer time = 15.42 GMT = 16.42 Central European Time = 17.42 German summer time. *Daily Digest of World Broadcasts*, Part I, No 1830 dated 21 July 1944 covering period 0001 Thursday 20 July – 0001 Friday 21 July, issued by Monitoring Service of the BBC. On German summer time see *Reichsgesetzblatt Teil I 1943* – p. 542, 1944 – p. 198; Helmut Sünder-

mann: *Deutsche Notizen 1945/1965*, pp. 63–4; Sündermann to the author 3 Dec. 1969.

CHAPTER 43

1 Verbal information from Ludolf Gerhard Sander (24, 25 April 1964) and Josef Wolf (27 February 1965).

2 See previous chapter, Note 134; [Percy Ernst Schramm:] 'Vorgänge im FHQu am 20.7.1944 (Attentat auf den Führer)' in Herbert Kraus: *Braunschweiger Remerprozess*, pp. 139–41.

3 [Schramm:] 'Mitteilungen des Stellv. Chefs WFSt 21.7.44 20 Uhr', ibid., pp. 142–5.

4 Eduard Wagner: 'Der Verlauf des 20. Juli (aus dem Gedächtnis)', typescript, [Zossen] 21 July 1944 IfZ ED 95. In the diary of the Head of the Army Personnel Office, [Rudolf Schmundt:] 'Tätigkeitsbericht des Chefs des Heerespersonalamts ...' pp. 164–5, NA microcopy T-84 roll 39. Schmundt's successor noted that by 2 p.m. it was known in the *Führer*'s headquarters that the leaders of the revolt proposed to appoint Witzleben as *Reich* Regent, Hoepner as C-in-C Replacement Army and Beck as Chief of OKW. He then says, however, (and on this point he must be well informed since he was on the spot himself) that an hour after the assassination attempt, in other words about 2 p.m., General Burgdorf came into 'Wolfschanze' to carry on the business of Schmundt, who had been severely wounded. Judging by the context, Field Marshal Keitel would have ordered him at that time or soon afterwards to call all *Wehrkreis* commanders and tell them in Keitel's name that all orders from the Bendlerstrasse or those signed by Hoepner, Witzleben, Olbricht or Fromm were invalid, that the only valid orders were those from the *Reichsführer-SS* and the Chief of OKW, that 'Valkyrie' measures were to be cancelled and that close touch was to be maintained with *Gauleiter* and Senior SS and Police Commanders [HSSPF] – in other words identical orders with those contained in Keitel's radio message quoted on p. 439 above. There is no evidence that these instructions were given before 4 p.m. or that 'Valkyrie' was launched before that time apart from the recollections of Remer, Harnack and others which are uncertain and in some cases inconsistent in themselves. The officer responsible for keeping up Schmundt's diary also gives much wrong information, quite apart from inaccurate timings.

5 See below, p. 460 and 696 Note 52.

6 Hans Bernd Gisevius: *Bis zum bittern Ende*, Vol. II, p. 391: Schramm, 'Vorgänge'; Wilhelm von Schramm: *Aufstand der Generale*, p. 75.

7 Original with marginal notes by Major Wolf and Lieutenant-Colonel Sander and authentication by a General Staff Colonel, in Major Wolf's papers.

8 Army Personnel Office lists, BA EAP 105/2; *Spiegelbild einer Verschwörung*, p. 372; Colonel Kandt (personnel officer *Wehrkreis* I) to the author 11 Feb., 13 Mar. 1964. In general see the author's 'Zum Ablauf des Staatsstreichversuches des 20. Juli in den Wehrkreisen' in *Wehrwissenschaftliche Rundschau* 14 (1964), pp. 377–97; some of the information therein has been completed or corrected as a result of further research but despatch timings can still not be regarded as altogether clear; see above, p. 681 Note 39. Timings given in the Army Signals report (*Spiegelbild*, pp. 63–5) were designed to shield those involved and confuse the *Gestapo* and so were not given correctly; they can only be established in certain cases (see copy of teleprint in Appendix). A *Wehrkreis* HQ was also the static corps HQ commanding Territorial and replacement units; as an example the full title of *Wehrkreis* I HQ was 'HQ *Wehrkreis* I and Rear HQ I Corps'; for simplicity's sake the second part of the title has been dropped in most cases.

9 General Albert Wodrig to the author 11 Mar. 1964. Wodrig refers to radio messages from Berlin and remembers receiving them 'somewhere about 4 p.m.' Colonel Kandt says that Thadden drove back to Königsberg 'immediately after the assassination attempt'; he had about an hour's drive. Even had he taken two hours Thadden would therefore have been back in Königsberg about 3 p.m. The orders, however, had already arrived when he got there. Since there is no other evidence that the teleprints announcing Hitler's death were received so early, General Wodrig's memory must be at fault. Colonel Kandt's calculations assume that Thadden left 'Wolfschanze' 'immediately after the assassination attempt' but 'immediately' is only Kandt's assumption or alternatively is based on a casual remark by Thadden; if the latter knew that Stauffenberg was under suspicion, it must have been at least 2 p.m. before he left. Thadden lunched with Streve, and lunch could not have started before 1 p.m. since Stauffenberg was to lunch with Streve after the midday situation conference. See *Spiegelbild*, p. 85. The fact that Wodrig returned before 6 p.m. is confirmed by Prince Louis Ferdinand of Prussia in *Als Kaiserenkel durch die Welt*, p. 357; just before 6 p.m. Field Marshal (retd) Küchler, with whom Louis Ferdinand was staying, telephoned General Wodrig who told him that he had orders from Berlin to arrest *Gauleiter* Koch and that Hitler was dead. He had, however, immediately telephoned Keitel and found that this was incorrect.

10 Kandt to the author 11 Feb. 1964; Louis Ferdinand, p. 357.

11 See the author's 'Der 20. Juli im Wehrkreis II' in *Aus Politik und Zeitgeschichte*, 14 July 1965 which supersedes the author's 'Ablauf', p. 386. Principal sources: Werner Kienitz: 'Der Wehrkreis II vor dem Zusammenbruch des Reiches', typescript, Hamburg 1953, BA Ost-Dok. 8 Po 22 and 'Bemerkungen zu den Bemerkungen des Herrn Oberst Staudinger . . .', typescript, Hamburg 1954, ibid.; Hans-Heinrich Staudinger: 'Bemerkungen zur Niederschrift von Herrn General Kienitz . . .', typescript, Schönböcken 1954, ibid.; Colonel von Uechtritz (Chief Signal Officer *Wehrkreis* II at the time) to Staudinger 2 June 1954, ibid.; Staudinger to the author 31 Oct. 1964, 28 Jan., 12 Feb., 24 Sept. 1965; Colonel Walther Schroeder (personnel officer *Wehrkreis* II at the time) to the author 9 Nov. 1964; Brigadier-General Klaus Schubert (Major, operations officer *Wehrkreis* II at the time) to the author 30 Sept. 1964; Major-General Siegfried von Stülpnagel (a regimental commander in *Wehrkreis* II at the time) to the author 1 Feb., 7 Apr. 1965. The author's '20. Juli im *Wehrkreis* II', p. 29 Note 19, is outdated by information from Wolfram Röhrig, signal traffic officer in the Bendlerstrasse and by *Trial of the Major War Criminals before the International Military Tribunal*, Vol. XXXIII, p. 362.

12 See *Trial*, Vol. XXXIII, p. 414; below see Kienitz 'Wehrkreis II', pp. 8–9.

13 In his letter to the author of 7 Apr. 1965 Major-General von Stülpnagel says that his reaction to Kienitz' reference to the orders from Berlin was: 'We'll go along with that.' In Kienitz's letter to Staudinger of 11 Jan. 1954 and Staudinger's to the author of 24 Sept. 1965 this is definitely denied.

14 In a letter to the Institut für Zeitgeschichte in Munich, dated 1 September 1965, the former forestry official nominated as Political Representative for Mecklenburg, Freiherr von Willisen, insists that shortly after midnight Kienitz told *Gauleiter* Hildebrand of Mecklenburg over the telephone that a teleprint from OKH had appointed Willisen Political Representative for Mecklenburg, in other words as the *Gauleiter*'s successor, and that Kienitz must have known 'what the implications of this call were'. Willisen's appointment could not be kept secret in any case, however; the contents of the teleprinter messages quickly became known to the authorities, many of them during the same night. Neither Kienitz's account nor that of Staudinger mentions the alleged call. Willisen was not arrested during the night although he was at the *Gauleiter*'s *after* the alleged telephone conversation between Kienitz and Hildebrand. Thus the implications

of this call did not become clear and effective until such time as the *Gauleiter* had been informed of Willisen's appointment from other sources, like Bormann's circulars to all *Gauleiter*, and when the *Gestapo* already knew the names of all Political Representatives.

15 On this point and below: Werner Bühlmann to the author 2 Mar. 1965; Dr Wilhelm Sommerlad (Colonel, personnel officer *Wehrkreis* IV at the time) to the author 5 Oct. 1964; Dr Ralph Jordan (in *Abwehr* office *Wehrkreis* IV at the time) to the author 12 Mar. 1965; Günther von Platen (Major in the same *Abwehr* office at the time) to the author 17 Mar. 1965; Kunrat Freiherr von Hammerstein: *Spähtrupp*, pp. 239–40. According to Dr Jordan a civil servant named Ley, also of *Wehrkreis* HQ and in a state of confusion and agitation similar to that of the duty officer, called the *Gestapo* as well.

16 Dr Sommerlad mentions Colonel Paul Huth, then commanding the Reserve Infantry Regiment in Dresden, in this connection but on 14 Jan. 1965 Huth told the author that, although woken by his supply officer during the night with the news of the assassination attempt, he did not alert any troops.

17 Because of his behaviour on 20 July according to Wolf Keilig in *Das deutsche Heer 1939–1945*, p. 211/348. This is contested by Adam and Tümpling, the main sources for the events in Stuttgart that evening – Kurt Adam to the author 5 Apr. 1964, 8 Jan. 1968; Walter Hindenach (Colonel, supply officer *Wehrkreis* V at the time) to the author 2 Mar. 1964; Wolf von Tümpling (Colonel, personnel officer *Wehrkreis* V at the time) to the author 4 Jan. 1968; *Spiegelbild*, p. 108. Max Waaser (intelligence officer *Wehrkreis* V at the time) told the author on 22 May 1971: 'General Veiel did not give any orders.' General Veiel and Colonel Adolf Steiger, his operations officer, are both dead.

18 The Gestapo report in *Spiegelbild*, p. 108 records a more or less meaningless conversation between Veiel and Hoepner, apparently on information from Hoepner: ' "Veil [sic] here; who's that?" Answer: "Hoepner here, Veil; what's up?" Veil: "It's all right." Hoepner: "What do you mean – it's all right?" Veil (ending conversation): "Well, it's all right." End of conversation.'

19 From Adam.

20 From Tümpling.

21 Martin Bärtels to the author 4 Sept. 1965; Friedrich Kuhn (Colonel, operations officer *Wehrkreis* VI at the time) to the author 25 Sept. 1964; Georg von Issendorf (Colonel, personnel officer *Wehrkreis* VI at the time) to the author Jan. 1964. Dr Hermann Pünder, who was then a Major on the staff of *Wehrkreis* VI and had connections with the opposition through his friendship with Goerdeler, is unfortunately not prepared to give information about his experiences on 20 July.

22 On this point and below: Max Ulich (Colonel, Chief of Staff *Wehrkreis* VII at the time) to the author 6 Apr., 1964; Bruno Grosser (Lieutenant-Colonel, operations officer *Wehrkreis* VII at the time) to the author 18 July 1964; *Spiegelbild*, p. 63; Otto Reheusser (telegraph construction official in General Post Office, Munich, at the time) verbally to the author 7 Aug. 1968.

23 Grosser says that he was asked to call Berlin 'at midday on 20 July'; Stauffenberg, however, did not arrive back in the Bendlerstrasse before 4.30 p.m. at the earliest, so it can hardly have been before 4 p.m.

24 On this point and below: Helmut Heiber: *Hitlers Lagebesprechungen*, p. 886 Note 1; Rudolf Koch-Erpach verbally to the author 28 Mar. 1964; Ludwig Freiherr Rüdt von Collenberg (Major-General, Chief of Staff *Wehrkreis* VIII at the time) to the author 3 and 15 Feb. 1964; Joachim Bergener (Colonel, personnel officer *Wehrkreis* VIII at the time) to the author 12 May 1964; Kurt Schindler (Lieutenant-Colonel, head of the *Wehrmacht* Recruiting Centre in Glatz at the time) to the author 19 and 24 Feb. 1964; Ger van Roon: *Neuordnung im Widerstand*, p. 120.

25 *Spiegelbild*, p. 68.

26 See pp. 459–60 below.

27 Circular from Bormann 20 July, in EAP 105/31.

28 Roon (pp. 120–1) records a statement by Lukaschek that Koch-Erpach had been ordered by the Bendlerstrasse to place himself under Lukaschek, which cannot be right. Moreover the commander only returned at 11 p.m.; the order nominating liaison officers and Political Representatives must have arrived considerably earlier but Koch-Erpach cannot have had time to read all the orders. He then handed the message over to the *Gauleiter*, Lukaschek continues, and Lukaschek was arrested late that evening. The *Gauleiter* received the messages, or at least all he needed to know of their contents, very quickly from the *Führer*'s headquarters (Bormann); in Berlin the *Gestapo* collected copies of all teleprints despatched and those awaiting despatch on which they could lay hands; during the next few days all available documents were confiscated from *Wehrkreis* HQs. Any impression, therefore, that Lukaschek was arrested because of (alleged) servility towards the *Gauleiter* on the part of Koch-Erpach is wrong.

29 On this point and below: Otto Schellert to the author 1 Feb. 1964, 2 Jan. 1968; Claus-Henning von Plate (Colonel, Chief of Staff *Wehrkreis* IX at the time) to the author 11 and 19 Aug. 1964, 14 Apr. 1966; Wilhelm Reutter (Colonel, personnel officer *Wehrkreis* IX at the time) to the author 13 Mar. 1964; Ludwig Kaiser: 'Was wissen wir vom 20. Juli?', typescript, Kassel 1964; Otto Schoener (Lieutenant-Colonel, *Wehrkreis* IX HQ at the time) to the author 21 July 1965; Ludwig von Nida (Major-General, Chief of Staff *Wehrkreis* IX until March 1944): 'Der 20. Juli 1944 in Kassel: Die Vorbereitungen', *Hessische Allgemeine* 18 July 1964; Hans Beck (Lieutenant-Colonel and *Wehrmacht* liaison officer with non-military official establishments in *Wehrkreis* IX): 'Der 20. Juli 1944 in Kassel: Unternehmen Walküre läuft an', *Hessische Allgemeine* 18 July 1964; report by Eisenach sub-station, SD Region Weimar, 26 July 1944, BA RG 1010–1602; report by District Leader of Eisenach to *Gauleiter* in Weimar 26 July 1944, ibid.; report by Jakob Sprenger, *Gauleiter* of Hesse, undated copy BA NS 19/188-F 42.

30 This would explain why neighbouring *Wehrkreise* were told at this time that nothing was being done in Kassel but a wait-and-see attitude adopted.

31 Colonel Reutter was not in Kassel on 20 July and his account is based solely on that of Schellert to him. After 20 July Schellert was undoubtedly trying to clear himself of any suspicion and this may be why Reutter's account differs from that of Plate in saying that on his return Schellert was faced with a fait accompli, the order for arrest of the *Gauleiter* having already been issued. Naturally, compared to other sources, Reutter's account contains numerous discrepancies and inaccuracies. General Schellert does not remember seeing the message – letter to the author 2 Jan. 1968. Plate must have told him of the contents without showing it to him.

32 Artur Wollschläger to the author 24 Nov. 1971.

33 On this point and below: Friedrich-Wilhelm Prüter to the author 10 Feb. 1964; activity report of *Wehrkreis* HQ written after the war by Major Bohnemeier and made available to the author on 3 Jan. 1965 by Lieutenant Colonel Hans Goverts; [Karl Kaufmann (*Gauleiter* in Hamburg at the time):] 'Der 20. Juli 1944 in Hamburg', typescript, [Bethel 1946]; Dr Werner Naumann to the author 9 Apr. 1970. When writing 'Ablauf' (pp. 386–7) Prüter's account was the author's only available source.

34 Prüter says that he was shown the teleprints in *Wehrkreis* HQ somewhat earlier, between 5 and 6 p.m. On the other hand Major Bohnemeier (Goverts to the author 3 June 1965) says that the first teleprint arrived about 6.15 p.m., the second about 6.45 and that Prüter did not come in until about 7 p.m. Copies of both messages received in Hamburg were in the files of the Schleswig-Holstein *Gauleiter*'s office and were sent for information to the Senior SS and Police Commander in

Hamburg on 21 July; they confirm Bohnemeier in that the receipt stamps read '18.17' and '18.38' respectively.

35 Peters (*Kreisleiter* and *Landrat* in Rendsburg): 'Bericht über den Verlauf des 20. Juli 1944 im Kreis Rendsburg', typescript, Rendsburg 21 July 1944, files of *Gauleiter*'s office Schleswig-Holstein (Kiel).

36 Dr Werner Naumann to the author 9 Apr. 1970.

37 Walter Görlitz in *Der deutsche Generalstab*, p. 664 (not in English translation) gives an unsupported and apparently exaggerated story that Prüter first drank a bottle of wine with the *Gauleiter*.

38 This is according to Kaufmann's account; he says that there was a telephone conversation with the *Führer*'s headquarters after the commander's arrival. Prüter, on the other hand, says that he telephoned General Burgdorf in the *Führer*'s headquarters before Wetzel's arrival and that he did not accept another call from Stauffenberg between 7 and 8 p.m. after the departure of the *Gauleiter* and other functionaries. From the timing point of view this cannot be right; probably Prüter is confusing the two conversations and for this reason I have followed Kaufmann's account which agrees with Prüter's in other respects – as opposed to my account in 'Ablauf', p. 387.

39 Kaufmann.

40 On this point and below: Benno Bieler: 'Bericht über die Vorgänge um den 20. Juli 1944 im *Wehrkreis* XI,' Ms, Dorfmark 1964. The other senior staff officers were all dead when I began my search for surviving witnesses in 1963.

41 Fritz Kober (Colonel, personnel officer *Wehrkreis* XII at the time) to the author 6 Sept. 1964. Information for this *Wehrkreis* is meagre because the chief actors (commander, operations officer for instance) are all dead.

42 On this point and below: Hans Liphart to the author 9 Sept. 1964; Eberhard Zeller: *The Flame of Freedom*, p. 437 Note 32, based on a report by 'K. Weller', not further identified. Sources are also scarce for the Nuremberg *Wehrkreis*: the commander and chief of staff are dead; Major Günter Oppenländer, the operations officer, was posted on 1 July 1944 and his successor, Lieutenant-Colonel Günther Wiegand, never took up his post owing to the effects of a wound from which he still suffers – Wiegand to the author 14 Oct. 1964.

43 Zeller, pp. 437–8 note 32 based on 'K. Weller', says that General Wiktorin showed the teleprinter messages to Major-General Johann Meyerhöfer, one of his divisional commanders, swearing him to secrecy but that the latter informed the *Gauleiter* who thereupon mobilized his forces. Meyerhöfer relieved Kolbe as Chief of Staff *Wehrkreis* XIII on 1 Aug. 1944 – Keilig, p. 211/220. Liphart also refers to suspicion and denunciation. This was not the reason for the collapse of the attempted revolt in Nuremberg, however. The *Gauleiter* and other functionaries had been informed by Bormann during the evening and they learned the contents of the radio bulletin. Nevertheless the incident is worth noting as indicating that *Wehrkreis* HQ would have encountered resistance had it tried to carry out the orders for the *coup*, as General Bieler felt sure would be the case in Hannover.

44 On this point and below: Julius Ringel to the author 5 Feb. 1964 and verbally 2 July 1965; Anton Glasl (Colonel, Chief of Staff *Wehrkreis* XVIII at the time) verbally to the author 4 Dec. 1964; Franz Rendel (Operations Officer *Wehrkreis* XVIII) verbally to the author 9 Dec. 1964 and letter 8 Mar. 1965; Edgar Ryll (Colonel, personnel officer *Wehrkreis* XVIII at the time) to the author 29 July 1964; Dr Wolfgang Laue (Governor of Salzburg and deputy *Gauleiter* at the time) verbally to the author 1 Sept. 1966; Hugo Manz (Lieutenant-Colonel, chief of intelligence *Wehrkreis* XVIII at the time) to the author 23 Oct. 1965; Dr Gustav Scheel (*Gauleiter* of Salzburg at the time) verbally to the author 14 Jan. 1965; Herbert Mader (SA leader and aide to the *Gauleiter* in Salzburg at the time) to the author 9 Mar. 1965. *Wehrkreise* XIV, XV, XVI and XIX did not

exist; *Wehrkreis* XVIII (Vienna) will be dealt with in the next chapter. Ludwig Jedlicka, *Der 20. Juli 1944 in Österreich*, despite the title of his book, says next to nothing about events in Salzburg.

45 Captain Heinz Eder, who was a regular attendant at these dicing parties and still lives in Salzburg, wrote to the author on 18 Jan. 1965 that he cannot remember anything particular or even that there was such a party on 20 July 1944; the hotel housing the mess, however, he says, was not the 'Excelsior', as Rendel says, but the 'Europa'.

46 Rendel's account is considerably different. In the Chief of Staff's absence, he says, he was representing him; he tried in vain to find Glasl who had gone out for a walk; Ringel had gone fishing; he called the *Gauleiter* and asked him to come to the headquarters at once. Rendel also presents himself as responsible for much else which Glasl and Ryll ascribe to Glasl; in other respects the accounts agree.

47 Accounts do not agree on the question whether the *Gauleiter* came to *Wehrkreis* HQ or whether Ringel and Glasl went to him; everybody did not know everything the others were doing and there are lapses of memory. Ringel and Ryll do not know of the contact between the *Gauleiter*'s office and the headquarters. Glasl says that he asked the *Gauleiter* to come and that he did so; Rendel says the same except that he claims to have done the asking. Dr Laue, the Governor, is not definite and cannot remember exactly. The *Gauleiter* himself says that on reaching his house on return from a journey, he found there Ringel, Glasl, Schulz representing the Senior SS and Police Commander, Dr Laue the Governor, and the Security Police Commander. Mader, the *Gauleiter*'s aide, says that Ringel called him first and then, after he had called back, came over to Scheel's house of his own accord. Mader also asked *SS-Gruppenführer* Erwin Rösener to come and he did so. With such contradictory reports (certainly not deliberately so) the course of events can no longer be reconstructed with certainty. It is therefore described in general terms only.

48 On this point and below: information from Frau Käthe von Boehmer to the 'Hilfswerk 20. Juli 1944'. Foundation in Frankfurt, 1 Jan. 1953; Arno Helling (Colonel, personnel officer *Wehrkreis* XX at the time) to the author 4 Sept. 1964; Army Personnel Office lists, OKH/HPA/P3, BA EAP 105/2. Colonel Hans Saal, the Chief of Staff, died in 1960.

49 Colonel Wolfgang Hassenstein, Chief of Staff *Wehrkreis* XXI, who was shot on 30 Jan. 1945, was probably not a member of the conspiracy – see NA microcopy T-78 roll 55.

50 Wedige von der Schulenburg (Colonel, personnel officer *Wehrkreis* XXI at the time) to the author 7 Dec. 1964; copies of teleprints received, BA EAP 105/31.

51 On this point and below: 'Aktenvermerk über die Ereignisse am 20./21.7.1944' by Abteilung Ic, *Wehrkreis* HQ Generalgouvernement, Krakau, 21 July 1944, typescript, BA-MA RH 53-23/V.34; Max Bork to the author 31 Jan. 1964; Horst Richter (Captain, personnel officer of the Defence District at the time) to the author 18 Aug. 1965; Richter thinks that the teleprints from Berlin arrived in Cracow between 2 and 3 p.m., but the author will follow the contemporary 'Aktenvermerk' cited at the beginning of this note, also on other points, thus correcting the descriptions given in the first and second German edition of the present work. See also the teleprints reproduced at Appendix, pp. 754–61.

52 *Spiegelbild*, pp. 297, 523; Frau Mertz von Quirnheim, diary 18 July 1945.

CHAPTER 44

1 Heinz Höhne: *The Order of the Death's Head*, pp. 494–6, based on Charles Wighton: *Heydrich: Hitler's Most Evil Henchman*, pp. 268–78.

2 On this point and below see: the author's 'Zum Ablauf des Staatsstreichversuches des 20 Juli 1944 in den Wehrkreisen' in *Wehrwissenschaftliche Rundschau* 14 (1964) which was based on the following main sources: Ferdinand Schaal: 'Der 20. Juli 1944 in Prag. . .', *Schwäbische Zeitung* (Überlingen) 26 July 1952; Dr Max Ziervogel (Major-General, Chief of Staff in Prague at the time) to the author 16 May 1964; *Spiegelbild einer Verschwörung*, pp. 106–7. Now supplemented by the following additional sources: Ziervogel to the author 29 July 1964; *SS-Gruppenführer* and Lieutenant-General of Police Ernst Hitzegrad to the author 23 Aug. 1964; Fritz Bollhammer (Captain, aide to commanding general, static corps HQ XVII, Vienna, at the time): 'Erinnerungsniederschrift über die Vorgänge in der Nacht vom 20./21. Juli 1944', in Ludwig Jedlicka: *Der 20. Juli 1944 in Österreich*, pp. 111–16.

3 Hitzegrad; Schaal.

4 Schaal; Ziervogel.

5 Lieutenant-General Ziervogel mentions an additional codeword 'Johannes' as part of the general alert arrangements – see also *Spiegelbild*, p. 106. According to Ziervogel and the *Gestapo*, Schaal issued the codewords 'Odin' and 'Johannes' after his telephone conversation with Berlin; Schaal says that he did so before it. Captain Bollhammer, duty officer in *Wehrkreis* HQ, Vienna, noted receipt of a telephone call from Prague at 19.48: 'Codeword "Odin" in force' – Jedlicka, p. 116.

6 Schaal; Ziervogel. If Schaal's memory and his account are correct, Stauffenberg perhaps mentioned the SD only, because he knew that a struggle between SS and army in Bohemia and Moravia would lead to loss of the German position there or to intolerable complications.

7 Schaal; Ziervogel; Hitzegrad.

8 Ibid.; *Spiegelbild*, p. 106.

9 Ibid.

10 Schaal; Ziervogel; *Spiegelbild*, pp. 106–7.

11 Schaal; Ziervogel; Hitzegrad; *Spiegelbild*, p. 107.

12 Schaal; Ziervogel; *Spiegelbild*, p. 107.

13 Schaal; Ziervogel.

14 Schaal.

15 The fact that Schaal heard nothing from 'Wolfschanze' perhaps resulted from Colonel Ruprecht's 'protection' of signal communications (Ziervogel); alternatively it may have resulted from the alleged blocking of *Wehrmacht* communications in the Protectorate by the *Waffen-SS* (*Spiegelbild*, p. 107). However these speculations can only be partially correct since Schaal telephoned to Berlin at 21.45 and to 'Wolfschanze' at 22.10.

16 Schaal; Ziervogel; *Spiegelbild*, p. 107.

17 This is the chronology given by Schaal and in *Spiegelbild*, p. 107. Hitzegrad says that the initiative for a meeting came from Frank earlier; Ziervogel says that it came from Schaal. In general, however, these sources agree; the same sources were drawn on below.

18 Schaal; Ziervogel; *Spiegelbild*, p. 107. In my 'Ablauf', p. 395, I gave the timings the other way round based on Ziervogel's account but in this case Ziervogel was basing himself on Schaal and had obviously made a mistake.

19 Schaal; Hitzegrad.

20 Ibid.

21 Schubert to the author 1 Feb. 1964. Main sources for events in Vienna are listed and in some cases reproduced in Jedlicka, pp. 50–70. Sources are: Robert Prince Arenberg: 'Der Befreiungsversuch des 20. Juli 1944 im Generalkommando Wien', copy of note of early 1945 in Jedlicka, pp. 125–35; Fritz Bollhammer, 'Erinnerungsniederschrift' in Jedlicka, pp. 111–16; Heinrich Kodré: '20. Juli 1944 in Wien', note on tape, Vienna 1962, Jedlicka, pp. 117–24; Karl Szokoll:

'Der 20. Juli 1944 in Wien', *Die Presse*, 31 Jan., 7 Feb. 1948 – also in Jedlicka, pp. 136–40 (incorrectly dated). Also Kodré to the author 22 Sept. 1964.

22 Wolf Keilig: *Das deutsche Heer 1939–1945*, p. 105.

23 According to Bollhammer in Jedlicka, p. 111, decoding took some twenty minutes; he must have been referring to copying, despatch and distribution. Manual decoding would have taken much longer and the automatic decoder produced the text in clear immediately on receipt. Jedlicka reproduced the beginning of the message on his p. 54; the sentence 'The Führer Adolf Hitler is dead' does not appear. Since Jedlicka does not give his source, this does not permit the conclusion that the first sentence was not transmitted to Vienna. What follows, and Kodré's account as given to Jedlicka (p. 118), and Szokoll in '20. Juli' tend to confirm that the opposite was the case. Szokoll explicitly states that the news of Hitler's death was given in the first message.

24 Bollhammer in Jedlicka, p. 111; Kodré in Jedlicka, p. 118. Szokoll in '20. Juli' gives a very abbreviated account: 'Somewhat after 5 p.m. Colonel Kodré, Chief of Staff *Wehrkreis* XVII, summoned me to the former War Ministry on the Stubenring and his first words were: "It's civil war." I looked at him knowingly and then hurried to my office and issued the codeword. The great wrought-iron gates of the old War Ministry clanged into place; the guard commander issued live ammunition and hand grenades. In front of me were copies of the telegram despatched half an hour before from the Bendlerstrasse in Berlin, the centre of the revolt, to all seventeen *Wehrkreise* and senior headquarters at the front . . . "The Führer Adolf Hitler is dead. An irresponsible clique . . ." '

25 Kodré in Jedlicka, p. 118.

26 Ibid.; Bollhammer, ibid., p. 112.

27 Bollhammer, ibid., pp. 112–13; Kodré, ibid., p. 119.

28 Szokoll, '20. Juli'.

29 Arenberg in Jedlicka, pp. 128–31; Bollhammer, ibid., p. 115; Ernst Wackerhagen to the author 24 Aug. 1969.

30 Kodré in Jedlicka, p. 119; Szokoll, '20. Juli'.

31 *Spiegelbild*, p. 105; Szokoll in '20. Juli' goes further and says 'Querner and Gotzmann declared themselves ready to side with the new rulers'. Later there was considerable disillusionment in Party circles over the attitude of the functionaries and leaders in Vienna – see report by a Party official [*Reichsamtsleiter*] Helmuth Friedrichs quoted by Jedlicka (pp. 68–9) which includes devastating comments by Scharizer on the personalities and capabilities of Querner (too quiet), Schumann (oozing whitewash), Gotzmann (played out – stupid policeman), Goedicke (old fogey), Hornung (*Waffen-SS* garrison commander – a civilian rather than a soldier). Since these reports were written by Party members, they criticized the SS leaders who were undoubtedly no kinder. From the regime's point of view the behaviour both of the SS and the Party had been spineless.

32 *Spiegelbild*, p. 80; Jedlicka, p. 61; Bollhammer and Kodré give no timing.

33 Kodré in Jedlicka, pp. 119–20.

34 *Spiegelbild*, pp. 105–6.

35 Kodré in Jedlicka, p. 120; Bollhammer, ibid., p. 115.

36 Kodré ibid.

37 Ibid., *Spiegelbild*, p. 70.

38 Kodré ibid., pp. 120–1; Bollhammer ibid., pp. 115–16.

39 Kodré ibid., p. 120.

40 Szokoll, '20. Juli'.

41 Bollhammer in Jedlicka, p. 116.

42 Ibid., pp. 115–16; Kodré ibid., pp. 120–1; *Spiegelbild*, pp. 105–6.

43 Kodré in Jedlicka, p. 121 gives the impression that they came to see him twice. This may be two accounts of the same incident; chronologically the story is not

entirely consistent. See also Bollhammer in Jedlicka, p. 115; Arenberg in
Jedlicka, p. 132, in so far as one can tell situates this incident around midnight
which would be about right.

44 Kodré in Jedlicka, p. 121: *Spiegelbild*, p. 36.
45 Wilhelm von Schramm: *Conspiracy among Generals*, pp. 22–4.
46 Ibid., p. 25; Günther Blumentritt: 'Der "20. Juli 1944" ', typescript, England Jan.
1946.
47 Schramm, op. cit., pp. 26–7.
48 Ibid., pp. 27–8; Hans Speidel: *We defended Normandy*, p. 130; Blumentritt.
49 Schramm, op. cit., pp. 29. 33–5.
50 Ibid., pp. 36–8. See also staff list at Appendix p. 766.
51 Schramm, op. cit., pp. 39–40 gives no time for the arrival of Boineburg-Lengsfeld
and does not point out the discrepancies in the sources he has used; later,
however, he quotes the timing (undoubtedly correct) given in the sources
referred to (pp. 66 et seq.). See also Karl Reichert: 'Der 20. Juli 1944 in Paris' in
Frankfurter Rundschau 20 July 1948 (interview with Boineburg-Lengsfeld); this
says that Boineburg was summoned to Stülpnagel at 6 p.m. Boineburg gave the
same information to Dr Helmut Pigge in 1970. Elmar Michel, on the other hand,
in 'Pariser Erinnerungen' (undated – before 1953 – in IfZ archives No 860/53)
says that Boineburg was already with Stülpnagel by 4.30. Friedrich Freiherr von
Teuchert (typescript notes, Munich 1946 in possession of 'Hilfswerk 20. Juli
1944' Foundation) says that Boineburg was with Stülpnagel soon after 5 p.m.
52 Schramm, op. cit., p. 40.
53 Ibid., pp. 42, 68–70; Reichert. According to Schramm (p. 67) the arrest operation
started punctually at 10.30 p.m.; Boineburg to Dr Pigge: 10 p.m.
54 Schramm, op. cit., p. 40.
55 Ibid., pp. 41, 43, 58; Walter Bargatzky: 'Persönliche Erinnerungen an die
Aufstandsbewegung des 20. Juli 1944 in Paris', roneoed, Baden-Baden 20 Oct.
1945 in possession of 'Hilfswerk 20 Juli. 1944' Foundation, p. 8 (less comprehen-
sively '20. Juli in Paris . . .' in *Stuttgarter Rundschau* 4 (1949), No 7, pp. 12–13);
Teuchert, p. 18. According to Schramm (p. 42) not only those on duty in the
Military Commander's staff who had nothing to do with the conspiracy had left
the building but also many who would have been needed later but had not been
informed. This does not apply, however, to the more important conspirators
(Bargatzky, Horst, Michel, Teuchert and Thierfelder).
56 Speidel, pp. 130–1. During numerous interrogations in 1945 Blumentritt gave
details of these and subsequent incidents to British and American officers – see
CSDIC (UK) GG Report – 'General der Infanterie Blumentritt', SRGG 1290
(C), typescript, 7 June 1945; CSDIC (UK) GG Report – 'General der Panzertruppen Eberbach, General der Infanterie Blumentritt', SRGG 1347, typescript,
19 Aug. 1945; both are hereafter referred to as 'Blumentritt'.
57 Speidel merely says 'between 6.0 and 7.0'. Schramm (p. 45) without quoting
evidence, gives a different story: Speidel told Kluge that Blumentritt had called
'about 3.30 p.m.' saying that there was no confirmation yet of the assassination
attempt or Hitler's death and no news had come from anywhere else. See also
Schramm, pp. 45–7, 50 based on notes by Captain Ernst Maisch, the duty officer
– also applicable below; see also Hans Bernd Gisevius: *To the Bitter End*, pp.
550–1. Beck's words – ' Herr Kluge, Germany is at stake now ' – were reported
by Hans K. Fritzsche verbally to the author on 14 July 1972.
58 Schramm, pp. 53–4 based on Maisch. See Stauffenberg's remark in Gisevius, *Bis
zum bittern Ende*, Vol. II, p. 391: 'Stieff has defected'; see also [Percy Ernst
Schramm:] Vorgänge im FHQu . . .' in Herbert Kraus: *Die im Braunschweiger
Remerprozess* . . . pp. 139–41.
59 Wilhelm von Schramm: *Aufstand der Generale*, pp. 75–6 (not in English
translation).

60 Alexander [Freiherr] von Falkenhausen: 'Bericht über meine Stellung zur N.S.D.A.P. und ihrem Regime', typescript, 15 Nov. 1946, NA record Group 338 MS No B 289; Schramm, *Conspiracy*, pp. 47, 48.

61 The author here follows on the whole the account given by Schramm, pp. 50–2, 55–6 which rests on a solid foundation of sources. It should be noted, however, that in 1946 Blumentritt reported to the effect that Kluge had not wavered again after his conversation with Stieff and had believed in Hitler's death only before this conversation. The arrival of Keitel's teleprint message that the *Führer* was alive and that any orders from Witzleben and Beck were not to be followed is also put before Kluge's conversation with Stieff by Blumentritt. Apparently the two conversations with Stieff became combined into one in Blumentritt's memory. Cf. below, pp. 473–4.

62 Blumentritt; Schramm, p. 52.

63 Schramm, pp. 52–4; Speidel, p. 131; Blumentritt.

64 Schramm, p. 54; Blumentritt.

65 Helmut Heiber (editor): *Hitlers Lagebesprechungen*, p. 618.

66 Schramm, pp. 55–6.

67 Ibid., p. 57; Blumentritt.

68 Schramm, pp. 58–9; Blumentritt.

69 Schramm, pp. 59–60; Blumentritt. Boineburg wrote to Dr Pigge that Stülpnagel had told him upon his (Stülpnagel's) return from La Roche-Guyon that Kluge had demanded time to consider until the next morning at 9 a.m.; cf. below, p. 476 and note 83.

70 Schramm, pp. 61–3; Blumentritt.

71 Speidel, p. 132 – 'as in a house just visited by death'.

72 Blumentritt; Schramm, pp. 63–5; at this point, as Hofacker later told his friends in Paris, Kluge is supposed to have said: 'It would be different if the swine were dead,' meaning that in this case he would have participated in the *coup*. Schramm does not give his source for this remark and does not say whether it is confirmed by Dr Horst.

73 Schramm, p. 64; Blumentritt.

74 Schramm, pp. 66–9. Schramm's comment (p. 71) that action went so smoothly in Paris because there it was not 'all desk work' is somewhat superficial. In Berlin new commanders tried to take over – Witzleben, Hoepner, Beck; the legally established commanders to whom everyone was accustomed disappeared without trace (or so it looked from outside); troops had first to be concentrated and only really arrived towards the end of the *putsch*; a Nazi 'Leadership Officer' and the Minister for Propaganda were able to 'switch round' the only troops available in Berlin. Conditions in Berlin and Paris were therefore very different and this had nothing to do with the question of 'desk work' or personal involvement. Admittedly many of the commanders in and around Berlin were not as resolute as those in Paris; on the other hand, on the day in question some were travelling and their deputies were naturally not so ready to take responsibility. Action in Paris, moreover, was being taken merely against the SS and SD, not against the government as in Berlin. Remer, for instance, who initially obeyed all the conspirators' orders certainly did not sit at his desk; in contrast to Boineburg-Lengsfeld, Brehmer and Unger, however, he and others soon received contrary orders. In any case, at the vital moment, the most senior officers in France were sitting, not at their desks, but at the dinner table.

75 Schramm, p. 67.

76 Boineburg to Dr Pigge.

77 Schramm, pp. 67–8.

78 Ibid., pp. 68–9.

79 Ibid., p. 69.

80 Ibid.

81 Ibid., pp. 115–16.

82 Ibid., p. 72.

83 Ibid., p. 95; Boineburg to Dr Pigge.

84 Ibid., pp. 89–90. These telephone conversations during the night, as recorded in the war diary of Naval Group Headquarters West, are given in 'Fuehrer Conferences on Naval Affairs, 1939–1945', *Brasseys Naval Annual* 59 (1948), pp. 410–12. Schramm uses the extracts given in Anthony Martienssen: *Hitler and His Admirals*, pp. 213–19. Schramm (p. 81) gives a figure of 5,000 marines under Krancke's command; details below and a correction of this figure in a letter from Krancke to the author 3 June 1970.

85 'Fuehrer Conferences', pp. 410–12; 'K.T.B. der Marine-Gruppe West' (war diary), pp. 6675—6682, BA-MA M 326 PG 37590, and Krancke – also applicable below.

86 Krancke thinks he can remember, however, that this was before Hitler's (and Dönitz's) speeches.

87 Schramm, p. 83.

88 Ibid., pp. 99–104.

89 Ibid., pp. 98–100; 'Fuehrer Conferences', p. 412; Boineburg to Dr Pigge.

90 Schramm, pp. 100–1.

91 Reichert.

92 'Fuehrer Conferences', p. 412; telephone conversations Kluge-Blumentritt 21 July 1944 in 'K.T.B. OB West', BA-MA H 11-10/39A; 'K.T.B. der Marine-Gruppe West'; Schramm, pp. 101–4, 106–8.

93 Krancke denies that Blumentritt paid a visit or that there was a celebration.

94 Blumentritt; Schramm, pp. 108–10.

95 Telephone conversations Kluge-Blumentritt 21 July 1944.

CHAPTER 45

1 Bruno Mitzkus: 'Um den 20 Juli und das Ende im Wehrkreiskommando III', typescript, Bad Homburg 1947.

2 Hans Bernd Gisevius: *Bis zum bittern Ende*, Vol. II, pp. 387–8; [Bruno] Mitzkus: 'Bericht über die Ereignisse im stellv. Generalkommando III', typescript, 9 Aug. 1945.

3 On this point and below: Hans Hagen: 'Bericht über meine Tätigkeit als Verbindungsoffizier . . .' in *Spiegelbild einer Verschwörung*, pp. 13–14; [Otto Ernst] Remer: 'Der Ablauf der Ereignisse am 20.7.1944 . . .' in *20. Juli 1944*, pp. 145–52.

4 About this time Goebbels called Speer, his voice 'excited and hoarse' (Albert Speer: *Inside the Third Reich*, p. 382); Speer was told to 'interrupt his work at once' and come to Goebbels.

5 See pp. 425 and 685 Note 74. Below see Speer, pp. 383–5.

6 From Frau von Hase; see pp. 429–30 above.

7 Remer, 'Ablauf'.

8 See Chap. 42 above, pp. 438–9.

9 Hagen's and Remer's accounts differ on this point. Hagen says that he penetrated as far as Hase's anteroom where he heard the general talking to Remer; mistrusting Hase, he did not go further and explained the situation to Siebert and Buck, two second lieutenants of the Guard Battalion; Buck was to tell Remer that Hitler was alive and government still in the same hands; Remer was to come to Goebbels at once and, if he did not arrive in twenty minutes, Hagen would get the SS to storm the Commandant's headquarters – *Spiegelbild*, pp. 14–15. Remer, on the other hand, says that he tried unsuccessfully to contact

Hagen; on return from his second tour of inspection he sat in Hase's anteroom, where Second Lieutenant Buck found him, called him outside and told him of Hagen's information – Remer, 'Ablauf'. Thus it is not clear when Hagen or Remer or both were in the Commandant's headquarters and failed to meet, nor how Hagen (allegedly) got into and out of the Commandant's headquarters and what circumstances or considerations led Remer to go to Goebbels.

10 Remer had allegedly forbidden Buck to refer to a military *putsch*. Remer does not say what Buck actually said to Hase and there is no other evidence – Remer, 'Ablauf'.

11 Remer, 'Ablauf'; [Wilhelm Grenzendörfer:] 'Notizen von der Schilderung . . .'; Korff verbally to the author 25 Feb. 1965. In his evidence to the Public Prosecutor of Oldenburg Provincial Court in 1949 Remer said (Ref. No 9 Js 164/49) that he had himself proposed that Hase send him to Goebbels to clarify the situation; in his book, *20 Juli 1944*, pp. 10–11, he says that he evaded carrying out Hase's order to arrest Goebbels when he (Remer) objected that this was impossible since Goebbels was Honorary Colonel of the Battalion. Both accounts contain both facts *and* omissions; Remer's report of 22 July 1944, however, makes it clear that, prior to his telephone conversation with Hitler, Remer was far less suspicious of the attitude and orders of Hase, the soldier, than of Goebbels and his entourage.

12 Remer, 'Ablauf'; confirmed by Siebert to the author 27 Oct. 1969 and 8 June 1970.

13 Ibid.

14 Remer, 'Ablauf'; Grenzendörfer; Hagen in *Spiegelbild*, p. 15. The timings given in Hagen's report seem too early. Remer cannot have reached Goebbels by 6.35 p.m. if his own report is correct.

15 Hagen in *Spiegelbild*, p. 15.

16 Grenzendörfer; Remer, 'Ablauf'; Speer, pp. 382–3.

17 In his report Remer used the words 'as a respectable National-Socialist officer'. At the latest by 4 p.m. Goebbels was able to telephone to 'Wolfschanze' without difficulty; he had certainly had news of the attempt soon after 1 p.m. Signals experts on duty at the points in question also reported that Goebbels was able to telephone freely *during* the black-out; according to Albert Praun in *Soldat in der Telegraphen- und Nachrichtentruppe*, p. 222, this was because the black-out was not complete, medium-level and junior personnel not being in the secret; according to Gerhart Goebel (Central Long-distance headquarters of the Post Office) in a letter to the author dated 21 Jan. 1966 it was because Goebbels had a direct line to the *Führer*'s headquarters routed through a special position in the trunk exchange, Berlin-Winterfeldstrasse. When the black-out was lifted, lines were monitored by officers involved in the conspiracy (Degner, Burchardt), by the RSD and by the *Gestapo*; this resulted in much interference. Even Goebbels' conversation with Hitler might have been interrupted by a 'technical hitch' if one of the conspirators had heard it and realized its significance – but only if he had known the secret routing of Goebbels' line.

Below see: Remer, 'Ablauf'; Grenzendörfer. Eberhard Zeller in *The Flame of Freedom*, pp. 339–40 gives the alleged wording of the conversation between Hitler and Remer but does not give his source; also Gisevius, *To the Bitter End*, pp. 556–7. Remer in 'Ablauf' gives the gist of the conversation and this tallies with Grenzendörfer's account. Another report comes from Hitler's valet, Linge in 'Kronzeuge Linge berichtet', *Revue* 24 Mar. 1956, p. 30; according to this the conversation took place about 5 p.m. which cannot be right, but the gist of it tallies with Remer's account. Both these accounts may have been based on the *Völkischer Beobachter* (Berlin edition) of 27 July 1944. Remer was suspicious because on the one side was Hase whom he regarded as an honest man and on the other Goebbels who was inclined to shoot off his mouth.

18 Paul Schmidt: *Hitler's Interpreter*, pp. 275–7; [Eugen] Dollmann: 'At FHQ After the Attempt', CSDIC/CMF/X 194 Interrogation Report, typescript 20 July 1945, and *Call Me Coward*, pp. 35–42.

19 Verbal information given to the author by Hans Hornbogen 14 Jan. 1965, Ernst John von Freyend 14 May 1965, Ludolf Gerhard Sander 24, 25 Apr. 1964, Josef Wolf 27 Feb. 1965.

20 Goebbels had certainly telephoned to Hitler's headquarters long before talking to Remer, though there is no direct evidence of this – Zeller (p. 338) gives none even though he gives the exact time as 5.30 p.m. See also Hagen in *Spiegelbild*, p. 14. Equally there is no evidence for Zeller's supposition (pp. 338–9) that Hitler had commissioned Goebbels to make an immediate radio announcement about the attempt. It seems reasonably certain, however, that Hagen's information produced an acceleration of the announcements and measures to protect radio installations against occupation. It seems likely that there was some connection between Hagen's report, made about 5.30 p.m. and the radio bulletin at 5.42.

21 Remer, 'Ablauf'; Hagen in *Spiegelbild*, p. 15; Goebbels' speech on the radio 26 July 1944, *Völkischer Beobachter* (Berlin edition), 27 July 1944, p. 1. Only Linge and Dollmann (*Coward*, p. 41) say that Remer was immediately promoted Colonel (Dollmann does not give rank); this can hardly be right since Hitler could not know how Remer would behave. Korff, who says that he was present in Goebbels' office while Remer was talking to Hitler, merely says that Remer was appointed *de facto* Commandant of Berlin, which meant that all units concentrated in the city were under his command or at least bound to obey his orders.

22 Jürgen von Kempski: 'Betrachtungen zum 20. Juli' in *Merkur* III (1949), pp. 807–16; Diagram at Appendix, p. 739. The question whether the *coup d'état* party in Berlin lacked resolute leadership (apart from Stauffenberg) is a very delicate one and there is no simple yes or no answer. The criticisms made by Gisevius in *Wo ist Nebe?* (p. 19) and by Wilhelm von Schramm in *Conspiracy among Generals*, p. 71 ('all desk work') are hardly fair. In Paris the counter-orders did not arrive almost simultaneously with the orders for the *coup*. Admittedly Hase, Olbricht, Thüngen and others did not place themselves at the head of their troops – no more did Stülpnagel or Speidel, just as a divisional commander does not lead a company into action.

23 Remer, 'Ablauf'; Hase in *Trial of the Major War Criminals before the International Military Tribunal*, Vol. XXXIII, p. 490.

24 Remer, 'Ablauf'; Speer, pp. 386–7.

25 Remer, 'Ablauf'; Korff; Maître to the author 19 Feb. 1965.

26 Remer, 'Ablauf'.

27 Remer, 'Ablauf'; Wolfgang Müller: 'Die Wehrmacht am 20, Juli' in *Main-Post* 21 July 1949 and 'Was geschah am 20. Juli 1944' in *Das freie Wort*, 19 July 1952; Siebert to the author 8 June 1970; Wolf Keilig: *Das deutsche Heer 1939–1945*, p. 211/38.

28 General Thomale to the author 11 Aug. 1971; Colonel Werner Mildebrath: '20. Juli 1944 in Berlin', typescript, Hannover 1971.

29 Remer, 'Ablauf'; Müller, 'Wehrmacht' and 'Was geschah'; Hagen in *Zwischen Eid und Befehl*, pp. 97–102, gives a somewhat different account which requires more detailed examination; see also Speer, p. 386. Heinrich V. Prinz Reuss to the author 15 May 1972 confirms that Glaesemer took up combat positions at Fehrbelliner Platz.

30 Frau Elli Tzschöckell (secretary to General Thomale at the time) to the author 18 Oct. 1971; Mildebrath.

31 See note 29 above.

32 Remer, 'Ablauf'; Grenzendörfer gives a somewhat different account (perhaps a misunderstanding); he says that Gehrke was immediately 'detained'.

33 Remer, 'Ablauf'; Grenzendörfer; confirmed by Stirius – letter to the author 2 Feb. 1967.

34 Rudolf Schlee: 'Bericht' in *20. Juli 1944*, pp. 152–5.

35 Remer, 'Ablauf'.

36 Schlee.

37 Report by Helmuth Cords, Heidelberg 18 Sept. 1946.

38 Schlee. According to Second Lieutenant Röhrig, signals officer in the Bendlerstrasse this captain must have been Captain Sieler, 'a merry adventurer type' who was inquisitive and shrewd rather than loyal. He was nevertheless given accelerated promotion to Major for his alleged part in suppressing the *coup* – Schlee was also given accelerated promotion, to captain (BA, Central Information Bureau PA 48231). For distribution procedure in the case of these orders see Chap. 42, p. 421. The term 'OKW building' is misleading; there were not many OKW offices in the Bendlerstrasse but a large number belonging to OKH, in particular those of the Replacement Army.

39 Schlee; Remer, 'Ablauf'.

40 Schlee says he set up a chain of sentries around the entire block of the Bendlerstrasse building; Cords had not (yet?) noticed such extensive measures when he left the building after giving instructions to the men from the Pyrotechnical School.

41 Schlee.

42 Heinz-Ludwig Bartram: '20. Juli 1944'; Schlee; Remer, 'Ablauf'. Remer says (wrongly) that Goebbels was in the Propaganda Ministry that evening, but both earlier and later refers to his flat; Hase in *Trial*, Vol XXXIII p. 493 also refers to the Ministry, as does Bruns but he then gives the lay-out of Goebbels' flat. Balzer's account clearly implies that Goebbels spent the entire evening in his flat; see also Hagen, *Zwischen Eid und Befehl*, passim.

43 On this point and below: Remer, 'Ablauf'; *Trial*, Vol. XXXIII, pp. 490–4; Mitzkus, 'Bericht' and 'Um den 20. Juli'.

44 [Percy Ernst Schramm:] '3. Aufzeichnung über die Vorgänge des 20.7.44' in Herbert Kraus: *Die im Braunschweiger Remerprozess . . .*, pp. 146–7.

45 After his talk with Hase Reinecke called the Bendlerstrasse and asked for Fromm, but Beck came on the line and said: 'Kluge, are you there?' Then he said that Fromm was not available and Reinecke would do better to keep out of the affair. Reinecke now knew that Beck was involved in the conspiracy and was torn between his friendship and respect for Beck and his orders which might involve having Beck shot. He was spared this decision, however, since he had no troops – Reinecke to the author 31 Jan. and 2 Feb. 1967. There is no question of Reinecke having suppressed the *putsch* or even being involved in its suppression. See Zeller, pp. 318–19; Rudolf Pechel: *Deutscher Widerstand*, p. 243. Not until after midnight did Reinecke, on orders from Keitel, give certain instructions regarding the withdrawal of teleprinter messages. See *Spiegelbild*, p. 65. Towards 1 a.m. on 21 July Reinecke went to the Bendlerstrasse and then to Goebbels.

46 *Trial*, Vol. XXXIII, p. 493; Remer, 'Ablauf'. Confirmed by Hermann Reinecke: 'Mein Erlebnis im Zusammenhang mit den Vorgängen des 20. Juli 1944', typescript, Hamburg 1964; Reinecke verbally to the author 30 Apr. 1965 and letters 31 Jan./2 Feb. 1967. It is not clear whether Hase acted on Reinecke's orders, as he said at his trial, or on his own initiative in order to do something towards carrying out the *coup d'état* measures.

47 Remer, 'Ablauf' and evidence to the Public Prosecutor, Oldenburg; Walter Bruns: 'Vor, am und nach dem 20. Juli 1944' papers of Otto John folio 5; Hagen, *Zwischen Eid und Befehl*, pp. 80–1; confirmed by Siebert.

48 Stirius to the author 2 Feb. 1967.

49 Wolfgang Müller: *Gegen eine neue Dolchstosslüge*, pp. 44–7; *Spiegelbild*, pp.

459–60. What follows is confirmed in complete detail by Hüttner (who was in Döberitz and opposed to the *putsch* from the outset) in a letter to the author 25 Jan. 1969.

50 See Chap. 42, pp. 432–3 and sources there given. According to Kurt Finker in *Stauffenberg und der 20. Juli 1944*, pp. 268–9 (first ed.) Corp. W. Keirath, who took part in the occupation of Broadcasting House, says that on his own initiative Jakob did not call 'General Olbricht's secret number' but *instead* telephoned to Goebbels and was dissuaded by him from taking any action to assist the conspirators. There is no confirmation of this.

51 According to Jakob's report repeated by Major-General Brühl (see p. 688 Note 100 above) after this altercation the SS withdrew; Karl Schober in 'Eine Chance blieb ungenutzt', pp. 56–61, refers to combined 'protection'. According to Schober the SS unit ordered to Broadcasting House on the intervention of Fritzsche, a civil servant [*Ministerialdirektor*] in the Ministry of Propaganda, was 200 men strong, whereas Jakob had a battalion of 400 men.

52 According to Remer's evidence to the Public Prosecutor, Oldenburg, Jakob was also given special instructions to allow no one to the microphone who did not appear in the programme. [Rudolf] Balzer: 'Aktennotiz für Chef OKW/WPr persönlich', 21 July 1944, BA NS 6/31, and Helmut Sündermann (*Deutsche Notizen*, pp. 65–6) confirm that Jakob was placed under Remer's orders and was instructed to allow no change in programme. See also Note 50 above.

53 Bruns; see pp. 436–7 above.

54 Bruns; see also Note 42 above.

55 Müller, *Dolchstosslüge*, p. 46; Corporal Helmut Nake in Finker, p. 281 (see also p. 379 Note 48).

56 Bruns; Nake in Finker, pp. 281, 379 Note 48 – also applicable below.

57 Kurt Hassel verbally to the author 11 Dec. 1964 – also applicable below; see also pp. 412–15 above and accounts (naturally incomplete) in *Spiegelbild*, pp. 226, 330, 377.

58 Hassel; *Spiegelbild*, p. 377; [Walter] Schellenberg (interrogation report), extracts recorded by H. R. Trevor-Roper in 1946; testimony by Walter Huppenkothen in answer to a question whether Schellenberg had been investigated after 20 July 1944, in a Nuremberg interrogation on 2 July 1948, in *Official Record, United States Military Tribunals Nürnberg* [sic], Case No 11, Tribunal IV (IV A), U.S. vs Ernst von Weizsaecker et al., Vol. 27, transcripts (English) 2–6 July 1948, p. 10950. According to Schellenberg Thiele said to him over the telephone about 6 p.m.: 'It's all gone wrong.'

59 Hassel. Kempe to the author 2 Jan. 1970, confirming Hassel's statements but giving different timings and including an expression of surprise that Hassel should have given him an order without insisting on its execution.

60 Eugen Gerstenmaier: 'Zur Geschichte des Umsturzversuches vom 20. Juli 1944', *Neue Zürcher Zeitung*, 23, 24 June 1945; see also pp. 488–9 above.

61 On this and below: Fritz Harnack: 'Bericht über die Vorgänge des 20. 7. 1944', typescript, Braunschweig 20 July 1948; Franz Herber: 'Was ich am 20. 7.44 in der Bendlerstrasse erlebte', typescript and undated (about 1948), BA H 90–3/4; B[olko] von der Heyde: 'Die Verschwörung des 20. Juli' in *Die Welt*, 31 July 1947, p. 2; Karl Pridun: 'Vermerk. Betrifft: 20. Juli 1944, Stellungnahme', IfZ ZS 1769; Harnack gives the timing of this first order as 'towards 2 p.m.' also that Mertz said at this point that Hitler had been assassinated. Herber does not mention this.

62 On this point and below: [Ernst Günter] von Roell (Colonel, head of Group II at the time): 'Bericht über die Ereignisse des Nachm. und Abends des 20.7.1944'; typescript, Berlin 21 July 1944 – BA H 90·3/2; Hoepner to People's Court, *Trial* Vol. XXXIII, pp. 407–8 – a shorter account. Joachim Kramarz in *Stauffenberg: The Life and Death of an Officer*, pp. 192–3, based on *Spiegelbild*, p. 191, says

that Beck also addressed the heads of section, but there is no other evidence of this.

63 Kleber later said that he was a member of Group II under Kennes; Roell, however, invariably refers to Kennes as head of Group III and says that Rohowsky and Kleber belonged to this group.

64 Volkmar Hoffmann: 'Nie wieder bin ich solch einem Menschen begegnet', *Frankfurter Rundschau* 18 July 1964; Kleist to the author 15 Sept. 1964, 2 Oct. 1968; Kunrat Freiherr von Hammerstein: *Spähtrupp*, p. 283.

65 [Eduard] Wagner: 'Der Verlauf des 20. Juli (aus dem Gedächtnis)' typescript, [Zossen] 21 July 1944, IfZ ED 95.

66 Gisevius, *Ende*, Vol. II, pp. 382–3; on what follows below also Rainer Graf von Kanitz verbally to the author 28 Aug. 1972.

67 Wagner, 'Verlauf'; evidence in *Trial*, Vol. XXXIII, pp. 370–1, 477–8; Ferdinand Prinz von der Leyen: *Rückblick zum Mauerwald*, p. 150. Witzleben and Graf Lynar came towards 7 p.m. and stayed for about fifteen minutes with General Wagner: Kanitz verbally to the author, Frau Elisabeth Wagner to the author 16 March 1972 based on information from Kanitz.

68 Kanitz says (verbally to the author) that Wagner still talked as if willing to help pull the *coup* through on the evening of 20 July, but also as if undecided about something; Wagner mentioned an aeroplane stationed at Staaken airfield; he wanted to get out of Zossen HQ, but in the end he stayed there.

69 Delia Ziegler: 'Wer schoss auf Stauffenberg?' in *Die Welt*, 21 Aug. 1947, p. 2; Lerche; Gisevius, *Ende*, Vol. II, pp. 382–3 apparently situates this scene (wrongly) in Stauffenberg's anteroom.

70 Gisevius, *Ende*, Vol. II, pp. 384–5 (*Bitter End*, pp. 544–5); [Walter] Huppenkothen: 'Der 20. Juli 1944', p. 1; Otto John: 'Zum Jahrestag der Verschwörung gegen Hitler' in *Wochenpost*, 18 July 1947. Huppenkothen's timings are about an hour too early; he says that the radio announcement was repeated about 4 p.m. and at about this time he ordered all RSHA officials not in their offices to go to them and tried to do the same himself but could get no further than the Potsdamer Platz by street-car. It must have been at least 5 p.m. by this time.

71 John, 'Jahrestag'.

72 Gisevius, *Ende*, Vol. II, p. 385, 393 (*Bitter End*, pp. 545, 549–50), and verbally to the author 8 Sept. 1972.

73 Gisevius, *Ende*, Vol. II, p. 386 (*Bitter End*, p. 553).

74 In his special edition (1964) Gisevius says 7 p.m. but in *Ende*, Vol. II, p. 387 6 p.m. (also in the 1954 edition, p. 625, and in *Bitter End*, p. 545).

75 Gisevius, *Ende*, Vol. II, pp. 387–8 (*Bitter End*, p. 546).

76 Gisevius, *Bitter End*, p. 547.

77 John, 'Jahrestag' and 'An Eye Witness's Account of the 20th July 1944 Plot against Hitler' typescript, London 1946, *Twice through the Lines*, pp. 148–9.

78 Otto John: 'Der 20. Juli 1944'.

79 John, 'Eye Witness', p. 8, 'Jahrestag', *Twice*, pp. 149–51.

80 See Chap. 44, p. 472; Gisevius (*Bitter End*, pp. 549–51) says that this conversation did not take place until about 8 p.m. but Schramm, based on his researches, does not accept this.

81 John, 'Eye Witness', pp. 8–11; 'Jahrestag'; 'Some Facts and Aspects of the Plot against Hitler.'

82 John, 'Eye Witness', p. 11; '20. Juli', p. 23; 'Jahrestag'.

83 John, '20. Juli', p. 23; 'Eye Witness', p. 11; 'Jahrestag'; 'Some Facts', p. 68. John is wrong in giving the time as 11 p.m. in '20. Juli', p. 24; in 'Some Facts' he is about right in saying between 9.30 and 9.45 p.m. All his accounts agree that he had left the building before counteraction began.

84 Gisevius, *Ende*, 1954 edition, p. 628.

85 Zeller, pp. 356–7.
86 Gisevius, *Bitter End*, pp. 547–8; Hassel; Wagner, 'Verlauf'.
87 *Trial*, Vol. XXXIII, pp. 410–11.
88 Gisevius, *Ende*, Vol. II, pp. 391–3 (*Bitter End*, p. 548).
89 Gisevius, *Ende*, Vol. II, p. 394 (*Bitter End*, p. 550).
90 Gisevius, *Ende*, Vol. II, pp. 396–7; extract from war diary of Army Group North in *20. Juli 1944*, p. 139.
91 Gisevius, *Ende*, Vol. II, pp. 396–8, 412 (*Bitter End*, pp. 551–2, 561–2); John, 'Facts', p. 67; Roell; Adolf Bernt: 'Der 20. Juli in der Bendlerstrasse' in *Die Gegenwart* II (1956), p. 598; Witzleben in *Trial*, Vol. XXXIII, pp. 360–70.
92 Cords to the author 11 Apr. 1971.
93 Gisevius, *Ende*, Vol. II, p. 397 (*Bitter End*, p. 558).
94 Gisevius, *Ende*, Vol. II, p. 412 (*Bitter End*, pp. 561–2); *Trial*, Vol. XXXIII, p. 370; Wagner, 'Verlauf'.
95 *Trial*, Vol. XXXIII, p. 409; [Percy Ernst] Schr[amm]: 'Mitteilungen des Oberst d.G. Meichsner, Abt.-Leiter der Abt. Org., 23.7., 9 Uhr' in Herbert Kraus: *Die im Braunschweiger Remerprozess . . .*, pp. 148–50; Kurt Rittmann: 'The Nature of an Insurrection', papers of Otto John folio 5, and with slight variations 'Erlebnisbericht über die Ereignisse am 20.07.44 im OKH in der Bendlerstrasse in Berlin'; Heinz-Ludwig Bartram: 'Der 20. Juli 1944', typescript [1954], BA H 90-3/4'; John, 'Eye Witness', p. 10; 'Some Facts', p. 66. The account of the episode with the three generals given in Zeller, p. 358 is based on unreliable and incomplete sources.
96 According to Schramm (information from Meichssner) Hoepner made these statements, coupling with them a request to the generals to mobilize their troops for the benefit of the new government.
97 Rittmann; Hoepner in *Trial*, Vol. XXXIII, p. 409; Schramm (from Meichssner) mentions a third general who may have been General Strecker.
98 On this point and below: Bartram; Roell; Rittmann; Hopf – report to Bormann on trial of Fromm 7 Mar. 1945.
99 According to Bartram Kennes thought him crazy and did not believe a word of his story.
100 This is Bartram's version; he says that 'heads of section', including Kennes, were briefed by Hoepner; Roell says that 'heads of groups' were briefed by Stauffenberg and this is confirmed by Hoepner in *Trial*, Vol. XXXIII, p. 407. Kennes, Sadrozinski and Roell were heads of groups, so in this respect Bartram's account is incorrect; Roell wrote on 21 July 1944, Bartram in 1954. The briefing may have been done by both Hoepner *and* Stauffenberg.
101 Roell.
102 Presumably an error; Burgdorf was, after all, in 'Mauerwald' or 'Wolfschanze'.
103 Major-General Langhaeuser remembers (Kramarz, p. 195; Langhaeuser verbally to the author 22 Aug. 1969 and letter 28 Nov. 1969) meeting Fromm in the passage about 6.20 p.m.; according to all other accounts it must have been somewhat later. Fromm told Langhaeuser that he had telephoned to Keitel and Hitler, who was alive; a *putsch* was in progress here; Langhaeuser should get away if he did not wish to become involved. Langhaeuser is sure that Fromm spoke out of genuine concern for him. He was due to go to Munich by night train and had merely come to the Bendlerstrasse to get his ticket from one of Fromm's staff.
104 Bartram; Rittmann; Schramm (from Meichssner) – also applicable below.
105 Bartram; *Trial*, Vol. XXXIII, p. 416.
106 On this point and below; [Fritz Harnack:] 'Bericht über die Vorgänge des 20. 7.44 in der Bendlerstrasse'; Herber: 'Was ich . . . erlebte' Pridun; *Trial*, Vol. XXXIII, pp. 415–18, 439; Heyde; Ziegler: 'Wer schoss'; Bernt, pp. 598–9; Peter

Boysen to the author 23 June and 6 July 1970 says Major Fliessbach had been the first to voice the suspicion that a *putsch* against the *Führer* was in progress; cf. Zeller, pp. 314–15, 435–6 Note 24; judgement of People's Court 17 Jan. 1945 on Captain Hermann Kaiser and Major Busso Thoma.

107 There is no direct evidence of this alleged radio bulletin; there may be confusion with radio or teleprinter messages concerning Himmler's appointment.

108 According to Herber his fellow-officers' demand for an explanation and Olbricht's order happened to coincide; Harnack, Pridun and Carl Adam (government architect, in AHA supply staff in the rank of major at the time) to the author 11 Aug. 1971, however, say that the meeting took place on Herber's initiative. Fräulein Lerche to Dr Gisevius 30 June 1946 gives its time as 10 p.m.

109 Cords, also applicable below; Bolko von der Heyde: 'Der 20. Juli 1944 im OKH-AHA in der Bendlerstr.'

110 After the war Herber, Heyde, Pridun and Fliessbach were upbraided for their part in the collapse of the *coup*; it was said that they first supported it and then, when they saw that it was not succeeding, stabbed their fellow-officers in the back – see, for instance, Ziegler, 'Wer schoss' and Zeller, pp. 360–1. Leyen (p. 153) has said much the same of Herber. As far as their alleged support for the *coup* is concerned I have discovered no evidence apart from Fräulein Ziegler's article, though this does not necessarily mean that they were not in favour of it or that the conspirators did not think so. Undoubtedly the question of involvement or non-involvement in an attempted revolt against the Nazi regime by senior staff officers possessing knowledge such as Herber, Heyde, Pridun and Fliessbach had, is in a very strict sense one of character. No light is shed on the course of events, however, by expecting more from non-conspirators than from the conspirators or by accusing people of treachery on the basis of one imprecise piece of evidence from someone who was not in the secret. These men were in a difficult position; had they done anything else they might subsequently have been accused of cowardice or sympathy with the conspirators. This does not alter the fact that their behaviour was unattractive. Moreover after the war they sometimes tampered with the truth, saying that they had not been promoted for the part they had played – see [Rudolf Schmundt:] 'Tätigkeitsbericht des Chefs des Heerespersonalamts' p. 223, microcopy T-84 roll 39 and Kunrat Freiherr von Hammerstein: *Flucht*, p. 51. On the other hand and quite apart from other understandable motives, they could not refuse promotion and at the same time continue to maintain that they had distinguished themselves by their loyalty. According to the personnel files available to me or which I have seen the following received *accelerated* promotion: Major Herbert Fliessbach to Colonel 1 Aug. 1944 with effect from 26 Aug. 1944; Lieutenant-Colonel Franz Herber to Colonel 1 Aug. 1944; Lieutenant-Colonel Bolko von der Heyde to Colonel 1 Aug. 1944; Lieutenant-Colonel Karl Pridun to Colonel 1 Aug. 1944.

111 Confirmed by Lerche and Adam. According to Heyde the weapons had been drawn from Küstrin; according to Bernt (p. 598) and Lt. Col. Christoph von Wildeiner gen. von Wildau (Chief, Section II/Personnel in OKH/Fz in Jüterbog at the time) to the author 20 July 1970 they came from the army ordnance depot in Spandau; according to Ziegler, 'Wer schoss', they came from Töpchin. According to Adam they were procured by Fliessbach.

112 Dr H. K. Fritzsche told Dr Helmut Pigge in 1970 that Heyde had burst into Olbricht's office even before the shooting, carrying a sub-machine gun, and saying (approximately): we note that something aimed against the *Führer* is taking place here; we remain loyal to him and we uphold our oath; I demand that you take us to Colonel-General Fromm. Olbricht had replied, according to Fritzsche (approximately): you are armed, I am not; but I ask you to go to Colonel-General Fromm with me first of all. In a letter to the author of 6 Aug. 1971 Fritzsche confirmed this account with the modification that he was not sure

which of these occurrences observed by him had taken place before and after the shooting.

113 Fritzsche to the author 6 Aug. 1971, similarly in his account given to Dr Pigge.

114 Ziegler, 'Wer schoss'; Alix von Winterfeldt verbally to the author 30 Aug. 1966. Rittmann confirms that Stauffenberg was wounded and retaliated, also Ludwig Freiherr von Hammerstein, who was present (*Spähtrupp*, p. 281); Dr Eugen Gerstenmaier verbally to the author 17 Aug. 1965. According to Heyde in *Der Spiegel*, 27 Jan. 1969, p. 10, Gerstenmaier also fired. According to Adam, Stauffenberg came into Olbricht's room just as Herber was declaring Olbricht under arrest; Stauffenberg had turned, going down the hall quickly towards Fromm's offices with Herber running after him; from the direction of where Stauffenberg was, a shot was then fired and Herber fired back an unaimed shot.

115 Winterfeldt.

116 Winterfeldt; Heinz Buchholz: 'Das Attentat auf Adolf Hitler am 20. Juli 1944'; Buchholz in Percy Knauth: *Germany in Defeat*, p. 177; Hans Karl von Hasselbach to the author 11 Oct. 1965; Heinz Pieper verbally to the author 24 July 1965; Helmuth Spaeter: *Die Geschichte des Panzerkorps Grossdeutschland*, Vol. II, p. 565; Dr Wilhelm Tobias Wagner verbally to the author 29 July 1965.

117 Winterfeldt.

118 Bernt, p. 599.

119 According to Bernt's and Bartram's accounts. Bartram says that he conducted Fromm from his apartment; Bernt, on the other hand, says that Bartram was standing near the apartment 'leaning against the wall, most upset'. Bartram's situation can easily be imagined: a *putsch* was collapsing on its own; during it his immediate master and commander had been removed from office and now that commander could not make up his mind to do anything.

120 Hoepner on 7 Aug. 1944 in *Trial*, Vol. XXXIII, p. 416; Herber in 'Was ich ... erlebte' says much the same; Bernt, pp. 599–600; Bartram.

NOTES/PART X/CHAPTER 46

1 *Trial of the Major War Criminals before the International Military Tribunal*, Vol. XXXIII, pp. 417, 505–8; [Fritz Harnack:] 'Bericht über die Vorgänge des 20.7.44 in der Bendlerstrasse', typescript, Braunschweig 20 July 1948; Adolf Bernt: 'Der 20. Juli in der Bendlerstrasse' in *Die Gegenwart* 11 (1956) pp. 599–600; Ludwig Bartram: '20. Juli 1944', typescript, [1954], BA H 90-3/4; Franz Herber: 'Was ich am 20.7.44 in der Bendlerstrasse erlebte', typescript, undated, BA H 90-3/4; Fabian von Schlabrendorff: *Revolt Against Hitler*, pp. 143–4.

2 *Trial*, Vol. XXXIII, p. 417; this imperfect copy of the equally imperfect record of proceedings shows 'Merz' and 'Lieutenant-Colonel von Haeften'. See also Rudolf Schlee: 'Bericht', typed copy, Berlin 23 July 1944, BA EAP 105/32, copy in *20. Juli 1944*, pp. 152–5; [Peter] Thelen: 'Revolution ohne Truppen', Frankfurt 1965 (draft of an unpublished article which Herr Thelen most kindly made available to the author); Karl Pridun: 'Vermerk, Betrifft: 20. Juli 1944 Stellungnahme' typescript, Bregenz 1953, IfZ ZS 1769; Bartram; Harnack.

3 Bernt, p. 600.

4 Karl Schweizer verbally to the author 18 June 1965.

5 Bernt, p. 600.

6 Bartram.

7 Schlee; [Otto Ernst] Remer: 'Der Ablauf der Ereignisse am 20.7.1944 ...', typed copy, Berlin 22 July 1944, BA EAP 105/32, copy in *20. Juli 1944*, pp. 145–52. Schlee and Remer say that Remer arrived in the Bendlerstrasse after the four had

been shot; Bartram probably errs in thinking that he met Remer on the stairs
earlier.

8 Schlee; Remer, 'Ablauf'.

9 This is what Bartram says; Dr Georg Kiessel in 'Das Attentat des 20. Juli 1944
und seine Hintergründe', signed typescript, Sandbostel (CIC camp) 6 Aug. 1946,
p. 28, also refers to the *coup de grâce*; on the version of Dr Kiessel's report
published as an 'SS report' see Chap. 40, Note 30. Bernt (p. 650) says: 'Later I
heard that someone had shot him [Beck].'

10 Schweizer; Thelen; see also Eberhard Zeller: *The Flame of Freedom*, p. 318
where a report is given by one of the drivers (identity unknown) who was present
at the executions.

11 The order in which they were executed is not certain; sources I have so far been
able to discover differ on this point. Schady was killed in action in 1945. On the
executions see: Thelen, who uses a report from Schweizer; Schweizer; Frau Alix
von Winterfeldt verbally to the author 30 Aug. 1966; Wolfram Röhrig verbally to
the author 29/30 June 1965; Schlee; Delia Ziegler: 'Bericht über den 20.7.1944',
typescript, about 1947, in possession of Gräfin Schwerin von Schwanenfeld;
Zeller, p. 318.

12 For the timing see: Schlee; Albert Speer: *Inside the Third Reich*, p. 388. According to the Army Signals report in *Spiegelbild einer Verschwörung*, p. 65, a
teleprinter message from Fromm to all *Wehrkreis* and Military Commanders
saying that the leaders of the *putsch* had been shot and that he, Fromm, had
reassumed command reached Lieutenant Röhrig, the Signals Traffic officer, at
12.10 a.m. and according to the same report he began despatch at once. The copy
in *Spiegelbild*, p. 76, carries a despatch time of 00.21. This despatch time is confirmed in [Percy Ernst Schramm:] 'Mitteilungen des Stellv. Chefs WFSt 21.7.44
Uhr', typescript, 22 July 1944, State Archives Nuremberg PS 1808, copy in
Herbert Kraus: *Die im Braunschweiger Remerprozess . . .*, pp. 142–5. As regards
timings of events from the arrival of Herber's group in Olbricht's office to the
executions only the beginning and end seem reasonably certain – 10.30
p.m.–12.30 a.m. The executions therefore may have taken place just before or
just after midnight.

Stauffenberg's call is that reported by Schweizer and he was only twenty yards
away; he, together with the other drivers, had had to illuminate the courtyard. Frau von Winterfeldt, Fromm's secretary at the time, remembers hearing
through the open window Stauffenberg call out: 'Long live sacred Germany.'
This is confirmed by Röhrig who, however, also thinks that Schweizer may be
right. Delia Ziegler in 'Bericht' remembers Stauffenberg calling 'Holy Germany.'
According to her Haeften also shouted 'Long live Germany.' According to an
NCO in the Bendlerstrasse signal centre, who heard it from others on 21 July,
Stauffenberg shouted 'Long live Germany' and Haeften 'Long live freedom' –
[Otto Weerth:] Interrogation Report on Otto Weerth, typescript, [Berlin] 23
Aug. 1945, BA/907/INT. Anni Lerche (one of Fromm's secretaries) says that she
was told by eye-witnesses that Stauffenberg called out 'Holy Germany'; this she
said in a letter to Dr Hans Bernd Gisevius dated 30 June 1946 which was in-
tercepted and translated by the British censorship office IRS 3 D.C.S. (typescript
17 July 1946); she also said that Mertz had thrown himself in front of
Stauffenberg and that Haeften had also died with a call to Germany on his lips.
Zeller (p. 318) gives Stauffenberg's call as 'Long live our sacred Germany' but he
quotes no evidence and this is apparently based on a report by one of the drivers
(Schweizer or Olbricht's driver?). Recently Gerstenmaier recalled having heard
these precise words – Eugen Gerstenmaier: 'Den Dolch im Lorbeerstrausse
tragen' in *Christ und Welt*, 19 July 1968, p. 22. Joachim Kramarz, Stauffenberg's
biographer, in *Stauffenberg: The Life and Death of an Officer*, p. 200 and Note
49, is unable to contribute anything on this point. In view of Stauffenberg's

membership of Stefan George's circle attempts have been made to establish some connection between Stauffenberg's last call and the 'secret Germany' of which, under his influence, there was some talk in opposition circles in 1943 and 1944 – see Edgar Salin: *Um Stefan George*, p. 324 Note 123. Theodor Pfizer: 'Die Brüder Stauffenberg' in *Robert Boehringer: Eine Freundesgabe*, edited by Erich Boehringer and Wilhelm Hoffmann, p. 490 says that the twelve men, including the three Stauffenberg brothers, who assembled round George's deathbed on 4 December 1933 felt themselves pledged to the true Germany which, since its prostitution by the Nazis, had become the 'secret Germany'. The figure of twelve is inaccurate and could well give birth to legend; actually there were eleven present round George's deathbed; not all were 'disciples' and the number was fortuitous – see Robert Boehringer (who was present): *Mein Bild von Stefan George*, pp. 188–91. In a letter to the author dated 11 Sept. 1968 Nina Gräfin von Stauffenberg says that only the words 'holy Germany' were in consonance with Stauffenberg's character; at a moment such as this no one would be thinking of any 'secret' or 'clandestine' circles.

13 Röhrig; Thelen; Otto Skorzeny: *Skorzeny's Special Missions*, p. 117.

CHAPTER 47

1 Otto John: 'Zum Jahrestag der Verschwörung gegen Hitler' in *Wochenpost*, 18 July 1947, p. 6; Anni Lerche to Dr Hans Bernd Gisevius, 30 June 1946.

2 Franz Herber: 'Was ich am 20.7.44 in der Bendlerstrasse erlebte', typescript, undated, BA H 90-3/4; Eberhard Zeller in *The Flame of Freedom*, pp. 316–17 gives the time as 11.05 p.m. but without giving source.

3 Kunrat Freiherr von Hammerstein: *Spähtrupp*, pp. 281–2, 285, based on reports by Ludwig von Hammerstein and Dr Fritzsche; Zeller, pp. 316, 435–6 Note 24, based on Fritzsche.

4 Hammerstein, op. cit., pp. 285–6.

5 Ibid., pp. 283–4.

6 Ibid., p. 284 based on report by Kleist; Eugen Gerstenmaier: 'Zur Geschichte des Umsturzversuches vom 20. Juli 1944' in *Neue Zürcher Zeitung*, 23, 24 June 1945. Zeller (p. 437 Note 29) gives an indirect quote from Skorzeny (*Skorzeny's Special Missions*, p. 117) which, however, does not mention the subject. There is hardly any other evidence to show whether Gerstenmaier is right in his belief or not. Fromm, however, with his rousing speech had more or less closed the action and he departed apparently without ordering further executions. Schlee and Remer, whose duty it would have been to carry them out, say nothing on the subject and the court martial only passed judgement on the officers specifically named; no one knows of any further sentences. Anything was possible, however, and the talk among those guarding them boded no good for the prisoners.

7 [Walter] Huppenkothen: 'Der 20. Juli 1944', typed copy, [1953], p. 1, IfZ ZS 249/II.

8 Treusch (? signature nearly illegible), *SS-Sturmbannführer*: 'Vermerk über den Ablauf der Ereignisse vom 20.7 auf 21.7.1944 . . .' typescript, Berlin 21 or 22 July 1944, Berlin Document Centre; Skorzeny, p. 117; Joachim Ruoff (Jüttner's operations officer) to the author 23 Nov. 1969.

9 Ibid.

10 The whole attitude of the SS, though neither very resolute nor energetic, was nevertheless plausible enough. It hardly supports the supposition that Himmler was waiting to see whether the *putsch* would succeed or not. Speculation on this subject is governed by the question how much Himmler knew about the *putsch* beforehand, and how far he was in sympathy with the conspirators for whatever reason. See pp. 377–9 above.

11 Skorzeny, pp. 113–16.
12 Ibid., pp. 115–17 Rudolf Schlee in 'Bericht', reproduced in *20. Juli 1944*, pp. 152–5 refers to 'the State Police under *Obersturmbannführer* Skorzeny'. Some *Gestapo* officials were already in the Bendlerstrasse – Achamer-Pifrader and his escort in particular; meanwhile 'Gestapo Müller' had sent an investigation squad to the Bendlerstrasse and finally, on hearing of the arrests and court martial, Kaltenbrunner had despatched a *Gestapo* detachment there. Huppenkothen (op. cit., p. 2) says that this took place on a telephone call from Achamer-Pifrader about 10 p.m. reporting the shootings, which cannot be right. The call might have come about 11 p.m., however, when Achamer-Pifrader could have heard that the executions had been *ordered*. In fact they took place a few minutes after midnight – according to Schlee, who was present as late as 'about 12.30 a.m. on 21.7.44'.
13 Skorzeny, p. 117; Fritz Harnack: 'Bericht über die Vorgänge des 20.7.44 in der Bendlerstrasse', typescript, Braunschweig 20 July 1948; Herber. Confirmation of the approximate timing in Albert Speer: *Inside the Third Reich*, pp. 387–8. Speer left Goebbels' house en route for the Bendlerstrasse 'shortly after midnight'; Remer and Bolbrinker were in the car with him. As they turned into the Bendlerstrasse they were stopped by SS men and found Kaltenbrunner and Skorzeny there; Speer said that he wanted to go to the Bendlerstrasse and stop Fromm's court martial but the two SS officers said that all was over already and the SS had no wish to be mixed up in it. Fromm then appeared.
14 Skorzeny, p. 117.
15 Hammerstein, op. cit., p. 284.
16 Skorzeny, pp. 117–18.
17 Adolf Bernt: 'Der 20. Juli in der Bendlerstrasse' in *Die Gegenwart* 11 (1956), p. 601; T[heodor] E[schenburg]: 'Die Rede Himmlers vor den Gauleitern am 3. August 1944', *VfZ* 1 (1953), p. 382; Dr Claus-Peter Goetzke (at the time Lieutenant, technical head of signal centre in the Bendlerstrasse building) to the author 14 July 1965; Zeller (p. 320) gives further details but without source; in the third German edition of his book published in 1956 (*Geist der Freiheit*, p. 261) he refers to 'a report for which there has hitherto been no confirmation'; this is presumably Hans Bernd Gisevius: *To the Bitter End*, pp. 565–6; Gisevius only revealed the source of this as being Helldorf when writing *Wo ist Nebe*, pp. 59–60.
18 Dr Peter Boysen (group chief in charge of army clothing in AHA at the time), who became a witness of the events, wrote to the author on 23 June 1970 that the bloody uniforms arrived at his office after a while with the order to incorporate them in a permanent uniform exhibition located in the basement of the Bendlerstrasse complex; Boysen did not carry out this assignment but merely had the wooden box with the uniforms deposited in a corner.
19 Bernt, p. 601.
20 *Spiegelbild einer Verschwörung*, p. 23.
21 Evidence by *SS-Standartenführer* Walter Huppenkothen, from files of Public Prosecutor, Provincial Court I, Munich, IfZ ZS 249–III; Dr Georg Kiessel 'Das Attentat des 20 Juli 1944 . . .', typescript, Sandbostel (CIC camp) 6 Aug. 1946, p. 31. Kiessel's report (p. 39) includes a signed addendum with the following figures and the comment 'All other figures are exaggerated': some 140 persons were condemned to death and executed in connection with 20 July 1944; some 700 [sic] were arrested; some 6,000 [sic] names were recorded and included in card indexes. The figures given in the 'SS-Bericht über den 20. Juli: Aus den Papieren des *SS-Obersturmbannführers* Dr Georg Kiessel' in *Nordwestdeutsche Hefte* 2 (1947), p. 33, – '7,000 arrested, 700 implicated officers condemned to death and executed' – are therefore wrong. All other officials involved in the investigations at the time give figures similar to those of Kiessel in 'Das Attentat' and all agree

that the number of executions connected with 20 July was under 200 and the number of arrests under 1,000 – see Willy Litzenberg: 'Der 20. Juli 1944', typescript, Nuremberg 4 June 1946; [Horst Kopkow-Cordes:] 'Kopkow's Account of the Plot of 20 Jul. 44', typescript, 9 Apr. 1946; 'Translation of Statement Submitted by Lischka' [civil servant (*Oberregierungsrat*), head of Group 2 in RSHA '20 July Special Commission'], on 1, 2 & 3 Apr. 46'; Walter Huppenkothen: 'Antworten', typescript, Hersbruck 17 May 1946. See also Gisevius, *Nebe*, pp. 155–60.

22 Heinz Ludwig Bartram: '20. Juli 1944', typescript, [1954], BA H 90-3/4; *Spiegelbild*, p. 18; Speer, p. 388.

23 Walter Bruns: 'Vor, am und nach dem 20. Juli 1944', typescript, undated (?1945-1948), in Otto John's papers folio 5, pp. 12–14; [Otto Ernst] Remer: 'Der Ablauf der Ereignisse am 20.7.1944 ...', BA EAP 105/32 (also *20. Juli 1944*, pp. 145–52).

24 On this point and below: [Bruno] Mitzkus: 'Bericht über die Ereignisse im stellv. Generalkommando III A.K. am 20 Juli 1944', typescript, 9 Aug. 1945, in possession of 'Hilfswerk 20. Juli 1944' Foundation and 'Um den 20. Juli und das Ende im Wehrkreiskommando III, Berlin', typescript, Bad Homburg, Apr. 1947, also in possession of Foundation; report by Amt V of RSHA 'Betrifft: Selbstmord des Majors Ulrich von Oertzen', typescript, 22 July 1944, BA R 58/1051; report by Chemical Section of Security Police Technical Institute to Nebe, head of Amt V, 23 July 1944, BA R 58/1051; Dr Martin Sobczyk (at the time Lieutenant-Colonel, senior *Abwehr* officer in *Wehrkreis* III) verbally to the author 27 Aug. 1965; Joachim von Wiese und Kaiserswaldau (at the time Colonel, Personnel Officer to Commander *Wehrkreis* III) to the author 10 Aug. 1964; Klaus Hentze to the author 10 Feb. 1970.

25 *Trial of the Major War Criminals before the International Military Tribunal,* Vol. XXXIII, p. 370; Schramm, information from Warlimont; *Spiegelbild*, pp. 36–7.

26 According to Skorzeny: *Geheimkommando Skorzeny*, p. 209 (not in English translation) Canaris was arrested about 10 p.m. on 20 July by Schellenberg in person. Schellenberg in *The Schellenberg Memoirs*, pp. 409–11, confirms that he made the arrest but says 'early August 1944'; he says the same in the extracts from his interrogation report made by H. R. Trevor-Roper in 1946. Dr Theodor Paeffgen testified in Nuremberg on 20 July 1948 that Schellenberg had told him he had been ordered by Kaltenbrunner via '*Gestapo* Müller' to arrest Canaris personally, and that he had done so; Official Record, United States Military Tribunal Nürnberg, Case No 11, Tribunal IV, Transcripts (English); pp. 12968, 12975, 12981–2. Gert Buchheit in *Der deutsche Geheimdienst*, p. 438 gives 23 July as the date and, surprisingly enough, quotes Schellenberg's memoirs as the source. See also *Spiegelbild*, p. 36 which gives 21 July and personal files of the 'Hilfswerk' Foundation which give 23 July.

27 *Spiegelbild*, p. 43.

28 Ibid., pp. 112, 33; Major Eckert: 'Meldung über Vorkommnisse im Stabe des Gen. Qu. am 21., 22. und 23.7.1944', [Zossen] 23 July 1944, IfZ ED 95; Ferdinand Prinz von der Leyen: *Rückblick zum Mauerwald*, p. 155; Eduard Wagner: *Der Generalquartiermeister*, pp. 237–43.

29 *Spiegelbild*, pp. 430–1; Franz Sonderegger (at the time *Gestapo* official [*Kriminalkommissar*]) to President of Provincial Court I, Munich, 14 Jan. 1951, copy in IfZ, also statements to representatives of 'Europäische Publikation' in Munich 15 Oct. 1952, copy in IfZ ZS 303 II; Christine von Dohnanyi: 'Aufzeichnungen', 1945/46, IfZ ZS 603, now reproduced in Eberhard Bethge: *Dietrich Bonhoeffer*, pp. 1096–1101 (not in English translation); Huppenkothen, '20. Juli' pp. 2–6.

30 On this point and below: Ludolf Gerhard Sander verbally to the author 24, 25

Apr. 1964; Chap. 36 above; Josef Wolf verbally to the author 27 Feb. 1965, 3 July 1971 and letter 18 Dec. 1968; [Hellmuth] Arntz: 'Account of the Twentieth of July Putsch by One of the Minor Conspirators' CSDIC (UK), S.I.R. 1610, 11 Apr. [sic] 1945 and verbally to the author 21 Nov. 1964; Zeller, pp. 348–9, based on another account by Arntz.

31 Wolf recalls that Keitel's order was instigated by Bormann and that Keitel personally gave it to Wolf shortly before or after midnight (Hitler's radio address was just about to begin). Sander also remembers having received the order from Keitel directly, and having passed it on to Wolf.

32 Arntz verbally and 'Account'.

33 Ibid.; almost word for word in Zeller, p. 349.

34 Hans Rothfels: *The German Opposition to Hitler*, p. 11.

35 *Spiegelbild*, pp. 91, 146. As eye-witness to the tortures Schweizer; Kiessel, 'Das Attentat', pp. 33–4 confirms them in circumlocutory terms; see also pp. 521–3 below.

36 Arntz verbally; Albert Beichele (at the time Major, head of Group III in OKH Signals) to the author 18 June, 31 Dec. 1967.

37 Albert Praun: *Soldat in der Telegraphen- und Nachrichtentruppe*, pp. 220–1; Beichele to the author 6 Feb. 1967.

38 Information from personal files on the victims in 'Hilfswerk' Foundation; *Spiegelbild*, p. 23. Before his arrest Stieff made unsuccessful attempts to warn members of the conspiracy, and possibly also to build himself an alibi. Cf. above, p. 690, Note 134.

39 Praun, p. 221.

40 *Spiegelbild*, p. 33.

41 Ibid., pp. 87–92.

42 Ibid., pp. 54–5; Army Personnel Office List No 1 ref. officers involved in 20 July, BA EAP 105/2.

43 Werner Wolf Schrader (son of Lieutenant-Colonel Schrader) to Graf von Hardenberg 16 Nov. 1946, in possession of 'Hilfswerk 20. Juli 1944' Foundation; *Spiegelbild*, p. 129.

44 Army Personnel Office, roll of General Staff officers, Ag P 3, 1943 (with subsequent additions), BA – Central Information Bureau.

45 *Spiegelbild*, pp. 100, 126–7, 128–34 and subsequent reports; Kiessel, op. cit., p. 31.

46 Gerhard Ritter: *Carl Goerdeler und die deutsche Widerstandsbewegung*, pp. 415, 557–8, Note 7, 416–19 (*The German Resistance*, pp. 289–91); *Spiegelbild*, p. 232; Elfriede Nebgen: *Jakob Kaiser*, pp. 192–4. See Paul Ronge: 'Warum ich Helene Schwärzel verteidigte' in *Nordwestdeutsche Hefte* 1 (1946) No 9, pp. 14–15.

47 *Spiegelbild*, pp. 63–5; Ritter, *Goerdeler*, pp. 419–24 (*Resistance*, pp. 293–7). This particular point is not affected by the statements made on 12 Oct. 1952 by the interrogating official, Franz Xaver Sonderegger, to Freiherr von Siegler, Dr Helmut Krausnick and to Dr Hermann Mau of Institut für Zeitgeschichte (IfZ ZS 303/I); Sonderegger said that Goerdeler revealed so much about so many people that it became embarrassing even to the interrogators; there seems to be no doubt, however, that many people were implicated who might otherwise have remained unmolested. Ritter (*Goerdeler*, pp. 420, 560 Note 19) quotes statements by Ernst Lautz, the Public Prosecutor on 17 June 1948 (see StA Nuremberg NG 5405) to the effect that as a result of Goerdeler's revelations 'numerous fresh arrests' were possible and 'numerous fresh proceedings initiated before the People's Court'. Lautz adds: 'Nevertheless only a few of these proceedings were completed.' In general, therefore, Goerdeler's idea seems to have worked out. Ritter however, gives no precise figures for the number of people affected or executed. According to Kunrat Freiherr von Hammerstein in *Flucht*, pp. 55, 76, 143 the only person executed as a result of Goerdeler's

revelations was Fritz Elsas with whom Goerdeler had spent a night while on the run and had then revealed the fact. Below see Nebgen, pp. 195–224.

48 This is the result of research by Walter Hammer in 'Die "Gewitteraktion" vom 22.8.1944' in *Freiheit und Recht* 5 (1959) No 8/9, pp. 15–18. A circular dated 16 Aug. 1944 from the *Gauleiter*'s office, Franconia, to all District Leaders (BA Schumacher collection 242) throws doubt on Hammer's categoric statements. This said that orders from the Head of the Party Chancellery prescribed the 'ruthless extermination of all traitors, defeatists and other lackeys of the enemy'. It continues: 'In order that all persons behind the affair may be apprehended, on orders from Security Headquarters I request you to inform me urgently of all individuals or circumstances possibly connected with 20 July 1944. I further request you to provide me urgently with the names of all other persons whose behaviour, either in the past or present, gives rise to doubts concerning their National-Socialist views or ideological integrity. Naturally, in addition to personal details, reasons must be given which would enable a subsequent check to be made or immediate action to be taken. On the *Gauleiter*'s orders I [Kunstmann, director of *Gau* headquarters] request you to list, if possible by return, all men and women who are not ideologically sound and constitute a danger. Lists should include in particular all former freemasons, Jewish lackeys and leaders or functionaries of former political parties.'

49 *Spiegelbild*, p. 346; information from 'Hilfswerk 20. Juli 1944' Foundation; Hammerstein, *Flucht*, p. 197.

50 *Spiegelbild*, pp. 563–73, gives records of proceedings and two of the sentences.

51 *Spiegelbild*, pp. 244–5; Lorenzen: submission to *Reichsleiter* Bormann, Ref: Proceedings of People's Court 20 July (Nebe's trial in this case), typed copy, Berlin 2 Mar. 1945 and Judgement of People's Court, 1st Chamber, Berlin 2 Mar. 1945 on *SS-Gruppenführer* and Lieutenant-General of Police Arthur Nebe, typed copy, Berlin 2 Mar. 1945 Az 1 L 54/45 O J 10/45 gRS, both in BA EAP 105/30. Gisevius in *Nebe*, pp. 160–74, describes in detail the odyssey of his friend Nebe.

52 According to the judgement of the People's Court Nebe had helped in the arrest of Helldorf; according to Gisevius in *Nebe*, pp. 160–74, Nebe was forced to agree to Helldorf's arrest at a conference in his, Nebe's, office and had no opportunity to warn him.

53 Gisevius, *To the Bitter End*, pp. 585–6 and *Nebe*, p. 54; Alexander Harder: *Kriminalzentrale Werderscher Markt*, pp. 399–413.

54 *Spiegelbild*, p. 36; Ludwig Jedlicka: *Der 20. Juli in Österreich*, p. 121.

55 Jedlicka, pp. 121–3.

56 Information from 'Hilfswerk 20. Juli 1944' Foundation; Ger van Roon: *Neuordnung im Widerstand*, p. 336; Friedrich Wilhelm Heinz: 'Von Wilhelm Canaris zur NKWD', typescript, ca. 1949, NA microfilm R 60.67, pp. 188–9. According to the Foundation Harbou hanged himself; according to H. H. von Pentz in a letter to the author dated 13 Nov. 1969 based on information from Bussche and Hammerstein he cut the veins in his wrists.

57 Wilhelm von Schramm: *Conspiracy among Generals*, pp. 108–11.

58 Ibid., pp. 113–14, 115–17, 120–1.

59 Ibid., pp. 123–8, 132–5, 152–4.

60 Ibid., p. 151.

61 Ibid., pp. 152–4, 156–7, 162–8, 172; see also judgements and reports of proceedings in BA EAP 105/31 (list of sources under 'Judgement', Hopf and Lorenzen); Dr Freiherr von Falkenhausen was released from arrest on 15 Feb. 1945 on condition that he be called up into the *Wehrmacht* forthwith – Kaltenbrunner to Graf Schwerin von Krosigk, the Finance Minister, 20 Feb. 1945, BA EAP 173-e-05.

62 Schramm, pp. 175–6.

63 Ibid., pp. 183–90, 194–206; Kiessel ('Das Attentat', p. 38) says that Kluge pointed to Avranches on the map and said: 'That's where I lost my reputation as a commander.' See also Speer, pp. 394–5. Kluge's suicide was at first declared a heart attack (Schramm, pp. 206–7). Nevertheless his body lay in state for close to two weeks in the church at Böhme (Altmark) where it was eventually buried in the family vault (Sondermann, propaganda director, to State Secretary in the Propaganda Ministry 5 Sept. 1944, BDC Sondermann file).

64 *Spiegelbild*, passim; see also Leyen, p. 167 which talks of 5,000 executed and 20,000 arrested in connection with 20 July.

65 Ulrich von Hassell: *The von Hassell Diaries*, p. 365; Gisevius, *Bitter End*, pp. 574–5; Ritter, *Goerdeler*, p. 414; Nebgen, pp. 195–218.

66 Eschenburg, p. 385; see also Isa Vermehren: *Reise durch den letzten Akt*, p. 152.

67 See files on the Stauffenberg 'clan' in BA EAP 105/34; Markwart Graf Schenk von Stauffenberg: 'Angaben . . .', typescript, Amerdingen 4 Jan. 1947 and similar 'Angaben' from Clemens Graf Schenk von Stauffenberg 27 Oct. 1946 – in files of 'Hilfswerk 20. Juli 1944' Foundation; also Alexander von Hase: 'Zur Sache "Remer" ' (evidence to Public Prosecutor, Oldenburg), typescript [1950] – in Otto John's papers, folio 1.

68 Ernst Kaltenbrunner, Chief of Security Police and SD, to Martin Bormann, Head of Party Chancellery, 25 Oct. 1944, BA EAP 105/34. In many cases the possessions of executed persons and their heirs were confiscated, especially when they had owned land. Confiscations did not stop short of the property of persons merely accused but not convicted or sentenced. See Himmler to Lammers 27 Aug. 1944, Finance Minister Graf Schwerin von Krosigk and Justice Minister Dr Thierack to Revenue Office Presidents etc. (*Oberfinanzpräsidenten*) 13 Nov. 1944, BA Schumacher collection 242. Many confiscations of land became meaningless quite soon as the Red Army began to overrun the German East; some confiscations were revoked before the end of the war or in subsequent litigation, and some had been moderated to begin with. SS-Lt. Gen. Breithaupt was commissioned by Hitler to administer fairly generous support of surviving family members and was given explicit authority to dispose of parts of their confiscated property for this purpose (see documents cited above). The principle of persecution and arrest of all family members was thus not followed consistently. The sufferings of the survivors should not be minimized in any way; financial hardships, the only ones, really, that could be repaired, were in some cases not compensated for at all, and in many cases compensation came after years of applications and litigation to restore pension rights, to regain a confiscated home etc. But for the sake of objectivity it should be noted that many suffered only very minor property losses. The Stauffenberg family were only temporarily unable to control their possessions. The authorities often carried out the orders they received with great moderation and with a mixture of rough humaneness and administrative inefficiency (though there were very painful exceptions to this). See also Thierack to Himmler 24 Oct. 1944, BA Schumacher collection 242; Hans Beck: 'Die Rettung der Sippe Stauffenberg', *Die Tagespost* (Augsburg) 17 Nov. 1949; Dr Benno Martin (*Höherer SS- und Polizei-Führer* in *Wehrkreis* XIII/Nürnberg at the time) verbally to the author 3 June 1971; Edward N. Peterson, *The Limits of Hitler's Power*, esp. pp. 285, 293–4.

69 Georg Thomas: 'Gedanken und Ereignisse' in *Schweizer Monatshefte* 25 (1945), pp. 554–5; Markwart Graf Schenk von Stauffenberg; Kurt von Schuschnigg: *Austrian Requiem*, English edition pp. 219–43, 238–41, US edition pp. 263–92, and in particular pp. 284–9. Nebgen's account (pp. 227–8) is based on the recollections of Frau Jakob Kaiser, who was there.

70 BA NS 19/34.

71 Ibid.

72 Ibid.

73 *Spiegelbild*, pp. 394–5; see also pp. 87–92, 175; Fabian von Schlabrendorff *Revolt against Hitler*, pp. 150–1.
74 Sonderegger (see Note 47); Alfred Heueck: 'Der Mann, der Roland Freisler sterben sah ...', *Frankfurter Rundschau* 27 Sept. 1955 (report on trial of Huppenkothen); Thomas, pp. 550–1; Schlabrendorff, op. cit., pp. 155–8 and *Secret War against Hitler*, pp. 311–13; also Schlabrendorff: 'Eine Quelle? Die "Kaltenbrunner Berichte" über das Attentat vom 20. Juli 1944', *Frankfurter Hefte* 17 (1962), pp. 18–19; Hans Rothfels: 'Zerrspiegel historischer Wahrheit', *Die Zeit*, 20 Oct. 1961, p. 3 and 'Zerrspiegel des 20. Juli', *VfZ* 10 (1962), pp. 62–7. On the tortures in general: Schweizer; Kiessel, 'Das Attentat', pp. 33–4.
75 Thomas, p. 552; Hedwig Freier and Annemarie Wolff: 'Erinnerungen an die Gefängniszeit von Walter Bauer 15.10.44–21.4.45', typescript, February 1971; Heueck; Schlabrendorff, *Secret War*, p. 313; Kurt Hassel verbally to the author 11 Dec. 1964; Kiessel, pp. 33–4; report by 'Hilfswerk 20. Juli 1944' Foundation concerning sentence on ex-*Kriminalkommissar* Josef Baumer, roneoed, Kronberg 1959; Dr Clemens Plassmann to Frau Annemarie Koch 10 Mar. 1947, copy in Foundation's files; judgement by Grand Criminal Chamber of Provincial Court in Siegen dated 15 Dec. 1953 on *Regierungsrat* Karl Neuhaus, roneoed, copy in possession of Foundation.
76 *Spiegelbild*, p. 249.

CHAPTER 48

1 Hubert Schorn: *Der Richter im Dritten Reich*, pp. 67–8 – also applicable below.
2 Deputy to '*Gestapo* Müller' as head of the '20 July Special Commission'.
3 Memorandum from Dr Sonnenhol to head of Group 'Inland II' in the Foreign Ministry, 11 Aug. 1944, Political Archives of *Auswärtiges Amt*, Inland II g 59.
4 Müller to Himmler 22 Dec. 1942, copy of teleprint in BA NS 19/416; Axel von Harnack: 'Arvid und Mildred Harnack ...' in *Die Gegenwart* 2 (1947), Nos 1/2, pp. 16–17; Günther Weisenborn: *Der lautlose Aufstand*, pp. 194–5, 199.
5 Law amending regulations of the general criminal code, the *Wehrmacht* criminal code and the penal code, 16 Sept. 1939, *Reichsgesetzblatt 1939 Teil I*, No 183, pp. 1841–3.
6 Schorn, pp. 171–2.
7 Hermann Reinecke (at the time General, head of General *Wehrmacht* Office [*Allgemeines Wehrmachtamt*] and associate member of People's Court) verbally to the author 30 Apr. 1965 and letters 1 and 16 Feb. 1966; [Rudolf Schmundt:] 'Tätigkeitsbericht des Chefs des Heerespersonalamts' NA microcopy T-78 roll 39, p. 187; Heinz Guderian: *Panzer Leader*, pp. 345–6; Georg Kiessel: 'Das Attentat des 20. Juli 1944 ...' typescript, Sandbostel 6 Aug. 1946, p. 32. Sometimes the 'court of honour' refused to expel an officer, generally on Guderian's initiative apparently – see Wolfgang Müller: *Gegen eine neue Dolchstosslüge*, p. 91. Eberhard Zeller in *The Flame of Freedom*, p. 444 Note 11, quoting Wilhelm Scheidt: 'Gespräche mit Hitler' in *Echo der Woche* 7 Oct. 1949, p. 5, records Hitler as saying to Scheidt: 'These criminals ... will be expelled from the *Wehrmacht* and brought before the People's Court. They are not to be given a respectable bullet but will hang like common traitors! ... And execution must take place within two hours of the sentence. They must hang at once without mercy. The important point is that they be given no time to make long speeches. But Freisler will see to that. He is our Vishinsky.' Vishinsky was prosecutor in the Russian set-piece trials of the 1930s. See also Eugen Dollmann: *Call me Coward*, p. 40.

8 Shorthand record of proceedings on 7 and 8 August in *Trial of the Major War Criminals before the International Military Tribunal*, Vol. XXXIII, pp. 299–530; on discovery of this record after the war see Allen Welsh Dulles: *Germany's Underground*, p. 83; Reinecke to the author 16 Apr., 15 Oct. 1964; Films 3023–1, 3023–2, 3179–1, 3179–3, 3179–4 with extracts of the proceedings in the People's Court in BA film library; camera man's report – Erich Stoll in *20. Juli 1944*, p. 214.

9 Reinecke to the author 15 Oct. 1964. The record of proceedings contains nothing on this point; there are also other omissions – see *Volksgerichtshof-Prozesse zum 20. Juli 1944*, passim.

10 *Trial*, Vol. XXXIII, p. 303–4.

11 Müller, p. 92. Zeller, pp. 363 and 444 Note 16 gives Müller as source for this remark; it also appears, without source but probably also from Müller, in Annedore Leber: *Das Gewissen entscheidet*, p. 233. Clearly no one had the temerity to include such remarks in the official record of proceedings.

12 Ursula von Kardorff, 'Zum Gedenken an Graf von der Schulenburg: Porträt eines Edelmannes', *Frankfurter Allgemeine Zeitung* 21/22 July 1956.

13 Films 3023–1 and 3179–2 in BA film library.

14 *Trial*, Vol. XXXIII, pp. 307–9, 315, 322.

15 Ibid., p. 424.

16 Film No 3179–1, BA film library.

17 Ibid.; Dr Heinz Boberach of BA to the author 24 Oct. 1968. Freisler quoted the statement in the trial of H. B. von Haeften: Haeften 'saw in the Führer the "Great Executor of Evil" '; see sentence of People's Court of 15 Aug. 1944 against B. Klamroth et al., NA microcopy T-120 roll 1038. Müller (p. 92) records the statements as follows: 'I stand by my friends of 20 July. I abhor murder because I am a Christian. But in Hitler I see evil personified in world history.' G[eorg] v[on] N[ostiz]: 'In memoriam Hans-Bernd von Haeften ...' in *Zeitwende* No 20 1948/9, p. 221, gives it as follows: 'For me and my friends Adolf Hitler was the incarnation of evil.' See Zeller, pp. 373 and 444 Note 16; Paul Sethe (who was present at the trial): 'Roland Freisler: Der Dämon der Justiz' in *Schwäbische Zeitung*, 7 May 1946 and in *In Wasser geschrieben*, pp. 21–2 gives it as follows: 'Because I regard the Führer as the executor of evil in history.'

18 Müller, p. 92.

19 Ulrich von Hassell: *The von Hassell Diaries*, p. 328; Müller, p. 92; as source for Maass' remark Zeller (p. 409 Note 10) gives an anonymous article 'Märtyrer der Freiheit: Die Angeklagten des 20. Juli vor Gericht' in *Schwäbische Zeitung* 10 May 1946 (Maass was tried by the People's Court on 24 October 1944 with Julius Leber and Adolf Reichwein). The editor of [Julius Leber:] *Ein Mann geht seinen Weg*, p. 293, relies on the report by Dr Paul Sethe, who was present at the trial (see Note 17 above). On Schulenburg Zeller quotes Ernst Jünger: *Strahlungen*, pp. 569–70. Zeller (p. 373) gives Fellgiebel's remark without quoting source. Reinecke in a letter to the author dated 16 Apr. 1964 confirms the courageous attitude of the defendants.

20 *20. Juli 1944*, pp. 207–8.

21 Ludwig Kaiser verbally to the author 6 July 1971.

22 Fabian von Schlabrendorff: *Revolt against Hitler*, pp. 159–60; Hopf to Bormann ref. trial before People's Court of Bolz, Pünder, Hermes, Kempner, Schlabrendorff and Staehle on 21 Dec. 1944, copy registered as received by *Führer*'s Headquarters, BA EAP 105/30.

23 Schlabrendorff, op. cit., pp. 164–5; Alfred Heueck: 'Der Mann, der Roland Freisler sterben sah ...', *Frankfurter Rundschau*, 27 Sept. 1955.

24 Schlabrendorff, op. cit., pp. 169–71, 173–5; Heueck.

25 Hopf to Bormann ref: trial held on 7 Mar. 1945 for treason committed on 20 July 1944 (Fromm's trial), typescript, Berlin 7 Mar. 1945, BA EAP 105/30.

26 [Wilhelm Leithold:] 'Vernehmung' police headquarters Wilmersdorf, typescript, Berlin-Wilmersdorf 16 July 1945 confirms that the first eight were strangled on 8 August and that films were taken of them on their way from their cells to the execution chamber *and* of the actual execution. According to Leithold some one hundred other conspirators were hanged *in the same way* – noose placed round the neck and drawn tight, then hung on the hook and the man left in that position for some twenty-five minutes. The production of the films is confirmed by Erich Stoll, the film operator who filmed the victims as they crossed the courtyard to the execution hut, to the author 18 June 1970, and by Heinz Sasse, who filmed the executions, verbally to the author 1 July 1971; also by Colonel Eduard Ackermann (at the time in General Buhle's office at *Führer* HQ) verbally to the author 20 Nov. 1964; by Dr Schmidt-Carell in Werner Maser: *Adolf Hitler*, pp. 255, 472; and by Gert Stegemann (at the time with German Newsreel service): 'Betr.: Filmmaterial zum Attentat auf Hitler am 20. Juli 1944', typescript, made available to the author by Deutsche Wochenschau GmbH 3 June 1970. Kiessel, p. 34 also confirms that films of the executions were taken and in addition says that Kaltenbrunner had protested but could not stop the photographs being taken; Graf von Helldorf, he says, was compelled to watch three other executions before his own. Geoffrey Fraser: 'Révélations sur l'exécution des conjurés antinazis', *XXᵉ Siècle* (Paris) 2 (1946) No 13, 3 Jan. 1946, based on information from a certain Hans Hoffmann who worked in Plötzensee Prison, gives these details: very bright filming lamps, film camera with two operators, on a small table a bottle of cognac with glasses, short thin cord, slow strangling, the executed completely nude, filming without interruption until the end of the hangings. On 18 August 1944 Albert Speer (*Inside the Third Reich*, p. 395) saw photographs of the hangings – Witzleben and others – lying on Hitler's maptable; he was invited to see the films of the executions that evening but did not go. Werner Vogel (verbally to the author 1 July 1971) also saw the photographs in 'Wolfschanze'; the executed were nude. Vogel remembers Hase and Stieff. In a letter to the author of 6 Jan. 1970 Walter Frentz (film reporter in the *Führer*'s headquarters and a frequent guest at Hitler's evening tea sessions) says that the films arrived in 'Wolfschanze' but only Fegelein went to see them. Speer saw many junior SS men going to the film show on 18 August but no *Wehrmacht* officers. After the war Frentz discovered that the films were definitely still in existence; Sasse (verbally to the author 1 July 1971) says they are no longer in existence. Harald Poelchau in *Die letzten Stunden*, pp. 53–4, 86–7, 100, 107–8, thinks it probable that certain of those condemned were named by Hitler to be slowly strangled; this must be on the basis of statements from eye-witnesses – he himself was not allowed to accompany the condemned men in these cases since spiritual aid was expressly forbidden. Ruth Andreas-Friedrich in *Berlin Underground 1938–1945*, pp. 169–70 says the same. Both Poelchau (p. 107) and Andreas-Friedrich (pp. 169–70) confirm that films were taken on 8 August; they opened with shots of the condemned men in their cells just before execution. John W. Wheeler-Bennett in *The Nemesis of Power*, p. 684, gives the result of enquiries made by the Allied intelligence services after the war (he himself belonged to the British service); he says that the victims were allowed to fall with the full weight of the body, but, since the noose was of specially thin cord, it did not break the neck but was merely drawn tightly round it resulting in a prolonged death agony. He confirms that films were taken but says that, although several copies were made, they have not been found. The American espionage service OSS had details of the method of execution (slow strangulation) and of the production of the films as early as 10 August 1944; OSS Research and Analysis Branch Summary L 48301, NA Record Group 226. One of the camera men reported that the victims were allowed to fall with their full weight and that in his view death must have come 'very soon'. Here again there is no question of

breaking the neck, in which case death would have been instantaneous – report by Sasse in *20. Juli 1944*, pp. 214–15. Sasse told the author on 1 July 1971 that he thought the neck was broken, but he also mentioned twisting and twitching of the executed that continued for quite some time. Walter Hammer: 'Dienst an der Wahrheit' in *Das freie Wort*, 13 Sept. 1952, says that the hangings were carried out in the normal way but he only knows details of the procedure used in Brandenburg prison. His statement that 'the agony of those hanged only lasted a short time' seems to exclude the possibility that the neck was broken. When dealing with the executions in Plötzensee in his book *Hohes Haus in Henkers Hand*, p. 17, Hammer refers to Zeller. Moltke used to tell his friends in the weeks before trial and execution when they were allowed to take walks in the prison yard: prepare yourselves, it takes twenty minutes until death; Hans K. Fritzsche verbally to the author 14 July 1972. The application of the 'Austrian method' is confirmed on the basis of diaries and information of Johann Reichart, the hangman, in Erich Helmensdorfer: 'Scharfrichter seit 200 Jahren', *Pitaval* (Munich) 1949 No 7, pp. 22–4. For details of methods of execution see also Kurt Rossa: *Todesstrafen*, passim, and on hanging in particular pp. 31–40. See also 'Der Henker des 20. Juli' in *Hannoversche Neueste Nachrichten*, 24 Aug. 1946 – an article on Wilhelm Friedrich Röttger, the executioner, and the methods of hanging which he used.

27 Friedrich Zipfel: *Plötzensee*, p. 21; Weisenborn, p. 268; Rossa, pp. 49–55.

28 Gerhard Ritter: *Carl Goerdeler und die deutsche Widerstandsbewegung*, pp. 420, 560 Note 23.

29 Lorenzen: memorandum to Bormann ref. proceedings of People's Court 20 July (in this case Nebe's trial 2 Mar. 1945), typed copy, Berlin 2 Mar. 1945, BA EAP 105/30.

30 Xerox copy of death certificate in the author's possession; Walter Hammer, who is particularly well informed on all events in Brandenburg prison, says in 'Das Ende des Generalobersten Fromm', *Rhein-Neckar-Zeitung* 17 Sept. 1946, that as he was shot Fromm called out 'Long live the Führer' – the standard cry for all those who had been granted death by shooting; cf. Himmler's speech of 3 Aug. 1944 in T[heodor] E[schenburg]: 'Die Rede Himmlers vor den Gauleitern am 3. August 1944', VfZ 1 (1953), p. 383.

31 Rudolf Pechel: *Deutscher Widerstand*, p. 328 (extract from the 'murder register' of the Ministry of Justice); *Spiegelbild einer Verschwörung*, p. 249.

32 Pechel, pp. 328–36.

33 Ritter, op. cit., p. 416 (*The German Resistance*, p. 312).

34 Pechel, pp. 335–6; Wilhelm von Schramm: *Aufstand der Generale*, pp. 241–7 reproducing a report of proceedings from a copy in Institut für Zeitgeschichte (IfZ) – not in English translation.

35 Hans Speidel: *We defended Normandy*, pp. 155–8; see also Zeller, pp. 377–9; Manfred Rommel: 'Erklärung', typed copy, Riedlingen 27 Apr. 1945; additional evidence on Rommel's death is provided by Keitel in Walter Görlitz (editor): *Generalfeldmarschall Keitel*, p. 332.

36 Weisenborn, p. 240.

37 Ibid.; see also Walter Hammer: 'Plötzensee' in *Das freie Wort* 20 Sept. 1952.

38 Walter Hammer: 'Die "Gewitteraktion" vom 22.8.1944 . . .' in *Freiheit und Recht* 5 (1959), No 8/9, pp. 15–18. 'Fuehrer Conferences on Naval Affairs, 1939–1945', *Brassey's Naval Annual* 59 (1948), p. 405: '. . . according to one source, based on names and places, more than 4,980 Germans were exterminated by the Nazis in the purge which followed July 20'. The authenticity of this figure is questionable. Hammer in 'Gewitteraktion', p. 15 and Zeller (pp. 445–6 Note 21) think that it refers to the total number of executions in 1944. See p. 712 Note 21 above for the incorrect figures given in the 'SS-Bericht über den 20. Juli',

Nordwestdeutsche Hefte 2 (1947), p. 33 and the more accurate figures given by Kiessel.

39 Harold C. Deutsch: *The Conspiracy against Hitler in the Twilight War*, pp. 181–2, 305 Note 155.

40 Letter dated 5 April 1945 from '*Gestapo* Müller' to *SS-Obersturmbannführer* Weiter, commandant of Dachau concentration camp reproduced in S. Payne Best: *The Venlo Incident*, between pp. 208 and 209. For a comprehensive account see Eberhard Bethge: *Dietrich Bonhoeffer* (English translation) pp. 824–31; Gert Buchheit: *Der deutsche Geheimdienst*, pp. 437–48, each using sources not available to the other. See also Hermann Bösch: *Heeresrichter Dr Karl Sack im Widerstand*, pp. 88–9; Schlabrendorff, op. cit., pp. 174–5.

41 A number of German courts examined Huppenkothen's case between 1951 and 1955. They ultimately came to the conclusion that in the prevailing circumstances such a sham judicial procedure was frequently employed to do away with a man and that Huppenkothen may well have considered his orders legal in view of current regulations and procedures – Buchheit, p. 475 Note 9. *20. Juli 1944*, pp. 215–16, gives a report by Max Geissler, a hospital orderly in Sachsenhausen camp, which is inaccurate in many respects.

42 According to Bethge, pp. 830–1 the camp doctor reported that death occurred 'after a few seconds'. The post-war trials showed that statements by camp doctors should be treated with scepticism but this does not mean that they are untrustworthy in every case. Bethge gives the report textually and without comment, principally because there is a complete lack of any other reliable evidence. Buchheit (pp. 445–6) gives no details. Bösch (p. 5) says, without giving source, that the prisoners were 'hung from piano wires'. E. A. Bayne: 'Resistance in the German Foreign Office' in *Human Events* No 14, 3 Apr. 1946, p. 7, says on the basis of secret service reports of which he gives no details, that Canaris was kept hanging until he was almost dead, then revived and hanged again and so on; he did not die until he had been strangled six times.

43 Kurt von Schuschnigg: *Austrian Requiem*, pp. 219–43. Alexander von Falkenhausen: 'Bericht über meine Stellung zur N.S.D.A.P. und ihrem Regime', typescript, 15 Nov. 1946, NA Record Group 338 MS No B-289.

44 Bethge, pp. 831–3.

45 In May and June 1945 Eberhard Bethge and Dr Heinz Haushofer instituted detailed and successful investigations on the fate of the inmates of this prison, some of whom were the last opposition martyrs. Then came reports from Helmuth Cords and Herbert Kosney, both of whom were in prison there and escaped with their lives. Kosney even survived his 'liquidation'. See: [Eberhard] Bethge: 'Bericht über die Sonderabteilung der ehem. Staatspolizei im Zellengefängnis Moabit Lehrterstr. 3, zusammengestellt am 14.7.1945', photostat copy in possession of 'Hilfswerk 20. Juli 1944' Foundation; Helmuth Cords: 'Brief an einen nahen Freund vom 18. Sept. 1946', photostat copy in possession of Foundation; 'Eingangsbuch über Häftlinge' (reception register for prisoners) of Lehrterstrasse prison, RUSI Mil. Mss 479 (the author is most grateful to the Council of the RUSI, London, for a copy of this register). These and other sources have been dealt with in detail by Peter Paret in 'An Aftermath of the Plot Against Hitler: the Lehrterstrasse Prison in Berlin, 1944–5', in *Bulletin of the Institute of Historical Research* 32 (1959), pp. 88–102. See also records of proceedings and sentences in BA EAP 105/30-31; Bethge, p. 832.

46 According to the report by H. Freier and A. Wolff (both were connected with Dr Bauer through their work and as friends) a common friend, Alfred Möllers, whose youngest son went to school with the son of '*Gestapo* Müller', had gone to see '*Gestapo* Müller' and offered to look after Müller Jr after the occupation of Berlin by the Red Army, and had asked that in return Dr Bauer be released. Dr Bauer's name was entered as the last one, in pencil, on the list of those to be

released, which was typed.

47 See Chap. 28 above.

48 Two days before, while still in the prison, some of the prisoners had been transferred by the *Gestapo* to the jurisdiction of the judicial authorities (according to the entry register); for this reason, presumably, papers and valuables had been returned.

49 Bethge (*Dietrich Bonhoeffer*, Annex 3 – German edition) thinks it possible that Dr Edmund Danecke, not Jennewein, was a member of this group; according to the entries in the register of prisoners Jennewein had been transferred to the judicial authorities on that day like the others who were shot on 23 April.

50 Information from 'Hilfswerk 20. Juli 1944' Foundation; Paret, p. 99 Note 6; see also *Spiegelbild*, p. 381.

51 On this subject Paret (p. 98) quotes Otto Lasch: *So fiel Königsberg*, p. 118.

52 Christa von Hofacker: 'Das schwere Jahr 1944/45', [Krottenmühl 1947], copy in possession of 'Hilfswerk 20. Juli 1944' Foundation; A. Gräfin von Üxküll: 'Bericht', undated copy in possession of Foundation, and *Aus einem Schwesternleben*.

53 Hofacker.

Appendices

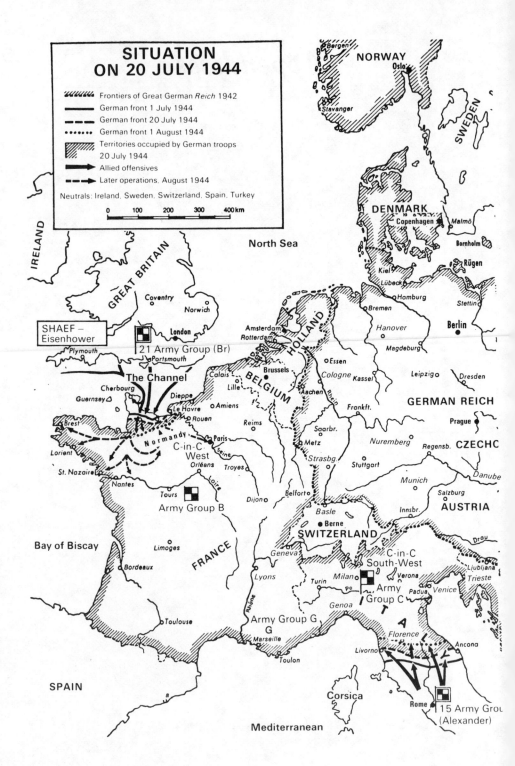

SITUATION
ON 20 JULY 1944

〰〰〰〰 Frontiers of Great German *Reich* 1942

──── German front 1 July 1944

- - - - German front 20 July 1944

• • • • German front 1 August 1944

▨▨ Territories occupied by German troops
20 July 1944

➡ Allied offensives

⇢ Later operations, August 1944

Neutrals: Ireland, Sweden, Switzerland, Spain, Turkey

0   100   200   300   400 km

IRELAND

North Sea

GREAT BRITAIN

Coventry

Norwich

SHAEF –
Eisenhower

London

21 Army Group (Br)

Plymouth

Portsmouth

The Channel

Cherbourg

Guernsey △

Brest

Dieppe

Le Havre

Rouen

Lorient

Normandy

C-in-C
West

Paris

Seine

St. Nazaire

Nantes

Orléans

Troyes

Bay of Biscay

Tours

Army Group B

Limoges

Bordeaux

FRANCE

Dijon

Lyons

Toulouse

Army Group G
G

Marseille

Toulon

SPAIN

Mediterranean

Corsica

NORWAY

Bergen

Oslo

Stavanger

SWEDEN

DENMARK

Copenhagen

Malmö

Bornholm

Rügen

Kiel

Lübeck

Stettin

Hamburg

Bremen

Hanover

Magdeburg

Berlin

Amsterdam

Rotterdam

HOLLAND

Calais

Lille

Amiens

Reims

BELGIUM

Brussels

Aachen

Cologne

Kassel

Essen

Rhine

Metz

Strasbg.

Saarbr.

Frankft.

Leipzig

Dresden

GERMAN REICH

Prague

CZECHO

Nuremberg

Regensb.

Stuttgart

Belfort

Basle

Berne

SWITZERLAND

Geneva

Munich

Salzburg

Innsbr.

AUSTRIA

Danube

Drau

Ljubljana

Trieste

C-in-C
South-West

Milan

Verona

Po

Army
Group C

Turin

Padua

Venice

Genoa

Florence

Livorno

Ancona

Rome

15 Army Group
(Alexander)

FINLAND

Helsinki

Leningrad

Narva

○Leningrad ⊞ Leningrad-Front

Novgorod

S
O
V
I
E
T

Volga

Stockholm

Reval

Estonia

Dagö

Dorpat

Ostrov

⊞ 3 Baltic Front

Üsel

Riga

⊞ Army Group North

Welikije-Luki

○ ⊞ 2 Baltic Front

Moscow

Oka

Libau

Baltic

Memel

Lithuania

Königsbg.

East Prussia

Kolberg

Danzig

Thorn

Vistula

Poznan

Warsaw

POLAND

Lodz

Breslau

Oder

SLOVAKIA

Brünn

Vilna

Kovno

Grodno

Minsk

Bialystok

Brest

Lublin

Kov el

Sandomir

Cracow

Przemysl

Lvov

Tarnopol

○ ⊞ 1 Baltic Front
Witebsk

Smolensk

⊞ 3 White Russian Front

⊞ 2 White Russian Front

⊞ ✠ Führer's Head quarters

⊞ Army Group Centre

⊞ 1 White Russian Front

Pripjet

Gomel

Desna

Brjansk

Orel

⊞ 1 Ukrainian Front

Rovno

○ ⊞ 4 Ukrainian Front
Shitomir

Kiev

Ukraine

Dnieper

Kharkov

Vinnitsa

⊞ 2 Ukrainian Front

Bug

⊞ 3 Ukrainian Front

Dnjepropetr.

Saporozhe

U
N
I
O
N

Košice

⊞ Army Group North Ukraine

Bratislava

Vienna

Budapest

H

HUNGARY

Graz

Szeged

Zag eb

Save

Cluj

⊞ Army Group South Ukraine

Sibiu

RUMANIA

Galati

Belgrade

Danube

YUGOSLAVIA
Partisans

Split

Sarajevo

evacuation of Balkans beginning Sept. 1944

Skoplje

ALBANIA

Tirana

Sofia

BULGARIA

Bucharest

Konstanta

Iasi

Prut

Dnjestr

Odessa

Sebastopol

Crimea

Black Sea

⊞ C-in-C South-East Army Group F

GREECE

Istanbul

TURKEY

Ankara

ip

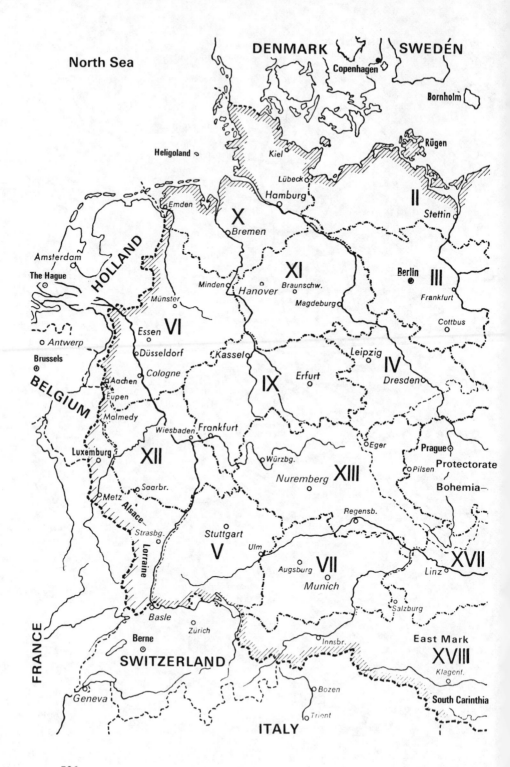

North Sea

DENMARK SWEDEN

Copenhagen

Bornholm

Heligoland

Kiel

Rügen

Lübeck

Hamburg

X

Bremen

II

Stettin

Amsterdam

The Hague

HOLLAND

Minden

Hanover

XI

Braunschw.

Berlin

III

Magdeburg

Frankfurt

Münster

Cottbus

Essen

VI

Antwerp

Düsseldorf

Kassel

Leipzig

IV

Brussels

Cologne

IX

Erfurt

Dresden

BELGIUM

Aachen

Eupen

Malmedy

Wiesbaden

Frankfurt

Würzbg.

Eger

Prague

Luxemburg

XII

Pilsen

Protectorate

Nuremberg

XIII

Bohemia—

Saarbr.

Metz

Alsace

Regensb.

Stuttgart

Strasbg.

Lorraine

V

Ulm

VII

XVII

Augsburg

Linz

Munich

Basle

Salzburg

Zurich

Berne

Innsbr.

East Mark

SWITZERLAND

XVIII

Klagenf.

Geneva

Bozen

South Carinthia

Trient

ITALY

FRANCE

726

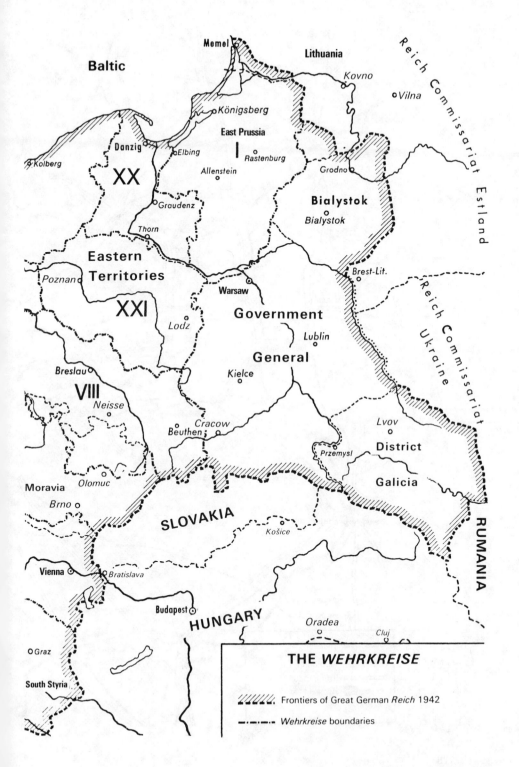

Baltic

Memel

Lithuania

Kovno

Vilna

Königsberg

East Prussia

Danzig

Elbing

Rastenburg

XX

Allenstein

Grodno

Kolberg

Graudenz

Bialystok

Bialystok

Thorn

Eastern

Poznan

Territories

Brest-Lit.

XXI

Warsaw

Government

Lodz

Lublin

General

Breslau

Kielce

VIII

Neisse

Cracow

Lvov

Beuthen

Przemysl

District

Moravia

Olomuc

Galicia

Brno

SLOVAKIA

Košice

Vienna

Bratislava

Budapest

HUNGARY

Oradea

Cluj

Graz

Reich Commissariat Estland

Reich Commissariat Ukraine

RUMANIA

South Styria

THE *WEHRKREISE*

////// Frontiers of Great German *Reich* 1942

—·—·— *Wehrkreise* boundaries

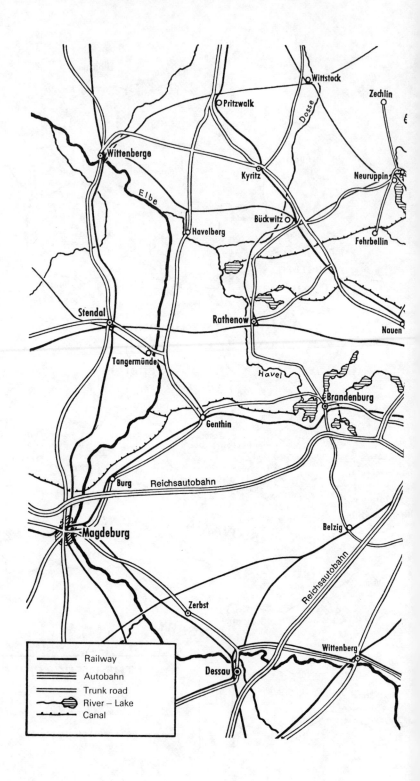

Railway
Autobahn
Trunk road
River – Lake
Canal

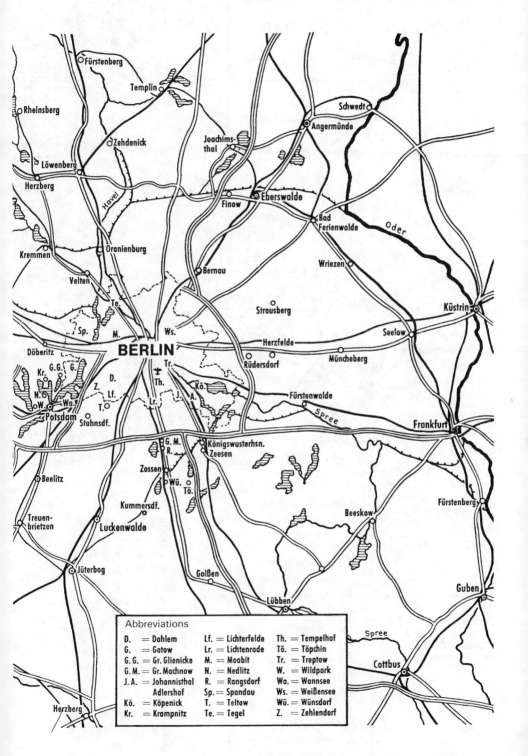

Abbreviations

D.	= Dahlem	Lf.	= Lichterfelde	Th.	= Tempelhof
G.	= Gatow	Lr.	= Lichtenrade	Tö.	= Töpchin
G. G.	= Gr. Glienicke	M.	= Moabit	Tr.	= Treptow
G. M.	= Gr. Machnow	N.	= Nedlitz	W.	= Wildpark
J. A.	= Johannisthal	R.	= Rangsdorf	Wa.	= Wannsee
	Adlershof	Sp.	= Spandau	Ws.	= Weißensee
Kö.	= Köpenick	T.	= Teltow	Wü.	= Wünsdorf
Kr.	= Krampnitz	Te.	= Tegel	Z.	= Zehlendorf

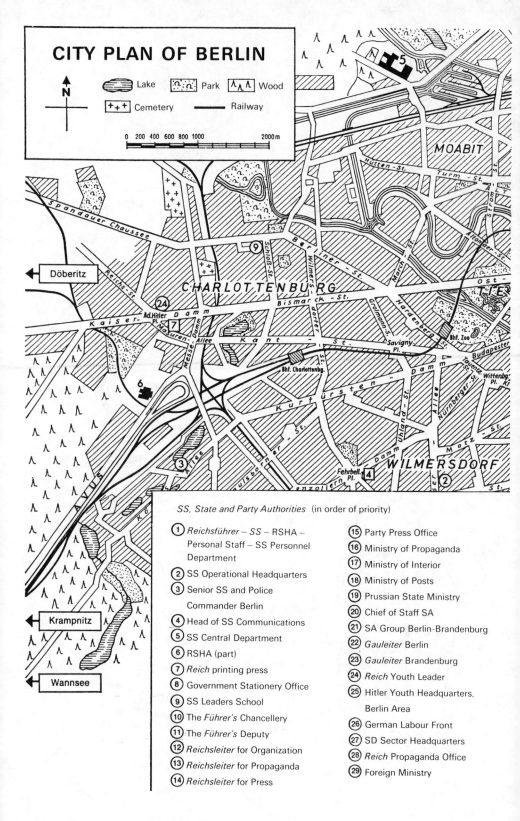

CITY PLAN OF BERLIN

N

Lake	Park	Wood
Cemetery		Railway

0 200 400 600 800 1000   2000 m

Spandauer Chaussee

Döberitz

Krampnitz

Wannsee

MOABIT

CHARLOTTENBURG

Bismarck-St.

Ad. Hitler Pl.

Kaiser-

Damm

Messe-Damm

Kurfürsten-

Kant-St.

Bhf. Charlottenbg.

Savigny-Pl.

Bhf. Zoo

Budapester

Wittenbg. Pl.

WILMERSDORF

Fehrbell. Pl.

Hardenberg

Grolmann-S.

Wilmersdorfer-St.

Berliner-St.

Schloß-St.

Hütten-St.

Turm-St.

Stroh

Alt-Moabit-St.

Reichs-St.

AVUS

TIE

SS, State and Party Authorities (in order of priority)

1 Reichsführer – SS – RSHA – Personal Staff – SS Personnel Department
2 SS Operational Headquarters
3 Senior SS and Police Commander Berlin
4 Head of SS Communications
5 SS Central Department
6 RSHA (part)
7 Reich printing press
8 Government Stationery Office
9 SS Leaders School
10 The Führer's Chancellery
11 The Führer's Deputy
12 Reichsleiter for Organization
13 Reichsleiter for Propaganda
14 Reichsleiter for Press

15 Party Press Office
16 Ministry of Propaganda
17 Ministry of Interior
18 Ministry of Posts
19 Prussian State Ministry
20 Chief of Staff SA
21 SA Group Berlin-Brandenburg
22 Gauleiter Berlin
23 Gauleiter Brandenburg
24 Reich Youth Leader
25 Hitler Youth Headquarters, Berlin Area
26 German Labour Front
27 SD Sector Headquarters
28 Reich Propaganda Office
29 Foreign Ministry

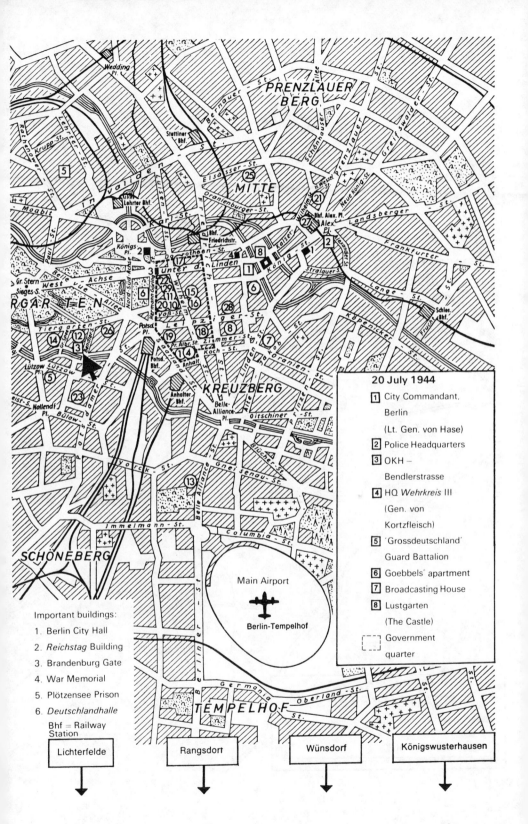

20 July 1944

1. City Commandant, Berlin (Lt. Gen. von Hase)
2. Police Headquarters
3. OKH – Bendlerstrasse
4. HQ *Wehrkreis* III (Gen. von Kortzfleisch)
5. 'Grossdeutschland' Guard Battalion
6. Goebbels' apartment
7. Broadcasting House
8. Lustgarten (The Castle)

Government quarter

Important buildings:

1. Berlin City Hall
2. *Reichstag* Building
3. Brandenburg Gate
4. War Memorial
5. Plötzensee Prison
6. *Deutschlandhalle*

Bhf = Railway Station

Main Airport

Berlin-Tempelhof

Lichterfelde

Rangsdort

Wünsdorf

Königswusterhausen

731

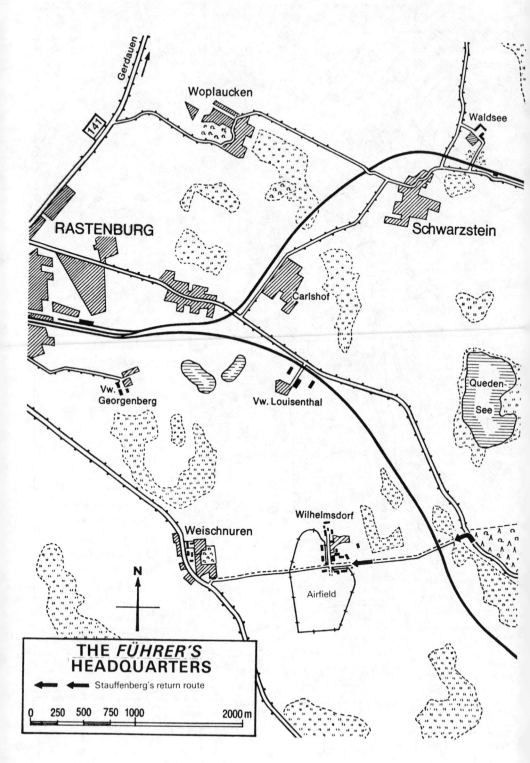

Gerdauen

141

Woplaucken

Waldsee

RASTENBURG

Schwarzstein

Carlshof

Vw. Georgenberg

Vw. Louisenthal

Queden- See

Wilhelmsdorf

Weischnuren

N

Airfield

THE *FÜHRER'S* HEADQUARTERS

Stauffenberg's return route

0   250   500   750 1000   2000 m

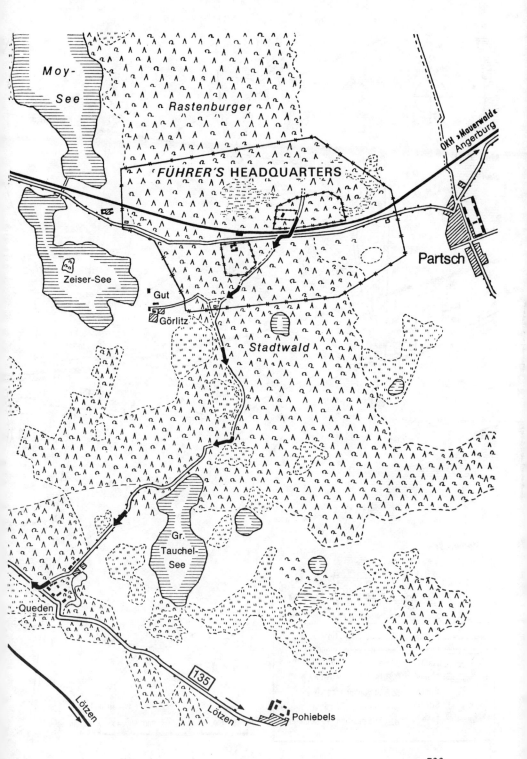

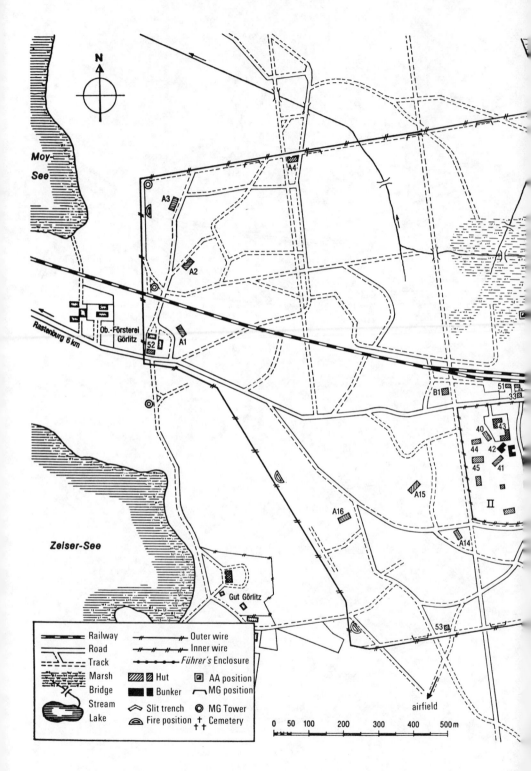

Moy-
See

N

A4

A3

A2

Rastenburg 6 km

Ob.-Försterei
Görlitz

52   A1

B1

51
33

40   43
44   42
45   41

II

A15

A16

A14

Zelser-See

Gut Görlitz

53

	Railway		Outer wire
	Road		Inner wire
	Track		*Führer's* Enclosure
	Marsh	▨ ▨	Hut
	Bridge		Bunker
	Stream		MG position
	Lake		AA position
	Slit trench	◉	MG Tower
	Fire position	† †	Cemetery

airfield

0   50 100   200   300   400   500 m

734

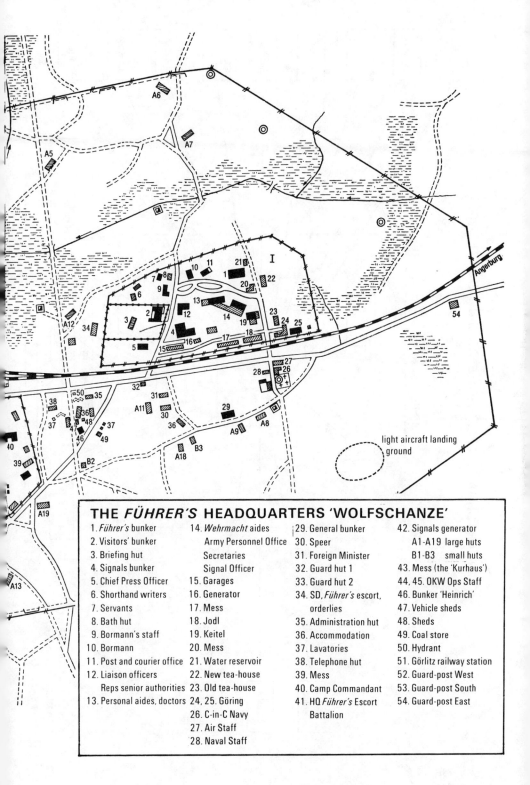

THE *FÜHRER'S* HEADQUARTERS 'WOLFSCHANZE'

1. *Führer's* bunker
2. Visitors' bunker
3. Briefing hut
4. Signals bunker
5. Chief Press Officer
6. Shorthand writers
7. Servants
8. Bath hut
9. Bormann's staff
10. Bormann
11. Post and courier office
12. Liaison officers
   Reps senior authorities
13. Personal aides, doctors

14. *Wehrmacht* aides
   Army Personnel Office
   Secretaries
   Signal Officer
15. Garages
16. Generator
17. Mess
18. Jodl
19. Keitel
20. Mess
21. Water reservoir
22. New tea-house
23. Old tea-house
24, 25. Göring
26. C-in-C Navy
27. Air Staff
28. Naval Staff

29. General bunker
30. Speer
31. Foreign Minister
32. Guard hut 1
33. Guard hut 2
34. SD, *Führer's* escort,
   orderlies
35. Administration hut
36. Accommodation
37. Lavatories
38. Telephone hut
39. Mess
40. Camp Commandant
41. HQ *Führer's* Escort
   Battalion

42. Signals generator
   A1-A19 large huts
   B1-B3 small huts
43. Mess (the 'Kurhaus')
44, 45. OKW Ops Staff
46. Bunker 'Heinrich'
47. Vehicle sheds
48. Sheds
49. Coal store
50. Hydrant
51. Görlitz railway station
52. Guard-post West
53. Guard-post South
54. Guard-post East

WOLFSCHANZE TELEPHONE COMMUNICATIONS
(as at 21 Jan. 1943)

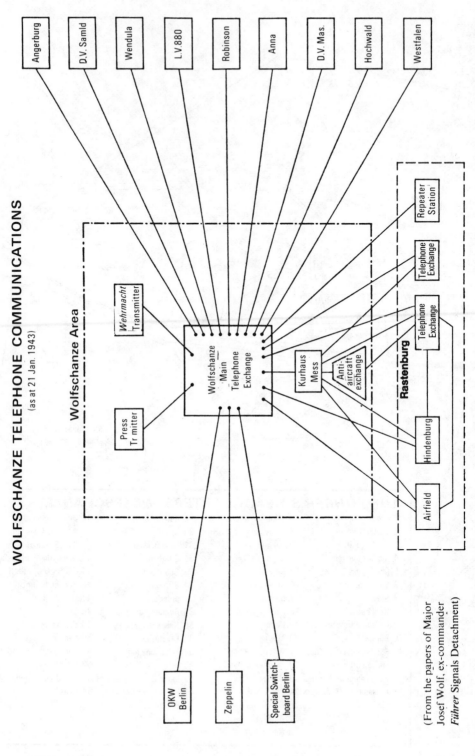

Wolfschanze Area

Angerburg
D.V. Samld
Wendula
L.V. 880
Robinson
Anna
D.V. Mas.
Hochwald
Westfalen

Wehrmacht Transmitter

Press Trmitter

Wolfschanze Main Telephone Exchange

Kurhaus Mess

Anti-aircraft exchange

Rastenburg

Repeater Station
Telephone Exchange
Telephone Exchange
Hindenburg
Airfield

OKW Berlin
Zeppelin
Special Switchboard Berlin

(From the papers of Major Josef Wolf, ex-commander *Führer* Signals Detachment)

736

WOLFSCHANZE TELEPRINTER COMMUNICATIONS

(position as at 21 Jan. 1943)

(From the papers of Major Josef Wolf, ex-commander *Führer* Signals Detachment)

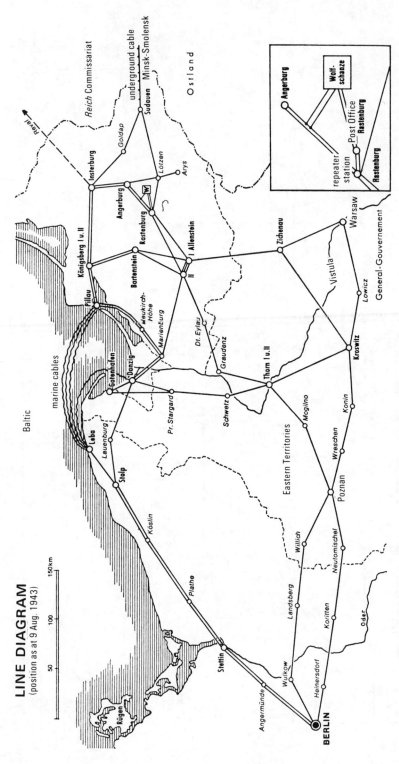

LINE DIAGRAM
(position as at 9 Aug. 1943)

Reich Commissariat

Reval

Ostland

underground cable Minsk-Smolensk

Sudauen

Goldap

Insterburg

Loizen

Angerburg

Arys

Rastenburg

Königsberg I u. II

Bartenstein

I Allenstein

Pillau

Neukirch-Höhe

II

Zichenau

Marienburg

Dt. Eylau

Warsaw

Graudenz

Vistula

General-Gouvernement

Gotenhafen

Danzig

Thorn I u. II

Lowicz

Baltic

marine cables

Pr. Stargard

Schwetz

Kroswitz

Leba

Lauenburg

Mogilno

Konin

Stolp

Wreschen

Köslin

Poznan

Eastern Territories

Willich

Neutomischel

Plathe

Landsberg

Koritten

Oder

Stettin

Wulkow

Heinersdorf

Rügen

Angermünde

BERLIN

0 50 100 150 km

[inset]

Angerburg

**Wolf-
schanze**

repeater
station

Post Office **Rastenburg**

Rastenburg

(From the papers of Major Wolf, ex-Commander *Führer* Signals Detachment)

CHANNELS OF COMMAND
(selected)

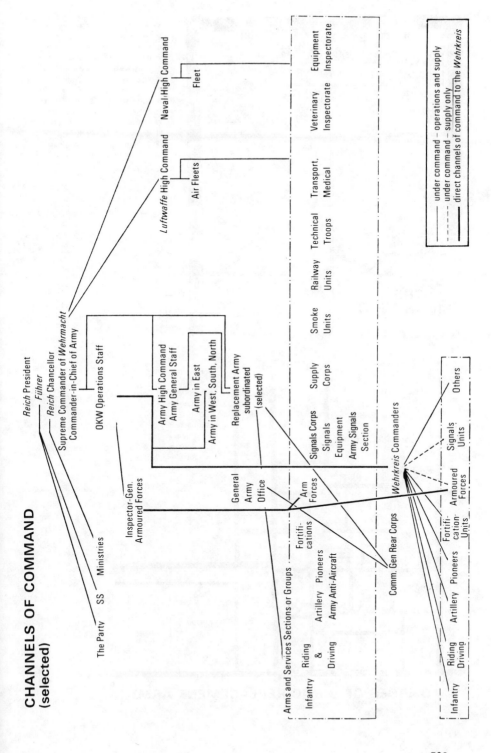

Reich President
Führer
Reich Chancellor
Supreme Commander of Wehrmacht
Commander-in-Chief of Army

The Party   SS   Ministries

OKW Operations Staff

Inspector-Gen. Armoured Forces

Army High Command
Army General Staff

Army in East

Army in West, South, North

Replacement Army subordinated (selected)

Luftwaffe High Command

Naval High Command

Air Fleets

Fleet

General Army Office

Arm Forces

Fortifications

Signals Corps
Signals Equipment
Army Signals Section

Supply Corps

Smoke Units

Railway Units

Technical Troops

Transport, Medical

Veterinary Inspectorate

Equipment Inspectorate

Comm. Gen Rear Corps

Wehrkreis Commanders

Arms and Services Sections or Groups

Infantry   Riding & Driving   Artillery   Pioneers   Army Anti-Aircraft   Fortifications

Armoured Forces

Infantry   Riding Driving   Artillery   Pioneers   Fortification Units   Signals Units   Others

under command – operations and supply
under command – supply only
direct channels of command to the Wehrkreis

739

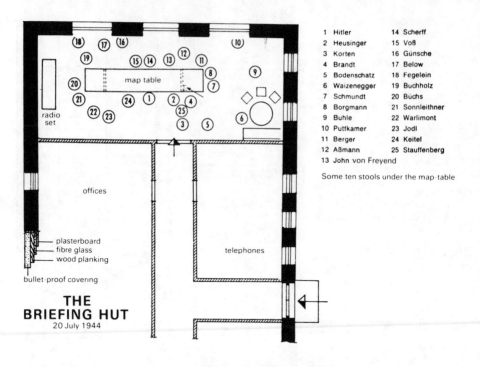

1	Hitler	14	Scherff
2	Heusinger	15	Voß
3	Korten	16	Günsche
4	Brandt	17	Below
5	Bodenschatz	18	Fegelein
6	Waizenegger	19	Buchholz
7	Schmundt	20	Büchs
8	Borgmann	21	Sonnleithner
9	Buhle	22	Warlimont
10	Puttkamer	23	Jodl
11	Berger	24	Keitel
12	Aßmann	25	Stauffenberg
13	John von Freyend		

Some ten stools under the map-table

map table

radio set

offices

plasterboard
fibre glass
wood planking

bullet-proof covering

telephones

THE BRIEFING HUT
20 July 1944

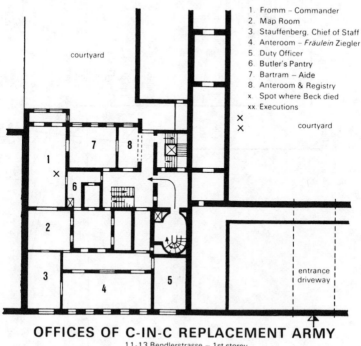

1. Fromm – Commander
2. Map Room
3. Stauffenberg. Chief of Staff
4. Anteroom – *Fräulein* Ziegler
5. Duty Officer
6. Butler's Pantry
7. Bartram – Aide
8. Anteroom & Registry
x. Spot where Beck died
xx. Executions

courtyard

courtyard

entrance driveway

OFFICES OF C-IN-C REPLACEMENT ARMY
11-13 Bendlerstrasse – 1st storey

0 1 2 3 4 5m

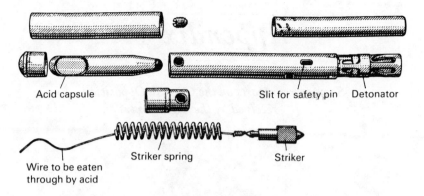

Acid capsule   Slit for safety pin   Detonator

Striker spring   Striker

Wire to be eaten
through by acid

British Chemical Time Fuse
of the type used by Tresckow/Schlabrendorff, Gersdorff and Stauffenberg

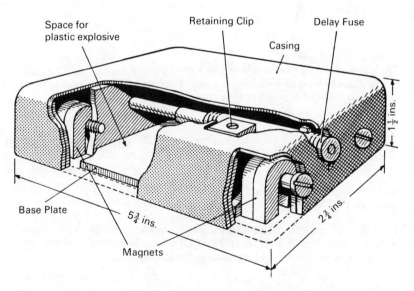

Space for
plastic explosive   Retaining Clip   Delay Fuse

Casing

$1\frac{1}{2}$ ins.

Base Plate

$5\frac{3}{4}$ ins.

$2\frac{3}{4}$ ins.

Magnets

British Adhesive Mine – 'The Clam' as used by Tresckow/Schlabrendorff and Gersdorff
(from 'Field Engineering and Mine Warfare – Pamphlet No 7: Booby Traps', London 1952)

Appendix 1

*Some secret reports on the German Opposition
received by the U.S. Govt.*

No. 1

COORDINATOR OF INFORMATION§

DATE:§

OFFICE MEMORANDUM§[1]

TO:§

FROM:§

SUBJECT:§

My dear Mr. President[2]
The attached is much like the information I relayed to you from Soong – 2 months ago
– Also it resembles the report from one of 'our people' which has come in by way of
Istanbul to the Navy – which you may have – if not I'll send it. Donovan

~~MOST CONFIDENTIAL~~

October 1, 1941

TO: Coordinator of Information[3]
FROM: W. D. Whitney

There is attached a detailed memorandum of our talk with *Stallforth* at 1647–30 St.,
N.W. on September 30, 1941, at 5:00 p.m. (His name is omitted from the attached
memorandum, in which he is referred to as the informant.)

---

* = rubber stamp
† = manuscript entry
‡ = manuscript deletion
§ = printed
[1] Originals of this and the following two documents are in PSF Safe Germany in Franklin D.
Roosevelt Library, Hyde Park, N.Y. Here and in all documents printed in the Appendix italics
were used only for what appeared underlined in the original.
[2] Text is manuscript.
[3] This note is typescript.

TO: Coordinator of Information[4]
FROM: W. D. Whitney

This is a memorandum of conference held at 1647–30 St., N.W., September 30, 1941, 5 o'clock p.m., between the informant (whose name is given on a separate memorandum), Colonel Donovan, and W. D. Whitney. The informant's story follows, using the first person singular:

In 1940, about the end of June or early July, I was in Berlin and had a personal conversation with Goering. He proposed a peace plan, after conferring with Hitler. The plan was:

1) British Empire in status quo, except certain colonies for Germany.
2) Political independence for France, Belgium, and Holland (except Alsace-Lorraine and Luxembourg to Germany).
3) Germany to have free hand in the East, including Poland and Czecho-Slovakia.

On August 12 I arrived in the United States and submitted this plan to Wilson of the State Department and to Drury, a British representative. I understand that it came to the attention of the Prime Minister and the President, and was of course turned down.

At the beginning of May, 1941, I was again in Germany, this time on the business of negotiating the sale of ships belonging to Axis-controlled countries in the Western hemisphere, and for which, although the ships were not German owned, German consent was necessary. I inquired for Goering, but this time he refused to see me. I was later advised that this was because Ribbentrop was in complete charge – and that all were confident of complete victory, so that Goering did not dare see me.

In talks with the Army, I was told that the plan to invade Russia had been fully agreed upon in early November and indeed the very day of June 22 had been set. There had been two disappointments:

1) That Russian tanks were three times as many as expected,
2) That the Russian troops were loyal to Stalin instead of showing the bad morale that had been expected,

but that the German General Staff still expected:

1) To annihilate the Russian armies by the end of October, this representing only a two months' delay beyond their original estimate of the end of August,
2) That the Russian political situation would be fully in hand by the spring of 1942.

Goering had recommended to Hitler that a boundary be put upon the German aims in Russia and that an all-out effort to conquer Russia should be abandoned. The next morning he found his home, the Kerinhalle, surrounded by SS men. He could not go out and his telephone wires had been cut. (I was informed of this by Frau Goering, who told me the whole story.) The basis of Goering's ideas on the Russian campaign was that the German people's morale would not stand up to it.

I was also reliably informed that Mussolini asked Hitler to make peace, saying that Italy must have peace. It was believed that Mussolini was the only man that could say this to Hitler without being locked up. But Hitler was merely rather amused by Mussolini, regarding him as sort of a naughty boy.

I also know that Von Pfeffer, who was the organizer of the Nazi party in Prussia, made the same recommendation to Hitler and was immediately arrested and ordered to be shot, but due to the intercession of Frau Von Pfeffer he was reprieved and put in solitary confinement.

Note by Whitney: I know that the informant was intimate with Von Pfeffer as I attended a private luncheon in informant's room with Von Pfeffer in a Berlin hotel

---

[4] The entire memorandum is typescript (spelling as in the original).

in 1936, at which Von Pfeffer outlined the then plans for an ultimate Russian campaign. This is the only corroboration that I can personally give to the informant's story.

I was called in by General Udet, Chief of the Luftwaffe, because I had had a long prior acquaintance with him, and through him I met Brauchitsch and Keitel and through them in turn many other officers. As a consequence I was invited to a rather formal luncheon at which were officers (not the top officers, but the second men) in each of the military establishments – General Staff, Army, Navy, and Luftwaffe. The course of the conversation ran as follows:

They:
> We are still confident that we will conquer Russia, but we are anxious at all costs to avoid war with the United States of America and wish to know what the USA wants.

I:
> We will make no peace with the present German government, and neither would Great Britain.

They:
> What if Hitler and Goering were to disappear or to resign.

I:
> That would not be enough. No party member would be accepted by the USA today, but I personally believe that the USA and Great Britain would likely make peace with a new constitutional government in which every private citizen would be recognized and have full normal rights.

They:
> How about a monarchy?

I:
> That would do, I think; if it were a constitutional monarchy on the English model.

A few days later, one of them came to me and the following conversation ensued:

He:
> Suppose – always suppose – that the army replaces the present regime and offers peace.

I:
> I think that it is possible that the USA and Great Britain would treat with the army under those circumstances.

He:
> The army's conditions would then be:
>
> 1) No double crossing of Germany, as happened after Germany's acceptance of Wilson's Fourteen Points;
> 2) The army to remain in control to avoid chaos and thus of course disarmament could not be immediate.

I:
> I think something could be arranged.

He:
> Whom would you suggest to meet with you.

I:
> I suggest Donovan, Willkie, and General Wood. (I thought of these three men to show that America was united, and to negative the idea that Willkie or Wood would not cooperate with the President.)

He further explained to me that they did not even ask who would be the emissary from England as they have full confidence in England, but indicated that they would prefer energetic men like Beaverbrook. They hate us more than the British, because we are spoiling their success; whereas they rather admire the British. He indicated that they would likely send Falkenhausen, Haltner, Stupnagel, and others of that type. They distrust Keitel; they believe that Brauchitsch will come over at the last. As a civilian member, they would probably send Von Hassel, son-in-law of old Tirpitz, and who, as a former ambassador to Rome, claims to be a friend of Phillips.

It was further explained to me that:

1) Everything against Hitler and the regime must originate from Germany. The German people must not get the idea that the disposition of Hitler has been organized from outside, as then they would line up to protect him.
2) If we consider their plan at all, we must do so very promptly, before hatred of the USA gets worse in Germany.
3) But as soon as it becomes plain to the German people that the change means peace, they will let Hitler go, as they put peace first in their affections and Hitler second.
4) The German army fears that the President or Churchill would kill any such plan, as they have been convinced by their own propaganda to the effect that the President and Churchill as individuals have a special and violent animosity against Germany while all the rest of the USA and Great Britain understand them. I of course explained that this was absurd and that the USA and the UK were definitely behind their two chiefs, but mere explanations do not surmount months of skillful propaganda. This does not of course mean that they would not be glad to deal with Churchill and the President, but they think that the President and Churchill would, for reasons of blind hatred, refuse even to consider reasonable solutions.

I showed them the eight points which they had not seen. (I got them from the Embassy in Berlin.) They read them over carefully and said they were satisfactory, except the last point about disarmament. They said there should be an economic union of Europe, but that politically they would be prepared to evacuate all territories, except only Austria. Germany and Austria should remain intact. They suggested the Kaiser's grandson as the new sovereign, because in the legitimate line.

They emphasized to me that I should make plain that they are making these suggestions, not because of fear, but to save the white race from further destruction.

No. 2

Memorandum by Brigadier General John Magruder, Deputy Director of Intelligence Service, Office of Strategic Services, to the Director of the Office of European Affairs (Dunn)[1]

WASHINGTON, 5 April, 1944.

Transmitted herewith for your information is a copy of a dispatch from the Bern office of this agency, giving reported German reactions to three major Allied propaganda lines.

JOHN MAGRUDER

BERNE, 31 March, 1944.

GERMANY: REACTION TO ALLIED PSYCHOLOGICAL WARFARE

On the basis of numerous reports and extended consultation, the OSS representative in Bern transmits the German reactions to three major Allied propaganda lines:

1. *The trend toward a German defeat is inescapable.* The Germans are certainly

---

[1] From *Foreign Relations of the United States, Diplomatic Papers, 1944,* Vol. I, pp. 505–7.

aware of this inescapable trend. Their hopes at present consist solely in: (*a*) diminution of Russian interest upon attaining the 1941 boundaries, or else friction between the USSR and the western Allies; (*b*) frustration of attempts to land in the Balkans or in France, added to war fatigue on the part of the western countries, the forthcoming elections in the US, and the degree to which the US views the war against Japan as its primary concern; (*c*) a miracle of some sort, such as a secret weapon, although this hope is fading; (*d*) an era of chaotic confusion throughout Europe, from which Germany would emerge in as good shape as any other country.

2. *Unconditional surrender does not mean total disaster.* The majority of Germans suspect that the Allies wish to ruin the economic as well as the military strength of Germany; 'unconditional surrender' therefore signifies to most of them total catastrophe for the country and for the individual German. We ourselves have done nothing to offer them a more hopeful meaning for this expression; we have never, for example, indicated that it refers only to military and party leaders. The Germans' pessimistic interpretation of 'unconditional surrender' is also supported by the widespread feeling that the Atlantic Charter has been discarded or at least does not hold good for Germany, and by Churchill's mention of compensation to Poland by giving her German territory. In the face of Goebbels' propaganda system, it would be difficult to 'sell' the German people on a new and more optimistic interpretation of 'unconditional surrender'; however, granting the issuance of authoritative and harmonizing proclamations from Churchill, Roosevelt and Stalin, it probably could be achieved in time. Thus far, back-handed encouragement from the Free German Committee in Moscow has been the only source of hope for the Germans, and many Germans regard this Committee as a trap.

3. *Overthrow of the Nazis by a minority group.* Unless Hitler and certain other Nazi leaders were murdered, and the Army takes over, most Germans believe that no minority faction could now seize authority over the existing ruler. Moreover, no effective opposition group, military or civilian, exists which favors the western powers. Most anti-Nazis who desire western orientation see no justification for risking their lives to promote any plans for Germany thus far submitted by the western powers. Other anti-Nazi elements in the Reich prefer to have the authority and responsibility maintained by the Nazi and military cliques until the ultimate debacle, so that the whole blame for the war and for Germany's downfall will rest for all time on the shoulders of Hitler and the military. The German Socialists, especially, do not intend to assume control, as they did the last time, and thus have to answer for the armistice and peace terms. The Catholics' point of view is much the same. The Communists possess no known leader. Of course, a new group probably would be created in case we chose to offer any indication that such a group could deal with us; until the capitulation, however, the strength of this group would be insignificant.

No. 3

Memorandum by Brigadier General John Magruder, Deputy Director of Intelligence Service, Office of Strategic Services, to Mr Fletcher Warren, Executive Assistant to the Assistant Secretary of State (Berle)[1]

WASHINGTON, 17 May, 1944.

Attention: Mr A. A. Berle, Jr.

Subject: Overtures by German Generals and Civilian Opposition for a Separate Armistice.

---

[1] From *Foreign Relations*, pp. 510–13.

There is enclosed herewith copy of a document[2] concerning the above subject, which has been prepared by this agency. The information contained therein was obtained from a series of cables from our Bern office, the most recent of which is dated May 13.

A copy of this document has been transmitted formally to the Secretary of State by the Acting Director, OSS.[3]

JOHN MAGRUDER

OVERTURES BY GERMAN GENERALS AND CIVILIAN OPPOSITION FOR A SEPARATE ARMISTICE

WASHINGTON, May 16, 1944.

1. Since early 1944 the OSS representative in Bern[4] has been approached periodically by two emissaries[5] of a German group proposing to attempt an overthrow of the Nazi regime. The group includes Leuschner, socialist leader and former Minister of Interior in Hesse; Oster, a general formerly the right-hand man of Canaris, arrested in 1943 by the Gestapo, kept under surveillance after his release, and recently discharged from official functions by Keitel; Goerdler, former Mayor of Leipzig; and General Beck. The last two men have been described by the OSS representative as leaders of the group; it is from them that the two emissaries have brought proposals for negotiation.

2. Early in April the emissaries talked with the OSS representative in Bern, conveying the suggestion of a deal between this German opposition group and the Western Allies. The group expressed their willingness and preparation to attempt ousting Hitler and the Nazis. They stated their belief that the time in which successful action could be carried out was rapidly shortening. They said they were the only group able to profit by personal approach to Hitler and other Nazi chiefs, and the only one controlling enough arms and enough influence in the Wehrmacht to accomplish the purpose of Nazi overthrow. The group stated that the German generals now commanding in the West – particularly Rundstedt and Falkenhausen – would be ready to cease resistance and aid Allied landings, once the Nazis had been ousted. They thought that similar arrangements might be worked out for the reception of Allied airborne forces at strategic points in Germany. While ready to attempt a coup, the group did not guarantee success.

3. The condition on which the group expressed willingness to act was that they would deal directly with the Western Allies alone after overthrowing the Nazi regime. As precedent for excluding the USSR from all negotiations they cited the recent example of Finland, which they said dealt solely with Moscow. This condition the group based on the conservative character of their membership and supporters. However, the group declared their willingness to cooperate with any leftist elements except the Communists; in February they had described Leuschner as an acceptable type of head for an interim government, assuming that neither the military nor the Communists would dominate during the transition period. The group feared political and ideological sway over Central Europe by Bolshevism, with a mere exchange of Nazi totalitarianism for a totalitarianism of the radical left accompanied by the submergence of democracy and

---

[2] The substance of the enclosed document was transmitted in aide-mémoire dated May 14 1944 (not printed), to the British and Soviet Embassies in Washington.
[3] G. Edward Buxton.
[4] Allen W. Dulles.
[5] Gisevius and Waetjen.

Christian culture. They stated that if capitulation were to be made primarily to the Soviet Union, it would have to be carried out by another group in Germany.

4. The OSS representative expressed to the emissaries his conviction that the United States and Great Britain would not act regarding Germany without the concert of Russia. In commenting on the opposition group's proposal, he expressed scepticism of their capability since Beck and Goerdler have been so prominently mentioned as potential leaders that the Gestapo must be aware of the situation and is only waiting to crack down until plans have gone farther or because the Gestapo may wish to keep an anchor to westward.

5. In May 1944, approximately one month after the April visit of the emissaries to the OSS representative, they received an oral message by courier from the opposition group. Now mentioned as members were also Halder, Zeitzler, Heusinger (chief of operations for Zeitzler), Olbr[i]cht (chief of the German Army Administration), Falkenhausen, and Rundstedt. The group was reported ready to help Allied units get into Germany if the Allies agreed that the Wehrmacht should continue to hold the Eastern Front. They proposed in detail: (1) three Allied airborne divisions should land in the Berlin region with the assistance of the local Army commanders, (2) major amphibious landings should be undertaken at or near Bremen and Hamburg, (3) landings in France should follow, although Rommel cannot be counted on for cooperation, (4) reliable German units in the area of Munich would isolate Hitler and other high Nazis in Ober Salzburg. The opposition group is reported to feel that Germany has lost the war and that the only chance of avoiding Communism in Germany is to facilitate occupation of as large a section of Europe as possible by American and British forces before collapse on the Eastern Front.

6. The emissaries, who had remained in Switzerland, replied to the courier that discussion of the plan would be unavailing because of the proviso concerning the USSR. Later the group dispatched to them a telegram advising no further action 'for the time being'. The emissaries think nevertheless that the subject is still open. They have characterized the group's proviso as unrealistic, and regard as the core of the proposal only the plan that American and British forces should become entrenched in Germany before the Russians; they urged that it was entirely a military matter if some of the German generals wish to assist the Allied invasion and try to take over the Nazi regime. The OSS representative reiterated to the emissaries that Great Britain and the United States would adhere to their Russian commitments. In answer to the objection that point (1) of the group's plan (paragraph 5, above, on page 3) might be regarded by the Allies as a trap, they stated that since they were not military men they could only say that sufficient opportunity for requisite precautions would be presented in the form of direct prior contact with German military authorities. The emissaries said that Zeitzler had been won over by Heusinger and Olbr[i]cht; they added that he was preoccupied in respect of military matters with the Eastern Front, that he would cooperate in any plan to bring about a systematic liquidation of that front in order to escape the blame for a military disaster there − which he greatly fears.

7. One of the opposition group's emissaries acknowledged his lack of confidence in the political courage of the German generals on the basis of past experience, and said the Allies might do well to ignore their propositions if there were assurance of early victory and a speedy Allied occupation of Germany. The OSS representative at Bern is convinced of the sincerity of this intermediary, as the result of investigation and of experience with him. The representative is of the opinion that there are some German generals who wish to liquidate their responsibility in the war by collaborating in the construction of an Anglo-American bulwark against the pressure of the USSR in Europe, and he is convinced that the two emissaries are in contact with such a group. Doubtful that the group would have the determination to act effectively at the appropriate time and sensitive to the problem of Soviet relations in the effectuation of

any plan in which the group might participate, he believes that the group's activities may nevertheless be useful to undermine the morale of the top echelon in the Wehrmacht.

No. 4[1]

SECRET*

Sec'y of State
Fletcher Warren
Joint Chiefs
Office of Strategic Services§ W.H. Map Room
Washington, D.C.§ L39970*

18 July 1944

'L' List†

Germany: Nazi Opposition Group Reports Progress

The following, transmitted by the OSS representative in Bern, is a sequel to a report dated 16 May concerning an opposition group in Germany, including some high military figures, which favors peace:

The objectives of this group have received new stimulus from the Soviet gains, the Soviet threat of invading German soil, and the Allied landings in Normandy. The group is receiving cooperation from another group composed of a number of anti-Hitler elements which are described as working independently of the Gestapo. The former group believes that the next few weeks represent the final opportunity to initiate steps to prove the desire of the German people to overthrow Hitler and his organization and to set up a 'respectable government'. It is the wish of the group that as much of Germany as possible be kept from falling into Soviet hands. The group's proposed plan of action would call for an ordered retreat from the west and the transfer of the best divisions to the defense of the eastern front.

The group also has been encouraged by their alleged acquisition of Colonel-General Fritz Fromm because he has charge of reserves in the Berlin area.

> [WASHINGTON COMMENT: General Fromm, Chief of the Home Command, is in charge of army equipment, and commander of replacement training for the army.]

According to the group, the OKW has shifted its headquarters from East Prussia to a locality near Berlin. The group views this transfer as favorable to its purposes, for General Frederich Olbricht [sic], Chief of the General Army Office, under General Fromm, and Colonel-General Kurt Zeitzler, Chief of Staff, as well as other generals supposedly in the opposition, are now accessible in the vicinity of Berlin.
(OSS Official Dispatches, Bern, 13 and 15 July)
BREAKERS Cables nos. 4110–4114 and 4111–12 (sic).

SECRET

---

[1] Typescript unless otherwise noted. Original in OSS Research and Analysis Branch Summaries, Record Group 226, NA.

No. 5[1]

SECRET*

STATE (Warren)
JCS (McGovern)
W.H. MAP ROOM
GEN. MARSHALL
(Gen. Magruder)
22 July 1944
L39971*

OFFICE OF STRATEGIC SERVICES§
WASHINGTON, D.C.§

22 July 1944

'L' List†

THE GERMAN COUP D'ÉTAT

The military *coup d'état* attempted on 20 July by strong elements of the German High Command is the outgrowth of political preparations of at least six months' duration. Although the *coup* is now believed to have failed, it has been felt worthwhile to review the composition and aims of the conspiring group, as known from OSS contacts with it, and to indicate the probable significance of the action taken.

I. *COMPOSITION AND AIMS:*

Two emissaries of the conspiring group first approached the OSS representative in Bern in January 1944. The group was then described as composed of various intellectuals from certain military and government circles gathered into a loose organization. The membership was said to be somewhat divided as to a course of action, some holding that Hitler and his cohorts should be made to shoulder all responsibility to the bitter end; while others favored an overthrow of Hitler and the organization of a new Government before the fighting stops, which might negotiate peace. The conspiring elements were united in their preference for a western rather than an eastern orientation of German policy. In general, they were characterized by their emissaries as well-educated and influential but not rightist individuals; such characterization may have been designed for Anglo-American consumption. The group as a whole apparently maintained its foreign contacts through the Canaris organization.

The following were said by the emissaries in February and April 1944 to be among the members of the group.

General Ludwig Beck, one of the two leaders of the group, former chief of the German General Staff, who retired 'at his own request' in 1938. General Beck, General Fritsch, and General Fromm [mentioned later as a member of this group] dominated the Reichswehr Ministry until 1938.

Carl Friedrich Goerdeler, co-leader of the group, a former Mayor of Leipzig, and one-time Nazi representative to business circles in the United States.

Brigadier-General Hans Oster, former right-hand man to Canaris, who was arrested by the Gestapo in 1943 and later released but kept under surveillance and was officially discharged by Keitel in early 1944.

Colonel-General Franz Ritter von Halder, a strong figure in Catholic circles, anti-Soviet, reported ousted in 1942, although thought under consideration by the Nazis for an important new post in late June, 1944.

General Thomas [probably General Georg Thomas, Chief of War Economy and Armaments in the OKW].

---

[1] Typescript unless otherwise stated. Original in NA, ibid.

Hans Leuschner, socialist leader and former Minister of the Interior in Hesse, a former anti-Nazi who may have made some sort of peace with the Nazis.

In early April the group's emissaries again approached the OSS representative, bearing a declaration said to represent the views of General Beck and Herr Goerdeler. This message stated that, with Germany's position coming to a head and the end of the war in Europe definitely in sight, the group was willing and ready to take steps to oust the Nazis and eliminate Hitler (see report dated 12 April 1944). The group claimed to be the only one with personal access to Hitler and other Nazi chiefs, with enough arms to accomplish its purpose, and with enough power in the army to make a *coup* feasible. Such action, however, would be contingent upon assurances from Britain and the United States that, once the Nazis had been overthrown, negotiations would then be carried out solely with the Western Powers and under no circumstances with the USSR. The essential conservatism of the group's planners was stressed, but also its willingness to cooperate with any available elements of the Left except for the Communists. The group expressed its anxiety to keep Central Europe from coming under Soviet domination. If capitulation were to be made primarily to the Soviet Union, the negotiations would have to be carried on by another group. Such Wehrmacht commanders in the West as von Rudstedt [sic] and Falkenhausen, the declaration maintained, would be ready to assist the Allied landings once the Nazis were removed from power.

To these overtures the OSS representative said little beyond expressing his strong conviction that the United States would never act without previous consultation with the USSR. He reported at that time that he had doubts as to the group's chances of success, since he said both Beck and Goerdler [sic] had been publicly mentioned as potential leaders of a *coup*, and since it could be taken for granted that the Gestapo was aware of this group. The representative thought that the Gestapo had not stepped in either because it planned to wait until the group's plans had been more nearly perfected, or because the Gestapo wished to have 'an anchor in the West'.

In early May the two emissaries forwarded to the OSS representative a further communication from the group. Its membership was said by this time to include important new members: Generals von Rundstedt [sic], Falkenhausen, Heusinger, Zeitzler, and Olbricht (see report dated 16 May). These generals were all reported ready to assist Anglo-American units to enter Germany provided the Western Allies would agree to allow them to continue the war on the eastern front.

A new plan of action was outlined in the May communication. The plan called for the landing of three Allied parachute divisions in the Berlin area with the help of local Army commanders; major amphibious landings at or near Bremen and Hamburg; the isolation of Hitler and high Nazi officials in Obersalzberg by trustworthy German units posted in the Munich region; and Allied landings on the French coast, though these in their early stages were thought difficult to plan as Rommel could not be counted upon for cooperation. In the communication the group reaffirmed its belief that Germany had lost the war, that the last hope of preventing the spread of Communism in Germany would be an Anglo-American occupation of the greatest possible portion of the Reich, and that the only means of accomplishing this would be to help the Anglo-American forces to enter Germany before military collapse in the East.

The two emissaries at this time expressed the opinion that the group's proviso with regard to the exclusion of the USSR was unrealistic; they regarded the plan for speedy American and British occupation of Germany as the core of the proposal. One of the emissaries admitted a lack of confidence in the political courage of the German generals, on the basis of past experience, and remarked that the Allies might do well to ignore their propositions if an early victory and speedy occupation of Germany appeared certain. The OSS representative reported his own doubts as to whether the group would possess the necessary determination to act effectively at the appropriate time.

In early July a courier arrived in Bern bearing a communication displaying new confidence in the strength of the group. (See report dated 18 July 1944.) This message reported that the movement had gained new vigor from the Soviet victories in the East, from the Allied landings in the West, and from certain developments in Germany. Colonel-General Fritz Fromm, Chief of the Home Command, who controlled the regular army within Germany, was said to have joined the group. Further strength was said to be acquired [sic] by the alleged transfer of OKW headquarters from East Prussia to a locality near Berlin and the resultant proximity to Berlin of General Olbricht, Chief of the General Army Office, Colonel-General Kurt Zeitzler, Chief of Staff, and other generals supposed to be in the opposition. Cooperation was also claimed from a group of Anti-Hitler elements [sic] headed by Wolff [sic] Graf Helldorf [sic], Berlin chief of police and an old-time Nazi. The message said that the group's plan of action called for an ordered retreat from the West and the dispatch of all crack divisions to defend the eastern front. Efforts would be made to convince the generals to wage a final struggle against Nazism.

On 12 July the OSS representative reported that a dramatic event might take place up north, if the information brought by the group's courier could be trusted, and warned that any news would be suppressed by violence, if necessary. This was the last word received before the news of the attempted *coup*.

II. *THE FAILURE OF THE COUP:*

A. *Nazi Countermeasures:*

By the first week in July it became amply clear that the National Socialist Government was aware of impending revolt in high military circles. In his funeral oration for General Dietl (2 July) Hitler extolled those who devoted themselves to the German cause with fanaticism as opposed to the lukewarm supporters of the war effort. On 7 July when the breakthrough in the East began and the western beachhead loomed as a firmly established threat, Goebbels wrote an editorial in *Das Reich* pointing out that the home front was the critical area in the German war effort and that all power should be given to 'the fanatics'. This article constituted a marked departure from the earlier propaganda line, which emphasized the participation of *all* Germans in the conduct of the war.

These official statements were harbingers of the Party's intention to seize all power in the state, including that over the military establishment. On 19 July news leaked out to Stockholm that Heinrich Himmler would shortly be named to a post of first importance in the German High Command. Himmler's powers, it was said, would include complete control over all military appointments both in the field and in the Home Command. As this report was received, telephone communications between Stockholm and Berlin were cut (1655, 19 July). The report therefore antedates the *coup* of 20 July.

B. *The Attempted Coup d'état:*

To the Army leadership the acquisition of such powers by Himmler clearly would be regarded as the end of their political power, domestic and international, which rested on their control of the armed forces. It may be assumed that the High Command felt its international bargaining strength to lie in its armies in the field. This was being weakened by enemy action and also by the removal of General von Rundstedt and the presence of Rommel on the Western front. The High Command's domestic strength, on the other hand, resided in General Fromm's home forces. As the armies in the field approached defeat the importance of the home army would increase. Only through control of the home army could Germany's military leadership eliminate the Nazis without exposing itself to social revolution.

It is therefore believed that the proposed appointment of Himmler [subsequently announced in Hitler's speech after the *coup*] precipitated the military conspirators into premature action. The actual attempt upon Hitler's life, hastily organized and ineffective as it was, had to be undertaken before the appointment of Himmler could take place.

With the failure of the assassination and the elimination or subordination of Generals Keitel, Zeitzler, Fromm, Rundstedt, and Beck, the Army High Command must be considered to have lost its opportunity to carry out its original plans. Press reports allege that mutinies are in progress in the Navy, and that civilian unrest is mounting. These reports are unconfirmed thus far. It is believed, however, that such revolutionary trends formed no part of the High Command group's plan.

Appendix 2

*Texts of the more important teleprinter messages
of 20 July 1944*

NOTE:
Unless otherwise stated the copies used are the original typed carbons in the possession
of Bernd Ruland, a sergeant in the Signals Corps at the time; he succeeded in removing
these from the Bendlerstrasse unnoticed on 20–21 July 1944. Three or four copies of
each message were required for the operators so that messages for *Wehrkreise I–V*, for
instance, could be despatched on one machine and those for *Wehrkreise* VI–XII on
another. In the general confusion the disappearance of one or two copies of the set was
able to pass unnoticed and, if necessary, could be explained later by saying that the conspirators, particularly those who had already been shot, had destroyed a great deal. Partial facsimiles of some of these messages are to be found in *Mitteilungsblatt der
Arbeitsgemeinschaft ehemaliger Offiziere* Nos 12 of 1968, pp. 9, 11; 1 of 1969, pp. 6–8; 2
of 1969, pp. 12–13. Use has also been made for reference of *Spiegelbild einer
Verschwörung,* pp. 66–82, and copies of the messages attached to the 'Kaltenbrunner
reports' in BA EAP 105/20-31 – only some of which are given in *Spiegelbild.*

* = rubber stamp
† = manuscript entry
‡ = manuscript deletion

MESSAGE NO 1

| stamp with delivery | I† | HOKW* 02160 † |
| details – mostly illegible] | | 20 July 1944* 1815† |

Secret* after receipt†
Top Secret*

Immediate*

To: Rear Corps Command HQs I–XIII (III by courier), XVII, XVIII, XX, XXI

1552

1 Valkyrie Stage 2 for Wehrkreis HQs I–XIII, XVII, XVIII, XX, XXI. All stores both
   of Field and Replacement Armies may be used including, if necessary, stocks in
   depots and parks.
   Hour 20.7   1800
2 Weapons, major items of equipment and motor vehicles drawn from OKH stocks in
   depots and parks to be reported forthwith by teleprint to AHA Staff (Supply).

3 Organization, strength and location of units mobilized to be reported to AHA Staff I through 'Immediate' teleprint by 1200 21.7.

4 Similar measures to be taken in *Wehrkreis* Bohemia/Moravia and Government-General. Units mobilized to be reported to AHA Staff I by 1200 21.7 as in 3 above.

OKH C-in-C Replacement Army
Chief Army Armaments and
AHA Staff I No 4996/44 Top Secret of 20.7.44

AHA Staff I	Copy No 1	by order
AHA Staff II	Copy No 2	Mertz†
AHA Staff Ib	Copy No 3	
Jn 3	Copy No 4	

MESSAGE NO 2

Secret*   Command Message II†   HOKW* 02165*
on receipt†
Top Secret*   20 July 1944*   1900†
                                                                              0590
                              Teleprint[1]   J2
                                                                              2030†

I The *Führer* Adolf Hitler is dead.
An irresponsible gang of Party leaders, far behind the front, has tried to exploit this situation to stab the hard-pressed army in the back and seize power for its own ends.

II In this hour of supreme danger the *Reich* government, to maintain law and order, has proclaimed a state of military emergency and has entrusted to me both supreme command of the armed forces and executive power in the *Reich*.

III I hereby order:

1 I transfer executive power, with right of delegation to territorial commanders:
In the Home Forces area to C-in-C Replacement Army who is at the same time appointed C-in-C Home Forces area
In western occupied territories to C-in-C West (C-in-C Army Group D)
In Italy to C-in-C South-West (C-in-C Army Group C)
In the south-eastern area to C-in-C South-East (C-in-C Army Group F)
In the occupied eastern territories to Cs-in-C of Army Groups South Ukraine, North Ukraine, Centre, North and the *Wehrmacht* Commander *Ostland,* each in their respective areas.
In Denmark and Norway to the *Wehrmacht* Commanders.

2 The following are placed under orders of the holders of executive power:
(a) all agencies and units in the area concerned of the armed forces including the *Waffen-SS,* the Labour Service and the Todt Organization;
(b) all official authorities (of the *Reich,* the *Länder* and of communities), in particular the entire regular police, security police and administrative police);
(c) all officials and branches of the National-Socialist Party and its affiliated organizations;
(d) all transport and supply agencies.

3 The whole of the *Waffen-SS* is incorporated into the Army with immediate effect.

4 The holders of executive power are responsible for the maintenance of public order and security. They will pay particular attention to:
(a) security of communications installations;
(b) elimination of the SD.
Any resistance to military authority will be ruthlessly suppressed.

---

[1] Text is in typescript. It has not so far been possible to establish whether this text was transmitted first or the version beginning with the words 'Internal Disturbances' instead of 'The Führer Adolf Hitler is dead' – the former carries time of receipt in signal centre as 1645. See Chapter 42 Note 39.

5 In this hour of supreme danger to the Fatherland the first necessity is the unity of the *Wehrmacht* and the maintenance of discipline.

I therefore order all Army, Navy and Air Force commanders to use all resources available to them to support those given executive power in their difficult task and to ensure that their orders are obeyed by all subordinate agencies.

The German soldier is confronted with a historic task. The salvation of Germany will depend on his energy and morale.

All territorial commanders, the High Commands of the Services and the Army, Navy and Air Force headquarters immediately subordinate to the High Commands have identical instructions.

The Supreme Commander of the *Wehrmacht*
(signed) v. Witzleben*
Field Marshal   M[1]

Chief Army Armaments and
C-in-C Replacement Army ‡
Staff, No 4500/44g   Berlin, 20 July 1944
                    Foregoing decree for information.
Return to AHA I Staff†   by order

MESSAGE NO 3

Teleprint[2]

HOKW 02155
20 July 1944   1800

To: *Wehrkreis* HQs I – XIII, XVII, XVIII, XX, XXI, Government-General, Bohemia-Moravia.

Secret!

1 By virtue of the authority granted me as Supreme Commander of the *Wehrmacht* I transfer executive power to *Wehrkreis* Commanders. The prerogatives of *Reich* Defence Commissars are also transferred to *Wehrkreis* Commanders.

2 The following measures are to be taken forthwith:

(a) Communications installations:

The most important buildings and installations of the Post Office and *Wehrmacht* communications networks (including wireless transmitters) will be taken systematically under military protection. Forces employed must be strong enough to prevent unauthorized action or demolitions. The more important communications installations will be occupied under officer supervision. In particular the following will be guarded: Repeater stations, army transmitting exchanges, main radio stations, telephone and telegraph offices carrying vital lines, amplifier and battery rooms, antennae, transmission current and emergency current rooms, traffic offices. The railway communications network will be protected in agreement with transport agencies. A radio network will be set up using own resources.

(b) Arrests:

Following will be relieved of their offices forthwith and placed in secure solitary confinement:

All *Gauleiter*, *Reichsstatthalter*, Ministers, Governors [*Oberpräsidenten*], Police Presidents, Senior SS and Police Commanders [HSSPF], heads of *Gestapo* and SD offices, heads of propaganda offices, *Kreisleiter*.

Exceptions only by my special order.

(c) Concentration Camps:

Concentration camps will be occupied at once, camp commandants arrested, guard personnel disarmed and confined to barracks. Political prisoners are to

---

[1] Initialled by Mertz von Quirnheim.
[2] From copy in BA EAP 105/24 folios 91–3 which carries the addition 'Despatched between 1800 and 2122 to Wehrkreis HQs I – VI, VII, XIII, XVII, XVIII, XXI'. See also *Spiegelbild*, pp. 66–7.

be instructed that, pending their liberation, they should refrain from demonstrations or independent action.

(d) *Waffen-SS*:

If compliance by commanders of *Waffen-SS* formations or by the senior *Waffen-SS* officers appears doubtful or if they seem unsuitable, they will be taken into protective custody and replaced by Army officers.

Waffen-SS formations whose unquestioned compliance appears doubtful will be ruthlessly disarmed. Firm action with superior forces will be taken to avoid further bloodshed.

(e) Police:

Gestapo and SD headquarters will be occupied.

Otherwise the regular police will be used as far as possible to relieve the *Wehrmacht*.

Orders will be issued by Chief of German Police through police channels.

(f) Navy and Air Force:

Contact will be maintained with naval and air force commanders.

Measures will be taken to ensure combined action.

3 To deal with all political questions I attach to each *Wehrkreis* Commander a Political Representative. Until further orders he will be responsible for administration. He will advise the *Wehrkreis* Commander on all political matters.

4 The headquarters of C-in-C Home Forces is the executive agency for all matters concerning the exercise of executive power. It will despatch a liaison officer to *Wehrkreis* Commanders for the exchange of information and views.

5 In the exercise of executive power no arbitrary acts or acts of revenge will be tolerated. The people must be made aware of the difference from the arbitrary methods of their former rulers.

Commander-in-Chief Home Forces
No 32160/44 secret
(signed) Fromm
Colonel-General
Graf Stauffenberg

Certifying accuracy: (signed)
v. Mertz, Colonel

MESSAGE NO 4

Most Immediate Radio Message[1]

To: Commander *Wehrkreis* IX
General Schellert, *Kassel*

Radio Message

The *Führer* is alive! In perfect health!

Reichsführer-SS C-in-C Replacement Army. Only his orders valid. Orders from Colonel-General Fromm, Field Marshal von Witzleben and Colonel-General Hoepner not to be executed!

Maintain contact with *Gauleiter* and Senior SS and Police Commander!

Wf. 20/7 1615†
[illegible] Wolf††

Keitel
Field Marshal
Chief OKW

Certifying accuracy†
[illegible]†
Colonel†

Acknowledge receipt!
Sdr.†[2]

---

[1] Typescript with manuscript notes. From Major Wolf's papers.
[2] Initialled by Lieutenant-Colonel Sander.

MESSAGE NO 5

HOKW 75853*
Secret*   Command Message/Rg†[1]
20.VII.44 19–47
Immediate Teleprint   20.7.44

To: *Wehrkreis* XX, XXI, Bohemia and Moravia, Government-General *Wehrmacht*
Commander Denmark.[2]
Broadcast communiqué not correct. The *Führer* is dead. Measures ordered to be
carried out with utmost despatch.

C-in-C Replacement Army
and
C-in-C Home Forces
Staff No 5000/44 secret

return to Staff Chief Army Armaments and C-in-C
Replacement Army   St†[3]

[Four despatch notes, ms,
inserted on stamps;
Times of despatch: 2015, 2020, 2030, 2105.
No time of despatch for Government-General.]

MESSAGE NO 6

Teleprint[4]

Received by Signals Officer†   20/7†   2035†[5.]
Command Message – *Wehrmacht* Sigs Offr 1336   20/7 2020

To: C-in-C South-West   Army Group Centre
Mil. Comdr. Italy   Army Group South Ukraine
C-in-C South-~~West~~‡ East†   Army Group North Ukraine
Army Group North   C-in-C West†

Submit immediately

With immediate effect the *Führer* has appointed *Reichsführer-SS* Himmler as C-in-C
Replacement Army and transferred to him all necessary powers over members of the
Replacement Army.
Only orders from the *Reichsführer-SS* or from me to be accepted.
Any orders from Fromm, Witzleben or Hoeppner invalid.

Chief of OKW – Keitel, Field Marshal

[Five despatch notes with partially illegible entries;
despatch times: 2230, 2238, 2255, 2305, 0050.][6]

---

[1] Initialled by Röhrig.
[2] The message was despatched to other *Wehrkreise* on other machines using other copies. The
copy in *Spiegelbild*, p. 70, was that for *Wehrkreis* XI, XII, XIII, XVII, XVIII, hence the
different ref. no HOKW 75851.
[3] Initialled by Stauffenberg.
[4] On 'In' message pad, text on tape, Ms receipt and transmission entries on top copy and
stamps. This was reception and transmission copy, the Bendlerstrasse being in this case only
a transmitting station. Cf. *Spiegelbild*, p. 75.
[5] Here follow certain entries and signatures, mostly illegible.
[6] Messages to the *Wehrkreise* were certainly not despatched as late as those to Army Groups
which were not under orders of C-in-C Replacement Army.

MESSAGE NO 7

[Teleprint][1]

[29.7.44] 2025, received 2034
To: *Wehrkreis* XXI
Political Representative for *Wehrkreis* XXI is Min. Dir. Colonel Vollert, Prague.
OKH Liaison Officer to *Wehrkreis* XXI is Major Kiessling, Tel: Trebnitz 406,
Silesia.
The above-named are to take up duties forthwith.

Chief of Home Forces Operations Staff
(signed) Hoeppner
Chief Army Armaments and C-in-C Replacement Army/AHA/Staff No 32161/44
secret

MESSAGE NO 8

[Teleprint][2]

[20.7.44] 2100, received 2111
Wehrkreis HQ XXI
I appoint Colonel-General Hoeppner as C-in-C Replacement Army and C-in-C
Home Forces
Certifying accuracy: (signed)   (signed) v. Witzleben
    Olbricht, Gen.   32201/44 secret

MESSAGE NO 9

[Teleprint][3]
20.VII.44 20–26*   HOKW 451902*
                                     Command Message
                                           1934

To: *Wehrkreis* HQ (Roman) 1–13, 17, 18, 20, 21,
Govt. Gen, Bohemia-Moravia[4].

Martial-Law Regulation No 1
I order that throughout the *Reich:*
1 Marches, demonstrations and concourses on streets and squares and assemblies in
enclosed areas are forbidden.
2 Only the *Wehrmacht*, the police when under its orders and other formations entrusted with official military or other guard duties are authorized to carry arms.
Within 24 hours of publication of this order all persons not authorized to carry arms
must report possession of weapons to the relevant police districts or, if these are not
accessible, to local police authorities.
3 It is forbidden to prepare and distribute leaflets.
4 Anyone contravening these instructions will be subject to martial law.

C-in-C Home Forces
(signed) Hoepner, Col-Gen M†

---

[1] Copy received by *Wehrkreis* XXI in files of *Gau* HQ Poznan – BA EAP 105/31. See
Spiegelbild, p. 81, where heading shows priority, origin, number, date and time of receipt in
Bendlerstrasse signals office – Immediate – HOKW 75864, 20.7.44 1949.
[2] Receipt copy of *Wehrkreis* XXI in files of *Gau* HQ Poznan – BA EAP 105/31. See
Spiegelbild, p. 69, with priority, origin, number, date and time of receipt in Bendlerstrasse
signal office – Immediate – HOKW 75866, 20.7.44 2008.
[3] Despatch copies for *Wehrkreis* XIII, XVII, XVIII, XX, XXI, Govt-Gen, Bohemia-Moravia.
According to Army Signals report in *Spiegelbild*, p. 64, this message was only despatched to
Wehrkreis I and X. Text is typed copy with stamps and initials.
[4] Messages for *Wekrkreise* XIII, XVII, XVIII, XX, XXI, Govt-Gen., Bohemia-Moravia are
numbered 1–7 in manuscript; this was presumably the intended order of despatch.

MESSAGE NO 10

Teleprint[1]

HOKW 451937†
Command Message†

21/7† 0021†

1 Army Group South Ukraine
2 Army Group North Ukraine
3 C-in-C South-East
4 Army Group Centre
Attempted *putsch* by irresponsible generals suppressed with bloodshed.
All leaders shot.
Orders from Field Marshal von Witzleben, Colonel-General Hoepner, General Beck and General Olbricht not to be obeyed.
I have resumed command after being temporarily held at gunpoint.

(signed) Fromm, Colonel-General.

MESSAGE NO 11

Teleprint[2]

HOKW 451946*
Command Message†

[21.7]
To: -all-‡ Wehrkreis HQs (Roman) 1–13, 17, 18, 20, 21
    Wehrmacht Commander Denmark, *Wehrkreis* Commander of Govt-Gen. and C-in-C Bohemia-Moravia
Ref: Valkyrie
    Teleprint AHA/Staff 4996/44 of 20.7.44 invalid for all HQs

Reichsführer-SS
(signed) Himmler

[Five despatch notes:
0200 to *Wehrkreis* XIII (Nuremberg),
0210 to *Wehrkreis* XI (Hannover),
0230 to *Wehrkreis* XVII (Vienna),
0230 to *Wehrkreis* XVIII (Salzburg),
0245 to *Wehrkreis* XII (Wiesbaden).]

---

[1] Monitor copy, tape on receipt form with manuscript despatch and address entries. See *Spiegelbild,* p. 76, which reproduces copy for Wehrkreis I–XIII, XVII, XVIII, XX, XXI, Govt-Gen., Bohemia-Moravia.
[2] On 'In' form. Text in typescript with stamps and entries in manuscript.

MESSAGE NO 12

Teleprint[1]

HOKW 453217*

21.VII.44 4* Command Message†

To: *Wehrkreis* (Roman) 1, 2, 3, 4, 5, 6, 7, 8, 9, 10, 11, 12, 13, 18, 20, 21, Bohemia-Moravia, C-in-C Denmark, C-in-C Govt-Gen.

To all according to distribution list and instructions.

Last paragraph of teleprint HOKW 451 937 from Colonel-General Fromm invalid. On orders from the *Führer* I have assumed command of Replacement Army. Only orders from me to be obeyed. Issue of codeword 'Valkyrie' cancelled with immediate effect.

Certifying accuracy: (signed) Himmler

(signed) Jüttner, *SS-Obergruppenführer*
and General of *Waffen-SS*

[Four despatch notes:
0431 to *Wehrkreis* V (Stuttgart),
0435 to *Wehrkreis* VI (Münster),
0448 to *Wehrkreis* VIII (Breslau),
0500 to *Wehrkreis* VII (Munich).]

---

[1] On 'In' form. Text in typescript with manuscript notes of issue.

Appendix 3

Report by Werner Vogel   26 June 1970

Ref: My Experiences on 20.7.1944

At about 11.40 a.m. on 20 July 1944 I walked over from the bunker of the Chief of
OKW to the office block. I found Lieutenant von Haeften in the visitors' waiting room
of this block. The waiting room was opposite the door connecting the bunker and the
office block.

As I went down the corridor I noticed against the left-hand wall just short of the
door of my office an object wrapped in camouflage material. Since this was unusual –
the passage was always empty – I went back to Lieutenant von Haeften and asked
whether it belonged to him. He said that it did and that Colonel Graf Stauffenberg
would need it for his briefing of the *Führer*. Thereupon I went to my office and started
work; while doing so I noticed that our visitor, Lieutenant von Haeften, seemed nervous – he was constantly walking up and down in the waiting room and in front of its
open door.

Just before midday I looked out into the passage again from my office and noticed
that the object mentioned was no longer there but did not like to ask Lieutenant von
Haeften about it again.

Soon afterwards, as far as I remember, the Chief, Field Marshal Keitel, Lieutenant-
Colonel John von Freyend and General Buhle with two other gentlemen came down the
corridor from the office of the Chief of OKW; they went towards the front exit, passing
my office and the waiting room. In this room at the time were Colonel Graf Stauffenberg
and Lieutenant von Haeften; they were whispering and working together on some
object, as I could see as I passed by towards the bunker. The five gentlemen mentioned
above were standing in front of the hut and, as I passed through the connecting door
back into the office block, Lieutenant-Colonel John von Freyend told me to ask the two
gentlemen in the visitors' waiting room to hurry. The door of the waiting room had been
closed again but I asked the two gentlemen (Stauffenberg and von Haeften) to come
along because Field Marshal Keitel was waiting. Both were still busy on the same
object. Colonel Graf Stauffenberg reacted very nervously and abruptly to my request
and said that he was coming at once. At that moment Lieutenant-Colonel John von
Freyend called again from the exit: 'Stauffenberg, you really must come.'

I left the door of the waiting room open and waited at the hut's exit. When Colonel
Graf Stauffenberg reached the exit Lieutenant-Colonel John von Freyend offered to
carry his briefcase which weighed heavily on the three fingers of his left hand. But the
Colonel almost snatched the briefcase away and looked at Lieutenant-Colonel John
von Freyend as if he had been insulted. I admired the energy and pride of Colonel Graf
Stauffenberg who had been very badly wounded in the war.

During this incident Lieutenant von Haeften had left, saying that he was going to
the visitors' hut.

After the gentlemen had left I locked the door of the visitors' room, noticing that there was now nothing unusual there, and then locked the door of the office block. Then I went to our area canteen for lunch.

After lunch, while I was talking to some of the others, there was an explosion, but we saw nothing unusual in this. But soon we heard people shouting 'explosion' or 'bomb' in the briefing hut. I ran back at once to our office block and opened up; Field Marshal Keitel soon arrived with Lieutenant-Colonel John von Freyend. Both were pretty agitated and looked in a bad way. Lieutenant-Colonel John von Freyend had to lie down at once and later, I think, was given an injection.

Field Marshal Keitel, whose uniform was blood-spattered and torn, asked for a fresh shirt and uniform. He washed and later had some of his wounds dressed (I cannot remember this part in detail because I had to run several errands and make several telephone calls at once).

A number of officers soon arrived in Field Marshal Keitel's office and hectic activity began. Our compound was hermetically sealed off by the SS. Sentries patrolled rooms and paths. The details of this, however, elude me.

I later talked over my experiences described above only with the aides — Lieutenant-Colonel John von Freyend and Major von Szymonski (who was absent on duty that day).

I was never questioned by the *Gestapo*.

I remember perfectly well the following incident:

On that day Himmler, the *Reichsführer-SS*, was appointed Commander-in-Chief of the Replacement Army. I typed the order which had been drafted by Field Marshal Keitel. I had to type this order five times because each time I made a serious typing error.

Field Marshal Keitel was standing in the door of my office waiting for me to finish so that he could take it straight to the *Führer* for signature. Unconsciously and without being in the least nervous, however, I made the same error each time. It was an odd occurrence.

[signed]   W. Vogel.

Appendix 4

Stauffenberg's Attendance at Briefings in the Führer's HQ in July 1944.[1]

Colonel Graf von Stauffenberg was present at the following conferences during the period 1–20 July:

Special conference on 6 July 1944 from 1705 to 1800 hours at the 'Berghof', concerning new units,

special conference on 6 July 1944 from 2355 to 0050 hours at the 'Berghof', concerning new units,

morning briefing on 11 July 1944 from 1307 to 1530 hours at the 'Berghof',

during the first part of the morning briefing on 15 July 1944 from 1310 to 1340 hours in 'Wolfschanze',

special conference on 15 July 1944 from 1340 to 1420 hours in 'Wolfschanze' concerning building of fortified positions and organization for front-stabilization,

special conference on 15 July 1944 from 1420 to 1425 hours in 'Wolfschanze' with Colonel-General Fromm,

morning briefing on 20 July 1944 in 'Wolfschanze'.

On 7 June 1944 there was held at the 'Berghof' from 1552 to 1652 hours a special conference with Colonel-General Fromm in which, if memory serves, Colonel Graf von Stauffenberg also participated. Precise determination of this is possible only by examining the minutes in the safe in Berlin.

Further, Colonel Graf von Stauffenberg was seen in the briefing room *before* the start of the morning briefing on 18 July 1944.

Dr Peschel

F.H.Qu., 22 July 1944
Stenographic Service
Dr. Pe/Dt.

---

[1] Original in BA EAP 105/34 (NA microcopy T-84 roll 21).

Appendix 5

Some of the more important Headquarters
(as at July 1944)

HQ Replacement Army (Chef H RüstuBdE)

Commander:	Colonel-General Friedrich Fromm
Aide:	Captain Heinz Bartram
Chief of Staff:	Colonel Claus Schenk Graf von Stauffenberg
Aide:	Lieutenant Werner von Haeften
Group I:	Colonel Rudolf Langhaeuser (until 30 June 1944)
	Lieutenant-Colonel Joachim Sadrozinski
Intelligence	Captain Harald Kriebitzsch
Group II:	Colonel Ernst Günther von Roell
Group III:	Major-General Werner Kennes
War Diary Officer:	Captain Hermann Kaiser

General Army Office, OKH [Allgemeines Heeresamt]

Commander:	General Friedrich Olbricht
Chief of Staff:	Colonel Hellmuth Reinhardt (1940–1943)
	Lieutenant-Colonel Claus Schenk Graf von Stauffenberg (October 1943 – June 1944)
	Colonel Albrecht Ritter Mertz von Quirnheim (June – 20 July 1944)
Operations:	Lieutenant-Colonel Bolko von der Heyde
Head of Ops Group:	Lieutenant-Colonel Karl Pridun
Desk Officer Ops:	Major Fritz Harnack
Supply:	Lieutenant-Colonel Franz Herber
Intelligence:	Colonel Willy Nürnberg
Personnel:	Lieutenant-Colonel Fritz von der Lancken

Wehrkreis III

Commander:	General Joachim von Kortzfleisch
Chief of Staff:	Major-General Günther von Rost (until May 1944)
	Major-General Otto Herfurth (from May 1944)
Ops (acting):	Lieutenant-Colonel Bruno Mitzkus
Intelligence:	Lieutenant-Colonel Martin Sobczyk
Personnel:	Colonel Joachim von Wiese und Kaiserswaldau
Commander *Wehrmacht* Patrol Service:	Lieutenant-Colonel Friedrich Wilhelm Heinz

City Commandant, Berlin

Commander:	Lieutenant-General Paul von Hase
Ops:	Lieutenant-Colonel Hermann Schöne

Ops/Org (Section Head):   Major Adolf-Friedrich Graf von Schack
Ops/Accn (Section head):   Major Wolf Freiherr von Massenbach-Salleschen
Personnel: Lieutenant-Colonel Holm Erttel

Commander-in-Chief West (St Germain)
Commander: Field Marshal Gerd von Rundstedt
    Field Marshal Günther von Kluge (from 2 July 1944)
    Chief of Staff:
    General Günther Blumentritt
Ops: Colonel Bodo Zimmermann
Intelligence: Major Reinhard Brink
Personnel: Colonel Richard Abé
Deputy Chief of Staff: Colonel Eberhard Finckh

Military Commander, France
Commander: General Karl-Heinrich von Stülpnagel
Chief of Staff: Colonel Karl-Richard Kossmann (until 10 May 1944)
    Colonel Hans-Ottfried von Linstow
Ops: Lieutenant-Colonel Hans Schwanbeck
Personnel: Colonel Günther von Scheven
Chief Signals Officer: Lieutenant-General Hans Oberhäusser

Military Administration, France
Head: Dr Elmar Michel – senior civil servant [*Ministerial-direktor*]
Subordinates: Dr Max Horst– civil servant [*Regierungsrat*]
    Friedrich Freiherr von Teuchert – military administrative official [*Kriegsverwaltungsoberrat*]
    Dr Rudolf Thierfelder – military administrative official [*Kriegsverwaltungsrat*]

Commandant of Greater Paris
Commandant: Lieutenant-General Hans Freiherr von Boineburg
Chief of Staff: Colonel Karl von Unger

Army Group B (La Roche-Guyon)
Commander: Field Marshal Erwin Rommel (1 January – 17 July 1944)
    Field Marshal Günther von Kluge
Chief of Staff: Lieutenant-General Hans Speidel
Ops: Colonel Hans-Georg von Tempelhof
Personnel: Colonel Lodegard Freyberg.

Ranks: Approximate Equivalents*

BRITISH ARMY	US ARMY	GERMAN ARMY (to 1945)	SS	GERMAN POLICE	NSDAP
Field Marshal	General of the Army	Generalfeldmarschall	Reichsführer		Reichsleiter Hauptbefehlsleiter
General	General	Generaloberst	Oberstgruppenführer (from 1942 only)	Generaloberst der Polizei	Reichsleiter Hauptbefehlsleiter
Lieutenant-General	Lieutenant-General	General (der Infanterie etc.)	Obergruppenführer	General der Polizei	Gauleiter Oberbefehlsleiter
Major-General	Major-General	Generalleutnant	Gruppenführer	Generalleutnant der Polizei	Gauleiter (or deputy) Befehlsleiter
Brigadier	Brigadier-General	Generalmajor	Brigadeführer	Generalmajor der Polizei	Gauleiter (or deputy) Hauptdienstleiter
Senior-Colonel	Senior-Colonel	Oberst	Oberführer	Oberst der Schutzpolizei or Gendarmerie	Gauleiter (or deputy) Oberdienstleiter
Colonel	Colonel	Oberst	Standartenführer	Reichskriminaldirektor	Gauleiter (or deputy) Oberdienstleiter
Lieutenant-Colonel	Lieutenant-Colonel	Oberstleutnant	Obersturmbannführer	Oberstleutnant der Schupo or Gendarmerie Oberregierungsrat and Kriminalrat	Kreisleiter Dienstleiter or Hauptbereichsleiter
Major	Major	Major	Sturmbannführer	Major der Schutzpolizei or Gendarmerie Regierungsrat and Kriminalrat Kriminaldirektor	a Kreisleiter Oberbereichsleiter or Bereichsleiter Hauptabschnittsleiter b Ortsgruppenleiter Oberabschnittsleiter
Captain.	Captain	Hauptmann or Rittmeister (Cav.)	Hauptsturmführer	Hauptmann der Schutzpolizei or Gendarmerie Kriminalrat	a Ortsgruppenleiter Abschnittsleiter b Zellenleiter Hauptgemeinschaftsleiter or Obergemeinschaftsleiter

*Ranks given in the text and notes are English translations but not necessarily equivalents of German ranks. In cases such as lieutenant, the British style (second lieutenant, lieutenant) was used for the two levels. See Note preceding Index.

BRITISH ARMY	US ARMY	GERMAN ARMY	SS	GERMAN POLICE	NSDAP
Lieutenant	First Lieutenant	Oberleutnant	Obersturmführer	Oberleutnant der Schutzpolizei or Gendarmerie Kriminalkommissar Kriminalinspektor	a Zellenleiter Gemeinschaftsleiter b Blockleiter Haupteinsatzleiter
Second Lieutenant	Second Lieutenant	Leutnant	Untersturmführer	Leutnant der Schutzpolizei or Gend. Kriminalsekretär Kriminaloberassistent	Blockleiter Obereinsatzleiter Einsatzleiter
Regimental Sergeant-Major	Sergeant-Major	Stabsfeldwebel Stabswachtmeister	Sturmscharführer	Meister Kriminalsekreär	Hauptbereitschaftsleiter
Sergeant-Major	Sergeant-Major	Hauptfeldwebel Hauptwachtmeister	Stabsscharführer (primarily a Waffen-SS rank)	Hauptwachtmeister Kriminaloberassistent	Hauptbereitschaftsleiter
Sergeant-Major	Master-Sergeant	Oberfeldwebel Oberwachtmeister	Hauptscharführer	Kompaniehauptwacht- meister Kriminaloberassistent	Oberbereitschaftsleiter
Quartermaster-Sergeant	Technical-Sergeant	Feldwebel Wachtmeister	Oberscharführer	Revieroberwachtmeister Kriminalassistent	Bereitschaftsleiter
Staff Sergeant	Staff Sergeant	Unterfeldwebel	Scharführer	Oberwachtmeister Kriminalassistent	Bereitschaftsleiter
Sergeant	Sergeant	Unteroffizier	Unterscharführer	Wachtmeister Kriminalassistentanwärter	Hauptarbeitsleiter
Corporal	Corporal	Stabsgefreiter Obergefreiter	Rottenführer	Rottwachtmeister	Oberarbeitsleiter
Lance Corporal	Corporal	Gefreiter	Sturmmann		
Senior Private	Private 1st Class	Oberschütze Obergrenadier etc.	Oberschütze	Unterwachtmeister	Arbeitsleiter Oberhelfer
Private	Private	Schütze Grenadier etc.	SS-Mann	Anwärter	Helfer

Abbreviations and Glossary

Abwehr	lit. defence. 'Military Intelligence'. The espionage, counter-espionage and sabotage service of the German Supreme Command (OKW/Amt Ausland/Abwehr).
AHA	Allgemeines Heeresamt – lit. General Army Office. The static organization dealing with personnel, training and equipment of the German Army.
Allgemeine SS	The general body of the SS composed of part-time, full-time and inactive or honorary members, distinct from the Waffen-SS.
Amt Ausland/Abwehr	OKW, Foreign countries division/Intelligence.
BA	Bundesarchiv (Federal Archives), Koblenz.
BA–MA	Bundesarchiv – Militärarchiv (Federal Archives – Military Archives), Freiburg i. Br.
BDC	Berlin Document Centre.
Bezirk	A district, an administrative unit.
Botschaftsrat	lit. Counsellor of Embassy. A rank in the German Foreign Service.
DBFP	Documents on British Foreign Policy, HMSO, London 1947 et seq.
DGFP	Documents on German Foreign Policy, HMSO and Washington 1949 et seq.
Einsatzgruppe	An operational group or task force of the Security Police and SD for special missions in occupied territory.
FBB	Führer-Begleit-Battaillon – the Führer's army escort battalion.
FBI	Federal Bureau of Investigation
FDR Library	Franklin D. Roosevelt Library, Hyde Park, N.Y.
FFA	Führer-Flak-Abteilung – the Führer's anti-aircraft detachment.
FHQ	Führerhauptquartier – the Führer's headquarters in the field.
FLNA	Führer-Luft-Nachrichten-Abteilung – the Führer's air reconnaissance detachment.
FNA	Führer-Nachrichten-Abteilung – the Führer's signal detachment.
FS	Fernschreiben – teleprinter message.
Gau	The main territorial unit of the Nazi Party, also civil defence region. Germany was divided into 42 Gaue.
Gauleiter	The highest-ranking Nazi Party official in a Gau, responsible for all political and economic activity, also

	for mobilization of labour and for civil defence.
Gemeinde	A municipality, community or parish.
Gestapo	Geheime Staatspolizei – secret state (political) police.
HNB	Heeres-Nachrichten-Betriebsleitung – Army Signals Traffic Directorate.
HNV	Heeres-Nachrichten-Verbindungen – Army Communications
HNW	Heeres-Nachrichten-Wesen Army Signals Service
Hochwald	Communications exchange in Himmler's East Prussian HQ, near Grossgarten.
HPA	Heeres-Personal-Amt – Army Personnel Office, responsible for all appointments.
HSSPF	Höherer SS- und Polizeiführer – Senior SS and Police Commander. Himmler's personal representative in each Wehrkreis and liaison officer with the Wehrkreis commander and other senior regional authorities.
IfZ	Institut für Zeitgeschichte – Institute of Contemporary History, Munich.
Kommissar	A senior rank in the government service or the police.
Kreis	An administrative district; the principal sub-division of a Gau.
Kreisleiter	The lowest salaried official of the Nazi Party. Responsible for a Kreis within a Gau.
Kriegsoberverwaltungsrat	A senior officer of Military Administration.
Kriegsverwaltungsrat	An official of Military Administration.
KTB	Kriegstagebuch – war diary.
Kurhaus	Communications exchange in 'Wolfschanze'.
Land	One of the fifteen territorial divisions of republican Germany, each with its independent government. From 1933 the central government controlled the Länder through Reichsstatthalter.
Landeshauptmann	Senior minister in a land (projected in Kreisau Circle plans).
Landrat	The chief authority in the administration of a Kreis; was frequently identical with the Nazi Party Kreisleiter.
Landwehr	A second-line military force roughly equivalent to the British Territorial Army.
Legationsrat	Legation or embassy counsellor in the Foreign Service.
Leibstandarte	'Leibstandarte SS Adolf Hitler' – the SS Bodyguard Regiment.
MFA	Militärgeschichtliches Forschungsamt – Military History Research Office, Freiburg i. Br.
Ministerialdirektor	Head of department in a Ministry. A senior official in the Civil Service roughly equivalent to Assistant Secretary.
Ministerialrat	A senior counsellor, usually head of a section in a ministry. Roughly equivalent to Principal.
NA	National Archives, Washington, D.C.
NSDAP	National-Sozialistische Deutsche Arbeiter Partei – National-Socialist German Workers Party – the official title of the Nazi Party.

NSKK	National-Sozialistisches Kraftfahr-Korps – National-Socialist Motor Corps. One of the para-military formations of the Nazi Party.
Oberpräsident	The senior administrative official in a Prussian province.
Oberregierungsrat	A senior government counsellor in the Higher Civil Service.
Oberstkriegs-gerichtsrat	A senior official or Judge-Advocate of the Military Legal Service.
OKH	Oberkommando des Heeres – the High Command of the German Army.
OKL	Oberkommando der Luftwaffe – High Command of the German Air Force.
OKM	Oberkommando der Kriegsmarine – High Command of the German Navy.
OKW	Oberkommando der Wehrmacht – High Command of the Armed Forces. Hitler's staff as Supreme Commander.
Ordnungspolizei	lit. 'Order Police'. The regular uniformed police.
OSS	Office of Strategic Services. The United States intelligence and sabotage organization formed during the war.
Regierungspräsident	The senior government official in a Bezirk.
Regierungsrat	Government Counsellor. The lowest rank in the Higher Civil Service.
Reich	lit. kingdom, realm. Territory and state of Germany to 1945.
Reichsführer-SS	Himmler's official title as head of the SS.
Reichsleiter	Title of the highest-ranking Nazi Party officials. Most also held ministerial and administrative posts.
Reichstag	Parliament. Shorn of legislative functions under the Hitler regime.
Reichsstatthalter	The Governor of a Land or Gau. Frequently identical with the Gauleiter.
RKPA	Reichskriminalpolizeiamt. Criminal Police headquarters.
RSD	Reichssicherheitsdienst. Hitler's personal criminal-police bodyguards.
RSHA	Reichssicherheitshauptamt. Central Security Department formed in 1939 and combining the Security Police (including Criminal Police and Gestapo) and the SD.
SA	Sturmabteilung – the 'Stormtroopers' or 'brownshirts'. The original para-military force of the Nazi Party.
Schutzpolizei	lit. Protection Police. The regular uniformed municipal or country constabulary.
SD	Sicherheitsdienst – Security Service. The intelligence organization of the SS.
Stahlhelm	The nationalist ex-servicemen's organization – absorbed into the SA in 1933.
SS	Schutzstaffel – lit. protection or guard detachment. The 'elite' of the Nazi Party para-military force and its most powerful branch.
VfZ	Vierteljahrshefte für Zeitgeschichte

Waffen-SS	The fully militarized formations of the SS which put nearly 40 divisions into the field during the war.
Wehrbezirk	Military Area, subordinate to a Wehrkreis – primarily concerned with recruiting.
Wehrkreis	A Military District, Roman numbered. In peacetime it contained the HQ and subordinate formations of an Army Corps carrying the same Roman numeral. When the corps went to war, rear Corps HQ remained and combined its duties with those of the District HQ.
WFSt	Wehrmachtführungsstab – OKW Operations Staff – the strategic section of OKW.
WNV	Wehrmacht-Nachrichten-Verbindungen – Wehrmacht Communications. The branch of the OKW Operations Staff responsible for all signals, radio and communications matters.
WNW	Wehrmacht-Nachrichtenwesen – the Wehrmacht (inter-service) signals service.
Zeppelin	Communications exchange 'Zeppelin' in 'Maybach' HQ (OKH) in Zossen.

Sources and Bibliography

I UNPUBLISHED SOURCES: Archive material*

[Adam, Wilhelm:] 'Colonel-General Wilhelm Adam', typescript, undated [England, pre-1949], Otto John's papers folio 3.

Adam, Wilhelm: 'Eidesstattliche Erklärung Nr. 2: betrifft: Stimmung unter den höheren Generalstabsoffizieren bald nach der "Machtergreifung" ', typescript undated, IfZ ZS 6.

'Aktenvermerk über die Ereignisse am 20./21.7.1944', Abteilung Ic, Wehrkreiskommando Generalgouvernement, typescript, Cracow 21 July 1944, BA – MA RH 53–23/V.34.

Albrecht, Heinz-Günther: 'Die militärischen Vorbereitungen der damaligen Führungsstelle der Widerstandsbewegung im Generalkommando Berlin im Hinblick auf den geplanten Regierungssturz', no place, 1946/47, typed copy June 1966.

Albrecht, [Karl-Friedrich]: 'Auswertung der Aufbauübung der Vermittlung "Zeltstadt" am 1. u. 2.10.43', typescript [Wolfschanze] 2 Oct. 1943, Josef Wolf's papers.

Amt V [RSHA]: 'Betrifft: Selbstmord des Majors Ulrich von Oertzen, Ia der Korps-Abteilung E der 2. Armee, im Dienstgebäude des Wehrkreiskommandos III', typescript, Berlin 22 July 1944, BA R 58/1051.

Anklageschrift see Indictment.

'Appendix "G". Eye Witness Account of One of the Trials of the Principal Conspirators. Information obtained from PW KP/229533 Fw Sonderführer Goetsch-Gyx, Fallschirm AOK (Propaganda Kompanie)', typescript, no place, undated, Otto John's papers folio 5.

Arntz, [Hellmuth]: 'Account of the Twentieth of July Putsch by One of the Minor Conspirators', C.S.D.I.C. (U.K.) S.I.R. 1610, typescript, no place, 11 Apr. 1945.

[Arntz, Hellmuth:] ['Bericht über General Erich Fellgiebel'], typed copy, no place, undated.

Balzer, [Rudolf]: 'Aktennotiz für Chef OKW/WPr persönlich', typed copy, [Berlin] 21 June 1944 [correctly: 21 July 1944], BA NS 6/31.

Bargatzky, Walter: 'Persönliche Erinnerungen an die Aufstandsbewegung des 20. Juli 1944 in Paris', roneoed, Baden-Baden 20 Oct. 1945, 'Hilfswerk 20. Juli 1944' Foundation.

Bartram, Heinz-Ludwig: '20. Juli 1944', typescript, no place [1954], BA H 90–3/4.

Beck, Ludwig: Papers, BA – MA H 08–28.

[Beck, Ludwig:] 'Zur Kriegslage nach Abschluss des polnischen Feldzuges', typescript, no place, undated, BA EAP 21-X-15/2 (now BA – MA N 104/2).

---

* Privately owned documents are included here, except information given to the author; unless otherwise stated the originals or copies are in the author's possession.

[Beck, Ludwig:] 'Das deutsche Friedensangebot vom 6.10.39 und der mögliche weitere Kriegsverlauf', typescript, no place, 10 Oct. 1939, BA EAP 21-X-15/2 (now BA – MA N 104/2).

[Beck, Ludwig:] 'Zwischenpause nach dem Misserfolg des deutschen Friedensangebotes', typescript, no place, 31 Oct. 1939 BA EAP 21–X–15/2 (now BA – MA N 104/2).

[Beck, Ludwig:] 'Eine Wendung im bisherigen Krieg?' typescript, no place, 20 Nov. 1939, BA EAP 21–X–15/2 (now BA – MA N 104/2).

[Beck, Ludwig:] 'Die russische Frage für Deutschland, eine Skizze', typescript, no place [autumn 1939], BA EAP 21–X–15/2 (now BA – MA N 104/2).

[Beck, Ludwig:] 'Betrachtung über die deutsche Lage um die Jahreswende 1939/40' typescript, no place, 2 Jan. 1940, BA EAP 21–X–15/2 (now BA – MA N 104/2).

Beck, Rudolf: 'Beiträge zur Lebensgeschichte und Charakteristik des Generaloberst Ludwig Beck', typescript, no place, undated, Otto John's papers folio 3.

Becker, Hellmut: 'Plaidoyer für Ernst von Weizsäcker', roneoed, Nuremberg Nov. 1948, StA Nuremberg.

Below, Nicolaus von: '032/Case No 0279', typescript, no place, 23 Jan. 1946.

'Bericht Nr. 28 [by Alfred Rosenberg's liaison officer with Hitler on a table talk by Hitler on 6 Sept. 1941]', typescript, Führer's HQ 7 Sept. 1941, BA R 6 o.Nr.

'Bericht der Stiftung "Hilfswerk 20. Juli 1944" über die Verurteilung des ehem. Krim.-Kom. Josef Baumer', roneoed, Kronberg i.T. 1959, 'Hilfswerk 20. Juli 1944' Foundation.

Bernard, [Curt]: ['Bericht'], typed copy, no place, 28 May 1945, IfZ ED 106 Archiv Walter Hammer Vol. 90.

Bertaux, Pierre: [Extracts from diary of 1938].

'Bescheinigung zur Vorlage beim Wirtschaftsamt, ausgestellt von der Geheimen Staatspolizei, Staatspolizeileitstelle für den Landespolizeibezirk Berlin', Berlin [Sept. 1944].

Bethge, [Eberhard]: 'Bericht über die Sonderabteilung der ehem. Geheimen Staatspolizei im Zellengefängnis Moabit, Lehrterstr. 3, zusammengestellt am 14.7.1945', typescript, no place, 14 July 1945, 'Hilfswerk 20. Juli 1944' Foundation.

'Beurteilungen von Gen. Stabs Offizieren bzw. Offizieren die zur Gen. Stabs Ausbildung kommandiert wurden', card file, no place [1944/45], NA microcopy T-78 roll R 52.

Bieler, [Benno]: 'Bericht über die Vorgänge um den 20. Juli 1944 im Wehrkreis XI', manuscript, Dorfmark 1964.

[Blumentritt, Günther:] 'C.S.C.I.C. (U.K.) G.G. Report: General der Infanterie Blumentritt, S.R.G.G.1290 (C)', typescript, no place, 7 June 1945.

[Blumentritt, Günther:] 'C.S.D.I.C.(U.K.) G.G. Report: General der Panzertruppen Eberbach, General der Infanterie Blumentritt, S.R.G.G. 1347', typescript, no place, 19 Aug. 1945.

Blumentritt, [Günther]: 'Stellungnahme zu dem Buch "Offiziere gegen Hitler". Nach einem Erlebnisbericht von Fabian v. Schlabrendorff bearbeitet und herausgegeben von Gero v. S. Gaevernitz 1946 Europa Verlag Zürich', typescript, [England] Nov. 1946, Otto John's papers folio 2.

Blumentritt, Günther: 'Der "20. Juli 1944" ', typescript, England January 1946, NA Record Group 338 MS No B-272.

[Bodenschatz, Karl:] 'S.R.G.G.1219 (C) C.S.D.I.C. (U.K.) G.G. Report', typescript, no place, 15 May 1945.

[Bodenschatz, Karl:] 'The Attempt as seen by eye-witnesses' (Summary of British interrogations), roneoed, no place, undated, Otto John's papers folio 5.

Boehmer, Käthe von: [Information given to 'Hilfswerk 20. Juli 1944' Foundation], typescript, no place, 1 Jan. 1953, 'Hilfswerk 20. Juli 1944' Foundation.

Boineburg-Lengsfeld, Hans Freiherr von: Letter to Dr H. Pigge, 1970.

Bormann, Albert and Schmundt, [Rudolf]: 'Rundschreiben', typescript,

[Wolfschanze] 20 Sept. 1943, BA EAP 105/33.

Bormann, M[artin]: Letter to Reich Treasurer of NSDAP, Munich 17 Jan. 1939, BDC.

Bormann, [Martin]: Teleprint circulars to Gauleiter, despatch copies from Führer's HQ, Wolfschanze 20 July 1944, BA EAP 105/31.

Bormann, M[artin]: Teleprint to Dr Friedrichs in Party Chancellery in Munich, despatch copy from Führer's HQ, [Wolfschanze] 20 Oct. 1944, BA EAP 105/32.

Brandt, Karl: 'Gedenkrede zum Gedächtnis der Toten des 20. Juli 1944 gehalten anlässlich der Feier am 20. Juli 1965 im Hof des früheren Reichskriegsministeriums in der Stauffenberg-Strasse zu Berlin', roneoed, Frankfurt/M. July 1965, 'Hilfswerk 20. Juli 1944' Foundation.

Brühl, [Ferdinand]: 'Niederschrift des Berichts von Major Jacob', manuscript, Bridgend 25 Apr. 1947, Otto John's papers folio 5.

Bruns, Walter: 'Vor, am und nach dem 20. Juli 1944', typescript, no place [between 1945 and 1948], Otto John's papers folio 5.

Buchholz, Heinz: 'Das Attentat auf Adolf Hitler am 20. Juli 1944: Augenzeugenbericht von Regierungsrat Heinz Buchholz, ehemaliges Mitglied des Stenographischen Dienstes im F.H.Qu.', typescript, Berchtesgaden 14 July 1945, University of Pennsylvania Library 46 M-25 Berchtesgaden Interrogations.

Burchardt, Heinz: 'Zugehörigkeit zur Widerstandsbewegung vom 20. Juli 1944', typed copy, Munich 1946.

Burchardt, Heinz: 'Eidesstattliche Erklärung', typescript, Munich 17 March 1947.

Burchardt, Heinz: 'Kurze Darstellung der Ereignisse', typescript, Bonn-Dottendorf 9 Feb. 1966.

[Burckhardt, Peter:] 'Gespräch mit dem früheren schweizerischen Militärattaché in Berlin, Burckhardt, heute Direktor in der Maschinenfabrik Bührle in Zürich-Oerlikon, Juli 1966, geführt von Herrn Peter Dietz', typescript, no place [1966].

Burgdorf, [Wilhelm]: Letter to HQ Wehrkreis IX dated 3 Oct. 1944, no place, typed copy in possession of H. Schwierz,

Conrad, Walter: 'Meine Besprechungen mit Generaloberst Halder über die Beseitigung Hitlers', typescript, no place, undated, BA – MA N 124/28.

Cords, Helmuth: Letter to an anonymous friend, no place, 18 Sept. 1946, 'Hilfswerk 20. Juli 1944' Foundation.

'Daily Digest of World Broadcasts (From Germany and German-occupied territory), Part I', No 1343 [for 21 March 1943], roneoed, [London] 22 March 1943.

'Daily Digest of World Broadcasts, Part I', No 1830 [for 20 July 1944], roneoed, [London] 21 July 1944.

'Deutsche Wochenschau' No 655/1943 (14/1943) BA film archive.

'Deutsches Fernkabelnetz (Maschenkarte), OKW/WFSt/AgWNV/KFA IIc, Stand vom 15. Feb. 1945', no place, 1945, Josef Wolf's papers.

Dietz, Peter: 'Telephonisches Gespräch mit Erich Kretz', typescript, Zurich 27 Feb. 1966.

Dohnanyi, Christine v[on]: 'Aufzeichnungen', typed copy, no place, undated, IfZ ZS 603.

Dollmann, [Eugen]: 'At FHQ After the Attempt: CSDIC/CMF/X 194 Interrogation Report', typescript, no place, 20 July 1945.

Donovan, William J.: 'Office Memorandum to President [Roosevelt]', manuscript, [Washington, D.C. 1 Oct. 1941] FDR Library PSF Safe Germany Box 2.

Donovan, William J.: 'Memorandum for the President [Roosevelt]', Washington, D.C. 20 March 1944, FDR Library PSF Safe File Box 4.

Eckert, [Max]: 'Meldung über Vorkommnisse im Stabe des Gen. Qu. am 21., 22. und 23.7.1944', typescript, [Zossen] 23 July 1944, IfZ ED 95.

Eicken, [Karl] von: Consultation notes concerning Adolf Hitler, typed copy, no place, 23 July 1944, NA ML 125, 125a, 131.

'Eingangsbuch über Häftlinge [des Zellengefängnisses Lehrterstrasse]', manuscript, Berlin 1944–1945, RUSI London Mil. Mss. 479.

'Einstellungsverfügung im Ermittlungsverfahren gegen Ewald Heinrich von Kleist, Georg Sigismund von Oppen und Hans Fritzsche wegen Hoch- und Landesverrats', Oberreichsanwalt beim Volksgerichtshof OJ 41/44 gRs, typed copy, Berlin 12 Dec. 1944, BA EAP 105/30.

[Etscheit, Alfred:] 'Die innere und äussere Lage', typed copy, Berlin 1 Jan. 1940, BA EAP 21–X–15/2 (now BA – MA N 104/2).

[Etzdorf, Hasso von and Kordt, Erich:] 'Das drohende Unheil', typescript, no place, [Oct. 1939], BA EAP 21–X–15/2 (now BA – MA N 104/2).

[Etzdorf, Hasso von:] 'Niederschrift der Unterredung zwischen Herrn Ministerialdirigent Dr v. Etzdorf, Bonn, Auswärtiges Amt, Länderabteilung (Ermekeilstrasse 27, Block E), und Herrn Dr H. Krausnick, im Auftrage des Instituts für Zeitgeschichte München, durchgeführt am 26. September 1953 in Bonn', typed copy, no place, 12 June 1958, IfZ ZS 322.

[Etzdorf, Hasso von] see also Krausnick.

'F-Verbindungen Wolfschanze: Stand vom 21.1.43', diagram, no place [1943], Josef Wolf's papers.

Fahrner, Rudolf: Letter to Professor Walter Baum 25 July 1962, IfZ ZS 1790.

[Falkenhausen, Alexander Freiherr von:] 'Vernehmung von Alexander von Falkenhausen durch Mr Ortmann auf Veranlassung von Mr. Dobbs SS-Section am 6. Nov. 1946 von 13.30–15.30 Uhr', Interrogation No 175, photostat of typescript, [Nuremberg 1946], IfZ ZS 888.

Falkenhausen, Alexander [Freiherr] von: ['Bericht über meine Stellung zur N.S.D.A.P. und ihrem Regime'], typescript, no place, 15 Nov. 1946, NA Record Group 338 MS No B–289.

'Fernsprechverzeichnis des OKH/Gen.St.d.H., Stand vom 1. März 1944', typed excerpt from copy in possession of A. Beichele.

Files on formation of 'Boeselager', Cavalry Regiment, Boeselager family archive, Schloss Kreuzberg/Ahr.

Files of SS anti-aircraft detachment Obersalzberg, NA microcopy T-405 rolls 11, 12.

Files on Stauffenberg family, BA EAP 105/34.

Films of proceedings of People's Court, Nos 3023–1, 3023–2, 3179–1, 3179–3, 3179–4, [Berlin 1944], BA film archive.

Freier, Hedwig, and Wolff, Annemarie: 'Erinnerungen an die Gefängniszeit von Walter Bauer 15.10.44–21.4.45', typescript, no place, Feb. 1971.

[Freytag-Loringhoven, Bernd Freiherr von:] 'Meine Begegnungen mit Wessel Freytag-Loringhoven während des Krieges', typescript, no place, undated, 'Hilfswerk 20. Juli 1944' Foundation.

[Frick, Wilhelm:] Letter to Ministers of Interior of Länder and Governors typed copy, [Berlin] 15 March 1936, BA RG 1010/3183.

Friedrichs, [Helmuth]: Teleprint to Reichsleiter Bormann, despatch copy from Party Chancellery in Munich, 24 Oct. 1944, BA EAP 105/32.

Fritzsche, Hans Karl: ['Bericht an Dr Helmut Pigge'], photostat of typescript, no place [1970].

[Fromm, Friedrich] 'Sterbeurkunde für den ehemaligen Generaloberst Friedrich Fromm, Nr. 853/1945', typed on printed form, signed (illegible), Brandenburg (Havel) 17 Apr. 1946.

'Führerinformation [des Reichsministers der Justiz] 7. Sept. 1942', typescript, [Berlin 7 Sept. 1942], BA R 22/4089.

'Führerinformation [des Reichsministers der Justiz] 1942 Nr. 131', printed, Berlin 14 Oct. 1942, BA R 22/4089.

'Führerinformation 1944 Nr. 181 des Reichsministers der Justiz vom 18. Juli 1944', StA Nuremberg NG 1249.

Gärtner-Strünck, Elisabeth: Letter to Dr H. Krausnick 27 March 1962, IfZ ZS 1811.

Gärtner-Strünck, E[lisabeth]: 'Aktennotiz', typescript, Frankfurt/M. 20 Apr. 1964, 'Hilfswerk 20. Juli 1944', Foundation.

Geheime Staatspolizei: Files of Staatspolizeileitstelle Munich, November 1939, BA RG 1010/3085.

Geheime Staatspolizei: Directive for telephone surveillance for Wilhelm Leuschner, typescript, Berlin 8 June 1938, BA II A 2/38g.

Geheime Staatspolizei (Gestapo) see also Staatspolizei.

Geisberg, [Wilhelm]: 'Meldung', typescript, [Wolfschanze] 23 July 1944, BA EAP 105/34.

[Geissler, Kurt:] 'Befragung [von Kriminaldirektor a.D. Kurt Geissler] über das Bürgerbräuattentat 1939', typescript, no place, 19 Dec. 1960, BA NS 20/65.

Gelpke, Alhard: 'Exposé Nr. 2: Über einige Comités, die während der Hitlerzeit im Dienste des Abendlandes wirkten', typescript, no place, May 1956, Hoover Library Ts Germany G 321.

Georgi, Friedrich: Memoir, manuscript, Bernau 21 July 1944.

Gersdorff, Rudolf-Christoph Freiherr von: Evidence on 16 Apr. 1948 to Military Court No V on Case XII (United States versus Leeb and others), roneoed, Record pp. 2120–2178, StA Nuremberg.

Gersdorff, [Rudolf-Christoph] Fr[ei]h[er]r v[on]: 'Beitrag zur Geschichte des 20. Juli 1944', typescript, Oberursel 1 Jan. 1946.

[Gersdorff, Rudolf-Christoph Freiherr von:] 'Unterhaltung mit General Rudolph v. Gersdorff am 15.1.1953, abends: Gedächtnisprotokoll', typescript, no place, undated, IfZ ZS 47/II.

Gersdorff, R[udolf-] Chr[istoph] [Freiherr von]: Letter to Dr [H.] Krausnick 19 Oct. 1956, typescript, IfZ ZS 47/II.

Gersdorff, R[udolf-] Chr[istoph] Fr[ei]h[er] v[on]: 'Bericht über meine Beteiligung am aktiven Widerstand gegen den Nationalsozialismus', typescript, Munich 1963.

Gersdorff, R[udolf-] Chr[istoph] Fr[ei]h[er]r v[on]: 'Richtigstellung von Behauptungen des Dr Max Domarus, die dieser in seinen Kommentaren zu dem von ihm herausgegebenen Dokumentationswerk "Hitler, Reden und Proklamationen 1932–1945" über den deutschen Widerstand gegen das nat. soz. Regime aufgestellt hat', typescript, Munich 1964.

'Gesamtliste der Generalstabsoffiziere des Heeres (1945)', OKH/HPA Ag P 3, typescript, no place, undated, NA microcopy T-78 roll 51.

[Grenzendörfer, Wilhelm:] 'Notizen von der Schilderung des Generalmajors Remer von den Vorgängen am 20. Juli 1944 in Berlin, gehalten am 24. Juni 1946 in dem englischen Internierungslager 2221/Q in Belgien', typescript, no place, undated, in possession of Dr P. Collmer.

Groppe, [Theodor]: 'Erlebnisse eines alten Soldaten während der Nazi-Zeit 1933–1945', typescript, Hanau 9 Nov. 1945, NA Record Group 338 MS No B-397.

[Groscurth, Helmuth:] 'Tagebuch Verb. Gruppe OKW Ausl. Abw. zu O.K.H. ab 1.9.39–26.9.39', manuscript, BA EAP 21–X–15/1 (now in BA – MA).

[Groscurth, Helmuth:] 'Kriegstagebuch Abt. z.b.V. [des OKA Amt Ausland/Abwehr beim OKH] 27.9.–14.11.39', manuscript, BA EAP 21–X–15/1 (now BA – MA).

[Groscurth, Helmuth:] 'Kriegstagebuch Abt. z.b.V. [des OKW Amt Ausland/Abwehr beim OKH] 15. November 1939 [–1. Feb. 1940]', manuscript, BA EAP 21–X–15/1 (now BA – MA).

Groscurth, [Helmuth]: Letter to Colonel-General von Witzleben, [Zossen] 31 Oct. 1939, BA EAP 21–X–15/2 (now BA – MA N 104/3).

Groscurth, [Helmuth]: Letter to Graf Schwerin von Schwanenfeld, [Zossen] 17 Feb. 1940, BA EAP 21–X–15/2 (now BA – MA N 104/2).

'Grundlagen für die Befehlserteilung bei der Abwehr von Fallschirmjägern', typescript, no place [1943/44], Josef Wolf's papers.

Hagen, Hans W.: 'Grössere und kleinere Fehler beim Bericht: "Remer und der 20.

Juli 1944" von Otto John', typescript, no place, undated, 'Hilfswerk 20. Juli 1944' Foundation.

[Halder, Franz:] 'C.S.D.I.C. (U.K.) G.G. Report: Report on information obtained from Senior Officer PW on 8–13 Aug. 45', G.R.G.G. 344, typescript, no place, 21 Aug. 1945.

[Halder, Franz] see also 'Protokoll . . .'.

'Handliste der Generalstabsoffiziere 1943', OKH/HPA Ag P3, NA microcopy T-78 roll R 57 (also BA – Zentralnachweisstelle).

'Handliste der Generalstabsoffiziere [1944]', OKH/HPA Ag P3, H 8/6a, NA microcopy T-78 roll R 48.

Hammerstein-Equord, Ludwig Freiherr von: Notes for Dr H. Pigge, typescript, no place, 6 Apr. 1970.

Hardenberg-Neuhardenberg, Carl-Hans Graf v[on]: 'Eidesstattliche Erklärung [über Generalmajor von Rost]', typescript, Kempfeld/Hochwald 12 Aug. 1946.

[Harnack, Fritz]: 'Bericht über die Vorgänge des 20.7.44 in der Bendlerstrasse', typescript, Braunschweig 20 July 1948.

[Hase, Alexander von:] 'Zur Sache "Remer" ' (statements to State Prosecutor's office in Oldenburg), typescript, no place [1950], Otto John's papers.

[Hassell, Ulrich von] Correspondence concerning Ulrich von Hassell between RSHA or Personal Staff of Himmler and Foreign Ministry, 6 Nov. 1941–15 Jan. 1942, with annexes, BA NS 19/414.

Haubach, Theodor: Letters, BA Nachlass Alma de l'Aigle.

[Haubach, Theodor:] Notes for his defence before People's Court, manuscript, no place, between 11 Oct. 1944 and 23 Jan. 1945, IfZ ED 106 Archiv Walter Hammer Vol. 48.

[Haushofer, Albrecht:] 'Gibt es noch Möglichkeiten eines deutsch-englischen Friedens?' Typescript, no place, 8 Sept. 1940, BA HC 833.

[Haushofer, Albrecht:] Letter to Rudolf Hess, no place, 19 Sept. 1940, carbon copy of typescript, BA HC 833.

H[aushofer], A[lbrecht]: 'Englische Beziehungen und die Möglichkeit ihres Einsatzes', typescript, Obersalzberg 12 May 1941, BA HC 833.

Heinz, Friedrich Wilhelm: 'Von Wilhelm Canaris zur NKWD', typescript, no place, [ca. 1949], NA microfilm No R 60.67.

Herber, Franz: 'Was ich am 20.7.44 in der Bendlerstrasse erlebte', typescript, no place [ca. 1948], BA H 90–3/4.

Hess, Rudolf: 'Anordnung Nr. 34/36', typed copy, no place, 9 March 1936, BA RG 1010/3183.

Heusinger, Adolf: Interview with Joachim Fest 17 Sept. 1970, magnetic tape, Bavaria Atelier GmbH Munich.

Heyde, Bolko von der: 'Der 20. Juli 1944 im OKH-AHA in der Bendlerstr.', typescript, [Gütersloh 1972].

Heydrich, [Reinhard]: Letter to heads of Gestapo offices, commanders of Security Police and SD (etc.) ref. 'intensified interrogation', carbon copy of typescript, Berlin 6 Oct. 1941, BA NS 19/34.

Heydrich, [Reinhard]: Letter to Foreign Minister von Ribbentrop, carbon copy of typescript with annexes and two additional letters, Berlin 6 Nov. 1941, BA NS 19/414.

Himmler, Heinrich: Telephone diary, manuscript, 21 Aug.–22 Nov. 1943, BA EAP 21–b/1–5.

Himmler, Heinrich: Engagement diary, manuscript, 2 Jan.–16 Dec. 1943, 3 Jan.–31 May 1944, BA EAP 21–b/1–5.

Himmler, Heinrich: Notes on conferences with Hitler and others, manuscript, May 1934–Dec. 1944, BA NS 19/275 and NS 19/331.

Himmler, Heinrich: Letter to Göring, 29 July 1942, BA EAP 104/3.

Hitzfeld, Otto: Letter to Gert Buchheit, carbon copy of typescript, 5 July 1966, IfZ ZS

1858.

Hitzfeld, Otto: Letter to Institut für Zeitgeschichte, Munich, typescript, 25 Sept. 1966, IfZ ZS 1858.

Hitzfeld, Otto: Letter to Wolfgang Müller dated 18 Oct. 1966, typed copy, IfZ ZS 1858.

[Hofacker, Christa von:] 'Das schwere Jahr 1944/45', typed copy, Krottenmühl 1947.

[Hofacker, Christa von:] 'Auszug aus Aufzeichnungen 1944/45 von Christa v. Hofacker, geb. 1931, die mit anderen Kindern nach dem 20. Juli 1944 in Bad Sachsa i.Harz interniert war', roneoed, Kronberg i.T. 1958.

Hoffmann, Heinrich: Photograph Archive, NA.

Hopf, [Werner]: Teleprint to Reichsleiter Bormann ref. trial before People's Court on 21 Dec. 1944 of Bolz, Pünder, Hermes, Kempner, Schlabrendorff and Staehle, receipt copy from Führer's HQ, 21 Dec. 1944, BA EAP 105/30.

Hopf, [Werner]: Teleprint to Reichsleiter Bormann ref. trial before People's Court on 18 Jan. 1945 of Klimpel and Palombini, typed copy, Berlin 18 Jan. 1945, BA EAP 105/31.

Hopf, [Werner]: Teleprint to Reichsleiter Bormann ref. trial before People's Court on 18 Jan. 1945 of H. Kaiser, Thoma, Lüdemann, Lösner, Schatter, Ulrich, Lehmann, Landwehr and Lilje, receipt copy from Führer's HQ 18 Jan. 1945, BA EAP 105/31.

Hopf, [Werner]: 'Vorlage an Herrn Reichsleiter Bormann. Betrifft: Prozess um den Verrat vom 20.7.1944 [gegen Lt. Lindemann am 22. Jan. 1945]', typescript, Berlin 22 Jan. 1945, BA EAP 105/31.

Hopf, [Werner]: 'Vorlage an Herrn Reichsleiter Bormann. Betrifft: Prozess um den Verrat vom 20.7.1944 [gegen Lüninck, Nieden, Maschke, Kossmann, Richter, Lenz, Zitzewitz, Noske, Korsch]', typescript, Berlin 19 Jan. 1945, BA EAP 105/31.

Hopf, [Werner]: Vorlage an Herrn Reichsleiter Bormann. Betrifft: Prozess um den Verrat am 20.7.1944 [gegen Fromm am 7. März 1945]', typescript, [Berlin 7 March 1945], BA EAP 105/30.

Huppenkothen, [Walter]: 'Der 20. Juli 1944', typed copy, no place [1953], IfZ ZS 249/II.

[Huppenkothen, Walter:] 'Aussage Huppenkothen: Personelle Zusammensetzung und Aufgabenverteilung der Sonderkommission 20. Juli 1944', typed copy from investigation files of Public Prosecutor, Land Court Munich I, photostated for IfZ 24 March 1953, IfZ ZS 249/III.

Indictment of Head Reich Prosecutor, People's Court, of 17 Sept. 1943 against Reinhold Mewes, typescript, Berlin 17 Sept. 1943, BDC.

Indictment of Head Reich Prosecutor Lautz of 20 Dec. 1944 against Dr Klaus Bonhoeffer, Dr Rüdiger Schleicher, Dr Hans John, Friedrich Justus Perels and Dr Hans Kloss, typed copy, 'Hilfswerk 20. Juli 1944' Foundation.

Jakob, Friedrich see Brühl.

'Jahresbeurteilungen 1945: Chefs der Gen. St. und Ia's der Generalkommandos, sowie Chefs d.Gen.St.Korück 583 u. 584[1944/45]', NA T-78 roll R 52.

Jesek, [Werner]: 'Schaltschacht Süd Wolfschanze', blue print, [Wolfschanze] 10 Nov. 1942, Josef Wolf's papers.

Jesek, [Werner]: 'Lage der Kabelschächte Wolfschanze', blue print, [Wolfschanze] 11 Nov. 1942, Josef Wolf's papers.

Jessen, Sydney: 'Aufzeichnung', typed copy, no place, 1946, 'Hilfswerk 20. Juli 1944' Foundation.

Jessen, Sydney: Letter to Professor Walter Baum of 20 Sept. 1957, IfZ ZS 1484.

Jodl, Alfred: Pocket diary for 1944 with manuscript entries, NA microcopy T-84 roll R 149.

[Jodl, Alfred:] 'Der 20. Juli im Führerhauptquartier', typescript, no place [1946], in possession of Frau Jodl.

John, Otto: 'Bericht. Betrifft: Spanien/Portugal', typed copy, no place, Feb./March 1944, Dr Walter Bauer's papers.

John, Otto: 'Bericht [aus Madrid für Oberst Hansen]', typed copy, no place, March 1944, Dr Walter Bauer's papers.

John, Otto: 'Remer und der 20. Juli 1944', typescript, no place, undated, BA H 91–1/2.

John, Otto: 'Der 20. Juli 1944', typescript, London, undated, Otto John's papers.

John, Otto: 'An Eye Witness's Account of the 20th July 1944 Plot against Hitler that Failed', typescript, [London] 1946, Otto John's papers.

John, Otto A.W.: 'Some Facts and Aspects of the Plot against Hitler', typescript, London 1948, Otto John's papers.

John, Otto: Letter to Dr Heinrich von zur Mühlen dated 11 June 1948, Otto John's papers folio 4.

Judgement of Grand Criminal Chamber of Land Court in Siegen on Regierungsrat Dr Karl Neuhaus 15 Dec. 1953, roneoed copy, no place, undated, 'Hilfswerk 20. Juli 1944' Foundation.

Judgement of People's Court 2nd Chamber on Reinhold Mewes 2 Nov. 1943, typescript, ref. no 9J70/42g 2H157/43, BDC.

Judgement of People's Court 1st Chamber on Thüngen 5 Oct. 1944, typed copy, ref. no. 1 L 348/44 OJ 6/44 gRs, [Berlin 5 Oct. 1944], BA EAP 105/30.

Judgement of People's Court 1st Chamber on Bolz and Pünder 21 Dec. 1944, typed copy, ref. no 1L 460/44 OJ 47 and 1 L 486/44 OJ 48/44 g Rs, [Berlin 21 Dec. 1944], BA EAP 105/30.

Judgement of People's Court 1st Chamber on Fischer and Frank 12 Jan. 1945, typed copy, ref. no 1 L 18/45 OJ 42/44 g Rs, [Berlin 12 Jan. 1945], BA EAP 105/31.

Judgement of People's Court 1st Chamber on Hahn, Menge and Stöhr 28 Feb. 1945, typed copy, ref. no 1 L 48/45 OJ 55/44 g Rs, [Berlin 28 Feb. 1945], BA EAP 105/30.

Judgement of People's Court 1st Chamber on Lüdemann 19 Jan. 1945, typed copy, ref. no 1 L 496/44 OJ 50/44 g Rs, [Berlin 19 Jan. 1945], BA EAP 105/30.

Judgement of People's Court 1st Chamber on H. Kaiser and Thoma 17 Jan. 1945, typed copy, ref. no 1 L 454/44 OJ 7/44 g Rs, [Berlin 17 Jan. 1945], BA EAP 105/30.

Judgement of People's Court 1st Chamber on Nebe 2 March 1945, typed copy, ref. no 1 L 54/45 OJ 10/45, [Berlin 2 March 1945], BA EAP 105/30.

Judgement of People's Court 1st Chamber on B. Klamroth, H.–G. Klamroth, Hayessen, Helldorf, Trott zu Solz and H. B. von Haeften 15 Aug. 1944, typed copy, ref. no 1 L 292/44 OJ 3/44 gRs, [Berlin 15 Aug. 1944] NA microcopy T-120 roll 1038.

Judgement of People's Court 1st Chamber on Nieden, Maschke and Kossmann 19 Jan. 1945, typed copy, ref. no 1 L 468/44 OJ 40/44 g Rs, [Berlin 19 Jan. 1945] BA EAP 105/30.

Judgement of People's Court 1st Chamber on Popitz and Langbehn 3 Oct. 1944, typed copy, ref. no 1 L 349–44 OJ 26/44 g Rs, [Berlin 3 Oct. 1944], 'Hilfswerk 20. Juli 1944' Foundation.

Judgement of People's Court 1st Chamber on Richter, Lenz and Korsch 19 Jan. 1945, typed copy, ref. no 1 L 510/44 OJ 53/44 g, [Berlin 19 Jan. 1945], BA EAP 105/30.

Judgement of People's Court 1st Chamber on Röchling and G. Freiherr von Falkenhausen 12 Jan. 1945, typed copy, ref. no 1 L 465/44 OJ 42/44 g Rs, [Berlin 12 Jan. 1945], BA EAP 105/31.

Kaiser, Hermann: Diary January–August 1943 in Ludwig Kaiser: 'Ein Beitrag zur Geschichte der Staatsumwälzung vom 20. Juli 1944 (Goerdeler-Bewegung), Teilbericht', typescript, no place, undated, NA Record Group 338 MS no B-285.

[Kaiser, Hermann:] Diary excerpts, see Judgement . . . on H. Kaiser.

Kaiser, Ludwig: 'Was wissen wir vom 20. Juli?' typescript, Kassel 1964, 'Hilfswerk 20. Juli 1944' Foundation.

Kaltenbrunner, Ernst: Letter to Head of Party Chancellery Reichsleiter Martin Bormann dated 25 Oct. 1944, BA EAP 105/34.

Kaltenbrunner, [Ernst]: Letter to Finance Minister Graf Schwerin von Krosigk, no place, Feb. 1945, BA EAP 173–e–05.

Kanitz, Rainer Graf von: Letter to Frau Elisabeth Wagner dated 23 March 1964.

[Kaufmann, Karl:] 'Der 20. Juli 1944 in Hamburg', typescript, [Bethel 1946].

Keitel, [Wilhelm]: Letter to Major-General Oster dated 16 Dec. 1943, carbon copy of typescript, BA – MA OKW 149.

Keitel, [Wilhelm]: 'Blitz-Funkspruch an den Befehlshaber im Wehrkreis IX, Gen.d.Inf. Schellert, Kassel', typescript, [Wolfschanze] 20 July [1944], Josef Wolf's papers.

Kessel, Albrecht von: 'Verborgene Saat: Das "Andere" Deutschland', typescript, Vatican City 1944/45, in possession of Gräfin Schwerin von Schwanenfeld.

Kienitz, Werner: 'Der Wehrkreis II vor dem Zusammenbruch des Reiches: Erlebnisse und Betrachtungen', typescript, Hamburg May 1953, BA Ost-Dok. 8 Po 22.

Kienitz, [Werner]: 'Bemerkungen zu den Bemerkungen des Herrn Oberst Staudinger über meine Ausarbeitung "Der Wehrkreis II vor dem Zusammenbruch des Reiches" ', typescript, Hamburg March 1954, BA Ost-Dok. 8 Po 22.

Kienitz, Werner: Letter to Colonel Staudinger dated 11 Jan. 1954.

Kiessel, Georg: 'Das Attentat des 20. Juli 1944 und seine Hintergründe', typescript, Sandbostel 6 Aug. 1946, signed.

[Kleist, Ewald Heinrich von] see 'Einstellungsverfügung . . .'; 'Vorlage . . .'.

[Kopkow-Cordes, Horst:] 'Kopkow's Account of the Plot of 20 Jul. 44', typescript, no place, 9 Apr. 1946.

Kordt, Erich see Etzdorf.

[Krausnick, Helmuth:] Note on contents of a fragment of Groscurth's diary of 14 Feb. 1940 read to him by Dr Hasso von Etzdorf, typescript, Bonn 26 Sept. 1953, IfZ ZS 322.

['Kriegstagebuch des Oberbefehlshabers West'] 1944, typescript, BA – MA H 11–10/39A.

'Kriegstagebuch Nr. 1, Band Dezember 1941, des Oberkommandos der Heeresgruppe Mitte, geführt von Hauptmann d.R.z.V. Petersen', Annex to p. 943, typescript, no place, 9 Dec. 1941, IfZ.

'Kriegstagebuch Nr. 1 [der Armee-Abt. A] 11. Sept. 1939–10 Okt. 1939' NA microcopy T-132 roll 1612.

'Kriegstagebuch Nr. 1: Führer-Hauptquartier 23. August 1939–9. Okt. 1939', NA microcopy T-77 roll 858.

'Kriegstagebuch Nr. 3: Führer-Hauptquartier 15. Feb, 1940–31. Juli 1940', NA microcopy T-78 roll 351.

'Kriegstagebuch Nr. 4: Führer-Hauptquartier 1. Aug. 1940–31. Dez. 1940', NA microcopy T-78 roll 351.

'Kriegstagebuch Nr. 6: Führer-Hauptquartier 1. Mai 1941–15. Juli 1942', NA microcopy T-78 roll 351.

'K.T.B. 1.1.41–30.6.41 [des] H.Gru.Kdo.D Ia', NA microcopy T-311 roll 12.

'K.T.B. (Text) 1.–31.7.44 der HGr D', NA microcopy T-311 roll 16.

'K.T.B., Tagesmeldungen 16.5.1944–31.12.1944, Befehlshaber im Heeresgebiet Generalgouvernement/Ia', NA microcopy T-501 roll 222.

Lahousen, [Erwin]: 'Tagebuch (OKW–Abwehr Aug. 1939–[3 Aug. 1943]', NA OKW 2280.

[Lahousen, Erwin:] 'Sidelights on the Development of the '20 July' in the Foreign Countries/Intelligence Service (Amt Ausland/Abwehr) for the Period of Time from the end of 1939 to the Middle of 1943', typescript, no place [ca 1945], NA Record Group 238.

Lahousen, Erwin: 'Zur Vorgeschichte des Anschlages vom 20. Juli 1944', carbon copy of typescript, Munich 1953, IfZ ZS 652.

Lanz, Hubert: 'Ein Attentatsplan auf Hitler im Februar 1943', typescript, Munich 1965.

781

Sources and Bibliography

[Lautz, Ernst:] 'Erklärung unter Eid', typescript, Nuremberg 17 June 1948, StA Nuremberg NG 5405.
[Leithold, Wilhelm:] 'Vernehmung, Polizei-Inspektion Wilmersdorf Abt. K/E/O', typescript, Berlin-Wilmersdorf 16 July 1945.
'Leitungsskizze [der Kabel zwischen Berlin und Wolfschanze]: Stand vom 9.8.1943', blue print, [Wolfschanze 1943], Josef Wolf's papers.
Lerche, Anni: Letter to Dr Hans Bernd Gisevius dated 30 June 1946, intercepted and translated by British censorship office IRS 3 D.C.S., typescript, no place, 17 July 1946.
[Liedig, Franz Maria:] 'Die Bedeutung des russisch-finnischen Zusammenstosses für die gegenwärtige Lage Deutschlands', carbon copy of typescript, no place, [December 1939], BA EAP 21–x–15/2 (now BA – MA N 104/2).
[Liedig, Franz Maria:] 'Special Interrogation Report (CSIR) No 6: Events of 20 July 44', typescript, no place [1945], Hoover Library Ts Germany USA 7 F 697.
Linge, Heinz: 'Record of Hitler's Activities 11 August 1943–30 December 1943', transcribed by Gerhard L. Weinberg, typescript, no place, 1952, NA Record Group 242 Misc. Box 13.
'Liste der besonderen Massnahmen gegen die Bekennende Kirche (Stand vom Dezember 1939)', carbon copy of typescript, no place, undated, BA EAP 21–X–15/1 (now BA – MA N 104/3).
'Liste der SS-Obergruppenführer bis SS-Standartenführer des Reichssicherheitshauptamtes, die einen Offiziersrang in der Polizei innehaben', after June 1940, EAP 173–b–10–05/43, NA microcopy T-175 roll 241.
Lists of General Staff officers arrested, released and sentenced, 1944–1945, OKH/HPA Ag P3, typescript, no place, undated, BA EAP 105/2.
Lists see also 'Beurteilungen . . .', 'Gesamtliste . . .', 'Handliste . . .'.
Litzenberg, Willy: 'Der 20. Juli 1944', typescript, Nuremberg 4 June 1946.
Lochner, Louis P.: Letter to Mr Lauchlin Currie dated 19 June 1942, FDR Library O.F. 198–a.
[Lochner, Louis P.:] 'Testimony of Mr Louis P. Lochner, taken at Berlin, Germany, on 25 July 1945, by Colonel John H. Amen, IGD', typescript, Berlin 25 July 1945, NA Record Group 238.
Loehning, Paul W.: 'Eidesstattliche Erklärung', typescript, Neu-Ulm 26 Aug. 1946, in possession of Graf von Strachwitz.
Lorenzen, [Sievert]: Teleprint to Reichsleiter Bormann ref. People's Court trial of Moltke, Delp, Reisert, Sperr and Fugger von Glött on 9 Jan. 1945, receipt copy from Führer's HQ [Wolfschanze] 9 Jan. 1945, BA EAP 105/31.
Lorenzen, [Sievert]: Teleprint to Reichsleiter Bormann ref. People's Court trial of Moltke, Gerstenmaier, Delp, Reisert, Sperr and Fugger von Glött on 10 Jan. 1945, receipt copy from Führer's HQ, [Wolfschanze] 10 Jan. 1945, BA EAP 105/31.
Lorenzen, [Sievert]: Teleprint to Reichsleiter Bormann ref. People's Court trial of Frank, Fischer, Röchling and G. Freiherr von Falkenhausen on 12 Jan. 1945, receipt copy from Führer's HQ, [Wolfschanze] 12 Jan. 1945, BA EAP 105/31.
Lorenzen, [Sievert]: Teleprint to Reichsleiter Bormann ref. sentencing by People's Court of Delp, Reisert, Sperr, Fugger von Glött, Moltke, Gerstenmaier, Hermes and Kempner on 12 Jan. 1945, receipt copy from Führer's HQ, [Wolfschanze] 12 Jan. 1945, BA EAP 105/31.
Lorenzen, [Sievert]: Teleprint to Reichsleiter Bormann ref. People's Court trial of Schwartz, Schwamb, Hermann and Timm on 13 Jan. 1945, receipt copy from Führer's HQ [Wolfschanze] 13 Jan. 1945, BA EAP 105/31.
Lorenzen, [Sievert]: Teleprint to Reichsleiter Bormann ref. People's Court trial of Haubach, Gross and Steltzer on 15 Jan. 1945, receipt copy from Führer's HQ, [Wolfschanze] 15 Jan. 1945, BA EAP 105/31.
Lorenzen, [Sievert]: 'Vorlage an Herrn Reichsleiter Bormann. Betrifft: Volksgerichtshofprozesse 20.7. [hier: gegen Nebe am 2. März 1945]', typed copy,

Berlin 2 March 1945, BA EAP 105/30.

Lorenzen, [Sievert]: 'Vorlage an Herrn Reichsleiter Bormann. Betrifft: Volksgerichtshofprozesse 20. Juli [hier: gegen Hahn, Menge and Stöhr am 27. Feb. 1945]', typescript, Berlin 7 March 1945, BA EAP 105/30.

Magee, Warren E. and Becker, Hellmut: 'Gesuch um Abänderung des am 14. April 1949 vom Amerikanischen Militärgericht Nr. IV im Fall 11 verkündeten Urteils gegen Ernst von Weizsäcker und sofortige Haftentlassung', roneoed, Nuremberg 28 Apr. 1949, StA Nuremberg.

Manstein, [Erich] von: 'Persönliche Notizen', typescript, Bridgend 20 May 1947, Otto John's papers folio 3.

Manstein, [Erich] v[on]: 'Richtigstellung zur Darstellung der Haltung des Feldmarschalls v. Manstein im Buch "Offiziere gegen Hitler" ', typescript, no place, undated, Otto John's papers folio 4.

Mertens, Emil: 'Tagebuch', manuscript, no place, 1944/45, IfZ ED 106 Archiv Walter Hammer Vol. 105.

Mertz von Quirnheim, Hilde: Diaries, manuscript, 1944–1945.

[Mertz von Quirnheim, Hilde:] 'Albrecht Ritter Mertz von Quirnheim, Oberst i.G.', typescript, no place, undated.

Michel, Elmar: 'Pariser Erinnerungen', typescript, no place, undated, IfZ Archiv Nr. 860/53.

Mildebrath, Werner: '20. Juli 1944 in Berlin', typescript, Hannover [1971].

'Militärischer Bericht Nr. 1217' (from Swiss intelligence service Hans Hausamann), [Berlin] 16 July 1944, typed copy in possession of P. Dietz.

'Minutenprogramm. Betr.: Führerbesuch beim Heer. 19. und. 20.8.38', typescript, Stettin 15 Aug. 1938, BA – MA WK XIII/240.

'Minutenprogramm für den Heldengedenktag in Berlin (10.3.1940)', typed copy, [Berlin 1940], BA NS 10/126.

'Minutenprogramm für den Gedenktag zu Ehren der Gefallenen im Zeughaus zu Berlin (16.3.1941)', typescript, Berlin 12 March 1941, BA – MA W 01–6/321.

Mitzkus, [Bruno]: 'Bericht über die Ereignisse im stellv. Generalkommando III. A.K. am 20. Juli 1944', typescript, no place, 9 August 1945, 'Hilfswerk 20. Juli 1944' Foundation.

Mitzkus, Bruno: 'Um den 20. Juli und das Ende im Wehrkreiskommando III, Berlin', typescript, Bad Homburg v.d.H. Apr. 1947, 'Hilfswerk 20. Juli 1944' Foundation.

'Mordregister', film of file card index on judicial executions, BA EC 941 N.

Morgenthau Jr, Henry: 'Diary', 1933–45, 864 Vols. FDR Library. Morgenthau Jr,

Morgenthau Jr, Henry: Presidential Diaries, 1938–45, 8 Vols., FDR Library.

Mühlen, Heinrich von zur: Letter to Otto John dated 28 May 1948, Otto John's papers folio 4.

Müller: Letter to SS-Sturmbannführer Sanders of RSHA ref. Remer dated 20 Oct. 1944, BA EAP 105/32.

Müller: 'Vermerk für Herrn Reichsleiter Bormann. Betreff: Oberst Remer', [Wolfschanze] 6 Nov. 1944, BA EAP 105/32.

Müller, Gotthold: 'Meine Beziehungen zum Grafen Fritz von der Schulenburg', carbon copy of typescript, Stuttgart 1961.

Müller, [Heinrich]: Teleprint to SS-Oberführer Hans Rattenhuber and Reichsführer SS and Chief of German Police Heinrich Himmler, typescript, Berlin 7 May 1942, BA NS 19/421.

Müller, [Heinrich]: Letter to all commanders of Security Police and SD (etc.) ref. 'intensified interrogation', carbon copy of typescript, Berlin 12 June 1942, BA NS 19/34.

Müller, [Heinrich]: Teleprint to Himmler dated 22 Dec. 1942, typed copy, BA NS 19/416.

[Müller, Josef:] Report on discussions in the Vatican 6–12 Nov. 1939, typescript, no place, 1939, BA EAP 21–X–15/2 (now in BA – MA N 104/2).

Müller, Max: Letter to 'Hilfswerk 20. Juli 1944' Foundation dated 31 Oct. 1967, with attached sketch of airfield near Rastenburg.

Müller, Ruth: Letter to Ricarda Huch dated 4 Apr. 1947.

Müller, Wolfgang: 'Erich Fellgiebel', typed copy, no place, undated.

Müller, Wolfgang: Letter to Otto Hitzfeld dated 15 Oct. 1966, typed copy, IfZ ZS 1858.

[Oertzen, Ulrich von] see Amt V; 'Selbstmord . . .'

Office of Strategic Services: 'Research and Analysis Branch Summaries', 1941–1946, index file and summaries, NA Record Group 226.

Personal files of 'Hilfswerk 20. Juli 1944' Foundation,

Peschel, [Kurt]: Note, typescript, signed, [Wolfschanze] 22 July 1944, BA EAP 105/34 (NA micrcopy T-84 roll 21).

Peters (Kreisleiter and Landrat of Rendsburg]: 'Bericht über den Verlauf des 20. Juli 1944 im Kreis Rendsburg', typescript, Rendsburg 21 July 1944, BA and BDC files of Gauleiter's office of Schleswig-Holstein (Kiel).

Pfuhlstein, Alexander von: 'Meine Tätigkeit als Mitglied der Berliner Verschwörerzentrale der deutschen Widerstandsbewegung vom 1. Oktober 1936–20. Juli 1944', roneoed, Kreuzwertheim/M. May 1946.

Pfuhlstein, Alexander von: '12 Abhandlungen über persönliche Erlebnisse', typescript, Kreuzwertheim/M. 1946, IfZ ZS 592.

Pieper, [Heinz]: 'Erziehungs- und Ausbildungs-Richtlinien für das Führer-Grenadier-Bataillon., roneoed, Führer's HQ 10 July 1944, Josef Wolf's papers.

Plassmann, Clemens: Letter to Frau Annemarie Koch dated 10 March 1947, typescript, 'Hilfswerk 20. Juli 1944' Foundation Persönliche Berichte I.

Posting card index file of OKH/HPA Ag P 3, NA microcopy T-78 roll R 55.

Pridun, Karl: 'Vermerk. Betrifft: 20. Juli 1944, Stellungnahme', typescript, Bregenz 30 Oct. 1953, IfZ ZS 1769.

'Protokoll aus der Verhandlung Halder [vor der] Spruchkammer X München [15.–21. Sept. 1948]', roneoed, [Munich 1948], BA – MA H 92–1/3.

Public Prosecutor, Leipzig: Letter to Reich Minister of Justice, Berlin, dated 1 June 1933 (with attachments), BA R 43 II/1519.

[Puttkamer, Karl-Jesko von:] 'Niederschrift zur Unterredung [von Dr Heinrich Uhlig] mit Konteradm.a.D.v.Puttkamer am 21.3.53', typescript, Cologne 21 March 1953, IfZ ZS 285.

Rantzau, Ehrengard Gräfin [von]: 'Erinnerungen an die Vorbereitungen zum 20. Juli 1944', typescript, no place, undated, 'Hilfswerk 20. Juli 1944' Foundation.

Reinecke, Hermann: 'Mein Erlebnis im Zusammenhang mit den Vorgängen des 20. Juli 1944', typescript, Hamburg 1964.

Remer, [Otto Ernst]: Letter to Army Personnel Office dated 8 Aug. 1944 ref. accelerated promotion for Lieutenant Schlee, BA – Zentralnachweisstelle PA 48231.

Remer, Otto: 'The 20 Jul. 44 Plot', interview, typescript, PW Camp No 26 15 Aug. 1945, NA Record Group 338 ETHINT 63.

[Remer, Otto Ernst:] Evidence to Public Prosecutor, Oldenburg, on 28 Oct. 1949, ref. no 9 Js 164–49, photostat, Otto John's papers folio 5.

Reproductions of photographs (remnants of detonator and explosive used on 20 July 1944, package of explosive discovered, pictures of damage), NA Record Group 242, EAP 105/14.

Richter, Bernt: 'In der Götzendämmerung: Querverbindungen und Holzwege der Anti-Hitler-Opposition zu Himmlers SS', broadcast by Süddeutscher Rundfunk Stuttgart on 18 July 1972, typescript, no place, undated.

Rieger, Franz Xaver: 'Schilderung des Aufgriffs des Georg Elser, Täter des Münchener Attentats vom 8. November 1939', typescript, Constance 15 Dec. 1939, BA – MA W 01–6/301 (OKW 788).

[Rittmann, Kurt:] 'The Nature of An Insurrection: Extract from Interim Report No.

6, 27 Aug. 1945', typescript, no place [1945], Otto John's papers folio 5.

Rittmann, Kurt: 'Erlebnisbericht über die Ereignisse am 20.07.44 im OKH in der Bendlerstrasse in Berlin', typescript, Munich 7 Feb. 1969.

Rode, Werner: Letter to Dr H. Pigge dated 24 July 1971, typescript.

Roell, [Ernst Günter] von: 'Bericht über die Ereignisse des Nachm. und Abends des 20.7.1944', carbon copy of typescript, Berlin 21 July 1944, BA H 90–3/2.

Rommel, Manfred: 'Erklärung', typed copy, Riedlingen 27 Apr. 1945.

[Rosenhagen, Werner:] Report on death of Colonel-General Freiherr von Fritsch on 26 Sept. 1939 in letter by Lt.-Col. Dr Hesse in OKW/W.Pr. IIe to OKW/W.Pr. dated 27 Sept. 1939, typed copy, BA EAP 21–X–15/1 (now in BA – MA N 104/3.

'Rundschreiben Nr. 43/44' of Gau head office Franken, staff office, typescript, Nuremberg 16 Aug. 1944, BA Sammlung Schumacher 242.

[Schaub, Julius:] 'Vernehmung des Julius Schaub am 12.3.1947 von 15.30–16.00 durch Dr. Kempner', typescript, [Nuremberg 1947], IfZ ZS 137.

Scheffler [?] (of office 'General of Artillery'): 'Bericht über die Angelegenheit Gen.d.Art. Lindemann', typescript, [Berlin 26 July 1944], NA microcopy T-84 roll 269.

[Schellenberg, Walter:] 'Testimony of Walter Schellenberg taken at Nurnberg, Germany on 13 November 1945, 1445–1710, by Lt. Col. Smith W. Brookhart, Jr. IGD, OUSCC. Also present: George A. Sakheim, interpreter: S/Sgt. William A. Weigel, Reporter', typescript, [Nuremberg 1945], NA Record Group 238 Box 6 (also StA Nuremberg NG 4718).

Schellenberg, [Walter]: Evidence, manuscript excerpts by H. R. Trevor-Roper from interrogation report, no place, 1946.

Schmidt, Friedrich: Letter to President of Denazification Court in Camp Hammelburg dated 21 Apr. 1947, carbon copy of typescript, in possession of F. Schmidt.

Schmundt, [Rudolf]: 'Befehl zur Verteidigung des Führerhauptquartiers Wolfsschanze' [Wolfschanze] 18 July 1944, typed copy, Josef Wolf's papers.

[Schmundt, Rudolf:] 'Tätigkeitsbericht des Chefs des Heerespersonalamts General der Infanterie Schmundt begonnen: 1.10.1942 [fortgeführt bis 29.10.1944]', NA microcopy T-84 roll 39.

Schrader, Werner Wolf: Letter to Graf von Hardenberg dated 16 Nov. 1946, 'Hilfswerk 20. Juli 1944' Foundation.

Schwerin von Schwanenfeld, Marianne Gräfin: 'Ulrich-Wilhelm Graf Schwerin von Schwanenfeld', typescript, Heidelberg, undated.

Schwierz, Helmuth: 'Bericht über meine Tätigkeit am 20. Juli 1944 und über meine nachfolgende Inhaftierung durch die Gestapo', typescript, Siegen i.W. [ca. 1963].

SD Sub-Region Koblenz to out-stations 28 Apr. and 1 Sept. 1938, typescripts, BA NS 29/vorl. 435.

SD out-station Eisenach of SD region Weimar: 'Bericht', typescript, Eisenach 26 July 1944, BA RG 1010/1602.

'Selbstmord des Majors Ulrich von Oertzen', report by Kriminaltechnisches Institut of Security Police, Chemical Department, carbon copy of typescript, [Berlin] 23 July 1944, BA R 58/1051.

'Selbstmordstatistik für das Deutsche Reich', RSHA, no place [1942–1944], BA EAP 173–a–10/64.

Sodenstern, [Georg] von: 'Zur Vorgeschichte des 20. Juli 1944', typescript, Frankfurt/M. March 1947, NA Record Group 338 MS no B-499.

Sonderegger, Franz [Xaver]: Letter to President of Land Court Munich I dated 14 Jan. 1951, copy in IfZ.

[Sonderegger, Franz Xaver:] 'Niederschrift der Unterredung des Herrn Franz Xaver Sonderegger, geboren 19. Juli 1898, wohnhaft in Alt-Leiningen/ü.Grünstadt/Pfalz, Obere Bahnhofstr. 124, derzeit Trier Paulinstr. 15/b. Michel, durchgeführt am 12. Oktober 1952 mit Dr Frhr.v.Siegler und Dr Helmut Krausnick, im späteren

Verlauf auch mit Dr Hermann Mau im Institut für Zeitgeschichte München', typescript, [Munich 1952], IfZ ZS 303/I.

Sonderegger, Franz [Xaver]: Record of statements made to representatives of 'Europäische Publikation e.V.' in Munich on 15 Oct. 1952, typescript, [Munich 1952], IfZ ZS 303/II.

Sonnenhol, [Gustav Adolf]: Memorandum to head of Group 'Inland II' in Foreign Ministry, typescript, Berlin 11 Aug. 1944, Auswärtiges Amt Pol. Archiv Inland II g 59.

Speidel, Hans: Statement, manuscript, Freudenstadt 19 May 1946, in possession of Graf von Strachwitz.

Speidel, Hans: 'Zur Vorgeschichte des 20. Juli 1944', typescript, Freudenstadt 16 June 1947, NA Record Group 338 MS no B-721.

Sprenger, [Jakob]: 'Bericht', typed copy, no place, undated, BA NS 19/188–F42.

Staatspolizei Oppeln: Letter to Geheime Staatspolizei Berlin dated 5 March 1937, typed copy, BA RG 1010/3183.

Staatspolizeileitstelle Koblenz: Letters to Landräte (etc.) dated 5 Apr., 13 May, 3 June and 1 July 1938, BA NS 29/vorl. 435.

Staudinger, Hans-Heinrich: 'Bemerkungen zur Niederschrift von Herrn Gen. Kienitz: "Der Wehrkreis II vor dem Zusammenbruch des Reichs" ', typescript, Schönböcken bei Lübeck 19 Feb. 1954, BA Ost-Dok. 8 Po 22.

Stauffenberg, Clemens Schenk G[raf] v[on]: 'Zu Anfrage zwecks Ergänzung der Kartothek über Zusammenhänge mit dem 20. Juli 1944', typescript, Jettingen 27 Oct. 1946.

Stauffenberg, Markwart Graf Schenk von: 'Angaben des Markwart Graf Schenk von Stauffenberg und seiner Familie über die Haft etc. anlässlich des 20. Juli 1944', typescript, Amerdingen 4 Jan. 1947.

[Stauffenberg] see also files.

[Stegemann, Gert:] 'Betr.: Filmmaterial zum Attentat auf Hitler am 20. Juli 1944', typescript, no place, undated, communicated by Deutsche Wochenschau GmbH with letter of 3 June 1970.

Steusch [?]: 'Vermerk über den Ablauf der Ereignisse vom 20.7. auf 21.7.44, soweit sie auf den mir erteilten Auftrag Bezug haben', typescript, [Berlin July 1944], BDC.

Strachwitz, Hyazinth Graf [von]: 'Aufzeichnung für die Personalakten', typed copy, Garmisch May 1945.

Strachwitz, Hyazinth Graf [von]: 'Ein Beitrag zur Geschichte des deutschen Widerstandes gegen das nationalsozialistische Regime', typescript, Allendorf Feb. 1947, NA Record Group 338 MS no B-340.

Streve, [Gustav]: 'Merkblatt über das Verhalten bei Alarm für die Belegschaft der Sperrkreise und Sonderzüge', roneoed, [Wolfschanze] 14 Oct. 1943, BA EAP 105/33.

Streve, [Gustav]: 'Merkblatt über das Verhalten bei Alarm für die Belegschaft der Sperrkreise und Sonderzüge während des Einsatzes in allen FHQu.-Anlagen', roneoed, no place, 5 May 1944, BA EAP 105/33.

Streve, [Gustav]: 'Zusatz zum Alarmbefehl für FHQu. Truppen und Merkblatt über Verhalten bei Alarm für Sprk.- und Sdr.-Zug-Belegschaft —gültig während Belegung "Wolfschanze"', roneoed, [Wolfschanze] 23 July 1944, BA EAPQ 105/33.

'T-Verbindungen Wolfschanze: Stand vom 21.1.43', blue print, no place, undated, Josef Wolf's papers.

Teuchert, Friedrich Freiherr von: [Aufzeichnungen über den 20. Juli 1944], typescript, Munich [1946].

Theil, Fritz: Letter to Marion Gräfin von Dönhoff dated Bukarest 28 May 1948, typed copy, 'Hilfswerk 20. Juli 1944' Foundation.

Theil, Fritz: ['Bericht'] typescript, Bad Godesberg, undated, 'Hilfswerk 20. Juli 1944' Foundation.

Thelen, [Peter]: 'Revolution ohne Truppen: Die letzten Stunden in der Bendlerstrasse am 20. Juli 1944', typescript, Frankfurt/M. 1965.

Thormaehlen, Ludwig: [Niederschrift über Claus Graf Schenk von Stauffenberg], typescript, [Bad Kreuznach 1946].

'T[räger-] F[requenz]-Skizze: Stand vom 12. Jan. 1945, [verbessert] auf den Stand vom 5. April 1945', blue print, no place, 1945, Josef Wolf's papers.

Uechtritz, [Karl-Ernst von]: Letter to H.-H. Staudinger dated 2 June 1954, BA Ost-Dok. 8 Po 22.

Uexküll[-Gyllenband], G[rä]f[i]n [von]: 'Bericht', typed copy, no place, undated, 'Hilfswerk 20. Juli 1944' Foundation.

Valkyrie see Walküre.

Vansittart, Robert Gilbert Baron: Affidavits ref. the brothers Erich and Theodor Kordt (in German), typescripts, London 12 and 31 Aug. 1948, StA Nuremberg NG 5786 and NG 5786–A.

'Verwendungsbereitschaft des Ersatzheeres', order by Chef H. Rüst u BdE, AHA Ia (I) Nr. 4810/42 g.Kdos., typescript, no place, 13 Oct. 1942, BA – MA RH 15/v.174.

'Vorlage an den Reichsleiter. Betrifft: Verhandlung vor dem Volksgerichtshof gegen weitere Verräter des 20. Juli 1944 [hier: am 23 Feb. 1945 gegen E.H.v.Kleist]', carbon copy of typescript, Berlin 23 Feb. 1945, BA EAP 105/30.

Voss, Hans-Erich: Letter to Professor Walter Baum dated 4 Apr. 1957, IfZ ZS 1786.

Wagner, [Eduard]: 'Der Verlauf des 20. Juli (aus dem Gedächtnis)' typescript, [Zossen] 21 July 1944, IfZ ED 95.

'Walküre[-Befehl mit Anlagen und späteren Zusätzen]', typescript, Berlin 31 July 1943, BA – MA WK XVII/91.

'Walküre II', order by Chef H Rüst u BdE, AHA Ia VII Nr. 1720/42 g Kdos, typescript, no place, 26 May 1942. BA – MA RH 15/v.175.

'Walküre[-Ergänzungsbefehl]', typescript, Berlin 6 Oct. 1943, BA – MA WK XVII/91.

Walz, [Hans]: 'Gedanken zur politischen Zielsetzung von Carl Goerdeler', typescript, [Stuttgart] 1968.

Warlimont, Walter: 'Circumstances of the Attempt of 20 July 1944', typescript, no place, 3 Aug. 1945, NA Record Group 238 ETHINT–5.

[Weerth, Otto:] 'Interrogation Report on Otto Weerth, BA/907/INT', typescript, [Berlin] 23 Aug. 1945.

[Weizsäcker, Ernst Freiherr von] 'Official Record, United States Military Tribunals Nürnberg, Case No. 11 Tribunal IV (IV A), U.S. vs Ernst von Weizsäcker et al', vol. 27, transcripts (English) 2–6 July 1948, roneoed, NA.

Wille, [Senor]: 'Niederschrift über die Vorgänge beim Postamt Zossen 10 am 20.7.1944', typescript, [Zossen ca. 9 Aug. 1944].

Willisen, Achim Fr[ei]h[er]r v[on]: Letter to Institut für Zeitgeschichte Munich dated 1 Sept. 1965, IfZ ZS 1857.

Wussow, Botho v[on]: 'Einige Sätze zu dem SS-Bericht über den 20. Juli 1944, der in den Nordwestdeutschen Heften veröffentlicht wurde u.z. 1947 Heft 1/2', typescript, no place, 1947.

Ziegler, Delia: 'Bericht über den 20.7.1944', typescript, no place, [ca. 1947].

Zipperer, Waldemar: 'Schilderung des Aufgriffs des Georg Elser, Attentäter des Münchner Anschlags vom 8. November 1939', typescript, Constance 15 Dec. 1939, BA – MA W 01–6/301.

II VERBAL AND WRITTEN INFORMATION TO THE AUTHOR (unless otherwise stated, records are in type, confirmed and signed by the originator; dates are those on which information was given)

Ackermann, Eduard, 20 Nov. 1964.

Ansorge, [Charlotte], 26 Feb. 1965 (unsigned).

Arntz, Hellmuth, 21 Nov. 1964.

Sources and Bibliography

Baur, Hans, 2 July 1965.
Beelitz, Dietrich, 21 Apr. 1964.
Below, Nicolaus von, 15 May 1964.
Berger, Gottlob, 21 Jan. 1965 (unsigned).
Bertaux, Pierre, 9 June 1965.
Boeselager, Philipp Freiherr von, 19 Nov. 1964.
Bothe, Karl Heinz, 25 June 1965.
Breitenbuch, Eberhard von, 8 Sept. 1966.
Büchs, Herbert, 1 July 1964.
Burchardt, Heinz, 13 July 1965 (unsigned).
Dangschat, Johannes, 18 July 1971.
Degner, Friedrich, 24, 25 Aug. 1965, corrected, amplified and signed 14 Oct. 1966.
Faber, [Walter], 2 July 1964.
Frentz, Walter, 1 June 1965.
Freundorfer, Otto, 18 Feb. 1965.
Georgi, Friedrich, 21 May 1973.
Gersdorff, Rudolf-Christoph Freiherr von, 25 May, 16 Nov. 1964.
Gerstenmaier, Eugen, 17 Aug. 1965.
Gisevius, Hans Bernd, 4 Aug. 1971, 8 Sept. 1972.
Glasl, Anton, 4 Dec. 1964.
Günsche, Otto, 6 Nov. 1972.
Haase, Kurt, 9 Aug. 1965.
Harnack, Fritz, 29 Aug. 1966.
Hase, Margarethe von, 31 Mar. 1964.
Hassel, Kurt, 11 Dec. 1964.
Herre, Heinz Danko, 9 Sept. 1972.
Herrlitz, Erich, 14 Jan. 1965.
Heusinger, Adolf, 6 Aug. 1964.
Hornbogen, Hans, 14 Jan. 1965.
Hummel Edler von Hassenfels, Helmut, 9 Sept. 1966 (unsigned).
Huth, Paul, 14 Jan. 1965.
Jalass, Erich, 24 June 1965.
Jesek, Werner, 24 May 1965.
John von Freyend, Ernst, 14 May 1964.
Kanitz, Rainer Graf von, 28 Aug. 1972.
Kaufmann, Karl, 15 Jan. 1965 (unsigned).
Kempka, Erich, 19 Aug. 1965.
Kleist, Ewald Heinrich von, 19 July 1964.
Knör, Hans, 6 Sept. 1966.
Koch-Erpach, Rudolf, 28 Mar. 1964.
Korff, Martin, 25 Feb. 1965.
Kretz, Erich, 29 Aug. 1965 (unsigned), 31 Aug. 1966.
Langhaeuser, Rudolf, 22 Aug. 1969.
Laue, Wolfgang, 1 Sept. 1966 (unsigned).
Lechler, Otto, 5 June 1964.
Maletzky, Hermann, 4 Aug. 1965.
Martin, Benno, 3 June 1971.
Meyer, [Ilse-Dörte], 21 June 1965 (unsigned).
Möller, Josef, 10 Dec. 1964.
Momm, Harald, 19 Aug. 1968.
Mylius, Helmuth, 21 Jan. [1969].
Oster, Achim, 26 May 1964 (unsigned).
Pieper, Heinz, 24 July 1965.
Poppe, Ulrich, 4 June 1971.
Puttkamer, Karl-Jesko von, 5 Mar. 1964.

Redlich, Friedrich, 3 July 1971.
Reheusser, Otto, 7 Aug. 1968 (unsigned).
Reinecke, Hermann, 30 Apr. 1965.
Reinhardt, Hellmuth, 1 July 1972.
Rendel, Franz, 9 Dec. 1964.
Ringel, Julius, 2 July 1965 (unsigned).
Röhrig, Wolfram, 29/30 June 1965.
Ruoff, Joachim, 3 June 1971.
Sander, Ludolf Gerhard, 24, 25 Apr. 1964.
Sasse, Heinz, 1 July 1971.
Scheel, Gustav Adolf, 14 Jan. 1965.
Schiffler, Maria, 7 Sept. 1966.
Schlabrendorff, Fabian von, 19 July 1964, 6 Aug. 1968.
Schmidt, Friedrich, 7 June 1973.
Schüler, Erich, 16 July 1965 (unsigned).
Schweizer, Karl, 18 June 1965.
Sobczyk, Martin, 27 Aug. 1965.
Sonnleithner, Franz von, 16 Jan. 1964.
Stauffenberg, Hans-Christoph Freiherr von, 28 July 1971, 5 July 1972.
Stauffenberg, Nina Gräfin von, 23 Aug. 1969.
Szymonski, Gerhard von, 2 July 1964.
Timm, Kurt, 7 Aug. 1968.
Tresckow, Arnold von, 5 Aug. 1968.
Vogel, Werner, 26 June 1970, 1 July 1971.
Waaser, Max, 22 May 1971.
Wagner, Wilhelm Tobias, 29 July 1965.
Waizenegger, Heinz, 9 Sept. 1963.
Warlimont, Walter: marginal comments on the author's 'Zu dem Attentat im Führerhauptquartier "Wolfsschanze" am 20. Juli 1944', *VfZ* 12 (1964), pp. 254–84, manuscript, Gmund am Tegernsee 30 Aug. 1964.
Widmann, Albert, 30 July 1968.
Winterfeldt, Alix von, 30 Aug. 1966.
Wolf, Josef, 27 Feb. 1965, 3 July 1971.

III LETTERS TO THE AUTHOR

Adam, Carl, 11 Aug. 1971.
Adam, Fritz, 21 Aug. 1971.
Adam, Kurt, 5 Apr. 1964, 8 Jan. 1968.
Albrecht, H[einz]-G[ünther], 11 May, 1 Aug. 1966, 27 Aug. 1967.
Albrecht, Kurt, 30 Jan. 1969.
Ansorge, Charlotte, 22 Aug. 1971.
Arntz, Hellmuth, 24 Nov. 1964.
Bärtels, Martin, 4 Sept. 1965.
Baur, Hans, 10 Jan. 1969.
Beelitz, Dietrich, 28 Apr. 1964.
Beichele, Albert, 18 June 1965, 14 Jan. 1966, 6 Feb., 31 Dec. 1967, 24 Apr. 1968.
Bergener, Joachim, 12 May 1964.
Bergeré, Günter, 15 Sept. 1971.
Bergschmidt, Robert, 9 Feb. 1965.
Boberach, Heinz, 24 Oct. 1968.
Boeselager, Philipp Freiherr von, 15 Jan. 1965, 28 Aug. 1969.
Bohnemeier – see Goverts.
Bork, Max, 31 Jan. 1964.

Bormann, Albert, 15 Nov. 1964.
Boysen, Peter, 23 June, 6 July 1970.
Brandt, Karl, 11 May, 6 Aug. 1968.
Breitenbuch, Eberhard von, 8 Nov. 1966.
British Broadcasting Corporation, 8 Dec. 1965.
Bühlmann, Werner, 2 Mar. 1965.
Bundesbahndirektion Nürnberg 11 June 1970.
Bussche, Axel Freiherr von dem, 9 Feb., 10 Feb., 1 Mar. 1966, 18 Sept. 1967, 22 Apr. 1970.
Cords, Helmuth, 11 Apr. 1971.
Darges, Friedrich, 10 Mar. 1965.
Degner, Friedrich, 1 Oct. 1968.
Delius, Kurt, 28 July 1965.
Dönitz, Karl, 5 Dec. 1964.
Dufring, Theodor von, 10 Aug., 29 Sept. 1971, 9 Jan. 1972.
Eder, Heinz, 18 Jan. 1965.
Erasmus, Johannes, 29 Aug. 1965.
Freiwald, [Kurt], 7 Jan. 1965.
Frentz, Walter, 6 Jan. 1970.
Fritzsche, Hans Karl, 6 Aug. 1971.
Froneberg, Walter, 3 May 1965.
Gaede, Wilhelm, 7 June 1971.
Gersdorff, E. K. Freiherr von, 2 Dec., 10 Dec. 1964.
Gersdorff, Rudolf-Christoph Freiherr von, 15 Jan. 1965, 23 Jan., 22 Mar. 1966.
Gigas, Ulrich, 28 Oct. 1969.
Gisevius, Hans Bernd, 10 Sept. 1972, [Dec. 1973].
Gnuva, Paul, 6 Apr. 1965.
Goebel, Gerhart, 21 Jan. 1966.
Goetzke, Claus-Peter, 14 July 1964.
Gottberg, Helmut von, 22 Apr., 16 June 1966.
Goverts, Hans, 3 June 1965.
Grosser, Bruno, 18 July 1964.
Günsche, Otto, 21 Jan. 1970.
Haaf, Oskar, 19 Dec. 1969, 15 Jan., 18 Apr. 1970.
Hase, Margarethe von, 3 Mar., 8 Mar. 1964.
Hasselbach, Hans Karl von, 11 Oct. 1965.
Heinz, Friedrich Wilhelm, 8 Mar., 22 Mar., 3 May 1966.
Helling, Arno, 4 Sept. 1964.
Hentze, Klaus, 10 Feb. 1970.
Herber, Franz, 25 Jan. 1966.
Herwarth von Bittenfeld, Hans, 28 Oct. 1969.
Heusinger, Adolf, 9 Sept. 1967.
Hindenach, Walter, 2 Mar. 1964.
Hitzegrad, Ernst, 23 Aug. 1964.
Hoch, Anton, 8 June 1970.
Hofmann, Christian, 16 Jan. 1965.
Hotzel, Wilhelm, Aug. 1965.
Hüttner, Hartmut, 25 Jan. 1969.
Issendorff, Georg von, Jan. 1964.
Jakob, Friedrich, 3 June 1969.
Jakob, Rudolf, 28 Jan. 1969.
John von Freyend, Ernst, 31 May 1965.
Jordan, Ralph, 12 Mar. 1965.
Kandt, Herbert, 11 Feb., 13 Mar. 1964.
Karl, Gregor, 18 May 1966, 17 Feb. 1968.

Kecker, Gottfried, 9 Jan., 27 Jan. 1969.
Kempe, Ludwig, 2 May 1965, 2 Jan. 1970.
Kessel, Albrecht von, 15 July 1970.
Kessen, Wilhelm, 13 Sept. 1970.
Kleist, Berndt von, 26 Feb. 1965.
Kleist, Ewald Heinrich von, 15 Sept. 1964, 14 Sept. 1967, 2 Oct. 1968.
Kober, Fritz, 6 Sept. 1964.
Koch-Erpach, Rudolf, 9 May 1964.
Kodré, Heinrich, 22 Sept. 1964.
Kohlhauer, Erich, 7 Mar. 1965.
Krancke, Theodor, 3 June 1970.
Küpper, Wilhelm, 28 Apr. 1965.
Kuhn, Friedrich, 25 Sept. 1964.
Kuhnert, Karl, 1 Dec. 1964, 17 Jan., May 1965.
Langhaeuser, Rudolf, 28 Nov. 1969.
Linge, Heinz, 15 Apr. 1969.
Liphart, Hans, 9 Sept. 1964.
Lochner, Louis P., 12 Jan., 9 Feb. 1967.
Lüthje, Karl, 15 Mar. 1971.
Mader, Herbert, 9 Mar. 1965.
Maître, Alexander, 19 Feb., 15 Mar. 1965.
Manz, Hugo, 23 Oct. 1965.
Maultzsch, Herbert, 10 May 1965.
Ministry of Defence, London, 23 Nov. 1964.
Moltke, Freya Gräfin von, 3 Feb. 1969.
Müller, Gotthold, 18 Nov. 1966.
Müller, Max, 16 Nov. 1967.
Naumann, Werner, 9 Apr. 1970.
Nettesheim, Kurt, 22 Aug. 1968.
Pantenius, H. J., 5 Mar. 1970.
Pentz, H. H. von, 13 Nov. 1969.
Pestinger, Emil, 20 Dec., 31 Dec. 1964, 19 Jan. 1965.
Plate, Claus-Henning von, 11 Aug., 19 Aug. 1964, 14 Apr. 1966.
Platen, Günther von, 17 Mar. 1965.
Prüter, Wilhelm, 10 Feb. 1964.
Raiber, R., 19 Sept., 20 Oct. 1969.
Reinecke, Hermann, 16 Apr., 31 May, 15 Oct., 16 Dec. 1964, 19 Apr., 20 Dec. 1965, 2 Feb., 7 Nov, 1967.
Reinhardt, Hellmuth, 12 Nov, 1967, 2 July 1972.
Rendel, Franz, 8 Mar. 1965.
Reumont, Alfred von, 14 Mar. 1965.
Reuss, Heinrich V. Prinz, 15 May 1972.
Reutter, Wilhelm, 13 Mar. 1964.
Richter, Horst, 18 Aug. 1965.
Ringel, Julius, 5 Feb. 1964.
Rode, Werner, 29 Aug. 1971.
Röhrig, Georg, 15 Mar. 1966, 6 Feb. 1969.
Rüdt von Collenberg, Ludwig Freiherr, 3 Feb., 15 Feb. 1964.
Ruoff, Joachim, 23 Nov. 1969.
Ryll, Edgar, 29 July 1964.
Sauermilch, Walter, 6 May, 13 May, 30 May 1970.
Schellert, Otto, 1 Feb. 1964, 2 Jan. 1968.
Schindler, Kurt, 19 Feb., 24 Feb. 1964.
Schlabrendorff, Fabian von, 22 Oct. 1966, 30 May 1968.
Schmidt, Friedrich, 8 Feb., 6 Oct. 1966, 4 Oct. 1967.

Schmidt-Salzmann, Walther, 14 Feb. 1966.
Schoener, Otto, 21 July 1965.
Schroeder, Walther, 9 Nov. 1964.
Schubert, Albrecht, 1 Feb. 1964.
Schubert, Klaus, 30 Sept. 1964.
Schulenburg, Wedige von der, 7 Dec. 1964.
Schulte-Heuthaus, Hermann, 20 Sept. 1965.
Schweizer, Karl, 2 Nov. 1967.
Schwierz, Helmuth, 25 Mar. 1965.
Sell, Augusta Freifrau von, 6 Jan. 1971.
Selle, Herbert, 24 Oct. 1970.
Siebert, Hans, 27 Oct. 1969, 8 June 1970.
Simonis, Susanne, 8 Mar. 1971.
Sinnhuber, Johann, 27 Jan. 1964.
Smart, Jacob-Edward, 22 Jan. 1969.
Sommerlad, Wilhelm, 5 Oct. 1965.
Speer, Julius, 22 Feb. 1966.
Speidel, Hans, 10 July 1965.
Staudinger, Hans-Heinrich, 13 Oct. 1964, 28 Jan., 12 Feb., 24 Sept. 1965.
Stauffenberg, Nina Gräfin von, 12 Feb. 1964, 30 July, 13 Aug., 1 Sept. 1968.
Stirius, Hans-Werner, 2 Feb. 1967.
Stoll, Erich, 18 June 1970.
Strachwitz, Hyacinth Graf von, 8 Jan. 1965, 20 Jan. 1966.
Stülpnagel, Siegfried von, 1 Feb., 7 Apr. 1965.
Sturm, Rolf, 1 Aug. 1971.
Sündermann, Helmut, 3 Dec. 1969.
Süsskind-Schwendi, Max Theodor Freiherr von, 22 Jan. 1966.
Thomale, Wolfgang, 11 Aug. 1971.
Thomas, Ewald, 16 Aug. 1972.
Thun-Hohenstein, Philippa Gräfin von, 24 Feb., 25 May 1970.
Tresckow, Arnold von, 17 Aug. 1968.
Tresckow, Eta von, 26 July 1971.
Tümpling, Wolf von, 4 Jan. 1968.
Tzschöckell née Ehlers, Elli, 18 Oct. 1971.
Ulich, Max, 6 Apr. 1964.
Utermann, Utz, Mar. 1965.
Voss, Gisela von, Sept. 1975.
Voss, Hans Erich, 17 Mar. 1964.
Waberseck, Alfons, 4 Feb. 1965.
Wackerhagen, Ernst, 24 Aug. 1969.
Wagner, Elisabeth, 16 Mar. 1972.
Wagner, Gerhard, 17 Nov. 1964.
Waldersee, [Alfred] Graf von, 21 July, 30 July 1965.
Warlimont, Walter, 30 Mar. 1964.
WASAG-Chemie A.G. 4 Dec. 1969, 17 Feb., 17 Mar. 1970.
Wehner, Bernd, 27 Oct. 1965, 4 Dec. 1967.
Weizsäcker, Richard Freiherr von, May 1970.
Wiegand, Günther, 14 Oct. 1964.
Wiese und Kaiserswaldau, Joachim von, 10 Aug. 1964.
Wildeiner gen. von Wildau, Christoph von, 20 July 1970.
Witzig. [Apr. 1973].
Wodrig, Albert, 11 Mar. 1964.
Wolf, Josef, 18 Dec. 1968.
Wollschläger, Artur, 24 Nov. 1971.

Zentralnachweisstelle des Bundesarchivs 29 June, 30 July, 23 Dec. 1965, 11 Aug. 1966, 22 Aug. 1968, 26 Mar. 1969.

Ziegler, Delia, 8 Jan. 1968.

Zielke, Erich, 20 July 1970.

Ziervogel, Max, 16 May, 29 July 1964.

IV PUBLISHED MATERIAL – PRIMARY SOURCES

'A.,G.': 'Letzte Begegnung mit Graf Stauffenberg', *Stuttgarter Zeitung* 20 July 1950.

Adressbuch für München und Umgebung 1930, 1931, 1932, Adressbuchverlag der Industrie-und Handelskammer München, Munich undated.

Adressbuch see also *Münchner Stadtadressbuch.*

Andreas-Friedrich, Ruth: *Berlin Underground 1938–1945,* translated by Barrows Mussey, Holt, New York 1947.

Arenberg, Robert Prinz: 'Der Befreiungsversuch des 20. Juli 1944 im Generalkommando Wien' in Ludwig Jedlicka: *Der 20. Juli 1944 in Österreich* (see below), pp. 125–135.

Assmann, Heinz: Account of 20 July 1944 in 'Wolfschanze' in Kurt Assmann: *Deutsche Schicksalsjahre* (see below).

Assmann Kurt: *Deutsche Schicksalsjahre: Historische Bilder aus dem zweiten Weltkrieg und seiner Vorgeschichte,* Eberhard Brockhaus, Wiesbaden,[2] 1952.

Astor, David: 'The Mission of Adam von Trott', *Manchester Guardian Weekly,* 7 June 1956, p. 7.

Astor, David: 'Why the Revolt against Hitler Was Ignored: On the British Reluctance to Deal with German Anti-Nazis', *Encounter* 32 (1969) no 6, pp. 3–13.

Ballestrem-Solf, Lagi Countess: 'Tea Party' in Eric H. Boehm (editor) *We survived,* (see below) pp. 132–49.

Bargatzky, Walter: '20. Juli in Paris: Die letzte Runde im Komplott gegen Hitler', *Stuttgarter Rundschau* 4 (1949), no 7, pp. 12–13.

Baur, Hans: *Ich flog Mächtige der Erde,* Verlag Albert Pröpster, Kempten 1962; *Hitler's Pilot,* translated Edward Fitzgerald, Frederick Muller, London 1958.

Beck, Hans: 'Der 20. Juli 1944 in Kassel: Unternehmen Walküre läuft an', *Hessische Allgemeine* 18 July 1964.

Beck, Ludwig: *Studien,* edited by Hans Speidel, K.F. Koehler Verlag, Stuttgart 1955.

Bell, George K.A.: 'Die Ökumene und die innerdeutsche Opposition', *Vierteljahrshefte für Zeitgeschichte* 5 (1957), pp. 362–78.

Below, Nicolaus von: 'Hitlers Adjutant über den 20. Juli im FHQ: Ein Augenzeugenbericht', *Echo der Woche* 15 July 1949, p. 5.

Bergsträsser, Ludwig: 'Erinnerungen an Wilhelm Leuschner', *Das Parlament,* 20 July 1954, p. 8.

Bernt, Adolf, 'Der 20. Juli in der Bendlerstrasse (Bericht eines Augenzeugen)' *Die Gegenwart* 11 (1956), pp. 597–601.

Best, S. Payne: *The Venlo Incident,* Hutchinson, London 1950.

Besymenski, Lew, A: *Der Tod des Adolf Hitler: Unbekannte Dokumente aus Moskauer Archiven,* Christian Wegner Verlag, Hamburg 1968.

Boberach, Heinz (editor): *Meldungen aus dem Reich,* Hermann Luchterhand Verlag, Neuwied 1965.

Bodenschatz, Karl: 'Hitler prophezeite Bruderkrieg', *Der Hausfreund für Stadt und Land* 26 June 1954, p. 2.

Boehm, Eric H. (editor): *We Survived: The Stories of Fourteen of the Hidden and the Hunted of Nazi Germany,* Yale University Press, New Haven, Connecticut 1949.

Böhm-Tettelbach, Hans: 'Ein Mann hat gesprochen', *Rheinische Post* 10 July 1948, p. 2.

Sources and Bibliography

Boelcke, Willi A. (editor): *Kriegspropaganda 1939–1941: Geheime Ministerkonferenzen im Reichspropagandaministerium*, Deutsche Verlags-Anstalt, Stuttgart 1966.

Boelcke, Willi A. (editor): *Deutschlands Rüstung im Zweiten Weltkrieg: Hitlers Konferenzen mit Albert Speer 1942–1945*, Akademische Verlagsgesellschaft Athenaion, Frankfurt/M. 1969.

Boineburg[-Lengsfeld], Hans von: 'Der 20. Juli 1944 in Paris' – see Reichert.

Bollhammer, Fritz: 'Erinnerungsniederschrift über die Vorgänge in der Nacht vom 20./21. Juli 1944' in Ludwig Jedlicka: *Der 20. Juli 1944 in Österreich*, pp. 111–16.

Bonhoeffer, Dietrich: *Gesammelte Schriften* (two vols) Chr. Kaiser, Munich 1958/59; *Letters and Papers from Prison*, enlarged edition, SCM Press, London 1971.

Bor, Peter: *Gespräche mit Halder*, Limes Verlag, Wiesbaden 1950.

[Bormann, Martin and Gerda]: *The Bormann Letters: The Private Correspondence between Martin Bormann and His Wife from January 1943 to April 1945*, translated R. H. Stevens, introduction H. R. Trevor-Roper, Weidenfeld and Nicolson, London 1954.

Brandt, Karl: 'Tenth Anniversary of the Assassination of the German Elite: A Memorial Address', U.S. Government Printing Office, Washington 1954.

Bumke, Oswald: *Erinnerungen und Betrachtungen: Der Weg eines deutschen Psychiaters*, Richard Pflaum Verlag, Munich 1952.

Burckhardt, Carl J.: *Meine Danziger Mission 1937–1939*, Verlag Georg D. W. Callwey, Munich 1960.

Bussche, Axel von dem: 'Eid und Schuld', *Göttinger Universitätszeitung* 7 Mar. 1947, pp. 1–4.

[Bussche, Axel Freiherr von dem]: Interview with Daniel Schorr in CBS Television Programme: *The Twentieth Century: The Plots Against Hitler*, Part II, shown on 1 Dec. 1964.

Bussche, Axel Freiherr von dem: Account on gramophone record – 'Der stille Befehl: Der Widerstand in Deutschland gegen Hitlers Tyrannei', Harmonia Mundi Record Society, No PL 50115, Münster W. undated.

Bussche, Axel Freiherr von dem: see also under 'Freiheitskämpfer gegen Hitler'.

Butler, Ewen: 'I talked of plan to kill Hitler', *The Times* 6 Aug. 1969. p. 1.

Churchill, Winston S.: *Blood, Sweat and Tears: Speeches*, compiled by Randolph S. Churchill, McClelland and Stewart Ltd, Toronto 1941.

Delp, SJ. Alfred: *Im Angesicht des Todes*, V. Joseph Knecht, Frankfurt/M.[4] 1954.

Dietrich, Otto: *Mit Hitler in die Macht: Persönliche Erlebnisse mit meinem Führer*, Verlag Frz. Eher Nachf., Munich[11] 1934.

Dietrich, Otto: *12 Jahre mit Hitler*, Isar Verlag, Munich 1955; *The Hitler I Knew*, translated Richard and Clara Winston, Methuen, London 1957.

Documents on British Foreign Policy 1919–1939, First, Second and Third Series, HMSO, London 1947 et seq.

Documents on German Foreign Policy 1918–1945, Series D (1937–1945), HMSO, London 1949 et seq.

[Dodd, William E.]: *Ambassador Dodd's Diary 1933–1938*, Victor Gollancz, London 1942.

Dollmann, Eugen: *Call Me Coward*, Wm. Kimber, London 1956.

Domarus, Max: *Hitler: Reden und Proklamationen 1932–1945* (two vols), Verlagsdruckerei Schmidt, Neustadt on Aisch 1962/63.

Dulles, Allen Welsh: *Germany's Underground*, Macmillan, New York 1947.

Dulles, Allen [Welsh]: *The Secret Surrender*, Weidenfeld and Nicolson, London 1967.

Elser, Johann Georg: *Autobiographie eines Attentäters*, Deutsche Verlags-Anstalt, Stuttgart 1970.

Emmenegger, Kurt: *QN wusste Bescheid: Erstaunliche Informationen eines Schweizer Nachrichtenmannes aus den Kulissen des Hitlerkrieges*, Schweizer Spiegel Verlag, Zurich 1965.

Erttel, Holm: ' "Meine Herren, es ist so weit!" Eine Erinnerung an den 20. Juli 1944', *Das freie Wort* 19 July 1952.

E[schenburg], T[heodor]: 'Die Rede Himmlers vor den Gauleitern am 3. August 1944' *VfZ* 1 (1953), pp. 357–94.

Evangelische Dokumente zur Ermordung der 'unheilbar Kranken' unter der nationalsozialistischen Herrschaft in den Jahren 1939–1945, Evangelisches Verlagswerk, Stuttgart 1964.

Field Engineering and Mine Warfare Pamphlet No. 7: Booby Traps, War Office, London 1952.

Fischer, Albrecht: 'Erlebnisse vom 20. Juli 1944 bis 8. April 1945' in Otto Kopp (editor): *Widerstand und Erneuerung* (see below), pp. 122–66.

Foertsch, Hermann: *Schuld und Verhängnis: Die Fritsch-Krise im Frühjahr 1938 als Wendepunkt in der Geschichte der nationalsozialistischen Zeit*, Deutsche Verlags-Anstalt, Stuttgart 1951.

Foote, Alexander: *Handbook for Spies*, Museum Press, London 1949, ³1953.

Foreign Relations of the United States, Diplomatic Papers: The Conferences at Malta and Yalta 1945, U.S. Government Printing Office, Washington 1955.

Foreign Relations of the United States. Diplomatic Papers: 1944, Vol. 1, U.S. Government Printing Office, Washington 1966.

Forschbach, Edmund: 'Edgar Jung und der Widerstand gegen Hitler', *Civis* 6 (1959), pp. 82–8.

'Freiheitskämpfer gegen Hitler', *Die Zeit* 22 July 1948, p. 3.

'Fuehrer Conferences on Naval Affairs, 1939–1945', *Brassey's Naval Annual* 59 (1948), pp. 25–538.

Furtwängler, Franz Josef: *Männer, die ich sah und kannte*, Auerdruck, Hamburg 1951

'Generäle: Neue Mitteilungen zur Vorgeschichte des 20. Juli', *Die Wandlung* 1 (1945–46), pp. 528–37.

German Explosive Ordnance (Bombs, Fuzes, Rockets, Land Mines, Grenades and Igniters), United States Government Printing Office, Washington 1953.

[Gerstein, Kurt:] 'Augenzeugenbericht zu den Massenvergasungen', *VfZ* 1 (1953), pp. 177–94.

[Gerstein, Kurt:] *Dokumentation zur Massenvergasung*, Bundeszentrale für Heimatdienst, Bonn 1955.

Gerstenmaier, Eugen: 'Zur Geschichte des Umsturzversuches vom 20 Juli 1944', *Neue Zürcher Zeitung* 23, 24 June 1945.

Gerstenmaier, Eugen: 'Entscheidende Stunden in der Bendlerstrasse: Der Ablauf der Ereignisse im Oberkommando der Wehrmacht', *Die Welt* 19 July 1946.

Gerstenmaier, Eugen: 'The Church Conspiratorial' in Eric H. Boehm (editor) *We Survived*, pp. 172–89.

Gerstenmaier, Eugen: 'Die Kreisauer und der 20. Juli ' in his *Reden und Aufsätze* (see below), Vol. II, pp. 238–43.

Gerstenmaier, Eugen: *Reden und Aufsätze* (two vols), Evangelisches Verlagswerk, Stuttgart 1956, 1962.

Gerstenmaier Eugen: 'Der Kreisauer Kreis: Zu dem Buch Gerrit van Roons "Neuordnung im Widerstand"', *VfZ* 15 (1967), pp. 221–46.

Gerstenmaier, Eugen: ' "Den Dolch im Lorbeerstrausse tragen": Stefan Georges Einfluss auf Stauffenberg und den 20. Juli', *Christ und Welt* 19 July 1968, p. 22.

'Gesetz gegen heimtückische Angriffe auf Staat und Partei und zum Schutz der Parteiuniform', 20 Dec. 1934, *Reichsgesetzblatt Teil I 1934*, Reichsverlagsamt, Berlin 1934, p. 1269.

Geyr von Schweppenburg, [Leo Frh.]: *The Critical Years*, Allan Wingate, London 1952.

Gisevius, Hans Bernd: *Bis zum bittern Ende* (two vols), Fretz & Wasmuth, Zurich 1946; *To the Bitter End*, translated Richard and Clara Winston, Jonathan Cape, London 1948.

Sources and Bibliography

Gisevius, Hans Bernd: *Bis zum bittern Ende*, Fretz & Wasmuth, Zurich [1954].

Gisevius, Hans Bernd: *Bis zum bitteren Ende*, vom Verfasser auf den neuesten Stand gebrachte Sonderausgabe, Rütten & Loening, Hamburg undated [ca. 1964].

Gisevius, Hans Bernd: *Wo ist Nebe? Erinnerungen an Hitlers Reichskriminaldirektor*, Droemersche Verlagsanstalt, Zurich 1966.

Goebbels, [Joseph]: *Tagebücher aus den Jahren 1942–43*, mit andern Dokumenten, edited by Louis P. Lochner, Atlantis Verlag, Zurich 1948; *The Goebbels Diaries*, translated and edited by Louis P. Lochner, Hamish Hamilton, London 1948.

'Dr Goerdeler an General Olbricht: Ein Dokument zur Vorgeschichte des Attentats vom 20. Juli 1944', *Die Wandlung* 1 (1945–46), pp. 172–5.

Görlitz, Walter (editor): *Generalfeldmarschall Keitel: Verbrecher oder Offizier? Erinnerungen, Briefe, Dokumente des Chefs OKW*, Musterschmidt-Verlag, Göttingen, Berlin, Frankfurt/M. [1961].

Greiner, Helmuth: *Die Oberste Wehrmachtführung 1939–1943*, Limes Verlag, Wiesbaden [1951].

Groppe, Theodor: *Ein Kampf um Recht und Sitte: Erlebnisse um Wehrmacht, Partei, Gestapo*, Paulinus-Verlag, Trier 1947.

Groscurth, Helmuth: *Tagebücher eines Abwehroffiziers 1938–1940* edited by Helmut Krausnick and Harold C. Deutsch assisted by Hildegard von Kotze, Deutsche Verlags-Anstalt, Stuttgart 1970.

Guderian, Heinz: *Erinnerungen eines Soldaten*, Kurt Vowinckel, Heidelberg 1951; *Panzer Leader*, translated Constantine Fitzgibbon, foreword Sir B. H. Liddell Hart, Michael Joseph, London 1952.

Guides to German Records Microfilmed at Alexandria, Va. No. 39: Records of the Reich Leader of the SS and Chief of the German Police (Reichsführer-SS und Chef der Deutschen Polizei) (Part III), The National Archives, Washington 1963.

Guides to German Records Microfilmed at Alexandria, Va. No. 52: Records of German Field Commands: Army Groups (Part II), The National Archives, Washington 1966.

Gun, Nerin E: *The Day of the Americans*, Fleet Publishing Corp., New York 1966.

Haetzel, Klaus: 'Die längste Schicht am Fernschreiber: "Telegraf"– Reporter sprach mit einer Augenzeugin des dramatischen Geschehens am 20. Juli 1944', *Telegraf* 19 July 1964, p. 8.

Hagen, [Hans W.]: 'Tatbericht über meine Tätigkeit als Verbindungsoffizier des Wachbataillons "Grossdeutschland" zum Reichsministerium für Volksaufklärung und Propaganda am 20. Juli 1944' in *Spiegelbild einer Verschwörung* (see below), pp. 12–15.

Hagen, Hans W.: *Zwischen Eid und Befehl: Tatzeugenbericht von den Ereignissen am 20. Juli 1944 in Berlin und 'Wolfsschanze'*, Türmer Verlag, Munich, [2]1959, [4]1968.

Halder, [Franz]: *Kriegstagebuch*, Vols. 1–3, W. Kohlhammer Verlag, Stuttgart 1962, 1963, 1964.

Hammerstein, Kunrat Freiherr von: *Spähtrupp*, Henry Goverts Verlag, Stuttgart 1963.

Hammerstein, Kunrat, Frh. v.: *Flucht: Aufzeichnungen nach dem 20. Juli*, Walter-Verlag, Olten-Freiburg i.Br. 1966.

Hanfstaengl, Ernst: *Unheard Witness*, Eyre & Spottiswoode, Philadelphia–New York 1957 (*Hitler: The missing Years*, Eyre & Spottiswoode, London 1957).

Hansard: *The Parliamentary Debates*, 5th Series, House of Commons, Vol. 351/2, HMSO London 1939.

Hassell, Ulrich von: 'Das Ringen um den Staat der Zukunft', *Schweizer Monatshefte* 44 (1964), pp. 314–27.

Hassell, Ulrich von: *Vom andern Deutschland: Aus den nachgelassenen Tagebüchern 1938–1944*, Fischer Bücherei, Frankfurt 1964; *The von Hassell Diaries 1938–1944*, Hamish Hamilton, London 1948.

Heiber, Helmut (editor): *Hitlers Lagebesprechungen: Die Protokollfragmente seiner militärischen Konferenzen 1942–1945*, Deutsche Verlags-Anstalt, Stuttgart 1962.

Heinz, F[riedrich] W[ilhelm]: 'Offener Brief an Herrn Remer', *Deutsche Wirklichkeit* I (1949) No 18, pp. 8–9.

Henk, Emil: *Die Tragödie des 20. Juli 1944: Ein Beitrag zur politischen Vorgeschichte*, Adolf Rausch Verlag, Heidelberg [2]1946.

Henk, Emil: 'Sozialdemokratischer Widerstand im Raum Mannheim' in *100 Jahre SPD in Mannheim: Eine Dokumentation*, Mannheimer Verlagsanstalt, Mannheim 1967, pp. 68–73.

Herwarth von Bittenfeld, Hans: 'Meine Verbindung mit Graf Stauffenberg', *Stuttgarter Zeitung* Nr. 162, 18 July 1969, p. 7.

Heueck, Alfred: 'Der Mann, der Roland Freisler sterben sah: Fabian v. Schlabrendorff berichtet vom Martyrium der Widerstandskämpfer', *Frankfurter Rundschau* 27 Sept. 1955.

Heusinger, Adolf: *Befehl im Widerstreit: Schicksalsstunden der deutschen Armee 1923–1945*, Rainer Wunderlich Hermann Leins, Tübingen 1950.

Heyde, B[olko] von der: 'Die Verschwörung des 20. Juli: Beteiligte sagen aus', *Die Welt* 31 July 1947, p. 2.

Heyde, Bolko von der: letter to the editor, *Der Spiegel*, No 5, 27 Jan. 1969, p. 10.

Hildebrandt, Rainer: *Wir sind die Letzten: Aus dem Leben des Widerstandskämpfers Albrecht Haushofer und seiner Freunde*, Michael-Verlag, Neuwied-Berlin [1949].

Hillgruber, Andreas (editor): *Staatsmänner und Diplomaten bei Hitler: Vertrauliche Aufzeichnungen über Unterredungen mit Vertretern des Auslandes 1939–1941*, Bernard & Graefe, Frankfurt 1967.

Himmler, Heinrich: *Geheimreden 1933 bis 1945 und andere Ansprachen*, ed. by Bradley F. Smith and Agnes F. Peterson, Proplyäen Verlag, Frankfurt/M., Berlin, Vienna 1974.

Himmler, Heinrich: See also Eschenburg.

'helmut hirsch 21.1.1916 – 4.6.1937', *schriften des bundes deutscher jungenschaften* 31 – Voggenreiter Verlag, Bad Godesberg [1970].

Hitler, Adolf: *Mein Kampf*, Verlag Franz Eher Nachf., Munich [3] 1930. (*Mein Kampf*, with an introduction by D. C. Watt, translated by Ralph Manheim, Hutchinson, London 1969.)

[Hitler, Adolf:] *Hitler's Table Talk 1941–1944*, translated by Norman Cameron and R. H. Stevens, Weidenfeld and Nicolson, London 1953.

[Hitler, Adolf:] see also Heiber, Hubatsch Picker, Treue.

Hofer, Walther: *Der Nationalsozialismus: Dokumente 1933–1945*, Fischer Bücherei, Frankfurt/M. 1957.

Hoffmann, Heinrich: *Hitler Was My Friend*, translated R. H. Stevens, Burke Pub. Co., London 1955.

Hoffmann, Volkmar: ' "Nie wieder bin ich solch einem Menschen begegnet": 20. Juli – 20 Jahre danach/Interview mit Stauffenbergs Sekretärin und anderen Beteiligten/ "Ich würde es wieder tun" ', *Frankfurter Rundschau* 18 July 1964, p. 3.

Hossbach, Friedrich: *Zwischen Wehrmacht und Hitler 1934–1938*, Vandenhoeck & Ruprecht, Göttingen [2]1965.

Hubatsch, Walther: 'Das dienstliche Tagebuch des Chefs des Wehrmachtsführungsamtes im Oberkommando der Wehrmacht, Generalmajor Jodl, für die Zeit vom 13. Okt. 1939 bis zum 30. Jan. 1940', *Die Welt als Geschichte* 12 (1952), pp. 274–87, 13 (1953), pp. 58–71.

Hubatsch, Walther: *Hitlers Weisungen für die Kriegführung 1939–1945: Dokumente des Oberkommandos der Wehrmacht*, Bernard & Graefe, Frankfurt/M. 1962; *Hitler's War Directives 1939–1945*, edited by H. R. Trevor-Roper, [translated Anthony Rhodes], Sidgwick and Jackson, London 1964.

Italiaander, Rolf: *Besiegeltes Leben*, Volksbücherei-Verlag, Goslar 1949.

Sources and Bibliography

Jacobsen, Hans-Adolf: *1939–1945: Der zweite Weltkrieg in Chronik und Dokumenten*, Wehr und Wissen Verlag, Darmstadt 1959.

Jedlicka, Ludwig: *Der 20. Juli 1944 in Österreich*, Herold-Verlag, Vienna-Munich 1965.

Jodl, [Alfred]: 'Dienstliches Tagebuch [4. Jan. 1937–25. Aug. 1939]' in *Trial of the Major War Criminals* . . . (see below), Vol. XXVIII, pp. 345–390.

Jodl, [Alfred]: 'Tagebuch General Jodl (WFA), umfasst Zeit vom 1.2. – 26.5.40', *Trial of the Major War Criminals* . . . (see below), Vol. XXVIII, pp. 397–435.

Jodl, Alfred: see also Hubatsch.

John, Otto: 'Männer im Kampf gegen Hitler', *Blick in die Welt* 2 (1947) No 6.

John, Otto: 'Männer im Kampf gegen Hitler (II)', *Blick in die Welt* 2 (1947) No 7.

John, Otto: 'Männer im Kampf gegen Hitler (IV): Wilhelm Leuschner', *Blick in die Welt* (1947), No 9, p. 20.

John, Otto: 'Männer im Kampf gegen Hitler (V): Helmuth James Graf von Moltke', *Blick in die Welt* 2 (1947), No 10.

John, Otto: 'Männer im Kampf gegen Hitler (VI): Carl Mierendorff, Theodor Haubach, Adolf Reichwein', *Blick in die Welt* 2 (1947), No 11, pp. 14–15.

John, Otto: 'Männer im Kampf gegen Hitler (VII): Hans von Dohnanyi', *Blick in die Welt* 2 (1947), No 12, pp. 16–17.

John, Otto: 'Zum Jahrestag der Verschwörung gegen Hitler – 20. Juli 1944', *Wochenpost* 18 July 1947, pp. 4–6.

John, Otto A.W.: 'Am achten Jahrestag der Verschwörung', *Das Parlament* 20 July 1952, p. 2.

John, Otto: *Zweimal kam ich heim: Vom Verschwörer zum Schützer der Verfassung*, Econ Verlag, Düsseldorf-Vienna 1969; *Twice through the Lines*, translated by Richard Barry, Macmillan, London 1972.

Jünger, Ernst: *Strahlungen*, Heliopolis-Verlag, Tübingen ³1949.

Der 20. Juli 1944: Beiträge zur Geschichte der deutschen Widerstandsbewegung Südverlag, Constance undated.

20. Juli 1944, edited by Bundeszentrale für Heimatdienst, Berto-Verlag, Bonn ⁴ 1961.

Kaiser, Hermann: diary – see 'Generäle . . .'.

Kaiser, Jakob: 'Kämpfer der Gewerkschaftseinheit: Zum Todestage von Wilhelm Leuschner – 29. September 1944', *Neue Zeit* 28 Sept. 1945.

Kaiser, Jakob: 'Der Aufstand des Gewissens', *Neue Zeit* 2 Feb. 1947, pp. 3–4.

Kaiser, Jakob: 'Deutschlands Teilung war vermeidbar', *Das Parlament* 20 July 1954, p. 2.

Kardorff, Ursula von: *Berliner Aufzeichnungen aus den Jahren 1942 bis 1945*, Biederstein Verlag, Munich 1962.

Keesing's Contemporary Archives: Weekly Diary of Important World Events, Keesing's Publications Ltd., Keynsham, Bristol – Vol. III 1937–1940, Vol. V 1943–1945.

Keilig, Wolf: *Das deutsche Heer 1939–1945: Gliederung – Einsatz – Stellenbesetzung*, loose-leaf, Verlag Hans-Henning Podzun, Bad Nauheim 1956 et seq.

Keitel, Wilhelm: see Görlitz.

Kielmansegg, Johann A. Graf [von]: ' "An jeden anderen Tag, nur heute nicht . . ." Am. 20. Juli 1944 im Hauptquartier/Ein Erlebnisbericht', *Die Zeit* 21 July 1949.

Kiesel, Georg: see 'SS Bericht . . .'.

Kleist, Peter: *Zwischen Hitler und Stalin 1939–1945: Aufzeichnungen*, Athenäum Verlag, Bonn 1950.

Kodré, Heinrich: '20. Juli 1944 in Wien' in Ludwig Jedlicka: *Der 20. Juli 1944 in Österreich*, pp. 117–24.

Kopp, Otto: 'Die Niederschrift von Hans Walz "Meine Mitwirkung an der Aktion Goerdeler" ' in Kopp's *Widerstand und Erneuerung*, pp. 98–120 (see below).

Kopp, Otto (editor): *Widerstand und Erneuerung: Neue Berichte und Dokumente vom inneren Kampf gegen das Hitler-Regime*, Seewald Verlag, Stuttgart 1966.

Kordt, Erich: *Nicht aus den Akten: Die Wilhelmstrasse in Frieden und Krieg*, Union Deutsche Verlagsgesellschaft, Stuttgart 1950.

Kraus, H[erbert] (editor): *Die im Braunschweiger Remerprozess erstatteten moral-theologischen und historischen Gutachten nebst Urteil*, Girardet Verlag, Hamburg 1953.

Kr[ausnick], H[elmut]: 'Goerdeler und die Deportation der Leipziger Juden', *VfZ* 13 (1965), pp. 338–9.

Kriegstagebuch des Oberkommandos der Wehrmacht (Wehrmachtführungsstab) 1940–1945, Vols I-IV, Bernard & Graefe Frankfurt/M. 1965, 1963, 1963, 1961.

Kursbuch der Deutschen Reichsbahn: Sommerfahrplan 15. Mai–7. Okt. 1939. Berlin 1939.

Lagevorträge des Oberbefehlshabers der Kriegsmarine vor Hitler 1939–1945, edited by Gerhard Wagner, J. F. Lehmanns, Munich 1972.

L'Aigle, Alma de: *Meine Briefe von Theo Haubach*, Hoffmann und Campe, Hamburg 1947.

Lang, Jochen von: *Adolf Hitler: Gesichter eines Diktators*, Christian Wegner, Hamburg 1968.

Lasch, Otto: *So fiel Königsberg: Kampf und Untergang von Ostpreussens Hauptstadt*, Gräfe und Unzer, Munich 1958.

Laternser, [Hans]: *Verteidigung deutscher Soldaten: Plädoyers vor alliierten Gerichten*, Girardet Verlag, Bonn 1950.

Leber, Annedore: 'Dr Leber und Stauffenberg', *Telegraf* 16 June 1946.

Leber, Annedore: *Den toten, immer lebendigen Freunden: Eine Erinnerung zum 20. Juli 1944*, Telegraf Verlag, Berlin 1946.

[Leber Julius:] *Ein Mann geht seinen Weg: Schriften, Reden und Briefe von Julius Leber*, Mosaik-Verlag, Berlin-Schöneberg Frankfurt/M. 1952.

Leiber SJ, Robert: 'Pius XII†', *Stimmen der Zeit* 163 (1958), pp. 81–100.

Leverkuehn, Paul: *Der geheime Nachrichtendienst der deutschen Wehrmacht im Kriege*, Bernard & Graefe, Frankfurt/M ²1957; *German Military Intelligence*, translated R. H. Stevens and Constantine FitzGibbon, Weidenfeld and Nicolson, London 1954.

Leyen, Ferdinand Prinz von der: *Rückblick zum Mauerwald: Vier Kriegsjahre im OKH*, Biederstein Verlag, Munich 1965.

[Linge, Heinz:] 'Kronzeuge Linge berichtet: F.H.Qu. 20. Juli 1944 1250 Uhr', *Revue* 24 Mar. 1956, pp. 26–30.

Lochner, Louis P.: *What about Germany?* Dodd Mead and Co., New York, Toronto, 1942.

Lochner, Louis P: *Tycoons and Tyrant*, Henry Regnery Co., Chicago 1954.

Lochner, Louis P: *Always the Unexpected*, Macmillan, New York 1956.

Löbe, Paul: ['Bemerkungen zum 20. Juli 1944'], *Der Tagesspiegel* 30 Apr. 1947.

Lonsdale Bryans, J[ames]: *Blind Victory (Secret Communications, Halifax-Hassell)*, Skeffington, London 1951.

Lonsdale Bryans, J[ames]: 'Zur britischen amtlichen Haltung gegenüber der deutschen Widerstandsbewegung', *VfZ* 1 (1953), pp. 347–56.

Louis Ferdinand, Prinz von Preussen: *Als Kaiserenkel durch die Welt*, Argon Verlag, Berlin 1952.

Mader, Julius: 'Dokumentenfund zum 20. Juli 1944', *Mitteilungsblatt der Arbeitsgemeinschaft ehemaliger Offiziere*, Nos 11 and 12 of 1968, 1 and 2 of 1969, pp. 13–15, 9–12, 5–8, 11–13.

Martienssen, Anthony: *Hitler and His Admirals*, Secker and Warburg, London 1948.

[Mason-Macfarlane, Noel:] 'Widerwillen gegen Morde', *Der Spiegel* No 32, 4 Aug. 1969, p. 18.

Messtischblatt 1994 Rastenburg (Stand v. 1.10.38), Reichsamt für Landesaufnahme, [Berlin] undated.

Messtischblatt 640 Gross Stürlack Neue Nr. 1995 (Stand v. 1.10.38), Reichsamt für Landesaufnahme, [Berlin] undated.

Moltke, Helmuth J. Graf von: *Letzte Briefe aus dem Gefängnis Tegel*, Karl H. Henssel, Verlag Berlin ⁹1963; *A German of the Resistance: The Last Letters of Count Helmuth James von Moltke*, Oxford University Press, London 1948.

[Müller, Josef:] 'Für das anständige Deutschland', *Telegraf* 15 Oct. 1952.

Müller, Vincenz: *Ich fand das wahre Vaterland*, Deutscher Militärverlag, Berlin 1963.

Müller, Wolfgang: *Gegen eine neue Dolchstosslüge: Ein Erlebnisbericht zum 20. Juli 1944*, Verlag 'Das andere Deutschland', Hannover ²1947.

Münchheimer, Werner: 'Die Verfassungs- und Verwaltungsreformpläne der deutschen Opposition gegen Hitler zum 20. Juli 1944', *Europa-Archiv* 5 (1950), pp. 3188–95.

Münchner Stadtadressbuch, 1933–1943, Adressbuchverlag der Industrie- und Handelskammer München, Munich [1932–1943].

Neubronn, Alexander Freiherr von: 'Als "Deutscher General" bei Pétain' *VfZ* 4 (1956), pp. 227–50.

Nida, Ludwig von: 'Der 20. Juli 1944 in Kassel: Die Vorbereitungen', *Hessische Allgemeine* 18 July 1964.

Niekisch, Ernst: *Hitler – ein deutsches Verhängnis*, Widerstandsverlag, Berlin 1932.

Niekisch, Ernst: *Gewagtes Leben: Begegnungen und Begebnisse*, Kiepenheuer und Witsch, Cologne, Berlin 1958.

N[ostiz], G[ottfried] v[on]: 'In memoriam Hans-Bernd von Haeften: Hingerichtet am 15. August 1944', *Zeitwende* 20 (1948/49), pp. 220–4.

Papen, Franz von: *Der Wahrheit eine Gasse*, Paul List Verlag, Munich 1952; *Memoirs*, translated Brian Connell, André Deutsch, London 1953.

Pfizer, Theodor: 'Die Brüder Stauffenberg' in *Robert Boehringer: Eine Freundesgabe*, edited by Erich Boehringer and Wilhelm Hoffmann, J. C. B. Mohr, (Paul Siebeck) Tübingen 1957, pp. 487–509.

Picker, Henry: *Hitlers Tischgespräche im Führerhauptquartier 1941–1942*, Seewald Verlag, Stuttgart ²1963.

Picker, Henry [and] Hoffmann, Heinrich: *Hitlers Tischgespräche im Bild*, edited by Jochen von Lang, Gerhard Stalling Verlag, Oldenburg and Hamburg 1969.

[Pius XI:] 'Official Abstract of Pope's Encyclical on Germany', *The New York Times* 23 Mar. 1937, p. 5.

Poelchau, Harald: *Die letzten Stunden: Erinnerungen eines Gefängnispfarrer aufgezeichnet von Graf Alexander Stenbock-Fermor*, Verlag Volk and Welt, Berlin 1949.

Praun, Albert: *Soldat in der Telegraphen- und Nachrichtentruppe*, published privately, Würzburg [1966].

Reichert, Karl: 'Der 20. Juli 1944 in Paris', *Frankfurter Rundschau* 20 July 1948.

Reichsgesetzblatt Teil I, 1934, 1935, 1938, 1940, 1942, 1943, 1944, Reichsverlagsamt, Berlin 1934, 1935, 1938, 1940, 1942, 1943, 1944.

Remer, [Otto Ernst]: 'Der Ablauf der Ereignisse am 20.7.1944 wie ich sie als Kommandeur des Wachbtl. Grossdeutschland erlebte' in *20. Juli 1944*, pp. 145–52.

Remer, Otto Ernst: *20. Juli 1944*, Verlag Hans Siep, Hamburg-Neuhaus/Oste 1951.

Rilke, Rainer Maria: *Briefe: Zweiter Band 1914 bis 1926*, Insel Verlag, Wiesbaden 1950.

Röhricht, Edgar: *Pflicht und Gewissen: Erinnerungen eines deutschen Generals 1932 bis 1944*, W. Kohlhammer Verlag, Stuttgart 1965.

Röhrig, Wolfram: 'Keine bewusste Initiative', *Zeitung* 16 Aug. 1965, p. 57.

R[othfels], H[ans] (editor): 'Ausgewählte Briefe von Generalmajor Helmuth Stieff (hingerichtet am 8. August 1944)', *VfZ* ²(1954), pp. 291–305.

R[othfels], H[ans] (editor): 'Zwei aussenpolitische Memoranden der deutschen Opposition (Frühjahr 1942)', *VfZ* 5 (1957), pp. 388–97.

R[othfels], H[ans] (editor): 'Adam von Trott und das State Department', *VfZ* 7 (1959), pp. 318–32.

Rothfels, Hans: 'Trott und die Aussenpolitik des Widerstandes', *VfZ* 12 (1964), pp. 300–23.

Saefkow, Aenne: 'Helden des antifaschistischen Widerstandes', *Neues Deutschland* 18 Sept. 1947.

Sander, Ludolf G.: 'Oberstleutnant Ludolf G. Sander zu den Vorgängen im Führerhauptquartier am 20. Juli 1944' in Annedore Leber und Freya Gräfin von Moltke: *Für und wider: Entscheidungen in Deutschland 1918–1945*, Mosaik Verlag, Berlin and Frankfurt/M. 1961, pp. 205–6.

Sauerbruch, Ferdinand: *Das war mein Leben*, Kindler Verlag, Munich 1951 (*A Surgeon's Life*, translated by Fernand G. Rainer and Anne Cliff, André Deutsch, London 1953).

Schaal, Ferdinand: 'Der 20. Juli 1944 in Prag: Der Attentatstag im Spiegel militärischer Befehle', *Schwäbische Zeitung* (Überlingen) 26 July 1952.

Schacht, Hjalmar: *Abrechnung mit Hitler*, Michaelis-Verlag Berlin, Frankfurt/M. [1949]; *Account Settled*, translated Edward Fitzgerald, Weidenfeld and Nicolson, London 1949.

[Schacht, Hjalmar] 'Der "Mann der Vernunft": Starke Entlastungsaussagen im Schacht-Prozess', *Die Welt* 24 April 1947.

[Schacht, Hjalmar] 'Ersing belastet Schacht', *Der Tagesspiegel* 24 April 1947.

[Schacht, Hjalmar] 'Entlastungs-Zeugen im Schacht-Verfahren', *Der Tagesspiegel* 25 April 1947.

[Schacht, Hjalmar] 'Für und wider Schacht: CDU-Vorsitzende Kaiser und Müller als Zeugen geladen', *Die Welt* 26 April 1947.

[Schacht, Hjalmar] 'Dokumente im Schacht-Verfahren', *Der Tagesspiegel* 26 April 1947.

[Schacht, Hjalmar] 'Schacht und der 20. Juli: Widersprüchliche Zeugenaussagen in Stuttgart', *Die Neue Zeitung* 28 April 1947.

[Schacht, Hjalmar] 'Kaiser über Schacht: Kein aufrichtiger Gefolgsmann Hitlers, aber umstrittene Rolle', *Die Welt* 29 April 1947.

[Schacht, Hjalmar] 'Für und wider Schacht: Beteiligung in der Widerstandsbewegung umstritten', *Die Welt* 30 April 1947.

Schärf, Adolf: *Österreichs Erneuerung 1945–1955*, Wiener Volksbuchhandlung, Vienna 1955.

Schärf, Adolf, *Erinnerungen aus meinem Leben*, Wiener Volksbuchhandlung, Vienna 1963.

Scheidt, Wilhelm: 'Wahrheit gegen Karikatur: Eine deutsche Antwort an Gisevius', *Neue Politik* 9 (1948), Nos 7–11, 1, 15, 29 Apr., 13, 27 May 1948, pp. 1–4, 1–3, 1–3, 1–3, 1–2.

Scheidt, Wilhelm: 'Gespräche mit Hitler', *Echo der Woche* 9 Sept. 1949. p. 5.

Schellenberg, Walter: *Memoiren*, Verlag für Politik und Wirtschaft, Köln 1956; *The Schellenberg Memoirs*, introduction Alan Bullock, edited and translated Louis Hagen, André Deutsch, London 1956.

Schlabrendorff, Fabian von: *Offiziere gegen Hitler*, Europa Verlag, Zurich 1946; *They almost killed Hitler*, Macmillan, New York 1947; *Revolt Against Hitler: The Personal Account of Fabian von Schlabrendorff*. Prepared and edited by Gero v.S. Gaevernitz, Eyre and Spottiswoode, London 1948.

Schlabrendorff, Fabian von: *The Secret War Against Hitler*, translated by Hilda Simon, Hodder and Stoughton, London 1966.

Schlabrendorff, Fabian von (editor): *Eugen Gerstenmaier im Dritten Reich: Eine Dokumentation*, Evangelisches Verlagswerk, Stuttgart 1965.

Schlee, Rudolf, 'Bericht' in *20. Juli 1944*, pp. 152–5.

Schlotterbeck, Friedrich: *Je dunkler die Nacht, desto heller die Sterne: Erinnerungen eines deutschen Arbeiters 1933 bis 1945*, Europa Verlag, Berlin, ²1948.

Schlotterbeck, Friedrich: . . . *Wegen Vorbereitung zum Hochverrat hingerichtet . . .*, Limes-Verlag, Stuttgart [²1946].

Schmid, Rudolf: 'Die Ereignisse des 22. Juni 1944: Wer kennt den Gestapospitzel Heim?', *Telegraf* 3 Jan. 1947.

SchmidNoerr, Friedrich Alfred: 'Dokument des Widerstandes: Entwurf einer deutschen Reichsverfassung (geschrieben im Sommer 1937)', *Voran und beharrlich* No 33/34, summer 1961.

Schmidt, Paul: *Statist auf diplomatischer Bühne 1923–45: Erlebnisse des Chefdolmetschers im Auswärtigen Amt mit den Staatsmännern Europas*, Athenänum Verlag, Bonn 1949; *Hitler's Interpreter*, edited R. H. C. Steed, William Heinemann, London 1951.

Schober, Karl: 'Eine Chance blieb ungenutzt' in *Darauf kam die Gestapo nicht: Beiträge zum Widerstand im Rundfunk*, Haude & Spenersche Verlagshandlung, Berlin 1966, pp. 52–66.

[Schramm, Percy Ernst] in Herbert Kraus: *Die im Braunschweiger Remerprozess . . .* 'Vorgänge im FHQu am 20.7.44 (Attentat auf den Führer), pp. 139–41. 'Mitteilungen des Stellv. Chefs WFSt 21.7.44, 20 Uhr', pp. 142–5. '3. Aufzeichnung über die Vorgänge des 20.7.44', pp. 146–7. 'Mitteilungen des Oberst d.G. Meichsner, Abt.-Leiter der Abt. Org, 23.7., 9 Uhr', pp. 148–50. 'Mitteilung des Oberst Frhr. v. Süsskind (Ic/Abwehr)', p. 150.

Schramm, Wilhelm Ritter von (editor): *Beck und Goerdeler: Gemeinschaftsdokumente für den Frieden 1941–1944*, Gotthold Müller Verlag, Munich 1965.

Schuschnigg, Kurt von: *Austrian Requiem*, translated Franz von Hildebrand, Victor Gollancz, London 1947.

Schwerin von Krosigk, Lutz Graf: *Es geschah in Deutschland: Menschenbilder unseres Jahrhunderts*, Rainer Wunderlich Verlag Hermann Leins, Tübingen and Stuttgart ³1952.

Semmler, Rudolf: *Goebbels – the man next to Hitler*, Westhouse, London 1947.

Sethe, Paul: 'Roland Freisler: Der Dämon der Justiz', *Schwäbische Zeitung* 7 May 1946.

Sethe, Paul: *In Wasser geschrieben: Porträts, Profile, Prognosen*, Verlag Heinrich Scheffler, Frankfurt/M 1968.

Shirer, William L: *Berlin Diary: The Journal of a Foreign Correspondent 1934–1941*, Hamish Hamilton, London 1941.

Skorzeny, Otto: *Geheimkommando Skorzeny*, Hansa Verlag, Hamburg 1950; *Skorzeny's Special Missions*, Robert Hale, London 1957.

Sommerfeldt, Martin Henry: *Das OKW gibt bekannt*, Westdeutsche Verlags- und Druckereigesellschaft, Frankfurt/M. 1952.

Speer, Albert: *Erinnerungen*, Propyläen Verlag, Berlin 1969; *Inside the Third Reich*, translated Richard and Clara Winstone, Weidenfeld and Nicolson, London 1970.

Speidel, Hans: *Invasion 1944: Ein Beitrag zu Rommels und des Reiches Schicksal*, Rainer Wunderlich Verlag Hermann Leins, Tübingen ³1950; *We defended Normandy*, translated Ian Colvin, Herbert Jenkins, London 1951.

Spiegelbild einer Verschwörung: Die Kaltenbrunner-Berichte an Bormann und Hitler über das Attentat vom 20. Juli 1944. Geheime Dokumente aus dem ehemaligen Reichssicherheitshauptamt, Seewald Verlag, Stuttgart 1961.

Spier, Eugen: *Focus: A Footnote to the History of the Thirties*, Oswald Wolff, London 1963.

Spranger, Eduard: 'Generaloberst Beck in der Mittwochsgesellschaft: Zu dem Buch: Ludwig Beck "Studien" ', *Universitas* 11 (1956), pp. 183–93.

'SS-Bericht über den 20. Juli: Aus den Papieren des SS-Obersturmbannführers Dr Georg Kiesel', *Nordwestdeutsche Hefte* 2 (1947), No 1/2, pp. 5–34.

Stauffenberg, [Claus] Graf Schenk von: 'Gedanken zur Abwehr feindlicher Fallschirmeinheiten im Heimatgebiet', *Wissen und Wehr* 19 (1938), pp. 459–76.

Steltzer, Theodor: *Von deutscher Politik: Dokumente, Aufsätze und Vorträge*,

Knecht, Frankfurt/M. 1949.

Steltzer, Theodor: *Sechzig Jahre Zeitgenosse*, List Verlag, Munich 1966.

Stieff, Helmuth – see Rothfels.

Sündermann, Helmut: *Deutsche Notizen 1945/1965: Erlebnis – Widerspruch – Erwartung*, Druffel-Verlag, Leoni am Starnberger See ²1966.

Szokoll, Karl: 'Der 20. Juli 1944 in Wien', *Die Presse* 31 Jan., 7 Feb. 1948.

Teske, Hermann: *Die silbernen Spiegel: Generalstabsdienst unter der Lupe*, Kurt Vowinckel, Heidelberg 1952.

Thomas, Georg: 'Gedanken und Ereignisse', *Schweizer Monatshefte* 25 (1945), pp. 537–59.

Thormaehlen, Ludwig: 'Die Grafen Stauffenberg, Freunde von Stefan George' in *Robert Boehringer: Eine Freundesgabe*, edited by Erich Boeheinger and Wilhelm Hoffmann, J. C. B. Mohr (Paul Siebeck), Tübingen 1957, pp. 685–96.

The Times, London 1936, 1944.

Topf, Erwin: 'Klaus Graf Stauffenberg', *Die Zeit* 18 July 1946.

Treue, Wilhelm (ed.): 'Rede Hitlers vor der deutschen Presse (10. November 1938)' *VfZ* 6 (1958), pp. 175–91.

Treue, Wolfgang: *Deutsche Parteiprogramme seit 1861*, Musterschmidt-Verlag, Göttingen ⁴1968.

Trial of the Major War Criminals before the International Military Tribunal: Nuremberg 14 November 1945 – 1 October 1946 (42 vols), Secretariat of the Tribunal, Nuremberg 1947–1949.

Trials of War Criminals before the Nuremberg Military Tribunals under Control Council Law No. 10 (15 vols), U.S. Government Printing Office, Washington 1949–1953.

Üxküll, A[lexandrine] Gräfin von: *Aus einem Schwesternleben*, Kohlhammer Verlag, Stuttgart 1956.

United States of America Congressional Record: Proceedings and Debates of the 76th Congress, Second Session, Vol. 85, Part I, U.S. Government Printing Office, Washington 1939.

Vermehren, Isa: *Reise durch den letzten Akt*, Christian Wegner Verlag, Hamburg 1947.

Visser 't Hooft, Willen, A.: *Die Welt war meine Gemeinde: Autobiographie*, R. Piper & Co. Verlag, Munich 1972.

Vogelsang, Thilo: 'Neue Dokumente zur Geschichte der Reichswehr 1930–1933' *VfZ* 2 (1954), pp. 397–436.

Völkischer Beobachter 1939–1944, Berlin edition.

Volksgerichtshof-Prozesse zum 20. Juli 1944: Transkripte von Tonbandfunden, Lautarchiv des Deutschen Rundfunks, [Frankfurt/M.] 1961.

'Vor fünf Jahren: 20. Juli 12.40 in der Wolfsschanze. Ein Augenzeuge berichtet über die Vorgänge in Hitlers Hauptquartier', *Neue Frankfurter Illustrierte* No 14 July 1949, pp. 9–11, 26–7.

Wagner, Eduard: *Der Generalquartiermeister: Briefe und Tagebuchaufzeichnungen*, Günther Olzog Verlag, Munich and Vienna 1963.

W[aizenegger], H[einz]: 'Der 20. Juli 1944 im "Führerhauptquartier" Von einem Augenzeugen', *Stuttgarter Zeitung* 20 July 1949, p. 3.

Walz, Hans – see Kopp.

Warlimont, Walter: *Im Hauptquartier der deutschen Wehrmacht 1939–1945: Grundlagen, Formen, Gestalten*, Bernard and Graefe, Frankfurt/M 1962; *Inside Hitler's Headquarters*, translated Richard Barry, Weidenfeld and Nicolson, London 1964.

Wedemeyer, Albert C.: *Wedemeyer Reports!* Henry Holt & Co., New York 1958 (*Der verwaltet Krieg*, Sigbert Mohn Verlag Gütersloh 1958).

Weinberger, Lois: *Tatsachen, Begegnungen und Gespräche: Ein Buch um Österreich*, Österreich Verlag, Vienna 1948.

Sources and Bibliography

Weizsäcker, Ernst von: *Erinnerungen*, Paul List Verlag, Munich 1950.

Welles, Sumner: *The Time for Decision*, Harper Bros, Hamish Hamilton, New York and London 1944.

Wengler, Wilhelm: 'Vorkämpfer der Völkerverständigung und Völkerrechtslehre als Opfer des Nationalsozialismus: 9. H. J. Graf von Moltke (1906–1945)', *Die Friedens-Warte* 48 (1948), pp. 297–305.

' "Widerstand ist vaterländische Pflicht": Aus den Akten des Schwedischen Ministerium des "Äusseren" ', *Politische Studien* 10 (1959), pp. 435–9.

Wiechert, Ernst: 'Der Dichter und seine Zeit', *Deutsche Blätter* (Santiago de Chile), 1 (1943), No 6, pp. 4–8.

Wiedemann, Fritz: *Der Mann der Feldherr werden wollte: Erlebnisse und Erfahrungen des Vorgesetzten Hitlers im I. Weltkrieg und seines späteren Persönlichen Adjutanten*, Blick & Bild Verlag, für politische Bildung, Velbert-Kettwig 1964.

Young, A. P.: *The 'X' Documents*, edited by Sidney Aster, André Deutsch, London 1974.

Ziegler, Delia: 'Wer schoss auf Stauffenberg?' *Die Welt* 21 Aug. 1947, p. 2.

Ziegler, Hans Severus: *Adolf Hitler aus dem Erleben dargestellt*, Verlag Ka.W. Schütz, Göttingen 1964.

Zoller, Albert: *Hitler privat: Erlebnisbericht seiner Geheimsekretärin*, Droste Verlag, Düsseldorf 1949.

V PUBLISHED MATERIAL – SECONDARY SOURCES

Abshagen, Karl Heinz: *Canaris: Patriot und Weltbürger*, Union Deutsche Verlagsgesellschaft, Stuttgart 1949; *Canaris*, translated A. H. Brodrick, Hutchinson, London 1956.

Almond, Gabriel A.: 'The German Resistance Movement', *Current History* 10 (1946), pp. 409–19, 519–27.

Aronson, Shlomo: *Reinhard Heydrich und die Frühgeschichte von Gestapo und SD*, Deutsche Verlags-Anstalt, Stuttgart 1971.

Balfour, Michael and Frisby, Julian: *Helmuth von Moltke: A Leader against Hitler*, Macmillan, London 1972.

Baum, Walter: 'Marine, Nationalsozialismus und Widerstand' *VfZ* 11 (1963), pp. 16–48.

Baumgärtel, Friedrich: *Wider die Kirchenkampflegenden*, Freimund-Verlag Neuendettelsau/Mfr. ²1959.

Baumgart, Winfried: 'Zur Ansprache Hitlers vor den Führern der Wehrmacht am 22. August 1939: Eine quellenkritische Untersuchung', *VfZ* 16 (1968), pp. 120–49.

Bayne, E. A.: 'Resistance in the German Foreign Office', *Human Events* III (1946), No 14, pp. 1–8.

Beck, Hans: 'Die Rettung der Sippe Stauffenberg', *Die Tagespost* (Augsburg) 17 Nov. 1949.

Bethge, Eberhard: *Dietrich Bonhoeffer: Theologe, Christ, Zeitgenosse*, Chr. Kaiser Verlag, Munich 1967; *Dietrich Bonhoeffer*, translated Eric Mosbacher [and others], Collins, London 1970.

Bierbaum, Max: *Nicht Lob, nicht Furcht: Das Leben des Kardinals von Galen nach unveröffentlichten Briefen und Dokumenten*, Verlag Regensberg, Munich ⁵1962.

Binder, Gerhart: *Epoche der Entscheidungen: Eine Geschichte des 20. Jahrhunderts*, Seewald Verlag, Stuttgart-Degerloch 1960.

Blond, Georges: *The Death of Hitler's Germany*, Macmillan, New York 1954.

Boehringer, Robert: *Mein Bild von Stefan George*, (2 vols) Helmut Küpper, previously Georg Bondi, Munich, Düsseldorf ²1967.

Bösch, Hermann: *Heeresrichter Dr Sack im Widerstand: Eine historisch-politische Studie*, Gotthold Müller Verlag, Munich 1967.

Boveri, Margret: *Wir lügen alle: Eine Hauptstadtzeitung unter Hitler*, Walter-Verlag, Freiburg i.Br. 1965.

Bracher, Karl Dietrich/Sauer, Wolfgang/Schulz, Gerhard: *Die nationalsozialistische Machtergreifung: Studien zur Errichtung des totalitären Herrschaftssystems in Deutschland 1933/34*, Westdeutscher Verlag, Köln & Opladen ²1962.

Braubach, Max: *Der Weg zum 20. Juli 1944: Ein Forschungsbericht*, Westdeutscher Verlag, Köln-Opladen 1953.

Brausch, Gerd: 'Der Tod des Generalobersten Werner Freiherr von Fritsch', *Militärgeschichtliche Mitteilungen* 1970 No. 1, pp. 95–112.

Brentano, [Heinrich] von: *Gedenkrede des Bundesministers Dr. von Brentano bei der Enthüllung der Ehrentafel für die Opfer des 20. Juli im Auswärtigen Amt am 20. Juli 1961*, [Auswärtiges Amt, Bonn] 1961.

Buchheim, Hans/Broszat, Martin/Jacobsen, Hans-Adolf/Krausnick, Helmut: *Anatomie des SS-Staates*, Walter-Verlag, Olten-Freiburg i.Br., 1965 (English edition see below under Krausnick).

Buchheit, Gert: *Ludwig Beck, ein preussischer General*, Paul List Verlag, Munich 1964.

Buchheit, Gert: *Der deutsche Geheimdienst: Geschichte der militärischen Abwehr*, Paul List Verlag, Munich 1966.

Buck, Gerhard: 'Das Führerhauptquartier: Seine Darstellung in der deutschen Literatur', *Jahresbibliographie der Bibliothek für Zeitgeschichte Weltkriegsbücherei Stuttgart*, 38 (1966) Bernard and Graefe, Frankfurt/M. 1968, pp. 549–66.

Bullock, Alan: *Hitler: A Study in Tyranny*, Odhams Books Ltd., London 1964.

Celovsky, Boris: *Das Münchener Abkommen 1938*, Deutsche Verlags-Anstalt, Stuttgart 1958.

Churchill, Rhona: 'Widow Strunk goes to Nuremberg', *Daily Mail* 28 Mar. 1946.

Churchill, Winston S.: *The Second World War* (Vol VI), Cassell and Co., London 1954.

Colvin, Ian: *Chief of Intelligence*, Victor Gollancz, London 1951 (*Master Spy: The Incredible Story of Admiral Wilhelm Canaris*, McGraw-Hill, New York 1951).

Colvin, Ian: *Vansittart in Office: An historical survey of the origins of the second world war based on the papers of Sir Robert Vansittart Permanent Under-Secretary of State for Foreign Affairs 1930–38*, Victor Gollancz London 1965.

[Conway, J[ohn] S.: *The Nazi Persecution of the Churches 1933–45*, Weidenfeld and Nicolson, London 1968.

Conway, John S.: 'The Vatican, Great Britain, and Relations with Germany, 1938–1940', *The Historical Journal* 16 (1973), pp. 147–67.

Dahrendorf, Gustav: 'Irrungen um Thomas', *Hamburger Echo* 4 Sept. 1946.

Dallin, David J.: *Soviet Espionage*, Yale University Press, New Haven, Oxford University Press, London 1955.

'Das Spiel ist aus – Arthur Nebe: Glanz und Elend der deutschen Kriminalpolizei', *Der Spiegel* No 12, 23 Mar. 1950, pp. 23–32.

Deutsch, Harold C.: *The Conspiracy against Hitler in the Twilight War*, University of Minnesota Press, Minneapolis, Oxford University Press, London 1968.

'Deutsche Gespräche über das Recht zum Widerstand' in *Vollmacht des Gewissens*, Vol. 1 (see below), pp. 13–136.

Dietz, P[eter]: 'Mut und Angst: Zum Attentat in der "Wolfsschanze" am 20. Juli 1944', *Allgemeine Schweizerische Militärzeitschrift* 130 (1964), pp. 442–4.

Dietz, P[eter]: 'Das Attentat auf Hitler am 20. Juli 1944', *Der Schweizer Soldat* 40 (1964), pp. 600–2.

Dietz, Peter: 'Das Attentat auf Hitler: Bilder und Gedanken in einem "Führerhauptquartier" ', *Schaffhauser Nachrichten* 18 July 1964.

Dietze, Constantin von: 'Die Universität Freiburg im Dritten Reich', *Mitteilungen der List Gesellschaft*, fasc. 3 (1960/61) No 3, pp. 95–105.

Donohue, James: *Hitler's Conservative Opponents in Bavaria 1930–1945: A Study of Catholic, Monarchist and Separatist Anti-Nazi Activities*, E. J. Brill, Leiden 1961.

Eder, Peter G.: 'Deutschland, deine Helden. 21 Jahre danach: Wer war was am 20. Juli 1944? Zeitung sprach mit Zeugen des Aufstandes', *Zeitung* 19 July 1965, pp. 17–21.

Ehlers, Dieter: *Technik und Moral einer Verschwörung: Der Aufstand am 20. Juli 1944*, Bundeszentrale für politische Bildung, Bonn 1964.

'Ein "Plan Lanz" war Rommel bekannt', *Passauer Neue Presse*, 21 July 1949, p. 3.

'Entscheidende Minuten am 20. Juli', *Hamburger Allgemeine Zeitung* 20 July 1949, pp. 1–2.

Erb, Alfons: *Bernhard Lichtenberg: Dompropst von St. Hedwig zu Berlin*, Morus Verlag, Berlin 1946.

Erfurth, Waldemar: 'Generaloberst a.D. Halder zum 70. Geburtstage (30.6.1954)' *Wehrwissenschaftliche Rundschau* 4 (1954), pp. 241–51.

E[schenburg], T[heodor]: 'Zur Ermordung des Generals Schleicher', *VfZ* 1 (1953), pp. 71–95.

'Fehlschlag', *Der Spiegel*, No 27, 30 June 1969, p. 105.

Finker, Kurt: *Stauffenberg und der 20 Juli 1944*, Union Verlag, Berlin, 1967, [4]1973.

Finker, Kurt: *Stauffenberg und der 20 Juli 1944*, Union Verlag, Berlin, 1967 [2]1971.

Fischer, Alfred Joachim: 'Retter der dänischen Juden: Einen Massenmord auf "Führerbefehl" verhindert', *Stuttgarter Zeitung* 20 April 1970, p. 3.

Flicke, W. F.: *Spionagegruppe Rote Kapelle*, Verlag Welsermühl, Wels 1957.

Foerster, Wolfgang: *Generaloberst Ludwig Beck: Sein Kampf gegen den Krieg*, Isar Verlag, Munich 1953.

Ford, Franklin L.: 'The Twentieth of July in the History of the German Resistance', *American Historical Review* 51 (1945/46), pp. 609–26.

Ford, Franklin L.: 'Der 20. Juli', *Die Amerikanische Rundschau* 3 (1947) No 11, pp. 5–17.

Franz, Helmut/Gerstein, Kurt: *Aussenseiter des Widerstandes der Kirche gegen Hitler*, EVZ Verlag, Zurich 1964.

Gallin, O.S.U. Mother Mary Alice: *Ethical and Religious Factors in the German Resistance to Hitler*, Catholic University of America Press, Washington 1955.

Gebhardt, Bruno: *Handbuch der deutschen Geschichte*, Vol. 4, Union Verlag, Stuttgart [8]1959.

The German Resistance to Hitler, translated by Peter and Betty Ross, B. T. Batsford Ltd., London 1970. German ed. see Schmitthenner.

Glondajewski, Gertrud/Schumann, Heinz: *Die Neubauer-Poser-Gruppe: Dokumente und Materialien des illegalen antifaschistischen Kampfes (Thüringen – 1939 bis 1945)*, Dietz Verlag, Berlin 1957.

Göhring, Rolf: 'General Fellgiebel: Leben, Wirken und Tod eines genialen Vorkämpfers der Nachrichtentruppe', *Impulse*, June 1960, pp. 8–10.

Görlitz, Walter: *Der deutsche Generalstab: Geschichte und Gestalt 1657–1945*, Verlag der Frankfurter Hefte, Frankfurt 1950; *The German General Staff*, translated Brian Battershaw, Hollis and Carter, London 1953.

Graml, Hermann: 'Die deutsche Militäropposition vom Sommer 1940 bis zum Frühjahr 1943' in *Vollmacht des Gewissens*, Vol. 2 (see below), pp. 411–74.

Graml, Hermann: 'Die aussenpolitischen Vorstellungen des deutschen Widerstandes' in Schmitthenner/Buchheim: *Der deutsche Widerstand gegen Hitler* (see below), pp. 15–72.

Graml, Hermann: 'Der Fall Oster', *VfZ* 14 (1966), pp. 26–39.

Haffner, Sebastian: ' "Beinahe": Die Geschichte des 20. Juli 1944', *Neue Auslese* 2 (1947), No 8, pp. 1–12.

Hammer, Walter: 'Das Ende des Generalobersten Fromm', *Rhein-Neckar-Zeitung* 17

Sept. 1946.

Hammer, Walter: 'Dienst an der Wahrheit', *Das freie Wort* 3 (1952), 13 Sept. 1952.

Hammer, Walter: 'Plötzensee', *Das freie Wort* 3 (1952), 20 Sept. 1952.

Hammer, Walter: 'Die "Gewitteraktion" vom 22.8.44: Vor 15 Jahren wurden deutsche Parlamentarier zu Tausenden verhaftet', *Freiheit und Recht* 5 (1959), No 8/9, pp. 15–18.

Hammer, Walter: *Hohes Haus in Henkers Hand: Rückschau auf die Hitlerzeit, auf Leidensweg und Opfergang Deutscher Parlamentarier*, Europäische Verlagsanstalt, Frankfurt/M. ²1956.

Harder, Alexander: *Kriminalzentrale Werderscher Markt: Die Geschichte des 'Deutschen Scotland Yard'*, Hestia Verlag, Bayreuth 1963.

Harnack, Axel v[on]: 'Arvid und Mildred Harnack: Erinnerungen an ihren Prozess 1942/43', *Die Gegenwart* 2 (1947), No 1/2, pp. 15–18.

Harnack, Axel von: *Ernst von Harnack (1888–1945): Ein Kämpfer für Deutschlands Zukunft*, Neckar Verlag, Schwenningen 1951.

Henderson, James L.: *Adolf Reichwein: Eine politisch-pädagogische Biographie* Deutsche Verlags-Anstalt, Stuttgart 1958.

Henk, Emil: 'Rede anlässlich der Gedenkfeier zum 20. Juli 1944 am 24.7.1960', mimeographed, 'Hilfswerk 20. Juli 1944' Foundation, Frankfurt/M. 1961.

'Der Henker des 20. Juli: Der Scherge Hitlers in Hannover festgenommen', *Hannoversche Neueste Nachrichten* 24 Aug. 1946.

Herfeldt, Olav: *Schwarze Kapelle: Spionagefall Berlin-Vatikan*, Verlag Welsermühl, Wels-Munich 1960.

Hobe, Cord v[on]/Görlitz, Walter: *Georg von Boeselager: Ein Reiterleben*, Verlag St. Georg, Düsseldorf 1957.

Hoch, Anton: 'Das Attentat auf Hitler im Münchner Bürgerbräukeller 1939', *VfZ* 17 (1969), pp. 383–413.

Höhne, Heinz: *Der Orden unter dem Totenkopf: Die Geschichte der SS*, Sigbert Mohn Verlag, Gütersloh 1967; *The Order of the Death's Head*, translated Richard Barry, Secker and Warburg, London 1969.

Höhne, Heinz: *Kennwort: Direktor. Die Geschichte der Roten Kapelle*, S. Fischer Verlag, Frankfurt/M. 1970. *Codeword Direktor,* translated Richard Barry, Secker and Warburg, 1971.

Hofer, Walther: *Die Entfesselung des Zweiten Weltkrieges: Eine Studie über die internationalen Beziehungen im Sommer 1939*, Fischer Bücherei, Frankfurt/M. and Hamburg 1960 (*War Premeditated 1939*, translated by Stanley Godman, Thames and Hudson, London [1955]).

Hoffmann, Peter: 'Zum Ablauf des Staatsstreichversuches des 20. Juli 1944 in den Wehrkreisen', *Wehrwissenschaftliche Rundschau* 14 (1964), pp. 377–97.

Hoffmann, Peter: 'Zu dem Attentat im Führerhauptquartier "Wolfsschanze" am 20. Juli 1944', *VfZ* 12 (1964), pp. 254–84.

Hoffmann, Peter: 'Der 20. Juli im Wehrkreis II (Stettin): Ein Beispiel für den Ablauf des Staatsstreichversuches im Reich', *Aus Politik und Zeitgeschichte* 14 July 1965, pp. 25–37.

Hoffmann, Peter C.: 'The Attempt to Assassinate Hitler on March 21 1943', *Canadian Journal of History/Annales Canadiennes d'Histoire* II (1967), pp. 67–83.

Hoffmann, Peter: 'Claus Graf Stauffenberg und Stefan George: Der Weg zur Tat', *Jahrbuch der Deutschen Schillergesellschaft* XII (1968), pp. 520–42.

Hoffmann, Peter: 'Hitler's Personal Security', *Journal of Contemporary History* 8 (1973) No 2, pp. 25–46.

Hoffmann, Peter: 'Maurice Bavaud's Attempt to Assassinate Hitler in 1938' in *Police Forces in History*, ed. by George L. Mosse, Sage Publications, London [1975], pp. 173–204.

Hoffmann, Peter: *Die Sicherheit des Diktators: Hitlers Leibwachen, Schutzmassnahmen, Residenzen, Hauptquartiere*, R. Piper & Co. Verlag, Munich, Zurich 1975.

Sources and Bibliography

Hoffmann, Wilhelm: *Nach der Katastrophe*, Rainer Wunderlich Verlag (Hermann Leins), Tübingen & Stuttgart 1946.

Irving, David: *Hitler und seine Feldherren*, Ullstein, Frankfurt/M., Berlin, Vienna 1975.

Italiaander, Rolf (editor): *In memoriam Albrecht Haushofer: Gedenkworte von Adolf Grimme, Carl F. v. Weizsäcker, Walter Stubbe*, Verlag Friedrich Oetinger, Hamburg 1948.

Jacobsen, Hans-Adolf: *Fall Gelb: Der Kampf um den deutschen Operationsplan zur Westoffensive 1940*, Franz Steiner Verlag, Wiesbaden 1957.

Jacobsen, Hans-Adolf: 'Das "Halder-Tagebuch" als historische Quelle' in *Festschrift Percy Ernst Schramm zu seinem siebzigsten Geburtstag von seinen Schülern und Freunden zugeeignet*, edited by Peter Classen and Peter Scheibert, Vol. II, Franz Steiner Verlag, Wiesbaden 1964, pp. 251–68.

Jacobsen, Hans-Adolf (editor): *20. Juli 1944: Die deutsche Opposition gegen Hitler im Urteil der ausländischen Geschichtsschreibung. Eine Anthologie*, Franz Steiner Verlag, [Wiesbaden 1969].

Jantar, Jerzy: *Wilczy Szaniec: Dawna Kwatera Hitlera*, Pojezierze, Olsztyn 1963.

Jedlicka, Ludwig: *Der 20. Juli 1944 in Österreich*, Verlag Herold, Vienna and Munich 1965.

Kardoff, Ursula von: 'Zum Gedenken an Graf von der Schulenburg: Porträt eines Edelmannes', *Frankfurter Allgemeine Zeitung* 21/22 July 1956.

Kempski, Jürgen von: 'Betrachtungen zum 20. Juli', *Merkur* III (1949), pp. 807–16.

Kielmansegg, [Johann A.] Graf [von]: *Der Fritschprozess 1938: Ablauf und Hintergründe*, Hoffmann und Campe Verlag, Hamburg 1949.

Kliem, Kurt: 'Der sozialistische Widerstand gegen das Dritte Reich dargestellt an der Gruppe "Neu Beginnen" ', typescript, dissertation, Marburg 1957.

Kluke, Paul: 'Der Fall Potempa', *VfZ* 5 1957, pp. 279–97.

Knauth, Percy: 'The Hitler Bomb Plot', *Life* No 22, 28 May 1945, pp. 17–18, 20–3.

Knauth, Percy: *Germany in Defeat*, Alfred A. Knopf, New York 1946.

Kosthorst, Erich: *Die deutsche Opposition gegen Hitler zwischen Polen- und Frankreichfeldzug*, Bundeszentrale für Heimatdienst, Bonn [3] 1957.

Kosthorst, Erich: *Jakob Kaiser: Der Arbeiterführer*, W. Kohlhammer Verlag, Stuttgart, Berlin, Köln, Mainz 1967.

Kramarz, Joachim: *Claus Graf Stauffenberg 15. November 1907 – 20. Juli 1944: Das Leben eines Offiziers*, Bernard und Graefe, Frankfurt/M. 1965; *Stauffenberg: The Life and Death of an Officer*, introduction H. R. Trevor-Roper, translated Richard Barry, André Deutsch, London 1967.

Krammer, Arnold: 'Germans against Hitler: The Thaelmann Brigade', *Journal of Contemporary History* 4 (1969), pp. 65–83.

Krausnick, Helmut: 'Vorgeschichte und Beginn des militärischen Widerstandes gegen Hitler' in *Vollmacht des Gewissens*, Vol. I (see below), pp. 177–99.

Krausnick Helmut/Buchheim, Hans/Broszat, Martin/Jacobsen, Hans-Adolf: *Anatomy of the SS State*, translated Richard Barry, Marian Jackson, Dorothy Long, Collins, London 1968.

Krebs, Albert: *Fritz-Dietlof Graf von der Schulenburg: Zwischen Staatsraison und Hochverrat*, Leibniz-Verlag, Hamburg 1964.

Krüger, Gabriele: *Die Brigade Ehrhardt*, Leibniz-Verlag, Hamburg 1971.

Langemann, Hans: *Das Attentat: Eine kriminalwissenschaftliche Studie zum politischen Kapitalverbrechen*, Kriminalistik Verlag für Kriminalistische Fachliteratur, Hamburg [1956].

Leasor, James: *Rudolf Hess: The Uninvited Envoy*, George Allen and Unwin, London 1962.

Leber, Annedore: *Das Gewissen steht auf: 64 Lebensbilder aus dem deutschen Widerstand 1933–1945*, Mosaik-Verlag, Berlin and Frankfurt [9] 1960; *Conscience in Revolt*, translated Rosemary O'Neill, Valentine Mitchell, London 1957.

Leber, Annedore: *Das Gewissen entscheidet: Bereiche des deutschen Widerstandes von 1933–1945 in Lebensbildern*, Mosaik-Verlag, Berlin and Frankfurt ⁴1960.

Leber, Annedore und Moltke, Freya Gräfin von: *Für und wider: Entscheidungen in Deutschland 1918–1945*, Mosaik-Verlag, Berlin and Frankfurt/M. 1961.

Leithäuser, Joachim G.: *Wilhelm Leuschner: Ein Leben für die Republik*, Bund-Verlag, Köln 1962.

Lindgren, Henrik: 'Adam von Trotts Reisen nach Schweden 1942–1944: Ein Beitrag zur Frage der Auslandsverbindungen des deutschen Widerstandes', *VfZ* 18 (1970), pp. 274–91.

Lorenz, Konrad: *On Aggression*, Harcourt, Brace and World, New York 1966.

Ludlow, Peter: 'Papst Pius XII, die britische Regierung und die deutsche Opposition im Winter 1939/40', *VfZ* 22 (1974), pp. 299–341.

Ludwig, Emil: *The Davos Murder*, translated by Eden and Cedar Paul, Methuen, London 1937.

Lühe, Irmgard von der: *Elisabeth von Thadden: Ein Schicksal unserer Zeit*, Eugen Diederichs Verlag, Düsseldorf and Köln 1966.

'Märtyrer der Freiheit: Die Angeklagten des 20. Juli vor Gericht', *Schwäbische Zeitung* 10 May 1946.

Maier, Hedwig, 'Die SS und der 20. Juli 1944', *VfZ* 14 (1966), pp. 299–316.

Maley, Alexander B.: 'The Epic of the German Underground', *Human Events* III (1946), No 9, 27 Feb. 1946, pp. 1–8.

Manvell, Roger and Fraenkel, Heinrich: *The July Plot*, Bodley Head, London 1964.

Manvell, Roger and Fraenkel, Heinrich: 'The Bomb Plot', *History of the Second World War*, Purnell Publ., London 1966–69, p. 1965.

Mastny, Vojtech: 'Stalin and the Prospects of a Separate Peace in World War II', *American Historical Review* 77 (1972), pp. 1365–88.

Matthias, Erich: 'Der Untergang der Sozialdemokratie 1933', *VfZ* 4 (1956), pp. 179–226, 250–86.

Mau, Hermann: 'Die "Zweite Revolution": Der 30. Juni 1934', *VfZ* 1 (1953), pp. 119–27.

Mau, Hermann and Krausnick, Helmut: *Deutsche Geschichte der jüngsten Vergangenheit 1933–1945*, Wunderlich Verlag Hermann Leins/J. B. Metzlersche Verlagsbuchhandlung, Tübingen/Stuttgart 1956; *German History 1933–45*, Oswald Wolff, London 1959.

McCloy II, John J.: *Die Verschwörung gegen Hitler: Ein Geschenk an die deutsche Zukunft*, Friedrich Vorwerk Verlag, Stuttgart 1963.

Melnikow, Daniil: *Der 20. Juli 1944: Legende und Wirklichkeit*, Christian Wegner Verlag, Hamburg ²[1968].

Michel, Karl: 'Stauffenberg: Der neue Dynamismus. Ein Beitrag zur Geschichte des Offiziersputsches gegen Hitler', *Die Tat* 25 Nov. 1946.

Michel, Karl: *Ost und West: Der Ruf Stauffenbergs*, Thomas Verlag, Zurich 1947.

Michel, Ursula: 'Albrecht Haushofer und der Nationalsozialismus: Ein Beitrag zur Zeitgeschichte', typescript, dissertation, Kiel 1964.

Miller, Max: *Eugen Bolz: Staatsmann und Bekenner*, Schwabenverlag, Stuttgart 1951.

Molden, Otto: *Der Ruf des Gewissens: Der österreichische Freiheitskampf 1938–1945*, Verlag Herold, Vienna & Munich 1958.

Mommsen, Hans: 'Der Reichstagsbrand und seine politischen Folgen', *VfZ* 12 (1964), pp. 351–413.

Mommsen, Hans: 'Gesellschaftsbild und Verfassungspläne des deutschen Widerstandes' in Schmitthenner/Buchheim: *Der deutsche Widerstand gegen Hitler* (see below) pp. 73–167.

Mommsen, Hans: 'Pläne und Träume zum Tag X', *Der Spiegel* No 36, 28 Aug. 1967, pp. 94–7.

Müller, Christian: *Oberst i.G. Stauffenberg*, Droste Verlag, Düsseldorf [1970].

Müller, Klaus-Jürgen: *Das Heer und Hitler: Armee und nationalsozialistisches Regime 1933–1940*, Deutsche Verlags-Anstalt, Stuttgart 1969.

Müller, Wolfgang: 'Die Wehrmacht am 20. Juli: Neue Forschungsergebnisse zu Deutschlands Schicksalstag vor fünf Jahren', *Main-Post* 21 July 1949.

Müller, Wolfgang: 'Was geschah am 20. Juli 1944?', *Das freie Wort* 3 (1952), 19 July 1952.

Nebgen, Elfriede: *Jakob Kaiser: Der Widerstandskämpfer*, W. Kohlhammer Verlag, Stuttgart, Berlin, Köln, Mainz 1967.

Norden, Albert: 'Die Bedeutung des 20. Juli', *Die Weltbühne* 2 (1947), pp. 553–60.

O'Neill, Robert J.: *The German Army and the Nazi Party, 1933–1939*, Cassell, London 1966.

Paetel, Karl O.: 'Deutsche im Exil: Randbemerkungen zur Geschichte der politischen Emigration', *Aussenpolitik* 6 (1955), pp. 572–85.

Paret, Peter: 'An Aftermath of the Plot Against Hitler: The Lehrterstrasse Prison in Berlin, 1944–5', *Bulletin of the Institute of Historical Research* 32 (1959), pp. 88–102.

Pechel, Rudolf: 'Tatsachen', *Deutsche Rundschau* 69 (1946), pp. 173–80.

Pechel, Rudolf: *Deutscher Widerstand*, Eugen Rentsch Verlag, Erlenbach and Zurich 1947.

Peterson, Edward Norman: *Hjalmar Schacht: For and Against Hitler. A Political-Economic Study of Germany 1923–1945*, Christopher, Boston 1954.

Peterson, Edward N.: *The Limits of Hitler's Power*, Princeton University Press, Princeton, N.J. 1969.

Pfeifer, Edda: 'Beiträge zur Geschichte der österreichischen Widerstandsbewegung des konservativen Lagers 1938–1940: Die Gruppen Karl Roman Scholz, Dr Karl Lederer und Dr Jakob Kastelic', typescript, dissertation, Vienna 1963.

Plesse, Werner: 'Zum antifaschistischen Widerstand in Mitteldeutschland 1939–1945', *Zeitschrift für Geschichtswissenschaft* 2 (1954), pp. 813–43.

Portmann, Heinrich: *Kardinal von Galen: Ein Gottesmann seiner Zeit*, Aschendorff Verlag, Münster i.W. [7/8]1959; (*Cardinal von Galen,* translated by R. L. Sedgwick, Jarrolds, London 1957).

Pross, Harry: *Literatur und Politik: Geschichte und Programme der politisch literarischen Zeitschriften im deutschen Sprachgebiet seit 1870*, Walter Verlag, Olten-Freiburg 1963.

Rehm, Max: 'Claus Schenk Graf von Stauffenberg: Generalstabsoffizier, Widerstandskämpfer gegen Hitler 1907–1944' in *Lebensbilder aus Schwaben und Franken*, Vol. 9, W. Kohlhammer Verlag, Stuttgart 1963, pp. 412–23.

Reichhardt, Hans J.: 'Möglichkeiten und Grenzen des Widerstandes der Arbeiterbewegung' in Schmitthenner/Buchheim: *Der deutsche Widerstand gegen Hitler* (see below), pp. 169–213.

Reventlow, Gräfin von: *Albrecht Bernstorff zum Gedächtnis*, privately produced, Altenhof 1952.

Richter, Bernt: 'In der Götzendämmerung: Querverbindungen und Holzwege der Anti-Hitler-Opposition zu Himmlers SS', typescript of broadcast, Süddeutscher Rundfunk, Stuttgart 1972.

Rieter, Fritz: 'Zwanzig Jahre nach dem Attentat auf Hitler', *Schweizer Monatshefte* No 44 (1964), p. 313.

[Ritter, Gerhard]: 'Lesson of the German Resistance: An Address by Dr Gerhard Ritter', *Wiener Library Bulletin* 9 (1955), No 1–2, p. 4.

Ritter, Gerhard: *Carl Goerdeler und die deutsche Widerstandsbewegung*, Deutsche Verlags-Anstalt, Stuttgart [3]1956; *The German Resistance: Carl Goerdeler's Struggle against Tyranny*, translated R. T. Clark, George Allen and Unwin, London 1958.

Rönnefarth, Helmuth K. G.: *Die Sudetenkrise in der internationalen Politik: Entstehung – Verlauf – Auswirkung* (2 parts) Franz Steiner Verlag, Wiesbaden

1961.

Ronge, Paul: 'Warum ich Helene Schwärzel verteidigte', *Nordwestdeutsche Hefte* 1 (1946), no 9, pp. 14–15.

Roon, G. van: 'Oberst Wilhelm Staehle: Ein Beitrag zu den Auslandskontakten des deutschen Widerstandes', *VfZ* 14 (1966), pp. 209–23.

Roon, Ger van: *Neuordnung im Widerstand: Der Kreisauer Kreis innerhalb der deutschen Widerstandsbewegung*, R. Oldenbourg Verlag, Munich 1967 (*German Resistance to Hitler: Count von Moltke and the Kreisau Circle* [abridged], translated by Peter Ludlow, Van Nostrand Reinhold Co., London 1971).

Roon, Ger van: *Wilhelm Staehle: Ein Leben auf der Grenze 1877–1945*, Gotthold Müller Verlag, Munich 1969.

Rossa, Kurt: *Todesstrafen: Ihre Wirklichkeit in drei Jahrtausenden*, Gerhard Stalling Verlag, Oldenburg and Hamburg 1966.

Rothfels, Hans: 'The German Resistance in Its International Aspects', *International Affairs* 34 (1958), pp. 477–89.

Rothfels, Hans: *Die deutsche Opposition gegen Hitler: Eine Würdigung*, Fischer Bücherei, Frankfurt/M. and Hamburg 1958 (new edition 1969); *The German Opposition to Hitler*, translated Lawrence Wilson, Oswald Wolff, London 1961.

R[othfels], H[ans]: 'Die Roten Kämpfer: Zur Geschichte einer linken Widerstandsgruppe', *VfZ* 7 (1959), pp. 438–60.

Rothfels, Hans: 'Zerrspiegel historischer Wahrheit', *Die Zeit* 20 Oct. 1961, p. 3.

Rothfels, Hans: 'Zerrspiegel des 20. Juli', *VfZ* 10 (1962), pp. 62–7.

Ruland, Bernd: 'Die Verschwörung des 20. Juli: Die Standrechtsverordnungen Stauffenbergs', *Die Welt* 2 (1947), 2 Aug. 1947, p. 2.

Ruland, Bernd: 'Die Verschwörung des 20. Juli 1944 nach Dokumenten: Standrechtsverordnungen im Falle des Gelingens der Erhebung', *Passauer Neue Presse*, Berlin, 23 Juli 1949.

Salin, Edgar: *Um Stefan George: Erinnerung und Zeugnis*, Verlag Helmut Küpper, Munich and Düsseldorf ²1954.

Salin, Edgar: 'Über Artur Sommer, den Menschen und List-Forscher', *Mitteilungen der List Gesellschaft* fasc. 6 (1967), No 4/5, pp. 81–90.

Schall-Riaucour, Heidemarie Gräfin: *Aufstand und Gehorsam: Offizierstum und Generalstab im Umbruch. Leben und Wirken von Generaloberst Franz Halder, Generalstabschef 1938–1942*, Limes Verlag, Wiesbaden 1972.

Scheurig, Bodo: *Freies Deutschland: Das Nationalkomitee und der Bund deutscher Offiziere in der Sowjetunion 1943–1945*, Nymphenburger-Verlagshandlung, Munich ²1961 (*Free Germany: The National Committee and the League of German Officers*, translated by Herbert Arnold, Wesleyan University Press, Middletown, Connecticut 1969.

Scheurig, Bodo: *Claus Graf Schenk von Stauffenberg*, Colloquium Verlag, Berlin 1964.

Scheurig, Bodo: *Ewald von Kleist-Schmenzin: Ein Konservativer gegen Hitler*, Gerhard Stalling Verlag, Oldenburg and Hamburg 1968.

Scheurig, Bodo: *Henning von Tresckow: Eine Biographie*, Gerhard Stalling Verlag, Oldenburg and Hamburg [1973].

Schmitt, Hejo: 'Bernhard Letterhaus: Porträt eines Widerstandskämpfers', *Deutsche Rundschau* 83 (1957), pp. 155–8.

Schmitthenner, Walter and Buchheim, Hans (editors): *Der deutsche Widerstand gegen Hitler: Vier historisch-kritische Studien*, Kiepenheuer and Witsch, Cologne, Berlin 1966 (Engl. ed. see *The German Resistance to Hitler*).

Schorn, Hubert: *Der Richter im Dritten Reich: Geschichte und Dokumente*, Klostermann, Frankfurt 1959.

Schorr, Helmut J.: *Adam Stegerwald: Gewerkschafter und Politiker der ersten deutschen Republik. Ein Beitrag zur Geschichte der christlich-sozialen Bewegung in Deutschland*, Kommunal-Verlag, Recklinghausen 1966.

Schramm, Wilhelm Ritter von: *Aufstand der Generale: Der 20. Juli in Paris*, Kindler-Taschenbücher, Munich [²] 1964; *Conspiracy Among Generals*, translated and edited by R. T. Clark, George Allen and Unwin, London 1956.

Sendtner, Kurt: 'Die deutsche Militäropposition im ersten Kriegsjahr' in *Vollmacht des Gewissens*, Vol. I (see below), pp. 385–532.

Siedler, Wolf Jobst: *Behauptungen*, F.A. Herbig, Berlin 1965.

Spaeter, Helmuth: *Die Geschichte des Panzerkorps Grossdeutschland*, Vol. II Selbstverlag Hilfswerk ehem. Soldaten für Kriegsopfer und Hinterbliebene e.V., Duisburg-Ruhrort 1958.

Späth, Alfred: 'Zum Andenken an Nikolaus Graf von Üxküll', *VfZ* 8 (1960), pp. 188–92.

Spuler, Bertold: *Regenten und Regierungen der Welt: Minister-Ploetz*, Part II, Vol. 4, A.G. Ploetz, Würzburg ²1964.

Stauffenberg, Alexander Graf von: 'Die deutsche Widerstandsbewegung und ihre geistige Bedeutung in der Gegenwart' mimeographed, no place [1951].

Stauffenberg, Alexander Graf von: *Denkmal*, Helmut Küpper previously Georg Bondi, Düsseldorf and Munich 1964.

Stockhorst, [Erich]: *Fünftausend Köpfe: Wer war was im Dritten Reich*, Blick und Bild Verlag, Velbert-Kettwig 1967.

Strauch, Rudi: *Sir Nevile Henderson: Britischer Botschafter in Berlin von 1937 bis 1939*, Ludwig Röhrscheid, Bonn 1959.

Strik-Strikfeldt, Wilfried: *Against Hitler and Stalin*, translated David Footman, Macmillan, London 1970.

Stubbe, Walter: 'In memoriam Albrecht Haushofer', *VfZ* 8(1960), pp. 236–56.

Stutterheim, Kurt von: *Die Majestät des Gewissens: In memoriam Albrecht Bernstorff*, Hans Christians Verlag, Hamburg 1962.

Sykes, Christopher: *Troubled Loyalty: A Biography of Adam von Trott zu Solz*, Collins, London 1968.

Theimer, Walter: 'Die Verschwörung des 20. Juli: Tragisches Versagen . . . in Berlin', *Die Welt* 19 July 1947, p. 3.

Theimer, Walter: 'Wilhelm Leuschner: "Einigkeit!" ', *Das Parlament* 20 July 1952, p. 3.

Trevor-Roper, Hugh Redwald: 'Hitlers Kriegsziele', *VfZ* 8 (1960), pp. 121–33.

Trevor-Roper, H. R.: *The Last Days of Hitler*, Macmillan, London and New York 1956.

Uhlig, Heinrich: 'Der verbrecherische Befehl' in *Vollmacht des Gewissens* 1956 Vol. 2 (see below), pp. 287–410.

Vogel, Heinrich: *Der Prediger von Buchenwald: Das Martyrium Paul Schneiders. Geboren am 20. August 1897, Gestorben am 18. Juli 1939*, Lettner-Verlag, Berlin ²1954.

Vollmacht des Gewissens (2 vols), edited by Europäische Publikation e.V., Alfred Metzner Verlag, Frankfurt/M., Berlin 1960, 1965.

Vyvyan, Michal: 'The German "Opposition" and Nazi Morale', *The Cambridge Journal* 2 (1948/49), pp. 148–68.

Walsh SJ, Edmund A.: 'Die Tragödie Karl Haushofers', *Neue Auslese* 2 (1947), No 3, pp. 19–29.

Walsh, SJ, Edmund A.: *Total Power: A Footnote to History*, Doubleday, Garden City, New York 1948.

[Wehner, Bernd:] 'Das Spiel ist aus' – see under 'Das Spiel . . .'.

Weingartner, Thomas: *Stalin und der Aufstieg Hitlers*, Verlag Walter de Gruyter & Co., Berlin 1970.

Weisenborn, Günther: *Der lautlose Aufstand: Bericht über die Widerstandsbewegung des deutschen Volkes 1933–1945*, 1953 (rororo Taschenbuch 1962). Rowohlt Verlag, Hamburg.

Weizsäcker, Carl Friedrich von: *Die Tragweite der Wissenschaft*, Vol. I, Hirzel,

Stuttgart [2]1966.

Wendt, Bernd-Jürgen: *München 1938: England zwischen Hitler und Preussen*, Europäische Verlagsanstalt, Frankfurt/M 1965.

Weniger, Erich: 'Zur Vorgeschichte des 20.VII.1944: Heinrich von Stülpnagel', *Die Sammlung* 4 (1949), pp. 475–92.

Wheeler-Bennett, John W.: *The Nemesis of Power: The German Army in Politics 1918–1945*, Macmillan, London, St Martin's Press, New York [2]1964.

Who's Who 1961: An Annual Biographical Dictionary with which is incorporated 'Men and Women of the Time', Adam and Charles Black, London and Macmillan, New York 1961.

Who's Who in America, Vol. 18, 1934–1935, A. N. Marquis Co., Chicago 1934.

Wiesenthal, Simon: *The Murderers Among Us*, McGraw-Hill, New York, Toronto, London, Sydney 1967.

Wilmot, Chester: *The Struggle for Europe*, Collins, London 1953.

Wirmer, E[rnst]: 'Ansprache am 20. Juli 1958 am Denkmal in der Stauffenbergstrasse anlässlich der Gedenkfeier in Berlin 1958', mimeographed, 'Hilfswerk 20. Juli 1944' Foundation, Kronberg i.T. 1958.

Wülcknitz, von: 'Was am 20. Juli 1944 wirklich geschah: Pläne, Rollen, Handlungen der Militärs', *Der Tagesspiegel* 20 July 1946.

Wunder, Gerd: *Die Schenken von Stauffenberg*, Müller & Gräff, Stuttgart 1972.

Yahil, Leni: *The Rescue of Danish Jewry: Test of a Democracy*, translated from the Hebrew by Morris Gradel, The Jewish Publication Society of America, Philadelphia 1969.

Zeller, Eberhard: *Geist der Freiheit: Der zwanzigste Juli*, Hermann Rinn, Munich 1954, [3]1956, Gotthold Müller Verlag, Munich [4]1963, [5]1965 (*The Flame of Freedom: The German Struggle against Hitler*, translated by R. P. Heller and D. R. Masters, Oswald Wolff, London 1967).

Zimmermann, F.: *Ludwig Freiherr von Leonrod: Ein Lebensbild aus der Tragödie unserer Tage*, privately produced, Waldsassen, undated.

Zipfel, Friedrich: *Plötzensee*, Landeszentrale für Politische Bildungsarbeit, Berlin [4]1963.

Zipfel, Friedrich: *Kirchenkampf in Deutschland 1933–1945*, Walter de Gruyter, Berlin 1965.

Zuckmayer, Carl: *Als wär's ein Stück von mir: Horen der Freundschaft*, S. Fischer Verlag, Frankfurt 1966.

Index

Note: Certain frequently occurring names and terms, e.g. Hitler, or *coup d'état,* have been included only selectively. German military ranks are generally given in linguistic translation, so that some ranks, such as captain and major, are identical with their English or American equivalents, but others, such as major-general, are not; see the comparative table on page 768. The abbreviations 'i.G.' (in the General Staff) and 'd.G.' (of the General Staff, serving in OKW) were dropped in the text but are given in the index as 'General Staff' and as 'General Staff/OKW'.

Index